The SAGE
Handbook of
Educational
Leadership

The SAGE Handbook of Educational Leadership

Advances in Theory, Research, and Practice

Fenwick W. English Editor

University of North Carolina at Chapel Hill

SAGE Publications
Thousand Oaks ▪ London ▪ New Delhi

For information:

Sage Publications, Inc.
2455 Teller Road
Thousand Oaks, California 91320
E-mail: order@sagepub.com

Sage Publications Ltd.
1 Oliver's Yard
55 City Road
London EC1Y 1SP
United Kingdom

Sage Publications India Pvt. Ltd.
B-42, Panchsheel Enclave
Post Box 4109
New Delhi 110 017 India

Printed in the United States of America

Library of Congress Cataloging-in-Publication Data

The Sage handbook of educational leadership: Advances in theory,
research, and practice / Fenwick W. English, general editor.
    p. cm.
Includes bibliographical references and index.
ISBN 0-7619-2979-7 (cloth)
   1. Educational leadership. 2. School supervision. 3. School administrators.
I. English, Fenwick W.
LB2805.S262 2004
371.2—dc222

2004014077

04 05 06 07 9 8 7 6 5 4 3 2 1

Acquiring Editor:	Todd Armstrong
Editorial Assistant:	Deya Saoud
Production Editor:	Diana E. Axelsen
Copy Editor:	Jacqueline A. Tasch
Typesetter:	C&M Ditigals (P) Ltd.
Indexer:	Mary Mortensen
Cover Designer:	Michelle Lee Kenny

Contents

Introduction: A Metadiscursive Perspective on the Landscape of
Educational Leadership in the 21st Century   ix
    Fenwick W. English, General Editor
    University of North Carolina at Chapel Hill

About the Editor   xvii

About the Contributors   xviii

PART I. MULTIPLE LENSES OF DEMOCRATIC LEADERSHIP   1

    Coeditors: Frances K. Kochan and Cynthia J. Reed, Auburn University

1. A History of Public School Leadership:
   The First Century, 1837–1942   7
       Ira E. Bogotch, Florida Atlantic University

2. Moral Leadership: Shifting the Management Paradigm   34
       Michael E. Dantley, Miami University of Ohio

3. Social Justice: Seeking a Common Language   47
       Alan R. Shoho, University of Texas at San Antonio
       Betty M. Merchant, University of Texas at San Antonio
       Catherine A. Lugg, Rutgers University

4. Collaborative Leadership, Community Building, and
   Democracy in Public Education   68
       Frances K. Kochan, Auburn University
       Cynthia J. Reed, Auburn University

PART II. MANAGEMENT, ORGANIZATION, AND LAW   85

    Editor: Charles J. Russo, University of Dayton

5. Leadership as Social Construct: The Expression of
   Human Agency Within Organizational Constraint   89
       Rodney T. Ogawa, University of California at Santa Cruz

6. Pivotal Points: History, Development,
   and Promise of the Principalship   109
       Kathleen M. Brown, University of North Carolina at Chapel Hill

7. The School Superintendent: Roles, Challenges, and Issues   142
   Theodore J. Kowalski, University of Dayton
   C. Cryss Brunner, University of Minnesota

8. The Role of Education Law in Leadership Preparation Programs   168
   Charles J. Russo, University of Dayton

PART III. EDUCATIONAL POLITICS AND POLICY: CREATING EFFECTIVE, EQUITABLE, AND DEMOCRATIC SCHOOLS   187

Editor: Gary L. Anderson, New York University

9. Educational Leaders as Policy Analysts   191
   Betty Malen, University of Maryland

10. Educational Leadership and the New Economy:
    Keeping the "Public" in Public Schools   216
    Gary L. Anderson, New York University
    Monica Pini, National University of San Martin, Argentina

11. A New Conception of Parent Engagement:
    Community Organizing for School Reform   237
    Eva Gold, Research for Action
    Elaine Simon, Research for Action
    Chris Brown, Cross City Campaign for Urban School Reform

12. Leading the School Through Culturally Responsive Inquiry   269
    Ruth S. Johnson, California State University, Los Angeles
    Lawson Bush, V, California State University, Los Angeles

13. Constructing a Democratic Foundation for School-Based Reform:
    The Local Politics of School Autonomy and Internal Governance   297
    Jesse Goodman, Indiana University and Harmony Education Center
    Daniel Baron, Harmony Education Center
    Carol Myers, Harmony Education Center

PART IV: THEORIES OF LEADERSHIP: RESEARCH PROBLEMS AND PRACTICES   333

Coeditors: Margaret Grogan, University of Missouri–Columbia and
Gary M. Crow, University of Utah

14. The Nature of Inquiry in Educational Leadership   337
    Michelle D. Young, University Council
    for Educational Administration
    Gerardo R. López, Indiana University

15. The Development of Leadership Thought
    and Practice in the United States   362
    Gary M. Crow, University of Utah
    Margaret Grogan, University of Missouri–Columbia

16. Leading in the Midst of Diversity: The Challenge of Our Times   380
    Carolyn M. Shields, University of British Columbia
    Anish Sayani, University of British Columbia

PART V: THE MICROPOLITICS OF SCHOOL LEADERSHIP   403

Editor: Larry E. Frase, San Diego State University

17. Curriculum Leadership: The Administrative Survival Skill in a
    Test-Driven Culture and a Competitive Educational Marketplace   407
    Fenwick W. English, University of North Carolina at Chapel Hill
    Betty E. Steffy, University of North Carolina at Chapel Hill

18. Refocusing the Purposes of Teacher Supervision   430
    Larry E. Frase, San Diego State University

19. Student Misbehavior and Violence:
    A Reexamination of the Enemy Within   463
    George J. Petersen, California Polytechnic
    State University, San Luis Obispo

20. Issues of Teaching and Learning   483
    Eric Haas, University of Connecticut
    Leslie Poynor, University of Connecticut

21. New Approaches for School Design   506
    Jeffery A. Lackney, University of Wisconsin–Madison

22. Unions, Collective Bargaining, and the Challenges of Leading   538
    Todd A. DeMitchell, University of New Hampshire

23. Finance, Planning, and Budgeting   550
    William K. Poston, Jr., Iowa State University

Author Index   571

Subject Index   589

Introduction

A Metadiscursive Perspective on the Landscape
of Educational Leadership in the 21st Century

FENWICK W. ENGLISH, GENERAL EDITOR
University of North Carolina at Chapel Hill

What happens when some of the most gifted and insightful researchers and practitioners are "let loose" to think creatively about educational leadership? The *Handbook of Educational Leadership: New Dimensions and Realities* is the product.

Each of the authors and coauthors involved in the production of the Handbook were commissioned to consider creative dimensions of educational leadership and practice in areas where they have spent a good deal of time doing research and scholarship. They were asked to probe widely and deeply: to connect to the past but not to be tied down by it. They were instructed to introduce the reader to the most resilient themes in their areas, trace their roots of development, and extend those themes into current contexts and challenges. Their line of responsibility was to think creatively without crossing over into fantasy. Nearly all of their efforts represent a kind of "close questioning" of existing forms of practice within carefully drawn portraits of where, how, and under what conditions the field of educational leadership might be advanced.

Of course, no promise was made that all of these themes *had* to go any particular place, or even that they had to become convergent at some arbitrary point. Each author was free to follow his or her thoughts and the research in whatever direction seemed most promising. And many took up the challenge of disagreeing with current directions and trends in education, pointing out the shortcomings and politicization of the field as it is bent by legislative mandate to forms of increasingly monolithic accountability, even as the content of those laws may be contradictory to the professed aims that formed them.

A perusal of the contributions of the scholars and researchers who contributed to the Handbook will reveal that educational leadership as a field, in the sense of a coherent body of accepted, undisputed content, is a fabrication. The fact that the authors in the Handbook came down on different sides of some disputes should not be surprising. When one considers the big issues facing educational leadership today on contested terrain, it would be a contrived artificiality to force a consensus.

The disputations described in the pages of the Handbook put an end to the idea that there is a single, uncontested knowledge base that informs practice in educational leadership today or at any time in the past. Any attempt to cloak over the serious challenges to a unitary knowledge base deserves the most serious skepticism. On this assumption of an uncontested knowledge base, national standards have been promulgated (Littrell & Foster, 1995). But it is an empty enterprise and full of unanticipated dangers, not the least of which is the idea that we can or should make schools as they now exist a permanent feature on the American landscape, thereby nipping in the bud any serious innovation that does not already look like the status quo.

A metadiscursive view of the perspectives and concepts explored in the Handbook will reveal some of the classic binaries (either/or dichotomies) that have become the shoals on which many discussions foundered in the past. Binaries represent junctures or paradoxes in a series of statements that are believed to be true but that seem contradictory and exclusive of one another (Fairclough, 1992, p. 222). A brief review of them may be instructive before the reader moves into the various parts of the Handbook and gets closer to the grounds of discussion and disputation. The deconstruction of binaries is one of the hallmarks of postmodern critique (English, 2003).

THE PUBLIC/PRIVATE BINARY

To Its Detriment, Educational Administration Is Already Captured by Business Mindscapes and Production-Function Metaphors

The public/privatization battle has been one of the most contested binaries in the educational leadership discourse over the years. At first, many professors in our fledging field were former superintendents, principals, and supervisors who had the task of bringing something of substance to the curriculum in newly founded schools of education. Their works attempted to bring order to this discourse. Infatuated as they were with the

signs of the times, and feeling the pressure to justify their existence apart from the classic arts and sciences models regnant in the larger university, they framed their efforts in the popular and very fashionable literature of scientific management at work in industry and business. This refuge enabled them to position themselves as distinct academic peers and to advance their claims of authority in the language of science as the uncontested arbiters of how to prepare educational leaders for the nation's schools. As the language of scientific management became more diffused into business and industrial management practices, educational leadership mimicked these approaches, promising better results; the idea was to mirror the growing success of improved industrial/business economic productivity, which was more easily gauged and popularized in the public eye.

Why can't education be run like a business? This platform remains an entrenched aspect of contested ground today. It is likely to remain a point of confrontation and friction well into this new century. The fact that educational leadership has been thoroughly infused with business management concepts has not been recognized in many circles. The intellectual founders of business, industrial, public, and educational management were often the same authors. Highly influential thinkers such as Frederick Taylor, Henry Fayol, Henry Gantt, Mary Parker Follett, Ralph Davis, Elton Mayo, Chester Barnard, Douglas McGregor, Herbert Simon, and W. Edwards Deming were not professors of education, nor even educators concerned with problems of school life. Yet, their thinking, ideas, assumptions, and mental models have exercised a pervasive and continuing influence in educational, business, industrial, and public spheres of management. The contrary proposition, advanced by Raymond Callahan (1962) more than 40 years ago, has not been recently explored in depth: that is, that educational leadership's problem has been and remains the fact that it has been run like a business and that the accountability models superimposed in educational settings reinforce and extend assumptions of business/industrial activities. Education is already being run like a business, and the nature of what is unique to the educational enterprise and the purpose of schooling in the larger society have been eroded in the continuing discourse regarding economic productivity. In addressing this problem, some of the authors of the Handbook raise the issue of social justice. If the schools keep reinforcing the existing social order, with its inequities and injustices perpetuated, what service has education rendered to such an unjust society? Has this not been a kind of disservice?

A business/industrial model works to maximize profit by excising all the factors that depress profit. Elaborate forms of standardization are advanced to eliminate all forms of variance that inhibit productivity. *Quality* is defined as the lowering of costs within the parameters of the production-function activity. The social impact is irrelevant to this model, as we see jobs outsourced to foreign countries and American workers unemployed at home. The so-called bottom line is all about profit.

Many of the authors in the Handbook take serious issue with a wide range of assumptions vigorously at work in education and in laws, policies, and regulations in which those assumptions are manifested. The problem of educational leadership is that it has been thoroughly saturated with the kind of thinking that has ignored social justice. One of the problems with educational leadership has been that its mental models are no different than those used by leaders in the private sector. These leaders remain largely indifferent to the social consequences of their operations (see O'Boyle, 1998). In any enterprise where greed, profit, and self-aggrandizement become the overriding motivations defining success, one should not be surprised to find the deep fissures in ethical conduct littered across the business landscape today (Fox, 2003; Jeter, 2003).

Similarly, when proposals are advanced to connect educational administrators' pay to so-called performance, the model that business provides is dismal and certainly counterproductive to an organization devoted to providing a public service (see Lauricella, 2004; Lublin, 2002; Morgenson, 2004).

The inculcation of the "for profit" business mind-set into education was described by Raymond Callahan (1962) as a calamity:

> The tragedy was fourfold: that educational questions were subordinated to business considerations; that administrators were produced who were not, in any true sense, educators; that a scientific label was put on some very unscientific and dubious methods and practices; and that an anti-intellectual climate, already prevalent, was strengthened. (p. 246)

The 21st century will see this binary continue to play out in the form of controversies regarding vouchers and creating a marketplace for schooling. But at the top of the hierarchy, there is little difference in the kinds of mind-sets business and educational administrators possess. The production-function model reigns supreme in both worlds.

THE MANAGEMENT/ LEADERSHIP BINARY

The Dissolution of a Dichotomy on a Continuum of Organizational Responsibility

The confusion between management and leadership continues to plague issues of preparation and performance in educational administration. Educational leaders do not perform in a social or organizational vacuum. Administrative positions exist within educational organizations, schools, colleges, and other related agencies. These positions are connected to other positions and to larger organizational boundaries and functions. The dichotomy between leaders and managers has become a point of contestation. Conventional wisdom attests that leaders are different than managers (Bennis, 1989, p. 25), but the line that separates them is indeed thin, perhaps nonexistent, especially so when both work inside organizations as in the case of educational administrators.

Contemporary leadership texts emphasize how leaders engage constituents in conversations regarding vision and mission (Fullan, 2001) and how they interact collaboratively in constructing communities of learners (Sergiovanni, 2000) and build positive organizational cultures (Deal & Peterson, 1999). Although these texts point to the work of leaders/managers within school organizations, none show an awareness of the fundamental fact that as leaders go about constructing what Barrows Dunham (1964) has called an "organizational ideology" (p. 15), they also cast themselves as defenders of orthodoxies.

Organizational ideologies have the purpose of constructing a rationale to "explain and justify their actions. They must do this for their own members, who otherwise might doubt the value of membership" (Dunham, 1964, p. 15). Dunham (1964) constructs an ideology divided into three parts, all of which are themes in a plethora of popular books about educational leadership today (Hoy & Hoy, 2003; Rebore, 2003) and are also embodied in national standards for school leaders connected to state licensure (see Hessel & Holloway, 2002).

The first act in creating an organizational ideology is to "describe the objective circumstances in which the organization acts and [state] the moral values which the organization regards as ultimate" (Dunham, 1964, p. 15). The second and third parts consist of indicating the purposes of the organization related to its structure and how such purposes are to be attained in a given array of circumstances. As Dunham (1964) makes clear:

> Without a description of objective circumstances, nothing can be explained; without a demonstrable system of values, nothing can be justified. Without a statement of purposes, it cannot be known how the purposes are to be attained. (p. 17)

An organization's ideology becomes a critical part of its *unity*. The importance of unity is to connect the actions of all members to the organization. Unity is intimately linked to intent, and as Dunham (1964) observes, "So long as this intent exists, unity will follow. What organizations fear is loss of the intent" (p. 17).

In constructing such unity, the activities and outcomes are subject to human miscalculation. As humans, we are subject to the prejudices of our times and Dunham (1964) prophetically explains, "we sometimes assert what we do not know, and we sometimes do not know what we assert" (p. 17). The important part of this observation is that such errors become part and parcel of the organization's ideology and undergird its unity. Because they are a source of such unity, removing errors, miscalculations, and unsupported claims "is not a mere scientific adjustment but a dislocation of the corporate body" (p. 18).

The first task of leadership within organizations is to create and preserve its unity. That involves the creation and perpetuation of its ideology. It doesn't matter if the ideology is true or false. What matters is the preservation of unity. At this juncture, Dunham (1964) separates orthodoxy and heresy, "for a doctrine is orthodox if it helps unite the organization; it is heretical if it divides" (p. 18). The first task of leadership within an organization is to preserve its unity, not to engage in a penetrating analysis of the truth or falsity of its organizational mythos. If the line that separates leadership from management is that managers can actually pause to consider purpose instead of simply being soldiers in the cause, then leaders cannot engage in the same activity without seriously jeopardizing the cohesiveness of the organization itself. Managers may not establish the strategic purposes of the organization because they accept them as is; so must leaders. Both managers and leaders within organizations are bound to some constraints, although the former may be more circumscribed than the latter. So, at least in an organizational context, the line that separates managers from leaders is not role difference but merely degrees of freedom. In bureaucracies, the degrees of freedom in roles remain hierarchically defined.

THE ART/SCIENCE BINARY

The Limitations of Scientific Research to Improve Educational Leadership

Many discussions of educational problems boil down to an argument that the field must become open to true scientific inquiry and embrace scientific standards of research to rise to a new level of legitimacy (Shavelson & Towne, 2003). Dictating the need for such scientific rigor is a definition that educational research is an applied field and that the function of research is "to add to fundamental understanding of education-related phenomena and events, and to inform practical decision making" (Shavelson & Towne, 2003, p. 83).

Reducing educational administration to a science has resulted in limiting the magnitude of the scope of such inquiry to existing sites and to existing practices, and this has voided any search for lines of inquiry that involve different epistemological assumptions than those supporting traditional notions of scientific inquiry. The continuing utilization of modernistic assumptions, which support only a unitary and largely linear idea of progress, is not going to produce revolutionary breakthroughs in approaching leadership, where the application has more to do with artistry than with scientific study. What seems not to have occurred to many researchers is that the research methods they embrace define the nature of the problems they pursue as well as the outcomes they obtain. To say that future research must focus on "significant" problems (Pounder, 2000, p. 465) is important only insofar as researchers understand the tautological and elliptical ways of knowing that bind inquiry to its own articles of faith. This limitation is illustrated by the first guiding principle advanced for conducting scientific research in education, namely that the researcher should "pose

significant questions that can be investigated empirically" (Shavelson & Towne, 2003, p. 55). The paradox here is that the guiding principle cannot be supported empirically, that is, by the methods it says are paramount. The assertion should be seen within the tradition of empiricism, which stipulates that anything not empirical is not "significant" (i.e., not worth considering), a value-laden proposition if there ever was one (see Feyerabend, 1995, p. 29). If science is consistently defined as empirical, then about all we can say is that nonempirical problems are not scientific, rather than that they are not significant. As a tradition, empiricism defines some problems as significant, and they are by definition approachable (defined and pursued) empirically.

Another guiding principle of "rigorous" research involves the ability to move "from evidence to theory and back again" (Shavelson & Towne, 2003, p. 67). This "chain of reasoning" provides a measure of consistency and coherency. This requirement excludes some theories that contain contradictions because the chain of logic would not be consistent as a researcher moves from observation to evidence and back again. Feyerabend (1993) demurs that noncontradiction is a necessity to perform research "only in rather simple logical systems" (p. 235). More complex systems can include inconsistencies and even contradictions. It is simply a matter of altering the rules of the game of research.

To do this is a matter of determining who has the privileged status to assert what the rules are. Not including the artistic in equations and portraits of leadership as legitimate ways of knowing is tantamount to sanctifying only one way of conducting inquiry.

> But a culture that centres on humans, prefers personal acquaintance to abstract relations (intelligence quotients, efficiency statistics) and a naturalists' approach to that of molecular biologists will say that knowledge is qualitative and will interpret quantitative laws as bookkeeping devices, not as elements of reality. (Feyerabend, 1993, p. 236)

The resolution of the art/science leadership binary will not be resolved by science alone because science is the doorjamb for the binary distinction. Rather, it will mean that as a tradition, science is only one way of knowing among many, and others must be pursued to fully engage the entire spectrum regarding the study of leadership. Accepting the idea of paradox in theory may be a very reasonable assumption in coming to grips with understanding the phenomenon of leadership (see Deal & Peterson, 1994, p. 9).

We should be guided by LeFanu's (1999) criticism of research in medicine using field trials and statistics as a guide.

> For medical science now recognizes only one source of knowledge, that which has "been proven" by statistics, and this too is a potent source of error. There are many ways of knowing and among the most powerful is the tacit knowledge that comes from experience and is best described as "judgement." (p. 362)

THE THEORY/PRACTICE BINARY

No Practice is "Theory-Less"

Few binaries have exerted greater attraction and exhortation than the theory/practice gap (English, 2002). It has become fashionable lately to bash university programs and professors for pursuing abstract theories that have little relation to the practical matters of running the schools (Fordham, 2003). This kind of "diss-ing" has punctuated efforts to disavow the importance of theory and to proffer the notion that new theories have nothing to add to the preparation of educational administrators concerned with the improvement of schooling (Murphy, 1999, p. 48).

The only way one can assume a position that no new theories are required is to assume that the current definitions of a field of practice are correct. Instead, what this perspective assumes is that what is needed are alternatives or innovations *within* such a field. Because all practice is theory embedded, this means that

the current practices being used require no radical change but merely enhancements. The posture of theory bashing displays a kind of smug satisfaction with things as they are and the roles and relationships that support the status quo. The satisfaction with the current paradigm carries with it a xenophobia about conceptual alternatives that are "out of paradigm." As Kuhn (1996) reminds us:

> No part of the aim of normal science is to call forth new sorts of phenomena ... indeed those that will not fit the box are often not seen at all. Nor do scientists normally aim to invent new theories and they are often intolerant of those invented by others. (p. 24)

One of the mistaken notions that have accompanied the idea of no new theories is that what is required to improve practice is to engage in the internship for longer time periods. This idea is the ultimate enshrinement of the status quo. Although it encourages refinement of existing practices, it also signifies the development of no new practices.

When one examines another applied field similar to educational administration, for example, one can see better evidence of the importance of theory breakthroughs that lead to better practices. For example, in medicine, no medical theory of the time could have produced penicillin or cortisone (LeFanu, 1999, p. 218). These discoveries were "out of paradigm." The continued use of current theories may actually block discovery in education as it has in medicine (LeFanu, 1999, pp. 135, 147).

Lakatos (1999) has criticized the development of theories in the social sciences, indicating they violate the logic of construction by using the same facts twice, once in their formulation and again in their validation. In this way, social science theory shows itself to be correlative but not predictive. The problem with much social science theory formulation can be attributed to what Lakatos has called *inductivism*, where theory construction is tautological (p. 36). By using the same facts twice, a theory is prevented from being able to predict novel events, the true test of its efficacy. Lakatos asserts that truly progressive theories will predict events or facts not known or not used in their initial construction. In this situation, there is no theory-practice gap. To resolve the theory/practice binary, one must envision a different way to construct a theory. If current theories used in educational administration are consistently being "patched up" to confirm new findings, they flunk the test of being predictive. They are regressive theories. With regressive theories, there is always a gap to practice. Practice leads an explanatory theory instead of being anticipated by it. This is the current situation in educational administration research. It lies at the heart of improving practice. The most sobering understanding is that there will be few innovative breakthroughs in practice as long as the current theory base remains unchallenged. By professing that no new theories are necessary, current practice is reified and fixed. Such a situation is profoundly detrimental to advancing any new discoveries to improve educational leadership.

SUMMARY

The Handbook is a provocative distillation of what we know and what we don't know about educational leadership. Of course, the latter category is enormous and the former a very thin sliver indeed. The complexities, ambiguities, and obstacles facing leaders in education could not be more ominous. But we ought to take comfort from one of the most revered of the ancient proverbs of Hippocrates, which refers to medical practice but may also befit education:

> Life is short, the Art is long, opportunity fleeting, experience delusive, judgment difficult. (Nuland, 1988, p.12)

In such circumstances, where there are few certainties and the challenges are immense, the exercise of judgment was correctly called "the Art" (Nuland, 1988, p. 12). A study of educational leadership and the contexts in which it is exercised is no less an art. No amount of research will ever change the necessity for art. Although research can be informative, it is not likely to be inspirational or decisive until it is applied by a human being with other human beings. Even in the 21st century, the art will be in great demand. To this end, the Handbook is proffered as a linchpin to the new century's continuing conversation.

REFERENCES

Bennis, W. (1989). *On becoming a leader.* Cambridge, MA: Perseus Books.

Callahan, R. (1962). *Education and the cult of efficiency: A study of the social forces that have shaped the administration of the public schools.* Chicago: University of Chicago Press.

Deal, P., & Peterson, K. (1994). *The leadership paradox: Balancing logic and artistry in schools.* San Francisco: Jossey-Bass.

Deal, P., & Peterson, K. (1999). *Shaping school culture: The heart of leadership.* San Francisco: Jossey-Bass.

Dunham, B. (1964). *Heroes and heretics: A social history of dissent.* New York: Knopf.

English, F. (2002, Winter). Cutting the Gordian knot of educational administration: The theory-practice gap. *UCEA Review, 44*(1), 1–3.

English, F. (2003). *The postmodern challenge to the theory and practice of educational administration.* Springfield, IL: Charles C Thomas.

Fairclough, N. (1992). *Discourse and social change.* Cambridge, UK: Polity Press.

Feyerabend, P. (1993). *Against method.* London: Verso.

Feyerabend, P. (1995). *Problems of empiricism.* Cambridge, UK: Cambridge University Press.

Fordham, T. (2003). *Better leaders for America's schools: A manifesto* (Thomas Fordham Institute). Retrieved from http://www.Edexcellence.net/fanifesto/manifesto.html

Fox, L. (2003). *Enron: The rise and fall.* Hoboken, NJ: John Wiley.

Fullan, M. (2001). *Leading in a culture of change.* San Francisco: Jossey-Bass.

Hessel, K., & Holloway, J. (2002). *A framework for school leaders: Linking the ISLLC standards to practice.* Princeton, NJ: Educational Testing Service.

Hoy, A., & Hoy, W. (2003). *Instructional leadership: A learning-centered guide*. Boston: Allyn & Bacon.

Jeter, L. (2003). *Disconnected: Deceit and betrayal at Worldcom*. Hoboken, NJ: John Wiley.

Kuhn, T. (1996). *The structure of scientific revolutions*. Chicago: University of Chicago Press.

Lakatos, I. (1999). Lectures on scientific method. In M. Motterlini (Ed.), *For and against method*. Chicago: University of Chicago Press.

Lauricella, T. (2004, January 8). Scandal reaches far and high. *The Wall Street Journal*, pp. R1, B14.

LeFanu, J. (1999). *The rise and fall of modern medicine*. New York: Carroll & Graf.

Littrell, J., & Foster, W. (1995). The myth of a knowledge base in educational administration. In R. Donmoyer, M. Imber, & J. Scheurich (Eds.), *The knowledge base in educational administration: Multiple perspectives* (pp. 32–46). Albany: SUNY Press.

Lublin, J. (2002, September 13). How CEOs retire in style. *The Wall Street Journal*, pp. B1, B6.

Morgenson, G. (2004, January 25). Explaining (or not) why the boss is paid so much. *New York Times*, Section 3, p. 1.

Murphy, J. (1999). *The quest for a center: Notes on the state of the profession of educational leadership*. Columbia, MO: UCEA.

Nuland, S. (1988). *Doctors: A biography of medicine*. New York: Knopf.

O'Boyle, T. (1998). *At any cost: Jack Welch, General Electric, and the pursuit of profit*. New York: Vintage Books.

Pounder, D. (2000, August). A discussion of the task force's collective findings. *Educational Administration Quarterly, 36*(3), 465–473.

Rebore, R. (2003). *A human relations approach to the practice of educational leadership*. Boston: Allyn & Bacon.

Sergiovanni, T. (2000). *The lifeworld of leadership*. San Francisco: Jossey-Bass.

Shavelson, R., & Towne, L. (Eds.). (2003). *Scientific research in education*. Washington, DC: National Academy Press.

About the Editor

Fenwick W. English is the R. Wendell Eaves Distinguished Professor of Educational Leadership at the University of North Carolina at Chapel Hill. He is author or coauthor of more than 20 books, including *The Postmodern Challenge to the Theory and Practice of Educational Administration* (2003). He has served as a middle school principal and superintendent of schools as well as a department chair, dean, and vice chancellor of academic affairs in higher education. In addition, he has served in the private sector as a partner (principal) in Peat, Marwick, Mitchell & Co. and as Associate Executive Director of the American Association of School Administrators.

About the Contributors

Gary L. Anderson is a Professor in the Educational Administration Department at New York University. He has published widely in the areas of educational leadership, critical theory, action research, and Latin American education. His most recent books are *Performance Theories in Education: Power, Pedagogy, and the Politics of Identity* (2004), coedited with Bryant Alexander and Bernardo Gallegos, and *The Action Research Dissertation: A Guide for Students, Faculty, and Institutional Review Boards* (2004, Sage), coauthored with Kathryn Herr. He is a former high school teacher and principal in New York City and Puebla, Mexico.

Daniel Baron is the Director of Outreach Services for the Harmony Education Center and also serves as National Coordinator and Senior Coach for the National School Reform Faculty as well for Accelerated Schools. He is a Senior Associate to the ATLAS Learning Communities and a Project Director for the Lucent Technologies Foundation. He has spent more than 25 years working in public, private, and Native American education, pre-K through college. He was a founder and teacher-coordinator of the Harmony Elementary School in 1977, and he has won awards for action research and excellence in teaching.

Ira E. Bogotch is Professor of Educational Leadership at Florida Atlantic University. He previously served for 10 years on the Educational Leadership faculty at the University of New Orleans. He has taught students from kindergarten to adults in New York City, Guatemala City, Miami, and Washington, D.C., and also administered programs in these cities. He is the Associate Editor for *The International Journal of Leadership in Education* and serves on the editorial boards of *Educational Administration Quarterly, The Journal of School Leadership,* and *Urban Education.*

Chris Brown is Director of the Schools and Community Program at the Cross City Campaign for Urban School Reform. The Schools and Community Program works with parent and community organizations to increase meaningful parent and community involvement in school reform. Before coming to Cross City, he served as Community Development Specialist at Chicago's United Way/Crusade of Mercy. Previously, he spent 7 years as Director of the ACORN Housing Corporation of Illinois, a nonprofit group providing home ownership opportunities for low- and moderate-income families in Chicago's Englewood community.

Kathleen M. Brown is Assistant Professor of Educational Leadership at the University of North Carolina at Chapel Hill. She brings 15 years of teaching and administrative experience to the professorate, including work as a middle-school teacher and as an elementary-middle school principal in the Philadelphia/Camden, New Jersey, area. In 2002, she coauthored the book *From the Desk of the Middle School Principal: Leadership Responsive to the Needs of*

Young Adolescents. This work, based on surveys and interviews with practicing middle school principals, was designed to impact practice at the school level.

C. Cryss Brunner is Associate Professor in the Department of Educational Policy and Administration at the University of Minnesota and Director of the UCEA Joint Program Center for the Study of the Superintendency. She was previously a teacher and administrator in public schools. For her academic work, including the publication of several books and research articles, she received UCEA's Jack Culbertson Award. She also was awarded a Spencer Fellowship by the National Academy of Education for study of the school superintendency.

Lawson Bush, V, is Associate Professor of Education in the Division of Administration and Counseling at California State University, Los Angeles. Some of his most recent publications include "Standing in the Gap: A Model for Establishing African American Male Intervention Programs Within Public Schools" (with K. Mitchell and E. Bush), appearing in *Educational Horizons;* "Magnet Schools: Desegregation or Resegregation? Students' Voices From Inside the Walls" (with H. Burley and T. Causey-Bush), appearing in *American Secondary Education;* and *Can Black Mothers Raise Our Sons?* (1999).

Gary M. Crow is Professor and Chair in the Department of Educational Leadership at the University of Utah. He is currently conducting comparative studies of the socialization of United Kingdom head teachers and U.S. principals. His most recent book is *Being and Becoming a Principal* (with L. Joseph Matthews), and his articles have appeared in *Educational Management and Administration* (UK), *Educational Administration Quarterly, Journal of School Leadership, Journal of Educational Administration,* and *Urban Education.* He is President-Elect of the University Council for Educational Administration.

Michael E. Dantley is an Associate Professor in the Department of Educational Leadership

at Miami University in Oxford, Ohio. He has written numerous papers and is the coauthor of an upcoming text on leadership, spirituality, and social justice. He has served as a teacher, principal, and central office administrator with the Cincinnati Public Schools. He is presently on the editorial boards of *Educational Administration Quarterly,* the *Journal of School Leadership,* and the *Scholar Practitioner Quarterly* and has recently become the editor of the *Journal of Cases in Educational Leadership.*

Todd A. DeMitchell is Professor of Education and Justice Studies and Chair of the Department of Education at the University of New Hampshire. He spent 18 years in the public schools prior to becoming a faculty member in higher education. He served as an elementary school teacher, lead teacher, vice principal, principal, director of personnel and labor relations, and superintendent. He has published two books and 90 articles and book chapters on the legal mechanisms that impact schools, including school law, collective bargaining, and policy analysis.

Larry E. Frase is Professor of Educational Administration in the College of Education, San Diego State University. He served as superintendent of schools in the Catalina Foothills School District in Tucson, Arizona, and as assistant superintendent in New York. He is the author of 80 journal articles and wrote or edited 20 books, including *Creating Learning Places for Teachers, Too; Maximizing People Power in Schools;* and *School Management by Wandering Around.* In addition, his research papers on the subject of flow have been presented at Division A of the American Education Research Association and the University Council of Educational Administration.

Eva Gold is Principal at Research for Action and has served over the last decade as primary investigator of numerous local and national studies examining the dynamics among parents, community, and schools. She is coauthor with

Elaine Simon and Chris Brown of the *Strong Neighborhoods, Strong Schools* series, which documents the contributions of community organizing for school reform. She also coauthored *Clients, Consumers, or Collaborators? Parents and Their Roles in School Reform During Children Achieving, 1995–2000,* a report that was part of the overall evaluation of Philadelphia's systemic reform effort.

Jesse Goodman is a Professor in the School of Education, Codirector of a master's level elementary teacher education program, and former Chair of the doctoral Curriculum Studies Program at Indiana University. In addition, he is one of three Codirectors of the Harmony Education Center, an organization committed to democratic school reform. He has received five national awards for distinguished research. His book, *Elementary Schooling for Critical Democracy* (1992), draws heavily on the works of John Dewey.

Margaret Grogan is Professor and Chair, Department of Educational Leadership and Policy Analysis, University of Missouri–Columbia. She is also President of UCEA 2003–2004. She edits a series on *Women in Leadership*. Recent publications include a chapter in the NSSE Yearbook, 2002, "Shifts in the Discourse Defining the Superintendency: Historical and Current Foundations of the Position," with Cryss Brunner and Lars Björk, and an article, "Influences of the Discourse of Globalisation on Mentoring for Gender Equity and Social Justice in Educational Leadership" in *Leading and Managing* (2003). She is the author, with Daniel Duke, Pam Tucker, and Walt Heinecke, of *Educational Leadership in an Age of Accountability* (2003).

Eric Haas is a lawyer and Assistant Professor in Educational Leadership at the University of Connecticut. He is the recipient of the Arizona State University Interdisciplinary Millennium Dissertation Fellowship. His dissertation examines the political, social, and economic representation of educational issues in major newspapers of the United States. He is the author of several forthcoming book chapters that address issues of law and media discourse as related to educational policy.

Ruth S. Johnson is Professor of Educational Administration at California State University, Los Angeles. She has been a classroom teacher, instructional consultant, director of elementary education, analyst, assistant superintendent of schools in the areas of curriculum and business, and superintendent of schools. She was a compensatory education consultant for the New Jersey Department of Education. Her book, *Using Data to Close the Achievement Gap: How to Measure Equity in Our Schools,* is being used in schools and colleges nationally.

Frances K. Kochan is Interim Dean and Professor of Educational Leadership in the Auburn University College of Education. She has had experience as an elementary teacher, a principal, assistant superintendent, and superintendent. She is past President of the University Council on Educational Administration and presently serves on the Executive Committee. She is editor of the Mentoring and Mentorship series and serves on numerous editorial boards, including *The Journal of School Leadership* and *Mentoring and Tutoring.*

Theodore J. Kowalski is the Kuntz Family Chair in Educational Administration at the University of Dayton. A former school superintendent, he served as Dean of the Teachers College at Ball State University from 1983 to 1993. He is the author of 15 books and more than 135 book chapters and journal articles, and he has given invited lectures at more than 80 universities.

Jeffery A. Lackney is an Assistant Professor in the Department of Engineering Professional Development at the University of Wisconsin–Madison. He is a registered architect specializing in the planning, design, research, and evaluation of school environments. In addition to consulting nationally as an educational facility planner advocating innovative vision-driven approaches to school design, he conducts research on school environments. Previously, he was founding director of the Educational Design Institute at Mississippi State University, a joint initiative between the College of Education and the School of Architecture.

Gerardo R. López is an Assistant Professor in the Department of Educational Leadership and Policy Studies at Indiana University. His areas of interest are parental involvement, school-community relations, and migrant education. He has published in the *American Educational Research Journal, Harvard Educational Review, Educational Administration Quarterly, International Journal of Qualitative Studies in Education, Qualitative Inquiry,* and *Educational Researcher,* and he is the coeditor (with Larry Parker) of *Interrogating Racism in Qualitative Research Methodology* (2003).

Catherine A. Lugg is Associate Professor of Education at the Graduate School of Education, Rutgers University. She is a former flute teacher in a community school of music. Her research has been published in *Educational Administration Quarterly, Education Policy, The Journal of School Leadership, Education and Urban Society, The American Journal of Semiotics,* and *Pennsylvania History.* She is also the author of two books, *For God and Country: Conservatism and American School Policy* and *Kitsch: From Education to Public Policy.*

Betty Malen is Professor of Education Policy and Leadership at the University of Maryland, College Park, and a former school administrator. Her research focuses on the politics of education reform. Her work appears in academic journals, edited volumes, and professional association yearbooks. Her most recent article was a coauthored study of school reconstitution, titled "Reconstituting

Schools: Testing the Theory of Action," in *Education Evaluation and Policy Analysis.*

Betty M. Merchant is Professor and Chair of the Department of Educational Leadership and Policy Studies at the University of Texas, San Antonio. She has taught in public schools, preschool through high school, and in tribally controlled, Native American schools in the Southwest. She has published in *Bilingual Research Journal Education Review, Educational Administration Quarterly, Educational Theory, Journal of Education for Students Placed at Risk, Journal of Research in Rural Education,* and *Urban Education.*

Carol Myers is the Associate Director of Outreach Services for the Harmony Education Center and has worked extensively in youth leadership, service learning, and organizational development projects. She has had several manuscripts on these topics published. She also serves as a consultant for a number of community development and anti-racist projects in the Midwest. Prior to her work at the Harmony Education Center, she taught courses in the School of Education at the University of Indianapolis and Butler University.

Rodney T. Ogawa is Professor and Chair of the Education Department, University of California, Santa Cruz. He is Vice President-Elect of Division A of the American Educational Research Association. His research focuses on school organization and educational leadership. His most recent work has been published in the *American Educational Research Journal, Teachers College Record,* and a volume entitled *Rethinking Educational Leadership.*

George J. Petersen is Associate Professor of Educational Leadership at California Polytechnic State University, San Luis Obispo. His research has been published in *Educational Administration Quarterly, Journal of*

School Leadership, Journal of Educational Administration, and *Educational Policy Analysis Archives.* He has a forthcoming book entitled *The District Superintendent and School Board Relationship: Trends in Policy Development and Implementation.* He also serves as Associate Director of the University Council for Educational Administration.

Monica Pini is Professor and Researcher at the National University of San Martin, Buenos Aires, Argentina, where she coordinates a master's degree program in education. She also works for the Ministry of Education in Argentina. Her dissertation was published in Spanish as *Escuelas Charter y Empresas: Un discurso que vende* (2003) (Charter Schools and Corporations: A Discourse That Sells), the first volume in a book series sponsored by the Public Policy Laboratory in Buenos Aires, directed by Pablo Gentilli.

William K. Poston, Jr., is Emeritus Associate Professor of Educational Administration at Iowa State University. He has served the public schools for 30 years as a math teacher and secondary school principal. He was a superintendent of schools in Arizona and Montana. He is the author and coauthor of such publications as *Effective School Board Governance* and *Making Governance Work.* He was the youngest international president ever to head Phi Delta Kappa.

Leslie Poynor is a lecturer at the University of Connecticut and has a PhD in Curriculum and Instruction from Arizona State University. She is coediting a book on the social, political, and economic contexts of literacy education, *Marketing Fear in America's Public Schools: The Real War on Literacy.* Her most recent book addresses the social, political, and economic contexts of pre-service and first-year teachers in schools with large populations of bilingual and English language learners. Her articles have appeared in the *Educational Researcher,* the *Bilingual Research Journal,* and the *TESOL Journal.*

Cynthia J. Reed is Director of the Truman Pierce Institute, a research, teaching, and outreach center in the College of Education at Auburn University, the Program Coordinator for Educational Leadership, and Associate Professor in Educational Leadership at Auburn University. She recently was awarded UCEA's Jack A. Culbertson Award. She has been an educator for more than 20 years, serving as a teacher, principal, and director of collaborative programs among K to 12 and higher education institutions, and now as an associate professor. She is coeditor of the *Southern Regional Council of Educational Administration Yearbook.*

Charles J. Russo is the Joseph Panzer Chair in Education in the School of Education and Allied Professions and Adjunct Professor in the School of Law at the University of Dayton, specializing in Education Law. The 1998–1999 President of the Education Law Association, he is the author of more than 150 articles in peer-reviewed journals and author, coauthor, or editor of 15 books and almost 450 total publications. He also speaks extensively on issues in education law in the United States and throughout the world.

Anish Sayani is currently working on his doctorate at the University of British Columbia. He also instructs pre-service teachers for the Faculty of Education at that university and consults as a staff developer for the San Juan School District in Utah. He has been a high school English and humanities teacher in British Columbia and Texas for 14 years. His master's paper won the 2002 research award of the Canadian Association for the Study of Educational Administration.

Carolyn M. Shields is Professor of Educational Leadership and Codirector of the School Leadership Centre at the University of British

Columbia. She is past President of the Canadian Association for Studies in Educational Administration, a board member of the Commonwealth Council for Educational Administration and Leadership, and a member of several ministry advisory committees. Her research and teaching interests relate to leadership for social justice and academic excellence in diverse settings nationally and internationally.

Alan R. Shoho is an Associate Professor in the Department of Educational Leadership and Policy Studies at the University of Texas at San Antonio. His research focuses on organizational cultures and how they affect the sense of alienation and ethical behavior of their stakeholders. He has published in the *Journal of School Leadership, The High School Journal, Research in the Schools, Theory and Research in Educational Administration, ERS Spectrum,* the *Journal of Special Education Leadership,* and *The International Journal of Educational Management.*

Elaine Simon is a Senior Research Associate at Research for Action, an anthropologist who has conducted ethnographic research and evaluation in the fields of education, employment and training, and community development. She is Codirector of Urban Studies in the School of Arts and Sciences and adjunct Associate Professor of Education in the Graduate School of Education at the University of Pennsylvania. She is coauthor with Eva Gold and Chris Brown of the *Strong Neighborhoods, Strong Schools* series. Her perspective on education is informed by her

background in urban studies and community development.

Betty E. Steffy has served as a Clinical Professor of Educational Leadership in the School of Education at the University of North Carolina at Chapel Hill. She served as a Superintendent of Schools in New Jersey as well as the Deputy Superintendent for Instruction in the Kentucky Department of Education when the Kentucky Education Reform Act (KERA) was implemented. She has also served as a professor and dean of the school of education at Indiana-Purdue University Fort Wayne and a professor at Iowa State University. She has authored or coauthored six books including *Career Stages of Classroom Teachers* (1989) and *The Kentucky Education Reform: Lessons for America* (1993).

Michelle D. Young is the Executive Director of the University Council for Educational Administration and a faculty member in Educational Leadership and Policy Analysis at the University of Missouri–Columbia. She serves on the editorial boards of the *Educational Administration Quarterly, Educational Administration Abstracts, Journal of Cases in Educational Leadership,* and *Education and Urban Society.* She also serves on the National Advisory Board for ERIC, the Wallace Reader's Digest Funds LEADERS Count Advisory Committee, the National Policy Board for Educational Administration, and the National Commission for the Advancement of Educational Leadership Preparation.

PART I

Multiple Lenses of Democratic Leadership

FRANCES K. KOCHAN
Auburn University

CYNTHIA J. REED
Auburn University

This section of the *Handbook of Educational Leadership* presents four chapters that emphasize the many lenses that today's educational leaders must use, and the considerations they must take into account, if we are genuinely interested in promoting democratic leadership. Individually, each chapter in this section prompts deeper thinking about the historical underpinnings and assumptions that often guide today's educational practices. These chapters have been written to challenge educational leaders to reclaim their rightful role as intellectual activists promoting a democratic way of life and reminding society of the essential roles that schools play in supporting democracy.

From its earliest days, an underlying assumption behind public education has been that a well-educated citizenry is vital if democracy is to survive (Dewey, 1933). As a result, fledgling communities on the frontiers of American civilization took great pride in their local school. Schools represented progress and possibilities, and people believed that a community that had a school was a good place to live (Mathews, 2003). Over the past two centuries, this sense of pride in public schools has become muted, especially in communities where there are inequitable opportunities and resources. Public education, once viewed as one of the most important resources fueling America's growth, has become contested and politicized (Tyack & Cuban, 1995), and educational leaders have born the brunt of this changing perspective (Lugg, Buckley, Firestone, & Garner, 2002). Some of this criticism was well deserved, and some was not.

In this section of the *Handbook of Educational Leadership*, the authors invoke a sense of hope. Each chapter builds on the previous, moving us from the individual to the collective, and exhorts educational leaders to reach out to diverse communities. In the first chapter, Ira E. Bogotch reminds us of the tendency to take "original, exploratory, and controversial interpretations" and frame them as "fixed and uncontested," ignoring the complexities of the contexts in which these ideas originated. Throughout history, there has been a tendency to minimize the influence of time and place on events. We have become comfortable with stories of educational leaders who were bureaucrats and managers, creating factory-like hierarchies that met the educational needs of few. Bogotch brings a fresh perspective to our thinking about the history of educational leadership.

In his chapter, "A History of Public School Leadership: The First Century, 1837–1942," Bogotch tells the stories of six school leaders who were "knowledgeable educators, social, political, and community activists, system builders, and democrats with a small 'd,'" locating their stories in the context of their time. Although these men and women faced immense personal and professional challenges, they made a difference in the lives of many. We can learn a great deal about the leadership needs of today from these six educators. The personal and professional stakes have always been high for educational leaders, but in today's pro-business and "take care of your own" climate, the renewal of support for public education is even more essential. One way to work toward this reclamation is to have educational leaders who are purposeful, moral, and courageous. Bogotch identifies eight historical dimensions of school leadership that have deep implications for those of us who prepare and help develop future and current educational leaders.

Michael E. Dantley's chapter, "Moral Leadership: Shifting the Management Paradigm," begins by exploring the impacts of scientific management and modernism on education. The underlying assumptions inherent in these paradigms suggest that the only purpose of school is academic achievement. During the scientific management and modernist heydays, there was a perception that schools were a "frictionless environment" for educators. Dantley explains that modernism offered a sense of certainty and the belief that one could find the truth through objective means. There was an intensified focus on self-interest as a driving force, and people no longer weighed the consequences of injustices.

Once postmodernism crept into our ways of viewing the world, questions were increasingly asked about the hidden meanings and intentions of curricula, as well as the processes and structures of schools. Postmodernism encouraged the questioning of all that had once been considered sacred.

Dantley suggests that our current educational crisis is one of meaning and that school leaders must grapple with the social, political, and cultural contexts in which their schools exist. Emerging out of his response to this crisis is his call for purpose-driven and moral leadership. Dantley believes that schools can be sites where social change is birthed, but critical self-reflection and strategizing will be needed to resist the persistent policies, procedures, and organizational behaviors that foster and perpetuate the undemocratic status quo. Dantley sees leadership as a balance of the technical and moral, whereby educators have a moral responsibility to everyone in society. When this type of leadership is implemented, social justice can thrive and the needs of all can be better met.

In the third chapter, Alan R. Shoho, Betty M. Merchant, and Catherine A. Lugg encourage readers to consider what social justice really includes and how it should be defined. They note that references to social justice and equity at major conferences have greatly increased in the past two decades, but that there is little consensus about what social justice is, and many of these references have emphasized proponents being pitted against each other rather than working together. In their chapter, "Social Justice: Seeking a Common Language," they point out that social justice implies a valuing of diversity but that there is currently no common reference point for engaging in scholarly and practical dialogue about social justice. Implied within the concepts of social justice is a tension between meeting individual needs and ensuring the betterment of life for all. The authors explore the historical roots of social justice as a coined term and challenge each of us to create meaningful dialogues with all stakeholders. They conclude by leaving the definition of social justice open for interpretation, stating that perhaps the process of discussing what it means to those involved is what is really most important.

The final chapter in this section, "Collaborative Leadership, Community Building, and Democracy in Public Education," explores ways that meaningful relationships can be built with all stakeholders. In this chapter, we (Frances K. Kochan and Cynthia J. Reed) provide a comprehensive look at collaborative leadership and community building. The growth of the current high-stakes accountability environment has arisen at least in part because of a disconnect between schools and their communities, and we suggest that a greater emphasis on collaborative leadership and community engagement is required if we are to restore a sense of public trust in public education. Educators must move beyond engaging in collaborative leadership to build internal and external communities to support schools and participate in rebuilding the communities in which our schools operate. The responsibility for accomplishing these goals rests not only with preschool through 12 schools and their leaders, but also with educational leadership faculty, who must integrate these strategies into our teaching, outreach, and research. We call for school leaders to be reframed as community builders who can work with others to transcend "what is" and to create "what might be." Factors that facilitate and hinder community building, the types of leadership skills required, and implications for educational leadership programs are shared.

Collectively, the chapters in this section remind us that as the public has lost faith in its educational systems, there has been an accompanying shift in control from local to state agencies. Most recently, the national government has intervened in public education at an unprecedented level. The roles for both public education and governmental institutions have undergone a sea change. At one time, community members felt able to influence the policies and practices that were important to them. Now, there is a feeling of disconnect and even helplessness regarding most public institutions.

All of the chapters in this section address some aspect of this disconnect and challenge us to think deeply about who is included and who is excluded within our communities. Bogotch's eight historical dimensions for school leaders remind us of the fundamental political and educational goals for public schools. There must be greater emphasis on the intellectual aspects of educational leadership. Educational leaders must take the time to reflect on their work and share their thoughts with one another, as well as those outside the field of education. Like those great leaders in Bogotch's chapter, we must reclaim our traditional roles as thinkers and social activists and, through our actions, gain greater respect from the community. However, at the same time, we must be careful not to appear to be too all-knowing and removed from our communities.

The chapters provide numerous methods for engaging the community. Our chapter suggestions provide ideas about how to collaboratively engage community members in dialogue and action with educators. We suggest that educators must redefine what it means to be a professional educator in a way that is inclusive, not exclusive. Shoho, Merchant, and Lugg help us to think differently about who is part of our communities. Dantley's discussion of the historical role of rebellion and resistance, along with Bogotch's eight historical dimensions of leadership and our call for transcendent leaders, reminds us of the need for educational leaders to be "bold activists." We must embrace the wholeness of our beings, living our beliefs and modeling our commitments. As critically reflective educational leaders, we must think deeply about what it means to be an educator in today's contextual setting rather than simply accepting the roles being imposed on us through mandates created by others.

We live in a world of paradox and distrust. Many of us have become too focused on preparing students for the workforce rather than embracing the multiple purposes that public schools once served—and could again. We need to move beyond this transactional view of education—be good, do your work, and you'll get a good job—to a greater acceptance of the civic responsibilities we each have to one another. We can begin this process of building trust by taking actions such as deliberating with community members about the purposes of education, broadening our circle of dialogue participants, and making an effort to engage those whose voices we may not want to hear.

Those of us who are charged with the preparation of educational leaders should think about how we can influence these future leaders to pursue and enact practices and policies for the common good while not overlooking individual needs. As faculty members responsible for the development of educational leaders, we need to ensure that these leaders will have strong communication skills and the necessary social skills to create a welcoming environment for all stakeholders, giving them the tools they will need to become more involved in purposeful deliberations about the functions and expectations of schooling. The chapters in this section of the book dare educational leaders and the faculty members who prepare them to confront these challenges, engaging in intellectual pursuits and inquiry and becoming social activists concerned with creating and sustaining democratic leadership.

REFERENCES

Dewey, J. (1933). *Experience and education.* New York: MacMillan.

Lugg, C. A., Buckley, K., Firestone, W. A., & Garner, C. W. (2002). The contextual terrain facing educational leaders. In J. Murphy (Ed.), *The educational leadership challenge: Redefining leadership for the 21st century* (pp. 20–41). Chicago: University of Chicago Press.

Mathews, D. (2003). *Why public schools? Whose public schools?* Montgomery, AL: New South Books.

Tyack, D., & Cuban, L. (1995). *Tinkering toward utopia: A century of public school reform.* Cambridge, MA: Harvard University Press.

1

A History of Public School Leadership

The First Century, 1837–1942

IRA E. BOGOTCH
Florida Atlantic University

History can be a great teacher and motivator. As an academic discipline, history has traditionally been about the interpretation of known facts rather than a debate over the facts themselves. For every event, there are multiple interpretations as to meanings, causes, and effects, and it falls to the historian to make the case explaining why his or her particular interpretation should be accepted. The final responsibility, however, rests with readers, who must decide whether the history they are presented with is either trustworthy or relevant.

The history of school leadership is largely based on three recognized masterpieces: *Education and the Cult of Efficiency* (Callahan, 1962), *The One Best System* (Tyack, 1974), and *The Managerial Imperative and the Practice of Leadership in Schools* (Cuban, 1988). Based on original and secondary sources, Raymond Callahan (1962) tested and confirmed his hypothesis that public school leaders have been vulnerable to powerful

business and governmental forces throughout history. His conclusion, however, was that business was "an inadequate and inappropriate basis for establishing . . . educational policy" (p. viii). David Tyack (1974) also used original and secondary sources to support his exploratory and interpretative history of urban education, describing the continuous pursuit for the one best system in terms of educational policies and practices. He was aware, however, that the historical and sociological methods he used "[did] violence to the kaleidoscopic surface and hidden dynamics of everyday life" (p. 4) and urged others to engage in historical research. In his book, Larry Cuban (1988) offered readers a persuasive argument that teachers and administrators have more in common—in terms of instruction, management, and politics—than is acknowledged by their different roles and images. He held out hope that our profession's future could be different.

All three of these scholars offered original, exploratory, and controversial interpretations of the facts. Once published, however, these histories were no longer read as exploratory or tentative. The ideas and conclusions became fixed and uncontested. The modest claims actually made by each of the authors were ignored. Instead, their conclusions were repeated, synthesized, and appropriated into taxonomies of historical eras. Decades of school leadership practices were categorized by a single phrase or metaphor, while the complexities of daily life, the material realities and struggles faced by earlier school leaders, have largely been ignored.

It is not a sign of good health for any academic field or discipline to have an uncontested and unexamined history, especially when that field is education. Discussion and debate, as well as actions, invigorate the policies and practices of school leadership. Practically every contemporary problem has had a long and rich history of discussion and debate. Yet, many of us today will not even consider consulting the hard-earned experience of our predecessors when faced with a problem, whether it be adopting a new reading curriculum or deciding on the role of classroom testing or the scheduling of classes. Our own history seems to have no place at the school leadership and policy tables.

This chapter is merely a tentative step in this new direction. It is neither a complete nor an original history; as such, it does not attempt to compete with the classic texts. What it offers to readers, however, is a series of individual narratives of several very successful school leaders who lived and worked during the first century of public education in the United States. Individually and collectively, these narratives directly challenge the depiction of school leaders as dependent and vulnerable. The school leaders portrayed here demonstrated practices that are worthy of consideration today, particularly in linking schools to communities and school leadership to public service. The narratives describe school leaders who are knowledgeable educators; social,

political, and community activists; system builders; and democrats with a small "d." During the first century of public education, they saw the future of education and society as differing from existing practices and from reforms originating outside education. As their schools and school systems grew, they incorporated the increasing demands of fiscal and managerial duties into educational frameworks and challenged the dominant industrial models promoting centralization and standardization. As civic as well as educational leaders, their primary objectives were to educate children while promoting the social, political, and economic welfare of their neighborhoods and society as a whole. To a person, their actions were attacked by powerful elites and tradition-bound authorities, and these men and women suffered considerable personal and professional stress as a result. More times than not, however, they emerged victorious.

Some of these school leaders are well-known: Horace Mann and Ella Flagg Young; others you may be meeting for the first time: Cyrus Peirce, Angelo Patri, William Maxwell, and T. H. Harris. Their lives come to us from biographies, autobiographies, and their own journal writings and speeches, as well as from other histories, including the classics mentioned above. I have presented these school leaders in terms of their personal narratives, following the advice of the historian Barbara Tuchman. In her book of essays, *Practicing History* (1981), she argued against beginning any study of history with a preconceived theory. Rather, she urged both authors and readers to come to their own conclusions, independent of what other historians had written. She was wary of academic historians who often began their research with a theory already in mind. Her concern was that the theory itself might influence, intentionally or not, the selection of facts or the telling of history to fit the facts. I have tried to follow her advice on both of these counts: The historical data are first presented within the personal narratives, and the tentative theories of educational leadership that emerge are presented at the end of the chapter.

As I learned more about these individuals, I found it impossible to ignore the material conditions they faced or their daily struggles. However, as an author, I had to choose the particular stories and events to include in this chapter. In making my selections, I relied heavily on these leaders' own words first, those closest in time to the school leaders second, historical observations third, and my own conclusions last. I followed the advice of both Larry Cuban (1988) and Roland Barth (1990), who described the distance and difference between educational researchers and school practitioners. Both indicated that only practitioners who are active participants can "put practice into prose." Even as skilled a researcher as Cuban observed that "leadership occurs more frequently than believed [and] is largely unexamined by researchers" (p. 224). Logically, it is the struggles of school leaders, not the interpretations of researchers who seek to understand practice, that matter most here.

Although chronology helps us organize the historical facts, history is not governed solely by the order of events. By focusing on the first century of public education, 1837 to 1942, it is relatively easy to distinguish school leadership actions that have continued into the present from those actions that have been displaced in current practices. In examining earlier debates and practices, we may come to rediscover political strategies that successfully disrupted the status quo and allowed these school leaders to advance their diverse goals for public education. Every generation of school leaders must confront the dominant forces of tradition to move schools and school systems in new directions. To accomplish this objective of rediscovery, the French historian Michel Foucault (1972) offers a method of historical analysis that can help us question the apparent inevitability and common sense of current practices.

Perhaps the most significant of all current practices has been the managerial trend toward business values that has dominated educational administration for some time. A search of historical records shows that from the outset, school leaders and university professors of educational leadership questioned the claims made by efficiency experts who were touting data-driven decision making and scientific management. During the first decades of the 20th century, New York City School Superintendent William Maxwell expressed fears that the new approach would turn teachers and administrators into mere record keepers. His views on education, and especially accountability, were pragmatic; if the information, including test data, was of no use to an experienced teacher, then why collect the data in the first place? Many of the educators you will meet in this chapter debated the merits of standardized teaching methods and testing regimes—recurring reforms throughout the history of education. These issues have been at the forefront of educational reform from the beginning. It is safe to say that today's emphasis on prescriptive pedagogical methods, standardized testing, and data-driven decision making would not have been favored by the school leaders you will meet here. What were their responses to similar situations? Would their strategies work today? Were they right? I will provide some of the historical evidence in this chapter; you, as educational leaders, will have to decide whether or not their actions will influence your future actions.

While the leadership-management debate has occupied the forefront of discussion and debate, what is also obvious about yesterday's school leaders is their intellectual mastery of curriculum and instruction. These individuals were first and foremost educators who used management as a tool in the service of teaching and learning. Their knowledge base was not centered on the latest business practices. They were articulate spokespeople for curricular reform across all subject areas and instructional methods. Toward the end of the first century of public schooling, however, they were beginning to deal with the emerging trends of business and management. Many fought back. In 1929, Clarence Stone, a disciple of Professor Ellwood Cubberley, wrote:

> In the midst of a multiplicity of managerial and professional duties the easiest road for one lacking in professional training and large vision is to give first attention to the managerial duties, and to the routine, the imperative, and the emergency duties. (p. 28)

The distinction Stone made between professional training and large vision on one hand and managerial duties on the other was not uncommon among principals and superintendents at the time. Even the most vocal advocate for applying the principles of scientific management to education, Dr. Franklin Bobbitt (1913), argued that to keep the profession of teaching fresh, teachers needed to become active participants in community affairs. The main purpose of scientific management, in his judgment, was to free up time during the day for teachers to visit other teachers, explore school neighborhoods, and learn about the outside lives of their students.

The writings of leaders such as Stone and Bobbitt indicate why it does not serve education well to limit ourselves to a fixed history based on unitary concepts (Foucault, 1972) or to see school leadership as having one definitive history (Zinn, 1998). In rejecting an ordered view of history, however, the academic discipline of history itself becomes more complex, making it difficult for readers to extract clear and exact lessons from past practices. That complexity is revealed in the multiple realities of school leaders' lives. It also may explain why school leaders within the same school or same school system may come to different conclusions when presented with the same evidence and why some support current practices, routines, and procedural rules while others do not. The essence of leadership always resides within the strategic and contextual choices made by individual school leaders. Without continual discussions and debates, policies and decisions fall victim to tradition and authority—the two sources of power challenged by first-century school leaders.

What is at stake here is more than a chapter on school leadership history. When a field of study believes that it already has a complete picture of itself, its members tend to justify their ideas and actions in relation to that fixed history. There is no pressing need to seek out alternative explanations or to ask questions critical of current practices so long as connections to the past are affirmed. Right actions and progress are thus understood in terms of past practices, traditions, and authority. Those in charge may become complacent, if not with details or technical improvement issues, then with the overall direction of the school or school system. Fewer questions are permitted; problems are seen as bumps in the road to be overcome, rather than as evidence of a need to consider new directions. These static dispositions are neither educational nor leader-like.

In contrast, one self-reflective public school leader you will meet in this chapter characterized his own leadership journey in the following self-reflective monologue:

> "How did you begin?"
> I don't know exactly how I began. I began as so many others did without realizing that I was beginning anything unusual. I began slowly, hesitatingly making many mistakes as I went.
> "How did you begin?"
> Does not the very question try to force a tabulated, logically arranged answer that may be applied like a formula to any situation? Is it not more important to know why the school began, and how the work grew, and the value of what the school learned while it was growing? (Patri, 1917, p. 85)

Here, then, are the lives of six very different public school leaders who built and rebuilt systems of education and understood the need to make educational changes and master politics. They embraced their social contexts and cultures and the importance of communities to children and schooling. For each of them, there could be no real school improvement without educating teachers, children, and their communities—all of society. These school leaders did not let tradition for the sake of tradition or school system structures constrain their actions. They refused to be "helpless in opposition," to quote T. H. Harris of Louisiana (1963, p. 169.). Each of these school leaders experienced political pressure, personal vendettas, and public ridicule. They fought back as educators, but when necessary they were prepared to walk away from a conflict when there was no room left to grow. Their lives were not studies in vulnerability, nor were they supplicants of a nameless, faceless system.

A SYSTEM OF PUBLIC SCHOOLS: THE FIRST CENTURY, 1837–1942

The first century, 1837 to 1942, was a century of dramatic growth and change for both schools and school leadership.[1] There were public schools in the United States prior to the 1830s, but they functioned locally and autonomously across the country. Towns and municipalities were responsible for hiring and firing teachers and for securing funds to build and support their own schools. It was common in towns and villages throughout the United States to see schoolteachers come and go every 10 months, sometimes more often (Butts & Cremins, 1962; Johnson, 1907). In the 1904 novel, *Jean Mitchell's School,* we read about 45 to 50 students, boys and girls of all ages and sizes, in a one-room schoolhouse.[2] "The windows were barricaded with heavy shutters. Through the open door glimpses of the dingy room within could be plainly seen from the road" (Wray, 1904, p. 18). Describing the same period, Harris (1963) reported that country schools were in a deplorable condition, "cheap and crude," with

ignorant teachers using "barbarous methods of teaching" (p. 158).

Newell Gilbert (1904), a professor at the DeKalb, Illinois, Normal School, wrote in his commentary to Wray's novel:

> The low ideals of the villagers and their failure to comprehend the teaching of children finds striking expression in the school premises. Barren and uninteresting without, dingy and forbidding within, the schoolhouse spoke of ignorance, of lack of thought, of abandonment to untoward conditions, that found reflection in the pupils' attitude. Rude, hostile, indifferent, disorganized, these children are altogether too sophisticated in the art of guile and deceit, in evasion and resistance, in disobedience and successful rebellion. Anarchy names correctly the condition which essentially exists. But this is not a condition native to these boys and girls; they are not innately bad. They are the inevitable product of the education to which they have been given over. (p. 8)

Even though public sentiment varied over the level of support for public schools, the principles of free schools, citizen education, and equitable taxation had been addressed in the framing of state constitutions, as well as in the U.S. Congress. The voices were contentious, however, especially when it came to taxes. In 1809, De Witt Clinton "argued against local taxation for the support of public schools on the ground that such taxation would set the people against education" (Maxwell, 1912, p. 306). In 1820, statesman and orator Daniel Webster argued that public schools serve all the people, not just those with children who benefit from public schools. "We hold every man subject to taxation in proportion to his property, and we look not to the question whether he himself have or have not children to be benefited by the education for which he pays" (Webster, cited in Butler, 1915, p. 338).

This politically contentious environment is where the story of school leadership began and continues to this day.

THE LIVES OF SCHOOL LEADERS

The Stories of Horace Mann and Cyrus Peirce

Like Thomas Jefferson before him, Horace Mann dreamed of something more than abstract principles of education. He left a career in law and politics to build a *system* of public schools, becoming the first Secretary of the State Board of Education in Massachusetts in June 1837. Most of his friends thought him a fool for taking up the cause of education, but to Mann, "The interests of a client are small compared to the interests of the next generation. Let the next generation be my client" (Tharp, 1953, p. 136). His earlier training, however, served him well, for as soon as he took up the cause of the *common schools,* Mann became the target of vicious personal and professional attacks that would continue as long as he remained in public education.

The first wave of controversy surrounded the doctrine of separation between church and state in public schools. Ten years before he took office, Massachusetts had passed such a law. Mann was a strong supporter and saw to it that the normal school curriculum and books in the first school libraries followed that doctrine. As a result, both he and his budding school system were attacked as being antireligious. According to educational historians Butts and Cremins (1962), "He was accused of conducting godless, immoral schools which bred delinquency and vice" (p. 273). Mann was savagely attacked by extreme orthodox religious leaders, who saw the future of secular schools as a threat to traditional ideas that equated morality with religion. Other attacks came from legislators, who believed that the entire common school experiment was too costly for the public to finance, and even from the Association of Masters of the Boston Public Schools, who vehemently disagreed with Mann's views on teaching, curriculum, and student discipline. Butts and Cremins (1962) wrote that the educational opposition believed that "authority . . . not love, must be the backbone of the teacher-student tie" (p. 220). As if this three-pronged attack was not enough, in an ironic turnabout, the very strata of society Mann hoped to serve, the poor immigrant groups, also opposed public education. Their opposition focused on the laws of compulsory attendance, which prevented their children from earning the extra money that these immigrant families so desperately needed.

In the face of all opposition, Mann persevered and continued to build a system of public education in Massachusetts. Structurally, it began with the building of the first normal school, that is, a school designed to board and train aspiring teachers. He found a vacant building in the village of Lexington that needed "carpentering, painting and whitewashing, all tasks to be completed by the first principal" (Tharp, 1953, p. 152). However, that was just the beginning. Mann not only had to lobby the state for public funding, but also had to raise additional private funds. In fact, throughout his career in public education, both he and his colleague, Cyrus Peirce, had to use their personal funds to keep various educational projects moving forward. Parenthetically, both men started (and ended) their careers earning the same state salary of $1,500 a year.

Mann hired Cyrus Peirce to be the first principal of the Lexington Normal School. Mann initially offered the position to several individuals with religious backgrounds. Although that might seem odd given his views on the separation of church and state, the candidates were highly esteemed educators who would be able to buffer the extreme orthodox attacks on public education. Mann first approached Thomas Gallaudet, a prominent educator and founder of a successful school for the deaf, but Gallaudet declined. Mann then offered the position to the Reverend Jacob Abbott, who also said no. Mann went on to offer the position to three other religious men, with the same negative responses, before turning to his longtime supporter and the principal of the

Nantucket High School, Cyrus Peirce—his sixth choice—to become the first normal-school principal in the nation. Peirce agreed to become not only the principal but also the sole lecturer, director of the model school, and janitor (Tharp, 1953, p. 152). As the date of the new school's opening approached, there were delays in the delivery of books, maps, and globes, along with a new innovation called a blackboard. Thus, instead of opening on April 19, the anniversary of the Battle of Lexington, the first normal school opened 2½ months late on July 2, 1839.

From Peirce's 1839 journal entries, his work-day combined teaching and teacher training. Peirce would teach at the normal school from 8 to 9 a.m., then go to the model school with his normal-school students and teach there from 9 to 11 a.m. At 11, the model school recessed until 1 p.m. The afternoon session went from 1 to 3 p.m. Normal school recessed from 11 a.m. until noon and then continued until 5 p.m.

> As for Cyrus Peirce, he recessed never. He rose before dawn to set the fires going in the cast-iron stoves in his little school building, and in winter he arose at intervals all night to keep the stoves going. He sat late over his desk, writing down the events of the day, and the progress of the great experiment. (Tharp, 1953, p. 156)

In another entry, Peirce described his students: "The school now consists of twelve scholars [all young ladies]. They seem industrious and interested; and nearly every one of *fair* [original emphasis] capacity. But many of them are yet backward . . . they want [i.e., lack] language—they want the power of generalization and communication" (Peirce's diary, quoted in Tharp, 1953, p. 154). The students were neither good readers nor good spellers, nor did they know much arithmetic and grammar. Still, it was Peirce's goal to educate them into becoming outstanding teachers.

In addition to opening the Lexington Normal School and two others in the state, Horace

Mann started a publication called the *Common School Journal*. Much of what we know about these first years of public schooling comes from Mann's writings and speeches, which were printed in the journal. However, the journal served a more immediate and important leadership function: Mann used communications and the media to fight back against his opponents, specifically through "public meetings, county institutes of teachers, annual reports to the legislature, and a biweekly publication" (Butts & Cremins, 1962, p. 256).

In the first issue (in November 1838), Mann wrote:

> None of you is so high as not to need the education of the people as a safeguard; none of you is so low to be beneath its lifting power. . . . There is a certainty about their [i.e., immigrants's] political and social powers—while there is a contingency depending upon the education they receive—whether these powers will be exercised for weal or woe. (quoted in Tharp, 1953, pp. 159–160)

In this journal issue, Mann referred specifically to the Irish railroad workers, people who, along with other hard-working but poor immigrants, helped build the country. "It is impossible for us to pay them in kind; but there is a compensation . . . which we have the ability to bestow. We can confer the blessing of education upon their children" (Tharp, 1953, pp. 159–160).

When it came to the topic of the common school, Horace Mann spoke with the same passion, if not religious fervor, as his opponents. In a speech in Boston on the Fourth of July, 1842, he said, "Select schools for select children should be discarded. Instead of the old order of nobility, a new order should be created—an order of Teachers, wise, benevolent, filled with Christian enthusiasm and rewarded and honored by all" (Tharp, 1953, pp. 177–178). Mann did not remain in public education until his retirement. He returned to politics and later became the president of Antioch College.

The Story of Ella Flagg Young

Ella Flagg Young began teaching in 1862 at the age of 17. The physical conditions of Chicago schools were not unlike those described for the rural schools of the period: poor equipment, lack of ventilation, and over-crowding.[3] Young's rise into administration, however, was rapid. By her second year, she was named head assistant and 2 years later became principal of a new "practice school" of the City Normal School. Like Peirce, Young took her duties in teacher training very seri-ously. Not every student was fit to become a teacher, she thought. Her actions eventually led to a conflict with a member of the school board, one of whose constituents objected to a student's dismissal from the practice school. In 1871, after 6 years as principal, Young requested a transfer back into teaching, this time at the high school level.

Her next opportunity as principal came in 1876. The leadership of her school, and later her district, focused on teaching methods and democratic decision making, aiming to raise teaching standards and build a broad, flexible curriculum. Based on her own experience, Young was convinced that teaching and testing could not be made into mechanical processes. "Many methods were like the mechanics in military drills but wholly unsuited to the play of thought" (Young, cited in McManis, 1916, p. 21). "Instead of having a 'method' of solving problems, a common practice among princi-pals, in teaching this subject, [Young] had as many methods as there were teachers in her school" (McManis, p. 60). As for classroom noise, "it never troubled her in a room if by it children were getting something done" (p. 68). "In faculty meetings, Mrs. Young insisted on discussions giving free play to ideas of each person, and never attempted to domi-nate minds and independence of the teacher" (pp. 60–61). She consulted, but did not direct:

[She] championed the cause of the teachers and democracy as opposed to methods which administered schools from the top, regardless of the ideas of the teachers. She refused to work under a regime which reduced school work to the lines of a busi-ness corporation and made mere tools and clerks of teachers and principals and assis-tant superintendents. (p. 96)

As principal, Young supported "newer" subjects, such as singing, drawing, clay model-ing, and gymnastics, and she insisted that her teachers participate in community activities; to Young, it was not enough that teachers knew their books if they "didn't know life outside" (McManis, 1916, p. 157). She herself was active in the surrounding neighborhoods promoting the benefits of elementary education and voca-tional guidance. Like Mann and John Dewey, she believed that schools had a larger role in society, and that meant she had to learn about political methods and engage in local city poli-tics (McManis, 1916).

In 1887, Ella Flagg Young was promoted to assistant superintendent in the Chicago school system. That year, she also gave an address, the first of many, at the conference of the National Educational Association, an organi-zation that brought together superintendents, professors, and college presidents to discuss the significant educational issues of the day. Young admired William T. Harris, school superintendent of St. Louis, and read his annual *Superintendent Reports* as her profes-sional literature. In fact, ever since the days of Horace Mann, annual reports of superinten-dents had been referred to as the most schol-arly discussions on education in the country. Young's own NEA addresses, monographs, and reports were no exception. Intellectually, she was the peer of Dewey and William James, both of whom she invited to speak to the teachers of the Chicago school district.

Just as some teaching methods had reduced the independent thinking of teachers, so, too, the centralization and business management practices reduced the independent thinking of public school administrators. These reforms came to Chicago in 1897. Two years later, Young once again resigned from a position "which hampered her and gave her no freedom for growth" (McManis, 1916, p. 51). Her critique of education was not limited to its mechanistic teaching methods and centralized business practices. Young recognized that public schools faced other obstacles: from parents, who wanted the same education for their children that they had received long ago; from taxpayers, who wanted the least expensive curriculum to ease their tax burdens; and from educators themselves, who wanted to keep schools "aloof from the life of society" (p. 82). Implicit in this criticism, however, was an understanding that schools were bound to past traditions and culture.

The Practitioner and the Professor: Two Scholars

Young's resignation from the Chicago school system in 1899 allowed her to accept an offer from Dewey to become both a student and instructor at the University of Chicago. She took courses in philosophy while at the same time advising Dewey on the development and operation of the university's laboratory school. Working together, these two great educators wrote six monographs. When Dewey left the University of Chicago because of a conflict with its president over the running of the laboratory school, so did Young. She returned to the Chicago school system to head the City Normal School. Once again, Young emphasized the free and independent judgment of faculty and students. That said, she had a reputation for being outspoken and would "not hesitate to tell the individual or the faculty what she thought on a question or issue" (McManis, 1916, p. 142).

Controversy as Superintendent

Her tenure as superintendent began in 1909 and ended in 1916. The last 3 years were stormy due to controversies ranging from textbook selection to teacher unions to the selection and purchase of building sites. Young actually resigned in 1913 but agreed to stay on when the school board refused to accept her resignation. In later years, she openly regretted that decision because as she wrote, "I violated one of my pet theories. . . . [W]hen a person resigns he should never go back to the position" (McManis, 1916, p. 166). In her last few superintendent reports, she returned to the most significant themes of her career: democracy, teachers, and a diverse curriculum. Young never would accept a

> school system [that] lacked confidence in the ability of the teachers to be active participants in planning its aims and methods. . . . Why talk about the public schools as an indispensable requisite of a democracy and then conduct it as a prop of an aristocracy? (p. 198)

At every level, Ella Flagg Young was a democratic leader. On her retirement, the *American School Board Journal* praised her leadership while acknowledging the prejudices she had encountered throughout her career as a woman:

> Mrs. Young was easily equal, if not superior, to the able men who preceded her in the Chicago Superintendency. She endured "personal political" conflicts. Beneath and behind many of the "school troubles" which arose, particularly during the past three years, there was a silent opposition and resentment that can only be explained as the basis of an unconscious assumption of male superiority. (1916, p. 26).

The Story of William Maxwell

For a quarter of a century, beginning in the 1890s, Dr. William H. Maxwell was a big-city district superintendent in Brooklyn and New York City. Like Mann and Young, he was of the generation of educators who combined leadership with both scholarship and public service. He wrote about all aspects of school and district leadership. Of one reformer who was advocating high-stakes standardized testing—the latest educational reform of that era—Maxwell wrote (in 1916): "One flash of Horace Mann's insight would be worth a thousand miles of your statistics" (cited in Callahan, 1962, p. 122). Like Young before him, Maxwell argued vigorously that scientific management (i.e., the cult of efficiency) and its excessive demands for data-driven decisions would turn teachers into bookkeepers. It was not that Maxwell opposed testing, accountability, and efficiency, but rather he opposed wasting teachers' time and importing the latest fashions in business practice into education. He believed that tests should be pragmatic; that is, he judged a test's value by whether or not it provided new information to experienced teachers. As for efficiency, Maxwell argued that the ultimate end or measure of a successful education was what a student went on to do in her or his adult life. T. H. Harris in Louisiana would later come to the same conclusion. However, according to Callahan (1962), few educational leaders at the time dared to speak out as vociferously as Maxwell did against big business and the direction being taken by school leadership. Maxwell wrote of the great problems facing education and the duties of school principals in an 1892 report (included in Maxwell, 1912) and his conclusions are summarized in the next section.

Problems Facing Education

Every solution proposed involved an increased expenditure of money. Immeasurably more effective, however, than money—vital though money is—to uplift the school, are the love and skill of the devoted teacher (Maxwell, 1912, p. 345). Love for children and teaching skill, to his mind, are the greatest things in a school.

Maxwell (1912) argued that it was a school leader's responsibility to communicate the function of public schooling to the general public. The responsibilities included

- providing educational opportunities for all citizens to enable them to make a living (p. 321);
- providing an education of the highest quality, by which he meant not an equal education, but rather an education appropriate to the differences in intellect among all children (p. 322);
- providing an education that reflects the spiritual inheritances of the different races and cultures, including the scientific, literary, artistic, institutional, and religious contributions that diverse communities make to our society. "As education is the work of the school, it is obviously, then, its function to introduce the child to his spiritual inheritances," Maxwell said (p. 333), both in mind and body.

As the school superintendent in New York City, Maxwell described the difficulties of providing adequate physical education where there is a lack of space. He related the problems of play and athletics to the lack of after-school activities, citing the crowded tenement house as an evil that "must be eradicated" (Maxwell, 1912, p. 326). As an educational leader, he argued passionately for better housing for the poor:

> The school should and must at all waking hours do all that its resources permit. To supply what the home, even under the most favorable conditions, loses by moving from agricultural to urban life; but if the home and its whole influences are not to be obliterated among the city poor, the city must see to it that the so-called working classes are enabled to live in homes where homely virtues have a chance to flourish and where children have space to play. (Maxwell, 1912, p. 328)

Although Maxwell may not have succeeded with every aspect of this ambitious agenda, he was successful in changing the physical structures of schools. The new schools in New York were "the finest in this or any other land—great, light, and airy structures, with playgrounds on the roof—all over the city . . . never one [school] shall be built without its playground (Riis, 1899/1957, p. 240). Maxwell's (1912) broad social agenda was open to the charge of paternalism. He responded, "It is justified when private initiative fails to root out an evil that is sapping the vitality of the nation at its root, the home life of the people" (p. 327). Of the many in-school programs he initiated, one was to feed school children: "What a farce it is to talk of the schools providing equal opportunities for all when there are hundreds of thousands of children in our city schools who cannot learn because they are always hungry!" (p. 328). In an era of extreme poverty, the policy should be to feed children "well-cooked food at cost price" (p. 402).

Maxwell (1912) attributed weaknesses in curriculum and instruction to two facts:

> first, that teachers were not as well educated or trained as they are today; and second, that in the absence of interesting subject matter, they required pupils to commit to memory dry and useless details in order to fill up the prescribed time. (p. 333)

He proposed a curriculum based on children having "a progressive knowledge of the outside world" (p. 333). From algebra to geometry, he thought the emphasis should be on solving problems and invention; from language and literature, art to manual training and physical exercises, the emphasis should be on real life experiences, not ordinary reading, writing, and drawing exercises. He also pushed for subject areas to be taught thematically.

But always, it was the lack of an adequate budget that created educational problems. Maxwell approached the budget from two perspectives: cost-effectiveness and educational value. Given his educational arguments that schools needed to function inside of society, he embraced the idea of keeping schools open longer hours. At first, he uncritically accepted the analogy of a factory: the longer the hours a factory is in operation, the higher the productivity. Why not schools? After implementing this reform in New York City, however, Maxwell found that this was not cost-effective. Factories could show a

definite increase in productivity for the added costs of staying open longer, but schools could not. In education, the costs resided always on the inputs, not outcomes. Thus, he reversed his position on this reform.[4]

During his tenure, Maxwell found himself in a serious budget controversy with the New York City comptroller. The issue was music education. Maxwell (1912) argued that:

> In a school that has good music are almost certain to be found good discipline, good results in other studies, and an inspiring school spirit. These statements are elementary. To abolish its teaching in the New York school, or even to reduce the small amount of time now devoted to it, would be a disgrace to our city. Perhaps, however, Comptroller Grout would not abolish it, but would simply discharge the special teachers of music. But experience has amply demonstrated that music cannot be successfully taught without the aid of specially trained music teachers. (p. 59)

Maxwell compared the costs of music instruction in New York (15 cents per pupil) with those in Boston (22 cents per pupil) and Providence (30 cents per pupil). He concluded:

> Under these circumstances, your committee cannot recommend either the abolition of the teaching of music or a reduction in the corps of music teachers. Comptroller Grout made no opposition last summer to the spending of $48,663.50 for music in the parks to entertain the public; why does he begrudge $72,000 to teach six hundred thousand children to sing? (p. 59)

A generation later, T. H. Harris of Louisiana would face a similar dilemma regarding the importance of teaching of music (and art) without receiving adequate funding.

Duties of the Principal

The roles of superintendents and principals are continuously changing, especially with respect to supervising instruction. Maxwell (1912) complained that "our schools are suffering from the presence of too many supervisors that are relieved from the work of teaching. And yet in many of our schools the supervision is neither of the right quality nor sufficient in quantity" (p. 16). By supervision, Maxwell meant:

> [The principal] should know the plan of work in every class. He should know exactly what every teacher is teaching and how she is teaching it. These two things he may find out by inspection and examinations; not stated examinations, but sporadic tests used as elements in teaching. The principal who has to wait until the end of a month or the end of a year to determine by a written examination whether a given stint of work has been accomplished, is lazy and inefficient. The stated monthly examination by the principal is probably responsible for more machine teaching, more injurious cramming, than all other causes combined. . . . The principal's inspection should be hourly, daily. In it, or in allied work, he should spend his entire time during school hours. . . . [T]he keeping of records and the like should be done outside of the regular school hours. (pp. 19–20)

The objective in every principal-teacher interaction was to instill in every teacher the ability to "think for herself and to discover truth for herself" (Maxwell, 1912, p. 22); otherwise, how can the teacher teach pupils to think for themselves? Maxwell asked. The greatest danger and the one Maxwell saw most frequently in principals' practice was when they turned teachers into "mere machines" by demanding that teachers do everything exactly as it is prescribed. Maxwell announced "the first duty of the superintendent," that is, to "step in and secure to the class teacher that reasonable liberty of thought and action, without which no teaching can be effective" (p. 24).

Although the managerial duties of the principal could not be ignored, especially school safety and sanitation, Maxwell saw human relationships and educational judgments as the primary duties of the principal. Principals must ensure that the children with special needs, physical or otherwise, were properly diagnosed and placed in appropriate classes.

> He should endeavor, with the aid of his teachers, to discover particular aptitudes and talents in his pupils and should advise with pupils and their parents as to the most fruitful course of education work. . . . There is no man in the community who can do so much to insure the right distribution of talent as the schoolmaster, if he will but study his pupils and give honest advice to parents. (Maxwell, 1912, pp. 17–18)

For Maxwell, educational accountability was a daily—if not hourly—school leadership responsibility, whose success could only be judged in terms of a productive citizen's life.

The Story of Angelo Patri

For most of his career, which covered the first half of the 20th century, Angelo Patri was an elementary and middle school principal in District 99 in New York City. Throughout his long, distinguished career, he demonstrated the ability to continuously learn on the job, to adapt to the changing dynamics inside and outside of his school, and to begin again.[5] His is a story of leadership as service as he worked to transform his school into the community's school.

Patri the Teacher

Patri's (1917) account of his first day as a teacher is chilling. His principal led him to a classroom:

> He opened the door and pushed me in saying, "This is your class." Then he vanished. There were sixty-six children in that room. Their ages ran from eight to fifteen. They had been sitting there daily annoying the substitutes who were sent to the room and driving them out of school. The cordial reception I had been given by the principal

held more of a relief for himself than of kindness for me. That first day passed.

"Coming back tomorrow?" a student asked.

"Yes, of course I am coming back. Why do you ask?" (p. 6)

Patri (1917) admitted that he was not strong in subject matter knowledge, pedagogy, or psychology. What he was strong in was discipline, which he had learned from his own experiences as a pupil, being disciplined "all the ten years of my life in school" (p. 7). Fortunately, that was (and often still is):

the standard for judging my work as a teacher. My continuance in the profession depended upon discipline. . . . At the end of my first month I was an assured success. My discipline of the class and the promptness with which I followed up the absentees gained recognition. I was promoted from teaching a fourth-year class to a fifth-year class. The new class was made for me especially because I was efficient. It was composed of all the children that the other teachers in approximate grades did not want. They were fifty misfits. (pp. 7–8)

Patri (1917) soon found that discipline, at least his methods of discipline, did not work with "those who defied discipline. . . . What was I to do?" (p. 9). He began, not unlike the fictional Miss Jean Mitchell (Wray, 1904), to tell the children stories of his childhood in the mountains of Italy. The pupils listened, and each day, Patri would end "so that more could be expected" (p. 10). Thus, he would bargain and trade: a story for a subject that the school said had to be taught.

"Then a new trouble arose," Patri (1917) said. It was the imposition of a "method book." The principal and supervisors would inspect and unless the class was taught in a specific way—that is, "'Class, open books to page 37.' . . . Two minutes later, 'Close books. Tell me what you learned'" (p. 11), the teacher would be criticized. Instead of teaching, the game became one of pleasing the supervisor.

After 2 years, Patri became depressed and left. Like Young, he turned to higher education, but all he received his first year were "words, words, words . . . so far away, so ineffectual, so dead" (Patri, 1917, p. 14). Then he took a course with Professor Frank McMurry, who used a text titled, *Ethical Principles*,[6] by John Dewey (1909). For the first time in Patri's life, he saw words that implied action, not the passivity defined by school learning. To him, action meant freedom, not compliance. Moreover:

The knowledge gained had to be used immediately and the worth of the knowledge judged by its fitness to the immediate needs of the child. . . . I realized then that the child must move and not sit still: that he must make mistakes and not merely repeat perfect forms: that he must be himself and not a miniature reproduction of the teacher. The sacredness of the child's individuality must be the moving passion of the teacher. . . . Under this leadership I came in touch with vital ideas and I began to work not in the spirit of passive obedience, but in one of mental emancipation. (Patri, 1917, pp. 14–16)

When Patri (1917) returned to the classroom, his supervisors objected. "You'll find those things may be all right in theory but they will not do in practice" (p. 16), they told him. Once again, Patri left. At his next school, his principal was the exact opposite—he "actually loved school children" (p. 18). Patri took inspiration from this principal, but he was quickly promoted to a high school where the teachers—not the students—moved from class to class for fear of noise and confusion. Within 2 months, Patri transferred schools again. On meeting Patri, his new principal said,

Why, this won't do, you don't want to come here. You are only a boy. You are not old enough nor strong enough! The boys in that corner room broke the teacher's eyeglasses and he was a bigger man than you are."[7] (p. 21)

The school was a failing school, where:

> The children were afraid of the teachers,
> and the teachers feared the children. . . . The
> antagonism between the school and the
> neighborhood was intense. Both came from
> mutual distrust found on mutual misunder-
> standing. . . . There was no attempt on the
> part of the school to understand the prob-
> lem and to direct the lives of the pupils.
> In fact, teaching the curriculum was the
> routine business of the day—no more. There
> was apparently little affection for the
> children, and no interest in the parents as
> co-workers in their education. (pp. 21–23)

Fortunately, the principal put Patri in charge
of assembly exercises and school discipline.
Here, at last, was an opportunity to put his
knowledge to practice and test himself as an
educator. Patri set up student discipline councils and gradually shifted the responsibility of
school discipline to the students themselves.
In so doing, he regained his confidence in
children, in the power of the school, and in
himself. His next promotion was to the position
of principal.

A Schoolmaster of the Great City[8]

The reality was not what Patri (1917)
expected:

> From six entrances the children surged
> through the halls and into their classrooms.
> I had a blurred impression of sound, and color
> and motion and many, many children and
> teachers all going swiftly by. I saw no individ-
> ual faces, no distinct forms, just the great mass
> surging past. Stunned and bewildered I stood
> where I was until I realized that a great silence
> had settled over the building. The big school
> had begun its day's work and begun it without
> me. I sat down at my desk because I didn't
> know what else to do. . . . The next day was
> the same—and the next! (pp. 25–26)

Patri (1917) found a uniformity of instruction as he moved from classroom to classroom. Student drawings were all alike (p. 45)

as were their compositions—all with the same
topic and the same number of paragraphs
(p. 43). All the subjects—the three R's—were
aligned and sequenced, formalized and logical.
It was not what Patri had envisioned. Nor did
he find any difference among the parents.
"Parents have been trained as [have] the
teachers, to think of school as a place where
the children are made to obey, to memorize,
made to repeat lessons" (p. 50).

As Patri (1917) became more accustomed to
being principal, he became aware of other serious problems: the horrific living conditions
inside the tenement buildings, the abject
poverty of the families and children, the lack
of jobs, truancy, gang violence in the neighborhood, convoluted feeder patterns and school
boundaries, little parental involvement, overcrowding, student discipline, student mobility,[9]
special classes,[10] and the regular fixed school
curriculum that never stayed "with a beautiful
idea long enough to have it become part of the
children's lives" (p. 162). He divided the problems into two categories: the community and
the school. In many instances, he saw that neither the community nor the school would own
the problem (p. 67), and if only one addressed
a problem, it could not solve it (pp. 83–84).

At first, Patri (1917) looked to the local
school board and central school officials for
help. He later recalled the advice of the school's
kindly old janitor: "Don't stir them up. . . . I've
been in this business for thirty years and I have
found stirring them up won't do. If they say it
is raining, put up your umbrella, but don't stir
them up" (p. 61). When Patri told a member of
the school board how the school boundaries
were causing hardships to many families with
multiple children, he was rebuked.

> What's the matter with you anyway? You're
> not playing the game. You knew this was
> a six-year school when you came to it. Then
> as soon as you get here you begin stirring
> up trouble. You're only a beginner, you'll
> get your full school when your turn comes.
> (pp. 61–62)

The First Parent Association

The next steps were political. Patri (1917) asked teachers and parents to form an association. He would organize a constituency and "get a reputation" (p. 104). But even that step was not enough. According to school law, an outside group could meet only four times a year at a school. To the parents, school issues demanded more frequent meetings. To persuade the board to change the rules, the association decided to put someone from the school on the board. Up until then, no member of the board had a child attending the school. Once that was accomplished, the association held their meetings monthly.

At first, Patri allowed the parents and the teachers to decide the agenda of the association. They set up committees according to individuals' interests. But soon, each committee came to him for his support, arguing that their particular issue was the most important one for the school. Because of the parent-community association, the school was now in danger of being pulled apart by competing interests. Patri's leadership lay in his ability to find a unifying answer that fit the demands of the moment—but then when conditions changed, he could begin again with a different unifying answer to meet the new conditions.

At the same time, other schools took notice of what was happening at Patri's school.

> This is getting to be a big thing, the President of the association said. A parent's association in every school! That's a big idea. I have been thinking of it for some time. What do you think of making a statement of policies? (Patri, 1917, p. 113)

The idea of parent associations had caught on in New York City.

Community Welfare

Perhaps the most far-reaching of the many standing committees of the association was one that "investigated cases of parental neglect, cases of need, [and] cases of truancy" (Patri, 1917, p. 108). It was called the relief committee, and its mandate ranged from providing parents with information on hygiene, clothes, medicine, groceries, and money (in the form of loans) to looking for jobs. The committee announcement read:

> Charity is not the primary object of the association. We are not here to make parents careless and dependent. Our object is to help children and this we try to do, though helping them we bring pressure to bear upon the parents to help their own. (p. 111)

Over time, the relief committee joined forces with a local branch of the settlement house. In a statement that summarizes Patri's educational philosophy, he wrote:

> We looked upon the settlement as a moving living force whose idea was one of service and not of power. Free from tradition, we felt that it would be the neighborhood social experimentation station, finding out, working out, and then beginning again, never stopping long enough to standardize. (p. 134)

As ever, Patri (1917) fought to release schools from "the grip of tradition, rules, records, and endless routine" (p. 196). His leadership was a dynamic and constant struggle to "vitalize the curriculum by means of first hand experiences or to push the classroom out into the world" (p. 157), constantly asking "Would the school be equal to the task of keeping the social forces working together, the children always as the center of the effort?" (p. 153).

The Story of T. H. Harris

T. H. Harris completed his memoirs in 1941, a year after his retirement as state superintendent of Louisiana, although they were not published until 1963 because it was not his intention to wound or embarrass anyone. He kept that part of his promise. For, whatever incident led to his resigning the Baton Rouge principalship and leaving education for the one and only time in his long and distinguished career goes unmentioned in these memoirs.

Education was not just his career. Harris was born into a family of educators and, aside from fishing and hunting, education was his life. Whereas many of his friends used teaching as a way to earn enough money to go on to study law, business, or medicine, Harris did not see those paths as realistic options for himself. Instead, he followed the traditional career path from teacher to principal-teacher to principal to superintendent, finally becoming the Louisiana state superintendent.

As Teacher and Principal

Looking back at the turn of the last century, Harris (1963) said, "Public officials in those pioneer days . . . had never seen any fine buildings and demanded none. They were accustomed to cheap wooden structures that cost only a few hundred dollars" (Harris, p. 66). Generally one or two teachers taught ungraded classes under primitive conditions, with uncomfortable furniture and no libraries. Teaching in the elementary field was barbarous, elementary textbooks were thoroughly bad, and library books for small children did not exist:

> [The] *McGuffey's Readers* were excellent from the standpoints of morals and literature. From the standpoint of child-interest they were very poor. There was little in them that appealed to the children who had to use them. They were, however, much better than the old *Blue Book Speller*, but they were not worthy to be mentioned in the same breath with the readers of today. (Harris, 1963, p. 43)

Harris (1963) considered the content and methods of teaching of science to be a waste of time:

> The time devoted to science was wasted. We studied physiology; but did not learn how

to play, keep vermin out of the house, the importance of personal cleanliness, ventilation, taking care of teeth, watching for bad tonsils, and what to do in case of bad cuts and broken bones. Instead we learned the names of the organs of the body, their functions, the names and functions of the bones, muscles and teeth—information of no value whatever to us. . . . The general science was more sensible than the physiology, but we gathered no specimens to make it real and interesting, as we could and should have done. (pp. 76–77)

Of a book on astronomy used in one high school where he worked, Harris (1963) wrote, "My deliberate judgment is that Professor Steele wasted his time writing the book, took money under false pretenses selling it, . . . and I should have been playing marbles or fishing instead of studying his book" (p. 77).

Professionalizing School Leadership

Up until the 20th century, public school leaders needed to have careers outside education in order to earn enough money to live. The low salaries (about $200 per year) prohibited a teacher from moving into administration. Therefore, school district superintendents were laymen. Generally speaking, they were honest, capable gentlemen; but they were ignorant of schools. The same was true for the position of state superintendent, Harris (1963) said:

> [The] office was a sinecure and the occupant of it a figurehead. He was selected by politicians for rounding out the ticket geographically and for his ability to make a noise in the campaign. He was not expected to do anything after election, and he proceeded faithfully to do nothing. (p. 94)

Teachers and principals could not look to the state for assistance in improving schools:

> I made my own course of study and selected the textbooks I desired to use. Of course, the children paid for them. The course of study was the result of bits of information picked

up at [my previous teaching positions]. The State Board of Education accepted it without question and placed its stamp of approval upon it. (p. 76)

When another principal asked Harris how his school had received high school accreditation:

I replied that all he had to do was to put down on paper a lot of junk about courses of study, textbooks, and teachers, and send it to Baton Rouge. I told him the State Superintendent reported at the office once a month to collect his salary; and that if he got to it on one of these visits, he'd open the application for approval and present it to the State Board of Education. (p. 91)

State school support was negligible; there was no state supervision, and no advice or suggestions for improvement came from state school authorities.

Principals had to both teach and supervise teachers, Harris (1963) said: "Time for supervision had to be stolen from my classes" (p. 89). In Baton Rouge, "I taught two or three classes and devoted the rest of the day to supervision, though the term was not in my vocabulary at the time. I made it a rule to visit every classroom in the system every day (not a good plan of supervision) and to have a few words with each teacher" (p. 106). The average educational level of public school teachers was probably not beyond the seventh grade.

Under Harris's state leadership (1908 to 1940) Louisiana established and enforced educational standards for school leaders: a bachelors' degree and 5 years of teaching experience for all superintendents. The State Board of Education passed a resolution requiring parish superintendents of education to earn certificates in examinations based on certain professional subjects and calling for full-time service on the part of these local officials, with a minimum salary of $600 per year. The purpose was to place local leadership in the hands of teachers. "One of the arguments advanced in

favor of the employment of successful teachers as parish superintendents of schools," Harris (1963) said, "was that these trained and experienced school men would be able to aid teachers in planning and executing their teaching routine in a successful manner" (p. 161).

Leadership and Management

Classroom supervision may not have been in Harris's vocabulary when he was a principal, but as state superintendent, he secured passage in 1914 of the Burke Act, which authorized the hiring of supervisors of instruction. Prior to this authorization, the practice was for parish/district superintendents to visit schools, observe classes, teach demonstration lessons, and hold clinics, teacher institutes, and staff development workshops. The superintendents, Harris (1963) said, "soon realized that there was a business side which demanded attention" (p. 161). Other duties involving finances, school tax elections, drafting school laws and regulations, transportation, discipline cases, misunderstandings, and correspondence were

too important to be neglected.... The parish superintendents, especially of the larger parishes, soon saw that they would have to choose between the professional and the business sides of their offices. They lacked the time to do both. And they naturally, and wisely, selected the business side. (pp. 161–162)

Concurrently, a decision was made that the high school principal "should be an executive, administrator, and supervisor instead of a teacher," Harris (1963) said. "Gradually, the principals of the large schools gave up teaching and devoted their time to administration and supervision" (p. 163). The new supervisory role in education was described as follows:

Usually a highly successful lady teacher would be employed as parish supervisor of classroom activities in the white schools.[11] The supervisor would visit schools and observe the teaching. She would point out to the faculty the important things she had seen in the teaching, especially the valuable things. She would aid the principal and teachers in developing a teaching program for the school. In cooperation with the teachers she would prepare desirable objectives to be attained in the various subjects and the out-of-class activities. In short, the supervisor was a *helping teacher* [emphasis in original]. Nagging and fault-finding were from the first taboo, and my impression is that these pernicious faults found but small place in the system of supervision. (p. 162)

School Improvement

Harris (1963) laid out an ambitious vision for his state superintendency. It was to establish a system of high schools; improve the physical plants of all schools; strengthen the courses of study; raise the standards and training for teachers, principals, and parish superintendents, as well as their salaries; improve vocational departments; consolidate several thousand one-teacher country schools; establish a state equalization formula for school financing; and create a state support system "to respond to the demands of public sentiment" (p. 114). His accomplishments were many, for both white and black schools, but Harris was also not afraid to admit his own mistakes. In perhaps the only first-person account we have of Louisiana's provision of free textbooks for school children, Harris opposed Governor Huey P. Long. Here is his account:

A few days after Governor Huey P. Long took over the office of Governor in May, 1928, he called me to his office and said he wished me to hear him dictate the free school book act. He proposed to furnish textbooks free to children attending elementary and high schools, both public and private, and to pay for the books out of the proceeds of a tax on natural products severed from the soil, such as oil, gas, salt, sulphur, sand, gravel, and lumber. I advised the Governor not to include children attending private schools, reminding him that practically

all private schools were affiliated with the Catholic Church and that the Constitution prohibited the use of public funds to aid religious institutions. Governor Long took the position that my viewpoint was unsound, that he was proposing to help *children* and not *schools* [emphases in the original]. I told him I was in sympathy with his purpose, but I believed the insertion of such a provision would destroy the act. He replied, "I am satisfied. I am a better lawyer than you are, and books for children attending private schools go in the act." And they did. (p. 159)

When parents and local school districts challenged the law, the appeal went all the way to the U.S. Supreme Court. In mid argument, Chief Justice Charles Evans Hughes stopped the opposing counsel, "asked a few questions and then stated that further arguments were unnecessary" (Harris, 1963, p. 160). The court upheld the Louisiana act. Harris, however, found one justification for his position. Taxes had not been collected prior to the opening of the school year, and thus, the state did not have the money to purchase or store the textbooks. Governor Long put pressure on the banks and had them loan the state $500,000 to purchase the books. Some of the local parishes still refused to accept the books, so Harris rented a warehouse to store them, figuring that people would choose a free book rather than pay for one. To smooth over relations with local parishes, the state agreed to buy back useable textbooks that parents had bought with their own money for one third the price. Politically the policy worked, but Harris called this an "economic mistake on our part" (p. 161).

Looking back on his state tenure, Harris (1963) would recall other mistakes. The curriculum issue was music and art education:

We decreed that *every* high school should employ music and art supervisors. We were too much on a bread and butter basis; we were neglecting the finer things in the nature of children. The scheme was ridiculous on its face, and I am surprised that I ever agreed to do it. In the first place, we did not have the specialists for these new fields of instruction. Usually only *one* specialist could be employed, and only in rare cases was one found who could handle both music and art. Generally speaking, she could not handle either. But she was required to look after both. In the second place, neither field was organized and our office was not prepared to set up standards and direct the work. We had made a blunder, but we were averse to admit it, and hung on till most of the superintendents and school boards asked us to lay off. The result of this experiment was to create a public sentiment against two important subjects and to postpone their introduction into the school system. (pp. 135–136)

In 1935, Harris (1963) had decided to retire. Huey Long, now a U.S. senator, called him and offered his support if he would run for office. Harris declined. Long persisted, asking for specific reasons for Harris's decision. Harris explained that while he was out of state attending the National Educational Association conference, Long had persuaded the state legislature to pass a law turning over the public school budget to the Governor's office, effectively making the state superintendency "helpless in opposition" (p. 169). Harris, who had fought to professionalize education, saw this move as relinquishing all employment decisions to partisan politics. Long argued the opposite view. He believed his budget act prevented local parish school boards from playing politics with principalship appointments. The two men talked and listened. At the conclusion of this Friday night telephone conversation, Long admitted that Harris was right and promised to help change the law in the next legislative session. For the last time, Harris agreed to run for the state superintendency. The decision was announced immediately. Two days later, on the following Sunday, Huey P. Long was assassinated. But in the next legislative session, the school budget law *was* changed.

THE HISTORICAL LESSONS OF PUBLIC SCHOOL LEADERSHIP

The history presented here challenges much of the thinking and practices that characterize today's 21st-century school leaders, as well as many of us involved in both the preparation of administrators and K–12 policy making. Previous histories may have left readers with the impression that past school leaders were more talk than action. Contemporary descriptions of leaders in the first century of public education label them *scholars, philosophers,* and *statesmen.* The personal narratives included here offer far richer perspectives of their lives. During that first century, school leaders' use of rhetoric was a significant aspect of their leadership roles, yet none of them remained aloof from any strata of society or above the political fray. Even when they argued to keep partisan politics out of their schools, their goals included building constituencies that would support their visions for public education.

Their use of rhetoric was not only political, however, but also intellectual and educational. They spoke continually of curricular concepts and instructional methods, and they advocated the need to revitalize the professions of teaching and administration. They publicly articulated the purposes of public education, emphasizing democratic ideals and practices along with community involvement, uniting concepts and actions. However, unlike philosophers, who seek universal meanings for their ideas, the concepts and actions of these school leaders differed according to the context: era, geography, and administrative role. In a material sense, their school leadership was unique, contextual, and in the process of being re-created.

The French historian Foucault (1972) reminds us that concepts—and especially the words used to describe them—change with time, relationships, and contexts. For example, the term *democracy* held a different meaning for each school leader. To Mann, democracy meant participating in public discourse through town meetings, newspapers, and professional journals as he attempted to educate the public on the responsibilities and benefits of public education. He viewed the intersection between democracy and public schools from a societal perspective. To Young, democracy was an essential process in teaching and curriculum development, as well as in educational decision making. She opposed organizational arrangements, such as centralization and standardization, that took power away from teachers and administrators. Maxwell and Harris used democratic forums to fight to keep education in the hands of educators rather than turning it over to businessmen or government officials. These two men relished their political exchanges with some of the most powerful business and government officials of their era. Angelo Patri's notion of democracy centered on building community support around his school and on giving teachers and parents voices in school-wide decision making. The retelling of history underscores the uniqueness of their concept and actions, which Foucault dubbed discursive practices.

Foucault (1972) described discursive practices in terms of strategic choices, which range from technical improvements, new notions, and conceptual transformations to discoveries. Each strategic choice is an autonomous event that reflects both the continuities and discontinuities found throughout history. This conceptual framework operates within, not apart from or above, the level of material conditions. Unfortunately, many of the material conditions revealed in these personal narratives are still problems today. A partial list of these continuities include: poorly prepared teacher candidates, inadequate funding and public support, overcrowded schools and classrooms, low salaries, low status, the predominance of women as teachers, a narrow "bread and butter" curriculum, authoritarian practices in teaching and administration, prescribed and mechanical methods of teaching, and the necessity of managing facilities and

finances while still attending to curricular and instructional issues. Despite enormous investments of time, energy, and dollars in trying to make technical improvements, these material realities persisted then, as they do today.

The school leaders we met in this chapter had to adjust to these realities. For instance, Cyrus Peirce had hoped to teach higher-order thinking and educational theory to the young female candidates at our nation's first normal school. Instead, he had to revise his curriculum and teaching to focus on basic arithmetic and grammar. Yet, in so doing, neither he nor Horace Mann ever gave up on turning these "young scholars" into outstanding teachers. Likewise, Ella Flagg Young set high standards for those entering the teaching profession. She continuously nurtured teachers' judgments rather than imposing her own methods on them. She spoke of the long silences at faculty meetings as she waited for teachers to come up with their own ideas. At the same time, she had to confront the hierarchical pressures to impose required teaching methods and programs that had been adopted by the district. Although she later expressed regret over her own compliance, she did not regret either her trust in teachers or her rigorous approach to teacher training—even after one such decision to weed out a candidate with political connections cost her her job. What that event taught her was that she needed to learn more about local city and school board politics.

Similar adjustments were evident in the other narratives. Both Young and William Maxwell continuously sought to minimize the impact that business practices and centralization had on their teachers and students. They became prolific writers and used professional forums, including the National Education Association, to win support for their ideas on curriculum and leadership. Maxwell and Harris worked to establish legal structures to support professional cultures by raising certification standards for both teachers and administrators. Although such restrictions today have been attacked, these school leaders witnessed far worse political abuses prior to certification requirements, especially in the area of personnel. When Angelo Patri was told to be patient and not stir up controversies, he began to organize student disciplinary councils, parent-teacher associations, and community welfare committees to provide both political and social support on behalf of his school's community. In each narrative, we saw how specific circumstances and contexts led school leaders to make their own strategic choices.

All of these school leaders encountered individuals bound by tradition,[12] from students, teachers, and administrators to parents and power elites. Yet, they persisted in working with these groups to create new structures, new curricula, unique teaching methods, and a new professional culture in education. Their leadership extended beyond making technical improvements and reforms; their practices challenged both tradition and externally imposed reforms. These school leaders recognized how important it was to build strong community-school relationships that respected the gifts that students and teachers brought to school.

When strategic choices are seen as autonomous events rather than a progressive evolution of ideas, then the concept of leadership shifts from the role of system maintenance to one of system building and rebuilding. Within this educational framework, every act is, in a sense, a creation and a discovery. Even re-creations are intentionally different and original, depending on the given material conditions of the specific era. These school leaders were efficient system builders, not loyal, obedient, and efficient system managers. They used their knowledge and skills concerning education and society to develop and implement new curricula and instructional methods. As advocates, they communicated the purposes of public education to constituents and engaged in politics. As civic leaders, they worked on behalf of their students, their families, and their local communities.

Collectively, their strategic actions may be characterized by eight historical dimensions of school leadership, detailed below.

1. School Leadership That Is Democratic With a Small "d"

Their democratic leadership was not just an espoused ideal but rather the necessary practices in and out of the school building. Each of the leaders brought democracy to classroom teaching and administration out of a "love for children" and an understanding that teachers need a democratic environment to grow, to learn, and, ultimately, to teach. The leaders built structures around their ideals including student councils, teacher councils, and parent committees that distributed decision-making powers. They fought against supervisory practices that promoted a single method of teaching or a test-driven or standardized curriculum. They opposed scientific management as a whole school/district/state reform. In contemporary terms, their democratic leadership incorporated knowledge, performance, and a disposition. It was *the* leadership standard.

2. In-Depth Knowledge of Curriculum and Instruction

Their knowledge of curriculum and instruction extended to the what (i.e., subject matter content) and the how (i.e., methods) of teaching and learning. In their various roles as teacher trainers, supervisors, principals, superintendents, or state superintendents, this knowledge was at the center of their fiscal decision making. Even the strongest proponent for modern business practices among the personal narratives, T. H. Harris, understood the importance of educators being able to make educational and management decisions about pupil progression, budgets, and personnel matters in schools and school systems.

Each of these school leaders worked to build trust among teachers so that they could think independently and bring interesting real-world social issues to their students. This trust in teachers' judgments was the basis for classroom and school accountability and the criteria for measuring student learning. Their views of school accountability rested on teachers' professional judgments and the quality of their students' adult lives after graduation[13]—which was intended to raise the level of society as a whole.

These school leaders believed that curriculum at every grade level should go beyond the Three Rs, enriched by courses in music, art, physical education, singing, literature, storytelling, science, and social studies. They certainly did not agree on any of the details regarding the grade-level configurations or subjects to be taught, or even the content of subjects; what they did agree on was that teachers, principals, and superintendents needed to experiment with ideas so as to engage students in learning. Thus, they developed and implemented diverse, flexible curricula and promoted differentiated instruction among teachers. They also argued for coursework that incorporated what Maxwell referred to as the "spiritual inheritances" among the races.[14] To accomplish this egalitarian mission, they sought to transform schools and those who taught in them into instruments of community activism and social change. Teachers and administrators needed more than book knowledge. Here, too, knowledge, performance, and dispositions converged around teaching and learning.

3. System Builders

Before Mann and Peirce, there were no normal schools to train teachers, no practice schools to experiment with teaching methods and curriculum, no organized political efforts to secure legislative votes for taxes and funding, and no forums to influence popular sentiment on behalf of public education. Other state-level educational leaders, such as James G. Carter in Massachusetts, Henry Barnard in

Connecticut, and later T. H. Harris in Louisiana recognized the need for a system, long before systems thinking took hold as a theory of educational leadership. For Young, Maxwell, and Patri, the challenges came as they transformed their schools and the systems within which they worked. As leaders, they could not accept the system as complete, finished, and just needing to be managed.

Running schools has always meant long hours and hard work; management was nothing new to these school leaders. Historically, a school leader

> bought the water pail, the dipper, and the broom; and he saw that the woodhouse was properly filled and the premises kept in repair. His position was not what the poet calls "a downy bed of ease," for he was the subject of much comment and criticism. (Johnson, 1907, p. 48)

The leaders described here learned organizational and management skills through doing the job. Management and administrative routines were the virtues of necessity, to be attended to on top of and outside of what has been depicted here as public school leadership. Harris wrote of this managerial turn with respect to the responsibilities of high school principals, school district superintendents, and his own role at the state level. But even in his advocacy of the "inevitability" of management, there was never the suggestion that management should replace education at the center of leadership and decision making. He may not have been the lawyer or politician that Huey P. Long was, but he was a strong educational leader who won Long's respect.

4. Community and Social Activism

Patri (1917) wrote, "The school alone could do nothing . . . the home alone could do nothing" (pp. 83–84). He told parents that by "acting together as a moral force in the neighborhood, you are more vital to the education of the children than is the school" (p. 100) and noted, "moral education meant group reaction" (p. 84). From Mann to Patri, these leaders understood the importance of schools being directly involved in community affairs: Teachers needed to become active participants in community life. This was not a philosophical position. During the first century of public schooling, teachers and administrators alike were involved with social issues such as housing, jobs, food, clothing, and hygiene, all of which impacted their students directly. Maxwell argued that the mission of the urban public school was to eradicate poverty in the tenement houses of New York City. He and Patri both described teachers and principals walking the streets of their communities, interacting with parents, students, and families. This practice was so deeply ingrained in the concepts of public school leadership during its early years that even the most vocal proponent of scientific management and business practices, Franklin Bobbitt (1913), called for teachers to be engaged in community work as it was essential to their professional development. He argued:

> It is becoming more and more apparent that the teacher of today, who is able to bear social responsibilities that the world is laying more and more upon our profession, must be a man or a woman of the world. . . . This is accomplished only by participation in the full, active life of the world of affairs. (p. 80)

Bobbitt encouraged teachers to leave their classroom, to visit other classes in their schools, in other cities, and states, and to attend concerts, theater productions, and lectures, declaring all to be "absolutely necessary" for sustaining the vitality of the profession.[15]

5. Politics

Beyond the borders of the school building, public school leaders practiced politics at the local, district, and state levels. Mann crisscrossed the state of Massachusetts on behalf of public schools, speaking at town meetings to everyone who would listen. He and Young used the print media and met with business and religious leaders, as well as state legislators, who were not always cordial. Mann faced constant political opposition to his ideas and programs. Young and Maxwell were the targets of both personal and professional attacks from opponents. As a matter of principle, Young refused to remain in a position that hampered her and "gave her no freedom for growth" (McManis, 1916, p. 51). Patri transferred to a different school on a number of occasions after getting into conflicts with teachers, principals, and school board members. As a principal, he encouraged teachers and parents to engage in local school board politics. Harris also experienced his share of private and public conflicts. On one occasion, he resigned his principalship of the Baton Rouge High School, never revealing the specific details. What he did write about were his pivotal meetings with Governor and later U.S. Senator Huey P. Long, particularly with regard to the historic textbook decision and the control of the education budget.

Whether the issues were the separation of church and state, free and reduced-cost lunches, free textbooks, or the budget to save music and art, these leaders engaged in political battles that were controversial—often at some considerable cost to their health and careers. Without exaggeration, these men and women are profiles in political courage. What sustained them was their belief in education, teachers, and children.

6. Communicators

Roland Barth (1990) devoted a chapter in *Improving Schools from Within* to the idea that practitioners should put their practice into prose. During the first century of public education, many of our school leaders did so.

Today, their words are our window into the history of leadership practice. With the exception of Harris, they wrote not so much for history, but rather to influence their colleagues, policymakers, and the public. Their willingness to share ideas created the professional literature of their day. The best of the annual superintendent reports were not self-promoting summaries of accomplishments but rather in-depth discussions on subject-matter teaching, innovations in curriculum, and managerial advice. What they did was to educate their own generation about the purposes of public schools. That responsibility resides with every generation of school leaders. By putting practice into prose, the leaders described did not leave this task to academicians, policymakers, consultants, or politicians.

7. Connections With Higher Education: Professional Community

During this first century of public education, educational leaders from public schools to higher educational institutions met regularly as fellow members of the National Educational Association or the National Society for the Study of Education. Today, however, every role has its own sphere of influence. Education has become fragmented. Professors of education have separated from practitioners. The field of educational leadership has separated from curriculum and instruction and from community educators.

Even as early as 1920, K–12 education was fragmented. According to a report published that year by the Carnegie Foundation for the Advancement of Teaching on the subject of professional preparation, the school system had become

> an elaborate hierarchical device that undertakes through successive gradations of textbook makers, superintendents, principals, and supervisors to isolate and prepare each modicum of knowledge and skill so that it may safely be entrusted to the humble

teacher at the bottom. (Report quoted by Rickover, 1963, pp. 16–17)

In contrast, Horace Mann ended his career as the president of Antioch College; Young joined Dewey for a time of study and teaching at the University of Chicago; Maxwell invited President and Professor Nicolas Murray Butler (1912) to write the introduction to his collected papers; Patri studied Dewey's work at Teachers College under Professor Frank McMurry; and Harris was offered the LSU presidency on three different occasions. If their writing had elevated the field of education as a whole, then their connections with higher education elevated these school leaders as individuals who valued learning for themselves. Then, as now, higher education provides a source of research ideas, a place to reflect on ideas and to experiment, and a respite from political strife and stress. That said, the connections of these leaders to higher education did not solve the persistent problems of K–12 schooling.

8. Radicalism as a Disposition

To many educators today, the term *radicalism* is unpopular. However, the word had a distinct meaning during the first century of public education. James Harvey Robinson (1921), a contemporary of these school leaders, described it as a disposition to believe that the future will look far different from the past (p. 229). When it comes to leadership, it is one thing to espouse a reform and quite another to take action and bring about change. The public school leaders in this chapter were activists who worked against the grain, distinguishing good practices from bad practices. At the same time, they understood that schools serve an important conservative function for society by transmitting knowledge, values, and culture from one generation to the next. They knew as practitioners that parents, taxpayers, lawmakers, and even other educators were essentially conservative individuals who based their ideas of good education on their own past experiences. However, all these public school leaders held their ground, opposing tradition for tradition's sake. To quote from Angelo Patri (1917), "I thought in terms of service, they thought in terms of tradition" (p. 62).

The public school leaders described in this chapter did not win over their opponents in each and every conflict, but they nevertheless made their educational and democratic positions clear to constituents and worked tirelessly on behalf of public schools and our profession. They left us their legacies for us to rediscover and re-create.

BACK TO THE FUTURE?

Toward the end of the first century of public education, educational leadership completed the managerial turn, whereby business values eclipsed the values of democracy in education. Governments, too, shifted their roles vis-à-vis public education from that of protecting the constitutional rights of all citizens to becoming the central authorities, dictating structural, curricular, and accountability policies for public schools. To a person, the school leaders you have met in this chapter would be opposed to today's 21st-century reforms—from vouchers, to prescriptive, drill-focused reading and writing programs, to the high-stakes role of standardized tests—because of what they believed to be fundamentally sound public education logic. Their opposition, however, would not have been limited to a debate of management versus instructional leadership; rather, first-century school leadership defined itself more broadly, encompassing democratic leadership, community education (Decker, 1975), and social justice (Furman & Shields, 2003). Mann, Peirce, Young, Maxwell, Patri, and Harris all saw public schools as essential to social change.

My reading of these school leaders' accounts optimistically suggests that today's narrow

reforms are more temporal and expedient than inevitable. But for change to occur, the field of educational leadership will have to travel back to the future. This chapter outlined *how* school leaders in the first century accomplished their goals, politically as well as educationally. The personal and professional stakes were as high for them as they are for us now. Yet, yesterday's school leaders found the time to reflect on education and write down their ideas. While we, generations later, are all in debt to them for their writings, they saw this intellectual activity as something more than providing a historical record; they understood how their words, written and spoken, were essential to their success as public school leaders.

NOTES

1. Outside of the school building, the century experienced a civil war, the beginnings of the industrial revolution, a massive wave of immigrants from southern and eastern Europe, World War I, the economic depression, and the rise of fascism in Europe and the Pacific leading up to World War II.

2. Teacher:student ratios mentioned in the various texts ranged from 1:77 in Chicago to 1:50 in a class of discipline problems in New York City.

3. According to the Superintendent's Report of 1860, the teacher:student ratio in Chicago was 1:77.

4. Later New York City superintendents implemented variations of the community school model, seeking to build closer relationships among the schools, civic groups, and public agencies (Seay & Wilkinson, 1953). By 1910, 55 cities "provided recreation through the use of schools and playgrounds" (Naslund, 1953, p. 261).

5. I have written about Angelo Patri's leadership before (Bogotch, 2002).

6. My 1909 edition is titled *Moral Principles in Education.*

7. According to Dr. Anthony Vihotti (undated), Angelo Patri was slightly taller than 5 feet and weighed about 100 pounds.

8. This is the title of his 1917 autobiography.

9. "Some years our transfer figures are larger than our register" (Patri, 1917, p. 135).

10. Special classes included: the atypical class, the anaemic class, the backward class, the posture class, the speech class, and the discipline class. At

one point, Patri (1917) became so frustrated with the proliferation of special classes that he wrote, "We're simply turning out more candidates for specials instead of making the specials useless" (p. 187).

11. It would be at least 10 years before the black schools had their own system of teacher supervision (Harris, 1963).

12. Throughout this chapter, I have tried to distinguish between two meanings of the term *tradition*. In the history of public education in the United States, democratic ideals and practices are part of our tradition and characteristic of U.S. school leadership in its first century. The word was also used, often by the school leaders themselves, to depict what they perceived to be unreflective existing practices that persist without educators critically questioning their effectiveness.

13. "I would judge the school by its product and dismiss questions of courses of study and methods" (Maxwell, 1912, p. 35). Harris stated similar beliefs.

14. That is, among European immigrants of different nationalities and ethnic and religious background. Throughout this century, American blacks were educated, if at all, in a number of public and private systems separate and not at all equal to the public schools described in this chapter.

15. In his 1955 Horace Mann lecture, "The education of free men," Ernest Melby described a proposal whereby "teachers divide their day or week between teaching children and youth in school and work with adults in the community. Think how vital and interesting the teacher would be were she to come to her schoolroom direct from facing community problems" (p. 56).

REFERENCES

American School Board Journal [25th anniversary issue]. (1916). *52*(1).

Barth, R. (1990). *Improving schools from within.* San Francisco: Jossey-Bass.

Bobbitt, F. (1913). The supervision of city schools. In S. C. Parker (Ed.), *The twelfth yearbook of the National Society for the Study of Education* (pp. 7–96). Chicago: University of Chicago Press.

Bogotch, I. (2002). Educational leadership and social justice: Practice into theory. *Journal of School Leadership, 12,* 138–156.

Butler, N. M. (1912). Introduction. In W. Maxwell, *A quarter century of public school development* (pp. vii–ix). New York: American Book Co.

Butler, N. M. (1915). *The meaning of education.* New York: Charles Scribner's Sons.

Butts, R. F., & Cremins, L. (1962). *A history of education in American culture.* New York: Holt, Rinehart & Winston.

Callahan, R. (1962). *Education and the cult of efficiency.* Chicago: University of Chicago Press.

Cuban, L. (1988). *The managerial imperative and the practice of leadership in schools.* Albany: SUNY Press.

Decker, L. (1975). *Foundations of community education.* Midland, MI: Pendell.

Dewey, J. (1909). *Moral principles in education.* Boston: Houghton Mifflin.

Foucault, M. (1972). *The archaeology of knowledge and the discourse on language.* New York: Pantheon Books.

Furman, G., & Shields, C. (2003, April). *How can educational leaders promote and support social justice and democratic community in schools?* Paper prepared for Division A of the American Educational Research Association (AERA) Task Force for the Development of an Agenda for Future Research on Educational Leadership and presented at the Annual Meeting of AERA in Chicago.

Gilbert, N. (1904). A commentary. In A. Wray, *Jean Mitchell's school* (Appendix, pp. 1–29). Bloomington, IL: Public-School Publishing.

Harris, T. H. (1963). *The memoirs of T. H. Harris.* Baton Rouge: Louisiana State University, College of Education, Bureau of Educational Materials and Research.

Johnson, C. (1907). *The country school.* New York: Thomas Y. Crowell.

Maxwell, W. (1912). *A quarter century of public school development.* New York: American Book Co.

McManis, J. (1916). *Ella Flagg Young and a half-century of the Chicago public schools.* Chicago: A. C. McClug.

Melby, E. (1955). *The education of free men: The Horace Mann Lecture, 1955.* Pittsburgh, PA: University of Pittsburgh Press.

Naslund, R. (1953). The impact of the power age on the community-school concept. In N. Henry (Ed.), *The community school: The 52nd yearbook of the National Society for the Study of Education* (Part II, pp. 251–264). Chicago: University of Chicago Press.

Patri, A. (1917). *A schoolmaster of the great city.* New York: Macmillan.

Rickover, H. G. (1963). *American education: A national failure.* New York: E. P. Dutton.

Riis, J. (1957). A battle with the slum. In E. Weeks & E. Flint (Eds.), *Jubilee: One hundred years of the Atlantic Monthly*. Boston: Little, Brown. (Reprinted from *Atlantic Monthly*, May 1899)

Robinson, J. H. (1921). *The mind in the making*. New York: Harper.

Seay, M., & Wilkinson, J. (1953). Overcoming barriers to the development of community schools. In N. Henry (Ed.), *The community school: The 52nd yearbook of the National Society for the Study of Education* (Part II, pp. 265–287). Chicago: University of Chicago Press.

Stone, C. (1929). *Supervision of the elementary school*. Boston: Houghton Mifflin.

Tharp, L. (1953). *Until victory: Horace Mann and Mary Peabody*. Boston: Little, Brown.

Tuchman, B. (1981). *Practicing history*. New York: Knopf.

Tyack, D. (1974). *The one best system: A history of American urban education*. Cambridge, MA: Harvard University Press.

Vihotti, A. (undated). *Dr. Angelo Patri*. Retrieved from http://home.earthlink.net/~m321/ap.html

Wray, A. (1904). *Jean Mitchell's school*. Bloomington, IL: Public-School Publishing.

Zinn, H. (1998). *The twentieth century: A people's history*. New York: HarperCollins.

2

Moral Leadership

Shifting the Management Paradigm

MICHAEL E. DANTLEY
Miami University of Ohio

INTRODUCTION AND OVERVIEW

Much of the thinking in the field of educational leadership has been shaped by the ideas and tenets of what is generally referred to as *scientific management*. Frederick W. Taylor is considered the father of this influential management theory. According to scientific management, the administration of organizations can be reduced to the replication of behaviors that have proved to be effective and efficient. Efficiency and effectiveness are evaluated by the use of hard data gained through quantifiable measurement. In fact, science and efficiency, according to the scientific management paradigm, serve as the quintessential elements of successful administrative behavior. *Taylorism,* as scientific management is sometimes called, stresses that there is always one best way to accomplish a job, and this is likely to be the fastest way to get the job done. Scientific management thus explores the quickest methods to accomplish a task, with the least number of body motions necessary to do a job efficiently. The role of the manager, then, is to discover the most time and cost-efficient way to accomplish tasks and then to provide specific training so that workers are able to reproduce the process. In this way, the results of workers' labor can always be predicted and quantified.

While the tentacles of scientific management remain firmly affixed to the leadership practices of institutions such as schools, many educators are beginning to sense an ontological and personal meaning disconnect between themselves and what happens in schools and are framing inquiries and discourses that are juxtaposed to the practices promoted through the auspices of a Taylorist management approach.

This chapter will examine the tenets of scientific management as the traditional leadership paradigm, its roots in modernist thinking, and the rise of the concept of moral leadership as an alternative to scientific management and an answer to the challenges that many in educational leadership now face. Moral or purpose-driven leadership is a way to situate school leadership in a broader social context. It not only is conscious of issues of race, class, and gender, but also perceives the work of schools as sites committed to social justice and more genuine demonstrations of democracy in our society. Moral and purpose-driven leadership takes seriously students' academic achievement, demands a deep investment of the school leader's genuine or authentic self, and dares to ask the hard questions regarding the purposes of schools and who are most ably served by them.

SCIENTIFIC MANAGEMENT AND EDUCATION

Scientific management holds that requiring workers to follow routine steps involving neither their imagination nor a great deal of their intellectual capability produces efficiency and effectiveness in accomplishing any task. In effect, each component of a specific task is clearly spelled out and monitored for accuracy in its execution by the manager. It thus becomes the responsibility of the organizational administrator to clearly delineate the discriminate steps essential to a task's completion, provide appropriate training for the workers who are to complete the tasks, and finally, to monitor the process of the workers' implementation. Management is seen as a rational way to sequence tasks so that predictable results occur. Inherent in the management paradigm is the assumed intellectual superiority of those who hold titular or positional power. Workers are considered to lack the internal motivation to get the work done. They are also assumed to lack the intellectual wherewithal to complete tasks without very close supervision or monitoring. Those who manage supposedly keep the ends of this mechanized process in mind and therefore create easy-to-implement steps

enabling the workers they supervise to complete their assignments, thus leading to the successful conclusion of the project. Clearly, as a result of this kind of mind-set, hierarchies are crafted, rules and processes for inclusion and exclusion are developed, and corporations and even schools are able to legitimatize and perpetuate society's prejudices and traditions within their very walls. Concomitantly, the properties of bureaucracies are firmly established through the clear delineation of managers' and workers' responsibilities.

Early in the 20th century, scholars in educational administration, who were bound by a modernist context, found the ideas of scientific management useful when applied to the work of schools. W. W. Charters has been cited as one of those responsible for introducing the tenets of scientific management to the work of schools (Maxcy, 1995). The goal was to measure efficiency in the manufacturing of schools' *products,* namely children. What seemed to be so appealing about scientific management was the way it embraced the concepts espoused by a positivist frame or perspective. Positivism, an offshoot of modernism, was founded on three primary principles: a preference for sanitized language, logical rigor, and value neutrality (Maxcy, 1995). Implicit in this acceptance of a positivist mind-set is the assumption that "peopled" endeavors are always linear in direction, rational, predictable, and consistent. Spencer Maxcy (1995) argues, "Where the scientific framework assumes that the interplay between concepts specified linguistically as variables matches point for point the interstices of human interaction in the life world, we have fallen heir to the fallacy of linguistic idealism" (p. 5). Essentially, Maxcy maintains that subscribing to notions such as sanitized language causes one to infer that the linguistic representation of life in schools is accurate and above discussion.

This is in keeping with the position of Herbert Marcuse (1898–1979), a German philosopher and central figure in the Frankfurt

School of critical theorists, who maintained that language is one of the most powerful weapons in the armory of the Establishment. In his writings, Marcuse argues that the language that represents hegemonic thought is a mixture of unprecedented brutality and sweetness (Kellner, 2001). He refers to it as an Orwellian language, which monopolizes communication and "stifles the consciousness, obscures and defames the alternative possibilities of existence, implants the needs of the status quo in the mind and body of men and makes them all but immune against the need for change" (p. 118).

A further examination of Marcuse's position on the power of language finds it contextualized in his deconstruction of the application of science in production and distribution. He admits that science has influenced social sciences, psychology, literature, and music, calling this a strange symbiosis of scientific humanistic thinking and a repressive society. He further notes that this symbiosis results in creativity and productivity actually serving the material culture, where imagination serves business and, ultimately, where scientific and humanistic thought actually serves as the driving force of social control.

SCIENTIFIC MANAGEMENT AND ITS RELATIONSHIP TO THE MODERNIST PARADIGM

Taylorism provides an extremely mechanized way to standardize the workplace (Foster, 1986). This standardization implies that there is a knowledge base that substantiates the creation of these standard ways of operation. The knowledge base of scientific management is found in what has been termed *modernity*. The idea of modernity defines a time in the early 20th century when life in Western civilization was characterized by capitalism, rationalism, individualism, and a move toward a secular culture. The fields of science, industry, and technology were perceived as arenas one needed to be conversant with if one were to achieve economic or social success. Cahoone (1996) considers that the self-image Western civilization portrayed through modernism was established on a scientific knowledge of the world and a rational knowledge of value. Inherent in modernist thinking was a belief in the virtue of rationality, control, individuality, and truth. Linear rationality was emphasized, and the validity of ideas was established only through empirical scrutiny. Patricia Hill-Collins (1998) defines modernity as a generally accepted new form of global social organization that developed when science and reason became the most important principles in European societies. She notes that philosophers tend to suggest that modernity originated during the 1600s, whereas many cultural critics would argue that the term *modernism* ought to be applied specifically to the literary and artistic productions of the early 20th century. Finally, Hill-Collins suggests that development theorists use modernization as a marker indicating a move toward industrialization, leading to capitalist market economies and political democracy in different societies.

Henry Giroux (1997) suggests a trinitarian approach to the definition of modernism, describing modernism through the context of three traditions: the social, the aesthetic, and the political. When articulating the tenets of modernism from the social tradition, Giroux states that modernism's notions of social progress were deeply tied to the dynamics of capitalist production and economic growth. Giroux further argues that modernism took on what he calls the epistemological project of elevating reason and rationality to an ontological status. Essentially, modernism became the hegemonic mind-set for circumscribing civilization. He concludes that "reason is universalized in cognitive and instrumental terms as the basis for a model of industrial, cultural, and social progress" (p. 184). Clearly, as modernism established the parameters of the hegemony, a systematic method of inclusion and exclusion of celebrated or legitimated thinking concomitantly constructed a grammar of dualisms that contextualized life at that time. The human subject became the ultimate source of meaning, according to Giroux, and "a notion of geographical and cultural territoriality is constructed in a hierarchy of domination and subordination marked by a center and margin legitimated through the civilizing knowledge/power of a privileged Eurocentric culture" (p. 184).

Modernism, as examined through the lens of the aesthetic tradition, according to Giroux (1997), was grounded in resistance. As displayed through art and literature, there was an expressed disdain for bourgeois values and traditions. Much of the creative work was a product of rebellion and critique that was best expressed, according to Giroux, "in avant-garde movements ranging from the surrealists and the futurists to the conceptualist artists of the 1970s" (p. 185). It is very interesting that the articulation of a different, resistant voice seems to have been the motivation for the modernist frame, although the systematic silencing of divergent voices, even to the new modernist discourse, also took place. For instance, modernism celebrated what had been termed high culture but denigrated or marginalized popular culture. It heralded a central truth as well as a central methodology by which the truth was unearthed. This notion of a universal truth was carried over into educational settings with the glorification of a core curriculum and a standard methodology or pedagogy with which to implement the core curriculum. Again, the modernist position demanded an epistemological high ground that promoted the passing on of accepted, hegemonic knowledge, while at the same time actively defaming any knowledge that was outside of the accepted canon. Indeed, critics of the modernist paradigm, including its emphasis on resistance, argued that its position simply celebrated an amalgam of the self and scientific technology, grounded in the reification of white European male notions of industrial technologies, rationalism, mastery, and even beauty.

Robert Starratt (2003) summarizes the tenets of modernity from a different perspective, maintaining that modernity assumed that science and technology were intrinsically good and that these two fields served as the drivers of society's engines. Furthermore, he maintains that the modernist frame contended that objective knowledge gleaned through scientific discovery and technological prowess was the only legitimate knowledge in the world. Starratt suggests that modernism held that "objective knowledge enables us to know all of life's realities" (p. 46). Modernity also emphasized, according to Starratt, the primacy of the individual: Modernist thinking held that any theory of society must begin with the sanctity of the individual and must celebrate the rights as well as the responsibilities of individuals. He considers that modernity defined society's happiness through the collective choices of reasonable and self-interested individuals, who were influenced by reason and self-interest to make certain economic choices. These economic choices were expected to combine to produce widespread societal happiness. Clearly, during the modernist era, happiness and economic well-being were almost synonymous.

Two other tenets of modernism also seem to have been exceptionally influential in shaping cultural thought. Starratt (2003) notes that modernist thinking particularly prized the contributions to progress made by an intellectual elite composed of those who were especially astute in the physical and social sciences and who were considered, because of their intellectual acumen, to be best suited to serve as managers in public affairs and private corporate institutions. Clearly, this was an age that celebrated cerebral activity, although only certain kinds of intellectual work were legitimated. Thought that was grounded in rationality and scientific, quantitative data was prized, whereas notions of intuition, perceptions, and "softer" mental musings were denigrated and presumed to be comparatively useless. The final tenet of modernism Starratt lists is the political context within which this thinking flourished, which applauded a democracy engaging capable elected representatives who were expected to pursue and enact the common good.

Those who subscribe to a modernist perspective where school leadership is concerned may question whether anything other than academic endeavors should take place in schools. There may be some doubt, on their part, as to the possible connection between student academic achievement and a sensitivity to issues of social class, race, gender, and "otherness." Many prospective as well as current school administrators see academic achievement as the only purpose for a school's existence. What they fail to appreciate through this myopic perspective is the friction that exists between what they are trying to do in their perceived pristine, antiseptic schoolhouse and what is taking place in the real social context in which the school functions. Within this frame of modernist thinking, however, is a perspective that takes into account the various aspects of the community in which the school is embedded. Some leadership and organizational theorists subscribe to an open systems frame of thinking that views the system of the school as situated in an environmental setting where the boundaries of the school are actually permeable. The environment provides inputs to the school such as the students themselves, community values, legislation, and funding. The open systems model sees those inputs as providing fodder for the transactions that take place in the school, after which the outputs, namely the students or graduates, re-enter the environment changed for the better.

OPPOSITION TO THE MODERNIST PARADIGM AND THE RISE OF MORAL IMPERATIVES IN LEADERSHIP

Those who opposed this modernist thinking condemned it as imperialist, anthropocentric, and replete with notions of class, gender, and race domination. In fact, these divergent thinkers saw the modernist paradigm and the resulting scientific management perspective as catalysts for the rise of alienation and the domination of the individual through bureaucracy. Max Weber (1864–1920), a German thinker and one of the founders of sociology, lamented that the modernist celebration of science implied that there were no incalculable forces at work in learning anything. That is, Weber (1996) argued, the early 20th century's penchant for empiricism meant that mastery came only through calculation:

> This means that the world is disenchanted. One need no longer have recourse to magical means in order to master or implore the spirits, as did the savage, for whom such mysterious powers existed. Technical means and calculations perform the service. (p. 170)

Cornel West (1982) suggests that the decline of modernism launched the culture into a postmodern frame of thinking. What West finds interesting are the results of this demythologizing of science, which places scientific explanations and theoretical perspectives of the self, world, and God in the same contested terrain of religious, artistic, and moral accounts of the self, world, and God. According to West, the demythologizing process resulted in a deep crisis in knowledge positions, which unraveled the heretofore hegemonic notions that science and truth were monogamous and actually formed the basis for the policies and actual practices in the marketplace. Another vestige of modernism is what West calls the degeneration of modern paganism into various forms of cynicism, fatalism, hedonism, and narcissism. West describes this degeneration as being represented by "impotent irony, barren skepticism, and paralyzing self-parody" (p. 42). He concludes: "It raises the prospect of a possible plurality of epistemic authorities on truth and reality as well as a frightening full-blown relativism or laissez-faire policy regarding access to truth and reality" (p. 42).

West (1982) characterizes the modernist period and the successive era of postmodernism as a time devoid of spiritual anchors. Along with scientific grounding and a concomitant critical interrogation of traditions and hegemonic forms came a vacuum in ontological and spiritual matters. The third indicator of a postmodern shift is what West calls philosophical attacks on the primacy of the subject, including the fact that the avant-garde has been absorbed or domesticated into the mainstream market. Market values, grounded in conspicuous consumption, undergird most of the thinking and behavior in this postmodern era. It is as if the thinking of the individual can only be legitimated if it can be viewed as leading to some market profitability. Radical voices, or ideas and images outside the status quo, become commodified or co-opted by burgeoning market forces determined to consume ideas, trends, and even movements that may portend a profit and enhance a capitalist position. West argues that a nihilistic sense pervades this era. Feelings of hopelessness and vanity are ubiquitous because so much value is placed on making a profit and enhancing the market. Those who are outside the mainstream thoughts or tenets of market values are assumed to be noncontributors and thus devalued by those who espouse this bias toward capitalism and profit. This is the context those who are in leadership positions in schools face every day.

Fortunately, the field of educational leadership currently must also contend with a more critical, progressive language that questions the hidden meanings and intentions of the curriculum and the other trappings of the American system of education. This questioning is framed in terms of a moral imperative that dares to include what happens in schools in the critical question of who ultimately benefits from what takes place in America's schools. This moral emphasis, embedded in a critical theoretical context, interrogates the American system of education through one of several fundamental inquiries, namely who actually profits or whose social capital is enhanced through what occurs in America's schools. This is a moral inquisition because it dares to assume that discrepancies and inequities abound among the thousands of schools and school districts in this country. It is moral because after asserting such a position, this sense of critique goes further, motivated by a spirit of possibility, to project that these undemocratic practices in places called schools can be altered. It is moral because this emphasis on matters of race, class, gender, and sexual orientation is bathed in what Paulo Freire (1998) calls the universal human ethic, that is, the ethic grounded in the liberation of all peoples from the bondage of systemic oppression and marginalization. As a result, moral educational leadership contextualizes the teaching and learning process in the societal realities where "otherness" and undemocratic practices are celebrated. Moral leadership is not complete in its ability to lodge critique but goes on to facilitate a creative environment where agendas for change and purer demonstrations of democratic principles are embedded in the curriculum and pedagogy of morally driven schools.

MORAL LEADERSHIP: A NECESSARY RESPONSE FOR THOSE TRAPPED IN THE MODERN/POSTMODERN CROSSFIRE

Educational leadership that is built on the tenets of scientific management is guilty of operating in an assumed frictionless environment that is fanciful at best. Wise students of educational leadership can place what happens in schools in a broader cultural context. They are also judicious if they realize that schools often serve as spaces for social reproduction. In fact, schools have historically been used either to solidify the status quo or to bring about societal change legislated by either federal or local governmental agencies, for example, school desegregation. Schools have become the purveyors of the culture that those who wield political and economic power deem legitimate. School leaders have been assigned to monitor pedagogical methods and curricula that convey these messages, which are often bathed in racist, sexist, and ageist language.

The whole notion of moral leadership moves educational administration from the realm of minimum competencies and high-stakes testing, which are grounded in a modernist frame, to a position of influence where the broader society is concerned. In *The Moral and Spiritual Crisis in Education*, David Purpel (1989) persuasively argues that educators have long emphasized the minutia of schooling to the neglect of weightier matters. Essentially, the more substantive, ontological discussions regarding American education focus on many of the moral issues Purpel outlines. He maintains that our cultural crisis is a crisis in meaning and that the current crisis in education is not appropriately localized in pedagogical technique, funding issues, and organizational or structural concerns. Rather, Purpel suggests that like the cultural crisis, the educational crisis is one of meaning. Some may misunderstand or not be familiar with the concept of meaning; when we have meaning in our lives, it satisfies an essential introspective inquiry centering on why we exist and why we are doing what we are doing. Having meaning in our lives ties our behavior to a purpose. It inextricably aligns our profession to an avocation and provides the reason why we adopt certain professional stances and practices. Meaning causes us to understand that our positions as educational leaders are not simply placeholders or the mechanisms by which we perpetuate commerce and the prevailing economic system but an active ingredient in defining what is significant to us and to what we have a heartfelt commitment. Educational leaders who grasp this fundamentally moral or spiritual concept also understand that schools are not merely places that are committed to

academic pursuits but are also spaces where human imagination and creativity can be used to re-create our world. Schools are terrains of struggle between the status quo, with all of its issues, and the fabrication of a different existence where undemocratic forms, structures, and rituals have been systemically denuded and have become the intentional focus of democratic projects of change. Purpel and others have voiced their displeasure over the fact that in the midst of a contemporary absence of meaning, with the culture crying out for more substantive ways to feel connected and to deal with the ills of poverty, drug addiction, legislative and judicial faux pas, child abuse, racism, gender disparities, and wars, schools are merely offering more measures of accountability and standardized tests as remedies to prevent any child being "left behind." There is hardly ever a discussion of substance that critically examines how schools perpetuate these societal diseases and how school leaders are compensated for leading the effort to maintain the hegemony.

When schools, school districts, and even individual school leaders attempt to implement scientific management or some other empirically based management system, without being cognizant of their social implications, then the kinds of successes they are looking for become few and far between. In fact, it is actively immoral for school leaders to attempt to embrace any genre of administration without first grappling with the social, political, and cultural contexts in which their schools exist. Foster (1986, p. 94) poses questions that school leaders must answer if they are to morally lead their schools. He asks administrators to reflect on a series of questions that address the radical reconstruction of schools:

1. How are society and culture reproduced through schooling?

2. Why are the sons and daughters of the underclass apt to be fathers and mothers of underclass children, too?

3. How is a culture of sexism and violence perpetuated?

4. Why can't schools break the cycle of class reproduction?

Parker and Shapiro (1993) argue that school leaders have to ground their work in theoretical frameworks that lend themselves to engaging questions such as those Foster raises. They maintain that the positivist framework that has traditionally informed the labor of school administrators is not open to such inquiries. In fact, the bureaucratic models of administration that celebrate logical positivism simply ignore the cultural realities experienced by their schools. What is needed is a more critical theoretical framework undergirding school leadership that dares to ask the moral questions about schools' agendas. Parker and Shapiro contend that "clearly, school leaders need to reflect upon social class issues within a changing economy and how these issues impact on curriculum, instruction, school culture, and the surrounding community" (p. 54). They believe that the moral thing for school leaders to do is to identify the detailed demographics of their school, school district, and community as they relate to social class. This demographic profile should be used to assist the school's administrators to ensure that there is an equitable representation on school committees, advisory teams, and other groups that inform what actually takes place in the schoolhouse. A leadership that engages these demographic issues can be described as purpose driven.

PURPOSE-DRIVEN MORAL LEADERSHIP

A school leader who is committed to purpose-driven moral leadership demythologizes the educational process and critiques, from a critical theoretical insight, the structures, forms, and rituals that have traditionally characterized life in schools. I (2003) argue:

The purpose of schools, especially for urban youth, is deconstructed by the purpose-driven leader who has the spiritual wherewithal to critically contextualize the conditions that define the lives of many of our youth from America's urban core. These leaders become a prophet of sorts in that the purpose-driven leaders ground their work in an effort to "bring an urgent and compassionate critique to bear on the evils of their day" (West, 1999, p.171). (p. 281)

Purposive leaders contend with the agenda of the hegemony while at the same time challenging those in the learning community "to rise above the nihilistic predispositions that are pervasive throughout the community" (Dantley, 2003, p. 281).

Purposive leaders are fully cognizant of the cultural issues that prevail outside the school's walls. They are also clearly aware of how class, race, gender, and other markers of difference play such a prominent role in what takes place in schools. These school leaders understand that in cooperation with other community agencies, the school is a site where the exigencies of societal change can be birthed. They see the work of schools as a moral imperative to serve as one of those critical voices addressing the meanings behind police and racial profiling, violence in the community, and the wholesale marketing and capitalist empire of drug trafficking, use, and abuse in many communities.

What this all means is that leaders who believe that their work should go beyond merely ensuring students' acquisition of academic accolades must position the work of the school in the forefront of societal accountability and responsibility. They see the work of schools and their leadership through the gaze of a moral imperative. That is, purpose-driven school leaders not only use epistemologies as instruments that craft knowledge but also accept the reality of their dynamic nature in "remembering, proving, imagining, inferring, perceiving, and reflecting" (Rebore, 2001,

p. 200). These leaders contextualize the work of the schoolhouse in an ever-changing, vibrant space. Furthermore, they understand a moral obligation to unravel and lay bare the often concretized notions of curriculum and pedagogy through a critical theoretical lens that keenly delineates the issues of power and culture and the asymmetrical power relationships that are often inherent in the teaching and learning process.

MORAL LEADERSHIP AND CRITICAL SELF-REFLECTION

It is thus clear that moral, purpose-driven leadership challenges educators to embrace much more than the rudiments of educational administration. Many preparatory programs of educational leadership do well in engaging prospective school leaders in the technocracy of administration but ignore what Ron Heifetz and Marty Linsky (2002) call the adaptive work, or challenges, that are also a part of school leadership. Heifetz and Linsky point out that leaders and organizations will find themselves in relatively safe and innocuous spaces if they simply contend with issues and problems for which they already know the answers. However, all leaders are bombarded with dilemmas for which they do not have a prepared technical solution. There is no adequate authoritative or procedural resolution to many of these issues. These are the challenges that Heifetz and Linsky call *adaptive*. These problems require that leaders and organizations such as school communities experiment with new ways of perceiving. They require examining and often relinquishing sedimented attitudes, values, and, ultimately, behaviors so that the essential changes needed to meet the demands may take place. Adaptive work dares to ask leaders to carefully examine values, attitudes, assumptions, and predispositions covering a whole host of issues. This process is a part of a leader's development of what is called an idiographic morality (Dantley, 2003), which

results from individuals' personal journeys as they grapple with the meanings of what is just and right and how they personally see or evaluate themselves in actualizing those definitions. It takes a keen introspective endeavor, essential for both current and prospective leaders, to unearth areas of dissonance that may exist between their demonstrated behavior and internal assumptions. That endeavor is critically reflective because it challenges leaders to engage themselves personally in issues of race, class, gender, ability, and markers of otherness. "Principled leadership is initiated when an individual questions the democratic efficacy of administrative decisions and procedures he or she is demanded to implement" (Dantley, 2003, pp. 187–188).

Contested terrains of thought for critical self-reflection could deal with issues such as the leader's assumptions about power and authority, his or her predispositions toward the labor of teachers, and issues of patriarchy and positional privilege. Critical reflection would compel prospective as well as current educational leaders to wrestle with how schools and potentially their administration would perpetuate racial and class divides. How do schools implement the notions of accepted social and cultural capital and penalize those who operate outside these hegemonic distinctions? Critical self-reflection, an essential part of developing idiographic morality, forces school leaders to contend with themselves in a serious ontological and axiological debate. This process challenges leaders to see themselves within the whole social, political, and economic context within which schools are mired.

Critical self-reflection has the potential to be reduced to inane "navel gazing" unless it is partnered with a serious effort to develop strategies designed to resist the persistent policies, procedures, and personal as well as organizational behaviors that diligently maintain an undemocratic status quo in schools. Certainly, school leaders are bombarded by immediate concerns that threaten to devour any time they may try to set aside for critical self-reflection; supervising lunchrooms, disciplining students, ordering books and supplies, and maintaining the budget are only a few of the areas clamoring for their attention. However, one of the main reasons that school transformation is so sporadic and often fleeting is that new technical devices are applied to deeply embedded adaptive issues while the underlying attitudinal and value challenges have never been addressed. For real change, moral change, to take place in our schools, leaders must seize the opportunity to situate themselves and what they have been asked to do outside the gated communities of hegemonic thinking when education is concerned. This whole notion of idiographic morality is generated as a result of leaders' embracing their spiritual selves. This idiographic challenge places the individual leader's personal sense of purpose and meaning within a system that often engages in immoral or undemocratic, marginalizing, and unethical behavior. Statistics on student achievement gaps and school dropout rates point to blatant discrepancies and unethical practices persistently tolerated in schools, practices that widen the academic achievement gap among students. Educational leadership preparatory programs would serve prospective school leaders well if they compelled them to undergo periods of critical self-reflection to equip them to deal forthrightly with those areas in their own attitudes and dispositions that may be problematic as they attempt to lead their schools in a democratic fashion. Rather than filling current school leaders' heads with more technical knowledge, professional development opportunities might include times of reflection where leaders are compelled to deal with critical issues in a nonthreatening environment. What is absolutely essential is a new way of perceiving the activities and responsibilities of school leadership in terms of purpose and learning.

DOUBLE-LOOP LEARNING AND PURPOSIVE LEADERSHIP

Although the open systems model, which is grounded in a modernist perspective, has some value and seems to offer some hope to schools touched by the exigencies of their communities, it is nonetheless laden with single-loop as opposed to double-loop thinking. Morgan (1997) defines single-loop learning as the ability to detect and correct errors in relation to a given set of operating norms. In open systems thinking about schools, those inputs that percolate through the permeable boundary of the school and are antagonistic to the hegemonic notions of school and its purpose are either dismissed or marginalized during the process of transaction. Such inputs are so divergent from the given set of operating norms that they must be corrected. Double-loop learning, however, depends on being able to take a second look at the situation by questioning the relevance of the operating norms. Morgan suggests that double-loop learning consists of sensing, scanning, and monitoring the environment, comparing this information against the traditional operating norms, questioning whether the operating norms are appropriate, and finally, initiating appropriate action. When comparing the two ways of dealing with contextual issues, Morgan argues:

> Many organizations have become proficient at single-loop learning, developing an ability to scan the environment, set objectives, and monitor the general performance of the system in relation to these objectives. The basic skill is often institutionalized in the form of information systems designed to keep the organization "on course." (p. 88)

In double-loop learning, the process of questioning whether the operating norms of an organization, and a school in particular, are appropriate allows for a moral interrogation to take place of schools and their administration. Such inquiries are grounded in ontological questions that penetrate to the heart of the purpose as well as the function of schools. This reflective process opens the rather closed system of schools to a deeply spiritual interrogation whose aim is to lay bare the various ways schools and school leaders perpetuate the asymmetric power relationships and undemocratic practices inherent in the very fiber of our society. Double-loop learning can potentially help educators, and particularly educational leaders, open their systems to inquiry and change:

> It also can assist educators in identifying deficiencies in the established norms of schools. In contrast to single-loop learning, double-loop processes embrace the need for an ongoing, reflective, and inclusive ethic of critique. Through double-loop learning, teachers and administrators use resistance or conflict arising within their schools as opportunities for inquiring into established norms and practices. For example, by critically examining the nonconforming and underperforming behaviors of students within our schools, as well as the context and circumstances in which those behaviors arise, educators can better determine the most appropriate and most ethically supportable institutional response. (Larson & Ovando, 2001, p. 183–184)

Double-loop learning is a reflective activity in which moral, purposive leaders (Dantley, 2003) engage.

BRINGING WHOLENESS TO LEADERSHIP

So what does this all mean? Clearly, given the social environment in which schools are presently operating, using a theory of administration that is grounded on predictability, rationalism, and linear processing is useless. The "messiness" of the educational endeavor militates against using a model that assumes education takes place in an antiseptic and frictionless space. Today's educators are faced with a plethora of social and political dilemmas. Ignoring them only deepens the

divide between schools and the realities of the everyday lived experiences of the students they serve.

Current school leaders are called to facilitate spaces where cultural difference is not only celebrated but concomitantly deconstructed through a process of critical self-reflection and an ongoing discourse on issues of power and privilege. The moral context of school leadership moves beyond merely holding educational leaders responsible for doing things right. Rather, it compels them to do the right thing. This clearly means that school leadership cannot afford to be built on the tenets of positivism or, indeed, any other theoretical framework that assumes linearity, predictability, and fact/value neutrality as its guiding conceptual framework. For years, the glorification of objectivity has resulted in schools where the whole person has not been welcome. The false sense of empirical purity and unalloyed policies and procedures has lulled current as well as prospective leaders into the gossamer security of rationality and prescience, both of which are fleeting and whimsical at best.

Sergiovanni (1999) is helpful in this regard as he describes the work of school leaders as being both technical and moral. The technical side of school leadership focuses on the accumulation of knowledge, orderliness, efficiency, and productivity. For years, those who entered the field of educational leadership have been bombarded with an array of lists, technical aids that purport to make them successful in their work. The technical side of school administration certainly must be dealt with, but not at the expense of the moral dimension. Textbooks must be ordered, budgets must be kept, teachers and staff must be employed. All of these technical ventures must, however, be couched in a moral context. Indeed, Sergiovanni argues that the technical and moral dimensions of school leadership cannot be separated in practice. The moral image of leadership embraces developing attitudes and dispositions within the learning community that undergird democratic practices, equity, and fairness in both the schoolhouse and society as a whole. Sergiovanni makes the point that every technical decision has moral implications and further delineates the essential differences in what he calls normative rationality and technical rationality. Although a critical theorist would problematize notions of empirical rationality, Sergiovanni's division of these two facets of a leader's work is nonetheless useful. Normative rationality involves behavior that is founded on what we believe and consider to be good. Technical rationality is concerned with behavior based on what is effective and efficient. Critical self-reflection, which is predisposed to examining the institution of education from a perspective of who has the power and how the maintenance of that power or status quo is operationalized, is one way to begin the work Sergiovanni outlines in normative rationality. He writes:

> Normative rationality influences the practice of leadership in schools in two ways. Principals bring to their job biases and prejudices, ways of thinking, personality quirks, notions of what works and what doesn't, and other factors that function as personal theories of practice governing what they are likely to do and not do, and school cultures are defined by a similar set of biases that represent the center of shared values and commitments that define the school as an institution. Both are sources of norms that function as standards and guidelines for what goes on in the school. (p. 28)

Moral leadership, then, accepts the arduous responsibility of sharing those predispositions and attitudes that form the basis of professional practice. These are examined through a critical theoretical lens that compels the person reflecting to consider the hegemonic ways schools and their leadership perpetuate undemocratic procedures and practices and marginalize those who are external to any accepted positionality, be it race, class, gender, or exceptionality.

The goal of moral leadership seems to be manifold. Unquestionably, academic achievement is one of the primary, overarching goals of educational leadership. A second goal, however, is the transformation of society so that democracy is operationalized. Clearly, this is not a task that the institution of education can accomplish by itself; it must partner with others in the community to see this goal come to pass. John Dewey (1859–1952) asserted that there cannot be two sets of ethical principles, one for life within the school and the other for life outside the school. Dewey argued that conduct is singular, and therefore, the principles on which conduct is based are also singular. He urged educators and others to recognize the moral responsibility of the school to society, saying:

> The school is fundamentally an institution erected by society to do a certain specific work—to exercise a certain specific function in maintaining the life and advancing the welfare of society. The educational system which does not recognize that this fact entails upon it an ethical responsibility is derelict and a defaulter. (quoted in Hickman & Alexander, 1998, p. 246)

Moral leadership, therefore, is broader than traditional school management. It demands a deep investment of the genuine or authentic self of the educational leader. Moral leaders have the courage to locate their work in a broader as well as deeper space as they work to bring about societal transformation. Moral leadership is problematic because it interrogates what school systems and communities have essentialized. It is problematic because it dares to demystify those structures and rituals that have become almost reified after so many years of acceptance. Moral leadership does not critique for the sheer pleasure of raising issues with the prevailing insights and practices in school systems; it does so with a sense of possibility that announces a more fair and democratic way to do school business. It offers alternatives to the marginalizing practices many schools use in selecting teachers, grouping students, and deciding which teachers they are assigned. Moral leadership is not timid about asking the hard questions of the purpose of schools and who are most ably served by them. It is a daunting task to be a moral school leader but one that must be embraced by more men and women in this 21st century.

REFERENCES

Cahoone, L. (Ed.). (1996). *From modernism to postmodernism: An anthology.* Malden, MA: Blackwell.

Dantley, M. E. (2003). Purpose driven leadership: The spiritual imperative to guiding schools beyond high stakes testing and minimum proficiency. *Education and Urban Society, 35,* 273–291.

Foster, W. (1986). *Paradigms and promises: New approaches to educational administration.* Buffalo, NY: Prometheus Books.

Freire, P. (1998). *Pedagogy of freedom: Ethics, democracy, and civic courage.* Lanham, MD: Rowman & Littlefield.

Giroux, H. A. (1997). *Pedagogy and the politics of hope: Theory, culture, and schooling.* Boulder, CO: Westview Press.

Heifetz, R. A., & Linsky, M. (2002). *Leadership on the line: Staying alive through the dangers of leading.* Boston: Harvard Business School Press.

Hickman, L. A., & Alexander, T. M. (Eds.). (1998). *The essential Dewey: Pragmatism, education, democracy.* Bloomington: Indiana University Press.

Hill-Collins, P. (1998). *Fighting words: Black women and the search for justice.* Minneapolis: University of Minnesota Press.

Kellner, D. (Ed.). (2001). *Towards a critical theory of society: Herbert Marcuse.* London: Routledge.

Larson, C. L., & Ovando, C. J. (2001). *The color of bureaucracy: The politics of equity in multicultural school communities.* Belmont, CA: Wadsworth.

Maxcy, S. J. (1995). *Democracy, chaos, and the new school order.* Thousand Oaks, CA: Corwin.

Morgan, G. (1997). *Images of organization.* Thousand Oaks, CA: Sage.

Parker, L., & Shapiro, J. R. (1993). The context of educational administration and social class. In C. A. Capper (Ed.), *Educational administration in a pluralistic society* (pp. 36–65). Albany: SUNY Press.

Purpel, D. E. (1989). *The moral and spiritual crisis in education: A curriculum for justice and compassion in education.* New York: Bergin & Garvey.

Rebore, R. W. (2001). *The ethics of educational leadership.* Upper Saddle River, NJ: Merrill Prentice Hall.

Sergiovanni, T. J. (1999). *Rethinking leadership: A collection of articles by Thomas J. Sergiovanni.* Arlington Heights, IL: SkyLight Training and Publishing.

Starratt, R. J. (2003). *Centering educational administration: Cultivating meaning, community, responsibility.* Mahwah, NJ: Lawrence Erlbaum.

Weber, M. (1996). Excerpt from the lecture, "Science as a vocation." In L. Cahoone (Ed.), *From modernism to postmodernism: An anthology* (pp. 169–176). Malden, MA: Blackwell.

West, C. (1982). *Prophesy deliverance: An Afro-American revolutionary Christianity.* Philadelphia: Westminster Press.

3

Social Justice

Seeking a Common Language

ALAN R. SHOHO
University of Texas at San Antonio

BETTY M. MERCHANT
University of Texas at San Antonio

CATHERINE A. LUGG
Rutgers University

INTRODUCTION AND OVERVIEW

Since the late 1980s, interest in social justice issues has increased among scholars in educational leadership preparation programs across the country. As recently as 5 years ago, Anderson (2002) noted, social justice and equity issues rarely appeared in the literature associated with educational leadership programs. Shoho and Broussard (2003) found increasing interest in social justice issues at the annual meetings of the University Council for Educational Administration (UCEA) over a 16-year period, 1987 to 2002. Whereas in the 1980s, few educational leadership scholars were working on social justice issues, the renaissance of social justice scholarship in other

educational areas has fueled growing interest in social justice and educational leadership at the dawn of the 21st century.

Although issues of social justice and equity are gaining legitimacy in the scholarly literature, there is still no broad-based agreement on a conceptual definition of social justice with respect to educational administration. For some scholars, social justice is restricted to issues associated with specific classifications such as race, ethnicity, gender, economic social class, sexual orientation, religion, and disability (Applebaum, 2001; Hutchinson, 1997; Mohr, 1989; O'Loughlin, 2002; Scheurich, 2002; Shakeshaft, 1989; Tyson, 2003; Weiner, 2001; White, 2002). Consequently, dialogues involving social justice issues often result in proponents working *against* rather than *with* one another. As Gonzalez (2002) noted, "The educational success of all children remains an untenable cause until all at the table realize that they are part of the solution" (p. 6). Similarly, Young, Petersen, and Short (2001) pointed out that laying the blame for perceived injustices on others is a waste of time.

The purpose of this chapter is to examine the historical and underlying aspects of social justice and propose a working conceptual framework for understanding it. To achieve this purpose, this chapter is organized into four sections. First, we will provide a rationale for investigating a definition of social justice and discuss why it is imperative that we start from a common reference in framing social justice discussions. Second, we will provide a historical overview to illustrate the roots of social justice and how this concept has fared in the educational administration profession. Third, we will scrutinize the literature to assess how other disciplines and scholars have defined social justice. Using this literature, we will construct a framework describing social justice and its guiding principles. Finally, we will discuss how educational leadership preparation programs can better prepare future school leaders to address social justice issues. In doing so, we will focus on the language that educational leadership programs use and how it may impede administrators' understanding and interpretation of social justice issues.

SOCIAL JUSTICE: THE IMPORTANCE OF A COMMON REFERENCE POINT

As with other popular social concepts, such as affirmative action, multiculturalism, and the provision of adequate school finance, social justice is a politically loaded term, subject to numerous interpretations. Like other abstract concepts, the exact meaning of social justice has been elusive and difficult to pinpoint. The meaning adopted for social justice greatly influences the perspective taken when

addressing an issue under examination. For example, some scholars view social justice strictly from a racial perspective (i.e., critical race/postmodern: see Scheurich, 2002), whereas others view it primarily from a gender perspective (i.e., feminist theory: see Shakeshaft, 1989; White, 2002). Although the term *social justice* implies a valuing of diversity, the variety of perspectives has created a situation where there is no common reference point from which to engage in scholarly and practical dialogue about the meaning and implications of social justice. Without a common language, it is difficult for scholars to engage school leaders in a meaningful dialogue on social justice issues. The multiplicity of social justice perspectives has produced an environment in which proponents of social justice often argue from narrow and mutually exclusive viewpoints regarding who should participate in addressing social justice issues (Mohr, 1989; Scheurich, 2002; Tyson, 2003; White, 2002).

This situation nullifies the very inclusiveness that social justice perspectives purport to espouse. This contradiction between the espoused theories (inclusiveness) and theories in action (exclusiveness) of social justice makes it difficult to reach consensus and forge alliances among all relevant stakeholders. Hence, because one of the purposes of social justice is to combat the societal ills experienced by those with the least voice in society, particularly children, it is imperative that those in positions of advocacy be able to communicate in a common language (i.e., have a shared understanding of what social justice is and means).

To gain an understanding of what social justice means and its semantic use in the English language, it is important to understand its roots. In Latin, *justice* comes from the word *equitas,* which means fairness, and *social* derives from the word *socius,* meaning companion. Combining these Latin roots produces a literal definition of social justice as being fair to one's companions. Although this definition appears to be straightforward and easy to comprehend, some basic assumptions underlie its simplicity. For example, to use this definition for social justice would entail a fundamental shift away from popular theories such as Maslow's hierarchy of needs, which places the individual above others, to a conceptual model such as that proposed by the Dalai Lama (1999) and McCalla (2002), where empathy and concern for others form the foundation for all social interactions. It is unlikely that in the foreseeable future, mankind will be able to evolve to a state where individual needs take a backseat to the needs of others. If individual needs continue to be the focal point of societal concerns, then a definition of social justice must take this into consideration.

As noted earlier, social justice is not a new concept for scholars in disciplines such as sociology, history, law, social work, curriculum, and, of course, theology, but it is a relatively new term to the field of educational administration. Social justice is deeply rooted in theology (Ahlstrom, 1972; Hudson, 1981) and social work (Koerin, 2003), with rich roots in educational disciplines like curriculum and pedagogy (Apple, 1996; Freire, 1970/1992, 1996). Despite this foundation, there is still great ambiguity about the term social justice and its underlying principles. In general, social justice has been linked to the concepts of equity and fairness. Beyond this simplified definition, however, there are varying perspectives on what social justice actually is. To gain a deeper appreciation of the underlying meaning of social justice, it is important to understand its historical roots. In the following section, we will trace the religious roots of social justice and its influence within the progressive education movement of the 1930s and 1940s. Subsequently, our historical analysis of social justice examines how educational administration programs have traditionally viewed social justice issues.

THE RELIGIOUS ROOTS OF SOCIAL JUSTICE

The roots of the educational social justice movement are found in the 19th-century religious traditions of the Protestant social gospel movement (1840s to 1914), as well as the Catholic Church's call for social justice (1890s through today). Both were responses to the rise of industrial capitalism and the dislocations it imposed on families and communities (Ahlstrom, 1972). What makes the social gospel movement striking is that it was a religious critique by Protestants of the very Protestant foundations of American capitalism (Hudson, 1981). At the time, the vast majority of American Protestants believed that the rich were rewarded by God for their good works; conversely, the poor were poor because they were being punished for some sin or personal failing (Hudson, 1981). As the income gap between industrial capitalists and industrial workers widened, however, poverty grew at rates never before seen. Millions of Americans lived in conditions marked by squalor and disease (Zinn, 1999). The long-standing biases regarding the "immoral" poor were thus called into question. Proponents of the social gospel, including some who were also political Progressives, advocated that "good Christians," meaning middle-class, white Protestants, needed to get involved in tackling the social ills of the day—taking action to ameliorate the conditions confronting the poor. They believed that like Christ, Christians should "visit prisoners, clothe the naked, and feed the hungry" (Armstrong, 2000, p. 169). Adherents were to rescue the poor workingman and his family from the vagaries of capitalism. As a result, activists rooted in the teachings of the social gospel worked to found settlement houses to serve recently arrived immigrants, expand public school offerings, establish minimum wage laws, establish a separate system of juvenile justice, and ban child labor (Kennedy, 1999;

Reese, 2002). Many of the educational innovations at this time—from playgrounds and school nurses to nascent lunch and breakfast programs, along with a greater focus on "child saving"—were legacies of religiously inspired Progressive reformers.[1] As numerous scholars have noted, most adherents of the social gospel were not socialists, as their political opponents were wont to allege (particularly after the 1917 Bolshevik revolution). Rather, they were religiously inspired reformers, working to soften the harsher edges of the capitalist status quo (see Ahlstrom, 1972; Kennedy, 1999; Lissak, 1989; Reese, 2002). Proponents also hoped to recruit workingmen, and particularly immigrant and Catholic workingmen, into their middle-class Protestant churches (Hudson, 1981). However, reformers had greater success in tackling the social ills of the day than in enticing working-class Catholics to join the congregations of the Protestant middle class.

The Catholic Church also reacted to these social and economic conditions and dislocations. In 1891, Pope Leo XIII issued *Rerum Novarum (On the Rights and Duties of Capital and Labor)*, which called for social justice, or a fairer distribution of society's economic resources (Ahlstrom, 1972). Like the social gospel, the 19th-century call for social justice was reformist, not revolutionary; *Rerum Novarum* contained explicit critiques of both socialism and broader revolutionary impulses:

> Justice, therefore, demands that the interests of the working classes should be carefully watched over by the administration, so that they who contribute so largely to the advantage of the community may themselves share in the benefits which they create—that being housed, clothed, and bodily fit, they may find their life less hard and more endurable. It follows that whatever shall appear to prove conducive to the well being of those who work should obtain favorable consideration. There is no fear that solicitude of this kind will be harmful to any interest; on the contrary, it will be to the advantage of all, for it cannot but be good for the commonwealth to shield from misery those on whom it so largely depends for the things that it needs. (Leo XIII, 1891)

However, it would be nearly 40 years until the Catholic Church in the United States embraced these teachings. As religious historian Aaron Abell tartly observed, "Though lip service was paid to Leo XIII's *Rerum Novarum*, leading Catholics . . . failed to emphasize its meaning; they expounded it as a 'bulwark' of the status quo and not as a charter of social justice" (quoted in Ahlstrom, 1972, p. 1004). Nevertheless, Leo XIII had laid a foundation that would be embraced later, when enthusiasm for the social gospel had largely faded in Protestant circles (Ahlstrom, 1972).

By the 1920s and 1930s, economic conditions were as dire for many Americans as they had been during the late 19th century. However, the depth and breadth of what eventually became a global depression touched far more people, not only disrupting families and communities but also bringing down several national governments and disrupting most others (see Hobsbawm, 1994; Kennedy, 1999). Such an overwhelming economic, social, and political disaster prompted various radical remedies, from the emergence of fascism in Italy, Germany, and eventually Spain to the forced collectivization in Stalin's Soviet Union (Hobsbawm, 1994). In the United States, both fascism and communism attracted followers, while more progressively minded Catholics—particularly those in the nascent Catholic Worker movement[2]—worked toward the greater economic social justice espoused in *Rerum Novarum* (Ahlstrom, 1972). Americans from diverse backgrounds continued to search for ways out of the expanding economic quicksand (Hobsbawm, 1994; Kennedy, 1999).

One of the most controversial social justice-oriented proposals of the era came from educators. In February 1932, in a speech at the Progressive Education Association's annual convention, George S. Counts asked the question, "Dare progressive education be progressive?" At the time, progressive education was largely the province of college professors and educators at schools—both public and private—for children of the upper middle class (Counts, 1932/1978; Cremin, 1961). Progressive education was noted for its commitment to child-centered education, but in Counts's Veblean worldview,[3] it was more of a benefit for the pampered children of the social elite than an instrument that could transform the political and economic status quo. The Depression provided an opportunity to return progressive education to its "progressive"—and potentially transformative—political roots. Counts insisted not only that educators should get involved with politics but that they needed to lead political change. He later observed in his seminal book, *Dare the School Build a New Social Order?*

We live in difficult and dangerous times—times when precedents lose their significance. If we are content to remain where all is safe and quiet and serene, we shall dedicate ourselves, as teachers have commonly done in the past, to a role of futility, if not positive social reaction. Neutrality with respect to the great issues that agitate society, while perhaps theoretically possible, is practically tantamount to giving support to the forces of conservatism. . . . To refuse to face the task of creating a vision of a future America immeasurably more just and noble and beautiful than the America of today is to evade the most crucial, difficult and important educational task. (Counts, 1932/1978, p. 51)

Counts, in his speech to the Progressive Education Association and in subsequent publications, called for educators to embrace political indoctrination of students and for teachers to work for the further democratization of American society by tackling the social, economic, and political issues of the day in their classrooms. This speech electrified the audience, which expected far blander rhetorical fare

(Cremin, 1961). In addition, it ignited a revival in progressive education that explicitly linked public educators to broader issues of economic justice and democracy.

Nevertheless, larger social and political issues eventually swamped educators' efforts at "social reconstructionism" (Cremin, 1961). First, progressive educators were an admittedly small minority within the profession. Second, without teacher tenure, most progressive public school educators needed the support of sympathetic administrators and board members even to attempt implementing these ideals. Third, World War II had an adverse impact on progressive education principles; educational reports like the Eight-Year Study found that progressive principles produced outcomes similar to traditional education. Finally, progressive educators were operating in an environment where many Americans increasingly equated progressive education with rampant classroom permissiveness. Progressive educators were also suspected of harboring communist sympathies. The 1957 launch of Sputnik, at the height of the Cold War, effectively marked the demise of progressive education (Cremin, 1961).

While progressive education and, more specifically, social reconstructionism receded from the educational landscape, the civil rights movement and subsequent women's, American Indian, Chicano, and nascent gay rights movements pushed educators and most Americans to rethink the basic meanings of *democracy, citizenship,* and *liberty.* Many people of faith were involved with these movements, particularly within the African American civil rights movement (Hudson, 1981). These experiences radicalized generations of social justice workers and theorists. By the 1970s, social justice-minded educational theorists drew selectively on the more emancipatory legacies from the Progressive Era and the theorizing generated by African American theologians and various political activists, as well as more radical notions.

Perhaps the most influential educational theorist of the current era is the late Paulo Freire, who combined liberation theology and Marxism (Freire, 1998). Freire was a long-time adult educator, working with illiterate peasants in rural Brazil. His involvement with education for social transformation resulted in his imprisonment and subsequent exile by a Brazilian junta in the late 1960s. He traveled throughout Latin American working with various educational and political organizations. He returned to Brazil after 16 years of exile (Allman, Mayo, Cavanaugh, Heng, & Haddad, 1998).

Freire employed a dialectical process as a means to critique traditional pedagogical practices, or what he called "banking education." But he went further, drawing on liberation theology to inspire students to engage in understanding and perhaps transforming their own social and political worlds. Through literacy, students would learn to read both the word and the world (Allman et al., 1998). Although some questioned Freire's embrace of both liberation theology and Marxist analysis, he saw no contradiction in his position:

> I began to read Marx and the more I did the more I became convinced that we should become absolutely committed to a global process of transformation. But what is interesting in my case . . . my "meetings" with Marx never suggested to me to stop "meeting" Christ. I always spoke to both of them in a very loving way. . . . Sometimes people say to me that I am contradictory. . . . I don't consider myself contradictory in this. . . . If you ask me then, if I am a religious man, I say no . . . they understand religious as religion-like. I would say that I am a man of faith. . . . I feel myself very comfortable with this. (quoted in Lange, 1998, p. 82)

Freire felt comfortable in claiming the faith in which he had been raised, namely Roman Catholicism, because Latin American theologians had been exploring very different notions of the Christian message of salvation. Developed at mid-century by clerics who could not reconcile the contradictions of European Catholicism with the harsh realities of life for many peasants in Latin America, liberation theology stated that the church had to take a prophetic role in addressing the historic injustices faced by the poor and dispossessed (Cleary, 1985; Peterson & Vasquez, 1998). The church had to have its own Easter. Like Christ, the church too had to be crucified, to die, and to be resurrected—this time siding with the poor (Lange, 1998; Peterson & Vasquez, 1998). Liberation theology differed from the earlier social gospel in that it explicitly drew on Marxist analyses of class to critique oppressive governmental and power structures (Allman et al., 1998; Lange, 1998).[4] Activists inspired by liberation theology worked against totalitarian regimes in Latin America throughout the 1960s, 1970s, and 1980s (Diamond, 1989).

Given Freire's combination of active political commitments, theorizing, and vast real-world experience, his writings have been embraced by many U.S. educators. Yet, the embrace of Freire by American educational theorists has been somewhat paradoxical. Although Freire was quite clear that religious faith inspired his work, many theorists, for whatever reasons, have stripped away his theological foundations. Religious educators have also found his works to be highly compatible, but they, of course, have retained one of his central features—liberation theology (see Prevost & Elias, 1999).

This paradox is not too surprising given the highly secular environments in which most U.S. academics work. In addition, an explicitly political theology has had a questionable political status—at least for white, middle-class Christians (see Dorrien, 1997). Fully embracing Freire, or for that matter the social gospel or social justice, would also present potential issues involving church and state, at least for public education (see Lugg, 2004). Nevertheless, by not mentioning these historic and religious roots, contemporary educators who are committed to promoting socially just practices in schools ignore an important legacy.

Although it is important to capitalize on the historical legacy of social justice and its advocates in education generally, it is also important to note that social justice does not have a long history in educational administration. This brief history and the reasons for it will be discussed in more detail in the next section.

SOCIAL JUSTICE AND EDUCATIONAL ADMINISTRATION: A PARADOXICAL PREMISE

Much of the history of educational administration as a profession and a discipline has been marked by a certain exclusionary zeal. This was particularly true for the early 20th-century administrative progressives, who embraced the nostrums of business efficiency to bolster their political and professional stature (Blount, 1998; Callahan, 1962; Tyack & Hansot, 1982). Not shy about promoting the cause of the efficient school administrator, professors of educational administration extolled the virtues that would flow to school districts that hired properly educated candidates, especially their own students (Blount, 1998; Callahan, 1962).

Furthermore, the truly professional administrator was appointed by the school board, not elected. As with the move toward a more professionalized school board, school districts, prodded by Progressive elites, increasingly dispensed with the practice of elected superintendents (Blount, 1998; Tyack & Hansot, 1982). This professionalized embrace was also calculated to push women out of the nascent profession, just at a time when more women were coming to the superintendency through the power of the ballot (Blount, 1998). Because educational administration programs either barred women or maintained strict quotas limiting their numbers, even if they were "properly trained," it was highly unlikely that female administrators would be selected by

a school board whose own membership was increasingly composed of businessmen (Blount, 1998; Bowles & Gintis, 1976; Callahan, 1962; Tyack & Hansot, 1982).

Religion also was an important informal criterion for choosing superintendents. For an aspiring superintendent, it helped to be Protestant and an active church member, especially in small or medium-size communities. For example, Fredrick Bair found in 1934 that among the 796 superintendents who responded to his survey, only 6 were Roman Catholic, none Jewish, and none agnostic. The remainder were Protestants of one form or another, and 93% of these were regular church attendees (in Tyack & Hansot, 1982).[5] This preference for "active" Protestants when selecting superintendents was continued well into the 1950s and beyond (Tyack & Hansot, 1982).

Similarly, race also shaped who could become and remain an administrator. Although segregated black schools typically hired African American principals, their work was likely to be overseen by a white superintendent, who might not be particularly sympathetic to the welfare of African American students, teachers, or administrators (Tyack & Hansot, 1982). By the 1960s and beyond, indifference and, at times, outright callousness and brutality led to clashes between African American communities and typically white school administrators (Tyack, 1974; Tyack & Hansot, 1982). Furthermore, when public school districts desegregated, black teachers and administrators generally lost their positions (Arnez, 1978).

As with race, class was also a defining feature, given the educational credentials and graduate education needed for entry, as well as the social expectations placed on many superintendents and principals (Callahan, 1962; Nasaw, 1979; Tyack & Hansot, 1982). Finally, with the growing awareness of homosexuality and homosexuals during the mid-20th century, administrators had to conclusively demonstrate their heterosexuality—that is, to be married. At the start of the Cold War, homosexuality was repeatedly linked with communism, and all manner of "gay purges" were carried out across the labor force (Blount, 1996, 1998, 2003; D'Emilio, 1983). Public school educators came under particular scrutiny, with single teachers and administrators viewed with suspicion (Blount, 1998, 2003). Lurid tales of "homosexual recruitment" were splashed across the front pages of newspapers (Alwood, 1996), and the State of Florida's Johns Committee spent several years in the early 1960s investigating such "infestation" within its public educational system (Sears, 1997). Consequently, one lingering Cold War legacy is that to remain in the field, public school administrators' "non-queer" credentials must still be unassailable (Blount, 2003; Lugg, 2003a, 2003b). By 1988, one study noted that "while fifty-seven percent of all households in this country are married couple households, ninety-four percent of superintendents and eighty-seven percent of public school principals are married" (Feistritzer, 1988, p. 17).

In each case—race, class, ethnicity, religion, gender, and sexual orientation—public school administrators have, at times, been expected to be the enforcers of oppressive societal and legal norms in a governmental institution that claims to espouse democratic values (Bowles & Gintis, 1976; Herr, 1999; Lugg, 2003b, 2003c; Nasaw, 1979; Rousmaniere, 1997). What this has meant in daily practice is that administrators have been charged with disciplining students and faculty into following proper social mores and, occasionally, punishing them (Foucault, 1979). This *policing* authority is both a historical legacy and a contemporary reality (Blount, 2003; Goodman, 2001; Lugg, 2003a, 2003b, 2003c). Superintendents and principals are expected to uphold a myriad of educational policies, which range from maintaining a drug-free zone (in all 50 states) to rooting out suspected "queer" educators (13 states),[6] to enforcing antibullying policies.

Public school administrators are also expected to enforce a complex mix of progressive and wildly socially regressive policies, which vary from district to district and from state to state (Lugg, 2003a, 2003b, 2003c).

Based on this brief history illustrating how educational administrators have reflected the values of the dominant society, it is unsurprising that educational administrators have often been the perpetuators of social injustices on those entrusted to their care (Bowles & Gintis, 1976; Lugg, 2003b, 2003c; Nasaw, 1979). At the same time, it is grossly unfair to characterize educational administrators as bankrupt individuals who mindlessly enforce socially unjust policies in a vacuum. For example, Leonard Covello was a high school principal working in New York City public schools, from 1934 to 1956. Drawing on his own experiences as an Italian immigrant boy attending the vastly overpopulated and occasionally anti-Catholic and anti-Italian public schools, he worked hard as a building principal to make his public school an oasis within an economically distressed and sociologically shifting community (Tyack & Hansot, 1982). As one former student recalled, "He filled a hero void for most of us, not a cowboy hero, not a blood and thunder hero, but a true hero. His dedication could show in his own quiet way . . . he was a real big brother and a real father" (Tyack & Hansot, 1982, p. 209). Another example was Miles Cary, principal at McKinley "Tokyo" High School in Honolulu from 1924 to 1948. Educated at Ohio State University under the supervision of Boyd Bode and other progressive educators, Cary reshaped an entire generation of mostly Japanese immigrant children into believing they could do anything they desired. As one former student said about Miles Cary's leadership:

> I think the generation of students that went through McKinley at the time he [Miles Cary] was principal all benefited from the sense that he was the one who was very much interested in their welfare and always

wanted the best for them in the sense that he wanted them to get an education to be able to cope with their society, to make a contribution to the society and to be active participants. (Shoho, 1990, p. 186)

However, in many ways, these two examples represent the exception rather than the rule (Shoho, 1990; Tyack & Hansot, 1982). Covello's commitment to ensuring his high school was a safe place entailed constant and heroic efforts that extended far beyond the regular hours of the position. Similarly, Cary's devotion to progressive principles like democracy was learned through his own experiences in school.

It has been shown that schools as organizations have powerful influences on the actions of individuals (Hoy & Miskel, 2001). Viewing social justice in schools from afar is often difficult during the heat of the moment. According to Beck (1994), moral dilemmas involving people are inherently difficult to resolve. Thus we must ask: To what degree have university programs contributed to the school administrator's lack of preparation to deal with social justice issues? And if preparation programs are part of the problem, then what can university administrative preparation programs do, beyond extolling the value of socially just policies and practices in schools?

SOCIAL JUSTICE AND EDUCATIONAL ADMINISTRATION PREPARATION PROGRAMS

From its inception, the position of school administrator was designed to attract individuals who were willing to comply with a view of schooling that validated rather than challenged existing norms (Blount, 1998; Callahan, 1962; Nasaw, 1979; Tyack & Hansot, 1982). School administrators were appointed as stewards of the communities in which they worked, charged with embodying and reinforcing the values of the power elites who hired them. Superintendents were expected to be responsive to the

demands of school trustees, to carry out their requests, and to ensure that teachers complied with their wishes (Cuban, 1988). As instructional leaders, principals were expected to supervise instruction, manage the curriculum, and assist teachers; as appointees of the school board, they were charged with executing the preferences of school trustees without controversy or dissent (Cuban, 1988).

The creation of formal, university-based administrator preparation programs at the beginning of the 20th century reflected Frederick Taylor's principles of scientific management as well as the increasing influence of the industrial-corporate sector with its emphasis on efficiency and effectiveness. This is reflected in the views of Franklin Bobbitt, an instructor in educational administration at the University of Chicago, whose work, *The Supervision of City Schools,* was published in 1913 as the 12th Yearbook of the National Society for the Study of Education (Callahan, 1962). According to Bobbitt, schoolmen would become "mechanics" whose task would be to implement policies and practices according to the dictates of business and industry (Callahan, 1962). With the rapid growth of cities in the mid-19th century, both the principalship and superintendency became increasingly important mechanisms for imposing order on a large and diverse student population (Nasaw, 1979; Pierce, 1935). The emphasis on principles of scientific management and the emulation of corporate values permeated the small circle of university professors who, through their role in the professional preparation of school administrators, exerted a powerful influence on the thinking of principals and superintendents in key positions across the country. This commitment to the values of efficiency and effectiveness is exemplified in Stanford School of Education Professor Elwood P. Cubberley's 1916 publication, *Public School Administration,* in a chapter entitled, "Efficiency Experts: Testing Results." As the influence of professional school managers grew, that of school boards decreased, a trend that was accelerated by turn-of-the-century reports of the illegal activities of many school board members, particularly those in urban areas (Guthrie, 1990). In an effort to improve the administration of schools, reformers in the Progressive Era were determined to separate the management of schools from the influence of politics, and by the third quarter of the 20th century, schools were bureaucracies character-ized by principals and superintendents as pro-fessional managers at the building and district levels and teachers as members of professional unions (Guthrie, 1990).

With the globalized economy that was in place by the end of the 20th century, Americans, fearful of losing their competitive edge, demanded that schools be held more accountable for improving the learning of all students, regardless of ascribed characteristics. The 1983 release of the publication, *A Nation At Risk: The Imperative for Educational Reform,* sparked a national effort to reform public schooling in the United States (National Commission on Excellence in Education, 1983). The demands for greater student achievement associated with this report were linked to calls for increased teacher participa-tion in matters of classroom instruction and the hiring and evaluation of teachers, as well as the allocation of resources and the devolu-tion of decision making to administrators, teachers, parents, students, and community members at the local school level (Guthrie, 1990).

Although the general trends in the evolu-tion of management-focused, university-based administrator preparation programs are clear, it is important to note countervailing perspec-tives that have argued for a social justice orientation in educational administration. During the 19th century, the populist move-ment and educational agenda provided the basis for contemporary democratic communi-tarianism, which espoused social construc-tivism (Haste, 1996; Johnson, 1995; Kahne, 1996; Macpherson, 1996; Singh, 1997;

Varlotta, 1997). In the latter half of the 20th century, critical theory and postmodern theory presented a challenge to the logical positivist paradigm, with its assumptions of an objective and measurable reality (Bhola, 2002). Springing from the neo-Marxist, criti-cal sociology of the Frankfurt School, "critical theory is a theory of participative democracy rooted in the analyses of social reproduction and resistance" (Bhola, 2002, p. 183). As such, it provides a powerful framework for a social justice orientation to educational administration (e.g., Kochan, 2002; Scheurich, 2002). Similarly, in its opposition to posi-tivism, the feminist critique has strong ties to critical theory, sharing with it "the emphatic themes of empowerment and emancipation" (Bhola, 2002, p. 183). It also serves as a useful framework for exploring issues of social justice in preparing educational leaders (see Grogan, 2000). Postmodernism challenges traditional notions of power and hierarchy and, as such, has played a significant role in exam-ining the intersection of social justice and edu-cational leadership (e.g., Sackney, Walker, & Mitchell, 1999). John Dewey's social recon-structivist philosophy resonates with postmod-ern perspectives and has been useful in conceptualizing educational administration and issues of justice (e.g. Bogotch, 2000; Maxcy, 1994). The concept of moral leader-ship has also played a critical role in discus-sions of social justice within leadership preparation (Beck & Murphy, 1994; Bogotch, Miron, & Murry, 1998; Greenfield, 1999; Hoyle, English, & Steffy, 1998; Leithwood & Duke, 1998; Sergiovanni, 1992; Wong, 1998).

Interest in understanding the nature of school leadership and the preparation of educational administrators has produced a substantial body of literature: descriptive (e.g., Beck & Murphy, 1993; Bolman & Deal, 2002; Daresh, 1997; Hallinger & Heck, 1998; Hart, 1993; Murphy, 2002), prescriptive (e.g., National Association of Elementary School Principals, 1994; Wilmore, 2002), and reform oriented (e.g. Barth, 2001; Blase & Anderson, 1995; Capper, 1993; Crow, Matthews, & McCleary, 1996; Duke, 1992; Goldring & Rallis, 1993; Institute for Educational Leadership, 2000; Jacobson, 1996; Lomotey, 1989; Murphy & Seashore, 1999). Within the past 15 years, numerous groups, including the National Commission on Excellence in Educational Administration, the National Commission for the Principalship, and the Danforth Foundation, have advocated reforms in educational administration preparation programs (Duke, 1992). The National Association of Secondary School Principals and the National Association of Elementary School Principals have also been active participants in the effort to improve the preparation of principals (Daresh, 1997).

In addition, the National Policy Board for Educational Administration, the Interstate School Leaders Licensure Consortium, and the University Council for Educational Administration (UCEA) have each played a key role in defining standards for the principalship and superintendency that acknowledge the importance of creating equitable educational environments in which all children can experience success. UCEA, in particular, has supported several important publications on the status of educational administration and the preparation of principals and superintendents (Jackson, 2001; Jacobson, Emihovich, Helfrich, Petrie, & Stevenson, 1998; Murphy, 1993; Wendel, 1991, 1992). Of the seven domains of knowledge in educational administration identified by UCEA, Domain I, identified as social and cultural influences on schooling, focuses on preparing administrators to respond more effectively to the needs of diverse student populations (for a critique of Domain I, see Lomotey, 1995; Merchant, 1995).

Because of their historic focus on management, departments of educational administration have not typically been associated with social justice issues, and consequently, most of the research in this area has originated

elsewhere. This is reflected in the ways in which colleges and schools of education tend to departmentalize their graduate degree programs, locating the professional preparation of school administrators in one department and educational policy studies, history, and sociology in one or several other departments (All Star Directories, 2003). When policy studies are incorporated into an educational administration department, social justice advocates and critics of the status quo (e.g., critical race theorists) tend to be in other departments, such as cultural studies or educational foundations. Such divisions may be perpetuated by faculty members who seldom, if ever, interact across these boundaries. In these environments, professors of educational administration may be stereotyped by their colleagues in other departments as stewards of the status quo, focused on preparing school administrators for conventional roles rather than equipping them to think reflectively, critically, and creatively about school reform from the perspectives of equity and fairness.

Although such stereotypes are unfair, it is true that for many years, professors of educational administration tended to be former public school superintendents (Cuban, 1988), increasing the likelihood that students would learn more about preserving rather than challenging the educational systems in which they worked. The last 20 years, however, have witnessed a shift in the hiring and outreach practices of colleges and universities, increasing the number of females and scholars of color who are faculty members (Antonio, 2002; Hargens & Long, 2002; "A JBHE Report Card," 2001–2002; Lindholm, Astin, Sax, & Korn, 2002; Pounder, 1990; Trower, 2002; Turner, 2000). Simultaneously, the traditional pipeline for professors of educational leadership has been severely limited by financial concerns. In many cases, principals and superintendents aspiring to the professoriate would incur a stark reduction in salary. As a result, departments of educational leadership are drawing professors from a broader range of academic disciplines, and they increasingly have little to no traditional practitioner leadership experience. These new professors have played a significant role in reshaping the dialogue regarding the preparation of principals and superintendents. Many of these new faculty members also bring with them a rich set of experiences with diverse populations across a variety of local, state, national, and international contexts. Part of the legacy of these new scholars is their deep commitment to applying the principles of equity and social justice to educational reform, so that public schools can become places in which all children are provided with the opportunities and resources to succeed academically and socially. Interest in incorporating a strong social justice component into the formal preparation of principals and superintendents is evidenced in the writings of increasing numbers of educational administration scholars (Beck, 1994; Capper, 1993; Donmoyer, Imber, & Scheurich, 1995; Gonzalez, Huerta-Macias, & Tinajero, 1998; Johnson & Shoho, 2002; Lomotey, 1989, 1995; Lugg, 2002; Marshall & McCarthy, 2002; Marshall & Scribner, 1991; Merchant, 1999a, 1999b; Merchant & Shoho, 2002; Reyes & Scribner, 1995; Reyes, Scribner, & Scribner, 1999; Rorrer, 2002; Skrla & Scheurich, 2001).

Incorporating a social justice orientation into the professional preparation of school administrators cannot be done without also acknowledging the importance of political action in making schools more equitable and just institutions:

> Principals, who, as a matter of habit, seldom consider whether managerial routines and instructional procedures are aligned with their values and beliefs and whose sense of organizational and personal goals are largely undefined or hidden would not be viewed as exercising an overtly political role. Yet, by enforcing district mandates and acting as agents of the superintendent, they would be engaging in tacit political activity through loyalty to existing arrangements. The

> consequences of a principal's actions are both political and moral in endorsing what an institution does. There is no such thing as nonpolitical behavior. (Cuban, 1988, p. 77)

While Blase and Anderson (1995) observe that "a central role of educational administrators traditionally has been to maintain the legitimacy of their institution by managing the various forms of critique and resistance that take place within it" (p. 138), they also urge administrators to direct their efforts toward understanding the relationship between schools and the broader social context, the difference between collaboration and collusion, and the ways in which institutional silencing occurs. The intersection of policy with issues of equity and social justice has powerful and at times conflicting implications for educational leaders (Jones, 2000; Larson & Ovando, 2001; Lomotey & Simms, 1996; Lopez, 2003; Lugg, 2003b; Marshall & Scribner, 1991; Merchant, 1999a).

Current efforts to reform the preparation of school administrators, whether university-based, emerging from the work of professional organizations, or influenced by special interest groups at the state and national levels, are occurring within a broader political context of increased accountability for student learning (Scheurich & Skrla, 2001; Scheurich, Skrla, & Johnson, 2000). While educational sociologists, policy analysts, historians, and educational researchers debate the merits and shortcomings of the various accountability efforts, professors of educational administration, albeit divided in their opinions about the effects of these efforts, are nonetheless obligated to prepare future administrators to work within these contexts. To address issues of fairness and equity, school administrators must be prepared to adapt, change, and, most important, challenge existing educational policies and practices, whether they originate at the building, district, state, or national level. The ways in which professors of educational administration integrate or reconcile their commitment to educational equity and social justice with local, state, and national accountability efforts will play a critical role in redefining the roles of public school administrators and in shaping their relationships with the staff members, teachers, students, and families with whom they work.

Since the 1990s, a growing movement within university administrative preparatory programs has focused on issues of social justice. Part of this growth has been fueled by concern for the growing number of public school students who are considered at risk for a host of dismal academic and life outcomes (Grogan, 2000). In addition, social justice concerns have received support from academics who are politically committed to shaping a more equitable society for all individuals, regardless of their race, ethnicity, sex, class, disability, sexual orientation, or religious affiliation. As Larson and Murtadha (2002) stated:

> Researchers and leaders for social justice . . . seek to define the theories and practices of leadership that are vital to creating greater freedom, opportunity, and justice for all citizens—citizens who, through public education, are better able to participate in and sustain a free, civil, multicultural, and democratic society. (p. 136)

Yet, it cannot be stressed firmly enough that a social justice approach is a marked departure from historic administrative practice in public schools, in that it acknowledges that public schools *can* and frequently *do* reproduce societal inequities (Bowles & Gintis, 1976; Larson & Murtadha, 2002; Nasaw, 1979; Shoho, Katims, & Meza, 1998; Shoho, Katims, & Wilks, 1997). In addition, some of the inequities, such as homophobia, are *mandated* by state statute in those states with laws barring consensual sodomy (Lugg, 2003c, 2004). One of the goals of a social justice approach is that when future educational administrators are schooled in theories and praxis of social

justice, they will be more aware of and work to both ameliorate and possibly eradicate the injustices and inequalities that arise within their buildings. An administrator using a social justice focus would also reach out to the larger community to build a network of support to redress these historic injustices. Although the goal of social justice-orientated educational leadership programs is to develop administrators who are sensitive to the lives and well-being of all children, these approaches may well mean that administrators are essentially conflicted in their daily practices.

For educational leadership programs to inculcate their students with a social justice framework implies a common understanding and definition of what the term means. However, one of the enduring problems arising out of the social justice literature is the ambiguity of the term itself. The next section lays out our proposed definition for the term social justice and identifies some of its guiding principles.

SOCIAL JUSTICE: GUIDING PRINCIPLES

As noted above, social justice has multiple meanings depending on who is asked. For some scholars, the multiple meanings associated with social justice are a positive feature that illustrates the inclusiveness of the term. In fact, Young (1990) and Novak (2000) felt it was impossible to have an agreed upon definition of social justice. As Novak noted, "The minute one begins to define social justice, one runs into embarrassing intellectual difficulties. It becomes . . . a term of art whose operational meaning is, 'We need a law against that'" (p. 11). Yet, one of the difficulties associated with this inclusiveness of meanings is the ambiguity it brings to communicating the language of social justice to others beyond the academic world. In this case, school practitioners, in general, do not use the term social justice in their daily language. They are more likely to use terms such as equity, equality, fairness, and adequacy.

In the literature, several perspectives have been taken when defining social justice. Some have taken an ethical perspective (Britz & Blignaut, 2001; Shapiro & Stefkovich, 2000) whereas others have used a power perspective (Ropers-Huilman, 1999) or a relational perspective (Young, 1990). In all of these treatments, social justice is framed from a distribution model, that is, allocation of resources. In other words, social justice was conceptualized from an economic model where financial resources were unevenly distributed among the masses. Another approach to defining social justice has been an anthropological viewpoint, where all human beings are considered to be of equal value (Rawls, 1973). Rawls identified four categories of social justice: (1) commutative justice, (2) retributive justice, (3) contributive justice, and (4) distributive justice. For Rawls, commutative justice means fairness in agreements between individuals or social groups. This type of justice is reflected in copyright laws and legal statutes. Similarly, retributive justice refers to just punishment for the guilty, effectively reflecting the "an eye for an eye" perspective. In contrast to commutative and retributive justice, contributive justice reflects a type of justice where an individual assumes responsibility and contributes to society without impairing any other individual's right to freedom and dignity. Contributive justice represents the closest ideal to the Dalai Lama's notion of a selfless ethic, whereby one's first concern is for others. The last element of Rawls's definition of social justice was distributive justice. For Rawls, distributive justice meant that information and access to information was to be fairly distributed to satisfy the basic needs of individuals. To a certain degree, distributive justice is aligned with Maslow's need to satisfy personal safety prior to addressing loftier goals.

From an educational perspective, Adams, Bell, and Griffin (1997) constructed five principles of social justice to overcome oppression in college classrooms. They urged educators to (1) balance the emotional and cognitive components of the learning process, (2) acknowledge and support the personal while viewing interactions systemically, (3) attend to the social needs of students, (4) use student reflection and experience as building blocks, and (5) value awareness, personal growth, and change.

Zollers, Albert, and Cochran-Smith (2000) went beyond mere principles to identify a continuum of prospective teacher beliefs based on fairness and equity. Their study of teacher perspectives of social justice illustrated the difficulties associated with exploring an abstract concept. As a result, they identified three categories of divergence around the meaning of social justice that encompassed a broad spectrum of perspectives. The three categories examined issues of (1) fairness and equity, (2) institutional versus individual understandings of social justice, and (3) the responsibility of individuals to advocate and promote social justice. Despite their conceptualization of social justice into three categories, Zollers et al. accepted the inherent difficulties associated with the range and complexity that social justice issues address, writing:

> Despite the fact that social justice is a fundamental mission of our institution and we are all committed to its pursuit, we could not assume that we were all committed to the same idea or shared fundamental meanings and assumptions of social justice. (p. 11)

The inherent difficulties associated with defining social justice in the literature notwithstanding, there has been widespread consensus on the guiding principles associated with social justice, with those cited most often being equality, equity, fairness, acceptance of others, and inclusiveness. The first three refer to the distribution of resources, whereas the last two principles involve a reframing of relationships. In particular, acceptance of others means to value and respect people who are different from you, that is, in terms of their race, ethnicity, gender, sexual orientation, disability, and so on.

As Malu Gonzalez (2002) noted in her 2001 presidential address at the UCEA annual meeting in Cincinnati, educational leadership and social justice involve scholars and leaders who are willing to transform traditional borders to a new path. She further called on professors of educational leadership to move away from alienated borderlands and toward an integrated borderland where people perceive themselves as part of an integrated whole. Congruently, inclusiveness refers to an environment where all stakeholders are brought to the table, that is, past perpetrators and victims of injustice. Although doing so may present the potential for further conflict, inequities are likely to remain unresolved until all parties involved in social justice issues are at the table. Inclusiveness may represent a new foundation on which all social justice issues should be framed.

However, until scholars and practitioners speak a common language and frame discussions from grounded reference points, any claim toward improving society through social justice is little more than meaningless rhetoric. For as George Counts wrote in 1932 (1978):

> Any individual or group that would aspire to lead society must be ready to pay the costs of leadership: to accept responsibility, to suffer calumny, to surrender security, to risk both reputation and fortune. If this price, or some important part of it, is not being paid, then the chances are that the claim to leadership is fraudulent. (p. 2)

If scholars of educational leadership programs are to be true advocates of social justice, then they must be willing to be all-inclusive, working with all stakeholders toward a common language in which to frame dialogues addressing issues of equity, fairness, and adequacy.

CONCLUSION

Based on its historical roots and literature, social justice is an elusive term to define. In this chapter, we traced the roots of social justice and elucidated a rationale for developing a common meaning. The task we undertook was greater than the sum of the individual efforts of the authors; like other academic quests for definition, we have been engaged with "nailing jelly to the wall" (Novick, 1988, pp. 1–17). Despite this, our quest brought forth several new insights. First, if social justice is to be true to its guiding principles, then advocates must create an inclusive environment where all relevant stakeholders are invited to participate, even those who may be perpetrators of injustices. Second, it may be more beneficial to focus on a common language of the guiding principles of social justice rather than on a common definition. Because diversity is one of the linchpins of social justice, attempting to force a common definition may be more counterproductive than helpful. Third, addressing social justice issues must go beyond mere awareness and using the latest buzzwords. Social justice encompasses life-altering experiences. This implies that professors of educational leadership need to reconceptualize the core technology of delivering the knowledge base of the field if social justice is to have any lasting effect on future school leaders.

If professors of educational leadership programs hope to imbue their students with a social justice foundation, then it is imperative to equip students who will be future school leaders with a lexicon they can use to span the boundary between the worlds of academics and practitioners. Otherwise, the gap between the two environments will continue to exist and issues of social injustice will continue unabated.

In attempting to define social justice, we discovered that the process may be more important than the outcome. Although a precise conceptual definition could not be constructed, the framework for a common language and shared understanding was developed. It is now up to scholars in educational leadership to advance the guiding principles of social justice, building a bridge that lets practitioners engage in dialogue and create socially just schools. Mirroring George Counts's challenge to educators in 1932, we end this chapter by asking scholars in educational leadership: Dare social justice advocates build a common language to create meaningful dialogues with all stakeholders?

NOTES

1. This does not imply that all Progressive Era social reformers were adherents of the social gospel, for many were not. Furthermore, many reformers were either of a differing religious faith (generally Catholic or Jewish), agnostic (Dewey), or avowed no faith at all. Nevertheless, the social gospel inspired a generation of reformers. Many of these would find a home in the early administration of Franklin Delano Roosevelt, as would adherents to the Catholic social gospel—most famously Frank Murphy (see Kennedy, 1999). The argument can be made that the Roosevelt New Deal drew heavily on both traditions because many of his policies had been piloted in New York State by Governor Alfred E. Smith.

2. Dorothy Day was the founder of the Catholic Worker Movement. A former "fellow traveler" in radical political circles, Day converted to Catholicism in the late 1920s. The Worker Movement, founded in 1933, drew like-minded politically progressive and radical Catholics to work directly to ameliorate the ills wrought by industrial capitalism. The movement was marked by direct social and political action coupled with "intense sacramental piety, self-abnegation, and prayer" (Ahlstrom, 1972, p. 1010).

3. George S. Counts is one of the most complex educational theorists and analysts. Largely influenced by both the social gospel and prairie progressivism (Kansas) of his youth, his outlook was rooted in the economic understandings of Thorsten Veblen rather than Marx. Although he did travel to the newly established Soviet Union, and even speaks well of its educational system (in 1932), he later expelled communists from the American Federation of Teachers because of their totalitarianism. Not only was he a lifelong unionist, he was also a life member of the NAACP and the American Civil Liberties Union, and he ran for the U.S. Senate on the Liberal Party's (New York) slate. Nevertheless, he was long vilified for "Dare the Schools" by those who believe he advocated a Soviet-style system of education. A senior colleague met Counts at an academic conference in the late 1960s; by that time, Counts confessed, the only way he was able to "make the program" was to submit his research proposals under the name of G. Sylvester Counts.

4. Many American conservatives viewed the rise of liberation theology with a good deal of worry. Prior to its advent, the Catholic Church in Latin America had largely been the supporter of oppressive regimes throughout the region. An embrace of truly revolutionary Christianity—that was Marxist to boot—was perceived as a direct threat to U.S. national and corporate interests. Although it makes for fascinating reading, the CIA's use of Protestant evangelical missionaries in Latin America during the 1980s is far beyond the scope of this chapter.

5. In Tyack and Hansot's work (1982, p. 291), they list Bair's study in a footnote (No. 7 for Section 12), but the footnote actually contains very little information regarding the scope of Bair's study.

6. The U.S. Supreme Court invalidated all laws criminalizing consensual sodomy in *Lawrence v. Texas* (2003). Consequently, the legal rationale (equating status with sexual behavior) for barring "avowed homosexuals" from working in public schools has evaporated. Nevertheless, at this writing, none of the 13 states that had criminalized sodomy have revised their public school codes to align with *Lawrence*.

REFERENCES

Adams, M., Bell, L. A., & Griffin, P. (1997). *Teaching for diversity and social justice.* New York: Routledge.

Ahlstrom, S. E. (1972). *A religious history of the American people.* New Haven, CT: Yale University Press.

Allman, P., Mayo, P., Cavanaugh, C., Heng, C. L., & Haddad, S. (1998). " . . . the creation of a world in which it will be easier . . . " *Convergence, 31*(1/2), 9–16.

All Star Directories, Inc. (2003). *All education schools online guide to education and careers.* Retrieved November 30, 2003, from http://www.alleducationschools.com/find/results.php?st = &prog = educational-leadership& submit=Find + a + School.

Alwood, E. (1996). *Straight news: Gays, lesbians, and the news media.* New York: Columbia University Press.

Anderson, G. L. (2002, November). *Can we effectively build credential programs for educational administrators on principles of social justice? A case study.* Paper presented at the meeting of the University Council for Educational Administration, Pittsburgh, PA.

Antonio, A. (2002). Faculty of color reconsidered: Reassessing contributions to scholarship. *Journal of Higher Education, 73*(5), 582–602.

Apple, M. W. (1996). *Cultural politics and education.* London: Open University Press.

Applebaum, B. (2001). Raising awareness of dominance: Does recognizing dominance mean one has to dismiss the values of the dominant group? *Journal of Moral Education, 30*(1), 55–70.

Armstrong, K. (2000). *The battle for God.* New York: Knopf.

Arnez, N. L. (1978). Implementation of desegregation as a discriminatory process. *Journal of Negro Education, 47*(1), 28–45.

Barth, R. (2001). *Learning by heart.* San Francisco: Jossey-Bass.

Beck, L. (1994). *Reclaiming educational administration as a caring profession.* New York: Teachers College Press.

Beck, L., & Murphy, J. (1993). *Understanding the principalship: Metaphorical themes 1920s–1990s.* New York: Teachers College Press.

Beck, L., & Murphy, J. (1994). *Ethics in educational leadership programs: An expanding role.* Thousand Oaks, CA: Corwin.

Bhola, H. (2002). A discourse on educational leadership: Global themes, postmodern perspectives. *Studies in Philosophy and Education, 21,* 181–202.

Blase, J., & Anderson, G. (1995). *The micropolitics of educational leadership: From control to empowerment.* New York: Teachers College Press.

Blount, J. M. (1996). Manly men and womanly women: Deviance, gender role polarization, and the shift in women's school employment, 1900–1976. *Harvard Educational Review, 68*(2), 318–339.

Blount, J. M. (1998). *Destined to rule the schools: Women and the superintendency, 1873–1995.* Albany: SUNY Press.

Blount, J. M. (2003). Homosexuality and school superintendents: A brief history. *Journal of School Leadership, 13,* 7–26.

Bogotch, I. (2000). *Educational leadership and social justice: Theory into practice.* Earlier version of paper presented at the Annual Meeting of the University Council for Educational Administration, Albuquerque, NM.

Bogotch, I., Miron, L., & Murry, J. (1998). Moral leadership discourses in urban school settings: The multiple influences of social context. *Urban Education, 33*(3), 303–330.

Bolman, L., & Deal, T. (2002). *Reframing the path to school leadership: A guide for teachers and principals.* Thousand Oaks, CA: Corwin.

Bowles, S., & Gintis, H. (1976). *Schooling in capitalist America.* New York: Basic Books.

Britz, J. J., & Blignaut, J. N. (2001). Information poverty and social justice. *South African Journal of Library & Information Science, 67*(2), 63–69.

Callahan, R. (1962). *Education and the cult of efficiency.* Chicago: University of Chicago Press.

Capper, C. (1993). Administrator practice and preparation for social reconstructionist schooling. In C. Capper (Ed.), *Educational administration in a pluralistic society* (pp. 288–315). Albany: SUNY Press.

Cleary, E. L. (1985). *Crisis and change: The church in Latin America today.* Maryknoll, NY: Orbis Books.

Counts, G. S. (1978). *Dare the school build a new social order?* Carbondale: Southern Illinois University Press. (Original work published 1932)

Cremin, L. A. (1961). *The transformation of the school: Progressivism in American Education, 1876–1957.* New York: Vintage Books.

Crow, G., Matthews, L., & McCleary, L. (Eds.). (1996). *Leadership: A relevant and realistic role for principals.* Larchmont, NY: Eye on Education.

Cuban, L. (1988). *The managerial imperative and the practice of leadership in schools.* Albany: SUNY Press.

Cubberley, E. P. (1916). *Public school administration: A statement of the fundamental principles underlying the organization and administration of public education.* Boston: Houghton-Mifflin.

Dalai Lama. (1999). *Ethics for the new millennium.* New York: Riverhead Books.

Daresh, J. (1997). Principals, schools, education, training, skills, curricula. *NASSP Bulletin, 81*(585), 3–8.

D'Emilio, J. (1983). *Sexual politics, sexual communities: The making of a homosexual minority in the United States, 1940–1970.* Chicago: University of Chicago Press.

Diamond, S. (1989). *Spiritual warfare: The politics of the Christian right.* Boston: South End Press.

Donmoyer, R., Imber, M., & Scheurich, J. (1995). *The knowledge base in educational administration: Multiple perspectives.* Albany: SUNY Press.

Dorrien, G. (1997). Communitarianism, Christian realism, and the crisis of progressive Christianity. *Cross Currents, 47*(3), 364–378.

Duke, D. (1992). The rhetoric and the reality of reform in educational administration. *Phi Delta Kappan, 73*(10), 764–770.

Feistritzer, C. E. (1988). *Profile of school administrators in the U.S.* Washington, DC: National Center for Education Information.

Foucault, M. (1979). *Discipline and punish: The birth of the prison.* New York: Vintage Books.

Freire, P. (1992). *Pedagogy of the oppressed.* New York: Seabury Press. (Original work published 1970)

Freire, P. (1996). *Letters to Christina.* New York: Routledge.

Freire, P. (1998). *Pedagogy of freedom: Ethics, democracy, and civic courage.* Lanham, MD: Rowman & Littlefield.

Goldring, E., & Rallis, S. (1993). *Principals of dynamic schools: Taking charge of change.* Newbury Park, CA: Corwin.

Gonzalez, M. L. (2002). Professors of educational administration: Learning and leading for the success of all children. *UCEA Review, 44*(1), 4–8.

Gonzalez, M., Huerta-Macias, A., & Tinajero, J. (Eds.). (1998). *Educating Latino students: A guide to successful practice.* Lancaster, PA: Technomic.

Goodman, R. (2001). Beyond the enforcement principle: Sodomy laws, social norms, and social panoptics. *California Law Review, 89,* 643–740.

Greenfield, W. (1999, April). *Moral leadership in schools: Fact or fancy?* Paper presented at the Annual Meeting of the American Educational Research Association, Montreal, Canada.

Grogan, M. (2000). Laying the groundwork for a reconception of the superintendency from feminist postmodern perspectives. *Educational Administration Quarterly, 36*(1), 117–142.

Guthrie, J. (1990). The evolution of educational management: Eroding myths and emerging models. In B. Mitchell & L. Cunningham (Eds.), *Educational leadership and changing contexts of families, communities, and schools: Eighty-ninth Yearbook of the National Society for the Study of Education* (Part II, pp. 210–231). Chicago: University of Chicago Press.

Hallinger, P., & Heck, R. (1998). Exploring the principal's contribution to school effectiveness: 1980–1995. *School Effectiveness and School Improvement, 9*(2), 157–191.

Hargens, L., & Long, J. S. (2002). Demographic inertia and women's representation among faculty in higher education. *The Journal of Higher Education, 73*(4), 494–506.

Hart, A. (1993). *Principal succession: Establishing leadership in schools.* Albany: SUNY Press.

Haste, H. (1996). Communitarianism and the social construction of morality. *Journal of Moral Education, 25*(1), 47–55.

Herr, K. (1999). Institutional violence in the everyday practices of school: The narrative of a young lesbian. *Journal for a Just and Caring Education, 5*(3), 242–255.

Hobsbawm, E. (1994). *The age of extremes: A history of the word, 1914–1991.* New York: Vintage Books.

Hoy, W. K., & Miskel, C. G. (2001). *Educational administration: Theory, research, and practice* (6th ed.). Boston: McGraw-Hill.

Hoyle, J., English, F., & Steffy, B. (1998). *Skills for successful 21st-century school leaders: Standards for peak performers.* Arlington, VA: American Association of School Administrators.

Hudson, W. S. (1981). *Religion in America* (3rd ed.). New York: Charles Scribner's Sons.

Hutchinson, D. L. (1997). Out yet unseen: A racial critique of gay and lesbian legal theory and political discourse. *Connecticut Law Review 29,* 561.

Institute for Educational Leadership. (2000). *Leadership for student learning: Reinventing the principalship. School leadership for the 21st century initiative: A report of the task force on the principalship.* Washington, DC: Author.

Jackson, B. (2001, September). *Exceptional and innovative programs in educational leadership.* Paper commissioned for the meeting of the National Commission for the Advancement of Educational Leadership Preparation.

Jacobson, S. (1996). School leadership in an age of reform: New directions in principal preparation. *International Journal of Educational Reform, 5*(3), 271–277.

Jacobson, S., Emihovich, C., Helfrich, J., Petrie, H., & Stevenson, R. (1998). *Transforming schools and schools of education: A new vision for preparing educators.* East Lansing, MI: Holmes Group.

A JBHE report card on the progress of blacks on the faculties of the nation's highest-ranked colleges and universities. (2001–2002). *Journal of Blacks in Higher Education, 34,* 10–14.

Johnson, B. C., & Shoho, A. R. (2002, November). *Social justice in educational administration preparation programs.* Paper presented at the Annual Meeting of the University Council for Educational Administration, Pittsburgh, PA.

Johnson, M. (1995). Nineteenth-century agrarian populism and twentieth-century communitarianism: Points of contact and contrast. *Peabody Journal of Education, 70*(4), 86–104.

Jones, B. (2000). *Educational leadership: Policy dimensions in the 21st century.* Stamford, CT: Ablex.

Kahne, J. (1996). *Reframing educational policy: Democracy, community, and the individual* (Advances in Contemporary Educational Thought, Vol. 16). New York: Teachers College Press.

Kennedy, D. M. (1999). *Freedom from fear: The American people in depression and war, 1929–1945.* New York: Oxford University Press.

Kochan, F. (2002). Hope and possibility: Advancing an argument for a Habermasian perspective in educational administration. *Studies in Philosophy and Education, 21,* 137–155.

Koerin, B. (2003). The settlement house tradition: Current trends and future concerns. *Journal of Sociology and Social Welfare, 30*(2), 53–68.

Lange, E. (1998). Fragmented ethics of justice: Freire, liberation theology, and pedagogies for the non-poor. *Convergence, 31*(1/2), 81–93.

Larson, C., & Murtadha, K. (2002). Leadership for social justice. In J. Murphy (Ed.), *The educational leadership challenge: Redefining leadership for the 21st century* (101st Yearbook of the National Society for the Study of Education, pp. 134–161). Chicago: University of Chicago Press.

Larson, C., & Ovando, C. (2001). *The color of bureaucracy: The politics of equity in multicultural school communities.* Stamford, CT: Wadsworth/Thomas Learning.

Leithwood, K., & Duke, D. (1998). Mapping the conceptual terrain of leadership: A critical point of departure for cross-cultural studies. *Peabody Journal of Education, 73*(2), 31–50.

Leo XIII, (1891). *Rerum Novarum.* Retrieved August 20, 2003, from http://www.vatican.va/holy_father/leo_xiii/encyclicals/documents/hf_l-xiii_enc_15051891_rerum-novarum_en.html

Lindholm, J., Astin, A., Sax, L., & Korn, W. (2002). *The American college teacher national norms for the 2001–2002 HERI faculty survey.* Los Angeles: Higher Education Research Institute.

Lissak, R. S. (1989). *Pluralism & progressives: Hull House and the new immigrants, 1890–1919.* Chicago: University of Chicago Press.

Lomotey, K. (1989). Cultural diversity in the urban school: Implications for principals. *NASSP Bulletin, 73*(521), 81–85.

Lomotey, K. (1995). Social and cultural influences on schooling: A commentary on the UCEA Knowledge Base Project, Domain I. *Educational Administration Quarterly, 31*(2), 294–303.

Lomotey, K., & Simms, J. (1996). Dispersing and employing knowledge on refashioning urban schools: Exacerbating the power relations dilemma. *Educational Policy, 10*(2), 297–303.

Lopez, G. R. (2003). The (racially neutral) politics of education: A critical race theory perspective. *Educational Administration Quarterly, 39*(1), 68–94.

Lugg, C. A. (2002, November). *Social justice and educational administration: No longer mutually exclusive?* Paper presented at the Annual Meeting of the University Council for Educational Administration, Pittsburgh, PA.

Lugg, C. A. (2003a). Our straight-laced administrators: The law, LGBT administrators, and the assimilationist imperative. *Journal of School Leadership, 13*(1), 51–85.

Lugg, C. A. (2003b). Sissies, faggots, lezzies, and dykes: Gender, sexual orientation, and a new politics of education? *Educational Administration Quarterly, 39*(1), 95–134.

Lugg, C. A. (2003c, November). *Still thinking about sodomy: Public school administrators as sexuality and gender police.* Paper presented at the Annual Meeting of the University Council for Educational Administration, Portland, Oregon.

Lugg, C. A. (2004). One nation under God? Religion and the politics of education in a post 9/11 America. *Educational Policy, 18*(1), 169–187.

Macpherson, R. (1996, November). *Reframing accountability policy research with postpositivism, pluralism, democracy, and subsidiarity.* Paper presented at the Annual Meeting of the American Educational Research Association, New York.

Marshall, C., & McCarthy, M. (2002). School leadership reforms: Filtering social justice through dominant discourses. *Journal of School Leadership, 12*(5), 480–502.

Marshall, C., & Scribner, J. D. (1991). "It's all political": Inquiry into the micropolitics of education. *Education and Urban Society, 23*(4), 347–355.

Maxcy, S. (1994). *Postmodern school leadership: Meeting the crisis in educational administration.* Westport, CT: Praeger.

McCalla, D. (2002). A theoretical framework of benign power in school sector decision making: A preface. *Discourse: Studies in the Cultural Politics of Education, 23*(1), 39–57.

Merchant, B. M. (1995). A reaction to Lomotey's article: "Social and cultural influences on schooling: A commentary on the UCEA Knowledge Base Project, Domain I." *Education and Urban Society, 31*(2), 304–312.

Merchant, B. M. (1999a). Ghosts in the classroom. Unavoidable(?) casualties of principals' commitment to the status quo. *Journal of Education for Students Placed at Risk, 4*(2), 153–171.

Merchant, B. M. (1999b). Now you see it; now you don't: A district's short-lived commitment to an alternative high school for newly-arrived immigrants. *Urban Education, 34*(1), 26–51.

Merchant, B. M., & Shoho, A. R. (2002, November). *Bridge people: Leaders for social justice.* Paper presented at the Annual Meeting of the University Council for Educational Administration, Pittsburgh, PA.

Mohr, R. D. (1989). Gay studies as moral vision. *Educational Theory, 39*(2), 121–132.

Murphy, J. (1993). *Preparing tomorrow's school leaders: Alternative designs.* University Park, PA: University Council for Educational Administration.

Murphy, J. (Ed.). (2002). *The educational leadership challenge: Redefining leadership for the 21st century* (Yearbook of the National Society for the Study of Education, Vol. 101, Part I). Chicago: University of Chicago Press.

Murphy, J., & Seashore, D. (Eds.). (1999). *Handbook of research on educational administration: A project of the American Educational Research Association* (2nd ed.). San Francisco: Jossey-Bass.

Nasaw, D. (1979). *Schooled to order: A social history of public schools in the United States.* New York: Oxford University Press.

National Association of Elementary School Principals. (1994). *Best ideas from America's blue ribbon schools: What award-winning elementary and middle school principals do.* Thousand Oaks, CA: Corwin.

National Commission on Excellence in Education. (1983). *A nation at risk: The imperative for educational reform.* Washington, DC: U.S. Department of Education.

Novak, M. (2000). Defining social justice. *First Things: A Monthly Journal of Religion & Public Life, 108,* 11–13.

Novick, P. (1988). *That noble dream: The "objectivity question" and the American historical profession.* New York: Cambridge University Press.

O'Loughlin, M. (2002). Is a socially responsible and critical psychology of difference possible? *Race, Gender, & Class, 9*(4), 177–192.

Peterson, A. L., & Vasquez, M. A. (1998). The new evangelization in Latin American perspective. *Cross Currents, 48*(3), 311–328.

Pierce, P. (1935). *The origin and development of the public school principalship.* Chicago: University of Chicago Press.

Pounder, D. (1990, November). *Educational megatrends and increased female leadership in schools.* Paper presented at the Annual Meeting of the University Council for Educational Administration, Pittsburgh, PA.

Prevost, R., & Elias, J. L. (1999). Whatever happened to Catholic philosophy of education? *Religious Education, 94*(1), 92–110.

Rawls, J. (1973). *A theory of justice.* Oxford, UK: Oxford University Press.

Reese, W. J. (2002). *Power and the promise of school reform: Grassroots movements during the Progressive Era.* New York: Teachers College Press.

Reyes, P., & Scribner, A. (1995). Educational reform, students of color, and potential outcomes. *High School Journal, 78*(4), 215–225.

Reyes, P., Scribner, J., & Scribner, A. (Eds.). (1999). *Lessons from high-performing Hispanic schools: Creating learning communities* (Critical Issues in Educational Leadership series). Williston, VT: Teachers College Press.

Ropers-Huilman, B. (1999). Social justice in the classroom. *College Teaching, 47*(3), 91–95.

Rorrer, A. (2002, November). *District leadership: Reinstitutionalizing equity in American public education.* Paper presented at the Annual Meeting of the University Council for Educational Administration, Pittsburgh, PA.

Rousmaniere, K. (1997). *City teachers: Teaching and school reform in historical perspective.* New York: Teachers College Press.

Sackney, L., Walker, J., & Mitchell, C. (1999). Postmodern conceptions of power for educational leadership. *Journal of Educational Administration and Foundations, 14*(1), 33–57.

Scheurich, J. (Ed.). (2002). *Anti-racist scholarship: An advocacy.* Albany: SUNY Press.

Scheurich, J., & Skrla, L. (2001). Continuing the conversation on equity and accountability: Listening appreciatively, responding responsibly. *Phi Delta Kappan, 83*(4), 322–327.

Scheurich, J., Skrla, L., & Johnson, J. (2000). Thinking carefully about equity and accountability. *Phi Delta Kappan, 82*(4), 293–300.

Sears, J. T. (1997). *Lonely hunters: An oral history of lesbian and gay southern life, 1948–1968.* Boulder, CO: Westview Press.

Sergiovanni, T. (1992). *Moral leadership: Getting to the heart of school improvement.* New York: Jossey-Bass.

Shakeshaft, C. (1989). The gender gap in research in educational administration. *Educational Administration Quarterly, 25*(4), 324–337.

Shapiro, J. P., & Stefkovich, J. A. (2000). *Ethical leadership and decision making in education: Applying theoretical perspectives to complex dilemmas.* Mahwah, NJ: Lawrence Erlbaum.

Shoho, A. R. (1990). *Americanization through public education of Japanese Americans in Hawaii: 1930–1941.* Unpublished doctoral dissertation, Arizona State University.

Shoho, A. R., & Broussard, C. (2003, November). *A content analysis of past UCEA conferences and the productivity of participating institutions.* Paper presented at the Annual Meeting of the University Council for Educational Administration, Portland, OR.

Shoho, A. R., Katims, D., & Meza, P. (1998). The alienation of special education teachers. *ERS Spectrum, 16*(4), 18–23.

Shoho, A. R., Katims, D., & Wilks, D. (1997). Perceptions of alienation among students with learning disabilities in inclusive and resource settings. *The High School Journal, 81*(1), 28–36.

Singh, B. (1997). Liberalism, communitarianism, and discussion methods as a means of reconciling controversial moral issues. *Educational Studies, 23*(2), 169–184.

Skrla, L., & Scheurich, J. (2001). Displacing deficit thinking in school district leadership. *Education and Urban Society, 33*(3), 235–259.

Trower, C. (2002, June). *What do we have to hide? Data and diversity.* Paper presented at the 42nd Annual Forum for the Association for Institutional Research, Toronto, Canada.

Turner, C. (2000). New faces, new knowledge. *Academe, 86*(5), 34–39.

Tyack, D. (1974). *The one best system: A history of American urban education.* Cambridge, MA: Harvard University Press.

Tyack, D., & Hansot, E. (1982). *Managers of virtue: Public school leadership in America, 1820–1980.* New York: Basic Books.

Tyson, C. (2003). Research, race, and an epistemology of emancipation. *Mid-Western Educational Researcher, 16*(1), 2–5.

Varlotta, L. (1997). Confronting consensus: Investigating the philosophies that have informed service-learning's communities. *Educational Theory, 47*(4), 453–476.

Weiner, G. (2001). Social inclusion, responsible citizenship, social justice, equal opportunities: Whatever happened to professional development? *Journal of In-service Education, 27*(3), 357–360.

Wendel, F. (Ed.). (1991). *Enhancing the knowledge base in educational administration* (University Council for Educational Administration Monograph Series). University Park, PA: University Council for Educational Administration.

Wendel, F. (1992). *Reforming administrator preparation programs.* University Park, PA: University Council for Educational Administration.

White, D. A. (2002). Gifted students and philosophy: Feminism and social justice. *Gifted Child Today Magazine, 25*(1), 40–46.

Wilmore, E. (2002). *Principal leadership: Applying the new Educational Leadership Constituent Council (ELCC) standards.* Thousand Oaks, CA: Corwin.

Wong, K. (1998). Culture and moral leadership in education. *Peabody Journal of Education, 73*(2), 106–125.

Young, I. (1990). *Justice and the politics of difference.* Princeton, NJ: Princeton University Press.

Young, M., Petersen, G. J., & Short, P. M. (2001, February). *The complexity of substantive reform: A call for interdependence among key stakeholders.* Paper commissioned for the National Commission for the Advancement of Educational Leadership Preparation, Racine, WI.

Zinn, H. (1999). *A people's history of the United States, 1492-present.* New York: Harper Collins.

Zollers, N. J., Albert, L. R., & Cochran-Smith, M. (2000). In pursuit of social justice: Collaborative research and practice in teacher education. *Action in Teacher Education, 22*(2), 1–14.

4

Collaborative Leadership, Community Building, and Democracy in Public Education

FRANCES K. KOCHAN
Auburn University

CYNTHIA J. REED
Auburn University

INTRODUCTION AND OVERVIEW

Schools are an integral part of the societies and communities in which they function (Sarason & Lorentz, 1998). The purposes of schooling and the demands made on schools and school leaders in the United States have shifted throughout history as the needs, mores, and demands of society have changed. A number of these changes were initiated by educators trying to enhance schooling, whereas others were implemented because of social, economic, or political pressures (Uline, 2001). Some, mandated by state or federal legislation, have even contained "contrary reform demands," whereas others have incorporated "strategies of accommodation, resistance, and hybridization" (Tyack & Cuban, 1995, p. 78).

The pace and intensity of the changes required of schools have increased in recent years and will probably continue to do so in the future, causing the job of educators to become yet more complex (Kochan, Jackson, & Duke, 1999). This complexity requires a leadership style that involves others in the process of problem solving and analysis, leading to calls for educational leaders to move away from bureaucratic to democratic leadership approaches (Barth, 1990; Rusch, 1998). Democratic leadership requires individuals to adopt a collaborative approach that includes building a sense of community with both internal and external stakeholders. It involves sharing power with others and involving multiple groups of stakeholders in decision making in meaningful ways. We agree with this notion of leadership. However, we also extend the concept to propose that educational leaders must become catalysts not only to reconnect with their communities but also to help rebuild the relationship between education and economic and community development.

Our chapter provides a comprehensive look at the terrain of collaborative leadership and community building. The chapter begins with an historical perspective describing the development of public schooling. We then examine the present relationship between schools and communities and the growth of the "accountability environment" in which we now exist. We posit that the rise in accountability demands has come about partly because of the separation of schools from their communities. The concepts of collaborative leadership and community as we perceive them are discussed, followed by an overview of how they are generally operationalized within and across schools and other organizational environments.

The next section of the chapter describes strategies that focus on rebuilding the communities in which our schools operate. We suggest that this responsibility rests not only with preschools through high schools and their leaders, but also with educational leadership faculty in higher education as a part of educational leadership preparation, outreach, and research. We offer an example of an initiative that focuses on rebuilding communities and engaging in "public making" (Mathews, 1996). The closing sections of the chapter discuss the factors necessary to be successful community builders, the factors that hinder success, and the implications for educational leadership preparation programs.

HISTORICAL PERSPECTIVES ON THE CONNECTIONS BETWEEN EDUCATION AND SOCIETY

One of the reasons public education was created was to foster and maintain the common structures and civilities needed to sustain our American democracy (Mathews, 2003). During the first half of the 19th century, education, along with numerous other social reforms, enjoyed widespread public support as demand for common schooling grew among the nation's expanding population (Mathews, 2003). Begun in and by communities, schools sprang up around the country and were viewed as a major asset. Having a school suggested that a community was progressive and a good place to live.

Disconnecting Schools and Communities

Beginning in the last quarter of the 19th century, schools were absorbed into state systems and began to operate according to scientific principles designed to increase efficiency as a primary endeavor (English, 2003). The rapid industrialization of the United States reinforced this production mentality of schools and leadership (Mathews, 2003). Leadership, whether in schools, corporations, or society as a whole, tended to focus on creating hierarchical structures in which the management of people, resources, and production was a primary focus (Tyack, 1974). The role of the principal was to efficiently manage the school and the people in it. As a result, the relationship between schools and their communities began to deteriorate as schools came to be viewed as more like factories than extensions of their communities.

In many settings, particularly in urban communities, large schools were built to increase efficiency. The trend toward efficiency continued to grow, and by 1986, more than half of the high schools in America had more than 1,000 students. Consolidation became a popular approach, based on the concept that big schools were better because they permitted differentiation of curriculum (Tyack & Cuban, 1995). The trend toward larger schools fostered an additional disassociation between educators, students, families, and communities (Mathews, 2003).

Other events also worked to enhance this disconnect between communities and schools. The professionalization of teaching and administration created an attitude that "teachers and principals know best," and parents and the community were excluded from the teaching and learning process (Doble & Higgins, 1998). New curricular innovations changed the way in which many students were taught, sometimes making it difficult for parents to assist their children in the learning process. Most Americans have been to school and know what a "real school" is like. When schooling departed too much from the consensual model of a "real school . . . trouble often ensue[d]" (Tyack & Cuban, 1995, p. 9).

As schools became larger and more services were provided, the costs per pupil rose accordingly. This increase in costs, combined with the decreased public involvement in public schools, created a lack of knowledge about what was occurring in schools and a public perception that schools were not performing adequately. This perception has grown in recent years, as noted by Tyack and Cuban (1995):

> Public perceptions and expectations of schools, well charted by Gallup polls, have so changed in recent decades that an institution once secure in the public confidence has regressed in public esteem to a point where the 1930s, 1940s or 1950s seem another world, to some even a golden age, despite the obvious gross inequities of those decades. Opinions about schools reflect a more general enchantment or disenchantment about institutions, both public and private. (p. 30)

A Decrease in Public Trust

In addition to the lack of connection between schools and their communities, other factors have contributed to the decrease in trust in the public schools. In the mid 1980s, the publication *A Nation at Risk* (National Commission on Excellence in Education, 1983), which criticized public education for not meeting the needs of students, increased demands that schools and school leaders "fix" education and society. Although people generally like the schools their children attend, reports such as this one, media coverage about educational problems and needs, and a decrease in trust in public institutions have helped to create a sense among the general public that public schools are not providing a good education for all students (Mathews, 2003).

This lack of trust may also be related to the societal trend that holds governments and public agencies more accountable for the expenditure of funds provided by taxpayers. The strained relationship between educators and the general public appears to be related to what Habermas (1975) has labeled the legitimation crisis. The major tenets of this concept are that modern society has replaced dependence on family and friends with a belief that governments and other institutions can and will solve individual and societal problems. This belief has severed people's connections with one another, robbing them of their "lifeworlds," and creating an emptiness within them (Foster, 1980). When governments and other institutions cannot deliver on promises, the government becomes more controlling of people and their lives. This shift in control causes people to become resentful and discontented with governmental institutions and agencies, resulting in a loss of trust and faith in these groups.

Foster (1980, 1986) has done an excellent job of applying Habermas's ideas on the legitimation crisis to educational administration. He discusses the many problems that families, schools, communities, and governments face, along with strategies that school administrators might use to deal with these issues (see also Kochan, 2002). Among these problems are the breakdown of the family and a lost sense of belonging within the community, a mistrust of public institutions, and a lack of effective communication between schools and their constituencies. Foster recommends that educational leaders reach out to their communities and engage their stakeholders in rebuilding connections and relationships.

The Accountability Environment

Public perceptions of failing schools, the disconnect between schools and communities, and a general reduction in the level of trust in public institutions have resulted in the advent of the "accountability age" (Leithwood, 2001). States have drastically increased the numbers and types of educational laws and regulations schools must adhere to, as if more of everything will improve educational outputs (Tyack & Cuban, 1995). There have also been more numerous demands to restructure schools and schooling and to change the face of public education in this country, including recommendations such as offering tuition waivers for individuals to attend private schools, creating private charter schools supported by public dollars, and allowing students who attend public schools that are classified as failing to attend private schools of their choice supported by public funding (Cook, 2004; Elementary & Secondary Education Act [ESEA], 2001).

Although there is no commonly accepted accountability approach for restructuring schools, state-mandated models of reform in the 1980s relied on what Richard Elmore called "standardization, central bureaucratic control, and externally imposed rules as a means of controlling the performance of schools" (as cited in Tyack & Cuban, 1995, p. 79). These models have created additional layers of paperwork and bureaucracy, causing educators to complain "about bureaucratic control, which seems to be spreading faster than kudzu. Regulations of every kind and from every source combine to entangle schools" (Mathews, 2003, p. 80).

Current accountability mandates call for highly quantifiable and "objective" data and processes that do not require educators to use their professional judgment (Reed & Ross, 2001). In the 19th century, education used many performance-based assessments, often having students engage in public demonstrations of their abilities (Mathews, 2003). There has been a shift away from such subjective and individualized assessments toward large-scale, impersonal methods for collecting achievement data, with a greater emphasis placed on how an entire school or district performs.

In the past, individual students were often held accountable by their parents, but schools in general were not held accountable. Today's accountability climate uses a high-stakes approach with schools, publicly reporting those schools that are "in need of improvement" (ESEA, 2001). Fueled by a growing sense of concern and media attention, increased calls for accountability have moved from local communities to state capitals, as well as to the national level, most recently with the passage of the No Child Left Behind legislation (ESEA, 2001).

Shifts in accountability strategies have paralleled a highly politicized approach to school reform, whereby noneducators have proposed or mandated "quick fix" approaches designed to appease a disgruntled public. The barrage of accountability measures aimed at schools has caused educators to focus on varied and questionable purposes, such as teaching to the tests and "dumbing down" the curriculum (McNeil, 2000) rather than preparing students to become useful and productive citizens.

Recent trends in education suggest two possibilities: Either greater control will be exerted over public schools and schooling, or conversely, educational autonomy will be expanded in the form of charter and independent schools, which would be unfettered by external controls and perceived as an alternative to public education (Goldring & Greenfield, 2002). No matter what the requirements or configurations of schools, educational leaders in the public sector will likely face greater stresses and increased demands for the successful performance of all students and for outcomes established by governmental and community groups. As the battle over public education continues, a common dilemma for school systems, leaders, and policymakers is how to find an appropriate balance between centralization and decentralization in order to fulfill their historical mandate to prepare citizens for participation in a democratic society (Retallick & Fink, 2002). We believe that the primary strategies for achieving success in addressing this mandate include collaborative leadership and community building.

EXPLORING COLLABORATIVE LEADERSHIP

Increased school reform and accountability demands, coupled with a shift away from the Industrial Age to a technological and global economy, have fostered calls for a move away from a hierarchical model of leadership to a collaborative one (Pounder, 1998). Although principal leadership is an essential element in school success, current research indicates that the complexities of schools require a new focus on collaborative leadership and creation of a sense of community in which leadership is shared (Retallick & Fink, 2002). A first step in becoming a collaborative leader is understanding the underlying philosophical nature and purposes of this strategy.

The Nature of Collaborative Leadership

There is currently no consensus on the definition of collaborative leadership, and this has led to varied interpretations of the concept (Fishbaugh, 1997). Collaborative leadership incorporates notions of reciprocity and working toward a common end. It is a "messy business: wrought with ambiguity and surprises" (Johnston, 1997, p. 118). As we conceptualize it, it encompasses moral purposes proposed generations ago by Dewey (1922) and more recently by Fullan (2003) and Furman and Starratt (2002). It is a relational experience that is defined in practice by those involved as they interrelate with one another and the context in which they operate. The ultimate goal of collaborative leadership is to create democratic learning communities in which power is shared and there is a mutual belief in working together for the common good.

Democratic learning communities create a common set of values, attitudes, and beliefs that bond people together to establish goals and objectives that will improve organizational cultures and outcomes (Sergiovanni, 1994). The focus is on empowerment rather than control and on the creation of dialogue, cooperation, and the fostering of democratic principles (Furman, 1998). There is an acceptance of what Strike (1999) labels "thick democracy" and fair decision making, which assigns "value to participation, civic friendship, inclusiveness, and solidarity" (p. 60).

Collaboration and Community Building in Educational Settings

Furman-Brown (1999) suggests that there are two strands involved in creating a sense of community in schools. The first strand deals with connecting to the broader community, whereas the second develops the structures and relationships within the school to create an internal community. These two strands generally have been the focus of school reform. We propose a third strand, closely related to Mathews's (1996) challenge to develop "public strategies" to reconstitute the relationship of the public to public education. This approach places the school in the position of aiding the community as it rebuilds itself and its relationship to the school. We have split our analysis of educational community building into these three strands, which we have labeled: (1) the reconstruction of the school organizational culture into a learning community, (2) the creation of partnerships and networks across organizations to form a community, and (3) the engagement of the school as a primary force in building the community and reconnecting with its public. Below, we will describe each strand in turn, providing examples and discussing the benefits of its implementation. Because the concepts related to the third strand are less familiar than those in the first two, the description of this strand and examples of its implementation will be more comprehensive than for the other two.

Reconstructing School Cultures

The rationale for creating a democratic community within the school is based on the concept that shared leadership and learning will increase the capacity of individuals, and thus the schools, to meet the needs of all students. Such communities can be internal, involving only those involved in the daily operations of the school (teachers, staff, administrators, students, and their families), or they can include external constituents, such as business and community leaders.

The effort to establish school- or site-based management (SBM), which has been popular in some circles during the past 20 years, is an example of creating school communities. An underlying basis for SBM is that those closest to the daily work of schools should be engaged in making decisions about the organization and its structure, management, goals, and objectives and should be engaged in a process of continuous learning about them (Silins, Mulford, & Zarins, 2002).

Some school communities might claim that individuals are engaged in joint decision making, but this tends to be espoused rather than practiced. In these situations, issues such as budgets, personnel, and organizational structures are mandated by the superintendent or other supervisors and/or the school principal. Well-developed learning communities that involve all members of the school, including parents and students, are engaged in developing the organization and in learning together to improve it (Barth, 1990).

An ideal learning community is organized in a way that fosters an open flow of thought; stimulates critical reflection about and analyses of ideas, policies, problems, and solutions; creates notions of the common good; and develops a concern for the rights and dignity of all people (Apple & Beane, 1995). In such a setting, teachers, staff, students, parents, and community members function together using democratic principles to improve the school and enhance learning (Murphy, 2002; Silins et al., 2002). This implies that the individual and the organization are actualized and considered in the learning process (Senge, 1990).

Leadership in these communities includes participatory democracy in all areas of school life, including a culturally diverse curriculum, a system of continuous whole-school renewal, and participatory teaching, learning, and assessment processes. Participatory school communities with a focused vision and shared goals have been shown to improve student learning (Kelly & Finnegan, 2003). They have successfully aided teachers in analysis and improvement of their practice, improved school environments, and enabled schools and individuals to balance "bottom-up processes" with "top-down regulations" (Veugelers & Zijlstra, 2002, p. 163).

Creating Partnerships and Networks

The expanded awareness of the value of collaboration in educational environments has led to an increase in the creation of partnerships and networks between and among teachers, leaders, schools, and other institutions. Teacher and educational leadership networks are usually built around a common purpose and tend to include continuous professional development along with an underlying focus on school improvement (Sergiovanni, 1994).

Examples of organizational partnerships or networks include professional development schools, which connect schools and universities through partnerships to enhance education from kindergarten through an undergraduate college degree (Kochan, 1999); networks of schools centered around common principles to enhance school improvement, such as the Goodlad Coalition for Essential Schools (Goodlad, 1990) and the Alabama Learning Coalition (Kochan & Kunkel, 1998); or initiatives such as full-service and community schools (Blank, Melaville, & Shah, 2003; Dryfoos & Maguire, 2002) focused on connecting the schools with their communities to enhance both. Such networks have reported many benefits, such as improving teacher education, developing collaborative communities, enhancing educational achievement, fostering professional development, and expanding research and inquiry (Kochan, 1998). Research on the Coalition for Community Schools, which connected community services with schools to enhance student learning, found that student learning was improved, family engagement was expanded, schools functioned more effectively, and community vitality was enhanced (Blank et al., 2003).

Engaging in Community Development

The importance of public support for public schools cannot be underestimated (Mathews, 1996). Fullan (1998) proposes that external constituents, which he describes as the "out there," are going to "get" schools anyway, so it is imperative that school leaders collaborate with them to gain their support. There are varied levels of support and involvement related to public education. Doble and Higgins (1998) identified five types of relationships that the public has with public schools. The first group, *consumers,* tends to comprise parents of school-age students, who view themselves as consumers of school services. Consumers are usually focused on their individual relationships with the schools, and as long as the school is attentive to their children's needs, consumers tend to be satisfied with the relationship. This may help to explain why many people say that their own

schools are fine but that the public education system as a whole is failing (Doble & Higgins, 1998). The relationship consumers have with public schools tends to be limited, fragile, and temporary, ending as soon as the consumer's children leave school. The other four types of relationships include: *partners,* who believe that they and their community are important education resources; *shutouts,* who feel blocked by school officials or regulations; *dropouts,* who have withdrawn their children from public education; and *inattentives,* who do not see education as a priority.

It is vital that educational leaders listen to the concerns voiced by all stakeholders and engage those who are not voicing their opinions or support, by forming relationships focused on the community and its needs as a starting point. Community development partnerships seek to connect the conditions of children and education with the conditions, needs, and resources of the community. These partnerships focus on the totality of the context of students and their school, seeking to enhance and improve it. Historically, the concept is grounded in Dewey's (1916) notion of finding a balance between the schools and the community; examples include the Community Schools Movement of the 1930s and the Cities in Schools program of the 1960s and 1970s. The notion is that these partnerships can build social capital and thus improve schools and communities (Kahne, O'Brien, Brown, & Quinn, 2001). In recent years, community building has experienced a renaissance as a result of the renewed desire to make connections and create bonds between schools and communities (Bryk & Driscoll, 1988).

Mathews (2002) refers to these types of initiatives as "public making" and suggests that they are essential to the survival of public education in the United States. Goldring and Greenfield (2002) advocate that social justice be the overarching concept around community building. In addition, they support the notion that schools should be the center of public discourse about these issues and that school personnel should engage the public in dealing with the critical connections between schooling and a "good society."

We concur with the belief that educational leaders must move beyond school communities and partnerships focused on institutions or organizations to become engaged in the community development process. We believe that the college faculty who prepare these leaders must also be involved in such activities. Our own experiences in such endeavors have led us to the conclusion that unless we become part of the process of enhancing the communities in which we work, we will not regain public trust, and this will result in more mandates, more control, and an increased move toward the privatization of schooling.

We believe that engaging in the work of rebuilding communities is a moral and ethical responsibility for educators. Below, we describe one such initiative we have engaged in that includes a community development process. It is presented to illustrate how this approach can work and to stimulate dialogue about the issues surrounding community engagement.

The West Alabama Learning Coalition

The West Alabama Learning Coalition (WALC) began as a Professional Development School (PDS) initiative and expanded to become a community development network. It comprises partnerships from eight highly isolated and impoverished communities across Alabama. Participating in the coalition are two research universities, two master's-granting colleges, two community colleges, and one technical school, each of which is partnered with a school or school system.

The aims of the WALC include the simultaneous renewal of education at the pre-K to 12 and university levels, as well as and economic and community development (Reed & Kochan, 2003a, 2003b). This purpose is based on the proposition that connecting the reform of

educational institutions to the needs and context of the community will enhance the transformational reform of both. Toward this end, WALC guidelines require each partnership to involve members representing a broad spectrum of the community, including partners from the public school or district, the college or university, community or social service agencies, and business enterprises. We continually ask: *Who is not at the table, but should be?* This keeps the group focused on bringing more voices to the table and thus increasing the problem-solving capacity of the group.

Partners meet periodically as individual partnerships at their own sites and attend meetings as a coalition of partnerships at least twice a year. Each partnership has a coordinator who maintains records, plans meetings, and generally keeps the partnership on track. The West Alabama Learning Coalition has been operating since Spring 1997, although some partnerships joined after the network was established.

Although our members have similar school populations and communities, they are also diverse in their needs and concerns. There is little infrastructure in place to support economic development in most of these communities, although several have established community leadership development programs as an outgrowth of their coalition activities. The school districts face many problems, including low test scores and difficulty recruiting and retaining teachers and administrators.

Our work has been guided by inquiry and the idea that ongoing evaluation can inform, reform, and transform institutions (Reed, Kochan, Ross, & Kunkel, 2001). Much of the evaluation work has focused on capacity building, helping personnel at each partnership to learn how to collect and analyze data in an ongoing manner so that a focus is continuous improvement and organizational learning (Reed, 1997; Senge, 1990). All team members are involved in internal and external accountability processes. External accountability is addressed through public reporting mechanisms (Ross, Reed, Kochan, & Madden, 2003) and through reports and displays at coalition meetings.

One goal of the WALC is to help others understand that educational improvement is closely linked to community and economic development. Although progress toward achieving this goal varies greatly by partnership, several communities have actively embraced the concept.

Our work with the coalition has taught us many lessons about sustainable reform in the educational and community development process. The first lesson we have learned is that there must be someone who is responsible for coordinating the initiatives at each site and who is given the time to do so. We have also found that it is important to have our partners geographically close enough so that we can meet and share together on a regular basis. Continuous planning and working on mutually agreed upon goals, while still remaining flexible and keeping stakeholders and the public informed, are other elements that we have found to be essential for our success. We have also learned that educational leaders must develop strategies for building mutually beneficial relationships with legislators and even lobby for policies that will enhance public schooling as a part of such deliberations, and we have built this into our partnership work (Reed, 2000; Reed & Kochan, 2001).

We have conducted several studies examining why participants made the decision to become part of a network focused on connecting schools, higher education institutions, and a diverse group of community stakeholders in a rural, impoverished area of the state. Initially, partners joined the network because they viewed it as matching their organizational goals and meeting organizational and personal needs. They remain in the network because these needs were met, and they view the coalition as a catalyst for organizational and personal change (Reed, 2000; Mullen & Kochan, 2000).

The coalition has promoted professional development and personal growth for its participants and has provided a framework for reform. Through the activities of the coalition and each of the PDS partnerships, we have been able to inform local stakeholders about the needs and goals of education and reform the ways of offering professional development and working for change, and we have thus begun to transform educational and other institutions in our region. Student achievement has improved in many schools, and new curricular programs have been instituted. Some partnerships have begun the process of conducting regular community forums on leadership and community needs. Others have created community development leadership councils to move reform from the school to the community, connecting them to one another.

The frustrations faced by partnership members have been many. Responding to changes in administration, finding effective ways to communicate with diverse stakeholders, and actually getting people to commit to being "at the table" have been challenging. The role of the coordinator in each partnership has been a key element of partnership success. Lacking money and time, getting higher education partners to deliver on their promises, and wrestling with state and federal mandates in addition to regional and partnership initiatives have placed difficult burdens on many participants.

Some progress has been made toward improving the economic development potential of these communities, although community and economic development are slow and difficult processes. Combining these with educational improvement makes sense, but it does add another dimension, at least initially, to the work of the group. However, we believe, and have seen clearly through our work, that by having all groups at the table working together, there is a much better chance for positive sustainable change.

FACTORS THAT FACILITATE AND HINDER COLLABORATIVE LEADERSHIP AND COMMUNITY BUILDING

Examining the literature on community building in the light of our own experiences, we have identified many factors that can either facilitate or hinder the process. We believe it may be valuable to examine these factors, and have organized our discussion around four topical areas: values, power, organizational elements, and transcendent leadership.

The Role of Values

Rusch (1998) found that values were more important than actual practices in sustaining democratic community. Within this value structure, there must be a sense of the "common good" (Furman & Starratt, 2002). Closely tied to values are the beliefs one possesses about teaching, learning, school, children, and all the myriad issues that impact one's actions.

When considering the issue of common values, Strike (1999) reminds us that the values on which democratic educational communities are built must be "thick" enough to hold people together, while at the same time supporting difference and inclusivity. He cautions us to remain aware of and understand the underlying power-related issues, such as how to come to consensus without creating conformity. Coming to consensus on values and purposes while still allowing for differences means that the group must have the capacity to engage in open dialogue on a consistent basis. Thus, it is essential that those involved engage in dialogue about their values and beliefs and come to a consensus about them as a part of the community-building experience (Stevenson & Doolittle, 2003). Participants must be able to engage in conversations where their "convictions are on display for all to see" (Johnston, 1997, p. 16).

To have open dialogue, shared values, and common goals, people must feel safe together.

There must be enough trust between them so they can speak about what they believe in, disagree, and come to consensus without fear (Kahne et al., 2001). We found trust to be an extremely significant factor in our coalition work. It took a long time to build such trust, and doing so required that people learn to listen to and accept one another.

Issues of Power

A primary aspect of school reform is political. Thus, one must deal with issues of power in relationships (Sarason, 1996). When seeking to build a community, the equalization of power must be addressed (Dewey, 1916; Fishbaugh, 1997). Members of the group need to understand where and how power is gained and lost and deal with who is being included and excluded in power relationships (Sergiovanni & Starratt, 1979). Participants must take time to assess the level at which power is or is not equalized. Creating structures and activities in which trust can be built is thus an essential part of community building (Kochan, 2002).

In school settings and other environments where the principal is often identified as "the leader," some administrators may find it difficult to give up power and control. Even when schools attempt to create empowering situations, barriers exist including language, positions, and attitudes implying that educators should not be questioned, that hinder the creation of equal power relationships. This is particularly true of parents, who may not be comfortable in a school or community setting and may feel unaccepted there. Such individuals may tend to feel intimidated by the situation and uncomfortable or distrustful because of past experiences (Seitsinger & Zera, 2002).

A related issue is that although collaboration is lauded as a democratic value in public education, research indicates that at times, creating involvement in schools actually reinforces traditional power structures and disenfranchises the groups it purports to serve. Collaboration can be used as a way to "play democracy [while ignoring] issues of race and gender to avoid conflict" (Smrekar, 1996, p. 100). For some groups, evoking democracy can sound like the imposition of white racial superiority over minority groups (Seitsinger & Zera, 2002). Thus, we must be reflective and cautious when using this term and open up our dialogue to deal with the underlying issues involved (Scheurich, 1998).

Organizational Factors

Whether engaging in building community on a broad scale or on a school level, the task is very time consuming and requires persistence. Speaking of this, one of our coalition members said, "You just have to keep trying. You keep plugging away, even when you feel like you are using a little toothpick on a giant iceberg. You have to keep going." (Reed & Kochan, 2003a). Community building requires a great deal of face-to-face interaction. Harsh words and hurt feelings can hinder these efforts, requiring that people have many opportunities to interact with one another (Johnston, 1997). This is time-intensive work, making it particularly difficult to implement in school-based settings because of the busy nature of the school leader's job. Principals' work is marked by variety, fragmentation, and brevity of activity, and much of their time is spent reacting to problems that others bring to them. The resultant pressure to deal with immediate and concrete problems tends to bias principals toward solution-oriented learning that fits into their hectic schedules.

The present accountability environment has exacerbated the time problem by adding bureaucratic demands, increased paperwork, and additional responsibilities for school leaders (Kahne et al., 2001). Mandates that dictate curriculum standards, performance assessments, and in some cases even teaching materials and instructional strategies can cause principals to focus on compliance with external demands rather than on the creative development of shared leadership through communities.

The responsibilities of the principal have been further complicated by increased demands from external constituencies, changing population demographics, the rapid growth in research on teaching and learning, and the expanded access to information resulting from the technological explosion (Leithwood, 2001). Thus, although accountability measures are often coupled with calls for school reform and change, the mandates that come with these measures make it unlikely that administrators will choose to engage in reflection, innovation, and risk-taking actions, concentrating instead on efficient ways to respond to legislative requirements (Bruckerhoff, 1995). These demands, coupled with traditional bureaucratic structures in schools, make it difficult for school leaders to establish their own ways of operating and to create democratic, jointly designed policies (Seitsinger & Zera, 2002).

To overcome these barriers, educational leaders must be determined and fully committed to the process of community building. Although leadership is a shared process, the person considered to be the leader must have the skills, knowledge, and disposition needed to work collaboratively and foster democratic community. We label such leaders *transcendent*, meaning that they can transcend circumstances, traditions, and barriers to create democratic environments as a natural part of their leadership role (Kochan, 2004). We believe that developing such leaders requires a change in the way leaders are prepared and in the way in which they view their roles. Throughout their preparation programs, there must be authentic opportunities to practice the work of community building. The section that follows provides some ideas for how that role can be conceptualized and taught.

Transcendent Leadership

Transcendent leaders are individuals who engage in visionary idealism, drawing from their whole selves and helping others to do the same. They are pragmatic and moral individuals who believe in and work for social justice and equity. They believe in the inherent value of public schools in a democratic society. Their leadership practice is based on a moral code that encompasses caring for others, fairness, integrity, and honesty (Fullan, 2003). An examination of the literature on individuals who have been successful in the task of democracy building suggests they have some common characteristics.

Transcendent leaders participate in transformative learning. Transformative learning implies that one is willing to engage in a deep change or transformation of one's tacitly acquired assumptions and the expectations that influence the way one thinks and acts. Transformative learning involves reflecting on assumptions in a critical way, being actively involved in dialogue about a problematic issue, taking reflective and critical action on the issue, and developing the practice of critical reflection about one's own assumptions and those of others (Sergiovanni, 1994).

Such leaders engage in self-development as a part of their role as principal and encourage others to do the same (Kochan, Bredeson, & Riehl, 2002). Professional growth is necessary so that principals can perform their jobs well, but there are also indications that principal learning has other important effects on teacher development, the school culture, systemic educational reform, and student learning (Bredeson & Scribner, 2000). The importance of the principal as learner led one educator to conclude that the litmus test for the selection of a school leader should be to "find the one man or woman most genuinely committed to

the professional development of himself and his colleagues" (quoted in Pohland & Bova, 2000, p. 137).

Transcendent leaders have the ability to build trust and high levels of communication skills (Schechter, 2002). They are not afraid of conflict but instead view it as a means of uncovering hidden meanings, beliefs, and mores that hinder the democratic process (Seitsinger & Zera, 2002). The process of envisioning and achieving what might be involves the ability and desire to engage in dialogue and critique for the common good (Johnston, 1997). Rapp (2002) defines this as

> refusing to let others do your thinking, talking, naming for you. . . . [It] means, you don't fall for shallow and easy solutions. . . . [It] means that you refuse to sell your talents and aspirations short, simply to avoid conflict and confrontation. . . . [It] means resisting the forces in society. . . . [It] means, therefore, the courage to be different. (pp. 177–178)

Schechter (2002) found that this type of leader was not overwhelmed by obstacles when working toward a goal and was willing to express doubts and vulnerability if necessary. This vulnerability causes others to have more trust in this type of leader and believe in his or her sincerity. This trust, in turn, results in more open dialogue and sharing. Sarason and Lorentz (1998) suggest that the desired role of such a leader be that of

> [An] honest broker. . . . A person who seeks an agreement fair to all parties. . . . A person who starts and ends with no power, an informed but selfless individual who seeks to help the parties enlarge or alter their view of their mutual interests. (p. 27)

Transcendent leaders must view community building as a continuous process of change, embracing uncertainty. They must be bold and courageous, willing to move beyond bureaucratic structures to achieve democracy (Seitsinger & Zera, 2002), and open to examining the need for continuity and change (Tyack & Cuban, 1995). This requires that they understand and recognize the context they are in and consider how to operate within it, while at the same time not giving in to it (Leithwood, 2001). Such leaders must be adaptable, flexible, able to deal with ambiguity, and not afraid of failure. Writing about such a leader, Schechter (2002) quoted a teacher as saying, "He is different from most of us. . . . He views failure as an opportunity for learning" (p. 118).

Building internal and external connections and relationships to transcend the context they are in also requires that leaders have a strong sense of personal identity and a high level of interpersonal skills. They must understand and reflect on their beliefs and continually question themselves about them (Stevenson & Doolittle, 2003). Without these elements, leaders can suffer high levels of burnout (Kremer-Hayon, Fraaj, & Wubbels, 2002).

Leaders of democratic schools must be equipped with the knowledge, skills, abilities, beliefs, and dispositions that will allow them to succeed. This requires that they become part of professional development and mentoring networks that will provide support while they serve in their role as educational leader. It also requires a change in their educational preparation programs and in the organizational structures in which they operate.

IMPLICATIONS FOR EDUCATIONAL PREPARATION PROGRAMS

Preparing educational leaders who believe in and can facilitate community building might be considered an overwhelming task. It is true that the responsibility for developing such leaders cannot fall solely on the faculty who prepare them because becoming a transcendent leader is a lifelong process requiring continuous engagement in the learning task. However, there are some strategies and activities that we believe will foster this type of leadership during the preparation period. These strategies and activities fall into three categories that overlap one another: curriculum and instruction, organizational structures, and partnerships and community involvement.

Curriculum and Instruction

The content and delivery of curricula that will prepare individuals to build democratic environments must be infused with readings, experiences, and structures that foster democratic ideals. Thus, classroom texts and readings must come from diverse perspectives so that dialogue and discussion can include opportunities to develop listening skills, challenge beliefs and values, and engage in critiques of one's own ideas and the ideas of others, questioning the status quo (Kochan, 2004; Stevenson & Doolittle, 2003).

Leadership preparation programs should be centered on values, with equity and social justice at the core (Sergiovanni, 1994). They should consider the whole person (intellect, emotion, and spirit) as they implement the curriculum in order to model the type of educational environment these educational leaders will be expected to create (Dantley, 2003).

Students must also be given opportunities to gain an understanding of the broader context in which they will be operating. Thus, they should be engaged in reading about and critiquing how leadership is viewed in various professions, such as the law, business, and public administration. These insights will assist them in understanding a wide range of perspectives and in working with diverse groups of people in the community.

Future educational leaders must also understand the political framework of schools and schooling and of working with the community. This requires that educational leadership programs involve students in forming mutually beneficial relationships with legislators and even engaging in policy advocacy as a part of their preparation program (Reed & Kochan, 2001).

Organizational Structures

In addition to the content of our curriculum, we must ensure that the environment in which we prepare leaders models democratic principles (Kochan & Sabo, 1995). Cohorts built around open dialogue and discussion are ideal groups in which to model collaboration (Stevenson & Doolittle, 2003). They can serve as a means of practicing trust building, effective listening, and other communication skills, allowing participants to critique issues and share leadership. We must also examine the relationships we have within our own departments to ensure that we are modeling the type of communities we are encouraging our students to create.

Partnerships and Networking

Higher education is as much a part of the community as is preschool to Grade 12 education. It is therefore imperative that we engage the public in our programs and that we form the kind of partnerships that we are expecting our students to develop. Our school partnerships should include not only placing interns in schools, but assisting with community building and the continuing professional development of educational leaders. Creating school and community partnerships such as the West Alabama Learning Coalition, which engage those traditionally forgotten in the community and educational development processes, should be a major part of our community-building endeavors. These partnerships are mutually beneficial, providing needed services to others while enriching our own experiences and practices.

We should also be communicating and partnering with others in our colleges, universities (Goldring & Greenfield, 2002), and wider communities, including such groups as chambers of commerce and social service agencies, working with them to foster partnerships within and across communities and schools. Our educational leadership students should be included in this relationship building while they are enrolled in their preparation programs so that they can develop the skills they will need to become transcendent, collaborative leaders. The more we engage in community building ourselves, the more credible we will be in assisting our students to become transcendent leaders and in becoming transcendent leaders ourselves (Kochan, 2004).

CONCLUSION

The complexity of the environment in which educators must operate and the escalating disengagement of the public from their schools have made it necessary for educational leaders to make internal and external community building a central priority of their leadership role. Educational leaders and the faculty that prepare them must work toward becoming transcendent leaders who are willing to challenge the status quo, build internal and external connections and relationships, and center their practice on the values of democracy and the common good. Collaborative leadership and community building beget collaborative leadership and community building. As Tyack and Cuban (1995) state, "[An] essential political task today is to renegotiate a pluralistic conception of the public good, a sense of trusteeship that preserves the best of the past while building a generous conception of a common future" (p. 11). As educational leaders, we must be aware of the past and build on it. We need to remember that "public schools were as much a foundation for American democracy as the Constitution and the Bill of Rights" (Mathews, 1996, p. 11). Thus, it is our responsibility to ensure that public education remains a central, respected, and treasured part of our American democracy. We can do nothing less.

REFERENCES

Apple, M. W., & Beane, L. A. (Eds.). (1995). *Democratic schools*. Alexandria, VA: Association for Supervision and Curriculum Development.

Barth, R. S. (1990). *Improving schools from within.* San Francisco: Jossey-Bass.

Blank, M. J., Melaville, A., & Shah, B. P. (2003). *Making the difference: Research and practice in community schools.* Washington, DC: Coalition for Community Schools.

Bredeson, P. V., & Scribner, J. (2000). A statewide professional development conference: Useful strategy for learning or inefficient use of resources? *Education Policy Analysis Archives, 8*(13). Retrieved from http://epaa.asu.edu/epaa/v8n13.html

Bruckerhoff, C. (1995, April). *School routines and the failure of school reform.* Paper presented at the Annual Meeting of the American Educational Research Association, San Francisco.

Bryk, A., & Driscoll, M. (1988). *The high school as community: Contextual influences and consequences for students and teachers.* Madison: University of Wisconsin-Madison, Wisconsin Center for Educational Research.

Cook, F. (2004). Vouchers, choice, and controversy. *American School Board Journal, 191*(1), 12–17.

Dantley, M. (2003). Principled, pragmatic, and purposive leadership: Reimagining educational leadership through prophetic spirituality. *Journal of School Leadership, 13*(2), 181–198.

Dewey, J. (1916). *Democracy and education: An introduction to the philosophy of education.* New York: Macmillan.

Dewey, J. (1922). *Human nature and conduct.* New York: Random House.

Doble, J., & Higgins, D. (1998). *How people connect: The public and the public schools* (A report prepared for the Kettering Foundation). Englewood Cliffs, NJ: Doble Research Associates.

Dryfoos, J., & Maguire, S. (2002). *Inside full-service community schools.* Thousand Oaks, CA: Corwin.

Elementary and Secondary Education Act (ESEA). (2001). No Child Left Behind Act. Available at the U.S. Department of Education website www.ed.gov

English, F. (2003). *The postmodern challenge to the theory and practice of educational administration.* Springfield, IL: Charles C Thomas.

Fishbaugh, M. S. E. (1997). *Models of collaboration.* Needham Heights, MA: Allyn & Bacon.

Foster, W. (1980). Administration and the crisis in legitimacy: A review of Habermasian thought. *Harvard Educational Review, 50*(4), 496–505.

Foster, W. (1986). *Paradigms and promises: New approaches to educational administration.* Amherst, NY: Prometheus Books.

Fullan, M. (1998). Leadership for the 21st century: Breaking the bonds of dependency. *Educational Leadership, 55*(7), 6–10.

Fullan, M. (2003). *The moral imperative of school leadership.* Thousand Oaks, CA: Corwin.

Furman, G. C. (1998). Postmodernism and community in schools: Unraveling the paradox. *Educational Administration Quarterly, 34,* 298–328.

Furman, G. C., & Starratt, R. J. (2002). Leadership for democratic community in schools. In J. Murphy (Ed.), *The educational leadership challenge: Redefining leadership for the 21st century* (101st Yearbook of the National Society for the Study of Education, pp. 105–133). Chicago, IL: University of Chicago Press.

Furman-Brown, G. (1999). Editor's foreword. *Educational Administration Quarterly, 35*(1), 6–12.

Goldring, E., & Greenfield, W. (2002). Understanding the evolving concept of leadership in education: Roles, expectations, and dilemmas. In J. Murphy (Ed.), *The educational leadership challenge: Redefining leadership for the 21st century* (101st Yearbook of the National Society for the Study of Education, pp. 1–19). Chicago: University of Chicago Press.

Goodlad, J. I. (1990). *Teachers for our nation's schools.* San Francisco: Jossey-Bass.

Habermas, J. (1975). *Legitimation crisis* (J. Viertel, Trans.). Boston: Beacon Press.

Johnston, M. (1997). *Contradictions in collaboration.* New York: Teachers College Press.

Kahne, J., O'Brien, J., Brown, A., & Quinn, T. (2001). Leveraging social capital and school improvement: The case of a school network and a comprehensive community initiative in Chicago. *Educational Administration Quarterly, 37*(4), 429–461.

Kelly, C. J., & Finnegan, K. (2003). The effects of organizational context on teacher expectancy. *Educational Administration Quarterly, 39*(5), 773–602.

Kochan, F. K. (1998). Benefits of professional development schools: The hidden message in the forest. *The Professional Education, xx*(4), 1–6.

Kochan, F. K. (1999). Professional development schools: A comprehensive view. In D. M. Byrd & D. J. McIntyre (Eds.), *Research on professional development schools* (Teacher Evaluation Yearbook, Vol. 7, pp. 173–190). Thousand Oaks, CA: Corwin.

Kochan, F. K. (2002). Hope and possibility: Advancing an argument for a Habermasian perspective in educational administration. *Studies in Philosophy and Education, 2*(2), 137–155.

Kochan, F. K. (2004). Leading, learning, and becoming in a kaleidoscopic universe. *UCEA Review, 46*(1), 1–6.

Kochan, F. K., Bredeson, P., & Riehl, C. (2002). Rethinking the professional development of school leaders. In J. Murphy (Ed.), *The educational leadership challenge: Redefining leadership for the 21st century* (101st Yearbook of the National Society for the Study of Education, pp. 289–306). Chicago: University of Chicago Press.

Kochan, F. K., Jackson, B., & Duke, D. (1999). *Voices from the firing line: A study of educational leaders' perceptions of their job, the challenges they face, and their preparation.* Columbia, MO: UCEA Press.

Kochan, F. K., & Kunkel, R. C. (1998). The learning coalition: Professional development schools in partnership. *Journal of Teacher Education, 49*(5), 325–333.

Kochan, F. K., & Sabo, D. (1995). Transforming educational leadership programs through collaboration: Practicing what we preach. *Planning and Changing, 26*(3/4), 168–178.

Kremer-Hayon, L., Fraaj, H., & Wubbels, T. (2002). Burn-out among Israeli Arab school principals as a function of professional identity and interpersonal relationships with teachers. *International Journal of Leadership in Education, 5*(2), 149–162.

Leithwood, K. (2001). School leadership in the context of accountability policies. *International Journal of Leadership in Education, 4*(3), 217–236.

Mathews, D. (1996). *Is there a public for public schools?* Dayton, OH: Kettering Foundation.

Mathews, D. (2002). *For communities to work.* Dayton, OH: Kettering Foundation.

Mathews, D. (2003). *Why public schools? Whose public schools?* Montgomery, AL: New South Books.

McNeil, L. M. (2000). *Contradictions of school reform: Educational costs of standardized testing.* New York: Routledge.

Mullen, C. A., & Kochan, F. K. (2000). Creating a collaborative leadership network: An organic view of change. *International Journal of Leadership in Education, 3*(3), 183–200.

Murphy, J. (2002). Reculturing the profession of educational leadership: New blueprints. In J. Murphy (Ed.), *The educational challenge: Redefining leadership for the 21st century*

(101st Yearbook of the National Society for the Study of Education, pp. 62–82). Chicago: University of Chicago Press.

National Commission on Excellence in Education. (1983). *A nation at risk: The imperative for educational reform* (A report to the Secretary of Education, U.S. Department of Education). Washington, DC: Author.

Pohland, P., & Bova, B. (2000). Professional development and transformative learning. *International Journal of Leadership in Education, 3*(2), 137–150.

Pounder, D. (1998). Introduction and overview of the book. In D. Pounder (Ed.), *Restructuring schools for collaboration: Promises and pitfalls* (pp. 1–8). Albany: SUNY Press.

Rapp, D. (2002). On lies, secrets, and silence: A plea to educational leaders. *International Journal of Leadership in Education, 5*(2), 175–185.

Reed, C. J. (1997). *Student leadership and restructuring: A case study.* Unpublished dissertation, University of Pittsburgh.

Reed, C. J. (2000). Preparing school leaders to be policy advocates: The role of educational leadership preparation programs. In F. K. Kochan (Ed.), *2000 Southern Regional Council for Educational Administration yearbook.* Auburn, AL: Truman Pierce Institute.

Reed, C. J., & Kochan, F. K. (2001). Preparing educational leaders for proactive involvement in policy development. *Journal of School Leadership, 11,* 264–278.

Reed, C. J., & Kochan, F. K. (2003a, April 21–25). *Educational improvement, economic development, and sustainability in rural professional development schools.* Paper presented at the Annual Meeting of the American Educational Research Association, Chicago.

Reed, C. J., & Kochan, F. K. (2003b, November 6–9). *Enhancing leadership capacity through scaffolding, collaboration, and advocacy.* Paper presented at the Annual Meeting of the University Council for Educational Administration, Portland, OR.

Reed, C., Kochan, F. K., Ross, M. E., & Kunkel, R. C. (2001). Designing evaluation systems to inform, reform, and transform professional development schools. *Journal of Curriculum and Supervision, 16*(3), 188–205.

Reed, C. J., & Ross, M. E. (2001). Investing in professional judgment-in-action: Negotiating relationships that enhance trust, responsibility, and efficacy. *Educational Considerations, 29*(1), 24–31.

Retallick, J., & Fink, D. (2002). Framing leadership: Contributions and impediments to educational change. *International Journal of Leadership in Education, 5*(20), 91–104.

Ross, M. E., Reed, C. J., Kochan, F. K., & Madden, J. (2003, Spring). Taking control of what counts in accountability: The context enriched report card. *Educational Considerations, 30*(2), 21–26.

Rusch, E. A. (1998). Leadership in evolving democratic school communities. *Journal of School Leadership, 8,* 214–250.

Sarason, S. B. (1996). *Revisiting the culture of school and the problem of change.* New York: Teachers College Press.

Sarason, S. B., & Lorentz, E. M. (Eds.). (1998). *Crossing boundaries: Collaboration, coordination, and the redefinition of resources.* San Francisco: Jossey-Bass.

Schechter, C. (2002). Marching in the land of uncertainty: Transforming school culture through communal deliberative process. *International Journal of Leadership in Education, 5*(2), 105–128.

Scheurich, J. J. (1998). The grave dangers in the discourse on democracy. *International Journal of Leadership in Education: Theory and Practice, 1*(1), 55–60.

Seitsinger, R. M., Jr., & Zera, D. A. (2002). The demise of parent involvement in school governance. *Journal of School Leadership, 12*(1), 340–367.

Senge, P. (1990). *The fifth discipline.* New York: Currency Doubleday.

Sergiovanni, T. (1994). *Building community schools.* San Francisco: Jossey-Bass.

Sergiovanni, T. J., & Starratt, R. J. (1979). *Supervision: Human perspectives.* New York: McGraw-Hill.

Silins, H. C., Mulford, W. R., & Zarins, S. (2002). Organizational learning and school change. *Educational Administration Quarterly, 38*(5), 613–642.

Smrekar, C. (1996). *The impact of school choice and community in the interest of families and schools.* Albany: SUNY Press.

Stevenson, R. B., & Doolittle, G. (2003). Developing democratic and transformational school leaders: Graduates; perceptions of the impact of the preparation program. *Journal of School Leadership, 13*(6), 666–687.

Strike, K. A. (1999). Can schools be communities: The tension between shared values and inclusion. *Educational Administration Quarterly, 35,* 46–70.

Tyack, D. (1974). *The one best system.* Cambridge, MA: Harvard University Press.

Tyack, D., & Cuban, L. (1995). *Tinkering toward utopia: A century of public school reform.* Cambridge, MA: Harvard University Press.

Uline, C. L. (2001). The imperative to change. *International Journal of Leadership in Education, 4*(1), 13–29.

Veugelers, W., & Zijlstra, H. (2002). What goes on in a network? Some Dutch experiences. *International Journal of Leadership in Education, 5*(2), 175–186.

PART II

Management, Organization, and Law

CHARLES J. RUSSO
University of Dayton

R ecognizing the essential role that leadership plays in the daily operation of
American schools, at both the building and district levels, this part of the
Handbook of Educational Research: New Dimensions and Realities consists of
four chapters that present contemporary research about educational leadership,
reflecting on the stresses and strains of practice. Viewed together, these chapters
challenge educational leaders, and those charged with their preparation, to reflect
on how the worlds of theory and practice must meld so as to best inform professionals who will take charge in the ever-evolving world of American schools.

More specifically, the first chapter sets the stage by presenting a broad
overview of organizational theory and its role in shaping educational leadership,
while the next two chapters examine the important jobs performed by principals
and superintendents, professionals who are charged with the day-to-day responsibility of leading educational systems. Further, insofar as the basis of organizational bureaucracy in public education is legal authority, the final chapter looks
at the role of school law as the anchor point in the development of public
education during the second half of the 20th century.

The first chapter, "Leadership as Social Construct: The Expression of Human
Agency Within Organizational Constraint," by Rodney T. Ogawa, explores various facets of organizational theory and how it has been used to shape and contain
ideas about leadership in school. In so doing, this chapter views the literature on
educational leadership through the interpretive lens provided by a heuristic device
highlighting issues that cut across scholarly treatments of this subject. The chapter
does not distill the wide-ranging literature on educational leadership to produce an
integrated, comprehensive theory, which has been attempted in previous literature
reviews. Rather, the chapter takes a step back and views educational leadership
from a broader perspective to rethink persistent issues, which often take the form
of conceptual ambiguities and tensions.

Chapter 6, "Pivotal Points: History, Development, and Promise of the Principalship," by Kathleen M. Brown, examines contemporary research on the school principalship, reviewing trends from 1840 through the year 2000. Acknowledging the inability to achieve scientific precision in documenting history, the chapter examines five pivotal points in the development of the principalship.

Point 1, the Emergence of the Principalship (circa 1840–1900), notes the shift from "head teacher" to "principal." Point 2, the Professionalization of the Principalship (circa 1900–1940), outlines the process of formal recognition and acceptance of the role. Point 3, the Anti-Intellectualism of the Principalship (circa 1940–1960), questions the transition from scientific management through the human relations movement to the theory movement. Point 4, the Constancy and Change of the Principalship (circa 1960–1980), highlights the intersection of normative pressures between those seeking stability and the maintenance of traditional values versus those that press for change. Point 5, the Reform and Restructuring of the Principalship (circa 1980–2000), charts the shift from demands for management and control with forced compliance to shared decision making and decentralized site-based management, namely from the implementation and maintenance of the status quo to staff development, program improvement, parent involvement, community support, and student growth. The chapter concludes with a discussion of the challenges and promises of the principalship for the 21st century.

"The School Superintendent: Roles, Challenges, and Issues," by Theodore J. Kowalski and C. Cryss Brunner, the third chapter in Part II, examines contemporary research on this vital position. The first two sections of this chapter provide historical perspectives by summarizing research on how the superintendency has evolved at its three different levels of operation, namely the state, intermediate district, and local district. The second part, which examines issues pertaining to the underrepresentation of women and minorities, is accompanied by a review of contemporary issues affecting the daily practices of superintendents. The chapter concludes with recommendations for research on this pivotal leadership position.

The final chapter in this section, "The Role of Education Law in Leadership Preparation Programs," by Charles J. Russo, reviews the place of education law, identifying how it has contributed to changing, restructuring, and redefining the nature of educational leadership. In light of the significant role that education law has assumed in the daily activities of educational leaders and in preparation programs, this chapter reviews three major areas that are important for all of those interested in elementary and secondary education. The chapter begins with a reflection on the centrality of education law in educational leadership preparation programs and practice; the chapter then examines key Supreme Court cases and federal legislation with regard to schooling. The chapter focuses on developments at the federal, rather than state, level since doing so provides a broader basis for understanding the wide range of legal issues that have an impact on preparation programs and the practice of educational leadership.

In sum, the chapters in this section recognize that in order for students to succeed, educational administrators, especially those in key building- and district-level positions, must be well grounded in both the theory and practice of leadership. Moreover, to the extent that so much of what has occurred in schools since the Supreme Court's monumental 1954 decision in *Brown v. Board of Education* is directed by the law, the section is rounded out with an examination of key developments in this important area because it has played a pivotal role in ensuring equity for all who are involved in public education.

As educational leaders seek to direct the activities of American schools in the 21st century, the chapters in this part remind them that they must take the time to reflect on the role that organizational theory and the law have played in shaping the professional activities of principals and superintendents. These chapters, written by faculty members in educational leadership programs who have served in a variety of capacities in schools, ranging from classroom teacher to principal to superintendent, encourage all of those interested in our common profession to think about the interrelatedness of the topics addressed herein so that all can work more effectively to improve the quality of education for all American children.

5

Leadership as Social Construct

The Expression of Human Agency Within Organizational Constraint

RODNEY T. OGAWA
University of California at Santa Cruz

INTRODUCTION

Throughout recorded history, humankind has been fascinated by its leaders. Everyone is familiar with stories of leaders who changed the destiny of neighborhoods, states, nations, and world affairs. Hollywood produces feature films that regale us with the impact of Gandhi, Malcolm X, General George S. Patton, Joan of Arc, Moses, and others who led their people. Leadership, it seems, is central to understanding historical and contemporary events, particularly in the West.

Thus, it is not surprising that over the past century, social scientists have developed a field of study around the subject of leadership (Yukl, 1998). Social scientists have studied leaders and leadership in numerous domains, including athletics, business, government, and education. In fact, the study of educational leadership has been so central to the field of educational administration that several attempts have been made to review the scholarly

literature on educational leadership, including chapters in both volumes of the *Handbook of Research on Educational Administration* (Immegart, 1988; Leithwood & Duke, 1999).

My purpose in this chapter is not to offer another comprehensive review of the development of theory and research on educational leadership. That purpose has been admirably served by previous syntheses (see, for example, Hoy & Miskel, 1996; Leithwood & Duke, 1999). Instead, I view the literature on educational leadership through the interpretive lens provided by a heuristic device to highlight issues that cut across scholarly treatments of this subject. Neither do I distill the wide-ranging literature on educational leadership to produce an integrated, comprehensive theory, which has been attempted in previous literature reviews, including the two *Handbook* chapters cited above. Rather, I step back and view educational leadership from a broader perspective to rethink persistent issues, which often take the form of conceptual ambiguities and tensions.

HUMAN AGENCY VERSUS
ENVIRONMENTAL DETERMINISM

In this chapter, I adopt the concept of human agency as a heuristic for examining theory and research on educational leadership. Agency involves the control that people exert over their destiny, which is matched against deterministic forces assumed to lie largely beyond their control. The struggle between human agency and external determinism is seemingly evident in every dimension of human experience, including the theological, biological, and social.

Humankind has, apparently since its origin, struggled with the question of whether its destiny is controlled by the supernatural or human will. For instance, Greek and Roman mythology often revolves around tensions between the dictates of gods and the choices of humans. The *Odyssey* recounts the tale of brave Ulysses, who struggled in a world shaped by the gods on Mount Olympus. Similarly, modern religious traditions historically have pondered the balance between the will of God and the will of people.

We have also wrestled with the question of whether the human condition has been influenced more by natural forces or by human intervention. For instance, theory and research seek to reveal the relative impact of biological determinants and human will on our capacity and actions. Commonly characterized as "nature versus nurture," this tension is exemplified by the long-standing debate over what factors shape human intelligence. Most recently, in the widely read volume *The Bell Curve*, Herrnstein and Murray (1995) explain that their analysis of a broad database strongly suggests that intelligence is largely genetically derived. Other scholars were quick to respond that because the same data suggest that intelligence is profoundly shaped by human experience, they are subject to planned intervention (Gould, 1994).

Humankind also confronts constraints of its own invention. We have developed elaborate systems of norms, rules, and regulations in an effort to establish and maintain social order. Institutions are societal rules that take the form of cultural theories and ideologies (Meyer, Boli, & Thomas, 1987). Formal organizations enact institutions, enabling collections of individuals to coordinate their activities to produce more than if they simply collected the products of their individual efforts or gain legitimacy with stakeholders in society or both (Meyer & Rowan, 1977). The structures that constitute organizations are "the patterned or regularized aspects of the relationships existing among participants in an organization" (Scott, 2003, p. 18). Weber (1947) characterized bureaucratic organization as an "iron cage," imagery that DiMaggio and Powell (1983) resurrected in their discussion of organizational structures that are adopted to conform to institutionalized rules. Whether organizational structures are intended to produce technical efficiencies or institutional legitimacy, they constrain human activity and relations. The organization of elementary schools by grade level and secondary schools by subject matter, for example, shapes the activities and relations of teachers and students in ways that affect both teaching and learning as well as the legitimacy of schools with parents, community groups, and state and federal regulatory agencies.

Just as humankind has pondered the theological bounds of free will and explored the biological limits of human intervention, we struggle with organizational constraints on individual discretion and autonomy. Among the enduring dilemmas that have been identified in educational organizations (Ogawa, Crowson, & Goldring, 1999), the four that concern internal relations all reflect the tension between organizational determination and individual will. One pits the overall goals of an organization against the needs of its individual members. The second involves the tension between formal structures, which are defined by the organization, and informal structures, which arise from day-to-day interactions of individuals. The third concerns the cross pressures between the uniformity of bureaucratic management and the judgments of individuals who possess specialized, professional knowledge and skills. The fourth contrasts hierarchical arrangements, where only top-level administrators make decisions for the entire organization, with decentralized structures, where individuals and workgroups make decisions based on their knowledge of local conditions.

LEADERSHIP AS AN EXPRESSION OF HUMAN AGENCY

In each type of dilemma, human agency is pitted against organizational control, revealing the centrality of this issue to scholarship on educational organizations, and suggesting its importance to the lived experiences of people in contemporary society. I propose that the concepts of organizational leadership, in general, and educational leadership, specifically, are potent expressions of human agency in response to a world that is increasingly controlled by large, formal organizations. Organizations have extended their reach in every human domain (Scott, 2003); education is not an exception. Despite growth in the home-schooling movement, large bureaucracies—whether in the form of schools both public and private, or in the form of corporations—provide instruction on everything from the three Rs to motorcycle repair, computer programming, and the taking of all manner of tests. In light of humankind's historical struggle with the determinism of forces beyond personal will, it is not surprising that we balk at being consumed by social "cages" of our own creation.

In a world controlled to a substantial degree by organizations, leadership highlights the capacity of individuals to shape the world and to have a say in determining their own destiny. This suggests that leadership has both substantive and expressive dimensions. That is, leadership is assumed to have an impact on organizations and thus bears important meanings for the people who inhabit organizations.

For the most part, scholarly work on educational leadership has emphasized the substantive dimension, attempting to define leadership and determine how it affects educational organizations and their outcomes. In this chapter, I focus on the expressive dimension, exploring how our aspirations for human agency in organizations have shaped our conceptualization of leadership.

Expressions of Leadership

The intriguing, expressive connection between leadership and organizations is reflected in the literatures on both leadership and organization. The literature on leadership includes a relatively small strand of work highlighting the symbolism of leadership. In explaining the difficulty of empirically linking leadership to organizational performance, Pfeffer (1978) concludes that leadership is symbolic. He argues that leadership provides a relatively simple explanation for the highly complex phenomenon of organizational performance. Thus, leaders are scapegoated when organizations fail and excessively praised when organizations succeed. Through a series of studies, Meindl, Ehrlich, and Dukerich (1985) confirm the tendency to "romanticize" leadership, to exaggerate its contribution in explaining the performance of organizations. They conclude that "a heroic version of what leaders and leadership are all about virtually guarantees that a satisfying understanding will remain beyond the grasp of our best scientific efforts" (p. 100), suggesting the importance of the expressive rather than purely substantive dimension of leadership.

The work of two foundational organization theorists reflects two sides of the expression of human agency lodged in notions of leadership. Weber (1947) began with leadership when he cast bureaucracy as the institutionalization of charisma. He noted that the legacy of a person whose authority, or legitimized power, is rooted in personal appeal is perpetuated not by relying on the possibility of finding another compelling figure but by developing formal, social structures that consolidate relationships and practices to pursue the ends originated by the charismatic leader. For example, when an educator with a compelling instructional vision establishes a charter school, the development of a curriculum, pedagogical approach, and governance structure reflecting that vision enables the faculty, parents, and students to continue the pursuit of the school's original purpose even after the founder leaves. Selznick (1957), on the other hand, began with organization in arguing that the conceptualization of leadership is necessarily rooted in a conceptualization of organization. He maintained that the function of leadership is to establish congruence between institutions, or societal rules, and organizations by either initiating organizational structures that conform to institutions or by shaping institutions to reflect organizational pursuits. As an illustration, the founder of a charter school can encourage faculty members to obtain teaching credentials from the state to gain legitimacy with the parents of current and prospective students and work with a local university to develop an alternative credentialing program through which the school's faculty can gain certification. Weber's and Selznick's treatments of the relationship between organization and leadership express two forms of human agency. By suggesting that organizations can, in a sense, be the embodiment of a particular type of leader, the first expresses a form of agency by which organizations pursue personal will. In depicting leadership as the vehicle by which organizations come to embody social values and norms, the second expresses a form of agency through which organizations pursue a social ethic.

Definitions of Leadership

The expressive quality of leadership is also reflected in a core feature of the literature on this subject: the seeming impossibility of agreeing on a definition. In completing a comprehensive survey of the literature, which

culminated his career-long study of leadership, Stogdill (1974) lamented, "there are almost as many definitions of leadership as there are persons who have attempted to define the concept" (p. 259). Many scholars continue to despair at ever arriving at a consensus on what precisely constitutes leadership. Yukl (1998), for instance, notes, "[The different definitions] reflect deep disagreement about identification of leaders and leadership processes. Researchers who differ in the conception of leadership select different phenomena to investigate and interpret the results in different ways" (p. 3). In his chapter in the first volume of the *Handbook of Research on Educational Administration,* Immegart (1988) agrees, "There really are no commonly accepted conceptualizations [of leadership], and there is very little of what could really be called leadership theory to guide inquiry" (p. 272).

In their chapter in the most recent volume of the *Handbook of Research on Educational Administration,* Leithwood and Duke (1999), citing McNeil and Frieberger (1993), speculate that the absence of an agreed-upon definition of leadership and the failure of many authors to define the concept may arise from the utter complexity of leadership, which makes "precise statements lose meaning and meaningful statements lose precision" (p. 46). Another possibility is that leadership defies definition not because of its conceptual complexity, but because it expresses a cultural ideal or aspiration. Bennis (1989) likens leadership to beauty, explaining that while it may be difficult to define, you know it when you see it. This view of leadership reinforces its expressive quality. But, what does it express? This chapter treats leadership as an expression of human agency pitted against external determinants, including the iron cage of organization and, thus, as a symbol of the efficacy of human action and interaction.

Viewed from this broader perspective, the great variety that is emphasized by authors seeking a singular definition gives way to recognition of broad, crosscutting themes that are consistent with leadership as an expression of human agency. Many, probably most, definitions of leadership emphasize individuals and their relationship to organizational structures both as constraints on and as the means of exerting agency, which typically takes the form of influencing the actions and interactions of other participants.

The emphasis that definitions of leadership place on the individual is self-evident. Many definitions explicitly locate leadership in the individual. For instance, Gardner (1990) starts his definition of leadership by indicating that it is a process "by which an individual . . . "; Hemphill and Coons (1957) assert that it is "the behavior of an individual . . . "; Fiedler (1967) begins, "The leader is the individual . . . " Other definitions imply that leadership lies with individuals. In his comprehensive treatment of organizational leadership, Yukl (1998) concludes, "Most definitions of leadership reflect the assumption that it involves a process whereby intentional influence is exerted by one person . . . " (p. 3). Katz and Kahn (1966) deepen the conceptualization of leadership as the province of individuals by defining it as "the influential increment over and above mechanical compliance with the routine directives of the organization" (p. 302). Thus, individuals do not lead when they gain the compliance of others by virtue of the organizational roles they occupy. Rather, leaders gain compliance by employing personal, rather than organizational, resources.

Definitions of leadership also highlight the relationship between leaders and organizational structures. Some authors treat organizations as constraints on leadership. Katz and Kahn (1966), as noted, locate leadership outside the bounds of organization's routine directives, or structures. Schein (1992) similarly characterizes leadership as "the ability to step outside the [organization's] culture" (p. 2), suggesting that leaders exceed the limits established by the norms and values embedded in existing organizational structures. Other authors view organizational structures as the means and ends of leadership. For instance, Lipham (1964) states directly, "Leadership is the initiation of structure . . . " (p. 122). Hosking (1988) adds that leaders "consistently make effective contributions to social order . . . " (p. 153).

Thus, definitions of leadership recognize both the agency of individuals and the limitations and opportunities for agency afforded by organizations. Leadership, then, expresses an inextricable relationship between agency and organization, reinforcing Selznick's (1957) position that the conceptualization of leadership is rooted in a conceptualization of organization. Specifically, the conceptualization of organization defines the limitations that existing structures place on agency, or leadership, but it also identifies opportunities for individuals to shape actions and interactions in organizational contexts. Consequently, different conceptions of organizations should produce correspondingly different conceptions of leadership.

CORRESPONDING CHANGES IN CONCEPTIONS OF ORGANIZATION AND LEADERSHIP

Indeed, as the conceptualization of organizations, generally, and school organizations, specifically, evolved over the past half-century, corresponding changes occurred in the conceptualization of leadership. This strongly suggests that the construction of leadership has been shaped, at least in part, by the prevailing view of the "iron cage," highlighting different sources of external control against and through which human agency works. In the following sections of this chapter, I chart a handful of developments in organization theory and explore parallel shifts in the focus of theory and research on educational leadership. The list of theoretical developments is not intended to be complete. Rather, the lists represent perspectives that have been important to the author's evolving view of organizations and are intended only to illustrate how leadership expresses aspirations for human agency in an organized world. The discussion begins by considering how the dominant, normative view of organizations of rational systems shaped early conceptualizations of leadership. I then examine three perspectives on organizations that depart from the rational frame, considering the implications of each for how we view leadership. Those perspectives are the following: the human relations approach; organizations as loosely coupled systems, with an emphasis on the new institutionalism; and organizations as cultures.

The Rational Perspective

The earliest modern conceptualization of organizations depicts them as rational systems. Rationality is meant in the narrow sense of technical rationality, whereby activities are arranged to attain a specific, predetermined goal with greatest efficiency. It does not concern the selection of goals, only their implementation. Thus, the technical-rational perspective on organizations highlights two dimensions: goals and formal social structure. Goals, which lie at the heart of organizations and serve as the reason for organizational being, have several related functions: They establish standards for assessing organizational performance, set criteria for evaluating and selecting among sets of alternative actions, and provide guides for developing organizational structures.

Formal social structure is the other dimension of organizations highlighted by the rational perspective. Formal structures are organizational rules that govern the behavior of actors by precisely and explicitly prescribing roles and role relations (Scott, 2003). From the rational perspective, organizations develop formal structures to enhance the efficiency of their core technologies and, hence, goal attainment. A central structure in organizations is

the arrangement of roles in a hierarchy, where the incumbents of successively more elevated positions establish structures to control the actions and interactions of subordinates with an eye to reducing the cost of organizational operations. Individuals ascend the hierarchy based on the merits of their job performance, which reflect their contributions to the attainment of organizational goals.

Early scholars in the field of educational administration embraced the technical-rational perspective in conceptualizing the management and operation of schools (Callahan, 1962). For example, Bobbitt (1913) adopted principles from scientific management, which were first developed by Frederick Taylor (1947), in conducting job analyses to identify component tasks, specify effective ways for completing tasks, and determine organizational arrangements that enhanced efficiency (Hoy & Miskel, 1996). Cubberley (1929) similarly applied tenets from the nascent field of administrative science to the management of schools (English, 2003), emphasizing the role of administrators as executives who engaged in such administrative functions as planning, organizing, staffing, directing, coordinating, reporting, and budgeting (Gulick & Urwick, 1937), all with an eye toward enhancing the performance and efficiency of schools. Thus, in keeping with a rational view of schools, early students of educational administration emphasized goal attainment (performance), the development of formal structures, ranging from the specification of tasks and definition of roles to the arrangement of administrative hierarchies, and the elevation of highly competent individuals to positions of authority. Recently, state and federal initiatives have held schools accountable for attaining either curricular standards or target scores on standardized achievement tests or both. In responding to these demands, school and district administrators adopted rationalistic strategies to control instructional content and practices that echo the earlier calls for invoking more centralized control over school and district operations (Fusarelli, 2002).

The determinacy of organization on human action and interaction are self-evident from the rational perspective: goals and formal structures, including a hierarchy, or chain of command, that heighten the effectiveness and efficiency with which goals are attained. In applying administrative science to schools, scholars purchased the image of organizations as "machines" that are engineered to maximize outcomes. The space for human agency in such a worldview is narrow. In fact, later conceptualizations of organizations emerged as scholars recognized the absence of agency in the rational perspective. But, the treatment of leadership corresponding with the rational perspective on organizations does reveal a form of agency, albeit one that is strictly confined by the "iron cage."

Agency from a technical-rational perspective begins with the ascent of individuals up the administrative hierarchy on the basis of personal merit. Individuals who perform well in their current roles and possess the qualifications for more elevated positions are promoted. Thus, human agency accounts, in part, for the rise of some individuals to positions of leadership. Hence, the earliest studies of leadership sought to identify traits that set leaders, individuals who hold high-level administrative posts, apart from other organizational participants. Stogdill (1948), in an early review of research on the traits of leaders, identified five categories: capacity, achievement, responsibility, participation, and status. In the end, though, he concluded that traits alone do not make leaders because different situations make different traits salient, essentially putting an end to the search for the definitive list of the traits that make leaders. Regardless of Stogdill's widely cited conclusion, the notion that certain people are destined to be leaders persists, suggesting that within the tight constraints emphasized by the rational perspective on organizations, an individual's

personal qualities are one of the few expressions of human agency. In his chapter in the first volume of the *Handbook of Research on Educational Administration,* Immegart (1988) wrote that four traits commonly set leaders apart from others: intelligence, dominance, self-confidence, and high energy.

As noted, since the technical-rational perspective assumes that organizations are structured to maximize the efficiency with which goals are reached, it emphasizes the implementation of goals, not their selection. Thus, goals would seem to place hard limits on the agency of organizational participants, constraining the potential for leadership. It is ironic, then, that much of the literature on organizational leadership depicts successful leaders as those whose organizations reach their goals. Many definitions of leadership emphasize the attainment of organizational goals. For example, Hemphill and Coons (1957) define leadership as "the behavior of an individual . . . directing the activities of a group toward a shared goal" (p. 7). Rauch and Behling (1984) similarly define leadership as "the process of influencing activities of an organized group toward goal achievement" (p. 46). So, taken on its face, the rational perspective allows for human agency, or leadership, only in that it contributes to the attainment of organizational goals. However, aspirations for agency in organizations would not be so bound, leading some scholars to move beyond the focus on simply implementing goals to a consideration of changing or even setting goals. Lipham (1964), for instance, writing to scholars of educational administration, begins by conventionally describing leadership as a "procedure for accomplishing an organization's goals and objectives . . . " but continues, "or for changing an organization's goals and objectives" (p. 122). Thus, conceptions of educational leadership would not be strictly bound by the constraints imposed in the rational perspective; Lipman adds that leaders not only contribute to goal attainment but also may shape the goals themselves.

Formal structure is the second feature of organizations that the rational perspective emphasizes. Here, again, strict constraints are placed on human agency. This is given clear expression in the literature on leadership by Kerr and Jermier (1978). They explain that the importance of leadership is reduced by the presence of "substitutes," which make leadership redundant or unnecessary by insuring that organizational participants, among other issues, understand their roles and tasks. Formal structures can accomplish both. In fact, a chief function of structures is to specify roles and their relations and to designate the tasks to be accomplished by incumbents of each role. Thus, there seems to be little room for agency from a perspective that emphasizes formal structures. Theory and research on leadership give expression to a highly constrained form of agency by treating formal structure as the means for exerting leadership. For instance, the Ohio State leadership studies that produced the Leader Behavior Description Questionnaire (LBDQ), arguably the most cited treatment of leadership in the educational administration literature, highlight two aspects of leadership. One, "initiating structure," involves the actions of leaders that define the formal structure of organizations (Halpin, 1966).

The rational perspective, with its emphasis on goals and formal structure, thus depicts organizations as systems that place tight constraints on participants, leaving little room for human agency. Leadership theory gives expression to whatever agency lies in the potential for individuals to change or determine goals and shape the formal structures that guide others' actions and interactions. However, leadership theory also reflects aspiration for the importance of the individual acting with the "cage" emphasized by the rational perspective by emphasizing that personal traits set leaders apart from others. Tellingly, the LBDQ pairs initiating structure

with "consideration," involving behaviors which engage subordinates on a personal level, expanding their importance in the conceptualization of leadership. This development in leadership theory was rooted in an emerging view of organizations that acknowledged their human dimension.

The Human Relations School

The human relations school grew out of the recognition that the rational perspective cast an overly narrow view of organizations, ignoring what McGregor (1960) characterized as the "human side of enterprise." As textbooks on educational administration note (Hoy & Miskel, 1996), the human relations school can be traced to Mary Parker Follett (1924, 1941), who explained that, on the one hand, social conflict can have positive consequences for organizations and, on the other hand, establishing and maintaining positive relations among individuals and groups is a central problem that organizations must solve. Ironically, the historic set of studies that marked the break from the technical-rational perspective was conducted at Western Electric's Hawthorne plant to determine conditions that heightened worker productivity (Roethlisberger & Dickson, 1939). Much to their surprise, the researchers discovered that the needs of individual workers and the informal arrangements that they established exerted a profound impact on their work. The human relations school is subsumed under the natural systems perspective on organizations (Scott, 2003), which emphasizes conditions that organizations share with all social groups, including both social conflict and consensus. The human relations school, then, highlights the multiple and sometimes competing goals of individuals and organizations and the informal structures that arise from the social interaction of organizational participants.

From the human relations perspective, individuals are motivated to achieve multiple goals by a variety of incentives, not all of which are material. By featuring individual participants, this view of organizations considers the alignment of organizational goals, which are emphasized by the rational perspective, with the goals of individuals. Additionally, the emphasis on individuals' goals focuses on incentives and organizational conditions that increase individuals' motivation levels, thereby influencing their job performances.

The human relations school also emphasizes informal social structures. Contrary to the rational perspective, under this approach individuals are not merely cogs in a machine. Rather, they possess knowledge, abilities, values, and expectations which are expressed in social interactions. Over time, these interactions shape informal structures, which provide relatively stable guides for action and interaction. Thus, from the human relations perspective, individuals act and interact as members of informal organizations, which may reinforce or contradict the formal organization and buffer members from formal organizational structures. For example, the Hawthorne studies found that informal group norms set performance standards and communication patterns and buffered workgroups from management.

The human relations school had a profound impact on scholars in the field of educational administration. The emphasis on individuals and their goals is reflected perhaps most clearly in the widespread attention given to issues of human motivation in educational organizations. The human relations focus on informal structure is evident in the many studies of school climate that pepper the educational administration literature.

For two decades, many prominent scholars in the field of educational administration studied work motivation in schools. Their research was based on leading theories of motivation (for comprehensive reviews, see Hoy & Miskel, 1996; Miskel & Ogawa, 1988). For example, Trusty and Sergiovanni (1966), utilizing Maslow's (1954) need hierarchy model, found that teachers and administrators perceived

their greatest needs lay in esteem, autonomy, and self-actualization, concluding that teachers drew little self-esteem from their school positions. Miskel (1973, 1974) conducted a pair of studies based on Herzberg, Mausner, and Snyderman's (1959) two-factor theory of motivation. His findings included the following: Principals had a greater tolerance for work-related pressure than teachers; educators who aspired to administration had a greater desire for risk and motivator rewards; and business managers in school districts had high-risk propensity with fewer concerns for hygiene factors (dissatisfiers), which is the opposite pattern exhibited by teachers.

During the same period, other highly visible scholars of educational administration conducted research and contributed to theory on the concept of school climate. Reflecting the importance of climate in educational administration, a chapter in the first volume of the *Handbook of Research on Educational Administration* noted "the large amount of literature on the organizational climate of schools" (Miskel & Ogawa, 1988, p. 290). Climate reflects the human relations school's emphasis on individuals and their informal social relations. For instance, among the elements of organizational climate identified by Tagiuri (1968) were milieu, which involves the presence of individuals or groups who possess particular attributes, and social system, which concerns social relations among individuals and groups. Research on school climate was based on prominent theories about organizational climate. For example, Hartley and Hoy (1972) employed Halpin and Croft's (1963) Organizational Climate Description Questionnaire (OCDQ) in a study of climate in high schools, which demonstrated an association between climate openness and the lack of student alienation. Willower and his colleagues developed a conceptualization of school climate, focusing on school-wide orientations to controlling student behavior (Willower, Eidell, & Hoy, 1967). They conducted numerous studies, employing variations of the Pupil Control Ideology (PCI) survey instrument. In fact, Hartley and Hoy's (1972) study of high schools supported the hypothesis that custodial climates are associated with high levels of student alienation.

In a sense, the human relations school marked the recognition of human agency within the constraints imposed by organizational goals and formal structures emphasized from the technical-rational perspective. It highlighted the individual and her/his goals as distinct from those of an organization and the informal structures that individuals and groups develop, sometimes in opposition to formal structures established by management. Developments in theory and research on leadership largely responded to this change in focus not by expressing new forms of agency within the constraints of informal organization, but by exploiting, for the purposes of management, the dimensions of organizations that were exposed by the human relations school. This took two basic forms: developing positive relations with subordinates, including the provision of salient incentives to enhance work motivation; and appropriating informal structures by making them formal.

The human relations school's emphasis on individuals and their attributes included the many and sometimes conflicting goals that people pursue, apart from the overall goals of an organization. Conceptualizations of leadership incorporated this recognition that individuals are more than the incumbents of well-defined roles, as described from the technical-rational perspective. The importance of individuals is reflected in the emergence of theories that included relations with subordinates as an important dimension of leadership. For instance, the Ohio State leadership studies added "consideration" to "initiating structure" as distinct dimensions of leader behavior (Halpin, 1966). Consideration involves behaviors that convey personal engagement, including trust, respect, and friendship. Similarly,

during the same period, researchers at the University of Michigan identified "relations-oriented" behavior as one of three types of behavior employed by effective leaders (Likert, 1967). Such behaviors built and maintained "human relations" by expressing consideration and support. Behavioral theories of leadership gave way to "contingency" theories that considered the interaction of leader behaviors and situational conditions. Despite the apparent theoretical advancement, these theories continued to balance the creation of work-related structure with attention to personal relations between leaders and subordinates. To this end, Fiedler's (1967) contingency model includes two leader tendencies: emphasis on the achievement of objectives, which reflects a technical-rational orientation, and emphasis on close, interpersonal relations with subordinates, which clearly resonates with the human relations school.

One aspect of the individual that the human relations school highlighted was the many and varied goals that people pursue through their involvement in organizations. This led to the emergence of work motivation as a central topic in the discourse of the human relations school, which subsequently became a tool of leaders. This is most evident in the path-goal theory of leadership, initially advanced by Evans (1970) and House (1971). While several authors elaborated on the original model, it essentially posits that "the motivational function of the leader consists of increasing personal payoffs to subordinates for work-goal attainment and making the path to these pay-offs easier to travel by clarifying it, reducing roadblocks and pitfalls, and increasing the opportunities for personal satisfaction en route" (House, 1971, p. 324).

Leadership theory also incorporated the human relations school's recognition that informal structures heavily influence the actions and interactions of organizational participants. Here, again, leadership was conceptualized to take advantage of an insight of the human relations school to increase the influence of managers over subordinates. In this case, leaders formalized structures and processes that otherwise might have developed and remained in the informal domain. Moreover, several scholars devised leadership theories centering on the ways in which decisions are made in organizations. The human relations roots of this work lie in the research of Coch and French (1948) who found that productivity was improved by involving employees in decision making, emphasizing the resources that individuals and groups can bring to bear on the work and relations of the workplace. Subsequently, several scholars offered theories regarding how leaders harness the knowledge and skills of subordinates and work groups, which were revealed by the human relations school, to control and enhance organizational performance by, in a sense, formalizing the informal. Yukl (1998) synthesized the work of several theorists (e.g., Heller & Yukl, 1969; Tannenbaum & Schmidt, 1958; Vroom & Yetton, 1973) in identifying four types of decision procedures: autocratic decision, consultation, joint decision, and delegation. These form a continuum from least to most participative. As Yukl (1998) notes, even delegation, the most openly participative decision-making procedure, can involve a manager's specifying "limits within which the final choice must fall" (p. 123). This suggests that, in addition to formalizing the involvement of subordinates in processes that might otherwise have taken an informal turn, participation in decision making can socialize subordinates to the norms of the formal organization and its managers.

The human relations school departed from the rational perspective by acknowledging that individuals possess attributes, including multiple and sometimes conflicting goals, and that individuals and groups shape informal structures that deeply affect work-related behaviors and social relations. Thus, the human relations school revealed a form of human agency that existed within the constraints presented by the organizational goals and formal structures featured from the rational perspective. However, rather than expressing agency, leadership was appropriated by managerial interests. Consequently, leadership was now conceptualized to include fostering positive relations with subordinates, employing salient incentives to motivate employees, and formalizing processes and structures that otherwise might develop in the informal domain beyond the control of management and the organization. The insights of the human relations school regarding the importance of individuals and informal structures to organizations were employed, somewhat ironically, to advance the technical-rational interests of organizations. Yet, later developments in organization theory continued to erode the technical-rational façade, perhaps reopening the conceptualization of leadership to expressions of human agency.

Schools as Loosely Coupled Systems

In the 1970s, a handful of prominent organization theorists coined the term "loose coupling" to raise questions about the extent to which organizations actually conform to assumptions of technical rationality. The concept of loose coupling can be traced to three sets of authors who explore what occurs in the presence of three conditions that undermine organizational rationality: goal ambiguity, technical uncertainty, and the absence of timely environmental feedback. Weick (1976), who perhaps is most closely associated with the concept, presented loose coupling as a "sensitizing device" to examine the linkages characterizing organizations in the absence of relationships intended to enhance the efficiency with which organizational goals are attained. Cohen, March, and Olsen (1972) proposed a theory of how organizations make decisions in conditions that they characterized as "organized anarchies," which do not provide the foundation for making decisions in a classically rational fashion: that is, conditions that produce decisions in which solutions do not solve problems.

Meyer and Rowan (1977) arguably provided the broadest organizational treatment of loose coupling, initiating what has become the "new institutionalism" in organization theory, otherwise referred to as institutional theory. They explained that under the three conditions listed above, organizations develop or adopt structures that reflect institutions, which incorporate general, societal rules that take the form of cultural theories, ideologies, and prescriptions (Meyer, Boli, & Thomas, 1987), to gain and maintain social legitimacy, not enhance technical efficiency. Consequently, organizations decouple administrative structures in order to respond to conflicting demands from the institutional environment and decouple structure from work activity to avoid the detection of the lack of consistency between structure and activity, which could lose social legitimacy. Yet, despite decoupling, structures that are adopted to mirror institutionalized forms may indirectly influence the work activity of organizational members. When people participate in activities surrounding institutionalized categories and practices, they can develop shared meanings and values that support the structural façade as well as informally coordinate the work itself (March & Olsen, 1984).

It was no coincidence that Meyer and Rowan's (1977) original essay focused on educational organizations that bear the three conditions that make it difficult to demonstrate the efficiency with which goals are attained. As such, much of the research derived from institutional theory has been conducted on educational organizations. The most recent *Handbook of Research on Educational Administration* includes a chapter on institutional theory (Rowan & Miskel, 1999). Most of this research focuses on

characterizing the institutional environment and examining its impact on the structure of organizations in particular domains. In this regard, Rowan (1982) demonstrated that the likelihood that innovations would spread among and be cemented in school districts was increased when state agencies, legislative bodies, and professional groups combined to form a "balanced" environment that supported the innovations. Strang (1987) traced the consolidation of American school districts over nearly a half century, noting that over 100,000 districts were dissolved due in large part to changes in societal norms about their appropriate sizes and structures. Focusing on a more recent educational reform strategy, Ogawa (1994) found that a network of political and professional organizations motivated the widespread adoption of school-based management as a means for improving schools.

More recently, research examined the impact of the institutional environment on the internal operation of school organizations. For example, a study of a school board's efforts to develop and implement a standards-based curriculum reveals that the district was heavily influenced by the state's adoption of standards and the promotion of standards by national groups (Ogawa, Sandholtz, Martinez-Flores, & Scribner, 2003). This study also indicates that the administration engaged teachers in developing standards and items for a criterion-referenced test not to benefit from their expertise but to encourage their "buy-in," suggesting ceremonial rather than substantive involvement.

It would not seem that the new institutionalism and the concept of loose coupling would offer much of a basis for conceptualizing leadership. As some critics argue, by placing such emphasis on the influence of institutional forces on the structure of organizations, institutional theory largely ignored human interest and agency (DiMaggio, 1988). In addition, by explaining that organizations decouple administrative structures from work activities, institutional theory notes the absence of an important link that many conceptualizations of leadership emphasize: the ability to shape formal structures, thus influencing the actions and interactions of other participants. However, institutional theory does reveal two other types of coupling through which agency, or leadership, may play a part: first, the impact of institutions, or cultural theories, on organizational structure; and, second, ceremonial activities surrounding institutionalized, or valued, categories and practices that produce commitment and coordination among organizational members. Both reveal the importance of social values, or a moral dimension, in organizations.

Two accounts of organizational leadership stemming from the institutional perspective suggest that leadership affects the moral dimension of organizations. Selznick (1957), an originator of institutional analysis (Rowan & Miskel, 1999), noted that leaders shape the structure and distinctive character of organizations. He explained that while a manager is concerned with executing technical operations, a leader defines an organization's mission by selecting and protecting its distinctive values, developing structures that embody them (Selznick, 1957). The shaping of an organization's character occurs at the intersection of "the interests of internal and external constituents of organizations and the changing social environments in which organizations are located" (Rowan & Miskel, 1999, p. 362).

Drawing on a tradition that reaches back to leadership research conducted at the University of Michigan (Cartwright, 1965; Tannenbaum, 1962), Ogawa and Bossert (1995) conceptualized leadership as an organizational quality. They noted that the new institutionalism sets the parameters of leadership at the organizational level by revealing that leadership develops structures to enhance the social legitimacy and, hence, the survival of organizations. Institutional theory also suggests the seeming contradiction between leadership and organizational roles by revealing both that leaders exert

influence by deploying resources available through their formal roles and that leadership is embedded in relations between the incumbents of different roles. Additionally, the neoinstitutional perspective explains that the medium of leadership is social interaction rather than action, as proposed by previous theories of leadership. Finally, drawing on Selznick's (1957) insights, Ogawa and Bossert (1995) explain that leaders operate in a largely cultural context, adopting organizational structures that reflect institutions and engaging organizational members in ceremonial activities that produce commitment and, thereby, contribute to coordinated activity.

In the mid to late 1970s, a small band of organizational theorists continued the assault on the technical-rational perspective begun by the human relations school. These scholars noted that organizational elements that should be tightly linked under assumptions of rationality are often only "loosely coupled." The new institutionalism in organization theory emerged during this period, declaring that, in the absence of precise goals, clear technologies, and timely feedback, organizations develop structures that reflect institutions, or cultural rules, to gain social legitimacy rather than to enhance technical efficiency. While not broadly recognized, the neoinstitutionalists' emphasis on the impact of social values on organizational structure reveals a moral dimension of organizing. Recall Selznick's (1957) observation that organizations are imbued with "value far beyond the value of the technical task at hand" (p. 17). In examining the interior of organizations, the new institutionalism again emphasizes values over technical rationality by noting that organizations engage in ceremonial activities around institutionalized categories and practices to engender the commitment of participants. Selznick's (1957) conceptualization of leadership indeed reflects the moral dimension of organizations, explaining that it shapes their distinct character. But, unlike previously discussed theories of leadership, Selznick offers that the character of organizations is shaped by the interests of internal and external constituents, thus broadening the range of individuals who affect organizations. This theme is extended by Ogawa and Bossert (1995), who argue that from an institutional perspective, leadership is not the domain of a few but a quality of entire organizations.

Organizational Culture

In the early 1980s, theorists invoked culture as a metaphor for organizations. Although scholars differed in how they employed the metaphor, some treating it as a variable (something that organizations have), others using it as a root metaphor (something that organizations are; Smircich, 1983), they agreed that organizational cultures shape participants' actions and interactions. Culture, much like leadership, has been defined in a variety of ways, emphasizing different elements. Schein (1992) offered the following, broadly quoted definition of culture as "a pattern of shared basic assumptions that the group learned as it solved its problems of external adaptation and internal integration . . . " (p. 12). Schein identified three cultural levels that form a continuum from the most easily observable and least determinant to the least easily observable and the most influential: artifacts, which provide easily apprehended manifestations of culture; espoused values, which are the statements that participants make to explain the culture; and basic assumptions, which are the taken-for-granted assumptions that lie at the core of culture. Many early examinations of culture treated it as a unitary quality of organizations, providing the bases for cohesion among all members (Firestone & Louis, 1999). Yet, others argued that organizations are multicultural and that conflicts can arise between cultures within an organization (Martin, 1992; Swidler, 1986).

The field of educational administration readily applied the cultural metaphor to educational organizations. The second volume of the *Handbook of Research on Educational Administration* features a chapter on "Schools as Culture" (Firestone & Louis, 1999). In their comprehensive literature review, Firestone and Louis noted that researchers have examined several aspects of school culture. For example, in describing an aspect of adult culture, Louis and Kruse (1995) reveal that school cultures vary in the extent to which educators focus on student learning. Metz (1978) documents a cultural split between two groups of teachers who hold very different pedagogical philosophies. While studies of school culture from the perspective of students are relatively rare, research documents student cultures that are oppositional (Foley, 1990) or disengaged (Steinberg, Brown, & Dornbusch, 1996) and describes the separation of students into cliques (Cusick, 1973).

The application of the cultural metaphor to organizations has produced congruent conceptualizations of leadership. Early works on the subject offered general observations that leadership shapes organizational cultures (Deal & Kennedy, 1982; Schein, 1992) and influences the meaning of organizational events for participants (Smircich & Morgan, 1983). From those beginnings, at least two conceptualizations of leadership have been advanced: transformational leadership and symbolic leadership.

Burns's (1978) historical analysis of great leaders identified two forms of leadership: transactional leadership, which involves instrumental exchanges between leader and followers, and transformational leadership, which raises the moral plane of both the leader and followers through the transcendence of self-interest. Bass (1985) extended Burns's conceptualization by offering a two-factor theory where transactional and transformation leadership mark two ends of a continuum. Leithwood (1994) further developed the concept and applied it to the study of leadership in schools. He identified seven dimensions of leadership, three of which concern the impact of leadership on goals and values: building school vision, establishing school goals, and modeling best practices and important organizational values. Leithwood thus marked the essentially cultural nature of transformational leadership, which he and his colleagues reinforced through their research, documenting that it changed the culture of high schools in Canada (Leithwood & Jantzi, 1990; Leithwood, Jantzi, & Fernandez, 1994). Two other aspects of transformational leadership align closely with conceptualizations of leadership rooted in institutional theory. Transformational leadership manages relations between the uncertainty and demands of the external environment and the integrity of the organization's culture (Deal & Peterson, 1991; Louis & Miles, 1990). And, in transformational leadership, "Authority and influence are not necessarily allocated to those occupying formal administrative positions. . . . Rather, power is attributed by organization members to whomever is able to inspire their commitment to collective aspirations. . . . " (Leithwood & Duke, 1999, p. 49).

Based on their studies of school principals, Deal and Peterson (1991, 1994) developed a theory of symbolic leadership. They explain that symbolic leaders maintain and strengthen the culture of their organizations by playing numerous roles: the historian, who interprets current events against the backdrop of the past; the anthropologist, who finds meaning in the behavior of organizational participants; the visionary, who projects aspirations for others; and the symbol for parallelism, who models and provides ceremonies and routines that reflect the organization's core values. Research has documented the importance of symbolic leadership. To this end, Reitzug and Reeves (1992) reveal how a principal employed language and allocated time and other resources to develop shared meanings among a school's staff. Similarly, Kelley and Bredeson's (1991) study demonstrates how principals of parochial and public schools reinforce and shape organizational culture.

By applying the cultural metaphor to organizations, theorists revealed that symbols and ceremonies express, and thus reinforce, core organizational values that shape the behavior and social relations of participants. Therefore, like previous developments in organization theory, the cultural perspective extended our understanding of the "iron cage" of organization beyond the goals and formal structures highlighted from the rational perspective to now include values and beliefs. Conceptualizations of leadership that grew from the cultural perspective on organizations emphasize the role of leaders in either transforming culture by raising the moral plane of all participants or managing culture by reinforcing values through the reliable use of symbols and ceremonies. Leithwood and Duke (1999) observe that much of the literature on transformational and symbolic leadership focuses on the incumbents of formal, administrative positions. However, owing to the diffusion of values throughout the membership of organizations, some scholars have proposed that neither transformational nor symbolic leadership is bound to roles. Rather, leadership flows to those individuals who can inspire others to overcome self-interest and commit to a higher good or who give clear and consistent expression to the organization's values.

CONCLUDING THOUGHTS

Having reached the end of this chapter, I realize that I have arrived at an unexpected destination. My conclusions do not match the original thesis that I described in the opening section. As I expected, the four stages in the development of organization theory that I reviewed broadened the identification of constraints that organizations place on participants' behaviors and relationships. The rational perspective highlighted organizational goals and formal structures. The human relations school, which grew out of research with the rational purpose of increasing worker productivity, discovered that individuals' attributes and informal structures shape work activity and group relations. The concept of loose coupling, while revealing ways in which organizations depart from norms of rationality, also uncovered other bases for connecting organizational elements. Specifically, institutional theory explained that in the absence of specific goals, clear technologies, and timely feedback, organizations tend to adopt structures that reflect institutions in the environment to gain social legitimacy, not enhance technical efficiency; and organizational members, by participating in activities surrounding institutionalized categories and practices, develop shared meanings and values that support the structural façade and generate commitments that result in coordinating work activities. The application of culture as a metaphor for organization revealed that deep and abiding organizational values, which are reinforced by consistent symbols and rituals, operate on a taken-for-granted level in shaping actions and relationships.

What I had not expected was that conceptualizations of leadership would exploit the organizational constraints identified from perspectives other than the rational to serve the rational purpose of increasing organizational effectiveness and efficiency. This most clearly occurred under the cloak of the human relations school. Knowing that individuals pursue personal goals and groups establish informal structures, leadership theorists identified mechanisms for increasing the motivation of employees to engage in work activities and appropriated the informal dimension of organizations by creating formal channels by which employees could organize their work. I had expected leadership theory to reveal avenues through which individuals could exercise agency within newly identified dimensions of the "iron cage" of organization. Instead, initially at least, it found ways to employ these newly identified constraints in furthering management's control over the behavior and relations of employees.

Leadership theory has never entirely escaped the influence of the rational perspective. This is evident in Leithwood and Duke's (1999) observation that most treatments of transformational and symbolic leadership focus on the incumbents of formal, administrative offices. However, the new institutionalism and the cultural metaphor revealed that organizations serve moral as well as technical purposes. Institutional theory explains that organizations develop structures that mirror cultural rules. Further, as Selznick (1957) pointed out, an organization is characterized by distinctive values that are embodied in its structures. The concept of organizational culture built on this observation, positing that organizations, reflected in their symbols and rituals, are an expression of core values. Scholars of more critical traditions have been even more pointed in advancing the moral nature of schools. For example, those writing from a postmodern perspective, which disputes the basic assumptions underlying modern science, claim that "modernism has depersonalized and dehumanized schools and the leaders who inhabit them by robbing them of any voice of morality or moral values" (English, 2003, p. 28).

Recognizing the moral side of enterprise, some students of leadership seemed to have taken a turn. While many, if not most, continue to emphasize how administrators could use newly revealed organizational constraints to influence subordinates, others focus on the diffusion of values across organizational members, thus conceptualizing leadership as the expression of agency and influence by any member of an organization. Thus, drawing on institutional theory, Ogawa and Bossert (1995) proposed that leadership is systemic rather than individual, that is, an organizational quality. Similarly, conceptualizations of transformational and symbolic leadership, which are rooted in the treatment of organizations as cultures, express an aspiration for all organizational participants to enact values to which others commit, that is, provide leadership.

The continued influence of the rational perspective on organizations and leadership, despite developments in theory and research, reflects the depth with which it is embedded in our collective psyche. Nowhere is this more apparent than in the current policy environment. Educational initiatives, including the No Child Left Behind Act (2001), bear all of the marks of technical rationalism. Goals are "precise": Raise scores on standardized achievement tests. Technologies are clear: Employ only "best practices" and programs whose effectiveness has been verified by "scientific research." Feedback is clear and timely: Schools will be held accountable; those that fail will be sanctioned. Predictably, school and district administrators are adopting rationalistic strategies to control instructional content and practices that echo earlier calls for invoking more centralized control over school and district operations. If nothing else, the evolution of theories of organization and leadership should remind us to be judicious in selecting the models we apply to schools. Based on what I learned from this interpretive review of the development of organization and leadership theory, it is unlikely that reliance on wholly technical approaches to educational improvement and leadership will loose the human agency necessary to close the achievement gap separating the nation's schools. Organizing and leading that emphasize both the human and moral sides of the educational enterprise hold greater promise for sustaining the agency and thus the leadership of the many stakeholders whose commitment and efforts will be required.

REFERENCES

Bass, B. M. (1985). *Leadership and performance beyond expectations.* New York: The Free Press.

Bennis, W. G. (1989). *On becoming a leader.* Reading, MA: Addison-Wesley.

Bobbitt, F. (1913). Some general principles of management applied to the problems of city school systems. In *The supervision of city schools, Twelfth Yearbook of the National Society for the Study of Education, Part I* (pp. 137–196). Chicago: University of Chicago Press.

Burns, J. M. (1978). *Leadership.* New York: Harper & Row.

Callahan, R. (1962). *Education and the cult of efficiency.* Chicago: University of Chicago Press.

Cartwright, D. (1965). Influence, leadership, control. In J. G. March (Ed.), *Handbook of organizations* (pp. 1–47). Chicago: Rand McNally.

Coch, L., & French, J. R. P., Jr. (1948). Overcoming resistance to change. *Human Relations, 1,* 512–532.

Cohen, M. D., March, J. G., & Olsen, J. P. (1972). A garbage can model of organizational choice. *Administrative Science Quarterly, 17,* 1–26.

Cubberley, E. P. (1929). *Public school administration.* Boston: Houghton Mifflin.

Cusick, P. (1973). *Inside high school: A student's view.* New York: Holt, Rinehart and Winston.

Deal, T. E., & Kennedy, A. A. (1982). *Corporate cultures.* Reading, MA: Addison-Wesley.

Deal, T. E., & Peterson, K. D. (1991). *The principal's role in shaping school culture.* Washington: Government Printing Office.

Deal, T. E., & Peterson, K. D. (1994). *The leadership paradox: Balancing logic and artistry in schools.* San Francisco: Jossey-Bass.

DiMaggio, P. J. (1988). Interest and agency in institutional theory. In L. G. Zucker (Ed.), *Institutional patterns and organizations: Culture and environment* (pp. 3–21). Cambridge, MA: Ballinger.

DiMaggio, P. J., & Powell, W. W. (1983). The iron cage revisited: Isomorphism and collective rationality in organizational fields. *American Sociological Review, 48,* 147–160.

English, F. W. (2003). *The postmodern challenge to the theory and practice of educational administration.* Springfield, IL: Charles C Thomas.

Evans, M. G. (1970). The effects of supervisory behavior on the path-goal relationship. *Organizational Behavior and Human Performance, 5,* 277–298.

Fiedler, F. E. (1967). *A theory of leadership effectiveness.* New York: McGraw-Hill.

Firestone, W. A., & Louis, K. S. (1999). Schools as cultures. In J. Murphy & K. S. Louis (Eds.), *Handbook of research on educational administration,* (Vol. 2, pp. 297–322). San Francisco: Jossey-Bass.

Foley, D. (1990). *Learning capitalist culture.* Philadelphia: University of Pennsylvania Press.

Follett, M. P. (1924). *Creative experience.* London: Longmans and Green.

Follett, M. P. (1941). In H. C. Metcalf & L. Urwick (Eds.), *Dynamic administration: The collected papers of Mary Parker Follett.* New York: Harper.

Fusarelli, L. D. (2002). Tightly coupled policy in loosely coupled systems: Institutional capacity and organizational change. *Journal of Educational Administration, 40,* 561–575.

Gardner, J. W. (1990). *On leadership.* New York: Free Press.

Gould, S. J. (1994, November 28). Curveball. *New Yorker, 70,* 139–149.

Gulick, L., & Urwick, L. (Eds.). (1937). *Papers on the science of administration.* New York: Institute of Public Administration, Columbia University.

Halpin, A. W. (1966). *Theory and research in administration.* New York: Macmillan.

Halpin, A. W., & Croft, D. B. (1963). *The organizational climate of schools.* Chicago: University of Chicago Press.

Hartley, M., & Hoy, W. K. (1972). Openness of school climate and alienation of high school students. *California Journal for Educational Research, 23,* 17–24.

Heller, F., & Yukl, G. (1969). Participation, managerial decision making, and situational variables. *Organizational Behavior and Human Performance, 4,* 227–241.

Hemphill, J. K., & Coons, A. E. (1957). Development of the leader behavior description questionnaire. In R. M. Stogdill & A. E. Coons (Eds.), *Leader behavior: Its description and measurement.* Columbus: Bureau of Business Research, Ohio State University.

Herrnstein, R. J., & Murray, C. (1995). *The bell curve: Intelligence and class structure in American life.* New York: Free Press.

Herzberg, F., Mausner, B., & Snyderman, B. (1959). *The motivation to work.* New York: John Wiley.

Hosking, D. M. (1988). Organizing, leading, and skillful process. *Journal of Management Studies, 25,* 147–166.

House, R. J. (1971). A path-goal theory of leader effectiveness. *Administrative Science Quarterly, 16,* 321–339.

Hoy, W. K., & Miskel, C. G. (1996). *Educational administration: Theory, research and practice* (5th ed.). New York: McGraw-Hill.

Immegart, G. L. (1988). Leadership and leader behavior. In N. J. Boyan (Ed.), *Handbook of research on educational administration* (pp. 259–277). New York: Longman.

Katz, D., & Kahn, R. L. (1966). *The social psychology of organizations.* New York: Wiley.

Kelley, B., & Bredeson, P. (1991). Measures of meaning in a public and in a parochial school: Principals as symbol managers. *Journal of Educational Administration, 29,* 6–22.

Kerr, S., & Jermier, J. M. (1978). Substitutes for leadership: Their meaning and measurement. *Organizational Behavior and Human Performance, 22,* 375–403.

Leithwood, K. (1994). Leadership for school restructuring. *Educational Administration Quarterly, 30,* 498–518.

Leithwood, K., & Duke, D. L. (1999). A century's quest to understand school leadership. In J. Murphy & K. Seashore Louis (Eds.), *Handbook of research on educational administration* (Vol. 2, pp. 45–72). San Francisco: Jossey-Bass.

Leithwood, K., & Jantzi, D. (1990). Transformational leadership: How principals can help reform school cultures. *School Effectiveness and School Improvement, 1,* 249–280.

Leithwood, K., Jantzi, D., & Fernandez, A. (1994). Transformational leadership and teachers' commitment to change. In J. Murphy & K. S. Louis (Eds.), *Reshaping the principalship* (pp. 77–98). Thousand Oaks, CA: Corwin.

Likert, R. (1967). *The human organization: Its management and value.* New York: McGraw-Hill.

Lipham, J. A. (1964). Leadership and administration. In D. Griffiths (Ed.), *Behavioral science and educational administration, sixty-third yearbook of the National Society for the Study of Education* (pp. 119–141). Chicago: University of Chicago Press.

Louis, K. S., & Kruse, S. D. (1995). *Professionalism and community: Perspectives on reforming urban schools.* Thousand Oaks, CA: Sage.

Louis, K. S., & Miles, M. B. (1990). *Improving the urban high school: What works and why.* New York: Teachers College Press.

March, J. G., & Olsen, J. P. (1984). The new institutionalism: Organizational factors in political life. *American Political Science Review, 78,* 734–749.

Martin, J. (1992). *Cultures in organizations: Three perspectives.* New York: Oxford University Press.

Maslow, A. H. (1954). *Motivation and personality.* New York: Harper & Row.

McGregor, D. (1960). *The human side of enterprise.* New York: McGraw-Hill.

McNeil, D., & Frieberger, P. (1993). *Fuzzy logic: The discovery of revolutionary computer technology and how it is changing our world.* New York: Simon & Schuster.

Meindl, J. R., Ehrlich, S. B., & Dukerich, J. M. (1985). The romance of leadership. *Administrative Science Quarterly, 30,* 78–102.

Metz, M. H. (1978). *Classrooms and corridors: The crisis of authority in desegregated secondary schools.* Berkeley: University of California Press.

Meyer, J. W., Boli, J., & Thomas, G. M. (1987). Ontology and rationalization in the western cultural account. In G. M. Thomas, J. W. Meyer, F. O. Ramirez, & J. Boli (Eds.), *Institutional structure: Constituting state, society and individual.* Beverly Hills, CA: Sage.

Meyer, J. W., & Rowan, B. (1977). Institutionalized organizations: Formal structure as myth and ceremony. *American Journal of Sociology, 83,* 440–463.

Miskel, C. (1973). The motivation of educators to work. *Educational Administration Quarterly, 9,* 42–53.

Miskel, C. (1974). Intrinsic, extrinsic, and risk propensity factors in the work attitudes of teachers, educational administrators and business managers. *Journal of Applied Psychology, 59,* 339–343.

Miskel, C., & Ogawa, R. (1988). Work motivation, job satisfaction, and climate. In N. J. Boyan (Ed.), *Handbook of research on educational administration* (pp. 279–304). New York: Longman.

No Child Left Behind Act of 2001, 20 U.S.C. §§ 6301 *et seq.* (2001).

Ogawa, R. T. (1994). The institutional sources of educational reform: The case of school-based management. *American Educational Research Journal, 31,* 519–548.

Ogawa, R. T., & Bossert, S. T. (1995). Leadership as an organizational quality. *Educational Administration Quarterly, 31,* 224–243.

Ogawa, R. T., Crowson, R. L., & Goldring, E. B. (1999). Enduring dilemmas of school organization. In J. Murphy & K. S. Louis (Eds.), *Handbook of research on educational administration* (Vol. 2, pp. 277–295). San Francisco: Jossey-Bass.

Ogawa, R. T., Sandholtz, J. H., Martinez-Flores, M., & Scribner, S. (2003). The substantive and symbolic consequences of a district's standards-based curriculum. *American Educational Research Journal, 40,* 147–156.

Pfeffer, J. (1978). The ambiguity of leadership. In M. W. McCall, Jr., & M. M. Lombardo (Eds.), *Leadership? Where else can we go?* (pp. 13–34). Durham, NC: Duke University Press.

Rauch, C. F., & Behling, O. (1984). Functionalism: Basis for an alternate approach to the study of leadership. In J. G. Hunt, D. M. Hosking, C. A. Schriesheim, & R. Stewart (Eds.), *Leaders and managers: International perspectives on managerial behavior and leadership.* Elmsford, NY: Pergamon Press.

Reitzug, U. C., & Reeves, J. E. (1992). Miss Lincoln doesn't teach here: A descriptive narrative and conceptual analysis of a principal's symbolic leadership behavior. *Educational Administration Quarterly, 28,* 185–219.

Roethlisberger, F. J., & Dickson, W. J. (1939). *Management and the worker.* Cambridge, MA: Harvard University Press.

Rowan, B. (1982). Organizational structure and the institutional environment: The case of public schools. *Administrative Science Quarterly, 27,* 259–279.

Rowan, B., & Miskel, C. G. (1999). Institutional theory and the study of educational organizations. In J. Murphy & K. S. Louis (Eds.), *Handbook of research on educational administration,* (Vol. 2, pp. 359–383). San Francisco: Jossey-Bass.

Schein, E. H. (1992). *Organizational culture and leadership* (2nd ed.). San Francisco: Jossey-Bass.

Scott, W. R. (2003). *Organizations: Rational, natural, and open systems* (5th ed.). Upper Saddle River, NJ: Prentice Hall.

Selznick, P. (1957). *Leadership and administration.* New York: Harper & Row.

Smircich, L. (1983). Concepts of culture and organizational analysis. *Administrative Science Quarterly, 28,* 339–358.

Smircich, L., & Morgan, G. (1983). Leadership: The management of meaning. *Journal of Applied Behavioral Science, 18,* 257–273.

Steinberg, L., Brown, B., & Dornbusch, S. (1996). *Beyond the classroom: Why school reform has failed and what parents need to do.* New York: Simon and Schuster.

Stogdill, R. M. (1948). Personal factors associated with leadership: A survey of the literature. *Journal of Psychology, 25,* 35–71.

Stogdill, R. M. (1974). *Handbook of leadership: A survey of the literature.* New York: Free Press.

Strang, D. (1987). The administrative transformation of American education: School district consolidation. *Administrative Science Quarterly, 32,* 352–366.

Swidler, A. (1986). Culture in action: Symbols and strategies. *American Sociological Review, 51,* 273–286.

Tagiuri, R. (1968). The concept of organizational climate. In R. Tagiuri & G. H. Lewin (Eds.), *Organizational climate: Explorations of the concept.* Boston: Division of Research, Graduate School of Business Administration, Harvard University.

Tannenbaum, A. S. (1962). Control in organizations: Individual adjustment and organizational performance. *Administrative Science Quarterly, 7,* 236–257.

Tannenbaum, R., & Schmidt, W. H. (1958). How to choose a leadership pattern. *Harvard Business Review, 36,* 95–101.

Taylor, F. W. (1947). *Scientific management.* New York: Harper.

Trusty, F. M., & Sergiovanni, T. J. (1966). Perceived need deficiencies of teachers and administrators: A proposal for restructuring teacher roles. *Educational Administration Quarterly, 2,* 168–180.

Vroom, V. H., & Yetton, P. W. (1973). *Leadership and decision making.* Pittsburgh, PA: University of Pittsburgh Press.

Weber, M. (1947). *The theory of social and economic organizations* (T. Parsons, Ed., A. M. Henderson & T. Parsons, Trans.). Glencoe, IL: Free Press.

Weick, K. E. (1976). Educational organizations as loosely coupled systems. *Administrative Science Quarterly, 21,* 1–19.

Willower, D. J., Eidell, T. L., & Hoy, W. K. (1967). *The school and pupil control ideology.* University Park: Pennsylvania State University.

Yukl, G. (1998). *Leadership in organizations* (4th ed.). Upper Saddle River, NJ: Prentice Hall.

6

Pivotal Points

History, Development, and Promise of the Principalship

KATHLEEN M. BROWN
University of North Carolina at Chapel Hill

"Almost all educational reform reports have come to the conclusion that the nation cannot attain excellence in education without effective school leadership." (Crawford, 1998, p. 8)

Given the importance of school administration, the role of educational leadership in school improvement, and the preparation of education leaders, it is essential to understand the history, development, and promise of the principalship. This chapter, which is intended to be illustrative rather than exhaustive, examines those pivotal points. Due to changing demographics, conflicting societal values, and shifting expectations, the principal's role is ever evolving. As such, this chapter briefly outlines the causes of some of those shifts before describing the effects on the role in general, on the preparation and certification of principals, and on the gender equity of career advancement opportunities.

Until the end of the 19th century and the beginning of the 20th century, full-time building administrators were not typically found in schools. Since then, the role of the principal has constantly been reshaped, redefined, and renegotiated. Because "the role of the principal is an extremely malleable one, shaped by a diverse set of concerns and events" (Beck & Murphy, 1993, p. 197), conceptualizations are problematic. Throughout the history of the modern American school, differences in political, social, and economic philosophies have had a major impact on the development and organization of education in general. Immigration, urbanization, the rise of great corporations, the traumas of two world wars, the Great Depression, the social upheavals of the 1960s and 1970s, and the high-stakes accountability movement of the 1990s influenced the values of society, reshaped the purpose of schooling, and increased the demands of the principalship. According to Ravitch (1983), expectations are high:

> Whether in the early 19th century or the late 20th century, Americans have argued for more schooling on the grounds that it would preserve democracy, eliminate poverty, lower the crime rate, enrich the common culture, reduce unemployment, ease the assimilation of immigrants to the nation, overcome differences between ethnic groups, advance scientific and technological progress, prevent traffic accidents, raise health standards, refine moral character, and guide young people into useful occupations. (p. xii)

Principals face a daunting task in trying to fulfill these unrealistic and often conflicting demands. According to Murphy and Beck (1994), principals are expected to "work actively to transform, restructure and redefine schools while they hold organizational positions historically and traditionally committed to resisting change and maintaining stability" (p. 3). From a critical perspective, this chapter chronicles trends from 1840 through the year 2000. Acknowledging the inability for precision when documenting history, the specific dates employed are somewhat arbitrary. Pivotal Point 1: The Emergence of the Principalship (circa 1840–1900) notes the shift from "head teacher" to "principal." Pivotal Point 2: The Professionalization of the Principalship (circa 1900–1940) outlines the process of formal recognition and acceptance of the role. Pivotal Point 3: The Anti-Intellectualism of the Principalship (circa 1940–1960) questions the transition from scientific management through the human relations movement to the theory movement. The intersection of normative pressures between those seeking stability and the maintenance

of traditional values versus those that press for change are highlighted in Pivotal Point 4: The Constancy and Change of the Principalship (circa 1960–1980). Pivotal Point 5: The Reform and Restructuring of the Principalship (circa 1980–2000) charts the shift from demands for management and control with forced compliance to shared decision making and decentralized site-based management (i.e., from implementation and maintenance of the status quo to staff development, program improvement, parent involvement, community support, and student growth). The conclusion discusses the challenges and promises of the principalship for the 21st century.

At times, there has been little relationship between the expressed goals of education and actual educational practices. Gaps between professional rhetoric and the reality of school administration are also present. Although role integration and persisting expectations are prevalent, conditions necessary for professional change to occur are often either absent or lacking important elements. For example, as the role of the principal evolved, certification of school leaders became an issue. Because most states require public school principals to have training in educational administration from state-approved programs, which often leads to a master's degree or other advanced degree in educational administration, the licensure issues section examines pivotal points in the formal preparation of principals. Farquhar (1977) points out that "the societal context for which we are preparing educational administrators is changing constantly and, accordingly, our efforts to improve our preparatory programs must continue indefinitely" (p. 337).

The gender equity section examines the inadequate representation of women among the ranks of the principalship. Recognizing that school administration was initially structured as a "manly" profession and that research historically reflected this androcentric bias (see Blount, 1998; Shakeshaft, 1989), it is important to compare and contrast the career advancement of female principals and their male counterparts. The assumption that leadership requires male characteristics has been disputed by research suggesting that factors such as gender and race predict the types of activities in which school administrators engage, their career paths, and their ultimate accomplishments in the field. For example, Andrews and Basom (1990) noted that female principals spend more time observing teachers in their classrooms, are more concerned with student accomplishments, and value teacher productivity more than their male counterparts. Smith and Andrews (1989) also noted that women administrators are more likely to be seen as instructional leaders in their schools by virtue of their greater years of experience as teachers and the different administrative and supervisory strategies they bring to the job. As such, this chapter explores issues such as these.

PIVOTAL POINT 1: THE EMERGENCE OF THE PRINCIPALSHIP (circa 1840–1900)

Introduction

The "head teacher" of the early 19th century was the first professional position in American schools to have administrative and supervisory responsibilities. As the nation's population grew and one-room schools became graded, multiroom schools with several faculty members, so the need for program coordination and internal management also grew. Although their role was hardly differentiated from teaching (Campbell, Fleming, Newell, & Bennion, 1987), "head teachers" were appointed to monitor students, teachers, and classroom procedures. Accountable to local school boards, "principal teachers" were expected to teach the highest class in their schools, to implement specific board policies, and to perform certain clerical and janitorial tasks. Over time, their duties became mainly administrative and less involved

with direct classroom instruction. The actual term *principal* appeared as early as 1838 in the Common School Report of Cincinnati and then again in 1841 in Horace Mann's (1842) report to the Massachusetts School Board, but the title did not become formally recognized and widely accepted until the latter part of the 19th century.

Causes of Pivotal Point 1

The title, role, and expectations of the "principalship" emerged between 1840 and 1900 due to the rapid growth of the nation's population, cities, and graded schools. As immigration, urbanization, and expansion increased, so did the purpose, structure, and number of schools along with the task of managing and maintaining schools. Americans began to believe that a public system of education was needed to build nationalism, to shape good citizens, and to reform society. Prior to this, education served mainly to prepare an individual to live a godly life and to confirm and confer status. During the second half of the 19th century, a pivotal shift in philosophy occurred. In viewing education as a government—as opposed to familial—function, education was brought into the service of public policy. The common schools movement established an organized system of public schooling whereby administrative decisions regarding personnel, finances, and daily operations of the schools were made by school boards, including the direct supervision of teachers and the delivery of instruction. Yet, by 1900, "there were school boards with as many as 500 members and, because boards of such size became unwieldy and ineffective, board members complained of the workload and impossibility of discharging their responsibilities effectively" (Reller, 1936, p. 17). The increased demands and complexity of rapidly changing student demographics yielded the need for a single person to assume site-based leadership responsibility. As communities grew in population, graded elementary classrooms were separated from high schools, superintendents were employed by boards of education to oversee districts, and full-time administrators called "principals" were hired to manage and transact the general business of each building.

The purpose of establishing a common or public school system in the United States included educating students for good citizenship and stimulating national economic growth. With its grassroots governance, consensual ideology, and universal curriculum, the "common schools movement" was one of the most significant social movements in American history. It mobilized the people in support of public education and attempted to create a common culture, morality, and political ideology. According to Spring (2001), "Common school reformers believed that education could be used to assure the dominance of Protestant Anglo-American culture, reduce tensions between social classes, eliminate crime and poverty, stabilize the political system, and form patriotic citizens" (p. 103). Administered by state and local governments for the purpose of achieving public goals, common schools became the central institution for the control and maintenance of social order. Advocates believed that mixing the rich and poor within the same schools would cause social-class conflict to give way to a feeling of membership in a common social class and so provide society with a common set of political and moral values.

Effects of Pivotal Point 1

During this time period, the role of the male principal emerged as "evangelical missionary" destined to establish the public school institution (Tyack & Hansot, 1982) and promote the basic moral doctrines of Christianity. Horace Mann, often referred to as the "father of the common school," listed these duties as instruction in piety, justice, love of country, benevolence, sobriety, industry, frugality, chastity,

moderation, and temperance. Principals were to ensure that teachers provided and children received a common religious and political education. Mann (1842) proclaimed that moral instruction was to be based on a nonsectarian use of the Bible and on common virtues, while political instruction was to include those articles of republican faith that were approved and believed in by all sensible, judicious, patriotic men. Viewed by some as a mechanism of social control and by others as a mechanism for gaining political and economic freedom and power, most agreed that common schools would help eliminate class distinctions and promote equality of economic opportunity. As men of good character, principals were responsible for ensuring that this happened.

The change from "head teacher" to "principal" signified the beginning of a critical movement toward professional leadership and administration in public education. The emergence of the "principalship" implied a pivotal shift in power from local lay administration to control by a single educational leader. Aside from teaching, the principal's duties included implementing state curriculum, keeping school attendance records, making reports to the school committee, overseeing the upkeep of the school building and grounds, and coordinating the use of instructional materials, equipment, and supplies. Over time, "the freeing of the principal from teaching duties to visit other rooms proved the opening wedge for supervision by the principal" (Pierce, 1935, p. 16). Luehe (1989) defined this early supervisory role as one of "inspector" in which the principal's responsibility was to weed out weak teachers and ensure school boards that standards were being met. Based on this, the principal's role increased in status and expectations.

> The closing decades of the nineteenth century found the principal in large cities well established, not to say entrenched, as the recognized administrative head of his

school. He gave orders, and enforced them. He directed, advised, and instructed teachers. He classified pupils, disciplined them, and enforced safeguards designed to protect their health and morals. He supervised and rated janitors. He requisitioned all educational, and frequently all maintenance, supplies. Parents sought his advice, and respected his regulations. Such supervisors, general and special, as visited his school usually made requests of teachers only with the consent, or through the medium, of the principal. (Pierce, 1935, p. 39)

Preparation and Licensure Issues

Insofar as schooling during this time was largely unbureaucratized and unprofessionalized, preparation requirements for educational leaders were likewise unspecified. Moreover, because early schools were simple organizations, their administration was not an arduous task. "Little had been written before 1900 on educational administration, and formal preparation programs for school administrators had not yet been developed" (Gregg, 1960, p. 20). As local elites, most "head teachers" and "principals" were Anglo-Saxon, Protestant males who shared a common religious and political conception of the role of public education in shaping a Christian nation. To the extent that school promoters tended to see themselves linked by a common moral earnestness and civic activism, Tyack and Hansot (1982) called them an "aristocracy of character." The minimal formal education required for teachers at the time was deemed sufficient for those who became administrators and learned their profession on the job by trial-and-error processes. "Formal training for administration included some basic pedagogy and lifelong search for the 'ideal' education, but not much self-consciousness or thought about their own roles as leaders, statesmen, or administrators. Hence, they attended no courses, received no credits, and applied for no licenses in educational administration" (Cooper & Boyd, 1987, p. 16).

Gender Equity Issues

Structured from the beginning as a male domain, the emergence of the principalship led to the emergence of what Tyack (1974) referred to as a "pedagogical harem" whereby men managed and women taught (i.e., men held superintendencies, principalships, and other positions of power, while women served as teachers). An understanding of how teaching became feminized, often referred to as a "pink-collar" profession, and the impact this had on educational administration is deeply rooted in the related histories of teaching and administration. By the 1850s, many women worked in schools in isolated, rural areas while men retained the majority of the higher-paid teaching positions in urban areas (Blount, 1998). Because urban schools were structured differently, teaching in cities and countrysides were, in many respects, different jobs. In the cities, teaching was a full-time job and teachers were paid two to three times more than their rural counterparts (Tyack & Hansot, 1990). Teachers in rural schools, however, enjoyed more autonomy, performing all the tasks associated with schooling, including instruction, administrative duties, and discipline. Motivated by economy, urban school boards cautiously began to hire women. Women quickly sought positions in urban areas and soon monopolized lower grades, while men worked in the higher grades and as managers (Tyack & Hansot, 1990). The escalating number of women teachers in the mid-1800s, coupled with the classification of students in self-contained, graded classrooms, particularly in urban schools, led directly to the birth of a new profession, created solely for men, called the "principalship." Blount (1998) commented,

Local and state officials created the domain of school administration, a realm reserved from the beginning for men. Just as communities eventually had welcomed women into schoolhouses to perform duties derived from the notion of republican motherhood, so too did school districts hire men to assume new authority positions configured suspiciously like institutionalized, idealized versions of the family man, husband, and father. (p. 26)

Social stereotypes reinforced the assumption that men are rational and objective and that women are governed by emotions and are prone to "petty" concerns with interpersonal relationships and responsibilities. This meant that women did not make good managers. Instead, the role of women in this type of organization was to be supportive of male leaders. As a result, sex bias was built into organizational models and the emergence of the principalship. John Philbrick, the first principal of the first graded school, the Quincy School, specified the following type of arrangement among staff members: "Let the Principal or Superintendent have the general supervision and control of the whole, and let him have one male assistant or sub-principal, and ten female assistants, one for each room" (In Cubberley, 1934, p. 312). According to Kanter (1975),

This "masculine ethic" elevates the traits assumed to belong to men with educational advantages to necessities for effective organizations: a tough-minded approach to problems; analytical abilities to abstract and plan; a capacity to set aside personal, emotional considerations in the interests of task accomplishment; and a cognitive superiority in problem-solving and decision-making. (p. 43)

Summary

While local control by elected school committees set a democratic stamp on public education, policy elites at the turn of the century complained that the efforts of rural school trustees fell short (Tyack, 2001, p. 6) and that the leadership in urban districts was poor. The development of the 8-year, graded elementary school, the uniform course of study, the district system, and the position of principal and

his accompanying "pedagogical harem," were all elements in the early development of the hierarchical, bureaucratic organization for the administration of American education. According to Spring (2001),

Many factors contributed to the development of this type of organization, including the real problems created by the increased size of schools and school districts, the common school ideal for a uniform curriculum for all children, the desire of the middle class and native groups to protect their values and power, and the need for the socialization of students for an industrial workplace. (p. 155)

The next Pivotal Point, The Professionalization of the Principalship, outlines the process of formal recognition and acceptance of both the title and the role.

PIVOTAL POINT 2: THE PROFESSIONALIZATION OF THE PRINCIPALSHIP (circa 1900–1940)

Introduction

The burgeoning role and new authority position of the principal was solidified in the early 1900s with the beginning of the progressive movement and the advent of scientific management (Knott & Miller, 1987). Scientific management, with its emphasis on efficiency, had dramatic and almost immediate effects on education, including the "professionalization" of the principalship. During this time period, executive, managerial functions were centralized and structured systematically at the top with specialized divisions in a hierarchical model intended to cause the entire school district and each school to run efficiently. The role of the principal shifted from evangelical missionary and values broker to scientific manager and dignified social leader (Beck & Murphy, 1993). Pierce (1935) noted that by the turn of the century, the principal had become the directing manager rather than the presiding teacher of the school. Charged with administering discipline, selecting, hiring, and evaluating teachers, determining the curriculum, monitoring pedagogical techniques, and overseeing other organizational tasks, the principal was quickly established as the school's administrative head and director of instruction.

Causes of Pivotal Point 2

The professionalization of the principalship developed during the first part of the 20th century as a result of massive change and progress in American society. Initiated by the Industrial Revolution and the emergence of the modern business corporation, early growth placed a premium on education as preparation for work. As industrial conditions grew between 1850 and 1900, so did the need for new and better forms of administrative organization and control. During this time, educational reformers grew dissatisfied with local self-rule and a shared curriculum. Their vision of democracy in the new urban and industrial society exalted experts and denigrated widespread lay participation. This newly founded, nationwide belief that professionals should be in charge caused lines of authority to be defined, organizational communications to be improved, data to be collected and analyzed, and structural and technical adjustments to be made. During this time, public schools became "instruments of democracy" run by apolitical experts who were charged with educating all children according to their abilities and destiny in life. "Such was the new vision of democracy in governance: a socially and economically efficient system that adapted schooling to different kinds of students, thereby guaranteeing equality of opportunity" (Tyack, 2001, p. 7).

Developed through time-and-motion studies, Frederick Taylor's principles of "scientific management" and industrial efficiency became the highly touted and widely accepted concept of "best practices" in administration.

Taylor's overall objective was "to improve the efficiency of the organization at its most fundamental level: the arrangement of individuals in the workshop, their supervisor, their materials, their incentive system" (in Knott & Miller, 1987, p. 56). Bureaucratic organizations would rely on uniform application of impersonal rules and standardized procedures to achieve managerial control. Employees would develop job specialization and be evaluated on the basis of adherence to approved standards of performance rather than by results (Guthrie, 1990). These developments had a terrific impact on school practices and educators' beliefs, including the managerial dimensions of educational leadership.

The notion of "one best way" of running organizations was born and adopted wholeheartedly by most institutions, including school systems. Education was to be centralized and standardized. Because small rural districts and one-room schools were not deemed cost-efficient, many were closed, consolidated, and restructured (Shakeshaft, 1989), with nearly 20,000 small schools closing between 1917 and 1922 (Thompson & Wood, 1998). As the trend of closing smaller schools continued, educational participation and school enrollment actually rose steadily.

> The schools developed an expanded economic role in the increasingly urban and industrial society of the late 19th century, and as this happened, the high school joined the elementary school as an institution at which attendance was considered essential for all people. (Spring, 2001, p. 164)

For example, in 1890 approximately 2,500 high schools served over 200,000 students, while by 1910 over 10,000 high schools served over 900,000 American students (National Center for Education Statistics, 1992). Between 1900 and 1940, compulsory schooling laws were enforced, the attendance age was raised to remove teenage workers from a depressed job market, and the standard

8–4 graded elementary and high school structure yielded to a new 6–3–3 structure with the creation of junior highs. The percentage of eligible students attending high school more than doubled between 1920 (27%) and 1940 (66%) and the curriculum shifted dramatically. Concerns with formal learning for the discipline of the mind were replaced with an emphasis on practical education for life and preparation for occupation.

The differentiated curricula of the junior high and senior high schools, together with vocational guidance, were to provide equal opportunity from the perspective of improving human capital. As millions of European immigrants were assimilated and millions of rural American citizens were prepared to assume roles in an emerging industrial nation, principals became key players in the formation of a new socioeconomic order. Efficiency experts advocated reform of schools based on the manufacturing analogy, with students as "raw materials" and schools as "factories" (Knott & Miller, 1987). These experts made numerous recommendations, including increasing class size, lessening "free" hours for teachers, abolishing certain courses, such as foreign languages, and providing different educations based on individual differences. "In essence, scientific management, combined with a differentiated curriculum, was to develop human capital by objectively controlling the provision of equality of opportunity" (Spring, 2001, p. 281). As a result, complex new bureaucratic structures in education emerged, including the formal creation of the school administration profession.

Effects of Pivotal Point 2

Just as the principalship was becoming a regular feature of most American schools and districts, the nature of education and the role of educational administrator changed dramatically due to Taylor's scientific management principles. Centralization, specialization, and the division of labor all reinforced the belief that the role of the principal should be separate from that of teaching. In 1900, rules and principles derived from research were established to guide practice. Further, because schools were under considerable pressure to produce results, teaching procedures and practices were greatly influenced by "experts" whose interest was primarily to improve organizational efficiency. Principals were assumed to be more like business executives using good management and social science research to run schools effectively and efficiently. They were expected to implement a standardized and regimented curriculum and monitor progress of teachers and students toward educational goals. A formal hierarchy of power was firmly established and schools increasingly became bureaucratized. "This scientific approach to administration emphasized a top-down approach to defining and communicating information concerning instructional practices, and the administrative personnel of a school or district became the legitimate experts" (Daresh, 2002, p. 82).

Defining school administration in terms of task areas was consistent with scientific management. For example, Gullick's (1937) master list of things managers did was abbreviated in the acronym POSDCoRB: planning, organizing, staffing, directing, coordinating, reporting, and budgeting. In addition to their administrative and managerial tasks, principals' supervisory activities included classroom visitation, teachers' meetings, tests and measurements, instruction in methods, pupil adjustment, and teacher rating (Pierce, 1935). Cubberley's (1916) highly influential textbook, *Public School Administration*, emphasized the principal as organizer, executive, and supervisor of work. While explaining the nature of state and local school governance and what building-level administrators are supposed to do to maintain balanced budgets, keep accurate student records, and oversee building maintenance, Cubberley claimed,

"As is the principal, so is the school" (p. 15). However, as the managerial dimensions of school leadership increased, the educational and pedagogical dimensions of the principal's role decreased. The shift from a political model to a hierarchical, bureaucratic model in governance, structure, and role meant that the instructional leadership role became submerged under the roles of manager and bureaucrat. Torn between administrative duties and instructional responsibilities, principals realized their precarious status in the hierarchy. To this end, Glanz (1998) wrote that "it was in response to mounting criticism that supervisors, in a concerted effort to gain control of their work, sought to professionalize as a means to counteract bureaucracy" (p. 42).

Cubberley (1923) also noted "the great spiritual importance" (p. 561) of principals' work and likened them to "the priest in the parish" (p. 26). Because religious involvement was an important requirement for selection as a leader in public schools, principals had to exude certain character traits linked to the community and to timeless truths and values. A very strong Protestant work ethic and principles such as thriftiness, efficiency mindedness, and high moral values were necessary for the role. Cubberley (1923) believed that a school leader "should know his community and be able to feel its pulse and express its wants, and the community should know him and believe in his integrity and honesty of purpose" (p. 153). The growth of centralized and bureaucratic control, as opposed to democratic localism, ensured the protection and dominance of a particular set of middle-class cultural and religious values. According to Tyack and Hansot (1982),

> In the Progressive era, school leaders retained much of this earlier moral earnestness and sense of mission, but they lost much of the specifically religious content of millennialism. Instead, they drew on a newer aspiration to control the course of human evolution scientifically through improving education. (p. 3)

Preparation and Licensure Issues

As teaching and administration developed into two separate vocations and the role of the principal became more complex, concerns were expressed that men being hired for the job had neither graduate work in educational administration nor the endorsement of experts. For example, in 1900, there were no professors of educational management and no subdepartments of school administration. Yet, between 1900 and 1940, "Colleges of education employed professors of school administration, textbooks giving advice on management of schools filled many shelves, and administration became a foremost area of graduate study in education" (Moore, 1964, p. 12). By the mid-1920s, in leading preparation programs "the pieces were all in place; the glow of 'science,' the language of 'management,' the goal of 'efficiency,' and finally the need for central control and authority" (Cooper & Boyd, 1987, p. 10) were present.

A large factor in the development of the modern principalship occurred in 1916 when the National Education Association (NEA) established the National Association of Secondary School Principals (NASSP). The National Association of Elementary School Principals (NAESP) was founded shortly thereafter, in 1921. The formation of these organizations marked a pivotal point in the professional leadership development of the principal. Matthews and Crow (2003) explained that during this time, the NEA was an umbrella organization for many groups of educators, including superintendents, teachers, professors, and educational researchers. "The creation of the school administrative departments signaled official recognition of the position of principal by a national body of professional educators" (p. 26). By establishing these departments, more scientific research was conducted, other principal associations became interested, and more professional publications and conferences appeared. The goal of this new organization was to make principals aware of their professional possibilities and responsibilities. Commenting on NAESP's role, Gross and Herriott (1965) wrote,

> Principals were urged to place greater emphasis on leadership of the instructional program and less on the routine and purely housekeeping facets of their work. They were encouraged to work closely with their staffs to improve the quality of teaching and the curriculum. Publications of their national association discussed research studies and new and improved practices in classroom organization and methods of teaching, and the principals were expected to introduce these new ideas into their own schools. (p. 4)

Professional organizations helped to persuade state legislatures to pass laws requiring certificates for the various specializations. Replacing earlier licenses based on examinations, new certificates were based on completion of professional training and legitimized specialists by level such as elementary, junior high, and high school, and by function such as teacher, principal, or counselor. According to Kowalski and Reitzug (1993), certification of school administrators during the 1920s was advocated primarily for two reasons: Many superintendents had not taken a single college course in school administration, and certification was perceived as one avenue for achieving professionalization of principals. By 1932, nearly half of the states adopted certification standards for administrators (Callahan, 1962). During this time, preparation programs were woven and rewoven to mirror high-status professions in the larger society (Button, 1966) with administrators being prepared to be business managers, school executives, and social agents.

State policies in certifying principals established particular educational requirements and stimulated the growth of university preparation programs. Although many principals were ministers or men trained in theology, little professional development and minimal

academic qualifications had been required for the role prior to this time. "Those who occupied school principal posts relied on their common sense, innate abilities, and teaching experience to perform largely management-related tasks" (Matthews & Crow, 2003, p. 25). As the role became more specialized and university training was more often required, the transition from being a teacher to being a principal required graduate work in educational administration. Yet, an 1890 survey of educational departments in 20 leading universities uncovered only two courses in educational administration. The scientific management movement pressured universities to broaden the education of school executives to include management techniques. Callahan (1962) reported that by 1917, offerings in educational administration at Teachers College of Columbia increased from two to eight courses.

Even with these changes, conditions were still less than ideal. Tyack and Cummings (1977) reported that in 1921, three quarters of leading graduate departments of education had fewer than 10 faculty members, and students, like the faculty, were almost all white males. University programs provided the opportunity for aspiring school administrators to receive professional training and, in the process, gain access to desirable positions. In their quest to create a well-ordered, scientifically managed society, faculties in graduate schools of education teamed up with the new breed of administrators using business management techniques, with elite school board members, and with experts in measurement. Transforming educational administration into a science and a recognized area of study allowed for both the professionalization of the principalship and competition with other prestigious fields such as law and medicine (Knott & Miller, 1987). Moore's (1964) study found that 42 of 47 institutions of higher education offered either a "major in educational administration or a sufficient number of classes in educational administration to equal a major"

(p. 630). Preservice education for aspiring principals tended to stress the technical and mechanical aspects of administration. "Program content was consistent with prevailing emphases of science on fact gathering, inductive reasoning, and empirical generalizations" (Culbertson, 1988, p. 9). Callahan and Button (1964) concluded that the average preparatory program of this era "was a fairly high-level service station which provided students with the practical skills (primarily in finance, business management, public relations, and 'plant' management) which enabled them to acquire and keep jobs in a business society" (p. 86).

Gender Equity Issues

During the early 20th century, women began to rebel against their subservient status in the educational hierarchy, seeking a greater voice in educational policy through unionization and participation in the administration of the schools. At the same time, the scientific label implied rational thought, objective logic, and masculine qualities. This notion ultimately reinforced the qualities of nurturance and caring as feminine and barred women from leadership roles in the school systems. Shakeshaft (1989) reported,

> Scientific management and, specifically, bureaucratization, then, helped keep women out of administrative roles because of the belief in male dominance that made it easier for both males and females to view women as natural followers and men as their leaders. (pp. 31–32)

As time passed, the division of teaching and administration became even clearer and men's claims to administration seemed secure. Tyack and Strober (1981) explained that because men enjoyed a higher status with the new science of administration, education in general received a higher social rating. In essence, prior to the efficiency era, education was "feminized" and had marginal social status; by

placing academically trained men in charge, the field was professionalized. As the dichotomy between school administration as a masculine endeavor and teaching as a womanly occupation grew, administrators gained prestige, power, and autonomy, while teachers lost in these areas. The emergence of an administrative layer shifted power upward such that principals controlled teachers' job security, certification, and tenure. Blount (1998) noted that school officials "lauded the notion of paid male school administrators who could monitor female teachers and keep them from getting out of line" (p. 26).

Some scholars refer to the early 1900s as "the golden age of women administrators" (Shakeshaft, 1989). However, a more accurate statement would be that a few women served in senior-level administrative positions during this era, including Ella Flagg Young, superintendent of Chicago schools and later the first female president of the NEA. Women made more significant gains in obtaining principalships, particularly in elementary schools. For example, in 1905, women held an impressive 61.7% of elementary principalships, but, between 1910 and 1930, they were principals in only 6% of high schools and 12% of junior high schools (Gotwalt & Towns, 1986). According to Shakeshaft (1989),

> a number of factors coalesced to allow both black and white women to claim positions in educational administration in the first 30 years of this century . . . the feminist movement, the organization of women teachers, the right to vote in local elections, and economic advantages . . . all worked to women's benefit during this period. (p. 35)

Although women obtained these positions, it was not with equal benefits, and gains were short-lived.

As schools became larger and more bureaucratic, there was even a gradual decline in the number of female elementary school principals as women "lost even their tenuous toehold on good jobs" in education (Tyack & Hansot, 1982, p. 181). Powerful elites subscribed to the belief that men should supervise men while women should teach children. This belief translated into the practice of hiring male superintendents to supervise male principals, who, in turn, managed a largely female faculty. Tyack and Hansot (1981) noted that boards sought men for leadership roles because "maleness gave the schools a higher social credit rating because of the higher general standing of men in society" (p. 13). Blount (1998) added that men who competed against women for superintendencies in the early 1900s were quick to denounce female leadership styles as being too curriculum-oriented. Women superintendents were more likely to have been teachers and naturally more inclined to focus on curriculum and classroom issues, but the growing expectation was that administrators should engage in supervisory duties not instructional matters. This expectation perpetuated the idea that supervision and administration required no background in teaching and men exploited these "unspoken gender differences" to their advantage (Blount, 1998, p. 53). In fact, a state superintendent informed his male subordinates he was "not going to send a person in petticoats to supervise your work" (Tyack & Hansot, 1982, p. 189). As Blackmore (1993) explained, "Top male administrators and male-dominated school boards continued to make certain that women administrators were concentrated in the lower administrative echelons and the male old-boys network was protected" (p. 35).

By the 1930s, women were virtually excluded from administrative positions, instructional or otherwise. Male domination of the NEA, state boards of education, and the American Federation of Teachers (AFT) thwarted women's efforts to retain the small gains they made during this time. Because of their size and supposed lack of physical strength, women were also viewed as incapable of maintaining the order and discipline

of a school. "Not only did women internalize these cultural norms, but official policies also barred married women from educational employment. . . . The situation grew worse during the Depression, as thousands of districts passed new bans" (Tyack & Hansot, 1982, p. 191).

Both women and people of color historically have been less likely than white males to be sponsored by other administrators to enter school leadership. Lacking mentors, it is difficult to gain entry and career advancement. School boards tended to hire what they themselves were—white, Protestant males (Shakeshaft, 1989). Male contenders for leadership positions also had greater accessibility to men at the top of district hierarchies and more opportunities to get to know powerful males in places that were inaccessible to and inappropriate for women (Tyack & Hansot, 1982). Shakeshaft (1989) argued that "century-old patterns of male dominance had solidified a number of beliefs about women that both men and women accepted" (p. 39). Regardless of whether they accepted these beliefs about male hegemony, women were forced to acknowledge the power that men wielded in the educational hierarchy.

Summary

In the 1920s, principals were considered to be a link among spiritual values, the "truths" of scientific management, and their schools. In the thirties, both the language and the content of educational writings suggest that the spiritual emphasis waned and that the principal came to be viewed as a business executive, a kind of manager within the school. (Beck & Murphy, 1993, p. 47)

This continued until the alliance between business managers and school administrators collapsed under the economic pressures of the Depression. Businessmen wanted the educational system to be inexpensive so that they could reduce their financial support. Administrators and professors of education, on the other hand, wanted to ensure the continued growth of educational services, resources, and opportunities. The two opposing views caused a serious rift in this long-held relationship. According to Murphy (1992), "The Depression, the New Deal that was undertaken to conquer it, and the Great War to free the world for democracy all brought an end to unbridled infatuation with the titans of business and with capitalistic-industrial values" (p. 26). Pivotal Point 3: The Anti-Intellectualism of the Principalship, charts the transition from the scientific movement through the human relations movement to the theory movement. The pendulum swings back and, once again, the principal is expected to link schools to societal values. Because of World War II and the ensuing Cold War, the values of the 1940s and 1950s were less religious than earlier and more concerned with democratic principles.

PIVOTAL POINT 3: THE ANTI-INTELLECTUALISM OF THE PRINCIPALSHIP (circa 1940–1960)

Introduction

From 1940 to 1960, there was a pivotal shift from a top-down managerial philosophy to more of a democratic facilitative process of developing, supporting, and coordinating cooperative group efforts as both an end and a means for reform in schools. As a result of World War II, the principal's role changed from authority figure to process helper, consultant, curriculum leader, supervisor, public relations representative, and leader on the home front (Beck & Murphy, 1993). Those occupying principalships were expected to demonstrate democratic rather than autocratic leadership, to be directly involved with a school's instructional program, and to communicate a school's practices and priorities of

their communities. According to Lucas (2001), "Just as our participation in World War II caused us to focus our attention on patriotic values, the principalship of the early 1940s and the early 1950s stressed the importance of education in a democratic and strong society" (p. 28). The business-management doctrine was abandoned, and the "social conscience" of administrators was awakened (Callahan & Button, 1964, p. 89). The purpose of schooling was now to promote democratic values.

After the war, communities began to rebuild, the economy began to rebound, and liberal progressive educators began to speak out. Although the *Brown v. Board of Education* decision occurred in 1954, its ramifications and the notion of inequitable schooling were not truly dealt with until the 1960s and 1970s. However, in 1957, when the Soviet Union launched Sputnik, the effects were immediate. As fear and panic gripped the nation, a major crusade against ignorance initiated the anti-intellectualism campaign against schools in general, and principals in particular. Beck and Murphy's (1993) metaphors for the 1950s include the principal as administrator, defender of educational practice, efficient manager of time, and overseer of minute details. In addition to merging the worlds of effective teaching with management of all tasks, principals were expected to prioritize and defend the work of educators by offering empirical evidence of effective performance.

Causes of Pivotal Point 3

One consequence of the scientific management era was the tendency to value organizational goals more than the interests and needs of the people who worked in an organization. During the 1940s and early 1950s, a human relations administrative philosophy took root. Principals were encouraged to use every means possible to stimulate employees by focusing on satisfying the personal and professional needs of individuals who worked in schools. In the transition from the scientific management era through the human relations era to the behavioral science era of the late 1950s, there was increasing dissatisfaction with "the economic view of administration and organization" (Culbertson, 1965, p. 5). Concurrent with the debate over the proper knowledge base and the role of values in principal preparation programs, criticisms were being leveled at practicing administrators for supposedly having "weakened" the academic training offered by schools, making it difficult for the United States to compete with the Soviet Union in developing military weapons for the Cold War. Preparation programs were also exhorted to develop stronger programs "to protect the public against ill-prepared or indifferent practitioners" (Goldhammer, 1983, p. 250). There is some evidence that by the late 1950s, "the almost complete lack of theory oriented research in the field of administration" (Griffiths, 1959, p. 4) was being addressed and that the theory movement was holding center stage among leading scholars in universities (Moore, 1964).

After World War II, ideological management in schools extended into the areas of military defense and the War on Poverty in the 1960s. The effects of the Cold War were played out in the schools in many ways. Believing that schooling could cure society's ills, postwar communities tried to rebuild themselves around their schools. Schools thus came to be seen as "the instrument for social change and the means by which the American warrior state could ready itself for the oncoming ideological and perhaps military conflict" (Shakeshaft, 1999, p. 111). By the 1950s, when anticommunism reached its peak, schools, movies, radio, and television were purged of teachers, actors, and ideas that sounded communistic. Under the influence of McCarthyism, many liberal, progressive, and so-called subversive educators were fired or silenced as pressures for ideological conformity became intense for students. High school students learned a curriculum based on strengthening

American military technology, while small children learned passive fear as an official way of life by participating in mock atomic attacks. The need to cultivate talent and compete with Soviet expertise generated a stream of educational policies designed to use schools to strengthen national defense. As increased federal aid to education entered in the National Defense Education Act of 1958, concerns with centralization of educational control at the federal level grew.

Effects of Pivotal Point 3

The early part of the 20th century suggested that administration was largely defined as the business of keeping organizations headed in the right direction by making certain that operational details, such as paying bills and evaluating staff, were addressed. Midcentury perspectives indicated that people were important and their needs were real. The new focus on faculty and staff morale caused the supervisory role of the principalship to shift from monitoring to providing assistance to teachers to improve instruction, from educational specialist and bureaucrat to facilitator and counselor. The era of human relations had principals become more involved with parents, community members, and teachers.

During World War II, Gregg (1943) reported the need for the principal to be a leader in the community for the war effort:

> Every leader . . . has not only the professional, but also the patriotic responsibility of an all out effort to make his school function in such a way that the nation and youth of his community will be served in the most effective way. (p. 7)

Principals were expected to serve as democratic leaders of schools that embodied the benefits of the American way of life. Commenting on the values of this era compared to the scientific management movement, Getzels (1977) concluded,

The work-success ethic was giving way to an *ethic of sociability;* the American ethos shifted from Main Street to Madison Avenue, and the model for our young changed from the hard-working Horatio Alger hero to the affable young man in the grey flannel suit. Future time orientation was giving way to *present time orientation;* the former national slogan "a penny saved is a penny earned" was replaced by the new slogan "buy now, pay later." Competitive individualism was giving way to *adaptive conformity;* inner-direction was transformed to other-direction; self-made man became organizational man. And Puritan morality gave way to moral relativism; morality became a statistical rather than an ethical concept; virtue was whatever the group one belonged to thought was virtuous. (pp. 6–7)

Scientists' authority in educational reform was fully established in 1958, following the launch of Sputnik. The glare of public scrutiny focused most intensely on American educational policy. In responding to both the public demand for action and the real needs of science education, plans were outlined to improve American education. The strong emphasis on mathematics and science did stir up resistance among those interested in the humanities. Critics called instead for a broad program of federal aid to update facilities, recruit teachers, and develop materials in all content areas. Principals were caught in the middle of this and other debates. Receiving messages concerning their roles and functions from a number of constituents, principals often vacillated between taking highly theoretical perspectives on their work and dwelling on mundane issues of practice.

Preparation and Licensure Issues

After World War II, when the social sciences began to come into their own, the theoretical literature in educational administration began to grow. People recognized that the preparation of successful educational administrators had to be based on more than just how to accomplish certain managerial tasks. Culbertson (1988) noted that the 1950s saw a "leap toward an administrative science" (p. 14) in education, a shift often termed the "theory movement in educational administration." He also noted the high value placed on the development of professional preparation programs that emphasized conceptual skills, "theory development and . . . the building of a 'science of administration'" (p. 16). *Administrative Theory in Education,* edited by Andrew Halpin (1958), and *Educational Administration as a Social Process,* by Jacob Getzels, James Lipham, and Roald Campbell (1968), served for many years as influential and visible statements of the belief that the world of administration was not simply about "doing" things but, more important, about being able to "understand and explain" things that happen in the daily lives of schools. Scientists, not businessmen, held center stage as the quest for a science of administration, and of school administration in particular, began.

During this time, a spirit of inquiry permeated the field. Hopes were high that a solid knowledge base was to be generated, that verified standards of practice would be established, and that knowledge of the behavioral sciences was the best choice (Button, 1966). As a result, milestones in the preparation of principals occurred. For example, the National Conference of Professors of Educational Administration (NCPEA) was formed in 1947. Then in 1955, the Committee for the Advancement of School Administration (CASA) was established. The committee, at the behest of the National Council for Accreditation of Teacher Education (NCATE), spent several years outlining both "important features of preparation programs for administrators which should be considered in any accreditation visit" (Moore, 1964, p. 28) and specific standards for review. The final "milestone" (Griffiths, 1959, p. 5) of this transition period occurred in 1956 when 34 programs in school administration at leading universities formed the University Council for Educational Administration (UCEA). The primary purpose of the association was "to improve graduate programs in educational administration through the stimulation and coordination of research, the publication and distribution of literature growing out of research and training activities, and the exchange of ideas" (Campbell et al., 1987, p. 182).

By the end of World War II, approximately 125 institutions offered programs to prepare school leaders, and by the 1950s, all states required some form of formal graduate course work and administrative certificate. Thirty-eight states actually "required a graduate degree in administration for superintendents and principals (Cooper & Boyd, 1987, p. 11). Moreover, although university course work and teaching experience requirements varied from state to state, veterans considering education as a career had an incentive: GI benefits. These benefits permitted veterans, largely men, to attend school to earn teaching and administrative credentials. The effects of this economic opportunity were long lasting. In 1971, nearly 70% of superintendents were assisted in their studies by the GI Bill (Blount, 1999). As even more states instituted certification requirements and advanced studies for administrators, the federal government "largely underwrote the training with G.I. Bill funding" (Blount, 1998, p. 118).

"At the end of WWII, training was still highly practical, a blend of plant management, scheduling and budgeting interspersed with courses on schools and the social order" (Cooper & Boyd, 1987, p. 11). In response to a rapidly changing environment, social foundations were introduced into preparation programs. "The industrial engineer had to become a human engineer as well" (Guba, 1960, p. 117). According to Silver (1982),

> the human factor found its way into preparation programs in educational administrations when readings by such leading authorities on

management as McGregor, Argyris, and Maslow became incorporated into course content. Issues such as employee satisfaction and motivation, job enrichment, and personal growth and development were added to the curriculum of educational administration in the form of courses in "the human factor," sensitivity or leadership training experiences, and emphasis on the development of human relations skills. (p. 52)

Gender Equity Issues

The advent of World War II meant that career paths for teachers and administrators became even more blatantly determined by gender. During the war, school boards actively sought and recruited married women to fill both teaching and administrative positions vacated by men serving in the military. Yet, as soon as the war ended, so too did women's educational career advancement opportunities. A combination of demographic, economic, and social factors drew women out of the labor market. During the postwar period of prosperity and low unemployment, women married earlier, fertility rates rose, suburbs grew, male college enrollments increased, and many women stayed home to raise children. As the baby-boom children entered school and the women who left teaching earlier for motherhood or higher-paying wartime industries did not return to the classroom, many districts experienced teaching shortages. Returning veterans, who were initially reluctant to consider teaching because of its being perceived as "woman's work," were enticed into the classroom with promises of rapid promotion to administration after they taught a few years. Women who remained in classrooms, on the other hand, did not have the same assurance. For women, teaching became a semi-profession, but for men, it became a springboard to a higher paying, more prestigious, full-fledged profession (Blount, 1998).

As GI Bill funds were available to pursue education and the promise of advancement, more men became teachers than before, in part reversing the trend toward feminization. Men filled 17% of teaching positions in 1945, 27% ten years later, and almost 32% in 1965 (Blount, 1998). Concomitantly, the percentage of women principals fell by nearly half. For example, in 1928, 55% of elementary school principals were women. By the 1970s, the number of women elementary school principals declined drastically to about 20% (Kalvelage, 1978). Lured into teaching, men were awarded administrative roles at the expense of women who were already serving in those positions (Blount, 1998). Women also lost positions in the 1950s when another wave of consolidation of small school systems took place (Shakeshaft, 1989).

Summary

The combination of higher education organizations such as UCEA upgrading credentialing programs for administrators, the flood of male war veterans seeking jobs, and the GI Bill providing free college education for the male war veterans, along with schools enforcing women proportion quotas of 2% or less, caused the period of female educational leadership to end. *Brown v. Board of Education* also ended the dual school system based on race and signaled the existence of an external force influencing and monitoring educational decision making. Pivotal Point 4: The Constancy and Change of the Principalship, highlights the tension between forces seeking stability and maintenance of traditional values and those pressing for change and the emergence of diverse values.

PIVOTAL POINT 4: THE CONSTANCY AND CHANGE OF THE PRINCIPALSHIP (circa 1960–1980)

Introduction

The Cold War, the launch of Sputnik during the late 1950s, and the social and political turbulence of the 1960s created a new focus for formal education. While school officials concentrated on academic excellence, particularly in mathematics and science, principals drew on empirically developed strategies for management and organization, working hard to maintain stability and a sense of normalcy. Nationwide trends toward school consolidation, education's emulation of corporate management, and the political nature of public schooling led the majority of principals to neglect the instructional arena as a domain of primary concern (Tyack & Hansot, 1982). According to Beck and Murphy (1993), the role of the principal during the 1960s shifted to that of bureaucrat, protector of bureaucracy, user of scientific strategies, accountable leader, and inhabitant of a role in conflict. While simultaneously living in a personal state of confusion regarding role definition due to conflicting expectations from stakeholders, principals were seen as members of a well-developed educational bureaucracy with clearly defined professional bases of power and responsibility. They were expected to guard the distribution of power within the hierarchy and handle those who challenged the system. Principals were also expected to use empirical data in planning and measuring the work of teachers and were held accountable for measurable outcomes in schools. In essence, principals were caught between the constancy of bureaucratic rational thought and the outcries for a "social revolution" (Campbell et al., 1987).

The growth of social problems in the 1970s, such as racial tension, substance abuse, and teen pregnancy, required principals to provide a wide variety of remedies that turned their primary attention away from academic leadership. *Community leader, imparter of meaning, juggler of multiple roles,* and *facilitator of positive relationships* are terms used by Beck and Murphy (1993) to describe a principal's role during this time period. These authors added that principals were expected to lead students, teachers, and the larger community, to impart meaning to educational efforts, to juggle a number of roles that often required competing skills, to relate well to persons, and to facilitate positive interactions between students and teachers. As public confidence in education declined in the 1970s, the theme of accountability surfaced for the first time.

Causes of Pivotal Point 4

While debates about schooling have included discussions of culture, race, and gender, a major theme in the history of schooling in the 20th century has been discrimination against minority groups and certain social classes. Following *Brown v. Board of Education,* reformers in the 1960s challenged the organizational structures introduced in the first half of the 20th century. The very idea of a meritocracy based on the sorting function of the school came under severe attack by the civil rights movement. Advocates argued that

> small schools are better, that big districts should be decentralized, that all students should be helped to meet the same high academic standards, that academic segregation of students into tracks limits their learning, and that schools can benefit from parents' involvement in educational reform. (Tyack, 2001, p. 7)

The changing concept of democracy with its concern about expanding democratic rights to a broader range of citizens meant that all people were to be involved, not just those in power. This placed new responsibilities on principals, including the task of correcting the inequities that resulted from segregation. Sociocultural concerns, including debates over financial disparities and the multicultural content of textbooks and the curriculum, greatly affected expectations for and the work of principals. Yet, according to Beck and Murphy (1993), principals seemed to deny the reality of these complex issues by avoiding

frank discussions of problems related to desegregation, poverty, and the general social unrest that pervaded American culture during this decade. "It seems that, as complex social problems expanded, the emphasis on the proper application of bureaucratic and scientific principles and the confidence that this focus would solve any educational problems also increased" (p. 114).

Effects of Pivotal Point 4

One result of the civil rights movement was the expansion of the federal role in education with the launching of the War on Poverty programs in the 1960s. During the 1960s and 1970s, principals became increasingly responsible for managing federally funded programs designed to assist special student populations. Compensatory education, bilingual education, education for the disabled, and other federal entitlements required implementation support from the school site administrator. Curriculum reform also took off in the early 1960s as an infusion of federal dollars stimulated widespread innovation in mathematics and science. In contrast to their earlier role of maintaining the status quo, principals were now expected to be involved with curriculum management and program improvement. As a result, change implementation functions ranged from monitoring compliance with federal regulations to assisting in staff development to providing direct classroom support for teachers.

At the same time, reform innovations were conceived and introduced by policymakers outside local schools. A principal's role was limited to managing the implementation of externally devised solutions to social and educational problems such as those whose goals, substance, and procedures were designed by others. This philosophy and practice limited ownership and responsibility assumed by local educators for the long-term institutionalization of program changes. While innovations were implicitly oriented toward educational improvement, researchers found that principals demonstrated greater concern for meeting criteria compliance than for program outcomes. Program implementation was often viewed as an end rather than a means of improving learning for students (Fullan, 1991).

The 1970s added further responsibilities. Principals were forced into the position of negotiator in matters of union demands and teacher contracts. In addition, principals were required to become more politically active and engaged in policy making, practices considered taboo in the 1900s. According to Castetter (1971), the principal was finding

> that he must compete with other public agencies for a share of the public tax dollar, that the schools are on the receiving end of strong group pressures, that he must find ways of recognizing the legitimate role of pressure groups and deal with their demands democratically and constructively, and that he is no longer the controlling force in the educational decisions. (p. 7)

The beginning of the accountability movement also affected principals' supervisory roles. Instead of being judgmental, principals became more clinical, analytical, and focused on curriculum development, viewing their new role as helping teachers be more effective by diagnosing teaching and learning problems.

Preparation and Licensure Issues

By 1964, Culbertson (1963) claimed that "the subject matter of school administration [had] undergone radical changes" (p. 35) and that training programs were employing "more encompassing and more rigorous types of content as bases for preparation" (Culbertson, 1964, p. 329). He listed these changes as "shifts from a practical orientation to a more theoretical one, from the use of one discipline to the use of several disciplines, [and] from a technical orientation to a more general one"

(Culbertson, 1963, p. 35). A 1964 study by the American Association of School Administrators (AASA) found that the integration of content from sociology, psychology, economics, political science, anthropology, and public administration represented a fundamental shift from the program content of the late 1950s (Farquhar & Piele, 1972).

The phenomena of growth, relevance, and democratization were a legacy from the 1960s. It was an era of change, high expectations, and expansion. Principals were concerned with the application and utilization of knowledge, with assessment and accountability, and with performance and competence, while preparation programs offered a fairly balanced treatment of conceptual, human relations, and technical skills in their certification requirements. There is some evidence that educational administration departments also expanded during the golden era of the 1960s and early 1970s. According to Farquhar (1977), the typical department had nearly doubled in size from 1964 to 1974 and contained nearly 10 full-time faculty members. Yet, departments remained overwhelmingly male and Caucasian; for example, in 1973, 98% of professors were male and 97% were white.

"The predominant trend during this era was the infusion of theoretical knowledge from the behavioral and social sciences—with related methodological perspectives—into programs of study for school administrators" (Murphy, 1992, p. 51). This was a movement "to produce a foundation of scientifically supported (hypothetico-deductive) knowledge in educational administration in place of the hortatory, seat-of-the-pants literature already in place" (Crowson & McPherson, 1987, pp. 47–48). This movement produced a view of school administration as "an applied science within which theory and research are directly and linearly linked to professional practice [and in which] the former always determines the latter, and thus knowledge is superordinate to the principal and designed to prescribe practice" (Sergiovanni, 1991, p. 4).

A further effect regarding preparation and licensure issues involved the collective bargaining tensions during the 1970s. As a result, specialty divisions of the NEA broke away from the national organization, and independent national organizations to serve the needs and interests of school administrators were formed. Superintendents tended to join the American Association of School Administrators, high school principals belonged to the National Association of Secondary School Principals, and elementary school principals became members of the National Association of Elementary School Principals. Middle school principals joined the NASSP, NAESP, and/or the National Middle School Association (NMSA). These associations adopted a code of ethics for school leaders and, along with the Association of Supervision and Curriculum Development (ASCD), continue to provide legal protection for members, conduct research, publish journals and newsletters, and provide development opportunities such as workshops and national conventions.

Gender Equity Issues

The 1950s and 1960s witnessed a revival of the prejudices against women that hindered their advancement into administration since the colonial period (Shakeshaft, 1999). Administrative positions were viewed as inappropriate for women, while teaching was seen as an acceptable occupation because they could combine their vocations with their home responsibilities. Summer vacations and shorter working days were compatible with the duties of wife and mother (Shakeshaft, 1999). If women did compete for administrative positions, they were seen as "masculine, aggressive, ambitious, and inappropriate" (Blount, 1998, p. 107). When women broached the question of gender inequities in leadership roles, responses included assertions that women were not motivated by money, were not professional, and tended to interrupt their careers by inconveniently having children (Blount, 1998). In essence, critics blamed women themselves for their lack of representation in educational administration.

Calls for more males in education were answered in the 1960s when many men entered teaching to avoid the draft (Shakeshaft, 1989), but the negative image of male teachers lingered. Teaching was acceptable for men only if they were on their way up the ladder to success. Thus, male teachers quickly positioned themselves for moves into administration. Tyack and Hansot (1981) noted,

> Often sensitive to the potential image of the teacher—especially the teacher of small children—as a sissy, men were more apt to teach in high school, to engage in publicly visible activities like sports that could attract esteem, and to interact socially with male power wielders in the community. Such a teacher might be marked as a principal-to-be. (p. 26)

Over the years, women's entry into administration most often has been through an elementary principalship; thus, the number of women elementary school principals is a useful barometer for measuring their progress. Women occupied a dominating 56% of elementary principalships in 1950. By 1960, this number plunged to 4% (Blount, 1998). In 1972, women retained 19.6% of elementary school principalships (Tyack & Hansot, 1981). Another report revealed that females accounted for 5% of elementary school principalships in 1928; 20 years later the number grew to 41%. In 1958, however, the number dropped to 38%, and in 1968 it again declined, to 22% (Ortiz, 1982). The elimination of segregated schools also resulted in fewer African Americans in the leadership hierarchy (Weinberg, 1977).

Summary

As the boundaries separating schools and the world outside them became blurred and permeable, principals, particularly during the 1970s, reached out to their communities, trying to help ameliorate academic, psychological, physical, and social problems. Pivotal Point 5: The Reform and Restructuring of the Principalship, outlines community efforts, led by politicians, business persons, academics, and others, to reach into schools in efforts to guide and shape both the educational processes and those who lead them (Murphy, 1990).

PIVOTAL POINT 5: THE REFORM AND RESTRUCTURING OF THE PRINCIPALSHIP (circa 1980–2000)

Introduction

During the reform stage of the 1980s and the restructuring stage of the 1990s, principals emerged as primary players in the improvement of school instructional programs. The instructional leadership role of the 1980s highlighted the centrality of the principal's role in coordinating and controlling curriculum and instruction. During this decade, principals were seen as problem solvers, resource providers, instructional leaders, visionaries, and change agents who managed people, implemented policies, solved problems, and provided resources to facilitate the teaching and learning process while guiding teachers and students toward productive learning experiences. Principals also developed and communicated a picture of the ideal school while facilitating needed changes in educational operations to ensure school effectiveness (Beck & Murphy, 1993). The motto of the 1950s shifted from "Happy employees are productive employees" to "Happy employees are productive employees if they work in a productive place."

In contrast, the transformational role of the 1990s emphasized the diffuse nature of school leadership and the role of principals as leaders of leaders. In 1993, Bredeson noted, "The traditional roles of principals and other educators in schools are changing and will continue to be reshaped, redefined and renegotiated as restructuring occurs" (p. 34). Restructuring of the 1990s brought the knowledge needed for school improvement back to the school and the role of principals back to the image of leader, servant, organizational architect, social architect, educator, moral agent, and person in the community. During this phase, principals were responsible to lead the transition from a bureaucratic to a postindustrial model of schooling. Principals were to provide direction for change while not offending the integrity of the hierarchical structure of school systems, find ways for schools to exist productively within their natural environments, assess the fit of the school in the larger societal fabric, return to an earlier image as the primary teacher in the schools, serve as values analyst and witness to lead the ethical formation of the school community, and lead the school as part of a caring and integrated community (Beck & Murphy, 1993).

Causes of Pivotal Point 5

With the rise of international economic competitors in the 1980s such as Japan and the publication of *A Nation at Risk* (National Commission on Excellence in Education, 1983), an unprecedented period of extensive school reforms began across America. Mandated by the states and boards to make schools more efficient and effective while retaining their basic features, policies were enacted to tighten educational standards, strengthen professional certification requirements, and increase accountability. The pressure on school principals to respond to the criticism increased from all quarters. Not only did citizens offer suggestions and advice to educators, but there were also many mandates requiring boards and superintendents to respond and principals to implement (Carter & Cunningham, 1997). One report (U.S.

Department of Education, 1984) estimated that 275 state and local task forces were formed to work on educational issues within 12 months of publication of *A Nation at Risk*.

The reforms, generally categorized as first-wave school reforms, dealt primarily with top-down reform efforts from the state legislatures, calling for educational leaders to refocus on academic achievement and the preparation of students for the workplace and for principals to engage more actively in leading the school's instructional program and in focusing staff attention on student outcomes. Activities were based predominantly on the belief that because school professionals had become "lax," increased supervision and regulation would improve the process and outcomes of schooling (Hallinger, Murphy, & Hausman, 1992). The American public's renewed interest in educational improvement and the documented importance of principal leadership united in the worlds of policy and professional practice. The problem of school leadership was framed by policymakers in terms of inadequate principal expertise in curriculum and instruction. Principals obviously lacked knowledge and skills, and they needed to be provided with the missing expertise. By the mid-1980s, professional norms deemed the principal's role of program management as unacceptable and instructional leadership became the new educational standard for principals (Murphy, 1991).

By the late 1980s, as educators and policymakers began to examine the structure of schools, they came to a growing awareness and consensus that centralized administrative structures were not resulting in meaningful improvement in teaching and learning at the school level (Hanson, 1991). Rigidly prescriptive reforms placed too much emphasis on policies, rules, and procedures and gave too little attention to results (Rebarber, 1992). The desired ends of schooling were defined for principals by policymakers as improved student achievement, while the means were specified in terms of selected models of

classroom instruction and school improvement. Work roles in schools tended to limit the effectiveness of teachers and principals, parents were excluded from participating in the decision-making process, and curriculum had little relevance for students.

Precipitated in 1989 by the Governors Education Summit, school reform was transformed into school restructuring, a process that focused, at least initially, not on repairs to the existing system as targeted under the earlier reform activities, but rather on the "reshaping of the entire educational enterprise" (Hallinger et al., 1992, p. 330). The term *restructuring* suggested that schools were now viewed as the units responsible for the *initiation* of changes, not just the *implementation* of changes conceived by others. This awareness led to the introduction of second-wave reforms that identified teachers and administrators as the solutions instead of the problem. The new wave called for a bottom-up approach to school improvement whereby teachers were viewed as important sources of expertise, rather than as the targets of others' efforts to improve schooling (Barth, 1990). Because restructuring empowered teachers rather than managed them, principals needed to learn new skills. As managerial functions shifted to leadership responsibilities, the importance of collegiality, experimentation, reflection, school-based staff development, and capacity building took on new meaning. According to Hallinger et al. (1992), "These facets highlight a new role for principals (and teachers) in problem finding and problem solving—a role increasingly referred to as *transformational leadership*" (p. 40). He further explained, "In restructured schools, the principal must not only assist staff in reaching their own conception of the problems facing the school, but also help generate and develop potentially unique solutions" (p. 42).

Effects of Pivotal Point 5

As educational authorities sought to reform the principalship in an image compatible with the popular conception of effective schooling, a pivotal shift in perspective implied a de-emphasis on the principal's role as a manager and greater stress on responsibilities for instructional leadership (Murphy, 1991). DeBevoise (1984) defined it as "those actions that a principal takes, or delegates to others, to promote growth in student learning" (p. 15). The instructional leader focus viewed principals as primary sources of knowledge for improving instruction, creating learning climates, and facilitating curriculum development. Smith and Andrews (1989) characterized strong instructional leaders as giving curriculum and instruction the highest priority, rallying and mobilizing resources to enable the accomplishment of those goals, and creating a climate of high expectations for high academic achievement and respect for all students.

For practitioners during this period, top-down orientation to change was implicit in most policy-driven translations of effective schools research. Assuming that principals lacked expertise and that the practices of effective teaching and leadership could be standardized and controlled, staff development programs outlined clear, sequential steps for managing school-based improvement teams. By the mid-1980s, while virtually every state boasted a substantial in-service effort aimed at developing the instructional leadership of principals (Hallinger, 1992), ironically few resources were actually allocated for coaching or on-site mentoring—necessary ingredients for change in practice at the school site (Murphy & Hallinger, 1987). Absent any significant technical assistance, adjustment in role expectations, or policies designed to support the use of new knowledge and skills, the role of instructional leader became more rhetoric than reality. Competing expectations required principals to assume a variety of managerial, political, and instructional roles with actual changes in administrative practice less evident than proclaimed or expected.

During the 1990s, concerns arose over the compatibility of the principal's role as an instructional leader with emerging conceptions of teacher leadership and professionalism (Barth, 1990). According to Grogan and Andrews (2002),

> The emergence of an increasingly competitive international economic reality, combined with rapidly changing social conditions in the United States—particularly changing family and student demographics—has caused many educators to speculate that the strict conceptualization of the principal as the only instructional leader in the school may be inadequate for today's contexts. (p. 240)

Policymakers, administrators, teachers, and parents recognized that the current system of education was not adequately preparing students, concluding that fundamental changes were needed in the organizational structure, professional roles, and goals of American public education. As a result, reformers recommended the decentralization of authority over curricular and instructional decisions from school boards to school sites, expanded roles for teachers and parents in the decision-making process, and an increased emphasis on complex instruction and active learning (Hallinger, 1992).

The pressure to restructure schools during the 1990s enhanced role overload and role ambiguity while increasing the complexity of school management tasks (Bredeson, 1993). Compounding the decision-making arena was the phenomenon Murphy (1994) referred to as "leading from the center," the necessity of obtaining input from many different groups before decisions were made, thus adding time and complexity to the principal's job. The restructuring move to site-based management called on principals to engage in expanding the leadership team or creating what Elmore (1999) referred to as distributed leadership. Empowerment became the motto, collaborative decision making became the norm, and facilitator, builder of collegial relationships, and resource provider became the principal's role.

By most contemporary accounts, the 1990s began an unprecedented level of public scrutiny regarding principals' jobs, expectations, and responsibilities. Proposed solutions to the notion of education for morality, citizenship, and economic growth combined moral instruction with the scientific efficiency techniques of accountability, testing, and standards. Charter schools, privatization, vouchers, decentralized governance, standardized testing, accountability, and youth social issues provoked new pressures and policies, including salary and contract sanctions and rewards based on gains in student achievement. In addition, other societal changes, including shifting demographics, the speed of communication, and the explosion of knowledge, rapidly changed the look of and the demands on schools (Marx, 2000). Beck and Murphy (1993) suggested that in the 1990s, "there [were] serious efforts developing to transform the principalship into an instrument of social justice" (p. 194). Other conceptual frameworks included principal as servant leader (Greenleaf, 1970), principal as transformational, moral agent (Burns, 1978), principal as ethical leader and shared follower (Sergiovanni, 1996), principal as political leader and coordinator of large administrative teams (Kimborough & Burkett, 1990), and principal as community builder and economic developer (Theobold & Nachtigal, 1995).

As the principal's role continued to evolve and become increasingly complex, increased expectations moving into the 1990s were accompanied by a loss of authority and an erosion of positional power. During this decade, state and local bureaucracies gained more control and influence over public education, while the nation's governors met to establish national performance goals to enhance the United States' global competitiveness. The "perception of a rising economic

challenge from highly industrialized nations" (Carter & Cunningham, 1997, p. 29) encouraged various citizen groups to seek input into educational policy making. As a result, principals were expected to administer a highly specialized, extensively regulated, and enormously complex human organization (Deal & Peterson, 1994).

Preparation and Licensure Issues

As the educational reform movement of the early 1980s began to mature, it became increasingly apparent that school administration, the role of educational leadership in school improvement, and the preparation of educational leaders would be pushed to the center of the educational reform stage. By 1983, all states required between 6 and 20 semester hours of college credit in educational administration for principal licensure with some requiring an M.Ed. or M.A. in the field, along with a practicum or internship. Yet, as late as 1985, Peterson and Finn reported "at a time when the nation is deeply concerned about the performance of its schools, and near-to-obsessed with the credentials of those who teach in them, scant attention has been paid to the preparation and qualifications of those who lead them" (p. 42).

In an effort to bring educational leadership in line with a postindustrial view of education and schooling, the administration-as-science perspective that dominated training programs from 1940 to 1980 came under severe attack. The theory movement failed to deliver on its promises, outcomes of the quest for a science of administration were considerably less robust than had been anticipated, and the knowledge base employed in preparation programs had not been especially useful in solving real problems in the field with, for example, the behavioral science knowledge base having little effect. Absent a conceptual unity, content tended to focus on the managerial and institutional dimensions of administration compared to teaching and the psychology of learning. Unfortunately, this is still true today.

Emerging views about a better future included the need to enhance the professional stature of school leaders. So, by 1988, virtually every state mandated a master's degree in administration or its equivalent for principal certification. By 1993, 71% of male principals and 58% of female principals had degrees in educational administration. However, the mere possession of a certificate does not automatically ensure quality or competency as a principal. In fact, many principals argued that their specified academic preparation was inadequate and unrelated to the realities of their jobs. Further, although many of the professional organizations concerned with principal preparation issued reports containing recommendations for training principals to function in reformed schools, research findings reveal that changes in the nature of principal preparation programs have been slow to follow the change in the conceptualization of the work of the principals such as the shift in perspective highlighting principals' role in the improvement of instruction and their greater impact on student performance. According to the National Commission for the Principalship (1990), "Clearly, the immediate task of our nation is to make certain that principals are competent for the changing school; that the new conditions facing school leaders are connected to redesigned programs for their preparation and certification. Today, those connections are incidental, even misaligned" (p. 9). Moreover, Spaedy (1990) wrote that "seeing the seriousness of poorly prepared school executives, we are now experiencing the demands for a total overhaul of university preparation programs" (p. 156).

In response to these requests, the National Policy Board for Educational Administration (NPBEA) published its highly visible report, *Improving the Preparation of School Administrators: The Reform Agenda* (1989). This report recommended that a common core of knowledge and skills in preservice programs be defined to include the following: societal and cultural influences on schooling, teaching and learning processes and school improvement, organizational theory, methodologies of organizational studies and policy analysis, leadership and management processes and functions, policy studies and politics of education, and moral and ethical dimensions of schooling. The content of these areas was to be grounded in the "problems of practice" and supported by an increased emphasis on clinical experiences.

Also, in answer to the certification dilemma, in the mid-1990s, 24 states and the District of Columbia united to form the Interstate School Leaders Licensure Consortium (ISLLC). In conjunction with the Council of Chief State School Officers, ISLLC generated a set of national standards for school leaders. The primary objective of this initiative was to strengthen the professional development of school leaders (Shipman, Topps, & Murphy, 1998). The standards serve two main purposes: first, to provide a model for university preparation programs to assist in assessing their curriculum, instruction, and assessment; and second, to provide the basis of the School Leaders Licensure Assessment (SLLA), a national test used by states as a licensing tool for initial principal certification. The ISLLC standards and their corresponding indicators in the areas of knowledge, disposition, and performance reflect what the two organizations feel are basic operating norms that successful principals employ. The six central standards are vision of learning; school cultural and instructional program; management; collaboration with families and community; acting with integrity, fairness, and ethics; and political, social, economic, legal, and cultural context.

Gender Equity Issues

Despite interest in the topic, the percentage of women in school administration was actually less in the 1980s than it was in 1905 (Shakeshaft, 1999). Some researchers labeled this phenomenon as the "vanishing woman administrator" while studies abounded in an effort to understand this topic. Weber, Feldman, and Poling (1980) proposed that it was because women did not have role models and were excluded from the "buddy system" or the male-affiliated "good old boy" network. The survey study of 600 women teachers and administrators in public and private school settings focused on women's choices to pursue or not to pursue a career in educational administration as it related to role definition, personal and family constraints, aspiration level, perception of discriminatory employment practices, and beliefs and attitude about educational administration. In testing four hypotheses, the researchers found that there was a perception among women teachers and administrators that it was very difficult to obtain a position due to sexist attitudes in personnel offices. The data also revealed that women teachers saw themselves "as traditionally more feminine than the characteristics that they attribute to administrators" (p. 21).

During the 1990s, when educational leadership grew much more complex and challenging, women made some progress in assuming leadership roles, particularly at the elementary school level. The National Center for Education Statistics (NCES) reported that the percentage of female principals rose from 21.4% to 34.5% from 1984 to 1994. By 1994, women comprised 41% of elementary school principalships, 20% of middle school principalships, but still less than 14% of secondary school principalships (NCES, 1998). While the increasing ratio of female to male principals in public schools is one indication of greater equity in school leadership, when comparing the number of women teachers with the number of women school administrators, inequities clearly still exist. Researchers examining the internal and external barriers women perceive in obtaining administrative posts,

named a lack of interest in administration, an unwillingness to relocate, and family/personal constraints as internal barriers. External barriers included politics, the "good old boy" network, lack of support from colleagues and mentors, and sexual discrimination. Women also cited race, age, and lack of experience as barriers to their obtaining administrative positions (DeFelice & Schroth, 1999).

Summary

The 1980s and 1990s witnessed the reform and restructuring of schools in general and the principalship in particular. Have we come full circle from 1840 to 2000? The role of "teacher of teachers" sounds very similar to the earlier role of "head teacher." The description of moral, ethical, and servant leadership echoes the earlier role of principal as evangelical missionary, values broker, and spiritual leader. And, the notion of goals, objectives, and benchmarks mirrors the earlier concept of efficiency, scientific management, and bureaucracy. As history continues to repeat itself, the concluding section discusses some of the challenges and promises of the principalship for the 21st century.

CONCLUSION: CHALLENGES AND PROMISES OF THE PRINCIPALSHIP (21ST CENTURY)

The 21st century presents new challenges and promises for principals. The once rational, objective leader of teachers and manager of conflict is quickly being replaced by the non-rational, subjective leader of leaders and advocate of conflict. Leadership at the top of the pyramid is being replaced by leadership within the center. And restructuring involving fundamental changes in roles and responsibilities is being replaced by reculturing involving the substitution of new beliefs, norms, and values for existing ones (Fullan, 1996). In definitions of the principalship for the 21st century, the emphasis has shifted from pointing out the processes that must be used by principals to more of a values-based, outcomes-based approach on what schools are supposed to accomplish. According to Rost (1991), leadership is "an influence relationship among leaders and followers who intend real changes that reflect their mutual purposes" (p. 102).

One task for tomorrow's school leader is to continue to address the very issues and challenges we have handled with insufficient success for the past century and a half. The challenge, not only for principals but for American society, is to change schooling to be responsive to the needs of historically disenfranchised and undereducated pupils rather than attempting to mold children to fit currently dysfunctional organizational forms. Vision-driven, action-oriented, and reflective confidence in our collective ability to instigate reform and stimulate success is needed for the goal of equality of educational opportunity to be truly achieved. In McPherson's (1990) opinion, the failed agenda of the last 50 years is still our appropriate agenda:

> The ones that will bedevil us are the ones we either have ignored or only partially addressed in the past—racial and social inequalities; failures in productivity and accountability's professional insularity; isolating, bureaucratic (rather than collegial) organizations; inadequate funding; little attention to human resource development of education professionals and non-professionals; misplaced authority and responsibility; and ignorance regarding the special needs of children emerging from generations of poverty. (pp. 94–95)

Another challenge asserts that the requirements of the profession are negatively affecting potential candidates' career development decisions (Cusick, 2003; McAdams, 1998). Long hours combined with low salaries and high stress are discouraging teachers and other graduate-level candidates from pursuing careers as principals. In other words, the future of the principalship is in jeopardy because the nature of the job is becoming less and less attractive and more and more burdensome. According to Educational Research Service (ERS) (2000), the United States is experiencing a dearth of interested, willing, and qualified candidates because the principal today is confronted with a job filled with conflict, ambiguity, and work overload. Given this, it is understandable that fewer and fewer qualified people aspire to the principalship, that good people *are* becoming increasingly harder to find, and that "bright, young administrators aren't appearing on the horizon" (McCormick, 1987, p. 4). The titles of two fairly recent front-page newspaper articles capture this point—*Washington Post* (January 5, 1999): "Wanted: A Few Good Principals (As the Job Becomes More Complicated, Schools Fear an Administrative Shortage)" and *Los Angeles Times* (June 23, 1999): "Principal: A Tougher Job, Fewer Takers."

The principalship has evolved into a complex role—far more complex than what it was a century ago. Factors dissuading those qualified as eligible for administrative posts from applying for positions range from higher teacher salaries, to more two-income households, to negative role perceptions, to balance-of-life questions. Several studies uncovered a myriad of factors contributing to the decline of potential principal candidates (Barker, 1997; ERS, 1998, 2000; Jones, 2001; McAdams, 1998; Portin, Shen, & Williams, 1998; Wulff, 1996):

- compensation, salary, and benefits not sufficient or commensurate with job responsibilities;
- stress, shifting organizational demands, huge workload, unending paperwork and phone calls, day-to-day mundane tasks, countless meetings, bureaucracy;
- time demands, long hours, late nights, supervision of events, little time for family or personal renewal, emotionally draining, demoralizing;
- pressing, complex societal problems, equity issues, increased discipline problems, safety issues, larger numbers of at-risk and ESL students, more special education issues, higher dropout rates;

- meeting students' and parents' affective and social needs rather than cognitive needs, difficulty focusing on instruction, teaching, learning, planning, evaluation, and reform;
- escalating standards, accountability pressures, high-stakes testing, accreditation requirements, school choice issues;
- lack of respect, erosion of authority and autonomy, shift in balance of power, decentralized decision making, higher expectations for immediate response, difficulty in satisfying parent and community demands, unrealistic standards;
- lack of support, isolation from colleagues, threats of litigation, absence of administrative tenure and job security, inadequate school funding;
- inadequate preparation, broader technical knowledge and collaboration skills necessary, little professional development, perplexity of information to know and share;
- negative press, increased public scrutiny, unreasonably high expectations;
- structure of state retirement systems;
- pervasively stressful political environments, roles, statutes, mandates, rewards and sanctions that dictate practice and benchmarks, legislated systemic change.

Factors such as these can be uncovered throughout the literature. Whitaker (1995), for example, interviewed principals to examine emotional exhaustion and depersonalization in their jobs. Four themes emerged that respondents indicated might prompt them to leave the principalship: increasing demands, lack of role clarity, lack of recognition, and decreasing autonomy. Duke (1988) conducted a similar qualitative study with principals who were considering leaving the principalship. The reasons these principals offered for wanting to escape to another line of work were grouped into four categories: fatigue, a growing awareness of self, a sense of career and timing, and lack of preparation for the realities of the job.

What are the realities of the job? Charged with the mission of improving education for all children, the principalship has become progressively more and more demanding and fraught with fragmentation, variety, and brevity (Peterson, 1982). McAdams (1998) explained that "the changing nature of school administration—in terms of professional status, complexity of tasks, time, demands, and accountability—is another deterrent to pursuing an administrative career" (p. 38). Frequently cited role changes in the literature are connected to the increased time associated with management tasks, shared decision making, site-based management, pressures to improve student achievement, students' changing demographics, special education issues, wearing the hat of "community leader," and issues associated with choice (Christensen, 1992; Murphy, 1994). Always adding to and never subtracting from the job description has led to excessively high expectations for principals. Wulff (1996) astutely pointed out, "Each new popular educational issue usually translates into another role for the principal" (p. 2). As a result, marketing that role has become problematic.

Murphy and Beck (1994) explain that principals fill a role replete with contradictory demands. They are expected to "work actively to transform, restructure and redefine schools while they hold organizational positions historically and traditionally committed to resisting change and maintaining stability" (p. 3). In addition to being first-rate instructional leaders, principals are being exhorted to be highly skilled building managers, outstanding human resource directors, and competent negotiators. They are expected to be change agents and problem solvers who provide visionary leadership, moral leadership, and cultural leadership while practicing transformational leadership, collaborative leadership, servant leadership, and distributive leadership. Deal and Peterson (1994) stated, "The role of the principalship has shifted toward administering a highly specialized, extensively regulated, and enormously complex human organization" (p. xi). Principals today must possess an "ever-expanding range of skills and knowledge and take responsibility for practically everything in the school" (Hurley, 2001, p. 4). In a sense, principals are expected to be all things to all students, to be everything to everyone. In fact, Copland (2001) calls them "superprincipals" and Yerkes and Guaglianone (1998) call them "heroes."

Challenges and obstacles to some are often viewed by others as promises and possibilities. For those with a deep sense of purpose and a strong desire to improve education, the principalship is a role replete with great potential. Being a leader of learners yields numerous opportunities for personal and professional growth and development. The shift in transformed schools from a power-over to a power-with approach signifies a reorientation toward moral leadership, professional empowerment, and collegial interdependence. Through collaboration, communication, and experimentation, principals for the 21st century can be learner-centered, vision-driven, action-oriented, and reflectively confident in their ability to instigate reform and stimulate success for all students.

REFERENCES

Andrews, R. L., & Basom, M. R. (1990). Instructional leadership: Are women principals better? *Principal, 70*(2), 38–40.

Annual Report of the Common Schools of Cincinnati. (1838).

Barker, S. L. (1997). Is your successor in your schoolhouse? Finding principal candidates. *NASSP Bulletin, 81*(592), 85–91.

Barth, R. (1990). *Improving schools from within: Teachers, parents, and principals can make the difference.* San Francisco: Jossey-Bass.

Beck, L., & Murphy, J. (1993). *Understanding the principalship: Metaphorical themes, 1920s– 1990s.* New York: Teachers College Press.

Blackmore, J. (1993). In the shadow of men: The historical construction of administration as a 'masculinist' enterprise. In J. Blackmore & J. Kenway (Eds.), *Gender matters in educational administration and policy.* London: The Falmer Press.

Blount, J. (1998). *Destined to rule the schools.* New York: State University of New York Press.

Blount, J. (1999, April). *W.W.II and the great gender realignment of school administration.* Paper presented at the annual meeting of the American Educational Research Association, Montreal, Canada.

Bredeson, P. V. (1993). Letting go of outlived professional identities: A study of role transition and role strain for principals in restructured schools. *Educational Administration Quarterly, 29*(1), 34–68.

Brown v. Board of Education, 347 U.S. 483 (1954).

Burns, J. M. (1978). *Leadership.* New York: Harper & Row.

Button, H. W. (1966). Doctrines of administration: A brief history. *Educational Administration Quarterly, 2*(3), 216–224.

Callahan, R. (1962). *Education and the cult of efficiency.* Chicago: University of Chicago Press.

Callahan, R., & Button, H. W. (1964). Historical change of the role of the man in the organization: 1865–1950. In D. E. Griffiths (Ed.), *Behavioral science and educational administration* (Sixty-third NSSE yearbook, Part II, pp. 73–92). Chicago: University of Chicago Press.

Campbell, R. F., Fleming, T., Newell, L. J., & Bennion, J. W. (1987). *A history of thought and practice in educational administration.* New York: Teachers College Press.

Carter, G., & Cunningham, W. (1997). *The American school superintendent.* San Francisco: Jossey-Bass.

Castetter, W. B. (1971). *The personnel function in educational administration.* New York: Macmillan.

Christensen, G. (1992, April). *The changing role of the administrator in an accelerated school.* Paper presented at the annual meeting of the American Educational Research Association, San Francisco.

Cooper, B. S., & Boyd, W. L. (1987). The evolution of training for school administrators. In J. Murphy & P. Hallinger (Eds.), *Approaches to administrative training* (pp. 3–27). Albany: SUNY Press.

Copland, M. (2001). The myth of the superprincipal. *Phi Delta Kappan, 82*(7), 528–533.

Crawford, J. (1998). Changes in administrative licensure: 1991–1996. *UCEA Review, 39*(3), 8–10.

Crowson, R. L., & McPherson, R. B. (1987). The legacy of the theory movement: Learning from the new tradition. In J. Murphy & P. Hallinger (Eds.), *Approaches to administrative training* (pp. 45–64). Albany: SUNY Press.

Cubberley, E. P. (1916). *Public School Administration*. Boston: Houghton Mifflin.

Cubberley, E. P. (1923). *The principal and his school*. Boston: Houghton Mifflin.

Cubberley, E. P. (1934). *Public education in the United States: A study and interpretation of American educational history*. Boston: Houghton Mifflin.

Culbertson, J. A. (1963). Common and specialized content in the preparation of administrators. In D. J. Leu & H. C. Ridman (Eds.), *Preparation programs for administrators: Common and specialized learnings* (pp. 34–60). East Lansing: Michigan State University.

Culbertson, J. A. (1964). The preparation of administrators. In D. E. Griffiths (Ed.), *Behavioral science in educational administration*. Sixty-third NSSE Yearbook, Part II (pp. 303–330). Chicago: University of Chicago Press.

Culbertson, J. A. (1965). Trends and issues in the development of a science of administration. In Center for the Advanced Study of Educational Administration, *Perspectives on educational administration and behavioral sciences* (pp. 3–22). Eugene: University of Oregon.

Culbertson, J. A. (1988). A century's quest for a knowledge base. In N. J. Boyan (Ed.), *Handbook of research on educational administration*. New York: Longman.

Cusick, P. (2003, May 14). The principalship? No thanks. *Education Week*, 44–34.

Daresh, J. (2002). *What it means to be a principal: Your guide to leadership*. Thousand Oaks, CA: Corwin.

Deal, T., & Peterson, K. (1994). *The leadership paradox: Balancing logic and artistry in schools*. San Francisco: Jossey-Bass.

DeBevoise, W. (1984). Synthesis of research on the principal as instructional leader. *Educational Leadership, 41*(5), 14–20.

DeFelice, M., & Schroth, G. (1999). Women in Texas who are certified but not employed as administrators. ERIC Issue: RIEJAN2001 ClearingHouse no: SPO39337 Texas. East Lansing, MI: National Center for Research on Teacher Learning. (ERIC Document Reproduction Service No. ED443787).

Duke, D. L. (1988). Why principals consider quitting. *Phi Delta Kappan, 70*(4), 308–313.

Educational Research Service. (1998). *Is there a shortage of qualified candidates for openings in the principalship? An exploratory study*. Arlington, VA: Author.

Educational Research Service. (2000). *The principal keystone of a high-achieving school: Attracting and keeping the leaders we need*. Arlington, VA: Author.

Elmore, R. (1999). *Leadership for large-scale improvements in American education*. Cambridge, MA: Graduate School of Education, Harvard University.

Farquhar, R. H. (1977). Preparatory programs in educational administration. In L. L. Cunningham, W. G. Hack, & R. O. Nystrand (Eds.), *Educational administration: The developing decades* (pp. 329–357). Berkeley, CA: McCutchan.

Farquhar, R. H., & Piele, P. K. (1972). *Preparing educational leaders: A review of recent literature*. (ERIC/CEM State-of-the-Knowledge Series, No. 14; UCEA monograph series, No. 1). Danville, IL: Interstate. (ERIC Document Reproduction Service No. ED069014).

Fullan, M. (1991). *The new meaning of educational change*. New York: Teachers College Press.

Fullan, M. (1996). Turning systemic thinking on its head. *Phi Delta Kappan, 77*(6), 420–423.

Getzels, J. (1977). Educational administration twenty years later, 1954–1974. In L. L. Cunningham, W. G. Hack, & R. O. Nystrand (Eds.), *Educational administration: The developing decades* (pp. 3–24). Berkeley, CA: McCutchan.

Getzels, J., Lipham, J., & Campbell, R. (1968). *Educational administration as a social process*. New York: Harper & Row.

Glanz, J. (1998). Histories, antecedents, and legacies of school supervision. In G. R. Firth & E. F. Pajak (Eds.), *Handbook of research on school supervision*. New York: Macmillan.

Goldhammer, K. (1983). Evolution in the profession. *Educational Administration Quarterly, 19*(3), 249–272.

Gotwalt, N., & Towns, K. (1986). Rare as they are, women at the top can teach us all. *The Executive Educator*, December, 13–14, 29.

Greenleaf, R. (1970). *The servant as leader*. Indianapolis: The Robert K. Greenleaf Center.

Gregg, R. T. (1943). The principal and his school in wartime. *Bulletin of the National Association of Secondary School Principals, 27*(112), 7–19.

Gregg, R. T. (1960). Administration. In C. W. Harris (Ed.), *Encyclopedia of educational research* (3rd ed., pp. 19–24). New York: Macmillan.

Griffiths, D. E. (1959). *Administrative theory*. New York: Appleton-Century-Crofts.

Grogan, M., & Andrews, R. (2002). Defining preparation and professional development for the future. *Educational Administration Quarterly, 38*(2), 233–256.

Gross, N., & Herriott, R. E. (1965). *Staff leadership in public schools.* New York: John Wiley and Sons.

Guba, E. G. (1960). Research in internal administration—What do we know? In R. F. Campbell & J. M. Lipham (Eds.), *Administrative theory as a guide to action* (pp. 113–141). Chicago: University of Chicago, Midwest Administration Center.

Gullick, L. (1937). Notes on the theory of organization. In L. Gullick & L. Urwick (Eds.), *Papers on the science of administration* (pp. 1–45). New York: Institute of Public Administration, Columbia University.

Guthrie, J. (1990). The evolution of educational management: Eroding myths and emerging models. In B. Mitchell & L. Cunningham (Eds.), *Educational leadership and changing contexts of families, communities, and schools* (pp. 219–231). Chicago: University of Chicago Press.

Hallinger, P. (1992). The evolving role of American principals: From managerial to instructional to transformational leaders. *Journal of Educational Administration, 30*(3), 35–48.

Hallinger, P., Murphy, J., & Hausman, C. (1992). Restructuring schools: Principals' perceptions of fundamental educational reform. *Educational Administration Quarterly, 28,* 330–349.

Halpin, A. W. (Ed.). (1958). *Administrative theory in education.* New York: Macmillan.

Hanson, E. M. (1991). *Educational administration and organizational behavior* (3rd ed.). Boston: Allyn and Bacon.

Hurley, J. (2001, May 23). The principalship: Less may be more. *Education Week on the Web.* http://www.edweek.org/ew.

Jones, B. A. (2001). *Supply and demand for school principals: A nationwide study.* Columbia, MO: Consortium for the Study of Educational Policy.

Kalvelage, J. (1978). *The decline in female elementary principals since 1928: Riddles and clues.* Eugene: University of Oregon.

Kanter, R. (1975). Women and the structure of organization: Exploration in theory and behavior. In M. Millman & R. Kanter (Eds.), *Another voice* (p. 43). Garden City, NY: Doubleday Anchor.

Kimborough, R. B., & Burkett, C. W. (1990). *The principalship: Concepts and practices.* Needham Heights, MA: Allyn and Bacon.

Knott, J., & Miller, G. (1987). *Reforming bureaucracy: The politics of institutional choice.* New Jersey: Prentice-Hall.

Kowalski, T. J., & Reitzug, U. C. (1993). *Contemporary school administration: An introduction.* New York: Longman.

Luehe, B. (1989). *The principal and supervision.* Bloomington, IN: Phi Delta Kappan Educational Foundation.

Lucas, C. J. (2001). *Teacher education in America: Reform agendas for the twenty-first century.* New York: St. Martin's Press.

Mann, H. (1842). *Fifth annual report of the secretary of the board.* Boston: Dutton and Wentworth, State Printers.

Marx, G. (2000). *Ten trends: Educating children for a profoundly different future.* Arlington, VA: Educational Research Service.

Matthews, L. J., & Crow, G. (2003). *Being and becoming a principal: Role conceptions for contemporary principals and assistant principals.* Boston: Allyn and Bacon.

McAdams, R. (1998). Governance: Who'll run the schools? *The American School Board Journal, 185*(8), 37–39.

McCormick, K. (1987, December). The school executive shortage: How serious is it? *The Education Digest, 55,* 2–5.

McPherson, R. B. (1990, September). *Reinventing school leadership* (pp. 94–96). Working memo prepared for the Reinventing School Leadership Conference. Cambridge, MA: National Center for Educational Leadership.

Moore, H. A. (1964). The ferment in school administration. In D. E. Griffiths (Ed.), *Behavioral science and educational administration* (Sixty-third NSSE Yearbook, Part II, pp. 11–32). Chicago: University of Chicago Press.

Murphy, J. (Ed.). (1990). *The education reform movement of the 1980s: Perspectives and cases.* Berkeley, CA: McCutchen Publishing.

Murphy, J. (1991). *Restructuring schools, capturing and assessing the phenomenon.* New York: Teachers College Press.

Murphy, J. (1992). *The landscape of leadership preparation: Patterns and possibilities.* Beverly Hills, CA: Corwin.

Murphy, J. (1994). Transformational change and the evolving role of the principal: Early empirical evidence. In J. Murphy & K. S. Louis (Eds.), *Reshaping the principalship: Insights from transformational change efforts.* Thousand Oaks, CA: Corwin.

Murphy. J. (1995). Rethinking the foundations of leadership preparation: Insights from school improvement efforts. *DESIGN for Leadership: The Bulletin of the National Policy Board for Educational Administration, 6*(1).

Murphy, J., & Beck, L. (1994). Restructuring the principalship: Challenges and possibilities. In J. Murphy and K. S. Louis (Eds.), *Reshaping the principalship: Insights from transformational reform efforts* (pp. 3–19). Thousand Oaks, CA: Corwin.

Murphy, J., & Hallinger, P. (1987). New directions in the professional development of school administrators: A synthesis and suggestions for improvement. In J. Murphy and P. Hallinger, (Eds.), *Approaches to administrative training in education* (p. xx). Albany: State University of New York Press.

National Center for Education Statistics. (1992). *The digest of education statistics 1992: Schools and staffing survey, 1987–1988.* Washington, DC: U.S. Department of Education.

National Center for Education Statistics. (1998). *The digest of education statistics 1998: Schools and staffing survey, 1993–1994.* Washington, DC: U.S. Department of Education.

National Commission for the Principalship. (1990). *Principals for our changing schools: Preparation and certification.* Fairfax, VA: Author.

National Commission on Excellence in Education. (1983). *A nation at risk.* Washington, DC: Government Printing Office.

National Policy Board for Educational Administration. (1989). *Improving the preparation of school administrators: The reform agenda.* Charlottesville, VA: Author.

Ortiz, F. I. (1982). *Career patterns in education.* New York: J. F. Bergin.

Peterson, K. D. (1982). Making sense of principals' work. *The Australian Administrator, 3*(3), 1–4.

Peterson, K. D., & Finn, C. E. (1985, Spring). Principals, superintendents and the administrator's art. *The Public Interest, 79,* 42–62.

Pierce, P. R. (1935). *The origin and development of the public school principalship.* Chicago: The University of Chicago.

Portin, B. S., Shen, J., & Williams, R. C. (1998). The changing principalship and its impact: Voices from principals. *NASSP Bulletin, 82,* 1–8.

Ravitch, D. (1983). *The troubled crusade: American education, 1945–1980.* New York: Basic Books.

Rebarber, T. (1992). *State policies for school restructuring.* Washington, DC: National Conference of State Legislatures.

Reller, T. L. (1936). The historical development of school administration in the United States. In C. M. Hill (Ed.), *Educational progress and school administration.* (p. 17). New Haven, CT: Yale University Press.

Rost, J. C. (1991). *Leadership in the twenty-first century.* New York: Praeger.

Sergiovanni, T. (1991). *The principalship: A reflective practice perspective* (2nd ed.). Boston: Allyn & Bacon.

Sergiovanni, T. (1996). *Leadership for the schoolhouse: How is it different? Why is it important?* San Francisco: Jossey-Bass.

Shakeshaft, C. (1989). *Women in educational administration.* Newbury Park, CA: Sage.

Shakeshaft, C. (1999). The struggle to create a more gender inclusive profession. In J. Murphy & K. Louis (Eds.). *Handbook of research on educational administration* (pp. 99–118). San Francisco: Jossey-Bass.

Shipman, N., Topps, B., & Murphy, J. (1998). *Linking the ISLLC standards to professional development and relicensure.* Paper presented at the annual meeting of the American Educational Research Association, San Diego.

Silver, P. F. (1982). Administrator preparation. In H. E. Mitzel (Ed.), *Encyclopedia of educational research* (5th ed., Vol. 1, pp. 49–59). New York: Free Press.

Smith, W. F, & Andrews, R. L. (1989). *Instructional leadership: How principals make a difference.* Alexandria, VA: Association for Supervision and Curriculum Development Press.

Spaedy, M. (1990, September). *Reinventing school leadership* (pp. 156–159). Working memo prepared for the Reinventing School Leadership Conference. Cambridge, MA: National Center for Educational Leadership.

Spring, J. (2001). *The American school: 1642–2000.* Boston: McGraw Hill.

Theobold, P., & Nachtigal, P. (1995). Culture, community, and the promise of rural education. *Phi Delta Kappan, 77*(October), 35.

Thompson, D., & Wood, R. (1998). *Money and schools: A handbook for practitioners.* New York: Eye on Education.

Thomson, S. E. (Ed.). (1993). *Principals for our changing schools: The knowledge and skill base.* Fairfax, VA: National Policy Board for Educational Administration.

Tyack, D. (1974). *The one best system: A history of American urban education.* Cambridge, MA: Harvard University Press.

Tyack, D. (2001). Introduction. In S. Mondale and S. Patton (Eds.), *School: The story of American public education* (pp. 1–8). Boston: Beacon Press.

Tyack, D., & Cummings, R. (1977). Leadership in American public schools before 1954: Historical configurations and conjectures. In L. L. Cunningham, W. G. Hack, & R. O. Nystrand (Eds.), *Educational administration: The developing decades* (pp. 46–66). Berkeley, CA: McCutchan.

Tyack, D., & Hansot, E. (1981). The dream deferred: A golden age for women school administrators. Washington: National Institute of Education (ERIC Document Reproduction Service No. ED207161).

Tyack, D., & Hansot, E. (1982). *Managers of virtue: Public school leadership in America, 1820–1980.* Boston: Basic Books.

Tyack, D., & Hansot, E. (1990). *Learning together: A history of coeducation in American schools.* New Haven, CT: Yale University Press.

Tyack, D., & Strober, M. (1981). Jobs and gender: A history of the structuring of educational employment by sex. In P. Schmuck, W. Charters, & R. Carlson (Eds.), *Educational policy and management* (pp. 131–150). New York: Academic Press.

U.S. Department of Education. (1984). *The nation responds: Recent efforts to improve education.* Washington: Government Printing Office.

Weber, M., Feldman, J., & Poling, E. (1980). *A study of factors affecting career aspirations of women teachers and educational administrators.* Paper presented at the annual meeting of the American Educational Research Association, Boston, Massachusetts.

Weinberg, M. (1977). *A chance to learn: A history of race and education in the U.S.* New York: Cambridge University Press.

Whitaker, K. (1995). Principal burnout: Implications for professional development. *Journal of Personnel Evaluation in Education, 9,* 287–296.

Wulff, K. (1996). The changing role of the principal. Project report, Executive Summary. Association of Washington School Principals and University of Washington.

Yerkes, D. M., & Guaglianone, C. L. (1998, November/December). Where have all the high school administrators gone? *Thrust for Educational Leadership, 28*(2), 10–14.

7

The School Superintendent

Roles, Challenges, and Issues

THEODORE J. KOWALSKI
University of Dayton

C. CRYSS BRUNNER
University of Minnesota

The purposes of this chapter are to detail the development of the office of school superintendent, to examine issues of gender and race, to identify contemporary issues affecting practice, and to identify future research topics. The first two sections provide historical perspectives summarizing how the position has evolved over the past 150 years at three different levels—state, intermediate district, and local district. A discussion of the position's history produces five role conceptualizations; having evolved over the past 150 years, these characterizations provide a mosaic of contemporary expectations. Next, considerable attention is given to the causes and implications of race and gender underrepresentation, and research on this topic is summarized. Contemporary challenges to practice are then presented in relation to education finance, school reform, social contexts of

schooling, and school board relationships. Last, suggestions for conducting research on the normative and actual roles, underrepresentation, and contemporary challenges are provided.

HISTORY OF THE OFFICE OF SUPERINTENDENT

State and Intermediate District Superintendents

Although the term *school superintendent* is most readily associated with local districts, the position also exists at two other levels of authority having jurisdiction over public education. One of them is the state government. The first state superintendent, appointed in New York in 1812, had three primary duties: plan a common school system for the state, report on the management of public funds, and provide school-related information to the state legislature. Over the next 40 years, every northern state and some southern states followed New York's lead in creating such a position (Butts & Cremin, 1953).

The creation of state departments was spawned by tensions between two basic and seemingly contradictory values, liberty and equality. The concept of local control, unique to the United States, is an expression of liberty; the intent was to allow residents of local school districts to participate in public school governance by influencing budget, curriculum, and personnel decisions. By the 1830s, however, state officials began to recognize that disparate educational opportunities existed among local schools. This perceived problem prompted them to embrace the common school concept. Spring (1994) identified this movement's three primary objectives as educating all children in a common schoolhouse, using schools as an instrument of government policy, and creating state agencies to control local schools.

Today, state-level superintendents are found in all 50 states.[1] While the overall responsibility of this position is to oversee education from a statewide perspective, the titles[2] and conditions surrounding the job certainly are not uniform. Variability exists in the following areas: method of selection (appointed versus elected); relationship to the state board of education (nonmember, nonvoting member, member, or chair); authority over the state board of education (high, moderate, or low); and required, desired, and actual qualifications (professional educators or noneducators). Despite such fundamental differences, the position of state superintendent focuses on several common purposes reflected in the activities of the Council of Chief State School Officers. This organization is composed of public officials who oversee elementary and secondary education in the states, U.S. extrastate jurisdictions (American Samoa, Guam, Northern Mariana Islands, Puerto Rico, and the Virgin Islands), the District of Columbia, and the Department of Defense's education activities. The council's mission is divided into four general activities: strategic partnerships and advocacy, professional development and capacity building, school performance and student achievement, and data collection, research, and technical assistance.

At a later time, most states established county-level agencies to act as liaisons between communities and state government. The executive officer of these units was commonly given the title of county superintendent. One of the responsibilities assigned to this position was to provide service and management to weak districts (Knezevich, 1971). Each state, however, has a somewhat unique history in the development of county-level districts (Campbell, Cunningham, Nystrand, & Usdan, 1990), partly because the number and size of local districts vary markedly across states. Some states, especially in the South, did not decentralize below the county level; by comparison, some states established separate school districts in virtually every town and township. Eventually, population increases and school consolidation reduced the number of small local districts, and the necessity of retaining a county-level agency in every county was challenged in some states. Typically, this scrutiny resulted in legislation that retained the concept but reduced the number of such agencies. Michigan and Illinois are two states that exemplify this type of reduction. Michigan's current 57 intermediate school districts were formed in 1962 when the state's 83 county school districts were reduced and renamed by state statute. A similar state law was passed in Illinois circa 1970. County-level education agencies were replaced by regional service centers while counties without sufficient population were forced to merge with neighboring counties.

These middle-level education agencies are frequently confederations, organizations in which the members have substantial control over the scope of activities (Knezevich, 1984). This control is exercised by virtue of a governance board composed of the local district superintendents or their designees. Differences across states exist in the following areas:

Funding. States differ with respect to how they fund these units. Typically, operating funds are a mix of state support and member district fees. In some states, these units have the authority to levy a local property tax.

Services. Middle-level units do not provide the same services across states. The nature and scope of services usually depend on the legal nature of the unit. Those that are legal extensions of state government perform delegated administrative functions (e.g., auditing or registering educator licenses) and also may engage in selected support services (e.g., technology, staff development, cooperative purchasing). Those that are independent confederations of local districts usually focus entirely on support services.

Relationship to local districts. Middle-level units that are legal extensions of state government are more likely to have authority in selected areas over local districts. Independent confederations, by comparison, are essentially controlled by the local districts they serve.

Appointment of the superintendent. Having the unit's governance board appoint the superintendent is the norm. In several states, however, the superintendent is elected. In Illinois, for example, the regional service center superintendents are elected on a partisan ballot.

Clearly, these differences make it impossible to provide a single definition of an intermediate-level superintendent that is universally accurate (Kowalski, 2003a). Most often, however, the individuals who hold this office are former local district superintendents, and their responsibilities include leadership, management, and facilitation.

School District Superintendents

The position of school district superintendent was created in the mid-1800s; between 1837 and 1850, 13 urban districts employed a person in this role. By most accounts, the first district superintendents were appointed in Buffalo, New York, and Louisville, Kentucky. (Grieder, Pierce, & Jordan, 1969). By the end of the 19th century, most city school boards had created this position. The need to do so was affected by a myriad of conditions including the development of larger city school districts, the consolidation of rural districts, an expanded curriculum, passage of compulsory attendance laws, demands for increased accountability, and efficiency expectations (Kowalski, 2003a). Historical accounts of the evolution of this position over the past 150 years reveal some discrepancies. Petersen and Barnett (2003) attribute this variance to differences in three conditions: literature sources, interpretations of historical accounts, and analytical approaches. Whereas some scholars (e.g., Tyack & Hansot, 1982) relied on a developmental approach, based on the premise that the superintendent's role matured over time, others (Callahan, 1966) employed a discursive analysis, relying on rhetoric and writings to determine role expectations. Noting the use of these two distinctively different approaches, Brunner, Grogan, and Björk (2002) concluded that the discursive approach resulted in a greater number of developmental stages.

Some authors (e.g., Carter & Cunningham, 1997; Petersen & Barnett, 2003) identify the earliest role conceptualization of the superintendent as being the school board's clerk. This role, thought to exist for several decades prior to 1850, was predicated on the belief that big-city school boards were compelled to employ a figurehead but reluctant to relinquish power. Hence, superintendents were relegated to performing simple clerical and practical tasks (Carter & Cunningham, 1997). The role of clerk proved to be temporary and was not sustained as the position matured; this may explain why some scholars have not included it in their writing. Five role conceptualizations are used here to discuss how the position of district superintendent has evolved since its inception. The first four were described by Callahan (1966) and the fifth by Kowalski (2001, 2003b): superintendent as teacher-scholar (1850 to early 1900s), manager (early 1900s to 1930), democratic leader (1930 to mid-1950s), applied social scientist (mid-1950s to mid-1970s), and communicator (mid-1970s to present). In practice, completely separating these five characterizations is impossible because practitioners often assume two or more of them at any time. Although all remain essential to effective practice, the importance of each varied based on social and philosophical conditions.

SUPERINTENDENT ROLE CONCEPTUALIZATIONS

Superintendent as Teacher-Scholar

From the time the position was created until the first decade of the 20th century, the primary foci of district superintendents were implementing state curricula and supervising teachers. The common school movement was intended to assimilate students into American culture by having public schools deliver a set of uniform subjects and courses. This strategy required centralized control and standardization to ensure compliance at the local level, and these responsibilities were assigned to state, county, and district superintendents.

Following the Civil War, rapidly developing urban school systems and their superintendents became the models of effective practice because their organizations were larger and more modern than others. The perception of these administrators as "master" teachers was predicated on the fact that they were former classroom teachers who were effective

in classrooms (Callahan, 1962) and devoted much of their time to instructional supervision, thereby assuring uniformity of curricula (Spring, 1994). Many big-city superintendents also authored professional journal articles about philosophy, history, and pedagogy (Cuban, 1988), whereas others moved on to become state superintendents, professors, and college presidents (Petersen & Barnett, 2003). The role of superintendent as teacher-scholar was summarized in an 1890 report on urban superintendents:

> It must be made his recognized duty to train teachers and inspire them with high ideals; to revise the course of study when new light shows that improvement is possible; to see that pupils and teachers are supplied with needed appliances for the best possible work; to devise rational methods of promoting pupils. (Cuban, 1976, p. 16)

In the late 1800s, teaching and administration were not viewed as separate professions. Superintendents identified themselves as members of the teaching profession, and they were the most influential members of the National Education Association. Often, these administrators used professionalism to protect themselves from powerful business and civic leaders who attempted to usurp their authority. Because they did not want to be perceived as politicians or managers, the business aspects of administration were often assumed by board members or subordinate officials (Callahan, 1966).

After 1910, the conceptualization of the district superintendent as teacher-scholar waned but did not become totally irrelevant. Over the past 100 years, expectations that superintendents should be instructional leaders have fluctuated. In recent decades, school reform initiatives and strategies heightened expectations that superintendents should provide the visionary leadership and planning necessary to produce academic gains at the school district level. Even so, policymakers often disagree over the extent to which superintendents require preparation and experience as professional educators, as evidenced by differing state licensing standards and by the credentials of superintendents employed in the nation's largest school systems.

Superintendent as Manager

At the beginning of the 20th century, America was becoming an industrial society. Social, economic, and political changes associated with this transition affected public education in two primary ways. First, industrialization encouraged urbanization. Large cities required large public school districts, which required managers to control material and human resources. Second, the philosophical underpinnings of the Industrial Revolution were widely accepted by public officials, including those who served on the school boards of rapidly growing cities (Callahan, 1962). Both factories and schools were thought to need scientific managers, individuals who could improve operations by concentrating on time and efficiency (Tyack & Hansot, 1982).

As early as 1890, reservations were expressed about the ability of traditional superintendents to administer large city districts. These concerns focused primarily on a perceived lack of managerial knowledge and skills. As Cuban (1976) noted, heated debates were waged on this topic, and "the lines of argument crystallized over whether the functions of a big-city superintendent should be separated in to two distinct jobs, i.e., business manager and superintendent of instruction" (p. 17). Such discussions were fueled by growing concerns that schools did not operate efficiently, at least not in comparison to successful businesses (Kowalski, 1999). Over the next 10 to 20 years, many leading education scholars, including Ellwood Cubberley, George Strayer, and Franklin Bobbitt, joined those advocating the adoption of scientific management in schools

(Cronin, 1973). Leading universities started offering courses in school management as many big-city superintendents tried to persuade policymakers and the general public that their work was separate from and more important than teaching (Thomas & Moran, 1992).

The primary management roles assigned to superintendents during this period included budget development and administration, standardization of operation, personnel management, and facility management. Yet, not everyone supported reshaping the superintendency into a management position. Some mayors, city council members, and other political bosses, for example, feared that the new role would increase the stature of superintendents, resulting in their acquiring more influence and power (Callahan, 1962).[3] Others, including some leading education scholars during that era, were apprehensive because they saw the role transition as a manifestation of a broader threat to grassroots participative democracy. More precisely, they feared that power elites in business, government, and public education would take control of the public schools, thus eradicating the concept of local community control (Glass, 2003). Although he recognized that an intricate set of social forces played some part in the adoption of scientific management in schools, noted historian Raymond Callahan (1962) pointed the finger of blame more deliberately at big-city superintendents. He concluded that their collusion was essential to this transformation, and he referred to them as dupes—powerless and vulnerable individuals unwilling to defend either their profession or their organizations. This conclusion, referred to as the "thesis of vulnerability," was accepted by many, but not all education scholars (Eaton, 1990). Burroughs (1974) and Tyack (1974), for instance, viewed these big-city superintendents as cunning, intelligent political pragmatists who responded to the societal realities surrounding their work. Thomas and Moran (1992), by comparison, decided that these superintendents embraced their new management role as a means of expanding their own legitimate power base.

The business executive perspective of school administration was increasingly criticized after 1930, largely for three reasons. First, the great economic stock market crash and subsequent Depression eroded much of the glitter captains of industry acquired by deploying scientific management during the previous three decades. Second, many local school district patrons began objecting to a perceived loss of liberty; they thought they were being excluded from the governance of their local schools (Kowalski, 2003a). Third, leading progressive educators, such as George Sylvester Counts, relentlessly criticized the infusion of business values into school administration, arguing that classical theory and scientific management were incongruous with the core values of a democratic society (Van Til, 1971). Although support for the conceptualization of superintendent as business executive diminished, the realization that management functions were essential became embedded in the culture of the education profession. Educators and policymakers became more accepting of the premise that effective administrators had to be both managers and leaders; the goal was not to eradicate management but rather to place it in its proper perspective (Kowalski, 1999).

Superintendent as Democratic Leader

The role of democratic leader is often equated with statesmanship. Björk and Gurley (2003) traced the origins of statesmanship from Plato to Alexander Hamilton. Plato believed that a statesman acted unilaterally and paternalistically to control and direct critical societal functions. Hamilton viewed a statesman as a true politician who juggled the interests of the common people and the interests of the economic elite while remaining an aristocrat. Callahan's (1966) conception of the superintendent as statesman was probably

not in total agreement with either of these perspectives, as his historical analysis of the period between 1930 and the mid-1950s appears to have been centered primarily on political leadership in a truly democratic context. After studying these perspectives, Björk and Gurley concluded that the term *statesman* "is not and may never have been an appropriate role conceptualization for the American superintendency, inasmuch as the role has never been about a stately, patriarch ubiquitously and benevolently guiding school systems single-handedly" (p. 35). Instead of statesman, they viewed this superintendent role as one of an astute political strategist.

The role conceptualization of superintendent as democratic leader is anchored in both political realities and philosophy. During and following the great economic Depression, resources for education were very scarce. Political activity was heightened as schools competed with other public services and with each other to secure financial support. Prior to this time, political involvement by superintendents was often deemed inappropriate and unprofessional (Björk & Lindle, 2001; Kowalski, 1995). However, in the highly turbulent environment of the 1930s, these convictions faded and were replaced by expectations that school administrators could function as lobbyists and political strategists. Simultaneously, critics of the preceding management era were still waging a battle to restore democracy in school districts that had become bureaucratic. A leading spokesperson for democratic administration was Ernest Melby, a former dean of education at Northwestern University and New York University (Callahan, 1966). Melby (1955) believed that the community was public education's greater resource, urging administrators to "release the creative capacities of individuals" and "mobilize the educational resources of communities" (p. 250). In essence, superintendents were urged to galvanize policymakers, employees, and other taxpayers to support a board's initiatives (Howlett, 1993).

By the mid-1950s, the idea of having superintendents engage in democratic administration also met with disfavor. Detractors argued that the concept was overly idealistic and insufficiently attentive to realities of practice. The everyday problems faced by superintendents were viewed largely as economic and political, and concerns mounted that administrators were not prepared properly to meet these challenges (Kowalski, 1999).

Superintendent as Applied Social Scientist

As with earlier role conceptualizations, the view of superintendent as applied social scientist was forged by several societal and professional conditions. Callahan (1966) noted four:

- Growing dissatisfaction with democratic leadership after World War II; critics charged that the concept was overly idealistic and ignored the realities of practice
- Rapid development of the social sciences in the late 1940s and early 1950s; much of the knowledge generated by this expansion was applicable to public organizations and administration (Callahan, 1966)
- Support from the Kellogg Foundation; during the 1950s, the foundation provided more than $7 million in grants, primarily to eight major universities that allowed school administration professors to conduct social science research
- A resurgence of criticisms of public education in the early 1950s; much like conditions leading to the management conceptualization, public dissatisfaction spawned reform efforts and heightened interest in the social sciences

At least two other factors were highly influential. Circa 1955, efforts to make school administration an established academic discipline equal to business management and public administration were intensifying (Culbertson, 1981). Redefining administrators as applied social scientists and infusing the social sciences into the curriculum for preparing school administrators were viewed as positive steps toward that goal (Crowson & McPherson, 1987). Second, prior to the 1950s, the practice of school administration focused largely on internal operations, but gradually, systems theory was employed to demonstrate how external legal, political, social, and economic systems affected the operation and productivity of public schools (Getzels, 1977). Consequently, administrators had to understand these external systems if they were to provide essential leadership and management.

The model of superintendent as social scientist encouraged professors and practitioners to emphasize empiricism, predictability, and scientific certainty in their research and practice (Cooper & Boyd, 1987). The intent was to rewrite the normative standards for practice; superintendents in the future were expected to apply scientific inquiry to the problems and decisions that permeated their practice. The study of theory was at the core of this normative transition, as evidenced by the changes in school administration textbooks. Textbooks written prior to 1950 never mentioned theory; virtually none written after 1950 omitted theory (Getzels, 1977).

In many ways, the development of the applied social scientist perspective paralleled the earlier development of the management perspective. Both changes occurred in the context of public dissatisfaction; both arguably benefited professors who prepared practitioners by elevating the status of their profession; and both separated administration from teaching, with administrators being viewed as having more demanding and more technical positions (Kowalski, 2003a).

Both management and social science cast superintendents as "experts" who possessed a knowledge base beyond teaching. More recently, the applied social scientist view captured the attention of critical theorists because knowledge associated with this role is highly cogent to eradicating social injustices in public institutions (Johnson & Fusarelli, 2003).

Superintendent as Communicator

The view of superintendent as communicator emerged in conjunction with America's transition from a manufacturing to an information society (Kowalski, 2001). Communicative expectations in this position reflect a confluence of reform initiatives and the social environment in which they are being pursued. Virtually every major school improvement concept and strategy encourages administrators to work collaboratively with teachers, parents, and taxpayers to build and pursue a collective vision. Yet, many schools retain cultures that promote work isolation as teachers and administrators work individually and in seclusion (Gideon, 2002) and in closed organizational climates where administrators attempt to avoid community interventions (Blase & Anderson, 1995).

Since the early 1990s, most policy analysts concluded that meaningful school reform requires revising institutional climates, including organizational structure and culture (Bauman, 1996). In addition, current reform efforts are largely predicated on the conviction that restructuring complex institutions necessitates a social systems perspective (Chance & Björk, 2004; Murphy, 1991; Schein, 1996). "Systemic thinking requires us to accept that the way social systems are put together has independent effects on the way people behave, what they learn, and how they learn what they learn" (Schlechty, 1997, p. 134). In this vein, the nature of public schools is influenced by human transactions occurring within and outside the formal organization, exchanges that are often driven by philosophical differences. Restructuring proposals that ignore the ubiquitous nature of political disagreements in public schools almost always fail, either because key implementers and stakeholders are excluded from visioning and planning or because the values and beliefs expressed in the reforms are incongruous with prevailing institutional culture (Schlechty, 1997).

Many scholars (e.g., Henkin, 1993; Murphy, 1994) believe that school improvement needs to be pursued locally and that superintendents must be key figures in the process. This assignment, however, is highly intimidating. Superintendents must openly discuss topics with stakeholders, topics that inevitably produce substantial conflict (Carlson, 1996), and they must assume assignments for which they have no or minimal preparation (Kowalski, 2003b). Most have become dubious about reform, having experienced a myriad of change failures during their careers (Sarason, 1996). Within existing school cultures, even new teachers and administrators often come to accept things as they are (Streitmatter, 1994).

Clearly, then, school restructuring is an especially intricate assignment because it usually requires long-standing values and beliefs to be identified, challenged, and changed. Institutional culture is central to school restructuring because it determines what individuals and groups truly believe and value about education (Trimble, 1996) and how they promote and accept change (Leithwood, Jantzi, & Fernandez, 1994). Many communication scholars concluded that communication and culture are inextricably linked. For example, Conrad (1994) wrote, "Cultures are communicative creations. They emerge and are sustained by the communicative acts of all employees, not just the conscious persuasive strategies of upper management. Cultures do not exist separately from people communicating with one another" (p. 27). Despite the fact that most organizational research categorized culture as a causal variable and communication as an intervening variable (Wert-Gray, Center, Brashers, & Meyers, 1991), scholars often describe the relationship between the two as reciprocal. Axley (1996), for instance, characterized this interdependence: "Communication gives rise to culture, which gives rise to communication, which perpetuates culture" (p. 153). As such, communication is a process through which organizational members express their collective inclination to coordinate beliefs, behaviors, and attitudes; in schools, communication gives meaning to work and forges perceptions of reality. Furthermore, culture influences communicative behavior, and communicative behavior is instrumental to building, maintaining, and changing culture (Kowalski, 1998). In the case of local districts, normative communicative behavior for superintendents is shaped largely by two realities: their need to assume leadership in the process of school restructuring (Björk, 2001; Murphy, 1994) and their need to change school culture as part of the restructuring process (Heckman, 1993; Kowalski, 2000).

Unfortunately, there is a disjunction between professional preparation and practice in the area of communication. As an example, communication skills are listed in standards for practice (e.g., standards developed by the American Association of School Administrators and standards used by the Interstate School Leaders Licensure Consortium) and routinely cited as required qualifications for superintendent vacancies. Yet, most administrators never complete a graduate-level course in communication. A nexus between effective practice and communication skills is not unique to education; recent studies of business executives revealed that most who were under attack were ineffective communicators (Perina, 2002). Communication has become especially important with respect to school improvement, open political dialogue, school district imaging, community support for change, information management, marketing programs, and human relations (Kowalski, 2004). Unquestionably, the ability of top-level administrators to access and use information to identify and solve problems encountered by their organizations is a primary criterion for evaluating effectiveness.

THE SCHOOL SUPERINTENDENCY: WOMEN AND PERSONS OF COLOR

In a chapter on the superintendency, it may strike the reader as odd to find a section on women and persons of color. People tend to believe that if men and women and persons of color are superintendents, then information on the superintendency applies to, and is related to, all of them. Such a belief is understandable, but it is not grounded in reality. Consider: Demographics alone establish that the school superintendency is a white man's position. In fact, white men have held 86% to 99% of all superintendencies, with the 99% figure occurring in 1980 (Blount, 1998; Brunner & Grogan, 2003; Glass, Björk, & Brunner, 2000), since the position was first created in the early 1800s (Butts & Cremin, 1953).

In terms of its representative nature, it can be said without equivocation that the superintendency represents white men. In national studies with aggregate findings from representative samples, the responses of white men dominate the conclusions so heavily that the responses of women and persons of color are virtually lost (Brunner, 2003). As Tallerico (1999) stated, "Of the approximately seventy-five years worth of extant scholarship relevant to the superintendency, most studies have either relied primarily on white, male samples, or have made no mention of the gender, racial, or ethnic backgrounds of their subjects" (p. 29). To be sure, only within the last 20 years have research and attention pointed specifically to women superintendents and superintendents of color. Without focused studies of women and superintendents of color, both groups may continue to lack appropriate and accessible role models; to believe themselves substandard because they do not fit the norms found in leadership and superintendency literature based on studies dominated by white men; to find themselves practicing in ways not mentioned in books on the superintendency; and indeed, to experience limited access to superintendency positions because criteria for hiring are based on white male norms.

To draw attention to the unique history of how women and persons of color have come to the superintendency, to establish that the norms grounded primarily in studies of white men do not necessarily fit women and persons of color, and to add additional perspectives and value to the superintendency and leadership literature, this section focuses on these two groups. The first part draws attention to historical patterns that created personal and professional space for women and persons of color in education. The second part follows the feminization of the teaching profession, which opened the doors for persons of color, and the third part describes the masculine nature of the superintendency. The last part poses the possibility that the superintendency is becoming feminized, a possibility that may create greater access and opportunity for women and persons of color.

Educational Settings for White Males Only

That women and persons of color would eventually be heads of school districts could not have been predicted during early America's colonial period; such a prediction could not have been made about persons of color as late as the 19th century. Beginning with religious teachings, the schooling of white male children was conducted almost exclusively by literate white men in communities. Women, girls, and persons of color of all ages were socialized to respect and rely on white men's authority and wisdom, and therefore, it was thought that the three groups had no need of education. This statement is not meant to imply that covert education was nonexistent. For example, Jackson (1999) reminds us, "We now know that even during slavery, black women had the courage to defy the law and teach slaves to read. They knew

that the very survival of their race depended on education" (p. 147). Thus, even as teaching became a differentiated role, white men, not women or persons of color, offered their "for pay" services to families who could afford them (Blount, 1998).

As early as the mid-17th century, Massachusetts passed laws requiring parents to ensure the education of their children. The gradually increasing demand for schooling in turn required more schoolmasters, a post that was viewed as unattractive or as a temporary position by most qualified white men (Waller, 1932). Yet, even as communities struggled to hire schoolmasters, they remained reluctant to hire women and persons of color for at least three reasons: White women were thought to be less intelligent than white men; because white women received little, if any formal schooling, they were not prepared to teach others (Blount, 1998); and persons of color were not considered at all, as historical evidence of their role in and experience of education is scarce as late as the mid-20th century (Jackson, 1999). On learning about historical attitudes toward women as teachers and toward persons of color generally speaking, one wonders how any ever became superintendents.

An Opportunity by Default: The Feminization of the Teaching Profession

At the same time that the demand for white male schoolmasters increased, there were noteworthy supporters, feminists of the time, of formal education for women, Abigail Adams for one (Blount, 1998). Catharine Beecher's promotion of women teachers was particularly effective because she argued that women should have dominion over the domestic sphere and any extension of the home, such as the education of children. Beecher believed that women made natural teachers (Blount, 1998; Gribskov, 1980). Her beliefs were later endorsed by

Horace Mann as he worked to address an impending teacher shortage. Furthermore, according to Blount, Benjamin Rush

> provided generally accepted rhetoric justifying education for females; women should receive education for the benefit of their sons, and by extension, the republic. Consequently, Rush's ideology of republican motherhood failed to challenge existing gender roles and relations deeply, perhaps a requirement for its acceptance at the time. (Blount, 1998, p. 13)

This ideology successfully rationalized and generated unprecedented formal education opportunities in seminaries, academies, and colleges for white women from 1790 to 1850 (Blount, 1998). History records almost nothing about persons of color during this time period.

During times when qualified white men found teaching less than appealing and numbers of primarily white women were educated for the benefit of their sons, women began schooling children, first in the home, next in dame schools, and eventually in local schools when men were unavailable. Persons of color provided their own teaching when and where they could outside the lives of whites (Jackson, 1999). Partially because of capable women teachers and activists like Emma Willard and Catharine Beecher, by the early 19th century, single and married white women slowly became acceptable sights in public schoolrooms across the nation.

For these and other reasons, including the fact that women's lack of work opportunities made them willing to take low wages, acceptance of women in teaching jobs grew, until in 1900 they accounted for about 70% of all teachers. After the Civil War, while most teachers were white, "Black men and women rapidly entered teaching, especially in schools built for Black children throughout the South. By 1900, as many as 20 percent of women teachers in the South were Black" (Blount, 1998, p. 37). Over a century later, women of all colors still significantly dominate the teaching

ranks, so much so that the profession is considered a feminized one, "feminized in that women constitute [a large] proportion of the teaching ranks, but also feminized in the sense that the work . . . fit[s] traditional notions of women's work" (Blount, 1998, p. 21).

The brief history provided here spans the years from the beginning of our nation to 1900. In summary, we purposely highlight the following points. First, only literate white men were teachers at the outset of the period. Women and persons of color, who were thought to be of lower intelligence than white men, were not educated. Teaching was a white and masculine occupation. Second, demand increased for teachers at the same time white, educated men were finding schoolhouse jobs too unsavory to do for long, if at all.[4] Third, advocates of women's education, the earliest of whom were feminists, justified it by suggesting that women should be teaching their sons. Indeed, such work was touted to be an extension of women's work at home. Fourth, because influential white men became convinced that educated women were the appropriate teachers of their sons, white women increasingly had opportunities to be educated. Once educated, some women were hired, usually when white men were unavailable. In addition, because teaching was the first public profession for women, they were willing to accept low wages to experience the benefits of financial independence. After the Civil War, African Americans moved into teaching jobs, primarily in the South.

By 1900, with 70% of teachers being women and 20% being women of color, the role was considered feminized. Being feminized meant that teaching was considered primarily women's work; it was a fairly low status role, making it also open to persons of color in the South; and wages remained relatively low. Although numerous historical elements are missing from this simplified story, these highlights help us catch sight of the feminization of a professional role.

The Superintendency: A Masculine Position

While teaching became feminized, administrative roles were masculinized. This point was painstakingly documented in historian Jackie Blount's (1998) *Destined to Rule the Schools: Women and the Superintendency, 1873–1995.* For the purposes of this chapter, suffice it to say that not all men left teaching, and those who remained felt pressure to maintain their masculinity. Along with others, Blount (1998) maintained

> that it was not coincidental that teachers' independence and decision-making powers were stripped away just as women dominated the profession numerically. The male educators who remained had to assert their masculine qualities somehow, thus many became administrators to control the labors of women just as fathers and husbands long had done in the home. Administrators did not appear in significant numbers until women began filling teaching positions. (p. 27)

Although white men have dominated administrative roles since their creation, women's presence as teachers assisted in their occasional transfers into administrative ranks (Shakeshaft, 1999). Once in teaching positions, white women activists slowly convinced individual state governments and state and national organizations headed by men (Reid, 1982) that women deserved to vote for school officials because they owned property and had the right, along with the men who taught and who could vote, to decide which school officials would determine their working conditions (Blount, 1998; Shakeshaft, 1999). Blount reminds us that by "1910, twenty-four states had granted women school suffrage" (p. 66). Regarding the importance of suffrage for women's entry into administration, Blount (1998) wrote,

> The women's suffrage movement had sparked the emergence of women school administrators for at least two reasons. First, the quest for women's rights had triggered the larger movement of organized women's groups, many of which actively supported the candidacy of women for school offices. Second, suffrage had given women power at the ballot box, which allowed them to affect the political process directly, to become, as some had hoped, a political constituency. (p. 81)

At the beginning of the 20th century, thousands of white women moved into school leadership positions, including the superintendency (Hansot & Tyack, 1981). Somewhat surprisingly, by 1930, 11% of all superintendents were women, with most having jobs at the county level (Blount, 1998). The percentage, however, began to plummet after the end of World War II as the women's movement lost its intensity and masses of men returned to postwar life and sought work in educational administration (Shakeshaft, 1989). By 1970, the proportion of women in the superintendency dropped to 3% and then declined even further in 1980 to about 1%. Not until the end of the 20th century did the proportion of women superintendents again increase to about 14% of all superintendencies (Brunner & Grogan, 2003; Glass et al., 2000). Over the course of one century, the numbers of women in the superintendency increased only 5%. In no small measure, the superintendency stubbornly remained a masculine role.

The story of superintendents of color is even more dismal. In fact, superintendents of color were practically nonexistent before the U.S. Supreme Court's *Brown v. Board of Education* decision of 1954. To be sure, there were notable exceptions. For example, Revere (1985) describes one African American woman, Velma Ashley, who served as superintendent in Oklahoma from 1944 to 1956. Three other African American women assumed superintendencies by the early 1970s (Blount, 1998; Jackson, 1999; Revere, 1985). In addition, a "black superintendent, Alonzo Crim, was appointed [in Atlanta] in 1972 as a condition of the court order [*Brown v. BOE*], demonstrating the expanding role of the court in school decisions. . . . Little was done, however, to desegregate the Atlanta schools until extensive court litigation forced action in the 1970s" (Jackson, 1995, p. 18).

The terse history in the preceding paragraph was a strong predictor of the numbers of superintendents of color as late as the 1970s. These numbers increased slightly over the decades following. In 1981–1982, about 2.2% of superintendents were persons of color, and by 1998, 5% of all superintendencies were filled by persons of color (Cunningham & Hentges, 1982; Hodgkinson & Montenegro, 1999). This percentage remained the same at the beginning of the 21st century (Glass et al., 2000). In no small measure, the current superintendency remains a position filled primarily by white men.

A DEARTH OF RESEARCH

In alignment with the sparse numbers of women and persons of color in the superintendency, the research on these aggregate groups has been missing, limited, and at times invisible. Also in keeping with the actual numbers of women and persons of color, research studies focused on women superintendents have outnumbered studies of superintendents of color. This section briefly discusses some of the literature on superintendents of color and then some of the slightly more extensive literature focused on women superintendents. Neither discussion should be considered a review of the literature. Rather, the intent of this section is to provide a sense of these literature sets for the reader.

Superintendents of Color: A Sampling of Literature

Although most historical and other data on superintendents of color have tended to focus on African Americans (see for example: Alston, 1999; Brunner & Peyton-Caire, 2000; Jackson, 1995, 1999; Lomotey, Allen, Mark, & Rivers, 1996; Murtadha-Watts, 2000; Revere, 1985; Sizemore, 1986), a few researchers studied

Hispanics in the role (see, e.g., Mendez-Morse, 1999, 2000; Ortiz, 1999, 2000; Ortiz & Ortiz, 1995) while others wrote more broadly about women superintendents of color (Arnez, 1982; Chase, 1995; Enomoto, Gardiner, & Grogan, 2000; Ortiz, 1982).

In general, early reports about superintendents of color are sparse, as the general population of the superintendency was often not disaggregated by race. Rare data reported that superintendents of color were predominantly employed in segregated black districts in southern states. A later report by the American Association of School Administrators (AASA) (Montenegro, 1993), *Women and Racial Minority Representation in School Administration*, revealed that superintendents of different racial backgrounds tended to serve in areas where people of the same race lived in significant numbers (Glass et al., 2000). This trend continues currently. Indeed, in the year 2000, in districts with enrollments of more than 25,000 students, 23% were superintendents of color (Glass et al., 2000). Table 7.1 shows the percentages and total numbers of superintendents within categories of ethnicity in the AASA study (which made use of representative sampling) (Glass et al., 2000, p. 104).

The AASA study (Glass et al., 2000) found some noteworthy differences between superintendents of color, men and women, and white superintendents, men and women. Examples include the following:

- 75% of superintendents of color have been in superintendencies for 9 or fewer years whereas 57.5% of white superintendents have been in their positions for 9 or fewer years.
- Twice as many superintendents of color (29.3% versus 13.1% of white superintendents) lived in large cities prior to college.
- Twice as many white superintendents (33.2% versus 17.5% of superintendents of color) considered themselves conservatives.
- In contrast to 10% of white superintendents, 47% of superintendents of color reported that discriminatory hiring and promotional practices limited career opportunities.

Table 7.1   Ethnicity by Gender

| | Gender | | | |
| | Men | | Women | |
Race	Number	Percentage	Number	Percentage
Black	38	2.0	15	5.1
White	1,833	95.3	272	91.5
Hispanic	27	1.4	4	1.3
Native American	15	0.8	2	0.7
Asian	3	0.2	2	0.7
Other	9	0.5	2	0.7
Total	1,947	100.0	297	100.0

SOURCE: Glass, T. E., Björk, L. G., & Brunner, C. C. *The Study of the American School Superintendent: A Look at the Superintendent of Education in the New Millennium.* © 2000 by American Association of School Administrators. Reprinted by permission of American Association of School Administrators.

- Whereas 41% of white superintendents reported that they were hired because of personal characteristics, 42% of superintendents of color reported that they were hired because of their potential to be change agents.
- About twice as many white superintendents (44% versus 29% of superintendents of color) believed that superintendents set policy.

As can be seen by this brief display of data, gaps exist between the perceptions of superintendents of color and those of white superintendents. This gap has been reported in other studies as well (see, e.g., Glass, 1992; Gleaves-Hirsch, 1997; Tallerico, 2000a, 2000b). As Tallerico (2000a) stated, "It's clear that the historically disenfranchised see things differently from the historically privileged" (p. 139).

Women Superintendents: Literature in Brief[5]

A little more than 20 years ago, a handful of researchers, primarily women, began to focus on women in administration (see, e.g., Adler, Laney, & Packer, 1993; Dunlap & Schmuck, 1995; Gardiner, Enomoto, & Grogan, 2000; Ortiz, 1982; Schmuck, 1975; Shakeshaft, 1989) and even later to study women in the superintendency (Bell, 1995; Brunner, 1999a, 1999b, 2000a, 2000b; Chase, 1995; Chase

& Bell, 1990; Grogan, 1996; Kamler & Shakeshaft, 1999; Maienza, 1986; Marietti & Stout, 1994; Pavan, 1999; Sherman & Repa, 1994; Skrla, Reyes, & Scheurich, 2000; Tallerico, 2000a, 2000b; Tallerico & Burstyn, 1996; Wesson & Grady, 1994). In addition, a few historians carefully chronicled the phenomenon of women in the superintendency (see Blount, 1998; Hansot & Tyack, 1981; Tyack & Hansot, 1982). In a review of literature on women superintendents, Tallerico (1999) conceptualized research on women in the superintendency in "terms of three interrelated and overlapping domains: profiles, patterns, and practice" (p. 30).

Tallerico (1999, p. 30) used the first domain, profiles, to refer to studies that focused on demographic characteristics and superintendents' attitudes, opinions, or perceptions on selected issues. Bell and Chase (1993), Blount (1998), Glass (1992), and Grady, Ourada-Sieb, and Wesson (1994) were a few included in this domain. The second domain, patterns, referred to examinations of career paths, mobility, and other issues related to access, mentoring, sponsorship, selection, retention, or exit. Researchers in this domain included but were not limited to Alston (1999), Beekley (1999), Brunner (1999a), Brunner and Schumaker

(1998), Chase and Bell (1990), Grogan (1996), Grogan and Henry (1995), Jackson (1999), Kamler and Shakeshaft (1999), Ortiz (1982, 1999), Ortiz and Ortiz (1993), Scherr (1995), Tallerico, Burstyn, and Poole (1993), and Tallerico and Burstyn (1996).

The third and largest domain, practice, referred to inquiry that seeks to understand the nature and experiences of superintendents' work. Researchers included in this domain were Banks (1995), Bell (1988), Chase and Bell (1990), Bell and Chase (1993, 1995, 1996), Brunner (1997, 1998a, 1998b, 1999a, 1999b, 1999c), Chase (1995), Grogan (1999), Helgesen (1990), Jackson (1999), Mendez-Morse (1999), Ortiz (1991), Ortiz and Marshall (1988), Ortiz and Ortiz (1995), Pavan (1999), Pitner (1981), Rosener (1990), Sherman and Repa (1994), and Wesson and Grady (1994, 1995).

In addition to the literature above, national studies of superintendents in recent years have disaggregated data by gender. For example, the AASA study (Glass et al., 2000) uncovered some noteworthy differences between women superintendents (all ethnicities) and men superintendents (all ethnicities). Examples include the following:

- Whereas 26.6% of men have 14 or more total years of superintendency experience, 74.9% of women have 9 or fewer total years of such experience.
- The educational background or undergraduate major for women superintendents was in education twice as often as for men (50% compared to 23.7%).
- Twice as many men superintendents (35% versus 16% of women superintendents) considered themselves conservatives.
- A greater percentage of women superintendents (57% versus 44% of men superintendents) held doctoral degrees.
- 43.8% of women superintendents held their first teaching position in elementary schools, compared to only 17% of men superintendents. The largest percentage of men superintendents (23.2%) were social studies teachers in their first teaching positions.
- More than 50% of men superintendents believed that there were no barriers for

women seeking superintendency positions other than a "lack of mobility." More than 50% of women superintendents reported numerous barriers to their access to superintendency positions, in addition to lack of mobility.

As with the data that compared superintendents of color to white superintendents, a gap exists between the perceptions of women superintendents and men superintendents. The fact that a gap exists between the perceptions of these two groups has been reported in other studies as well (see, e.g., Glass, 1992; Glass et al., 2000; Tallerico, 2000a). As with superintendents of color when compared to white superintendents, the "historically disenfranchised see things differently from the historically privileged" (Tallerico, 2000a, p. 139). Interestingly, in this particular data set, the data from and perceptions of women and persons of color are in agreement much of the time.

CONTEMPORARY CHALLENGES FOR DISTRICT SUPERINTENDENTS

Generalizing about problems facing superintendents is difficult for at least two reasons. First, the severity of most problems varies both within and among local school districts. For example, compliance with state mandates may be a taxing issue in a district until necessary compliance actions are completed or until a state rescinds or modifies the pertinent law. Likewise, the most critical problems identified by urban district administrators are not necessarily the same problems identified by rural administrators. Second, research questions used to obtain data on perceived problems have not always separated individual and organizational problems. What a superintendent identifies on an individual level may be substantially different from what he or she identifies on an organizational level. For these reasons, discussing problems categorically is preferable to discussing them individually. The most enduring struggles are examined here under the following headings: fiscal support, social contexts, school reform, and school board relationships.

Fiscal Support

Superintendents often identify inadequate finances as their most pressing problem (e.g., Glass, Bjork, & Bruner, 2000). Inadequate financing is both an economic and political issue entangled in an intricate mix of adequacy and equity concerns (King, Swanson, & Sweetland, 2003). From an economic perspective, school finance focuses on the allocation of fiscal resources. For example, what portion of school funding comes from the state versus the local property tax? How often and in what manner are tax payments made to local districts? From a political perspective, the problem focuses on competition for scarce resources. That is, how much of a state's revenue is used to fund public education? Has the education lobby been competitive in securing state funds?

Policy decisions in the area of public school funding are guided by several metavalues that are widely accepted by American society. Two of them, adequacy and equity, frame the concerns that face the contemporary superintendent. Adequacy is an imprecise standard that may pertain to quality issues or quantity issues. Most often, policy addressing adequacy contains minimum standards, such as minimum revenue per pupil or the minimum expenditure per pupil. Basically, this value is expressed in the following question: How much money is necessary to provide an adequate level of schooling? Superintendents and state policymakers often have dissimilar answers, because they disagree both as to what constitutes an adequate level of education and as to the amount of money necessary to provide adequate education. Adequacy tends to be a more pervasive concern than equality among superintendents because it is cogent for

all types of districts regardless of fiscal ability (i.e., wealth as measured by taxable property per student). Equality, on the other hand, tends to be a primary concern among superintendents in districts characterized by low wealth or declining wealth (Kowalski, 1999).

Equality is often defined politically as the equal right to participate in a political system and economically as access to equal wealth (Fowler, 2004). In public education, the concept has been analyzed most often as reasonably equal opportunities. If equality were defined as a fair and just method of distributing resources among students, equality could be measured by looking at variations in revenue and spending across local districts (Crampton & Whitney, 1996). In essence, an equitable state system would produce low or moderate variation in revenue and spending among local districts. Insofar as state governments are ultimately responsible for ensuring equality, disparities in wealth and spending have resulted in litigation in nearly 90% of the states. Plaintiffs are often low-wealth districts, or residents thereof, seeking favorable revisions in state funding formulas. Despite all this litigation, the issue remains unresolved in many states. In part, this is due to the fact that the courts have defined equality in three different ways:

1. Resource accessibility: a condition achieved when average educational practice or the estimated needs of students are fully funded (Sielke, 1998)

2. Ex post fiscal neutrality: a condition achieved when the negative effects of local wealth on revenues and spending are neutralized (Thompson, Honeyman, & Stewart, 1988)

3. Ex ante fiscal neutrality: a condition achieved when there is an equal yield for equal effort (Crampton & Whitney, 1996)

The first two approaches focus on equal access and opportunities for students whereas the third focuses on equal treatment of taxpayers. In addition, courts almost always mandate state legislatures to provide remedies to inequities. When this occurs, the decision-making process is again politicized. Even in the face of court mandates, some legislatures have refused to enact sweeping reforms. Finally, state supreme courts have often ruled that some degree of inequality is acceptable to preserve liberty, as in, for example, the authority of local school boards to make some fiscal decisions (King et al., 2003).

Clearly, financing public education is a problem, but it is especially disconcerting for superintendents who work in states with less than adequate standards for revenue and spending; in low-wealth districts in states that have not provided sufficient district equalization; and/or in districts with declining taxable property values in states where sufficient adjustments for this factor have not been adopted. Problems also arise when the number of special needs pupils is unusually high and state supplemental funding for these needs is inadequate and when enrollment increases are much greater than property value increases.

Social Contexts

The demographic profile of the typical school district today is considerably different than it was in 1950, and for the most part, the changes have made the superintendent's responsibilities more complex and demanding. Fewer taxpayers have children enrolled in the public schools; growing numbers of school-aged children are being reared in poverty; most communities have become increasingly diverse, ethnically, religiously, and culturally. At the same time that more students are entering school with emotional, physical, and psychological problems, the curriculum continues to expand. These realities, however, have not deterred some critics from demanding that superintendents do more with less (Glass, 2004).

Perhaps the most relevant social condition affecting public education has been the erosion of community life. Historically, many public schools enjoyed a symbiotic relationship with their communities. Parents and neighborhood groups were often highly involved with or even in the schools. Today, many taxpayers know little or nothing about their local schools; some do not even know their next-door neighbors. Yet, children need strong and purposeful communities providing them human and social capital (Sergiovanni, 1994).

For the typical superintendent, the negative aspects of current social conditions get expressed in several ways. These include but are not limited to intense philosophical and political disagreements, parental apathy, lack of community involvement and support, and a growing number of at-risk students (Glass et al., 2000). In the most divided communities, superintendents are increasingly facing divided school boards.

School Reform

Over the past few decades, citizens across the entire spectrum of political persuasions have criticized public education. Most Americans fortunately continue to believe that better schools result in a better society (Tyack & Cuban, 1995), but their values and preferences affecting school reform have been less than uniform. At one end of the spectrum are those who want schools to compensate for a variety of social ills such as poverty, abuse, and dysfunctional homes; they favor increased fiscal resources, even if more funding results in a further erosion of local control. At the other end are those who view schools as being inefficient and insufficiently attentive to academic standards; they favor creating competition through concepts such as vouchers, tax credits, and charter schools (Kowalski, 1999). Such ideological differences also exist within individual districts and have the potential of polarizing communities and school boards (Keedy & Bjork, 2002).

Since about 1990, the locus of school reform has shifted from state government to local districts. This transfer has been based on observations such as these:

1. Because of philosophical and political differences, a substantial portion of the population is likely to oppose any national and state-initiated reform (Kowalski, 2001).

2. Schools are more likely to change imposed reforms than imposed reforms are likely to change schools (Cuban, 1998).

3. Educators have tended to be indifferent toward or opposed to centralized mandates that are in conflict with their values and beliefs (Fullan & Stiegelbauer, 1991).

4. State-imposed reforms have often lacked clear objectives, were difficult to implement, and failed to achieve their goals (Madsen, 1994).

Consequently, most policymakers now accept the premise that school improvement is more feasible at the district and individual school levels. This strategic shift has made superintendents and school boards key school reform figures (Wirt & Kirst, 1997).

Many superintendents, however, are concerned that state deregulation and district decentralization have contributed to role conflict in two important ways. First, the public is being led to believe that administrators have considerable latitude to improve local schools when, in fact, state government is still highly influential in setting the reform agenda. Even as deregulation is being embraced, state legislatures are imposing higher accountability standards and setting the criteria for district evaluations. To the extent that both decentralization and evaluation involve the exercise of power, conflict between the two variables is inevitable (Weiler, 1990). Second, residents in local districts often express disparate expectations. They want visionary superintendents who can lead and be trusted while they seek superintendents who will listen to them and implement their agendas (Wirt & Kirst, 1997).

School Board Relationships

The topic of superintendent and school board relations arguably is not new. During the first half of the 20th century, problems in

this arena were often framed in terms of formal roles. That is, conflict often was observed between the policymaking role of school boards and the administrative role of superintendents (Kowalski, 1999). More recently, attention has shifted to issues such as political alignments, the use of power, and tensions between professionalism and democracy (Keedy & Bjork, 2002).

Scholars (e.g., Iannaccone & Lutz, 1970; McCarty & Ramsey, 1971) have long recognized a nexus between community power structures and school board power structures. As expected, districts with homogeneous populations have been less likely than districts with heterogeneous populations to be divided over issues such as political ideology and religious values. In the past, superintendents faced the basic question of whether to align themselves with a community's dominant power structure; today, they often face the difficult task of discerning how political power is divided within a community and how they might work effectively with all groups (Keedy & Bjork, 2002).

Arguably, superintendents and board members contribute to the tensions that surround their relationship. Many school administrators were socialized to accept bureaucratic and individualistic behaviors that inhibit them from maturing as collaborative leaders (Dunn, 2001). Often, "being in charge" remains more important than building and mobilizing support for a coherent reform plan. For these superintendents, deregulation and decentralization are threatening because legitimate authority is challenged.

Ideally, school board members are expected to be public trustees who should make objective policy decisions in the best interests of their entire communities. Yet, in reality, many of them function as political delegates, making both policy and administrative decisions on the basis of the narrower interests of their supporting political factions. Even when school board members acknowledge that their intended role is to develop policy, few are able to agree on the nature of policy. So, rather than setting a cogent and visionary policy agenda, they react to a constant stream of problems as if they were administrators (Shibles, Rallis, & Deck, 2001).

In summary, problems surrounding superintendent and school board relations are both constant and evolving. Although the two groups have never really accepted a clear separation of policymaking and administration, they must now deal with their differences in a more politically intense environment, one that often induces reaction rather than pro-action. In this context, superintendents receive mixed messages. They are told to be bold risk takers, but they remain fearful that they will not receive support and rewards from the school board if they are (Shibles et al., 2001).

AN AGENDA FOR FUTURE RESEARCH

Much has been written about the school district superintendent over the past 100 years. Nevertheless, many aspects of this pivotal position merit further study. This is true in large measure because practice in all administrative positions is influenced substantially by context, that is, the conditions under which a practitioner applies his or her knowledge. Issues affecting education are fluid, and consequently, the parameters of effective practice are not constant.

Role Expectations

As noted earlier, superintendents not only are expected to assume at least five distinct roles, they must know when to shift emphasis from one role to another. Relatively little is known about the variables that may be associated with a practitioner's ability to do this. Likewise, relationships between context and role spawn several critical questions. For example, are certain types of districts more likely to encourage or discourage specific

roles? To what extent do superintendents seek positions that match their strengths and weaknesses with respect to role expectations?

Academic preparation, professional experience, and licensing also offer fertile ground for role research. To what extent are practitioners being adequately prepared to assume each role? Does professional experience prior to entering the superintendency enhance role competency? To what extent are states emphasizing role expectations in their licensing standards?

Gender and Race

On reviewing the history and current status of women and persons of color in the superintendency, one question comes distinctly to the fore: Are there signs that the superintendency is becoming feminized? Does the history of women teachers (white and of color) provide us with a pattern of how disadvantaged groups infiltrate and later even dominate a profession? To begin a response, one can point out several similarities between women and teaching and women and the superintendency. First, teaching, in early stages of American history, was dominated by white men, and the superintendency is dominated by white men. Second, at one time women and persons of color, for various reasons, were thought to be inappropriate candidates for teaching positions. The same is true for the superintendency. Third, an increased demand for teachers occurred at the same time that white men were finding the role less desirable. In parallel fashion, recently there has been a focused concern about the dearth of superintendency candidates (see, e.g., Anthony et al., 2000; Houston, 1998; McAdams, 1998). At the same time, men indicate that the job has less or about the same status than it once did, while women and persons of color report that it has a greater amount of status (Glass et al., 2000). Women and persons of color have also noted a greater amount of self-fulfillment from the role than men (Glass et al., 2000).

Fourth, advocacy in the form of research and publications for women superintendents and superintendents of color now exists that did not exist as little as 15 years ago. Perhaps the recent, although not large, increase of women and persons of color in the superintendency has been the result of this literature and the need for qualified candidates. Fifth, research has pointed to the existence of feminine attributes (Brunner, 2000a, 2000b; Helgesen, 1990; Rosener, 1990; Sherman & Repa, 1994; Wesson & Grady, 1994, 1995), such as a predisposition toward collaborative work and a focus on instruction, at a time when men, by and large, in government continue to mandate collaborative decision-making. Sixth, women dominate educational administration programs currently, and persons of color, who were once denied an education, have unprecedented access.

As stated earlier, the feminization of teaching meant that the role was considered primarily women's work; it was a fairly low-status role, making it also open to persons of color in the South; and wages remained relatively low. Consider, then, that feminine attributes of leadership have become valuable, whether this means that the superintendency is women's work, that the status of the superintendency appears to be dropping, and that salaries for women (white and of color) superintendents are not much higher than salaries for women central office administrators (Brunner & Grogan, 2003), and whether this makes women and persons of color more attractive superintendency candidates.

These questions have yet to be answered. However, if the superintendency is becoming more feminized by virtue of the attributes that are necessary to perform the required work, then such jobs may become more broadly open to women and persons of color, just as teaching did.

Contemporary Issues

A host of political, economic, social, and professional issues are affecting school superintendents. Many are centered on long-standing concerns such as relationships with school board members and job security. The following topics are especially noteworthy with respect to contemporary problems:

- The effects of state deregulation and district decentralization on the superintendency
- Superintendent influence on school district performance
- Practice in districts experiencing high rates of leadership instability (e.g., large, urban districts)
- Best practices in school reform, visioning, and planning
- Building coalitions and partnerships for improving education

Studies in these and related areas would broaden the professional knowledge base and deepen perspectives about the contextual nature of contemporary practice.

NOTES

1. Hawaii has only one school system and the superintendent is appointed by the State Board of Education.

2. In some states, this position has a different title. The title "commissioner of education" is used in about one fourth of the states (e.g., Kentucky, Minnesota, New Jersey, New York); other states use titles such as *secretary of education* (Pennsylvania) and *director of education* (Iowa).

3. This power could be expressed through activities such as making employment decisions, awarding contracts, and doling out favors to segments of the community.

4. Several reasons for the decline of male teachers have been advanced by historians and others of the time: (a) low wages made the job unattractive to capable men, (b) the status of teaching was considered "belittling" to men because it was poor work (Bardeen, 1908; cited in Blount, 1998), (c) arguments that teaching was women's work made it less appealing, (d) men did not like working with women, and finally, (e) during the Civil War, thousands of men left teaching

to fight, and not many returned to the role after the war (Blount, 1998).

5. Portions of this section were taken from C. C. Brunner, 2000, "Unsettled Moments in Settled Discourse: Women Superintendents' Experiences of Inequality. *Educational Administration Quarterly, 36*(1), 76–116.

REFERENCES

Adler, S., Laney, J., & Packer, M. (1993). *Managing women: Feminism and power in educational management*. Philadelphia: Open University Press.

Alston, J. A. (1999). Climbing hills and mountains: Black females making it to the superintendency. In C. C. Brunner (Ed.), *Sacred dreams: Women and the superintendency* (pp. 79–90). Albany: SUNY Press.

Anthony, R., Roe, J., & Young, M. D. (2000). *Selecting new administrators for tomorrow's administration*. Iowa City, IA: Educational Placement Consortium.

Arnez, N. (1982). Selected black female superintendents of public school systems. *Journal of Negro Education, 51*(3), 309–317.

Axley, S. R. (1996). *Communication at work: Management and the communication-intensive organization*. Westport, CT: Quorum Books.

Banks, C. M. (1995). Gender and race as factors in educational leadership and administration. In J. A. Banks & C. A. McGee Banks (Eds.), *Handbook of research on multicultural education* (pp. 65–80). New York: Macmillan.

Bardeen, C. W. (1908, April). Why teaching repels men. *Educational Review, 35*, 351.

Bauman, P. C. (1996). *Governing education: Public sector reform or privatization*. Boston: Allyn & Bacon.

Beekley, C. (1999). Dancing in red shoes: Why women leave the superintendency. In C. C. Brunner (Ed.), *Sacred dreams: Women and the superintendency* (pp. 161–176). Albany: SUNY Press.

Bell, C. (1988). Organizational influences on women's experience in the superintendency. *Peabody Journal of Education, 65*(4), 31–59.

Bell, C. S. (1995). "If I weren't involved in schools, I might be radical": Gender consciousness in context. In D. Dunlap & P. Schmuck (Eds.), *Women leading in education* (pp. 288–312). Albany: SUNY Press.

Bell, C. S., & Chase, S. E. (1993). The underrepresentation of women in school leadership. In C. Marshall (Ed.), *The new politics of race and gender: Yearbook of the Politics of Education Association* (pp. 141–154). Washington, DC: Falmer Press.

Bell, C. S., & Chase, S. E. (1995). Gender in the theory and practice of educational leadership. *Journal for a Just and Caring Education, 1*(2), 200–222.

Bell, C. S., & Chase, S. E. (1996). The gendered character of women superintendents' professional relationships. In K. Arnold, K. Noble, & R. Subotnick (Eds.), *Remarkable women: Perspectives on female talent development* (pp. 117–131). Cresskill, NJ: Hampton Press.

Björk, L. (2001). Institutional barriers to educational reform: A superintendent's role in district decentralization. In C. Brunner & L. Björk (Eds.), *The new superintendency* (pp. 205–228). Oxford, UK: JAI, Elsevier Science.

Björk, L., & Gurley, D. K. (2003, April). *Superintendent as educational statesman*. Paper presented at the Annual Meeting of the American Educational Research Association, Chicago.

Björk, L., & Lindle, J. C. (2001). Superintendents and interest groups. *Educational Policy, 15*(1), 76–91.

Blase, J., & Anderson, G. (1995). *The micropolitics of educational leadership: From control to empowerment*. New York: Teachers College Press.

Blount, J. (1998). *Destined to rule the schools: Women and the superintendency, 1873–1995*. Albany: SUNY Press.

Brown v. Board of Education, 347 U.S. 483 (1954).

Brunner, C. C. (1997). Working through the riddle of the heart: Perspectives of women superintendents. *Journal of School Leadership, 7*(1), 138–164.

Brunner, C. C. (1998a). Can power support an "ethic of care?" An examination of the professional practices of women superintendents. *Journal for a Just and Caring Education, 4*(2), 142–175.

Brunner, C. C. (1998b). Women superintendents: Strategies for success. *Journal of Educational Administration, 36*(2), 160–182.

Brunner, C. C. (1999a). "Back talk" from a woman superintendent: Just how useful is research? In C. C. Brunner (Ed.), *Sacred dreams: Women and the superintendency* (pp. 179–198). Albany: SUNY Press.

Brunner, C. C. (1999b). Power, gender, and superintendent selection. In C. C. Brunner (Ed.), *Sacred dreams: Women and the superintendency* (pp. 63–78). Albany: SUNY Press.

Brunner, C. C. (1999c). Taking risks: A requirement of the new superintendency. *The Journal of School Leadership, 9*(4), 290–310.

Brunner, C. C. (2000a). *Principles of power: Women superintendents and the riddle of the heart.* Albany: SUNY Press.

Brunner, C. C. (2000b). Unsettled moments in settled discourse: Women superintendents' experiences of inequality. *Educational Administration Quarterly, 36*(1), 76–116.

Brunner, C. C. (2003). Invisible, limited, and emerging discourse: Research practices that restrict and/or increase access for women and people of color to the superintendency. *Journal of School Leadership, 13,* 428–450.

Brunner, C. C., & Grogan, M. (2003, April). *The American Association of School Administrators' study of women superintendents and central office administrators.* Paper presented at the Annual Meeting of the American Educational Research Association, Chicago.

Brunner, C. C., Grogan, M., & Björk, L. (2002). Shifts in the discourse defining the superintendency: Historical and current foundations of the position. In J. Murphy (Ed.), *The educational leadership challenge: Redefining leadership for the 21st century* (pp. 211–238). Chicago: University of Chicago Press.

Brunner, C. C., & Peyton-Caire, L. (2000). Seeking representation: Supporting black women graduate students who aspire to the superintendency. *Urban Education, 35*(5), 532–548.

Brunner, C. C., & Schumaker, P. (1998). Power and gender in "New View" public schools. *Policy Studies Journal, 26*(1), 30–45.

Burroughs, W. A. (1974). *Cities and schools in the gilded age.* Port Washington, NY: Kennikat.

Butts, R. F., & Cremin, L. A. (1953). *A history of education in American culture.* New York: Henry Holt.

Callahan, R. E. (1962). *Education and the cult of efficiency: A study of the social forces that have shaped the administration of public schools.* Chicago: University of Chicago Press.

Callahan, R. E. (1966). *The superintendent of schools: A historical analysis.* (ERIC Document Reproduction Service No. ED 0104 410)

Campbell, R. F., Cunningham, L. L., Nystrand, R. O., & Usdan, M. D. (1990). *The organization and control of American schools* (6th ed.). Englewood Cliffs, NJ: Prentice Hall.

Carlson, R. V. (1996). *Reframing and reform: Perspectives on organization, leadership, and school change.* New York: Longman.

Carter, G. R., & Cunningham, W. G. (1997). *The American school superintendent: Leading in an age of pressures.* San Francisco: Jossey-Bass.

Chance, P. L., & Björk, L. G. (2004). The social dimensions of public relations. In T. J. Kowalski (Ed.), *Public relations in schools* (3rd ed., pp. 125–148). Upper Saddle River, NJ: Merrill, Prentice Hall.

Chase, S. (1995). *Ambiguous empowerment: The work narratives of women school superintendents.* Amherst: University of Massachusetts Press.

Chase, S., & Bell, C. (1990). Ideology, discourse, and gender: How gatekeepers talk about women school superintendents. *Social Problems, 37*(2), 163–177.

Conrad, C. (1994). *Strategic organizational communication: Toward the twenty-first century* (3rd ed.). Fort Worth, TX: Harcourt Brace College.

Cooper, B. S., & Boyd, W. L. (1987). The evolution of training for school administrators. In J. Murphy & P. Hallinger (Eds.), *Approaches to administrative training in education* (pp. 3–27). Albany: SUNY Press.

Crampton, F., & Whitney, T. (1996). *The search for equity in school funding* (NCSL Education Partners Project). Denver, CO: National Conference of State Legislatures.

Cronin, J. M. (1973). *The control of urban schools: Perspective on the power of educational reformers.* New York: Free Press.

Crowson, R. L., & McPherson, R. B. (1987). The legacy of the theory movement: Learning from the new tradition. In J. Murphy & P. Hallinger (Eds.), *Approaches to administrative training in education* (pp. 45–64). Albany: SUNY Press.

Cuban, L. (1976). *The urban school superintendent: A century and a half of change.* Bloomington, IN: Phi Delta Kappa Educational Foundation.

Cuban, L. (1988). *The managerial imperative and the practice of leadership in the schools.* Albany: SUNY Press.

Cuban, L. (1998). How schools change reforms: Redefining reform success and failure. *Teachers College Record, 99*(3), 453–477.

Culbertson, J. A. (1981). Antecedents of the theory movement. *Educational Administration Quarterly, 17*(1), 25–47.

Cunningham, L., & Hentges, J. (1982). *The American school superintendency 1982: A summary report.* Arlington, VA: American Association of School Administrators.

Dunlap, D., & Schmuck, P. (Eds.). (1995). *Women leading in education.* Albany: SUNY Press.

Dunn, R. J. (2001). Community and control in the superintendency. In C. C. Brunner & L. G. Björk (Eds.), *The new superintendency: Advances in research and theories in school management and educational policy* (Vol. 6, pp. 153–168). Oxford, UK: JAI Press.

Eaton, W. E. (1990). The vulnerability of school superintendents: The thesis reexamined. In W. E. Eaton (Ed.), *Shaping the superintendency: A reexamination of Callahan and the cult of efficiency* (pp. 11–35). New York: Teachers College Press.

Enomoto, E. K., Gardiner, M. E., & Grogan, M. (2000). Notes to Athene: Mentoring relationships for women of color. *Urban Education, 35*(5), 567–583.

Fowler, F. C. (2004). *Policy studies for educational leaders: An introduction* (2nd ed.). Upper Saddle River, NJ: Merrill, Prentice Hall.

Fullan, M. G., & Stiegelbauer, S. (1991). *The new meaning of educational change* (2nd ed.). New York: Teachers College Press.

Gardiner, M., Enomoto, E., & Grogan, M. (2000). *Coloring outside the lines: Mentoring women into school leadership.* Albany: SUNY Press.

Getzels, J. W. (1977). Educational administration twenty years later, 1954–1974. In L. Cunningham, W. Hack, & R. Nystrand (Eds.), *Educational administration: The developing decades* (pp. 3–24). Berkeley, CA: McCutchan.

Gideon, B. H. (2002). Structuring schools for teacher collaboration. *Education Digest, 68*(2), 30–34.

Glass, T. E. (1992). *The study of the American school superintendency 1992: America's education leaders in a time of reform.* Arlington, VA: American Association of School Administrators.

Glass, T. E. (2003, April). *The superintendency: A managerial imperative?* Paper presented at the Annual Meeting of the American Educational Research Association, Chicago.

Glass, T. E. (2004). Changes in society and schools. In T. J. Kowalski, (Ed.), *Public relations in schools* (3rd ed., pp. 30–46). Upper Saddle River, NJ: Merrill, Prentice Hall.

Glass, T. E., Björk, L. G., & Brunner, C. C. (2000). *The study of the American school superintendent: A look at the superintendent of education in the new millennium.* Arlington, VA: American Association of School Administrators.

Gleaves-Hirsch, M. (1997, September 28). Council takes on racism. *Syracuse Herald American,* pp. B1, B7.

Grady, M., Ourada-Sieb, T., & Wesson, L. (1994). Women's perceptions of the superintendency. *Journal of School Leadership, 4*(2), 156–170.

Gribskov, M. (1980). Feminism and the woman school administrator. In D. K. Biklen & M. B. Brannigan (Eds.), *Women and educational leadership* (pp. 77–91). Lexington, MA: D. C. Heath.

Grieder, C., Pierce, T. M., & Jordan, K. F. (1969). *Public school administration* (3rd ed.). New York: Ronald Press.

Grogan, M. (1996). *Voices of women aspiring to the superintendency.* Albany: SUNY Press.

Grogan, M. (1999). A feminist poststructuralist account of collaboration: A model for the superintendency. In C. C. Brunner (Ed.), *Sacred dreams: Women and the superintendency* (pp. 199–216). Albany: SUNY Press.

Grogan, M., & Henry, M. (1995). Women candidates for the superintendency: Board perspectives. In B. Irby & G. Brown (Eds.), *Women as school executives: Voices and visions* (pp. 164–174). Austin: Texas Council for Women School Executives.

Hansot, E., & Tyack, D. (1981, May). *The dream deferred: A golden age for women school administrators* (Policy Paper No. 81-C2). Palo Alto, CA: Stanford University Institute for Research on Educational Finance and Governance.

Heckman, P. E. (1993). School restructuring in practice: Reckoning with the culture of school. *International Journal of Educational Reform, 2*(3), 263–272.

Helgesen, S. (1990). *The female advantage: Women's ways of leadership.* Garden City, NY: Doubleday.

Henkin, A. B. (1993). Social skills of superintendents: A leadership requisite in restructured schools. *Educational Research Quarterly, 16*(4), 15–30.

Hodgkinson, H., & Montenegro, X. (1999). *The U.S. school superintendent: The invisible CEO.* Washington, DC: Institute for Educational Leadership.

Houston, P. (1998). The ABCs of administrative shortages. *Education Week, 17*(38), 32–44.

Howlett, P. (1993). The politics of school leaders, past and future. *Education Digest, 58*(9), 18–21.

Iannaccone, L., & Lutz, F. W. (1970). *Politics, power, and policy.* Columbus, OH: Merrill.

Jackson, B. L. (1995). *Balancing act: The political role of the urban school superintendent.* Washington, DC: Joint Center for Political and Economic Studies.

Jackson, B. L. (1999). Getting inside history—against all odds: African American women school superintendents. In C. C. Brunner (Ed.), *Sacred dreams: Women and the superintendency* (pp. 179–198). Albany: SUNY Press.

Johnson, B. C., & Fusarelli, L. D. (2003, April). *Superintendent as social scientist.* Paper presented at the Annual Meeting of the American Educational Research Association, Chicago.

Kamler, E., & Shakeshaft, C. (1999). The role of the search consultant in the career paths of female superintendents. In C. C. Brunner (Ed.), *Sacred dreams: Women and the superintendency* (pp. 179–198). Albany: SUNY Press.

Keedy, J. L., & Bjork, L. G. (2002). Superintendents and local boards and the potential for community polarization: The call for use of political strategist skills. In B. Cooper & L. Fusarelli (Eds.), *The promises and perils facing today's school superintendent* (pp. 103–128). Lanham, MD: Scarecrow Education.

King, R. A., Swanson, A. D., & Sweetland, S. (2003). *School finance: Achieving high standards with equity and efficiency* (3rd ed.). Boston: Allyn & Bacon.

Knezevich, S. J. (1971). *The American school superintendent.* Arlington, VA: American Association of School Administrators.

Knezevich, S. J. (1984). *Administration of public education: A sourcebook for the leadership and management of educational institutions* (4th ed.). New York: Harper & Row.

Kowalski, T. J. (1995). *Keepers of the flame: Contemporary urban superintendents.* Thousand Oaks, CA: Corwin.

Kowalski, T. J. (1998). The role of communication in providing leadership for school reform. *Mid-Western Educational Researcher, 11*(1), 32–40.

Kowalski, T. J. (1999). *The school superintendent: Theory, practice, and cases.* Upper Saddle River, NJ: Merrill, Prentice Hall.

Kowalski, T. J. (2000). Cultural change paradigms and administrator communication. *Contemporary Education, 71*(2), 5–10.

Kowalski, T. J. (2001). The future of local school governance: Implications for board members and superintendents. In C. Brunner & L. Bjòrk (Eds.), *The new superintendency* (pp. 183–201). Oxford, UK: JAI, Elsevier Science.

Kowalski, T. J. (2003a). *Contemporary school administration* (2nd ed.). Boston: Allyn & Bacon.

Kowalski, T. J. (2003b, April). *The superintendent as communicator.* Paper presented at the Annual Meeting of the American Educational Research Association, Chicago.

Kowalski, T. J. (2004). Contemporary conditions. In T. J. Kowalski (Ed.), *Public relations in schools* (3rd ed., pp. 3–29). Upper Saddle River, NJ: Merrill, Prentice Hall.

Leithwood, K., Jantzi, D., & Fernandez, A. (1994). Transformational leadership and teachers' commitment to change. In J. Murphy & K. S. Louis (Eds.), *Reshaping the principalship* (pp. 77–98). Thousand Oaks, CA: Corwin.

Lomotey, K., Allen, K., Mark, D., & Rivers, S. (1996, April). *Research on African American educational leaders: The state of the art.* Paper presented at the Annual Meeting of the American Educational Research Association, New York.

Madsen, J. (1994). *Educational reform at the state level: The politics and problems of implementation.* Bristol, PA: Falmer Press.

Maienza, J. (1986). The superintendency: Characteristics of access for men and women. *Educational Administration Quarterly, 22*(4), 59–79.

Marietti, M., & Stout, R. (1994). School boards that hire female superintendents. *Urban Education, 8*(4), 4–11.

McAdams, R. (1998). Who'll run the schools? The coming administrator shortage. *American School Board Journal, 185*(8), 37–39.

McCarty, D., & Ramsey, C. (1971). *The school managers: Power and conflict in American public education.* Westport, CT: Greenwood Press.

Melby, E. O. (1955). *Administering community education.* Englewood Cliffs, NJ: Prentice Hall.

Mendez-Morse, S. E. (1999). Redefinition of self: Mexican American women becoming superintendents. In C. C. Brunner (Ed.), *Sacred dreams: Women and the superintendency* (pp. 179–198). Albany: SUNY Press.

Mendez-Morse, S. E. (2000). Claiming forgotten leadership. *Urban Education, 35*(5), 584–595.

Montenegro, X. (1993). *Women and racial minority representation in school administration.* Arlington, VA: American Association of School Administrators.

Murphy, J. (1991). *Restructuring schools.* New York: Teachers College Press.

Murphy, J. (1994). The changing role of the superintendency in restructuring districts in Kentucky. *School Effectiveness and School Improvement, 5*(4), 349–375.

Murtadha-Watts, K. (2000). Cleaning up and maintenance in the wake of an urban school administration tempest. *Urban Education, 35*(5), 603–615.

Ortiz, F. I. (1982). *Career patterns in education: Women, men, and minorities in educational administration.* New York: Praeger.

Ortiz, F. I. (1991). An Hispanic female superintendent's leadership and school district culture. In N. Wyner (Ed.), *Current perspectives on the culture of school* (pp. 29–43). Cambridge, MA: Brookline Books.

Ortiz, F. I. (1999). Seeking and selecting Hispanic female superintendents. In C. C. Brunner (Ed.), *Sacred dreams: Women and the superintendency* (pp. 179–198). Albany: SUNY Press.

Ortiz, F. I. (2000). Who controls succession in the superintendency: A minority perspective. *Urban Education, 35*(5), 584–595.

Ortiz, F. I., & Marshall, C. (1988). Women in educational administration. In N. Boyan (Ed.), *Handbook of research on educational administration* (pp. 123–141). New York: Longman.

Ortiz, F. I., & Ortiz, D. J. (1993). Politicizing executive action: The case of Hispanic female superintendents. In C. Marshall (Ed.), *The new politics of race and gender: Yearbook of the Politics of Education Association* (pp. 155–167). Washington, DC: Falmer.

Ortiz, F. I., & Ortiz, D. J. (1995). How gender and ethnicity interact in the practice of educational administration: The case of Hispanic female superintendents. In R. Donmoyer, M. Imber, & J. Scheurich (Eds.), *The knowledge base in educational administration: Multiple perspectives* (pp. 158–173). Albany: SUNY Press.

Pavan, B. N. (1999). The first years: What should a female superintendent know beforehand? In C. C. Brunner (Ed.), *Sacred dreams: Women and the superintendency* (pp. 105–124). Albany: SUNY Press.

Perina, K. (2002). When CEOs self-destruct. *Psychology Today, 35*(5), 16.

Petersen, G. J., & Barnett, B. G. (2003, April). *The superintendent as instructional leader: History, evolution, and future of the role.* Paper presented at the Annual Meeting of the American Educational Research Association, Chicago.

Pitner, N. (1981). Hormones and harems: Are the activities of superintending different for a woman? In P. Schmuck, W. Charters, & R. Carlson (Eds.), *Educational policy and management: Sex differentials* (pp. 273–295). New York: Academic Press.

Reid, R. L. (Ed.). (1982). *Battleground: The autobiography of Margaret A. Haley.* Urbana: University of Illinois Press.

Revere, A. B. (1985). *A description of black female school superintendents.* Unpublished dissertation, Miami University of Ohio.

Rosener, J. (1990). Ways women lead. *Harvard Business Review, 68*(6), 119–125.

Sarason, S. B. (1996). *Revisiting the culture of the school and the problem of change.* New York: Teachers College Press.

Schein, E. H. (1996). Culture: The missing concept in organization studies. *Administrative Science Quarterly, 41*(2), 229–240.

Scherr, M. (1995). The glass ceiling reconsidered: View from below. In D. Dunlap & P. Schmuck (Eds.), *Women leading in education* (pp. 313–326). Albany: SUNY Press.

Schlechty, P. C. (1997). *Inventing better schools.* San Francisco: Jossey-Bass.

Schmuck, P. (1975). *Sex differentiation in public school administration.* Arlington, VA: American Association of School Administrators.

Sergiovanni, T. J. (1994). *Building community in schools.* San Francisco: Jossey-Bass.

Shakeshaft, C. (1989). *Women in educational administration.* Newbury Park, CA: Sage.

Shakeshaft, C. (1999). The struggle to create a more gender-inclusive profession. In J. Murphy & K. Seashore Louis (Eds.), *Handbook of research on educational administration* (2nd ed., pp. 99–118). San Francisco: Jossey-Bass.

Sherman, D., & Repa, T. (1994). Women at the top: The experiences of two superintendents. *Equity and Choice, 10*(2), 59–64.

Shibles, M. R., Rallis, S. F., & Deck, L. L. (2001). The new political balance between superintendent and board: Clarifying purpose and generating knowledge. In C. C. Brunner & L. G. Björk (Eds.), *The new superintendency: Advances in research and theories in school management and educational policy* (Vol. 6, pp. 169–182). Oxford, UK: JAI Press.

Sielke, C. C. (1998). Michigan school facilities, equity issues, and voter response to bond issues following finance reform. *Journal of Education Finance, 23,* 309–322.

Sizemore, B. (1986). The limits of the black superintendency: A review of the literature. *Journal of Educational Equity and Leadership, 6*(3), 180–208.

Skrla, L., Reyes, P., & Scheurich, J. (2000). Sexism, silence, and solutions: Female superintendents speak up and speak out. *Educational Administration Quarterly, 36*(1), 19–43.

Spring, J. H. (1994). *The American school, 1642–1993* (3rd ed.). New York: McGraw-Hill.

Streitmatter, J. (1994). *Toward gender equity in the classroom: Everyday teachers' beliefs and practices.* Albany: SUNY Press.

Tallerico, M. (1999). Women and the superintendency: What do we really know? In C. C. Brunner (Ed.), *Sacred dreams: Women and the superintendency* (pp. 29–48). Albany: SUNY Press.

Tallerico, M. (2000a). *Accessing the superintendency: The unwritten rules.* Thousand Oaks, CA: Corwin.

Tallerico, M. (2000b). Gaining access to the superintendency: Headhunting, gender, and color. *Educational Administration Quarterly, 36*(1), 18–43.

Tallerico, M., & Burstyn, J. N. (1996). Retaining women in the superintendency: The location matters. *Educational Administration Quarterly, 32,* 642–664.

Tallerico, M., Burstyn, J. N., & Poole, W. (1993). *Gender and politics at work: Why women exit the superintendency.* Fairfax, VA: National Policy Board for Educational Administration.

Thomas, W. B., & Moran, K. J. (1992). Reconsidering the power of the superintendent in the progressive period. *American Educational Research Journal, 29*(1), 22–50.

Thompson, D. C., Honeyman, D. S., & Stewart, G. K. (1988, September). *Achievement of equity in capital outlay funding for Kansas schools: A policy critique.* Paper presented at the National Rural Education Research Forum, Bismarck, North Dakota.

Trimble, K. (1996). Building a learning community. *Equity and Excellence in Education, 29*(1), 37–40.

Tyack, D. (1974). *One best system: A history of American urban education.* Cambridge, MA: Harvard University Press.

Tyack, D., & Cuban, L. (1995). *Tinkering toward utopia: A century of public school reform.* Cambridge, MA: Harvard University Press.

Tyack, D., & Hansot, E. (1982). *Managers of virtue: Public school leadership in America, 1820–1980.* New York: Basic Books.

Van Til, W. (1971). Prologue: Is progressive education obsolete? In W. Van Til (Ed.), *Curriculum: Quest for relevance* (pp. 9–17). Boston: Houghton-Mifflin.

Waller, W. (1932). *The sociology of teaching.* New York: John Wiley.

Weiler, H. N. (1990). Comparative perspectives on educational decentralization: An exercise in contradiction? *Educational Evaluation and Policy Analysis, 12*(4), 433–448.

Wert-Gray, S., Center, C., Brashers, D. E., & Meyers, R. A. (1991). Research topics and methodological orientations in organizational communication: A decade of review. *Communication Studies, 42*(2), 141–154.

Wesson, L., & Grady, M. (1994). An analysis of women urban superintendents: A national study. *Urban Education, 8*(4), 412–424.

Wesson, L., & Grady, M. (1995). A leadership perspective from women superintendents. In B. Irby & G. Brown (Eds.), *Women as school executives: Voices and visions* (pp. 35–41). Austin: Texas Council for Women School Executives.

Wirt, F. M., & Kirst, M. W. (1997). *The political dynamics of American education.* Berkeley, CA: McCutchan.

8

The Role of Education Law in Leadership Preparation Programs

CHARLES J. RUSSO
University of Dayton

INTRODUCTION AND OVERVIEW

Fifty years ago, the U.S. Supreme Court handed down *Brown v. Board of Education* (1954; *Brown I*),[1] undoubtedly the most important education-related decision in the nation's history and perhaps its most important judgment ever. With *Brown I* providing a major impetus, over the past half century, the nation has undergone a myriad of educational, legal, and social transformations. In striking down racial segregation in public schools, *Brown I* not only ushered in an era of equal educational opportunities for all children but, in a very real sense, also signaled the birth of the field known as education law or school law.

Prior to *Brown I*, the Court addressed only a handful of education-related cases, all of which concerned some aspect of religion. Yet, now hardly a year passes when the Court does not decide at least one case that originated with a dispute in the schools. In fact, since 1947, the Court has resolved more than 30 cases in each of the two controversial areas of school desegregation and religion alone.

In light of the significance that education law has assumed in the daily activities of educational leaders, this chapter reviews three major areas that are, or should be, important for preparation programs and practitioners focusing on issues affecting elementary and secondary education. The article begins with a reflection on the centrality of education law in educational leadership preparation programs and practice before examining key Supreme Court cases and federal legislation with regard to schooling. Furthermore, the chapter focuses on developments at the federal level in light of the fact that they provide a much broader basis for legal issues that impact on preparation programs and the practice of educational administration than do developments at the state level.

THE CENTRALITY OF EDUCATION LAW IN EDUCATIONAL LEADERSHIP

The centrality of education law in educational leadership is reflected in a comprehensive study conducted on behalf of the University

168

Council for Educational Administration (UCEA). The survey revealed that 87.5% of UCEA's members offering courses in education law (Pohland & Carlson, 1993), making it the second most commonly taught subject in leadership programs. In addition, because many universities offer a variety of graduate and undergraduate classes in education law (Gullatt & Tollett, 1997), it is likely to remain a crucial element in curricula, clearly indicating that as an applied rather than purely theoretical discipline, it is essential for educators at all levels.

From the perspective of those who are deeply committed to the study of education law, the UCEA study and other indicators support the proposition that specialists in education law must help clarify the law so that it remains such a valuable tool. Faculty members who specialize in education law can help to preserve the importance of education law by teaching students to focus on such basic concepts as due process and equal protection, essential elements in the development of sound policies and best practices. In other words, as important as abstract legal principles or theories are, faculty members who teach education law must concentrate on ways to help practitioners apply these concepts broadly rather than having them memorize case holdings apart from their application in day-to-day, real-life situations. Faculty members who fail to present the law as a practical discipline deny its real meaning in the daily professional activities of educational practitioners.

Education law presents a unique intellectual challenge and a strategy for preparing educational practitioners, whether board members, superintendents, principals, teachers, or other personnel such as counselors, to be more proactive. Working in a discipline that tends to be reactive, faculty members teaching education law need to present their subject matter as a tool that should be applied in advance to help ensure that school officials meet the needs of all of their constituents, ranging from students and parents to faculty, staff, and the local community. Yet, the goal of making the law proactive becomes complicated because most changes generated by education law indeed prove to be reactive to this extent: The status of the law is typically modified only after a real case or controversy has been litigated or a legislative body has responded to a need that had yet to be addressed or resolved. To this end, *Brown I* is a typical example of how the law can be seen as reactive insofar as there would not have been a need for *Brown I* if the schools in Topeka, Kansas, and elsewhere had been meeting the needs of African American students.

Along with balancing the tension present between the proactive and reactive dimensions of education law, law classes in educational leadership programs should not become "Law School 101." Rather than trying to turn educators into lawyers equipped to deal with such technical and procedural matters as jurisdiction, statutes of limitation, and the service of process, courses in education law should provide a broad understanding of the law that will allow practitioners to accomplish two important goals.

First, classes in education law should provide educators with enough awareness of the legal dimensions of a situation that they can better frame questions for their attorneys to answer, performing a kind of triage to limit problems when a legal controversy arises. To this end, educators must be taught to recognize the great value in making their attorneys equal partners not only in problem solving after the fact, but also in developing responsive, proactive policies before difficulties can arise. Such a proactive approach is consistent with the notion of preventative law, wherein knowledgeable educators can identify potential problems in advance and, in concert with an attorney, can work to ensure problems do not develop into crises. Moreover, when educational leaders select attorneys for their boards, for example, they would be well advised to hire individuals with specialized practices in education law, thereby avoiding potential gaps in critical knowledge and ensuring that their legal advice includes the most up-to-date perspectives on legal matters.

Second, classes in education law must teach educators how to rely on their substantive knowledge of the law and where to look to update their sources of information through professional organizations such as the Education Law Association, so they can develop sound policies to enhance the day-to-day operations of schools. Education law is a dynamic, intellectually stimulating discipline that is constantly evolving to meet the needs of educational leaders as they direct the daily activities in schools. The merits of the decisions aside, and the impact that they are likely to have on educational leaders aside, one has only to read recent Supreme Court opinions in such areas as sexual harassment, religion, and special education, among others, all of which are discussed below, to recognize how important it is to keep abreast of legal changes. In light of these cases, educators are charged with the task of developing and implementing policies that will enhance the school environment for students, faculty, and staff.

In sum, perhaps the only constant in education law is that as it is ever evolving to meet the demands of a constantly changing world, it is likely to remain of utmost importance for all of those who are interested in schooling. In fact, the seemingly endless supply of new statutes, regulations, and cases speaks of the need to be ever vigilant regarding how legal developments impact the law. The challenge for all educators, then, is to harness their knowledge of this ever-growing field so that we can make the schools better places for all of our children. With this in mind, the next section of this chapter reviews landmark cases in education law that have helped to shape the practice of educational leadership.

KEY SUPREME COURT CASES IN EDUCATION LAW

Rather than focus on a "top 10" compilation of Supreme Court cases (see Russo, Underwood, & Cambron-McCabe, 2000), this section focuses on areas often reviewed by the Court, identifying the leading cases in each. Such a compilation highlights the key role that the Supreme Court has played in shaping American education and policy throughout the 20th century. Overall, the Supreme Court has left few aspects of public education untouched. In highlighting landmark cases, it is important to note that education law as a separate legal specialty did not truly develop until the mid 1950s after the Supreme Court's monumental decision in *Brown v. Board of Education (Brown I)* (1955).

Equal Educational Opportunities

Race and Ethnicity

Brown v. Board of Education's (1954) significance lies not only in its having addressed race but also in its having opened the door for later developments in the areas of civil rights and equal educational opportunities, culminating specifically with special education and gender equity. In *Brown I,* the Court ruled that de jure segregation in public schools on the basis of race deprived minority children of equal educational opportunities, in violation of the equal protection clause of the Fourteenth Amendment. A year later, in *Brown v. Board of Education (Brown II)* (1955), the Court began dismantling segregated school systems.

In *Brown I*, the Supreme Court unanimously struck down de jure segregation in public schools on May 17, 1954. As a prelude to its ruling, the Court noted that "education is perhaps the most important function of state and local governments" (p. 493). The Court next framed the issue in the form of the question: "Does segregation of children in public schools solely on the basis of race, even though the physical facilities and other 'tangible' factors may be equal, deprive the children of the minority group of equal educational opportunities?" The Court succinctly answered, "We believe that it does" (p. 493).

For the first time in its history, the Court relied on social sciences data in considering the harmful effects of racial segregation and reaching its judgment. Although stopping short of an outright reversal of *Plessy v. Ferguson* (1896), the Court unequivocally repudiated the "separate but equal" doctrine espoused in that earlier ruling, a case involving public railway accommodations, holding "that in the field of public education the doctrine of 'separate but equal' has no place. Separate educational facilities are inherently unequal" (p. 495).

As important as *Brown I* was, it did not address remedies. Rather, the Court ordered further arguments to consider relief. While the Court intended *Brown II* to lead "with all deliberate speed" (p. 301) to the racially nondiscriminatory admission of African Americans to formerly segregated public schools, it neither mandated an immediate end to school segregation nor set a timetable for its elimination. However, the Court did offer general guidance to the lower courts, directing them to fashion their decrees on equitable principles characterized by flexibility. Aware of the far-reaching impact of its decision, involving such matters as administration, school transportation, personnel, admissions policies, and changes in local laws, the Court reasoned that once progress was under way, the lower courts could grant more time to implement its ruling.

In *Bolling v. Sharpe* (1954), decided on the same day as *Brown I*, the Court unanimously struck down the law calling for school segregation in the District of Columbia. The difference between the cases was that since the equal protection clause of the Fourteenth Amendment applies only to the states, the Court based its judgment in *Bolling* on the due process clause of the Fifth Amendment.

Over the ensuing 50 years, the Court has handed down decisions in a wide array of areas dealing with desegregation (Russo, Harris, & Sandidge, 1994). Among its actions, the Court permitted bussing to achieve integration (*Swann v. Charlotte-Mecklenburg Board of Education,* 1971) and addressed the status of Mexican Americans (*Keyes v. School District No. 1, Denver, Colorado,* 1973). More recently, the Court reflected its lack of interest in desegregation by holding that desegregation orders are not meant to operate in perpetuity, and the judiciary had to consider whether a board acted in good faith in doing all that it could to eliminate the vestiges of past discrimination (*Board of Education of Oklahoma City Public Schools v. Dowell,* 1991). The Court also found that judicial supervision of a desegregation order can be achieved incrementally (*Freeman v. Pitts,* 1992).

On the related matter of ethnicity, in *Plyler v. Doe* (1982), the Court held that under the equal protection clause, Texas could not deny a free public school education to undocumented school-age children whose parents were from Mexico. In so doing, the Court struck down a statute that would have deprived local boards of state funds for the education of children who were not legally admitted to the United States and that authorized officials to refuse to enroll such students. In declaring that equal protection applies to children, the Court wrote that the constitutionality of the classification depended on whether it could be viewed as fairly furthering a substantial state interest. According to the Court, the uniqueness of education distinguishes it from general forms of social welfare, thereby triggering a demand that the state offer a more substantial justification than the usual rational relationship test if it wants to withhold education. The Court concluded that Texas failed to meet this test in the reasons given for its statute and that although the children were innocent of the conduct of their parents, the law's impact severely punished them while they were in the United States.

A year later, in a second case from Texas, *Martinez v. Bynum* (1983), the Court rejected a challenge to the constitutionality of a residency requirement that denied tuition-free admission to public schools to minors who lived apart from their parents if they were in the districts primarily to obtain free education. In affirming that the statute violated neither the Fourteenth Amendment nor interfered with the right of interstate travel, the Court declared that "a bona fide residence requirement, appropriately defined and uniformly applied, furthers the substantial state interest in assuring that services provided for its residents are enjoyed only by residents" (p. 328).

Special Education

Board of Education of the Hendrick Hudson Central School District v. Rowley (1982) was the first Supreme Court case involving special education. In *Rowley*, parents of a kindergarten student in New York who was hearing impaired challenged their school board's refusal to provide their daughter with a sign-language interpreter. The Court, recognizing that the child achieved passing marks and advanced academically without the sign-language interpreter, reversed earlier rulings in favor of the parents. In effect, the Court interpreted the Education for All Handicapped Children Act (EAHCA), now the Individuals with Disabilities Education Act (IDEA), as providing a floor on opportunities rather than a vehicle to maximize a child's potential. An appropriate education was one that met the IDEA's procedures, the Court ruled, and was "sufficient to confer some educational benefit" (p. 200) on the child. Insofar as the Court was convinced that the child received "some educational benefit" without the sign-language interpreter, the Court maintained that she was not entitled to one, even though she might have achieved at a higher level had officials provided her with such assistance.

In its only case on discipline and special education, *Honig v. Doe* (1988), a dispute from California, the Court addressed two major issues. First, the Court affirmed that the case was moot with regard to one of the two students because he was already over the age of 21. Second, in refusing to write in a "dangerousness" exception, the Court affirmed that the IDEA's stay-put provisions prohibit school officials from using dangerous or disruptive conduct that manifests their disabilities as a reason to unilaterally exclude students with disabilities from school during the pendency of review proceedings. The Court added that officials could impose normal, non-placement-changing procedures, including temporary suspensions for up to 10 school days, for students who posed an immediate threat to the safety of others. Furthermore, the Court recognized that if educators and parents agreed, students could be given interim placements as proceedings went forward. If this approach failed, the Court acknowledged that officials could file suit for injunctive relief to remove children. The 1997 reauthorization of the IDEA and its 1999 regulations clarified a number of gaps left following *Honig*.

Most recently, in *Cedar Rapids Community School District v. Garrett F.* (1999), the Court interpreted the IDEA as requiring a school board to provide and pay for, regardless of cost, a full-time nurse while a student, who was rendered quadriplegic due to a motorcycle accident involving his father, was in school because his medical condition required constant monitoring. This decision expanded the Court's earlier ruling in *Irving Independent School District v. Tatro* (1984), wherein it decided that a procedure such as catheterization that can be performed by a school nurse or trained layperson is a required related service for students with disabilities under the IDEA.

Gender

Franklin v. Gwinnett County Public Schools (1992) was the first Supreme Court case to address sexual harassment in a school setting. In *Franklin,* a former high school student unsuccessfully sued her school board for monetary damages under Title IX of the Education Amendments of 1972 because officials failed to take proper action when she informed them that one of her male teachers coerced her into engaging in sexual relations. The Court reversed in favor of the student and ruled that she could pursue money damages under Title IX.

In *Gebser v. Lago Vista Independent School District* (1998), the Court rejected a suit filed by a student in Texas against her school district after she had a sexual relationship with one of her teachers. In light of the board's promptly engaging in corrective actions in firing the teacher and taking steps to have his teaching license revoked, the Court held that the school board was not liable under Title IX for sexual harassment unless administrators in positions of authority were notified of the situation but failed to act.

Most recently, in *Davis v. Monroe County Board of Education* (1999), a case from Georgia, the Court set the standards for peer-to-peer sexual harassment. The Court was of the opinion that a school board can be accountable for peer-to-peer sexual harassment only if educators, who have substantial control over the students and the context within which the harassment occurred, are deliberately indifferent to harassment of which they have actual knowledge and if the harassment is so severe, pervasive, and objectively offensive, that it deprives the victim of access to the educational opportunities or benefits.

Church-State Issues

The Court's first two cases involving religion and education did not involve the establishment clause of the First Amendment, according to which "Congress shall make no law respecting an establishment of religion or prohibit the free exercise thereof." Rather, the Court decided both cases on the basis of the due process clause of the Fourteenth Amendment.

Pierce v. Society of Sisters (1925) is perhaps the most important case dealing with nonpublic schools. At issue in *Pierce* was the constitutionality of an Oregon statute that required parents or guardians to send their children to public schools in order to satisfy the state's compulsory attendance law. In *Pierce,* the Court ruled in favor of two nonpublic schools that challenged the law on the ground that it violated their Fourteenth Amendment due process rights to not have their property, in the form of the ownership of their schools, taken away without due process of law. If the Court had upheld the law, then it would have been up to individual states to determine whether nonpublic schools satisfied compulsory attendance laws. The Court also recognized that while the state has the right to regulate nonpublic schools, it cannot do so to any greater extent than it does with public education and that the law at issue unreasonably interfered with the rights of parents to direct the education of their children.

In *Cochran v. Louisiana State Board of Education* (1930), the Court again relied on the due process clause of the Fourteenth Amendment in upholding a state statute that provided textbooks for students, regardless of whether they attended public or nonpublic schools.

State Aid

Everson v. Board of Education (1947) is the first in a long series of Supreme Court cases examining the contentious issue of state aid to students who attend religiously affiliated nonpublic schools, based on the merits of claims under the establishment clause in the First Amendment. Over the years, the Court limited, and expanded, the availability of such aid.

In *Everson,* the Court upheld a statute from New Jersey that permitted local boards of education to reimburse parents of children who attended religiously affiliated non-public schools for the cost of transportation. Although not actually using the words *child benefit,* the Court essentially found that because education satisfies a secular state purpose, and because transportation fits in the general category of public services that are available to all, such as police and fire protection, the benefit primarily accrued to the children and not their religiously affiliated schools. Under this test, the Court determined that states, if they wish, may—but are not required to—provide benefits to students in nonpublic schools.

Debates about its continuing viability aside, the most significant case involving aid to nonpublic schools was *Lemon v. Kurtzman* (1971), wherein the Court considered the constitutionality of programs from Rhode Island and Pennsylvania. The disagreement from Rhode Island centered on a state statute that paid salary supplements to certified teachers in nonpublic schools who taught only subjects that were offered in the public schools. Similarly, the dispute from Pennsylvania involved a state law that provided reimbursements for teachers' salaries, textbooks, and instructional materials for courses, as long as they did not contain "any subject matter expressing religious teaching, or the morals or forms of worship of any sect" (p. 610). The Court, invalidating both programs, created a tripartite test that it has since relied on in virtually all subsequent cases involving the establishment clause. The Court maintained that

> every analysis in this area must begin with consideration of the cumulative criteria developed by the Court over many years. Three such tests may be gleaned from our cases. First, the statute must have a secular legislative purpose; second, its principal or primary effect must be one that neither advances nor inhibits religion; finally, the statute must not foster "an excessive government entanglement with religion." (pp. 612–613)

Prior to *Lemon,* the Court had set the outer limits of the child benefit test in *Board of Education of Central School District No. 1 v. Allen* (1968), when it upheld a New York statute, challenged under the establishment clause, that authorizes the loaning of textbooks in secular subjects to students who attend nonpublic schools. Similarly, the Court upheld state textbook loans, where appropriate safeguards were in place, in *Meek v. Pittenger* (1975) and *Wolman v. Walter* (1977). Conversely, the Court struck down loans of other instructional materials in these last two cases. In *Mitchell v. Helms* (2000), however, a plurality (meaning that a majority of justices did not agree on the Court's rationale, thereby weakening its value as precedent) of the Court overturned the parts of those two cases that were inconsistent with its permitting public officials to loan materials such as computers and projectors to religiously affiliated nonpublic schools.

In *Agostini v. Felton* (1997), arguably its most important establishment clause case since *Lemon,* the Court expanded the parameters of the child benefit test for the first time since *Allen* by taking the unusual step of following through on its promise to repudiate its earlier decision in *Aguilar v. Felton* (1985). In *Aguilar,* the Court banned the on-site delivery of remedial educational services under Title I of the Elementary and Secondary Education Act for economically disadvantaged students in religiously affiliated nonpublic schools in New York City. In *Agostini,* the Court reasoned that the New York City Board of Education's Title I program did not violate the establishment clause because there was no governmental indoctrination, there were no distinctions between recipients based on religion, and there was no excessive entanglement. More specifically, the Court was satisfied that because Title I is a federally funded activity that offers supplemental, remedial instruction to disadvantaged children on a neutral basis and because appropriate safeguards were in place in the nonpublic schools, the program did not run afoul of the establishment clause. *Agostini* modified the *Lemon* test by reviewing only its first two parts, dealing with an enactment's purpose and effect, while recasting entanglement as one criterion in determining a statute's effect.

Most recently, in *Zelman v. Simmons-Harris* (2002), the Court upheld the constitutionality of an Ohio voucher program. Relying on *Agostini*, the Court considered "whether the government acted with the purpose of advancing or inhibiting religions [and] whether the aid has the 'effect' of advancing or inhibiting religion" (p. 649). Lacking real disagreement over the program's valid secular purpose in providing programming for poor children in a failing school system, the Court considered whether the program had the forbidden effect of advancing or inhibiting religion. The Court was convinced that the voucher program was constitutional because, as part of the state's far-reaching attempt to provide greater educational opportunities in a failing school system, it allocated vouchers on the basis of neutral secular criteria that neither favored nor disfavored religion, was made available to both religious and secular beneficiaries on a nondiscriminatory basis, and offered assistance directly to a broad class of citizens, who might direct the aid to religious schools based entirely on their own genuine and independent private choices. The Court was not concerned by the fact that almost all participating schools were religiously affiliated; this situation arose because surrounding public schools refused to participate in the program. The Court concluded that because it was following an unbroken line of cases supporting true private choice that provided benefits directly to a wide range of needy private individuals, its only choice was to uphold the voucher program.

Prayer and Religious Activity

Unlike cases involving aid to students who attend religiously affiliated nonpublic schools,

wherein the Court's attitude has shifted over the years since its first case involving religion in the schools, the Court has largely adopted the Jeffersonian metaphor calling for "building a wall of separation between Church and state" (Jefferson, 1903, p. 281), language that is not in the Constitution. In *People of State of Illinois ex rel. McCollum v. Board of Education of School District No. 71, Champaign County* (1948), the Court vitiated a program under which religious leaders entered public schools and offered religious instruction for students whose parents agreed to have their children attend the classes. The Court ruled that tax-supported public school buildings cannot be used to disseminate religious doctrine and that state officials acted impermissibly in affording religious groups invaluable aid in helping them to engage students via the state's compulsory education machinery.

Engel v. Vitale (1962) was the Court's first case involving school prayer. At issue was a prayer the New York State Board of Regents had offered for suggested use in public schools to inculcate moral and spiritual values in students. When a local school board adopted the prayer as part of a policy that required it to be recited in class each day, a group of parents challenged the action even though the board's policy permitted children to be exempted from participation if their parents objected in writing. The Court reversed lower court rulings in favor of the school board, holding that the daily classroom practice of having students recite prayer was a religious activity wholly inconsistent with the establishment clause.

A year later, in the companion cases of *School District of Abington Township v. Schempp* and *Murray v. Curtlett* (1963), the Court addressed the appropriateness of Bible reading and/or the use of the Lord's Prayer/Our Father in public schools in Pennsylvania and Maryland, respectively. *Abington* and *Murray* are important because the Court expanded the limits of its First

Amendment jurisprudence by enunciating the first two parts of what would develop into the so-called *Lemon* test. In so doing, the Court vitiated both programs in light of its test, which maintained that "to withstand the strictures of the Establishment Clause there must be a secular legislative purpose and a primary effect that neither advances nor inhibits religion" (p. 222). Applying this test, the Court subsequently reached such far-reaching decisions as striking down the posting of the Ten Commandments in public schools in Kentucky (*Stone v. Graham,* 1980) and a statute from Alabama that would have mandated the observance of a "moment of silence" in every public school classroom (*Wallace v. Jaffree,* 1985).

In something of an exception, *Board of Education of Westside Community Schools v. Mergens* (1990), the Court upheld the Equal Access Act, a federal statute that permits student-sponsored prayer or Bible study clubs to meet in schools during noninstructional time. The Court later expanded this rational to allow nonschool groups access to public school facilities in *Lamb's Chapel v. Center Moriches Union Free School District* (1993) and *Good News Club v. Milford Central School* (2001).

Lee v. Weisman (1992) was the Supreme Court's first ruling on school-sponsored prayer at public school graduation ceremonies. In *Lee,* a middle school student in Providence, Rhode Island, and her father objected to prayer at her graduation, where school officials invited a rabbi to deliver the invocation and benediction. The rabbi was asked to follow guidelines outlined in a pamphlet on public prayer in a pluralistic society, published by the National Conference on Christians and Jews. The Supreme Court agreed with the earlier rulings in striking the prayer down as violating the establishment clause. In eschewing the tripartite *Lemon* test, the Court contended that the state, through school officials, had a pervasive role not only by selecting who would offer the prayer but also by directing the content of the prayer. The

Court was also of the view that the role of the school *qua* government in permitting prayer at the graduation created possible psychological coercion of the students. The Court found the prayer impermissible because students were a captive audience: forced to participate, possibly against their wishes, insofar as they were not free to absent themselves from the graduation ceremony.

In *Santa Fe Independent School District v. Doe* (2000), the Court affirmed that a policy permitting student-led prayers prior to the start of high school football games in Texas violated the establishment clause. The Court reviewed the status of prayer from the perspective of whether its being permitted at football games was an impermissible governmental approval or endorsement, rather than a form of psychological coercion that subjected fans to values or beliefs other than their own. In striking down the prayer policy, the Court rejected the school board's three main arguments. First, it rejected the board's contention that the policy furthered the free speech rights of students. Second, the Court disagreed with the board's stance that the policy was neutral on its face. Third, the majority rebuffed the board's defense that a legal challenge was premature because prayer had not been offered at a football game under the policy.

As this book goes to press, in something of a surprise, the Court upheld the constitutionality of the words "under God," which were added to the Pledge of Allegiance in 1954, on the basis that the child's noncustodial father lacked standing—the ability to file suit (*Elk Grove Unified School District v. Newdow,* 2004). Unfortunately, the way in which the Court resolved this dispute failed to clarify the place of religion in the marketplace of ideas (Russo, in press).

Student Rights

As important an area as this is, there are relatively few Supreme Court cases dealing with student rights. This section highlights the major cases in this regard.

Student Speech and Expression

Tinker v. Des Moines Independent Community School District (1969) is the first case involving the First Amendment free speech rights of students in public schools. *Tinker* arose when junior and senior high school students were suspended for refusing to remove the black armbands they wore to protest American involvement in Vietnam. The students challenged their being disciplined pursuant to a 2-day-old policy that the local school board adopted in anticipation of the protest.

The Supreme Court ruled in favor of the students, noting that wearing armbands as a form of passive, nondisruptive protest was the type of symbolic act that placed the students' actions within the free speech clause of the First Amendment. As such, the Court reasoned that because school officials lack absolute power and pupils do not "shed their constitutional rights to freedom of speech or expression at the schoolhouse gate" (p. 506), limits can be placed on the extent to which educators may regulate student speech. The Court ruled that absent a reasonable "forecast [of] substantial disruption of or material interference with school activities" (p. 514), educators cannot infringe on students' constitutional right to freedom of expression. In not negating educators' duty to maintain discipline, the Court emphasized the need to recognize the constitutional expression rights of pupils in acknowledging that "students in schools as well as out of schools are 'persons' under our Constitution. They are possessed of fundamental rights which the state must respect" (p. 511). The Court added that public schools are a particularly appropriate place to instill a respect for First Amendment freedoms.

Tinker represents the turning point in the law of students' rights. Prior to *Tinker,* many educators were of the opinion that children are

in school to learn, not to express their own political opinions. After *Tinker,* school officials have had to consider students' constitutional rights in all of their practices.

In *Bethel School District No. 403 v. Fraser* (1986), the Court restricted the reach of *Tinker* in acknowledging that school officials in Washington state could discipline a student for violating school rules by delivering a lewd speech at a school assembly. In its analysis, the Court distinguished the speech from *Tinker,* where the armbands were a passive, nondisruptive expression of a political position, from the lewd and obscene speech, totally lacking in any political viewpoint, which was incident to a student election and delivered to an unsuspecting, captive audience. In recognizing that school officials have the duty to inculcate habits and manners of civility and teach students the boundaries of socially appropriate behavior, the Court decided that "the determination of what manner of speech in the classroom or in school assembly is inappropriate properly rests with the school board" (p. 683).

Hazelwood School District v. Kuhlmeier (1988) is the Court's only case involving school-sponsored publications. *Hazelwood* arose when a principal in Missouri deleted two articles, one on teenage pregnancy and the other about divorce, from a newspaper that was written and edited by members of a journalism class as part of the school's curriculum. In declaring that the newspaper was neither an open forum nor had become one by any past practice, the Court found that the principal acted reasonably, based on factors such as possible identification of unnamed pregnant students in the first article, references to sex activity and birth control that were inappropriate for some of the younger students, and a student's unilateral criticism of her father in the second article. Even though the student's name was deleted, the principal was unaware of that fact when he acted.

The Court distinguished *Hazelwood* from *Tinker* in that *Hazelwood* involved not the right of students to speak on a particular matter but rather the right of school authorities not to promote particular student speech. The latter area concerns educators' authority over school-sponsored publications, theatrical productions, and other expressive activities that could reasonably be perceived to bear a school's imprimatur. The Court reasoned that "educators do not offend the First Amendment by exercising editorial control over the style and content of student speech in school-sponsored expressive activities so long as their actions are reasonably related to legitimate pedagogical concerns" (p. 273).

Discipline/Due Process

Goss v. Lopez (1975) is the leading case on the due process rights of students in public schools who face short-term suspensions due to their misbehavior. *Goss* was filed on behalf of high school students in Ohio, who successfully challenged their being suspended without hearings for a variety of infractions. Affirming in favor of the students, the Court explained that because the state conferred a property right on students to receive an education, that right could not be withdrawn due to misconduct, absent fundamentally fair procedures to determine whether the misbehavior had, in fact, taken place. As such, the Court posited that because a short-term suspension was not a minimal deprivation of their right to an education, students could not be excluded from school for up to 10 days unless they received, at the least, notice of the charges against them and had an opportunity to respond. At the same time, aware of educators' need to maintain a safe and orderly learning environment, the Court asserted that there was no reason to delay the time between giving notice and students' responses. The Court also noted that students who pose a continuing danger to persons or property or who disrupt the educational process can be removed immediately but must be provided with due process as soon as is practicable.

Fourth Amendment

The Supreme Court first addressed search and seizure in a school context in *New Jersey v. T.L.O.* (1985). When a 14-year-old student in New Jersey, identified as T.L.O., and a friend were accused of violating school rules by smoking cigarettes in a lavatory in their high school, they were questioned by a teacher. After T.L.O. denied smoking, the teacher brought her to the assistant principal's office. On opening T.L.O.'s purse, the assistant principal discovered that she possessed cigarettes; the assistant principal removed them and accused the girl of lying. He also found cigarette rolling papers, some marijuana, a pipe, plastic bags, a substantial quantity of one dollar bills, an index card that appeared to be a list of students who owed T.L.O. money, and two letters implicating her in dealing marijuana. After a trial court adjudicated T.L.O. delinquent, the state Supreme Court reversed in her favor.

On further review, the Supreme Court reversed in favor of the state and upheld the search. Finding that the Fourth Amendment's prohibition against unreasonable searches and seizures applies to public school officials, the Court devised a two-part test to evaluate the legality of a search. "First, one must consider 'whether the . . . action was justified at its inception;' second, one must determine whether the search as actually conducted 'was reasonably related in scope to the circumstances which justified the interference in the first place'" (p. 341). According to the Court, a search is ordinarily justified at its inception when school officials have reasonable grounds to suspect that a search of a student will uncover evidence that the pupil has violated or is violating either school rules or the law. Regarding scope, the Court held that a search is permissible if its goals are reasonably related to its objectives and the search is not excessively intrusive in light of the age and sex of a student and the nature of an infraction.

For example, school officials will have to adopt less intrusive methods when searching younger students and may act in a more invasive manner if they are looking for a gun rather than a child's missing lunch. Following *T.L.O.*, courts have upheld the majority of searches in a variety of settings, ranging from strip searches to sniff dogs to student lockers to backpacks to metal detectors.

Ten years after *T.L.O.*, the Supreme Court revisited the Fourth Amendment in a dispute over drug testing of student athletes in Oregon in *Vernonia School District 47J v. Acton* (1995). In *Acton,* the Court applied a three-part balancing test in affirming the constitutionality of the policy. First, conceding that students have a lesser expectation of privacy than ordinary citizens, the Court reasoned that student athletes, in particular, experience diminished privacy because they are subject to physical examinations before becoming eligible to play and they dress in open areas of locker rooms. Second, the Court pointed out that urinalysis was minimally intrusive because it was coupled with safeguards that allowed little encroachment on students' privacy. Third, given the perception of increased drug use, the Court was satisfied that there was a significant need for a policy to eliminate drug use and that the one in place was an effective means for doing so.

Seven years later, in *Board of Education of Independent School District No. 92 of Pottawatomie v. Earls* (2002), the Court applied the test from *Acton* and upheld a board policy from Oklahoma that required all middle and high school students to consent to urinalysis testing for drugs in order to participate in extracurricular activities. In practice, the policy applied only to students who took part in competitive extracurricular activities sanctioned by the state's secondary schools activities association. The Court was satisfied that in light of the minimally intrusive way in which urine samples were collected, along with the limited uses for the test results and the

significance of the need to deter drug use, the invasion into the privacy rights of students was within constitutional limits.

Employee Rights

Free Speech

Pickering v. Board of Education of Township High School District 205 (1968) is the first Supreme Court case to address the free speech rights of teachers in public schools. In *Pickering*, a teacher in Illinois successfully challenged his being fired for sending a letter, which contained erroneous statements that criticized the board's allocation of funds for educational and athletic programs and the superintendent's presentation of proposals to raise revenue for these items, to a local newspaper. The Court held that the First Amendment protects the free speech rights of a public employee when he or she speaks on a matter of public concern. The Court added that the duty of the judiciary is to balance the interest when a teacher, as private citizen, speaks up on a matter of public concern against the interest of the state as employer to promote the efficiency of services that it provides through its employees. As such, the Court concluded that absent proof that a public employee knowingly or recklessly makes false statements on matters of public concern, then his or her speech is protected by the First Amendment.

In later cases, the Court further refined the *Pickering* balancing test into a three-step process (*Mt. Healthy City School District Board of Education v. Doyle*, 1977; *Connick v. Myers*, 1983). First, a public employee must show that the speech was protected. Second, an employee must prove that the protected speech was a substantial or motivating factor in the adverse employment decision. Third, an employee must demonstrate that the employer would have taken the adverse employment action even if he or she had not engaged in the protected activity.

Due Process

In *Cleveland Board of Education v. Loudermill* (1985), the Court clarified the minimum requirements of constitutional due process that must be afforded before boards can terminate the employment of teachers with tenure or continuing contract status who have property interests in their jobs. Specifying that teachers are entitled to some kind of hearing prior to being discharged, the Court noted that such informal pretermination hearings need not be elaborate because posttermination hearings would follow at which educators could present their cases.

Collective Bargaining

A major issue involving school employees is collective bargaining, a practice that is legal in more than 30 states. A major topic, from the point of view of unions, is agency or fair-share fees, which allow them to charge nonmembers a fair share for the services that the union provides on employees' behalf in negotiating employment contracts.

In *Abood v. Detroit Board of Education* (1977), the first of four cases involving fair share agreements, the Court held that the Constitution does not prohibit agency fee provisions in bargaining agreements, as long as unions do not use these funds to support ideological activities that members and nonmembers oppose and that are unrelated to the negotiations process. The Court explained that because individuals who object to how their funds are being spent must notify unions of their concerns, they should do so in general terms that do not necessitate their having to reveal their positions on particular matters.

Six years later, in a noneducation case that arose in California, the Court decided that agency fees could be used for conventions, business meetings, occasional social activities, and publications that communicate about nonpolitical activities (*Ellis v. Brotherhood*

of Railway, Airline and Steamship Clerks, Freight Handlers, Express and Station Employees, 1984). The Court also approved of advanced reductions of fees for nonmembers. Yet, the Court forbade the use of agency fees for organizing activities and litigation not connected to bargaining while disapproving of using rebates in dealing with fees, even if unions paid interest on these funds.

The Court next examined procedures established to effectuate the preceding decisions. In *Chicago Teachers Union, Local No. 1, AFT, AFL-CIO v. Hudson* (1986), the Court disapproved a rebate system because it did not avoid the risk that funds of nonunion members might have temporarily been used for improper purposes, a system whereby unions offered inadequate information to justify the amount of agency fees, and a system that did not afford a reasonably prompt decision regarding expenditures and fees by an impartial third-party decision maker.

In a case from Michigan involving a faculty union in a public institution of higher learning, *Lehnert v. Ferris Faculty Association* (1991), the Court reviewed which activities a union can charge to nonmembers. The Court decided that chargeable items must be germane to bargaining, be justified by the government's vital policy interest in labor peace and avoiding "free riders," and not significantly burden the free speech inherent in allowing an agency or union shop. The Court thus permitted a local union to bill nonmembers for costs associated with otherwise chargeable activities of its state and national affiliates, even when those activities—such as publications dealing not only with bargaining but with teaching and education generally, professional development, employment opportunities, and miscellaneous matters neither political nor public in nature, along with delegate participation in state and national conventions—were not performed for its benefit or that of its members. The Court refused to permit the union to charge nonmembers for the costs associated with lobbying and general public relations activities.

Funding

San Antonio Independent School District v. Rodriguez (1973) is the only school finance case that the Supreme Court has accepted. Parents in Texas filed a class action suit alleging that the state's system of funding, based on the value of taxable property in local school districts, was unconstitutional in that it violated the equal protection clause because it resulted in disparities in per-pupil expenditures based on wealth. Ruling in favor of the state, the Court held that the system neither discriminated against a definable class of poor people on the basis of wealth nor impermissibly interfered with a fundamental right or liberty. In rejecting the equal protection claim, the Court unambiguously declared that "education, of course, is not among the rights afforded explicit protection under our Federal Constitution. Nor do we find any basis for saying it is implicitly so protected" (p. 35). Even though the Court reaffirmed the importance of education, it refused to find a basis for declaring it a federal right. In the absence of a federal right to equality in funding, the remaining substantial inequities have led to dozens of cases based on state equal protection provisions.

Summary

As extensive as the authority of state and local school officials is to regulate public schools, the cases discussed above reflect that policies and practices must not impair federal constitutional rights unless justified by overriding public interests. Although the Supreme Court does not create law in the same way as legislative bodies or administrative agencies, preparation programs must help educators to recognize its pervasive influence on educational practices by interpreting constitutional

and statutory provisions as exemplified by these cases. In this way, the Court renders the U.S. Constitution a living document that is continually shaped to meet the needs of our changing society.

FEDERAL STATUTES

Brown I marked the beginning of the federal government's active involvement in education. The federal government took an even bigger step in sharing responsibility for education in 1958, when Congress passed, and President Eisenhower signed into law, the National Defense Education Act (NDEA). The NDEA, enacted in response to the Soviet Union's launching of Sputnik, made federal funds available to schools, from elementary through graduate programs, to focus on areas such as mathematics, science, and foreign languages that were believed to be critical to national defense. Although the NDEA no longer exists as an independent statute because many of its programs were consolidated under the Elementary and Secondary Education Act of 1965, its impact remains until this day. In light of the far-reaching consequences of federal statutes, this section summarizes major federal statutes dealing with education so educational leaders will have a handy guide to major laws impacting on education. As voluminous as regulations may be, filling in details that legislative actions leave to administrative agencies, this section focuses on federal statutes because they set the tone that regulations must follow.

Students/Educational Programming

The Elementary and Secondary Education Act of 1965. Enacted in 1965 as part of President Johnson's Great Society programs at the height of the civil rights movement, the Elementary and Secondary Education Act of 1965 (ESEA), the most expansive federal education statute, is now divided into 14 subtitles, more commonly referred to as titles. In the

ESEA, Congress was able for the first time to provide large-scale support for education, both public and nonpublic. In addition, the ESEA created a pool of federal funds that could be, and were, used to withhold support for those states that failed to comply with the Civil Rights Act of 1964.

Title I is the best-known section of the ESEA. Title I provides compensatory education in the form of remedial services, typically in mathematics and language instruction for specifically identified children from poor families. Other key provisions in Title I cover basic grants (including a comprehensive school reform demonstration program); Even Start Family Literacy Programs (to integrate early childhood education, adult literacy, or adult basic education and parenting education into a unified family literacy program for low-income families); migrant education; and programs for children and youth who are neglected, delinquent, or at risk of dropping out of school.

No Child Left Behind Act. In its most recent reauthorization, signed into law by President Bush in 2002, Congress expanded Title I of the ESEA to include the No Child Left Behind Act. A far-reaching federal statute, the act's major provisions include language holding local school boards accountable for student performance and for hiring teachers who are "highly qualified," meaning that an educator who is not at the entry level meets state competencies for certification in particular subject areas. The act also has ramifications for testing and placing students with disabilities.

Educational Amendments of 1972, Title IX. Title IX is designed to bar programs that feature gender-based discrimination from receiving federal financial assistance. The Supreme Court has significantly expanded the scope of Title IX by applying it in three cases, discussed earlier, involving sexual harassment in school settings.

The Individuals with Disabilities Education Act. Enacted in 1975 as the Education for All Handicapped Children Act, the Individuals with Disabilities Education Act (IDEA) guarantees each student with a disability a free appropriate public education in the least restrictive environment. The IDEA also provides parents with unprecedented procedural due process rights. More specific in terms of eligibility requirements (students must be between the ages of 3 and 21, have a specifically identified disability, and be in need of a special education program directed by an individualized education program) than Section 504 of the Rehabilitation Act of 1973, the IDEA has arguably had the most profound impact on education of any federal law.

Section 504 of Rehabilitation Act of 1973. Section 504 of the Rehabilitation Act of 1973, the first federal civil rights law to protect the rights of people with disabilities, is more expansive than the IDEA because it covers students, staff, and even parents and visitors in school settings. According to Section 504, an otherwise qualified individual with a disability (meaning that he or she can participate in a program receiving federal financial assistance despite his or her disability) cannot be denied the benefits of the program or be subjected to discrimination if he or she can complete it by means of a reasonable accommodation.

Family Educational Rights and Privacy Act. The Family Educational Rights and Privacy Act (1975) (FERPA), also known as the Buckley Amendment after its sponsor, New York Senator James Buckley, clarifies the rights of students and their parents to educational records. FERPA's two main goals are to grant students and their parents access to their educational records and to limit the access of outsiders to the educational records of students.

Stewart B. McKinney Homeless Assistance Act. This statute, last reauthorized in 2002, requires states to ensure that homeless children have equal access to the same public school education as other children.

Employment

Title VI of the Civil Rights Act of 1964. Title VI prohibits discrimination on the basis of race, color, or national origin in any program that receives federal financial assistance.

Title VII of the Civil Rights Act of 1964. Title VII, arguably the most important federal employment statute, prohibits discrimination on the basis of an individual's race, color, religion, sex, and/or national origin. Title VII, which recognizes an array of exceptions for religious organizations, covers all employers regardless of whether they receive federal financial assistance.

Age Discrimination in Employment Act of 1967. The Age Discrimination in Employment Act (ADEA) of 1967 prohibits employment discrimination against individuals who are 40 years of age or older with regard to hiring, firing, job classifications, and wages.

Age Discrimination in Employment Act of 1975. The ADEA of 1975 differs from its counterpart, the 1967 ADEA, essentially to the extent that it applies to programs that receive federal financial assistance.

Americans with Disabilities Act of 1990. The Americans with Disabilities Act of 1990 prohibits state and local governments from discriminating based on disabilities in employment and in public accommodations.

Equal Pay Act of 1963. The Equal Pay Act, part of the larger Fair Labor Standards Act, prohibits discrimination in pay based on gender.

Family and Medical Leave Act. The Family and Medical Leave Act, enacted in 1993, protects working parents who may be forced to choose between their families and jobs when they need extended leave to care for personal and family medical needs.

Additional Remedies

Along with the remedies that may be available under each of these categories, two additional antidiscrimination laws can be applied in cases involving students, their parents, and employees.

Section 1981 of the Civil Rights Act of 1866. Section 1981 prohibits discrimination on the basis of national origin and race in the making of contracts.

Section 1983 of the Civil Rights Act of 1871. Section 1983 does not contain discriminatory categories of its own but is a vehicle for seeking damages for violations of federal constitutional and statutory rights. More specifically, Section 1983 makes it unlawful for anyone who acts "under color of law," meaning with the apparent authority to act on behalf of the state, to deprive another citizen of the United States or person within its jurisdiction of any rights, privileges, or immunities protected by the Constitution and laws.

CONCLUSION

As important as the cases and statutes discussed above are, schools are also covered by a wide assortment of other federal and state laws, and educational leadership preparation programs and practitioners should keep this in mind. To this end, faculty members in leadership programs and educational leaders who are responsible for ensuring the sound management of their schools would be wise to update their knowledge of education law regularly not only by attending professional development presentations but also by retaining the services of an attorney who specializes in the area of education law. Although compliance with the law does not guarantee that one will be completely immune from litigation, the more carefully that educators understand and follow these cases and statutes, the more likely that they can avoid the threat of unnecessary lawsuits.

NOTE

1. This chapter uses the typical legal shorthand in second references to cases: for example, *Brown v. Board of Education* would become *Brown*. In this case, because there were two cases by the same name, I refer to this one as *Brown I* and the 1955 case as *Brown II*.

REFERENCES

Abood v. Detroit Board of Education, 431 U.S. 209 (1977).

Age Discrimination in Employment Act of 1967, 29 U.S.C. §§ 621 *et seq.*

Age Discrimination in Employment Act of 1975, 42 U.S.C. §§ 6102.

Agostini v. Felton, 521 U.S. 203 (1997).

Aguilar v. Felton, 473 U.S. 402 (1985).

Americans with Disabilities Act of 1990, 42 U.S.C. § 12101 *et seq.*

Bethel School District No. 403 v. Fraser, 478 U.S. 675 (1986).

Board of Education of Central School District No. 1 v. Allen, 392 U.S. 236 (1968).

Board of Education of Independent School District No. 92 of Pottawatomie v. Earls, 536 U.S. 822 (2002).

Board of Education of Oklahoma City Public Schools v. Dowell, 498 U.S. 237 (1991).

Board of Education of the Hendrick Hudson Central School District v. Rowley, 458 U.S. 176 (1982).

Board of Education of Westside Community Schools v. Mergens, 496 U.S. 226 (1990).

Bolling v. Sharpe, 347 U.S. 497 (1954).

Brown v. Board of Education, 347 U.S. 483 (1954).

Brown v. Board of Education, 349 U.S. 294 (1955).

Cedar Rapids Community School District v. Garrett F., 526 U.S. 66 (1999).

Chicago Teachers Union, Local No. 1, AFT, AFL-CIO v. Hudson, 475 U.S. 292 (1986).

Cleveland Board of Education v. Loudermill, 470 U.S. 532 (1985).

Cochran v. Louisiana State Board of Education, 281 U.S. 370 (1930).

Connick v. Myers, 461 U.S. 138 (1983).

Davis v. Monroe County Board of Education, 526 U.S. 629 (1999).

Elementary and Secondary Education Act (ESEA) of 1965, 20 U.S.C. §§ 6301–8962.

Elk Grove Unified School District v. Newdow, 2004 WL 1300159 (2004).

Ellis v. Brotherhood of Railway, Airline and Steamship Clerks, Freight Handlers, Express and Station Employees, 466 U.S. 435 (1984).

Engel v. Vitale, 370 U.S. 421 (1962).

Equal Pay Act of 1963, 29 U.S.C. § 206(d).

ESEA, Subchapter I, 20 U.S.C. §§ 6301 *et seq.*

Everson v. Board of Education, 330 U.S. 1 (1947).

Family and Medical Leave Act of 1993, 29 U.S.C. §§ 2611 *et seq.*

Family Educational Rights and Privacy Act of 1975, 20 U.S.C. § 1232g.

Franklin v. Gwinnett County Public Schools, 503 U.S. 60 (1992).

Freeman v. Pitts, 503 U.S. 467 (1992).

Gebser v. Lago Vista Independent School District, 524 U.S. 274 (1998).

Good News Club v. Milford Central School, 533 U.S. 98 (2001).

Goss v. Lopez, 419 U.S. 565 (1975).

Gullatt, D. E., & Tollett, J. R. (1997). Educational law: A requisite course for preservice and inservice teacher education programs. *Journal of Teacher Education, 48*(2), 129–135.

Hazelwood School District v. Kuhlmeier, 484 U.S. 260 (1988).

Honig v. Doe, 484 U.S. 305 (1988).

Individuals with Disabilities Education Act of 1975, 20 U.S.C. §§ 1400 *et seq.*

Irving Independent School District v. Tatro, 468 U.S. 883 (1984).

Jefferson, T. (1903). *Writings of Thomas Jefferson: Vol. 16* (A. Andrew, Ed.). Washington, DC: Thomas Jefferson Memorial Association of the United States.

Keyes v. School District. No. 1, Denver, Colorado, 413 U.S. 189 (1973).

Lamb's Chapel v. Center Moriches Union Free School District, 508 U.S. 384 (1993).

Lee v. Weisman, 505 U.S. 577 (1992).

Lehnert v. Ferris Faculty Association, 500 U.S. 507 (1991).

Lemon v. Kurtzman, 403 U.S. 602 (1971).

Martinez v. Bynum, 461 U.S. 321 (1983).

Meek v. Pittenger, 421 U.S. 349 (1975).

Mitchell v. Helms, 530 U.S. 793 (2000).

Mt. Healthy City School District Board of Education v. Doyle, 429 U.S. 274 (1977).

Murray v. Curtlett, 374 U.S. 203 (1963).

New Jersey v. T.L.O., 469 U.S. 325 (1985).

No Child Left Behind Act of 2002, 20 U.S.C. §§ 6301 *et seq.*

People of State of Illinois ex rel. McCollum v. Board of Education of School District No. 71, Champaign County, 333 U.S. 203 (1948).

Pickering v. Board of Education of Township High School District 205, 391 U.S. 563 (1968).

Pierce v. Society of Sisters, 268 U.S. 510 (1925).

Plessy v. Ferguson, 163 U.S. 537 (1896).

Plyler v. Doe, 457 U.S. 202 (1982).

Pohland, P. A., & Carlson, L. T. (1993). Program reform in educational administration. *UCEA Review, 34*(3), 4–9.

Russo, C. J. (in press). The Supreme Court and pledge of allegiance: Does God still have a place in American schools? *Brigham Young University Education and Law Journal.*

Russo, C. J., Harris, J. J., & Sandidge, R. (1994). Brown v. Board of Education at 40: A legal history of equal educational opportunities in American public schools. *Journal of Negro Education, 63,* 297.

Russo, C. J., Underwood, J., & Cambron-McCabe, N. (2000). The top ten education law cases: The Supreme Court's impact on schooling. *International Journal of Educational Reform, 9*(1), 21–31.

San Antonio Independent School District v. Rodriguez, 411 U.S. 1 (1973).

Santa Fe Independent School District v. Doe, 530 U.S. 290 (2000).

School District of Abington Township v. Schempp, 374 U.S. 203 (1963)

Section 504 of Rehabilitation Act of 1973, 29 U.S.C. § 504.

Section 1981 of the Civil Rights Act of 1866, 42 U.S.C. § 1981.

Section 1983 of the Civil Rights Act of 1871, 42 U.S.C. § 1983.

Stewart B. McKinney Homeless Assistance Act of 2002, 42 U.S.C. §§ 11431 *et seq.*

Stone v. Graham, 449 U.S. 39 (1980).

Swann v. Charlotte-Mecklenburg Board of Education, 402 U.S. 1 (1971).

Tinker v. Des Moines Independent Community School District, 393 U.S. 503 (1969).

Title VI of the Civil Rights Act of 1964, 42 U.S.C. § 2000d.

Title VII of the Civil Rights Act of 1964, 42 U.S.C. § 2000e.

Title IX of the Educational Amendments of 1972, 20 U.S.C. § 1681.

Vernonia School District 47J v. Acton, 515 U.S. 646 (1995).

Wallace v. Jaffree, 472 U.S. 38 (1985).

Wolman v. Walter, 433 U.S. 229 (1977).

Zelman v. Simmons-Harris, 536 U.S. 639 (2002).

PART III

Educational Politics and Policy

Creating Effective, Equitable,
and Democratic Schools

GARY L. ANDERSON
New York University

Perhaps more than at any other time in American educational history, leaders need to understand their policy environment and the politics of policy making. The omnibus No Child Left Behind educational reform legislation, signed by President Bush on January 8, 2002, represents a massive attempt to use policy as a form of social engineering. Like most political documents, it represents not a rational plan but a series of political compromises. Whether it will be an effective "stick" to pressure schools into becoming more effective and equitable remains to be seen. Most scholars of organizational and social change would be skeptical of such a theory of change. This section of the *Handbook* aims at providing researchers and practitioners with conceptual tools to help them put this new policy context into perspective, while providing the conceptual and practical tools to move schools in more effective, equitable, and democratic directions.

It is safe to say that most of the authors in this section are skeptical that No Child Left Behind will result in more effective, democratic, and equitable schools. Some believe this because, regardless of how well intentioned some of those supporting the legislation are, many aspects are ill conceived and will lead to perverse incentives and unintended negative outcomes. Others see the legislation as a way to ignore the social investments that are needed in areas like health care, urban investment, and family policy, along with a less regressive tax code and the provision of other forms of social welfare. These authors believe that it takes more than school reform to help all children succeed; it takes a just society that provides all citizens with certain inalienable rights like health care, shelter, a living wage, and so on. The authors in Part III do not discount using those aspects of the No Child Left Behind Act that work toward noble goals, but neither do they assume that this legislation is the last word. To borrow two concepts from critical theory, No Child Left Behind may be a case of the systemworld colonizing the lifeworld of schools (Habermas, 1987; Sergiovanni, 2000).

The systemworld consists of the management designs, policies, rules, and schedules that provide a framework for students and teachers to engage in the practice of teaching and learning. The lifeworld is the culture of the school and is represented by the values, norms, and beliefs that determine the social interactions among students, teachers, and administrators.

The lifeworld and systemworld are both essential to school organization. When they are in balance, they function symbiotically to create schools and classrooms in which system efficiency is in harmony with the lifeworld where teaching and learning take place. However, increasingly, the systemworld dominates the lifeworld of schools. A dominant systemworld destroys the fabric of the school culture, creating isolation, alienation, and a loss of professional efficacy. The chapters in this section focus on maintaining this balance by strengthening the lifeworld of school communities, of low-income children and children of color, and of collaborative, democratic decision making among teachers, students, and parents. As Gold, Simon, and Brown argue in Chapter 11, strengthening this lifeworld is also an alternative way of achieving public accountability for public schools.

This section is an attempt to provide an accessible primer on policy and politics in education while also discussing them with an eye toward building and sustaining more democratic and just organizations. Chapter 9 is written by Betty Malen, a policy researcher who has produced some of the most cogent and creative policy analyses in the field. Malen has done research on state policy making, site-based management, and reconstitution of schools, among other topics. Chapter 9 provides an overview of the primary theoretical approaches to understanding policy and its effects. As every educator knows, it is impossible to be playful and creative with knowledge until you have some foundational knowledge of a field. Malen provides this foundation, describing both rational and political approaches to policy and discussing their strengths and limitations. She also addresses how these approaches can provide administrators with a solid framework for understanding both the policies that they have to generate in their own settings and the ones that they must respond to from their policy environment. She cautions leaders that policies nearly always have unintended consequences, that they are often driven more by political utility than research, and that leaders and followers may variously implement, accommodate, subvert, or resist policies.

Subsequent chapters look at how school policies and politics impact schools at the societal, community, and organizational levels. Since the era of effective schools research, there has been an emphasis on the school as a unit of analysis to the detriment of the community and society. Reforming schools will do no good if there are few economic opportunities awaiting students when they graduate. In Chapter 10, Gary L. Anderson and Monica Pini discuss how a neoliberal economic model is radically changing educational policy and the nature of public education and other social institutions. They discuss the impact on education of four tendencies:

1. *Corporatization* or a greater role for business—particularly the corporate sector—not only in education but in society at large

2. *Marketization* or a tendency to view individual choice in a marketplace as a more efficient and effective way to allocate resources and values in society, as well as a more effective form of accountability for public institutions

3. *Privatization* or the transfer of public institutions into private hands

4. *Commercialization* or the opening up of public schools to commercial exploitation

According to Anderson and Pini, school reform is too often analyzed in the absence of an analysis of how the political economy impacts education. As Tyack and Cuban (1995) have pointed out, education reformers throughout recent history have colluded in "blaming schools for not solving problems beyond their reach. More important, the utopian tradition of social reform through schooling has often diverted attention from more costly, politically controversial, and difficult societal reforms" (p. 3).

School reform will not help low-income communities unless they have sufficient influence to help determine how their children are educated. Leaving this work to school professionals will result in reforming schools around the well-meaning but often pathologizing views that white, middle-class professionals have of other people's children. In Chapter 11, Eva Gold, Elaine Simon, and Chris Brown describe a 3-year study of community organizing for school reform. Using an interfaith group, Oakland Community Organizations, as a case study, they present a model for the politics of parent and community involvement that decenters the school professional and makes the school community a more influential player in school reform. The work of community-organizing groups offers a conception of the role of parents and community members in school reform that moves beyond the traditional rhetoric about parents as partners to a discourse of parents as citizens engaged in decision making in their children's schools and in the community at large.

At the organizational level, leaders need to understand the ways that schools are structured to systematically advantage some students and disadvantage others and to learn how to intervene in ways that make schools more equitable in their structures and practices. The organizational politics of race, class, gender, and disability have been largely overlooked by scholars of the politics of education. In Chapter 12, Ruth S. Johnson and Lawson Bush, V, argue that culturally responsive pedagogies in classrooms require culturally responsive schools. This chapter discusses how to build a collaborative culture through leadership teams and how to monitor equity in schools though the use of equity-sensitive data.

Finally, leaders need to understand how to push beyond the rhetoric of participation and site-based management to genuine forms of participation in schools, forms in which the collective wisdom of teachers, students, and community members is allowed to inform the education of children. In Chapter 13, Jesse Goodman, Daniel Baron, and Carol Myers describe the new structures and norms that must be created to democratize school cultures. Based on years of working with schools, the authors provide practical examples from schools that have created authentically democratic cultures.

We hope these chapters are useful to scholars of policy and politics as well as practitioners at all levels of the school system who are committed to more democratic and equitable schools. The authors provide accessible but intelligent accounts that not only push current thinking in policy and politics of education, but also provide detailed case examples and practical tools for change.

REFERENCES

Habermas, J. (1987). *The theory of communicative action: Vol. 2. Lifeworld and system: A critique of functionalist reason* (T. McCarthy, Trans.). Boston: Beacon Press.

Sergiovanni, T. (2000). *The lifeworld of leadership: Creating culture, community, and personal meaning in our schools.* San Francisco: Jossey-Bass.

Tyack, D., & Cuban, L. (1995). *Tinkering toward utopia: A century of public school reform.* Cambridge, MA: Harvard University Press.

9

Educational Leaders as Policy Analysts

BETTY MALEN
University of Maryland

INTRODUCTION AND OVERVIEW

Whether charged with the responsibility to implement mandates enacted in more distant arenas or to invent alternatives for their more localized contexts, educational leaders are continuously involved in efforts to forge policies that might effectively address a wide range of serious social problems. The classic but artificial distinctions between policy, administration, and teaching blur as educators who occupy a range of roles in public school systems, knowingly or inadvertently, influence policy developments in myriad ways (Cuban, 1998; Honig, 2003). Often cast as both targets and agents of policy activity, educational leaders can elect to be relatively "passive recipients of a sequence of policy surprises" (Fowler, 2000, p. 22) or relatively active participants in the search for policy successes.

For those who seek to be active, effective policy agents, the challenges are daunting. Public school systems are complex political

systems currently under enormous, if not unprecedented, pressures. Nested in governmental structures, confronted by multiple competing demands, and dependent on diverse constituencies for essential support if not ultimate survival, public schools face the "dual challenge" of conflict management and institutional legitimation (Weiler, 1993), as well as the fundamental problem of organizational performance. Determining whether and how a public school system might develop and implement policies that individually or collectively attend to all three critical functions can be a daunting, mind-boggling task. The sheer volume of education-related, reform-oriented initiatives that have been enacted over the last 3 decades makes it difficult to keep track of the dizzying array of policy directives, make sense of their implications for school systems, and make use of whatever "policy learning" occurs (Jenkins-Smith, 1988) to invent more robust approaches to urgent social and educational problems. While the proliferation as

Author's Note: I am indebted to Tim Mazzoni, Jackie Cossentino, Jennifer King Rice, and Gary Anderson for their thoughtful reviews of early versions of this chapter.

well as the intensification of education policy making complicates our ability to systematically and critically examine education policy developments, these trends also underscore the importance of policy analysis for education leaders.

For instance, both federal and state policymakers have enacted legislation that embodies graduated but strident sanctions for school systems that fail to meet various sets of standards (Fuhrman, 2001; Ladd, 1996). Calls for reconstitution, privatization, and other "performance based" rewards and punishments have become prevalent features of the education policy landscape (Fuhrman, 2001). These dramatic approaches to school reform magnify some of the salient stakes embedded in education policymaking generally because they stress overturning organizational arrangements, redefining fundamental responsibilities, reallocating scarce human and fiscal resources, and infusing market mechanisms into the governance and operations of school systems (Galvin, 2000; Jones & Malen, 2002). These and other attempts to advance policies that cut deep into the structures and operations of school systems provide poignant reasons to be engaged in policy analysis, for they remind us that education policymaking is directly and inextricably linked to our interests and our ideals.

For this author and for many others, the most compelling reasons to be engaged in policy analysis reside in the persistence of educational inequities, the intensification of socioeconomic inequities, and the commitment to the creation of a just, compassionate society. To be clear, public schools are not the sole determinants of students' life chances (Stier & Tienda, 2001); but they can have a profound influence on the aspirations and the accomplishments of the students who rely on them for access to quality educational experiences (Croninger & Lee, 2001; Lee, Smith, & Croninger, 1997). Furthermore, important dimensions of complex educational problems and prevalent school practices may lie beyond

the reach of even the most carefully crafted education policies (Glazer, 1988; Rothstein, 2002; Stier & Tienda, 2001). But a recognition of the limitations of public policy as a transformative force need not stifle our pursuit of sound initiatives that hold promise for addressing more effectively the challenges confronting public school systems. However imperfect, public policy remains a major force that we can draw on to tackle the underlying causes of educational problems, to improve the quality and equity of educational opportunities in public schools (Anyon, 1997; Rothstein, 2002; Schorr, 1988), and to advance broader social ideals.

Given the salience and centrality of education policy as a force that is affecting, for better or worse, the priorities and practices of public schools, educational leaders are surrounded—at times, bombarded—by intense policy demands, consequential policy choices, and disconcerting policy effects. This chapter seeks to help educational leaders deal with some of the policy-based aspects of their work. It provides an overview of the broad field of education policy analysis and a rationale for the particular focus of the chapter, then concentrates on a description of conceptual tools that educational leaders might draw on to think through some of the knotty policy predicaments that permeate, and at times dominate, their work. It concludes with a discussion of the strengths and limitations of these conceptual tools as aids for educational leaders.

OVERVIEW OF EDUCATION POLICY ANALYSIS AS A FIELD OF STUDY

Like public policy analysis, education policy analysis has been variously characterized as a way of "speaking truth to power" (Wildavsky, 1979) as well as a way of altering truth to acquire or accommodate power; as an impartial, rational effort to inform policy debates as well as a partisan, ritualistic effort to short-circuit policy deliberations and control policy decisions (Cooper & Randall, 1999; Heineman, Bluhm, Peterson, & Kearny, 1997; Radin, 2000). Although there are multiple, competing views of the purpose, scope, relevance, and significance of the field, this chapter views education policy analysis as a potentially constructive and consequential form of "disciplined inquiry" (Shulman, 1988) that focuses on the systematic, even-handed, evidence-based examination of alternative approaches to prevalent public problems. The purpose is "both enhanced understanding and improved input into the policy process" (Heineman et al., 1997, p. 6). Education policy analysis is an eclectic field that draws on different theoretical orientations, research designs, and dissemination strategies; as defined here, it does not embrace the polemics, editorials, anecdotal testimonials, or other unsubstantiated interpretations of policies that have become prevalent in the media and in the professional and popular literature on education reforms.

Typically characterized as an applied, interdisciplinary field that seeks to "improve" an intensely human enterprise, education policy analysis, like other types of social policy analysis, is necessarily value laden (Callahan & Jennings, 1983). Policy choices affect and reflect social values; they transmit "messages about what government is supposed to do, which citizens are deserving (and which are not), and what kinds of attitudes and participatory patterns are appropriate in a democratic society" (Schneider & Ingram, 1993, p. 334); they allocate and legitimate the distribution of benefits and burdens in educational systems and in the broader society. Given this terrain, education policy analysis is a complicated, contested field of study. The conditions that education policy is expected to address are often tangled webs of problems whose symptoms, causes, and "solutions" are neither readily apparent nor reliably addressed by policy provisions (Glazer, 1988; Rothstein, 2002). The sheer number of diverse policy interventions, as well as the multiple aims freighted

upon them and the inconsistent effects attributed to them, makes it hard to know whether policy will "work" as anticipated (Malen & Knapp, 1997). The pressure to oversimplify issues, underestimate problems, and overpromise results confounds policy analysis in governmental arenas (Allison & Zelikow, 1999; Heineman et al., 1997; Moynihan, 1969) and in public school systems (F. M. Hess, 1999; Jones & Malen, 2002). For these and other reasons, well-intentioned architects of education policy, like well-intentioned architects of other types of public policy, often find themselves saying, with varying degrees of frustration and consternation, "That is not what we meant to do" (Gillon, 2000).

Focus of This Chapter

As earlier noted, this chapter concentrates on two conceptual orientations or analytic frameworks that education leaders (and other interested parties) can draw on to think through some of the perplexing policy challenges facing public schools and the people who seek to exercise leadership in those systems. This chapter also draws on select, research-based analyses of prevalent policy issues and initiatives just to illustrate the utility of these frameworks, not to render verdicts about either the efficacy of various policy options or the character of the political dynamics that fuel particular policy developments. In short, this chapter provides an illustrative discussion of select conceptual tools, not a comprehensive review of the relevant research on prevalent policy topics.

Generally speaking, to adopt a conceptual emphasis means recognizing that analytic frameworks (be they explicit, literature-based models or more implicit, individually developed orientations) shape how we think about policy (Allison & Zelikow, 1999). These frameworks can help us identify questions, organize information, interpret policy developments, and create new courses of action.

Because alternative frameworks may "open minds a little wider and keep them open a little longer" (Allison & Zelikow, 1999, p. 8), they can both bring into view and call into question our taken-for-granted assumptions about the policies we create or confront. If deployed with intelligence and integrity, alternative frameworks can help us develop more deliberative habits of mind and more thoughtful plans of action.

Because analytic frameworks are transportable devices that can be applied to different issues and different contexts, they may enable educational leaders occupying a wide range of roles in a wide range of settings to examine policy developments that are of particular interest to them. For example, educational leaders could use various frameworks to guide their own research projects, to coordinate commissioned research projects, and to aggregate, assess, and interpret research findings and other types of information generated or disseminated by the various policy institutes, research centers, philanthropic foundations, issue networks, professional associations, consultants, and academicians that make up what Kingdon (1995) terms "the policy community." Frameworks can also be used to raise issues, to diagnose developments in local schools and their broader institutional contexts, and to inspect the basis of policy-oriented judgments and actions.

The two conceptual frameworks emphasized here are rooted in rational and political traditions of policy analyses. These two prisms provide distinct but valid ways of thinking about key dimensions of education policy. Taken together, they help unpack the many ways that education policies may affect and reflect the ever-present pressures to address organizational performance, social conflict, and institutional legitimacy. Although other frameworks could have been selected, the two discussed below may be especially useful to educational leaders.[1] They undergird much of the work that has been done in the field of education policy. Thus, they provide a sensible, arguably essential foundation for educators who may be conducting or coordinating policy studies in their own systems or trying to aggregate, assess, and interpret policy studies carried out by others.

RATIONAL TRADITIONS

Rational traditions of analysis cast policy as a value-maximizing choice, an optimal solution to a carefully defined and accurately diagnosed social problem or set of social problems (Malen & Knapp, 1997). While many variations of rational models have been advanced, they generally emphasize systematic, data-driven, "cost-benefit" assessments of policy options (Moe, 1984). In their pure, arguably rigid form, rational perspectives presume actors can secure all the information required to identify the symptoms and discern the causes of social problems; develop comprehensive, comparative examinations of all the conceivable intervention options; discover the "best" choice; and determine whatever midcourse corrections may be necessary to institutionalize a consistent course of action.

More relaxed versions of rational models recognize that policy choices are often, if not always, made under "conditions of partial ignorance" (Kerr, 1976, p. 126); that policy actors rarely if ever engage in the vigorous, linear, logical appraisals that this classic model calls for; and that characterizations more in line with Lindblom's (1959) treatise on policy making as "the science of muddling through" come closer to capturing the realities of policy analysis in most organizational and governmental contexts. Many policy scholars and policymakers have long recognized and readily acknowledged that even if all relevant information could be secured, human beings do not have the cognitive capacity or the organizational support required to carry out such complete and definitive analyses (Kingdon, 1995; Lindblom, 1959). Even relatively rigorous analyses rarely result in the tight agreement about the "best" or even the "acceptable" course of action that rational perspectives espouse. As Henig (1994) explains,

> No matter how many the studies or how sophisticated their design, experience indicates that evidence about the likely effects of public policies is rarely definitive. The step from evidence to policy is always a problematic one. The uncertainty of social science techniques means that important decisions about what should be done inevitably require that decisions be made in the face of incomplete and conflicting evidence, competing values, unselfconscious assumptions and shifting contexts. . . . [T]he evidence can inform, but it cannot define our move. (p. 148)

Critics not only question the central tenets of the classic rational model, but also debate the likely impact of this approach to policy analysis on democratic decision-making processes. Some argue that rational models may precipitate "technocratic tunnel vision" (Kahne, 1996, p. 2), the tendency to focus only on the means of achieving various goals rather than on the virtues of pursuing these goals. Critics also warn that the model may reify certain forms of knowledge and thereby enable insular policy elites, armed with the legitimacy of systematically acquired information that may not be so systematically acquired, to procure a privileged edge in policy deliberations (Jenkins-Smith, 1990; Lynn, 1999). Others maintain that policy analysis anchored in rational traditions can be used to carry out research that is designed in conjunction with diverse stakeholders, shared with broad publics, and used to inspire, expand, and elevate public debate about both the ends we pursue and the means we employ (Sebring & Bryk, 1993; Smith & Ingram, 2002). This author concedes that rational models of policy analysis have their limitations and liabilities but argues that rational traditions of policy analysis offer potentially fruitful ways of thinking about how various policy options

might alleviate substantive problems, improve organizational performance, and advance societal ideals.

Analytic Orientation: Policies as Hypotheses To Be Tested and Trade-offs To Be Assessed

Because the relationship between the social conditions that have been identified as policy problems and the particular solutions that may be attached to them is often tenuous, it is appropriate and prudent to view education policies as hypotheses to be tested (Elmore & Sykes, 1992; Wildavsky, 1979). Policies represent choices among alternative courses of action; therefore, it is also appropriate and prudent to view policies as sets of trade-offs. If policy analysts adopt these general orientations, their task is to untangle and inspect the causal connections and means-ends linkages embedded in policies, to identify the costs and consequences of alternative courses of action, and to array the probable or actual gains and sacrifices that are part and parcel of investments in and choices among policy options.

Key Constructs

The constructs defined and illustrated below can be used separately or in various combinations to develop rationally rooted analyses of policy alternatives. Each construct is defined and illustrated through brief references to studies that indicate how it can be used to guide the analysis of education policy issues.

Theories of Action

This concept is frequently associated with Argyris and Schon (1982), who maintain that individuals espouse "theories of action," or sets of principles and propositions to describe, assess, and defend the effectiveness of their behavior. Although these theories of action may be incomplete, untested, or even contradictory, they constitute a framework that individuals use to guide, interpret, or justify their actions. This concept is also fairly prevalent in program evaluation research (Weiss, 1998) because it helps clarify "how program staff believe what they do will lead to desired outcomes" (Patton, 1990, p. 107). Evaluators have capitalized on Argyris and Schon's (1982) distinction between "espoused theories" and "theories in use" to compare "the official version of how the program or organization operates" with "what really happens" (Patton, 1990, p. 107) and to array the immediate and long-term objectives of a program and all of the linkages that must hold for these sets of objectives to be realized. Some writers have suggested that like particular programs, broad policy initiatives embrace theories of action, or sets of principles and propositions, orientations, and related assumptions that can be used to illustrate and assess the efficacy of these interventions (Elmore & Rothman, 1999; Malen, Ogawa, & Kranz, 1990). In applying this concept to broad policy initiatives, scholars have derived a policy's theory of action from both the particular rationales articulated by policy actors and the internal logics of the policy identified by the analyst (Malen et al., 1990).

The theory of action concept is a useful sensitizing device for unearthing and interpreting information about the substantive promise of policy. It directs attention to the often implicit sets of assumptions about the nature of the problem to be addressed and the causal linkages or means-end connections that must hold for a policy or genre of policies to ameliorate the problems to which it has been attached. In addition, the theory of action concept provides an analytic mechanism for tracking policy effects and comparing them to policy intents, a mental map for unpacking the underlying logic that links the policy action taken with the policy outcomes sought. Thus, it can be helpful to those who design, enact, and implement education policies and to those who wish to "test"

the central tenets of the theory of improvement embodied in a particular policy or genre of policies. Studies of prominent education issues illustrate the utility of this concept.

For example, policy scholars have identified and inspected the underlying assumptions embedded in definitions of policy problems and discussed the implications of those findings for the selection of policy interventions. In so doing, they expose and test different, albeit often implicit, theories of action. Ingersoll's (1999, 2001) analyses of teacher supply, teacher turnover, out-of field teaching patterns, and the organizational factors that affect teacher retention show how prevalent but unfounded assumptions about the scope and causes of "teacher shortages" can lead to "policy solutions" that miss the mark. In a similar vein, scholars have identified factors that shape teacher effectiveness and student achievement. For instance, scholars have examined the relationship between teacher attributes and teacher effectiveness (Rice, 2003b) and between class size and student achievement. These streams of work can inform judgments about whether "qualified teachers [are] really quality teachers," about "what teacher attributes really contribute to desired educational outcomes" (Rice, 2003b, p. 1), and about what combinations of policies are likely to have the greatest impact on the availability and distribution of quality teachers in school systems (Rice, 2003b). This research can inform judgments about whether the gains in student achievement that may be attributed to reductions in class size hold across student groups, academic subjects, and organizational contexts (Nye, Hedges, & Konstantopoulos, 2002). Also, the research can be used to gauge whether the assumptions undergirding policies governing the qualifications of teachers and the numbers of students assigned to classrooms withstand empirical scrutiny.

More explicit applications of the theory of action concept are evident in studies that examine the major assumptions regarding how particular policy solutions are supposed to alleviate prevalent policy problems. For example, efforts to examine the various theories of action embedded in site-based management initiatives revealed that basic assumptions about how site-based management can democratize school governance, foster organizational renewal, enhance school effectiveness, and equalize educational opportunities are not dependable; that multiple factors associated with the design of the policy and the context of schools can converge to preempt authentic participation and to restrict the ability of these initiatives to achieve their stated aims (Bryk, Easton, Kerbow, Rollow, & Sebring, 1993; Bryk, Sebring, Kerbow, Rollow, & Easton, 1998; Fager, 1993; Handler, 1996; Leithwood & Menzies, 1998; Lewis & Nakagawa, 1995; Malen et al., 1990).

Similarly, an attempt to test the theory of action embedded in school reconstitution reforms revealed that the strategy rests on three major interrelated premises: (a) that reconstitution will replace incumbents of administrative, teaching, and support positions with individuals who are more capable and committed; (b) that changes in the composition of the faculty and staff will result in redesigned schools; and (c) that the redesigned schools will improve student achievement. Evidence acquired from a 2-year study of a particular reconstitution reform indicated that in a context characterized by persistent teacher shortages and scarce fiscal and informational resources, this particular theory of action appeared to be seriously if not fatally flawed (Malen, Croninger, Muncey, & Jones, 2002).

Ongoing efforts to test "the seemingly straightforward theory of action regarding how standards-based reforms can enhance academic achievement and equalize educational opportunities" (Ogawa, Sandholtz, Martinez-Flores, & Scribner, 2003, p. 147) further demonstrate the utility of this construct as a vehicle for mapping essential linkages and arraying the evidence about the durability of those connections. For example, a recent synopsis of the literature on standards-based reforms identified three key interrelated assumptions of this genre of reforms: (a) "standards now offer to students, teachers, and principals a consistent and coherent guide;" (b) the specification of knowledge and skills conveys the instructional practices teachers are to emulate; and (c) "if the attainment of standards is assessed . . . teachers and administrators will receive timely and specific feedback on student performance and thus on their own instructional effectiveness" (Ogawa et al., 2003, pp. 147–148). This analytic breakdown provided a mechanism for gauging what extant information reveals about the prospects for policy success. For instance, previous experience suggests that education reforms of various sorts do not penetrate classroom practices in a particularly poignant, let alone uniform fashion (Cuban, 1993; Elmore, Peterson, & McCarthy, 1996); that the imposition of standards and tests can dilute instruction (McNeil, 2000) as well as enhance it (Cohen & Hill, 2001); and that the implementation of policies is shaped by a host of individual and institutional factors such as teachers' beliefs, knowledge, and experience, professional norms and networks, and district supports (Ogawa et al., 2003; Spillane, 1996). By exposing these and other complexities, the theory of action concept helps analysts inspect simplistic proclamations and develop more accurate understandings of the conditions under which particular policies would be more or less likely to operate as espoused. In short, the concept encourages analysts to render more measured judgments regarding the potential efficacy and relative effectiveness of various policy options.

Costs of Interventions

This concept recognizes that all education policies, programs, and practices carry costs. That seemingly obvious statement involves much more than adding up the funds required by or dedicated to various policy interventions.

The cost of an intervention is the value of *what is given up* when resources are dedicated to support the goals of the initiative. As Levin and McEwan (2001) express it, "all costs represent the sacrifice of an opportunity that has been foregone. . . . By using resources in one way, we are giving up the ability to use them in another way, so a cost has been incurred" (p. 44).

Assessing the total cost of any policy involves identifying and assigning a value to the full array of resources that are required to realize the goals of the initiative. In some cases, like the direct purchase of a good or a service, the costs of an action can be represented accurately in terms of monetary expenditures. However, educational interventions generally require a variety of resources, including time and effort, facilities and infrastructure, and materials and equipment, that can be difficult to value (Rice, 1997, 2002a). For example, education reforms tend to require substantial time and effort, resources that are not readily convertible to dollar estimates of worth. Reforms may also impose consequential human tolls that cannot be expressed in financial terms (Rice & Malen, 2003). Even though cost analyses are riddled with these and other messy measurement matters, understanding the full opportunity cost of a policy intervention entails recognizing and valuing all of the resources required to accomplish the goals of the initiative, arraying the full range of costs incurred, and mapping how those costs are distributed. Because the costs as well as the effects of education interventions are often distributed across a variety of individuals and organizations, analyses that reveal the distribution of costs are essential components of efforts to understand the "who pays" side of the policy ledger and to determine whether policy interventions are feasible, let alone desirable.

For instance, accurate information about the range of costs that may be incurred and the manner in which these costs are distributed across individuals and organizations is necessary to make informed judgments about whether a community has the appropriate levels of the various types of resources required to implement policy (Rice, 2002b). Suppose a reform pivots on parent involvement; a community lacking adequate pools of parents who are willing and able to contribute and an opportunity structure to support their participation may be well advised to consider other alternatives whose resource requirements better match the available resources. In the case of reconstitution, because a primary resource is capable and committed teachers and administrators, this reform may not be appropriate for communities that do not have or cannot secure this resource in abundant supply. In the case of class size reductions, essential resources include not only the funds required to fill new positions but also an adequate supply of quality teachers and an adequate amount of space to accommodate the increase in the number of new classes created (Rice, 2002b).

Because a comprehensive cost analysis is a critical step in gauging whether a policy is feasible and a critical ingredient in judging whether a policy is worth the costs incurred, this type of analysis warrants more attention than it has received (Rice, 1997). Although cost analyses have been underutilized in education, scholars have developed rubrics for estimating the cost of teacher professional development (Rice, 2003a); the "cost of working together" to develop "comprehensive support systems for children" (Rice, 2001); the cost of alternative comprehensive school reform models for at-risk students (King, 1994; Rice 2002b); the financial cost of reducing class size (Brewer, Krop, Gill, & Reichardt, 1999), equalizing state education finance systems, and providing "adequate" levels of revenue for education programs (Chambers & Parrish, 1983); the human costs of reconstitution reforms (Rice & Malen, 2003); and the educational costs of state testing policy (McNeil, 2000). In so doing, cost analyses have documented the value of the cost construct as a vehicle for (a) uncovering the wide range of visible and hidden, tangible and intangible costs that education policies may impose; (b) revealing the manner in which those costs are distributed across individuals and organizations; (c) gauging the extent to which the multiple costs of particular interventions are more or less aligned with the cost-carrying capabilities of local school systems; and (d) addressing the cost side of the various cost-effectiveness calculations and comparisons that can be developed to inform policy decisions.

Webs of Policies

This concept directs attention to the relationships within and across sets of policies. Because education policy initiatives can undermine as well as complement one another, policy analysts have underscored the importance of examining how existing policies interact and how new initiatives might be reinforced by or offset by other policies that schools are to follow (Fuhrman, 1993; Mitchell & Encarnation, 1984). For example, personnel policies and professional development directives may or may not support curriculum and instruction initiatives, which in turn may or may not be aligned with accountability policies and revenue policies. If policies governing the major dimensions of the system are not congruent, they may fragment organizational energies and undermine efforts to strengthen organizational performance. Conversely, if policies are in concert, then they may support the coordination of organizational energies and enhance efforts to improve organizational performance. The calls for "systemic reform" (Smith & O'Day, 1990) and "coherent policy" (Fuhrman, 1993) reflect this view. Because educational problems and policy successes interact with and, at times, are contingent on a host of social circumstances and opportunity structures (Glazer, 1988; Rothstein, 2002; Stier & Tienda, 2001), examining policies not only in education but also in related

domains such as health, housing, income maintenance, taxation, and employment may generate insights regarding how policies within and across sectors might be tethered to create more powerful, multiplier effects or at least might be aligned to reduce the incidence of offsetting effects.

The appeals for policy coherence within education have been supported by research that documents how various types of policy initiatives may precipitate or exacerbate organizational dynamics that undercut the capacity—and hence the prospects—for organizational improvements. For example, policies may contribute to levels of stress and to patterns of accommodation that deny organizations and those who work in them the opportunity as well as the ability to concentrate on essential tasks and to integrate those tasks in ways that might enhance the performance of the organization (Hatch, 2002; F. M. Hess, 1999; Newman, Smith, Allensworth, & Bryk, 2001). The rapid proliferation of distinct, disjointed, and at times inconsistent education reform initiatives makes it hard for educational leaders to figure out how they are to work amid, rather than to be trapped within, the web of policies they are to follow (Knapp, Bamburg, Ferguson, & Hill, 1998; Malen & Rice, 2003). What's more, schools and school systems may be inclined to respond to policy pressures for major and immediate improvements in school performance by rapidly and indiscriminately adopting a host of programmatic initiatives that end up being only partially or symbolically implemented (Bryk et al., 1993, 1998; Hatch, 2002; F. M. Hess, 1999; Malen & Rice, 2003; Newman et al., 2001). This tendency to respond frenetically can further confound the prospects for developing robust instructional programs and supportive organizational environments (Bryk et al., 1998; Newman et al., 2001). As one analyst put it, "The cumulative demands and resulting fragmentation and incoherence can undermine the capacity of schools to make the very improvements so many desire" (Hatch, 2002, p. 626).

On a more optimistic note, research documents how some local districts selectively and strategically use policies imposed on them to advance their local agendas and priorities (Firestone, 1989b; Fuhrman & Elmore, 1990). These "active users of reforms" are often ahead of the curve; that is, they are engaged in developing policies and practices in advance of state requirements. Situated to capitalize on the influx of "new policy" to energize and extend their priorities and programs, these districts avoid some of the chaos and confusion that policy initiatives can engender. These exceptional cases offer insights regarding how public school systems might engender coherence and retain focus amid the proliferation of education policy overtures.

Although the call for more coherent policy has been issued and examined, the task has not been accomplished within the domain of education, let alone across other related sectors of social policy (Fuhrman, 2001). Various organizational partnerships launched to foster collaboration between public schools and other social service agencies have received some attention as have other efforts to cultivate school-community connections that might strengthen opportunities for teaching and learning (Honig, Kahne, & McLaughlin, 2001; White & Wehage, 1995). But systematic efforts to map how social policies and education policies might be harnessed to more comprehensively address the multiple conditions that shape students' life circumstances and learning experiences are few and far between (Rothstein, 2002).

Because policies take many twists and turns as they are enacted and implemented, untangling the web of policies and the web of responses to them is an ongoing, taxing process. For reasons discussed later in the section on political traditions of policy analysis, the web of policies that we inherit and create will never be perfectly consistent and coherent, but reasonable efforts to articulate the relationships within and across sets of policies in education and related domains would enable us to discover connections and contradictions and to see ways to align select policies so that they might complement and reinforce more than undermine and offset each other.

Contexts of Schools

As the preceding discussion makes clear, policies do not operate in a vacuum. Their efficacy is influenced significantly, at times decisively, by the contexts of schools. Although references to the "contexts of schools" permeate the prior discussion, this cross-cutting construct is set out here because it is such an essential, albeit slippery, component of policy analysis. The intent here is to highlight dimensions of school contexts that may help educational leaders gauge whether and how policies "fit" schools and identify the types of adjustments and supports that may be required for policy to take hold in schools.

The webs of policies that guide and govern action operate in organizational and environmental settings that condition how policies play out. Like other complex organizations, school systems have habits and histories, norms and traditions, rhythms and routines that can reduce or reinforce the ability of policies to alter organizational priorities and practices. Moreover, schools are made up of people who bring different orientations and dispositions, views and values, talents and energies to the education enterprise. Thus, school systems are mixtures of individual and organizational ingredients that interact to mediate policy purposes, provisions, and effects. Situated in state and local communities that have distinctive resource configurations, cultural customs, social conventions, and "civic capacity" (Stone, Henig, Jones, & Pierannunzi, 2001), school systems or individual schools within those systems may respond to similar policies in markedly different ways (Fuhrman, 2001; Mintrop, Gamson,

McLaughlin, Wong, & Oberman, 2001; Muncey & McQuillan, 1998).

As the previous discussions of site-based management and standards-based reforms illustrate, individual dispositions, knowledge, and skill, along with organizational norms, networks, and relationships between individual schools, their districts, and state agencies, affect policy implementation (see also Fuhrman, 2001; Malen & Muncey, 2000). As the previous discussion of cost indicates, the efficacy of various education reforms may pivot on the degree to which the resource requirements of the policy coincide with the resources available in the local school community (Mintrop et al., 2001; Rice, 2002b). These examples illustrate how the context of schools construct can direct attention to and help organize information about the dimensions of the organizational and environmental context that may reduce or reinforce the efficacy of policy interventions. The examples indicate how a nuanced analysis of school contexts can inform judgments about how policy alternatives fit various school settings, direct attention to a contextualized search for "the best fit model" (Rice, 2002b), and expose adjustments that may be required for policy to realize its stated aims in particular settings.

POLITICAL TRADITIONS

Political traditions of policy analysis rest on the premise that policy is more than an attempt to ameliorate the substantive conditions that powerful sectors of society deem worthy of public attention and policy intervention. Because all compelling demands on the political system cannot be addressed, given limited resources and finite carrying capacities, powerful pluralistic interests seek to influence the tough, contentious choices that must be made. To foster stability and ensure survival, political systems must manage the actual and anticipated conflicts surrounding these difficult choices in ways that preserve public confidence

in the system's right to make binding decisions about how societal resources will be allocated. Policy is the major vehicle that political systems rely on to regulate social conflict over the distribution of scarce materials and symbolic resources in ways that affirm the legitimacy of the system. Analyses anchored in political theories take many forms (Dodd & Jillson, 1994; Easton, 1985; Sabatier, 1999); generally speaking, political perspectives recognize these multifaceted policy functions, bring the contests surrounding policy to the fore, and direct attention to the manner in which policy choices and outcomes affect and reflect the patterns of power and privilege in particular systems and in the broader society (Clegg, 1989; Easton, 1985; Malen & Knapp, 1997; Weiler, 1993).

The analytic approach outlined here casts policy as the product of the play of power, a *resultant* that mirrors the diverse interests and unequal power of the various actors who seek to influence policy developments (Allison & Zelikow, 1999). The focus is on how actors operating in various formal and informal arenas use their power to influence what social conditions get attended and neglected, what policy options get selected and rejected, and whether policies get implemented, reformulated, or circumvented. Because context situates and mediates the play of power, this approach also seeks to gauge how institutional and environmental forces (a) shape actors' conceptions of problems and priorities, (b) fix the opportunity structures within which actors vie for influence, and (c) convey the normative boundaries that political systems and their subunits must appear to respect in order to be seen as legitimate entities (Jones & Malen, 2002; Malen, 1994; March & Olsen, 1989; Mazzoni, 1991; Portz, Stein, & Jones, 1999). Political models like the one emphasized here are credited for openly acknowledging that pressures to manage conflict, accommodate powerful interests, and maintain legitimacy infiltrate and, at times, dominate policy deliberations and decisions in governmental and organizational settings (Allison & Zelikow, 1999; Fischer, 1999; Weiler, 1993). But the models also are criticized for their tendency to emphasize the pursuit of private parochial interests at the expense of public transcendent ideals and the tactical more than the principled use of power (Burns, 1978; Hoy & Tarter, 2004; Morgan, 1986); for their focus on the dynamics of conflict and competition more than the development of consensus and cooperation (Bolman & Deal, 1991); and for their inability to resolve the classic disputes about the relative strength of structural forces and human agency in explanations of political developments (Clegg, 1989; Howlett & Ramesh, 1995).

This author grants that political models have shortcomings but argues that this does not require analysts to adopt anemic views of political processes or to endorse endemic abuses of power. Rather, the models provide potentially constructive ways of thinking about how various policy options affect the capacity of the system to regulate conflict and retain legitimacy as well as to improve performance. They may permit policy analysts to see how actors holding different conceptions of the public good seek to advance their interests and their ideals through cooperative and competitive exchanges that reflect the more principled as well as the more instrumental and injurious aspects of power-based transactions in public school settings and in the broader governmental institutions that house them. Like any analytic lens, political models can be called on to serve noble as well as base purposes.

Analytic Orientation:
Policies as Products of
Power and Symbols of Legitimacy

Because policy is not only an attempt to solve substantive problems but also an attempt to address the two-fold challenge of conflict regulation and system legitimation, it is valid and instructive to view policies as products of power and as symbols of legitimacy. If policy analysts adopt these general orientations, their task is to untangle the interest-driven, power-based interactions that significantly affect, if not ultimately determine, policy choices and outcomes; to examine how policy alternatives affect the stability and legitimacy as well as the performance of the system; and to assess how policy affects the distribution of valued outcomes.

Key Constructs

The key constructs associated with politically anchored analyses constitute a set of categories, all of which must be invoked in order to carry out a political analysis. For that reason, this section unfolds differently than the section on rational traditions of policy analysis. Here, all of the constructs will be defined, then the full set of constructs will be illustrated with studies that show how these concepts, taken together, contribute to our understanding of the select policy issues highlighted in the section on rationally rooted policy analyses.

Actors, Interests, and Arenas

These terms refer to the participants involved in formulating and implementing policy in the multiple formal and informal sites in which policy-related activity occurs (Firestone, 1989a; Mazzoni, 1991). The participants may be highly "visible" or more "hidden" clusters of players (Kingdon, 1995) who interact within and across the different levels of the policy system in an effort to influence what issues get considered, how those issues get framed, what policy choices get selected, and how those choices are (or are not) altered in implementation. The initial analytic aim is to identify the full cast of characters involved with particular policy issues; that is, to array the relevant authorities (those organizational actors who have the formal power to make binding decisions in particular arenas of the system) and other individuals and well-established or loosely aligned groups, foundations, organizations, corporations, or policy networks who are or may become involved in the policy process. The second aim is to develop an understanding of these actors; that is, to figure out their interests and the interests of those they represent as well as their positions on issues and the views and values that give rise to those positions. The third aim is to map the alignments and linkages these actors have with each other and the connections they have with policy elites, political parties, mass media, and broad publics. Such a layout enables the analyst to become more cognizant of who is absent as well as who is present; that is, to recognize who is, by design or default, left out of the process as well as who is let in. It allows the analyst to become acquainted with the "perennially neglected populations" as well as the "reputedly powerful networks" (Malen, 2001).

Although arraying actors and the interests they represent is important, it is not sufficient. Different arenas may be more or less open, accessible, and receptive to different players and their points of view; also, different arenas have their own, often tacit, "rules" of participation and accommodation. As a result, developing an understanding of how the locus of decision making may affect the prospects for gaining access and influence is central to any examination of the political landscape (Firestone, 1989a; Mazzoni, 1991). Studies of how relatively private arenas that are open to established actors and larger, more public arenas that permit a wider range of actors and interests to enter the fray affect the prospects for enacting and implementing redistributive reforms underscore the importance of the arena notion and provide some guidance in analyzing this aspect of power transactions (Jones & Malen, 2002;

Mazzoni, 1991). Studies of more general policy developments further reinforce the need to understand how different arenas alter the prospects for policy influence. Governing systems are made up of multiple venues wherein critical policy decisions can be made. As Baumgartner and Jones (1991) explain,

> Each venue carries with it a decisional bias, because both participants and decision-making routines differ. When the venue of a public policy changes, as often occurs over time, those who previously dominated the policy process may find themselves in the minority, and erstwhile losers may be transformed into winners. (p. 1047)

Developing an understanding of the actual and potential participants within and across arenas is always an empirical task. Knowing who is involved or may become involved with particular issues in particular settings "cannot be delineated *a priori*. All that we can say with certainty is that the policy actors come from within the machinery of the state and from the society at large" (Howlett & Ramesh, 1995, p. 52). But the particular configuration of players who may be involved with policy issues in various arenas and the manner in which features of the arena shape the patterns of participation and the style of play are matters that analysts must determine empirically.

Studies that seek to identify the major actors who seek to influence education policy tend to focus on the more obvious candidates, namely teachers, administrators, parents, school boards, mayors, community-based organizations, business groups, the professional and parent-based associations that are part of the public school lobby, governors, state legislatures, and the organized interests that shape education policy in federal arenas. Sets of less obvious actors, such as foundations, research centers, policy institutes, think tanks, reform organizations, academicians, consultants, and others who make up what

Kingdon (1995) terms the "policy community" have received less attention (Malen, 2001). Patterns of nonparticipation and the economic and structural arrangements that affect the opportunity, capacity, and inclination to become politically active have been addressed more in the broader literature on political participation than in the subfield of education politics (Gamson, 2002; Malen, 2001; Walker, 1991). Still, numerous works, only a few of which are noted here, provide useful information on the prominent clusters of actors who seek to influence education policy in individual schools and school districts (e.g., Henig, Hula, Orr, & Pedescleaux, 1999; Malen, 1994, 1995; Muncey & McQuillan, 1998; Orr, 1999; Shipps, 1997; Tallerico, 1992), in state arenas (e.g., Mazzoni, 1991, 2000), and in federal sites (e.g., Miskel & Song, 2003; Sroufe, 1995).

Power Sources and Influence Strategies

These terms refer to the actors' sources of power and the tactics they use to convert those power bases into policy influence. Put differently, the terms are used to help reveal the actors' political capital and the manner in which they expend that capital to advance their interests and ideals.

Taking stock of the actors' political currency involves identifying their assets (e.g., positional authority, money, time, expertise, experience, information, connections, constituencies, savvy, leadership) and their liabilities (e.g., forms of financial, informational, social, and cultural capital that may be necessary to wield influence in particular arenas but are unavailable to or not under the control of the actors). These steps are taken to gauge the actors' relative capacity to exert influence (Bolman & Deal, 1991; Dahl, 1984; Dahl & Stinebrickner, 2003; Mazzoni, 1991; Morgan, 1986).

Examining strategies involves identifying the range of activities that actors engage in to influence policy developments. Here, classic as

well as contemporary treatments of political strategies can be particularly helpful. For instance, an analysis of strategies involves unpacking how actors may gain access and keep it from others (Truman, 1951); exercise their voice and silence the voices of others (Cobb & Ross, 1997; Gaventa, 1980); define problems, frame issues, and regulate participation; exchange, slant, and control information and invoke symbols (Edelman, 1964); manage the "scope of conflict" (Schattschneider, 1960); forge coalitions; create "policy images," "shop" for "policy venues," and shift issues to more favorable decision arenas (Baumgartner & Jones, 1993); and otherwise work to affect policy-making dynamics and developments (Bolman & Deal, 1991; Mazzoni, 1991; Morgan, 1986; Schneider & Ingram, 1993).

Because the relative potency of power sources and strategies varies across issues and arenas, political *skill*, the capacity to figure out how to capitalize on the available political currency to secure and sustain influence, and political *will*, the commitment to convert power bases into policy influence, are among the most prized political commodities (Allison & Zelikow, 1999; Burns, 1978; Dahl, 1984). Indeed, "policy entrepreneurs" (Kingdon, 1995) who are willing to invest heavily and who are able to connect policy proposals to pressing problems in persuasive ways at opportune moments can be valuable assets, if not indispensable allies, in many governmental and organizational arenas (Kanter, 1983; Levin, 2001; Malen, 1994; Mazzoni, 1991; Mintrom, 2000; Roberts & King, 1996).

Institutional and Sociocultural Contexts

These categories recognize that political dynamics do not play out in a vacuum. Indeed, "politics often unfolds in an institutional context and always in a sociocultural context."[2] These contexts become more than the stage on which political dramas are carried out. They become elements of the drama itself, as actors both draw on the "windows of opportunity" (Kingdon, 1995) that arise to promote their interests and ideals and move within the mesh of fiscal, ideological, and structural constrains that converge to restrict their discretion, modify their aims, and adjust their strategies. Treated here in very abbreviated terms, notions of context are elusive but essential ingredients of political analyses.

Generally speaking, institutions and their broader environments "generate rules, regulations, norms and definitions of the situation" (Rowan & Miskel, 1999, p. 359) that affect how actors think and behave (see also Portz et al., 1999, p. 24). These institutional scripts are manifest in the political system's formal structures of authority and in its embedded habits, routines, and repertoires. They are also manifest in the broader sociocultural values, traditions, and predispositions and in the reigning ideologies that shape our conceptions of legitimate social problems and appropriate policy interventions (Dahl, 1984; Easton, 1985). The institutional and sociocultural contexts are never neutral (Mazzoni, 1991; Rowan & Miskel, 1999). They infuse the political system with presumptions, preferences, and prejudices that operate to advantage some and disadvantage others; and, they convey the images that political systems like public school systems must try to project in order to be perceived as legitimate entities.

The institutional texts and the broader sociocultural forces transmit the core values, prevailing expectations, innovative impulses, and status-enhancing images that vulnerable organizations might emulate to strengthen legitimacy. They signal what public schools and their governmental sponsors might do to replenish the reservoir of favorable sentiments regarding the "rightness" of actions and to accumulate the symbolic reserves required to deflect criticism and maintain confidence in the system. Because policy is a vehicle for signifying that a political system is aligned with (or making a concerted effort to become aligned with) these normative forces, actors may advance initiatives to foster the legitimacy of the system and its current regime, even though there is little evidence the initiatives will improve the performance of the system or subunits of it (Jones & Malen, 2002; Malen, 1994; Malen et al., 1990; Ogawa et al., 2003).

Interactions and Outcomes

These concepts direct attention to the manner in which actor relationships and contextual forces interact to explain decision outcomes. The analytic intent is to identify the critical influence relationships and the critical contextual forces that converge to produce policy choices and mediate policy outcomes.

Identifying the influential forces that impinge on the system and the influential actors who affect policy developments in the system is not a simple, straightforward process. There are no foolproof formulas or precise prescriptions for measuring either (a) the relative power of the contending actors or (b) the relative strength of the broad forces that structure political dynamics and the human agents who seek to influence those dynamics (Clegg, 1989; Dahl, 1984). But analysts can render well-reasoned judgments about the relative power of players by looking at (a) the content of specific decisions to see whose interests are served; (b) the clusters of actors who are reputed to be influential on particular issues, in particular arenas, at particular points in time; and (c) the dynamics that unfold to see whether the attributions of power constitute plausible explanations of the policy decisions and related developments (Dahl, 1984: Geary, 1992). Taken together, these indicators can help analysts avoid the pitfalls of global assessments of influence, which are often misleading (Kingdon, 1995), and examine the basis for contextualized judgments, which are often more accurate appraisals of the influence players wield on particular policy issues in various formal and informal arenas during different phases of the policy process.

Gauging the impact of context is even more problematic than gauging the influence of key actors. The process involves observing how these broad forces structure opportunities, and how they operate to augment the power, strategies and incentives of some players and diminish the same for other actual or potential participants. It also involves listening to actors' perceptions of the relevance and significance of contextual forces on the political dynamics and policy developments. These imprecise orientations recognize that contextual forces may be potent, but they need not be deterministic. Although there are competing points of view, the analytic framework emphasized here assumes that actors who are powerful, tenacious, and astute can ease constraints and seize opportunities in ways that permit them to exert substantial influence on policy developments.

Some would argue that such an assumption underestimates the power of broad forces and overestimates the power of human agency. That risk is one this author accepts in part because lenses that give the nod to human agency (as opposed to lenses that treat context as deterministic) hold greater promise for discovering the types of power configurations and strategic actions required to enact and implement policies that might rectify the stark inequities in our nation's schools and communities.

Policy Issue Illustrations

Various studies demonstrate how the set of constructs highlighted here can be applied to unravel and interpret "the politics of policy" within and across arenas and over time.[3] This section returns to some of the same policy issues discussed under the rational traditions of analysis in an effort to provide especially telling illustrations of how political lenses add to our understanding of policy as a mechanism for managing power relations and legitimating educational and related governmental institutions.

Studies of site-based management councils uncovered poignant and persistent disparities between (a) the promises of empowerment and the parameters of authority and levels of resources granted these groups; (b) the promises of greater teacher and parent influence on school policy and the patterns of principal control of council processes; and (c) the promises of improved educational outcomes for all students and the realization that educational gains are not easily expanded or readily redistributed (Lewis & Nakagawa, 1995; Malen, 1995, 1999). Studies that focused on the politics of site-based management were able to unpack council dynamics and uncover the resources, strategies, and broader economic and institutional constraints that contributed to the disappointing discrepancies between policy promises and policy outcomes (Lewis & Nakagawa, 1995; Malen, 1995, 1999; Shipps, Kahne, & Smylie, 1999). These studies were also able to demonstrate that although these councils typically did not operate as model centers of democratic governance or potent agents of school improvement, they appeared to serve a number of important political functions.

For example, in some settings, site-based management was enacted to diffuse conflict, that is, to create more organizational bins into which contentious issues could be channeled and add new buffer zones that might insulate districts and states from the ramifications of divisive decisions, such as revenue cutbacks and employee layoffs (Malen, 1994; Malen & Muncey, 2000; McLeese, 1992). Site-based management was also enacted because it enabled states and districts to embrace democratic ideals, mimic the innovative practices of high-status corporations, transmit images of bureaucratic accessibility and responsiveness, and otherwise enrich their stock of legitimating capital, albeit not always in dependable and durable ways (Malen, 1994, 1999; Shipps et al., 1999). Although other justifications were advanced, the political utilities of site-based management were very appealing to state and district officials, particularly in settings where various crises of confidence were evident or imminent (Malen, 1994; Shipps et al., 1999). Once in place, some site-based councils functioned as cooling mechanisms, as forums to vent and assuage concerns, as symbols of teachers' and parents' right to a voice in decisions, and as structures to disperse the influence of parent and community activists "who wish to say something about the pattern of resource inequities [or uneven accomplishments] across schools" (Shipps, 1997, p. 103). In these and other ways, site-based councils may be vehicles to deflect demands and maintain rather than alter the governance and operations of schools. There are different takes on this reform movement, particularly on the efforts to decentralize and recentralize decision-making authority in the Chicago public schools (see, e.g., Chambers, 2002–2003; G. A. Hess, 1999; Shipps et al., 1999). Studies of site-based management, however, illustrate how political perspectives may deepen our understanding of policy choices, functions, and outcomes on multiple dimensions of interest, including the impact of policies on the distribution of power in school systems and their broader communities (Chambers, 2002–2003).

An analysis of a very different type of reform, a district-mandated reconstitution initiative (Malen et al., 2002), not only casts doubt on this reform's theory of action but also generates insights about its political utilities (Jones & Malen, 2002). Confronted with intense state regulatory pressures and growing local concerns about school performance and state takeovers, the superintendent launched a reconstitution initiative as a dramatic gesture that might restore confidence in the district's willingness to take decisive action and thus preempt further state intervention. Enacted through a series of low-key conversations in private arenas, the initiative engendered intense negative reactions when educators and parents were told their schools would be reconstituted. Despite efforts to quell resistance, the superintendent could not regain control of the initiative or contain the damage

created as veteran teachers departed, new staffs struggled to reestablish basic organizational routines, and public promises regarding the provision of opportunities and resources to redesign schools were not fulfilled. Ironically, an initiative enacted to bolster confidence in the system by embracing a reform that held currency among state officials failed to preempt further state intervention in the district, relieve local pressures for school improvement, or secure the superintendent's position. Instead, the initiative imposed serious political tolls (the exodus of teachers, the alienation of employees, the loss of legitimacy among internal audiences). These outcomes are particularly costly consequences for a reform that was advanced to improve organizational performance and enhance the autonomy and legitimacy of the district. They suggest that despite its currency in state and federal arenas, on multiple counts, reconstitution may be a particularly precarious approach to education reform.

Politically oriented analyses of the state-directed standards and accountability movement have yielded competing views of the extent to which this movement has altered the balance of power between state governments and local school systems. For example, an early study suggests that local districts retained considerable discretion, despite the high volume of state-initiated legislation (Fuhrman & Elmore, 1990). Indeed, some local units were able to exert considerable influence on policy in their immediate settings as well as in state arenas. A more recent review of research suggests that during the 1980s and 1990s, states not only imposed new obligations, expectations, rules, and regulations on schools but also significantly altered the balance of power between state government and local school systems (Malen & Muncey, 2000). The broadly accepted view that educators at the district and site have the incentive, opportunity, and ingenuity required to effectively unmake or remake policy faster than policy can alter organizational priorities and practices was called into question by evidence suggesting that state policy is restricting the autonomy of local schools, in highly visible as well as in more subtle ways. Legitimated by a heavy reliance on results-oriented rhetoric and public pledges of achievement gains for all students, the standards and accountability movement is a dramatic illustration of how policy can affect the balance of power among governmental authorities, transmit strong messages about the legitimate roles and responsibilities of units within the education policy system, and produce effects that are not readily captured by looking only or primarily at the impact of policies on indicators of organizational performance.

Viewed through a political lens, efforts to develop coherent policy within and across education-related domains and efforts to coordinate human service agencies are more than attempts to spot inconsistencies within and across webs of policy or to envision technically complementary approaches to social problems. They are, at their core, efforts to reconcile conflicting if not incompatible views of both the problems to be attended and the solutions that are or could be attached to them. A political take suggests that because policy is a settlement that mirrors the unequal power and diverse interests of key actors, ambiguous, even contradictory policies are virtually inevitable. Despite the rhetorical appeal of consistent coherent policy, even the most ardent advocates of this approach recognize that a political system's penchant for innovation, its impatience with reforms that do not register immediate results, and its inclination to focus more on the symbols of institutional legitimation than the substance of school improvement all work against the realization of this goal (Fuhrman, 1993). Whether actors can develop the durable bridging strategies and consensus-building structures required to approach this goal remains an open, empirical question (Fuhrman, 1993, 2001). What can be said is that efforts to secure greater coherence will require ongoing political negotiation

as well as ongoing technical searches for complementary policy alignments.

Likewise, efforts to engender collaborative relationships between social service agencies and public schools vividly illustrate that "the technical is often highly political" (White & Wehage, 1995, p. 25), particularly when actors within and across these organizations hold divergent views, seek to protect their respective turfs, and try to wend their way through a maze of local, state, and federal policies governing their organizational operations and collaborative possibilities. The intra- and interorganizational conflicts can be debilitating (Smrekar, 1998). Moreover, efforts to coordinate services and "clientize" populations (Smrekar, 1998) may undermine the ability of human service agents to provide appropriate, empowering assistance and may mask the importance of redistributing resources directly to communities so they can develop the social capital, political infrastructure, and economic opportunities associated with vibrant community settings.

SUMMATIONS, APPLICATIONS, AND LIMITATIONS

This chapter has identified and illustrated conceptual frameworks that educational leaders (and other interested parties) can draw on to think through some of the critical policy issues confronting public school systems. Employing these frameworks to analyze policy developments, however, is not an easy undertaking under the best of conditions. Educational leaders may find it particularly difficult to engage in policy analyses. Because political systems, including public school systems, have a strong penchant for action, they tend to be impatient with the time it takes to carry out responsible analyses of policy options and to be frustrated by the uncertainties that such analyses expose. The pronounced tendency to cast politics as an unprofessional and unsavory enterprise (Hoy & Tarter, 2004) makes it hard to examine, systematically and empirically, the political dynamics that undergird policy developments. For these and other reasons, it is not easy for educational leaders to be policy analysts. Yet, the policy challenges confronting schools summon educational leaders to hone their analytic skills, and the conceptual perspectives offered here can contribute to that end. As both producers and consumers of policy-relevant research, educational leaders might use these perspectives to guide research that is being carried out under their jurisdiction as well as to integrate and interpret information generated by others. As pivotal policy agents and reflective professional practitioners, educational leaders might use these perspectives to foster the development of more deliberative habits of mind and more promising plans of action.

For example, the "policies as hypothesis to be tested" stance can encourage educational leaders to be cognizant of the fragile connections between policy aims, provisions, and effects; to be open to conflicting information about the substantive viability of various policy interventions; and to be mindful of the hazards associated with guaranteeing and overpromising results. Recognizing that the efficacy of policy options is mediated by the context of schools, educational leaders can use the theory of action and webs of policy constructs to examine what we might expect to accomplish with various policy options or combinations of policy initiatives and who might reap the actual or anticipated benefits. The costs of action construct can be used to uncover what we give up when we make policy choices and who bears the various costs incurred. Taken together, the constructs provide ways to gauge what we might gain and what we might sacrifice through different policy options or different combinations of policy initiatives.

The "policies as products of power and symbols of legitimacy" stance can encourage educational leaders to recognize the multiple functions of policy; to understand the "enduring differences" (Bolman & Deal, 1991), as well as the overlapping interests of actors; to unpack the power transactions and the legitimacy pressures that undergird policy developments; and to generate insights regarding the resources required and the strategies available for influencing those developments in various arenas and contexts. Taken together, this set of constructs can help explain how the distribution of benefits and burdens gets determined and rationalized and how those distributional choices reinforce or redefine existing patterns of power and privilege. Although they are often cast as competing traditions of analysis, rational and political orientations are essential components of an educational leader's analytic repertoire. Because policy is called on to serve multiple functions, educational leaders who can examine policy alternatives in light of their prospects for addressing substantive problems, social conflicts, and system legitimation may be better prepared to develop policies that address these fundamental, interrelated challenges. Indeed, research on policy entrepreneurs who have exercised considerable influence on education policy developments suggests that these key actors are rational and political; that is, they act "as purposive agents who seek solutions to complex problems based on their analysis and study . . . [and as] political actors who engage in power struggles with the dominant advocacy coalition they seek to displace" (Roberts & King, 1996, p. 243). Research on education reform ventures as well as on other organizational change initiatives also documents how policy entrepreneurs effectively combine sound policy proposals with astute political strategies to influence public policy and enhance organizational performance (Kanter, 1983; Levin, 2001). These streams of research suggest that conceptual frameworks that unpack rational and political dimensions of education policy may be quite useful tools for educational leaders.

However helpful these conceptual orientations may be, they have serious shortcomings.

The most glaring is their lack of explicit attention to the normative dimensions of policy and the ethical responsibilities of policy analysts and agents in a democratic, pluralistic society. Unfortunately, a discussion of how educational leaders or other interested parties might couple data, reason, power, and politics with principles of equity, justice, and compassion falls well beyond the scope of this chapter and the expertise of this author.[4] What is offered here is a modest primer on rational and political traditions of policy analysis, which educational leaders (and other interested parties) can use to develop more thoughtful, informed judgments about how policies affect the distribution of benefits and burdens in school systems and in the broader society. Hopefully, with that foundation in place, educational leaders, like other interested parties, may be better equipped to develop and sustain policies that foster the creation of a more equitable, just, and compassionate society.

NOTES

1. For discussions of alternative perspectives, see, for example, Kahne, 1996; Malen & Knapp, 1997; Schneider & Ingram, 1993; and Yanow, 1996.

2. This statement was drawn from personal communications with Tim Mazzoni.

3. For example, Zimmerman's (2002) account of the curriculum disputes and "cultural wars in the public schools" demonstrates how actors of different persuasions capitalized on broad social developments as well as localized opportunities to reframe the public debate and to advance their conceptions of what ought to be taught in the nation's public schools. Murphy's (1971) analysis of Title I legislation reveals how actors at all levels of the loosely coupled governmental system operated to adapt this law to their interests, constituencies, and contexts. Mazzoni's (2000) analysis shows how "contextual influences *upon* systems" and "actor influence *within* systems" (p. 148) converged to intensify education policy-making in state arenas. It examines how governors, individual legislators, representatives of big business, and national policy networks including

foundations, teacher unions, and subject-matter organizations interacted around a range of policy initiatives (e.g., school finance reforms, teacher professionalism, school restructuring, outcome-based education, standards-based reforms) during the decade following the infamous *A Nation at Risk* report and explains why states have assumed an increasingly aggressive policy posture. Wells and Serna's (1996) study of detracking reforms indicates how deeply ingrained, often unspoken stereotypes surrounding race, intelligence, and entitlements for "gifted" children and fears evoked by the threat of "white flight" enabled elite parents to deploy a range of strategies that operated to derail detracking initiatives. Marsh's (2002) study of how power imbalances, institutional norms, organizational contexts, and levels of interpersonal and institutional trust shape the efforts of education professionals and community members to "[co-construct] goals, roles and relationships" (p. vi) helps identify the conditions under which the ideals of deliberative democracy might be approximated in local school systems.

4. For assistance with these crucial matters, see, for example, the classic work of James MacGregor Burns (1978) and thoughtful writings by Callahan and Jennings (1983) and Kahne (1996).

REFERENCES

Allison, G., & Zelikow, P. (1999). *Essence of decision* (2nd ed.). New York: Longman.

Anyon, J. (1997). *Ghetto schooling: The political economy of urban educational reform.* New York: Teachers College Press.

Argyris, C., & Schon, D. A. (1982). *Theory in practice.* San Francisco: Jossey-Bass.

Baumgartner, F., & Jones, B. (1991). Agenda dynamics and policy subsystems. *Journal of Politics, 53,* 1044–1074.

Baumgartner, F., & Jones, B. (1993). *Agendas and instability in American politics.* Chicago: University of Chicago Press.

Bolman, L. G., & Deal, T. E. (1991). *Reframing organizations.* San Francisco: Jossey-Bass.

Brewer, D. J., Krop, C., Gill, B. P., & Reichardt, R. (1999). Estimating the cost of national class reduction under different policy alternatives. *Educational Evaluation and Policy Analysis, 2,* 179–192.

Bryk, A. S., Easton, J. Q., Kerbow, D., Rollow, S. G., & Sebring, P. A. (1993). *A view from the elementary schools: The state of reform in*

Chicago. Chicago: Consortium on Chicago School Research.

Bryk, A. S., Sebring, P. A., Kerbow, D., Rollow, S. G., & Easton, J. Q. (1998). *Charting Chicago school reform*. Boulder, CO: Westview Press.

Burns, J. M. (1978). *Leadership*. New York: Harper Colophon Books.

Callahan, D., & Jennings, B. (1983). *Ethics, the social sciences, and policy analysis*. New York: Plenum Press.

Chambers, J., & Parrish, T. (1983). *The development of a resources cost model funding base for education finance in Illinois*. Stanford, CA: Associates for Education Finance and Planning.

Chambers, S. (2002–2003). Urban education reform and minority political empowerment. *Political Science Quarterly, 117(4)*, 643–665.

Clegg, S. R. (1989). *Frameworks of power*. Newbury Park, CA: Sage.

Cobb, R. W., & Ross, M. H. (1997). *Cultural strategies of agenda denial: Avoidance, attack, and redefinition*. Lawrence: University of Kansas Press.

Cohen, D. L., & Hill, H. C. (2001). *Learning policy: When state education reform works*. New Haven, CT: Yale University Press.

Cooper, B. F., & Randall, E. V. (1999). *Advocacy or accuracy: The politics of research in education*. Thousand Oaks, CA: Corwin.

Croninger, R. C., & Lee, V. E. (2001). Social capital and dropping out of high school: Benefits to at-risk students of teachers' support and guidance. *Teachers College Record, 103(4)*, 548–581.

Cuban, L. (1993). *How teachers taught: Constancy and change in American classrooms, 1890–1990* (2nd ed.). New York: Teachers College Press.

Cuban, L. (1998). How schools change reforms: Redefining reform success and failure. *Teachers College Record, 99*, 453–477.

Dahl, R. A. (1984). *Modern political analysis* (4th ed.). Englewood Cliffs, NJ: Prentice Hall.

Dahl, R. A., & Stinebrickner, B. (2003). *Modern political analysis* (6th ed.). Upper Saddle River, NJ: Prentice Hall.

Dodd, L. C., & Jillson, C. (1994). *The dynamics of American politics: Approaches and interpretations*. Boulder, CO: Westview Press.

Easton, D. (1985). Political science in the United States: Past, present, and future. *International Political Science Review, 6*, 133–152.

Edelman, M. (1964). *The symbolic uses of politics*. Champaign–Urbana: University of Illinois.

Elmore, R. F., Peterson, P. L., & McCarthy, S. J. (1996). *Restructuring in the classroom: Teaching, learning, and school organization*. San Francisco: Jossey-Bass.

Elmore, R. F., & Rothman, R. (1999). *Testing, teaching, and learning: A guide for states and school districts*. Washington, DC: National Academy Press.

Elmore, R. C., & Sykes, G. (1992). Curriculum policy. In P. W. Jackson (Ed.), *Handbook of research on curriculum* (pp. 185–215). New York: Macmillan.

Fager, J. (1993). *The 'rules' still rule: The failure of school-based management/shared decision-making in the New York City public schools*. New York: Parents Coalition for Education in NYC.

Firestone, W. A. (1989a). Education policy as an ecology of games. *Educational Researcher, 18(7)*, 18–24.

Firestone, W. A. (1989b). Using reform: Conceptualizing district initiative. *Educational Evaluation and Policy Analysis, 11(2)*, 151–164.

Fischer, F. (1999). *Technocracy and the politics of expertise*. Thousand Oaks, CA: Sage.

Fowler, F. C. (2000). *Policy studies for educational leaders*. Upper Saddle River, NJ: Prentice Hall.

Fuhrman, S. H. (1993). *Designing coherent education policy*. San Francisco: Jossey-Bass.

Fuhrman, S. (2001). *From the capital to the classroom: Standards-based reform in the states*. Chicago: University of Chicago Press.

Fuhrman, S. H., & Elmore, R. F. (1990). Understanding local control in the wake of state education reform. *Educational Evaluation and Policy Analysis, 12(1)*, 82–96.

Galvin, P. (2000). Organizational boundaries, authority, and school district organization. In N. D. Theobald & B. Malen (Eds.), *Balancing local control and state responsibility for K-12 education* (pp. 279–310). Larchmont, NY: Eye on Education.

Gamson, W. A. (2002). *Talking politics*. Cambridge, UK: Cambridge University Press.

Gaventa, J. (1980). *Power and powerlessness, quiescence and rebellion in an Appalachian valley*. Oxford, UK: Clarendon.

Geary, L. S. (1992). *The policymaking process resulting in fiscal policy for special education in Utah*. Unpublished doctoral dissertation, University of Utah, Salt Lake City.

Gillon, S. M. (2000). *That's not what we meant to do: Reform and its unintended consequences*

212EDUCATIONAL POLITICS AND POLICY

212212EDUCATIONAL222222

in twentieth century America. New York: W. W. Norton.

Glazer, N. (1988). *The limits of social policy.* Cambridge, MA: Harvard University Press.

Handler, J. F. (1996). *Down from bureaucracy: The ambiguity of privatization and empowerment.* Princeton, NJ: Princeton University Press.

Hatch, T. (2002, April). When improvement programs collide. *Phi Delta Kappan,* 626–639.

Heineman, R. A., Bluhm, W. T., Peterson, S. A., & Kearny, E. N. (1997). *The world of the policy analyst: Rationality, values & politics* (2nd ed.). Chatham, NJ: Chatham House.

Henig, J. R. (1994). *Rethinking school choice.* Princeton, NJ: Princeton University Press.

Henig, J. R., Hula, R. C., Orr, M., & Pedescleaux, D. S. (1999). *The color of reform: Race, politics, and the challenge of urban education.* Princeton, NJ: Princeton University Press.

Hess, F. M. (1999). *Spinning wheels: The politics of urban school reform.* Washington, DC: Brookings Institute.

Hess, G. A. (1999). Expectations, opportunity, capacity and will: The four essential components of Chicago school reform. *Educational Policy, 13*(4), 494–517.

Honig, M. (2003). Building policy from practice: School district central office administrators' roles and capacity for implementing collaborative education policy. *Educational Administration Quarterly, 39*(3), 292–338.

Honig, M., Kahne, J., & McLaughlin, M. M. (2001). School community connections: Strengthening opportunity to learn and opportunity to teach. In V. Richardson (Ed.), *Handbook of research on teaching* (4th ed., pp. 998–1028). Washington, DC: American Educational Research Association.

Howlett, M., & Ramesh, M. (1995). *Studying public policy.* Oxford, UK: Oxford University Press.

Hoy, W. K., & Tarter, J. C. (2004). *Administrators solving the problems of practice: Decision-making concepts, cases, and consequences.* Boston: Pearson Education.

Ingersoll, R. M. (1999). The problem of underqualified teachers in American secondary schools. *Educational Researcher, 28*(2), 26–37.

Ingersoll, R. M. (2001). Teacher turnover and teacher shortages: An organizational analysis. *American Educational Research Journal, 38*(3), 499–534.

Jenkins-Smith, H. C. (1988). Analytical debates and policy learning: Analysis and change in the federal bureaucracy. *Policy Sciences, 21,* 169–211.

Jenkins-Smith. H. C. (1990). *Democratic politics and policy analysis.* Pacific Grove, CA: Brooks/ Cole.

Jones, D. R., & Malen, B. (2002). Sources of victory, seeds of defeat: Linking enactment politics and implementation developments. In W. Hoy & C. Miskel (Eds.), *Theory and research in educational administration* (Vol. 1, pp. 41–76). Greenwich, CT: Information Age Publishing.

Kahne, J. (1996). *Reframing educational policy.* New York: Teachers College Press.

Kanter, R. M. (1983). *The change masters.* New York: Simon & Schuster.

Kerr, D. (1976). *Educational policy.* New York: Davis McKay.

King, J. A. (1994). Meeting the educational needs of at-risk students: A cost analysis of three models. *Educational Evaluation and Policy Analysis, 16,* 1–19.

Kingdon, J. W. (1995). *Agendas, alternatives, and public policies* (2nd ed.). New York: Harper Collins.

Knapp, M. S., Bamburg, J. D., Ferguson, M. C., & Hill, P. T. (1998). Converging reforms and the working lives of frontline professionals in schools. *Education Policy, 12*(4), 397–418.

Ladd, H. (1996). *Holding schools accountable: Performance-based reform in education.* Washington, DC: Brookings Institution.

Lee, V. E., Smith, J. B., & Croninger, R. C. (1997). How high school organization influences the equitable distribution of learning in mathematics and science. *Sociology of Education, 70,* 128–150.

Leithwood, K., & Menzies, T. (1998). Forms and effects of school-based management: A review. *Educational Policy, 12,* 325–346.

Levin, B. (2001). *Reforming education: From origins to outcomes.* New York: Routledge Falmer.

Levin, H. M., & McEwan, P. (2001). *Cost-effectiveness analysis* (2nd ed.). Thousand Oaks, CA: Sage.

Lewis, D. A., & Nakagawa, K. (1995). *Race and educational reform in the American metropolis: A study of school decentralization.* Albany: SUNY Press.

Lindblom, C. (1959). The science of muddling through. *Public Administration Review, 14,* 79–88.

Lynn, L. E. (1999). A place at the table: Policy analysis, its postpositive critics, and the future of practice. *Journal of Policy Analysis and Management, 18,* 411–425.

Malen, B. (1994). Site-based management: A political utilities analysis. *Education Evaluation and Policy Analysis, 16,* 249–267.

Malen, B. (1995). The micropolitics of education: Mapping the multiple dimensions of power relations in school polities. In J. Scribner & D. Layton (Eds.), *The study of educational politics* (pp. 147–167). New York: Falmer Press.

Malen, B. (1999). The promise and perils of participation on site-based councils. *Theory into Practice, 38*(4), 209–216.

Malen, B. (2001). Generating interest in interest groups. *Educational Policy, 15*(1), 168–186.

Malen, B., Croninger, R., Muncey, D., & Jones, D. (2002). Reconstituting schools: Testing the theory of action. *Education Evaluation and Policy Analysis, 24*(2), 113–132.

Malen, B., & Knapp, M. (1997). Rethinking the multiple perspectives approach to education policy analysis: Implications for policy-practice connections. *Journal of Education Policy, 12,* 419–445.

Malen, B., & Muncey, D. (2000). Creating "a new set of givens"? The impact of state activism on site autonomy. In N. D. Theobald & B. Malen (Eds.), *Balancing local control and state responsibility for K-12 education* (pp. 199–244). Larchmont, NY: Eye on Education.

Malen, B., Ogawa, R. T., & Kranz, J. (1990). What do we know about site-based management? A case study of the literature—a call for research. In W. H. Clune & J. F. Witte (Eds.), *Choice and control in American education: Vol. 2. The practice of choice, decentralization, and school restructuring* (pp. 289–342). New York: Falmer Press.

Malen, B., & Rice, J. K. (2003, March). *Strengthening incentives, diluting capacity: An analysis of the initial effects of high stakes accountability initiatives on local schools.* Paper prepared for the annual meeting of the American Education Finance Association, Orlando, FL.

March, J. G., & Olsen, J. P. (1989). *Rediscovering institutions: The organizational basis of politics.* New York: The Free Press.

Marsh, J. A. (2002). *Democratic dilemmas: Joint work, education politics, and community.* Unpublished doctoral dissertation, Stanford University, Palo Alto, CA.

Mazzoni, T. L. (1991). Analyzing state school policymaking: An arena model. *Educational Evaluation and Policy Analysis, 13*(2), 115–138.

Mazzoni, T. L. (2000). State politics and school reform: The first decade of the "education excellence" movement. In N. D. Theobald & B. Malen (Eds.), *Balancing local control and state responsibility for K-12 education* (pp. 147–196). Larchmont, NY: Eye on Education.

McLeese, P. (1992). *The process of decentralizing conflict and maintaining stability: Site council enactment, implementation, operation, and impacts in the Salt Lake City School District 1970–1985.* Unpublished doctoral dissertation, University of Utah, Salt Lake City.

McNeil, L. M. (2000). *Contradictions of school reform: Educational costs of standardized testing.* New York: Routledge.

Mintrom, M. (2000). *Policy entrepreneurs and school choice.* Washington, DC: Georgetown University Press.

Mintrop, H., Gamson, D., McLaughlin, M., Wong, P. L., & Oberman, I. (2001). Design cooperation: Strengthening the link between organizational and instructional change in schools. *Educational Policy, 15*(4), 520–546.

Miskel, C., & Song, M. (2003). *Passing reading first: Prominence and processes in an elite policy network.* Unpublished paper, University of Michigan.

Mitchell, D. E., & Encarnation, D. J. (1984). Educational policy analysis: The state of the art. *Educational Administration Quarterly, 20*(3), 129–160.

Moe, T. (1984). The new economics of organization. *American Journal of Political Science, 28,* 739–777.

Morgan, G. (1986). *Images of organizations.* Beverly Hills, CA: Sage.

Moynihan, D. P. (1969). *Maximum feasible misunderstanding.* New York: Free Press.

Muncey, D., & McQuillan, P. (1998). *Reform and resistance in schools & classrooms.* New Haven, CT: Yale University Press.

Murphy, J. T. (1971). Title I of ESEA: The politics of implementing federal education reform. *Harvard Educational Review, 41*(1), 35–63.

Newman, F. M., Smith, B., Allensworth, E., & Bryk, A. S. (2001). Instructional program coherence: What it is and why it should guide school improvement policy. *Educational Evaluation and Policy Analysis, 23*(4), 297–321.

Nye, B., Hedges, L. V., & Konstantopoulos, S. (2002). Do low-achieving students benefit more from smaller classes? Evidence from the Tennessee class size experiment. *Educational Evaluation and Policy Analysis, 24*(3), 201–217.

Ogawa, R. T., Sandholtz, J. H., Martinez-Flores, M., & Scribner, S. P. (2003). The substantive and symbolic consequences of a district's standards' based curriculum. *American Educational Research Journal, 40*(1), 147–176.

Orr, M. (1999). *Black social capital: The politics of school reform in Baltimore, 1986–1998.* Lawrence: University of Kansas Press.

Patton, M. Q. (1990). *Qualitative evaluation and research methods* (2nd ed.). Newbury Park, CA: Sage.

Portz, J., Stein, L., & Jones, B. B. (1999). *City schools and city politics: Institutions and leadership in Pittsburgh, Boston, and St. Louis.* Lawrence: The University of Kansas Press.

Radin, B. A. (2000). *Beyond Machiavelli policy analysis comes of age.* Washington, DC: Georgetown University Press.

Rice, J. K. (1997). Cost analysis in education: Paradox and possibility. *Educational Evaluation and Policy Analysis, 19*(4), 309–317.

Rice, J. K. (2001). The cost of working together: A framework for estimating the costs of comprehensive support systems for children. *Administration & Society, 33*(4), 455–479.

Rice, J. K. (2002a). Cost analysis in education policy research: A comparative analysis across fields of public policy. In. H. M. Levin & P. McEwan (Eds.), *Cost-effectiveness analysis in education: Progress and prospects* (pp. 21–36). Larchmont, NY: Eye on Education.

Rice, J. K. (2002b). Making economically grounded decisions about comprehensive school reform models: Considerations of costs, effects, and contexts. In K. K. Wong & M. C. Wang (Eds.), *Efficiency, accountability, and equity issues in Title I schoolwide program implementation.* Greenwich, CT: Information Age Publishing.

Rice, J. K. (2003a). Investing in teacher quality: A framework of estimating the cost of teacher professional development. In W. Hoy & C. Miskel (Eds.), *Theory and research in educational administration* (Vol. 2, pp. 209–233). Greenwich, CT: Information Age Publishing.

Rice, J. K. (2003b). *Teacher quality: Understanding the effectiveness of teacher attributes.* Washington, DC: Economic Policy Institute.

Rice, J. K., & Malen, B. (2003). The human costs of education reform: The case of school reconstitution. *Educational Administration Quarterly, 39*(5), 635–661.

Roberts, N. C., & King, P. J. (1996). *Transforming public policy: Dynamics of policy entrepreneurship and innovation.* San Francisco: Jossey-Bass.

Rothstein, R. (2002). *Out of balance: Our understanding of how schools affect society and how society affects schools.* Chicago: Spencer Foundation.

Rowan, B., & Miskel, C. G. (1999). Institutional theory and the study of educational organizations. In J. Murphy & K. Seashore Louis (Eds.), *Handbook of research on educational administration* (2nd ed., pp. 359–383). San Francisco: Jossey-Bass.

Sabatier, P. A. (1999). *Theories of the policy process.* Boulder, CO: Westview Press.

Schattschneider, E. E. (1960). *The semi-sovereign people.* New York: Holt, Rinehart & Winston.

Schneider, A., & Ingram, H. (1993). Social construction of target populations: Applications for politics and policy. *American Political Science Review, 87*(2), 334–347.

Schorr, L. B. (1988). *Within our reach: Breaking the cycle of disadvantage.* New York: Anchor Press.

Sebring, P. A., & Bryk, A. S. (1993). Charting reform in Chicago schools: Pluralistic policy research. *New Directions for Program Evaluation, 59*, 13–28.

Shipps, D. (1997). The invisible hand: Big business and Chicago school reform. *Teachers College Record, 99*, 73–116.

Shipps, D., Kahne, J., & Smylie, M. (1999). The politics of urban school reform: Legitimacy, city growth, and school improvement in Chicago. *Educational Policy, 13*(4), 518–545.

Shulman, L. S. (1988). Disciplines of inquiry in education: An overview. In R. M. Jaeger (Ed.), *Complementary methods for research in education* (pp. 3–17). Washington, DC: American Educational Research Association.

Smith, M., & O'Day, J. (1990). Systemic school reform. In S. Fuhrman & B. Malen (Eds.), *The politics of curriculum and testing* (pp. 233–267). New York: Falmer Press.

Smith, S. R., & Ingram, H. (2002). Rethinking policy analysis: Citizens, community, and the restructuring of public services. *The Good Society, 11*(1), 55–60.

Smrekar, C. (1998). The organizational and political threats to school-linked integrated services. *Educational Policy, 12*(3), 284–304.

Spillane, J. P. (1996). School districts matter: Local educational authorities and state instructional policy. *Educational Policy, 10*, 63–87.

Sroufe, G. E. (1995). Politics of education at the federal level. In J. D. Scribner & D. H. Layton (Eds.), *The study of educational politics* (pp. 75–88). New York: Falmer Press.

Stier, H., & Tienda, M. (2001). *The color of opportunity: Pathways to family, welfare, and work.* Chicago: University of Chicago Press.

Stone, C. N., Henig, J. R., Jones, B. O., & Pierannunzi, C. (2001). *Building civic capacity: The politics of reforming urban schools.* Lawrence: University Press of Kansas.

Tallerico, M. (1992). The dynamics of superintendent-school board relationships. *Urban Education, 24,* 215–231.

Truman, D. B. (1951). *The governmental process.* New York: Knopf.

Walker, J. L., Jr. (1991). *Mobilizing interest groups in America: Patrons, professions, and social movements.* Ann Arbor: University of Michigan Press.

Weiler, H. (1993). Control versus legitimation. In J. Hannaway & M. Carnoy (Eds.), *Decentralization and school improvement* (pp. 55–83). San Francisco: Jossey-Bass.

Weiss, C. H. (1998). Nothing as practical as good theory: Exploring theory-based evaluation for comprehensive community initiatives for children and families. In J. P. Connell, A. C. Kubisch, L. B. Schorr, & C. H. Weiss (Eds.), *New approaches to evaluating community initiatives* (pp. 65–92). Washington, DC: The Aspen Institute.

Wells, A. S., & Serna, I. (1996). The politics of culture: Understanding local political resistance to detracking in racially mixed schools. *Harvard Educational Review, 66,* 93–118.

White, J. A., & Wehage, G. (1995). Community collaboration: If it is such a good idea, why is it so hard to do? *Educational Evaluation and Policy Analysis, 17,* 23–38.

Wildavsky, A. (1979). *Speaking truth to power.* New Brunswick, NJ: Transaction Books.

Yanow, D. (1996). *How does a policy mean? Interpreting policy and organizational actions.* Washington, DC: Georgetown University Press.

Zimmerman, J. (2002). *Whose America? Culture wars in the public schools.* Cambridge, MA: Harvard University Press.

10

Educational Leadership and the New Economy

Keeping the "Public" in Public Schools

GARY L. ANDERSON
New York University

MONICA PINI
National University of San Martin, Argentina

INTRODUCTION AND OVERVIEW

Most school leaders are currently immersed in a new policy environment that is driven by standards and standardization through high-stakes testing. They are also experiencing what some are calling policy overload, particularly in California, where the usual state legislative policies are supplemented with the latest ballot initiatives. Perhaps less noticed but growing rapidly is a shift toward school choice, privatization of services and school management, and the popularity of "business models." Charter schools and more lenient student transfer policies in most states have altered the educational landscape for principals and superintendents, as schools increasingly compete for students and teachers. The massive increase in outsourcing of school and district services to private companies, pressures to supplement revenues by opening up schools to commercial exploitation, and the arrival of for-profit Educational Management Organizations (EMOs) is altering the ways districts structure their finances and collective bargaining agreements.

These new trends toward privatization are moving ahead so rapidly that our current notions of leadership, school law, finance, and educational policy fail to adequately capture what is going on in statehouses, school districts, schools, and classrooms. Few educational leaders understand the extent to which these changes are related to a corporate-led shift in the goals of schooling to an almost exclusive emphasis on the creation of human capital for the "new world economy." In this

216

chapter, we will attempt to bring some conceptual clarity to these tendencies by describing four areas of influence that have impacted education in the last two decades. In some cases, these areas of influence represent relatively new phenomena, and in others, they are an intensification of social phenomena that have been around for more than a century. The four overlapping influences that are having a powerful impact on education are

1. *Corporatization:* a greater role for business, particularly the corporate sector, not only in education but in society at large

2. *Marketization:* a tendency to view individual choice in a marketplace as a more efficient and effective way to allocate resources and values in society, as well as a more effective form of accountability for public institutions

3. *Privatization:* the transfer of public institutions into private hands

4. *Commercialization:* the opening up of public schools to commercial exploitation

Although these four areas of influence overlap considerably, we find it useful to discuss them separately because the implications of each for school leaders are different. At times, we take a strong cautionary tone toward the increased marriage of business and schooling, in part because corporate money has financed a network of think tanks, foundations, and lobbyists to convince Americans that "the business model" or privatization is the answer to nearly every social problem. Our basic premise is that any time we transfer ideas and perspectives from one sector to another, we must look carefully at whether the fit is appropriate and carefully analyze the motivations behind such a transfer. Not only are some attempting to argue that what is good for business is also good for education, but also some suggest that democratic public institutions are obsolete and need to be replaced by more market-oriented, private ones (Chubb & Moe, 1990).

Gelberg (1997) argues that the tendency of education to ape business can be traced back to the administrative progressives of the early 20th century, and some scholars trace it back much further (Welch, 1998). Although the interest of the business community in education waned somewhat in the postwar years, its presence during the last two decades of the 20th century has been powerful, although, as we will see, not necessarily speaking in a unified voice. The recent World Trade Organization protests, filmmaker Michael Moore's popular corporate exposés, and the Enron debacle have made a small chink in the commonsense notion that many Americans hold of the benign corporation whose interests reflect our own. This growing attention to corporate control has opened up a relatively hidden history of the growth of corporate influence worldwide. The following section will review this history and its implications for the public sector and public schooling in particular.

THE CORPORATIZATION OF SOCIETY AND EDUCATION

A Short History of the American Corporation

Few Americans are aware that the first corporations in America were chartered by the King of England. The notion widely held today that corporations are private enterprises would have appeared nonsensical to any American up to the end of the 19th century. Corporations under the British monarchy were formed to promote the interests of the monarchy, and they were held on a short leash. Many of the original American colonies, such as the Massachusetts Bay Company, were in fact British corporations chartered to stake claims in the New World. After the American Revolution, corporations were chartered by the American states in the interests of their citizenry, which at the time was limited to white, propertied males.

At least legally, then, corporations were public institutions created by special charters of incorporation granted by state legislatures to serve the common good. Although many corporations chartered to build such things as canals or colleges also created wealth for individuals, the primary function of the corporation was to serve the public interest. People, through their legislature, retained sovereignty over corporations, and legislatures dictated rules for "issuing stock, for shareholder voting, for obtaining corporate information, for paying dividends and keeping records. They limited capitalization, debts, landholdings, and sometimes profits." (Grossman & Adams, 1995, cited in Derber, 1998, p. 124)

However, popular sovereignty and legislative control over corporations began to unravel during the late 19th century. The 14th Amendment of the U.S. Constitution, created to protect the equal rights of freed slaves, was used as a legal tool to provide corporations with the legal rights of a person. Much like today, conservative judges during the Gilded Age of the early 20th century were cynically allied with powerful corporate friends. These judges and corporate leaders colluded to turn public control over corporations into a violation of the 14th Amendment, which holds that no state "shall deprive any person of life, liberty, or property, without due process of law." Thus, the courts of the Gilded Age broke with the state grant theory of public accountability over corporations and supported instead a conception of corporations as a voluntary contract among private people. In this way, a public institution, created and controlled by a sovereign people, became a private institution or "enterprise" whose existence was independent of the state *and largely immune from public accountability*. In recent years, courts have used the First Amendment to the Constitution to view massive corporate contributions to political campaigns as an expression of free speech, thus supporting the notion that a corporation is the equivalent of a human being under the law.

What is perhaps even more remarkable is that this history of the shift of corporations from publicly accountable, chartered enterprises to private enterprises is virtually unknown among the general public in the United States. Such accounts do not appear in high school history texts, nor are they taught in colleges of education, in spite of the current attempts to privatize schools.

Why should we care whether a corporation is state controlled or not? This question goes to the heart of the debate about public school privatization. What are public institutions, and what makes them different from private ones? Increasingly, corporations are taking over many public functions and impacting public policy. Corporations affect political outcomes with their campaign contributions and lobbyists. "More than 500 corporations maintain political offices in Washington and, along with trade associations, employ thousands of lobbyists who often end up writing the bills that affect their industries" (Derber, 1998, p. 24). Many see the growing economic influence of corporations and their control of major media as a threat to American democracy.

How Public Schools Subsidize Corporations

Although many school administrators and teachers think that corporations generously help to subsidize public education, the truth is actually quite the opposite. Corporations are constantly in search of tax breaks that take public money away from education. Because they are mobile, they can pit communities, states, and even countries against each other by requiring tax concessions and other favorable legislative changes in return for their presence and the jobs they may bring to the community. Then, having wrested concessions, increased the local population's taxes, and saved millions of their own dollars, corporations can turn around and make "philanthropic" contributions that build positive public relations for the company. Although many local politicians are aware that they are essentially being blackmailed, they often feel they have to play the game or lose jobs. In reality, many of these companies only stay for the period of their tax breaks, and most transfer or import higher paid workers from outside the community (Shuman, 1998).

Unfortunately, the extent to which the public subsidizes corporations is far greater than tax breaks. U.S. business has been subsidized on a grand scale by public schools since the late 19th century. Welch (1998) describes how U.S. business turned to the public schools to subsidize its training of workers through vocational education.

> U.S. business interests, having consistently failed to invest in the training of apprentices, became increasingly alarmed at the paucity of skilled personnel that was available to serve the needs of an industrializing economy. Given this lack, two strategies suggested themselves: either to import foreign labor (particularly from Germany, whose technical and industrial education was universally admired) or to train the future workers in the US. However, the industrialists did not wish to adopt the financial burden of training US youth themselves. Thus, the tactic adopted was to press the state to adopt the burden. (Welch, 1998, p. 8)

Thus, the burden of training workers for industry was shifted from corporations to the public schools through vocational education programs. The irony of this turn of events is that at the same time that manufacturers succeeded in unloading this financial burden onto the taxpayer, they have over the years criticized schools for not preparing workers to the specifications of industry. The constant complaints of the corporate sector that U.S. public schools are doing a poor job of producing human capital are hypocritical, given this monumental and little acknowledged shift of costs to the taxpayer. Callahan (1962) puts it this way:

> As a first step to secure their [corporations'] ends, they and their agents in unmeasured terms denounced the public schools as behind the age, as inefficient, as lacking in public spirit. And why? Because the public schools are not training artisans—doing the work that had been done by employers of labor for thousands of years. The arrogance of the manufacturers was two-fold, first, in condemning the schools for not doing what . . . had never before been considered the duty of the schools to do; and second, in demanding that the state, after . . . fill[ing] the pockets of the manufacturers [through tariff protection], should then proceed to pay the bills for training their workmen. (pp. 13–14)

That corporations are private entities with the rights of people and that the public schools should subsidize the training of corporate workers are notions that are now taken for granted by most Americans and are therefore beyond critique. Having established this level of hegemony in American society, corporations are now moving on to demand more concessions. Some of these will be discussed in the following sections.

The Corporate Impact on Cities, Districts, and Schools

So far, we have discussed how corporations play cities off each other for tax concessions; however, recent research indicates that the impact of corporations on cities, school districts, schools, and classrooms is deleterious in other ways. Some of these will be discussed in the remaining sections of this chapter. Mickelson (1999) has provided perhaps the most extensive overview of corporate influence on education. Her typology of corporate influence helps to provide some theoretical handles on a complex social phenomenon. Mickelson (1999) describes six types of corporate actors with different types of involvement and motivation:

Type I: Large independent foundations whose boards of directors are from the highest ranks of the corporate world. These foundations help to conceptualize and fund reform initiatives that reflect their political and economic worldview. Many task forces, conferences, research grants, and think tanks are funded by these foundations.

Type II: Corporate leaders who serve on national task forces or use their visibility and resources to promote reform initiatives at the national, state, and local levels.

Type III: Mid-level corporate actors who do much of the day-to-day labor on task forces. They serve as links to local and state school personnel as reforms are implemented and, occasionally, as executives-on-loan to a school system or education foundation.

Type IV: Corporate employees who volunteer as tutors or mentors in particular schools. They sometimes are guest speakers, or they may hard-wire schools for the Internet. They often volunteer in schools their children attend.

Type V: Educational decision makers, often business leaders in elected or appointed positions, most commonly school board members. They often are appointed or run for these offices to provide a perspective different from professional educators.

Type VI: For-profit companies that sell their products or services. Here, Mickelson (1999) does not refer to vendors who sell specific services such as bus driving or maintenance or products such as paper or sports equipment, but rather EMOs like the Edison Project or media productions like Channel One. However, the increased prevalence of outsourcing of services, costly test and textbook purchases, and special contracts with soda and sneaker companies constitute an often overlooked dimension of privatization that we will discuss below.

Another set of actors that Mickelson neglects to mention are the Business Roundtable and many local chambers of commerce, which have presented proposals for school reform in many state legislatures. Thus, corporate influence is pervasive, coming from multiple sources, levels, and media.

Mickelson (1999) also provides a case study of the impact of a single corporation (IBM) on a single community (Charlotte, North Carolina). Her case study demonstrates how IBM worked to create policy changes in Charlotte that would help provide high-quality, racially segregated schools for their incoming professional and executive families. The Charlotte community approved an $82 million bond initiative to fund a state-of-the-art, four-school magnet cluster named Education Village. Meanwhile, IBM executives, working directly with the Charlotte school superintendent, John Murphy, received verbal permission to set aside one third of the seats for IBM employees. Mickelson documents the significant influence IBM was given because of a $2 million contribution it promised to the new magnet cluster. Ultimately, the school board, under pressure from the community, successfully challenged the deal, which enraged the IBM executives. A local business leader (quoted in Mickelson, 1999) wrote in an editorial published in the *Charlotte Observer*:

> These companies [which donate money to schools] do not need to have their motives questioned. They do not need to be hassled. They do not need to be set straight by public officials. They need to be persuaded to offer even more support. Like me, people in other businesses are watching the Education Village situation unfold. If our school board can't understand the grant's purpose, won't honor agreements and can't act graciously, other companies will think twice before extending new offers of support. (p. 10)

The corporatization of Charlotte schools involved an intensification of social class and racial segregation in a community that had previously been viewed as a national model of desegregation. Corporations sought to provide not only an elite public education for incoming professional workers and executives, but also an educational environment that was racially segregated.

Shipps (1997) documents corporate influence in Chicago (see also Lipman, 2002). In 1988, Chicago experimented with a democratic community-based reform that gave greater control over schools to local community boards. She documents the battle between business interests and community-based advocacy organizations and the resultant corporate reforms of 1995. According to Shipps,

the view of the two reforms that emerges when the business role is understood focuses less on the growth of parent power and democratic revitalization than on the replacement of centralized professional control with decentralized business management. (p. 3)

The 1995 legislation in Chicago "gave sweeping new powers to a school district management team whose titles read more like those of a Fortune 500 corporation than an urban public school system" (Shipps, 1997, p. 1). The superintendent's cabinet, all appointed by the mayor of Chicago, now had names like chief executive officer (superintendent), chief financial officer, chief operations officer, and so on.

Together they have authority to determine which schools require intervention; to dismiss, lay off, or reassign any and all personnel in them; and to dissolve elected Local School Councils (LSCs). They are also empowered to cut costs, privatize work usually performed by employees, and abrogate many collective bargaining agreements. (Shipps, 1997, p. 1)

In many ways, the corporate-led reforms in Chicago were more sweeping than in Charlotte because they resulted in profound structural changes that made the school district operate on the principles of a private business rather than

those of a school district. That relatively few people see this as a problem is an indication of how successful the corporate community has been at promoting its worldview. Other case studies of corporate influence at the local level are being produced by researchers around the world (Gewirtz, 2002; White, 2002).

The Corporate Influence on Educational Administration and Teaching

Much of the new language that has entered the lexicon of educational administration came from an army of workshop leaders and professors who taught the principles of Total Quality Management (TQM), which became popular in the 1980s and 1990s. In reality, TQM had already been critiqued within the corporate world, when educators picked it up. Terms like *continuous improvement, teaming, customer, quality,* and so on became in this period part of administrators' vocabulary. TQM principles were even promoted in classrooms through the Baldridge approach, which applied TQM principles to classroom instruction.

TQM devolved decision making to workers, promoting teaming and site-based decision making. However, while important strategic decisions were made by management, workers were allowed to make relatively insignificant operational decisions. This essentially becomes a new, more sophisticated motivation theory in which workers—or teachers—have the illusion of control over their workplace, while real control is consolidated at higher levels of the system. Thus, teachers, according to this business model, are encouraged to "take ownership" and "buy into" someone else's agenda. Anderson (1998) has argued that workers are becoming increasingly aware that while they are being "empowered" on the shop floor through participation in selected work-related decisions, their unions are being busted, their companies downsized, their jobs moved overseas, and their salaries and benefits slashed. A similar trend can be seen in education, where funding is slashed and top-down testing regimes coexist with teacher "empowerment" and "autonomy" through site-based decision making.

Edelman (1978) put it more bluntly:

> Participation in group meetings has often been obligatory: in China, in Russia, and in Nazi Germany, just as it usually is in mental hospitals, in prisons, and in high schools that emphasize student self-government; for it helps evoke popular acquiescence in rules that would be resisted if authorities imposed them by fiat. (p. 121)

The other aspect of TQM that has infused education is the notion of statistical control and the elimination of variance. In most businesses, it makes sense to want to produce products that eliminate variance. A quality product is one that does not vary, such as a McDonald's hamburger or an air filter for an automobile. Any variation is viewed as a defect, and the use of statistical control helps to eliminate variation. This notion has essentially been lifted from business and applied wholesale to education through current testing regimes that exert statistical control over student achievement. The only problem is that the core technologies of business and education are fundamentally different. Successful student achievement depends on addressing variation in students, and the essence of education is helping each student find his or her own individual and unique self-actualization.

As we have tried to indicate in this section, corporate influence in education, while not new, is stronger today than at any time in our history. Corporations have given us much that is good. Business as a social enterprise is a cherished foundation of our economy and society. Few economists today would argue that any country can prosper without a vibrant private sector. However, humans are not merely *homo economicus,* and our schools were never meant merely to serve the needs of business. Corporations have a place in our

society, but sovereignty belongs to the public. Without a government and public spaces independent of corporate control, the notion of "public" in public schooling is called into question.

MARKETIZATION: TRANSFERRING MARKET PRINCIPLES INTO THE PUBLIC SPHERE

The ascendancy of corporations in American society during the 20th century was accompanied by a transfer of business ideology from the private sector to the public sector. This process is often referred to as *marketization.* Transferring market principles to the public sphere means a shift in language and values that replaces a concern with the common good with values of competition and self-interest. Before getting into the specific impact of a market mentality on schools, it is important to understand the mechanisms through which such ideological shifts take place in society. Many accounts give the impression that these shifts are part of a linear march of progress toward ever purer forms of free-market capitalism. In fact, such shifts have everything to do with Machiavellian political maneuver and, in modern times, control of media and other apparatuses that control how people think. Among political scientists, Murray Edelman (1988) has perhaps best described how the way people think about social issues is influenced through what he calls the construction of a political spectacle.

Edelman argues that an understanding of the following elements is crucial for an understanding of how the political spectacle is constructed. We have briefly related each element to how business interests have been legitimized in the United States over the past several decades.

1. *The importance of language and discourse.* In his book, *Political Language: Words That Succeed and Policies That Fail,* Edelman (1978) focused on the relationship between language

and politics and what he called "the linguistic structuring of social problems" (p. 26). He provides a methodology for studying policy based on the notion that "how the problem is named involves alternative scenarios, each with its own facts, value judgments, and emotions" (p. 29). A simple example is the current trend of describing students and parents in schools as customers or superintendents as CEOs. Once the corporate language of the market becomes dominant, the market logic follows.

2. *The definition of events as crises.* "A crisis, like all news developments, is a creation of the language used to depict it; the appearance of a crisis is a political act, not a recognition of a fact or a rare situation" (Edelman, 1988, p. 31). Crises, according to Edelman, "typically rationalize policies that are especially harmful to those who are already disadvantaged" (pp. 31–32). By promoting a view of public schools as in crisis, the business community can provide solutions to the crisis, such as market-oriented educational policies or high-stakes, standardized testing.

3. *A tendency to cover political interests with a discourse of rational policy analysis.* A crisis is often created through an appeal to scientific, rational, neutral discourses. For example, political advantage is gained not through political rhetoric, but rather through privately funded, ideologically driven think tanks that sponsor and disseminate ideology couched as "objective" research. The vast majority of Washington think tanks are heavily funded by corporations and promote a probusiness ideology.

4. *The linguistic evocation of enemies and the displacement of targets.* Those with the power to manage meaning can cast tenured radicals, the welfare state, social promotion, progressive teaching methods, teachers unions, and so on as the villains of educational reform. All displace attention from other possible actors and events. Limiting the demand for accountability

to the public sector and, specifically, public schools also displaces other targets that escape attention (e.g., corporations, military spending). Greater public accountability is advanced for the public sector, while deregulation (or less public accountability) is advanced for the private sector.

5. *The public as political spectators.* Democratic participation is limited to such reactive rituals as voting or being polled: "An individual vote is more nearly a form of self-expression and of legitimation than of influence" (Edelman, 1988, p. 97). School choice in a quasi-market is promoted as being more democratic than school boards for parent participation. The concept of *citizen* is reduced to *consumer*.

6. *The media as mediator of the political spectacle.* Edelman (2001) gave news reporting and other forms of media a central place in the construction of the political spectacle. A handful of corporations now own nearly all newspapers and major TV stations. Battles are currently being waged over the control of new media such as the Internet.

From his earliest work, such as *The Symbolic Uses of Politics* (1967), to his later work, *Constructing the Political Spectacle* (1988), Edelman acknowledged the traditional venues elites have used to gain and maintain power, but his work was an attempt to help political scientists and the public understand the less visible ways that power is wielded and the specific symbolic strategies used by dominant groups to promote their interests.

Intellectual Roots of Marketization

The very groups that constructed a political spectacle portraying a public school system in crisis were largely the same groups that proposed solutions. Certain elements of current school reform, such as high-stakes testing, outcomes-based evaluation, data-based decision-making, and leadership teams, rely on social engineering to steer the school system and have borrowed heavily from the corporate sector. However, more conservative economists see in this manufactured crisis an opportunity to promote their neoliberal, free-market, ideological aims. In the years after World War II, a group of University of Chicago economists promoted a view of human nature as *homo economicus,* based on assumptions of individuality, rationality, and self-interest. Milton Friedman, Gary Becker, and George Stigler had prepared the intellectual groundwork for what Peters (2001) calls the "imperialistic" form of free-market economics in which

> neoclassical economics was deemed to provide a *unified* approach to the study of human behavior. This approach was to be extended into areas that are traditionally the preserve and prerogative of political science, sociology, and the other social science disciplines. (p. 15)

As Mickelson (1999) suggested above, think tanks funded by private foundations are a key vehicle for the dissemination of the new neoliberal market gospel and neoconservative moralizing about values, choice, and standards. The Heritage Foundation, the Hudson Institute, the Manhattan Institute, and the American Enterprise Institute are the most important bases of neoliberal and neoconservative analysts such as Denis Doyle, Chester Finn, Jr., Diane Ravitch, and Bruno Manno, who, along with others, use these foundations as a platform to disseminate ideas and influence public opinion. Doyle is a member of the advisory board of *The Education Industry Report,* Finn was an Edison consultant, and all of them have combined public positions in Republican administrations with strong pro-school choice activism.

These groups see the logic of the market as appropriate for all aspects of society and as the solution to all problems. As a form of accountability, the market is viewed as complementing current testing regimes. Using private schools as a model, neoliberals and neoconservatives argue in true Darwinian fashion that opening up schools to consumer choice will force schools to improve or "go out of business." Unfortunately, this "free market" system does not exist in the real world of business (Kuttner, 1996), and research is demonstrating that it doesn't work in education either (Gewirtz, 2002; Wells et al., 1999).

The market is also seen as a replacement for politics and democracy. Chubb and Moe (1990), in *Politics, Markets, and America's Schools,* argue that

> the most basic cause of ineffective performance among the nation's public schools is their subordination to public authority. . . . The school's most fundamental problems are rooted in the institutions of democratic control by which they are governed. (p. 267)

According to advocates of marketization, the downside of participation in the form of school boards or school-level shared governance is inherent ineffectiveness, making choice in a quasi-market preferable to voice in a politicized environment. However, it is important to understand the differences between participation as consumerism and participation as citizenship. In a marketized environment, the role of citizens is limited to that of passive consumers of "products" provided by others. If consumer-citizens don't like the product, there is no need to become involved in changing it; they can merely—in theory, at least—select another one. They become passive spectators of a political spectacle in which they rarely participate directly. The political spectacle of school reform based on market principles is profoundly antipolitical and leads to the atrophy of skills and dispositions for political participation (Boggs, 2000).

Liberal democrats since John Stuart Mill, and more recently rational choice theorists, have portrayed the individual as autonomous and fully developed, assuming that the individual enters into a choice situation with externally constituted goals. On the other hand, radical democrats would argue that individuals and their goals are, in fact, constituted through the very processes of participation and deliberation.

> Although favored liberal institutions—market and ballot box—are praised as sensitively attuned to expressing the wills of consumers and citizens, this sensitivity fails to extend to a most central area of personal control; that is, the choices determining how individuals are to develop their preferences, their capacities for social participation, and their abilities to make informed decisions. Liberalism claims that the marketplace and the ballot box allow people to get what they want. But liberalism is silent on how people might get to be what they want to be, and how they might get to want what they want to want. (Bowles & Gintis, 1987, p. 125)

Radical democrats argue that democratic participation is justifiable on the grounds that it is educative and provides a developmental process in which social actors become more knowledgeable about their choices and aware of their own best interests.

Frank (2000) calls the conflation of democracy with market principles *market populism*.

> From Deadheads to Nobel-laureate economists, from paleoconservatives to New Democrats, American leaders in the nineties came to believe that markets were a popular system, a far more democratic form of organization than (democratically elected) governments. This is the central premise of what I will call "market populism": that in addition to being mediums of exchange, markets were mediums of consent. Markets were a friend of the little guy; markets brought down the pompous and the snooty; markets gave us what we wanted; markets looked out for our interests. (p. xiv)

More recently, marketization has been promoted as a solution to the plight of poor urban parents who want to escape mediocre neighborhood schools. For example, some have pointed out the hypocrisy of white middle-class parents who critique voucher plans for poor parents while using their resources to obtain choices for their own children (Fuller, 1997). Brantlinger, Majd-Jabbari, and Guskin (1996), in interviews with white, middle-class mothers, demonstrate how politically liberal discourses were often used as a cover for the protection of self-interest when it came to their own children's schools. Why not give poor and working-class parents, disproportionately from communities of color, the same choices that middle- and upper-class parents have?

Parker and Margonis (1996) counter that market-based plans underestimate the complexity of the decision-making processes engaged in by urban minority parents, as well as their access to transportation, information, and the cultural and social capital required to finesse the system. More important, they document the patterns of urban racial and socioeconomic containment practices (housing, occupational, and school segregation as well as housing and employment discrimination) and their devastating impact on people of color in economically depressed urban areas. Parker and Margonis argue that market-driven responses to these conditions are not a break with past racist policies, but rather consistent with the lack of national commitment to urban issues. In light of the Reagan-Bush conservative political era and its dismantling of federal aid to the cities, school choice is viewed as a simplistic solution that ignores the structural constraints poor urban residents face. This is another case of the spectacle's displacement of targets, focusing on "choice" while ignoring the larger and more costly infrastructural neglect of poor neighborhoods. In this way, the political spectacle steers the public's attention away from neglect in more costly social sectors and toward others where educational "reform" can replace real social investment.

The point here is not to defend the inequitable public school system we have, nor to eschew choice in all cases, but rather to promote a view of public schools in a strong and healthy public sector that is being undermined by neoliberal economic policies. There is nothing wrong per se with providing choices for children and parents, just as there is nothing wrong with exchanging goods in a marketplace. However, as Deborah Meier (1995) argues,

> We must shape the concept of choice into a consciously equitable instrument for restructuring public education so that over time all parents can have the kinds of choices the favored few now have, but in ways that serve rather than undercut public goals. (p. 99)

The current school reform spectacle, while claiming to improve the education of all children, too often appears to undercut those very goals.

THE GROWING PRIVATIZATION OF EDUCATION

Privatization in American education is not new. In fact, private schools predate public schools, and vendors have sold textbooks to schools at least since the McGuffy Reader. What is new is the increasing pace of privatization and the extent to which it has expanded beyond its traditional boundaries. Levin (2001), in setting out a research agenda for privatization, suggests that the following areas are key to understanding where major shifts are occurring in privatization:

- How education is financed
- Whether schools are sponsored by the private or public sector
- Who operates schools
- Who benefits from schools
- How for-profit providers benefit

In asking who benefits from schools, Levin (2001) suggests that even public schools can have private benefits, and private schools can have public benefits.

Labaree (1997) argues that the ambivalence about whether to consider education primarily a public or private good has manifested itself historically as a continuous conflict over the relative weight assigned to three competing goals for education: democratic equality (schools should focus on preparing citizens), social efficiency (they should focus on training workers), and social mobility (they should prepare individuals to compete for social positions). These goals represent the educational perspectives of, respectively, the citizen, the taxpayer or employer, and the consumer.

Labaree's (1997) first two goals conceive of education as a public good while the third conceives of education as a private good: "The increasing hegemony of the mobility goal and its narrowly consumer-based approach to education has led to the reconceptualization of education as a purely private good" (p. 51). For Labaree, education as a public good is inclusive and provides shared societal benefits while education as a private good is exclusive and provides selective individual benefits. Given the previous discussion on corporatization, one could also question whether Labaree's social efficiency goal better serves societal or corporate interests and to what extent these overlap in the context of globalization. Increasingly, the goal of preparing democratic citizens has taken a back seat both to the development of human capital for industry and to the maximization of individual gain, resulting in serious implications for our democratic society.

The corporate or business sector does not have a monolithic position with respect to this issue. Some companies see the convenience of maintaining the current public school system as "a vital part of their personnel development" (Sipple, 1999, p. 21) and adapting curricula to the future needs of corporations. Partnerships and sponsorships are the most common strategies used by private companies to influence public schools. A similar trend is the involvement of business roundtables and corporately funded foundations involved in issues of educational reform at state and national levels; similarly, local chambers of commerce are actively involved in educational policy. Although all of these areas deserve exploration, in this section, we will deal most in depth with the emerging trend of for-profit schooling or EMOs.

Unlike those corporate interests that see school reform of the existing system through business models as the answer, others want private, for-profit management of schools. Among these, we find those entrepreneurs who run their own private schools and those who want to operate schools using public funds through vouchers or charters (Pini, 2000). After all, education is a $650 billion industry, making it America's second-largest economic sector, and a growing body of research is documenting the movement to privatize America's public schools (Boyles, 2000; Engel, 2000; Lancaster Dykgraaf & Kane Lewis, 1998; Levin, 2001; Lubienski, 2002; Miron & Applegate, 2000; Morando Rhim, 2001; Murphy, 1999; Murphy, Gilmer, Weise, & Page, 1998; Saltman, 2000).

One of the primary publications for education entrepreneurs is a monthly newsletter founded in the early 1990s, titled *The Education Industry Report,* which can be found at Eduventures.com. Most educators do not read corporate newsletters, and they will find it instructive to see what the corporate sector is saying about education. *The Education Industry Report's* advisory board is composed of presidents and executives of important educational organizations and private firms. The educational organizations are: The Center for Education Reform, an important advocate of school choice, whose president is Jeanne Allen (a former member of the Reagan administration); the School of Education of the University of Southern California, whose dean is on the board; the National School Boards Association; and the

Association of Educators in Private Practice. Also on the advisory board are executives of important private firms, like Children's Comprehensive Services and Doyle Associates, and well-known financial firms like Merrill Lynch and Allied Capital. The newsletter slogan reads, "Covering private investment in the $650 billion education industry, America's second-largest economic sector."

This 12-page publication is expensive, costing $399 per year for a subscription. Until the beginning of 2000, *The Education Industry Report* was published by The Education Industry Group, L.L.C. In March 2000, it was acquired by Eduventures.com, a Boston-based market-research firm. Eduventures' executive vice-president, Peter Stokes, is a business analyst and the author of *E-learning: Education Businesses Transform Schooling.* There he describes how e-learning will transform education and why public-private partnerships must lead the way (Stokes, 2000).

In the mid-1990s, two major EMOs, Alternative Inc. and Edison Project, were on the verge of collapse. Less than 5 years later, with new names—Tesseract and Edison Schools—they were prosperous and expanding. In 2000, Tesseract encountered financial trouble again. Meanwhile, several other new companies emerged and spread throughout the United States, marketing both educational and administrative services to public schools. They offered everything from "news" programs (Channel One), to contracts to govern public schools. As of 2002, they managed schools or districts in at least 24 states, and the list has since grown. For many years, corporations have been involved in education—managing different auxiliary services and providing textbooks, tests, job training, program assessment, custodial services, and even instructional programs (Boyles, 2000; Molnar, 1996). But the phenomenon of for-profit corporations taking on the actual administration and management of schools and districts is more recent.

As early as 1995, the Reason Foundation sponsored a conference called: "Making Schools Work: Competitive Contracting for School Services." The Reason Public Policy Institute defines *contracting* as "a form of public-private partnership that breaks the mold of one-size-fits-all education programs and introduces lower cost opportunities for schools and students" (Seder, 1999, p. 2). Commenting on this conference, *The Education Industry Report* affirmed that "the era of outsourcing instruction and management was just beginning" ("K–12 Contracting," 2000, p. 1). In 1999, the Reason Public Policy Institute hosted a second conference, "Making Schools Work II: Public-Private Partnerships Supporting Public Education." Sponsoring these conferences is one of the foundation's strategies to expand the market for contracting (Seder, 1999).

The expansion of the best-known and largest EMO, Edison Schools, founded by Chris Whittle, is instructive. Whittle began targeting charters as a solution to his financial troubles when school vouchers were no longer on the front burner of the federal agenda. The 1992 presidential election, which removed the elder George Bush from office, ruined his plan to use vouchers to fund his private schools (Spring, 1997). He had founded Edison Project "to capture some voucher money by designing a conservative and technologically advanced school that could be franchised across the country" (p. 62). This would allow him to acquire capital to create a large number of for-profit, private schools. Whittle offered Benno C. Schmidt, Jr., former president of Yale University, an annual salary of about $1 million to head Edison Project, a position that he has had since 1992 (Spring, 1997). Whittle's strategy has been to save money by reducing bureaucracy and the number of credentialed teachers and by increasing voluntary work by parents and students (Weiss, 1999). It is worth noting that Whittle, who has contracted in areas with large numbers of

low-income students of color, was instrumental in promoting the 1998 publication of *The Disuniting of America* by Arthur Schlesinger. According to Spring (1997), Whittle sent free copies of this attack on multicultural education to business leaders.

In its public relations texts online, Edison (2004) claims to offer a "comprehensive" school design, professional expertise, and important political connections. The following text is from "People Behind Edison":

> Edison's school design is the result of a comprehensive research and development effort involving professionals from the worlds of education, technology, government, communications, and business. Among those who worked to create the Edison school design and who now are guiding its implementation in schools across the country are the following individuals. Together they represent many years of education and management experience.

The text tells us that Edison team members "represent many years of education and management experience." What the text does not say is that Chris Whittle, Benno C. Schmidt, Jr., and John Chubb, who head the list, are advocates for the privatization of public education and, in some cases, for principles that replace democracy with markets (Chubb & Moe, 1990).

Another person behind Edison is Chester Finn, Jr., of the conservative Hudson Institute. Finn is a former U.S. Department of Education assistant secretary under William Bennett (in the Reagan administration), coauthor with Bennett of *The Educated Child* (Bennett, Finn, & Cribb, 2000), president of the Thomas B. Fordham Foundation, and member of the board of a new Bennett venture, K12.[1] He was also a member of the transition advisory team for the Department of Education during the presidential campaign of George W. Bush and has a long career as a scholar backed by a network of foundations that advocate right-wing causes (Robelen, 2001; Spring, 1997; Walsh, 2001).

Business Week dedicated the cover of its February 10, 2000, issue to "For-Profit Schools," with reports from Massachusetts, Michigan, Philadelphia, and Arizona (Symonds, 2000; Symonds, Palmer, Lindorff, & McCann, 2000). The theme of this and previous articles on for-profit schools argued that the new knowledge economy and increasing dissatisfaction with public schools was leading to growing opportunities for for-profit companies. For such companies, education is just like any other industry: To make a profit, they have to attract consumers and lower costs. But as an "education analyst" tells *Business Week:* "The major competitor is the government," because "education is the last big bastion of the economy largely controlled by the government" (Symonds, 2000, p. 35).

The Facts about EMOs

Pini (2001) analyzed the claims made in EMO corporate Web pages and compared them to the reality of EMOs in practice and found the following: EMOs claim to be innovative, but they use mostly standardized curricula and other programs typically found in public schools. They claim to decrease bureaucracy, but they are large, impersonal organizations with centralized decision making from corporate headquarters, which are generally located out of state. EMOs are not accountable to the public. They enjoy corporate confidentiality and do not have to make budgets and other data public. Teachers work longer hours for the same or less pay. EMOs often take advantage of probusiness and antiunion school board members to gain exemptions from negotiated union contracts. Education is highly labor intensive, and the only way for-profit corporations can make high profits in the long run is to decrease teacher salaries, benefits, and pensions. Therefore, EMOs tend to hire younger, less experienced teachers whom they can pay less. Finally, there is no evidence that EMOs have better student achievement

outcomes when compared to comparable public schools. (For a summary of the research that analyzes EMOs claims, see Table 10.1.)

Another, often overlooked aspect of EMOs is their failure rates and their propensity to engage in the same questionable accounting practices that sent Enron under. For-profit charter schools often go bankrupt midyear, taking the children's education and the yearly fiscal allocation with them. Recently, Edison, the largest EMO, made headlines nationally for being under scrutiny for allegedly inflating its profit statements to attract investors.

> In an informal inquiry concluded last Tuesday, the Securities and Exchange Commission said that Edison had omitted crucial information from its filings, allowing it to report revenues from 1999–2002 that were 41% to 48% higher than it actually generated. The company had been counting teachers' salaries and other expenses paid by its client school districts and charter-school boards as revenue, even though none of the cash entered Edison's coffers. Because Edison also reported the funds as expenses, its bottom line was accurate, the SEC said, and the reporting procedures did not violate generally accepted accounting rules. Still, the SEC said, Edison should have told investors how it was tabulating its impressive revenue growth. (Winters, 2002, p. 1)

THE COMMERCIALIZATION OF SCHOOLS AND THE PROMOTION OF CONSUMERISM

Like the other tendencies discussed in this chapter, the commercialization of schools is not new, but it has intensified in the past two decades. In his 2003 book, *Educating the Consumer-Citizen*, Joel Spring traces the history of how a consumerist ideology has been promulgated in the United States through the advertising industry and the media, but also to a surprising extent through our schools. Perhaps the most striking example was the role of home economics classes in presenting

Table 10.1   A Different Version of Educational Management Organization (EMO) Practices

What EMOs Say They Do	What EMOs Do
• Innovate in education	• Apply programs already implemented in public schools; no innovation (Apple, 2000; Berliner & Biddle, 1995; Kolbert, 2000; Olson, 2000; Rothstein, 1998; Wells et al., 2000)
• Address students and community needs	• Address companies' needs: growing school systems with centralized organizations, uniform school organization and curriculum (EMO Web pages), and segregation (Cobb, Glass, & Crockett, 2000; Harris Bowman, 2000; Horn & Miron, 1999; Miron & Nelson, 2002; WestEd, 1999; Wong & Shen, with Novacek, 2001)
• Increase efficiency and cost-effectiveness	• Increase bureaucracy and use voluntary work of parents and teachers to cut costs (Edison, Mosaica, Heritage Web pages), evidence of mismanagement (Advantage, Tesseract), no evidence of cost savings (Henig, Moser, Holyoke, & Lacireno-Paquet, 1999)
• Promote school-based decision making	• Centralize decisions, hierarchic structure, scale operations (EMOs Web pages; Mander, 1997; van Gelder, 2001)
• Provide a good job environment	• Overwork, longer work day, lower salaries, no unions (Cobb, Barden, McMillen, O'Sullivan, & Noblit, 2000; EMO Web pages; Henig et al., 1999; Horn & Miron, 1999; Wells et al., 2000; WestEd, 1999)
• Hire experienced teachers	• Research evidence shows that a high percentage of teachers are younger and have less experience (Miron & Nelson, 2002; Morando Rhim, 2001; Wells et al., 2000)
• Achieve academic excellence and better test scores	• Research evidence does not show that EMO students have better results when compared to public school students in the same district (Henig et al., 1999; Horn & Miron, 1999; Miron & Applegate, 2000; Miron & Nelson, 2002; Wells et al., 2000; WestEd, 1999)
• Provide public accountability	• Corporate confidentiality (Lloyd, 2000)
• Transform public education	• Privatize and profit from public education, in some cases introducing Christian values in public schools

to generations of women new fashion trends and the wonders of processed foods and brands like Jell-O, Crisco, and Wonder Bread. Although some of the arguments for replacing homemade bread with "factory bread" were feminist, the advertisers took an increasing interest in the captive audiences that home economics classes represented. Today, this interest is far more pervasive as schools are deluged with a variety of marketing schemes that expose students not only to brand names, but

to the products themselves. The incursion of advertising into schools has become far more sophisticated and bold.

Perhaps the best-known example of this type of classroom invasion by advertising is Channel One, a 12-minute daily newscast (including 2 minutes of advertising) that is required viewing for 8 million school children across the country. Schools receive free televisions and satellite equipment for their participation in the program. A more recent example is

ZapMe! Corporation, which offers schools free computer equipment and services. Every ZapMe! computer features a frame around the screen with advertisements in it. Through the software in use, corporations are able to collect demographic information on the students who choose to view an ad.

Molnar (1996) has provided an overview of the ways commercialization has become manifested in American schools. In this earlier work and in subsequent work through the Commercialization in Education Research Unit (CERU) of the Education Policy Studies Laboratory at Arizona State University, Molnar has identified the following different types of commercialization in schools:

Sponsorship of programs and activities. Businesses give all or part of the money needed to hold a school event (such as an academic contest or athletic tournament) for the right to associate their name with the event.

Exclusive agreements. Corporations give schools or districts a percentage of their profits in exchange for the right to be the sole provider of a product or service (such as beverages, athletic wear).

Incentive programs. A school receives funds, products, or services when the school community (staff, students, parents) takes part in a specific activity, such as collecting box tops, labels, or grocery store cash register receipts.

Appropriation of space. In exchange for advertising space—on textbook covers, school rooftops, buses, and scoreboards—businesses reciprocate with funds. Each year, students in more than half of U.S. classrooms receive free book covers that are filled with advertisements; 6 million students choose from cafeteria menus that include advertising.

Sponsored educational materials. Businesses or trade associations offer free curricular materials that are tied to their corporate message or ideology.

Electronic marketing. Electronic equipment (computers, satellite dishes, televisions) and/or programming is provided in exchange for the right to advertise to those who use it.

Privatization. Schools and school programs— such as for-profit charter schools—are managed by private, for-profit corporations or other nonpublic groups.

In response to this increased corporate practice of marketing to children in schools, several organizations and most school districts have developed a set of principles and policy guidelines with regard to corporate involvement. The following are a set of principles recommended by the National Parent Teachers Association (1991):

School-business relationships based on sound principles can contribute to high-quality education. However, compulsory attendance confers on educators an obligation to protect the welfare of their students and the integrity of the learning environment. Therefore, when working together, schools and businesses must ensure that educational values are not distorted in the process. Positive school-business relationships should be ethical and structured in accordance with all eight of the following principles:

1. Corporate involvement shall not require students to observe, listen to, or read commercial advertising.
2. Selling or providing access to a captive audience in the classroom for commercial purposes is exploitation and a violation of the public trust.
3. Since school property and time are publicly funded, selling or providing free access to advertising on school property outside the classroom involves ethical and legal issues that must be addressed.
4. Corporate involvement must support the goals and objectives of the schools.

Curriculum and instruction are within the purview of educators.

5. Programs of corporate involvement must be structured to meet an identified need, not a commercial motive, and must be evaluated for effectiveness by the school/district on an ongoing basis.

6. Schools and educators should hold sponsored and donated materials to the same standards used for the selection and purchase of curriculum materials.

7. Corporate involvement programs should not limit the discretion of schools and teachers in the use of sponsored materials.

8. Sponsor recognition and corporate logos should be for identification rather than commercial purposes. (National Parent Teachers Association, 1991,[2] reprinted with permission from the National Parent Teachers Association, © 1999)

Many school administrators may feel that in these times of decreased funding for education, they need to take advantage of any source of income or "free" technology that comes their way. However, the "gifts" come from the same corporations that want to make money off our public schools and lobby against taxes and social spending. This, in addition to the tax breaks they wrest from communities, contributes to public schools' inability to fund many programs.

One of the justifications of corporate partnerships with schools is that corporations contribute much-needed funds. However, Molnar (1996, cited in Saltman, 2000) argues that the amount of money that corporations actually give public schools is tiny compared to the tax breaks they receive and compared to the amount they give to private schools.

In 1989, total corporate contributions to public elementary schools totaled $156 million. Corporate contributions to private schools and to colleges and universities totaled $2.4 billion in the same year.

Considered from another angle, $156 million is a tiny fraction of the $1 billion plus in tax breaks that Wisconsin corporations alone received each year from the state of Wisconsin in the later 1990's. By one estimate, total corporate contributions to kindergarten through twelfth-grade (K–12) education in 1990 would run the nation's schools for less than two hours. (p. 7)

Commercialization and corporate tax breaks leave cities on the horns of a dilemma. They want the jobs corporations bring, but the tax breaks they give to attract corporations rob the city of needed resources. Administrators experience similar dilemmas: Take much-needed corporate money to increase school resources, and deliver kids to corporate exploitation. Reject the money, and leave kids with fewer resources. As researchers have discovered, dilemmas are a central theme of administrators' work (Jacobson, Hickcox, & Stevenson, 1996). The new corporate policy environment has created a new set of dilemmas. These dilemmas won't go away, but being informed can help administrators better understand the trade-offs they are making.

CONCLUSION

Although future educational leaders have no choice but to deal with the realities of corporatization, marketization, privatization, and commercialization, they do not have to buy into the corporate myths that the business community is promoting. Several of these myths have been debunked in this chapter:

1. *The myth that what is good for business is good for education.* Because the core technology of corporations (producing products and services for a profit) and schools (educating children and youth) is fundamentally different, transferring ideas from one sector to another must be done with great caution. Much unexamined "baggage" tends to slip in through the metaphors we use.

2. *The myth of market populism, or the belief that markets are democratic.* Consumer choice in a marketplace is not a replacement for participating in a democracy. In a marketized environment, the role of citizens is limited to that of passive consumer. Furthermore, some "consumers" have greater resources to take advantage of choices the market provides, leading to increased inequities.

3. *The myth of corporations as private enterprise.* As documented above, corporations function as mini-governments, influencing national and local policy, receiving public money through tax breaks and protections ("corporate welfare").

4. *The myth of the private sector as more efficient and effective.* As discussed above, Edison schools are not more innovative than public schools, nor are their achievement scores higher. They increase bureaucracy, and their lack of accountability encourages mismanagement and fraud. There is no evidence of cost savings over public schools.

5. *The myth of corporate accountability.* Not only have corporations become less accountable to the public over the past century, their status as private enterprises exempts them from having to make budgets and other information public. In an age of increasing accountability in education, it is inconceivable that the private sector could serve as an example in this area.

According to Morgan (1997), "The ability to read and understand what is happening in one's organization is a key managerial competency" (p. 355). The same can be said for learning to read and understand the larger social and policy environment in which administrators work. Our goal here is not to overwhelm administrators and leave them feeling paralyzed and helpless before these large social forces that are shaping schools. Administrators have always figured out ways

to tiptoe through the political land mines that are part of their world. The political context, however, has shifted over the past 30 years, and administrators will need new perspectives to locate the new land mines. Serving the needs of their students will mean resisting the temptations of corporate ideology and corporate resources with strings attached. Unfortunately, most administrators are being exposed to relatively little social critique and large doses of business ideology. David Berliner (1997) is worth quoting at length as he cautions educational administrators to beware of getting too cozy with business:

> Obviously business people and educators need to sit at the same table and work together on issues of schooling and employment. But I don't think school administrators should believe that they have the same agenda as the business community. I think they are naïve and may sell out our children when they believe this. The primary goal of business, and rightly so in our capitalist society, is return on investment to stockholders. To be true to that goal requires paying as little as possible in local taxes, keeping school budgets in check so that general state taxes do not have to increase, getting trained workers from the schools so that on-the-job training costs are minimized, and for most of the jobs in the contemporary economy, insuring that workers sent by the schools are docile thinkers. These are not the goals of educators. Too many of the school administrators I have met like to think of themselves as managers or chief executive officers, and their personal models are successful business leaders in the nation. So they feel at ease among the business community and seem to have lost their voice as educators. Without remembering who they speak for they are in danger of becoming pawns of the business community. (p. 14)

Berliner argues that administrators need "voice lessons." They need to rediscover the wisdom that resides in the best practitioners and in our best thinkers: John Dewey, Ella Flagg Young, Carter Woodson, Jesse Newlon, and others. These educators promoted many of the things that the business community is promoting, but with the goal not of increasing productivity and profits but rather of democratizing society and fostering critical thinkers. Local, democratic, decision making; engaging in cycles of data gathering and analysis; creating learning organizations; using teams; replacing supervision with coaching—these are not inherently bad ideas, but they must be understood in the context of the host organization and the goals they are attempting to achieve. Once educators find their own voice, they will be in a position to adopt and adapt ideas and methods from the private sector if they so choose, but on their own terms. They will also be in a position to insist that corporations pay their fair share of the social cost of educating future democratic citizens and their future employees.

NOTES

1. K12 is an online-learning venture started in 2001 by William J. Bennett. However, his co-authored book, *The Educated Child* (Bennett et al., 2000) claims that there is no evidence that computer use improves learning significantly. In his new venture, Bennett will pair current technology with a traditionalist view of learning. The for-profit venture is backed by the Knowledge Universe Learning Group, an affiliate of the education and training company led by the former financier Michael Milken (initial $10 million). The Web-based school plans to provide a full curriculum from kindergarten through 12th grade, supplementary courses, and assessments. One major target is home-schooling families, but the Web school also will provide courses to public schools, and it will also form online charter schools in some states, which would allow tuition costs to be covered by taxpayer dollars. Board members include Lowell Milken, brother and a partner in Knowledge Universe, and Chester E. Finn, Jr. (Walsh, 2001).

2. National Parent Teachers Association. (1991). *National PTA guidelines for corporate involvement in the schools.* © 1999 by the National Parent Teachers Association; reprinted with permission.

REFERENCES

Anderson, G. L. (1998). Toward authentic participation: Deconstructing the discourse of participatory reforms. *American Educational Research Journal, 35*(4), 571–606.

Apple, M. (2000). *Official knowledge: Democratic education in a conservative age* (2nd ed.). New York, Routledge.

Bennett. W., Finn, C., & Cribb, J. (2000). *The educated child: A parents' guide from preschool through eighth grade.* New York: Free Press.

Berliner, D. (1997). Voice training. *UCEA Review, 39*(2), 9–14.

Berliner, D., & Biddle, B. (1995). *The manufactured crisis: Myths, fraud, and the attack on America's public schools.* New York: Longman.

Boggs, C. (2000). *The end of politics: Corporate power and the decline of the public sphere.* New York: Guilford Press.

Bowles, S., & Gintis, H. (1987). *Democracy and capitalism: Property, community, and the contradictions of modern social thought.* New York: Basic Books.

Boyles, D. (2000). *American education and corporations: The free market goes to $chools.* New York & London: Falmer Press.

Brantlinger, E., Majd-Jabbari, M., & Guskin, S. L. (1996). Self-interest and liberal educational discourse: How ideology works for middle-class mothers. *American Educational Research Journal, 33*(3), 571–598.

Callahan, R. (1962). *Education and the cult of efficiency.* Chicago: University of Chicago Press.

Chubb, J., & Moe, T. (1990). *Politics, markets, and America's schools.* Washington, DC: The Brookings Institute.

Cobb, C., Barden, M. A., McMillen, B., O'Sullivan, R., & Noblit, G. (2000, April). *A profile of North Carolina charter schools.* Paper presented at the Annual Meeting of the American Educational Research Association, New Orleans, LA.

Cobb, C. D., Glass, G. V., & Crockett, C. (2000, April). *The U.S. charter school movement and ethnic segregation.* Paper presented at the Annual Meeting of the American Educational Research Association, New Orleans, LA.

Derber, C. (1998). *Corporation nation.* New York: St. Martin's.

Edelman, M. (1967). *The symbolic uses of politics.* Urbana: The University of Illinois Press.

Edelman, M. (1978). *Political language: Words that succeed and policies that fail.* New York: Academic Press.

Edelman, M. (1988). *Constructing the political spectacle*. Chicago: University of Chicago Press.

Edelman, M. (2001). *The politics of misinformation*. Cambridge, UK: Cambridge University Press.

Edison Schools. (2004). *People behind Edison*. Retrieved from http://www.edisonschools.com/overview/ov04.html

Engel, M. (2000). *The struggle for control of public education: Market ideology vs. democratic values*. Philadelphia: Temple University.

Frank, T. (2000). *One market under God: Extreme capitalism, market populism, and the end of economic democracy*. New York: Doubleday.

Fuller, H. (1997, April). *The crisis in urban education*. Paper presented at the Annual Meeting of the American Educational Research Association, Chicago.

Gelberg, D. (1997). *The "business" of reforming American schools*. New York: SUNY Press.

Gewirtz, S. (2002). *The managerial school: Post-welfarism and social justice in education*. London: Routledge.

Grossman, R., & Adams, R. (1995). *Taking care of business: Citizenship and the charter of incorporation*. Cambridge, MA: Charter, Ink.

Harris Bowman, D. (2000, February 28). Charter closings come under scrutiny. *Education Week*, pp. 1, 14–15.

Henig, J., Moser, M., Holyoke, T., & Lacireno-Paquet, N. (1999). *Making a choice, making a difference? An evaluation of charter schools in the District of Columbia*. Washington, DC: George Washington University, Center for Washington Area Studies.

Horn, J., & Miron, G. (1999). *Evaluation of the Michigan public school academy initiative*. Kalamazoo: Western Michigan University, Evaluation Center.

Jacobson, S., Hickcox, E., & Stevenson, R. (Eds.). (1996). *School administration: Persistent dilemmas in preparation and practice*. Westport, CT: Praeger.

Kolbert, E. (2000, February 20). Unchartered territory. *The New Yorker*, pp. 34–41.

K–12 contracting: Assessing progress. (April, 2000). *The Education Industry Report*, 8(4), pp. 1–2.

Kuttner, R. (1996). *Everything for sale*. Chicago: University of Chicago.

Labaree, D. (1997). *How to succeed in school without really learning: The credentials race in American education*. London & New Haven: Yale University Press.

Lancaster Dykgraaf, C., & Kane Lewis, S. (1998). For-profit charter schools: What the public needs to know. *Educational Leadership*, 56(2), 51–53.

Levin, H. (2001). Studying privatization in education. In H. Levin (Ed.), *Privatizing education: Can the marketplace deliver choice, efficiency, and social cohesion?* (pp. 3–19). Cambridge, MA: Westview Press.

Lipman, P. (2002). Making the global city, making inequality: The political economy and cultural politics of Chicago school policy. *American Educational Research Journal*, 39(2), 379–419.

Lloyd, M. (2000, September 24). Full disclosure for charters. *The Grand Rapids Press*, p. A8.

Lubienski, C. (2002). Reconstructing public education as a private good: Strategies and implications from Michigan charter schools. In G. Miron & C. Nelson (Eds.), *What's public about charter schools?* Thousand Oaks, CA: Sage.

Mander, J. (1997, December). The rules of corporate behavior. *The Sun*, pp. 14–20.

Meier, D. (1995). *The power of their ideas: Lessons from a small school in Harlem*. Boston: Beacon Press.

Mickelson, R. (1999). International business machinations: A case study of corporate involvement in local educational reform. *Teachers College Record*, 100(3), 476–506.

Miron, G., & Applegate, B. (2000). *An evaluation of student achievement in Edison Schools opened in 1995 and 1996*. Kalamazoo: Western Michigan University, Evaluation Center.

Miron, G., & Nelson, C. (2002). *What's public about charter schools?* Thousand Oaks, CA: Sage.

Molnar, A. (1996). *Giving kids the business: The commercialization of America's schools*. Boulder, CO: Westview Press.

Morando Rhim, L. (2001, April). *School privatization in practice: A case study of strategies to increase efficiency in an Edison charter school*. Paper presented at the Annual Meeting of the American Education Finance Association, Cincinnati, OH.

Morgan, G. (1997). *Images of organization*. Thousand Oaks, CA: Sage.

Murphy, J. (1999, April). *Governing America's schools: The shifting playing field*. Paper presented at the Annual Conference of the American Educational Research Association, Montreal, Canada.

Murphy, J., Gilmer, S., Weise, R., & Page, A. (1998). *Pathways to privatization in education*. Greenwich, CT: Ablex.

National Parent Teachers Association. (1991). *National PTA guidelines for corporate involvement in the schools*. Retrieved from

Education Policy Studies Laboratory Website, http://www.asu.edu/educ/epsl

Olson, L. (2000, April 26). Redefining "public" schools: Charter and voucher programs bring lots of choices, little consensus. *Education Week, 19*(33), 1, 24–27.

Parker, L., & Margonis, F. (1996). School choice in the U.S. urban context: Racism and policies of containment. *Journal of Education Policy, 11*(6), 717–728.

Peters, M. (2001). *Poststructuralism, Marxism, and neoliberalism: Between theory and politics.* Lanham, MD: Rowman & Littlefield.

Pini, M. (2001, April). *Moving public schools toward for-profit management: Privatizing the public sphere.* Paper presented at the Annual Meeting of the American Educational Research Association, Seattle, WA. (ERIC Document Reproduction Service No. ED453603)

Robelen, E. W. (2001, January 10). A changing of the guard: Bush promises swift action on education. *Education Week, 20*(16), 1, 42–43.

Rothstein, R. (1998, July/August). Charter conundrum. *The American Prospect,* pp. 46–60.

Saltman, K. J. (2000). *Collateral damage: Corporatizing public schools—A threat to democracy.* Maryland: Rowman & Littlefield.

Schlesinger, A. (1998). *The disuniting of America.* New York: W. W. Norton.

Seder, R. (1999, April). Contracting opportunities in K–12 education. *The Education Industry Report, 7*(4), 2.

Shipps, D. (1997). The invisible hand: Big business and Chicago school reform. *Teachers College Record, 99,* 73–116.

Shuman, M. (1998). *Going local: Creating self-reliant communities in a global age.* New York: Free Press.

Sipple, J. (1999, Fall). Institutional constraints on business involvement in K-12 education policy. *American Educational Research Journal, 36*(3), 447–454.

Spring, J. (1997). *Political agendas for education: From the Christian Coalition to the Green Party.* Mahwah, NJ: Lawrence Erlbaum.

Spring, J. (2003). *Educating the consumer-citizen: A history of the marriage of schools, advertising, and media.* Mawah, NJ: Lawrence Erlbaum.

Stokes, P. J. (September, 2000). How e-learning will transform education. *Education Week, 20*(2), 55.

Symonds, W. C. (2000, January 10). Industry outlook 2000—Services. Education. *Business Week.* Retrieved 3/24/00 from http://www.businessweek.com/

Symonds, W., Palmer, T., Lindorff, D., & McCann, J. (2000, February 7). For-profit schools. *Business Week,* p. 44.

van Gelder, S. R. (2001). What to do when corporations rule the world: An interview with David C. Korten. *Yes Magazine.* Retrieved 9/2/01 from http://www.yesmagazine.com/18 Commons/korten.htm

Walsh, M. (2001, January). Former education secretary starts online-learning venture. *Education Week, 20*(19), 8.

Welch, A. R. (1998). The cult of efficiency in education: Comparative reflections on the reality and the rhetoric. *Comparative Education, 34*(2), 157–175.

Weiss, M. (1999). La microeconomía de la educación [Microeconomy of education]. In H. Munin (Ed.), *La autonomia de la escuela: Libertad y equidad?* [School autonomy: Freedom and equity?]. Buenos Aires: Aique.

Wells, A. S., Artiles, L., Carnochan, S., Wilson Cooper, C., Grutzik, S., Jellison Holme, J., Lopez, A., Scott, J., Slayton, J., & Vasudeva, A. (1999). *Beyond the rhetoric of charter school reform: A study of ten California school districts.* Los Angeles: UCLA.

WestEd. (1999, April). *The findings and implications of increased flexibility and accountability: An evaluation of charter schools in Los Angeles Unified School District* [Cross-site report.]. Paper presented at the Annual Meeting of the American Educational Research Association, Montreal, Canada.

White, R. E. (2002, April). *The anatomy of a corporate transaction: A study of corporate involvement in two Canadian school districts.* Paper presented at the Annual Meeting of the American Educational Research Association, New Orleans.

Winters, R. (2002, May 27). Trouble for Schools Inc. *Time.*

Wong, K., & Shen, F., with Novacek, G. (2001, April). *Institutional effects of charter schools: Innovation and segregation.* Paper presented at the Annual Meeting of the American Educational Research Association, Seattle, WA.

11

A New Conception of Parent Engagement

Community Organizing for School Reform

EVA GOLD
Research for Action

ELAINE SIMON
Research for Action

With

CHRIS BROWN
Cross City Campaign for Urban School Reform

During the 1990s, schools changed for the better in Chicago's Logan Square neighborhood, where there were significant increases in student achievement by the end of the decade.[1] In response to overcrowding in this low- to moderate-income community, the district has built five elementary school annexes and two new middle schools, with plans for a new high school in the works. A program for parents trains them in pedagogy and leadership skills and brings them into classrooms, where they provide extra social and academic help to children.[2] Since this parent-teacher mentor program was initiated in 1995, more than 840 parents have participated. Teachers in the neighborhood's schools credit the program for increases in the individualized attention their students get, the level of

Author's Note: We would like to thank the Cross City Campaign for Urban School Reform and especially Anne Hallett, for her support of this study. A number of Research for Action staff participated on the research team, and we would like to especially note the contributions of Sukey Blanc. Leah Mundell contributed to reviewing the literature for this chapter. Last but not least, we thank the organizers and parent leaders of the community groups we studied, who have shared with us the work of education organizing and introduced us to their neighborhoods, cities, and schools.

parent-teacher communication, and their own ability to understand their students' neighborhood and Latino cultural backgrounds. With parents' presence in the schools, school climates are more orderly and respectful. Parent representatives on the local school council are more knowledgeable and capable leaders. School-based community centers have been established, and a neighborhood-wide literacy initiative is under way.

What provided the impetus for school improvement in the Logan Square neighborhood? Why were schools with a majority of low-income, Latino students the beneficiaries of new resources and innovative programs? Education reform groups, local teachers and principals, and the Chicago Public Schools (CPS) contributed to the efforts to improve these neighborhood schools, but a neighborhood group, the Logan Square Neighborhood Association (LSNA), initiated and has sustained the school improvement effort. LSNA is a 40-year-old association of businesses, schools, congregations, and individuals in Chicago's Logan Square neighborhood that has worked to improve local housing and economic well-being through community organizing. LSNA became more involved in education in 1988, when the Chicago School Reform Act created the opportunity for increased parent and community involvement in local schools. In the course of obtaining the central office's commitment to build new school facilities, LSNA developed strong relationships with local principals and teachers. The parent-teacher mentor program, designed and run by LSNA, was one outcome of these strong relationships. Parents trained through the program have been instrumental in starting and staffing the community centers and in running the literacy program, which reaches parents and community members throughout the neighborhood.

Across the country, groups like LSNA have been turning their attention to improving public education for their members, and the number of community organizing groups working on education issues has grown significantly in the last decade (Gold & Simon with Brown, 2002c; Mediratta, Fruchter, & Lewis, 2002; see Box 11.1 for the characteristics of community organizing groups). These groups work at the neighborhood and policy levels to address the range of issues urban public schools face, such as overcrowding, deteriorating facilities, inadequate funding, high turnover of staff, lack of up-to-date textbooks, and the low test scores of students at these schools. Students attending these schools too often are shut out of high-quality academic programs, discouraged from going to college, and short-changed in their employment opportunities. In the dozen years that community organizing for school reform has taken hold and spread, community groups have begun to address these issues and to see their efforts pay off.

For 4 years, a partnership of Research for Action and the Cross City Campaign for Urban School Reform documented the education organizing activities of five groups from across the country: the Alliance Organizing Project or AOP (Philadelphia), Austin Interfaith (Austin, Texas), LSNA (Chicago), New York ACORN (New York City), and Oakland Community Organizations or OCO (Oakland, California).[3] Our purpose was to develop a way to show the education reform accomplishments of community organizing and to explain how these accomplishments lead to improving schools and student achievement.

Our examination of the groups in this study revealed that their efforts are bringing new resources to schools with the highest need, improving school climate and creating better conditions for teaching and learning. Nonetheless, within the discourse of school reform, community organizing groups and their accomplishments remain largely unacknowledged, while the families in these low-income communities continue to be characterized as lacking in the skills and values necessary

---

Box 11.1   **The History and Characteristics of Community Organizing**

Almost all community organizing groups trace back to Saul Alinsky, whose community organizing in the 1930s was the first to take the methods union organizers used to develop power and apply them to solve issues affecting neighborhoods. Over the years, community organizing has been influenced by the experiences of the civil rights movement, as well as by new leaders from within Alinsky's own Industrial Areas Foundation and other national community organizing networks.

Community organizing groups:

- Build relationships and collective responsibility by identifying shared concerns among neighborhood residents and creating alliances and coalitions that cross neighborhood and institutional boundaries
- Build a large base of members who take collective action to further their agenda
- Develop leadership among community residents to carry out agendas that the membership determines through a democratic governance structure
- Build power for residents of low- to moderate-income communities, which results in action to address their concerns using the strategies of adult education, civic participation, and public negotiation and action
- Work to strengthen public institutions to make them more equitable and accountable to low- and moderate-income communities

Read more about community organizing:

Alinsky, Saul D., *Rules for Radicals: A Practical Primer for Realistic Radicals*

Cortés, Ernesto, Jr., "Reweaving the Fabric: The Iron Rule and the IAF Strategy for Power and Politics"

Delgado, Gary, *Organizing the Movement: The Roots and Growth of ACORN*

Kahn, Si, *Organizing: A Guide for Grassroots Leaders*

Medoff, Peter, and Sklar, Holly, *Streets of Hope: The Fall and Rise of an Urban Neighborhood*

Payne, C., *I've Got the Light of Freedom: The Organizing Tradition and the Mississippi Freedom Struggle*

Ransby, B., *Ella Baker and the Black Freedom Movement: A Radical Democratic Vision*

Warren, M., *Dry Bones Rattling: Community Building to Revitalize American Democracy*

NOTE: Complete publication information is found in the reference list.

to support their children's education. Our research expands the work of others who have pointed to the importance of new conceptions of parent engagement that challenge the discourse of deficit when considering the role of communities and parents in supporting

children's educational experience. This new conception is linked to the growing body of work on the relationship between schools and communities.

In this chapter, we provide an indicators framework for understanding the contributions

---

Box 11.2   **Research Approach to Developing the Indicators Framework for Education Organizing**

To develop an indicators framework, Research for Action and the Cross City Campaign used a research design with four levels of investigation:

- Conducting a broad search and creating a database of 140 community organizing groups working on school reform nationwide
- Selecting 19 groups for lengthy telephone interviews

Analysis of those interviews yielded a preliminary indicators framework:

- Selecting five groups for case studies, with the advice of a national advisory group
- Sending research teams and staff on two site visits of 3 days each in spring and fall of 2000 to each of the five sites, to collect data through: interviews with a wide array of public school stakeholders, including parents, teachers, administrators, elected officials, and education reform groups; and observations of community and school events relevant to local organizing

These interviews and observations, in combination with feedback sessions with the local groups in a third site visit and with a national advisory group, helped us to refine the preliminary indicators framework.

---

of community organizing to school reform. (See Box 11.2 for our research approach to developing an indicators framework for education organizing.) We show that community organizing is an effective vehicle for building community capacity, which plays a critical role in school reform. When school staff, parents, and community together engage in democratic decision making, they develop a sense of joint ownership of local schools. Voices external to schools and school systems are necessary to create the political will needed for genuine school improvement. Furthermore, when teachers value the knowledge parents and community members bring to children's learning, they can design challenging and culturally responsive curriculum.

In addition to an indicators framework for education organizing, we present a theory of change model that shows the link between school improvement and the work these groups do to improve community capacity. By looking at the work of community organizing for school reform, we have found that when school reform goes hand-in-hand with building strong communities, the institution of schooling itself changes fundamentally, increasing the chances that reform efforts will be carried out and sustained.

RETHINKING PARENT ENGAGEMENT AND SCHOOL REFORM

How come because we live in a lower income neighborhood do we have to get less? Our children have to drink out of lead fountains; our kids got to play in dirt. We don't have music lessons; we don't get gym until the second half of the year. But if you travel up the road to one of these prestigious schools, their kids [have these things]. But not mine.

—Parent leader, Alliance Organizing Project, Philadelphia

By almost any measure, urban public schools are failing to provide an adequate education to their students. Such indicators of school well-being as student achievement, promotion rates, and retention of teachers have all continued to decline relative to schools in suburban and more affluent areas. The job of improving schools has been left primarily to professional educators and the education policy community. Yet, the persistence of urban school failure has confounded the professionals, as well as civic leaders and government officials. In this context of the widening disparity between the education schools can provide and what most urban public schools actually do provide, low- to moderate-income parents have turned to community organizing to make schools work for their children.

Much of the recent school reform literature has focused on the importance of tapping a community's assets and creating links between schools and communities. Some of this literature has begun to erode the professional paradigm that elevates professional expertise and overlooks the contributions of low-income families and communities to the educational process. In general, however, research still focuses on the ways that educational professionals involve parents and does not address the ways that parents themselves might gain influence in public education to best serve their children. Chicago's local school councils have offered researchers the opportunity to examine parent-professional relationships in which parents and community members are in the majority, an intentional strategy meant to counterbalance the power advantage professionals have from their position as school insiders. Although a number of these studies note the importance of social trust in the school setting, they offer little discussion of the possibilities for building social trust across asymmetrical lines of power, including when parents are in a position of authority (Bryk & Schneider, 2002). This discussion has been taken up by the literature on community organizing for school reform, which, in the words of Dennis Shirley (1997), distinguishes between "*accommodationist* forms of parental *involvement* and *transformational* forms of parental *engagement*" (p. 73; emphasis in original). Community organizing serves two purposes that stand in productive tension: to challenge school power structures that exclude parents and community *and* to develop the social trust between school professionals and parents that is so crucial for long-term school improvement.

Parent Involvement Versus Parent Engagement

Despite the challenges involved in building bridges between schools and communities, many educators have come to embrace the value of parental involvement in schools. Henderson and Mapp (2002) provide a comprehensive overview of the literature on connections between schools and communities, highlighting evidence that parental involvement not only improves the school climate but also is linked to higher student achievement (see also Marcon, 1999; Miedel & Reynolds, 1999). While indicators such as family income and educational level are associated strongly with children's educational outcomes, studies now acknowledge that despite the challenges of poverty and lack of formal education, families of all backgrounds have the potential to encourage high achievement for their children and will become involved in education if schools reach out to engage them (Clark, 1993; Epstein & Sanders, 2000; Henderson & Mapp, 2002). If parents are to feel welcome in the school environment, at a minimum, schools must become more culturally responsive to families and communities. Researchers who have examined the role of culture in schooling have shown that local knowledge can also enrich curriculum and pedagogy (Au, 1980; Delgado-Gaitan, 1987;

Erickson & Mohatt, 1987; Heath, 1983; McConnell, 1989; Moll, Amanti, Neff, & Gonzalez, 1992; Valdés, 1996).

Too many studies of parent involvement show how the professional paradigm limits the role of parents to serving the priorities of professionals. In this sense, parents contribute by reinforcing teachers' work through activities such as reading to children at home, showing an interest in children's school achievement, providing enrichment activities, and volunteering in school (Chall & Snow, 1982; Epstein, 1995; Henderson & Berla, 1994; Snow, 1998). Nancy Chavkin (1993) highlights the ways that parental involvement might particularly benefit minority students, who lag behind majority students in educational achievement and whose families are often excluded from traditional parent-involvement programs directed at middle-class, educated parents (see also Lareau, 1989). Nonetheless, Chavkin also notes that educators have a somewhat limited vision of the role that parents might play in schools. Chavkin reports that educational professionals participating in a study in the southwestern United States were overwhelmingly interested "in parents performing roles of school-program supporter, home tutor, and audience" (p. 3; see also Williams & Chavkin, 1985). Although such studies provide examples of an expanded role for parents as active partners in their children's education, they focus on parents as listeners and supporters, rather than as advocates for equity or decision-makers.

The community organizers and parent leaders discussed in this chapter acknowledge the importance of parental involvement for individual student success; in fact, these parent leaders are deeply involved in their own children's education. As community leaders, however, their concerns for quality education extend beyond the needs of their own children to the needs of all children in their community. This commitment to equity in education helps to combat what Lareau and Shumar (1996) call the "individualist approach to family-school relationships," which keeps parents isolated from one another and inhibits them from taking collective action on behalf of their community's children (see also Giles, 1998).

Novella Keith (1999) describes these conceptions of the role of parents as the difference between a "partners for improvement" discourse, as in Chavkin (1993), and a "new citizenship" discourse of decision making and advocacy. The "partners for improvement" discourse is reflected in late 1990s federal education policy, which placed a renewed emphasis on community partnerships and family involvement. However, as Keith points out, this discourse "cast[s] schools and educators in the role of agents, while families are left largely to respond to their initiatives" (p. 228).[4] The "new citizenship" discourse stems from community organizing and the work of researchers such as Harry Boyte (Boyte & Kari, 1996) and Dennis Shirley (1997). These organizations and scholars critique the "partners for improvement" model in part because its service orientation reinforces a deficit approach to parents (for an explanation of the deficit approach, see Delpit, 1995; Hidalgo, 1992; Lightfoot, 1978). As Keith (1999) notes, the problem with the "partners for improvement" discourse is "that schools, by treating parents, students, and community members as clients and consumers, are reneging on their historic responsibility as sites for education in democracy and thus further contribute to the erosion of public life" (p. 230). Community organizing is consonant with the work of scholars who advocate the democratization of both the governance structures and the curriculum of schools (Apple & Beane, 1995; Bastian, Fruchter, Gittell, Greer, & Haskins, 1986; Wood, 1988). Whereas educators focus on the internal functioning of schools, community organizations believe that democratizing a school also means building the capacity of the community to inform and participate in the work of schooling.

Extending Social Trust

Literature on school reform and school change has taught us that one source of schools' resistance to reform is their insularity, the ingrained nature of their culture and power structure (Fullan, 1999; Sarason, 1982, 1990). This entrenchment of school power structures means that educational reform designed to make schools more inclusive of parents is often ineffective, serving instead as "a form of public relations to create greater institutional legitimacy for current educational practices" (Anderson, 1998, p. 571; see also Malen & Ogawa, 1988, on local school councils). Nonetheless, school districts have undertaken systemwide attempts to alter their governance structures, most fundamentally in Chicago, where the 1988 school reform act authorized the creation of local school councils, composed of parents, teachers, and community representatives with the power to hire and fire principals (Hess, 1999; Katz, 1992; Rollow & Bryk, 1993). Research on this model of democratic localism demonstrated the contribution of parent and community participation to curriculum and instruction and to raising student achievement (Bryk, Sebring, Kerbow, Rollow, & Easton, 1998; Moore, 1998). But some of these researchers also found that decentralization efforts of this kind sometimes fail if they do not take into account the importance of social trust within the school environment. They suggest that the human resources of schools—culture, climate, and interpersonal relationships—may be more critical to school success than the structural arrangements under which the school operates (Bryk & Schneider, 1996; Kruse, Louis, & Bryk, 1995; Useem, Christman, Gold, & Simon, 1997).

Payne and Kaba (2001) have written convincingly that school-driven strategies of parent involvement, which are believed to create better parent-teacher relations, often result in the converse. In their observations of Chicago schools operating under the Comer model, they found that the Comer staff worked hard to combat teacher stereotypes of parents by actively involving parents in the life of the school (for an explanation of the Comer model, see Comer, Haynes, Joyner, & Ben-Avie, 1996). Contrary to the findings of other researchers (Epstein & Sanders, 2000), however, Payne and Kaba (2001) found that the increased parental involvement actually *raised* the tension between parents and teachers: "Merely interacting more didn't change the deeply-ingrained tendency of one group to interpret the behavior of the other group in the most negative way possible" (p. 5; see also Payne, 2003). Social trust was absent, and without it, parents remained outside the accepted professional culture of the school.

Payne and Kaba's (2001) observations of the "social impediments to reform" remind us that social trust cannot be based only on increased visibility of parents or a school's declaration that it is "welcoming" to the community. Instead, social trust requires the development of what community organizers call accountable relationships, where trust is established through parties' mutual agreement about their obligations to one another. In this conception, no single institution or individual holds unilateral power over another; nor is power a zero-sum game. Parent leaders who seek a role in school governance, for example, are not seeking "power over" school professionals but "power to" create school change in relationship with teachers and administrators.[5] At times, achieving this power shift might require confrontational tactics. Community organizing groups, however, aim not simply to provoke confrontation but to develop new "sites of power" at the school level, including parents, community, teachers, and administrators (Bowles & Gintis, 1987, as cited in Rollow & Bryk, 1993).[6]

Social trust is one indicator of what sociologists and political scientists are today calling social capital, the "features of social organization such as networks, norms, and social trust that facilitate coordination and cooperation for mutual benefit" (Putnam, 1995, p. 67; see also Coleman, 1988). As Sandefur and Lauman (1998) point out, however, accounts of the consolidation of social capital do not always explain "the mechanisms through which social capital has its effects" (p. 483, as cited in Goddard, 2003). In this chapter, we contribute to a growing body of scholarship showing the ways that community organizing helps develop both bonding social capital—within existing social or cultural groups—and bridging social capital—across-group relationships (Shirley, 2002; Warren, 2001; Wood, 2002). We found that bridging social capital is especially important in moving organizing campaigns forward because it builds accountable relationships that generate the political will to override individual and private interests.

UNDERSTANDING STORIES OF COMMUNITY ORGANIZING FOR SCHOOL REFORM: AN INDICATORS FRAMEWORK

In the 4 years that we followed the five case study groups, we gathered many stories of education organizing.[7] We came to understand, from many different perspectives—those of parents, organizers, teachers, administrators, elected officials, and school board members—the impacts the groups were having and the challenges they face. As we gathered and reviewed stories of community organizing, we categorized their work into eight areas. These categories of work, which we call indicator areas, are leadership development, social capital, community power, public accountability, equity, school/community connections,

curriculum and instruction, and school climate. (See Box 11.3 for definitions of the eight indicator areas.) We show the work of community organizing by specifying the primary strategies groups use and their results within each of the indicator areas. In each area, we suggest a set of possible measures or indicators of the group's accomplishments. We developed what we call an *indicators framework for education organizing* as a tool for understanding the contributions and accomplishments of community organizing for education reform.[8] The framework consists of a set of charts that detail the strategies and results for each indicator area, as well as data sources for documenting the results. These charts are included in two reports, *Successful Community Organizing for School Reform* (Gold & Simon with Brown, 2002c) and *The Education Organizing Indicators Framework: A User's Guide* (Gold & Simon with Brown, 2002a).[9]

The work of community organizing groups in each of the eight indicator areas is important, but the outcomes that are most important to everyone from parents to politicians are those related to students and their school achievement. Stories of community organizing for school reform should create confidence that ultimately student learning will improve. To investigate the relationship between the indicator areas and improving student learning, we returned to each of the five case study sites to follow up selected education organizing campaigns. By looking across the many organizing stories we gathered, we were able to see the ways in which the eight indicator areas work together in a change process that underlies education organizing, illustrated in a theory of change model (Figure 11.1 on page 247). The theory of change model shows how community organizing builds community capacity, which leads to improving schools and higher student achievement.

On the far right of the model are the indicator areas: *curriculum and instruction* and

Box 11.3   **Definitions of the Eight Indicator Areas**

Leadership Development

- Builds the knowledge and skills of parents and community members (and sometimes teachers, principals, and students) to create agendas for school improvement
- Empowers parents and community members to take on public roles
- Heightens leaders' civic participation and sharpens their skills in leading meetings, interviewing public officials, representing the community at public events and with the media, and negotiating with those in power

Community Power

- Helps residents of low-income neighborhoods gain influence to win the resources and policy changes needed to improve their schools and neighborhoods
- Emerges when groups act strategically and collectively to build a large base of constituents and form partnerships for legitimacy and expertise
- Uses its clout to draw the attention of political leaders and the media to the community's agenda

Social Capital

- Activates networks of mutual obligation and trust, both interpersonal and inter-group, to leverage resources to address community concerns
- Means bringing together people—beginning with relationships among neighborhood residents and within local institutions—who might not otherwise associate with each other, either because of cultural and language barriers (e.g., Latinos, African Americans, and Asian Americans) or because of their different roles and positions, such as teachers, school board members, and parents
- Requires community organizing groups to create settings for these "bridging relationships" in which issues are publicly discussed, as the key to moving a change agenda forward

Public Accountability

- Seen in a broad acknowledgement of and commitment to solving the problems of public education
- Built on the assumption that public education is a collective responsibility
- Requires community organizing groups to create public settings for differently positioned school stakeholders—educators, parents, community members, elected and other public officials, the private and nonprofit sectors, and students themselves—to identify problems and develop solutions for improving schools in low- to moderate-income communities
- Holds officials accountable to respond to the needs of low- to moderate-income communities

(Continued)

Box 11.3 (Continued)

Equity

- Guarantees that all children, regardless of socioeconomic status, race, or ethnicity, have the resources and opportunities they need to become strong learners, to achieve in school, and to succeed in the work world
- Aims to provide equitable opportunities, which may require more than equalizing the distribution of resources
- Requires community organizing groups to push for resource allocation that takes into account poverty and neglect, so that schools in low-income areas receive priority
- Also means groups must work to increase the access of students from these schools to strong academic programs

School/Community Connection

- Requires that schools become institutions that work with parents and the community to educate children
- Means institutional change in which professionals come to value the skills and knowledge of community members
- Envisions parents and local residents serving as resources for schools, and schools extending their missions to become community centers offering the educational, social service, and recreational programs local residents need and desire

Positive School Climate

- Lays a basic foundation for teaching and learning, in which teachers feel they know their students and families well and in which there is mutual respect and pride in the school
- May begin when community organizing groups move for school improvement by addressing safety in and around the school and the need for improved facilities
- May include reducing school and class size

High-Quality Instruction and Curriculum

- Exists when classroom practices provide challenging learning opportunities that also reflect the values and goals of parents and the community
- Requires community organizing groups to create high expectations for all children and to provide professional development for teachers to explore new ideas, which may include drawing on the local community's culture and involving parents as active partners in their children's education

school climate, both strongly associated with school improvement. High-quality instruction and curriculum connote classrooms where teaching is content rich and academically rigorous and students are engaged (Newmann, Secada, & Wehlage, 1995). Positive school climate is evidenced through well-maintained facilities and a social environment characterized by orderliness, safety, low incidence of discipline problems, and good teacher/student

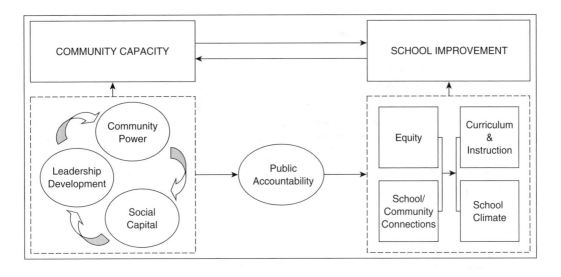

Figure 11.1 Theory of Change: Relationship of Community Capacity and School Improvement

rapport and respect (Cash, 1993; Corcoran, Walker, & White, 1988; Emmons, 1996). Both of these indicator areas are directly associated in the research literature with raising student achievement.

The work of community organizing groups represented on the far left of the model under community capacity—*leadership development, community power,* and *social capital*—work interactively to build *public accountability.* Through leadership development, community members learn the skills of civic participation and gain education expertise. They augment social capital by building new relationships and networks among people within a community as well as across differently positioned stakeholders around shared educational concerns. Through the power of numbers and strategic alliances and actions, community residents are able to bring public officials into accountable relationships for improving schools (Shirley, 1997; Warren, 2001; Wood, 2002.)

The change process hinges on public accountability. This kind of accountability is the result of commitments made in public settings that obligate a wide range of stakeholders—parents, educators, community

members, officials, and others—to follow through on their promises to improve schools (Gold & Simon, 2004; Gold & Simon with Brown, 2003).[10] By broadening accountability for public education, community organizing advances issues of *equity* and *school/community connection* and brings new influences to bear on curriculum and instruction and on school climate. With broad acknowledgement that equity and school/community connection are important goals, resources for schools in low-income areas become more plentiful; schools often turn into centers of the community. Respectful relationships among parents and teachers and students expand ownership for the educational experience of children. Teachers' expectations for children's academic achievement rise as they come to understand community concerns, including parents' interest in their children's education. Curriculum and instruction that are both more rigorous and culturally responsive can result (Comer, 1984; Hatch, 1998; Shirley, 1997).

As noted earlier, some researchers and educators acknowledge the importance of the connection between schools and communities. The theory of change presented here fills in the story of how what happens outside the school connects to what happens inside the school, showing the pathway that connects the community and school domains and that ultimately leads to students' academic success. To make the indicators framework presented above come alive, and to illustrate the underlying structure of change in the education organizing process, in the next section we recount a story about education organizing in Oakland, California.

EDUCATION ORGANIZING IN ACTION: OAKLAND COMMUNITY ORGANIZATIONS' SMALL SCHOOLS CAMPAIGN[11]

Oakland Community Organizations (OCO), an affiliate of the Pacific Institute for Community Organizing (PICO), is a federation of 31 congregations and 40,000 members. It has been working in Oakland neighborhoods for 30 years, the first 20 on neighborhood issues such as housing, drugs, and crime prevention. OCO began working on education in the early 1990s because of its members' concern with school overcrowding and their children's low scores on standardized tests. By the time OCO began its education organizing, it already had established its reputation in Oakland as a political player representing the interests of low- to moderate-income neighborhoods. OCO's early efforts in the school reform arena, which included afterschool programs, a school-to-career curriculum, charter schools, support for reduced classroom size, and the attempt to establish a small school within a larger Oakland elementary school, introduced the organization to the possibilities and barriers to improving schools. These experiences led OCO to conclude that for low- to moderate-income families to have good school choices, the organization needed to find a systemwide approach, rather than continue with programs or individual school change initiatives. Tying together members' concern about

school overcrowding with a growing awareness of the benefits of small schools, OCO began a campaign for small autonomous schools that addressed overcrowding in neighborhood schools and the need to improve public education in Oakland.

We divide the story of the OCO small schools campaign into three parts corresponding to the change process illustrated in our theory of change model. Boxes 11.4, 11.5, and 11.6, below, highlight the strategies that community organizing groups employ in each of the indicator areas in which they work.

Building Community Capacity: Leadership Development, Community Power, and Social Capital

In 1986, Montgomery Ward abandoned its mail order warehouse in Oakland, and the building began to deteriorate with disuse.[12] By 1993, OCO leaders who had been conducting individual and house meetings with residents in the immediate neighborhood began hearing complaints about the building. The empty building was a neighborhood eyesore. The windows were broken. People who lived near the building reported that they heard gunshots coming from the building at night. One leader explained, "There was graffiti inside and out and . . . certain gangs were there. . . . It was very scary."

During the same time period, leaders in all the neighborhoods where OCO was working were learning about parents' concerns with school overcrowding. As a result, the OCO board decided that school overcrowding would be a focus for the whole organization, and leaders began research into the issue. Their research revealed a huge difference in student achievement between crowded schools in their neighborhoods and smaller schools in more affluent areas of Oakland. They began to study the effect of school size on student learning, and this led them to develop a small-schools campaign. The campaign for small

---

Box 11.4   **The Building Blocks of Community Capacity: Leadership Development, Community Power, and Social Capital**

Leadership Development

- Identify and train parents and community members (and sometimes teachers, principals, and students) to take on leadership roles
- Develop parents and community members (teachers, principals, and students) as politically engaged citizens
- Promote individual, family, and community empowerment

Community Power

- Create a mass-based constituency within communities that results in deep membership commitment and large turnout
- Form partnerships for legitimacy and expertise
- Create a strong organizational identity
- Draw political attention to the organization's agenda

Social Capital

- Build networks
- Build relationships of mutual trust and reciprocity
- Increase participation in civic life

---

schools brought them back to the Montgomery Ward site. One leader told us, "All these research meetings . . . and the work and training they necessitated became a veritable leadership 'classroom' for new and emerging leaders, as well as for experienced leaders."

Gentrification had increased the value of the Montgomery Ward site, and residents found themselves in the middle of competing interests regarding how the site should be used. Residents wanted the land for two small schools and a neighborhood playground. Whenever OCO leaders thought they were close to having the building torn down to make way for small schools, they would meet new obstacles, often in the form of lawsuits launched by developers who wanted to use the property for commercial purposes or for new middle-class housing.

To increase their clout, OCO leaders continuously met with neighborhood residents to build and replenish the ranks and keep the effort going. They needed to create a strong base for action. One leader commented, "We kept pulling together hundreds and thousands of people." OCO sent 1,500 petitions to Montgomery Ward's Chicago headquarters. Leaders made regular phone calls to mobilize people to accompany the city inspector into the building or keep track of the proceedings of lawsuits in courtrooms. They held citywide and neighborhood public actions in which thousands of residents turned out.

Leadership development, community power, and social capital are the building blocks of community capacity. Through work in these areas, community organizing groups increase civic participation and build relationships and partnerships within and across communities as well as with those in positions of authority.

Box 11.5   **The Bridge to School Change: Public Accountability**

Public Accountability

- Create a public conversation about public education and student achievement
- Monitor programs and policies
- Participate in the political arena
- Create joint ownership/relational culture

Box 11.6   **The Pressure for Equity and School/Community Connection Enhances School Climate and Instruction and Curriculum**

Equity

- Increase funding and resources to underresourced schools
- Maximize access of low-income children to educational opportunities
- Match teaching and learning conditions with those in the best schools

School/Community Connection

- Create multiuse school buildings
- Position the community as a resource
- Create multiple roles for parents in schools
- Create joint ownership of schools and school decision making

Climate

- Improve safety in and around the school
- Create respectful school environments
- Build intimate settings for teacher/student relations

High-Quality Instruction and Curriculum

- Identify learning needs, carry out research, and implement new teaching initiatives and structures
- Enhance staff professionalism
- Make parents and community partners in children's education
- Hold high expectations

Through neighborhood meetings, OCO organizers and leaders helped residents see their shared concerns about blight and overcrowded schools. Through research, reflection, and participation in civic life, community residents developed the knowledge, expertise, strategic thinking, and sense of empowerment that leaders need to move their agendas forward. The countless individual and group meetings built and strengthened networks, forming the basis for collective action. The large turnout of parents and community members at public actions contributed to OCO's reputation as a powerful voice of the community and drew political attention to the organization's agenda.

The Bridge to School Change: Public Accountability

To succeed in demolishing the Montgomery Ward building and acquiring the space for small schools, it was necessary for leaders to meet with elected and nonelected officials at city, school district, and state levels to make their concerns known and enlist their support. As one leader commented,

> At our annual meeting in May 1997, we publicly talked for the first time to city representatives and the school district and got their support for three badly needed schools in Oakland, including one at the Montgomery Ward site. So it was out there publicly that this is what we were working towards.

In the following years, OCO and its community partners turned out members to several large citywide and neighborhood actions where they publicly asked officials for their commitment to tear down Montgomery Ward and put small schools at the site. "An important piece of our organizing was making sure the school district, the city, and the community were on the same page constantly and trying to keep that number one priority." OCO leaders also met with Montgomery Ward's corporate leaders to confront the claim that the department store chain, which was buying up new stores throughout the Northeast, lacked the financial resources to tear down the building.

Finally, in February 2001, despite a last-ditch effort by developers to get the court to grant a stay on demolition, the city tore down the Montgomery Ward building and put temporary classrooms in place while plans

moved ahead for new small schools. An OCO leader commented,

> [We were] armed with all the facts, willing to do the work and to testify on our own behalf, and strengthened with the knowledge that none of us stands alone. Through our organized efforts we know we can win many victories.

Public accountability is the bridge that connects community capacity with school improvement. Community organizing groups seek to broaden accountability to include an array of public school stakeholders who assume responsibility for public education. Public accountability generates the political will necessary for public officials to take action on behalf of children from low- to moderate-income families.

By bringing their agenda into the public arena, OCO challenged the bureaucratic culture, in which decision makers often pass responsibility off one to the other, and took a first step in holding public officials accountable. OCO leaders were laying the groundwork for making decisions regarding the public schools through a public process, rather than one that takes place behind closed doors. This public discourse about issues of concern to low-income community residents influenced elected officials to take up the interests of the community over those of powerful economic players.

School Improvement: The Pressure for Equity and School/Community Connections Enhances School Climate and Instruction and Curriculum

During the 8 years it took to have the Montgomery Ward building torn down and the land designated for new small schools, OCO recorded a number of significant accomplishments furthering its overall small-schools initiative. In 1999, OCO and the Bay Area Coalition of Equitable Schools (BayCES), a local school reform group, joined together in a powerful partnership. Together, they hired an organizer to work directly with teachers around the idea of small schools. As a result of the partnership, the support of hundreds of teachers, and the systematic one-on-one meetings OCO leaders had with school board members and other elected leaders, in Spring 2001, the district adopted a policy supporting small autonomous schools. That summer, a new superintendent created a school reform office charged to implement the small-schools policy. OCO also helped to win passage of a $300 million bond issue for school facilities targeted to low- to moderate-income neighborhoods, facilitating the construction of new small schools. The Gates Foundation awarded a grant for nearly $16 million to BayCES to implement small schools, stating that Oakland had been selected as the first small-schools grantee. At a public event where the Gates Foundation awarded the grant, a Gates representative noted, "because of the great leadership in the school, city, the non-profits and the community, the necessary groundwork [for success] has been laid." Finally, OCO and BayCES, along with the school district and the teachers union, sat at the table where successful designs for new small schools were selected. With these accomplishments, OCO turned its attention to the central office, pressuring it to develop the capacity to support small schools. The group continued to work with parents and teachers to develop the capacity to work collaboratively in the design and implementation of small schools.

Although school autonomy is a part of the plan for small schools, so is accountability. An evaluation of the effectiveness of the Oakland Unified School District (OUSD) policy supporting small autonomous schools, completed in 2003, showed that the schools are meeting the policy's goals in five key areas: equity, teacher quality, parent involvement, student achievement, and school climate (Little & Wing, 2003). The new small schools are serving students

from the most overcrowded and lowest performing schools, are more successful in attracting and retaining credentialed teachers than comparison schools, are involving parents in ways that go "well beyond having mandated parent representation on the official School Site Council" and other school bodies (Little & Wing, 2003, p. 2), are maintaining parent involvement even at the middle and high school levels, and are lowering incidences of graffiti and vandalism. The new small schools are exceeding expectations for academic achievement. New small schools are more likely than comparison schools to increase their academic performance index (API). Students in the new small schools who were at the lowest performance levels when they entered are more likely to increase their performance to the middle range. For the past 2 years, attendance in the new small schools ranks them at the top of the district. Finally, 100% of the seniors in the new small high school that opened in 2001–2002 graduated, "far surpassing district averages" (Little & Wing, 2003, p. 3).

The effort to maintain the partnership with the OUSD, however, took a critical turn in Spring 2003. As the result of a fiscal crisis, the state took over the OUSD and assigned a state-appointed administrator as a condition of additional funding. Despite the loss of a superintendent who had backed its efforts, the OCO/BayCES partnership was intent on sustaining the small-schools reform initiative through the turbulence of state takeover. OCO leaders, along with BayCES, immediately organized meetings with the new district administrator to inform him about the small-schools reform and the support the initiative had garnered from the local community and from foundations.

At the state level, the 17 affiliates of the California project of the national PICO network organized support for a Small Schools Incentive for Construction bill forwarded by a state legislator representing Oakland. That bill, which has passed the House and is now in the Senate, sets aside $20 million for the construction of small high schools. It provides targeted incentives for school districts to construct small high schools by adding a provision to the construction bond that would lower the local match when the construction is for a small high school. Success of such a state-level measure could further ensure the sustainability of the Oakland small-schools reform initiative, as well as give a boost to PICO organizing for small schools throughout the state and nationwide.

The campaign for new small autonomous schools finally addressed the significant and long-standing inequities in school size and resource allocation across the Oakland district. The targeted funding for new small schools in low-income neighborhoods of Oakland, which OCO helped to obtain, is beginning to relieve overcrowding in some of the OUSD's largest elementary and high schools. At both the elementary and high school levels, parents' and community members' engagement with school staff in planning the new small schools has created the basis for strong school-community connections. Since the new small schools opened, parents have continued to play a role in their evolution.

From their research, OCO members had learned that the relationship between students, families, and their teachers was closer and more supportive in small schools, positively shaping school climate. The evidence from research on small schools is that stronger relationships can also result in fewer discipline problems and higher academic motivation (Fine & Somerville, 1998). Evaluation results of the new small schools in Oakland show that school climate has improved, resulting in higher academic motivation as evidenced by safer schools and increases in attendance and retention rates. At the same time, OCO's small-schools campaign intended to influence curriculum and instruction to improve academic performance. Although test scores are only one measure of student learning, early results indicate that the small schools are having an impact on student achievement.

The story of the small-schools campaign in Oakland illustrates the theory of action and how work in each of the indicator areas can contribute to improving the conditions for teaching and learning, which is likely to increase student performance. The next two sections of this chapter discuss variation across organizing sites and the unique contribution of community organizing to school reform.

MAKING SENSE OF VARIATION AMONG GROUPS

We have used the story of one community organizing group, OCO, to explain the areas in which community organizing groups work and to illustrate the change process and the theory of change. Yet, no two organizing efforts look exactly alike. Here we identify the influences on organizing activity that make sense of the variation among groups and that explain how a snapshot of activities taking place at a particular moment relates to a larger effort. (Using the 19 groups we interviewed, we show some of the variation among community organizing groups in Figure 11.2.) There are four important influences to consider: local context, organizational characteristics, the phase of an organizing campaign at a particular moment in time, and the scale at which the group is aiming its effort.

Local Context

The overall region, state, city, and district context in which a community organizing group is working shapes how it defines the problem, the strategies it adopts, and, to some extent, its outcomes. Factors such as school district size, dominant educational policies, local and state politics, demographics, economic and social conditions, and the local area's history of civic engagement are factors to consider in understanding the priorities that a community organizing group sets, the targets of its work, and the particular strategies it chooses. The importance of context is further

Organization Name and State	Location		Affiliation			Constituency				Focus	
	Urban	Rural	National	Network	Independent University	African American	Latino	Caucasian	Other	Multi Issue	Single Issue
All Congregations Together, LA	•		PICO			•		•		•	
Alliance Organizing Project, PA	•			•		•	•	•			•
Austin Interfaith, TX	•		IAF			•	•	•	•	•	
Blocks Together, IL	•		NPA				•	•		•	
Bronx ACORN, NY	•		ACORN				•	•		•	
Challenge West Virginia, WV		•		•				•			•
Logan Square Neighborhood Association, IL	•			•			•			•	
Lowell Alliance for Families and Neighborhoods, MA	•			•		•	•		•		
Metro New York, NY	•		IAF			•	•	•		•	
Milwaukee Inner City Congregation Allied for Hope (MICAH), WI	•		Gamaliel			•	•	•		•	

Figure 11.2 Theory of Change: Relationship of Community Capacity Building and School Improvement

Organization Name and State	Location		Affiliation			Constituency				Focus	
	Urban	Rural	National	Network	Independent University	African American	Latino	Caucasian	Other	Multi Issue	Single Issue
Mothers on the move (MOM), NY	•			•		•				•	
Oakland ACORN, CA	•		ACORN			•	•			•	
Oakland Community Organizations, CA	•		PICO			•	•			•	
People Acting for Community Together, FL	•		DART			•	•	•	•	•	
Powerful Schools, WA	•			•		•		•	•		
Programs for Academy and Cultural Enhancement of rural schools (PACERS), AL		•			•	•	•	•		•	
San Diego Organizing Project, CA	•		PICO				•	•		•	
Southeast Education Task Force, MD	•				•	•		•	•	•	
Southern Echo, MS		•		•		•				•	
Summary	16	3	10	7	2	14	13	13	5	14	5

underscored by the fact that members' concerns, forged in neighborhood settings within particular city and regional environments, define the problems that community organizing groups take on. The outcomes that are possible and worthwhile also vary depending on factors in the local environment. Furthermore, local environments can influence the course of events and the progress of a group toward its goals.

Organizational Characteristics

Although the case study groups share a common organizing heritage, there is a range of organizational characteristics among community organizing groups, from how they recruit members to their role in implementing programs, with implications for the size of their constituent base and the kinds of training and expertise needed for their education work. These characteristics influence a group's capacity to carry out its work as well as its strategy and the resources available to it. One critical way in which groups differ is in terms of whether they work on several issues at the same time, such as housing, economic development, or public health, or whether they work only in education. Most of the groups that we studied were multiple-issue groups, and they benefited from a strong and dense set of relationships with politicians, government officials, and other key community players whom they could then call on for support in their education work.

Another organizational characteristic that distinguishes groups is whether they are independent or part of a larger network. Several national and regional organizing networks, as well as intermediary organizations, work with organizing groups. Being part of a national network affords access to resources such as training, guidance from the experiences of others, and a broad base of members across the state or region that can be mobilized for larger scale policy efforts.

A third organizational characteristic that differentiates how groups carry out their work is whether they use an institution-based or individual-member strategy of recruitment. In an institution-based recruitment strategy, members of congregations, schools, and other nonprofits are the members of the organizing group because their institution is a member. An individual recruitment strategy is carried out by going door to door or seeking individual members in a neighborhood or school catchment area. Building a base of members through individual recruitment appears to require great effort when compared to building a base through recruiting institutional members.

Phase of an Organizing Campaign

There are multiple phases of an organizing campaign, and recognizing where an activity fits into a campaign is critical for seeing its relevance to a wider effort with larger goals. Organizing campaigns take place over a long period of time, and generally, organizing groups work on more than one campaign at a time. As a result, it is important to see how different campaigns at different periods in an organization's history or concurrent campaigns relate to each other. A current campaign may have emerged from an earlier one or may represent a new approach based on past experience.

The organizing group also takes on different roles in its relationship to political officials, educators, and others at different points in an organizing process. The group may work in partnership with its allies during one phase of a campaign and act independently during another phase, for example, in obtaining commitments. As an organizing group moves closer to its goals, such as policy change or alliances with schools, it may move into a collaborative relationship with educators to see these efforts through. Relationships change over time as an organizing group balances the increasingly "insider status" that comes with collaboration with an "outsider" position that allows them to continue to hold schools and school systems accountable for following through on their commitments. The tensions in this insider/outside role echo our earlier discussion of the constructive tension that community organizing groups bring to relationships in the school community.

The phase of organizing should be considered when setting expectations for the nature and scale of impact of a group's work. Over time, some initiatives endure and continue to mature. The efforts of several of the groups that we studied had reached a mature phase and were beginning to have an impact on student achievement. Other campaigns may be at an earlier phase, and the accomplishments are more appropriately measured by indicators of community capacity or public accountability. Organizing is not a quick fix. Problems created over decades require a long-term commitment to correct.

Scale

Community organizing groups usually work on multiple levels, from the local neighborhood or individual school to citywide or even statewide efforts. Furthermore, working at multiple levels is critical to their success. Gains at the local level are important for building and sustaining the base of constituents, but accomplishments at the local level often require having an impact on policies at the city, district, or state levels. Therefore, groups must work at multiple levels at once, with some efforts geared to building and maintaining the local base through concrete wins and others aimed at working through networks or in coalitions to reach larger policy levels. The local level is also the stage for building leadership and community power, which contributes to the capacity of parents, teachers, and administrators to effectively carry out reform efforts and programs.

THE ADDED VALUE OF COMMUNITY ORGANIZING TO SCHOOL REFORM

We have explained that education organizing is distinct from the forms of parent involvement most familiar to educators, such as efforts by the school to recruit parent volunteers, get parent assistance in raising funds, increase parent attendance at school events, and boost parental guidance over homework. Education organizing is also different from efforts of nonprofits and legal services to bring needed supports for families into schools or to advocate for students and families. How does the work of community organizing groups complement the work of educators, and what difference does community organizing make for schools and students?

Community organizing is not a prescription for a particular educational program or a restructuring approach. Education research and its application in the development of effective practices are essential to improve classroom instruction and curriculum and school climate, as are the technical assistance, family services, and advocacy offered by many external groups. Community organizing plays a unique role in education reform by building community capacity and linking that to school improvement through public accountability. The work of community organizing associated with building community capacity and public accountability, however, is almost totally absent in the work of school reform as it is usually defined. Even where there is overlap between the work of community organizing and the work of educators and reform experts—in the areas of equity, school/community connections, school climate, and curriculum and instruction—community organizing adds a critical dimension.

Community organizing for school reform adds value in four ways: (a) sustaining the vision and momentum for change over time, (b) persisting in working toward change despite obstacles and setbacks, (c) building political capital and creating the political will that motivates officials to take action, and (d) producing authentic change in policies and programs that reflect the concerns of parents and community members.

Sustaining the Work Over Time

School reform is a long-term enterprise, yet many factors in the larger context, such as short-term funding patterns and turnover of politicians and school and city administrations, mean that reforms often come and go without taking hold (Cuban & Usdan, 2003; Hess, 1999). Community organizing groups are committed to the neighborhoods where their members live and serve as an antidote to the political churn that often undercuts school reform. They are an external force that can keep up the momentum for improvement over time and with a changing cast of players. Key to the ability of community organizing groups to sustain reform efforts over time are their practices of holding one-on-ones and house meetings for maintaining a strong base of members ready to act collectively around shared interests. These members monitor the progress of reform to be sure efforts stay on track.

Bringing in new members is a critical part of the work of community organizers and leaders. A common argument is that schools cannot depend on parents because they are only interested and involved during the time their children are attending a school. Organizing practice, however, involves continually renewing the base of members. Almost any organizing campaign extends over several years, and although some neighborhood residents or parents are part of an effort for the entire time, newer constituents or those who had been working in other issue areas are able to replenish the group of participants.

Community organizing also contributes to sustainability by nurturing education professionals who come to share concerns and beliefs about the central role of parents and community in improving schools. In several of the sites we studied, teachers who were working with community organizing groups became principals in other schools and were instrumental in developing the next generation of reform educators. Even when they remained as teachers in the school setting, they would often play an important role in keeping up strong school/community connections by socializing incoming principals and teachers. In both cases, the assumptions and practice of these teachers and administrators changed as they began to value the community/school connection. In one instance, professionals who considered themselves part of the community organizing effort moved up to central office positions, bringing a community-oriented perspective to the district level.

Persistence

Without persistent champions, the strong counterforces of entrenched bureaucracy and competing political and economic interests can derail reforms. The high level of passion and commitment of community residents most directly affected by failing neighborhood schools motivates them to find ways around obstacles. Education organizing adds value to school reform because of the unique and important vantage point that community members and organizers bring to their efforts. Community organizing groups are rooted in a neighborhood and have a long-term commitment and a deep understanding of what it takes to support local families. For example, in our study, four of the groups have been organizing in their settings for 20 years or more. They see schools as tied to other community concerns that need attention. Their members are deeply affected and angry when public institutions are ineffective or corrupt. Organizers tap constituents' anger and motivation and help them build the skills and power to become formidable and uncompromising in working for institutional change. Every school district we studied had a turnover of superintendent at least once during the 4 years of this project. Community organizing groups, because of their commitment to neighborhoods, are a force external to the schools and school system that can sustain the vision and momentum for change over time and with a changing cast of school district players.

Another way that education organizing adds persistence to school reform efforts is through its tradition of research and reflection, which enables community members to circumvent bureaucracy's often-used subterfuge of misinformation. Education organizers publicize their research so it can be used as the basis for community-wide problem identification and problem solving, thereby counteracting excuses by public figures for inaction. Organizers' research and reflection also lead to learning from past experience, thereby helping them avoid previous mistakes.

A third aspect of education organizing that generates persistence in school reform is the organizing group's reputation through its strong base of members and strategic alliances. Having a strong base of constituents can discourage officials from raising obstacles in the first place. Strategic alliances add expertise and strengthen the organization's reputation and legitimacy to work in the education arena. In several cities, education reform groups sought out community organizing groups as partners because of their reputations as powerful organizations with strong community bases that could be counted on to persist in their efforts to improve the local schools.

Political Will

Bureaucracies, such as city government and urban school systems, are known for inaction, corruption, and resistance to change or conversely for reform overload, which virtually guarantees that efforts will have "shallow roots" (Cuban & Usdan, 2003; Hess, 1999). In addition, school and public officials manage competing interests, and they often act in their own best interest—avoiding the risk of losing power. Three features of education organizing mitigate these impediments to action. Through community organizing, which builds bridging social capital, community members establish relationships of trust with school and elected officials. Through these relationships, all parties become aware of each other's concerns and agendas and make commitments for follow-through.

Second, powerful community organizations can counter competing economic and political interests, for example, by providing political cover that allows officials to act in the interests of low-income communities. Making discussions public is a third way that education organizing creates the political will that can bring public officials to take action. Without back-door deals, it is more difficult for officials to dodge responsibility.

Authentic Change
That Represents the Perspectives
of Parents and Community Members

By adding the perspectives of families and communities to the school reform equation, education organizing reflects the essence of the new generation of work in engaging parents, which values local knowledge and takes into account the dynamic between schools and their external environments. Parent and community voices can strengthen school reform efforts by making curriculum more challenging and congruent with community life, raising issues that otherwise would not come up, revealing how schools and the community can be resources for each other, and creating joint ownership of schools and reform.

The bottom line for parents, regardless of their circumstances, is making sure their children get what they need to be successful at the next level of school or in life. When low-income parents and community members gain sophistication with education issues and politics, they are more likely to make the kinds of demands on schools that their middle-class, suburban counterparts do. They demand that their children are challenged and that the curriculum reflects their values and culture. As a result, school reforms with strong community engagement are likely to result in more challenging teaching that addresses students' learning needs, as well as curriculum that taps into student and community knowledge. Such a curriculum is more connected to community values and can better support student achievement.

A second way in which the addition of community voices contributes to reform is by raising issues that would not have come up otherwise and then developing initiatives to address them. Issues that are important from the vantage point of parents or community members are often invisible from inside the school walls—for example, the need for a health clinic in a school to improve attendance—and can reveal taken-for-granted assumptions about school practices and policies, such as the absence of Spanish-language books in a school library where Spanish is the home language of many students.

Third, community voices add value to reform in making the walls between schools and communities more permeable. In some cities, schools have become a resource to the community by remaining open after school hours for child care or adult education courses. The community also becomes a resource to the schools, offering cultural, experiential learning opportunities and other experiences that can enrich the curriculum.

Finally, the addition of parent and community voices to school reform creates joint ownership of programs, providing needed support for their continuity and effectiveness. When schools value parents' and community members' knowledge and traditions, the continuity between students' homes and school is stronger. Continuity between home and school strengthens parents' ability to support their children and children's ability to make positive choices about their own commitment to their academic pursuits

(Coleman, 1988; Portes & Rumbaut, 2001; Putnam, 2000). Responsiveness to community interests shapes reform in ways that make the school program more effective in motivating and challenging students, as well as in activating external support systems to work for children's school success.

CONCLUSION: THE NECESSITY TO STRENGTHEN COMMUNITIES AND BUILD CITIZEN PARTICIPATION FOR SCHOOL REFORM

This chapter contributes to the "new citizenship" (Keith, 1999) discourse on the role of parents and community members in public schools. This new citizenship discourse challenges the predominant discourse of parent involvement, which narrowly defines parents' role as supporting the work of school professionals. Our research shows the process by which parents, taking action as citizens, can contribute to school improvement. The methodology of community organizing specifically focuses on democratic participation through its commitment to build community capacity and use it as the basis for improving schools. Community capacity promotes citizenship as parents gain the skills for civic participation, engage in the political arena, and form networks that enable them to gain power both through numbers and through relationships with powerful allies.

Community capacity defined in this way influences schools by creating accountability for public institutions. In publicly accountable relationships, whether they are at the school level or at the policy level, commitments and obligations serve wide community interests. Several authors have described the contours of a new paradigm of parents' roles in schools, and our use of an indicators framework and theory of change shows how this new paradigm actually links to school improvement. We have shown how the methods of community organizing build community capacity, which in turn creates the public accountability necessary to advance school improvement. For example, the work of these groups to address equity issues by bringing new and necessary resources to low- to moderate-income neighborhood schools and their efforts to forge deeper connections between schools and their communities to create joint ownership and greater communication and understanding are linked to factors that ultimately affect student achievement: high-quality curriculum and instruction and positive school climate.

The vignette about LSNA that we used to open this chapter and the OCO story that we tell at length both illustrate the process by which community organizing contributes to an interrelated series of outcomes that together lead to students performing better in school. Box 11.7 illustrates the range of accomplishments of the five case study groups in our study.

Box 11.7   Major Accomplishments of the Five Case Study Groups

Financing

Austin Interfaith and Oakland Community Organizations	Redirected city bonds to benefit schools in low-income neighborhoods, e.g., Oakland Community Organizations obtained a $300 million bond issue that is now contributing to construction of new small schools

Improved Facilities and Program

Alliance Organizing Project, Austin Interfaith, Logan Square Neighborhood Association, New York ACORN, and Oakland Community Organizations	Obtained district and/or city allocations for facility improvements and/or afterschool programs that provide academic enrichment, e.g., Austin Interfaith was instrumental in gaining funds to establish afterschool programs in 28 schools

New Schools

New York ACORN, Logan Square Neighborhood Association, and Oakland Community Organizations	Leveraged funding to build new schools and facilities in overcrowded districts, e.g., Logan Square Neighborhood Association won five new annexes at elementary schools and two new middle schools, and New York ACORN opened three new high schools

School Environment and Safety

Alliance Organizing Project and Austin Interfaith	Increased school safety by obtaining more crossing guards, better lighting, and improved traffic patterns in school areas, e.g., Alliance Organizing Project won an increase in funding for 37 additional traffic guards

(Continued)

Box 11.7 (Continued)

Quality Education

Alliance Organizing Project, New York ACORN, and Oakland Community Organizations	Worked for smaller class sizes and/or smaller schools that create more intimate settings for teaching and learning and closer relationships between students and teachers
Austin Interfaith	Negotiated district policies that open access for low-income students to challenging academic programs and bilingual instruction
Austin Interfaith, Logan Square Neighborhood Association, New York ACORN, and Oakland Community Organizations	Sponsored new kinds of professional development for teachers and principals, including visits to other schools with parents to observe innovative programs, in-service training driven by the needs of teachers and principals, home-visit training, and workshops with parents to design schools and/or curriculum

Parent Engagement

Alliance Organizing Project, Austin Interfaith, New York ACORN, Logan Square Neighborhood Association, and Oakland Community Organizations	Increased the presence of parents in schools and the roles parents are playing, making parent-professional exchange and collaboration a reality

The research on community organizing (see Box 11.8 for some recommended reading) is particularly relevant in light of the growing recognition among policymakers that parent involvement is an important element of school reform, as evidenced by the parent involvement provision in the federal No Child Left Behind legislation and by the investment that funders and school districts are willing to make in the name of school-community relationship building. The reform effort under way in the New York City schools offers a case in point. As part of a sweeping reform of schools in New York City, Chancellor Joel I. Klein launched a program intended to hire a parent coordinator for every New York City school with the purpose of encouraging parents to "participate in their children's education." With 1,200 schools in the city and a salary range of $30,000 to $39,000, the cost represents the largest investment in parent involvement to date—$43 million. The 1,200 new parent coordinators are receiving training from several nonprofit organizations in New York City on cultural sensitivity and avoiding conflict (Gootman, 2003a, 2003b). The desire is to make schools more welcoming, or to move away from the idea of "school as walled fortress . . . and break open the walls of those fortresses" (Gootman, 2003b, p. B6). But to do this without repeating past models requires a new conceptualization of parents' roles, and it is not clear whether such an effort can be achieved as a school-driven program. At the very least, without a good deal of thought, it is likely that the strategies to involve parents in the school-driven effort will reflect the "partners for improvement" discourse rather than the "new citizenship" discourse discussed above. It is not clear that power relations will

---

Box 11.8   **Recommended Reading on Education Organizing**

Although this field is still new, several important accounts of the work of education organizing exist. To explore the development of the work of community organizing groups for school reform, the issues they face as well as their struggles and successes, we recommend the following:

Hollyce Giles (1998), "Parent Engagement as a School Reform Strategy"

Eva Gold and Elaine Simon with Chris Brown (2002c), *Successful Community Organizing for School Reform*

Kavitha Mediratta, Norm Fruchter, and Anne C. Lewis (2002), *Organizing for School Reform: How Communities are Finding their Voices and Reclaiming their Public Schools*

Dennis Shirley (1997), *Community Organizing for Urban School Reform*

Dennis Shirley (2002), *Valley Interfaith and School Reform: Organizing for Power in South Texas*

Mark Warren (2001), *Dry Bones Rattling: Community Building to Revitalize American Democracy*

Richard I. Wood (2002), *Faith in Action: Religion, Race, and Democratic Organizing in America*

Eric Zachary and Shola Olatoye (2001), *A Case Study: Community Organizing for School Improvement in the South Bronx*

---

change in any way while efforts concentrate on making schools more welcoming. Without a dimension that builds the capacity of parents to be education leaders in their schools and communities, these school-driven efforts, regardless of how sincere they are, are likely to replicate previous unsuccessful parent involvement efforts (Fine, 1993).

What can educators learn from community organizing that would follow a "new citizenship" approach and make these efforts to engage parents more successful? First, it is important for school professionals to recognize that a power difference between parents and school staff shapes the opportunities and interactions that parents have in the school and potentially can discourage parent engagement. For parents to feel their engagement is worthwhile, opportunities and structures for parent and community participation must balance power asymmetries and permit the building of joint ownership and two-way communication.

Second, school professionals can acknowledge and value parents' and community members' expertise and knowledge. When teachers are aware of and appreciate the neighborhoods and social environments in which their students live and are willing to bring into their classrooms the complexity and contradictions of students' daily lives, they can be more effective educators and supporters (Fine, 1991). When parents and community members are admitted to domains that professionals traditionally have controlled—for example, the classroom and curriculum—students benefit from extra attention; with more adult eyes on them—especially community eyes—they often are more orderly. Students can be more academically motivated when they are learning from a curriculum that reflects their interests and backgrounds as well as the tensions of their social situations.

Finally, it is important for educators to be aware that the institution of schooling privileges the perspectives and priorities of professionals over those of parents and community members. As a result, educators may fail to understand the underlying problems affecting schools, bypass factors that affect students' academic performance, and fail to procure needed programs or new resources because they do not have the external support necessary to persuade officials to provide required funding. It can be a challenge for school professionals to recognize the validity of parents' and community members' concerns when these include issues that seem to them to have only indirect influence on the classroom, for example, safety, overcrowded schools, or culturally appropriate learning materials. Recognition of the parent perspective and the centrality of issues such as these from the vantage point of community members can be potentially rewarding to the entire school community.

The "new citizenship" model of parent engagement is best achieved by efforts that are driven by schools and communities together. The indicators framework and theory of change we provide shows the link between building capacity in local communities and improving schools. In this paradigm for school reform, strengthening community capacity is directly related to improving schools (Mathews, 1996). We suggest a way of seeing parents and community members, not as the source of urban school failure but rather as part of the solution to improving urban public schools.

NOTES

1. Information on student achievement for 1997 to 2003 is available on the Chicago Public Schools database, www.research.cps.k12.il.us.

2. We use *parents* in this chapter to refer to all child caregivers including biological parents, foster parents, grandparents, and others.

3. Case studies that illustrate the accomplishments of the groups include Gold and Pickron-Davis with Brown (2002); Simon and Gold with Brown (2002); Blanc, Brown, and Nevarez-LaTorre with Brown (2002); Simon and Pickron-Davis with Brown (2002); and Gold and Simon with Brown (2002b). The case studies are available from www.crosscity.org.

4. Keith locates the partners for improvement discourse in two U.S. Department of Education policy documents in particular: *Strong Families, Strong Schools* (Ballen & Moles, 1994) and *New Skills for New Schools* (Shartrand, Weiss, Kreider, & Lopez, 1997).

5. These terms are common in community organizing groups' discussions of relational power. A fuller discussion of relational power is found in Cortés (1993).

6. Rollow and Bryk (1993) explain that Chicago school reform's "democratic localism" created such sites of power, balancing the relations among parents, teachers, and administrators. Nonetheless, they conclude that in communities that lack social resources, the new decentralized governance structure has been much less successful. They suggest that outside assistance may be needed to empower parents and community members as full participants in school reform. We recommend that community organizations such as those discussed in this chapter are perfectly positioned to play such a role.

7. In referring to education organizing *stories,* we are adopting the language used by community organizing groups for the narratives that describe their campaigns, leadership development, and successes. Stories are the way community organizing groups create a record of their history. They serve as the memory of the role of organizing in bringing about change, which too often is lost as the accomplishments of the groups are absorbed within the system. This institutional memory is important for both inspiring and instructing future leaders and organizing efforts.

8. Our charge from the sponsors of this research was to develop indicators of the contributions of community organizing to school reform; the sponsors saw this approach as helping several audiences—funders, educators, and organizing groups themselves—to understand and be able to assess the value of education organizing as a strategy for school improvement. Indicators are generally categorized within a set of conceptual areas authenticated by both research and popular consensus. Indicators studies use three types of

approaches, often in concert: convening stakeholders, conducting empirical research, and drawing on existing studies in the literature. We used all three strategies to develop an indicators framework applicable to community organizing for school reform.

(1) *Convening stakeholders*: We asked staff members at each site to set up an advisory group that would include not only organizational members but also key players in the community. We met with the advisory group during each site visit to gain a variety of local perspectives on what counted as significant accomplishments of the group's work. In addition, the Cross City Campaign convened a national advisory group of funders, academics, and community organizers that met twice annually during the 4 years of the study.

(2) *Empirical research*: Both in the 19 sites where we conducted telephone interviews and in the case study research, we used a variety of field research techniques to understand education organizing and the outcomes that could be associated with it.

(3) *Using existing research*: We conducted a literature review that included research on school reform and community development. We looked for empirical research that connected school improvement to parent and community participation in school reform, and as we developed the indicator areas, we continued to look for literature that would link each to community capacity, school improvement, and student achievement.

9. Both of these reports are available from the Cross City Campaign for Urban School Reform Website, www.crosscity.org.

10. Mediratta and Fruchter (2003) and Zachary and olatoye (2001) also address the ways in which community organizing contributes to accountability that has a community focus.

11. Some of the material in this section is adapted from Gold, E., and Simon, E., with Brown, C. (2002b), *Strong Neighborhoods, Strong Schools: Case Study: Oakland Community Organizations*, pp. 18–22. © by Cross City Campaign for Urban School Reform. Reprinted by permission of Cross City Campaign.

12. See Gold and Simon with Brown (2002b) and Wood (2002) for a more complete rendition of the story to have the Montgomery Ward warehouse torn down.

REFERENCES

Alinsky, S. D. (1972). *Rules for radicals: A practical primer for realistic radicals*. New York: Random House.

Anderson, G. L. (1998). Toward authentic participation: Deconstructing the discourses of participatory reforms in education. *American Educational Research Journal*, *35*(4), 571–603.

Apple, M. W., & Beane, J. (1995). *Democratic schools*. Alexandria, VA: Association for Supervision and Curriculum Development.

Au, K. (1980). Participation in structures in a reading lesson with Hawaiian children: Analysis of a culturally appropriate instructional event. *Anthropology and Education Quarterly*, *11*(2), 91–115.

Ballen, J., & Moles, O. (1994). *Strong families, strong schools: Building community partnerships for learning*. Retrieved June 20, 1998, from http://eric-web.tc.columbia.edu/families/strong/

Bastian, A., Fruchter, N., Gittell, M., Greer, C., & Haskins, K. (1986). *Choosing equality: The case for democratic schooling*. Philadelphia: Temple University Press.

Blanc, S., Brown, J., & Nevarez-La Torre, A., with Brown, C. (2002). *Strong neighborhoods, strong schools: Case study: Logan Square Neighborhood Association*. Chicago: Cross City Campaign for Urban School Reform.

Bowles, S., & Gintis, H. (1987). *Democracy and capitalism: Property, community, and the contradictions of modern social thought*. New York: Basic Books.

Boyte, H. C., & Kari, N. N. (1996). *Building America: The democratic promise of public work*. Philadelphia: Temple University Press.

Bryk, A. S., & Schneider, B. (1996). *Social trust: A moral resource for school improvement*. Chicago: Consortium on Chicago School Research.

Bryk, A. S., & Schneider, B. L. (2002). *Trust in schools: A core resource for improvement*. New York: Russell Sage Foundation.

Bryk, A. S., Sebring, P., Kerbow, D., Rollow, S., & Easton, J. Q. (1998). *Charting Chicago school reform: Democratic localism as a lever for change*. Boulder, CO: Westview Press.

Cash, C. (1993). *A study of the relationship between school building conditions and student achievement and behavior*. Unpublished doctoral dissertation, Virginia Polytechnic Institute and State University, Blacksburg.

Chall, J. S., & Snow, C. (1982). Families and literacy: The contributions of out of school experiences to children's acquisition of literacy. *The Harvard Families and Literacy Project final report*. Washington, DC: National Institute of Education.

Chavkin, N. F. (1993). *Families and schools in a pluralistic society*. Albany: SUNY Press.

Clark, R. (1993). Homework-focused parenting practices that positively affect student achievement. In N. F. Chavkin (Ed.), *Families and schools in a pluralistic society* (pp. 85–105). Albany: SUNY Press.

Coleman, J. (1988). Social capital in the creation of human capital. *American Journal of Sociology, 94*(Supplement), S95–S120.

Comer, J. (1984). Home-school relationships as they affect the academic success of children. *Education and Urban Society, 16*, 323–337.

Comer, J., Haynes, N., Joyner, E., & Ben-Avie, M. (1996). *Rallying the whole village: The Comer process for reforming education*. New York: Teachers College Press.

Corcoran, T., Walker, L., & White, J. L. (1988). *Working in urban schools*. Washington, DC: Institute for Educational Leadership.

Cortés, E., Jr. (1993). Reweaving the fabric: The iron rule and the IAF strategy for power and politics. In H. G. Cisneros (Ed.), *Interwoven destinies: Cities and the nation*. New York: W. W. Norton.

Cuban, L., & Usdan, M. (2003). *Powerful reforms with shallow roots: Improving America's urban schools*. New York: Teachers College Press.

Delgado, G. (1986). *Organizing the movement: The roots and growth of ACORN*. Philadelphia: Temple University Press.

Delgado-Gaitan, C. (1987). Traditions and transitions in the learning process of Mexican children: An ethnographic view. In G. Spindler & L. Spindler (Eds.), *Interpretive ethnography of education: At home and abroad* (pp. 333–359). Hillsdale, NJ: Lawrence Erlbaum.

Delpit, L. (1995). *Other people's children*. New York: New York Press.

Emmons, C. (1996, Spring). The SDP school climate surveys. *School Development Program Newsline*.

Epstein, J. (1995). School/family/community partnerships: Caring for the children we share. *Phi Delta Kappan, 76*(9), 701–712.

Epstein, J. L., & Sanders, M. G. (2000). Connecting home, school, and community: New directions for social research. In M. T. Hallinan (Ed.), *Handbook of the sociology of education* (pp. 285–306). New York: Kluwer Academic/Plenum.

Erickson, F., & Mohatt, G. (1988). Cultural organization of participation structures in two classrooms of Indian students. In G. Spindler (Ed.), *Doing the ethnography of schooling: Educational anthropology in action* (pp. 132–174). Prospect Heights, IL: Waveland Press.

Fine, M. (1991). *Framing dropouts: Notes on the politics of an urban public high school*. Albany: SUNY Press.

Fine, M. (1993). [Ap]parent involvement. *Equity and Choice, 9*(3), 4–8.

Fine, M., & Somerville, J. I. (Eds.). (1998). *Small schools, big imaginations: A creative look at urban public schools*. Chicago: Cross City Campaign for Urban School Reform.

Fullan, M. (1999). *Change forces: The sequel*. Philadelphia: Falmer Press.

Giles, H. C. (1998). Parent engagement as a school reform strategy. *ERIC Clearinghouse on Urban Education Digest, 135*.

Goddard, R. D. (2003). Relational networks, social trust, and norms: A social capital perspective on students' chances of academic success. *Educational Evaluation and Policy Analysis, 25*(1), 59–74.

Gold, E., & Pickron-Davis, M., with Brown, C. (2002). *Strong neighborhoods, strong schools: Case study: Alliance Organizing Project*. Chicago: Cross City Campaign for Urban School Reform.

Gold, E., & Simon, E. (2004). Public accountability. *Education Week, 23*(18).

Gold, E., & Simon, E., with Brown, C. (2002a). *The education organizing indicators framework: A user's guide*. Chicago: Cross City Campaign for Urban School Reform.

Gold, E., & Simon, E., with Brown, C. (2002b). *Strong neighborhoods, strong schools: Case study: Oakland Community Organizations*. Chicago: Cross City Campaign for Urban School Reform.

Gold, E., & Simon, E., with Brown, C. (2002c). *Successful community organizing for school reform*. Chicago: Cross City Campaign for Urban School Reform.

Gold, E., & Simon, E., with Brown, C. (2003). Reframing accountability for urban public schools. *The Evaluation Exchange, 9*(2). Cambridge, MA: Harvard Family Research Project.

Gootman, E. (2003a, August 30). In gamble, New York schools pay to get parents involved. *The New York Times*, p. A1.

Gootman, E. (2003b, August 21). 1,200 parents prepare to take on role as paid liaisons in schools. *The New York Times*, p. B6.

Hatch, T. (1998). How community action contributes to achievement. *Educational Leadership, 55*(8), 16–19.

Heath, S. B. (1983). *Ways with words: Language, life, and work in communities and classrooms.* New York: Cambridge University Press.

Henderson, A. T., & Berla, N. (Eds.). (1994). *A new generation of evidence: The family is critical to student achievement.* Washington, DC: The Center for Law and Education.

Henderson, A. T., & Mapp, K. L. (2002). *A new wave of evidence: The impact of school, family, and community connections on student achievement.* Austin, TX: Southwest Educational Development Laboratory.

Hess, F. M. (1999). *Spinning wheels: The politics of urban school reform.* Washington, DC: Brookings Institution Press.

Hidalgo, N. M. (1992). *I saw puerto rico once: A review of the literature on Puerto Rican families and school achievement in the United States* (Report No. 12). Baltimore: Johns Hopkins University, Center on Families, Communities, Schools and Children's Learning.

Kahn, S. (1991). *Organizing: A guide for grassroots leaders.* Washington, DC: National Association of Social Workers Press.

Katz, M. B. (1992). Chicago school reform as history. *Teachers College Record, 94*(1), 56–72.

Keith, N. Z. (1999). Whose community schools? New discourses, old patterns. *Theory Into Practice, 38*(4), 225–234.

Kruse, S. D., Louis, K. S., & Bryk, A. S. (1995). An emerging framework for analyzing school-based professional community. In K. S. Louis & S. D. Kruse (Eds.), *Professionalism and community* (pp. 23–42). Thousand Oaks, CA: Corwin.

Lareau, A. (1989). *Home advantage: Social class and parental intervention in elementary education.* London: Falmer Press.

Lareau, A., & Shumar, W. (1996). The problem of individualism in family-school policies. *Sociology of Education* [Extra issue], 24–39.

Lightfoot, S. L. (1978). *Worlds apart: Relationships between families and schools.* New York: Basic Books.

Little, J. W., & Wing, J. Y. (2003). *An evaluation of the effectiveness of Oakland Unified School District's new small autonomous schools policy (2000–2003).* Retrieved October, 2003, from http://www.bayces.org/pdf/NSASEx_Summary.pdf

Malen, B., & Ogawa, R. T. (1988). Professional-patron influence on site-based governance councils: A confounding case study. *Educational Evaluation and Policy Analysis, 10*(4), 251–270.

Marcon, R. A. (1999). Positive relationships between parent school involvement and public school inner-city preschoolers' development and academic performance. *School Psychology Review, 28*(3), 395–412.

Mathews, David (1996). *Is there a public for public schools?* Dayton, OH: Kettering Foundation Press.

McConnell, B. (1989). Education as a cultural process: The interaction between community and classroom in fostering learning. In J. Allen & J. M. Mason (Eds.), *Risk makers, risk takers, risk breakers: Reducing the risks for young literacy learners* (pp. 201–221). Portsmouth, NH: Heinemann Educational Books.

Mediratta, K., & Fruchter, N. (2003). *From governance to accountability: Building relationships that make schools work.* New York: The Drum Major Institute for Public Policy.

Mediratta, K., Fruchter, N., & Lewis, A. C. (2002). *Organizing for school reform: How communities are finding their voice and reclaiming their public schools.* New York: New York University, Institute for Education and Social Policy.

Medoff, P., & Sklar, H. (1994). *Streets of hope: The fall and rise of an urban neighborhood.* Boston: South End Press.

Miedel, W. T., & Reynolds, A. J. (1999). Parent involvement in early intervention for disadvantaged children: Does it matter? *Journal of School Psychology, 37*(4), 379–402.

Moll, L. C., Amanti, C., Neff, D., & Gonzalez, N. (1992). Funds of knowledge for teaching: Using a qualitative approach to connect homes and classrooms. *Theory Into Practice, 31*(2), 132–141.

Moore, D. R. (1998). *What makes these schools stand out? Chicago elementary schools with a seven-year trend of improved reading achievement.* Chicago: Designs for Change.

Newmann, F. M., Secada, W. G., & Wehlage, G. G. (1995). *A guide to authentic instruction and assessment: Vision, standards, and scoring.* Madison: University of Wisconsin, Wisconsin Center for Education Research.

Payne, C. M. (1995). *I've got the light of freedom: The organizing tradition and the Mississippi freedom struggle.* Berkeley: University of California Press.

Payne, C. M. (2003). "I don't want your nasty pot of gold": The Comer school of development process and the development of leadership in urban schools. In A. Datnow & J. Murphy (Eds.), *Leadership for school reform: Lessons from comprehensive school reform designers*. Thousand Oaks, CA: Corwin.

Payne, C. M., & Kaba, M. (2001). *So much reform, so little change: Building-level obstacles to urban school reform*. Unpublished manuscript.

Portes, A., & Rumbaut, R. G. (2001). *Legacies: The story of the immigrant second generation*. Berkeley: University of California Press.

Putnam, R. (1995). Bowling alone: America's declining social capital. *Journal of Democracy, 6*(1), 65–78.

Putnam, R. (2000). *Bowling alone*. New York: Simon & Schuster.

Ransby, B. (2003). *Ella Baker and the Black Freedom Movement: A radical democratic vision*. Chapel Hill: University of North Carolina Press.

Rollow, S., & Bryk, A. (1993). The Chicago experiment: The potential and reality of reform. *Equity and Choice, 9*(3), 22–33.

Sandefur, R. L., & Lauman, E. O. (1998). A paradigm for social capital. *Rationality and Society, 10*, 481–501.

Sarason, S. B. (1982). *The culture of the school and the problem of change* (2nd ed.). Boston: Allyn & Bacon.

Sarason, S. B. (1990). *The predictable failure of educational reform*. San Francisco: Jossey-Bass.

Shartrand, A. M., Weiss, H. B., Kreider, H. M., & Lopez, M. E. (1997). *New skills for new schools: Preparing teachers in family involvement*. Cambridge, MA: Harvard Family Research Project.

Shirley, D. (1997). *Community organizing for urban school reform*. Austin: University of Texas Press.

Shirley, D. (2002). *Valley Interfaith and school reform: Organizing for power in South Texas*. Austin: University of Texas Press.

Simon, E., & Gold, E., with Brown, C. (2002). *Strong neighborhoods, strong schools: Case study: Austin Interfaith*. Chicago: Cross City Campaign for Urban School Reform.

Simon, E., & Pickron-Davis, M., with Brown, C. (2002). *Strong neighborhoods, strong schools: Case study: New York ACORN*. Chicago: Cross City Campaign for Urban School Reform.

Snow, C. (1998). *Preventing reading difficulties in young children*. Washington, DC: National Academy Press.

Useem, E., Christman, J. B., Gold, E., & Simon, E. (1997). Reforming alone: Barriers to organizational learning in urban school change initiatives. *Journal of Education for Students Placed at Risk (JESPAR), 2*(1), 55–78.

Valdés, G. (1996). *Con respeto: Bridging the distances between culturally diverse families and schools*. New York: Teachers College Press.

Warren, M. (2001). *Dry bones rattling: Community building to revitalize American democracy*. Princeton, NJ: Princeton University Press.

Williams, D. L., Jr., & Chavkin, N. F. (1985). *Final report of the Parent Involvement in Education Project*. Washington, DC: U.S. Department of Education.

Wood, G. (1988). Democracy and the curriculum. In L. Beyer & M. Apple (Eds.), *The curriculum: Problems, politics, and possibilities*. Albany: SUNY Press.

Wood, R. L. (2002). *Faith in action: Religion, race, and democratic organizing in America*. Chicago: University of Chicago Press.

Zachary, E., & Olatoye, S. (2001). *A case study: Community organizing for school improvement in the South Bronx*. New York: New York University Institute for Education and Social Policy.

12

Leading the School Through Culturally Responsive Inquiry

RUTH JOHNSON
California State University, Los Angeles

LAWSON BUSH, V
California State University, Los Angeles

The school leadership team and the principal had spent a considerable amount of time collecting and disaggregating data by student racial, ethnic, language, and income groups and preparing a presentation for teachers about the achievement in their school. They were excited about their work and felt that the faculty would be eager to see and address the issues related to the data. They presented the findings at the monthly faculty meeting. Achievement gap patterns among student groups were apparent. On every indicator of achievement, there were disparities by race, ethnicity, and income. African American, Latino, Native American, and low-income students did less well on standardized tests and other indicators of achievement than their middle-income, white, and Asian peers did. African American and Latino students were disproportionately placed in lower-level groupings and special education, and they also were consistently on lists for disciplinary infractions. However, all groups in the school had similar attendance rates.

After the presentation, the team asked the faculty to examine and discuss the data in small groups and to propose some solutions to improve student achievement and to close the gap. The teams had allotted about 30 minutes for discussion. This was the first time the staff had looked at such comprehensive disaggregated data, and most of the faculty members were clearly uncomfortable with the information. Instead of breaking into groups, some challenged data accuracy; others said that the achievement disparity had to do with poverty and that there was enough research to prove it, and still others claimed that the parents did not care and that the kids were uncooperative.

Others had silver-bullet solutions such as this or that program or creating another remedial course. Some resented the fact that the data were disaggregated and felt that doing so was racist. They claimed that they did not see color and that this presentation was divisive. There were others, however, who saw the data as confirming their assumptions about what they thought was happening to different groups in the school. They were glad that there would be an opportunity to have dialogue around these patterns and to pose some solutions. They had heard about schools with similar demographics that were significantly closing the gap, and they believed that the data picture in their school could change.

Unfortunately, the faculty was not able to begin the data dialogue because the time for the faculty meeting had ended, so they would have to take this up at another time. The leadership team was disappointed and frustrated because its members often were not able to address the challenges posed by their colleagues at this meeting, and they had no idea as to when they could schedule a follow-up meeting.

OVERVIEW

This chapter is about how school communities can become responsive to all students and their cultures by implementing inquiry strategies. We argue that the infusion of culturally responsive inquiry strategies into the school's culture offers powerful opportunities to build capacity in schools to alter low student-achievement scenarios. These strategies promise to create significantly positive outcomes for students. Our focus is on schools where low-income students and many students of color have historically been underachievers. We have organized our chapter in the following ways. First, we provide contextual information on current achievement patterns in America. These patterns illustrate differential achievement levels associated with race, ethnicity, and income. Second, to address these achievement patterns, we discuss how teaching and student achievement are linked. We argue that culturally responsive teaching, learning, and schools are a necessary response to systemically reverse patterns of low achievement. Next, we discuss the need to build on the culturally responsive teaching model by using whole-school inquiry. This requires multiple layers of reflection and investigation by the school community. Furthermore, it allows schools to build the capacity to continually measure the responsiveness of the school to all students and their cultures. We provide some suggestions and tools about stages, issues, and benefits to students when schools engage in this approach. Finally, we discuss implications for leaders in schools that use whole-school inquiry. We hope to create a sense of urgency in the school community so that members will challenge inequitable systems and fundamentally transform them to be effective learning environments for all students.

The research on cultural responsiveness informs us that it should be central to the conversations on school improvement and not an afterthought. Any discussion of whole-school inquiry as a transformation strategy should be situated within the current discourse on culturally responsive and appropriate pedagogy (Delpit, 1988; Hale, 2001a, 2001b; Irvine, 1990; Ladson-Billings, 2001). Whole-school inquiry could become the essential strategy to demonstrate the need for culturally responsive and appropriate pedagogy to those involved in the educational enterprise. When well implemented, this approach provides educators with the powerful knowledge, capacity, and skills to influence and address institutional barriers to achievement such as: persistent structural inequalities, differential treatments and opportunities to learn for diverse student populations, curriculum content and cultural relevancy, and effective and ineffective instructional and whole-school practices. Ultimately, as with all educational reform efforts, including those implementing a culturally relevant model, whole-school inquiry must influence and have a sustained impact on the ongoing effectiveness of the institutional culture for all students and their outcomes.

THE CONTEXT: CURRENT PATTERNS OF ACHIEVEMENT

Public education is in an era of accountability, standards-based reform, high school graduation requirements, and high-stakes testing. One of the major requirements of the federal No Child Left Behind Act is that schools demonstrate targeted achievement levels for all groups of students, levels that are measured against rigorous standards. If any student group (e.g., African American, English language learners) does not meet the target, the school is considered low performing. These are major challenges given the persistent patterns of low achievement present in most schools attended by students of color and low-income students.

The College Board's National Task Force on Minority Achievement (1999) offers compelling evidence about the persistent gaps between African American, Latino, and Native American students and their white and Asian counterparts, gaps that begin in elementary school and continue through the postsecondary levels of education:

- The gaps are found among these groups regardless of socioeconomic level.
- At second and third grade, African American, Latino, and Native American youngsters are scoring much lower than their white and Asian counterparts are. African American, Latino, and Native American 12th graders made up only about 1 in 10 of those students scoring at the proficient level on the 1996 National Assessment of Educational Progress (NAEP) math and science tests, although they represented about one third of the population who took the test. They did somewhat better in the 1998 reading tests, but their scores were not comparable to those of their white and Asian counterparts.
- There are gaps in other measures of achievement, such as grades and class rank.
- Achievement gaps are evident in the Advanced Placement and SAT exams.
- Although college-going rates are increasing for all groups, African American, Latino, and Native American students earn much lower grades than do white and Asian students with similar admission test scores. Data for 1995 show that they represented only 13% of the bachelor's degrees, 11% of the professional degrees, and 6% of the doctoral degrees earned, although they make up 30% of the under-18 population.

High-stakes testing and graduation requirements receive a great deal of attention. However, other gap measures related to student achievement are significant and need attention. The first is the overrepresentation of some groups in special education programs, and second, the technology divide. These areas have long-term consequences for students' life opportunities and therefore need careful monitoring.

A report on special education by the Civil Rights Project at Harvard University (cited in Fine, 2001) found that African American youngsters are more often classified as needing special education, and once they are so classified, they are not likely to be placed in mainstream classrooms or returned to regular classes. African American students were more often given labels such as *mentally retarded* and were provided with a less rigorous curriculum. U.S. Department of Education data for 1997, which was cited in the project report, found:

> Black students were 2.9 times more likely than whites to be identified as having mental retardation. They were 1.9 times more likely to be identified with an emotional problem, and 1.3 times more likely to be identified with a specific learning disability. (Fine, 2001, p. 6)

The study indicates that bias plays some role in the overrepresentation of African American students in special education.

Likewise, the technology divide has the potential to perpetuate "have and have nots" by denying large numbers of students exposure not only to hardware, but more important to the kinds of software that give students access to high levels of knowledge. Although more students at all income levels and in all groups have access to computers today, access is less common among low-income students, females, low-achieving students, minority students, students whose primary language is not English, students who live in rural areas, and students with disabilities than it is among higher-income and white students (Bushweller &

Fatemi, 2001; Scoon Reid, 2001). Other factors contributing to the technology divide, observed in many urban schools, are woefully old buildings that do not have the space, the up-to-date wiring, or the security equipment for supporting computer hardware. In these schools, computers are often gathering dust or are still in the boxes.

The other technology divide concerns the type of computer programs students use. Kohl (quoted in Scoon Reid, 2001) states:

> Schools with predominantly minority enrollments are more likely to use their state-of-the-art technology for drill, practice, and test-taking skills. Meanwhile, white students in more affluent communities are creating Web sites and multimedia presentations. The computers become nothing much more than trivial workbook and control mechanisms for kids in the heavily minority schools. . . . In other communities, they are instruments used toward the success and the futures of kids. (p. 16)

There is also a gender divide. Young women are not choosing technology majors, and the College Board reported that only a small percentage of the almost 20,000 students who took the Advanced Placement exam in computer science were females (Gehring, 2001).

The picture is not all bleak; hopeful indicators are emerging that defy the myths about low achievement by certain groups. These indicators show that increasing numbers of students from African American, Latino, and low-income backgrounds are passing high-stakes tests and taking college preparatory courses and Advanced Placement and college entrance tests—at levels comparable to higher income and white students. These encouraging signs usually have underpinnings in schools where students are supported by systems that provide not only access but appropriate preparation, adult support, and responsiveness to all students, the use of data for monitoring, and resources for success (Johnson, 2002).

CULTURALLY RESPONSIVE TEACHING, LEARNING, AND SCHOOLS

Another accountability measure of the No Child Left Behind Act is the requirement to place high-quality teachers in all classrooms. The National Commission on Teaching and America's Future (1996) report strongly argues that teachers' content knowledge and pedagogical strategies absolutely affect student achievement, particularly for students in low-achieving, low-income urban and rural schools. The effect of poor teaching is more devastating for low-income students. Their parents are least able economically to ameliorate the effects of ineffective teaching. Parents at higher income levels are more able to have access to private tutors and other academic support services for their children. These parents often know how to negotiate the schools and how to put demands on the system relative to which teacher their child receives.

The Education Trust in Washington, D.C., issued a report on research related to teachers and student achievement. The report clearly illustrates that across the nation, students in low-income schools are more likely to be taught by unqualified teachers. For example, Figure 12.1 demonstrates that low-income students are more frequently taught by teachers who lack a minor or major in the content area that they are teaching.

Studies done in Tennessee, Dallas, and Boston all link teacher quality to student achievement. The teacher effectiveness study in Dallas by Jordan, Mendro, and Weerasinghe (cited in Haycock, 1998) shows the cumulative effect on students who were taught by effective or ineffective teachers over 3 years. Students who began at similar starting points in fourth grade experienced very different outcomes 3 years later. Those with three very effective teachers in a row rose to the 76th percentile from the 59th percentile by the end of sixth grade, whereas those with three ineffective

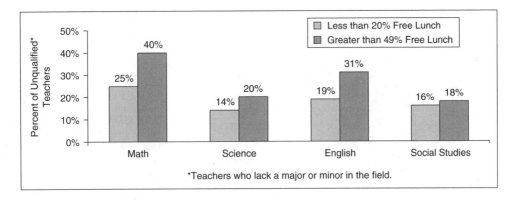

Figure 12.1   Classes in Low-Income Schools Are More Often Taught by Underqualified[a] Teachers

Source: The Education Trust Inc. *Achievement in America* (2000) (Slide No. 46); also in National Commission on Teaching and America's Future (1996), *What Matters Most: Teaching for America's Future*, p. 16.

a. *Unqualified* usually means not having a credential—teachers who have emergency certificates and those who lack the experiences and competencies to teach in their assigned field.

teachers had fallen to the 27th percentile by the end of Grade 6 (see Figure 12.2).

These disparities in educational outcomes underscore the need for students to be in schools where they are consistently taught by teachers who show evidence of being able to effect high academic achievement regardless of students' background and income. The research cited thus far may lead us to conclude that teachers' content knowledge is the only condition we need to consider in improving teacher quality. Although teachers' content knowledge may be a necessary ingredient in looking at teacher quality, it may not be a sufficient condition in looking at effective teaching for racially and ethnically diverse students. The research related to culturally responsive teaching and learning needs to be central to our discussion on how schools need to respond to all students (Darder, 1991; Ladson-Billings, 1995). With this in mind, our task here is not to present the research on culturally responsive teaching and learning in its entirety—there are now volumes of works in this area. Rather, we aim to give the reader a synopsis of its ideological underpinning and a review of its basic tenets to better understand

its implications for culturally responsive whole-school inquiry.

A pedagogy that demands high academic achievement must stress cultural competence, and the ability to function effectively in one's culture of origin[1] and an emphasis on a sociopolitical critique of society are quintessential components of culturally responsive teaching (Darder, 1991; Ladson-Billings, 1995, 1998). However, the call for and practice of such a pedagogy did not have its genesis in the early 1970s as commonly noted in the culturally responsive discourse (see Gay, 2000). We would argue that, just to name a few, the writings of Marcus Garvey in the early 1900s (see Hill, 1987; also see Bush, 1997), the work of Carter G. Woodson (1933/1977), and the scholarship of W. E. B. DuBois (1903/1969) clearly maintained that the mainstream educational system had deleterious psychological, social, and academic consequences for those we now call students of color. In addition, these early pioneers also declared that effective schools, specifically where African Americans are concerned, should be situated in the African American historical and sociopolitical experience. However,

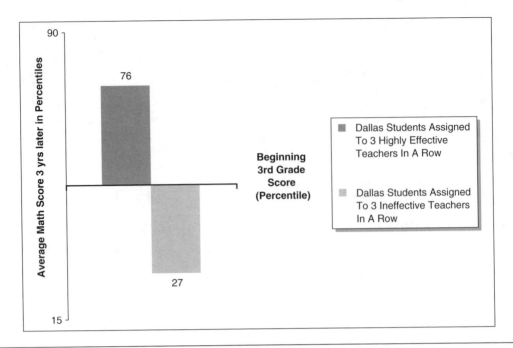

Figure 12.2   Effects on Students' Math Scores in Dallas (Grades 3–5)

Source: The Education Trust. Slide No. 49, "Effects on Students' Math Scores in Dallas." *Achievement in America* (2000). Reprinted by permission. Secondary Source: Jordan, H., Mendro, R., & Weerasinghe, D. (1997). *Teacher effects on longitudinal student achievement.* Paper presented at the Annual Meeting of CREATE, Indianapolis, IN.

these sentiments can be generalized to other historically excluded groups.

Building on their predecessors, scholars in the early 1970s added to the voices proclaiming the necessity of a different educational experience for students of color in order to produce successful educational outcomes. Gay's (2000) work reminds us that the culturally responsive teaching approach has its ideological beginnings in the early discourse on cultural diversity and multiculturalism. Abrahams and Troike (1972, cited in Gay, 2000) argue that teachers must examine their own issues, biases, and cultural differences that prevent them from teaching students of color effectively. Chun-Hoon (1972, cited in Gay, 2000) contends that teaching cultural diversity has positive educational outcomes for Asian Americans and society in general. Carlson (1976, cited in Gay, 2000) cautions educators to acknowledge and address the

fact that cultural differences affect educational outcomes, and not to evade or ignore this situation. Forbes (1973, cited in Gay, 2000), who constructed an educational program centered on Native American ontological traditions, concludes that such a program fosters academic success and perpetuates cultural traditions unique to native peoples.

Today, those who prescribe and practice in schools a pedagogy that is aligned with the cultural traditions and knowledge of students and draws on, affirms, and validates prior experiences, language, frame of references, and performance styles of bicultural peoples now fit under the culturally responsive teaching umbrella. Culturally responsive teaching has also been called "culturally relevant," "congruent," and "synchronized" teaching (Gay, 2000). We would add under the culturally responsive teaching and learning umbrella closely related pedagogies such as critical multiculturalism (see McLaren, 1993; also see Tejeda, Martínez, & Leonardo, 2000), African-centered education (Lee, 1994; Murrell, 2002), and critical pedagogy (Freire, 1995).

We will describe what we view as the main components of culturally responsive teaching, learning, and schools and add some additional aspects drawn from the literature (Edmonds, 1979; Gay, 2000, 2002; Hale, 2001a; Ladson-Billings, 1995, 1998, 2001). Culturally responsive teaching, learning, and schools do the following:

- Demand high academic achievement
- Have high expectations of teachers and students
- Provide the space for students to critique the dominant culture and power relations
- Recognize and validate color, relationships, ways of being, and culture of bicultural students
- Bring students closer to who they are as defined in their community, culture, and history
- Draw heavily on and affirm the cultural knowledge, language, prior experience, frame of reference, and performance styles of diverse populations
- Ensure that cultural relevance permeates and informs classroom management and discipline procedures, instructional strategies and methods, classroom environment, student-teacher and parent-teacher relationships, and curriculum content
- Exhibit strong leadership
- Monitor student progress continually

The outcome of practicing culturally responsive teaching is a pedagogy that is transformative (Gay, 2000) and liberating (Lipman, 1995; Shujaa, 1994). Of great significance in the current results-oriented climate, culturally responsive teaching and learning produces academic success as well (Au, 1993; Coggins, Williams, & Radin, 1997; Foster, 1997; Hilliard, 1991; Howard, 1991; Ladson-Billings, 1994; Tharp & Gallimore, 1988; also see Gay, 2000). Moreover, some studies report improvements in dropout rates, grade point average, and attendance, particularly in "at risk" populations (see Mitchell, 2003). The challenge is for culturally responsive teaching to be happening systematically throughout schools and school systems, rather than being episodic.

Space and our focus on entire schools do not allow us to provide examples of what culturally responsive teaching and learning looks like in the classroom. The works of Cooper (2003), Gay (2000), Ladson-Billings (1994), and Murrell (2002) provide ample cases and illustrations. Beyond these texts, however, we recommend that educators visit and spend time with the students, teachers, and parents who are involved in successful culturally responsive programs and settings. It has been our experience that these culturally responsive spaces look and feel different than most traditional places where historically excluded students reside.

We will build on the culturally responsive teaching and learning model to answer the question that many of us are beginning to ask: What would a culturally responsive school (or community) look like? As we move in this direction, we must add a necessary component and step: whole-school inquiry. Whole-school inquiry, among other things, helps to clarify and illuminate the data, issues, and challenges that need to be addressed on a school site. Thus, it gives both teeth and direction to culturally responsive practices as it moves to permeate a school community.

COMPONENTS OF WHOLE-SCHOOL INQUIRY

Few members of the school staff understand the need to analyze the organizational context and the underlying assumptions on which classroom and school practices are based. It appears that the system is more successful in finding ways to contain young people than to educate them. Principals and other administrators receive high marks for good control, and therefore, they tend to focus little attention on the connection between culturally responsive practices to teaching and learning, on the one hand, and student behaviors and academic achievement. Many are not consciously aware of the hidden curriculum. This curriculum may be defined as the norms, beliefs, and attitudes reflected in the school's practices and the behavior of teachers and administrators.

Broad-scale improvement in culturally insensitive schools where student outcomes are low necessitates the challenging process of changing whole systems—and the cultures within them. Under the microscope, actual institutional behaviors often appear very different than what we say we believe or want for students. Data can be a foundation for school-wide examination of these patterns. Properly implemented, whole-school inquiry can be a compelling means of launching, sustaining, and institutionalizing a reform effort. We are highlighting whole-school inquiry because it enables a school to know whether it is culturally responsive to all groups of students.

Whole-school inquiry is a paradigm shift from a data provider culture to a data user culture. It replaces a culture that provides data to external requesters, such as the state, the district, or a funder, with a culture that is able to define indicators of progress including the distribution of learning opportunities, to test assumptions about students and their experiences, and to encourage more provocative inquiry about institutional practices that contribute to performance. This new paradigm includes constant internal monitoring of progress toward goals. The data generated from whole-school inquiry not only can act as a lever to describe student outcomes, but also can facilitate knowledge about students' access to meaningful content and effective teaching. Rich dialogue can provide early opportunities to assess and understand the beliefs and values that drive norms of behavior in the school culture.

Some of the major stages for organizing the school to engage in whole-school inquiry are

building leadership and/or data teams, killing myths about student achievement, building dissatisfaction (where needed), creating the culture of inquiry, creating the vision, and monitoring progress. Although these stages are described in a certain order, some schools may organize their approaches in a different way depending on where the school is relative to transformation. The stages are described below.

1. Building leadership and data teams. Transformation begins with individuals within the school, the district, and the community. Many times, an outside catalyst, such as an external review or federal or state measuring and funding requirements (e.g., the No Child Left Behind Act) identifies the need for major reform. Whatever the reason, individuals must recognize from the beginning the value of an inclusive and culturally responsive reform process and the possible uses of data as a fundamental tool in the process. The leadership and data teams must be trained with the proper knowledge and skills and allowed adequate professional time to collect and analyze data for the school.

2. Killing the myth/building dissatisfaction. Schools are socializing agencies for both educators and students, and the content and context of that socialization are very powerful. As a result of a series of educational practices, educational outcomes are affected. When practices manifest a nonrelevant cultural context, low expectations, watered-down curricula, and inappropriate instructional strategies, low achievement is the likely outcome. Such practices can become time-honored and institutionalized, as administrators, teachers, parents, and students become accustomed to and participate in them. In the end, if these ingrained institutional behaviors are allowed to persist, a cultural pedagogy of low achievement will also continue (Haberman, 1991).

Culturally responsive educators, therefore, must set about killing the myth that low-income children and children from some racial or ethnic groups are incapable of anything but low outcomes. The school community must review national data to examine the long-term consequences of these outcomes, such as the economic outlook for students who receive an inferior education. Teachers and school leaders need to see, examine, and dialogue about data from schools that have defied the myth that low-income, African American, Latino, and Native American students cannot achieve at high levels. Also, they need to see the broad discrepancies between rhetoric and actual teaching practices at schools like their own. This is one way to help build a momentum of dissatisfaction, hope, and inquiry among colleagues and thus ignite a commitment to change (Johnson, 2002).

3. Assessing where you are, why you are there, and what needs to change. Willingness to ask the hard questions related to equity issues—and to look for the real answers—gets to the heart of how data can stimulate the school change process. School communities and districts need to evaluate the practices and services offered to students and how both are delivered. Creating a culture of inquiry involves analyzing relevant data, probing perceptions about why things are as they are, and examining the academic culture, classroom cultures, and issues of access, equity, and opportunities to learn.

4. Creating a vision and plan for your school. Once the school community understands its possibilities and its needs through the inquiry process, it is time to begin envisioning the future. What should institutional practices look like? How will people be behaving and interacting? What types of student outcomes are desired? And what do we want the school to look like in 3 to 5 years? This planning stage requires long-term intensive collaboration among the implementers of the change. Schoolwide priorities must be identified,

responsibilities assigned, resources allocated and reallocated, measures of progress determined, and timelines established.

5. Monitoring progress. Monitoring must become part of the school culture. Not only do test scores not tell the whole story, they may tell an entirely wrong story when used irresponsibly. At one level, the quest must be to evaluate whether planned programs or practices have been implemented faithfully, whether reforms are appropriate for different groups of students, and finally, whether they are raising student achievement to the desired level. A plan to monitor the progress of every goal should be devised. In addition to objective indicators of progress, changes in the academic culture of the institution or district need to be monitored.

To measure student progress, schools must create ways and systems that are continuous, immediate, and responsive. Teachers should use such data continuously. Schools should not wait for test results to gauge how students are achieving. Some schools have designed their own internal systems using technology (Excel spreadsheets), logs, and assessment formats. They also build in time for reflection related to information from data.

SOME TOOLS FOR WHOLE-SCHOOL INQUIRY

The school community ought to develop inquiries that are linked to the goals of creating and sustaining an authentic culturally responsive school where indicators of equity, access, learning opportunities, and outcomes can be measured. Developing knowledge bases in these areas is essential. Here are some questions that need to be asked and answered:

- Are students from different racial, income, and gender groups receiving the same opportunities for higher learning?
- What are the cultural factors that are influencing students' opportunity? What types of

outcomes are evident for different groups of students?

- What institutional conditions affect placement patterns, policies, and the distribution of resources?
- How are teachers teaching, and how effective are different pedagogical approaches for different groups of students?
- How is progress monitored and evaluated?
- Which groups of students are in gifted programs?
- Which are in special education?
- Who teaches which students?

Multiple types and layers of information are needed to look at how well the school is doing at the task of creating a culture that responds effectively to diverse student groups. Members of the school community will need to have professional development so they can become skilled in seeing the culturally relevant nuances in gathering, analyzing, and interpreting information. Some suggestions regarding implementation are provided in a later section of this chapter. Data should include information on outcomes, programs, processes, and policies.

1. Measure outcomes.

These data include outcome accountability measures such as indicators from standardized and standards-based tests as well as grades, teacher assessments, and graduation and college-going rates. Nonacademic indicators such as referrals, suspensions, and expulsions are needed to examine and assess how different groups of students are experiencing school.

Disaggregated outcome data need to be compared to expectations for all students. If all students are expected to achieve on grade level or above or are expected to be eligible for college enrollment, the gaps or lack of gaps in matching those expectations need to be noted for each student group (by race, ethnicity, income, gender, and special program groups, e.g., gifted and talented). The next step is to measure how close or far from the standard

each group places. Simply measuring gap information from group to group can be short-sighted if the highest group is achieving at a below-level standard. We have seen instances in which every group was below the desired standard. Although some groups were closer to the standard than others were, there was an achievement gap for every group relative to the achievement expectation.

In examining outcomes, schools and districts should set up systems to look at both short- and long-term outcomes. Looking at snapshot data at isolated points in time—by teacher, by student, by grade level, or by school—gives some—but insufficient—information about a school or district. Coherent decision making will depend on a systemic examination and analysis of patterns and reform efforts. Systems should be set up so the data can be gathered at the institutional, teacher, and student level over time. Inquiries should include the following: What happens to students as they move through the system? Who stays, who leaves, and for what reasons? What does the picture look like in kindergarten and at 12th-grade graduation for different students? Do students leave the system better off than when they entered? What do we expect our students to be able to do when they leave the system? For example, our expectation may be that all students should be prepared to complete high school and enter a baccalaureate degree-granting institution.

The levels of data that might be examined are:

- District
- K–12 feeder patterns
- School level
- Grade level
- Programs and tracks
- Classroom/teacher/student

The ways to look at data might include:

- Aggregate data (district, school, and classroom, using means and medians)

- Quartile data (looking at four different percentile bands)
- Cohorts over time (the same group of students as they move through the system)
- Disaggregated data (looking at data by student groups, teachers, program)
- Individual teacher
- Individual student
- Content cluster strengths and weaknesses (school, grade, class, student)
- Content cluster alignment to the curriculum
- Over time

2. Assess the academic culture, policies, practices, and programs.

The central focus of school reform must be the creation of academic environments that produce high-level achievement outcomes for all students, regardless of background. Procedures, processes, and practices affect student outcomes, but little time is spent in systematically looking at the everyday workings of the institution. Most of the explanations as to why outcomes look like they do are embedded in norms and practices. Research gives clues about what are effective and ineffective institutional practices. We also have lots of information on how certain institutional structures and practices contribute considerably to inequitable outcomes.

Discussing what impact reform may bring to the work lives of key participants can help to crystallize the real need for reform and the potential for lasting effects for students. This deeper level of reflection must continue as the school or district evolves its visions, sets goals, and develops strategies.

Assessing where your school is involves probing perceptions about why things are as they are. It means asking the hard questions: What are we doing? What is working? What is not working, and for which students? Educators need to evaluate the services they offer students and how they are performed.

Questions should lead not to pointing the finger at parents or students as the problem, but to identifying institutional policies and practices

that affect student achievement. This requires individual and collective reflection. Saavedra (1996) suggests using teacher study groups to create changes in teachers' beliefs and practices. Teachers study in context. This provides a rich opportunity for teachers to examine their own cultural, social, and political identities. Saavedra states, "In other words, through understanding their world and themselves with their world, teachers engage in the process of creating and shifting knowledge, meanings, ideologies and practices and thus transform themselves and conditions of their lives" (p. 272). As a result of this participation, teachers were able to change their practices and beliefs about diverse groups of students and their parents.

A climate of urgency, trust, risk taking, and action must be fostered. Sometimes, schools use an external facilitator with expertise to begin the process. However, the school community must ultimately make a commitment to ask and answer questions such as the ones posed throughout this chapter. This becomes at once a continual schoolwide assessment effort and an ongoing individual effort because transformation is ultimately personal and may require deep-seated behavioral change. To move this process forward, it will be important to ask reflective questions and provide information and processes that provoke professionals to evaluate some entrenched underlying assumptions (e.g., low income is solely responsible for low achievement, the system is fair) and beliefs. To do this, schools will need to assess how they are doing in areas that count: expectations, teacher quality and professionalism, teaching and learning, curriculum and instructional practices, learning opportunities, leadership and planning, and parent and community involvement.

An example of an assessment instrument is *Assessing Institutional Reforms in the Academic Culture of Schools* (Figure 12.3). This instrument was designed to reflect the research in each of the areas indicated (see Johnson, 2002). Using instruments like this one can move staff away from simply placing blame on parents and communities and build an awareness that the academic culture of the school contributes to the achievement patterns of children. The instrument described here should be used in schools where the focus is on student achievement and where there is a commitment to look at institutional practice. However, it can also be used as a wake-up call for schools to better understand how their institutional practices contribute to high or low achievement.

Prior to using the instrument shown in Figure 12.3, it is important to go over the categories and terms so there are clear operational definitions. For example, the staff may need to review the literature defining "rigorous, balanced curriculum" in the curriculum area. Time and information must be dedicated to defining and describing what culturally responsive behaviors look like in each of the areas assessed. This will assure that the staff has some grounding in this area. Examples of some of the desired culturally responsive behaviors are found on page 275 of this chapter. Descriptors of levels of reform may be used instead of numerical ratings. After the staff has done its own internal analysis, the school may want an outside evaluator(s) to assess the school, using the same instrument. This will offer additional grounding about where the school stands. The information can then be analyzed and decisions made for school development. This instrument can also be used for baseline data about the reform in school culture; if carefully done, such analysis can serve as a progress indicator of reforms that can lead to advances in student achievement.

3. Examine school documents.

Rich sources of data exist in schools. These documents can describe compelling information related to equitable and inequitable institutional structures and behaviors. Looking at existing everyday documents in a school can help to pinpoint how the school distributes and allocates its most valuable resources: people, time, material resources, space, and money. Examples include the master schedule; student and teacher schedules; time allocations and how time is used; teacher assignments by experience, credentials, and student outcomes; and counselor practices. Crawford and Dougherty (2000) demonstrate powerful ways for high schools to examine their master schedules and school calendars. This strategy shows how information from these documents can reveal meaningful information about the equity and student achievement. Table 12.1 on pages 288–289 gives examples of the types of documents, the purposes they can be used for, and the information that can be gained.

4. Establish multiple and combination quantitative and qualitative indicators of the school's or district's academic health.

One of the most powerful possibilities for uses of data exists in combining indicators to reveal patterns, practices, and processes of schools and districts. These combinations can provide insights and access to knowledge that would otherwise go undiscovered. Assumptions can be tested and challenged. For example, in one school district where work was being done to increase access and equity for African American and Latino students' college enrollment, many assumptions were being made about students' and parents' aspirations related to attending college. Administrators, teachers, and counselors thought that these groups had low aspirations for postsecondary education.

When the data on the parents' aspirations for college going and the actual enrollment rates in 2-year and 4-year colleges were combined and compared, an interesting picture emerged. Only 11% of African American parents and 13% of Latino parents expected their children to attend 2-year colleges. Only 16% of African

(text continued on p. 287)

Assessing Institutional Reforms in the Academic Culture of Schools

Name (optional): _____   School: _____

Position: _____   Date: _____

(Fill in for post assessment *only*.)
Filled out instrument in 2004 ____?   *Yes* _____ *No* _____

Directions: Please fill in the circle under the number that you believe best represents your school. One (1) is the lowest rating and five (5) is the highest.

Area	Underachievement	Rating					Higher Achievement
Leadership/ Planning/ Decision Making	* Little or no collaboration between administrators and teachers about strategies to raise student achievement	1 -O-	2 -O-	3 -O-	4 -O-	5 -O-	* Frequent and regular collaboration and joint problem solving to design and evaluate strategies to raise student achievement with a focus on access and equity
	* Mostly top-down style of leadership; leadership teams function in isolation from colleagues; roles and commitment unclear	1 -O-	2 -O-	3 -O-	4 -O-	5 -O-	* Frequent collaboration with administrative leaders; teams skillfully engage with each other; planning and decision making involve all major stakeholders
	* No use of data	1 -O-	2 -O-	3 -O-	4 -O-	5 -O-	* Regular planning and use of data for inquiry; disaggregation of data
	* No vision or strategic planning; add-on fragmented programs; no inclusion of stakeholders	1 -O-	2 -O-	3 -O-	4 -O-	5 -O-	* Consensus on shared vision for school; focus on systemic issues that reform institutional policies and practices
	* Meetings focus solely on operations, adult agenda	1 -O-	2 -O-	3 -O-	4 -O-	5 -O-	* Meetings and activities have a clear focus on instruction

What evidence supports your assessment? _____

©Johnson, R. (2002). *Using Data to Close the Achievement Gap.* Thousand Oaks, CA: Corwin Press.

Area	Underachievement	Rating					Higher Achievement
Professionalism/ Responsibility	* Low achievement and poor school functioning blamed on others	1 -O-	2 -O-	3 -O-	4 -O-	5 -O-	* Staff views improved achievement and school functioning as its responsibility; analyzes institutional practices; highly committed staff; includes the entire school community

Figure 12.3   Assessing Institutional Reforms in the Academic Culture of Schools

(Continued)

Figure 12.3 (Continued)

Area	Underachievement		Rating				Higher Achievement
Professionalism/ Responsibility	* 20% or more teachers lack credential	1 -O-	2 -O-	3 -O-	4 -O-	5 -O-	* 90% to 100% of the teachers are fully credentialed
	* Few teachers, counselors, and administrators are engaged in continuous meaningful professional development that will result in improved academic achievement	1 -O-	2 -O-	3 -O-	4 -O-	5 -O-	* All professionals are continuously developing their professional skills
	* Most professionals are not up-to-date in fields	1 -O-	2 -O-	3 -O-	4 -O-	5 -O-	* Staff experiments; keeps up-to-date in field; experiments with new strategies; evaluates progress and regularly uses data; teacher is a researcher; visitations to other sites with successful practices
	* Nonrelevant, isolated, sporadic, or nonexistent staff development; in-service is the only form of staff development	1 -O-	2 -O-	3 -O-	4 -O-	5 -O-	* Development is systematic, comprehensive, and tied to diverse student and staff needs—up to date, culturally responsive strategies, peer teaching, coaching, assessment, collegiality

What evidence supports your assessment? _____

©Johnson, R. (2002). *Using Data to Close the Achievement Gap.* Thousand Oaks, CA: Corwin Press.

Area	Underachievement		Rating				Higher Achievement
Standards/ Curriculum	* Curriculum and courses are not aligned with state/national standards	1 -O-	2 -O-	3 -O-	4 -O-	5 -O-	* Curriculum and courses are aligned with state/national standards
	* Few students are engaged in standards-based tasks	1 -O-	2 -O-	3 -O-	4 -O-	5 -O-	* All students are engaged in rigorous standards-based tasks; 90% to 100% of students score at levels demonstrating mastery
	* Little or no agreement on consistent process to measure and report student performance	1 -O-	2 -O-	3 -O-	4 -O-	5 -O-	* Consensus and commitment to ensuring standards-based rigor in curriculum and coursework for all students; consistent framework for measuring student progress and providing feedback

Area	Underachievement	Rating					Higher Achievement
Standards/ Curriculum	* Curriculum actually taught is thin, fragmented, and not culturally responsive	1 -O-	2 -O-	3 -O-	4 -O-	5 -O-	* Students are taught a culturally responsive, rigorous, balanced curriculum, rich in concepts, ideas, and problem solving
	* Remedial instruction is isolated to low-level skills based on discrete facts	1 -O-	2 -O-	3 -O-	4 -O-	5 -O-	* All students are taught a curriculum that is at or above grade level; students pushed toward higher-order thinking
	* No technology included in the curriculum	1 -O-	2 -O-	3 -O-	4 -O-	5 -O-	* Students have technology integrated into curriculum

What evidence supports your assessment? _____

©Johnson, R. (2002). *Using Data to Close the Achievement Gap.* Thousand Oaks, CA: Corwin Press.

Area	Underachievement	Rating					Higher Achievement
Instruction	* Mostly lecture format; students passive; emphasis on low-level skills	1 -O-	2 -O-	3 -O-	4 -O-	5 -O-	* A variety of successful, challenging, and interactive instructional strategies are used, such as cooperative learning, directed lessons, extended engagement time for learners; use of high-quality technology and software programs
	* Cultural knowledge, frames of reference, and issues and concepts are not integrated into standards-based instruction; no use of students' authentic learning outside of school to connect what is being taught in school	1 -O-	2 -O-	3 -O-	4 -O-	5 -O-	* Culturally responsive content, issues, and concepts are integrated into standards-based instruction; use of students' authentic learning outside of school to connect what is being taught in school
	* Repetitive low-level drills; heavy use of workbooks	1 -O-	2 -O-	3 -O-	4 -O-	5 -O-	* Higher level skills taught; progress assessed frequently; production rather than reproduction of knowledge is encouraged

(Continued)

Figure 12.3 (Continued)

Area	Underachievement	Rating					Higher Achievement
Instruction	* Lots of pullout programs isolated from regular classroom instruction; emphasis on remedial instruction	1 -O-	2 -O-	3 -O-	4 -O-	5 -O-	* Students taught all subjects that lead to college entrance; addresses needs of diverse student populations
	* Student abilities and achievement assessed solely on standardized skill-based tests	1 -O-	2 -O-	3 -O-	4 -O-	5 -O-	* A variety of indicators are used to measure student performance
	* No use of standards-based assessments	1 -O-	2 -O-	3 -O-	4 -O-	5 -O-	* Appropriate and frequent use of standards-based assessments

What evidence supports your assessment? _____
©Johnson, R. (2002). *Using Data to Close the Achievement Gap*. Thousand Oaks, CA: Corwin Press.

Area	Underachievement	Rating					Higher Achievement
Expectations	* Academic goals are unfocused; no attention to access and equity	1 -O-	2 -O-	3 -O-	4 -O-	5 -O-	* Goals are clearly focused on student achievement, access, and equity
	* Students from low-income and certain ethnic backgrounds are viewed as not having the potential to gain high-level knowledge and skills	1 -O-	2 -O-	3 -O-	4 -O-	5 -O-	* All students viewed as potential high achievers—staff believes all students are capable of mastering high-level knowledge and skills
	* Students considered not capable of taking required courses for 4-year postsecondary institutions	1 -O-	2 -O-	3 -O-	4 -O-	5 -O-	* All students have access and are supported and prepared for 4-year postsecondary institutions
	* Staff conversation reflects much negativity about children; staff assumes no responsibility for low levels of achievement	1 -O-	2 -O-	3 -O-	4 -O-	5 -O-	* Staff constructively focuses on institutional and instructional practices that need changing and engages in discussions about culturally responsive ways to help students learn at high levels
	* Students are informally and formally labeled in negative ways, e.g., slow, remedial, dropouts	1 -O-	2 -O-	3 -O-	4 -O-	5 -O-	* All students are viewed and treated as high achievers

What evidence supports your assessment? _____
©Johnson, R. (2002). *Using Data to Close the Achievement Gap*. Thousand Oaks, CA: Corwin Press.

Area	Underachievement	Rating					Higher Achievement
Learning Opportunities Grouping/ Tracking/ Labeling	* Students separated by perceived ability into rigid homogeneous groups	1 -O-	2 -O-	3 -O-	4 -O-	5 -O-	* Flexible grouping for short periods of time; most/all instruction in heterogeneous groups
	* Lower level and remedial groups get least prepared, culturally insensitive teachers, watered-down curriculum	1 -O-	2 -O-	3 -O-	4 -O-	5 -O-	* All students have opportunities to be taught by best-prepared, culturally responsive teachers
	* Only high-achieving students taught advanced-level information/ skills/technology	1 -O-	2 -O-	3 -O-	4 -O-	5 -O-	* All students get same rigorous core curriculum—variety of strategies including technology is used
	* Few options for low-achieving students	1 -O-	2 -O-	3 -O-	4 -O-	5 -O-	* Students form study groups; extended days are provided; other student supports are introduced and implemented; practices are altered when necessary to better serve students
	* Level that students function at is seen as unalterable	1 -O-	2 -O-	3 -O-	4 -O-	5 -O-	* All students viewed as having the capacity to achieve at higher levels

What evidence supports your assessment? _____

©Johnson, R. (2002). *Using Data to Close the Achievement Gap.* Thousand Oaks, CA: Corwin Press.

Area	Underachievement	Rating					Higher Achievement
Parent Involvement	* Parents are considered indifferent toward child's achievement	1 -O-	2 -O-	3 -O-	4 -O-	5 -O-	* Staff, parents, and leaders use a variety of culturally responsive strategies to motivate and accommodate parents as partners in their children's education; families learn to become effective advocates for their students
	* Education viewed as a domain of professionals; little or no collaboration between staff and parents	1 -O-	2 -O-	3 -O-	4 -O-	5 -O-	* Collaborative process where staff and parents assume joint responsibility for student performance, homework, communication

(Continued)

Figure 12.3   (Continued)

Area	Underachievement	Rating					Higher Achievement
Parent Involvement	* Parent involvement limited to a few persons; insensitivity to cultural differences hinders participation	1 -O-	2 -O-	3 -O-	4 -O-	5 -O-	* Parents, leaders, and staff use effective culturally responsive strategies to achieve broad involvement and representation of all racial, ethnic, and income groups in activities
	* Parents, students, and other community members are not aware of and rarely provided with information about preparing students for higher education	1 -O-	2 -O-	3 -O-	4 -O-	5 -O-	* Parents, students, and community partners actively participate in planning and implementing programs
	* Information rarely translated into the parents' dominant languages; communications seldom relate to achievement	1 -O-	2 -O-	3 -O-	4 -O-	5 -O-	* Translation to parents' dominant languages consistently provides for effective school communication (oral and written) focused on student achievement

What evidence supports your assessment? _____

©Johnson, R. (2002). *Using Data to Close the Achievement Gap.* Thousand Oaks, CA: Corwin Press.

Area	Underachievement	Rating					Higher Achievement
Support Services for Students	* Few or no tutoring services; tutoring usually in the form of a homework club; limited number of students use services	1 -O-	2 -O-	3 -O-	4 -O-	5 -O-	* Ample support services closely integrated with instructional program; variety of tutoring programs offered with a flexible schedule, coordinated with core curriculum; regular participation of students who need assistance
	* Little coordination among special programs; no mechanism to catch students "falling through the cracks"	1 -O-	2 -O-	3 -O-	4 -O-	5 -O-	* Special programs integrated into regular instruction; counseling programs aligned

Area	Underachievement		Rating				Higher Achievement
Support Services for Students	* No agreed-upon plan for handling attendance, discipline, vandalism problems; uncaring environment; no review of implications on academic achievement	1 -O-	2 -O-	3 -O-	4 -O-	5 -O-	* Agreed-on culturally responsive procedures for handling attendance and discipline problems; reduced referrals, suspensions; caring environment; impact on academic achievement is monitored by racial, ethnic, gender, and income groups

What evidence supports your assessment? _____

©Johnson, R. (2002). *Using Data to Close the Achievement Gap.* Thousand Oaks, CA: Corwin Press.

SOURCE: Johnson, R., *Using Data to Close the Achievement Gap*, pp. 144–147, copyright © 2002 by Corwin Press. Reprinted by permission of Corwin Press, Inc.

American students and 22% of Latino students expected to go to 2–year colleges. In contrast to this enrollment rates were much higher. African American enrollment in 2-year colleges was 42%, and Latino enrollment was 38%. In this case, actual enrollment exceeds expectations; a starkly different picture emerged in the 4-year college aspirations and enrollments. A high percentage (55%) of African American parents and 49% of African American students desired 4-year college enrollment; however, only 8% of African Americans students had enrolled in 4-year colleges in the previous year. Similarly, 39% of Latino parents and 38% of Latino students aspired to a 4-year college; the actual enrollment in 4-year colleges for Latinos was 9%. (See Figure 12.4, page 290)

As a result of analyzing these data, the school leadership and counselors had to acknowledge that they had made false assumptions about the aspirations of African American and Latino parents and students. They needed to drastically transform some existing practices and develop ways to respond to these groups of students.

Another example of how combination indicators can help reveal information about practices is related to course content. The research (Adelman, 1999; College Board's National Task Force on Minority Achievement, 1999) tells us that schools need to assess whether content is masquerading as being on grade level or college preparatory when it is in fact below grade level or remedial. When this happens, we are setting students up for academic ridicule by making them less academically competitive. Abt Associates (1993, cited in Education Trust, 2001) found that when test scores are compared to grades students receive, an A in a low-income school would be a C in a high-income school. Similarly, when comparing SAT-9 test score results in an urban high school, the Principals Exchange in California found that many students in a low-income urban high school who were receiving grades of A to C nevertheless scored below the 50th percentile on both the reading and math tests (see Figure 12.5, page 291).

Another use of combination data is to dispel myths about meritocracy. When school personnel are asked why a disproportionately low number of African American and Latino students enroll in courses like algebra that would prepare them for college, they typically

Table 12.1 Analyzing School Documents

Documents	Types of Possible Equity Information	Comments
Master schedule	Increases and decreases in the number of students, number and levels of courses offered, course enrollments at different points in time, number of and types of teacher assignments	The schedule must be analyzed at key times during the year to assess progress toward equity goals. Determining when the master schedule is finalized for each semester can indicate how much instructional time might be lost. Some schools report that it takes up to 6 weeks to finalize a master schedule.
Teacher schedules	Distribution of teacher quality: Which students get the most effective teachers? How is time used? How is academic and nonacademic time distributed for all and different groups? Which subjects or courses get more or less time?	Should be combined with student achievement outcomes. Many ninth graders have school adjustment problems. Are they receiving the most effective teachers?
Student schedules	Which students get what courses, which teachers, and when? How much time is nonacademic?	Also need to look at student athlete schedules—many skip the last period for away games: What classes are scheduled? What about ESL students?
School calendar	What is the instructional flow? Are there lots of breaks in instruction? How is allotted time being used?	Many schools have empty times when little or no quality instruction is occurring. Assess all activities that interrupt the calendar. Are these activities compromising academic achievement?
Subject time and homework time allocations	Find inconsistencies in the amount of subject matter time from teacher to teacher. What amount of homework is done at home or in school?	Inconsistencies and time allocations should be examined. What relationship does this have to academic achievement?
Teacher plan books	Review planned content to be taught. Are teachers planning instruction to meet standards, and at what level? What is the amount of time spent on different subjects? What types of materials and culturally responsive approaches are being used?	Analysis should be compared to student outcomes.
Counselor record keeping	How do counselors keep records on students? What kinds of counseling are different groups of students receiving?	Analyze access to information, the types of information, and when students receive information.

(Continued)

Table 12.1 (Continued)

Documents	Types of Possible Equity Information	Comments
Disciplinary records	Which students get referred and disciplined? When and who does the referring and disciplining? For what infractions? How do students respond? What are the patterns related to race, ethnicity, gender, and income? What are the long-term consequences?	It is important to examine patterns and their relationship to how different groups of students are treated. Another issue to assess is the relationship to academic achievement.
Budgets	How are resources used? Has it had an effect on student achievement, or has there been more fragmentation of programs?	New programs and resources need constant evaluation. Which programs get the most resources? Are they linked to student needs?
Agendas of meetings	What does the school focus on? Do agendas reflect a culture that focuses on student achievement or routines? Do they reflect the written goals or the informal goals?	Analyze agendas over a period of time to find out the amount of time spent on routine items v. discussions that are focused on teaching and learning.

SOURCE: Johnson, R., *Using Data to Close the Achievement Gap*, pp. 144–147, copyright © 2002 by Corwin Press. Reprinted by permission of Corwin Press, Inc.

respond that placement is based on test scores. They believe their system is bias-free and based on merit. But an examination of actual school practices reveals interesting differences. For example, in one school district, a look at algebra placements for students who scored in the top quartile on standardized mathematics tests revealed very different placement practices for different groups. Proportionally, Asian and white students had higher placement rates than did African American or Latino students, even when achievement on tests indicated that the placements should be similar. The educators in the district were most startled by these data because they exposed systemic biases. Use of these data, as represented in Figure 12.6 (p. 291), helped to accelerate changes in practices. Over and over, cases are reported of low-income students and students of color who are not placed in higher level classes regardless of how they achieve (Spring, 2000).

These are only a few examples of the many types of combination indicators that can be examined to highlight school practices. Data and leadership teams will need to develop inquiries that require more than one indicator to describe conditions in schools.

5. Utilize the voices of students and parents to improve access to academic courses and college-going opportunities.

Parents and students may have very different perceptions than educators about why things are the way they are. There is often a cultural dissonance between the school, the parents, and the students in the manner that information, knowledge, and access get communicated (Nieto, 2000). The following scenario is based

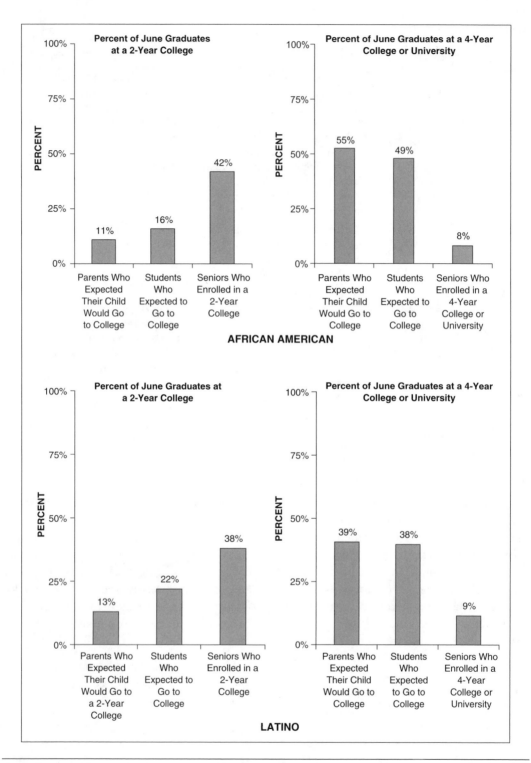

Figure 12.4 Comparison of Students' and Parents' Expectations for College Enrollment to Percent of June High School Graduates Enrolled in College

SOURCE: These figures were obtained from an urban school district.

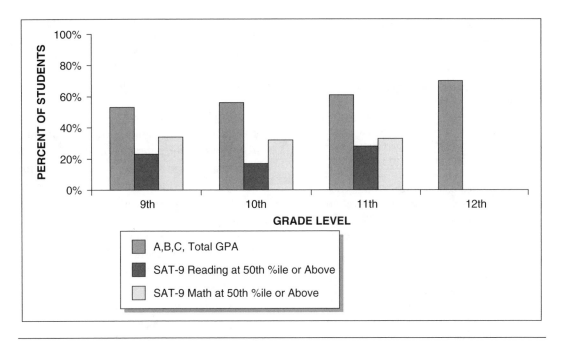

Figure 12.5 Number of Students on Grade Level: Comparison of Grade Point Average and SAT-9 Performance

SOURCE: Courtesy of the Principals Exchange, Whittier, California.

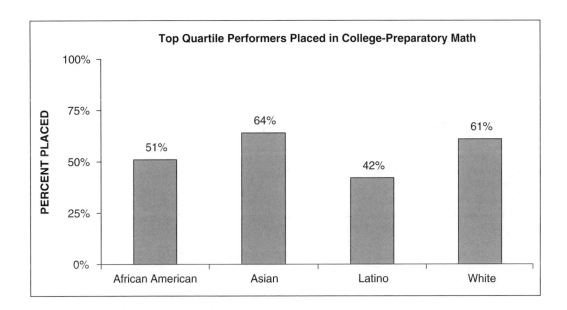

Figure 12.6 Middle School Students' Performance on Standardized Tests and Course Placement by Ethnicity: How Many Well-Qualified Students Don't Get Placed in Algebra?

SOURCE: Johnson, R., *Using Data to Close the Achievement Gap*, pp. 144–147, copyright © 2002 by Corwin Press. Reprinted by permission of Corwin Press, Inc.

on a school that was dealing with the issue of parent involvement and homework.

> At a staff meeting where teachers, counselors, and administrators are deliberating the low achievement of students in their school, the subject of parent involvement surfaces. There are comments such as, "If the parents showed more interest and came to school more often, the kids would do better. They don't care about their child's academic achievement. The students have no ambitions. They don't want to do the work. They don't turn in the homework, so why bother to assign it?"
>
> At a meeting with parents whose children attended this school, the following comments are heard: "The homework is never checked by teachers. We need homework directions in Spanish. Kids should have homework every night. Teachers need to explain homework. More homework—20 to 30 minutes for K–2 and one hour for grades 3–5. My child has too many substitutes, and they don't follow the plans the teachers leave. My child enjoys reading. We want evening classes for parents. The school needs to jump-start the program and be consistent from teacher to teacher. Tutoring needs to be done by a qualified person with a focus on the area for remediation—not old homework. Videos should not be shown during the week. How much time goes to special events and draws away from regular instruction? There are inconsistent standards at a grade level—and inconsistent expectations for students. Office personnel need to be more approachable. Perfect attendance breakfast was great! I want my child to go to college. Will he be prepared?"
>
> In a meeting with students, the following comments are heard: "We don't do homework because no one checks it. I don't understand the homework. I do my homework in class. I want harder work. I ask for help, but the teacher has no time to help me. She leaves right after school. We can't bring our books home

> because we have to share them with another class. The work is too easy. I'm bored. I am tired of watching videos all day long. We always do projects in a group. I am tired of that."

Repeated evidence indicated that assumptions that teachers, counselors, and administrators hold about parents and students from diverse backgrounds need to be tested for accuracy. Their voices contain essential data for shaping reform strategies.

Culturally responsive schools create data by continually seeking out and talking to students and by actively listening and responding to their voices. Doing this can often be more powerful than mounds of quantitative data. The example below is the voice of an urban student who experienced course content misrepresentation firsthand. She represents the voices of many students.

Melony Swasey, an African American female student, was in a college preparatory program and had received a "top ten" academic rank in her senior year. She left her urban high school for a year and attended a suburban high school, where she discovered that her new student colleagues were being challenged by a more rigorous college preparatory curriculum. This shocking experience caused her to realize that she should expect more of her school and herself. She states,

> I have realized that many of the clubs and classes that Kennedy offers bear respectable names or titles, but don't carry the weight or the full challenge that they should. In the supposedly challenging classes that I have, we aren't working at the capacity of students in those same classes on a national level. . . . I believe, because of our inadequate preparation, many of us will naively go out as confident soldiers and be knocked down before we even reach the front lines. (Swasey, 1996–1997, pp. 5–6)

She also makes the point that this cycle includes parents, who may lack the educational background, as well as the students who have been socialized to a *pedagogy of poverty* (Haberman, 1991).

For more examples and ways to measure the academic health and the cultural responsiveness of your school or district, we suggest you read Johnson (2002), *Using Data to Close the Achievement Gap: How to Measure Equity in Our Schools.*

IMPLICATIONS, ISSUES, AND CHALLENGES: WHERE THE RUBBER MEETS THE ROAD

There has been a continuous stream of literature focusing on the critical role of leadership in whole-school transformation (Barth, 1990; Edmonds, 1979; Elmore, 2000; Evans & Teddlie, 1995; Sergiovanni, 2001). Leaders of culturally responsive schools need competencies in several domains. Lindsey, Nuri Robins, and Terrell (1999) describe the culturally proficient leaders:

> [They are] guided by theory in developing first a vision and then a mission that serves the needs of all students. In addition, they recognize the formal and nonformal systems in the school, know about the cultural issues that affect learning, and have access to the resources necessary for an appropriate learning environment within the school. (p. 53)

In moving the school forward, these culturally proficient leaders must have the skills and knowledge to persuade and influence those that they lead to challenge their assumptions about current practices in schools. Then, they must lead and organize in ways that have the school measure current conditions and move into planning appropriate strategies that are embedded in culturally responsive practice.

Using whole-school inquiry will require a shift in the current practices of most schools; thus, engaging the school community in the whole-school inquiry process can appear to be a daunting task. In schools where expectations are low; where content is weak; where practices are ineffective; and where students' race, ethnicity, and culture are not acknowledged or valued, using such components of whole-school inquiry as study groups and professional development through dialogue can play a much-needed role in fostering an environment of critique and growth. Creating cultures to transform beliefs and practices will bring richer analysis, interpretations, and implications for data. Becoming skilled in dialogue and using guiding questions such as those in the templates given here bring meaningful problem solving and solutions.

Whether we are proponents or opponents of the No Child Left Behind Act, there is an impetus for schools to engage in the whole-school inquiry process. Moreover, because this new federal law reportedly calls for the "success" of all students, school data must be disaggregated according to subgroups. This provides opportunity for school leaders to begin meaningful conversations around race, class, gender, and privilege.

Implementation of the whole-school inquiry process requires that all members of the school community examine their own issues, biases, and cultural differences. In a connected way, this process makes them constantly aware of their positionality—the "identity that is shaped by power, status, rank, and sense of privilege in a given social context" (Murrell, 2002, p. 42). Last, Murrell (2002) cautions that we should not be tricked into believing that learning the history of particular populations is the key to providing a culturally responsive pedagogy; rather, teachers must become expert cultural learners. We contend that both phases are necessary: the history reminds us of the possibilities of a people while we learn their culture; that is, being an expert cultural learner informs teachers how to create the space for students to achieve those possibilities. In other words, history shows you Point B, and culture tells you how to facilitate the conditions for individuals to move from Point A to Point B.

Dialogue is critical. Yet, its effectiveness is highly dependent on what the conversation is about. We have found that many schools fail to have meaningful dialogue concerning gender, class, and particularly race. School leaders have been reluctant to lead organizations down a sometimes messy and uncertain path that these conversations bring—this is where the rubber meets the road. Culturally responsive teaching and learning cannot exist in a school where there are no conversations about power relations and no analysis of data along the lines of race, class, and gender. Carefully selected literature must be read, discussed, and linked to the issues and implementation. It is particularly important also to include literature that describes how negative conditions for students can be reversed by creating culturally responsive policies and practices.

Handing out and presenting data without a plan for structuring meaningful dialogue can be dangerous and counterproductive. One of the most important goals of data is to stimulate dialogue in the school community. Whenever data are presented, time, and ideally facilitation, must be invested. Inevitably, some of the discoveries that the school and district make regarding their beliefs, practices, and outcomes will be painful. How do we begin to have conversations that can result in some deeper reforms that make a difference for students?

Dialogue is useful to identify how different stakeholders in the school or district community perceive success. Some may want to eliminate all remedial groupings, some may want all children placed in algebra, and others may be satisfied with incremental increases. These perceptions have an impact on how the changes are implemented and can also affect the levels of commitment to the change. Although these discussions can produce some conflict, the problem solving that ensues can be healthy for the process. If this open dialogue does not occur—or is not allowed to occur—problems from differential expectations will surface later in ways that may not be possible to resolve or remediate.

It is essential to pay careful attention to the timing, structure, and facilitation of the dialogues. Having rushed conversations in an afterschool meeting is sure to derail the process. Existing use of time will probably need to be reallocated. Acquiring new skills and knowledge bases is required to create the inquiries and solutions that lead to institutionalizing a culturally responsive school. Therefore, most schools must develop appropriate professional development. This will involve setting aside the resources to implement the work.

Whole-school inquiry must not become another symbolic exercise, the latest buzzword, or a fad with limited possibilities for affecting young people's lives. What one has to bring—and to cultivate—is a vision, a passion, and a belief that all children are capable of achieving at high academic levels regardless of background. Therefore, in many cases, accomplishing these outcomes for students will mean dismantling long-held values, beliefs, and practices. This will cause great discomfort and pain for many, but the goal of creating a culturally responsive school for students must be kept at the forefront. Leaders of these schools will need the belief, the skills, the passion, the endurance, the will, and the persistence to make this happen. Risk taking is needed. Leaders will need to balance patience and impatience. In the end, they have to believe that young people are worth the investment and that they deserve no less than the best—that is the bottom line.

NOTE

1. In fact, many (Akbar, 1982; Foster, 1992; also see Bush, 1997) define education—a process that should make people more capable of manifesting who they are as defined by their cultural and community norms—in the same manner cultural competence is defined.

REFERENCES

Adelman, C. (1999). *Answers in the tool box: Academic intensity, attendance patterns, and bachelor's degree attainment.* Washington, DC: U.S. Department of Education.

Akbar, N. (1982). *Miseducation to education.* Jersey City, NJ: New Mind Productions.

Au, K. H. (1993). *Literacy instruction in multicultural settings.* Fort Worth, TX: Harcourt Brace Jovanovich.

Barth, R. S. (1990). *Improving schools from within: Teachers, parents, and principals can make the difference.* San Francisco: Jossey-Bass.

Bush, L. (1997). Independent black institutions in America: A rejection of schooling, an opportunity for education? *Urban Education, 32,* 98–116.

Bushweller, K., & Fatemi, E. (Eds.). (2001, May). *Technology counts 2001: The new divide* [Special issue: 2001 Editorial Projects in Education]. *Education Week, 20*(35).

Coggins, K., Williams, E., & Radin, N. (1997). The traditional tribal values of Ojibwa parents and the school performance of their children: An exploratory study. *Journal of American Indian Education, 36,* 1–15.

College Board's National Task Force on Minority Achievement. (1999). *Reaching the top: A report of the National Task Force on Minority High Achievement.* New York: Author.

Cooper, L. (2003). *Effective teachers of African American students: A case study of observed behavioral indicators.* Unpublished doctoral dissertation, Claremont Graduate University, Claremont, CA.

Crawford, M., & Dougherty, E. (2000). *Updraft/downdraft: Class, culture, and academic achievement in high school.* Unpublished manuscript prepared for the National Association of System Heads.

Darder, A. (1991). *Culture and power in the classroom: A critical foundation for bicultural education.* New York: Bergin & Garvey.

Delpit, L. (1988). The silenced dialogue: Power and pedagogy in educating other people's children. *Harvard Educational Review, 58,* 280–298.

DuBois, W. E. B. (1969). *The souls of black folk.* New York: Fawcett World Library. (Original work published 1903)

Edmonds, R. (1979). Effective schools for the urban poor. *Educational Leadership, 37*(1), 15–23.

Education Trust. (2001). *Education in America 2001* [PowerPoint presentation]. Washington, DC: Author.

Elmore, R. F. (2000). *Building a new structure for school leadership.* Washington, DC: The Albert Shanker Institute.

Evans, L., & Teddlie, C. (1995). Facilitating change in schools: Is there one best style? *School Effectiveness and School Improvements, 6*(1), 1–22.

Fine, L. (2001, March 14). Studies examine racial disparities in special education. *Education Week,* p. 6.

Foster, M. (1992). Education for competence in community and culture: Exploring the views of exemplary African American teachers. *Urban Education, 27,* 370–390.

Foster, M. (1997). *Black teachers on teaching.* New York: New Press.

Freire, P. (1995). *Pedagogy of the oppressed.* New York: Continuum.

Gay, G., (2000). *Culturally responsive teaching: Theory, research, & practice.* New York: Teachers College Press.

Gay, G., (2002). Preparing for culturally responsive teaching. *Journal of Teacher Education, 53,* 106–116.

Gehring, J. (2001, May). Not enough girls. *Education Week, 20*(35), 18–19.

Haberman, M. (1991). The pedagogy of poverty versus good teaching. *Phi Delta Kappan, 73*(4), 290–294.

Hale, J. E. (2001a). Culturally appropriate pedagogy. In W. H. Watkins, J. H. Lewis, & V. Chou (Eds.), *Race and education: The roles of history and society in educating African American students* (pp. 173–189). Needham Heights, MA: Allyn & Bacon.

Hale, J. E. (2001b). *Learning while black: Creating educational excellence for African American children.* Baltimore: Johns Hopkins University Press.

Haycock, K. (1998). Good teaching matters a lot. *Thinking K–16, 3*(2), 4–13.

Hill, R. (Ed.). (1987). *The Marcus Garvey and Universal Negro Improvement Association.* Berkeley: University of California Press.

Hilliard, A., III. (1991). Do we have the will to educate all children? *Educational Leadership, 49*(1), 31–36.

Howard, J. (1991). *Getting smart: The social construction of intelligence.* Lexington, MA: Efficacy Institute.

Irvine, J. J. (1990). *Black students and school failure: Policies, practices, and prescriptions.* New York: Greenwood Press.

Johnson, R. S. (2002). *Using data to close the achievement gap: How to measure equity in our schools.* Thousand Oaks, CA: Corwin.

Ladson-Billings, G. (1994). *The dreamkeepers: Successful teachers of African American children.* San Francisco: Jossey-Bass.

Ladson-Billings, G. (1995). Toward a theory of culturally relevant pedagogy. *American Educational Research Journal, 42,* 465–491.

Ladson-Billings, G. (1998). Teaching on dangerous times: Culturally relevant approaches to teacher assessment. *Journal of Negro Education, 67,* 255–267.

Ladson-Billings, G. (2001). The power of pedagogy: Does teaching matter? In W. H. Watkins, J. H. Lewis, & V. Chou (Eds.), *Race and education: The roles of history and society in educating African American students* (pp. 73–88). Needham Heights, MA: Allyn & Bacon.

Lee, C. (1994). African-centered pedagogy: Complexities and possibilities. In M. Shujaa (Ed.), *Too much schooling too little education: A paradox of black life in white societies* (pp. 295–318). Trenton, NJ: Africa World Press.

Lindsey, R. B., Nuri Robins, K., &Terrell, R. D. (1999). *Cultural proficiency: A manual for school leaders.* Thousand Oaks, CA: Corwin.

Lipman, P. (1995). "Bringing the best out of them": The contribution of culturally relevant teachers on educational reform. *Theory and Practice, 34,* 202–208.

McLaren, P. L. (1993). *Schooling as a ritual performance: Towards a political economy of symbols & gestures.* New York: Routledge.

Mitchell, K. (2003). *Standing in the gap: A critical case study of the Maat academy.* Unpublished doctoral dissertation, Claremont Graduate University, Claremont, CA.

Murrell, P. (2002). *African-centered pedagogy: Developing schools of achievement for African American children.* Albany: SUNY Press.

National Commission on Teaching and America's Future. (1996). *What matters most: Teaching for America's future.* New York: Author.

Nieto, S. (2000). *Affirming diversity: The sociopolitical context of multicultural education* (3rd ed.). New York: Longman.

Saavedra, E. (1996). Teacher study groups: Contexts for transformative learning and action. *Theory Into Practice, 35,* 271–277.

Scoon Reid, K. (2001). Racial disparities. *Education Week, 20*(35), 16–17.

Sergiovanni, T. J. (2001). *The principalship.* Needham Heights, MA: Allyn & Bacon.

Shujaa, M. J. (1994). *Too much schooling, too little education: A paradox of black life in white societies.* Trenton, NJ: Africa World Press.

Spring, J. (2000). *American education.* White Plains, NY: Longman.

Swasey, M. (1996–1997, Winter). School shock. *Rethinking Schools,* pp. 5–6.

Tejeda, C., Martínez, C., & Leonardo, Z. (Eds.). (2000). *Charting new terrains of Chicana(o)/ Latina(o) education.* Cresskill, NJ: Hampton Press.

Tharp, R. G., & Gallimore, R. (1988). *Rousing minds to life: Teaching, learning, and schooling in social context.* Cambridge, UK: Cambridge University Press.

Woodson, C. (1977). *The mis-education of the Negro.* New York: AMS Press. (Original work published 1933)

13

Constructing a Democratic Foundation for School-Based Reform

The Local Politics of School Autonomy and Internal Governance

JESSE GOODMAN
Indiana University and Harmony Education Center

DANIEL BARON
Hormony Education Center

CAROL MYERS
Harmony Education Center

INTRODUCTION AND OVERVIEW

This chapter portrays and explores several aspects of our work as external change agents who have been involved in numerous comprehensive, school-based educational reform efforts in the United States. School-based reforms are primarily conceptualized, initiated, and acted on by a particular school community (e.g., administrators and teachers with additional involvement from support staff, parents, community leaders, and, to some degree, students) rather than from other locations of power such as government agencies, corporations, or district administration (e.g., Barth, 1990; Fullan, 1993; Glickman, 1993; Hofenberg & Levin, 1993; Sarason, 1990).

While many think of school reform solely in terms of standards, curriculum, approaches to teaching, and/or discipline techniques, much of what goes on during these efforts is also political (e.g., Anderson, 1996; Dow, 1991; Mirel, 1994; Muncey & McQuillan, 1992). *Micropolitics* refers to the use of formal and

Authors' Note: This project was supported from a grant by the Josephine Bay Paul and C. Michael Paul Foundation.

informal power to achieve goals within a given school or district (Blase, 1998).

> Schools and school systems are political organizations in which power is an organizing feature. Ignore [power] relationships, leave unexamined their rationale, and the existing system will defeat efforts at reform. This will happen . . . because recognizing and trying to change power relationships, especially in complicated, traditional institutions, is among the most complex tasks human beings can undertake. (Sarason, 1990, p. 7)

From this perspective, one aspect of educational reform concerns altering the political relationships and dynamics of power within a given school or district.

Although the school community controls the content and nature of school-based reform, it is not uncommon for external change agents to provide temporary leadership, guidance, and assistance. Fortunately, there is a plethora of scholarship that addresses the processes of this work (e.g., Comer, Haynes, Joyner, & Ben-Avie, 1996; Elmore, 1990; Fullan, 1993; Glickman, 1993; Murphy, 1991) and more important, a small but significant discourse concerning the nature and struggles of these efforts in the United States, Canada, Australia, and Europe (e.g., Goodman, 1994; Hargreaves, 1994; Hatch, 1998; Korostoff, Beck, & Gibb, 1998; Smyth, 1995; Sulla, 1998). This chapter contributes to this latter body of scholarship by exploring the way we (the Harmony Education Center) and several schools[1] during the last dozen years have worked together on comprehensive school-based reform projects. The focus of this particular chapter is on issues related to school autonomy and internal governance. As White (1992) stated, "While nearly everyone concerned about education is talking about school restructuring and the need for school-based management, little is known about how school decentralization actually works, how authority is relocated, and how school decentralization affects teachers" (p. 69). Prior to this

exploration, it is important to provide some background of who we are and the nature of our work.

HARMONY EDUCATION CENTER AND SCHOOL-BASED REFORM WORK

About 15 years ago, the first author of this chapter conducted an interpretive study of Harmony, an independent school serving children and adolescents (Goodman, 1992). The stated purpose of Harmony School is to create an education that fosters the development of a critical, liberal, social democracy. The term *critical* is used in the sense that it is unwise to take a given notion of democracy for granted; *liberal* refers to beliefs in individual freedom, privacy, and opportunity; and *social* means that, as Dewey (1927) argued, democracy is best viewed as a "way of life" rather than merely a set of political rituals (e.g., voting) and governmental structures (e.g., congress, president). Social democracy emphasizes values such as equity, social justice, and the common good. As the title of this chapter suggests, the primary focus of our work is to bring democratic values, structures, and habits of interaction to schools for the purpose of facilitating meaningful educational reform.

Shortly after research on Harmony School was completed, the Harmony Education Center (HEC) was established as a collaboration between Harmony School and Indiana University, with the goal of supporting progressive educational reform in the United States. We view this work as engaging in a variety of discourses (Gee, 1990). As a center, we seek to participate in conversations among scholars committed to democratic reform (through university seminars, journals, books, conferences, etc.), school practitioners (e.g., administrators, teachers, staff, parents, children), educational change agents (e.g., Coalition of Essential Schools, ATLAS, League of Professional Schools), and philanthropic institutions (e.g., the Bay Foundation, the Gates Foundation, the Philanthropic Initiative, the Lucent Foundation). HEC consists of three integrated components:

1. An *early childhood to 12th grade school,* which is committed to democratic education and serves as a demonstration site for school visits and debriefing sessions. Harmony teachers and students also get involved in the reform efforts of interested schools (e.g., establishing critical friends groups, demonstrating lessons and democratic student meetings, arranging student exchange visits and projects).

2. An *Office for Outreach Services,* which provides assistance to schools engaged in substantive reform projects; offers staff development activities on topics of progressive, democratic education; organizes meetings and conferences on topics of school reform; and collaborates with organizations that share our pedagogical and social ethos.

3. An *Institute for Research,* which is responsible for contributions to educational scholarship, supports the inquiry work of young scholars and Harmony teachers, and provides resources (e.g., books, articles, films, speakers) to educators working with the HEC.

Since its creation, the Office for Outreach Services has worked with hundreds of schools in all parts of the United States. Our involvement ranges from one-day faculty development sessions to intensive, multiyear partnerships in which the entire center is involved. Shortly after the creation of HEC, we came to the conclusion that these intensive partnerships offered great potential for fostering substantive school reform, and as a result, we prioritized this type of work for many years.[2]

In our initial meetings, we assumed two primary roles.[3] First, as constructivist/ transformational leaders (e.g., Anderson, 1990, 1996; Blase & Anderson, 1995; Quantz, Rogers, & Dantley, 1991), we facilitated the reform process. We typically began by conducting introductory interviews with the faculty,[4] 20 to 30 parents, and 100 or more students in small groups and whole classes (Spradley, 1979).[5] The purpose was to elicit "stories," which, in turn, illuminated the nature of a given school's culture. Based on these data, plus information that emerged from several structured conversations with the faculty on a variety of topics (e.g., rationale for educational reform; nature and difficulties of organizational change; purposes of education; perceptions of children and their families, issues of student, teacher, and school assessment; concepts of intelligence and learning styles; relationship between schools and society), the faculty generated a vision of their ideal school. During the next 6 to 18 months (depending on the specific situation), the school community created study groups, which explored areas of concern related to their vision. Based on this study, the school generated a plan (e.g., goals and strategies) to make its vision a reality. During the next 1 to 4 years, the school implemented its plan, reflected on these efforts, and in light of this reflection, affirmed or altered its strategies, goals, and/or the original vision.[6]

The ideas examined in this chapter are based on reviewing fieldnotes we generated from 1990 to 2000. In addition, from June 1997 until June 1998, we kept extensive fieldnotes of our planning sessions, our intensive partnerships with five "high poverty" elementary schools, and our subsequent debriefing sessions. A graduate assistant interviewed about 75% of the faculty in these five schools at the conclusion of or at least one year after their planning year was initiated.

Throughout the 1997–1998 academic year, conversation and observation notes were reviewed daily. Incidents and bits of information were at first coded into tentative conceptual categories. As these categories emerged, questions arose that were used to guide further investigation. The findings from subsequent observations and conversations were then compared to the initial categories. Through this "constant comparison"

(Glaser & Strauss, 1975) of data, the analytical themes explored in this chapter crystallized. As the process continued, special attention was given to data that seemed to challenge original conceptualizations (Erickson, 1973). This return to the field followed by modification of ideas continued until the ideas could be discussed in some detail. It is important to note that we are not attempting to present our work as a "model" for others to emulate. Rather, our goal is to portray our work and say something worthwhile about educational reform in ways that others will find engaging and meaningful.

NEGOTIATING FOR SCHOOL AUTONOMY

One of the key principles of school-based reform is that the faculty will have the power to identify, conceptualize, and implement the curricular, instructional, and structural alterations that are deemed necessary to significantly improve their students' education. Unfortunately, Bullough and Gitlin's (1985) observation remains true even after more than a decade of efforts to promote school-based reform:

> Following a model common to many businesses and institutional bureaucracies, school reform efforts have been directed from the top down. That teachers need to be told what to do and how to do it has come almost to be taken for granted. (p. 219)

In spite of the efforts of politicians and business people to control what happens in schools, many continue to argue that significant decisions about educational reform should be made by the people who work on a day-to-day basis with children, and this view has gained acceptance among many educators. As a result, building a school's autonomy is a necessary prerequisite for meaningful school reform (e.g., Barth, 1990; Darling-Hammond, 1997; Fullan, 1993; Glickman, 1993; Sarason, 1990).

> Autonomy is a concept that institutions define in a variety of ways. Essentially it is a measure of an institution's independence and self-directedness, and the degree to which it is free of interference by outside authority. . . . The greater the school's autonomy, the more it is free from institutional regulation and supervision. (Shank, 1994, p. 286)

It is important to remember that autonomy does not mean that a school can do whatever it wants. A school's autonomy is always a matter of degree because an individual school must operate within the context of other external powers. Central to negotiating greater school autonomy within a well-established external power structure is the issue of control. That is, who has the power to make what types of decisions that affect the education of children in a particular school? As discussed below, we have focused much of our work with faculty in helping them understand and negotiate the distribution of power in their districts and how to increase their realm of control and influence. In this work, schools typically have had to negotiate with four external sources of power.

District Administration

One of the most obvious external powers is the district administration. As Chubb and Moe (1990) point out, public schools are controlled by elected boards that hire administrators to manage their schools. These individuals are responsible for the education in a specific district. It would be naive to think that central administrators will completely abandon their control over what occurs in individual buildings as a result of these schoolwide reform projects. Nevertheless, establishing a building's autonomy is so important, it is often the first topic of discussion in our work.

> Since this district has a reputation of micromanaging its schools, we wanted to clarify the need for building autonomy with the district's

Title I Coordinator and the Assistant Superintendent for Elementary Education. These two individuals stated their commitment to this school-based reform project. They both recognized that over the years, there has been a lot of mistrust generated between the "central office" and individual schools.

Their main concern was that the education of the children *really* improve. They expected higher scores on the state standardized tests within a few years; however, they also wanted to see significant "improvement" in the quality of curriculum and instruction, and "more positive" attitudes of both teachers and students towards schooling. They agreed that the schools, themselves, needed to have control over all reforms related to curriculum (content and resources), instructional strategies, internal school governance, building atmosphere, and parent/community relations.

This district's administration was so supportive of the project that its leaders were mandating (over the next 5 years) it for all their high-poverty elementary schools. The irony of this mandate didn't escape our attention, and it has been subsequently a topic of discussion in our meetings with building faculty.

(Summary of fieldnotes)

At a minimum, several of the schools with which we have worked negotiated considerable autonomy over the types and substance of internal reforms that emerged from their deliberations related to curriculum and instruction (e.g., purchasing their own curriculum materials rather than having to use district-wide textbooks; determining topics of study, instructional strategies, and student assessments), internal decision making and structure (e.g., realigning building hierarchy, creating multiage versus graded classes, eliminating tracking), use of the building and grounds (e.g., eliminating classroom desks, creating gardens), and staff development funds and activities.

In addition, a few schools have negotiated power over matters such as hiring new faculty, conducting teacher evaluation, and establishing their own relationships with district-wide programs (e.g., special education).

This is the third year we've worked with this school. During our meeting today, we discussed the faculty's desire to initiate a "peer evaluation project" of their teaching. One of the teachers asked, "Wouldn't it be nice to have this [peer evaluation] instead of the usual process" [i.e., district supervisor observations and checklist]? A decision was made to write a memo to the superintendent asking if this "peer evaluation project" could substitute for the traditional teacher evaluations.

Some time was spent discussing the rationale and description of the process with the school's Title I Coordinator, who volunteered to write the memo. At the end of the meeting, one of the teachers said, "They'll [central administration] never go for it." A week later, the faculty was informed that they would be allowed this substitution, and the only request was that records of the project's usefulness be kept so that it could be treated as a potential "pilot" for the entire district.

(Summary of fieldnotes)

Another school in a different district proposed the establishment of a "year-round" calendar, but difficulties of student mobility and busing for a single school on a different calendar from the rest of the district prevented the idea from being implemented. Several schools tried to negotiate faculty control over the hiring of building administrators. We've encouraged these proposals due to the important role faculty and principals play in reform efforts.

It's been 2 months into the second year of reform in this school. Last August, we were told that Betty [all proper names are fictitious], the principal, was being transferred to another school. Her absence seems to have dramatically slowed the pace of reform. The new principal feels "out of the loop," and perhaps threatened by the power of the school's Leadership Team, which was created last year. She rarely comes to its meetings, and when she is there, she rarely speaks.

In response to her lack of enthusiasm and involvement, several teachers have told us how the decision to transfer principals confirms their view that central administration doesn't really care about their school, and they resent it. When we discussed this transfer with the district's Title I Coordinator, she shrugged her shoulders, rolled her eyes, and mentioned the long history of autocratic control by the central administrators in this district.

(Summary of fieldnotes)

Although we advocate for school communities to have an authentic voice in hiring building administrators, only one school in our years of work has been successful in doing so. A comment by one administrator helped us understand the difficulty of this goal.

You need to understand. Up until recently, this district had an unwritten policy that principals had to be transferred every 3 years to keep them from building a strong base of support in the local community and thus be[ing] in a position to challenge decisions made by central administrators. Superintendents and their assistants are in a very vulnerable position. If somebody—and it doesn't take a lot of somebodies—doesn't like what's going on in schools, central administrators get the heat. Their only real connection to the schools is through the principal. They see the principal as *their* representative in the building. It's hard for them to let go of controlling who this person will be, even if it's ultimately good for the school to have this power for itself.

Given this orientation, it is easy to see the difficulties of expanding a school's autonomy to include the hiring of building administrators. Negotiating with central administrators over the degree of a school's autonomy is central to substantive school reform. Schools need to know "where they stand" vis-à-vis their district administration. Without overtly addressing these questions of control, educational reformers set themselves up for possible misunderstandings and subsequent frustrations and potential resentment that arise from these misunderstandings.

Unions

Although most individuals think of central administration as being juxtaposed against a school's independence, in our work, we have found teacher unions to be even more concerned about the implications of school autonomy. Our perception is not unique. Unions have, at times, been portrayed as the primary obstacle to improving the education of young people. Some school reformers (e.g., Casner-Lotto, 1988; Chubb & Moe, 1990; Finn & Clements, 1989) have called for a complete reassessment of union representation under the auspices of school restructuring.

In the school districts in which we work, the unions have not been a bulwark against school autonomy, but this resistance might occur if we failed to negotiate our school reform plans with union representatives. Unlike central administrators, who were chiefly interested in controlling certain decisions such as the hiring and removal of building principals, unions in these districts focused their concerns primarily on protecting teachers' workloads.

Today, we met with union representatives. Unlike the case in Berryville, where the union and district administration have developed a collaborative relationship, the union and management in Sharptown have had a long history of distrust and conflict. Four years ago, this community had a bitter and protracted teachers' strike that damaged both the union and school board/administration, and there continues to be significant mistrust between these groups.

As the meeting began, we soon learned that the union was particularly concerned about reform efforts that would require teachers to work extra hours without compensation. From their perspective, schools that had "gone school-based" in the previous 2 years seemed to expect their teachers to volunteer hours during the process of reform. We did not deny that some teachers had volunteered their time. Authentic change requires that teachers study and communicate with their colleagues on a regular basis, and we understood the difficulty of finding time to do this during the academic year.

As we further explored each other's concerns and desires for improving the education of the children, we reached an understanding. The contract stipulates that teachers must be available for an hour every day after school, but each school could (with faculty approval) alter the scheduling of these hours so that a block of time could be set aside for reform work.

Another concern of the union was that teachers might be expected to assume administrative responsibilities (such as a newly created position of "team leader") without the recognition or compensation for these new responsibilities. We responded by saying that no structural changes would occur in any building unless the faculty reached consensus on it. Given this understanding, the representatives agreed that any specific aspect of the current contract could be waived if 90% of the teachers in a given building agreed to the change. As we talked more, the union representatives' concern that these efforts would weaken their members dissipated.

(Summary of fieldnotes)

This concern for protecting teachers' workloads is a potential, but not a necessary, obstacle for reform. However, it has required schools to develop creative schedules. For example, the teachers in one school decided to start work 30 minutes early each day of the week, provide extracurricular activities for the students who could not leave early, and thus freed Wednesday afternoons for the faculty to engage in school reform work. In another school, the faculty decided to leave school immediately after class on Fridays but stayed for 2 hours on Thursday for reform discussions. A third school met once each week after school for 2 hours but gave each faculty member the option of leaving after the first hour.

Another major concern of unions is seniority. In particular, questions of hiring and transferring faculty between schools are extremely problematic.

In our discussion with the principal, we emphasized the importance of hiring future teachers who will agree with the new vision of the school. If newly hired teachers do not agree with the vision, then it would be difficult to implement the school's plans for change. We also encouraged him to give his faculty a voice in hiring any new teachers. He responded that he had little or no choice in selecting new faculty.

The contract between the union and the school board stipulated that he could only hire a new faculty member if no teachers already employed by the district wanted to transfer to his school. He only had a choice if more than one teacher requested a transfer to fill a position. Only if no one requested a transfer could he hire a new teacher from outside the district, and in those situations, all the principals who needed faculty met to decide on (or as this principal told us, "compete" for) which candidates were offered jobs in which buildings.

(Summary of fieldnotes)

Protecting the jobs of its members is central to the union's mission, and one cannot criticize the union for negotiating these types of policies into their contract. However, under many circumstances, schools were prevented from selecting their own colleagues, which we viewed as problematic. These schools spent considerable effort generating the ideas on which their alterations were based. If schools could not select future teachers who share these ideas, then it placed the long-term possibilities for reform in jeopardy. However, no school with which we have worked has been successful in negotiating a hiring process that replaces seniority with educational ideology as a basis for hiring or transferring teachers.

Although these contracts limit a school's autonomy, it is important to remember that unions have played an meaningful role in the development of our nation's schools (Murphy, 1991; Urban, 1982). In many situations, they have advocated for progressive policies such as collective bargaining, the equalization of pay between male and female teachers, limits on class size, health and pension benefits, safety regulations, tenure, and grievance procedures. On the other hand, teacher unions have also succumbed to conservative and at times even reactionary stances, such as the expulsion of "communist" members during the Red Scare of the late 1940s and early 1950s and resistance to "community control of schools" as in the Ocean Hill-Brownsville conflict in 1968. These latter tensions still exist in many urban areas and, as illustrated above, regularly emerged in our work with schools.

The issue of teacher unions and school autonomy is complex. Teacher unions historically have followed the structure and interests of the industrial trade union movement. That is, the welfare of their members supercedes the production of a company's product. Although it is not difficult to value the lives of workers over the production of an object, teacher unions occasionally *seem* to pit the welfare of their members over the welfare of a community's children. These conflicting interests often emerged as altercations among the faculty in several of the schools in which we have worked.

Government

Another external power that places limits on these schools' autonomy is the federal and state Departments of Education. For instance, each school is required by law to follow curricular, safety, equal access, and other regulations established by the state legislature. Several years prior to our involvement with these schools, these regulations clearly served as a fetter against a school establishing more building autonomy. Each Department of Education published lists of "essential" reading, writing, and math skills for each grade level and required students to take a competency test of these skills. Unlike standardized competency exams in the past, which were used for individual assessment, these reforms initiated what several scholars (e.g., Herman & Golan, 1993; Madaus, 1990; Shepard &

Doughtery, 1991) have called "high stakes" tests, in that a school's scores are made public, and government funding (and now punitive measures) is partially determined by students' scores.

As these scholars have noted, high-stakes competency tests and the setting of "standards" have significantly narrowed the range of potential curriculum and instructional strategies. Specifically, these exams focus the content of schools on discreet minimum skills through drill work and practice testing. In districts where we have worked, these regulations were interpreted in ways that left little room for meaningful school-based curricular reform. In response to the state's regulations, district administrators bought comprehensive instructional programs specifically designed to raise children's scores on these standardized tests. These programs came complete with all materials needed for instruction (often including written dialogue of what teachers should say to students), step-by-step lessons for each day and each "subject" (i.e., skill area), individualized worksheets for remediation of particular skills, review lessons and quizzes, and tests (which could often be graded by computers).

As we noted (Goodman, 1988) over a decade ago, several scholars warned that during the 1980s, elementary teachers were becoming increasingly "deskilled." Today, more than ever, teachers are not being viewed as reflective practitioners who are capable of establishing a relevant and meaningful education for their students. These instructional programs have transformed educators into little more than instructional technicians who merely coordinate the day's work to ensure that students "get through the material" on time. During the last two decades, most staff development in schools has focused on helping teachers become more efficient at managing these programs.

Perhaps due to the limited success of these instructional programs, the districts in which we worked (especially those located in high-poverty areas) have been open to other options, including school-based reform, as a way to improve their students' education. As a result, these schools were no longer required to use these instructional programs if they found or developed more promising curricula for their students. However, scoring well on the state standardized test was still *essential* in the minds of district and building administrators, the school boards, and teachers.

> We were discussing the rationale for this school's reform, and Betty mentioned improving the children's scores on the state's test. "I know there are more important things about education than this test. I know it doesn't measure everything or even the most important things children need to know in life. I know that the test is biased in many ways and too much emphasis is placed on it. But it's a reality we all have to live with. I hate that they now give the test at the beginning of the year. I know the scores aren't a reflection of what I do with them in class, but it's my name that gets listed when they publish the class scores, and so getting these scores up is damn important to me."
>
> (Summary of fieldnotes)

Many individuals, especially in light of the No Child Left Behind legislation, now expect reform efforts to eventually result in higher test scores.

Several states had other regulations besides the standardized test and the listing of skills to be taught in each grade, such as the number of days in each academic year, minimum number of minutes devoted to each subject per week, and minimum teacher/child ratio. Although individual schools have received waivers from some regulations if they requested them (e.g., minutes per subject), none have been able to obtain a waiver from taking the state's standardized test.

As might be expected, we have engaged in numerous discussions of testing and skill-focused curriculum with the faculty in these schools. Ironically, one government regulation that came with Title I schoolwide funding assisted faculty in reconsidering the value of a skills-based curriculum. Although the federal government's Title I schoolwide reform guidelines during the Clinton administration addressed issues of the reform process (i.e., conducting a comprehensive needs assessment of the school, developing long-term educational goals, identifying strategies needed to reach these goals, planning staff development activities, and establishing a process for yearly assessment), one regulation did address the issue of academic skills. Specifically, this regulation stated that essential skills should be taught in "an enriched and accelerated curriculum." This statement, along with the fact that children's test scores improved in each of the schools after reforms were begun, provided faculty with a powerful basis for not automatically associating higher scores on standardized tests with a skills-based curriculum.

Nevertheless, in most of the schools in which we have worked, the power of the state's high-stakes test and list of grade-level skills, as well as the difficulty of knowing whom to talk to about these governmental regulations, greatly undermined the autonomy a school was able to obtain. One might rightfully question if any meaningful school autonomy could take place, given the power of these tests and skill lists to determine what (and how) content should be taught. However, after much discussion (see pp. 319–320), many of these schools found the civic courage to move substantially away from, as one teacher stated, "the skill, drill, and kill" practices that had prevailed in these schools for well over a decade.

External Change Agents

A final outside power with whom these schools need to negotiate their autonomy is external change agents such as ourselves. As previously mentioned, most of these schools have had a plethora of "staff developers" come into their schools in an effort, as one teacher stated, "to fix us. They come, do their thing, and then leave. They don't really understand us or our kids. All they really care about is whatever they happen to be pushing [instructional program]." Anyon (1997) points out that many faculty, especially in high-poverty schools, are suspicious of these "outsiders."

Several of our inaugural activities help to mitigate these initial attitudes of distrust. In our first meetings with a given school community, we clearly explain the intensive partnership being offered by HEC and, in particular, our roles as facilitators and informed participants in the reform project. Throughout these meetings, we are extremely sensitive to the negative history of staff developers being hired to "change schools" and overtly express our desire not to impose a "model" of education on their school. The school community is given assurance that *its members* will determine the reforms necessary to create the school *they* want. In those cases where central administrators had required high-poverty schools to go through our reform project, we spent considerable time with the school community discussing ways to make this process as meaningful as possible, given the irony of this mandate.

In the cases we discuss here, these initial meetings have been helpful in establishing a tentative working relationship between us and the school community; however, trust often did not begin to develop until we conducted introductory ethnographic interviews with teachers. Although these interviews were structured around a few "grand tour questions" (Spradley, 1979; see note 5), what emerged from them were the stories of a school. Each member of a school community had a story to tell, and in telling it to us, trust slowly emerged. At the end of our interviews, several teachers expressed views similar to Martha's: "I never realized how much [frustration] was built up in me. Just talking about it, finally, I feel like a big weight has

been lifted from my shoulders." This trust was often supported when we shared with the school community our findings, which were filled with (anonymous) quotes from the interviews. At the conclusion of these reports, it was not uncommon for someone to say something similar to this teacher's comment: "Well, one thing for sure, you really know who we are and what this school is like." The rapport developed through these interviews helped us overcome much of the historical antipathy faculty feel about external change agents.

However, this early rapport did not completely resolve the issue of trust. At some point in the process, and in nearly every school in which we worked, there came a time when our motives and even our integrity were questioned by at least a few members of the school community. In one school, this challenge came from an administrator, in another from a few teachers, and in another from a parent or concerned community member. Whenever our involvement with a given school is contested, we have found it best to deal with it directly.

> Dorothy, the school's Title I coordinator, called us last night extremely upset. It seems as if a few of the teachers have been questioning the legitimacy of our partnership with their school. In response, we altered the agenda for tomorrow's meeting with the faculty so we could discuss these teachers' concerns.
>
> We began the meeting by stating, "Recently, we heard through the grapevine that some of the faculty had some questions about our involvement with the school." After a minute or two of silence, finally one of the teachers said, "Several teachers were wondering who is paying you for your time. Is it the school?" We explained that about 50% of the funds were coming from the state's Title I School-wide Initiative and the rest from the district and local funding agencies.
>
> As we continued explaining the details, one teacher asked how much we were earning as "consultants," and the teachers were surprised that we earned less than many of them. They wanted to know why we would

want to work in their school. As one person asked, "What are you getting out of it?" We reiterated what we told them at our first meeting several months ago. Namely, our motives were, for the most part, ideological. "Like you, we want to do what we can to help improve the education of children, especially children who are marginalized in our society."

We once again told them the history and the reasons why the Harmony Education Center was established in the first place. After about an hour, the discussion ended with us applauding them for raising these questions. "In lots of schools, teachers wouldn't say anything, but would instead be resentful and angry with us. Discussing these types of issues, no matter how difficult, is better than the alternative [keeping silent]." We concluded by encouraging them to raise any concerns they might have about our work.

(Summary of fieldnotes)

After this conversation and others like it, our emotional connection to the school was often deepened. Our willingness to deal with these types of issues increased the level of trust and commitment between us and these schools. As a result, we have, ironically, come to value having our motives questioned.

At times, the politics associated with our involvement with a given school was more complex and highly charged. As we discuss later in this chapter (see pp. 314-317), one of the major, initial problems facing many of these schools is the existence of building antagonisms. In all but one or two schools in which we have worked, the school community has been divided into conflicting factions. As the case below illustrates, it has been difficult at times to avoid being caught between competing factions.

Jane, the principal and a strong advocate for children, asked for this meeting with us and the district's Title I Coordinator to discuss our role in her school. During our initial interviews at Jane's school, we became aware of the deep hostility between Jane (and her supporters) and a group of teachers in the building who were very active in the union. From the various stories we heard, it seems that when Jane became principal last year, she did so with a great deal of fanfare about "improving" or "fixing" Bradley Elementary School. Several teachers believed that Jane implied that the teachers in this school were not working hard or didn't know how to teach low income children. During her first year as principal, this group of teachers filed numerous grievances against her. In response, Jane eventually filed a lawsuit for harassment against these teachers.

In this meeting, Jane accused us of either being allies with this group of teachers or being "used" by them to take control of the school, and thus she wanted to end our partnership. She described several situations that she felt illustrated her concerns. Fortunately, we were able to indicate to her how our actions in these circumstances were a result of either simple misunderstandings or poor communication, and we agreed to several changes in our work to avoid these problems in the future. More important, we were able to help her see the benefits (e.g., higher level of commitment from teachers to reform, sense of ownership and pride in the school, accountability for the education of their children, resolution of conflicts) that comes from distributing power more equally in the schools through the establishment of the leadership team and the study groups.

(Summary of fieldnotes)

Although Jane's concerns were resolved in this meeting, in another school in which there was extreme mistrust, disrespect, and animosity between most of the teachers and the principal, we were not able to maintain our neutrality. As we began to establish structures such as a leadership team and rituals (e.g., feedback norms, standards of communication, consensus decision making) to democratize and redistribute power in the building, our involvement was terminated by the principal (see pp. 320-321).

In summary, we have learned that our position as external change agents cannot be taken for granted. It would be naive to think that we could request from a given school community a year or more of hard work, the redistribution of power, a serious study and thoughtful reconsideration of their students, and the implementation of a comprehensive plan to significantly improve this education and not have *our* status and function at some point questioned and challenged.

Reflections on Autonomy

As we reflect on our experiences, we are left with several matters worthy of continued contemplation. The first matter concerns the definition of organizational autonomy. Some imply that only individuals can claim to be autonomous and that institutions by their nature cannot exercise autonomous action (Gaylin & Jennings, 1996). If autonomy is not applicable to organizations, then much of our work may be futile. However, as Kant noted (Cassirer, 1981), autonomy is a state of potential existence available to all "free rational agents," that is, beings or subjects who are capable of rational thought, informed decision making, and moral empathy (i.e., their acts are based on the categorical imperative). He also points out that organizations, institutions, and even nations are best viewed as a collective subject or being; thus, they qualify for autonomy under his previous definition (Cassirer, 1981). From this perspective, it is useful to view organizational autonomy as a state of mind. We have found that, like individuals who wish to be autonomous, school communities must develop their sense of existential freedom (see pp. 317–320) to develop confidence and self-reliance. Given this conception, organizational autonomy is not an object that can be just "given" to a school nor does it appear like magic from the sky. Similarly, autonomy is not an "event" that takes place in one moment of time: One minute an organization lacks autonomy, and the next it has it. School autonomy is, in part, a function of its ongoing collective self-perception.

Our experience suggests that until a given school community no longer sees itself as victimized (see pp. 317–320) by the numerous constraints and problems it faces, it will not generate the sense of efficacy to effectively confront those in superordinate positions of power.

Second, Kant also notes that autonomy is not synonymous with license or the freedom to do whatever one wants, what several social theorists refer to as "negative freedom" (Gaylin & Jennings, 1996). Rather, to be autonomous means to be self-ruled or self-governed. It connotes that one has the aptitude to establish values, rules of conduct based on those values, and the self-discipline to act accordingly (Cassirer, 1981). An autonomous individual or organization does not have the license to act without regard to the impact these actions may have on other free, rational agents. From this perspective, autonomy is a state of power that can only really exist in relation to other subjects (individuals and/or organizations) who operate within the same legal domain.

Autonomous schools must learn how to negotiate with others who have power and responsibility for the education of our children. In our work, schools typically have negotiated with their district administrators, union representatives, state and federal government workers, and ourselves, as external change agents. As we have discussed, these negotiations often focus on issues of curricular content and materials, instructional strategies and learning activities, internal governance, workloads, hiring procedures, the role of external change agents, evaluations of children and teachers, and staff development. Although we have begun to explore the nature and substance of these negotiations in our own work, additional scholarship is sorely needed. In particular, because we assume the power necessary to set up a democratic structure and decision-making process needed to initiate the task of reforming a given school's culture and because we openly share our views on numerous educational issues, we would find especially beneficial scholarship that explores the negotiations between school communities and openly ideological external change agents.

CREATING A DEMOCRATIC CULTURE FOR SCHOOL-BASED REFORM

It is extremely important to emphasize that increasing a school's autonomy will not automatically improve the education of children. It is not hard to imagine a school gaining more power and using this power unwisely or inappropriately. School autonomy is a crucial first step in a very long journey. It is equally important to help schools create a democratic ethos and "culture" within which to generate conversations about pedagogical and curricular reforms.

As Anderson (1998) observed, the notion that decisions about educational reform should be made by the people who work on a day-to-day basis with children has gained some acceptance in the United States.

> Viewed in education as an antidote to entrenched bureaucracy, hierarchy, and excessive specialization, [school-based reform] appears to have strong support among superintendents, principals, teachers, and the general public, regardless of their political ideologies. (p. 572)

However, Anderson (1998) and others (e.g., Anderson & Grinberg, 1998; Barker, 1993; Campbell & Neill, 1994; Campbell & Southworth, 1990; Hargreaves, 1994; Katz, 1995; Lipman, 1997; Malen, 1994) point out that school-based reform is extremely challenging. With this difficulty in mind, this section of our chapter is organized around three emerging goals of our work: (a) establishing democratic structures, (b) promoting the voices in a given school community, and (c) providing ways to work through conflict. Finally, we explore several issues in light of our work as external educational change

agents committed to improving the education within a democratic ethos.

Establishing Democratic Structures

At the heart of school-based reform is the disruption of conventional ways that power is distributed within a given building. In most of the schools in which we have worked, official power flowed from the principal down to teachers and staff, and then to students and their parents. However, as in all complex organizations, the flow of power is more multifaceted than the previous statement would imply. One of the common themes that has emerged during our introductory interviews with teachers is the fact that all of these schools, to some degree, were "loosely coupled systems" (Weick, 1988). Either by direct opposition with the assistance of their unions or through indirect noncompliance, subordinates in these schools often found ways to ignore or alter many superordinate directives. However, without exception, the vast majority of faculty in these schools initially expressed deep feelings of powerlessness. Several faculty expressed sentiments similar to those Beverly, a fourth-grade teacher with 19 years of experience, shared during an introductory interview: "I'll believe it [the faculty having an authentic role in reforming her school] when I see it. This school can't change. A year from now you [Harmony Education Center] will be a distant memory."

Given this situation, we have found it necessary to set up a structure to maximize participation in all aspects of the reform project. Ironically, our power to establish this structure was given to us initially for being the project facilitators. The governance restructuring that took place in Elletstown Elementary School was similar to what occurred in each of the schools where we have worked.

Once the introductory interviews were completed and the findings reported to the faculty, the building administrators (e.g., principal, assistant principal, Title I Coordinator), teachers, parents, and support staff formed a leadership team (LT). We suggested the following criteria to the principal for selecting teachers: (1) willingness to work, (2) grade-level representation, and (3) diverse representation regarding: race, gender, age, and seniority in the building/profession.

At the first LT meeting, we explained that the team's primary responsibility was to encourage, articulate, communicate, and coordinate the ideas of the school community, and we then asked if anyone else should be included. A few suggestions were made, and the principal agreed to ask these individuals to join. At our first meeting with the entire faculty, the LT was introduced, and we asked each teacher to internally identify at least one individual on the LT whom they trusted to represent their interests. If a given faculty member did not feel represented, he or she was invited to join the LT or recommend someone else who would have his or her trust. One teacher accepted our invitation.

(Summary of fieldnotes)

The question of who participates in making school reform decisions, however, cannot be fully satisfied through representative governance. As many educational change agents have noted (e.g., Anderson, 1998; Barth, 1990; Fullan, 1993; Glickman, 1993; Sarason, 1990), unless the faculty are directly involved in making the reforms for their school, the likelihood of noncompliance and/or sabotage is greatly increased. In addition, given the complexity of school-based reform, ideas from the entire school community are essential. Therefore, in addition to the LT, study groups (SGs) similar to those at Westview Elementary (described in the passage that follows) were created in each school where we have worked.

Today's LT agenda was to identify topics [based on a collective analysis of the introductory interviews and several structured dialogues with the school community] to be studied in preparation for writing the

school's vision and reform plan. After a lengthy conversation, the LT generated three SGs: (1) Curriculum, Instruction, and Assessment, (2) Student/Parent Empowerment, and (3) School Climate. Members of the LT then selected which SG they wanted to join, making sure at least two members of the LT were on each SG for the purpose of coordinating ideas and minimizing duplication of work.

At the next faculty meeting, each individual joined one of the SGs. The LT explained that the SGs would generate proposals rather than establish regulations to be imposed on their colleagues. The SGs' primary purpose was to study (e.g., read and discuss relevant literature, make site visits to Harmony and other schools, arrange for discussions with individuals who have special knowledge of their topic). Once their inquiry was completed, each SG would generate one or two goals and several specific strategies for each goal to be included in the school's reform plan. The LT ended by asking the SGs to increase their membership with people (e.g., parents, community volunteers, students, support staff) who might be interested in the topic.

(Summary of fieldnotes)

Through the establishment of these SGs, each member of the school community had the opportunity to directly influence the type of school they wanted to see emerge from this project.

Although creating a democratic structure to enhance the potential participation of all members of the school community in reforming the education and culture of their building was essential, it was not viewed as the ultimate goal. Significant reform was best manifested in schools that, along with the above structure or one similar to it, established ways of making decisions through which members of the community not only were physically present but also felt as if their ideas were heard and valued. As a result, we built on the previously described structure and established a ritual of decision making in these schools that maximized the voices within the school community.

Expanding Voices

Being represented or even physically present at meetings does not automatically translate into an experience of being heard. Faculty meetings have a long history of inattention by those present. In addition, individuals rarely speak their minds in these meetings. If they disagree with what is being said, the usual reaction is to remain quiet and either become apathetic and resentful, or ridicule the idea with one's colleagues once the meeting is adjourned. In a follow-up interview, one fourth-grade teacher told us:

> The thing that has changed the most is that we really talk to each other now. Before, when we had meetings nobody listened. If something was said you didn't like, you kept quiet and put it down afterwards to your friends.

We heard similar comments from faculty in each of the schools at the end of their planning year. To contest this culture of silence, it was necessary to engage in several strategies.

Perhaps the most important response to this culture of silence was to ensure that everyone had an opportunity to speak and be heard. To meet this challenge, we encouraged schools to give those individuals who were directly affected by a particular decision an unmediated voice in making that decision. To facilitate this goal, we encouraged school communities to make decisions by consensus, defined in ways similar to what we did at Yellowspring Elementary.

> Before a decision becomes policy, a call for consensus will be made. You can consent to a decision if you can say "yes" to the following questions: (1) I can "live" with the decision, that is, the implementation of this recommendation does not make working in this school impossible for me; (2) I will enthusiastically support those colleagues who want to act on this recommendation, even if I am not excited about it myself; (3) I will do *nothing* to subvert this decision once it has been agreed on. Before calling for consensus, we will ask for questions, comments, or concerns. This call provides one last opportunity to voice your opinions.
>
> If subsequently you have misgivings about a decision, you can always bring it up in future meetings. In fact, all decisions will be regularly reviewed, so there will always be opportunities to raise concerns. Before a recommendation that impacts everyone can become school policy it must obtain consensus from the appropriate SG, then it goes to the LT, and if the LT reaches consensus, it finally goes to the whole faculty. If the LT cannot reach consensus, then the recommendation goes back to the SG with suggested alterations from the LT. This continues until both groups reach consensus.
>
> [At this point someone asked why not just vote and let the majority rule.] From our experience, the problem with voting is that someone always ends up losing, and potentially this feeling of loss can too easily lead to subversion of the decision through noncompliance or worse.
>
> (Summary of fieldnotes)

As a school community became familiar with consensus decision making, it learned to treat disagreements and problems as concerns to work through, rather than dividing lines around which cliques fight.

> The purpose of today's retreat is to review and approve all of the proposed goals and strategies that have emerged from the SGs and the LT. The final approval of the reform plan went smoothly with one exception. One goal was to engage students in more intellectually challenging activities, and the proposed strategy was to teach at least one lesson each day that calls on students to use their powers of observation, speculation, analysis, synthesis, and/or imagination. At this point, the three first-grade teachers did not consent to the proposal. When asked why, they pointed out their responsibilities to "teach the basics," which left no time to teach these types of lessons, and they said young children could not easily engage in these types of intellectual activities.
>
> Several teachers questioned these assertions. One teacher stated, "We're not

talking about a complete revamping of your curriculum. Certainly, you could find time to do a science experiment, something as simple as having students observe what happens to an ice cube when placed on a plate in the room. The kids could keep notes of what happens, speculate on why it happens, and discuss their speculations, couldn't they?"

After several exchanges, the first-grade teachers were still not convinced. As a result, the plan was altered to excuse the first-grade teachers from agreeing to participate in this particular strategy. After the plan was changed, consensus was reached.

(Summary of fieldnotes)

Making decisions by consensus minimized the likelihood of teachers' noncompliance to or subversion of agreed-on actions. Commitments made under this process generally seemed to be taken seriously by each school community. Most important, consensus decision making avoided the feelings of exclusion and of being silenced that occur to those who are on the losing side of a given vote. Once a school began making decisions by consensus, it often provided skeptical faculty with new hope, as described in this excerpt from an informal conversation with a teacher.

I think the turning point came with the resolution of the paper crisis. [He is asked to explain.] After about a month of school, the principal unilaterally told us we could no longer take any paper from the storage room. Some teachers, she claimed, had used too much causing this "crisis." Several teachers were so upset that they wanted to file a grievance against her. It seemed as if the principal was hoarding paper and only giving it to those teachers she felt were "worthy."

At Carol's [Carol is a member of the Harmony Center team] request, the teachers held off on filing the grievance and turned the matter over to the LT. The LT team created a committee composed of teachers who were perceived as the principal's "friends and foes" to study the problem and recommend a solution to the LT, with the stipulation that any solution had to be reached by consensus.

About a month later, the LT met with this committee to discuss its recommendations and, after several minor modifications, reached consensus on this proposal. The following week, the full faculty met to discuss the recommendations, and they, too, reached consensus. I've been working at this school for 15 years, and this was the first time we ever collectively made a decision about anything. When I first heard about this [school reform], I was doubtful, but maybe something good will come of it after all.

It usually takes time to teach a school community how to operate by consensus; however, as one teacher stated in a follow-up interview, "Making decisions this way makes working here much better. This is the first job I've had where I felt that what I say really counts."

In addition to making decisions by consensus, we have discovered that the individual voices of a school community need to be actively sought out. Overtly seeking ideas from individuals is rarely done in schools or discussed in reform literature. Faculty with whom we have worked are unaccustomed to seeking out the ideas of their colleagues or having requests made for their input into discussions. In virtually every school, we have incorporated this type of activity into our work. Our efforts to elicit ideas have taken place in several different contexts.

First, our introductory interviews provide an opportunity for each school community member to articulate his or her ideas and concerns. These half-hour interviews establish a precedent for school community members to "speak their minds." In reporting the findings from these interviews, we read numerous quotes. (Each interviewee is told that his or her comments will remain anonymous but not confidential.) As a result, faculty, often for the very first time in their careers, actually hear their voices and the voices of their colleagues. In a follow-up interview, a third-grade teacher said: "The first thing that impressed me [about the school's reform project] was hearing everyone's comments when Carol reported the results of the interviews. Just hearing what people *really* thought about the school, the kids, and what we are doing here got to me." Emphasizing the right to be heard is central to our work.

Ms. Randolf, a black third-grade teacher, was speaking. After a couple of minutes, we noticed that a small group of white teachers were whispering, rather than listening. After she finished talking, Daniel [a member of the Harmony team] said, "Something that just happened reminded me of a conference session I attended on African American issues in education. I was the only white person, and before the session started, someone asked if I should stay. This person explained that often when whites and blacks are in a discussion, whites tend to dominate the conversation. When blacks do speak, their comments are ignored, and if a white person later makes the same point, people then respond. I was allowed to stay, but was reminded that this particular session was to give blacks an opportunity to speak. I told you this story because I noticed that a group of teachers weren't paying attention to Ms. Randolf while she was speaking, and it reminded me of that session. One of the things we need to work on is creating an atmosphere in which everyone's voice is heard."

After the meeting was over, Daniel spoke to the white teachers who had been whispering and asked them if they were offended by what he had said. Ms. Arnold replied, "God, no. As a special education teacher, I often feel the regular ed teachers don't pay attention when I speak. It [listening to each other] is something we really do need to establish as a norm."

(Summary of fieldnotes)

A second context occurred in meetings. Specifically, we often asked individuals who were silent for their comments, and when concerns came to our attention, we encouraged their public disclosure.

The Parent Coordinator (PC) asked us to help her with a parent who was convinced that her child's teacher was racist. She accused the teacher of denigrating him and other black children in the class. The teacher was white, and the only children who received her verbal belittlement were black. When the parent confronted the teacher she denied the accusation. The parent felt as if the teacher was completely unresponsive to her concerns. The PC was not sure how to proceed.

We suggested she invite the parent to speak with (and perhaps even join) the Parent Involvement Study Group [of which the PC was a member]. We suggested that at this time, not to single the teacher out, but to work with the SG and to develop some goals that would help minimize the likelihood that teachers would continue to respond to parents in this fashion and to plan some strategies to explore the dynamics of racial differences between teachers, students, and parents.

We also suggested that she begin to keep records of parents' concerns regarding the way this teacher interacts with her black students, in case a direct confrontation would be necessary at a later date. We also suggested that she try to establish a working relationship with this teacher to develop trust as the basis for giving her more direct feedback about this or other situations that might emerge in the future.

(Summary of fieldnotes)

In most public schools, when individuals become aware of situations that need alteration, they often do not have a structure through which their voice can be heard. After many years of working in these types of schools, people forget that they even have a voice.

A final context for seeking out voices occurred during brief and unplanned moments. Whenever possible, we consciously reached out to those community members who rarely spoke. During breaks or after a given meeting, we asked individuals who had been silent for feedback regarding what had been said by various colleagues. If the feedback seemed significant, we encouraged them to articulate their ideas at the next opportunity. In those cases in which people had reason to remain silent, we offered to share their ideas anonymously. In addition, we visited each classroom and established student leadership teams (SLTs) as a way to facilitate children's voices in reforming their schools.[7] Helping people "find their voice" is central to our work. If and when we notice members of a given school community seeking out each other's ideas, we know that this school is well on its way to establishing a foundation for substantive reform discourse.

Confronting Conflict

Our final goal toward establishing a school culture in which substantive educational reform can be fostered is to make it possible for a given community to work through its differences in public and in ways that minimize the potential for subsequent feelings of marginalization and the sabotage that often accompanies conflicts. One of the central problems facing many of the schools where we worked was the existence of building antagonisms. For example, in one school, the faculty was divided between the upstairs (Grades 4–6) and the downstairs (Grades K–3). Here's how a third-grade teacher described the situation during a follow-up interview.

> Before we began working on this [reform project], the upstairs and downstairs [teachers] wouldn't speak to each other. The upstairs thought the downstairs did nothing but play games with the kids, and so they weren't prepared for the upper grades. The downstairs thought the upstairs were too lazy to individualize their instruction to meet the needs of the kids. There was a lot of tension.

In another school, the tension existed between the African American and Hispanic teachers. The former were upset at the district's extra funding for bilingual education programs, which they saw as benefiting the Latino children at the expense of African American children in their school. Racial strains between black and white faculty and parents were also present in many of these schools. In several buildings, there was hostility between the administrators (and their supporters) and a particular group of teachers. To overcome these antagonisms, it was necessary to initiate several conversations.

The first conversation typically focused on the moral purposes of school reform. One question we asked during our initial interviews was: "In what ways does your school help prepare students to live in a democratic society?" In several early discussions, we asked faculty to consider ways in which school reform might help their students break the cycle of poverty in their community. However, most of our references to the moral purpose of school reform focused on the lives of the students in their building. Early in and throughout our relationship, we encouraged faculty to put the existential quality of their students' lives in school at the center of our work. We have often suggested that although the faculty cannot do much, if anything, about the quality of their students' lives on the street or in their homes, they do have an opportunity to create a culture in the school that is safe for everyone's bodies and feelings and honor, for example, by nurturing the students' intellectual, communicative, kinesthetic, and artistic talents. Fortunately, this call to significantly improve the existential lives of their students in school seems to have resonated with all but the most cynical individuals. Most important, this moral appeal provided a strong rationale for working through conflicts in mutually respectful ways. In all the years of our work, only one school has failed to respond positively to our request to put aside acrimony for the sake of the students. As illustrated below, the power of this moral rationale for reform work should not be underestimated.

> Baker Elementary has been plagued by bitter disputes along racial, gender, and hierarchical lines for several years, and we

were asked to work with this school by the superintendent to avoid firing the principal and the subsequent public controversy. The principal has had many conflicts with teachers who see him as dictatorial, disrespectful, and vindictive. The principal and the few teachers who support him view the teachers' concerns as an indication of racism because his most vocal critics are white and the principal is black.

Due to this animosity, we asked members of the school community (during our initial interviews) if these conflicts had any impact on their students. Over and over again, the faculty said no. When we read numerous statements to the contrary from interviews we had with their students, the room went silent. Over and over we read statements that indicated not only the students' awareness of the faculty's conflicts but also their anguish regarding these conflicts. Many teachers were shocked and surprised by the students' insights into how these conflicts hurt the school's reputation and their collective identity. Perhaps for the first time, the faculty realized the importance of working through their disagreements.

(Summary of fieldnotes)

Contextualizing reform work in terms of students' existential experiences has been propitious in addressing the ways in which these schools have traditionally resolved or failed to resolve conflicts.

A long-standing problem emerged in our meeting today. Like many schools, teachers were assigned to monitor the halls prior to the start of the day. However, several teachers complained, "They [the students] get all juiced up and come to class ready to rock and roll, instead of ready to work." In response, one of the teachers who had this responsibility said that she has tried to keep the students from acting out, but that there are too many of them. It was noted that this situation has been a problem for several years. No one wanted to be the hall monitor.

At this point, we asked what would be the best way to begin the school day *for the students*. One teacher shared her vision of children being welcomed into the school and into each classroom. Several said it should be a time for relaxed conversations and activities. After several more minutes of conversation, a proposal emerged that received consensus: Instead of having a floor monitor, all teachers would stand outside their doors 15 minutes prior to the beginning of school and personally welcome each child into their rooms. At the same time, the principal and other staff members would wander the halls welcoming students to school. In this way, each child would receive some personal attention as he or she entered the classroom.

(Summary of fieldnotes)

Once teachers internalized this rationale (putting students' quality of life first), they seemed to be able to move beyond their acrimonious histories.

Additional conversations focused on the nature and dynamics of conflict in the reform process. As several school reformers mentioned at the beginning of this chapter noted, we suggested that faculty reconceptualize and embrace conflict as a natural and positive aspect of people working together for common purposes (i.e., the thoughtful education of children). Unfortunately, the lack or avoidance of conflict was often viewed as a desirable goal. However, without conflict, there can rarely be growth. As we shared with the faculty at Baker Elementary School, "People of goodwill have legitimate differences, and differences always hold the potential for conflict. If we are afraid of conflict, we will not be able to honestly explore or do what we need to do" (summary of fieldnotes). At the same time, it has been important to stress that the resolution of disagreements should not mean a victory by some faculty at the expense of others.

We also initiated conversations on rituals of personal interaction among the faculty. In nearly every school in which we have worked, these interactions were often counterproductive.

Due to the antagonisms among the faculty, it was necessary to discuss what we called "standards of interaction." That is, we initiated a discussion about how colleagues should communicate. Out of this discussion, the faculty reached consensus to: (1) never talk negatively about a colleague "behind his/her back," (2) focus on the issue rather than the individual who expresses a contrary point of view, (3) instead of finding blame, focus on what needs to be done to correct or improve the situation, (4) avoid expressing hearsay information as if it came from direct experience, (5) speak only for oneself (e.g., avoid saying, "Several of us think . . ."), (6) listen carefully and understand what someone has said or done before responding or reacting, and (7) give "gentle reminders" to individuals who forget to follow these standards of interaction.[8]

(Summary of fieldnotes)

In an action closely related to our conversations about these standards of interaction, we found it useful in many schools to initiate discussions around giving and receiving feedback. These conversations often began with exploring with faculty times when they received or gave inappropriate feedback (e.g., receiving "put-downs," irrelevant information, embarrassing feedback in public). From deconstructing these autobiographies, we generated insights into what the faculty wanted to avoid. Next, these discussions usually focused on constructing a list of "feedback norms" similar to the ones at Columbus Elementary School.

After a long discussion that began with sharing "feedback nightmares," followed by an analysis of these stories, the faculty reached consensus on the following feedback norms: (1) before giving negative feedback, be sure to identify something positive about a colleague's work, (2) give negative feedback in private, (3) whenever something worthwhile is noticed, be sure to tell the individual, (4) ask for permission before giving negative feedback, and (5) if inappropriate feedback is given, "gently" remind the individual of the previously agreed-upon feedback norms.

(Summary of fieldnotes)

We have found that accepting and learning how to address conflict in ways that promote rather than tear apart a school's sense of community was a crucial aspect of these reform efforts.

A final conversation related to conflict involves issues of jurisdiction. At the core of our efforts to create a more democratic culture within these schools, we have encouraged them to carefully consider the principle of making certain that those who are most affected by a given decision have a direct voice in making that decision. This has led to conversations about who has the power to make what types of decisions. For example, decisions that directly affect only a given classroom should ideally be made by the teacher and his or her students. A decision that impacts only the lower grades should be made by those teachers (and if appropriate their students) who teach Grades 1 to 3. At the same time, there are often decisions that may not directly impact one's colleagues but nevertheless do have some effect on them. For example, the lower elementary teachers could make a decision that might have some impact on the teachers (and students) in higher grades or the school administrators. In these situations, it has been necessary to discuss the importance of notifying these secondary stakeholders so they have an opportunity to discuss any concerns they might have about a particular decision. In a few schools, we have helped sort out this question of jurisdiction by identifying potential "spheres of influence" in their school, along with the primary and secondary stakeholders associated with each of these "spheres," in ways similar to Table 13.1, which was the outcome of discussions at Jason Elementary School.

To summarize, our efforts to create a democratic culture for the purpose of substantively reforming the education of children in these schools focused primarily on three goals. As leaders of these projects, we redistributed power within a given school by establishing

Table 13.1   Spheres of Influence

Spheres of Influence	Primary Stakeholders	Secondary Stakeholders	Realm of Decisions (Examples)
Classroom	Teachers	Students, parents, program director, other teachers, principal	Curriculum, instruction, student learning, assessment, classroom rules, atmosphere, and layout
Elementary program	Program director, teachers, counselor, aides	Principal, parents, students	Coordinated projects and rituals, safety rules, graduation criteria, new faculty hiring
Secondary program	Program director, teachers, counselors	Principal, parents, students	Same as above
Academic departments	Department chair, faculty	Principal, program director, students	Same as above
Faculty assembly	Five elected teachers/staff, principal, assistant principal, program directors	Faculty, staff, students, parents	Campus-wide policies (e.g., discretionary funds, grievance procedures, hiring criteria)
Central administration	Principal, assistant principal, program directors	Central administration, faculty	Building and grounds policies; administrative paperwork; new faculty hiring; communication with central office, board of education, and state department of education; community relations

several democratic structures for making policy (e.g., creation of LTs and SGs), devised rituals for helping all school community members find their voices and hence experience a sense of efficacy (e.g., consensus decision making, seeking out those who are silent), and fostered communication patterns to help community members work through conflicts. We now turn our attention to struggles we continue to confront.

STRUGGLES AND DILEMMAS

Space does not allow for a full discussion of the numerous struggles we have faced in our efforts to alter the culture of the schools where we worked. However, we have found three aspects of this work to be particularly challenging and thus worth supplemental attention.

Victimization

Many educators view people who live in poverty as victims who are battered by their socioeconomic circumstances. As several scholars (Anyon, 1997; Pakalov, 1993; Payne, 1995; Shannon, 1998) have illustrated, these children are routinely victimized in school. However, children are not the only victims in these schools. Perhaps more disturbing has been the expressions of victimization that emerged from school faculty. For example, Anyon (1997) notes that faculty often feel battered by poor administrative support, lack of sufficient funding, overcrowding, poor physical facilities, lack of parental involvement, students who are not well prepared and often alienated, the public's perception that they are inadequate, and staff development that promises relief but rarely remains involved long enough to even know—let alone seriously address—their problems. As one veteran teacher stated in a follow-up interview:

> Before Dr. Orlando [the superintendent], Ms. Black [the principal], and you guys came, this school was a mess. No one cared. I mean it, no one—not the principal, not the central administrators, not the parents, not the kids, not the Department of Education, no one. A lot of teachers would say, "If they don't care, why should I." For years, this school was a pit. If you had a problem, there was no one to help. If you tried to do something worthwhile, everyone else would look at you like you were nuts. "What's the point?" they'd say. No one gave a damn, so why should you work your butt off for nothing?

Although there are many obvious reasons why faculty in high-poverty schools are overwhelmed by external constraints and thus can be viewed as victims of their circumstances, we have found it necessary to challenge the perception of these limitations as excuses for complacency.

As the quote above suggests, the most devastating ramification of victimization is the sense of powerlessness that comes with it. Being a victim drastically undermines a faculty's sense of efficacy. As long as teachers view themselves as victims, as impotent people working against overwhelming forces, real school reform will remain an illusion. As a result, one of our most important struggles has been to help faculty alter this corrosive self-perception. Although we often agree with their assessment of the difficulties of their occupation, we have found it necessary to challenge their sense of powerlessness. Here's what one Title I Coordinator told us during a follow-up interview:

> I'd say the most important event came during the first year. Several teachers started to blame Daniel [a member of the Harmony team] for the tensions in the building that had been brought out into the open. Some suggested that what we were doing was a waste of time and that the only person benefiting was Daniel. I can't remember exactly what he said but it was something like, "Listen, you can blame me if you want, or the parents, central administrators, or kids. You can't change the type of children who come to this school, you can't change their parents, you can't change their neighborhoods, you can't change their histories, but you ask me to leave. It's up to you. Only *you* can improve what really happens inside this school for the 6 hours children are here each day. Think about what you want to do, and let me know if you still want to work with me when I return next week." He wasn't defensive or angry when he said that, and it really got us thinking. It was at that moment when we, or at least the majority of us, realized that if we weren't going to make this school better, no one was.

In addition to directly challenging their sense of victimization, we typically initiated conversations that explored their power, conversations similar to the following one at Union Elementary School.

> The discussion with the faculty addressed spheres of power or what some scholars call "locus of control." We asked them to identify those types of decisions that they had control over, those they had influence over, and those they had, from their perspective, no influence over. At first, they felt they had no control over anything, but with a little prodding everyone realized that, at the least, they make decisions over much of what happens in their own classrooms especially concerning how they respond to students' ideas, attitudes, and behavior.
>
> We did not contradict their perceptions of powerlessness, but rather asked them to focus the work of their three SGs (e.g., School Climate/Culture, Curriculum/Instruction, and Community/Parent Involvement) on two types of decisions. Namely, those realms of decisions that they clearly have control over and those they can reasonably expect to have some influence over. By focusing on what they had control over and what they might reasonably be able to influence, rather than what they couldn't do, their perception of their own power

gradually increased throughout the year. Now there are very few issues they see outside of their sphere of influence.

For example, in an effort to spend more time working together, they wrote a memo to the central administration asking if they could leave the districtwide workshop at noon on Martin Luther King's holiday to work together on their reform plan. What we found most impressive was their response to the administration's denial. Instead of blaming and complaining about being thwarted and thus victimized again, they merely turned their attention to finding another afternoon to meet.

(Summary of fieldnotes)

Slowly, over time, many faculties began to question limitations placed on them by external agencies.

The faculty at Highland Elementary School decided to eliminate, for the most part, phonics-centered language arts and traditional memory/recall-based science and social studies lessons. In its place, they had developed: (1) a process-based writing program that emphasizes fluency of expression and teaches mechanics as a process of copy editing, (2) integrated thematic units of study based on the natural and social sciences, and (3) a literature-based reading program. However, several faculty expressed serious concerns about the school's scores on the state's competency test.

An animated discussion ensued around this issue. Some teachers felt the proposed changes might be too drastic and if the students didn't perform well on the test, the school standing would be in jeopardy. Others thought it was worth the risk, given their previous discussions. Someone suggested we meet with the Department of Education's testing office to see what they thought before moving ahead.

A meeting was set up, and to our surprise, the representatives enthusiastically supported this school's plan. One stated, "Our studies have indicated that children in literature-rich classrooms where lots of writing occurs do best on our test. Spelling, for example, is not really a spelling test. It's a word recognition test. Children who read

and write a lot do better on this test than those who merely memorize spelling words. Kids who are asked to make what they read meaningful score much better on the comprehension test than those who have been taught to identify the 'main idea or character' of a paragraph or story."

(Summary of fieldnotes)

Ultimately, faculty are encouraged and supported to develop a sense of existential freedom as discussed in Sartre's (1956) *Being and Nothingness*. Although they are "born" into a world not of their own making and thus are not free to do whatever they want, they are free to determine *their experience* of this world. As teachers working in high-poverty schools, they face many substantive constraints. They can view impediments as absolute limits to complain about, as excuses for not being more proactive, as examples of why nothing ever changes, as reasons for their cynicism, or as challenges toward which they can apply their creativity, moral courage, and determination. Although we encouraged faculty to adopt the latter of these dispositions, this type of change could not be simply mandated. It took significant time and only really began to change once a given faculty honestly *experienced* the expansion of their "realms of influence." In schools that have gone through this transformation, we have noted that faculty take greater responsibility for the way in which they live their occupational lives.

Since this was the first LT meeting of the year (third year of our partnership), we asked each member to share his or her reflections from the summer break.

One teacher said something especially noteworthy. "I went to a workshop on thematic curriculum, and after the overview of the process, we were put into groups to work on the development of a thematic unit. Our group spent the first 15 minutes complaining about how the speaker's ideas wouldn't work in their school because of whatever. Finally, I told them to stop complaining and just start working. All that bellyaching really brought me back to our first year, and all the excuses we used to make why we couldn't do this or that."

Another teacher then stated, "The same thing happened to me. I went to a workshop on discipline. We also broke up into groups, and my group started off just complaining how this wouldn't work and that wouldn't work, and I was the one who finally stopped them. I said, 'Let's get on with it.' All that wasted energy."

(Summary of fieldnotes)

Assuming this existential responsibility helped faculty avoid getting distracted by the countless ordeals they faced as teachers in urban settings. Most important, developing this existential responsibility often provided faculty with more power than they previously thought possible. It seemed that teachers first had to experience having significant influence over their own occupational lives before they were able to help their students and families break the oppressive cycle of intergenerational poverty. Without these experiences, it was very difficult for teachers to design a learning community that could in turn prepare young people to meaningfully influence the circumstances of their own lives. Although we are gratified by the many teachers who have altered the way in which they come to view their occupational position, addressing the issue of victimization remains a major struggle in our work.

Leadership

As previously mentioned, we initially assumed the primary role of leadership for the purposes of facilitating these school-based reform projects. Given this position, we have been confronted with two concerns related to leadership in these schools.

As previously noted, the creation of LTs and SGs results in a redistribution of power, and we found it necessary to address the ramifications of this reallocation when it was noticed by building administrators. Although

several of the principals appreciated the broadening distribution of power within their buildings, many others had difficulty adjusting to their new status.

The principal shared that he was confused and somewhat "lost." He didn't know if he was really needed anymore, now that the LT had taken over so much of the running of the school. In response, we first reviewed why he felt this way. It was true that many of his former responsibilities were now shared among his faculty, but that might not be the real cause of his "extra time." We reminded him that most of his time prior to these reforms was spent in "crisis management," which now needed little of his attention. We recalled the special role he plays on the LT for initiating and supporting the reform efforts. Although our comments of support seemed to ease his concerns, we realized that we haven't given enough thought to helping building administrators make this transition. We agreed to continue our discussion during our next visit.

(Summary of fieldnotes)

As our previous discussion of Jane, the principal of Bradley Elementary School (see p. 307) illustrates, some principals came to view our participation as infringing on their domain.

In any case, asking principals to adjust their leadership role is difficult, and this was especially true because of past animosities that existed in many of these buildings. For example, in one school (in a correctional facility), we were asked to leave specifically due to our efforts at redistributing power among the faculty.

The principal told us he did not like the way "things" were going, and our services were terminated. We are not surprised by his decision. The hierarchy of this school is deeply entrenched and long-standing. There is little respect between the faculty and administration. We remembered that during our debriefing meeting with the principal and superintendent following the first meeting with the faculty, the principal said he agreed with everything we said *except* when we told the faculty that they would determine what reforms to make in the school, that no policies would be imposed on them as a result of our work.

We remembered him telling us that the faculty needed to change their values and practices. Our response was to point out that while the teachers needed to change, this would not occur through imposition from superordinates, but only through meaningful discourse. Nevertheless, from the beginning, the principal was uncomfortable with the power being distributed to the faculty.

(Summary of fieldnotes)

In the years we have been involved in these projects, this was the only time we were asked to terminate our participation prior to the end of the planning year. Nevertheless, as external change agents, we have not devoted enough attention to the ramifications of this work for building administrators. As Talbot and Crow (1998) pointed out, the transition from a conventional to a democratic principal can be rough on one's occupational perception, and clearly, more can be done to make this conversion smoother.

The second leadership issue needing more attention in our work concerns the problem of transference of leadership from ourselves to the school community. Although we assume the authority necessary to initiate and maintain these projects, one of our struggles is to eventually withdraw, leaving behind a culture that can sustain ongoing, substantive reform discourses. Thus, transferring the leadership required to make reform discourse an integral facet of occupational life in these schools is perhaps one of the most important and difficult aspects of our work. If we could not facilitate this relocation of leadership in a given school, then our ultimate goal went unfulfilled.

In those schools that had dynamic, thoughtful, and communicative principals, this transfer of power was relatively smooth and easy. However, although most principals in these schools were adequate managerial leaders, they often did not have the talents necessary for transformative leadership. In addition, many principals were highly mobile, never staying in one building for more than a few years. As a result, it has been reassuring to note that most of these schools maintained their LT and transformed their SGs into standing committees for the purpose of school governance beyond the initial planning year. In these schools, many issues were brought to the LT instead of just the building administrators. The work of Norris Elementary School's LT was similar to other schools that permanently modified their governance structure.

The next agenda item was a proposal to stop the practice of selling candy to children. The LT reviewed several concerns such as: physical and dental health of the children, the negative effect (hyperactivity) that sugar has on several of the children, and the ethical dilemma of making it easy for children who do not have much money to spend it on candy.

At this point, a representative from the kitchen staff raised a financial concern. She noted that selling candy has been a practice for many years at the school and has become an important supplement to the low wages of the women who work in the kitchen. After a lengthy discussion, the LT agreed to support a proposal to allow candy to be sold only to those students who have parental permission, to limit the amount of candy each child can buy, and to revisit the issue in 2 months to assess the impact of their action.

(Summary of fieldnotes)

The previously discussed democratic structures and rituals were particularly valuable in those schools in which the principal left the building prior to the completion of the reform project.

At the LT meeting today, we noticed that once again, Ms. White, the new principal, was not present. However, we were impressed that 2 months into their second year of the project, this LT and thus the school were operating effectively. We left the meeting and found Ms. White in her office.

In our conversation, she shared her feelings of "not being needed" and "out of the loop." She wondered if this school really needed a principal and thought her presence might be resented. We encouraged her to get involved in spite of these feelings and told her we would help her move into the flow of events. We emphasized the crucial role the principal plays in times of substantive change. After discussing her situation, she agreed to become more involved.

We then went back into the LT meeting and discussed ways to bring the principal into the process. Several teachers empathized with Ms. White, and others apologized if their actions implied that she wasn't needed. The meeting ended with two members of the LT agreeing to "bring her up to speed."

(Summary of fieldnotes)

Ideally, this leadership structure served as a foundation on which schools could continue their reform work.

At today's meeting, the Curriculum Committee discussed the progress of the school's goal to use more inquiry-based pedagogy. Specifically, we discussed their stated strategy to develop a science curriculum that would include at least one "hands on" experiment each week. After a few minutes of discussion, it was clear that little had been accomplished. Only a few teachers had by this time (end of October) implemented this strategy.

After several people speculated on the causes for this failure (e.g., no time, concern over the state's standardized test, lack of science knowledge, fear of failure), the committee members decided to identify and interview the teachers who were implementing this goal to find out what they are doing. The Committee then decided to publicize this information so that others will have some ideas of how to start. Finally, it was decided that the primary agenda item for the next meeting would be to review the results from their interviews. In the meantime, a few members volunteered to explore staff

development resources to help the faculty meet this goal.

(Summary of fieldnotes)

Establishing democratic structures made the transference of power possible, but it could not, by itself, promote the ongoing reflection and action we hoped would emerge from our work. It was also necessary to locate those individuals in each school who would assume responsibility for continuing reform discourses.

Fortunately, once LTs and SGs were firmly established beyond the initial planning year, this structure allowed for individuals who had leadership talents to manifest them, regardless of their official position in these schools. As Quantz and his colleagues (1991) have stated,

Transformative leadership theory, however, must argue that leaders can and should be located at all levels of an organization, for transformative leadership achieves its power and authority not through domination but through democracy and emancipation. And democracy requires individuals at all levels to assume responsibility for constructing a democratic community. Leadership theory must back away from the assumption that the administrators are the only leaders in the school and must focus on how leadership is to be fostered at all levels of a school. (p. 104)

Although we provided leadership during the planning year, as the work continues, we took note of those teachers, parents, support staff, and, of course, building administrators who assumed leadership.

During our debriefing session today, we tried to identify school community leadership potential for the future. In particular, we discussed Ms. Bove, the school counselor, and Ms. Jackson, a fifth-grade teacher, who had the respect of their colleagues, who were honest, who could speak in public forums, and who were committed to the project. We made plans to nurture their leadership potential.

(Summary of fieldnotes)

During our work in these schools, we identified and supported classroom teachers; school counselors, parents, Title I Coordinators, and, in one case, a substitute teacher as "unofficial" school leaders.

To summarize, all too often, reform efforts die once "the leader" leaves the building. As a result, establishing a structure that encourages participation of the entire school community is crucial for any serious effort to promote ongoing school-based reform discourse. However, in our work, these structures were not enough. We also had to consciously identify and support those individuals in a given school who seemed to possess qualities of "transformational leadership," that is, people who had vision, the respect and admiration of their colleagues, a commitment to participatory democracy, talent for facilitating their colleagues' work, and an optimistic work ethic (Quantz et al., 1991; Yukl, 1994). Unfortunately, our effort to locate and support these individuals was only partially successful. It remains an aspect of our work that demands more from us than we give in most instances. It continues to be an area of concern that we, reformers and scholars, need to pay more attention to in the future.

Authenticity

As several scholars (e.g., Anderson & Grinberg, 1998; Barker, 1993; Beare, 1993; Campbell & Southworth, 1990; Chapman & Boyd, 1986; Gitlin & Margonis, 1995; Hargreaves, 1994; Lipman, 1997; Malen, 1994; Smyth, 1993) have noted, discourses located in many school-based reform projects are often inauthentic.

> Shared governance structures may not result in significant participation in decisions but, instead, result in contrived collegiality, reinforced privilege, and even create a tighter iron cage of control for participants. . . . From the grassroots level, teachers in schools are increasingly complaining that

participation is often bogus, takes time from their interactions with students, and intensifies an already heavy workload leading in many cases to teacher burnout. (Anderson, 1998, p. 572)

Anderson (1998) goes on to suggest that, "In many cases, attempts at increased participation are sincere but poorly conceived and implemented or caught up in a larger institutional and societal logic that is antithetical to norms of participation" (p. 586). In response, several scholars have tried to identify what they consider to be the characteristics of authentic collaborative work among school communities.

Hargreaves (1994, pp. 192–193) suggests that bona fide, collaborative cultures are often spontaneous as opposed to administratively regulated, voluntary rather than compulsory, development oriented rather than implementation oriented, pervasive across time and space instead of fixed in time and space, and unpredictable rather than predictable. Anderson (1998, pp. 586–595) identifies democracy and equity, broad inclusiveness of school community members, few restrictions on what topics are open for school-based decision making, open communication without regard to position within the school, and contested relationships with external powers as elements in genuine participatory, school-based reform.

We agree with the sentiments expressed by these scholars. Without authenticity, school-based reforms are a sham and thus not worthy of our time and energy, or the time and energy of the school communities in which we work. Perhaps the most important goal of our work is to provide a context in which the school community can authentically discuss the education of their children. Although discussion of authenticity has been instructive and comprehensive, we have, in light of our work, a few additional comments to make regarding this extremely important aspect of school-based reform.

Given these previously mentioned characteristics, our work in these schools seemed to be both authentic and inauthentic depending on the individuals involved, the topics and perceived progress of our discourses, and the timing of these discourses. For example, several of these reform projects were initiated by the district administration. At times, these projects were started against the expressed wishes of the school's faculty. As a result, our work in these locations clearly began as inauthentic projects. One might conclude that anything we might have done, therefore, was inappropriate, especially given our commitment to the previously discussed democratic principles. However, we have drawn a different conclusion, namely that authenticity has less to do with the manner in which particular projects might get initiated and developed and more to do with being willing to openly address the way in which members of a school community existentially experience the process of reform at any given time.

> Our very first conversation with the faculty focused on their request [which was denied by the district administration] to *not* participate in this school-based reform project. We asked them to share with us why they did not want to participate. Many noted the long history of central administration's desire to "micromanage" what happens in schools. In addition, concerns were raised about the time needed to participate, the potential additional work, the discomfort of working through conflicts, fear of the unknown, and skepticism regarding who would make final decisions.
>
> After each of these concerns was addressed, we challenged the faculty [in a very warm and friendly way] to think of ways in which this work could be meaningful in spite of the administration's "directive" as the primary focus of our next meeting.
>
> (Summary of fieldnotes)

Several schools entered into these reform projects with the expectation that ours would be no different and no more authentic than any other "staff development" program in which they were required to participate. Ironically,

these difficult beginnings did not taint the entire process. To the contrary, these onerous beginnings often created an opportunity to develop authentic trust and communication.

Another aspect of this discourse concerns the implication that if a project is to be authentic, participating individuals must feel free to openly express themselves during discussions. Although this is an extremely worthwhile situation, we have come to believe that authenticity has less to do with verbal expression and more to do with the reasons behind a person's decision to participate in a given interchange.

> Today, we discussed Gloria Ladson-Billings' book, *The Dreamkeepers*. Given that 98% of the students and 50% of the faculty are of African American heritage, we thought this book would engage the faculty. However, this was not the case.
>
> Even before the discussion, Ellen, a black teacher, told us she hated the book. When we asked her why, she said it was filled with nonsense but wouldn't elaborate. During the discussion she seemed not to be listening. The teachers who did speak endorsed Ladson-Billings's central thesis, and when we consciously tried to generate more diverse reactions, we were confronted with silence. Despite numerous efforts to solicit the faculty's reactions, this conversation did not generate a diversity of responses.
>
> Afterward, we asked some teachers why they didn't participate. Most avoided the question, but Julie, a novice African American teacher, said she was inspired but also angered by the book because she saw many examples of teaching in this school that were not "culturally responsive." She didn't speak during the discussion because she didn't want to offend her colleagues by expressing this thought.
>
> (Summary of fieldnotes)

What does this conversation tell us about authenticity? Was Ellen's refusal to speak publicly about her negative reaction to this book inauthentic? If her silence was because she hadn't read the book or was alienated from the project as a whole, then her initial criticism and subsequent silence might be an example of inauthentic involvement. If Ladson-Billings's descriptions of "culturally relevant teaching" were too contrary to the way she taught and thus the subject matter was personally threatening, then her silence might have been an effort to avoid being put on the defensive. In this latter case, our failure, as facilitators of this discussion, to critique rather than merely neutrally present Ladson-Billings's ideas might have contributed to an inauthentic situation for Ellen. On the other hand, it is important to remember that Ellen's level of authenticity is ultimately her own decision. As Sartre (1956, pp. 47–70) notes in his discussion of this issue (which he refers to as "bad-faith"), Ellen might merely have made a decision to "go through the motions" of being a teacher. If so, our facilitation of this discussion would probably have not made a difference to her.

Certainly, some of the teachers in this discussion were not authentic participants. However, to say that Julie was inauthentic would be problematic from our perspective. Perhaps her silence was not a sign of spuriousness but one of self-protection due to her lack of seniority; perhaps it was her inability at that moment to express herself without being angry and thus embarrassed; or perhaps it was because she was sensitive to her colleagues' feelings of defensiveness and recognized that forcing this issue would be counterproductive at this particular time. Regardless of her reasons, her silence did not represent a lack of authenticity or genuine engagement. In this discussion, she was an authentic participant who was engaged in an active—but internal—dialogue. It is important not to equate public verbosity with authenticity. No matter how carefully a school reform project might manifest the previously mentioned characteristics, each individual decides for him- or herself whether or not to participate authentically.

Finally, it is important to note, as Buber (1958) did in *I and Thou*, the role that reciprocity plays in questions of authenticity.

It has been our experience that authenticity attracts itself. People who approach life (in this case, occupational life) in an authentic manner seem to gravitate to others who also are living authentically. As a result, the issue of authenticity, from a change agent's perspective, is largely a matter of self-authenticity. By focusing on being authentic ourselves, rather than playing a particular role of "change agent," we connect with those members of a given school community who are also interested in working authentically to improve the education of their children.

However, what about those individuals who resist authentic engagement in these projects? Do we ignore these individuals, marginalize them, and hope they leave for another school, or pretend that they are participating when they are only "going through the motions"? Clearly, it is useless to try and convince someone to become authentically involved if they do not want to be. As previously mentioned, one of the characteristics of authentic participation is its voluntary quality. However, initially, we required faculty to attend regular school reform meetings that were negotiated as part of their "work day" but made it clear that no one was required to volunteer their time.

Exactly at 4:15, two teachers who had been sitting by the windows got up and walked across the entire library during the middle of a conversation and left the building. Since the meeting was only half over, it was a clear statement of resistance. These teachers had expressed their lack of enthusiasm at the first faculty meeting, in which we determined when and how often the faculty would participate. At that time, we expressed the importance of having everyone at these meetings so that no one felt marginalized by the final decisions. However, the teachers' contract limited meetings to 1 rather than the 2 hours needed. As a result, we agreed that anyone who wanted to leave these meetings could do so, and this bold walk across the library was a clear indication of these teachers' unwillingness to participate in what they saw as "just another program."

(Summary of fieldnotes)

After about 6 weeks, in which we consciously sought their input on a variety of topics, these teachers began to participate authentically in these and SG meetings. Developing honest relationships with individuals who are initially suspicious of any "change efforts" has been one of our most important, creative challenges. As one fifth grade teacher told us in a follow-up interview,

> At first I refused to participate. I made it clear to everyone that I wanted nothing to do with this whole business. In response, they [the rest of the school] allowed me to supervise students in the building [along with community volunteers] while the faculty met [each Wednesday afternoon]. What I really appreciated was the perception that my helping the volunteers was a *real* contribution. No one looked at my withdrawal as a put-down to me or the reform. Eventually, I was drawn into it, mostly because Daniel [a member of the Harmony team] kept at me, and showed me how my involvement was needed.

The importance of generating authenticity through reciprocity is an often overlooked and yet crucial aspect in understanding this phenomenon. Perhaps the most crucial implication is that questions of authenticity need to be openly and honestly addressed whenever the need arises during these projects.

CONCLUSION

Micropolitics of School Reform

This chapter has described the ways in which we, as external change agents, have worked with various educational communities in their effort to transform the culture of their schools and thus improve the education of their students. These efforts have focused on two vitally important aspects concerning the

micropolitics of school reform. First, we have concluded that it is extremely important to assist schools in building greater autonomy. Schools seeking to generate authentic reforms need to learn how to effectively negotiate with various external powers, such as central administrators, unions, government agencies, and external change agents. Second, we have found it vital to focus much of our effort on the internal governance of schools. Establishing democratic rituals and structures, expanding the voices of all school community members, and addressing conflict within a given building have emerged as particularly significant tasks. In addition, we have discussed issues of victimization, leadership, and authenticity with which we continue to struggle. However, a few final issues warrant further discussion.

The first issue concerns the place of pedagogy in these school reform projects. Specifically, some time ago, at a meeting of "educational reformers," our approach to school-based reform was criticized by an individual who questioned our initial emphasis on micropolitics rather than pedagogy. Although discourses about the education of children are central to our work (Goodman, Baron, & Myers, 2001), the criticism is well deserved. Within a few years of working as external change agents, we soon realized that until a school community could work together as genuine colleagues, discussions of pedagogy were of little value. Until a school community is able to make important decisions, pedagogical talk remains just that—talk. Fullan (1993) is correct in his observation that changing the substance of education depends on creating an organizational culture that fosters faculty ownership over and commitment to whatever changes would be made through honest, open, and comprehensive dialogue. As Yankelovich (1999) notes and we have observed, dialogue (rather than debates or disputes) in which people come together as equals, listen with empathy and seek to understand each other, and are willing to examine assumptions and ideas without judging their own or others' self-worth can transform the nature of an occupational situation from one of conflict, mistrust, and isolation to one of community and collaboration. Only after a school community is able to develop such communicative patterns of interaction can pedagogical talk become transformed into actual changes in what children learn, the way in which they learn, and the climate in which they learn. For those reformers who, like us, place critical, liberal, social democracy at the center of children's education (Goodman, 1992), it soon becomes apparent that unless teachers learn to work with each other toward these goals, they will rarely work toward them with the students in their classrooms. Educational leaders involved in school-based reform projects make a mistake if they ignore what on the surface might seem as "procedural" or "decision-making protocols" in favor of delving directly into issues of pedagogy. It is important to remember that school-based reform discourses are significantly different from graduate seminars. Whereas the latter need not strive for consensus or directly result in alterations of specific children's schooling, the former must be focused and lead to definite decisions that the school community supports.

Second, it is important to briefly address the relationship between democracy and values of social justice and equity. Some might well argue that developing more autonomy and democratic structures, rituals, and values in a school does not guarantee the promotion of a more socially just and equitable school or society. Might not a school that gains autonomy and creates a democratic ethos and structure for adults have the option to create an unjust and demeaning educational experience for children and thus perpetuate the inequities currently found in the United States? If the answer to the above question is "yes" (and we believe it is), then what if any responsibility do democratic-minded external change agents have in this situation?

Space does not allow for an adequate discussion; however, a few comments in response to this concern are necessary. Our commitment to democracy is not rooted in idealist essentialism. Rather, it is deeply connected to Dewey's (1920) pragmatism. As Rorty (1989) suggests, the primary value of democracy lies in its ability to resolve conflicts and make decisions in ways that minimize cruelty among those who are members of a given community. It does not guarantee any particular sort of outcome or type of decision. Nevertheless, we have noticed that often the adults in these schools draw meaningful connections to their pedagogy as a result of their participation in these democratic discourses. For example, in each school, teachers have been encouraged, and many have opted, to establish democratic conversations with students (i.e., town meetings) about their classroom experiences on a regular basis. As teachers begin to internalize the standards of interaction or norms for giving feedback in their work with each other, they have indicated to us how these communication patterns have transformed their work with students. Similarly, as issues of racism, patriarchy, poverty, and other forms of marginalization are discussed in SGs and faculty retreats, several teachers have expressed sensitivity to these issues in relation to their students and their families. Democracy provides the potential for reducing cruelty and humiliation within a given school, but it provides no warranties.

As we (Goodman, 1994) have explored elsewhere, our responsibility as external change agents is not to impose decisions on a school but to provide space for open discourse and deliberation. On the other hand, as previously mentioned, we do not mute ourselves, and we assume responsibility for expressing our own ideas and values. However, in the end, it is the school community that must make all final decisions. Although imposing change might alter school or societal structures, it also distorts human intelligence and empathy. As Dewey (1946, p. 139) insightfully noted,

> Doctrines, whether proceeding from Mussolini or Marx, which assume that because certain ends are desirable therefore those ends and nothing else will result from the use of force to attain them is but another example of the limitations put on intelligence by any absolutist theory. In the degree in which mere force is resorted to, actual consequences are themselves so compromised that the ends originally in view have in fact to be worked out afterwards by the method of experimental intelligence.

Dewey goes on to argue that it is only through democratic, inclusive discourses that a given community (e.g., a school or society) can genuinely become more socially just and humane. To critique democracy for failing to rectifying social injustice in the short run is to miss the point. Although we, as educational leaders of school-based reform, have often been disappointed with many of the specific goals or strategies that a given school adopts as a result of these reform projects, our optimism remains intact as long as this community continues its commitment to study, discuss, and use democracy as a means to develop and grow.

Finally, it is important to conclude this chapter with a reflection on the process from which our discussion emerged. As mentioned at the beginning, the purpose of this chapter was not to evaluate the effectiveness of our work, to measure our success, or to identify our strengths and weaknesses. Rather, it was to identify and portray the substance of our work and examine significant ideas and issues in relation to this work that others might find engaging. However, there is an obvious danger in conducting self-reflective studies. In particular, there is always the risk that the authors will conduct their analysis in ways that are self-serving. This potential for conducting a self-serving study might easily have influenced all aspects of our inquiry: taking observation notes, asking certain types of interview and follow-up questions, reviewing fieldnotes, making decisions about what aspects of our work to portray, selecting the ideas and issues related to this portrayal, and generating the final analysis. This potential for self-interest is especially problematic when those who conduct the study authentically have confidence in what they do and find their work personally and socially meaningful. Given this experience, one might ask, how likely are we to publicly disclose our failings or analyze our work from an antagonistic perspective? This question becomes particularly important if there is a covert purpose to use this or other articles as a way to generate "business."

Unfortunately, we are not metacognitive enough to know for sure if this potential self-interest has corrupted the analytical portrayal of our work. We do know that our involvement in schools has never been initiated by knowledge obtained from any of the scholarly articles we have written. All of our work, to date, has come to us through "word of mouth," and our purpose for engaging in scholarly discourse is pedagogical, not financial. That is, we conducted this self-reflection as a means to learn and grow from our work and to share what we have learned with, in this case, other scholars, school reformers, and educational leaders. We have found this process of self-study intellectually stimulating and challenging. Nevertheless, educational leaders who wish to pursue this particular method of inquiry (and we strongly encourage others to do so) should take the issue of self-interest seriously and recognize the embedded risks involved in such endeavors.

NOTES

1. Over the last decade we have worked with many different schools at all grade levels and in all regions of the continental United States. However, the vast majority of our work has been in elementary schools located in high-poverty urban and rural communities. As a result, with the exception of one middle/high school located in a correctional

facility, the portrayal of experiences and discussion of ideas were generated from work in these elementary schools located in the Midwestern/ Great Lakes region of the United States.

2. Recently, the Office for Outreach Services merged with the National School Reform Faculty (NSRF), a loosely coupled organization of 40,000 to 60,000 educators working toward academic achievement and equity in schools (see Goodman, forthcoming).

3. As discussed elsewhere (Goodman, 1994), we have played a wide variety of roles in these projects.

4. For the purposes of this chapter, the term *faculty* refers to all building teachers, administrators, and classroom support staff (e.g., Title I coordinators, school social workers, teacher aides, counselors, regular substitute teachers, and classroom volunteers). The term *school community* refers to the previous individuals as well as building secretaries, kitchen staff, bus drivers, parents, and other community volunteers.

5. Interview questions were modified, given the particular school in which we work, but generally included: (1) Does your school have a guiding philosophy and if so what is it? If not, what do you think should be its guiding philosophy? (2) What, in a positive sense, makes your school special? (3) What are some of the obstacles your school deals with on a regular basis? (4) If you had a magic wand that could change anything in your school, what would it be? and (5) In what ways, if at all, does your school help prepare young people to live in a democratic society?

6. Typically, our involvement was extensive during the first 2 years (e.g., about one day each week in each school) but tapered off during the next 3 years.

7. Student Leadership Teams (SLTs) were created with representatives from each classroom. Unlike "student councils," which plan parties and bake sales, the purpose of the SLTs was similar to SGs. Students chose topics to study (with the assistance of an adult volunteer) and made proposals to improve the school. All proposals from the SLTs go directly to the LT in each school for consideration, in the same way as proposals from the other SGs. If SLT proposals did not achieve consensus in the LT, then a dialogue was initiated to work out differences until there was consensus from both the LT and the faculty as a whole.

8. In each school, we have had to carefully monitor compliance to these standards of interaction during meetings and when informed of noncompliance by others. In almost every case, we have assumed the responsibility for initially demonstrating the way "gentle reminders" can be expressed. Once we became aware of an instance of noncompliance, we brought it to the attention of all concerned so that over the course of the first year, these standards were internalized by most faculty.

REFERENCES

Anderson, G. (1990). Toward a critical constructivist approach to school administration: Invisibility, legitimization, and the study of non-events. *Educational Administration Quarterly, 26*(1), 38–59.

Anderson, G. (1996). The cultural politics of schools: Implications for leadership. In K. Leithwood (Ed.), *International handbook of educational leadership and administration* (Part 2, pp. 741–763). Boston: Kluwer Academic.

Anderson, G. (1998). Toward authentic participation: Deconstructing the discourses of participatory reforms in education. *American Educational Research Journal, 35*(4), 571–603.

Anderson, G., & Grinberg, J. (1998). Educational administration as a disciplinary practice: Appropriating Foucault's view of power, discourse, and method. *Educational Administration Quarterly, 34*(3), 329–353.

Anyon, J. (1997). *Ghetto schooling: A political economy of urban educational reform.* New York: Teachers College Press.

Barker, J. (1993). Tightening the iron cage: Coercive control in self-managing teams. *Administrative Science Quarterly, 38*(3), 408–437.

Barth, R. (1990). *Improving schools from within: Teachers, parents, and principals can make a difference.* San Francisco: Jossey-Bass.

Beare, H. (1993). Different ways of viewing school-site councils: Whose paradigm is in use here? In H. Beare & W. Boyd (Eds.), *Restructuring schools: An international perspective on the movement to transform the control and performance of schools* (pp. 200–217). London: Falmer Press.

Blase, J. (1998, April). *The micropolitics of educational change.* Paper presented at the Annual Meeting of the American Educational Research Association.

Blase, J., & Anderson, G. (1995). *The micropolitics of educational leadership: From control to empowerment.* New York: Teachers College Press.

Buber, M. (1958). *I and thou.* New York: Scribner.

Bullough, R., & Gitlin, A. (1985). Schooling and change: A view from the lower rung. *Teachers College Record, 87*(2), 219–237.

Campbell, J., & Neill, S. (1994). *Curriculum at stage one: Teacher commitment and policy failure.* Harlow, UK: Longman.

Campbell, J., & Southworth, G. (1990, April). *Rethinking collegiality: Teachers' views.* Paper presented at the Annual Meeting of the American Educational Research Association, Boston.

Casner-Lotto, J. (1988). Expanding the teacher's role: Hammond's school improvement process. *Phi Delta Kappan, 69*(5), 349–353.

Cassirer, E. (1981). *Kant's life and thought.* New Haven, CT: Yale University Press.

Chapman, J., & Boyd, W. (1986). Decentralization, devolution, and the school principal: Australian lessons on statewide educational reform. *Educational Administration Quarterly, 22*(4), 28–58.

Chubb, J., & Moe, T. (1990). *Politics, markets, and America's schools.* Washington, DC: The Brookings Institute.

Comer, J., Haynes, N., Joyner, E., & Ben-Avie, M. (1996). *Rallying the whole village: The Comer Process for reforming education.* New York: Teachers College Press.

Darling-Hammond, L. (1997). *The right to learn: A blueprint for creating schools that work.* San Francisco: Jossey-Bass.

Dewey, J. (1920). *Reconstruction in philosophy.* New York: Henry Holt.

Dewey, J. (1927). *The public and its problems.* New York: Henry Holt.

Dewey, J. (1946). *The problems of men.* New York: Philosophical Library.

Dow, P. (1991). *Schoolhouse politics: Lessons from the Sputnik era.* Cambridge, MA: Harvard University Press.

Elmore, R. (1990). *Restructuring schools.* San Francisco: Jossey-Bass.

Erickson, R. (1973). What makes school ethnography "ethnographic?" *Anthropology and Education Quarterly, 4*(2), 10–19.

Finn, C., & Clements, S. (1989). *Reconnoitering Chicago's school reform efforts: Some early impressions.* Washington, DC: Educational Excellence Network.

Fullan, M. (1993). *Change forces: Probing the depths of educational reform.* London: Falmer Press.

Gaylin, W., & Jennings, B. (1996). *The perversion of autonomy: The proper uses of coercion and constraints in a liberal society.* New York: Free Press.

Gee, J. (1990). *Social linguistics and literacies: Ideology in discourses.* New York: Falmer Press.

Gitlin, A., & Margonis, F. (1995). The political aspect of reform: Teacher resistance as good sense. *American Journal of Education, 103,* 377–405.

Glaser, G. & Strauss, A. (1975). *The discovery of grounded theory: Strategies for qualitative research.* Chicago: Aldine Press.

Glickman, C. (1993). *Renewing America's schools: A guide for school-based action.* San Francisco: Jossey-Bass.

Goodman, J. (1988). The disenfranchisement of elementary teachers and strategies for resistance. *Journal of Curriculum and Supervision, 3*(3), 201–220.

Goodman, J. (1992). *Elementary schooling for critical democracy.* Albany: SUNY Press.

Goodman, J. (1994). External change agents and grassroots school reform: Reflections from the field. *Journal of Curriculum and Supervision, 9*(2), 113–135.

Goodman, J. (forthcoming). *Reforming schools: Working within a progressive tradition during conservative times.*

Goodman, J., Baron, D., & Myers, C. (2001). Talking back to the neo-liberal agenda from the ground floor: School-based reform discourses in difficult times. *International Journal of Educology, 12–15*(1), 1–38.

Hargreaves, A. (1994). *Changing times: Teachers' work and culture in the postmodern age.* New York: Teachers College Press.

Hatch, T. (1998). The differences in theory that matter in the practice of school improvement. *American Educational Research Journal, 35*(1), 3–31.

Herman, J., & Golan, S. (1993). The effects of standardized testing on teaching and schools. *Educational Measurement: Issues and Practice, 12*(4), 20–25, 41–42.

Hofenberg, W., & Levin, H. (1993). *The accelerated schools: Resource guide.* San Francisco: Jossey-Bass.

Katz, M. (1995). *Improving poor people: The welfare state, the "underclass," and urban schools as history.* Princeton, NJ: Princeton University Press.

Korostoff, M., Beck, L., & Gibb, S. (1998, April). *Supporting school-based reform: Lessons from the work of the California Center for*

School Restructuring. Paper presented at the Annual Meeting of the American Educational Research Association.

Lipman, P. (1997). Restructuring in context: A case study of teacher participation and the dynamics of ideology, race, and power. *American Educational Research Journal, 34*(1), 3–37.

Madaus, G. (1990). The distortion of teaching and testing: High-stakes testing and instruction. *Peabody Journal of Education, 65*(3), 29–46.

Malen, B. (1994). Enacting site-based management: A political utilities analysis. *Educational Evaluation and Policy Analysis, 16*(3), 249–267.

Mirel, J. (1994). School reform unplugged: The Bensenville new American school project. *American Educational Research Journal, 31*(3), 481–518.

Muncey, D., & McQuillan, P. (1992). The dangers of assuming consensus for change. In G. Hess, Jr. (Ed.), *Empowering teachers and parents: School restructuring through the eyes of anthropologists*. Westport, CT: Greenwood Press.

Murphy, J. (1991). *Restructuring schools: Capturing and assessing the phenomena*. New York: Teachers College Press.

Pakalov, V. (1993). *Lives on the edge: Single mothers and their children in the other America*. Chicago: University of Chicago Press.

Payne, R. (1995). *Poverty: A framework for understanding and working with students and adults from poverty*. Baytown, TX: RFT.

Quantz, R., Rogers, J., & Dantley, M. (1991). Rethinking transformative leadership: Towards democratic reform of schools. *Journal of Education, 173*(3), 96–118.

Rorty, R. (1989). *Contingency, irony, and solidarity*. Cambridge, UK: Cambridge University Press.

Sarason, S. (1990). *The predictable failure of educational reform*. San Francisco: Jossey-Bass.

Sartre, J. (1956). *Being and nothingness: An essay on phenomenological ontology*. New York: Philosophical Library.

Shank, B. (1994). Must schools of social work be freestanding? Yes. *Journal of Social Work Education, 30*(3), 273–294.

Shannon, P. (1998). *Reading poverty*. Portsmouth, NH: Heinemann Press.

Shepard, L. & Doughtery, K. (1991, April). *Effects of high-stakes testing on instruction*. Paper presented at the meeting of the American Educational Research Association and the National Council on Measurement in Education.

Smyth, J. (1993). *A socially critical view of the self-managing school*. London: Falmer Press.

Smyth, J. (1995). *Critical discourses on teacher development*. London: Cassell Press.

Spradley, J. (1979). *The ethnographic interview*. New York: Rinehart & Winston.

Sulla, N. (1998, April). *Maximizing the effectiveness of external consultants in the educational reform agenda*. Paper presented at the Annual Meeting of the American Educational Research Association.

Talbot, D., & Crow, G. (1998, April). *When the school changed, did I get a new job? Principals' role conceptions in a restructuring context*. Paper presented at the Annual Meeting of the American Educational Research Association.

Urban, W. (1982). *Why teachers organized*. Detroit: Wayne State University Press.

Weick, K. (1988). Educational organizations as loosely coupled systems. In A. Westoby (Ed.), *Culture and power in educational organizations*. Philadelphia: Open University Press.

White, P. (1992). Teacher empowerment under "ideal" school-site autonomy. *Educational Evaluation and Policy Analysis, 14*(1), 69–82.

Yankelovich, D. (1999). *The magic of dialogue: Transforming conflict into cooperation*. New York: Simon & Schuster.

Yukl, G. (1994). *Leadership in organizations*. Englewood Cliffs, NJ: Prentice Hall.

PART IV

Theories of Leadership: Research Problems and Practices

MARGARET GROGAN
University of Missouri–Columbia

GARY M. CROW
University of Utah

> *There are more things in heaven and earth, Horatio,*
> *Than are dreamt of in your philosophy.*
>
> *Hamlet*, I, v

At the beginning of a new century, it is appropriate for academics to take stock of what we know and how we know what we know. Periodic assessments of knowledge are important for they allow us to step back and pay attention to political, economic, social, and technical changes that often shape research and scholarship unobtrusively. Our endeavor is particularly timely because the field of educational leadership has come under close public scrutiny in this modern era of accountability. Educational leadership does not have a long history, although it draws, in part, from a wide narrative about political and corporate leadership. Thus, it is important for us in academe to examine our credos and canons carefully if we are to respond well to the challenges we are currently facing.

The three chapters in this section of the *Handbook* take a critical look at the knowledge base of educational leadership. Authors question how research has been conducted to arrive at the body of knowledge experts in the field hold dear: What assumptions and beliefs have guided such research? Authors ask whether the theoretical foundations of the knowledge base are too limited, and whether this knowledge is still robust enough to inform us in the increasingly global 21st century. The critique does not negate the worth of the research and scholarship on which our knowledge of this field has been built. On the contrary, the authors are very aware of the legacy of this previous work. However, they have accepted the charge of determining what new directions research and scholarship in educational leadership might take.

In Chapter 14, *The Nature of Inquiry in Educational Leadership*, Michelle D. Young and Gerardo R. López reflect on what philosophies, theories, methodologies, and research questions have framed research in educational leadership. They take the position that the field has been constrained theoretically and methodologically because most studies thus far have used a traditional rationalist framework. Therefore, we do not yet have a comprehensive understanding of the phenomena under research. They argue that "our commonly accepted research and theoretical frameworks provide a partial heuristic for understanding the epistemological and ontological 'baggage' of the field as a whole" (p. 339).

Citing many scholars who have criticized the field for its traditionally white, male, middle class, heteronormative approaches to research and knowledge production, the authors contend that leadership practice is necessarily limited as a result. Quoting Heck and Hallinger (1999), they assert that the field suffers from a number of "blind spots," which prevent researchers and practitioners alike from understanding issues of leadership that have not been identified or problematized. Our taken-for-granted assumptions about leadership consequently reflect a narrow set of lived experiences.

This knowledge base has not gone uncontested. Young and López review recent work in educational leadership, using critical race theory, queer theory, and feminist poststructural theory. They offer these perspectives as a means to expand the theoretical frames for research in the field and to capture more varieties of experience.

Gary M. Crow and Margaret Grogan follow this discussion with a chapter on the development of leadership thought and practice. Chapter 15 calls into question the traditional ways the history of leadership thought and practice has been formulated and expressed here in the United States. They argue that the sources of leadership knowledge have been limited to concepts from industrial psychology, corporate management literature, human relations theories, political science, and social science theories. Missing from these accounts are insights into leadership gained from the humanities—the arts, literature, philosophy, and history.

Moreover, our sources have been entirely grounded in Western traditions and thought, although leadership has been a subject for study in most world cultures, with different assumptions and values guiding it on the various continents. Drawing on Rost (1991), the authors show that there are a number of weaknesses in the way our texts account for the development of leadership. Not only have the theories emphasized dyadic relationships instead of organizational and societal relationships, they have also reflected male, heroic images and have been excessively rationalistic and materialistic in their assumptions.

The chapter offers a glimpse into a few different possible sources for understanding leadership. Some of Shakespeare's histories and tragedies, along with other ancient and medieval literature, are referenced. African and East Asian philosophies of leadership are touched on in an effort to enrich our knowledge of leadership. The value of this approach is to further the knowledge base with new ideas and old ones that have been forgotten. In this postmodern era, we are reminded that knowledge is not fixed and stable. Practitioners in our schools and districts are facing conditions undreamed of in some of our theories, so we need to seek more widely and in heretofore unlikely places for new knowledge.

Finally, to conclude this section, Carolyn M. Shields and Anish Sayani wrote Chapter 16, "Leading in the Midst of Diversity: The Challenge of Our Times." The authors set their remarks against a description of the turbulent new century. They argue that the world of education is besieged by multiple pressures, conflicting goals, and diverse interpretations of the desired ends of education. Schools themselves are entirely unlike schools in the past. They are diverse in ways we have not encountered before. For example, the authors contend that "few schools in previous decades were what might be called 'majority-minority' schools—schools in which the . . . white or Caucasian [group] constitutes a numerical minority . . . and in which 'other,' often minoritized populations together constitute the numerical majority." (p. 381).

The authors consider the emerging notion of cross-cultural leadership as an approach to educational leadership that is better able to deal with this diversity. Preferring Ryan's (2002) term, "leadership in a context of diversity," they offer some different philosophical foundations for a more relevant attitude to educational leadership that will help the principal or superintendent steer a course amid the dynamic tensions existing in these schools today.

Their suggestions for school leaders include creating spaces for students and faculty to hear each other and to celebrate difference—cultural, ethnic, linguistic, religious, and so on. In the spirit of Martin Buber (1970), Shields and Sayani encourage meaningful dialogue among individuals in schools. They make the point that true learning about difference cannot take place until the learner finds a way to incorporate the new idea or new belief into her or his lived experience. Building relationships among students and between students, faculty, and staff founded on active listening and dialogic exchange will facilitate this understanding.

Shields and Sayani are concerned particularly with bridging the theory-practice divide. Illustrating their ideas with a couple of vivid vignettes, they place their remarks within the context of practice. They advocate critical multiculturalism, which becomes a transformative project through active learning about others rather than passive acceptance of others' difference. The authors warn against taking a position of supposed neutrality or "color blindness." By integrating some of the existing strands of research into a coherent model of leadership for diversity, they emphasize the goals of such leadership as striving to promote academic excellence, social justice, and deeply democratic citizenship.

All three chapters provide opportunities for educational leaders, professors, students, and policymakers to reexamine leadership from new and exciting frameworks. Although the leadership practice, theory, and research that have gone before have provided a useful foundation, it is time to question those assumptions, reflect on their application to a postmodern world, and critically examine how we think and practice leadership. These important activities are vital for educational leadership to respond to the education of all students in a diverse and dynamic world.

REFERENCES

Buber, M. (1970). *I and thou.* New York: Charles Scribner's.

Heck, R. H., & Hallinger, P. (1999). Next generation methods for the study of leadership and school improvement. In J. Murphy & K. Seashore Louis (Eds.), *Handbook of research on educational administration* (2nd ed., pp. 141–162). San Francisco: Jossey-Bass.

Rost, J. C. (1991). *Leadership for the twenty-first century.* New York: Praeger.

Ryan, J. (2002). Leadership in contexts of diversity and accountability. In K. Leithwood & P. Hallinger (Eds.), *Second international handbook of educational leadership and administration* (pp. 979–1002). Boston: Kluwer.

14

The Nature of Inquiry
in Educational Leadership

MICHELLE D. YOUNG
University Council for Educational Administration

GERARDO R. LÓPEZ
Indiana University

INTRODUCTION AND OVERVIEW

Over the past decade, national professional associations—as well as state departments of education—have made tremendous efforts to upgrade standards for the preparation of school and school system leaders. In 1994, the Council for Chief State School Officers (CCSSO) received a grant from the Pew Charitable Trusts to develop a set of national standards for school administrators. This effort brought about the most widely accepted set of leadership standards in the United States: the Interstate School Leaders Licensure Consortium (ISLLC) Standards for School Leaders (Murphy & Shipman, 2002). Currently, the ISLLC standards have been adopted by approximately 40 states and by the National Council for the Accreditation of Teacher Education's (NCATE) specialty area review group, the Educational Leadership Constituent Council.

The scale of the ISLLC standards' acceptance across the country is rather extraordinary. The story of the ISLLC standards, as told by Joseph Murphy (2000, 2002; see also Murphy, Yff, & Shipman, 2000), goes something like this: Practitioners, professors, and other stakeholders came together, worked together, compromised, and created the standards. Because a "professional consensus" (Murphy 2000, p. 412) was reached between all parties, Murphy concluded that the ISLLC standards represented the most comprehensive set of tenets and principles grounded in "research on successful schools and wisdom of the field" (p. 412).

Once the standards were developed, the CCSSO and its ISLLC team worked diligently to gain state acceptance of the standards, to develop leadership licensure exams based on the ISLLC standards, and to become connected with organizations like NCATE.

Today, the ISLLC standards are used as the foundation of countless educational leadership programs and professional development institutes (English, 2000a). Moreover, in many states, the ISLLC standards are used as the basis for both the licensure of school leaders and the accreditation of university-based leadership preparation programs (Schneider, 2002).

Indeed, the wide acceptance of the ISLLC standards is remarkable, particularly given the profound disagreements that exist regarding the very nature of educational leadership, as well as the knowledge base from which ideas about leadership are typically born (Anderson, 2001; Anderson et al., 2002; Donmoyer, Imber, & Scheurich, 1995; English, 2000a, 2000b, 2002a, 2002b, 2003). In this chapter, we discuss one issue of contention concerning the knowledge base in our field: the nature of inquiry in educational leadership scholarship. Our argument emerges from a perception of educational leadership as constrained by both its theoretical and methodological tools. In support of our argument, we begin this chapter with a review of the historical development of research in educational leadership and demonstrate that this research has taken place within a traditional rationalist or functionalist[1] frame. Moreover, we argue that the findings of these studies do not provide a comprehensive understanding of the phenomena being researched and, thus, should not be considered as the basis for an uncontested knowledge base or national standards (for either practice or preparation). In the second part of this chapter, we respond to this predicament by arguing in favor of expanding the theoretical frames used in educational leadership research.

Having been schooled in an educational administration department, we are aware of the traditional literature that has been written about leadership in various textbooks. Moreover, in our reviews of literature in the field, reaching from the 1950s to the present, we have become familiar with the development of various aspects of the knowledge base in educational leadership and management. In our own research in education leadership, management, and policy, we have found different perspectives useful in expanding our understanding of phenomena and in helping us to challenge taken-for-granted beliefs and concepts. Although we believe there are many theoretical frameworks that could provide helpful perspectives and approaches to developing our knowledge of leadership in education, we limit our discussion to three such frameworks: critical race theory, queer theory, and feminist poststructural theory.

THE ROOTS OF INQUIRY IN EDUCATIONAL LEADERSHIP

The acknowledgement of blind spots in the field means that at best we have developed an incomplete and distorted view of the role of school leaders in school improvement.

Heck & Hallinger, 1999, p. 143

In their review of the various theoretical and methodological strands used to explore issues of school leadership, Heck and Hallinger (1999) made a distinction between theoretical *blank spots* and *blind spots* in the field. The former referred to research areas in need of further investigation: areas in our knowledge base that need to be pursued to expand our understanding of school leadership and related organizational phenomena. These areas, often taken for granted, include important questions in the field that can only be answered through "sustained, narrowly focused inquiry" (p. 142).

Heck and Hallinger (1999) also suggested that the field suffered from a number of blind spots, knowledge that is unknown or curtailed because of our limited theoretical lenses. Just like the scientists in Kuhn's (1970) *The Structure of Scientific Revolutions,* Heck and Hallinger argued that researchers in educational administration tend to overrely on a single ontological and epistemological[2] framework that "impede[s] us from seeing other facets of phenomena under investigation" (p. 141). It is not until we switch our framework (or our paradigm) that we can also shift our vantage point and shed light on these proverbial blind spots. In effect, our theoretical lenses function as both lens and blinder, providing a discursive space to know or understand a particular "truth" at the same time they act as a blinder to hide competing "truth regimes" (Foucault, 1970, 1972, 1980).

To be certain, researchers in educational leadership tend to rely on logical positivism as their preferred lens or method of scientific inquiry (Griffiths, 1988). The adoption of this tradition in our field was heavily influenced by the "theory movement" of the 1950s through 1970s—in part, to justify educational leadership as a "legitimate" area of scholarship (Campbell, Fleming, Newell, & Bennion, 1987; Willower, 1994) and in part to "professionalize" our field within the academic community (Willower, 1996). This mode of inquiry searches for consistent, generalizable, and predictable empirical laws that explain behavioral regularities (Hoy & Miskel, 1996; Willower, 1975). Not only does this method of inquiry emerge from a specific ontological and epistemological framework, but it also reifies a particularly functionalist view of the organization: where human behavior is not only predictable, but somewhat malleable (Burell & Morgan, 1979).

The historical place of logical positivism in the field has strongly influenced our theoretical and methodological approaches. Over time, scholarship in educational leadership has led to the development of "big tent" thinking (Donmoyer, 1999), where alternative and competing theories, frameworks, and research findings are downplayed or marginalized. One result of this condition is a narrow and bounded set of research findings—a collective blind spot in our field (Marshall, 1997; Nagel,

1984; Scheurich, 1994; Young, 1999). Because our research methods largely dictate the phenomena we study, another result is the production and reification of blank spots.[3] In effect, the framework through which scholarship on educational leadership operates has resulted in time-worn assumptions, norms, and traditions about the appropriate way to conduct research, as well as the appropriate phenomena or concepts on which our research should focus. In this regard, there is a circular relationship between the tools of inquiry we use and our commonly accepted ideas of what we know or need to know.

This, however, does not suggest that educational leadership scholars cannot, or do not, subscribe to other philosophical and methodological traditions in their scholarship. Nor are we suggesting that the methodologies used in our field are entirely unidimensional. We simply argue that our commonly accepted research and theoretical frameworks provide a partial heuristic for understanding the epistemological and ontological "baggage" of the field as a whole (Denzin & Lincoln, 1994; Lincoln & Guba, 1985).

As Denzin and Lincoln (1994) argue, researchers within a field inquire about their world "with a set of ideas, a framework (theory, ontology) that specifies a set of questions (epistemology) that are then examined (methodology, analysis) in specific ways" (p. 11). Therefore, as researchers, we enter and exit the process of inquiry somewhat problematically (Tierney & Lincoln, 1997; Wolcott, 1995). This problematic position results in a gap that leaves open the possibility—or impossibility—of truthfully capturing reality. Although some scholars believe more rigorous methods of scientific inquiry and empirically tested evidence can yield better theoretical concepts and generalizable assumptions that can help us fill this gap of knowledge (Callahan, 1962; Campbell et al., 1987; Culbertson, 1988), other scholars believe that the search for "truth" is a falsity because it subscribes to a particular worldview that silences or further marginalizes competing perspectives (Donmoyer et al., 1995).

In the past, disagreements over the knowledge base in educational leadership have certainly been contentious (Donmoyer, 1999). In the past decade alone, an unprecedented number of researchers questioned the beliefs and practices associated with traditional methods of inquiry in our field. For example, Ball (1994), English (2002a, 2002b, 2003), Scheurich (1994), and Young (1999) have challenged the rational model in educational leadership and policy research as being overly mechanistic and controlling. Grogan (1996, 2003), Shakeshaft (1989, 1999), Tallerico (1997, 2000a, 2000b), and Marshall (1993, 1997) have also critiqued research and practices in educational administration as being male centered (see also Brunner, 1999, 2000a, 2000b, 2002; Skrla, 2000; Skrla, Reyes, & Scheurich, 2000). Scholars such as Anderson (1990, 2001; Anderson & Grinberg, 1998) have critiqued the traditional view of leadership as a deliberate process undertaken by a known and bounded set of actors, who use research and reason to ensure best practice. Koschoreck (2003), Blount (1998, 1999, 2003), Lugg (2003a, 2003b), and Capper (1999; Fraynd & Capper, 2003) have collectively questioned the ingrained heteronormativity in our field as well as the blatant homophobia on which our field was established. Moreover, the scholarship of Stanfield (1985, 1993, 1994), Banks (1993), Gordon, Miller, and Rollock (1990), López and Parker (2003), and Scheurich and Young (1997, 1998) has questioned the traditional approach to educational research, arguing that our epistemologies and ways of knowing are racially biased. In short, there is a wealth of scholarship in our field that consistently documents the failure of traditional educational research to adequately explain, understand, and change educational practice (Sirotnik & Oakes, 1986).

Like the scholars described above, we contend that most research in educational leadership takes place within—and is constrained by—traditionally accepted positivist research frameworks. This circumscription results in a number of serious limitations, including the following:

1. A failure to critique rational decision-making models that view research problems as "natural" (Scheurich, 1994; Young, 1999)

2. Viewing the findings of research as "value-free" (Marshall, 1997)

3. Viewing issues of organizational planning and implementation as processes that can or should be effectively and efficiently managed (Forester, 1993)

4. Viewing the knowledge necessary for planning, evaluation, and implementation as obtainable, objective, and shared (Adams, 1991)

In addition, we believe the traditional approach to research in educational leadership has legitimated specific types of behavioral and organizational norms that many researchers—and users of research—endeavor to regulate (Adams, 1997; Marshall, 1997).[4] Moreover, we believe our limited frameworks fail to help us recognize and understand how research reshapes the lived worlds of different populations and how it restructures contexts in ways that can alter opportunities, capacities to act, and self-concepts (Fine, 1996; Forester, 1993; Pillow, 1997). Finally, we believe that the vast majority of research in our field fails to provide a robust, dynamic, and multifaceted description of leadership and the work of educational leaders (Forester, 1993; Hamilton, 1991; Young, 1999).

Such omissions, individually and collectively, lead to ignorance of issues that arise from alternate theoretical perspectives—issues that have the potential not only to strengthen the knowledge base in educational leadership but also to address the concerns held by members of nonmajority populations.[5] Like

Heck and Hallinger (1999), we contend that the field suffers from a number of serious blind spots, and we argue that because most educational leadership studies take place within a limited theoretical and methodological framework, the knowledge base within our field is severely curtailed.

Inquiry in educational leadership has historically been undertaken within a narrow framework. What are needed are broader frameworks for understanding leadership, organizational life, and the role and purpose of leaders in a changing social context. By expanding our theoretical and methodological lenses to include perspectives that stand outside traditional discursive configurations, we will not only create an opportunity to expose the field to different understandings of leadership and organizational phenomena, but also disrupt our taken-for-granted assumptions of what leadership is, what it can be, and what purposes it ultimately serves.

BROADENING THE VISTA OF INQUIRY IN EDUCATIONAL LEADERSHIP

The key position of this chapter is that scholarship in educational leadership needs to include a broader range of perspectives. To be certain, the research framework one uses dictates—to a large extent—the way one identifies and describes research problems, the way one researches these problems, the findings that are highlighted, the implications that one considers, and the approach(es) one takes to planning and implementation. However, there are many perspectives and frameworks from which educational researchers may choose, such as the cultural perspective (Kingdon, 1995), critical race theory (Crenshaw, Gotanda, Peller, & Thomas, 1995; Parker, Deyhle, & Villenas, 1999; Solorzano, 1998; Solorzano & Villalpando, 1998; Tate, 1997), First Nations/Indigenous (Bishop, 1998; Hermes, 1998; Rains, Archibald, & Deyhle, 2000), feminist

(Ferguson, 1984), Black feminist (Collins, 1991; Dillard, 2000), Chicana (Delgado Bernal, 1998; Trujillo, 1998; Villenas, 1996, 2000), feminist critical policy analysis (Marshall, 1997), spirituality (Capper, Hafner, & Keyes, 2002; Dantley, 2003; Thompson & Johnson, 2000), poststructural policy archaeology (Scheurich, 1994), policy reconstruction (Forester, 1993), and queer theory (Britzman, 1995; Pinar, 1998; Sedgwick, 1990)—just to name a few. Indeed, as we expand our theoretical understanding of what we know and how we know, so too must we expand our understanding of the relationship between research methods (i.e., tools of inquiry), methodology (i.e., theories about how inquiry should proceed), and epistemology (i.e., ways of seeing and knowing).[6]

In this section, we will illustrate our position by highlighting three alternative frameworks for conducting research in our field—critical race theory, queer theory, and feminist poststructural theory—while discussing their ontological and epistemological underpinnings. This task, however, is not a simple one. Although we present these frameworks as unitary and all-encompassing, most researchers who work with or in these and other research traditions often borrow heavily from different theoretical strands of research (Donmoyer, 1999; Willower & Forsyth, 1999; Young, 1999). As such, our aim is not to totalize or homogenize these approaches, but rather to highlight other discourses of inquiry that have been largely marginalized within our field, as well as to interrogate how such frameworks illuminate alternate understandings of leadership and organizational life.

Critical Race Theory Approaches to Scholarship in Educational Leadership

Critical race theory (CRT) emerged from the critical legal studies movement of the 1970s and became widely popular in subsequent years following the success of crossover books such as Derrick Bell's (1987) *And We Are Not Saved,* Patricia Williams's (1995) *The Alchemy of Race and Rights,* and Richard Delgado's (1995a) *Critical Race Theory: The Cutting Edge.* Since its inception, CRT has gained increased momentum in both legal (Crenshaw et al., 1995; Delgado, 1995a; Delgado & Stefancic, 2001; Valdés, Culp, & Harris, 2002) and educational circles (Delgado Bernal, 2002; Ladson-Billings, 1999, 2000; Ladson-Billings & Tate, 1995; López & Parker, 2003; Parker et al., 1999; Solorzano, 1997, 1998; Solorzano & Yosso, 2001, 2002; Tate, 1997; Villalpando & Delgado-Bernal, 2002). The emerging scholarship in this area has resulted in poignant accounts, analyses, narratives, and "counterstories" (Delgado, 1995b) of the various faces of racism in both law and society.

Generally speaking, CRT unapologetically insists that issues of race and racism are not sociological aberrations but permanent social conditions because they are endemic components of our social fabric (Crenshaw et al., 1995; Delgado, 1995a; Delgado & Stefancic, 2001; Matsuda, 1996; Matsuda, Lawrence, Delgado, & Crenshaw, 1993; Valdés et al., 2002). As such, racism is seen as both an individual construct as well as a social and "civilizational" construct (Scheurich & Young, 1997). By placing race at the center of its discourse, CRT analyzes both overt and hidden manifestations of racism in the political, legal, organizational, and social arenas and argues that racism is a normal part of everyday life—the usual way "society does business" (Delgado & Stefancic, 2001, p. 7). By focusing on the permanence of racism (Bell, 1987), CRT contends that beliefs about neutrality, equal opportunity, democracy, objectivity, color blindness, and equality "are not just unattainable ideals, they are harmful fictions that obscure the normative supremacy of whiteness in American law and society" (Valdés et al., 2002, p. 3). In effect, CRT scholars argue that claims of social neutrality not only hide the economic, political, and legal interests of dominant groups but also serve to reify social relations by masking issues of racial power and privilege in society.

According to Solorzano and Yosso (2001, 2002; see also Solorzano, 1997, 1998), CRT centers around five fundamental points: (a) the centrality and intersectionality of race and racism, (b) the challenge to the dominant ideology of racial neutrality, (c) the commitment to social justice, (d) the importance of experiential knowledge, and (e) the reliance and use of interdisciplinary perspectives. These five tenets are briefly described below.

The first tenet of CRT places issues of race and racism at the center but also views its intersections with other forms of oppression such as gender (Iglesias, 1998; Luna, 2001; Montoya, 2000), sexual orientation (Valdés, 1998, 2000, 2002), class (Ansley, 1989; Powell, 1993), language (Pabón López, 2001; Perea, 1992), and immigration status (Johnson, 1998, 2002) among other areas of difference. As Valdés et al. (2002) argue, an intersectional perspective is necessary because "race itself is the product of other social forces—for example as the product of heteropatriarchy in a post-industrial, post-colonial, capitalist society" (p. 2). In effect, CRT claims that the struggle against racism is tightly interwoven with the struggle against other forms of oppression and subordination. Therefore, to understand racism conceptually, theoretically, and methodologically, one must understand how it influences—and is influenced by—an interlocking "system of ignorance, exploitation, and power" (Marable, 1992).

The second tenet of CRT challenges the notion of neutrality common in popular U.S. ideology—where racism is perceived as an *individual* and *irrational* act in a world that is otherwise neutral, rational, and just. In the traditional view, racism is not necessarily connected to the larger "distribution of jobs, power, prestige, and wealth" (Crenshaw et al.,

1995, pp. xiv) but is viewed as an individual or personal construct. Critical race scholars argue that such a slippage only serves to protect the idea of a neutral social order by moving the focus away from the barriers and inequities that exist in society and refocusing it on the "ignorant" individual. In effect, the belief in neutrality is protected, and white privilege and power are camouflaged (see also Scheurich & Young, 1997; Young & Laible, 2000).

The third aspect of CRT is the commitment to social justice: a deep commitment to end racial oppression and eliminate other interlocking systems of subordination such as sexism, homophobia, language discrimination, and economic exploitation. In this regard, CRT has a critical or transformative purpose, as well as a political and ethical commitment toward antiracist scholarship and political action (Méndez-Morse, 2003).

The fourth tenet of CRT privileges experiential knowledge, particularly the stories and counterstories of people of color (Delgado, 1995b, 1995c). CRT scholars believe there are two differing accounts of reality: the dominant reality, which "looks ordinary and natural" (Delgado, 1995a, p. xiv) to most individuals, and a "racial reality" (Bell, 1995), which has been filtered out, suppressed, and censored. The counterstories of people of color are those stories that are not told, stories that are consciously or unconsciously ignored or downplayed because they do not "fit" socially acceptable notions of "truth." By highlighting these "subjugated" accounts, CRT hopes to demystify the notion of a racially neutral society and tell another story of a highly racialized social order: a story where social institutions and practices serve the interest of white individuals (Oliva, 2000).

The final CRT tenet relies on interdisciplinary perspectives to understand the lived reality of people of color as well as the racist structures they must navigate on an everyday basis. As such, the use of a single, ahistorical,

and "monocular" lens (Bakhtin, 1968) is discarded in favor of multiple lenses that provide a more binocular and historical tapestry to assist in understanding issues of race and racism in society. This includes the use of lenses that are more sociological, psychological, and historical in nature as well as the use of postmodern, poststructural, and postcolonial theories, lenses, and frameworks.

Queer Theory Approaches to Scholarship in Educational Leadership

Queer theory—a cultural study, a philosophy, a political analysis, and social critique—disturbs taken-for-granted assumptions of "normality" by examining the processes, structures, discourses, and cultural texts that inscribe meaning in a culturally and historically situated subject (Britzman, 1995, 1997; Dilley, 1999; King, 1999; Pinar, 1998; Sedgwick, 1990; Tierney, 1997, 1999). By examining identities, especially—although not exclusively—sexual identities, queer theory aims to identify how such identities get constructed through language and discourse (Halperin, 1995; Sedgwick, 1990). Because, as Derrida (1967/1974) suggests, there is nothing outside the text, the text of queer theory is quite broad; it could be a "book or film . . . a conversation, a life story, a memory, sexual activity, history, a gathering place, or a social trend" (Dilley, 1999, p. 459). In effect, queer theory aims to understand why and how specific discourses, structures, behaviors, and actions become inscribed, normalized, and reproduced through linguistically codified and culturally sanctioned rules and norms.

The word *queer,* for example, is infused with specific social meaning. For many, queer is a term used largely as a derogatory slur aimed at individuals who are not heterosexual or individuals whose apparent (hetero)sexuality is called into question (i.e., people whose sexuality, gender, physical appearance, or actions "place them outside of society's idea of 'normal;'" Dilley, 1999, pp. 457–458). Not only does this definition accept as its organizing premise the notion of heterosexual "normality," but it simultaneously positions those considered queer as lacking or deficient and therefore less than normal or abnormal (Honeychurch, 1996). By reappropriating the term to signify not a lack of something but the presence of something else (e.g., same-sex desires, fondness for drag, genital ambiguity, etc.), queer theory undermines the homo/hetero, masculine/feminine, male/female binaries, while inverting traditional assumptions of what one considers to be normal. As such, it places queerness—both as an essence and a social construction—at the center of the discourse: It celebrates the normality of queerness while questioning the queerness of normality.

Although an emphasis on sexual orientation[7] is central in queer theory, it is not its principal focus. To be certain, sexual orientation intersects, in profound and complex ways, with other areas of identity such as sex, sexuality, gender,[8] and other markers of difference such as race, ethnicity, and class (Honeychurch, 1996). In this regard, queer theory reminds us of the simple fact that *all* individuals—gays, lesbians, bisexuals, transgendered, and heterosexuals alike—are shaped by a power and knowledge regime that structures and shapes our desires, behaviors, and actions. In effect, sexual identity functions as a window through which to understand how interlocking systems of power become normalized in the larger social order.

According to Tierney (1997), queer theory revolves around five central tenets: (a) It seeks to understand sexual identity over time, (b) it seeks to uncover norms and deconstruct ideological practices within social institutions, (c) it is confrontational rather than consensual, (d) it seeks to understand sexual identity as being more than sexuality, and (e) it sees society and culture as interpretive and political (see also Britzman, 1995; Dilley, 1999; Sedgwick, 1990).

The first tenet of queer theory contends that sexual orientation is not a stable or stagnant entity across time and space because different social discourses give rise to different understandings of sexual identity. For instance, history has documented same-sex relations, as well as stable same-sex relationships, since antiquity. The societal meaning of homosexuality, however—that is, how the broader society views same-sex relations, as well as how individuals interpret and give meaning to those sexual acts—has shifted throughout time. Foucault (1977) has traced the notion of modern hetero/homo sexuality, as a category of identity, to the late 19th century when sodomy was first forbidden and when the sodomite became an outcast or deviant (see also Katz, 1995). Prior to this period, Foucault argues, hetero/homo identities did not reside in the sexual act but in other social criteria. Tracing the history of sexuality over time—its archaeology, its embeddedness in popular discourse, its regulations by social institutions—is a critical first step in understanding how society normalizes and regulates issues of sexuality writ large, and same-sex relations in particular.

In this regard, the first tenet of queer theory is closely related to its second tenet: It seeks to uncover social norms around issues of sexuality and to deconstruct heterosexist ideological practices that are often taken for granted on an everyday basis. For example, in the introduction to *Academic Outlaws: Queer Theory and Cultural Studies in the Academy,* Bill Tierney (1997) explains how something as simple as a book's dedication reflects heterosexist assumptions: Whereas readers rarely question a male author's dedication to "my loving wife" or assume a male author is married (to a female) when the dedication reads "to Pat," they are often disturbed, or at least momentarily taken aback, when the male author's dedication reads "to Bill, with love" or "to Jim—my friend, my partner, my life." Although some readers may interpret the latter book dedications as political, or perhaps ostentatious, such understandings only assume that the former dedications were not political or ostentatious in any way. By uncovering such examples of heterosexual privilege in everyday life, queer theory helps us understand that heterosexism is deeply ingrained and rampant in society: It permeates our practices, discourses, and ways of thinking about the world.

The third tenet of queer theory is that it is confrontational rather than consensual, meaning that it is not satisfied by status quo or facile understandings of homophobia and heterosexual privilege. Rather, queer theory aims to critically interrogate how power is manifested in all realms of life: What is often taken for granted as normal is really a by-product of social discourses and how they discipline and control identities and individual behavior. Queer theory provides an important theoretical space that reveals the promises and problematics of power while providing a forum for understanding how a direct confrontation of normality exposes the arbitrariness of the social world as well as the systems of power that order our world.

The fourth tenet of queer theory insists that sexual identity involves much more than the sexual act. By deconstructing sex/sexuality/sexual orientation/gender interrelationships and focusing more on the *meaning* people give to their sexuality, queer theory opens up a wide number of possibilities for sexual identities within the homo/hetero spectrum. To be certain, as Sedgwick (1990) asserts, "even identical genital acts mean very different things to different people" (p. 25). Moreover, there are individuals of various sexual identities who do not find significant meaning in sexual acts with others but find more pleasure in autoeroticism, inanimate objects, or pure fantasy. In this regard, queer theory seeks to move the discourse away from sexual acts as the basis for sexual identity and highlight the ways in which society prescribes identities for individuals.

The last tenet of queer theory views society and culture as interpretive and political, suggesting that ways of knowing and experiencing the world are socially constructed, and certain voices, perspectives, and worldviews are circulated and privileged over others (Honeychurch, 1996; Tierney, 1999). Queer theory takes an impenitent stance in identifying and deconstructing the discourses and regimes of truth that normalize certain perspectives and "realities" while marginalizing, silencing, and disparaging others. Therefore, in queer theory, the struggle is not over *who* is (or is not) queer—but rather, *how* one is made queer and who benefits by such a categorization (Dilley, 1999). Queer theory reminds us that there is, indeed, a real struggle in the world: a struggle over discourse, a struggle over political interests and power, a struggle over identity, a struggle to make visible the politics of the invisible, and a struggle to define and defend what we come to see, experience, and believe to be normal and natural.

Feminist Poststructural Approaches to Scholarship in Educational Leadership

In recent years, feminist researchers in the field of educational leadership have found an ally in poststructuralism. Researchers like Ortiz and Marshall (1988) and Shakeshaft (1989), who began to make use of feminist perspectives in their analyses of educational leadership and management in the early 1980s, have found their work being taken to another level by combining the concerns and insights of feminism with those of poststructuralism.

Grounded in such disciplines as philosophy, sociology, psychology, and history, feminism (although certainly not a unitary category) primarily explores the significance of gender relations and other "distinctively feminist issues [which are] the situation of women and the analysis of male domination" (Flax, 1990a, p. 40; see also the work of: Belenky, Clinchy, Goldberger, & Tarule, 1986; Britzman,

1991; Chodorow, 1989; Collins, 1991, 1995; Ellsworth, 1997; Flax, 1990b; Gilligan, 1993; Harding, 1987; Hartsock, 1985; Pillow, 2000, 2002; St. Pierre, 1997, 2000; Scott, 1986). According to Flax (1990a) feminist theory aims "to analyze gender relations: how gender relations are constituted and experienced and how we think or, equally important, do not think about them" (p. 40). Moreover, feminist scholarship has at its core a praxis. It advocates action that results in a more equitable distribution of resources and opportunities for those who have been marginalized.

Like feminism, poststructuralism embraces concepts that enable us to understand educational leadership in terms different from those that have been used in the past. Poststructuralism—a continuation of the French philosophical movement of the 1960s that fed the intellectual curiosity of theoretical luminaries such as Foucault, Derrida, Boudrillard, and de Beauvoir[9]—has gained increased significance in academic circles as a vehicle to understand concepts such as discourse, subjectivity, power and knowledge, and resistance.

Feminist poststructuralism, as the name suggests, combines both feminist and poststructural perspectives. Working from poststructural conceptions of discourse, subjectivity, power and knowledge, and resistance, feminist poststructuralism focuses these concepts on issues of concern to feminists (e.g., gender roles, inequity, oppression). The work of Benhabib (1990), Davies (1994), Flax (1990a, 1990b), Grogan (2003), Haraway (1990), Lather (1992), Nicholson (1990), Skrla (2003), and Weedon (1997) exemplifies this perspective.

Foucault (1980) uses the term *discourse* to communicate how we are positioned as subjects in different relationships with others (e.g., daughter, father, employee, supervisor, wife, husband). Thus, our conceptions of proper behavior, rules, and speech in the various discourses within which we are

positioned are dependent on our relative position within each discourse. Using a feminist-poststructural lens to examine discourse on educational leadership research, for example, one would find that those who have had the power to define good research have primarily been white male researchers; their experiences and perspectives have traditionally provided the basis for most research texts, research funding, publishing opportunities, and so on.

Subjectivity is a term used to signify the thoughts and emotions of an individual (both conscious and unconscious), how one understands oneself, and how one understands one's relationship with and within larger society (Weedon, 1997). Poststructuralism posits that what we come to know and believe as normal and natural is not accidental (Foucault, 1972) but an age-old by-product of humanism (St. Pierre, 2000). As such, humanism is the lens with which we see, experience, and come to know the world. As St. Pierre (2000) suggests:

> Humanism is the air we breathe, the language we speak, the shape of the homes we live in, the relations we are able to have with others, the politics we practice, the map that locates us on the earth, the futures we can imagine, the limits of our pleasures. Humanism is everywhere, overwhelming in its totality; and, since it is so "natural" it is difficult to watch it work. (p. 478)

Key to understanding the concept of subjectivity is that humanism and its localized discourses "systematically form the objects of which they speak" (Sarup, 1988, p. 70)—in other words, we are subjectified by discourse. Thus, as Grogan (2003) points out, "a man or woman who becomes superintendent is shaped by the discourse of the superintendency" (p. 19). He or she will learn to make meaning of his or her experiences according to the dominant values and beliefs expressed within that particular discourse. The goal of poststructuralism regarding subjectivity is to critically engage the limits of humanism by examining the structures and processes it creates and normalizes (as well as those that are created and are normalized by it). It specifically aims to bring into question what is typically considered normal (i.e., the norm) by disrupting and exposing the categories, structures, and processes that give it meaning and thereby open up new avenues for understanding and knowing the world (Foucault, 1972).

Conceptions of knowledge and power are central to poststructural (and feminist-poststructural) thought. The notion of universalizing truths (i.e., theories that purport to provide comprehensive explanations) is strongly rejected. Instead, poststructuralism suggests that social reality can be known only locally and contemporaneously.

> This approach respects knowledge and understanding that comes from local stories, for instance, that comes from a critical awareness of the particular historical situatedness of the set of conditions that contribute to the local context. Instead of seeing a local context as *merely* representative of wider social, political, and economic trends and forces, it allows us to pay attention to the distinctive features of a local context and to hear the local players in their particular places and times. (Grogan, 2003, p. 20)

Moreover, poststructuralism reminds us that knowledge (even local knowledge) and truth are neither fixed nor stagnant—they are slippery, unstable, and open to a multitude of readings or inscriptions. Indeed, all knowledge is contested; what counts as knowledge depends on who creates it, anoints it, and communicates it (Foucault, 1980).

Yet, the problem remains that certain "truths" tend to be circulated over others. Foucault (1972) suggests that the reason this happens is because power, knowledge, and truth are intricately connected: Truth does not exist "out there" but is actively produced and proliferated within discourse. The reason why specific truths are privileged is because other truths are actively constrained, controlled, and afforded a different status. Truth, hence, is not "objective" or "waiting to be discovered" but is pregnant with the "values, politics, and desires" (St. Pierre, 2000, p. 484) of society. As such, poststructuralism is not preoccupied with a search for truth; it is more interested in understanding the relationship between knowledge and power as well as *how* and *why* certain truths are enabled and proliferated.

The fourth and final concept of feminist poststructuralism is the notion of resistance. If knowledge and truth, as suggested above, are to be challenged or expanded to include many voices (rather than the voices of the powerful alone), then one can expect that the "new" knowledge and truths that emerge will include a resistance to the formerly accepted claims to knowledge and truth (Grogan, 2003). Moreover, as questions arise and doubt grows, a productive lack of certainty about "the way things are" as well as a constructive appreciation of multiple perspectives may emerge. Thus, feminist poststructuralism encourages a cognitive resistance that enables individuals to take action. How and whether cognitive resistance is translated into action depends on the individual actor and what power is at her or his behest.

In sum, the fundamental aims of feminist poststructural theory are to identify how patriarchy functions in the world, to understand how women and men are impacted—linguistically, socially, materially—within humanism's discourse, to reveal the relationship between power and knowledge, and to open opportunities for resistance (see also St. Pierre & Pillow, 2000). As St. Pierre (2000) suggests:

> Once these questions can be asked of the specific, local, everyday situations that oppress women, and once the working of patriarchy is made intelligible at the level of micropractice, women can begin to make different statements about their lives. Once they can locate and name the discourses and practices of patriarchy, they can begin to refuse them. (p. 486)

THE APPLICATION OF ALTERNATIVE PERSPECTIVES IN EDUCATIONAL LEADERSHIP RESEARCH AND SCHOLARSHIP

Our examination of the theoretical roots of inquiry in educational leadership revealed the strong influence that logical positivism has had on the base of knowledge and theories that have developed around the practice of school and school system leaders. Over time, this knowledge base has been criticized, although the criticisms were rarely related to its theoretical narrowness (e.g., Donmoyer et al., 1995; English, 2002a). Rather, scholars criticized the knowledge base in educational administration as underdeveloped—full of blank spots and blind spots (Heck & Hallinger, 1999). Our critique builds on these understandings but pushes past the issue of what the knowledge base does or does not contain to a consideration of *why* it has blank and blind spots. We contend that the answer to this question, in large measure, lies in the theoretical and methodological tools used in educational leadership scholarship.

In the section above, we presented three perspectives that are seldom used by researchers in our field: critical race theory, queer theory, and feminist poststructural theory. We consider these three perspectives to be powerful alternatives to the perspectives typically used in educational leadership research, alternatives that hold the potential of expanding knowledge, pushing theory, and revealing complexity. In reflecting on the value of critical race theory, Ladson-Billings (2000) notes:

> The point of working in racialized discourses and ethnic epistemologies [including other areas of difference] is not merely to "color" the scholarship. It is to challenge the hegemonic structures (and symbols) that keep injustice and inequity in place. The work also is not about dismissing the work of European and Euro-American scholars. Rather, it is about defining the limits of such scholarship. (p. 258)

Indeed, the implications of using alternative perspectives in research on leadership are powerful. In the following three subsections, we demonstrate, through examples, how critical race theory, queer theory, and feminist poststructural theory have been applied by colleagues in our field.

Applying CRT to Research in Educational Leadership

Several scholars in the field of education have already discussed the blatant and persistent problem of race and racism in both our theories as well as our methodologies (e.g., Banks, 1993; Collins, 1991; Gordon, 1990; Sleeter, 1992; Sleeter & Grant, 1987, 1999; Tatum, 1992, 1997). Although some scholars have addressed race and racism in the specific area of educational leadership (e.g., Allen, Jacobson, & Lomotey, 1995; Laible & Harrington, 1998; Larson, 1997; Lomotey, 1989, 1995; Ortiz & Ortiz, 1995; Parker & Shapiro, 1992; Reyes, Velez, & Peña, 1993; Rizvi, 1993; Young & Laible, 2000; Young & Rosiek, 2000), only a handful of researchers have used CRT as a theoretical lens in their work (e.g., Ladson-Billings, 2000; Ladson-Billings & Tate, 1995; López, 2003b; López & Parker, 2003; Parker, 1998, 2003; Parker & Lynn, 2002; Scheurich & Young, 1997; Smith-Maddox & Solorzano, 2002; Solorzano & Delgado Bernal, 2001; Solorzano & Yosso, 2001, 2002; Tate, 1997; Tillman, 2002; Tyson, 1998; Villalpando & Delgado Bernal, 2002).

López (2003a), for example, uses CRT to critically engage the limits of the discourse surrounding the politics of education by placing race at the center of his analysis. Through the use of counterstorytelling, he exposes the color-blind and racially neutral assumptions within this area of scholarship while highlighting the notion that the knowledge base in educational leadership largely fails to engage issues of race and racism head-on. López suggests that the "important stuff" in the leadership arena is often relegated to a political knowledge consisting of leadership theory, organizational theory, school finance, school law, and other staple and politically safe topics. He suggests that these theories are insufficient because they often downplay, or altogether ignore, the centrality of race, class, gender, and sexual orientation in the daily life of schools. Such invisibility, López asserts, only serves to institutionalize racism by failing to probe and analyze how it permeates the landscape of education. Moreover, the invisibility of race in our field only serves to relegate racism to a "theoretical footnote" (p. 70) within the larger discourse of educational leadership and fails to equip future school leaders with the tools to understand how race and racism function in schools and society at large (see also Parker & Shapiro, 1992; Young & Laible, 2000). In short, López challenges us to embrace the tenets of CRT and begin the process of "naming and dismantling racism in our ranks as well as in the work we do" (p. 87).

To be certain, CRT can be used to investigate the counternarratives of principals, superintendents, teachers, parents, students, and community members of color at school or district—particularly those counterstories that highlight the multiple ways in which racism functions in daily life (cf. Dunbar, 1999, 2001; Foster, 1993, 1997; Henry, 1998; López, 2003a). It can be used as a theoretical lens to understand the apparent racial neutrality of organizational structures (cf. Parker & Lynn, 2002; Solorzano & Yosso, 2001, 2002). It can be used to better understand the limited nature of our knowledge base—especially the knowledge of what educational leaders should know and be able to do (cf. Parker & Shapiro, 1992; Scheurich & Skrla, 2003; Young & Laible, 2000). In short, when issues of race and racism are placed at the center of analysis, it opens up new possibilities for understanding leadership and organizational life, while disrupting our taken-for-granted assumptions of the apparent apoliticality of the field.

Applying Queer Theory to Research in Educational Leadership

Catherine Lugg and James Koschoreck coedited a special issue of the *Journal of School Leadership* (2003) that focused specifically on issues, contexts, and lives of lesbian, gay, bisexual, and transgendered (LGBT) educators. Most, if not all, of the articles in this issue (Blount, 2003; Fraynd & Capper, 2003; Koschoreck, 2003; Lugg, 2003a) used tenets of queer theory to foreground the blatant homophobia and heteronormativity in educational leadership and schools, while describing the structures, processes, and discourses that reify and reproduce sexual hierarchies in society at large.

Blount (2003), for example, traces the history of sexuality and gender in educational administration since its inception, finding that educational leadership was built around conventional norms of marriage, heterosexuality, and "appropriate" gender roles that directly paralleled the roles of men and women in traditional married households (see also Blount 1998, 1999; Lugg, 2003a, 2003b). Her research not only identified why men were relegated to the role of administrators and women to the role of teachers but also showed how these roles patrolled both gender and sexuality in men and women. In effect, Blount finds that although both men and women could "cross" into the other profession, their gender roles could not: Female administrators and male teachers could not "cross" the bounds of socially proscribed gender roles, modes of interaction, styles of dress, and so on—lest they run the risk of being labeled lesbian or gay. In this regard, Blount's research demonstrates how school administration normalizes gender roles for both men and women and how these gender roles, in turn, rely on as well as reproduce the hetero/homo binary (see also Butler, 1990).

Lugg (2003a, 2003b) uses queer legal theory—a fusion of critical legal theory and queer theory—to foreground how state sodomy laws regulate individual behaviors, forcing LGBT educators to hide a critical component of their identity to "fit in" to the fold of educational organizations. In this regard, Lugg highlights how the law not only punishes people for "bad" behavior but also rewards them for seemingly "good" behavior (see also Foucault, 1980). The law, as a regulative, disciplinary body, not only reproduces the proverbial closet but forces LGBT educators to weigh the costs and benefits of being out against the costs and benefits of not being out—ultimately forcing them to regulate and check their own behaviors and actions (see also Capper, 1999; Fraynd & Capper, 2003; Koschoreck, 2003). It also forces straight educators to play and uphold appropriate gender roles in schools—as well as check their own behaviors and actions—or they run the risk of being labeled queer.

In short, queer theory can be used in educational leadership to disrupt our taken-for-granted assumptions of how administrators, teachers, students, and community members—of any gender or sexual orientation—"should" behave and act with or in educational organizations and society at large (Tierney, 1997; Tierney & Dilley, 1998). It can be used to analyze how structures—both organizational and ideological—regulate and are regulated by a heteronormative social order (Britzman, 1995; Butler, 1990; Lugg, 2003b; Tierney, 1997). And it can be used to open spaces of possibility in schools—where educators, gay and straight alike, struggle to "break down the walls of ignorance" (Koschoreck, 2003, p. 46) and create an organizational climate of respect for all individuals regardless of their sexual orientation, gender, physical appearance, or actions.

Applying Feminist Poststructural Theory to Research in Educational Leadership

In the time that has passed since Shakeshaft (1989) published her book questioning the

androcentric bias in educational leadership, feminist researchers have developed a significant body of research on gender and educational administration. Within this literature base, several scholars have contributed pieces that made use of feminist poststructural theory (e.g., Brunner, 1999, 2002; Grogan, 1996, 2003; Skrla, 2000, 2003; Young, 2003). This research has considered educational leadership in a different way than either feminist or traditional research in our field. In other words, feminist poststructural theory has opened up the discourse toward understanding leadership from a radically different perspective.

Grogan (2003), for example, uses constructs from feminist and postmodern thought to examine the current conception of the superintendency. Fully recognizing that "knowledge of [the superintendency] is partial and limited by gender" (p. 21), she uses feminist-poststructural theory to raise different questions about the position and role of today's superintendent:

> We know little about how the superintendency has been linked to issues of social justice. Has the position been thought of as one from which equitable policies must emerge? We learn that superintendents have been encouraged to think and behave in ways that have been dictated by a white, male dominated discourse shaped by a different age. Most important for the possibility of future change, we become aware that superintendents retain a great deal of power despite the intrusions of local, state, and federal politics. (p. 21)

As a result of her use of this alternative perspective, she has identified several paradoxes (e.g., the finding that successful reformers need not reform) that must be negotiated by superintendents and educational leaders. The alternative approaches that emerged out of questioning the current superintendency include: (a) be comfortable with contradiction, (b) work through others, (c) appreciate dissent, (d) develop a critical awareness of how children are being served, and (e) adopt an ethic of care. Grogan argues that while "traditional educational leadership theories did not necessarily prevent superintendents from adopting these approaches in the past, the theories did not advocate them as I define them" (p. 22).

Skrla (2003) also uses feminist poststructural theory in her research on the superintendency. However, in her work, she makes use of Popkewitz and Brennan's (1998) definition of power as deployment to propose an alternative lens for studying sexism in the superintendency. This view of power, which is based on the work of Foucault, focuses on the effects of power

> as it circulates through institutional practices and the discourses of daily life. . . . Strategically, the study of the effects of power enables us to focus on the ways that individuals construct boundaries and possibilities. . . . Foucault enables us to understand that such reasoning has multiple trajectories and to explore the various strategies through which individuality is constructed as both disciplining and productive of power. The productive elements of power move from focusing on the controlling actors to the systems of ideas that normalize and construct the rules through which intent and purpose in the world are organized. The effects of power are to be found in the production of desire and in dispositions and sensitivities of individuals. (pp. 18–19)

This type of power, according to Skrla (2003), is circulated and reinforced and actually produces normative thoughts, rules, and behaviors. In the public school superintendency, Skrla found multiple normalizations (e.g., race, professionalism, expertise) at work, although the most powerful was gender. These normalizations include a tendency for women superintendents: (a) to remain silent about issues of gender, (b) to deny any past ambition to become a superintendent, (c) to reinforce the idea that there is an essential difference in

the leadership styles of men and women, and (d) to redefine their power as "power to" collaborate and empower others. Skrla argues that by participating in and reinforcing these norms, "women are able to maintain appropriately feminine roles in their organizations while in leadership roles" (p. 259).

Scholars like Skrla (2003), Grogan (2003), Brunner (2000a, 2000b), and others who have been using feminist-poststructural theory in their work are unpacking and challenging taken-for-granted understandings about educational leadership. They have demonstrated how educational administration as a field has reinforced particular leadership discourses, rules, rituals, expectations, relationships, and practices, and they have provided standpoints from which leadership might be otherwise viewed and enacted.

Unfortunately, the body of feminist-poststructural research, like much of the research undertaken from a CRT or queer theory perspective, has remained on the margins of mainstream educational leadership literature. As a result, it has had little if no effect on the preparation and practice of school and school system leaders. This is unfortunate. The understandings provided by alternative perspectives like feminist poststructuralism, CRT, and queer theory offer our field potentially important contributions. They provide the opportunity to challenge our taken-for-granted assumptions about research, to expand our knowledge base, to push theory, and to reveal the complexity of educational leadership. Moreover, these perspectives provide opportunities for understanding leadership differently and spaces to reconstruct our world—as well as our relation to that world—differently (Britzman, 1991; Ellsworth, 1997; Lather, 1996; Peters, 1996; St. Pierre, 1997).

CONCLUSION

It has been argued in this chapter that research in the field of educational leadership and management is limited by its overreliance on a single theoretical frame: logical positivism. The profound shifts taking place in contemporary social life require a shift in our research traditions. They require leadership scholars to broaden their approaches to exploration and understanding. When multiple theoretical frameworks and epistemological perspectives come to bear on the knowledge base in educational leadership, the usefulness of that knowledge base will be broadened. Researchers will know more about the phenomena they are examining, and they will know more deeply.

Beyond having positive effects on the findings of research and informing the knowledge base in educational leadership, using different frameworks would also affect the ways research is conducted and the ways researchers are trained. While some would argue the incommensurability of research paradigms and theories (see Kuhn, 1970), others have recognized that "incommensurable languages can be compared and rationally evaluated in multiple ways" (Bernstein, 1993, p. 65). Thus, researchers can learn to make use of more than one theory, framework, or paradigm in an effort to understand phenomena. In fact, Bernstein (1993) argues that researchers have an obligation to understand and use more than one framework in their research endeavors.

> The plurality of rival incommensurable traditions imposes a universal responsibility upon reflective participants in any tradition— a responsibility that should not be confused with an indifferent superficial tolerance where no effort is made to understand and engage with the incommensurable otherness of "the Other." (p. 66)

This would of course require that leadership scholars study paradigms and theories that differ from their own. It would also obligate institutions that train educational researchers to encourage their students to explore alternative theoretical frames as well as alternative research methods. Furthermore, it would

enjoin leadership scholars to think carefully about the framework and methodology they choose when conducting research.

To be certain, the use of alternate theoretical and epistemological lenses provides a new perspective for looking at the world of educational leaders. It opens up new possibilities for understanding leadership and organizational life and provides a more holistic viewpoint that recognizes the partiality of the theories and perspectives we use in our field. We are not suggesting that our present knowledge base is wrong or entirely unfounded. Rather, we are merely pointing out that it is partial, limited, and ambiguous at best (English, 2002a). The use of alternative perspectives helps us realize that knowledge is not closed or finite but open to a wide range of possibilities. As such, the notion of relying on a single test or set of standards to gauge leadership knowledge is highly problematic and suspect.

Taken holistically, the use of alternative frameworks has a number of important implications for research in educational leadership. These implications concern the preparation of scholars for field research, the way research is carried out, the contribution such research makes to the educational literature, and the direction of future research. Most important, however, would be the potentially positive effect that an expanded and enhanced knowledge base in educational leadership could have on leadership preparation and practice.

NOTES

1. Heck and Hallinger (1999) note that functionalism "emphasizes systems and contingency theory, rational models of decision making, and a positivist, or so-called 'objective,' view of science" (p. 142). Historically, research in educational leadership has overrelied on a scientific framework that is functionalist in nature—in part, to justify its legitimacy as a social science (Campbell et al., 1987; Willower, 1994) and in part, to "become a more professionalized field of study and preparation" (Willower, 1996, p. 345). This is not to suggest that the field is entirely homogenous

or unidimensional, nor does it suggest that scientific inquiry is unimportant or unnecessary. Rather, it merely suggests that positivist, scientific inquiry has been the foundation that has overwhelmingly defined "accepted modes of research" in the field (Heck & Hallinger, 1999, p. 142; see also Culbertson, 1988). Such a declaration, however, does not intend to "blur" the distinction between science, positivism, and functionalism. Indeed, as Willower (1996), Hoy (1996), and Evers and Lakomski (1991, 1996) argue, functionalism—of the Fredrick Taylor variety—is an organizational philosophy, whereas positivism is but one form of scientific inquiry. Notwithstanding, few would disagree that both functionalism *and* positivism have left a strong imprint on the field (Culbertson, 1988; Griffiths, 1988). To be certain, our goal is not simply to disparage science or functionalism but to examine the problem of overwhelmingly relying on a single framework of inquiry in our research.

2. The ontological nature of a research project is identified by answering the question: "What is the nature of reality, and therefore, what is there that can be known about it?" (Denzin & Lincoln, 1994, p. 108). In traditional research, it is assumed that there is a reality. However, scholars may disagree about whether or not that reality is directly apprehensible (positivism) or not (post-positivism). Epistemology is the study of the relationship between the knower and what can be known (Denzin & Lincoln, 1994). Epistemology is related to ontology in that if the researcher believes in a real and apprehensible reality, then her or his relationship as a knower to what can be known will be objective.

3. For example, in their discussion, Heck and Hallinger (1999) describe how their own blank spots about the role of the principal in school effectiveness influenced their understanding of who the primary player was in this effort (i.e., the principal), as well as how this person demonstrated success in this position (i.e., student achievement). Their frameworks or lenses bar them from seeing things differently. Their lenses reinforced particular understandings.

4. These norms emerge from widely accepted views of who the leader is, what he or she is supposed to "do" within the organization, and the types of practices that are more effective than others. To be certain, the notion of best practices within our field has taken on a particular life of its own—engendering behavioral and organizational norms that are often prescriptive in nature.

5. The strength or relevance of the traditional perspective is not at issue here; traditional methods have proven their productiveness. However, as Apple (1996) notes, the usefulness of theories depends "on the *work* they enable us to do" (p. 20, emphasis in original).

6. For a more detailed discussion of these three concepts, see Harding (1987) and Pillow (2003).

7. Lugg (2003b) defines sexual orientation as the sexual object of choice, or the sex of the person with whom one falls in love. Sexual orientation may or may not be related to sexual activity, although modern culture often conflates this distinction (Sedgwick, 1990).

8. *Sex* is a biological category that is often defined in chromosomal terms: females having an XX chromosomal makeup and males having an XY chromosomal makeup (Sedgwick, 1990). This, however, does not suggest that sex is necessarily dichotomous or irreducible because biological variations in individuals are both common and widespread (Lugg, 2003b). *Sexuality* is the "array of acts, expectations, narratives, pleasures, identity formations, and knowledges, in both women and men, that tend to cluster most densely around certain genital sensations but is not adequately defined by them" (Sedgwick, 1990, p. 29). In effect, sexuality may or may not be related to sexual activity or to chromosomal sex. *Gender* is a complex set of roles and behaviors that constitute male and female identities. It is socially constructed, meaning that those roles and behaviors are defined by culture, tradition, race, ethnicity, and societal norms (Blount, 1998, 1999; Butler, 1990; Sedgwick, 1990).

9. The French poststructuralist movement was itself heavily influenced by the structuralist underpinnings of Marx, Nietzsche, Sartre, Sasurre, and Levi-Strauss, who collectively sought to identify how societal structures "create" the individual by shaping a person's understanding, meaning, relationships, and knowledge of the world. In effect, structuralism argued that one was not "free" to think outside of societal structures because the structures themselves framed an individual's existence and worldview. Whereas Marxism placed more emphasis on the economic superstructure as a dominant organizing force, linguistic structuralists such as Levi-Strauss believed that language systems were more important in shaping human thought because everything with/in the world was signified in (and through) language and, therefore, imbued with a specific meaning.

REFERENCES

Adams, D. (1991). Planning models and paradigms. In R. V. Carlson & G. Awkerman (Eds.), *Educational planning: Concepts, strategies, and practices* (pp. 5–20). New York: Longman.

Adams, N. (1997). Toward a curriculum of resiliency: Gender, race, adolescence, and schooling. In C. Marshall (Ed.), *Feminist critical policy analysis: A perspective from primary and secondary schooling* (pp. 153–164). London: Falmer Press.

Allen, K., Jacobson, S., & Lomotey, K. (1995). African American women in educational administration: The importance of mentors and sponsors. *Journal of Negro Education, 64,* 409–422.

Anderson, G. L. (1990). Toward a critical constructivist approach to school administration: Invisibility, legitimation, and the study of non-events. *Educational Administration Quarterly, 26*(1), 38–59.

Anderson, G. L. (2001). Disciplining leaders: A critical discourse analysis of the ISLLC national examination and performance standards in educational administration. *International Journal of Leadership in Education, 4*(3), 199–216.

Anderson, G. L., Creighton, T., Dantley, M., English, F., Furman, G., Gronn, P., & Marshall, C. (2002). *Invited commentary: Problematizing the ISLLC standards and exam* [online]. Retrieved from http://www.aera.net/divisions/a/anews/spring02.htm

Anderson, G. L., & Grinberg, J. (1998). Educational administration as a disciplinary practice: Appropriating Foucault's use of power, discourse, and method. *Educational Administration Quarterly, 34*(3), 329–353.

Ansley, F. L. (1989). Stirring the ashes: Race, class, and the future of civil rights scholarship. *Cornell Law Review, 74,* 993.

Apple, M. (1996). *Cultural politics and education.* New York: Teachers College Press.

Bakhtin, M. M. (1968). *Rabelais and his world* (H. Isowolsky, Trans.). Cambridge: MIT Press.

Ball, S. (1994). *Education reform: A critical and poststructural approach.* Buckingham, UK: Open University Press.

Banks, J. A. (1993). The canon debate, knowledge construction, and multicultural education. *Educational Researcher, 22*(5), 4–14.

Belenky, M., Clinchy, B., Goldberger, N., & Tarule, J. (1986). *Women's ways of knowing: The development of self, voice and mind.* New York: Basic Books.

Bell, D. A. (1987). *And we are not saved: The elusive quest for racial justice.* New York: Basic Books.

Bell, D. A. (1995). Racial realism after we're gone: Prudent speculations on America in a post-racial epoch. In R. Delgado (Ed.), *Critical race theory: The cutting edge* (pp. 2–8). Philadelphia: Temple University Press.

Benhabib, S. (1990). Epistemologies of postmodernism: A rejoinder to Jean-Francois Lyotard. In L. Nicholson (Ed.), *Feminism/postmodernism* (pp. 107–132). New York: Routledge.

Bernstein, R. J. (1993). *The new constellation: The ethical-political horizons of modernity/postmodernity.* Cambridge, UK: Polity Press.

Bishop, R. (1998). Freeing ourselves from neo-colonial domination in research: A Maori approach to creating knowledge. *International Journal of Qualitative Studies in Education, 11*(2), 199–219.

Blount, J. M. (1998). *Destined to rule the schools: Women and the superintendency, 1873–1995.* Albany: SUNY Press.

Blount, J. M. (1999). Manliness and the construction of men's and women's work in schools, 1865–1941. *International Journal of Leadership in Education, 2*(2), 55–68.

Blount, J. M. (2003). Homosexuality and school superintendents: A brief history. *Journal of School Leadership, 13*(1), 7–26.

Britzman, D. (1991). *Practice makes practice: A critical study of learning to teach.* Albany: SUNY Press.

Britzman, D. (1995). Is there a queer pedagogy? Or, stop reading straight. *Educational Theory, 45*(2), 151–165.

Britzman, D. (1997). The tangles of implication. *Qualitative Studies in Education, 10*(1), 31–37.

Brunner, C. (1999). *Sacred dreams: Women in the superintendency.* Albany: SUNY Press.

Brunner, C. (2000a). *Principles of power: Women superintendents and the riddle of the heart.* Albany: SUNY Press.

Brunner, C. (2000b). Unsettled moments in settled discourse: Women superintendent's experiences of inequality. *Educational Administration Quarterly, 36*(1), 76–116.

Brunner, C. (2002). A proposition for the reconception of the superintendency: Reconsidering traditional and nontraditional discourse. *Educational Administration Quarterly, 38*(3), 402–431.

Burell, G., & Morgan, G. (1979). *Sociological paradigms and organizational analysis.* London: Heinemann.

Butler, J. (1990). *Gender trouble: Feminism and the subversion of identity.* New York: Routledge.

Callahan, R. E. (1962). *Education and the cult of efficiency: A study of the social forces that have shaped the administration of the public schools.* Chicago: University of Chicago Press.

Campbell, R. F., Fleming, T., Newell, L. J., & Bennion, J. W. (1987). *A history of thought and practice in educational administration.* New York: Teachers College Press.

Capper, C. A. (1999). (Homo)sexualities, organizations, and administration: Possibilities for in (queer)y. *Educational Researcher, 28*(5), 4–11.

Capper, C. A., Hafner, M. M., & Keyes, M. W. (2002). The role of community in spirituality-centered leadership for justice. In G. Furman (Ed.), *School as community: From promise to practice* (pp. 77–94). Albany: SUNY Press.

Chodorow, N. (1989). Feminism and psychoanalytic theory. New Haven, CT: Yale University Press.

Collins, P. H. (1991). *Black feminist thought: Knowledge, consciousness, and the politics of empowerment.* New York: Routledge.

Collins, P. (1995). Black women and motherhood. In V. Held (Ed.), *Justice and care* (pp. 117-135). New York: Teachers College Press.

Crenshaw, K., Gotanda, N., Peller, G., & Thomas, K. (Eds.). (1995). *Critical race theory: The key writings that formed the movement.* New York: New York Press.

Culbertson, J. A. (1988). A century's quest for a knowledge base. In N. J. Boyan (Ed.), *Handbook of research on educational administration* (pp. 3–26). New York: Longham.

Dantley, M. E. (2003). Critical spirituality: Enhancing transformative leadership through critical theory and African American prophetic spirituality. *International Journal of Leadership in Education, 6,* 1–15.

Davies, B. (1994). *Poststructuralist theory and classroom practice.* Geelong, Victoria: Deakin University.

Delgado, R. (Ed.). (1995a). *Critical race theory: The cutting edge.* Philadelphia: Temple University Press.

Delgado, R. (1995b). Legal storytelling: Storytelling for oppositionists and others: A plea for narrative. In R. Delgado (Ed.), *Critical race theory: The cutting edge* (pp. 64–74). Philadelphia: Temple University Press.

Delgado, R. (1995c). Rodrigo's chronicle. In R. Delgado (Ed.), *Critical race theory: The cutting edge* (pp. 346–354). Philadelphia: Temple University Press.

Delgado, R., & Stefancic, J. (2001). *Critical race theory: An introduction.* New York: New York University Press.

Delgado Bernal, D. (1998). Using a Chicana feminist epistemology in educational research. *Harvard Educational Review, 68*(4), 555–579.

Delgado Bernal, D. (2002). Critical race theory, Latino critical theory, and critical race-gendered epistemologies: Recognizing students of color as holders and creators of knowledge. *Qualitative Inquiry, 8*(1), 105–126.

Denzin, N., & Lincoln, Y. (Eds.). (1994). *Handbook of qualitative research.* Thousand Oaks, CA: Sage.

Derrida, J. (1974). *Of grammatology* (G. C. Spivak, Trans.). Baltimore, MD: Johns Hopkins University Press. (Original work published 1967)

Dillard, C. (2000). The substance of things hoped for, the evidence of things not seen: Examining an endarkened feminist epistemology in educational research and leadership. *Qualitative Studies in Education, 13*(6), 661–681.

Dilley, P. (1999). Queer theory: Under construction. *Qualitative Studies in Education, 12*(5), 457–472.

Donmoyer, R. (1999). The continuing quest for a knowledge base: 1976–1998. In J. Murphy & K. S. Louis (Eds.), *Handbook of research on educational administration* (2nd ed., pp. 23–44). San Francisco: Jossey-Bass.

Donmoyer, R., Imber, M., & Scheurich, J. J. (Eds.). (1995). *The knowledge base in educational administration: Critical perspectives.* Albany: SUNY Press.

Dunbar, C. (1999). Three short stories. *Qualitative Inquiry, 5*(1), 130–140.

Dunbar, C. (2001). *Does anyone know we're here? Alternative schooling for African American youth.* New York: Peter Lang.

Ellsworth, E. (1997). *Teaching positions: Difference, pedagogy, and the power of address.* New York: Teachers College Press.

English, F. W. (2000a). A critical interrogation of Murphy's call for a new center of gravity in educational administration. *Journal of School Leadership, 10*(5), 445–463.

English, F. W. (2000b). Psssst: What does one call a set of non-empirical beliefs required to be accepted on faith and enforced by authority?

[Answer: A religion, aka the ISLLC standards]. *International Journal of Leadership in Education, 3*(2), 159–167.

English, F. W. (2002a). Cookie-cutter leaders for cookie-cutter schools: The teleology of standardization and the de-legitimization of the university in educational leadership preparation. *Leadership and Policy in Schools, 2*(1), 27–46.

English, F. W. (2002b, October). *The ELCC standards: The teleology of standardization and the fundamental threat to the professoriate and academic freedom.* Paper presented at the Annual Meeting of the University Council for Educational Administration, Pittsburgh, PA.

English, F. W. (2003). *The postmodern challenge to the theory and practice of educational administration.* Springfield, IL: Charles C Thomas.

Evers, C. W., & Lakomski, G. (1991). *Knowing educational administration: Contemporary methodological controversies in educational administration research.* Oxford, UK: Pergamon Press.

Evers, C. W., & Lakomski, G. (1996). Science in educational administration: A postpositivist conception. *Educational Administration Quarterly, 32*(3), 379–402.

Ferguson, K. E. (1984). *The feminist case against bureaucracy.* Philadelphia: Temple University Press.

Fine, M. (1996). Preface. In D. Kelly & J. Gaskell (Eds.), *Debating dropouts: Critical policy and research perspectives on school learning* (pp. xi-xviii). New York: Teachers College Press.

Flax, J. (1990a). Postmodernism and gender relations in feminist theory. In L. Nicholson (Ed.), *Feminism/postmodernism* (pp. 39–62). New York: Routledge.

Flax, J. (1990b). *Thinking fragments: Psychoanalysis, feminism, and postmodernism in the contemporary West.* Berkeley: University of California Press.

Forester, J. (1993). *Critical theory, public policy, and planning practice: Toward a critical pragmatism.* Albany: SUNY Press.

Foster, M. (1993). Educating for competence in community and culture: Exploring the views of exemplary African American teachers. *Urban Education, 27*(4), 370–394.

Foster, M. (1997). *Black teachers on teaching.* New York: The New Press.

Foucault, M. (1970). *The order of things: An archaeology of the human sciences.* New York: Vintage Books.

Foucault, M. (1972). *The archaeology of knowledge* (A. M. Sheridan Smith, Trans.). New York: Pantheon Books.

Foucault, M. (1977). *Discipline & punish: The birth of the prison* (A. Sheridan, Trans.). New York: Pantheon.

Foucault, M. (1980). *Power/knowledge: Selected interviews and other writings by Michel Foucault, 1972–1977* (C. Gordon, Ed.). New York: Pantheon.

Fraynd, D. J., & Capper, C. A. (2003). "Do you have any idea who you just hired?" A study of open and closeted sexual minority K–12 administrators. *Journal of School Leadership, 13*(1), 86–124.

Gilligan, C. (1993). *In a different voice: Psychological theory and women's development.* Cambridge, MA: Harvard University Press.

Gordon, E. W. (1990). The necessity of African American epistemology for educational theory and practice. *Journal of Education, 172*(3), 88–106.

Gordon, E. W., Miller, F., & Rollock, D. (1990). Coping with communicentric bias in knowledge production in the social sciences. *Educational Researcher, 19*(3), 14–19.

Griffiths, D. (1988). Administrative theory. In N. Boyan (Ed.), *The handbook of research on educational administration* (1st ed., pp. 27–52). New York: Longman.

Grogan, M. (1996). *Voices of women aspiring to the superintendency.* Albany: SUNY Press.

Grogan, M. (2003). Laying the groundwork for a reconception of the superintendency from feminist postmodern perspectives. In M. D. Young & L. Skrla (Eds.), *Reconsidering feminist research in educational leadership* (pp. 9–34). New York: SUNY Press.

Halperin, D. (1995). *Saint Foucault: Towards a gay hagiography.* London: Oxford University Press.

Hamilton, D. N. (1991). An alternative to rational planning models. In R. V. Carlson & G. Awkerman (Eds.), *Educational planning: Concepts, strategies, and practices* (pp. 21–47). New York: Longman.

Haraway, D. (1990). A manifesto for cyborgs: Science, technology, and socialist feminism in the 1980s. In L. Nicholson (Ed.), *Feminism/postmodernism* (pp. 190–233). New York: Routledge.

Harding, S. (1987). *Feminism & methodology.* Bloomington: Indiana University Press.

Hartsock, N. (1985). *Money sex, and power.* Boston: Northeastern University Press.

Heck, R. H., & Hallinger, P. (1999). Next generation methods for the study of leadership and school improvement. In J. Murphy & K. Seashore Louis (Eds.), *Handbook of research on educational administration* (2nd ed., pp. 141–162). San Francisco: Jossey-Bass.

Henry, A. (1998). *Taking back control: African Canadian women teacher's lives and practice.* Albany: SUNY Press.

Hermes, M. (1998). Research methods as a situated response: Towards a First Nations methodology. *Qualitative Studies in Education, 13*(4), 155–168.

Honeychurch, K. G. (1996). Researching dissident subjectivities: Queering the grounds of theory and practice. *Harvard Educational Review, 66*(2), 339–355.

Hoy, W. K. (1996). Science and theory in the practice of educational administration: A pragmatic perspective. *Educational Administration Quarterly, 32*(3), 366–378.

Hoy, W. K., & Miskel, C. G. (1996). *Educational administration: Theory, research, and practice* (5th ed.). New York: McGraw-Hill.

Iglesias, E. M. (1998). Maternal power and the deconstruction of male supremacy. In R. Delgado & J. Stefancic (Eds.), *The Latina/o condition: A critical reader* (pp. 508–515). New York: New York University Press.

Johnson, K. (1998). Citizens as foreigners. In R. Delgado & J. Stefancic (Eds.), *The Latina/o condition: A critical reader* (pp. 198–201). New York: New York University Press.

Johnson, K. (2002). Race and the immigration laws: The need for critical inquiry. In F. Valdés, J. M. Culp, & A. P. Harris (Eds.), *Crossroads, directions, and a new critical race theory* (pp. 187–198). Philadelphia: Temple University Press.

Katz, J. N. (1995). *The invention of heterosexuality.* New York: Dutton.

King, J. R. (1999). Am not! Are too! Using queer standpoint in postmodern critical ethnography. *Qualitative Studies in Education, 12*(5), 473–490.

Kingdon, J. W. (1995). *Agendas, alternatives, and public policies.* New York: Harper Collins.

Koschoreck, J. W. (2003). Easing the violence: Transgressing heteronormativity in educational administration. *Journal of School Leadership, 13*(1), 27–50.

Kuhn, T. (1970). *The structure of scientific revolutions.* Chicago: University of Chicago Press.

Ladson-Billings, G. (1999). Just what is critical race theory and what's it doing in a nice field like education? In L. Parker, D. Deyhle, & S. Villenas (Eds.), *Race is . . . race isn't: Critical race theory and qualitative studies in education* (pp. 7–30). Boulder, CO: Westview Press.

Ladson-Billings, G. (2000). Racialized discourses and ethnic epistemologies. In N. Denzin & Y. Lincoln (Eds.), *Handbook of qualitative research* (2nd ed., pp. 257–277). Thousand Oaks, CA: Sage.

Ladson-Billings, G., & Tate, W. F. (1995). Toward a critical race theory of education. *Teachers College Record, 97,* 47–68.

Laible, J., & Harrington, S. (1998). Leaders with alternative values. *International Journal of Leadership in Education, 1,* 111–135.

Larson, C. (1997). Is the land of Oz an alien nation? A sociopolitical study of school community conflict. *Educational Administration Quarterly, 33*(3), 312–350.

Lather, P. (1992). Critical frames in educational research: Feminist and post-structural perspectives. *Theory into Practice, 31*(2), 87–99.

Lather, P. (1996). Troubling clarity: The politics of accessible language. *Harvard Educational Review, 66*(3), 525–545.

Lincoln, Y. L., & Guba, E. G. (1985). *Naturalistic inquiry.* Beverly Hills, CA: Sage.

Lomotey, K. (1989). *African American principals: School leadership and success.* New York: Greenwood Press.

Lomotey, K. (1995). Social and cultural influences in schooling: A commentary of the UCEA knowledge base project, Domain I. *Educational Administration Quarterly, 31,* 294–303.

López, G. R. (2003a). Parent involvement as racialized performance. In G. R. López & L. Parker (Eds.), *Interrogating racism in qualitative research methodology* (pp. 71–96). New York: Peter Lang.

López, G. R. (2003b). The (racially neutral) politics of education: A critical race theory perspective. *Educational Administration Quarterly, 39*(1), 68–94.

López, G. R., & Parker, L. (Eds.). (2003). *Interrogating racism in qualitative research methodology.* New York: Peter Lang.

Lugg, C. A. (2003a). Our straightlaced administrators: The law, lesbian, gay, bisexual, and transgendered educational administrators, and the assimilationist imperative. *Journal of School Leadership, 13*(1), 51–83.

Lugg, C. A. (2003b). Sissies, faggots, lezzies, and dykes: Gender, sexual orientation, and a new politics of education? *Educational Administration Quarterly, 39*(1), 95–134.

Lugg, C. A., & Koschoreck, J. W. (Eds.). (2003). The final closet: Lesbian, gay, bisexual, and transgendered educational leaders [Special issue]. *Journal of School Leadership, 13*(1).

Luna, G. T. (2001). La causa Chicana and communicative praxis. *Denver University Law Review, 78*(4), 553–573.

Marable, M. (1992). *Black America: Multicultural democracy in the age of Clarence Thomas and David Duke.* Westfield, NJ: Open Media.

Marshall, C. (1993). *The new politics of race and gender: The 1992 yearbook of the Politics of Education Association.* Washington, DC: Falmer Press.

Marshall, C. (1997). Dismantling and reconstructing policy analysis. In C. Marshall (Ed.), *Feminist critical policy analysis: A perspective from primary and secondary schooling* (pp. 1–39). London: Falmer Press.

Matsuda, M. J. (1996). *Where is your body? And other essays on race, gender, and the law.* Boston: Beacon Press.

Matsuda, M. J., Lawrence, C. R., Delgado, R., & Crenshaw, C. W. (1993). *Words that wound: Critical race theory, assaultive speech, and the First Amendment.* Boulder, CO: Westview Press.

Méndez-Morse, S. (2003). Chicana feminism and educational leadership. In M. D. Young & L. Skrla (Eds.), *Reconsidering feminist research in educational leadership* (pp. 161–179). New York: SUNY Press.

Montoya, M. E. (2000). Máscaras, trenzas, y greñas: Un/masking the self while un/braiding Latina stories and legal discourse. In R. Delgado & J. Stefancic (Eds.), *Critical race theory: The cutting edge* (2nd ed., pp. 514–524). Philadelphia: Temple University Press.

Murphy, J. (2000). Commentary: A response. *International Journal of Leadership in Education, 3*(4), 411–414.

Murphy, J. (2002). *Invited commentary: The ISLLC standards at work* [online]. Retrieved from http://www.aera.net/divisions/a/anews/winter02.htm

Murphy, J., & Shipman, N. (2002). The interstate school leaders licensure consortium (ISLLC) story: A brief narrative. In K. Hessel & J. Holloway (Eds.), *A framework for school leaders: Linking the ISLLC standards to practice.* Princeton, NJ: Educational Testing Service.

Murphy, J., Yff, J., & Shipman, N. (2000). Implementation of the interstate school leaders licensure consortium standards. *International Journal of Leadership in Education, 3*(1), 17–39.

Nagel, S. S. (1984). *Contemporary public policy analysis.* Birmingham: University of Alabama Press.

Nicholson, L. (1990). Introduction. In L. Nicholson (Ed.), *Feminism/postmodernism* (pp. 1–16). New York: Routledge.

Oliva, M. (2000, April). *Bakhtin.* Paper presented at the Annual Meeting of the American Educational Research Association, Montreal, Canada.

Ortiz, F., & Marshall, C. (1988). Women in educational administration. In N. Boyan (Ed.), *Handbook of research on educational administration* (pp. 123–141). New York: Longman.

Ortiz, F. I., & Ortiz, D. J. (1995). How gender and ethnicity interact in the practice of educational administration: The case of Hispanic female superintendents. In R. Donmoyer, M. Imber, & J. J. Scheurich (Eds.), *The knowledge base in educational administration: Multiple perspectives* (pp. 158-173). Albany: SUNY Press.

Pabón López, M. (2001). The phoenix rises from El Cenizo: A community creates and affirms Latino/a border cultural citizenship through its language and safe haven ordinances. *Denver University Law Review, 78*(4), 1017–1048.

Parker, L. (1998). Race is . . . Race ain't: An exploration of the utility of critical race theory in qualitative research in education. *Qualitative Studies in Education, 11*(1), 43–55.

Parker, L. (2003). Critical race theory and its implications for methodology and policy analysis in higher education desegregation. In G. R. López & Parker L. (Eds.), *Interrogating racism in qualitative research methodology.* New York: Peter Lang.

Parker, L., Deyhle, D., & Villenas, S. (Eds.). (1999). *Race is . . . race isn't: Critical race theory and qualitative studies in education.* Boulder, CO: Westview Press.

Parker, L., & Lynn, M. (2002). What's race got to do with it? Critical race theory's conflicts with and connections to qualitative research methodology and epistemology. *Qualitative Inquiry, 8*(1), 7–22.

Parker, L., & Shapiro, J. P. (1992). Where is the discussion of diversity in educational administration programs? Graduate student voices addressing an omission in their preparation. *Journal of School Leadership, 2*(1), 7–33.

Perea, J. F. (1992). Demography and distrust: An essay on American languages, cultural pluralism, and official English. *Minnesota Law Review, 77,* 285–286.

Peters, M. (1996). *Poststructuralism, politics, and education.* Westport, CT: Bergin & Garvey.

Pillow, W. S. (1997). Decentering silences/ Troubling irony: Teen pregnancy's challenge to policy analysis. In C. Marshall (Ed.), *Feminist critical policy analysis: A perspective from primary and secondary schooling* (pp. 134–152). London: Falmer Press.

Pillow, W. S. (2000). Exposed methodology: The body as a deconstructive practice. In E. St. Pierre & W. S. Pillow (Eds.), *Working the ruins: Feminist poststructural research and practice in education* (pp. 199–219). New York: Routledge.

Pillow, W. S. (2002). When a man does feminism should he dress in drag? *Qualitative Studies in Education, 15*(5), 545–554.

Pillow, W. S. (2003). Race-based methodologies: Multicultural methods or epistemological shifts. In G. R. López & L. Parker (Eds.), *Interrogating racism in qualitative research methodology* (pp. 181–202). New York: Peter Lang.

Pinar, W. F. (Ed.). (1998). *Queer theory in education.* Mahwah, NJ: Lawrence Erlbaum.

Popkewitz, T. S., & Brennan, M. (1998). Restructuring of social and political theory in education: Foucault and a social epistemology of school practices. In T. S. Popkewitz & M. Brennan (Eds.), *Foucault's challenge: Discourse, knowledge, and power in education* (pp. 3-35). New York: Teachers College Press.

Powell, J. A. (1993). Race and poverty: A new focus for legal services. *Clearinghouse Review, 20,* 299.

Rains, F. V., Archibald, J. A., & Deyhle, D. (Eds.). (2000). Through our eyes and in our own words: The voices of indigenous scholars [Special issue]. *Qualitative Studies in Education, 13*(4).

Reyes, P., Velez, W., & Peña, R. (1993). School reform: Introducing race, culture, and ethnicity into the discourse. In C. Capper (Ed.), *Educational administration in a pluralistic society* (pp. 66–85). Albany: SUNY Press.

Rizvi, F. (1993). Race, gender, and the cultural assumptions of schooling. In C. Marshall (Ed.), *The new politics of race and gender: The 1992 yearbook of the Politics of Education Association* (pp. 203–217). Washington, DC: Falmer Press.

St. Pierre, E. (1997). Nomadic inquiry in the smooth spaces of the field: A preface. *Qualitative Studies in Education, 10*(3), 363–383.

St. Pierre, E. (2000). Poststructural feminism in education: An overview. *Qualitative Studies in Education, 13*(5), 477–515.

St. Pierre, E., & Pillow, W. S. (Eds.). (2000). *Working the ruins: Feminist poststructural research and practice in education.* New York: Routledge.

Sarup, M. (1988). *An introductory guide to poststructuralism and postmodernism.* New York: Harvester Wheatsheaf.

Scheurich, J. J. (1994). Policy archaeology: A new policy studies methodology. *Journal of Education Policy, 9*(4), 297–316.

Scheurich, J. J., & Skrla, L. (2003). *Leadership for equity and excellence: Creating high-achievement classrooms, schools, and districts.* Thousand Oaks, CA: Corwin.

Scheurich, J. J., & Young, M. D. (1997). Coloring epistemologies: Are our research epistemologies racially biased? *Educational Researcher, 26*(4), 4–17.

Scheurich, J. J., & Young, M. D. (1998). In the United States of America, in both our souls and our sciences, we are avoiding white racism. *Educational Researcher, 27*(9), 27–32.

Schneider, J. (2002). NCATE accepts NPBEA standards for educational leadership programs. *UCEA Review, 43*(2), 7–8.

Scott, J. (1986). Gender: A useful category of historical analysis. *American Historical Review, 91,* 1053–1075.

Sedgwick. E. K. (1990). *Epistemology of the closet.* Berkeley: University of California Press.

Shakeshaft, C. (1989). *Women in educational administration.* Newbury Park, CA: Sage.

Shakeshaft, C. (1999). The struggle to create a more gender inclusive profession. In J. Murphy & K. Seashore Louis (Eds.), *Handbook of research on educational administration* (2nd ed., pp. 99–118). San Francisco: Jossey-Bass.

Sirotnik, K. A., & Oakes, J. (1986). Critical inquiry for school renewal: Liberating theory and practice. In K. A. Sirotnik & J. Oakes (Eds.), *Critical perspectives on the organization and improvement of schooling* (pp. 3–93). Boston: Kluwer Nijhoff.

Skrla, L. (2000). Mourning silence: Women superintendents (and a researcher) rethink speaking up and speaking out. *Qualitative Studies in Education, 13,* 611–628.

Skrla, L. (2003). Normalizing femininity: Reconsidering research on women in the superintendency. In M. D. Young & L. Skrla (Eds.), *Reconsidering feminist research in educational leadership* (pp. 247–264). New York: SUNY Press.

Skrla, L., Reyes, P., & Scheurich, J. J. (2000). Sexism, silence, and solutions: Women superintendents speak up and speak out. *Educational Administration Quarterly, 36*(1), 44–75.

Sleeter, C. E. (1992). *Keepers of the American dream.* London: Falmer Press.

Sleeter, C. E., & Grant, C. A. (1987). An analysis of multicultural education in the USA. *Harvard Educational Review, 57,* 421–444.

Sleeter, C. E., & Grant, C. A. (1999). *Making choices for multicultural education: Five approaches to race, class, and gender.* Columbus, OH: Merrill.

Smith-Maddox, R., & Solorzano, D. G. (2002). Using critical race theory, Paulo Freire's problem posing method, and case study research to confront race and racism in education. *Qualitative Inquiry, 8*(1), 66–84.

Solorzano, D. G. (1997). Images and words that wound: Critical race theory, racial stereotyping, and teacher education. *Teacher Education Quarterly, 24*(3), 5–19.

Solorzano, D. G. (1998). Critical race theory, racial and gender microaggressions, and the experience of Chicana and Chicano scholars. *Qualitative Studies in Education, 11*(1), 121–136.

Solorzano, D. G., & Delgado Bernal, D. (2001). Examining transformational resistance through a critical race and LatCrit theory framework: Chicana and Chicano students in an urban context. *Urban Education, 36*(3), 308–342.

Solorzano, D., & Villalpando, O. (1998). Critical race theory, marginality, and the experience of minority students in higher education. In C. Torres & T. Mitchell (Eds.), *Emerging issues in the sociology of education: Comparative perspectives* (pp. 211–224). Albany: SUNY Press.

Solorzano, D. G., & Yosso, T. J. (2001). Critical race and LatCrit theory and method: Counterstorytelling Chicana and Chicano graduate school experiences. *Qualitative Studies in Education, 14*(4), 471–495.

Solorzano, D. G., & Yosso, T. J. (2002). Critical race methodology: Counterstorytelling as an analytic framework for educational research. *Qualitative Inquiry, 8*(1), 23–44.

Stanfield, J. (1985). The ethnocentric basis of social science knowledge production. *Review of Research in Education, 12,* 387–415.

Stanfield, J. (1993). Epistemological considerations. In J. Stanfield & R. Dennis (Eds.), *Race and ethnicity in research methods* (pp. 16–36). Newbury Park, CA: Sage.

Stanfield, J. (1994). Ethnic modeling in qualitative research. In N. Denzin & E. Lincoln (Eds.), *Handbook of qualitative research* (pp. 175–188). Newbury Park, CA: Sage.

Tallerico, M. (1997). Gender and school administration. In B. Bank & P. Hall (Eds.), *Gender, equity, and schooling* (pp. 187–210). New York: Garland.

Tallerico, M. (2000a). *Accessing the superintendency: The unwritten rules.* Thousand Oaks, CA: Corwin.

Tallerico, M. (2000b). Gaining access to the superintendency: Headhunting, gender, and color. *Educational Administration Quarterly, 36*(1), 18–43.

Tate, W. F. (1997). Critical race theory: History, theory, and implications. *Review of Research in Education, 22,* 195–247.

Tatum, B. D. (1992). Talking about race, learning about racism: The application of racial identity development theory in the classroom. *Harvard Educational Review, 62*(1), 1–24.

Tatum, B. D. (1997). *"Why are all the black kids sitting together in the cafeteria?" And other conversations about race.* New York: Basic Books.

Thompson, C. M., & Johnson, R. A. (2000). *The congruent life: Following the inward path to fulfilling work and inspired leadership.* San Francisco: Jossey-Bass.

Tierney, W. G. (1997). *Academic outlaws: Queer theory and cultural studies in the academy.* Thousand Oaks, CA: Sage.

Tierney, W. G. (1999). Praxis at the millennium: Epistemological authority, voice, and qualitative research. *Qualitative Studies in Education, 12*(5), 451–457.

Tierney, W. G., & Dilley, P. (1998). Constructing knowledge: Educational research and gay and lesbian studies. In W. F. Pinar (Ed.), *Queer theory in education* (pp. 49–71). Mahwah, NJ: Lawrence Erlbaum.

Tierney, W. G., & Lincoln, Y. S. (1997). Introduction: Explorations and discoveries. In W. G. Tierney & Y. S. Lincoln (Eds.), *Representation and the text: Re-framing narrative voice.* Albany: SUNY Press.

Tillman, L. C. (2002). Culturally sensitive research approaches: An African American perspective. *Educational Researcher, 31*(9), 3–12.

Trujillo, C. (Ed.). (1998). *Living Chicana theory.* Berkeley, CA: Third Women Press.

Tyson, C. (1998). Coloring epistemologies: A response. *Educational Researcher, 27*(9), 21–22.

Valdés, F. (1998). Notes on the conflation of sex, gender, and sexual orientation: A queercrit and Latcrit perspective. In R. Delgado & J. Stefancic (Eds.), *The Latina/o condition:*

A critical reader (pp. 543–551). New York: New York University Press.

Valdés, F. (2000). Sex and race in queer legal culture: Ruminations on identities and interconnectivities. In R. Delgado & J. Stefancic (Eds.), *Critical race theory: The cutting edge* (2nd ed., pp. 334–339). Philadelphia: Temple University Press.

Valdés, F. (2002). Outsider scholars, critical race theory, and "outcrit" perspectivity: Post-subordination vision as jurisprudential method. In F. Valdés, J. M. Culp, & A. P. Harris (Eds.), *Crossroads, directions, and a new critical race theory* (pp. 399–409). Philadelphia: Temple University Press.

Valdés, F., Culp, J. M., & Harris, A. P. (Eds.). (2002). *Crossroads, directions, and a new critical race theory.* Philadelphia: Temple University Press.

Villalpando, O., & Delgado Bernal, D. (2002). A critical theory analysis of barriers that impede the success of faculty of color. In W. Smith, P. Altbach, & K. Lomotey (Eds.), *The racial crisis in American higher education* (2nd ed.). Albany: SUNY Press.

Villenas, S. (1996). The colonizer/colonized Chicana ethnographer: Identity, marginalization, and co-optation in the field. *Harvard Educational Review, 66,* 711–731.

Villenas, S. (2000). This ethnography called my back: Writings of the exotic gaze, "othering" Latina, and recuperating Xicanisma. In E. St. Pierre & W. S. Pillow (Eds.), *Working the ruins: Feminist poststructural research and practice in education* (pp. 74–95). New York: Routledge.

Weedon, C. (1997). *Feminist practice and poststructuralist theory* (2nd ed.). New York: Basil Blackwell.

Williams, P. J. (1995). *The alchemy of race and rights: Diary of a law professor.* Cambridge, MA: Harvard University Press.

Willower, D. J. (1975). Theory in educational administration. *Journal of Educational Administration, 13,* 77–91.

Willower, D. J. (1994). *Educational administration: Inquiry, values, practice.* Lancaster, PA: Technomic.

Willower, D. J. (1996). Inquiry in educational administration and the spirit of the times. *Educational Administration Quarterly, 32*(3), 344–365.

Willower, D. J., & Forsyth, P. B. (1999). A brief history of scholarship on educational administration. In J. Murphy & K. S. Louis (Eds.), *Handbook of research on educational administration* (2nd ed., pp. 1–23). San Francisco: Jossey-Bass.

Wolcott, H. F. (1995). *The art of fieldwork.* Walnut Creek, CA: AltaMira Press.

Young, M. D. (1999). Multifocal educational policy research: Toward a method for enhancing traditional educational policy studies. *American Educational Research Journal, 36*(4), 677–714.

Young, M. D. (2003). Troubling policy discourse: Gender, constructions, and the leadership crisis. In M. D. Young & L. Skrla (Eds.), *Reconsidering feminist research in educational leadership* (pp. 202-231). New York: SUNY Press.

Young, M. D., & Laible, J. (2000). White racism, antiracism, and school leadership preparation. *Journal of School Leadership, 10*(5), 374–415.

Young, M. D., & Rosiek, J. (2000). Interrogating whiteness. *Educational Researcher, 29*(2), 39–44.

15

The Development of Leadership
Thought and Practice in the United States

GARY M. CROW
University of Utah

MARGARET GROGAN
University of Missouri–Columbia

INTRODUCTION AND OVERVIEW

Leadership is one of the most discussed, examined, and yet elusive ideas in the social sciences in general and educational leadership in particular (Bennis & Nanis, 1986). In spite of the innumerable definitions of leadership and claims made about it, we continue to seek greater understanding in both theory and practice. The history of leadership thought is itself a complicated and treacherous journey that has implications not only for how we understand the meaning of leadership but for what definitions and claims about leadership are regarded as appropriate, valued, and honored.

In this chapter, we call into question the traditional ways the history of leadership thought and practice has been formulated and expressed, and we seek to broaden and enrich perspectives on leadership history. We begin with a critique of these traditional accounts of the history of leadership. Our purpose is neither to present these accounts—they are well known to any leadership student—nor to provide an exhaustive report of the development of leadership thought. Rather, we will present some of the features of these historical accounts and identify some weaknesses. Following this critique, we will identify several sources of leadership thought and practice that have been ignored in the traditional accounts and explore their value for understanding and practicing leadership. A comprehensive discussion of all those sources that have been ignored would be impossible. However, by offering a few examples of some of these sources, we hope to stimulate discussion of how leadership thought could benefit from other sources. We end the chapter with a discussion of the implications for changing the way we describe the history of leadership theory for research, practice, and preparation.

A CRITIQUE OF THE HISTORY OF LEADERSHIP THOUGHT

Probably every student of educational leadership can recite the traditional account of the development of leadership thought. Although these stories vary slightly, they tend to reflect the same progression. Beginning with trait theory, they move to behavioral theory and contingency theory, then continue with excellence and transformational theories. This history is influenced by another account originating in the industrial psychology and management literature, namely, scientific management, human relations, and social science theories (Getzels, 1977).

These traditional accounts have several features. First, as we mentioned previously, they are influenced strongly by the industrial psychology and management literature. In addition, sociology, political science, and other social sciences have contributed to leadership thought. The humanities, including arts, literature, and philosophy, have played a very minor role, if any, in these accounts. Because of this, aspects of leadership such as aesthetic and ethical dimensions have been largely ignored in the traditional U.S. history of leadership thought. Second, the traditional accounts are chronicled in a way that suggests linear progression toward clarity. For example, we are told that the original trait theories were discredited because of research that found that leadership behaviors differed among leaders. Moreover, the accounts tell us that the original task-versus-relationship behavior theories were improved through the identification of various situational factors that influenced leader effectiveness. These renditions of the history of leadership thought tend to ignore detours and obstacles on the historical journey and assume a steady progression toward greater precision. Third, these

accounts have become the sacred texts of the field. They are taught to students, reflected in the literature reviews of research reports, and used to argue for what the next stage of leadership investigations should be. Rost (1991) states that

> These summaries of leadership theory movements are ritualistically repeated by author after author, especially textbook writers. As with other things that are repeated over and over, people begin to accept them as facts. These movements are part of the folklore of leadership studies and, like other folktales and myths, they are believed because leadership high priests have told us they are true. (p. 17)

These features suggest weaknesses in the traditional account that are important to acknowledge. In so doing, we wish to strengthen the discussion of leadership thought and practice by looking outside its traditional sources. Our critique is organized in three areas: how the traditional accounts are found wanting in terms of their own claims; how these accounts use a narrow slice of thought and disciplines to develop their ideas; and how the narratives of leadership thought do not reflect the context of a postmodern world.

Critique Based on Their Own Claims

Rost (1991) argues that the traditional leadership narratives suggest that the theories are separate and distinct, but in fact, they all are based on a structural-functionalist view. As he puts it, "All leadership theories [presented in the narratives] have a structural-functionalist frame of reference in the hierarchical, linear, pragmatic, Newtonian background assumptions of what makes the world go around" (p. 27).

Rost's (1991) critique of the leadership theories is based on five characteristics of these theories. The leadership theories are:

1. Oriented toward goal-achievement

2. Emphasize face-to-face, dyadic relationships rather than larger organizational and societal relationships

3. Representative of male, even macho, heroic images

4. "Utilitarian, short-term, and materialistic in their ethical base" (p. 27)

5. "Excessively rationalistic, technocratic, quantitative, and scientific in their background assumptions" (p. 27)

Rost's critique may be attacked for ignoring more recent leadership theories, including leadership as an organizational quality, spirituality in leadership, feminist approaches, and critical theories. However, his critique seems appropriate in that little mention is made of these more recent theories in most traditional accounts of leadership thought, which still dominate many of the conversations about leadership practice.

Rost (1991) also criticizes the leadership narratives as assuming that the theories had distinct beginnings and endings.

> A much more accurate interpretation of these theories as a saga of popular movements is that there were periods of heightened popularity for certain theories, but when that popularity waned, the theories remained in the minds and hearts of scholars and practitioners alike because they appealed to the structural-functionalist frame within which most researchers operated and to the managerial psyche of most practitioners. (p. 29)

Rost's third critique is that the leadership narratives maintain that progress has been made in leadership thought. However, even traditional leadership theorists themselves suggest that leadership continues to be an elusive concept (Sheive & Schoenheit, 1987). An argument could be made that the leadership theories have contributed to identifying new questions for debate. However, to suggest that the theories have progressed to greater explanatory or predictive power is to overstate the case.

Critique Based on a Narrow Set of Disciplines

As mentioned previously, researchers and theorists in two fields of inquiry, namely industrial psychology and managerial science, have essentially written the history of leadership thought. Given these sources, it is not surprising that one of the critiques of the larger field of educational leadership is that it has been overly influenced by corporate models (Callahan, 1962; English, 1992, 2003).

The assumption behind these traditional leadership narratives is that no alternative work in leadership has occurred. Yet, leadership has been a frequent topic in biography (Preskill, 1992), literature, theater, philosophy, religion, and art—Western and non-Western. These areas, however, have not influenced the traditional U.S. narratives and, therefore, the accepted ways of understanding and describing, perhaps even explaining, leadership behavior. English (1997) asserts that the scientific management movement kidnapped the study of leadership found in the liberal arts. In doing so, the result was that "it debunked narratives embedded in history, theatre, and biography as 'unscientific,' and hence untrustworthy sources to become an educational leader" (p. 7). In the second section of this chapter, we will provide examples of how some of these areas could benefit our understanding and practice of leadership.

In addition to a restricted use of disciplines, the history of leadership thought in the United States and some other Western countries has ignored contributions from other countries. One dramatic example of this lack of awareness of leadership thought in other societal contexts lies in the U.S. emphasis on the status of cultural heroes and the rational economic actor assumption. The heroic image attributed by this society to corporate leaders such as Chrysler's Lee Iacocca or military leaders such as Gen. H. Norman Schwarzkopf is rarely seen in non-Western narratives of leadership. Blunt and Jones (1997) point out that the status that U.S. leadership thought gives to cultural heroes is not enjoyed by people in most other countries, even industrialized nations such as Germany and Japan. Furthermore, Blunt and Jones argue that the rational economic actor assumption in Western views of leadership contradicts

> important values held by people in 80 percent of the countries of the world and by an even higher percentage of people in developing countries. Most non-Western cultures do not place high value on overt individual and group competition; they are collectivist in nature, that is, they value the group over the individual. (pp. 4–5)

As has been pointed out, we are skeptical of the claim that the traditional leadership narratives on leadership thought have developed toward greater precision and clarity. However, in suggesting that other fields of inquiry, beyond industrial psychology and managerial science, and views of leadership from other countries would benefit our understanding and practice of leadership, we are not implying that considering these fields and cultural differences will provide greater precision in our thinking and examining of leadership. Rather, we argue that recognizing these alternatives will enrich our understanding of leadership. In other words, instead of narrowing leadership study so that we achieve more exactness, opening the narratives of leadership thought to include leadership accounts provided by other fields and cultures broadens our viewpoints to consider larger leadership images and perspectives. Such breadth will enable us to conceive of and practice leadership differently from the ways our traditional accounts suggest.

Critique Based on a Postmodern World

Narratives of any type, far from being value free, are attempts to define what is accepted, appropriate, and even sacred (English, 2003). In the case of leadership narratives, these traditional accounts intentionally or unintentionally are used to define the knowledge base of the field. As Peter Gronn (2003) and others have argued, these attempts restrict the understanding and practice of leadership to what could be called "designer leadership." Several have complained that recent accountability attempts, such as the almost religious adoption of ISLLC standards, reflect corporate models clothed with educational jargon. In educational leadership, these attempts have recently been called into serious question (English, 1997, 2003). The theories used in the traditional narratives of leadership thought are based on causal relationships, views of a single reality, and other features of positivism that have been critiqued in regard to their value for understanding leadership in a postmodern world. Educational leadership in a postmodern world, where there are multiple realities, shifting perspectives, a rejection of absolute cause-effect relationships, and a broadening of inquiry methods beyond the scientific, technical, and rational, calls into question the confident, seemingly coherent narrative of leadership we have inherited. The debate on leadership needs to be broadened and enriched with alternative perspectives (Furman, 2003).

This postmodern context shuns the absolutism and singularity of traditional accounts of leadership theories and rejects the sacredness with which theorists, writers, and researchers have held them. Such a critique, far from being damaging to the understanding of leadership, provides exciting prospects for our understanding, examining, and practicing of leadership in schools. In the next section, we hope to contribute to that process by identifying and discussing several ways that accounts of leadership can be expanded.

NONTRADITIONAL SOURCES FOR LEADERSHIP THOUGHT

In this section, we will identify two major sources for leadership thought that have traditionally been ignored in the history of leadership. Our purpose in this section is not to identify all the sources of leadership thought but rather to give two examples, Western classical literature and non-Western political thought, which we believe are valuable sources and which exemplify how nontraditional sources may be useful in broadening our understanding of leadership. We do not put forward a detailed and exhaustive discussion of Western classical literature or non-Western political thought, but we provide both specific literature and broad outlines that exemplify these alternative and enriching sources.

Leadership Themes From Western Classical Literature

By looking closely at some ancient plays, some medieval writings, and some of Shakespeare's history plays and tragedies, we gain broader and deeper perspectives on leadership. The dramatist's art, in particular, allows us to read (or better yet watch) the prince, king, elected ruler, or usurper navigate his[1] way through the minefields of political intrigue and constraints of personal limitations. The hero's success or failure, and the successes or failures of the major characters who serve as his foils or his supporters, help us to understand the human side of leadership. Through literature, we are informed intellectually and emotionally. By tapping into any of the arts, we understand a subject like leadership more fully because our emotions are engaged. This dimension of understanding is entirely lost in theorizing and in learning from theories.

To get a glimpse of some famous characters and their contexts, this section of the chapter draws on Shakespeare's *Richard II, King John,* *Richard III, Julius Caesar, Macbeth, and King Lear.* Machiavelli's *The Prince* and Sophocles' *Oedipus the King* are referenced. Some of Aristotle's ideas from *The Politics* and *Nichomachean Ethics* are also included. Brief mention is made of Chaucer, as well. Along with our own interpretation of the texts mentioned, we have also drawn on the ideas of a number of literary critics to support the points made. Because we have gleaned ideas about leadership only from the primary works and the secondary commentaries about them, we do not attempt to deal fully in the literary sense with any of the plays or essays.

Leadership is rarely mentioned by name in these works. Rather the business of leading or ruling is their subject. Common themes found in them, as in many other works of their times, include: (a) the road to tyranny and the right of lawful resistance to or overthrow of the tyrant, (b) the moral obligation of kings to rule with the common good in mind, (c) the practical art of ruling versus the moral ideals of leadership, and (d) the value of knowledge of self and others for a ruler. Traditional leadership thought has been concerned with some of these themes—the right to lead (or who should lead) and the survival of the leader; the practical art of leading—and, to some extent, the idea of the common good has been translated into the achievement of common goals. However, we find little in the traditional U.S. theories of leadership about the moral and ethical dimensions of leadership (except for Burns's 1979 notion of transforming leadership[2]) and very little on the value of knowledge of self and others beyond learning how to manipulate others. So to get a better idea of how classical Western writers dealt with their leadership issues, we delved into the works themselves. In this endeavor, we hope to whet the appetites of others interested in expanding the knowledge base on leadership. The following discussion reveals but a tiny tip of the great iceberg of Western classical literature, and it does not begin to take account of any modern literature. We are aware, therefore, that in this literature section, we are still writing about white male notions of leadership.

Tyrant Versus Good King

Although Shakespeare set many of his plays in the ancient world or in premodern times, his views on kingship and governance were strongly influenced by the prevailing theories of Elizabethan England. Shakespeare's plays were most likely written between 1585 and 1611 (Staunton, 1979). Two main theories of kingship were popular in England at that time: the contractual or resistance theory and the providentialist theory (Carroll, 2003).

The latter theory was the most popular and is known more familiarly as the "divine right" of kingship.

> At the heart of the providential theory of kingship is the concept of the monarch ruling as the chosen vice-regent of God, independent of the consent of the commons, unfettered by ecclesiastical authority, outside of and prior to the laws of the kingdom. (Carroll, 2003, p. 127)

The resistance theory was not yet as clearly formulated but had grown out of experiences with the excesses of rulers such as Catholic Queen Mary. Although resistance was contemplated, the legitimate overthrow of an unpopular king was considered a counter-discourse in Shakespeare's time. "The radical concepts of royal limitation . . . were rarely if ever heard during Queen Elizabeth's reign; articulating the logic of deposing a lawful king was one thing during Queen Mary's reign, but not at all relevant or permissible [in Elizabethan England]" (Carroll, 2003, p. 134).

Thus, Shakespeare crafted his plots carefully, making sure his tales of the deposition of ruler or regicide (e.g., *King John, Richard II, Macbeth, Julius Caesar*) revolved around tyrants or showed the negative consequences of such violence.[3] For instance, after killing

the rightful ruler Duncan, Macbeth's guilty conscience renders him virtually incapable of carrying out his plans. At the end of *King John*, which is set in medieval England, there is a call for unity, for a contract between king and subjects that echoes England's concern in the 1590s with the need for legitimate succession after the Virgin Queen. Unlike some of the other tragedies or history plays, there is no sense of victory at the conclusion. Instead, there is a practical call for a limited monarchy in the body of the young Henry III. Those left standing will "accept the king's legitimacy and subscribe to his 'just and lineal descent,' and he will build a functioning government on their acceptance of his claim" (Vaughan, 2003, p. 392). Vaughan argues that Shakespeare underscores the idea that "legitimacy is conferred by the people's assent" (p. 393). The people agree to accept the notion of a body politic ruled by a leader whose individual values and emotional needs give him (or her) the right to rule. The people will accept rule from a human being who has gained their trust rather than from an ideology such as the divine right of kings.

Even in medieval times, there was a strong belief that a lord or ruler was given power for the good of the people. "Some writers even went so far as to state explicitly: the right of lordship is based on the consent of the governed. It is subordinate to the laws, to which legitimate rulers are themselves subject" (Schlauch, 1945, p. 134).[4] Chaucer made clear that the purpose of lordship must be the welfare of all classes. Tyranny occurs when a leader neglects that duty out of self-indulgence and ambition. For Chaucer, the ideal king should cultivate "mercy, peace, observance of law and just severity against rebels" (Schlauch, 1945, p. 136). He admonished Richard II for arbitrary rule and exhorted him to greater steadfastness. Chaucer believed regard for the law and attention to justice were the hallmarks of a good ruler. "Pity, benignity, mercy, accessibility to petitioners are among the royal virtues listed in the [*Prologue* to the *Legend of Good Women*]" (Schlauch, 1945, p. 152). In looking out for the common good, or the *bonum commune,* the king must exercise those powers rooted in the law to ensure equity for all his subjects.

Meron (1998) makes the point that by refusing to account for their acts, arrogant rulers abuse power. To illustrate, he quotes Lady Macbeth, who urges her husband to evil with the taunt: "Fie, my lord, fie, a soldier and afeard? What need we fear who knows it when none can call our power to account?" (*Macbeth,* 4.1.34–36, in Meron, 1998, p. 2). In another example is Goneril, who claims absolute rule with her haughty assurance: "Say if I do, the laws are mine, not thine./Who can arraign me for't?" (*King Lear,* 5.3.149, in Meron, 1998, p. 2). By using these words and the beliefs they illuminate, Shakespeare shows that the social compact between subject and king has been shattered.

When Richard II seizes Bolingbroke's lands and prevents him from receiving his hereditary rights, he too descends into the murky realm of the ruler who believes he is not beholden to the laws. That excess along with his unjust taxation and his own political incompetence demonstrates that Richard is not fit to be king. But is rebellion and overthrow (and in the end assassination) justified? Meron (1998) argues that, in *Richard II,* the question remains unanswered. Others believe that since the blood of Richard is on the hands of his successor, Bolingbroke, soon to be Henry IV, the evil will be perpetuated. Henry IV is doomed to rule in Richard's tyrannous image (Roe, 2002, p. 60).

By contrast, Shakespeare does approve of the rebellion against and removal from office of such despots as Richard III and Macbeth. "[Richard's] ascent to the throne and reign are ruthless and devoid of ethical standards, his power, survival and security the only goals. Anyone who is, or could be, a threat must be eliminated" (Meron, 1998, p. 36). Both

Richard III's and Macbeth's murderous acts and their usurpation of the crown made them legitimate targets for elimination. In many plays, rebellion leads to disorder and instability, which for Shakespeare is exactly the opposite of a desirable state of affairs. Therefore, to justify any kind of uprising, the character of the ruler or king had to sink to a level of evil that, in the case of Richard III, for instance, seems to have been inspired by the archetype of scheming and amorality: Machiavelli's Prince (Meron, 1998, p. 37).

Leadership for the Common Good

Concern for the welfare of their subjects is one of the strongest attributes of good leaders. This duty exists alongside the other Aristotelian virtues of physical bravery, frankness in speech, and pioneering initiative (Lindsay, 2000). Both the character and the capacities of a ruler are important. King Oedipus, for instance, a noble, brave, and forthright ruler, is especially beloved by his people for ridding Thebes of the Sphinx and bringing safety and stability to the city-state. The Priest praises him and tells him that the people "judg[e] him as the first of men/in all the chances of this life" (lines 32–33 in Grene & Lattimore, 1960, p. 112). As the play opens, the people entreat Oedipus, as someone who has their best interests at heart, to help them out of their current misfortunes just as he did in the past. He acknowledges how he feels for them.

> Your several sorrows each have single scope
> and touch but one of you. My spirit groans
> for city and myself and you at once.
> You have not roused me like a man from sleep;
> know that I have given many tears to this . . .
> (lines 62–66 in Grene & Lattimore, 1960, p. 113)

From the literature of ancient Greece and Rome through medieval tales to Shakespeare, we see the same emphasis on care for those governed.

Respect for the common weal as the objective of a true king appears in several of Chaucer's passages (Schlauch, 1945). The notion that discord and unrest were enemies of the well-being of the people is clear in his work. The king should wisely bring rest and ease to his subjects. Thus, peace was always sought, even in eras of conquest and continual strife that have characterized much of history. Julius Caesar's personal ambition suggesting a return to absolute rule threatens the fledgling Republic of 45 B.C. Brutus takes part in the conspiracy to murder Caesar because he is afraid that Caesar will no longer be good for his people. At the end, Antony says of Brutus:

This was the noblest Roman of them all:
All the conspirators save only he
Did that they did in envy of great Caesar.
He only, in a general honest thought
And common good to all, made one of them.
(*Julius Caesar*, 5.5, 68–72; in Staunton, 1979)

Brutus represents the most "noble" of them all because he, somewhat naively, acted out of the belief that he was serving the best interests of the Romans. He wanted also to preserve the Republic, which his actions ironically helped to destroy. But friend and loyal soldier to Caesar, he would never have committed murder had he not considered Caesar's growing power as threatening the liberty of the people. An honest man, he kills Caesar openly and puts himself before the people for their judgment. Brutus wanted to safeguard the people's freedom, but Roe (2002) argues that this play "posits notions of freedom while expressing reserve over the prospect of its being truly exercised" (p. 154).

This helps us to understand that the concept of ruling for the common good or leading with the best interests of the people in mind is a very contextual one, and one that necessarily depends on the skill of the ruler as well as his or her moral consistency. Much blood has been shed in the name of the common good. Wars are fought for the purpose of bringing about a more stable social order in *King John, King Lear,* and *Macbeth,* to mention but a few of the plays on this theme.

Aristotle's virtues of warrior courage and the ruler's duty to look after his subjects as a father looks after his family do not always happily coexist. Aristotle acknowledges that the "manly daring" he so values also places a people at risk. Violence and warfare harm both subjects and leader alike. Lindsay (2000) argues that although Aristotle admired the kind of spiritedness that defines a leader, through his story of the 4th-century tyrant Jason, he illustrates the personal dangers of such behavior. Like *Julius Caesar,* this story shows that "while insatiable ambition is doubtless a threat to political life, it is no less, and perhaps more a threat to the ambitious. Jason, as all Aristotle's audience knew, was assassinated by his own men" (Lindsay, 2000, p. 439). Therefore, even if the arrogant ruler disregards the common welfare, he ought to desist for his own good at least.

The Practical Art of Ruling Versus the Moral Ideals of Leadership

In many of the plays discussed in this section, Shakespeare frequently juxtaposes the moral with the amoral—often in quite subtle and ambiguous ways. There are distinct Machiavellian themes and characters. Machiavelli lived and wrote in Florence from the late 15th to mid 16th centuries. He is described as articulating a shockingly pragmatic view of ruling and rulers that had not been voiced until then, although others might have thought it.

[His] view is that the world in its operations is amoral, that none of the laws held to be essential for the governing of ethical behavior exists in fact, and that the sole effective determinant in human affairs is the ability to exercise power. (Roe, 2002. p. ix)

Shakespeare had ample opportunity to see Machiavellian ideas brought to life in the theater of his time and possibly to read Machiavelli's works. Machiavelli's cynicism has been widely debated. He advocates dissembling and deceit. The following excerpt gives a flavor of his beliefs.

A prudent prince neither can nor ought to keep his word when to keep it is hurtful to him and the causes which led him to pledge it are removed. If all men were good, this would not be good advice, but since they are dishonest and do not keep faith with you, you, in return, need not keep faith with them. (Machiavelli, 1513/1992, p. 60)

Throughout *The Prince*, he offers practical advice to rulers based on his observations and experience as a public official for a time during the various struggles associated with the Medici family's quest for power in Florence. Shakespeare demonstrates the deleterious effects of many of these ideas through several of his characters' actions and words. The obvious villains in the plays under discussion here, such as King Richard III, Claudius (from *Hamlet*), and Edmund (from *King Lear*), are clear examples. But apart from illustrating that evil ultimately does not pay, these characters are not as interesting as those who have some Machiavellian inclinations but who are not really evil men because they are capable of reflection and moral reasoning. King Richard II, Hamlet, and King John are examples of the latter.

Richard II reveals his political scheming early on in the play by "the giving of 'blank charters' to his ministers to appropriate money from the wealthy . . . and by his callous reaction to the grave illness of . . . his uncle John of Gaunt" (Grady, 2002, p. 72). Then, upon John of Gaunt's death, Richard appropriates

Bolingbroke's inheritance: "The lining of his coffers shall make coats/To deck our soldiers for these Irish wars (*Richard II*, 1.4.60–61 in Staunton, 1979).

Wrong though these acts are, they would not have met with the approval of Machiavelli. Richard "is a poor Machiavellian who needs to study the details of his *Prince* much more closely" (Grady, 2002, p. 73). Richard has not understood the Machiavellian principle that rulers should give the appearance of virtue and honesty. In revealing his stratagems this way, he loses all support. Carried along through most of the play by his (ultimately disastrous) scheming, Richard displays little sense of reflection until he is imprisoned after his abdication.

Hamlet, by contrast, spends most of his time contemplating the murder of his father, King Hamlet, and his possible courses of action in response. He questions his own beliefs and values and comes to believe that traditional moral and ethical principles are no longer revered in the modern world. But despite his tortured soul, his capacity for princely cunning surfaces on several occasions. For example, in place of the decree for his own execution, he substitutes orders for the killing of Rosencrantz and Guildenstern, and he plans and carries out the performance of the "play-within-the-play" revealing the regicide committed by his uncle Claudius, who then married Hamlet's mother and became king. "Despite the metaphysical bewilderment for which he is celebrated, Hamlet shows an astuteness that would have won the praise of Cesare Borgia[5] himself in his successful reversal of the plot against him involving his treacherous old school friends" (Roe, 2002, p. 21).

Clearly both *Hamlet* and *Richard II* offer opportunities for the protagonists and their characters to illustrate the tension between accepting a ruler's ruthless action—understood, if not excused, for political reasons—and fearing possible moral consequences in an essentially Christian England. The same can be said of *King John*, especially regarding the king's complicity in the killing of the young Prince Arthur, whom John viewed as a threat to his throne. Indeed, when it is known that Arthur is dead, "The nobles, whose silent presence propped up John's claim to the throne [earlier], . . . question the monarch's actions and integrity, and rush off to spark rebellion" (Vaughan, 2003, p. 389). John realizes that he has lost the consent of the governed. But despite his Machiavellian capacity to plot and scheme, John has a conscience, although it does him little good. He knows his deeds were wrong and ponders his moral responsibility. "Although they attribute Arthur's possibly accidental death to John, the barons understand that John is not made of wholly immoral fabric. . . . His struggles pit his conscience against his political ambition" (Meron, 1998, p. 24). Thus, powers of reflection and a conscience are highly valued in a leader although they are not always predictive of a successful rule. Shakespeare seems to regard a ruler's well-developed moral capacity as a necessary but not sufficient condition for survival.

The Value of a Leader's Knowledge of Self and Others

King Lear, Richard II, and King Oedipus are good examples of leaders who are brought to better knowledge of themselves and others through extreme adversity. The message is that their leadership, while appearing to be virtuous at times, is built on false premises. It is clear that in all three cases (and also in the parallel case of the Duke of Gloucester in *King Lear*), the leaders' suffering is intense. It is not only mental anguish: Lear and Gloucester are thrust outdoors in the freezing wilderness, and Gloucester and Oedipus lose their eyes violently. It is suggested that these leaders, like Lear, "hath ever but slenderly known [themselves]" (*King Lear*, 1.1.297; in Staunton, 1979). As kings and noblemen, they have passed judgment on their subjects, made decisions deeply affecting others' lives, influenced

the course of events in their own realms, and managed their own affairs—all in ignorance of who they are and who many others are, as well.

Richard II makes the serious mistake of trusting in lords who do not have his best interests at heart. Instead of advisers, they are flatterers who abandon him as his ambition leads him to miscalculation and as Bolingbroke grows in strength. Roe (2002) makes the point that Shakespeare demonstrates a Machiavellian concept by highlighting Richard's ineptitude. Sound knowledge of others is key to the prince's success. "A prince's wisdom does not come from having good policies recommended to him; on the contrary, good policy, whoever suggests it comes from the wisdom of the prince" (Machiavelli, quoted in Roe, 2002, p. 47). The key is to know whether to value the opinions of those giving advice or not. Oedipus, Lear, and Gloucester all fall into similar traps.

In his arrogance, Oedipus misses the importance of the blind seer, Teiresias, who tells him, "You have your eyes but see not where you are/In sin" (*King Oedipus* in Grene & Lattimore, 1960, pp. 413–414). Lear rejects his beloved daughter Cordelia, falling prey to the shallow flattery of his other daughters, Regan and Goneril. And, blind Gloucester, having been betrayed by Edmund, at the height of his misery echoes Sophocles' imagery of sight: "I have no way, and therefore want no eyes;/I stumbled when I saw" (*King Lear*, 4.1.23–24 in Staunton, 1979). Gloucester's evil son Edmund has arranged for his father's eyes to be put out and for his brother Edgar's banishment.

Whereas Richard II and Gloucester are both somewhat flawed characters from the outset, Lear and Oedipus are depicted as having been good kings. Not only are they characterized as honest and just rulers, but we are told they have brought peace and stability to their kingdoms as the plays open. It is important to understand through these plays that self-knowledge and knowledge of others exist independently of other virtues. But we cannot help imagine that they would have been better rulers had they had such knowledge in the first place. According to Machiavelli, such leaders would have survived longer, but in Shakespeare, those governed would have been better off. Although the characters themselves would surely have benefited, most important, the instability and violence that accompanied their downfall could possibly have been avoided.

Shakespeare, in particular, clearly depicts the value of the inner self, which can see better or understand the human condition more fully once the political persona is cast off. In losing their public place in the world, Lear, Gloucester, and Richard all come to understand moral and social issues in much greater depth. There is a suggestion in these plays (and others) that "the qualities that make for a successful king . . . are the qualities that detract from the values of humanity" (Grady, 2002, p. 90). Grady (2002) highlights the quality of self-reflection associated with the capacities to suffer and to dream, which all the characters learn to value in these plays. Grady points out "the 'inner man' is of fundamentally greater moral importance than the mere external man of action" (p. 90).

A related point is that all these characters also learn the value of their emotions once they have been stripped, physically and metaphorically, of their titles and prestige. Lear is perhaps the best example of this, as he learns pity for Poor Tom, for Gloucester, and for those whose offenses he should have pardoned while he was king. Shakespeare suggests here and elsewhere that he does not accept the traditional male heroic conventions uncritically (Wells, 2000). By showing the feminine side of princes and kings such as Lear, Hamlet, and Richard II, he creates characters whose human qualities render leadership a much more complicated endeavor than fighting wars and subduing rebellion suggests.

"Charismatic heroes are dangerous because they are capable of causing us to suspend rational judgment and revert to the values of heroic society where the honour (*sic*) code is a substitute for the rule of law" (Wells, 2000, p. 206). Thus, in following the development of self-understanding and understanding of others in these plays, we gain sympathy for the manly king, the warrior or statesman whose masculinity is softened by compassion. Learning to identify with their fellow sufferers, Richard and Lear both explore the experience of nothingness, which serves as a direct contrast to their having been "something" as king. The worth of decisive action and political scheming disappears as both men grasp for spiritual understanding.

Leadership Themes in Non-Western Political Thought

Although few of the above themes have found their way into the history of leadership thought in quite the way illustrated by the literature, the leadership accounts are strongly influenced by Western concepts, especially from United Kingdom and U.S. industrial psychology and management science. However, the idea of leadership did not originate in the West, and to assume that only Western theorists have been discussing leadership is arrogant and narrow. In this section, we will look at two non-Western contexts for leadership, Africa and East Asia, in particular China, to examine non-Western examples of leadership thought. Our intent is not to present an extensive review and discussion of leadership thought in these two contexts but to identify some key ideas that highlight differences with traditional Western leadership thought and the history that has been traditionally expressed. It is important to acknowledge that although we present general themes of leadership in these two contexts, there are important differences within the African and East Asian contexts. A more in-depth discussion would need to recognize the important differences within and among African and East Asian nations and cultures, as well as the larger contextual factors that influence how leadership is viewed and practiced.

Leadership in African Contexts

The African context is important for reminding us that leadership is not an exclusively Western concept. The early history of leadership thought in Africa includes the emphasis placed in early Egyptian culture on organization and administration; famous philosophers from Benin and Ife in Nigeria and other African empires such as Ghana, Mali, Songhai, and Oyo; and the powerful Obas ruling class, which "applied management as a hierarchical, large-scale organization" (Nzelibe, 1986, p. 8). Early African models and principles of leadership, such as the emphasis on harmony and communalism, are rarely included in the traditional U.S. history of leadership thought.

Nzelibe (1986) points to the intrusion of Western forms of leadership and management during the colonial period in Africa, which had consequences for the subsequent independence era. During the colonial period, these earlier models of communalism and traditionalism were devalued. Moreover, indigenous people were ignored for corporate management positions, with the result that few Africans had managerial experience at the beginning of the independence era. In addition, Western forms of leadership—many of which remained during the independence era—conflict with African management thought. "Whereas, Western management thought advocates Eurocentrism, individualism, and modernity, African management thought emphasizes ethnocentrism, traditionalism, communalism, and cooperative teamwork" (Nzelibe, 1986, p. 11).

Although a discussion of African leadership thought could identify many elements, we will

focus on three that seem to distinguish it from traditional Western leadership narratives. First, African leadership thought includes the guiding principle of a "quest for equilibrium with other human beings and with the supernatural" (Blunt & Jones, 1997, p. 9). Rather than a focus on constant change and reform, African leadership thought seeks to engender stability and harmony among individuals. Blunt and Jones (1997) argue that "the preferred type of leader who emerges . . . is more likely to be seen as offering a degree of assurance and security than would the thrusting, demanding, driven creature of the Western model" (p. 12).

Second, the connection with the supernatural promotes a spiritual focus, which until recently has been all but ignored in U.S. leadership thought. Nzelibe (1986) emphasizes the importance of the family as the primary socializing force that "encourages the belief in the relation to Nature and supernatural beings and important connections between the individual and his ancestors" (pp. 11–12). This connection with the past and with the supernatural is all but excluded in Western corporate models of leadership and in the traditional history of leadership thought.

Third, in contrast to the Western emphasis on individual achievements, African leadership thought places importance on interpersonal loyalty and communalism. "In many circumstances, ceremony, ritual, interpersonal relations, reciprocity, and the distribution of scant resources to clan and ethnic affiliates are therefore natural responsibilities of leadership in Africa" (Blunt & Jones, 1997, p. 10). In light of this, traditionalism becomes an element of African leadership that involves the "adherence to accepted customs, beliefs, and practices that determine accepted behavior, morality, and the desired characteristics of the individual in African society" (Nzelibe, 1986, p. 11). Blunt and Jones (1997) argue that African leadership contrasts "a leader who is kindly, considerate, and understanding to one who is too dynamic and productive and, possibly, too demanding" (p. 11).

These three elements of stability based on connections with others, importance of the human connection to the supernatural, and communalism point to leadership concepts that have received less emphasis in U.S. leadership thought. Although these concepts have certainly found their way into some U.S. discussions of leadership, they are secondary to ideas such as competition, achievement, and vision.

Leadership in East Asian Contexts

Like the history of African leadership thought, leadership narratives in East Asian contexts have been significant and long-term. Blunt and Jones (1997) identified two general characteristics of leadership in East Asian contexts. First, in line with higher levels of power distance[6] (Hofstede, 1991), leadership in East Asia is "contingent on non-utilitarian qualities of leader[s]" (Blunt & Jones, 1997, p. 8) rather than dependent on the level of support from followers. East Asian leaders maintain their position through structures that are internal and external to the organization and may have deep historical roots. Such leadership focuses on larger purposes and values rather than on immediate follower satisfaction.

Second, Blunt and Jones (1997) argue that East Asian thought focuses on the responsibility of the leader to maintain harmony. Similar to African leadership, East Asian leadership focuses on collectivism and interpersonal harmony rather than the elements of Western functionalism that emphasize "autonomy, competition between individuals and groups, performance and self-assertion" (p. 9). The current emphasis, in the United States and other countries, on organizational change, improvement, and reform has eclipsed the important role of the leader in establishing and maintaining harmony.

These two elements are especially obvious in the particular case of Chinese leadership. In the remainder of this section, we will identify elements of Chinese leadership that emerge from the history of Chinese leadership thought. In our discussion, we draw heavily from the work of Guo (2002), who provides a historical perspective to understand the personalities of ideal Chinese political leaders.

According to Guo (2002), the history of Chinese political leadership thought includes three traditions: Confucian *junzi* (nobleman), Daoist *shengren* (sage) and *zhenren* (authentic person), and Legalist *mingjun* (enlightened leader). Different leadership ideals emerge from these traditions. In the case of Confucianism, leaders are expected to exemplify three concepts: humaneness, which involves sympathy and empathy; ritualism, where the leader is expected "to comply with established social norms and to set himself as a model for the populace" (p. x); and moralism, where the leader is expected to provide a role model for establishing moral order. In the Confucian ideal, morality and politics are inseparable.

In the Daoist tradition, the ideals of sage and authentic person are emphasized. The leader as sage exemplifies the belief that "political order and social harmony can be achieved and maintained by following Nature" (Guo, 2002, p. xi). At times, this tradition encourages the doctrine of inaction, which discourages intervention. Inaction is a leadership strategy ignored in the traditional heroic imagery of Western thought. Also in the Daoist tradition, leaders are expected to be authentic persons. This expectation involves shunning glory and wealth in order to keep the spirit free. By diminishing reliance on position, fame, fortune, and so on, the leader is able to reach a purer and clearer focus for followers.

The Legalism tradition, like all Chinese political thought, emphasizes wisdom but combines this with cunning. Based on the assumption that individuals are evil and that human interactions are focused on exchange relationships, the Legalist tradition expects leaders to use political technique, political authority, and penal law to maintain control. However, Chinese political thought "does not favor an institutionalized political system to control bureaucracy, but rather relies on a ruler's personal qualities to master officialdom" (Guo, 2002, p. xiii).

These three traditions and the ideals they emphasize suggest, according to Guo (2002), five characteristics of ideal Chinese political leadership. First, this leadership emphasizes Confucian humaneness (*ren*). "The ideal political personality in Confucianism is a heroic figure motivated by a sense of historic mission, socially intuitive knowledge, and a desire to uphold the Way to change the world and manifest humanness" (p. 232). In contrast to many Western conceptions, the heroic orientation is focused not on personal achievement nor on specific organizational improvement but on commitment and valiant efforts for the benefit of the larger society.

Second, Chinese leadership promotes a strong tendency toward ritual (*li*). "Compared with the Christian concept of law, *li* is more inclusive and relates to personal conduct, social relations, and political organizations" (Guo, 2002, p. 233). This tendency toward ritual means that leaders are more likely to depend on social norms and ceremonies than on fear to establish social control.

Third, these traditions emphasize a strong moral obligation of leaders. This moral obligation is interpreted differently by the different traditions. The Confucian *junzi* (nobleman) is seen as a sage emphasizing humanness, altruism, sympathy, and so on. As Guo (2002) points out, however, this moral obligation is not individualistic but rather seeks to promote social harmony and cohesion. For the Daoist, this social harmony is achieved through union with Nature. A recent study of Chinese educational leaders found that leader effectiveness was conceptualized differently in China than in the West. Cheng and Wong (1996) found that leader effectiveness focused more on the moral dimension, including the role of the leader in moral education.

Fourth, Chinese political leadership possesses a transcendent attitude toward political pursuits. The ideal leader is not dependent on political authority, office, glory, and possessions and in fact must remain free of these in order to provide leadership.

Fifth, the ideal leader is a strategist. "The ideal Daoist sages . . . were those who could employ traits such as softness, darkness, receptivity, tranquility, and weakness to overcome hardness, lightness, exclusiveness, agitation, and dominance to protect themselves and pursue an advantage" (Guo, 2002, p. 237).

These characteristics of the ideal Chinese political leader suggest a picture of leadership that includes moral obligation, humanness, wisdom, cunning, freedom from distracting glory, and even the ability to lead by inaction. Many of these characteristics and traits are very different from those found in the traditional Western leadership models. While acknowledging the importance of culture, these non-Western leadership characteristics can be useful in identifying features of leadership that may provide alternative approaches (Walker & Dimmock, 2002).

IMPLICATIONS OF A CRITICAL HISTORY OF LEADERSHIP THOUGHT

By critiquing the traditional history of leadership thought and identifying some alternative sources, we seek not only to contribute to the academic conversation but also to say something that can benefit practice. In this final section, we identify several implications of this discussion for the practice of school administration. Also, we will present implications for both leadership research and the improvement of leader preparation programs that can promote creative leadership practice.

Implications for Practice

Broadening and enriching the understanding of the development of leadership thought beyond the traditional U.S. accounts offers school and district leaders the opportunity to create images of leadership that are not limited to a corporate model. Instead of viewing leadership exclusively as a series of activities to achieve organizational goals, some of the sources we have identified suggest the value of seeing leadership, for example, in moral terms and in societal terms. Interestingly, several authors (Beck & Murphy, 1993; Tyack & Hansot, 1982) have identified historical eras in the history of U.S. school leadership in which a more societal view of the leader's role was promoted. For example, during World War II, schools and their leaders were urged to contribute to the efforts to create a more democratic society. Whether or not one agrees with the reasons for this endeavor, it is important to realize that school leaders were seen as having societal responsibilities beyond their school buildings. In contemporary society, school leaders can make an important contribution by viewing their leadership responsibilities as including contributing to a larger global vision (Furman & Starratt, 2002). One way school leaders can accomplish this is to encourage the recognition, value, and use of diverse ideas and to place importance on increasing student and faculty diversity in order to promote a sense of global awareness.

The moral qualities of leadership that we identified in classical Western literature, that is, tyrant versus good king, and non-Western political thought, that is, the Confucian nobleman image, suggest that school leaders should expand their view of leadership to include a sense of moral obligation. For example, instead of viewing their commitment to the learning of all children as an accountability motto, school leaders should see it as a moral obligation that pervades school goals and actions.

In addition to helping school leaders expand their leadership conceptions, these alternative sources also provide a way for principals and other school leaders to examine the assumptions of reform plans. In an era of obsessive focus on reform, being a critical observer and skeptic can be a very practical and useful leadership function. For example, suggesting that inaction and maintaining stability are, at times, appropriate leadership responses would probably be considered by many as taboo. But in some contexts, these leadership functions may create an environment in which not only harmony but also creativity and moral purpose can flourish. The current incessant reform mentality burns out teachers and administrators, discourages students, and creates more harm than good. However, maintaining stability without acknowledging moral purpose only preserves a status quo that damages underserved populations in our schools. One of a leader's first moral responsibilities is to provide equity of access to rigorous education, of opportunity to learn, and of resources that influence authentic learning outcomes.

In a similar vein, expanding the notion of the development of leadership thought permits school leaders to be self-reflective about their roles, commitments, passions, anxieties, and disappointments. Just as Oedipus missed the value of the blind seer, Teiresias, who told him, "You have your eyes but see not where you are/In sin" (*King Oedipus* in Grene & Lattimore, 1960, pp. 413–414), school leaders caught up in the maddening pace created by accountability pressures may be blinded to those aspects of students' lives that are not reflected in test scores. When school leaders lose the ability or opportunity to be self-reflective, they cease to be leaders and become blind followers.

Implications for Research

Broadening our understanding of leadership beyond the traditional account suggests at least three implications for research. First, many of the themes we have identified move us beyond the simple, causal, and positivistic examinations of leadership research. For example, variables such as connecting with the past and the spirituality of leadership are not likely candidates for causal analysis. Yet, these non-Western and Western literary sources suggest the power of these factors. Moreover, the inherent necessity in some positivistic and structural-functionalist examinations of leadership to narrow the variables to a manageable number makes a more holistic analysis of leadership impossible.

Second, in a similar holistic manner, the methods we use to research leadership need to be broadened to look at the entire person of the leader and the larger context of leadership rather than a few behaviors. African leadership thought emphasizes the communal nature of leadership and the importance of the family or community. The authenticity stressed in Daoist thought argues for cultural methods to examine leadership in a holistic way. And the Shakespearean plays remind us that those on the receiving end of leadership (a very different notion from the idea of followers) must be part of any research on leadership.

Third, both Western literary and non-Western political thought identify themes involving the emotions, the interpersonal, and other features of leaders that are ignored in much of Western educational leadership research. More attention needs to be paid to leaders' human capacity for empathy and unqualified respect for others unlike themselves. A growing number of theorists and researchers are beginning to focus on such issues as trust, integrity, and emotional development; we hope this trend will continue.

Several authors have maintained that using cultural perspectives from other societies contributes to research on a variety of educational problems confronting U.S. schools. Heck (2002) identifies research problems such as implementation of educational standards, comparison of educational progress, and the decentralization of educational decision making as three issues in which research could benefit from an international and comparative focus. Limiting our research to Western countries prohibits the use of conceptions and frameworks from non-Western cultures that may provide insight into our own national educational problems.

Implications for Leader Preparation

Critiquing the traditional history of leadership thought and practice and using alternative sources to broaden our understanding of leadership is vital for school leader preparation. Several of the implications we previously presented connect to preparation. By using these nontraditional sources and others, including biography, drama, and art, we encourage aspiring school leaders to expand their conceptions of leadership, for example, to include societal responsibilities and the importance of viewing leadership in terms of the common good defined broadly enough to encompass all young people regardless of color, race, religion, gender, sexuality, or socioeconomic status. Also, using these sources can help aspiring leaders to develop the skills of self-reflection and self-knowledge. Moreover, several of the literary examples we have presented could be used to provide opportunities for students to struggle with the many ethical dilemmas that face school leaders daily.

Recognition of the limitations of traditional accounts of leadership history and the use of alternative sources also helps to move us beyond "designer leadership" models of preparation (Gronn, 2003). In part, these alternative sources emphasize the contextual nature of leadership, but also the importance of recognizing the variety in leadership practice and potential. Instead of trying to narrow leadership to the least common denominator, preparation programs can open up the conceptions of leadership available to these aspiring candidates in a way that will encourage creativity rather than conformity.

CONCLUSION

In this chapter, we have provided a critical examination of the traditional history of leadership thought. In no way are we arguing that the many contributions that make up these traditional accounts are without value. Rather, we argue for expanding our understanding of the history of leadership thought in such a way that these traditional perspectives are enriched by other, frequently ignored perspectives. Perhaps such a critical reflection on the history of leadership thought and practice can help facilitate conversations that acknowledge that the elusive nature of leadership can be valuable instead of regrettable.

NOTES

1. The heroes of the classical literature mentioned here were all men. Where women played a part, even a royal part, they were rarely illustrating important, positive lessons on leadership.

2. In the alternative or emerging narratives of leadership, there is a greater emphasis on the moral and ethical underpinnings of leadership (see, e.g., Beck, 1994; Begley, 1999; Noddings, 1992; Shapiro & Stefkovich, 2001; Starratt, 1994, 2003).

3. However, some of Shakespeare's plays *did* create the conditions under which the overthrow of a leader would be desirable. None of our modern theories ever attend to this possibility. To read a theory versus a play underscores a curious focal difference between the two: The former is developed to aid the leader's access to and maintenance of power, whereas the latter shows the followers how power, can be abused and gives them ideas of what they can do about it.

4. As an interesting aside, it is noteworthy that no mention is made in this article, published in 1945, of any contemporary absolute rulers such as Hitler or Mussolini—not even in the notes. This points to the fact that it is far safer and more palatable to make points about excesses of leadership if the comments refer to a different age.

5. One of Machiavelli's "heroes" described in *The Prince*.

6. Power distance is one of the dimensions of Hofstede's (1991) categorization of national or societal cultures. Power distance refers to the degree of equality or inequality of power in a culture. A high power distance means that there is high inequality within a culture.

REFERENCES

Beck, L. (1994). *Reclaiming educational administration as a caring profession.* New York: Teachers College Press.

Beck, L., & Murphy, J. (1993). *Understanding the principalship: Metaphorical themes, 1920s–1990s.* New York: Teachers College Press.

Begley, P. (Ed.). (1999). *Values and educational leadership.* Albany: SUNY Press.

Bennis, W., & Nanis, B. (1986). *Leaders.* New York: Harper & Row.

Blunt, P., & Jones, M. L. (1997). Exploring the limits of Western leadership theory in East Asia and Africa. *Personnel Review, 26*(1), 6–23.

Burns, J. M. (1979). Leadership. New York: Harper & Row.

Callahan, R. E. (1962). *Education and the cult of efficiency.* Chicago: University of Chicago Press.

Carroll, W. (2003). Theories of kingship in Shakespeare's England. In R. Dutton & J. E. Howard (Eds.), *A companion to Shakespeare's works* (pp. 125–145). Malden, MA: Blackwell.

Cheng, K., & Wong, K. (1996). School effectiveness in East Asia: Concepts, origins, and implications. *Journal of Educational Administration, 34*(5), 32–49.

English, F. (1992). *Educational administration: The human science.* New York: Harper Collins.

English, F. (1997, March 24–28). *The recentering of leadership from the jaws of management science.* Paper presented at the American Educational Research Association, Chicago.

English, F. (2003). *The postmodern challenge to the theory and practice of educational administration.* Springfield, IL: Charles C Thomas.

Furman, G. (2003). The 2002 UCEA presidential address. *UCEA Review, 45*(1), 1–6.

Furman, G., & Starratt, R. J. (2002). Leadership for democratic community in schools. In J. Murphy (Ed.), *The educational leadership challenge: Redefining leadership for the 21st century* (pp. 105–133). Chicago: National Society for the Study of Education.

Getzels, J. (1977). Educational administration twenty years later, 1954–1974. In L. L. Cunningham, W. G. Hack, & R. O. Nystrand (Eds.), *Educational administration: The developing decades.* Berkeley, CA: McCutchan.

Grady, H. (2002). *Shakespeare, Machiavelli, and Montaigne*. Oxford, UK: Oxford University Press.

Grene, D., & Lattimore, R. (Eds.). (1960). *Greek tragedies*. Chicago: University of Chicago Press.

Gronn, P. (2003). *The new work of educational leaders*. London: Paul Chapman.

Guo, X. (2002). *The ideal Chinese political leader*. Westport, CT: Praeger.

Heck, R. (2002). Issues in the investigation of school leadership across cultures. In A. Walker & C. Dimmock (Eds.), *School leadership and administration: Adopting a cultural perspective*. New York: Routledge-Falmer.

Hofstede, G. H. (1991). *Cultures and organizations: Software of the mind*. London: McGraw-Hill.

Lindsay, T. (2000). Aristotle's appraisal of manly spirit: Political and philosophic implications. *American Journal of Political Science, 44*(3), 433–448.

Machiavelli, N. (1992). *The prince* (N. H. Thomson, Trans). New York: Quality Paperback Book Club. (Original work published 1513)

Meron, T. (1998). Crimes and accountability in Shakespeare. *The American Journal of International Law, 92*(1), 1–40.

Noddings, N. (1992). *The challenge to care in schools*. New York: Teachers College Press.

Nzelibe, C. O. (1986). The evolution of African management thought. *International Studies of Management and Organization, 16*(2), 6–16.

Preskill, S. (1992, October 30–November 1). *Biography and leadership: Exploring issues of race and gender*. Paper presented at the University Council for Educational Administration, Minneapolis, MN.

Roe, J. (2002). *Shakespeare and Machiavelli*. Rochester, NY: D. S. Brewer.

Rost, J. C. (1991). *Leadership for the twenty-first century*. New York: Praeger.

Schlauch, M. (1945). Chaucer's doctrine of kings and tyrants. *Speculum, A Journal of Mediaeval Studies, 20*(2), 133–156.

Shapiro, J., & Stefkovich, J. (2001). *Ethical leadership and decision making in education: Applying theoretical perspectives to complex dilemmas*. Mahwah, NJ: Lawrence Erlbaum.

Sheive, L. T., & Schoenheit, M. B. (1987). *Leadership: Examining the elusive*. Alexandria, VA: Association for Supervision and Curriculum Development.

Starratt, R. J. (1994). *Building an ethical school*. London: Falmer Press.

Starratt, R. J. (2003). *Centering educational administration*. Mahwah, NJ: Lawrence Erlbaum.

Staunton, H. (Ed.). (1979). *The complete illustrated Shakespeare*. New York: Park Lane.

Tyack, D., & Hansot, E. (1982). *Managers of virtue: Public school leadership in America, 1820–1980*. Boston: Basic Books.

Vaughan, V. M. (2003). King John. In R. Dutton & J. E. Howard (Eds.), *A companion to Shakespeare's works* (pp. 379–394). Malden, MA: Blackwell.

Walker, A., & Dimmock, C. (2002). *School leadership and administration: Adopting a cultural perspective*. New York: Routledge-Falmer.

Wells, R. H. (2000). *Shakespeare on masculinity*. Cambridge, UK: Cambridge University Press.

16

Leading in the Midst of Diversity

The Challenge of Our Times

CAROLYN M. SHIELDS
University of British Columbia

ANISH SAYANI
University of British Columbia

We all carry worlds in our heads, and those worlds are decidedly different. We educators set out to teach, but how can we reach the worlds of others when we don't even know they exist? Indeed, many of us don't even realize that our own worlds exist only in our heads and in the cultural institutions we have built to support them.

Delpit, 1993, p. xiv

At the beginning of the 21st century, the worlds of educators are besieged by multiple pressures, conflicting goals, and diverse interpretations of the desired ends of education. Educational policy seems increasingly driven by economic rather than social goals, by a strong emphasis on the development of a highly skilled workforce, and by knowledge production for the global economy (Codd, 2003). As the influence of market forces expands, educators are also faced with calls for accountability, high-stakes testing, higher expectations for parental participation, and more opportunities for e-learning. In addition, educators on the ground are challenged by changing enrollment patterns, a growing number of international fee-paying students, and increased diversity within their local communities.[1] For these and many other reasons, the issue of what is often called *cross-cultural leadership* is one of the most important challenges facing educational leaders today.

At the same time, we are not sure that *cross-cultural* is actually the best way to describe the leadership needed to create school communities in which the myriad of competing individual and group needs may be addressed. Although on occasion we use (and have used) the term,[2] we would prefer a term like *intercultural* or *intracultural* or perhaps even the less compact but more accurate term *leadership in a context of diversity* (see, e.g., Ryan, 2002). Although diversity is often equated with the concept of cultural diversity, one must define culture broadly to be inclusive of all influences that contribute to the dynamic identity formation of an individual or group. Within a school, diversity of class, gender, and ability must also be included in one's definition of culture if the term cross-cultural leadership is to have meaning. Moreover, according to this definition, all leaders are cross-cultural. Hence, for the most part, we simply write about "leaders in the midst of diversity" to emphasize the wide applicability of our discussion.

To state the obvious, schools today are highly diverse. Some of the differences have always existed—differences in physical and intellectual abilities; differences in wealth and advantage; differences in family structure, with many children living with a single parent, another relative, or a court-appointed guardian; or differences in gender and sexual orientation. But few schools in previous decades were what might be called "majority-minority" schools—schools in which the largest single group in the school (sometimes the white or Caucasian students) constitutes a numerical minority and in which "other," often minoritized groups, together constitute the school's numerical majority. Here, we use the term *minoritized* to denote groups that, although in the numerical majority, have been excluded from full participation and access to decision making through the perpetuation of structures and cultures that either covertly or overtly (intentionally or unintentionally) perpetuate deficit thinking, pathologizing, and even neocolonial hegemony. It is perhaps the increasing frequency of this phenomenon that has brought diversity—in its multiple facets—to the forefront of thinking about school leadership.

It is little wonder that there are insistent voices calling for a renewed sense of moral and purposeful leadership in education (Furman, 2003; Shields, 2003), leadership that takes into account the need for social inclusion, for new and heterogeneous school communities, and for democratic citizenship. Yet, even these terms lack clarity and thus provide little guidance for educational leaders wanting to take account of difference in meaningful and appropriate ways.

How does one create learning environments that are socially just and academically excellent and that meet the myriad needs of diverse learners? How does one attend to difference without singling people out or reducing difference to a solitary, essentialized trait? How does one lead morally and purposefully without losing one's way amid the multiple and competing goals? Thomson (cited in Bates, 2003) identifies some of the tensions in this way:

> In significant ways the expectations pull in different directions. Consider whether it is really possible to simultaneously achieve high standards, educate all children to the fullest and give out credentials, the value of which depends at least in part on their scarcity and their capacity to rank and create hierarchy. Sorting, selecting and distributing social and cultural capitals to those that matter are significantly at odds with ideas of equity, justice, and entitlements. They move in different directions. (p. 6)

Let us say, at the outset, that we do not believe these expectations necessarily pull in opposite directions; rather, with some careful attention to how each is framed and understood in the context of the other, all may be successfully addressed by educational leaders in public schools.

The purpose of this chapter is to develop an approach to educational leadership that will help leaders steer a course amid the dynamic tensions that exist within a school environment.

We are familiar with, and supportive of, the literature that advocates increasing the proportion of educational leaders from underrepresented groups and with studies of the particularly strong efforts of many leaders of color in achieving student success in multicultural communities (see Ah Nee-Benham & Cooper, 1998; Baber, 1995; Dillard, 1995; Murtadha-Watts, 1999). In this chapter, we take a different approach, looking primarily beyond the literature in leadership studies (such as Riehl, 2000;[3] Strodl & Johnson, 1994; Vadasy & Maddox, 1992) for additional perspectives to inform the complex task of leading diverse schools. In doing so, we hope to help bridge the traditional theory-practice divide by presenting a framework that will be useful to school-based educational leaders and robust enough theoretically to satisfy the most demanding academic context. To accomplish this, we integrate our review of some existing strands of research and theory into a coherent approach to educational leadership for schools with diverse populations. We conclude by demonstrating how our framework can help the educational leader to bring together what are often seen as competing demands: academic excellence, social justice, and deeply democratic citizenship. Before delving into the various strands of literature that seem to us to be relevant, we provide two illustrative narratives, an explanation of the term *cross-cultural leadership*, and an overview of the argument we will be developing.

SETTING THE SCENE

To ensure that the argument we develop in this chapter brings together theory and practice, we present here two vignettes that will serve to illustrate many of the issues raised and will permit us to develop a complex and nuanced perspective on educational leadership.

One typical approach to cross-cultural leadership is expressed in the following anecdote:

One November morning in 2003, during the feast of *Diwali* (a Hindu festival that leads "into Truth and Light"[4]) a national radio show was broadcast from a large, local secondary school whose majority population was South Asian. The principal of the school had set aside the day for professional development; classes were cancelled, national and internationally renowned performers had been invited, local restaurants had donated food, and all members of the community were invited to participate in the festival activities—food, fashion, cultural performances—a true celebration of light. The broadcaster interviewed a student, asking how he felt about the day. He responded, "I have attended this school for several years, and this is the first time that my culture has been acknowledged." The principal, Randy (a pseudonym), was next. "How did the event come about?" the broadcaster asked. The response was surprising: "We don't see difference in this school. We're color-blind!"

What dissonance! The celebration was wonderful. The excitement was palpable. People came together in new ways. Students felt recognized and valued. The principal had responded to the large Hindu population by staging the celebration at the school. Yet, he purported not to see difference.

Consider a second incident narrated by Anish (one of the authors):

Every December 13, Shia Ismaili Muslims around the world celebrate the birthday of their living Imam (spiritual leader). Earlier in December, another Ismaili parent, Ashifa, my wife Noorjean, and I had discussed the religious significance of the day with our sons' day care staff. Recognizing the importance of this event for us as Muslims, the day care supervisor immediately created space for us to share and celebrate our special day. As we talked, we decided that the structure of the children's morning would remain constant, but the art, reading activities, circle, and snack times would revolve around the theme of Khushiali Mubarak.

After reading two books about Muslim festivals, the children began creating

Khushiali Mubarak cards. The art materials—scissors, glue, paper, and sparkles—were familiar, but the art created that day reflected the diversity and strength of the religious community of which several of the preschool children were also members.

After sharing *samosas* (Indian savories) and juice, the children assembled for circle time, where Noorjean and Ashifa demonstrated how Ismaili Muslims exchange a Khushiali Mubarak greeting. Before the children began practicing the "hand and kiss" gesture, Jennifer, a newly enrolled toddler acknowledged my silence and chirped, "Who's he? Why isn't he speaking?"

As all heads turned toward me, another toddler quipped, "He's Santa Claus." Laughter erupted. More kids parroted, "He's Santa!" Someone asked, "If you're Santa, where is your beard?" To which I responded, "I shaved." Laughter ensued. Ethan asked, "Why aren't you wearing your red suit?" I replied that it was being washed. After more waves of laughter had subsided, a voice from the circle, confident and resolute, exclaimed, "He's not Santa; he's a black man."

In this case, the starting point was the same: the celebration of a festival important to some members of the school community. Yet, we would argue that there were subtle, yet highly significant differences. In the second case, the celebration was not disconnected from the rest of the curriculum. It did not remain outside of the experiences of those who were not "from" that culture but was integrated in unpredictable ways. Who could have known that it would be skin color—not the lack of a flowing white beard, not the absence of a stuffed red suit—that would convince a child that Anish was not Santa? Here there was no denial of difference, but a space to explore it in ways that connected to the daily lives and experiences of the preschoolers.

Clarifying Cross-Cultural Leadership

Cross-cultural leadership is a term used by various theorists but rarely defined. For the most part, *cross-cultural* refers to the position

"that inter- and intra-cultural variations can be better understood by taking context into account" (Hong & Mallorie, 2004, p. 60) and, furthermore, that cultures, defined as "systems of shared meaning among members of different cultural groups" (p. 63) are of particular relevance. In the last two decades, the concept of cross-cultural leadership has gained prominence in education as a way of highlighting the importance of culture and cultures as powerful influences in school communities (see Hofstede, 1991; Kakabadse, Myers, McMahon, & Spony, 1997). The term commonly refers to attempts to lead *across* cultures, in other words, to find some generic approaches to leadership that hold across time, place, and sociocultural contexts. Robertson and Webber (2000), for example, studied a "cross-cultural exchange" intended to "foster participant understandings of educational issues that are prevalent in education internationally" (p. 317).

Sometimes, the emphasis is simply to understand how a given topic is constructed and perceived from within a given culture, with a view to finding similarities and differences across cultures. Hallinger and Leithwood (1996) and Leithwood and Duke (1998), for example, provide extensive studies of leadership models prevalent in various countries, and Walker and Dimmock (2002) examine the "influence of societal culture on leadership and organizational behavior" (p. 167) and identify some of the strengths and weaknesses of the approach. Some other studies examine child rearing of Sami and Norwegian parents (Javo, Ronning, & Heyerdahl, 2004), social work personality psychology (Hong & Mallorie, 2004), aggressive driver attitudes (Lajuenen, Parker, & Summala, 2004), and so forth.

Studies of leadership in different cultural contexts, despite their utility for a macrocomprehension of how schools operate throughout the world, are not the same as understanding how a school leader might address the pluralistic and diverse cultures and needs of students in a given school or district. For this purpose, the influence of culture and cultures is perhaps better illuminated by the twin concepts of hybridity[5] and diversity (Gutierrez, Baquedano-Lopez, & Tejeda, 1999). These ideas (to be elaborated later) suggest that "learning contexts are immanently hybrid, that is, poly-contextual, multivoiced, and multiscripted. Thus conflict, tension, and diversity are intrinsic in learning spaces" (Gutierrez et al., 1999, p. 287).

Although conflict is inherent in multivoiced learning spaces, the treatment of tension in much of the leadership literature suggests that it is something to be avoided or resolved rather than understood (see Greenberg-Walt & Robertson, 2000; Moxley, 2000; Spreitzer & Cummings, 2001). An undue focus on conflict results in perceptions of diversity as a problem, as needing resolution and solution. Yet, because diversity is simply a fact of life, a social reality, it is dangerous and damaging to equate it with difficulties; rather, we would propose embedding discussions of diversity in concepts of possibility and opportunity.

For school leaders, trying to understand all of the various cultures and perspectives of all students and their families seems an impossible and unending task. The need to deal with conflict and tension as well as all of the other competing demands seems overwhelming. Thus, it often seems easier and perhaps most effective to ignore differences, claiming not to see difference but to be color-blind—tolerant and respectful of all. To be sure, human beings share numerous characteristics; however, bell hooks (1992) has called this "homogenizing" approach *racial erasure*, the "sentimental idea . . . that racism would cease to exist if everyone would just forget about race and see each other as human beings who are the same" (p. 12). This approach typically leads to the kind of denial of difference expressed by the principal in the first vignette. Alternatively, people celebrate without further exploration

of the significance of the event to participants or to others. Too often, trying to find generic approaches to leadership results in a disavowal of the richness of the community one is leading. Hence, by cross-cultural leadership, we mean something quite different. For us, the term requires that leaders take a stand in the midst of diversity, helping all members of the community to understand it and to translate those understandings into positive and respectful action.

We maintain first that it is the role of (cross-cultural) leaders to create spaces in which meaningful dialogue may occur, dialogue that helps students to make sense of the formal, informal, and/or hidden curricula (see Delpit, 1993; English, 1992; Macedo, 1995) as students and teachers are encouraged to bring the totality of their lived experiences into the educational context. As understanding is deepened through conversations that permit the exploration of such issues as race, ethnicity, color, class, sexual orientation, or academic ability, relationships are forged, and the groundwork is laid for the development of deeply democratic communities. Thus, we will make the case that the fundamental task of cross-cultural leaders is to transform the institution of learning so that difference becomes part of the daily conversations of the school—in the classroom, teachers' lounge, parent council, formal and informal meetings—so all members of the school community learn to interact in relational and dialogical ways; and so all students will make the connections necessary for them to learn successfully to high levels.

THE LITERATURE

To develop the argument outlined above, we provide an overview of literature that enhances our understanding of the following concepts: space, community, dialogue, identity, difference, and critical multiculturalism. Throughout, we refer to the two vignettes presented earlier to clarify our interpretation of the various literatures. It is important to note here that it is not our intention (neither would it be possible in the space allocated to us) to explore thoroughly each of the theoretical components of the framework that we develop for leading within diversity. Instead, we bring together concepts that are rarely integrated, ideas from various branches of philosophy and disparate strands of intellectual inquiry, to develop an argument for a more robust way of thinking about (and doing) *educational leadership in contexts of diversity*.

Creating Spaces of Encounter

Various theorists have explored the concept of space—both as a physical and a metaphorical construct—as one critically important component of how we understand ourselves and others. Bourdieu (cited in Swingewood, 1998) defines social context as a

> multidimensional space differentiated into distinct fields, networks of objective positions occupied by agents through their possession of different forms of capital—economic (material skills, wealth), cultural (knowledge, intellectual skills) and symbolic (accumulated prestige and sense of honour). (p. 92)

Moreover, Bourdieu employs the notion of *habitus*, or "socialized subjectivity," to suggest the persistence and durability of the dispositions that allow agents to understand, interpret, and act in the social world.

As students (as agents) bring their unique perspectives into the school, spaces become rich, inevitably complex, and potentially contested. Bakhtin (1973), highlighting the need for understanding in such spaces, writes about the importance of carnivalesque spaces in bringing differences into a place where they may be elucidated and better understood. For this, he argues, that "all things that are distant and separated must be brought together in a single 'point' in space and time. And for this the *freedom* of carnival and carnival's artistic conception of space and time are needed"

(p. 148). Bakhtin defines *carnival* as "an attitude toward the world which liberates from fear, brings the world close to man and man close to his fellow man (all is drawn into the zone of liberated familiar contact)" (p. 133). The carnivalesque attitude, he claimed, liberates people from dogmatic and absolutizing attitudes that divide us.

Creating spaces in which one can be liberated from fear is central to understanding difference and living joyfully together. Thus, carnival is one way to overcome the function of the school as a space that, as Gur-Ze'ev (2003) explains, functions as "one of the cultural, social, and economic reproduction apparatuses in service of the dominant group and/or the hegemonic master signifiers and their realm of self-evidence" (p. 21).

Maxine Greene (1992) relates the notion of spaces for freedom and possibility to the goal of education itself: "Progressive education is and will be education for reflective practice and for wide-awakeness and for social concern. It will be carving out wider and wider spaces for freedom and the bite of possibility" (p. 18). Bhabha (1990) proposes the concept of a third space: "one that is *new*, that emerges through cultural encounters and one that cannot be defined in advance" (quoted in Greenwood, 2001, p. 194).

An educational leader must consider the spaces of the school, both physical and metaphorical, as locations for inclusion, acceptance, and respect, or alternatively as locations of marginalization, exclusion, and despair. Palmer (1998) clarifies his use of the term *space* in these words:

> By *space* I mean a complex of factors: the physical arrangement and feeling of the room, the conceptual framework that I build around the topic my students and I are exploring, the emotional ethos I hope to facilitate, and the ground rules that will guide our inquiry. The space that works best for me is one shaped by a series of paradoxes. (p. 73)

He goes on to outline some of the paradoxes: The space should be bounded and open, hospitable and charged; invite the voice of the individual and the voice of the group; honor the "little" stories of the students and the "big" stories of the disciplines and tradition; support solitude and surround it with the resources of the community; and welcome both silence and speech (p. 74).

The burgeoning literature on space clearly suggests the importance of creating spaces in which individuals and groups within a school may encounter and come to understand one another. To facilitate this exploration, school leaders must create spaces of respect, spaces in which each person is treated with "absolute regard" (Starratt, 1991) and in which each not only is encouraged to share his or her personal stories and lived experiences but also perceives the environment to be safe enough to do so.

Anish's experience with Noah's preschool took account of many of these paradoxes. Into the bounded space of the classroom, the big idea and multiple voices of Islam were introduced and honored. But the space also took account of little student stories and individual voices as Jennifer and Ethan explored possible connections between their understanding of Santa and the one who embodied the new ideas of Islam that had been shared. In contrast, the Diwali festival, with all of its excitement, occurred within the physical space of the school but left the conceptual space unexplored. The Diwali celebration (at least as reported to us) provided no opportunities for dialogue or encounter between non-Hindu members of the community and Diwali celebrants.

Creating Communities of Difference

The foregoing discussion of space and its importance in creating a positive atmosphere for all members of the school community implies that more traditional, positivistic, and homogeneous understandings of community are inadequate as a basis for leadership in pluralistic contexts. To those on the margins, understandings of community centered around existing shared norms, beliefs, and values appear to be exclusive and exclusionary, leaving little room for new perspectives and changed norms.

Instead of examining underlying assumptions, one strand of current literature on community focuses on school-community relations (Devlin-Scherer & Devlin-Scherer, 1994; Epstein, Coates, Salinas, Sanders, & Simon, 1997; Van Meter, 1993). The notion of school-community recognizes that the school is not a separate entity but one that is embedded in the social, economic, cultural, and political realities of the wider society (see Strike, 1999). This body of literature acknowledges the importance of partnerships and relationships with parents and community groups—whose roles in supporting the activities of the school are incontrovertible. Nevertheless, its focus is more external than internal, and it does not directly address the need for school leaders to create spaces *within* the school in which all students and teachers feel that they belong.

The literature related to professional learning communities (Mitchell, 1999; Mitchell & Sackney, 2000; Toole & Louis, 2002) may be found under various headings, such as collegiality, teacher networks, or collaboration. It focuses not only on "discrete acts of teacher-sharing, but in the establishment of a school-wide culture that makes collaboration expected, inclusive, genuine, ongoing, and focused on critically examining practice to improve student outcomes" (Toole & Louis, 2002, p. 247). Creating a culture focused on teaching and learning is one necessary component of effective leadership for pluralistic contexts, but it requires careful definition and clarification. If learning communities are organized around transformational rather than transformative leadership,[6] they may promote better overall results but ignore inequities and injustices that continue to marginalize some members of the school community. Moreover, care must be taken to ensure that improving student outcomes is not defined in terms of narrow, test-driven accountability mechanisms, as has been the case of much reform literature, particularly in the wake of the U.S. No Child Left Behind legislation (2001).

While educational leaders must attend both to school-community relations and to the creation of a professional learning community in which teachers are not left to work in isolation behind the closed doors of their classrooms, it also behooves them to look for guidance to the more paradoxical concepts of community that acknowledge difference as well as commonality. Furman-Brown (1999) expressed concern about the dilemma or paradox of "community building in public schools with diverse populations, given that a widely held assumption about community is that it is based in commonalities such as shared values" (p. 7). She used the term *community of otherness* as a postmodern way of thinking about community; subsequently, others have used the term *community of difference* to emphasize the need for educational leaders to take account of difference in meaningful ways (see, e.g., Fine, Weis, & Powell, 1997; Furman & Starratt, 2002; Murtadha-Watts, 1999; Shields, 2000; Shields & Seltzer, 1997; Tierney, 1993). This literature is unabashedly normative, advocating a new kind of community—one that does not try to homogenize or assimilate its members into an established set of shared values, common beliefs, and preferred practices but is inclusive, respectful, equitable, and mutually beneficial. It acknowledges that schooling is not a neutral concept but a profoundly moral ideal to be achieved by educational leaders with a deeply grounded sense of moral purpose. A *community of difference*, like other models of community, is a socially constructed concept. There is no prescription for this type of community because it emerges from strong personal commitments to dialogue, reflection, critique, and social justice and to the basic values of inclusion and respect.

It could be argued that both the Diwali and the preschool incident enhanced school-community relations by welcoming parents into the school's activity. The Diwali celebration, however, maintained traditional boundaries; its parameters were predictable and defined in advance. The Khushiali presentation was more spontaneous; no one could have predicted or orchestrated the response of the children to Anish. For that reason, it had more potential to foster a deeply democratic community of difference—the kind of community that evolves when spaces for encounter, dialogue, and collaborative action are created within the school, spaces that permit people to come together in new ways to best address the needs of all members. In turn, this leads to a fluid and dynamic unity rather than a fixed and irrevocable one.

Facilitating Dialogue

Although many people today use the term *dialogue* to suggest an approach that fosters a sense of community, better understanding, and perhaps even shared vision, there is little clarity about what constitutes meaningful dialogue. First and foremost, it is clear that dialogue is not just talk (see Shields & Edwards, in press); it is not simply an exchange—verbal or otherwise—of ideas or information. Indeed, dialogue begins, as Buber (1970, p. 69) says, with relationship. His differentiation between *I-it* and *I-Thou* relationships is well known. For true dialogue to occur, one must be cognizant of the nature of that relationship. If we interact with another without a genuine desire to know and understand that person, then dialogue is not occurring. Buber explains: "The relation to the You is unmediated. Nothing conceptual intervenes between I and You, no prior knowledge and no imagination" (p. 62). Moreover, Buber makes it clear that in order to enter into relation, I must not *become* Thou but *meet* Thou. Thayer-Bacon (2003), writing more recently, restates the position:

I begin with the assumption that all *people are social beings*. Our lives begin and are lived in relationships with others. The quality of these relationships directly affects our abilities to become knowers. This is because *we develop a sense of "self" through our relationships with others*, and *we need a sense of self in order to become potential knowers.* (p. 7, italics in original)

Indeed, *I-Thou* relationships with others are so important that several thinkers (Buber, 1970; Margonis, 1998; Noddings, 1984; Shields & Edwards, in press; Sidorkin, 1999, 2002) consider them to be ontological: a way of life. Dialogic interaction is the foundation of the educational leader's ability to lead in a context of diversity. We must meet the other, in the fullness of his or her identity, experience, emotions, and actions, in order to develop the relationships that lead to sharing within diversity. We do not become the other, but we are frequently changed in the process in some fundamental and powerful ways as we encounter and learn to understand the other. Once again, we turn to Martin Buber (1970):

He who takes his stand in relation shares in a reality, that is, in a being that neither merely belongs to him nor merely lies outside him. All reality is an activity in which I share without being able to appropriate for myself. Where there is no sharing there is no reality. (p. 64)

When one accepts relation and dialogue as ontological, as starting points for educational leadership, there is a basis for coming into the spaces of schooling. We can share, not with the hegemonic goal of imposing our wants, desires, and beliefs on another, but in a deeply human and respectful manner. We learn to recognize both hybridity and diversity.

Once educational leaders understand relationship as the basis for dialogue, they can proceed to explore some of the complexities of the dialogic relationship. Burbules (1993) picks up on Gadamer's (1960/2002) notion of dialogue

as a *to and fro* between people and describes dialogue as a sort of "game" with some basic "rules"[7] or principles. He suggests that dialogue requires participation, commitment, and reciprocity (pp. 80–81). Participation must be active and voluntary; commitment is aimed at the pursuit of intersubjective understanding; and reciprocity requires that the interaction occur "in a spirit of mutual respect and concern" (p. 82).

While Burbules (1993) focuses on the processes of dialogue, others such as Bakhtin have elaborated both the processes and the outcomes. For Bakhtin (1973), dialogue is so fundamentally basic that it is both the vehicle for all genuine thought and the threshold of action. If we do not encounter the other in the fullness of his or her reality (and yes, difference), then Bakhtin would maintain that there can be no real thinking, no progress or understanding. He writes:

An idea does not *live* in one person's *isolated* individual consciousness—if it remains there it degenerates and dies. An idea begins to live, i.e., to take shape, to develop, to find and renew its verbal expression, and to give birth to new ideas only when it enters into genuine dialogical relationships with other, *foreign,* ideas. Human thought becomes genuine thought, i.e., an idea, only under the conditions of a living contact with another foreign thought, embodied in the voice of another person, that is, in the consciousness of another person as expressed in his word. (p. 71)

Bakhtin (1973) reiterates and reframes the concept a little later in his discussion of the poetics of Dostoevsky by saying, "The truth is not born and does not reside in the head of an individual person; it is born of the dialogical intercourse *between people* in the collective search for truth" (p. 90). Later, he goes further, suggesting that dialogue is not only the basis for action, but "the action itself." For Bakhtin, "to be means to communicate dialogically. When the dialog [sic] is finished, all is finished. Therefore the dialog, in essence, cannot and must not come to an end" (p. 213).

For school leaders, an understanding of dialogue as ontological and deeply relational, leading to meaningful communication and understanding, provides the focus for creating spaces and a sense of community in which all members of the school feel accepted, respected, and valued. If the principal had taken on the task of moving a celebration such as Diwali into the conceptual spaces of the school, facilitating both formal and informal conversations focused on the experiences of both participants and observers, true dialogue might have occurred, understanding have happened, and meanings have changed. If, however, as occurred here, Diwali remains at the level of an *it*—a celebration, a festival—then much of the potential for creating shared meanings as a basis for community remains untapped. On the other hand, when the kinds of conversation that Anish and his family initiated in the preschool classroom become the norm, then the Other is no longer an exoticized or foreign *It*. The dialogue has led to new understandings and deeper, more inclusive relationships. Poignantly here, even a young child noted Anish's silence and took steps to draw him, in her unique way, into the dialogic relations of the circle where others were permitted to ask about his appearance.

Understanding Identity and Difference

In the last few decades, educational interest in issues of identity and difference has grown (McCarthy & Crichlow, 1993; Pinar, 1993; Taubman, 1993); yet the topics are still largely ignored in leadership literature. Without a fundamental understanding of these concepts, educational leaders risk falling into the traps of exoticizing or essentializing difference, of assuming that one salient feature defines a student or entitles him or her to *represent* a particular culture or position.

Dolby (2000, p. 991) states that "difference is not a static, immobile, 'reality,' but a discursively constructed set of practices that reverberate throughout a society; difference is always constructed within, expresses, and produces power." Rather than difference being conceived as a fixed and static quality that distinguishes self from other, it is fluid. As Stuart Hall asserts, "difference does not exist outside of the particular conditions that produce it" (cited in Dolby, 2000, p. 992). Hence, when all students within a school population are accepted as members of the community, there is neither insider nor outsider. Power relations are diminished. The boundary is circumscribed around everyone, rather than drawn between groups of students, dividing them because of specific academic ability, skin color, religious persuasion, and so forth.

This notion of difference is integral to understanding the construction of identities. School leaders must take pains to ensure that the conversations and actions manifest within the school avoid false binaries such as self and other, we and they, insider and outsider, or white and brown. Such binaries lead to the privileging of an "in" group and the marginalization and pathologization of an "out" group, that is, the ones who are different (Hall, 1997). Identities are, as we have said before of the learning context, "polycontextual, multivoiced, and multiscripted" (Gutierrez et al., 1999). Not only are identities formed from a multiplicity of sources (including ethnicity, social class, sexuality, gender, nationality, daily interactions, preferred activities, and so forth), they are also fragmented and often internally contradictory.

Equating a person's identity with a single, often observable characteristic ignores the richness and complexity of human nature, reducing the person so characterized to a caricature, a flat and one-dimensional entity, an *it*, rather than a *Thou* with whom it is instructive to enter into dialogue and relation. Hybridity, another central feature of our understanding of both individual and group identities, emphasizes that identities are constantly changing, grafting new features onto traditional ways of thinking and acting, responding to changes in the environment in innovative and creative ways, and initiating change in a proactive way because of the catalytic effect of a novel idea.

Understood in this way, identity is dynamic and thus depends no longer on superficial or assumed commonalities with a specific person or group, but on the creation of meaningful relationships, conversations, and interactions within the learning environment. Just as identity is not fixed, the meanings constructed from dialogic interactions within diverse populations are also fluid. As Derrida (1982) suggests, "the signified concept is never present in and of itself" (p. 11). Meaning, as Derrida's concept of *différance* suggests, is produced through a process of deferral; our understanding of difference is constantly being expanded, transmuted, and nuanced. Together, as Bakhtin suggested, we simultaneously create meaning and understanding through dialogue.

As presented to the school population, Diwali was fixed. It was showcased and enacted, offered as an artifact, without opportunity for meaning-making on the part of observers. Anish as Santa, however, constituted an exemplar of meaning deferred. As the children began to develop an understanding of Khushiali, a festival outside of many of their experiences, they were permitted to introduce their own sense of the season, overcoming the potential for conflict or binary we-they thinking. Although the preschoolers likely failed to attain even a rudimentary understanding of the importance of the Imam in Islam, stronger relationships were forged, new ideas planted, and the potential for fuller understanding achieved, albeit deferred.

Considering Multiculturalism

One of the current educational challenges, as we see it, is that educators have commonly tried to address issues of identity and difference by instituting multicultural education without understanding the foregoing concepts.

In recent years, multicultural awareness programs have been introduced in many schools; at the same time, numerous theorists have offered various critiques of the superficiality of many of the approaches to multiculturalism in education. (See, e.g., Banks, 1991; Derman-Sparks, 1995; May, 1999; Moodley, 1995; Nieto, 2000; Sleeter & McLaren, 1995). We build on their insight and on the comprehensive critique offered by Kincheloe and Steinberg (1998) that provides a systematic approach to understanding some of the difficulties inherent in various approaches to multiculturalism.

Kincheloe and Steinberg (1998) identify five variants of multiculturalism: conservative, liberal, pluralist, left-essentialist, and critical (pp. 3–26). In general, their critique is that common approaches to multicultural education err in several ways. They either recognize difference but attempt to overcome it, reject difference in favor of "common humanity," emphasize and celebrate difference without disrupting "the dominant Western narratives" (p. 15), or attribute essentializing characteristics to specific cultures, "failing to appreciate the historical situatedness of cultural differences" (p. 19). As an alternative to the first four approaches, Kincheloe and Steinberg propose *critical multiculturalism*, a process they claim is "based on an emancipatory commitment to social justice and the egalitarian democracy that accompanies it" (p. 26). In challenging the inequities of power, critical multiculturalism becomes a "transformative project" (p. 26).

Multicultural education in the form of diversity celebration is, therefore, not the answer. Neither is attempting to infuse the curriculum with units of "cultural relevance" that are either disconnected from the "conversations that make sense of things" or offered as add-on or enrichment exercises if time permits. Aside from some innovative curricular approaches that critically examine how racism, sexism, and class bias (for example) are produced and perpetuated (Craft, 1984; DeVillar, Faltis, & Cummins, 1994; Harrison, Smith, & Wright, 1999; Henderson & Hawthorne, 1995; Rader & Sittig, 2003; Takaki, 2001), dominant North American educational activities have grown out of the first four types of multiculturalism summarized by Kincheloe and Steinberg (1997). Although critical multiculturalism has the potential to disrupt inequities and affect underlying assumptions, narratives, and hegemonic positionings, it has remained largely at the theoretical level, difficult for most educators to translate into practice. Grounded in theoretical understandings of critical theory, the pedagogical utility has been elusive.

Carolyn (one coauthor), in listening to the radio broadcast of the school's Diwali celebration, was a cultural tourist, listening to world-class performers as they played "Indian" instruments for the amusement and entertainment of the listening audience. Like so many multicultural activities introduced into our classrooms, the performances were fixed, recorded, and available for future generations to access and enjoy. Anish, although initially silent, was brought into the midst of the sense-making conversation because of Jennifer's question. The process was not fixed but deferred; not completed and replicable but dialogical. Although both activities hold the potential for increased understanding and further exploration, the preschool conversation had begun a process of co-construction of meaning[8] that had not yet been realized in the Diwali celebration.

We maintain that understanding critical multiculturalism in this light can support a theory of educational cross-cultural leadership, or leadership for contexts of diversity, that is firmly embedded in the lived experiences of children, making possible spaces of encounter, dialogue, relationship, and understanding, where each voice can contribute to the sense-making process of the whole community.

DIALOGUE IN COMMUNITY SPACES ABOUT DIFFERENCE

Once educational leaders have begun to understand recent theorizing about identity and difference, they must find ways to bring this comprehension to the educational context. We take as a starting point Madeleine Grumet's discussion of curriculum (formal, informal, and hidden). Grumet (1995) emphasizes that our "relationships to the world are rooted in our relationships to the people who care for us" (p. 19). She claims that "curriculum is never the text, or the topic, never the method or the syllabus"; but curriculum is "the conversation that makes sense of ... things. ... It is the process of making sense with a group of people of the systems that shape and organize the world we can think about together" (p. 19).

Effective educational leaders in contexts of diversity will create open yet bounded spaces within which people may find acceptance, begin to come together in community, encounter one another, and engage in meaningful dialogue. They will explore ways to understand identity and difference that are less essentializing and more nuanced than multicultural approaches generally promote. Then, they will seek to facilitate, model, and initiate conversations to make sense of things, perhaps using some of the following concepts as starting points for teaching and learning in diverse educational settings.

Rejecting Deficit Thinking

The vast literature on deficit thinking (see the discussions of Gould, 1996, and Valencia & Solórzano, 1997), pathologizing the lived experiences of children (Bishop & Glynn, 1999; Nash, 1997; Palmer, 2000; Shields, Bishop, & Mazawi, in press), and blaming the victim (see McLaren's 2003 critique) convinces us that to make sense of things, participants in the conversation must first reject deficit thinking.

Where individuals or groups have been successful in school, they have been held up as examples—as proof—that hard work leads to success, thus perpetuating the sense that those who have not succeeded have simply failed to apply themselves. Alternatively, in many developed countries, those who are seen as different in some way, whose reality is not congruent with the fundamentally white, middle-class norms of education, have been marginalized, minoritized, and pathologized. Deficit thinking or pathologizing the lived experiences of children may be defined as Shields, Bishop, and Mazawi (in press) have done:

> Pathologizing is a process where perceived structural-functional, cultural, or epistemological deviation from an assumed normal state is ascribed to another group as a product of power relationships, whereby the less powerful group is deemed to be abnormal in some way. Pathologizing is a mode of colonization used to govern, regulate, manage, marginalize, or minoritize primarily through hegemonic discourses. (p. 2)

Although it is never possible to completely overcome inequitable power relationships, a focus on the other as *Thou* certainly permits one to reject the myth of abnormality and to encounter one another in dialogue with "absolute regard." To ensure the dialogic encounter becomes the norm in a school community, one must focus both on the processes we have already described and also on the content of the discourse.

Wagstaff and Fusarelli (1999), for example, found that the single most important factor in the academic achievement of minority children was the *explicit* rejection of deficit thinking by the school-based administrator. Bishop and colleagues (Bishop, Berryman, & Richardson, 2001; Bishop, Berryman, Tiakiwai, & Richardson, 2003) have found that when teachers were trained to avoid deficit thinking, the academic achievement of Maori students increased within months; moreover, both researchers and respondents report that the conversations in staff rooms have changed to the extent that teachers gently correct each other. "You're in deficit thinking, now," they feel free to say. School leaders who want to be effective cross-cultural leaders will need to listen carefully for the implicit and explicit messages being given to children in the school by their peers, teachers, or other members of the community.

Incorporating Lived Experiences

The conversation must also permit each individual to bring the fullness of his or her lived reality into the spaces we call school. Much has been written in recent years about the dissonance between the values, beliefs, and practices of the school and those of the homes of many children. Macedo (1995), for example, asserts that at present, the dominant curriculum "is designed primarily to reproduce the inequality of social classes, while it mostly benefits the interests of the dominant class" (p. 54). Drawing on Foucault's work, he emphasizes the role of power in defining what counts as knowledge and, hence, in shaping the official curriculum. Macedo urges that power in education be examined through a discussion of the politics of "which content gets taught, to whom, in favor of what, of whom, against what, against whom" (p. 43). These are other conversations in which educational leaders would want to engage if the curriculum of our schools is to make sense to all children. They will ask what metaphors and images they use in their instruction that require specific kinds of social, political, and cultural knowledge to participate fully in the conversations. For, as Freire (2000b) states, "To read the word is to read the world" (p. 163).

Using the definition of curriculum as sense-making conversations and relationships, educators will find ways to connect the content, knowledge, values, and perspectives of the formal curriculum to the lived experiences of students. We will no longer rely on a narrow repertoire of images, sounds, and smells that are common to middle-class experiences but broaden our perspectives to be more reflective of the ranges of experiences lived by the children in our schools (for further discussions of social class, see Brantlinger, 2003; Davies, 1999; hooks, 1992, 2000; Knapp & Woolverton, 1995).

Acknowledgment that current conversations and the curriculum that results are relatively narrow helps us to understand that ability to learn and opportunity to learn are not synonymous (see Larson & Murtadha, 2001). Children whose prior experiences are most like those represented and valued in our curricula are advantaged and readily able to make connections, whereas other children with different experiences also have equally valid knowledge and experiences that can form the basis for legitimate connections. It is important not only to acknowledge and build on the experiences of children who have traveled with their families or attended local cultural activities but also to acknowledge those children who have learned to be self-reliant at a young age—to ride the bus, to do the shopping, meal planning, and home care for younger siblings. Educators must consider not only the traditional two-generation family often reflected in the narratives and texts of schools in developed countries but the wider support networks of children whose cultures value the wisdom and contributions of grandparents, great-grandparents, aunts, and uncles, all living under one roof.

The message is that children must be able to bring the totality of their lived experiences to the conversation that makes sense of things without shame and without fear of ridicule. Note, this does not mean that as educators we either accept or value abusive or dysfunctional situations, only that we do not blame the children or make them more fearful, ashamed, and vulnerable than they already are. It is important for all children, as they make sense

of things in age-appropriate ways, to confront the unpleasant reality that in our society some people face very difficult physical and emotional circumstances whereas others live in relative ease and comfort (for good examples of such conversations, see Vibert, Portelli, & Leighteizer, 1998).

Rejecting Color Blindness

We return to the story of the Diwali celebration presented earlier in this chapter to address head-on the concept of color blindness, another topic that must be included in the sense-making conversation. Here, we use color blindness as a sort of metaphor for rejection of, or silence about, any kind of diversity represented in our schools. The discussion is therefore about more than color; indeed, it is equally applicable to how we address such realities as class, poverty, advantage, physical and intellectual abilities and disabilities, and gender orientation, as well as race, ethnicity, and ethnoculture.

Principal Randy insisted that in his school, people did not see color; yet, it was the presence of a large visible minority student body that had precipitated the cancellation of classes for the Diwali celebration. Indeed, his assertion convinces us of the separateness of that celebration. If the shared norm of the school is one that overtly ignores difference, relating it to special moments rather than integrating it into the conversations that make sense of things, then we are led to ask about the nature of the encounter, understandings, and dialogue that might result. We maintain that it was the recognition of difference (color, ethnicity, and religion) that prompted the celebration in the first place. Why then, if it was important enough to warrant a full day, was it kept outside, maintaining an image of Other, rather than becoming part of the fabric of the conversation? We contend (with Kincheloe & Steinberg, 1998, and many others, e.g., Akintude & Cooney, 1998; Holcomb-McCoy,

1999; Johnson, 1999; Roman, 1993) that advocating color blindness, although perhaps well intentioned, perpetuates hegemonic *I-It* power relations, in that only the one who purports to be color-blind has the luxury of denying the fact that was the impetus for the statement in the first place. Given the splendor of diversity, why would anyone want to choose color blindness, reducing brightly colored and richly textured hues to a bland shade of gray?

On the other hand, the conversation between Anish and the young preschoolers in the second anecdote is an excellent example of addressing difference. Anish did not raise the topic. He did not go into the classroom intending to make color (or race or ethnicity) a focal point; yet, he is brown. This is an undeniable fact. To deny it or brush it off with a comment about everyone being the same would have been to shut down conversation, eliminating an opportunity for connection and understanding.

Diversity is a fact. Diversity is not to be celebrated as an exotic manifestation of otherness but to be enjoyed and appreciated as the gift of life itself. Hence, purporting to be color-blind (or ignoring differences of any other kind) is neither caring nor appropriate. Effective school leaders, wanting to lead with sensitivity and strength in a pluralistic community, will ensure that the conversations that make sense of things do not artificially draw boundaries that exclude legitimate elements of the lived experiences of either teachers or students.

Rejecting Spiritual Blindness

Because of its unique position in law and in the sensitivities of many people, we want to specifically address the need to make sense of spirituality and spiritual differences in education. We define spirituality using the words of Starratt (2003): "being present to the most profound realities of one's life" (p. 1).[9] Our position is consistent with the legal status of religion and religious instruction in the United States, Canada, and many other developed countries.

We are not advocating any form of religious teaching (except in organized classes about world religions and denominations) in schools. Yet, we are deeply concerned about any actions or policies on the part of educators that deny children or adults the ability to make connections to the deepest realities of their lives. We have been profoundly troubled when we have heard media reports that a young child from a Christian family has been forbidden to quietly say her own prayer of thanks at snack time in kindergarten, that parents such as Anish and Noorjean have been refused the opportunity to share something of their traditions, or that children have been instructed not to use the word *God* in any of their conversations while at school. And we are dismayed when the head of a department, seeking to console a colleague on the death of his parents, is censured for saying "our prayers are with you."

Although specific instruction may be inappropriate, asking people to deny what constitutes the deepest realities of their lives is a way of rejecting the very real and legitimate knowledge perspectives they bring to the school community. We cannot lead effectively in diverse school communities if, by our silence, we either pretend that we all believe the same thing or we marginalize and essentialize those who hold alternative beliefs or faith perspectives.

We return to Palmer's (1998) notion of a space that is both bounded and open to suggest that while the appropriate boundaries must be negotiated within each community, they must always make room for both big and little stories of life and faith. The acceptable boundaries will proscribe proselytizing but will not prohibit natural connections. When we draw the boundaries too narrowly around spirituality or any other difference, our very silence suggests something unnatural, exotic, perhaps even fearful, and helps to create and perpetuate myths like some of the current representations of all Muslims as fanatics and terrorists.[10]

In this section, we have provided a brief overview of some literature that demonstrates the importance of rejecting deficit thinking as a basis for sense-making conversations. Furthermore, we have argued that ignoring difference is one way of denying the lived realities of children. We have also posited that by purporting, for example, to be color-blind or by denying the legitimate right of all members of the school community to express their deepest beliefs and values, we convey the clear message that the community is made up of distinct groups: powerful insiders and minoritized and marginalized outsiders. One task of educational leaders, working in contexts of diversity, is therefore to create safe spaces in which meaningful dialogue may occur.

IMPLICATIONS FOR EDUCATIONAL LEADERS

To this point, we have developed a framework for what we believe to be an appropriate and effective way of thinking about cross-cultural educational leadership for schools that are inevitably diverse. We have claimed that educational leaders must create spaces in which all members of the community are respected, in which relationships of "absolute regard" prevail, spaces in which diversity (including cultural differences) is not essentialized but encountered dialogically. We have suggested some concepts that must be addressed rather than silenced, either due to their potential for conflict or because educators are unfamiliar with them and unable to predict or control the conversation.

We conclude this chapter with a brief examination of some of the implications of our model for school leaders and their communities. In short, we believe that the approach we have outlined will help school leaders to bring together what are often conceived as separate and competing goals and to achieve academic excellence grounded in a socially just vision of education and in a deep sense of democratic citizenship that promotes not only the unity of the school community

but also a better understanding of global citizenship (see, e.g., Barber, 2001; Furman & Shields, 2003; Goodlad, 2001). Our claims seem grandiose, and there is no sense in which we believe this particular model of leadership will achieve these ends perfectly; nevertheless, we are persuaded that it will help all members of the school—parents, educators, and students—to move toward these desired ends.

Our vision of leadership for diverse communities is fundamentally relational. It is holistic, taking difference seriously as part of the wonderful rich reality of human existence, but not focusing narrowly or unduly on difference. It is an approach that eschews binaries—we–they, us–other—and one that is careful not to essentialize or pathologize the very complex, always dynamic lived realities of individuals and groups.

Educational Outcomes

One of the most significant pressures facing educational leaders in this decade is the need for accountability for student outcomes. Many current approaches to accountability equate academic success with high scores on standardized tests, reducing the concept of academic excellence to an almost meaningless statistic. We therefore argue strenuously for a more meaningful definition of academic excellence, one that takes into account various student outcomes, demonstrated in multiple ways and using multiple measures. Nevertheless, we accept the strong message coming from many accountability movements that success must be for all children (see Adams & Karabenick, 2000; Raivetz, 1992), that no sociocultural group should be disadvantaged because its members have had less opportunity to learn those outcomes that are measured, when they have equal ability to learn (Skrla & Scheurich, 2001).

We believe that research demonstrates convincingly that helping students to make connections between what is taught and their lived experiences makes more meaningful neural connections (Caine & Caine, 1991), facilitates student engagement (see Newmann, 1992; Smith, Donahue, & Vibert, 1998), increases their opportunity to learn (Caine & Caine, 1991; Larson & Murtadha, 2001; Shields & Vibert, 2003), and hence, results not only in greater academic success but in academic excellence more broadly defined.

Socially Just Outcomes

Farrell (1999) asserts that for academic outcomes to be equitable and socially just, educators must attend to equality of access, sustainability, outcomes, and outputs. When children who have previously been marginalized or minoritized are encouraged to bring to the curricular conversations their own stories that help them to "make sense of things," they feel a greater sense of belonging, a sense of acceptance as legitimate and participating members of the school community. In turn, they are less likely to be pathologized or segregated into lower level, less challenging courses. Moreover, as they participate as co-creators of meaning, they are less likely to drop out; rather, as Bishop et al. (2003) have clearly demonstrated, they begin to achieve to the same high levels as their peers who were previously separated into more challenging academic programs. As students who were previously considered unable to complete graduation requirements or to proceed to university programs demonstrate their abilities, longer term outcomes for them and for society become more optimistic. By being more inclusive, more meaningful, more respectful, and more sensitive, education can open doors of opportunity and windows of understanding for all students.

Deeply Democratic Outcomes

Maxine Greene (cited in Banks, 1991) asks: "What does it mean to be a citizen of the free world?" She concludes that it is "having the capacity to choose, the power to act to attain one's purposes, and the ability to help transform a world lived in common with others" (p. 32). The model we have advanced of leadership in contexts of diversity prepares students for life in a world in common, but not in conformity, with others. It helps to break down barriers and binaries, it overcomes essentializing and stereotypical myths about the other and about difference, and it overthrows balkanization by demonstrating the empowerment that comes from being part of a community of difference.

Judith Green (1999) writes about *deep democracy* as opposed to formal systems; she describes it as a "conception of democracy that expresses the experience-based possibility of more equal, respectful, and mutually beneficial ways of community life" (p. vi). Our model of leadership has emphasized the importance of creating school communities in which relationships of equality, respect, and mutuality are facilitated and fostered as everyone is able to make sense of their formal educational experiences in the light of the totality of their lived experiences.

LEADING IN THE MIDST OF DIVERSITY

To lead effectively in the midst of the diversity that exists in all schools, educators must come to understand their beliefs, values, assumptions, and positionings—the worlds they carry in their heads. They must also, as Delpit (1993) suggested, find ways to acknowledge, understand, and "reach" the worlds of others. We have proposed, based on the literatures related to spaces, community, dialogue, identity, difference, and multiculturalism, some starting point for making connections with the worlds carried by others in our organizations. The creation of safe, open (yet bounded) spaces—physical, psychological, emotional, social, and conceptual—in which others may share their lived experiences is essential.

Establishing dialogic relations based on absolute regard for each member of the community is a necessary complement. As stated earlier, we conceptualize dialogue as fundamentally ontological, the basis for understanding difference: Dialogue is not just talk. Thus, the ability and willingness to acknowledge and understand difference and to engage in dialogue about difference are essential to leading in the midst of diversity.

As we have shown in our discussion of the Diwali festival, we cannot ignore difference; moreover, it is not adequate (although it is certainly important) to celebrate it. We must encounter difference and diversity, bring them into our educational spaces, and engage in the conversations that make sense of other worlds, changing our understandings, and ultimately ourselves in the process. We are not rejecting the possibilities inherent in shared celebrations (Anish and Noorjean shared samosas and juice with the children); we are suggesting that educational leaders must integrate celebrations like Diwali and Khushiali into the central spaces of institutional learning.

The model we have developed is beguilingly simple. It does not ask leaders to know enough about the diversity in their schools to *teach* it; rather, we are asking that each educator acknowledge the existence of other worlds and encourage their exploration, taking seriously the potential of dialogic relations as fundamentally ontological.

Freire (2000a) described the relationship of dialogue to education in this way: "Dialogue is an I–Thou relationship, and thus necessarily a relationship between two Subjects. Each time the "thou" is changed into an object, an "it," dialogue is subverted and education is changed to deformation" (p. 89). When difference is objectified, celebrated in *I-it* ways, it is robbed of its transformative potential, and dialogue is subverted. When we encounter difference dialogically, it holds the potential for transformation, for meaningful relationships and deeply democratic learning communities. The challenge, as we see it, for educational leaders who lead in the midst of diversity in this decade, is to lead so that schools may fulfill their potential for transforming the education we offer our children as well as the society in which they will live and work.

NOTES

1. We acknowledge that schools have always been diverse. Nevertheless, in terms of demographics alone, according to the Organization for Economic Cooperation and Development's statistics, in 2001–2002 the United States admitted more than 1 million permanent residents who now represent roughly 10% of the total population. Canada and New Zealand admitted unprecedented numbers, and France, Austria, and Switzerland admitted 15% more than in previous years (*Vancouver Sun,* January 22, 2004).

2. The term was used by Shields (2003), for example; but increasingly as educators are involved in the quest for similarities and differences across cultures, we are concerned about the potential for essentializing constructs and hence prefer to avoid the label *cross-cultural.*

3. For an excellent review of extant literature, see also Riehl (2000).

4. For a fuller description of the origins and significance of the festival, see Bisen (2004).

5. Hybridity, in sociology, as in biology, refers quite simply to "something of mixed origin or composition" (*The American Heritage Dictionary,* 2002, Houghton Mifflin Co.). We use the term to suggest the fluidity of sociological constructs such as culture, identity, or difference.

6. See the discussion and clarification in Shields (2003). *Transformational* leadership tends to focus on internal organizational qualities, whereas *transformative* leadership moves beyond to address inequities and injustices that may occur within and outside of the organization.

7. Burbules (1993, p. 66) indicates that he uses the term *rule* with ambivalence. We join him in this, wishing he had selected a term with less prescriptive and more playful connotations.

8. We want to emphasize here that we are talking about the co-construction of *meaning,* each one taking his or her understanding based on his or her cultural positioning; this does not necessitate or imply a change in the fundamental ceremony, a change that can only legitimately be made by adherents to the position itself.

9. For a more thorough investigation of the implications of this definition, see C. M. Shields, M. M. Edwards, & A. Sayani (in press), *Inspiring Practices: Spirituality and Educational Leadership.*

10. For further exploration of this issue, see Sayani (in press).

REFERENCES

Adams, L., & Karabenick, S. A. (2000). *Impact of state testing on students and teaching practices: Much pain, no gain?* (ERIC Document Reproduction Service No. ED443870)

Ah Nee-Benham, M. K. P., & Cooper, J. E. (1998). *Let my spirit soar! Narratives of diverse women in school leadership.* Thousand Oaks, CA: Sage.

Akintude, O., & Cooney, M. H. (1998). *On confronting white privilege and the "color-blind" paradigm in a teacher education program.* Laramie, WY: University of Wyoming, College of Education.

Baber, C. R. (1995). Leaders of color as catalysts for community building in a multicultural society. *Theory and Research in Social Education, 23*(4), 342–354.

Bakhtin, M. (1973). *Problems of Dostoevsky's poetics.* Ann Arbor, MI: Ardis.

Banks, J. A. (1991). Multicultural education: For freedom's sake. *Educational Leadership, 49*(4), 32–36.

Barber, B. (2001). An aristocracy of everyone. In S. J. Goodlad (Ed.), *The last best hope: A democracy reader* (pp. 11–24). San Francisco: Jossey-Bass.

Bates, R. (2003, December). *On the governance of public education.* Paper presented to the NZARE/AARE Joint Conference, Auckland, NZ.

Bhabha, H. (1990). The third space. In J. Rutherford (Ed.), *Identity: Community, culture, difference* (pp. 207–221). London: Lawrence & Wishart.

Bisen, M. (2004). *Diwali.* Retrieved January 2004 from http://www.bawarchi.com/festivals/diwali1.html

Bishop, R., Berryman, M., & Richardson, C. (2001). *Te Toi Huarewa. Report to the Ministry of Education.* Wellington, NZ: Ministry of Education.

Bishop, R., Berryman, M., Tiakiwai, S., & Richardson, C. (2003). *Te Kōtahitanga: The experiences of Year 9 and 10 Māori students in mainstream classrooms* (Report to Ministry of Education. Wellington, NZ). Retrieved from www.minedu.govt.nz/goto/tekotahitanga

Bishop, R., & Glynn, T. (1999). *Culture counts: Changing power relations in education.* Palmerston North, NZ: Dunmore.

Brantlinger, E. (2003). *Dividing classes.* London: RoutledgeFalmer.

Buber, M. (1970). *I and thou.* New York: Charles Scribner's Sons.

Burbules, N. C. (1993). *Dialogue in teaching.* New York: Teachers College Press.

Caine, R. N., & Caine, G. (1991). *Making connections: Teaching and the human brain.* Alexandria, VA: Association for Supervision and Curriculum Development.

Codd, J. A. (2003, December). *Reconnecting education policy to social polity: Towards a new agenda.* Paper presented to the NZARE/AARE Joint Conference, Auckland, NZ.

Craft, M. (1984). Education for diversity. In M. Craft (Ed.), *Education and cultural pluralism.* London: Falmer Press.

Davies, S. (1999). Stubborn disparities: Explaining class inequalities in schooling. In R. F. Arnove & C. A. Torres (Eds.), *Comparative education: The dialectic of the global and the local* (pp. 138–150). New York: Rowman & Littlefield.

Delpit, L. (1993). *Other people's children: Cultural conflict in the classroom.* New York: The New Press.

Derman-Sparks, L. (1995). How well are we nurturing racial and ethnic diversity? In D. Levine et al. (Eds.), *Rethinking schools: An agenda for change.* New York: The New Press.

Derrida, J. (1982). *Margins of philosophy* (A. Bass, Trans.). Chicago: University of Chicago Press.

DeVillar, R., Faltis, C. J., & Cummins, J. P. (1994). *Cultural diversity in schools: From rhetoric to practice.* New York: SUNY Press.

Devlin-Scherer, R., & Devlin-Scherer, W. L. (1994). Do school boards encourage parent involvement? *Education 114*(4), 535–542.

Dillard, C. B. (1995). Leading with her life: An African American feminist for an urban high school principal. *Educational Administration Quarterly, 31*(4), 539–563.

Dolby, N. (2000). Changing selves: Multicultural education and the challenge of new identities. *Teacher College Record, 102*(5), 898–912.

English, F. W. (1992). *Deciding what to teach and test.* Newbury Park, CA: Corwin.

Epstein, J. L., Coates, L., Salinas, K. C., Sanders, M. G., & Simon, B. S. (1997). *School, family, and community partnerships.* Thousand Oaks, CA: Corwin.

Farrell, J. P. (1999). Changing conceptions of equality of education: Forty years of comparative education. In R. F. Arnove & C. A. Torres (Eds.), *Comparative education: The dialectic of the global and the local* (pp. 149–177). Lanham, MD: Rowman & Littlefield.

Fine, M., Weis, L., & Powell, L. C. (1997). Communities of difference: A critical look at desegregated spaces created for and by youth. *Harvard Educational Review, 67*(2), 247–284.

Freire, P. (2000a). Education for critical consciousness. In A. M. A. Freire & D. Macedo (Eds.), *The Paulo Freire reader* (pp. 80–110). New York: Continuum.

Freire, P. (2000b). Literacy: Reading the word and the world. In A. M. A. Freire & D. Macedo (Eds.), *The Paulo Freire reader* (pp. 111–163). New York: Continuum.

Furman, G. (2003). The 2002 UCEA presidential address. *UCEA Review, 45*(1), 1–6.

Furman, G. C., & Shields, C. M. (2003, November). *How can educational leaders promote and support social justice and democratic community in schools?* Paper prepared for the American Educational Research Association, Division A, research agenda task force, and presented to the Annual Conference of the University Council for Educational Administration, Cincinnati, OH.

Furman, G. C., & Starratt, R. J. (2002). Leadership for democratic community in schools. In J. Murphy (Ed.), *The educational leadership challenge: Redefining leadership for the 21st century* (pp. 105–133). Chicago: National Society for the Study of Education.

Furman-Brown, G. (1999). Editor's foreword. *Educational Administration Quarterly, 35*(1), 6–12.

Gadamer, H. G. (2002). *Truth and method* (2nd, rev. ed.) (J. Weinsheimer & D. Marshall, Trans.). New York: Continuum. [Original work published 1960]

Goodlad, S. J. (2001). *The last best hope: A democracy reader.* San Francisco: Jossey-Bass.

Gould, S. J. (1996). *The mismeasure of man.* New York: W. W. Norton.

Green, J. M. (1999). *Deep democracy: Diversity, community, and transformation.* Lanham, MD: Rowman & Littlefield.

Greenberg-Walt, C., & Robertson, A. G. (2000). The evolving role of executive leadership. In W. Bennis et al. (Eds.), *The future of leadership.* San Francisco: Jossey-Bass.

Greene, M. (1992). Perspective and diversity: Toward a common ground. In F. Pignelli &

S. W. Pflaum (Eds.), *Celebrating diverse voices: Progressive education and equity.* Newbury Park, CA: Corwin.

Greenwood, J. (2001). Within a third space. *Research in drama education, 6*(2), 193–205.

Grumet, M. R. (1995). The curriculum: What are the basics and are we teaching them? In J. L. Kincheloe & S. R. Steinberg (Eds.), *Thirteen questions: Reframing education's conversation.* New York: Peter Lang.

Gur-Ze'ev, I. (2003). Critical theory, critical pedagogy, and the possibility of counter-education. In M. L. Peters & C. M. Olssen (Eds.), *Critical theory and the human condition* (pp. 17–35). New York: Peter Lang.

Gutierrez, K. D., Baquedano-Lopez, P., & Tejeda, C. (1999). Rethinking diversity: Hybridity and hybrid language practices in the third space. *Mind, culture, and activity, 6*(4), 286–303.

Hall, S. (1997). The spectacle of "the Other." In S. Hall (Ed.), *Representation: Cultural representations and signifying practices.* London: Sage.

Hallinger, P., & Leithwood, K. (1996). Culture and educational administration: A case of finding out what you didn't know you don't know. *Journal of Educational Administration, 34*(5), 98–116.

Harrison, J., Smith, N., & Wright, I. (1999). *Critical challenges in social studies.* British Columbia: Critical Thinking Cooperative.

Henderson, J. G., & Hawthorne, R. D. (1995). *Transformative curriculum leadership.* Englewood Cliffs, NJ: Prentice Hall/Merrill.

Hofstede, G. (1991). *Cultures and organizations: Software of the mind.* New York: McGraw-Hill.

Holcomb-McCoy, C. C. (1999, April). *Understanding "whiteness" in academia: A black woman's perspective.* Paper presented at the Annual Meeting of the American Educational Research Association, Montreal.

Hong, Y., & Mallorie, L. M. (2004). A dynamic constructivist approach to culture: Lessons learned from personality psychology. *Journal of Research in Personality, 38,* 59–67.

hooks, b. (1992). *Black looks: Race and representation.* Cambridge, MA: South End Press.

hooks, b. (2000). *Where we stand: Class matters.* New York: Routledge.

Javo, C., Ronning, J. A., & Heyerdahl, S. (2004). Child-rearing in an indigenous Sami population in Norway: A cross-cultural comparison of parental attitudes and expectations. *Scandinavian Journal of Psychology, 45,* 67–78.

Johnson, L. (1999, April). *"My eyes have been opened": White teachers coming to racial consciousness.* Paper presented at the Annual Meeting of the American Educational Research Association, Montreal.

Kakabadse, A., Myers, A., McMahon, T., & Spony, G. (1997). Top management styles in Europe: Implications for business and cross-national teams. In K. Grint (Ed.), *Leadership.* Oxford, UK: Oxford University Press.

Kincheloe, J. L., & Steinberg, S. R. (1997). *Changing multiculturalism.* Philadelphia: Open University Press.

Kincheloe, J. L., & Steinberg, S. R. (1998). Reconfiguring white identity in a pedagogy of whiteness. In J. L. Kincheloe, S. R. Steinberg, N. Rodriguez, & R. Chenault (Eds.), *White reign: Deploying whiteness in America.* New York: St. Martin's.

Knapp, M. S., & Woolverton, S. (1995). School class and schooling. In J. A. Banks & C. A. McGee Banks (Eds.), *Handbook of research on multicultural education* (pp. 548–569). New York: Macmillan.

Lajuenen, T., Parker, D., & Summala, H. (2004). The Manchester Driver Behaviour Questionnaire: A cross-cultural study. *Accident Analysis and Prevention, 36,* 231–238.

Larson, C. L., & Murtadha, K. (2001, November). *Leadership for social justice.* Paper presented at the Annual Meeting of the University Council for Educational Administration, Cincinnati, OH.

Leithwood, K., & Duke, D. L. (1998). Mapping the conceptual terrain of leadership: A critical point of departure for cross-cultural studies. *The Peabody Journal of Education, 73*(2), 31–50.

Macedo, D. (1995). Power and education: Who decides the forms schools have taken, and who should decide? In J. L. Kincheloe & S. R. Steinberg (Eds.), *Thirteen questions: Reframing education's conversation.* New York: Peter Lang.

Margonis, F. (1998). The demise of authenticity. *Philosophy of education 1998.* Retrieved from http://www.ed.uiuc.edu/EPS/PES-yearbook/1998/argonis_2.html

May, S. (1999). Critical multiculturalism and cultural difference: Avoiding essentialism. In S. May (Ed.), *Critical multiculturalism: Rethinking multicultural and antiracist education.* Philadelphia: Falmer Press.

McCarthy, C., & Crichlow, W. (Eds.). (1993). *Race, identity, and representation in education.* New York: Routledge.

McLaren, P. (2003). *Life in schools: An introduction to critical pedagogy in the foundations of education* (4th ed.). Boston: Pearson.

Mitchell, C. (1999). Building learning communities in schools: The next generation or the impossible dream? *Interchange, 30*(3), 283.

Mitchell, C., & Sackney, L. (2000). *Profound improvement: Building capacity for a learning community.* Lisse, Netherlands: Swets & Zeitlinger.

Moodley, K. A. (1995). Multicultural education in Canada. In J. A. Banks & C. A. Banks (Eds.), *A handbook of research on multicultural education* (pp. 801–820). New York: Macmillan.

Moxley, R. S. (2000). *Leadership and spirit.* San Francisco: Jossey-Bass.

Murtadha-Watts, K. (1999). Spirited sisters: Spirituality and the activism of African American women in educational leadership. In L. Fenwick (Ed.), *School leadership: Expanding horizons of the mind and the spirit.* Lancaster, PA: Technomic.

Nash, R. (1997). *Inequality/difference: A sociology of education.* Palmerston North, NZ: Massey University Printery.

Newmann, F. M. (Ed.). (1992). *Student engagement and achievement in American secondary schools.* New York: Teachers College Press.

Nieto, S. (2000). Multicultural education in practice. In S. Nieto (Ed.), *Affirming diversity: The sociopolitical context of multicultural education* (3rd ed., pp. 349–369). New York: Longman.

No Child Left Behind. (2001). Official U.S. Department of Education Website. http://www.nochildleftbehind.gov/start/facts/achievement_native.html (Accessed Sept. 1, 2003)

Noddings, N. (1984). *Caring: A feminine approach to ethics and moral education.* Berkeley: University of California Press.

Palmer, D. (2000). Identifying delusional discourse: Issues of rationality, reality, and power. *Sociology of Health & Illness, 22*(5), 661–678.

Palmer, P. J. (1998). *The courage to teach: Exploring the inner landscape of a teacher's life.* San Francisco: Jossey-Bass.

Pinar, W. (1993). *Understanding curriculum as racial text: Representations of identity and difference in education.* Albany: SUNY Press.

Rader, D., & Sittig, L. H. (2003). *New kid in school: Using literature to help children in transition.* New York: Teachers College Press.

Raivetz, M. J. (1992). Can school districts survive the politics of state testing initiatives? *NASSP Bulletin, 76*(545), 57–65.

Riehl, C. J. (2000). The principal's role in creating inclusive schools for diverse students: A review of normative, empirical, and critical literature on the practice of educational administration. *Review of Educational Research, 70*(1), 55–81.

Robertson, J. M., & Webber, C. F. (2000). Cross-cultural leadership development. *International Journal of Leadership in Education, 3*(4), 315–330.

Roman, L. G. (1993). White is a color! White defensiveness, postmodernism, and anti-racist pedagogy. In C. McCarthy & W. Crichlow (Eds.), *Race, identity, and representation in education*. New York: Routledge.

Ryan, J. (2002). Leadership in contexts of diversity and accountability. In K. Leithwood & P. Hallinger (Eds.), *Second international handbook of educational leadership and administration* (pp. 979–1002). Boston: Kluwer.

Sayani, A. (in press). Allah-consciousness: A meta-meaning system to understand Muslim spirituality in an educational context. In C. M. Shields, M. M. Edwards, & A. Sayani, (Eds.), *Inspiring practices: Spirituality and educational leadership*. Lancaster, PA: Proactive.

Shields, C. M. (2000). Learning from difference: Considerations for schools as communities. *Curriculum Inquiry, 30*(3), 275–294.

Shields, C. M. (2003). *Good intentions are not enough: Transformative leadership for communities of difference*. Lanham, MD: Scarecrow.

Shields, C. M., Bishop, R., & Mazawi, A. E. (in press). *Pathologizing practices: The impact of deficit thinking on education*. New York: Peter Lang.

Shields, C. M., & Edwards, M. (in press). *Dialogue is not just talk: A new ground for educational leadership*. Lanham, MD: Scarecrow.

Shields, C. M., & Seltzer, P. A. (1997). Complexities and paradoxes of community: Toward a more useful conceptualization of community. *Educational Administration Quarterly, 33*(4), 413–439.

Shields, C. M., & Vibert, A. B. (2003). Approaches to student engagement: Does ideology matter? *McGill Journal of Education, 38*(2), 221–240.

Sidorkin, A. M. (1999). *Beyond discourse: Education, the self, and dialogue*. Albany: SUNY Press.

Sidorkin, A. M. (2002). *Learning relations*. New York: Peter Lang.

Skrla, L., & Scheurich, J. J. (2001). Displacing deficit thinking in school district leadership. *Education and Urban Society, 33*(3), 235–259.

Sleeter, C., & McLaren, P. (Eds.). (1995). *Multicultural education, critical pedagogy, and the politics of difference*. New York: SUNY Press.

Smith, W. J., Donahue, H., & Vibert, A. B. (Eds.). (1998). *Student engagement in learning and school life*. Montreal: McGill University, Office of Research in Education.

Spreitzer, G., & Cummings, T. (2001). The leadership challenges of the next generation. In W. Bennis et al. (Eds.), *The future of leadership*. San Francisco: Jossey-Bass.

Starratt, R. J. (1991). Building an ethical school: A theory for practice in educational leadership. *Educational Administration Quarterly, 27*(2), 185–202.

Starratt, J. R. (2003, November). *Spirituality of educational leadership*. Paper presented at the Annual Meeting of the University Council of Educational Administration, Cincinnati, OH.

Strike, K. A. (1999). Can schools be communities? The tensions between shared values and inclusion. *Educational Administration Quarterly, 35*(1), 46–70.

Strodl, P., & Johnson, B. (1994). Multicultural leadership for restructured constituencies. *Reports*, p. 14. (ERIC Document Reproduction Service No. 375 190)

Swingewood, A. (1998). *Cultural theory and the problem of modernity*. New York: St. Martin's.

Takaki, R. (2001, April). *Multiculturalism: The disuniting or the reuniting of America?* Paper presented to the Annual Meeting of the American Educational Research Association, Seattle, WA.

Taubman, P. (1993). Separate identities, separate lives: Diversity in the curriculum. In L. Castenall & W. Pinar (Eds.), *Understanding curriculum as a racial text: Representing identities and difference in education* (pp. 289–307). New York: SUNY Press.

Thayer-Bacon, B. J. (2003). *Relational "(e)pistemologies."* New York: Peter Lang.

Tierney, W. (1993). *Building communities of difference: Higher education in the twenty-first century*. Toronto: Ontario Institute for Studies in Education.

Toole, J. C., & Louis, K. S. (2002). The role of professional learning communities in international education. In K. Leithwood & P. Hallinger (Eds.), *Second international handbook of educational leadership and administration* (pp. 245-279). London: Kluwer.

Vadasy, P., & Maddox, M. (1992). *Building bridges: The Yakima equity study. The conditions of success for migrant, Hispanic, and*

Native American students in the Yakima Valley. (ERIC Document Reproduction Service No. ED359 009)

Valencia, R. R., & Solórzano, D. G. (1997) Contemporary deficit thinking. In R. R. Valencia (Ed.), *The evolution of deficit thinking.* Washington, DC: Falmer Press.

Van Meter, E. J. (1993). Setting new priorities: Enhancing the school-community relations program. *NASSP Bulletin, 77*(554), 22–28.

Vibert, A. B., Portelli, J. P., & Leighteizer, V. (1998). Nova Scotia: NS1. In W. J. Smith, H. Donohue, & A. B. Vibert (Eds.), *Student engagement in learning and school life: Case reports from project schools* (Vol. 1, pp. 119–160).

Montreal: McGill University, Office of Research on Educational Policy.

Wagstaff, L., & Fusarelli, L. (1999). Establishing collaborative governance and leadership. In P. Reyes, J. Scribner, & A. Scribner (Eds.), *Lessons from high-performing Hispanic schools: Creating learning communities.* New York: Teachers College Press.

Walker, A., & Dimmock, C. (2002). Moving school leadership beyond its narrow boundaries: Developing a cross-cultural approach. In K. Leithwood & P. Hallinger (Eds.), *Second international handbook of educational leadership and administration* (pp. 167–202). Boston: Kluwer.

PART V

The Micropolitics of School Leadership

LARRY E. FRASE
San Diego State University

Part V presents a comprehensive overview of day-to-day and micropolitical challenges facing school leaders. In this section, the authors tackle critical issues involving curriculum, teaching and learning, instruction, student behavior and violence, personnel motivation and quality of work life, school architecture, negotiations, and budgets. The seven chapters in this section are unique in that they are designed to give not only tried-and-true advice about practice but also the related theory and research that give the advice academic credibility. The latter illustrates the authors' viewpoint that it is their obligation to share information that is useful on a day-to-day basis and that is backed by sound theory and research and not fanciful notions.

The purpose of schooling is student learning—this contention is front and center in Chapter 17, by Fenwick W. English and Betty E. Steffy. Based on this premise, they expand the thinking about schooling and learning with a discussion about how the goals and objectives define student outcomes and how they are packaged into what we call a curriculum. Another underlying premise is that if curriculum developers do not understand the context in which we think about and develop curriculum, the status quo regarding learning and inequities will be reinforced. This premise is deftly framed within the context of accountability laws that reinforce bureaucracy and hyperrationalization. Both can interfere in the attainment of desired learning results.

The authors present a review of how curriculum development was attempted in the past and how that task must now, in these days of high-stakes testing, be accomplished via curriculum back-loading. It is clear that the ultimate value of these practices remains to be seen. Initial research results, however, are promising. A complicating factor in student achievement and curriculum development is the bureaucratic nature of school districts, and school bureaucracies are renowned for absorbing financial and human resources—depleting these resources that can promote greater student learning. The ideas presented in this chapter can work well in bureaucracies, but they will not debureaucratize schools.

The authors advance pedagogical thinking about curriculum design and the ethics involved in serving all students well, regardless of their home life and the cultural capital they bring to school. These advances are bolder and more progressive than those in the curriculum literature published to date and provide the theory and experiential bases for curriculum design and delivery.

In Chapter 18, Larry E. Frase deals with supervision and carefully analyzes two areas: instruction and teacher satisfaction and motivation. Frase uses Einstein's theory of the cosmological constant or negative gravity in an analogy that highlights what the research has repeatedly illustrated: Teacher satisfaction and motivation are at an all-time low while teacher attrition is at an all-time high. The reasons for these unacceptable conditions and what they mean to student learning are discussed in light of teacher motivation and satisfaction research.

One new theory still on the fringe of the field of teacher supervision and educational leadership is the psychological concept of flow. Flow has been called the most powerful source of job motivation a person can experience, a claim that is well substantiated in the literature (Csikszentmihalyi, 1990, 1996). A summary of the uses of flow theory in the educational leadership research is provided, and practical applications of this concept are detailed with the purpose of providing readers ideas for establishing work environments where teachers have more opportunities to find flow experiences. The author asserts and expounds on the idea that teacher and administrative supervisors must be deeply knowledgeable about flow and its application in supervisory practice as a tool for reversing the trend of rapid teacher attrition and low satisfaction levels.

There is considerable research today indicating which instructional techniques result in more learning than others. This information is crucial to professional development personnel and supervisors as they go about their daily supervisory practices. Research on the following topics is reviewed: teacher verbal ability; teacher academic subject matter training; pre-service pedagogical training; and professional in-service training; and instructional behaviors, including instructional strategies, classroom management, and curriculum instructional design.

In Chapter 19, George J. Petersen provides the reader with an overview of the extant literature exploring the complex and enigmatic issues that contribute to student misbehavior and violence in our nation's schools. He argues that both school and family (social) issues in the lives of children actually work in combination to influence and, at times, compound the problem of misbehavior and violence; they also impair a school leader's ability to adequately and equitably address disruptive and aberrant behaviors in substantive and effective ways. Petersen then examines some of the most pertinent risk factors faced by children, their families, and schools through the lens of social capital. The idea of social capital focuses on the importance of developing "dense networks" among all key stakeholders with the intention of building equitable and credible schools. This chapter also provides a generative discussion of how the development of such social capital among the key stakeholders—students, families, community members, and school personnel—can actually lead to building high-quality, participatory, credible, and equitable social institutions. The chapter ends with an insightful discussion of current violence prevention models and suggests that action research be used to create social capital and to adequately and more accurately identify and address the problems of student misbehavior and violence. Petersen expands the conversation by addressing some of the limitations inherent in commercial violence prevention models. He asserts that action research will also help practitioners and researchers frame and identify the most pressing problems for those wrestling with these issues on a daily basis—namely, teachers, administrators, and students—with the intent of offering an investigative tool that will permit key stakeholders to identify and institute strategies that will resolve issues leading to misbehavior and violence within the context in which they are found.

In Chapter 20, Eric Haas and Leslie Poynor provide an engaging treatment of some of the basic issues involved in teaching and learning. They begin by asserting that the manner in which teaching and learning are conducted in a classroom depends in large part on how well the teacher, his or her fellow educators, and the larger community understand the processes involved in learning. This chapter examines teaching and learning practices from two vantage points—a traditional transmission perspective and a progressive transaction perspective. The former is based on behaviorist learning theory and hierarchal social models featuring top-down directives as well as classroom teacher dominance (e.g., testing for comparison purposes, transmitting information to students, encouraging a climate of competition and comparison, treating students as incapable and deficient if they do not meet a standard, rejecting and penalizing students for errors, and fostering dependence on external authority). The latter is based on social-constructivist learning theory and cooperative social models and promotes teacher and student communal development of curriculum, group work, group performance assessments, and teacher service as mentor and facilitator. In this scenario, the teacher treats students as being capable and shares the responsibility of developing curriculum with them. Teachers adopting traditional transaction teaching practices should expect to fit in well with the dominant school and social structures pontificating the virtues of standardized tests. The authors posit that teachers adopting progressive transaction practices will likely find their work to be often misunderstood, at odds with the current school and social structures, and even actively opposed.

In Chapter 21, Jeffrey A. Lackney asserts that educational leaders and decision makers need to recognize that school facilities are, in effect, a policy statement on the relative importance placed on education and students in a community. This chapter posits that school design is a critical and integral component in education and introduces educational leaders to the vital role that school design plays in supporting teaching and learning. The author discusses the continuing powerful effect on students and teachers of the one-room school house; the fact that innovations have frequently driven school facility design, for example, open space schools; and the idea that engaging community in the design of schools is fundamental to building a healthy school community. He asserts that school facilities must now be oriented to meet the personalized needs of individual learners. An outline of the relationship between school design and educational reform is presented, and Lackney places this relationship in a historical context. Five emerging issues are discussed: school designs for smaller learning communities, collaborative learner-centered environments, extending learning into the community; technology and school design, and high-performance school design. Regarding the latter, Professor Lackney clearly illustrates the need to make school environments more thermally, visually, and acoustically comfortable and healthful while at the same time accommodating advanced technology. A framework for assessing the educational suitability of a school, the first critical step in defining the specific school design problem, is offered as a tool to educational leaders. Finally, the process through which school facilities are delivered and the role of the educational leader in that process are outlined.

In Chapter 22, Todd A. DeMitchell offers an insightful analysis of teacher unions and their impact on schools. He begins with the commonsense assertion that administrators must understand union and collective bargaining. He further offers a historical perspective on the role of unions and how this knowledge can and should be used today. Historical accounts take on significant importance in that there is very little reliable research on unions; hence, current actions must be based on logic, context, and historical issues.

The industrial labor model defines teaching as labor and not as a professional service. DeMitchell notes that this is a disservice to teachers and the profession. Furthermore, there is a mismatch between the industrial union model codified into public sector bargaining laws and the delivery of professional educational services. Bargaining laws have bred a massive number of grievances and are generally viewed as problematic. Professor DeMitchell cleverly illustrates that grievances can and should be the administrators' friend.

In Chapter 23, William K. Poston, Jr., provides a solid grounding in principles of school finance—a topic that provides momentous challenges to both prekindergarten through Grade 12 schools and to education administrators and teachers. He approaches this most important problem area with an emphasis on the problems facing educators today.

Revenue sources and amounts are delineated, revenue distribution and equalization plans are examined, and comparisons are drawn to illustrate the tremendous differences in financial support. The perplexing challenge to provide needs-based allocation systems is addressed, and the tools for educational equity are described. Moreover, obstacles to sound cost-benefit analyses and financial management are confronted, and the model for building community economic confidence in schools is introduced.

Budgeting technologies and levels are described, and the impact of rapid institutional change on financial planning and budgeting is addressed to enable systems to tackle more powerful and productive budgeting processes. The chapter includes definitive means for addressing the leadership challenges in finance, planning, and budgeting to help the educational leader determine how to grasp and solve the problems of school funding.

REFERENCES

Csikszentmihalyi, M. (1990). *Flow: The psychology of optimal experience.* New York: Harper & Row.

Csikszentmihalyi, M. (1996). *Creativity: Flow and the psychology of discovery and invention.* New York: Harper Collins.

17

Curriculum Leadership

The Administrative Survival Skill in a Test-Driven Culture and a Competitive Educational Marketplace

FENWICK W. ENGLISH
University of North Carolina at Chapel Hill

BETTY E. STEFFY
University of North Carolina at Chapel Hill

INTRODUCTION AND OVERVIEW

What it means to be an instructional leader in today's schools is inextricably connected to sound curriculum leadership. With the current accountability movement, disaggregated test scores have become the focal point for hiring, firing, rewarding, and punishing school administrators and staff. Although the use of test scores as a measure of how well the educational community is performing its job is not new, current state and federal legislation has brought new meaning to the word *accountability*. One result of this movement has been to more narrowly define what it means to be educated. Another has been to erroneously assume that teachers are pliable and willing to give up their freedom to make choices about what curriculum to teach and how to teach it.

When it becomes necessary to improve test scores yearly—as required by the No Child Left Behind Act of 2001, which became Public Law 107–110 in 2002—the school system must respond by creating more tightly connected relationships among the functions of curriculum development, assessment/testing, and staff development. In so doing, there is a need for a great deal of reorientation within the system. This reorientation becomes intrusive to classroom dynamics, personal interrelationships, and general operations. Effective curriculum leaders have found ways to provide the necessary instructional program coherence and to support teacher collaboration in decision making. Growing evidence suggests that principal visibility in classrooms is becoming critical.

It is undeniable that schools are linked to the existing social order, so any attempt to restructure them must also include consideration of how the larger society has impacted the schools. This is not to say that the status quo must be accepted. Rather, the astute curriculum leader will find ways to work within the present structure to make needed changes so as not to reproduce existing socioeconomic inequities.

Educational leadership in the arena of curriculum and instruction has surged to the forefront as *the* survival skill for school administrators in the high-stakes testing and accountability context facing schools in America. Best epitomized by the controversial federal legislation, No Child Left Behind Act of 2001, school administrators find their jobs tightly lashed to improved achievement as measured by test scores. Test scores are not new to the educational scene, having been first used on a mass scale in American schools as early as 1895 (see Kliebard, 1986, p. 22). Even earlier, in 1845, test scores were used as political weapons to challenge the dominant power base in schooling: in Boston by none other than Horace Mann, the father of American public education (see Messerli, 1972, pp. 418–419).

What is new to many practicing administrators is that test scores must be disaggregated by major racial and ethnic groups, English language proficiency status, students with disabilities as compared to all other students, economically disadvantaged students as compared to students not economically disadvantaged, migrant status, and gender. These breakout points for test results mean that it is extremely difficult to hide groups of students who are not doing well on tests within reported larger group mean scores. Educational practices that were previously found acceptable, such as tracking and other forms of not so subtle resegregation of students, are called into question as never before, viewed as regressive practices that lower expectations of student test achievement for some groups of students.

School administrators and the general public considering the role of curriculum in the schools typically think of the subjects to be taught in classrooms as "the curriculum." *Curriculum* is math, science, English, social studies, physical education, foreign language, and perhaps some electives. Considered as subjects to be taught, curriculum is transparently a repository of a series of decisions about what should be taught within each of these areas across and within grade levels, that is, "sixth grade mathematics," or "ninth grade English."

The popular idea of curriculum as *ordered subjects* is traced by Hamilton (1989) to records of the University of Leiden in 1582; the development was related to the movement for standardizing university curricula in Europe. As Jackson (1992) has noted, in the 16th century, the idea of curriculum was a response to needed organizational requirements "imposed by authorities for the purpose of bringing order to the conduct of schooling" (p. 5). Bennett (1917) traces the notion of a course of study to 1528, when the Electorate of Saxony adopted a graded plan of studies for a uniform state system of schools. In 1599, the Jesuits adopted the *Ratio Studiorum*, which was a course of study and the concepts regarding daily routines of pupils and teachers (Bennett, 1917, p. 109).

To this day, it is hard to discuss curriculum without also dealing with matters of administration, control, and organizational structure in schools and universities. This intersection is clearly evident in very early books about education. For example, Dutton's (1908) book, *School Management,* included a full chapter on the school curriculum. Commenting on the notion that good teaching may not have occurred in some schools, Dutton observed, "The fault is in the selection, arrangement, and method of interpretation of the curriculum. . . . Here, then, we have a very practical part of school management" (p. 113). Thorndike's (1912) text, *Education: A First Book,* made a similar point, linking school organization to curricular structure (p. 264), as did Bennett's (1917) almost century-old definition of the scope of school management:

The field of this subject lies anywhere between the specific problems of instruction in the narrow sense and the broad questions of administration and supervision. The lines of demarcation will necessarily fluctuate and overlap, rendering any definition of the subject arbitrary and of little use. Any topic may be regarded as legitimately in this field which aims to guide the teacher in securing school conditions, spiritual or material, favorable to the educative progress. We may discuss anything from sanitary finger nails to national ideas, provided we are thereby clarifying our conceptions of the school conditions under which real educative results are best attained. (p. 1)

Perhaps the intersection of curriculum, management, and leadership was best summarized by McKinney and Westbury (1975), when they said, "In all cases the curriculum can be seen as an *idea* that becomes a thing, an entity that has institutional and technical form" (p. 6).

Developing the curriculum or sequencing subjects involves a subjective determination of complexity and learning difficulty of subject matter content. The more complex and conceptually harder concepts are taught at higher grade levels while simpler and easier concepts are taught at lower grade levels. Within these notions of sequencing a curriculum lie such practices as grouping (forms of tracking by ability or interest) and generic ideas of instruction: lecturing to whole groups or having students work in smaller groups or individually. Overlay these ideas with accountability concepts and laws, along with high-stakes testing, and the importance of selecting the content within curricular subjects is apparent.

Pay schemes such as so-called valued-added plans used in Tennessee (Sanders & Horn, 1994) and Georgia (Archer, 2000) rest on these ideas, traditions, and historic practices. However, as research by Heck (2000) has shown,

Reasonable evaluation of differences between schools, therefore, should emphasize appraisal that is context based; that is any evaluation of the school must take into consideration its unique setting (student composition, school factors, community) [because] [s]chools should not be penalized for problems such as poverty that are beyond their control. (pp. 539–540)

A critique of the value-added model used in Tennessee has revealed some severe shortcomings, not the least of which is that it remains sensitive to the impact of wealth in assessing student progress. Kupermintz (2003) comments about other assumptions it makes about activities going on in schools, not the least of which is a specific orientation toward curriculum:

The TVAAS [Tennessee Value Added Assessment System] model represents teacher effects as independent, additive, and linear. Educational communities that value collaborations, team teaching, interdisciplinary curricula, and promote student autonomy and active participation in educational decisions may find little use for such information. (p. 290)

Despite such admonitions, various state legislatures and state departments of education are coming more and more to incorporate simplistic accountability assumptions in laws and regulations, coupled with the federal legal requirements for No Child Left Behind. It is within this continuing context for improved educational productivity that we examine the role of curriculum and curriculum leadership. At the outset, the importance of aligning or matching curriculum content with tested content is almost universally recognized as central to improving pupil performance (Cohen, 1987; English, 2000; English & Steffy, 2001; Moss-Mitchell, 1998; Newmann, 1993; Scalafani, 2001; Webb, 1997, 1999, 2002; Wixon, Fisk, Dutro, & McDaniel, 1999).

At the root of concepts of efficiency in all of these notions is the idea of "covering the curriculum." Translated into matters of practice in most accountability schemes, covering the curriculum refers to the ability of any given teacher in any given year with any group of students to transmit to them the content contained in a textbook and/or a curriculum guide in the shortest time possible as measured by the tests in use. Learning "mastery" is thus test defined, test correlated, and test contained.

That many of these practices are detrimental to students has been discussed ever since 1917, when Henry Bennett commented:

> "We have to get over the ground" is perhaps the commonest excuse for all the sins of inefficient teachers; as though covering ground were in any sense a function of the school. . . . In fact, the best educative results are attained, if conditions of organization permit, when the division of the pupils' work into subjects is largely lost in the correlations and concentrations of better teaching. (pp. 110–111)

By 1990, the National Commission on Testing and Public Policy estimated that each year across the nation, about 20 million school days were consumed by children taking tests. With this in mind, it becomes important to examine current curriculum/testing practices if for no other reason than because of their growing intrusion at every level and the cost of them in national schooling.

This chapter examines the role of curriculum leadership in the context of the current accountability movement. Three main themes are discussed: first, the idea that the current accountability movement has led to the expansion of educational bureaucratic structures, particularly at the state level, a condition referred to by Wise (1979) as hyperrationalization; second, the notion that this increased hyperrationalization means greater focus on rationality, efficiency, and effectiveness, which impacts relationships among the school system, school, and classroom and has some detrimental consequences. Within this context, the effectiveness of curriculum leadership is explained as contextual. Finally, ideas that point to curriculum reconceptualism and alternative views of curriculum leadership are explored.

CURRICULUM AS A TOOL FOR HYPERRATIONALIZATION OF SCHOOLS

The application of current accountability schemes that embody these ideas and practices was described by Wise (1979) as *hyperrationalization*, a process that "causes more bureaucratic overlay without attaining the intended policy objectives" (pp. 47–48). As an effect of treating educational organizations as high rational structures in which means and ends are clearly related, there are unintended results.

Faulty Assumptions

To begin with, the assumptions that support nearly all accountability plans are that both children and teachers are pliable. Pliability applied to children refers to the assumption not only that they come to school within a "normal" range of aptitude, but that they will be and remain compliant about the schooling process (Wise, 1979, p. 57). The subordination of children to the established schooling process and the relationship of the school to society are reinforced. In this conception, schools are not seen as transformative agents for social change. Rather, they are seen as foundational to the existing social order. Kincheloe, Slattery, and Steinberg (2000) explain:

> Schools have traditionally used white, Anglo-Saxon, middle-class, Judeo-Christian, heterosexual, able-bodied, English speaking male norms to identify what it means to be educated . . . [and they] present the belief systems, definitions of citizenship, views of success and histories of members of this group as privileged while they devalue the perspectives and histories of other groups. (p. 253)

Darling-Hammond and Post (2000) reinforced the idea of privilege when they observed,

> Few Americans realize that the U.S. educational system is one of the most unequal in the industrialized world, and students

routinely receive dramatically different learning opportunities based on their social status. (p. 127)

Children are supposed to "fit in" to the social order and not challenge it. Children who do not fit the norms are marginalized or silenced (see LeCompte, 1993). Those who resist are considered aberrations and deviants by those in control of the institutions. They are threats and are subjected to either disciplinary/ normative or therapeutic remedies to make them become compliant. The large number of expulsions and disciplinary remedies imposed on African American males in schools has long been disproportionate to their actual numbers (Banks, 1989, p. 2; Osborne, 1999). This disparity is also reflected in the nation's prisons. For example, whereas 1.6% of white men in the age group 20 to 34 are in prison, 12% of African American males of the same age are similarly incarcerated. The Bureau of Justice Statistics has indicated that 28% of all black men will spend time in jail (Butterfield, 2003, p. A12). The assumption of student pliability is limited to those students from the social class structure most compatible with the dominant, white, middle-class cultural norms. In a study of student engaged time in schools, Yair (2000) found that "African American and Hispanic students exhibit high rates of disengagement in traditional teacher-centered instruction . . . [because] African American and Hispanic students prove to be more vulnerable to mediocre instruction" (p. 506). Tracking and other means of segregating minority students have shown that the latter are more apt to be cordoned off into classes and curricula where they are much less likely to receive high-quality instruction (Oakes, 1985; Oakes, Gamoran, & Page, 1992).

Teacher Pliability

Teacher pliability connotes not only a docile workforce but one that will be responsive to changes in policies and administrative directives. Such an assumption completely ignores the role teachers have played in the reform drama in U.S. education over an extensive time period and is incredibly naïve about teacher power today. The Chicago Teachers Federation was organized in 1897 by Margaret Haley and Catherine Goggin (Spring, 1986, p. 259) and became an active and militant force in the history of Chicago school reform (Tyack, 1974, p. 169).

Margaret Haley, speaking before the National Education Association's 1904 meeting, declared,

> There is no possible conflict between the interest of the child and the interest of the teacher. . . . For both the child and the teacher, freedom is the condition of development. . . . The same things that are a burden to the teacher are a burden also to the child. (Donley, 1976, p. 20)

Haley quoted John Dewey, who had urged in 1903 that

> the public school system [be] organized in such a way that every teacher has some regular and representative way in which he or she can register judgment upon matters of educational importance with the assurance that this judgment will somehow affect the school system. (Donley, 1976, p. 21)

Teachers were similarly involved in the politics of the New York City schools (see Ravitch, 1974, p. 195) long before teacher unionism embraced the use of the strike in the 1960s (Spring, 1986, p. 328).

The rise of the National Education Association has been described as "phenomenal" by Lieberman (1997) who indicated that, "Since 1961, membership in the NEA has increased from 766,000 to 2.2 million, almost 300 percent" (p. 1). Similarly, the NEA and American Federation of Teachers (AFT) together have dues revenue of more than $1 billion annually, of which their political operatives spend more than $100 million each year (Lieberman, 1997, p. 4). Are they active on education issues? "Indisputably, the NEA/ AFT are the main political opponents of privatization" says Lieberman (p. 7). Poole's (2001) study challenged Lieberman's negativity regarding unions. After studying the behavior of two unions in Canada and the United States as it pertained to educational reform, Poole (2001) found that "the unions demonstrate an openness to entertain and sometimes to embrace educational reform" (p. 194).

The influence of the NEA led to the creation of the federal Department of Education in 1976 (Bell, 1988, p. 96). Part of conservative opposition to a Cabinet-level position was that it afforded a leverage point for educational lobbyists. If educational programs were scattered throughout the federal government, "educational organizations would be forced to report to and work with several cabinet agencies, and this would complicate and frustrate their efforts" (Bell, 1988, p. 91). After studying the effects of state-mandated changes on schools in Maryland, Wilson and Rossman (1993) observed that;

> Today . . . conceptions of change are neither linear nor context free. Instead the focus [is] on the centrality of local context and [valuing] the talents of individual teachers to modify, adapt, and individualize new ideas to better suit the diversity of the students present in their classroom. (p. 191)

These observations were echoed by Coburn (2003), who observed that part of the success in transferring educational reforms from one site to another to expand school reform hinged on the ability to think about the *enacted curriculum*, that is, the "ways that students and teachers engage with particular materials or activities over time" (p. 5) and ways in which this interaction was transformative. Successful reform transfer involved coming to an understanding of the "beliefs, norms, and pedagogical principles as enacted in the classroom" (p. 5). Recent research by Newmann, Smith, Allensworth, and Bryk (2001) examined the relationship between student achievement and program coherence in 222 Chicago elementary schools. Data indicated that even when the principal developed a framework to create such coherence, if the principal ignored the need of teachers "to exercise expertise or raise questions about selected methods or programs," the ameliorative effect of focus was effectively negated (p. 313).

Another reason for understanding how teachers engage in change concerns the idea of reform ownership. Many reforms are initiated externally to schools and classrooms. Obtaining teacher "buy in" so that a reform becomes "self-generative" is critical (McLaughlin & Mitra, 2001). If this shift does not occur, any reform ultimately fails. Recognizing the importance of the teacher as an active rather than a passive participant is pivotal because as Murnane (1975) observed nearly 30 years ago in a study of what school resources impacted pupil achievement, "What matters in the classroom is the way that students and the teacher interact" (p. 80). Interaction is in part a matter of belief and commitment. Without commitment an educational reform dependent on teachers and principals for implementation in schools and classrooms is not likely to succeed (see Borman & Hewes, 2002, p. 260).

A Science of Education

Another critical assumption cited by Wise (1979) regarding hyperrationalization is that a true science of education exists (p. 57). Such a science would enable one to order inputs and decide processes that were most efficient based on a calculus of results obtained. The difficulty of doing this was underscored by Wise's quoting of John Goodlad (1975), who indicated that a science of education "is an idea whose time has not yet come" (p. 110), and James Guthrie (1976), who noted that "the complexity of a human endeavor such as learning defies simple cost-effectiveness measures" (pp. 260–261).

The methodological difficulties of calculating inputs to outputs, called by Murnane (1975) "the production function concept," is found to be "not entirely appropriate for a study of schools" (p. 93). One example Murnane (1975) cited was that when teachers were considered as inputs, it was not possible to unbundle some of their characteristics from all of the rest of their characteristics. Murnane (1975) found the lack of a well-developed theory of learning on which to base the allocation of school resources a significant problem (p. 94).

Murnane (1975) noted the following problems with producing a database that could be used in determining the effectiveness of allocating school resources. First, it is very hard to fully randomize "treatments" when comparing the use of different resources (p. 91). This deficit means that "differences in achievement may be attributed to differences in treatments while the actual causes are other factors which, due to the selection mechanism, are correlated with the treatments" (p. 92). Another problem was missing data when, because of poor attendance, two test scores could not be found to use in calculating achievement gains. Still another problem posed was the lack of information on school-specific variables, for example, any data on the school principal (p. 98). The lack of information regarding how school resources, along with family influence, impacted achievement was also noted (p. 100). Murnane called this study, done nearly 30 years ago, "exploratory" because it was not "testing a set of explicit hypotheses within the framework of a well defined, tightly structured model" (p. 101).

Moving into more recent times, it is instructive to examine similar studies and see how educational researchers are still constrained by the lack of a science of education. Hamilton et al. (2003) studied 11 sites involved in the National Science Foundation's Systemic Initiatives (SI) to change classroom instructional practices and found a small but positive relationship between student achievement and teachers' reported use of reform practices (p. 18). The study was unable to use a true experimental design, and the sites were in different states and localities. Because of the lack of randomization, the researchers said they "cannot be certain that the relationships observed can be attributed solely to classroom practices" (p. 22). There was the lack of a common outcome measure for comparison purposes, and in some sites, there were no test scores for prior years. The relationship between achievement and student background characteristics could not be detected due to measurement error (p. 18). The study reported the frequency of some practices used by teachers, but it was unable to address the ways such practices were employed or their overall quality (p. 19). Finally, lacking multiple outcome measures, the study relied solely on state tests using multiple-choice questions. It is clear that although testing is more common and some advances have been made in new statistical techniques in tracking school resources, there is still no science of education.

Cost-Effective Behavior Will Be Preferred

The final assumption that supports hyperrationalization as cited by Wise (1979) is that if people are shown the ways in which practices can become cost-effective, these ways will be chosen over ways that are not cost-effective (p. 57). Part of the dilemma in this assumption is that there are many ways to approach the task of engaging in a determination of costs. Stone (1992) reviewed a model for determining costs, using a three-dimensional frame for categorizing costs. The dimensions referred to the value of the inputs, the time when the inputs occurred, and their distribution (p. 2). Value is indicative of the marketplace price paid for an input. However, in education, such a determination is not always possible, so proxy measures have to be developed. A proxy value is the assumed value of equivalent input. Stone (1992) proffers that in education, there are inputs for which it is impossible to find an assumed value (p. 2).

A determination of costs depends as well on a calculation of whether such costs are internal or external to the frame employed and whether they are recurrent such as salaries and fringe benefits or related to capital expenditures such as the purchase of equipment. With equipment, a decision has to be made about how to calculate depreciation and obsolescence. This can be built into the budget as costs for a period of years, or "annualized."

Some costs have to be prorated because they are used by more than one program, grade level, or school site. Such a cost would be affiliated with expenditures for central administration. Other costs are those that Stone (1992) labels "opportunity costs." These are costs connected to student time in school.

> The cost value of time a student spends in school is identified as the "average amount of money students of different ages could be expected to earn if they were gainfully employed instead of spending time on their studies." (Benson, 1988, p. 357)

Another example might be parents volunteering to help in schools. But the most contentious of the cost issues is how to attribute value to costs that are not confined to one program. For example, the cost of school buildings may have to be spread out over "generations of students" (Stone, 1992, p. 5).

We see many of these problems in a study by Borman and Hewes (2002), who tried to assess the cost of a popular reading program, *Success for All*. Once again, the evaluators were unable to use a true experimental design because of the lack of randomization and control (p. 261). In examining the results of their costing process, various aspects represent key assumptions made along the way that reveal the complexities involved and make problematic the claim that when shown the "facts," humans will prefer the most cost-effective alternative. For example, in reducing costs,

it becomes necessary to reallocate existing resources such as personnel from one project to another. So to ensure that a certain innovation is "costless," a series of administrative decisions must be rendered to ensure that new costs are offset with such tactics. The potential "loss" of services redeployed from one area to another was not part of the cost calculations in *Success for All* (p. 252). Whether one would "prefer" a pursuit of cost-effectiveness then depends on the values one desires to obtain. What is cost-effective depends on where one's priorities are placed.

In addition, determining costs often rests on the kinds of accounting decisions decision makers employ. For example, when calculating a per-pupil expenditure, a decision has to be made whether to use total expenditures versus current expenditures. Current expenditures include all the day-to-day expenses of operations, whereas total expenditures include costs associated with capital outlay, debt repayment, and preschool programs. Calculation of costs using total expenditures is more subjective and hence includes more variability. Still another decision pertains to the time to count students. In determining per-pupil costs, does one use enrollment at a specified time, or does one use average daily attendance? (Borman & Hewes, 2002, p. 263). In this more contemporary study, the researchers cautioned that

> although we have standardized the cost-effectiveness results for the four model interventions as an effect per $1,000 investment in each program, these cost-effectiveness ratios do not necessarily suggest that spending on one of the less expensive approaches could be increased to produce the larger effects of the more expensive models. (Borman & Hewes, 2002, p. 261)

It is clear, then, from nearly 30 years of efforts at cost calculations in education that no one has been able to rid the process of subjective decisions regarding how, when, and under what conditions cost is calculated. As Borman and Hewes (2002) note,

> We suggest that decisions among the interventions be driven by more complex decision-making processes and by careful analysis of the local context in which the program is to be implemented. (p. 260)

If cost determination is for the most part a locally dependent phenomenon, then there are no universally agreed upon measures to determine what they are. How then can people prefer "cost-effective" versus "non-cost-effective" behaviors apart from their preferences and biases? If this is not possible, then all we can say about cost-effectiveness efforts is that a person's preferences are usually selected over their nonpreferences.

ACCOUNTABILITY, BUREAUCRATIZATION, AND CURRICULUM LEADERSHIP CHALLENGES

The theory of education that undergirds current accountability efforts such as No Child Left Behind leads to greater school bureaucratization rather than less. Wise (1979) cites the work of Corwin (1975), which describes the assumptions supporting bureaucratic structure. These are that (1) organizations have or should have clear-cut goals that are understood and supported by constituents, (2) activities should be planned, (3) activities should be closely coordinated, (4) information should be available by which decisions are shaped, and (5) administrative officers should have sufficient control over the organization to ensure adherence with extant plans (p. 89). Reliance on these aspects of organizations ensures their rationality as means to identified ends.

Silver (1983) identified organizational rationality as consisting of three elements: (1) *rationality,* which is the extent to which an organization is goal directed; (2) *efficiency,*

which is represented by cost-effectiveness; and (3) *effectiveness,* which is the extent to which the organization attains its goals (p. 77). The more rational the organization becomes, the more bureaucratic it is likely to be. Bureaucracies are marked by hierarchical offices, rules and regulations, task specialization (the division of labor), impersonality, a reliance on written records, salaried personnel, and control of resources by the organization's officers (pp. 75–77). Nearly all government-imposed accountability plans assume that school systems and schools are rational. The requirement for plans and insistence on results as evidenced by student outcomes are firmly rooted in assumptions about bureaucratic structure and behavior. Most accountability plans, therefore, do not reform educational structure in that they are not antibureaucratic antidotes. Rather, they reinforce and extend bureaucratic structure. This is Wise's (1979) hyperrationalization concept.

Effective curriculum leadership in contemporary schools must be evaluated in the context in which schooling is defined and regulated. A determination of effectiveness is, therefore, situated in a public context overlaid with a three-tiered governmental structure that is simultaneously federal, state, and local. The allotment of influence among these levels is not always clear or consistent. While a discussion of alternatives may be interesting and eventually fruitful if it leads to alternative policies and practices, contemporary curriculum leadership has to be examined within these parameters if it is not going to be utopian (see Stanley, 1992; Wraga, 1999, 2002).

Implications for School District Curriculum Leadership

English (2003a) examined the impact of high-stakes testing on school district leadership concepts and practices and weighed its impact on organizational structure. High-stakes testing is a discourse that has already generated much controversy (Kohn, 2000; Neill, 2000). Issues concerned with high-stakes testing have been accelerated within the confines of No Child Left Behind.

The data consisted of an analysis of responses from recent curriculum management audits (see English, 1987, 1988; English et al., 2002; Frase, English, & Poston, 1995; Poston et al., 2001; Steffy et al., 1999) and one national study of urban school systems undertaken by the Manpower Demonstration Research Corporation for the Council of Great City Schools (Snipes, Doolittle, & Herlihy, 2002).

The idea of examining the challenges to school district curriculum leadership is based on the notion of *work texts*. This concept is a derivative of a *text* as the basic unit of discourse analysis (Olshtain & Celce-Murcia, 2003, p. 708). A text includes not only the written words but also the *context* or situation in which communication occurs. There are pragmatic features of any specified situation that must be understood to grasp the meaning of communication. Work text is about the pragmatics of designing the work in a social service organization—in this case a school system. Figure 17.1 shows these relationships in a typical school district.

Work text applied to a school system includes three levels: system, unit (school), and subunit (classroom). In typical systems, these elements may be completely independent. They are all together, but they don't work together. Working together requires knitting a system of interdependencies and, in the case of high-stakes testing, dependencies. Dependencies are unusual because they connote largely one-way relationships. The creation of dependencies works against the tendency of units and subunits to develop autonomy from the system to protect their functions (sometimes called "buffering"; see Thompson, 1967, p. 20). Extreme buffering, which results in independent subunits or units operating at the expense of the larger system,

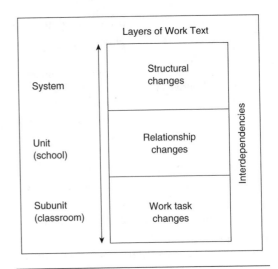

Figure 17.1   Work Text/Work Task Unit/Subunit Interdependencies/Dependencies

is called *suboptimization* (Thompson, 1967, p. 94).

The challenges of high-stakes testing place unusual demands on school system structure. The current structure consists of loosely coupled functions (Weick, 1976), sometimes connected and sometimes not connected. Functions may come together at certain times and operate independently at other times. The most critical system functions required to be responsive to a high-stakes testing scenario are: curriculum development, staff development, and assessment and testing.

Figure 17.2 shows three views of these functions. Successful school system operations require greater specificity in school work plans (curriculum), greater use of testing feedback to improve pupil performance over successive iterations of the test, and a training program that shows principals how to create classroom interdependencies laterally and vertically within their schools. Staff development is also necessary to refocus teachers on the use of test data in the delivery of instruction. This requires the creation of teaching/test dependencies sometimes called *data-driven decision making*. Once again, teachers, like all people

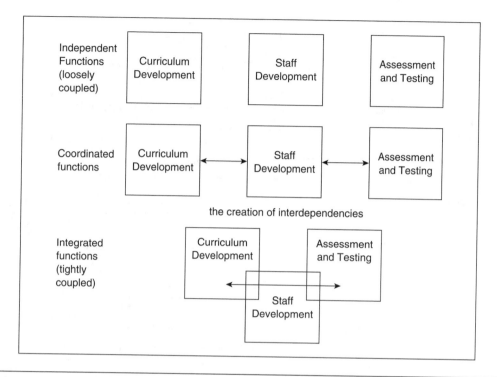

Figure 17.2   Three Views of System-Level Changes in Work Text

in various units and subunits in social systems, have created independencies over time. This kind of self-containment, so characteristic of school instruction (see Bidwell, 1965), is a major physical (temporal-spatial) and psychic block to work task changes that are required across units and within the subunits. The work of teachers has to become more tightly lashed from classroom to classroom, vertically and laterally, and centered on test content and feedback. Of course, bad tests will exert a detrimental impact on students as they are taught better (an anomaly but a distinct possibility in so-called data-driven cultures, where tests are given to the lowest bidder). One has to be careful about the tests that are being used if this trend is not to become counterproductive.

Figure 17.3 shows the necessary changes in the units and subunits when they become data driven. In systems responding to high-stakes testing, performance is always defined by the test (the boundaries and content of performance

definitions) and *not* by the curriculum. There is a great deal of slippage between the curriculum in most local school systems and the content of state tests (English & Steffy, 2001, pp. 55–86; Webb, Horton, & O'Neal, 2002). *Slippage* here refers to test/curriculum/classroom ambiguities that result in teaching that is "off" the test. This creates many false impressions so that a teacher may believe something has been taught when, in reality, it has not been taught.

The necessary changes within the units and subunits to create work dependencies stemming from the three functions, now coordinated or integrated at the system level, will require a great deal of reorientation within the school district. The creation of dependencies and interdependencies can be stoutly resisted by those who heretofore have been independent from such pressures. There is no way around the fact that high-stakes testing is *intrusive* in system structure, operations, and relationships.

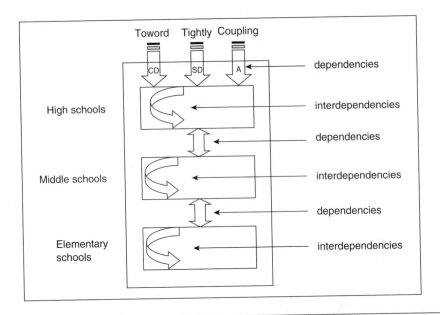

Figure 17.3   Work Text/Work Task Unit/Subunit Interdependencies/Dependencies

Note: CD = curriculum development; SD = staff development; A = assessment.

To meet the challenges imposed by high-stakes testing requires a different set of organizational relationships. It also requires what Deming (1986) called *constancy of purpose*. Once the structure has been changed, forging the integration of the key functions, and new dependencies and interdependencies are put into place along with changes in the curriculum, then the "new" structure and functions must be held constant. To put it another way, borrowing a term from tests and measurement, school system *reliability* must be enhanced and maintained. The drift toward independence will be seductive and strong. The desire for autonomy, and hence buffering, will always be around. It will take tending and monitoring to combat it.

The Key Elements

The key elements in this process are the following:

- *Leadership*: Strong leadership focused on the results required by the tests is necessary at all levels. Leadership and focus are required to engage in the necessary system changes. Leadership has to be vigilant about being concerned with the "right" functions and tasks.

- *Monitoring*: Leadership must also monitor the changes and exert effort to maintain constancy of purpose (intrasystem reliability) by ensuring that organizational drift is resisted.

- *Curriculum*: The curriculum must be changed to include greater specificity and alignment with the assessed content embraced by the tests. This usually means a curriculum must be developed or rewritten so that tighter linkages are forged between the written, taught, and tested curricula (English, 1987; English & Larson, 1996; English & Steffy, 2001; Smith & O'Day, 1991).

- *Anticipating resistance*: The necessary changes are not trivial. It should be recognized at the outset they will be profound and intrusive. They cannot be superimposed overnight. Change must be initiated on a broad front, but always with a focus on the critical functions and necessary interconnectivity.

- *Maintenance*: Once put into place, the new relationships and practices must be maintained. Doing so will require a good deal of organizational resources. Such organizational factors as student, teacher, and administrative turnover also "churn" the system and erode constancy of purpose. Continuing staff development is necessary to counteract organizational churning. Like dieting, improved performance on high-stakes tests is not a fad but a change in the way a school system functions and how the people in it interact and work together over an extended time period. There are no short cuts or quick fixes. Although topological alignment can produce some quick test score gains (English & Steffy, 2001, pp. 87–114), on the longer haul, such gains cannot be maintained or enhanced without deeper organizational changes.

Effective School Site Curriculum Leadership Practice

Insights into effective curriculum leadership at the school site level are provided by a research study of 222 Chicago elementary schools by Newmann et al. (2001). The study included multiple years of data gathering, including information from more than 5,000 teachers and 80,000 students (p. 302). Student outcomes were measured by a standardized achievement test.

The study showed that student achievement was related to *instructional program coherence*. This critical attribute was defined by the researchers as

> a set of interrelated programs for students and staff that are guided by a common framework for curriculum, instruction, assessment, and learning climate and that are pursued over a sustained period. (Newmann et al., 2001, p. 297)

In many ways, these characteristics mirror those deemed important at the school district level.

The person responsible for the creation and implementation of this common framework was the school principal. Not only was the principal crucial to the success of program coherence, but the site leader had to ensure continuity and stability.

A feature that distinguished the high- and low-coherence schools was

> significant investment in instructional materials and programs, including staff development, that were grounded in a particular concept of instruction and perhaps more importantly—implemented school wide. (Newmann et al., 2001, p. 311)

But higher scoring schools not only showed tighter coordination of instruction around a common curricular framework, they also exhibited strong communication networks among teachers that were centered in such a framework (p. 312). Although these high-scoring schools enabled teachers to exercise some discretion within a common framework, it definitely was not a kind of "anything goes" where teacher autonomy reigned supreme. These researchers noted that the presence of "voluminous lists of discrete skills and items of knowledge," which were often a product of so-called standards for curriculum and assessment, might "fail to communicate a common framework for instruction" (p. 315).

The lesson for successful curriculum leadership at the site level is that, "School principals [should] focus their improvement plans, professional development, and acquisition of instructional materials on a few core educational goals pursued through a common instructional framework" (Newmann et al., 2001, p. 315). To create a school environment in which teachers within a grade level use common learning goals and instructional and assessment strategies, and across grade levels avoid repetition and present to students more complex aspects of subject matter, principals must know what is going on in their schools. A key strategy to ensure continuity of instruction within a stable curriculum is classroom observation, but such observation has to be more than ensuring instructional congruence to "ideal" lessons. Without ensuring congruence to a common curricular framework, classroom observation cannot be a tool to provide focus and continuity.

There are two primary components of this focus and connectivity, a design component and a delivery component (English, 2000). The design component refers to the written documents placed in the hands of teachers, which become the basis for their instructional planning. The delivery component refers to how the principal monitors the implementation of the designed curriculum.

Principals must be able to review design documents and evaluate their effectiveness as planning tools for teachers. With the exception of Iowa, all of the states now have some sort of state standards ("Quality Counts," 2004). *Education Week* annually conducts a survey to determine the status of individual states on a variety of indicators. One of these indicators is the quality of the state standards, and individual states are given a grade. Because Iowa has no state standards, it traditionally receives a grade of F. In the 2004 listing of states, 10 received a grade of A or A-, 21 received a grade of B+, B, or B-, 14 received a grade of C+, C, or C-, and six received a grade of D or D-. Principals cannot assume that because a grade of A was received for the state standards, these standards are of sufficient specificity to serve as quality design documents for teachers. For example, the Ohio K-12 English Language Arts Academic Content Standards (Center for Curriculum and Assessment, 2001) list standards, benchmarks, and indicators by strand and grade level. The standards are broad statements of what students should know and be able to do. The benchmarks are more specific and provide direction for a range of grade levels. The indicators are grade level-specific by strand. The following is a listing of grade-level indicators dealing with setting for the area of Reading Applications: Literary Text (Center for Curriculum and Assessment, 2001, pp. 89–95).

Grade Four: Identify the influence of setting on the selection

Grade Five: Explain the influence of setting on the selection

Grade Six: Identify the features of setting and explain their importance in literary text

Grade Seven: Analyze the features of the setting and their importance in a text

Grade Eight: Analyze the influence of setting in relation to other literary elements

Grade Nine: Analyze the influence of setting in relation to other literary elements

Grade Ten: Analyze the features of setting and their importance in a literary text

Grade Eleven: Analyze the historical, social, and cultural context of setting

Grade Twelve: Analyze the historical, social, and cultural context of setting

Even at the indicator level, these statements do not provide teachers with enough specificity to know exactly what students should know and be able to do at a given grade level. The Ohio standards received a rating of A by *Education Week*. Even though state departments of education profess quite explicitly that these state standards documents are not to take the place of locally developed curriculum guides, many school systems develop local guides using the same language that appears in the state documents. Curriculum leadership at the district and building level must provide the direction necessary to produce quality curriculum guides. Downey et al. (2002) outlined nine specific strategies to attain a quality guide (p. 7).

1. Ensure external assessment target objectives are embedded in the written content standards and are linked to state expectations

2. Have clear and precise district objectives: content, context, cognitive level

3. Deeply align objectives from external assessments

4. Sequence objectives for mastery well before they are tested

5. Provide a feasible number of objectives

6. Identify specific objectives as benchmark standards

7. Place objectives in a teaching sequence

8. Provide access to written curriculum documents and direct the objectives to be taught

9. Conduct staff development in curriculum and its delivery

Quality curriculum guides are the basis providing for continuity of instruction.

Once quality curriculum guides are in the hands of teachers, the next emphasis for the building principal is on the implementation of the curriculum. Because of the legal mandates attached to school accountability, the principals must be active and diligent in monitoring classroom instruction. Principals are critical to developing the type of positive school culture that supports the changes required for accountability and school reform. As stated by Freedman and LaFleur (2002):

> To address current reform challenges, administrators must acquire new skills to serve as change agents, rather than act as mere conduits of externally mandated changes. Administrators must become more visible in their school, know what is happening in classrooms, assess the alignment between the written, taught and tested curriculum, promote reflective practice, encourage public conversations about teaching and learning, support collaboration, articulate system and school vision, and have a comfort with creative tensions and ambiguities. (p. 1)

There is growing recognition that meeting all of these expectations requires that principals be more visible in classrooms. It has become popular to describe these classroom visits as walk-throughs. The information that principals learn from these walk-throughs can include everything from classroom management techniques to instructional strategies. For some, the walk-through is an informal way to gauge the level of student involvement. For others, it is a way to determine the type of activities teachers plan. Frase has linked a variety of benefits to frequent classroom visits (Downey, Steffy, English, Frase, & Poston, 2004; Frase, 2001; Frase & Hetzel, 1990). These include: improved teacher self-efficacy, improved teacher attitudes toward professional development, improved teacher attitude toward appraisal, increased perceived teacher efficacy of other teachers, improved classroom instruction, improved teacher perception of principal effectiveness, improved student discipline and student acceptance of advice and criticism, and improved teacher perception of the effectiveness of the school. Other researchers have linked principal visibility in classrooms with building capacity, support for teachers, and a more accurate picture of the learning that is taking place (Carr, 2002; Fullan, 1991; Glickman, 2002).

Although a variety of walk-through models exist, one that combines classroom visits with opportunities to engage with teachers in reflective dialogue was created by Downey (Downey et al., 2004). This model presents a template for gathering a multitude of information from a brief 2- to 3-minute classroom visit. The principal learns to quickly ascertain the following information: whether the students appear to be engaged in learning, the content objective(s) the teacher is teaching, the process the teacher is using to teach to the objectives, the complexity of the cognitive learning taking place, the type of pedagogy being used, examples of past student learning evidenced by classroom artifacts, and whether there are health or safety issues that need to be addressed. Based on a number of classroom visits, principals are encouraged to engage in reflective conversations with teachers in such a way that the conversation promotes teacher growth over time. The goals for this particular model include developing teachers who (1) are self-analyzing and self-critical learners, (2) implement the district's curriculum, and (3) consistently grow over time. Research on the benefits of using this model is beginning to be reported (Freedman, 2003; Freedman & LaFleur, 2002). Whatever the model employed, principals are now being held accountable for improved student achievement of state standards as measured by state accountability assessments.

ALTERNATIVE CONCEPTIONS OF CURRICULUM LEADERSHIP

Current conceptions of curriculum leadership have been thoroughly consumed with notions of management efficiency best epitomized by Frederick Taylor's (1911) scientific management principles (see Callahan, 1962) and contemporary notions of total quality management (TQM) as advanced by Deming (1986, 1993), heavily overlaid with bureaucratic structure (Weber, 1946). The driving and dominant force in school leadership, characterized by Goodson (1994) as "massively powerful" (p. 27), remains the relentless pursuit of standardization in a variety of forms and guises aimed at cost reduction, that is, efficiency as measured by standardized outputs (see Anderson, 2001; Dantley & Rogers, 2001; English, 2003b, 2003c; Gronn, 2002; Marshall & McCarthy, 2002). Current concepts of leadership as grounded in management and bureaucratic theories inevitably reproduce schools as they are in American society. Alternatives to curriculum leadership must begin there.

Grounding curriculum in societal concerns is not a new approach. One of the most influential books about curriculum appeared in 1918. This seminal work was Franklin Bobbitt's *The Curriculum,* which has left a lasting imprint on curriculum thinking today (Apple, 1979, p. 47; Beauchamp, 1975, p. 65; Giroux, 1981, p. 150; Kliebard, 1986, pp. 97–99; Schubert, 1980, p. 5; Tanner & Tanner, 1990, pp. 180–183). Bobbitt (1918/1971) stressed the need for a very practical approach to thinking about curriculum, indicating that the purpose of education was

"to look primarily and consciously to efficient practical action in a practical world" (p. 3). Education was conceived as the basis for preparing to live in a world of work (p. 20).

Bobbitt (1918/1971) was enamored with scientific management. He saw the scientific method being applied in many spheres in schools with the exception of curriculum development (p. 41). To correct this, he advocated a "scientific technique" (p. 42) that consisted of analyzing social activities in the real world of work and having these become the objectives of a curriculum. Bobbitt specifically said that the range of activities to be analyzed should be "total" (p. 43) and included the "habits, skills, abilities, forms of thought, valuations, ambitions, etc., that its members need for the effective performance of their vocational labors" (p. 43).

Bobbitt's lasting legacy was the idea of making curriculum "relevant" and "practical" by examining its impact in the world of work, with emphasis on the elimination of waste as an important factor for determining schooling effectiveness (Kliebard, 1986, p. 98). He had a penchant for developing lists of specific objectives as an antidote to excessive "theorizing" and as preparation for life (Tanner & Tanner, 1990, p. 188), and his thinking about schooling used factory metaphors involving the production-function concept. These streams of thought are still present in the national accountability discourse of contemporary times.

In a penetrating and trenchant critique of Bobbitt's (1918/1971) approach to "curriculum discovery" (pp. 41–52), Bode (1930) pointed out that using the current social order to derive curricular objectives from tasks was antidemocratic at its core because it assumed that the existing social order was static and desirable. Bode (1930) said:

> Any scheme of education that fails to make provision for this element of progress is . . . hostile to the democratic purpose of humanizing both education and life. (p. 79)

The notion that life consists of specific activities may have some sort of validity in a society that is stratified in fixed classes. It has no place in a democracy. (p. 111)

In a prescient moment, Bode anticipated the rise of the curriculum reconceptualists some 40 years later (see Pinar, 1975) when he observed, "I wish to repeat that the appeal to the social environment for educational objectives must have back of it a social program or philosophy" (p. 91).

Macdonald (1975) began his criticism of *curriculum engineering,* as embodied in Bobbitt's approach and later manifested in the work of Ralph Tyler (1949), by stipulating that the idea of curriculum development as purely a "technical model" rested on "an acceptance of contemporary social values (thus eliminating the value question of what to teach" (p. 7). This penetrating criticism of the field of curriculum studies, as adopted by the reconceptualists, remains a potent force today (see Lincoln, 1992, pp. 79–97). Any purely technical approach to curriculum development that avoids asking questions about what schools do in the larger society to reproduce current social inequalities may actually do an injustice to teachers and students in them. Schools are linked to the existing social order. They act to reproduce that order as it is. The rampant racism, sexism, and homophobia that pervade the larger social system are perpetuated in the nation's schools (Bowles & Gintis, 1976; Lopez, 2001; Lucas, 1999; McLaren, 1994; Sapon-Shevin, 1994). The realization that powerful social and structural relationships in the larger society are embedded in school curricula is largely due to the work of the reconceptualists, who have elevated the discussion of curricular leadership from the purely technical to the larger sociopolitical domain (Giroux, 1983; Stanley, 1992).

Reconceptualism has come in for its share of criticism, however. Perhaps the most pungent has been that in an effort to distance theory from practice in order to think more clearly about theory and the educational experience in general (Pinar, 1975, pp. xi–xiv), curriculum theorizing has nearly nothing to say to those people in the schools who are developing or implementing curriculum (Wraga, 1999). Therefore, its ideas cannot be the base for notions of leadership. Curriculum theorizing is not about action. It is about thinking about action, or perhaps thinking about thinking. The fact that it hasn't done much to resolve the theory-practice gap has been the topic of serious incrimination (Wraga, 2002).

Despite these shortcomings, curriculum reconceptualism has been able to influence the mainstream of curriculum thought along several dimensions. First, as a result of reconceptualist writing, curriculum developers and leaders are much more aware of the importance of social and cultural differences in constructing curriculum. Second, the idea of incorporating the topic of critical thinking within curriculum as an aim of schooling has been generally accepted. Third, there has been an acceptance of the idea that the school must become an active agent for social change, although there are differences about how this should occur (Stanley, 1992, p. 90).

On this latter point, the reconceptualists have succeeded in discrediting the idea, advanced by Bobbitt (1918/1971), that

To begin with, he [the superintendent] should accept the situation in his city as it is. He should look upon it as the normal, and therefore proper, result of the institutional growth-influences that have been operative in that city. (p. 285)

. . . If he is to make mistakes, it is better for him to continue the old mistakes than to invent a new series. (pp. 286–287)

The idea that school leaders should sit by and accept the status quo is no longer acceptable because of the inherent and implicit inequalities that exist in the larger sociopolitical arena and that will continue to produce inequalities if not acted on. The extent to which such actions are radical becomes the hinging point. Professor Debra Meyerson of Harvard University indicates that leaders who engage in systematic changes over a long time which result in significant improvement are *tempered radicals*: "They want to rock the boat, and they want to stay in it" (Church, 2002, p. C1). Leaders who are so radical they get themselves expelled from practice are of little use in serious school reform efforts. Ultimately, the value of curriculum theory is the extent to which curriculum practice is changed in actual school settings. Theories must be tested in practice, not divorced from practice. Without a connection between the two, curriculum theorizing is an academic exercise (see Wraga, 2002, p. 17).

In 1908, Samuel Dutton wrote:

> The value of anything consists in the way it is used. . . . This is especially true of such educational means as a curriculum, which, in itself is a dead thing, and must be clothed before it has meaning and value. The teacher must put energy and life into it, in order to make it yield its proper fruit. Education is a vital process, and is largely accomplished by one living soul acting upon another. (p. 118)

In arguing for the centrality of focusing on practice in curriculum arguments, Wraga (2002) cites the work of Snyder, Bolin, and Zumwalt (1992) as being interested in *curriculum enactments* (pp. 418–427). The idea of curriculum enactments is that the living curriculum is the one that arises in the interactions between teachers and students, hopefully in democratic school settings so that different social relationships can be experienced in the school instead of just the existing arrangements of power in the general society. Students are more likely to engage in social change when the school curriculum has prepared them for a different kind of life, one that is not merely discussed, but lived.

Alternative forms of curriculum leadership begin with understanding that the current penchant for producing educational improvement based on elaborate forms of standardization are bound to fail if teachers and students are reduced to the calculus of actors who cannot do anything but mechanically read the lines written for them by legislative playwrights. If curriculum is a "dead thing" as pronounced by Dutton (1908) nearly a century ago, and only comes alive when "one living soul [acts] upon another," great care must be taken to center the enacted curriculum as pivotal in an act of enlightened implementation of curriculum change. Such recognition is nearly always potentially radical in spirit, if not in form. The diffusion of power is therefore central to the success of curriculum leadership as an alternative to "effective" as opposed to standardized practice. There is evidence that standards do not always lead to standardization and that it is possible to work within the standards-based movement and still recognize the centrality of the enacted curriculum (see Newmann et al., 2001; Scheurich & Skrla, 2003, pp. 54–56).

Such a recognition shifts the idea of effective leadership from an exclusive focus on one individual, in most cases the school principal, to the notion of distributed leadership, where the principal is acting in concert with significant others, in this case teachers and students. This concerted action may arise spontaneously in the school environment or may develop out of close working relationships based on intuitive understandings. More rarely, it could be created in formal institutional arrangements regarding actual school governance (see Gronn, 2003, pp. 27–50).

The current research on exactly how a school leader impacts teaching has been deemed inadequate (Stein & Spillane, 2003, p. 9). The so-called "direct effects model" of examining the influence of principals on student outcomes has been labeled "too simple a representation of what is an exceedingly complex phenomenon" (Stein & Spillane,

2003, p. 9). Discovering that administrative behaviors impact achievement "reveal[s] little about how leadership operates" (Hallinger & Heck, 1996, p. 18). What is currently being recommended as a more promising tack is *leadership content knowledge* (Stein & Nelson, 2002). This intersection of knowledge about leadership and curriculum "would equip administrators to be strong instructional leaders" (Stein & Spillane, 2003, p. 29). Such knowledge would enable school administrators to know competent instruction when they observe it; to see what to do if it is not present, and to establish school norms that promote increased instructional competence among any given school faculty.

Irrespective of the form taken, the emerging competitive marketplace in education, with its reliance on test scores as the arbiters of "quality," has elevated curriculum leadership to the forefront in determining effective curriculum practices in schools. Such matters are highly complex and intensely contextual. Viewing the concept of school success as more than a simple production function problem may avoid the outcome of increased hyperrationalization of education. To this end, confronting the unintended consequences of reform mandates is as much a part of leadership as being accountable for the fidelity of their implementation.

REFERENCES

Anderson, G. (2001, September). Disciplining leaders: A critical discourse analysis of the ISLLC national examination and performance standards in educational administration. *International Journal of Leadership in Education: Theory and Practice, 4*(3), 199–216.

Apple, M. (1979). *Ideology and curriculum.* London: Routledge & Kegan Paul.

Archer, J. (2000, March 1). Georgia legislators pass accountability plan. *Education Week, 19*(25), 20.

Banks, J. (1989). Multicultural education: Characteristics and goals. In J. Banks & C. Banks (Eds.), *Multicultural education* (pp. 2–25). Boston: Allyn & Bacon.

Beauchamp, G. (1975). *Curriculum theory.* Wilmette, IL: Kagg Press.

Bell, T. (1988). *The thirteenth man: A Reagan Cabinet memoir.* New York: Free Press.

Bennett, H. (1917). *School efficiency: A manual of modern school management.* Boston: Ginn and Company.

Benson, C. (1988). Economics of education. In N. Boyan (Ed.), *Handbook of research in educational administration* (pp. 355–372). New York: Longman.

Bidwell, C. (1965). The school as a formal organization. In J. G. March (Ed.), *Handbook of organizations* (pp. 972–1022). Chicago: Rand McNally.

Bobbitt, F. (1971). *The curriculum.* New York: Arno Press. (Original work published 1918)

Bode, B. (1930). *Modern educational theories.* New York: Macmillan.

Borman, G., & Hewes, G. (2002, Winter). The long-term effects and cost-effectiveness of success for all. *Educational Evaluation and Policy Analysis, 24*(4), 243–265.

Bowles, S., & Gintis, H. (1976). *Schooling in capitalist America.* New York: Basic Books.

Butterfield, F. (2003, April 7). Prison rates among blacks reach a peak, report finds. *New York Times,* p. A12.

Callahan, R. (1962). *The cult of efficiency.* Chicago: University of Chicago Press.

Carr, M. (2002). The principal: An authority, an educator, an advocate. *Newsleader* (NASSP), *49*(7), 3.

Center for Curriculum and Assessment. (2001). *Academic content standards: K-12 English language arts.* Columbus: Ohio Department of Education.

Church, E. (2002, February 11). Tempered radicals aim to rock the boat—and stay in. *Globe and Mail,* p. C1.

Coburn, C. (2003, August/September). Rethinking scale: Moving beyond numbers to deep and lasting change. *Educational Researcher, 32*(6), 3–12.

Cohen, S. (1987). Instructional alignment: Searching for a magic bullet. *Educational Researcher, 16*(8), 16–20.

Corwin, R. (1975). Models of educational organizations. *Review of Research in Education, 2,* 247–295.

Dantley, M., & Rogers, R. (2001, January). Including a spiritual voice in the educational leadership and school reform discourse. *International Journal of Educational Reform, 10*(1), 87–101.

Darling-Hammond, L., & Post, L. (2000). Inequality in teaching and schooling: Supporting high-quality teaching and leadership in low-income schools. In R. Kahlenberg (Ed.), *A notion at risk: Preserving public education as an engine for social mobility*. New York: Century Foundation.

Deming, E. (1986). *Out of the crisis*. Cambridge: MIT Press.

Deming, E. (1993). *The new economics*. Cambridge: MIT Press.

Donley, M. (1976). *Power to the teacher*. Bloomington: Indiana University Press.

Downey, C., English, F., Frase, L., Melton, G., Poston, W., & Steffy, B. (2002). *50 ways to raise students' test scores*. Johnson, IA: Curriculum Management Systems.

Downey, C., Steffy, B., English, F., Frase, L., & Poston, Jr., W. (2004). *The three-minute classroom walk-through*. Thousand Oaks, CA: Corwin.

Dutton, S. (1908). *School management: Practical suggestions concerning the conduct and life of the school*. New York: Charles Scribner's Sons.

English, F. (1987). *Curriculum management for schools, colleges, business*. Springfield, IL: Charles C Thomas.

English, F. (1988). *Curriculum auditing*. Lancaster, PA: Technomic.

English, F. (2000). *Deciding what to teach and test: Developing, aligning, and auditing the curriculum*. Thousand Oaks, CA: Corwin.

English, F., et al. (2002). *A curriculum management audit of the Anchorage school district*. Bloomington, IN: Phi Delta Kappa.

English, F. (2003a). *Changing work texts: A non-judgmental analysis of altering school system structure and mechanics as a response to high stakes testing*. Unpublished paper, University Council for Educational Administration, Portland, OR.

English, F. (2003b). The ISLLC standards: The de-skilling and de-professionalization of educational administration. In F. English, *The postmodern challenge to the theory and practice of educational administration* (pp. 102–131). Springfield, IL: Charles C Thomas.

English, F. (2003c). Tsar khorosh, boyary polkhi—The ISLLC standards and the enshrinement of mystical authoritarianism as anti-change doctrine in educational leadership preparation programs. In F. Lunenburg & C. Carr (Eds.),

Shaping the future: Policy, partnerships, and emerging perspectives (pp. 112–133). Lanham, MD: Scarecrow Education.

English, F., & Larson, R. (1996). *Curriculum management for educational and social service organizations* (2nd ed.). Springfield, IL: Charles C Thomas.

English, F., & Steffy, B. (2001). *Deep curriculum alignment: Creating a level playing field for all children on high-stakes tests of educational accountability*. Lanham, MD: Scarecrow Press.

Frase, L. (2001, April 10–14). *A confirming study of the predictive power of principal classroom visits on efficacy and teacher flow experiences*. Paper presented at the Annual Meeting of the American Educational Research Association, Seattle, WA.

Frase, L., English, F., & Poston, W. (1995). *The curriculum management audit*. Lancaster, PA: Technomic.

Frase, L., & Hetzel, R. (1990). *School management by wandering around*. Landham, MD: Technomic.

Freedman, B. (2003, January 5–8). *Principal visibility and classroom walk-throughs: Supporting instructional leadership and school improvement*. Paper presented at the International Congress of School Effectiveness and School Improvement Annual Conference, Sydney, Australia.

Freedman, B., & LaFleur, C. (2002, April). *Making leadership visible and practical: Walking for improvement*. Paper presented at the Annual Conference of the American Educational Research Association, New Orleans, LA.

Fullan, M., with Steigelbauer, S. (1991). *The new meaning of educational change*. New York: Teachers College Press.

Giroux, H. (1981). *Ideology, culture, and the process of schooling*. Philadelphia: Temple University Press.

Giroux, H. (1983). *Theory and resistance in education: A pedagogy for the opposition*. South Hadley, MA: Bergin & Garvey.

Glickman, C. (2002). *Leadership for learning: How to help teachers succeed*. Alexandria, VA: ASCD.

Goodlad, J. (1975, October). A perspective on accountability. *Phi Delta Kappan, 57*(2), 109–110.

Goodson, I. (1994). *Studying curriculum*. New York: Teachers College Press.

Gronn, P. (2002, September). Designer leadership: The emerging global adoption of preparation standards. *Journal of School Leadership, 12*(5), 522–578.

Gronn, P. (2003). *The new work of educational leaders. Changing leadership practice in an era of school reform.* London: Paul Chapman.

Guthrie, J. (1976). Social science, accountability, and the political economy of school productivity. In J. McDermot (Ed.), *Indeterminacy in education* (pp. 260-261). Berkeley, CA: McCutchan.

Hallinger, P., & Heck, R. (1996). Reassessing the principal's role in school effectiveness: A review of empirical research, 1980–1995. *Educational Administration Quarterly, 32*(1), 5–44.

Hamilton, D. (1989). *Toward a theory of schooling.* London: Falmer.

Hamilton, L., McCaffrey, D., Stecher, B., Klein, S., Robyn, A., & Bugliari, D. (2003, Spring). Studying large-scale reforms of instructional practice: An example from mathematics and science. *Educational Evaluation and Policy Analysis, 25*(1), 1–30.

Heck, R. (2000, October). Examining the impact of school quality on school outcomes and improvement: A value-added approach. *Educational Administration Quarterly, 36*(4), 513–552.

Jackson, P. (1992). Concepts of curriculum and curriculum specialists. In P. Jackson (Ed.), *Handbook of research on curriculum* (pp. 1–40). New York: Macmillan.

Kincheloe, J., Slattery, P., & Steinberg, S. (2000). *Contextualizing teaching.* New York: Longman.

Kliebard, H. (1986). *The struggle for the American curriculum 1893–1958.* Boston: Routledge & Kegan Paul.

Kohn, A. (2000). *The case against standardized testing: Raising the scores, ruining the schools.* Westport, CT: Heinemann.

Kupermintz, H. (2003, Fall). Teacher effects and teacher effectiveness: A validity investigation of the Tennessee value added assessment system. *Educational Evaluation and Policy Analysis, 25*(3), 287–298.

LeCompte, M. (1993). A framework for hearing silence: What does telling stories mean when we are supposed to be doing science? In D. McLaughlin & W. Tierney (Eds.), *Naming silenced lives* (pp. 9–28). New York: Routledge.

Lieberman, M. (1997). *The teacher unions.* New York: Free Press.

Lincoln, Y. (1992). Curriculum studies and the traditions of inquiry: The humanistic tradition. In P. Jackson (Ed.), *The handbook of research on curriculum* (pp. 79–97). New York: Macmillan.

Lopez, G. (2001, January-February). Re-visiting white racism in educational research: Critical race theory and the problem of method. *Educational Researcher, 30*(1), 29–33.

Lucas, S. (1999). *Tracking inequality: Stratification and mobility in American high schools.* New York: Teachers College Press.

Macdonald, J. (1975). Curriculum theory. In W. Pinar (Ed.), *Curriculum theorizing: The reconceptualists* (pp. 5–14). Berkeley, CA: McCutchan.

Marshall, C., & McCarthy, M. (2002, September). School leadership reforms: Filtering social justice through dominant discourses. *Journal of School Leadership, 12*(5), 480–502.

McKinney, W., & Westbury, I. (1975). Stability and change: The public school of Gary, Indiana, 1940–70. In W. Reid & D. Walker (Eds.), *Case studies in curriculum change.* London: Routledge & Kegan Paul.

McLaren, P. (1994). *Life in schools: An introduction to critical pedagogy in the foundations of education.* New York: Longman.

McLaughlin, M., & Mitra, D. (2001). Theory-based change and change-based theory: Going deeper and going broader. *Journal of Educational Change, 2*(4), 301–323.

Messerli, J. (1972). *Horace Mann.* New York: Knopf.

Murnane, R. (1975). *The impact of school resources on the learning of inner city children.* Cambridge, MA: Ballinger.

Moss-Mitchell, F. (1998, May). *The effects of curriculum alignment on the mathematics achievement of third-grade students as measured by the Iowa Test of Basic Skills: Implications for educational administration.* Unpublished doctoral dissertation, Atlanta, GA: Clark University.

National Commission on Testing and Public Policy. (1990). *Reforming assessment: From gatekeepers to gateway in education.* Chestnut Hill, MA: Boston College.

Neill, M. (2000, Spring). State exams flunk test of quality. *The State Education Standard, 1*(2), 31–35.

Newmann, F. (1993). Beyond common sense in educational restructuring: The issues of content and linkage. *Educational Researcher, 22*(2), 4–13, 22.

Newmann, F., Smith, B., Allensworth, E., & Bryk, A. (2001, Winter). Instructional program coherence: What it is and why it should guide school improvement policy. *Education Evaluation and Policy Analysis, 23*(4), 297–322.

Oakes, J. (1985). *Keeping track: How schools structure inequality.* New Haven, CT: Yale University Press.

Oakes, J., Gamoran, A., & Page, R. (1992). Curriculum differentiation: Opportunities, consequences, and meaning. In P. Jackson (Ed.), *Handbook of research on curriculum* (pp. 570–608). New York: Macmillan.

Olshtain, E., & Celce-Murcia, M. (2003). Discourse analysis and language teaching. In D. Schriffin, D. Tannen, & H. Hamilton (Eds.), *The handbook of discourse analysis* (pp. 707–724). Malden, MA: Blackwell.

Osborne, J. (1999). Unraveling underachievement among African-American boys from an identification with academics perspective. *Journal of Negro Education, 68*(4), 555–563.

Pinar, W. (Ed.). (1975). *Curriculum theorizing: The reconceptualists.* Berkeley, CA: McCutchan.

Poole, W. (2001, April). The teacher unions' role in 1990s educational reform: An organizational evolution perspective. *Educational Administration Quarterly, 37*(2), 173–196.

Poston, W., English, F., Boris, V., Chernosky, C., Nichols, B., Reed, J., Stevenson, Z., Busch, J., Cannie, M., Ellsberry, J., McKennan, C., & Mitchell, J. (2001, December). *An external audit of the Georgia quality core curriculum for the Georgia State Board of Education.* Bloomington, IN: Phi Delta Kappa.

Quality counts. (2004, January 8). *Education Week,* p. 104.

Ravitch, D. (1974). *The great school wars: New York City, 1805–1973.* New York: Basic Books.

Sanders, W., & Horn, P. (1994). The Tennessee value-added assessment system (TVASS): Mixed-model methodology in educational assessment. *Journal of Personnel Evaluation in Education, 8,* 299–311.

Sapon-Shevin, M. (1994). *Playing favorites: Gifted education and the disruption of community.* Albany: SUNY Press.

Scalafani, S. (2001). Using an aligned system to make real progress for Texas students. *Education and Urban Society, 33*(3), 305–312.

Scheurich, J., & Skrla, L. (2003). *Leadership for equity and excellence.* Thousand Oaks, CA: Corwin.

Schubert, W. (1980). *Curriculum books: The first eighty years.* Washington, DC: University Press of America.

Silver, P. (1983). *Educational administration: Theoretical perspectives on practice and research.* New York: Harper & Row.

Smith, M., & O'Day, J. (1991). Systemic school reform. In S. Furhrman & B. Malen (Eds.), *The politics of curriculum and testing* (pp. 233–268). Bristol, PA: Falmer Press.

Snipes, J., Doolittle, F., & Herlihy, C. (2002, September). *Foundations for success: Case studies of how urban school systems improve student achievement.* Washington, DC: Council of Great City Schools.

Snyder, J., Bolin, F., & Zumwalt, K. (1992). Curriculum implementation. In P. Jackson (Ed.), *Handbook of research on curriculum* (pp. 402–435). New York: Macmillan.

Spring, J. (1986). *The American school 1642–1985.* New York: Longman.

Stanley, W. (1992). *Curriculum as utopia.* Albany: SUNY Press.

Steffy, B., English, F., Lewis, L., McLendon, D., Proffitt, E., Heard, D., Mattox-Hall, D., Perkins, H., & Wilkerson, D. (1999). *A curriculum management audit of the Rockford public schools.* Bloomington, IN: Phi Delta Kappa.

Stein, M., & Nelson, B. (2002). *How subjects matter in school leadership.* Paper presented at the University Council for Educational Administration, Pittsburgh, PA.

Stein, M., & Spillane, J. (2003). *Research on teaching and research on educational administration: Building a bridge.* Paper presented at Division A Task Force on Future Research on Educational Leadership, American Education Research Association, Chicago.

Stone, M. (1992, December). Cost analysis in an educational setting. *Studies in Educational Administration,* pp. 1–12.

Tanner, D., & Tanner, L. (1990). *History of the school curriculum.* New York: Macmillan.

Taylor, F. (1911). *The principles of scientific management.* New York: Harper and Row.

Thompson, J. (1967). *Organizations in action: Social science bases of administrative theory.* New York: McGraw-Hill.

Thorndike, E. (1912). *Education: A first book.* New York: Macmillan.

Tyack, D. (1974). *The one best system: A history of American urban education.* Cambridge, MA: Harvard University Press.

Tyler, R. (1949). *Basic principles of curriculum and instruction.* Chicago: University of Chicago Press.

Webb, N. (1997). *Criteria for alignment of expectations and assessments in mathematics and science education* (NISE Research Monograph No. 6). Madison: University of Wisconsin-Madison, National Institute for Science Education; Washington, DC: Council of Chief State School Officers.

Webb, N. (1999). *Alignment of science and mathematics standards and assessment in four states* (NISE Research Monograph No. 18). Madison: University of Wisconsin-Madison, National Institute for Science Education; Washington, DC: Council of Chief State School Officers.

Webb, N. (2002, April). *An analysis of the alignment between mathematics standards and assessments for three states.* Paper presented at the American Education Research Association, New Orleans, LA.

Webb, N., Horton, M., & O'Neal, S. (2002, April). *An analysis of the alignment between language arts standards and assessments for four states.* Paper presented at the American Education Research Association, New Orleans, LA.

Weber, M. (1946). Bureaucracy. In H. Gerth & C. Mills (Eds. & Trans.), *From Max Weber: Essays in sociology* (pp. 196–264). New York: Oxford University Press.

Weick, K. (1976). Educational organizations as loosely-coupled systems. *Administrative Science Quarterly, 23*, 1–19.

Wilson, B., & Rossman, G. (1993). *Mandating academic excellence: High school responses to state curriculum reform.* New York: Teachers College Press.

Wise, A. (1979). *Legislated learning: The bureaucratization of the American classroom.* Berkeley: University of California Press.

Wixon, K., Fisk, M., Dutro, E., & McDaniel, J. (1999). *The alignment of state standards and assessments in elementary reading* (A report commissioned by the National Research Council's Committee on Title 1 Testing and Assessment). Ann Arbor: University of Michigan.

Wraga, W. (1999). Extracting sun-beams out of cucumbers: The retreat from practice in reconceptualized curriculum studies. *Educational Researcher, 28*(1), 4–13.

Wraga, W. (2002). Recovering curriculum practice: Continuing the conversation. *Educational Researcher, 31*, 17–19.

Yair, G. (2000, October). Not just about time: Instructional practices and productive time in school. *Educational Administration Quarterly, 36*(4), 485–512.

18

Refocusing the Purposes of Teacher Supervision

LARRY E. FRASE
San Diego State University

Persons attempting to find a motive in this narrative will be prosecuted; persons attempting to find a moral in it will be banished; persons attempting to find a plot in it will be shot.

(Mark Twain, *The Adventures of Huckleberry Finn*, 1884/1948, p. i)

Contrary to Twain's decree to readers of his highly prominent and poignant book, all readers of this chapter are challenged to become "meaning makers." You are encouraged to actually use this information and implement these ideas. In this way, it is hoped that supervision will improve at all levels to further the personal success of each school administrator and teacher in the noble quest to produce student learning. This is what this chapter is all about—its motive, its moral orientation—the plot, if you will.

Teacher morale is at an all-time low and attrition at an all-time high. This chapter exposes the dinosaurs that continue to drive current supervisory practices, with the result of unacceptable workplace conditions for teachers.

To help refocus supervision, the chapter includes a review of current research on teacher variables, and teacher instructional practices related directly to improved student learning are provided. Delving into the depths of workplace quality, we investigate flow theory as a new overriding focus for administrators as they attempt to improve conditions for their teachers. Flow is described, research results are provided, and implications for how school administrators can build workplace conditions more conducive to teacher flow experiences are detailed.

INTRODUCTION AND OVERVIEW

Einstein used the term *cosmological constant* to describe his conjecture that all of space is bubbling with an invisible form of energy that creates a mutual repulsion between objects normally attracted to each other—*negative gravity*. Scientists recently discovered proof of this theory by viewing exploding stars (Glanz, 2001). Negative gravity describes the current gravitational status between educators and schools. For decades, teaching and administrative jobs attracted high numbers of applicants. These people were driven by a powerful desire to do the job, and they believed they would be successful—they could help young people achieve. They found satisfaction in doing so. But teacher satisfaction levels have plummeted. Recent studies show that teachers' desire to stay in teaching and their overall satisfaction and morale have dropped dramatically over the past two decades (Perie & Baker, 1997; Public Agenda Foundation, 2000; Scholastic, Inc., 2000). This is education's negative gravity: schools and teachers repulsing each other. Schools repulse teachers because of poor working conditions, and teachers depart due to the fact that they find so little success in achieving their noble and No. 1 goal—helping students learn.

Few can argue against the fact that budget shortages and the pressures of high-stakes testing result in great pressure on educational systems and teachers. These forces derive their power from national and state governments and are therefore outside of the schools' control. My conjecture is that school administrators must focus on what they can control. They can control and ensure high-quality curriculum and instructional design and delivery. They also can and must produce high-quality teacher workplace environments. Variations in the quality of curriculum and instruction are a result not so much of funding levels as of management's lack of focus and commitment to them and to the concomitant supervising practices.

School districts' treatment of teachers seems more consistent with La Mettrie's (1748/1994) machine model, in which he claimed that the universe consists of a single substance, and therefore, that men and machines are identical. Furthermore, a great many work-life problems are related to supervisors' fascination with mechanized models of management—in other words, treating people like machines—the theory espoused by 18th-century philosopher Julien Offray de La Mettrie's (1748/1994) essay, *Man A Machine*. In this tradition, teachers, especially in inner-city schools, are isolated in classrooms; they receive little training that they value; scant, if any, feedback from others on the quality of their work; few opportunities to confer with other teachers; deficient amounts of time to reflect on their practice; and little assistance in dealing effectively with the many problems they face in their classrooms (Choy, 1993; Public Agenda Foundation, 2000; Scholastic, Inc., 2000). The bottom line is that they receive little assistance that they can use to improve the quality of their work (Blair, 2000; Fullan, 2002). The sad result of this is that their potential for further increasing their success is severely limited. For the most part, teachers have not been treated as the schools' internal clients, as Deming (1986) espouses.

The picture of overcrowded classrooms, inadequate materials, noncompetitive salaries, poor working conditions, and a sense of distrust is very clear and alarming (Eisner, 2002). As a result, the past 20 years have seen a mass exodus of teachers from the profession and an all-time low morale level (National Center for Education Statistics, 1999; National Education Association, 1992; Public Agenda Foundation, 2000). Based on the current teacher morale levels and attrition rates, the frank reality is that organizations must focus on building work environments where teachers have greater opportunities to find success and, thereby, greater motivation and satisfaction.

Archer (2003) analyzed the teacher attrition problem by examining school communities with lower and higher socioeconomic status (SES) and comparing teacher retention rates to the degree of support provided to the teachers. A general finding was that attrition was lower and teacher morale was higher in higher SES school districts; one specific finding was that the few high schools serving poor, inner-city students that do provide motivating environments have managed to attract and keep the same percentage of teachers as schools serving the wealthy communities. This result supports the thesis that the quality of teachers' work lives and the level of their success in helping students learn are powerful factors in increasing teacher retention rates.

Fallacious Philosophies of Supervision and Motivation

The deplorable conditions of school work environments are surprising considering the proclaimed purpose of supervision. The purpose of supervision in education is quite noble and humanistic and has remained relatively consistent since its inception in America's public schools. As early as 1875, educational leaders stated that the purpose of supervision was to improve teaching (Bolin, 1987; Payne, 1875). Since then, other historians have amassed citations illustrating the longevity of this purpose (Ayer, 1954).

- "[Supervision] is the foundation upon which all programs for the improvement of teaching must be built." (Barr & Burton, 1927, cited in Ayer, 1954)
- "Supervision is an expert technical service primarily concerned with studying and improving the condition that surrounds learning and pupil growth." (Barr, Burton, & Brueckner, 1947, cited in Ayer, 1954)
- "Supervision is a service activity that exists to help teachers do their job better." (Wiles, 1950, cited in Ayer, 1954)
- "The terms 'supervisor,' 'supervision,' and 'supervisory program' relate to the instructional phases of school plans and activities." (Melchior, 1950, cited in Ayer, 1954)
- "To supervise means to coordinate, stimulate, and direct the growth of the teacher." (Briggs & Justman, 1952, cited in Ayer, 1954)

This view of supervision remains popular today. Sullivan and Glanz (2000) chose the title of their book to reflect this idea—*Supervision That Improves Teaching*. This definition has been widely accepted, and the importance of supervision has been established. In 1957, the American Association of School Administrators wrote in its 35th yearbook, "The superintendent of schools knows his most important task is that of improving instruction" (p. 167). Since then, hundreds of books and articles have been written on the topic, but to what end?

Although the original purposes and intents of supervision were to improve teaching and student growth, there is little evidence of success in attaining this purpose. Gambrill (1929) searched for the scientific foundation and justification of the principles of supervision and concluded that little research data existed to guide its practice. She further commented that opinions are freely espoused, but with few facts to back them up. Glanz (1998) drew similar conclusions from his study of current supervision literature. Although the findings from these studies appear to be artifacts of logical positivism, the deplorable condition of America's workforce remains. Supervision has been ineffective in alleviating these adverse conditions, and it is a likely cause. I contend in this chapter that the primary factor accounting for the status quo is the failure to build supervisory practices on proper human motivation and satisfaction theory and research-based supervisory practices.

Although human motivation theories are contradictory, a substantive body of research supports what is known as Theory Y, which posits that people want to work, want to do a good job, and are motivated by doing their job well (Drucker, 1974). Unfortunately, teacher supervisory practices have been modeled after the opposing theory of the day, Theory X, which espouses that people must be coerced into doing a good job, do not want to work, are lethargic, and lack internal motivation. This theory drove the Industrial Revolution, in which efficiency was the target. Reliance on external rewards and coercive practices gave rise to great unrest and a need for workers to unionize to protect themselves and bring about a better quality work life, but it has not succeeded (Streshly, 2001). Theory X was build on the fundamental belief that people are like machines and that the only effective means of motivating them is through coercion and external rewards (Drucker, 1974). This theory was built on the assumptions not only that using external motivation and inculcating fear is proper, but that it is the only source of human motivation.

The machine metaphor and the Theory X philosophy greatly influenced school administrators, supervisors, and legislators as they designed and mandated teacher evaluation programs. Over the last 50 years, each state has enacted laws or legal codes requiring regular teacher evaluations, and the widely stated purpose of this was to improve teaching. In some cases, states have gone so far as to prescribe the evaluation instrument and procedure. The result has been failure. Teacher evaluation as a practice has been labeled deficient (Frase & Streshly, 1994; Haefele, 1993), chaotic (Medley, Coker, & Soar, 1984; Soar, Medley, & Coker, 1983), inadequate (Scriven, 1981), of little value in assisting teachers in improving classroom instruction (Duke, 1995; Frase & Streshly, 1994, 2000; Nevo, 1994), and unjust in consideration of the extraordinary cost (Scriven, 1988).

A quotation from long ago rings so true today: "The attitude of the teacher will be determined by the kind of supervision that is attempted" (Newlon, 1923, p. 548). Newlon's quotation was prophetic; today, most teachers find supervisory practices ineffective and some even say worthless. They are treated as chattel, not as people with internal drive and devotion to their craft. The results, as illustrated earlier, are high attrition and depressed satisfaction levels.

The Theory X top-down, I'll-tell-you-what-to-do strategy was present from the beginning

of supervision. As early at the 17th century, townsmen inspected classrooms to inform themselves of the methods being used, and they issued requirements for change (Boston Town Records, 1710). A vivid example of this deficient citizen inspectional practice was even experienced by the brilliant Luther Martin. After the school inspector found Martin's students shooting mark (target shooting) and lacking the knowledge to properly answer his questions, Martin was reprimanded in front of the class and was forced to leave the school. Luther Martin then went on to become a lawyer and famously defended Aaron Burr (Tanner & Tanner, 1987). Most authors espouse improvement of teaching as the purpose of supervision. In Luther Martin's case, the mission was not accomplished. The same is true today.

Dinosaurs and Insights in Supervision

The "machine" has been the primary work metaphor for the past 300 years. In this century, the practices it encouraged have been called *scientific management* and have been likened to the *scientific method*. Modernism offered unsubstantiated assurances that following the scientific steps of inquiry would result in truth and the security of being "right," a binary approach that loses sight of individuals and the human spirit but that is considered synonymous with progress (Maxcy, 1994). Since World War II, structuralism's nearly singular focus on efficiency has become the sine qua non of schools. State requirements for growth plans and for teacher evaluation generally based on a rating scale are the embodiment of this modernistic approach to supervision.

The past 30 years have witnessed a steady flow of innovations designed to motivate teachers and improve education—site-based management, restructuring, merit pay, shared decision making, situational leadership, management by objectives, and total quality management, to name a few. Superintendents and legislatures began to mandate highly intensive supervision as a means of determining teacher quality ratings and justifying merit pay. On the other end of the spectrum, some scholars and school districts ruled that the principal cannot be both an instructional leader and evaluator, and therefore teacher mentors were assigned to perform evaluations. This belief is foundationless (Downey, Steffy, English, Frase, & Poston, 2004). Regardless, each strategy has failed to make substantive changes in schools, and this serves as yet another denouncement of the tenets of logical positivism and modernism, which hold that the key to enlightened leadership, high productivity, and job satisfaction lies in an esoteric, static ratio of mechanistic ingredients in the management brew.

This atomistic thinking took a heavy toll on the confidence of teachers and on the public's opinion regarding schools. Wisdom accumulated over the centuries (Cutler, 2003; Fox, 1994) and a steady stream of research (Caouette, 1995; Csikszentmihalyi, 1990; Csikszentmihalyi & Csikszentmihalyi, 1988; Hackman & Oldham, 1980; Herzberg, 1959; Sheldrake, 1994; Zhu, 2001) deny legitimacy to La Mettrie's view that men and machines function alike. Logical positivists believe they can find the keys or the secret ratios to nearly any topic through empirical means. They also believe that their current ideologies must not be questioned until their next discovery is revealed (Feyerabend, 1993). An excellent example of logical positivism in action is operations research, a structuralistic attempt to apply scientific method to decision making using mathematics, systems, and machines. The belief is that given enough well-organized quantitative data, the answers to a problem or dilemma will be inescapable. Marshall Dimock (1958) recounted the story of the U.S. government's plan to build a new, modern city during the New Deal. All data available were used—for example, facts regarding employment, climate, terrain, transportation facilities, and so on—and they were appropriately weighted. One site earned 95 out of 100 points—much more than the other sites. This site was located on the banks of a river. In the first year, the city was flooded and completely destroyed (p. 143). The fallacies of the logic of this operations research are obvious. The interpreters of the research data failed to realize that decisions should be made in consideration of the context of the geographical area and community; they should have realized that not all valuable information is meaningfully quantifiable. The point made by Dimock is reminiscent of a statement by Foucault: "People know what they do; they frequently know why they do what they do; but what they do not know is what they do does" (Foucault, quoted in Dreyfus & Rabinow, 1983, p. 221).

This sort of superficial tinkering and the ideological practices of modernity have been affecting American schools for more than 200 years. Wheatley's (1992) notion that organizations rise and fall on the quality of relationships has been largely excluded in the development of innovations, as has ancient wisdom and recent research that links success at work with optimal life experiences (Csikszentmihalyi, 1990; Csikszentmihalyi & Csikszentmihalyi, 1988; Fox, 1994; Hackman & Oldham, 1980; Sheldrake, 1994). St. Thomas Aquinas said it perfectly: ". . . when we delight in our work and the whole life of a person is ordered to it, then it is called our life" (cited in Fox, 1994, p. 107).

To the chagrin of those who have attempted to move beyond the constraints of modernism, those who create educational innovations have paid little attention to the actual needs of teachers and administrators, never really considering the inherent potential of human motivation or its sources. Modernity dictates conceiving of organizations as concrete objects embedded in artifacts such as policies and buildings (Gephart, Thatchenkery, & Boje, 1996, p. 2); far more desirable is Mauws's (1995) idea of using social actors in contextually embedded social discourse as a model to interpret the social world—in this case, the workplace. As Gergen (1992) argues, the hallmark of an organization theory should be whether it supports patterns of relationships that have potential for positive rather than negative consequences for social life. And the social life of an organization cannot be distilled into numbers. As Gergen proffered, the ultimate value of a theory must be derived from its pragmatic implications rather than from its level of truth as defined by levels of statistical significance or dogma. In doing so, theoretical voice is restored to significance.

Workplace Intangibles

Like those in private industry, educators have discussed the virtues of intangibles such as worker satisfaction; they have suggested that these intangibles are important to workers and their work life and that these intangibles are closely linked to the quality of the work they produce. We have tinkered with the concept of worker satisfaction and have developed formulae for determining the proper ingredients. Attempting to establish these causal relations is walking on a slippery slope indeed. Educators have focused on teacher satisfaction—how to make teachers happier and more satisfied—thinking that such an emphasis will lead to better and greater student learning. The reality is that this supposed casual link has not been adequately demonstrated, either empirically or experimentally. Teacher satisfaction has been viewed, and in some cases is still viewed, as the ultimate purpose of an organization; in reality, it is but a poor proxy for the primary product of schooling—student learning. The evidence for a relationship between teacher satisfaction and the production of student learning is not prima facie. The research base linking teacher satisfaction to student learning is very shallow. Furthermore, only a few studies have

directly analyzed how satisfaction levels or teaching practices contribute to variations in student engagement (Meece, 1991; Shernoff, Schneider, & Csikszentmihalyi, 1999).

Few people deny that teachers are the most important element in the formal education of a child. In the mechanistic tradition, however, schools attended to what Herzberg (1959) originally named "hygiene needs"—the extrinsic parts of employment, such as policy and salary—rather than the job itself, for example, achievement and doing a job well. Witness the energy and resources expended on contract negotiations rather than on what the district could do to create a work environment where teachers are more likely to be successful (and thereby find satisfaction and motivation to attain even greater success in their work). Herzberg's research results have been replicated repeatedly in many professions, and they make sense. We have strong evidence that people come to the teaching profession with the primary purpose of helping students learn. Research also reveals that they leave because they have failed to achieve that goal.

Due to the unionized milieu of school districts and lack of insight into discovering how to do better, boards and union leaders tend simply to battle over money and management rights (Streshly, 2001). These external factors are important to the well-being of teachers and must be adequate to prevent dissatisfaction on the job, but beyond the hygiene level, more pay does not lead to sustained satisfaction or motivation (Herzberg, 1959; Sergiovanni, 1967). This point is brought clearly into focus in the Public Agenda Foundation (2000) report. Its survey of 900 new teachers and about the same number of college graduates who did not choose teaching as a career found that "teachers do believe that they are underpaid"; however, higher salaries would not likely alleviate the teacher shortage because considerations other than money are "significantly more important to most teachers and would-be teachers."

The focus on external motivational factors and management gimmickry—site-based management, sprinkles of quality circles, management/union negotiations—has missed the target. The target, the important stuff that defines quality work life, is all the internal elements of the job—such as achievement, recognition, responsibility, advancement (Herzberg, 1959), task identity, feedback, skill variety (Hackman & Oldham, 1980), and the quality of work life. As discussed earlier, teachers who find themselves isolated and in deplorable conditions and those who have little contact or support from others tend to leave the field. As Archer (2003) found, although retention is generally higher and attrition lower in higher SES schools, when low SES schools provide motivating work environments (as characterized by a focus on the work itself, e.g., presence of administrative support, high-quality training, and opportunities to reflect on their work with other teachers), they also attract and keep the same percentage of teachers as the high SES schools. Other research has demonstrated that lack of administrative or supervisory support is a primary reason for teacher attrition (Jenkins, Jenkins, Hall, Ware, & Heintzleman, 1998; Natale, 1993; National Center for Education Statistics, 1995). Furthermore, the teachers most likely to leave are the beginners (Archer, 2003; Chance & Chance, 1999; Olson, 2003a, 2003b). Teachers in one study gave the following prioritized list of reasons for departing the profession:

1. Conditions of the work and the work environment

2. Heavy workload—increased paperwork and additional nonteaching demands

3. Lack of parental support and negativity from parents

4. Lack of administrative support

5. Low professional status and salary. (Archer, 2003; Olson, 2003a, 2003b)

All of the above contribute to the primary reason for most teachers leaving the profession: dissatisfaction and failure to achieve their No. 1 goal—to help their students learn. School boards, superintendents, and legislative bodies are failing either to notice or to alleviate these problems. Instead, these entities have tightened the screws on teachers and schools; the bar of expectations for teachers has been raised.

In contrast, the advantage of focusing on the internal aspects of work rather than the external elements has been supported over the years by many theorists and researchers (Darling-Hammond, 2000; Deming, 1986; Frase, 1989; Hackman & Oldham, 1980; Herzberg, 1959; Kohn, 2003; Sergiovanni, 1967).

This problem is not new. More than 42 years ago, *Life Magazine* carried an article on teachers' work conditions. A quotation from that article could have been written today: "Too many will quit permanently because they are fed up. Their ambition and self-respect will take them into business or other professions. . . . They leave behind an increasing proportion of tired time-servers." Failure to address the problems that prevent teachers from accomplishing their No. 1 goal of helping students learn has led to the current abysmal teacher work-life situation and, in many ways, to low student achievement levels.

Based on the current teacher morale levels and attrition rates, the frank reality is that organizations must focus on building work environments where people have greater opportunities to find success and, thereby, motivation and satisfaction. It is well past time that legislatures, union leaders, school boards, and school superintendents learn that the workers on the front lines, teachers, are the more important elements in the education process. It follows, then, that creating work and learning places where teachers can perform their craft well is absolutely imperative. Gephart and his colleagues (1996) support this view from a postmodern perspective:

"A positive reconstruction necessarily focuses on the underlying assumptions made by social actors when they construct organizations and other features of society. The focus should be on examination of assumptions, presentation of alternatives, and consideration of choices" (p. 365).

This chapter presents an alternative for viewing the work environment of teachers. My belief in this alternative view is based on the theoretical perspective and research results showing that when work is successfully completed, this results in satisfaction and the motivation to perform work even more successfully; it is also based on the conviction that management has both the ability and the responsibility to provide work environments and conditions that give workers the best opportunity to do their jobs well and that these factors will result in worker satisfaction and create the motivation necessary to do even higher quality work. As Marshall Dimock wrote in 1958, "If every administrator looked upon every employee as something separate and special and to be dealt with as a conscientious trustee would, remarkable things would begin to happen to group morale, institutional accomplishment, and the happiness of individuals" (p. 160). This is the supervisor's true challenge, and this should be every supervisor's goal.

An Obvious Obstacle to Increased Teacher Motivation and Satisfaction

There is a very practical obstacle to focusing on teacher motivation and satisfaction. Today's emphasis on high-stakes testing makes it difficult to convince school boards, unions, and legislatures to devote the financial resources necessary to improve workplace conditions. Instead, school boards and other educational leaders continue to march in compliance with Bismarckian or Prussian efficiency to gain higher test scores. Although this reflects an obvious myopia, people still believe that the school principal in particular and the

organization in general can have positive or negative influences on human growth, development, satisfaction, and motivation (Bass, 1998; Deming, 1986; Dimock, 1958; Drucker, 1974; Hackman & Oldham, 1980; Herzberg, 1959).

SUPERVISION: REFINING THE FOCUS

Socioeconomic Status Versus Teaching: Which Matters Most?

The importance of teachers to the educational process has seldom, if ever, been seriously questioned by either academicians or lay people; however, over the past four decades it has become increasingly clear that the SES of students is also a major contributing factor. Beginning with what became known as the Coleman Report (Coleman et al., 1966), SES was touted as the primary factor that predicted student achievement, to the exclusion of all school variables included in his study. Coleman estimated that SES accounted for 90% of the variations in achievement test scores. His reanalysis of his research methodology and a study on school policy persuaded Coleman to revise his conclusion. In his second study (Coleman, 1997), he found that school policy and teacher quality also had significant effects on student achievement. In the 1990s, studies by the National Center for Education Statistics (1993) began to reveal a reduction in the predictive power of SES. The Center's work attributed about 79% of the variation in student test scores to SES. Although they use a different type of analysis, international studies such as the Third International Mathematics and Science Study (TIMSS) revealed that teacher practices and other factors such as school policy and curriculum construction and alignment have major impact on student learning (Schmidt, McKnight, & Raizen, 1997; Stevenson & Stigler, 1992; Stigler & Hiebert, 1999). A more recent analysis data from the 1993–94 Schools and Staffing Surveys (SASS) and the

National Assessment of Educational Progress (NAEP) revealed that teacher practices contribute greatly to student achievement as illustrated by the following conclusion:

> Policy investments in the quality of teachers may be related to improvement in student performance [and] measures of teacher preparation and certification are by far the strongest correlates of student achievement in reading and mathematics, both before and after controlling for student poverty and language status. (Darling-Hammond, 2000, p. 1–2)

Offering further evidence that Coleman was mistaken and that individual teachers can have the most significant impact on student learning, Wright, Horn, and Sanders (1997) wrote that "the most important factor affecting student learning is the teacher. . . . The immediate and clear implication of this finding is that seemingly more can be done to improve education by improving the effectiveness of teachers than by any other single factor" (p. 63).

Regarding the effects of the differing quality of teacher practices, Sanders, Collins, and Rivers (1996) concluded that students assigned to a series of several ineffective teachers had significantly lower achievement and achievement gains than those who were assigned to several highly effective teachers. The positive effects of high-quality educational practices and teaching are now clear; there is little doubt expressed by lay people, academicians, or practitioners that teachers are in the position to substantially improve student academic achievement.

The question now becomes: What characteristics of teachers and educational practices will achieve the desired differences? Academic and pedagogical preparation? Instructional techniques? Professional development while in service? In the next section, we turn to a discussion of research results that provide some answers and that also have implications for teacher supervision.

Supervision Research Results: Scant Beginnings and Powerful Developments

W. W. Charters (1918, cited in Tanner & Tanner, 1987) once wrote,

> Once upon a time the classroom teacher was required to provide school buildings, pupils, books, materials and instruction. Since those primitive days there was developed a department of school activity called administration whose primary function is to provide everything which will improve classroom teaching. (p. 3)

Charters concluded that supervision is a function of school administration for improving instruction and, further, that its potential is yet to be realized.

Eleven years later, Gambrill (1929) furthered the search for fulfillment of this potential. She narrowed Charters's search and, with a focus derived from logical positivism, sought to answer the question "[To what] extent have we a factual basis for the theory and practice of supervision?" (p. 279). In her study, she reviewed the extant literature in professional journals and categorized the articles on the basis of whether they were scientific or editorial in orientation. She concluded that the beginnings of a scientific knowledge base were fruitful but that the movement was still young and the actual knowledge base meager. She went on to declare that a very small proportion of the content of the textbooks on supervision was based on research data.

In 1998, Harris presented an exhaustive review of supervision literature, including that which was found in professional journal articles, dissertations, and theses. He assessed hundreds of studies from the early 1980s through the early 1990s. In general, he found these studies lacked focus and yielded little data-driven theory.

Despite a long history of widely recognized responsibilities, an extensive literature in published sources, and legal provisions in many countries and U.S. states, the field "remains

Table 18.1   Research Findings and Implications

Summary Finding	Implication
Teacher verbal ability is positively correlated with student achievement	Improving the verbal ability of teachers should become a target of supervision in school and school district professional development programs; verbal ability could also be used as one criterion in the hiring of teachers
Training in academic subject matter does, in general, positively affect student achievement in the same subject matter	Subject-matter knowledge and subject matter-specific methodology training should be a focal point of school and school district professional development training
High-quality pre-service pedagogical training is positively correlated with subjective measures of teacher effectiveness and student learning	High-quality training in methodology should become a focus of school and school district pedagogical training
How in-service professional development training is designed and delivered makes a difference in teacher effectiveness and student achievement; selection and quality of teacher instructional methods is related to higher student achievement	Schools and school districts should weave the design and delivery of the curriculum and subject matter to be taught into sustained professional development programs, and these should be the foci of supervisors; teacher training should be grounded in subject matter-specific methodologies

one that is full of controversy and uncertainty" (Harris, 1998, p. 1).

Educators and researchers are now attempting to help fulfill the unfulfilled potential to which Gambrill (1929) referred. The 1990s and the first 3 years of the 21st century have been productive, giving the profession a strong set of research-based findings regarding instructional techniques. We now turn to research findings regarding SES, teacher verbal ability, teacher knowledge of subject matter, teacher pedagogical skills, professional development, instructional behaviors, classroom management, and instructional design as they relate to supervision.

SUPERVISION RESEARCH FINDINGS FOR TODAY'S SCHOOLS

Contrary to Coleman et al. (1966) and later Jencks et al. (1972), who claimed that SES is the only variable that predicts differences in student achievement, recent evidence suggests that better qualified teachers may be a much more important factor in improving student learning at the classroom, school, and district levels. Recently, much of this research has focused on the effectiveness of teacher training institutions. Here, however, we will examine the research on teacher factors and behaviors that can be influenced during hiring and instilled or improved in schools via high-quality supervisory practices. The research results and implications for supervision are provided in Table 18.1 and a discussion of each follows.

Teacher Verbal Ability

Some see teacher verbal ability as a predictor of student achievement (Bowles & Levin, 1968; Coleman et al., 1966; Hanushek, 1971, 1992). Of course, teachers with high verbal ability by definition convey ideas more clearly to students. Hanushek's (1992) analysis of Murnane and Phillips's (1981) data revealed that student gains on reading scores (but not vocabulary scores) were highly correlated with a teacher's verbal ability. Although verbal ability is also highly correlated with SES, teachers and administrators can increase these skills through training (Laflamme, 1997; Luckham, 1991). Wenglinsky (2000) also found a strong relationship between teacher verbal ability and student achievement.

Teacher Knowledge of Subject Matter

Although the results of studies assessing the effects of subject matter training on student achievement are mixed, many well-crafted studies show a positive correlation. Monk and King's (1994) research showed student test scores in mathematics increased when teachers had higher levels of mathematics training. Monk (1994) also found that the teaching of five mathematics courses was the threshold level; there was a negative correlation between student achievement and teachers who had more than five university mathematics classes Goldhaber and Brewer (2000, cited in Wenglinsky, 2000) found similar results for English and history.

In studies with adequate variability in the level of subject matter training in the subject being taught, student achievement was positively correlated with teacher training in subject matter. Byrne (1983) arrived at the same conclusion from a review of 31 studies. Of these, 17 studies showed a student achievement difference favoring teacher training in academic subject matter while 14 showed no difference. Rowan, Chiang, and Miller (1997) found that 10th- and 12th-grade mathematics students achieved higher scores on the mathematics section of the 1988 National Educational Longitudinal Study (NELS) when their teachers correctly answered a mathematics test item and when the teachers were determined to be more highly motivated. In another study, Ferguson and Ladd (1996) revealed that Alabama teacher scores on the ACT were positively correlated with student gains on reading scores from Grade 3 to 4.

Furthermore, a review of research by Bridge, Judd, and Moock (1979) showed an interesting difference between teachers with majors in education and those with majors in the subject matter they taught. Their results showed lower scores for students whose teachers majored in education. Darling-Hammond, Berry, and Thoreson (2001) drew a similar policy conclusion regarding teacher degrees; however, they report that training in education is also positively related to student achievement. Furthermore, Hawk, Coble, and Swanson (1985) and Druva and Anderson (1983) found that student achievement was greater in higher level science classes when their teachers also had higher levels of science training.

A school-level path model using the NAEP database found that teacher preparation in student matter taught is associated with student academic achievement (Wenglinsky, 2002). In a study in England, McBer (2000) found a strong relationship between student achievement and teacher content knowledge.

Knowledge of Pedagogy and Teacher Effectiveness

Results from numerous studies demonstrate a strong positive relationship between full certification and teacher effectiveness (Ashton & Crocker, 1987; Begle, 1979; Evertson, Hawly, & Zlotnik, 1985). The criterion used in these studies was teacher effectiveness as determined by various instruments and methods rather than by learning (which served as the criterion variable in the previous section on the effects of subject matter training). Other studies have linked levels of certification and subject-related methodology with student achievement (National Center for Education Statistics, 1994). In this study, students whose teachers were fully certified, who held training in literature-based instruction, and who had master's degrees scored higher in reading skills than other students. Other studies (Knoblock, 1986; Sanders, Skonie-Hardin, & Phelps, 1994) show similar outcomes. These studies, however, did not consider the effects of other school variables or of student backgrounds such as SES. In studies comparing the effects of variables on student achievement, particularly those aggregated at the classroom level, variables measuring teacher knowledge and skills were far more influential than static variables such as teacher experience or class size. However, top-scoring states on the NAEP usually have very small average school sizes (Feistritzer, 1993; Fowler & Walberg, 1991).

Quality of Instruction and Professional Development

Although professional development is generally considered ineffective nationwide (Culbertson, 1996; Fullan, 1995; Public Agenda Foundation, 2000) research studies reveal that the delivery style of professional development programs can make a substantial difference in teacher effectiveness. Studies found that higher levels of student achievement in mathematics were associated with mathematics teachers' participation in sustained training that was grounded in subject matter-specific methodology and that was also linked to a specific curriculum they were required to implement (Brown, Smith, & Stein, 1995; Cohen & Hill, 1997; Wiley & Yoon, 1995).

Although these findings and implications give some new direction for supervision, they fail to specify which instructional techniques result in higher student learning. As the evidence demonstrating the importance of teaching and schools in student learning continues to mount, it becomes important to specify what exactly effective teachers do. The good news is that this work has begun, and the results are very powerful. This information is crucial to effective supervision. The following section deals with the research on this topic.

TEACHER INSTRUCTIONAL BEHAVIORS

Effective Instructional Practices

An effective instructional practice is one that produces relatively more learning than other instructional practices. Having a strong working knowledge of these practices is crucial to supervisor effectiveness. In regard to the importance of teacher effectiveness and the importance of supervision, Marzano (2003) concluded that "if teachers exhibit average performance and a school is willing to do all that it can to be most effective, then students in that school will demonstrate remarkable gains" (p. 75). Marzano borrowed findings from previous research (Brophy, 1996; Cotton, 1995; Creemers, 1994) to create three teacher-level factors that have high impact on student learning. These are instructional strategies, classroom management, and classroom instructional design.

High-Impact Factor 1: Instructional Strategies

Numerous summaries of research on instructional strategies exist, and it is helpful to sort them into three groups. The first group of research summaries is the generic "I think" type. These typically appear in teacher and administrator trade journals and are expressions of the authors' ideas about the effectiveness of certain instructional strategies. Frequently, these articles expound on the worth and value of a program the authors are familiar with and do not deal with research results.

The second group of research summaries highlights instructional strategies backed by one or more research studies that indicate their effectiveness. Examples include Hattie (1992), Bennett (1986), Creemers (1994), and Good and Brophy (1986). These researchers found that the following teacher behaviors have been positively related to higher student learning:

- Teacher clarity
- Teacher enthusiasm
- Student task-oriented behavior
- Variability of lesson approaches
- Student opportunity to learn criterion material

In another example of this second group, Berliner and Tikunoff (1976), Doyle (1986), Schalock (1979), McBer (2000), and Walberg and Waxman (1983) show that a teacher's ability to use varying instructional strategies with student groups and individual students takes on great importance because no one instructional strategy is unvaryingly successful. The call for use of multiple instructional strategies has been made for many years.

It is interesting to note student perceptions of teacher effectiveness also. In one study, students were asked to identify characteristics of the "best" and "worst" teachers; the students responded that the No. 1 characteristic of good teachers was their sense of humor, and the No. 1 characteristic of the "worst" teachers was that they were dull and boring ("Students Say," 1997).

The third type of research summaries is different from the second in that it ratchets up the level of research sophistication. These studies include the result known as effect size. For example, in addition to saying that one strategy is significantly more effective than another, conclusions about effect size tell us *how much more* the students learn. Work by Marzano, Pickering, and Pollock (2001) and Marzano (2003) falls into this category. Marzano and his team analyzed the extant research on instructional strategies and summarized the findings into nine categories. These, along with examples of the behavior, are provided in Table 18.2.

High-Impact Factor 2: Classroom Management

Classroom management means maintaining a classroom environment where effective instruction can occur, where students attend to the lesson, and where learning actually does occur. Classroom management is a major problem in many classrooms across the United States, particularly in low SES schools, and it has been identified as the variable having the most impact on student achievement (Wang, Haertel, & Walberg, 1993). Furthermore, teachers who perform poorly attributed this to their lack of classroom management and to inadequate preparation (Miller, Ferguson, & Simpson, 1998). So, as we can see, classroom management skills are crucial to both teacher and student success. That is why it is imperative for supervisors to be knowledgeable and skillful in conveying techniques that help teachers establish and maintain effective classroom management.

Rules and procedures established by teachers and administrators provide a beginning in the endeavor to attain good classroom management. Evertson and colleagues (1985) found that well-defined rules and procedures that communicate expectations for specific behaviors were present in all effectively managed classrooms. But all of us with experience in preK–12 classrooms or even graduate classrooms know that the best laid plans—in this case, classroom management rules and procedures—are not always followed. Students do break rules, and teachers should monitor behavior and react appropriately.

The following list summarizes key research findings on the most effective classroom management and student discipline techniques. Supervisors can use this list as they work with teachers in professional development, discussion groups, and actual day-to-day supervision. These ideas should become common knowledge among teachers and administrators and should be translated into action in the classroom. Teachers demonstrating effective classroom management and student discipline techniques:

1. Minimize discipline time and accentuate instructional time

2. Realize that time spent disciplining students inversely affects student achievement outcomes

3. Realize that the least effective strategy is not dealing with discipline and rule breaking

Table 18.2   Instructional Categories Divided Into Specific Behaviors

General Instructional Category	Specific Behaviors
Identifying similarities and differences	Assigning in-class and homework tasks that involve comparison and classification Assigning in-class and homework tasks that involve metaphors and analogies
Summarizing and note taking	Asking students to generate verbal summaries Asking students to generate written summaries Asking students to take notes Asking students to revise their notes, correcting errors and adding information
Reinforcing effort and providing recognition	Recognizing and celebrating progress toward learning goals throughout a unit Recognizing and reinforcing the importance of effort Recognizing and celebrating progress toward learning goals at the end of a unit
Homework and practice	Assigning homework for the purpose of students practicing skills and procedures that have been the focus of instruction
Nonlinguistic representations	Asking students to generate mental images representing content Asking students to draw pictures or pictographs representing content Asking students to construct graphic organizers representing content Asking students to act out content Asking students to make physical models of content Asking students to make revisions in their mental images, pictures, pictographs, graphic organizers, and physical models
Cooperative learning	Organizing students in cooperative groups when appropriate Organizing students in ability groups when appropriate
Setting objectives and providing feedback	Setting specific learning goals at the beginning of a unit Asking students to set their own learning goals at the beginning of a unit Providing feedback on learning goals throughout the unit Asking students to keep track of their progress on learning goals Providing summative feedback at the end of a unit Asking students to assess themselves at the end of a unit
Generating and testing hypotheses	Engaging students in projects that involve generating and testing hypotheses through problem-solving tasks Engaging students in projects that involve generating and testing hypotheses through decision-making tasks Engaging students in projects that involve generating and testing hypotheses through investigation tasks Engaging students in projects that involve generating and testing hypotheses through experimental inquiry tasks Engaging students in projects that involve generating and testing hypotheses through systems analysis tasks Engaging students in projects that involve generating and testing hypotheses through invention tasks

(Continued)

Table 18.2 (Continued)

General Instructional Category	Specific Behaviors
Questions, cues, and advance organizers	Prior to presenting new content, asking questions that help students recall what they might already know about the content
	Prior to presenting new content, providing students with direct links with what they have studied previously
	Prior to presenting new content, providing ways for students to organize or think about the content

SOURCE: Marzano et al., 2001 (pp. 82–83) Used with permission.

4. Realize that the most effective strategy is using a combination of punishment and reinforcement

5. Interpret and respond to inappropriate behaviors promptly

6. Maintain clear rules and procedures and establish credibility with students through fair and consistent implementation of discipline

7. Reinforce and reiterate the expectations for positive behavior

8. Scan the room frequently, particularly when working with a small group or with an individual (Berliner, 1986; Brophy, 1996; Kounin, 1983)

9. Monitor their own attitudes about specific students by mentally reviewing their students before class, noting those with whom they anticipate having problems, forming a mental picture of these students demonstrating appropriate behavior, and then keeping positive expectations when interacting with these students (Good, 1982; Rosenshine, 1983; Rosenthal & Jacobson, 1968)

In cases where rules are broken, what actions are recommended by research? A meta-analysis by Stage and Quiroz (1997) found that a variety of interventions resulted in reducing disruptive classroom behavior among 78% of the treated subjects. The strategy yielding the largest effect size was use of a combination of punishment and reinforcement, the second-largest effect size was reinforcement, and the third was punishment. The least effective strategy was using no immediate consequence. The work of Miller, McKenna, and McKenna (1998) also supports these findings.

High-Impact Factor 3:
Classroom Instructional Design

Classroom instructional design is perhaps the most important factor in student learning, and the reason has become quite clear. In these days of high-stakes testing, we are required to prepare students to perform well on these tests. This means that districts, administrators, and teachers must deconstruct the test items to determine the skills required to attain mastery of the item and the context in which competence is to be demonstrated. All of this then becomes the curriculum. Without doing this first, no amount of inspired or instructionally sound teaching of content and context of the test is going to help students perform well. *The teaching must be focused on the skills required by the test.*

Marzano (2003) provides an excellent discussion of lesson construction. For a robust and straightforward discussion of how curricula can be built from tests and why, readers are referred to Chapter 1 in this book, English and Steffy (2001), and English (1992).

Caveats on Research

We have made a strong attempt here to cite findings and opinions based on high-quality research. We are professional pedagogues whose work rests on a strong research base that we use to promote learning. To illustrate the point, physicians are also professionals who use a strong research base. We ask rhetorically, would you take advice from a physician who dreams up treatments that do not have a sound experimental base? Of course not. Hence, our need to use the quality research at hand—and its strength and substance is growing. Improved student learning and enhanced public perception of education is at stake.

Now for the caveat. Be cautious of your expectations of research and what it means. A research study may show that students experiencing Treatment A scored .5 standard deviation points higher than students experiencing Treatment B and that the level of significance is .01. Does that mean that using Treatment A will always have those effects? The answer is no. Statistics simply report probabilities, and the probabilities are diluted when we consider the contextual differences in the experiment and in the application setting. A better way to interpret the research is to think that there is a higher probability that students will learn more if we use Treatment A rather than B, if the contexts are as similar as possible. It is important to remember that research results are never guaranteed. They do not equate to fact. This strategy for interpreting research results is important information for all professional educators and particularly for supervisors.

It is also important to note that much research can be debunked on methodological grounds. As in car sales, let the buyer beware. To facilitate greater teacher effectiveness, it is incumbent on supervisors to be very knowledgeable about instructional strategies, the related research, and techniques for effectively sharing this information. For a full discussion of how to use and interpret research, see McEwan and McEwan (2003).

The research on supervision reported here is solid, but not perfect. It should be used to influence supervision and instruction, but further research is needed. In this sense, it is worth considering the quote by 19th-century educator and researcher Mark Pattison (as cited in Firth & Pajak, 1998): "In research the horizon recedes as we advance . . . and research is always incomplete" (p. xiii). Remember, our research base is good, and it will get better—possibly contradicting current findings.

Summary

This chapter offers academic legitimacy to what educators and laypeople have believed for years. First, supervision can have highly positive effects on the quality of teaching and schooling; thus, supervisory direction should be informed by research. Second, teachers and what they do are the most important factors in the formal education of students. Third, the quality of a teacher's work life, their success in helping students learn, their motivation and satisfaction, and their attrition rates are tightly bound. This is a logical conclusion that sets a straightforward focus for school boards and legislatures and sets the tone and purpose of what teacher supervision should be.

THE QUALITY WORK ENVIRONMENT: THE FUNCTION OF "FLOW" IN SUPERVISION

Educators need a new perspective on the intricacies of work life in schools in terms of what motivates and satisfies teachers in their workplace. Because teachers are the ones who actually do the most important work in schools—teaching kids—it is imperative that we investigate what will make their job more rewarding. Here, I will focus on a concept I believe can help accomplish that goal. It is from the field of psychology, but it has recently been receiving some discussion in educational circles. The concept is *flow* (Csikszentmihalyi, 1990). Csikszentmihalyi indicates that the experience of flow represents a distinct state of consciousness that integrates high but effortless concentration, intrinsic motivation, loss of awareness of self and time, facile response to challenge, and feelings of competence and freedom.

This section of the chapter presents (1) a discussion of the concept of flow and its potential as an indicator of a quality workplace, (2) an examination of variables that research has connected to flow environments, (3) a discussion of the conditions of flow environments, and (4) an interpretation of the principal's role in creating school work environments where teachers have greater opportunities to experience flow. These form a new set of themes on which to base supervision.

Several assumptions have guided my work in this area. First, I believe that successful completion of high-quality work results in greater motivation and increased work satisfaction. Another assumption is that management has the ability and responsibility to provide work environments and conditions that give workers the best opportunity to do their jobs well and that doing so will result in satisfaction and the motivation to do even higher quality work. These assumptions have been espoused throughout the ages (Fox, 1994) and have been supported in scientific work over the past 40 years (Deming, 1986; Hackman & Oldham, 1980; Herzberg, 1959). Unfortunately, educational management has not acted on this research in an effective or sustained manner.

Consideration of Flow Experiences as a Crucial Ingredient in Quality of Work Life

Flow is a feeling of intense involvement in an activity that tests but does not overpower one's abilities; it has been established as a legitimate psychological concept in the literature, with powerful implications for improving the quality of workplaces and productivity

(Csikszentmihalyi, 1990; Csikszentmihalyi & Csikszentmihalyi, 1988). Flow theory has been confused with the personal experience theories—for example, peak experience and peak performance—popularized in lay literature; however, flow is conceptually and distinctly different and has a strong psychological research base (Csikszentmihalyi, 1990; Privette, 1983).

Flow experiences are periods of deep, intense involvement in activities that, as stated above, challenge but do not overwhelm one's skills. As opposed to the feeling of being buffeted by anonymous external forces, flow is a state in which people feel in control of their actions and feel a deep sense of exhilaration that is long cherished and that becomes a landmark in memory for what life should be like (Csikszentmihalyi, 1990). As further characterized by Csikszentmihalyi (1990), flow is the key to intrinsic motivation; it is "the state in which people are so involved in an activity that nothing else seems to matter; the experience itself is so enjoyable that people will do it even at a great cost, for the sheer sake of doing it" (p. 4).

Does flow happen in classrooms? Csikszentmihalyi (1997, p. 33) asserted his opinion that it is easier for students to be in flow when the teacher is in flow. This statement is based on his many research articles theorizing about flow and underscores the importance of a teacher's psychological state. However, this assertion is not based on empirical evidence directly derived from a study of teachers. According to Csikszentmahalyi, the mid-1990s marked the beginning of research on teacher flow experiences. Based on reviews of the literature from that time forward, I conclude that only seven studies have directly investigated the existence and nature of teacher flow experiences.

Caouette (1995) was one of the first researchers, if not the first, to analyze teacher flow experiences. Her study involved in-depth interviews with six teachers who were read narratives of flow experiences and were asked to describe similar experiences. Caouette's subjects described flow in many ways. One of the participants reported on the internal cues accompanying the phenomenon of flow. She saw it as a feeling of "being able to get lost in my work with the kids because I'm so focused on them. . . . I only had two minutes left and I forgot. I didn't know, and the bell went off" (p. 73). This same participant explained flow as the moment "you realize you've got them, like they're with you—and I honor that experience and wonder. It's a feeling of wonder" (p. 74). Another participant explained her sense of flow as

[a] sense of [a] relaxing, fulfilled, self-fulfilling feeling. I think of walking around these kids [who] are so focused into what they're doing. I feel almost like a little stuffed kitty at the end of a big meal. You sit back and you relax and you enjoy what has been prepared here. It's a wonderful sense. (p. 99)

Another responded, "I will be presenting something to the students and I will see every eye on me and not a sound in the room. And I just—I almost—it's scary" (p. 299).

In a more recent study, Frase and Gray (2003) asked 18 teachers in a large urban area to describe when they felt flow occurred and what caused it to occur. All but 1 of the 18 teachers answered with examples of times they felt students were engaged during instruction. Teachers perceived either that their flow caused students to be engaged or that the engagement of students in what the teacher was doing caused the teacher's flow experience. As one teacher explained,

To watch them discuss, it felt like they were having so much fun—but they were getting so many good ideas at the same time. . . . I could have done that forever and not stopped because it was—everybody was so involved, but yet I felt like I was watching it [on] a movie screen where I can let go of it. (Frase & Gray, 2003)

When asked about how being in flow made them feel, one participant stated, "I mean time stops. I'm not bored. I'm feeling very challenged. I know that I can make this work" (p. 8). Another indicated, "Personally, it makes me feel good because I feel like I'm doing a good job and I might be a good teacher" (p. 77).

When in flow, teachers report they are connected to their students; they have eye contact, they feel that students are attending to the lesson, and they sense that learning is happening (Frase, 2003). Helping teachers find success in helping students learn is a powerful method for stimulating more frequent teacher flow experience.

The impact of teacher flow experiences continues to expand. Zhu (2001) used the experience sampling method in classrooms to check teachers' flow experiences. He used beepers, which sounded five times a day, at which times teachers recorded whether or not they believed they were experiencing flow. He found that the frequency of teacher flow experiences predicted student levels of cognitive engagement. His research reported that 25% more students were cognitively engaged in their academic lessons when teachers were experiencing flow. This finding offers strong insight to supervisors.

Focusing supervision and mentoring on teacher self-examination of their teaching strategies may increase the possibility of student cognitive engagement. Such a process can facilitate instructional improvement by involving an experienced educator working with a less experienced teacher collaboratively and nonjudgmentally to study and deliberate on ways to improve classroom instruction (Sullivan & Glanz, 2000). These practices are nonthreatening and may increase the likelihood that teachers will experience flow as recorded by Zhu (2001).

The evidence that flow experiences can mean greater teacher satisfaction and motivation and greater student cognitive engagement provides a powerful rationale for investigating and building the concept of flow into supervisory practice. Research evidence and a discussion of variables that lead to teacher flow experiences follow.

Administrative Variables Conducive to Flow Experiences

Due to the previously cited low teacher morale level and high attrition rates, along with the legislative demands for higher test scores, it becomes critical to examine variables in the culture of schools that might have a relationship to teachers experiencing flow. A review of the literature indicates that the following may be related to teacher job satisfaction and flow experiences: (a) frequency of school principals' visits to the classroom; (b) teacher self-efficacy and perceived efficacy of other teachers and the school; (c) teachers' value of professional development, including well-designed mentor programs; and (d) teachers' views on the value of performance evaluations. Each is addressed in more depth below.

School Principal Classroom Visits

Literature on how principals spend their day leads us to conclude that they spend very small portions of their time in classrooms or working with teachers on curriculum and instructional problems (Frase & Streshly, 1994; Howell, 1981; Kmetz & Willower, 1982; Martin & Willower, 1981). A synthesis of these studies indicates that principals spent from 40% to 80% of their time in their office or office area, 23% to 40% in hallways and playgrounds, 11% off campus, and only 10% in classrooms. The number of principal visits (of any duration) to each classroom in their school per month was very low. Studies have shown that although some principals visit each classroom frequently (twice a week or more), others never visit or do so only once a semester or once a year (Frase & Streshly, 1994; PricewaterhouseCoopers, 1998). Numerous teachers interviewed in this same study, however, said that the principal was never in the classroom when students were present or that some visit the classroom once per semester or only once a year.

Evidence of the positive influence of principal presence in classrooms is mounting. Research studies (Frase, 1998, 2001, 2003) conducted in two low socioeconomic inner-city school districts of about 19,000 students each and one study in a suburban middle-class school district of 30,000 students offered the following findings, as illustrated in Figure 18.1. Frequency of classroom visits positively predicted (a) teacher self-efficacy, (b) teacher-perceived school efficacy, (c) teacher-perceived efficacy of other teachers, (d) teacher-perceived organizational effectiveness, (e) teacher opinions on the value of evaluations and professional development programs, and (f) the frequency of teacher flow experiences.

On another note, teacher self-efficacy, perceived efficacy of other teachers, and perceived school efficacy predicted the frequency of teacher flow experiences. Also, the frequency of teacher flow experiences correlated with and predicted student cognitive engagement levels, as reported by Zhu (2001).

Numerous other studies focusing on the degree of the principal's attention to curriculum and instruction, frequency of classroom visits, and visibility in the school show all of these factors lead to higher student achievement (Andrews, Soder, & Jacoby, 1986; Heck, 1991, 1992; Heck, Larsen, & Marcoulides, 1990). In a recent qualitative study, researchers found that teachers actually liked and requested more frequent visitations from the principal when the Downey Walk-through with reflective questions (Downey et al., 2004) was used (Freedman & Lafleur, 2003). In Frase and Gray's (2003) study, when teacher's were asked about classroom visits by the principal, one teacher responded, "For me it also checks

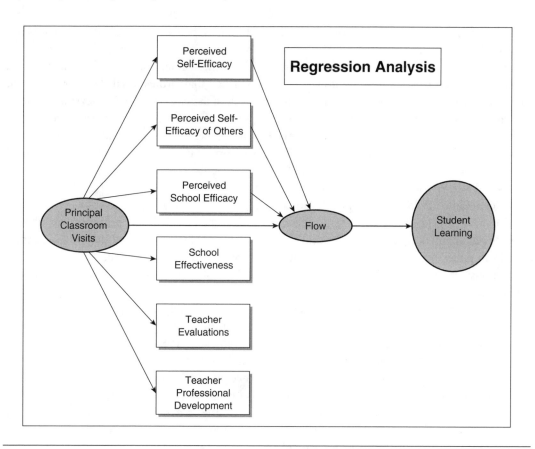

Figure 18.1   Relationship Between Principal Classroom Visits and Other Variables That Predict Flow

SOURCE: Frase, 2003.

me in and kind of gives me a feeling like somebody cares about what's going on in my room and [is] noticing that" (p. 7). Others responded that "I value it quite a bit because I get specific feedback" (p. 5) and "It's a sign that he [the principal] cares" (p. 6). Yet another stated that "When I've got it in the back of my mind that somebody can walk in at any particular time, that is a motivating factor for me to try to make sure that my students are on task" (p. 7).

It is important that even nonmanagers with a tradition of emphasizing teacher classroom autonomy believe in frequent principal classroom visits. Elliot Eisner (2002), one of America's most highly esteemed thinkers in pedagogy and one who comes from a nonmanagement leadership background, said that

in the kind of schools America needs, principals would spend about a third of their time in classrooms in order to know what is going on.

Professional Development

Many teachers, administrators, and researchers express little belief in the value of professional development (Culbertson, 1996; Public Agenda Foundation, 1995). Annunziata (1997) characterized professional development as one-shot deals, superficial and faddish programs, feel-good sessions, "make and takes" or "bags of tricks," and consultant-driven presentations. The National Staff Development Council (cited in Culbertson, 1996) reported that current practices are inadequately designed to be the bridge that takes teachers from where they are to where they need to be in order to guide student learning. Furthermore, Orlich, Remaley, Facemyer, Logan, and Cao (1993) found scant evidence that professional development was linked to student achievement. Furthermore, the evidence that did link professional development to increased student achievement was spurious, due to use of inappropriate measurement techniques and research designs. Darling-Hammond and McLaughlin (1995) described professional development as crucial to educational success and offered guidelines for policy formation to transform policy practices from the status quo to a robust enterprise that benefits students and teachers.

There is some evidence that teachers believe professional development is important. Blase and Blase (2004) found that teachers noted that effective principals promote teachers' professional development to increase student achievement by talking with them, by promoting their professional growth opportunities, and by fostering their self-reflection on instruction. A survey of teachers by Parsad, Lewis, and Farris (as cited in Holloway, 2003) found a link between the amount of professional development in which teachers participated and teachers' feelings of competence. Collaborative activities seemed to be the most effective in promoting competence.

> Teachers who participated in regularly scheduled collaboration with other teachers, networked with teachers outside the school, and mentored another teacher were more likely than those who did not participate in these activities to report feeling very well prepared for the overall demands of their classroom assignments. (p. 87)

Huling and Resta (2001) would agree. They believe that professional growth opportunities should include access to good mentoring programs. Mentoring programs create a structure that allows experienced teachers to work with novice teachers in ways that will ultimately benefit the students of novices and mentors as well as the overall organization.

On the whole, it appears that there is some evidence that professional development could result in increased student achievement, but the policies for developing effective professional development practices and the research to support their efficacy are lacking at this time.

Teacher Evaluation

Teacher evaluation practices are labeled deficient (Haefele, 1993), chaotic (Soar et al., 1983), inadequate (Scriven, 1988; Soar et al., 1983), of little value in assisting teachers in improving classroom instruction (Duke, 1995; Frase & Streshly, 2000; Nevo, 1994), and unjust, in consideration of their extraordinary cost (Scriven, 1988). Moreover, principal training in effective supervision and professional development practices is generally viewed as being absent, grossly ineffective, or divorced from the teacher evaluation (Annunziata, 1997; Duke, 1995; Haefele, 1993).

Teacher Self-efficacy and Perceived Efficacy of Other Teachers

Ashton and Webb (1986) demonstrated that teacher efficacy has a strong predictive link with student achievement. In their study, students of teachers with high self-efficacy levels consistently had higher achievement levels than students of teachers with lower self-efficacy levels. Evidence of the importance of self-efficacy to personal esteem and job effectiveness has been mounting for many years (Bandura, 1997; Locke, 1997). Higher teacher efficacy enhances student mastery of both cognitive and affective goals (Guskey, 1994; Ross, 1992, 1994; Turgoose, 1996; Watson, 1991). Studies by Frase (1998, 2001, 2003) and Frase and Gray (2003) found that the frequency of principal classroom visits predicted teacher-perceived organizational efficacy, perceived efficacy of others, and teacher value of teacher evaluation, while teacher self-efficacy and teacher-perceived efficacy of other teachers predicted frequency of teacher flow experiences (see Figure 18.1). Based on these studies, I believe that teacher efficacy is a key ingredient in the determination of the frequency of flow experiences and student achievement.

It is also important to note a current effort to make the self-efficacy subject-specific rather than general across all subjects and organizational variables. This approach is viable and offers promise of further understanding efficacy as a construct. This calls for the incorporation of Shulman's (1986) work on pedagogical content knowledge (see also Roberts & Moreno, 2003) in the development and use of efficacy instruments. These newer developments serve to limit the use of self-efficacy findings derived from current instruments.

Collective efficacy is another crucial aspect of efficacy as it relates to group work. Perceived collective efficacy is concerned with the performance capability of a social system as a whole. Goodard, Hoy, and Hoy (2000) found that collective teacher efficacy was positively associated with important institutional variables, including student achievement in both reading and mathematics; for example, a group of teachers is generally more likely to accomplish a mission when they believe they are able than when they do not. The concept of collective efficacy also relates to Deutsch's (1949) work on social interdependence and is supportive of it. In his theory and research, he found that groups have greater success when the individuals in the group perceive that others in the group can also reach their goals. This is similar to Kurt Lewin's (1952) belief regarding teamwork: that the whole is greater than the sum of the parts.

Student Cognitive Engagement

Given that a person must focus to learn complex knowledge and skills, student cognitive engagement can be seen as a proxy variable for learning (Zhu, 2001). Wehlage, Rutter, Smith, Leski, and Fernandez (1989) define cognitive engagement as the "psychological investment required to comprehend and master knowledge and skills" (p. 177). Goodlad (1983), Glasser (1993), and Shernoff et al. (1999) offer a strong rationale for increasing student engagement. Cothran and Ennis (2000) reported that two thirds of the high school populations in their study were disengaged from prescribed learning. They found that students believed their engagement levels vary and are responsive to their teachers' actions. The students also believed that engaging teachers communicate, care, and enthusiastically present active learning opportunities. These characteristics are also related to the behaviors teachers demonstrate when experiencing flow (Caouette, 1995). This need for engaging and stimulating teachers is illustrated by the fact that it is a central issue in educational literature and constructivist learning theory as well as in mentoring theory and practice.

The recent research is encouraging because it shows that gains in student achievement can be attributed to variables that administrators can control—classroom visits, the type of professional development offered, and teacher evaluations. These variables also appear to offer strong potential to help teachers become more competent instructors (Guskey & Huberman, 1995). This same research, however, suggests that these variables are currently performed poorly, and teachers are consequently deprived of their greatest reward—doing an important job well by more effectively helping young people learn.

These are powerful findings. If, indeed, flow experiences predict student levels of cognitive engagement, then we need to make certain that principals' behaviors that support flow experiences are performed more systematically. How do principals create work environments in which teachers experience

Table 18.3   Comparison of Environmental Flow Criteria and Job Characteristics Model Criteria

Flow Criteria	Job Characteristics Model Criteria
Concrete goals and manageable rules	Task identity Task significance
Opportunities to adjust task	Skill variety Autonomy
Clear feedback on how well the work is progressing	Feedback
Environments that minimize distraction, making concentration possible	Addressed indirectly from the perspective that the required job characteristics provide a setting for great concentration and thereby less influence from distraction

SOURCE: Frase (1995), p. 511.

more flow experiences and thus increase the probability that students will be cognitively engaged more frequently?

The Flow Work Environment

Although it has been found that individuals must find flow experiences for themselves (Csikszentmihalyi, 1990), administrators should use the research to design work environments more conducive to teachers' finding flow. This concept is based on the philosophy and theoretical underpinnings of worker motivation (Hackman & Oldham, 1980; Hertzberg, 1959). Hackman and Oldham (1980) identified five job characteristics in their Job Characteristics Model (JCM) that lead to worker motivation. Later, Csikszentmihalyi (1990) identified four criteria required in a flow-facilitating work environment. Table 18.3 shows a comparison of Csikszentmihalyi's work and Hackman and Oldman's (1980) Job Characteristics Model.

The fact that these two research efforts arrived at virtually the same conclusion using different assumptions and different research techniques makes the findings particularly interesting and substantive. Caouette's (1995) study also reported finding that similar criteria in work environments foster flow experiences (see Table 18.3).

Concrete Goals

"Do I know what's expected of me?" Buckingham and Coffman (1999) describe this as a basic question that all employees must address before they can be productive. This strongly implies that the administration should make it known at the policy level and school level that the teacher's job is to teach, above all other peripheral duties and to the exclusion of other nonteaching duties such as committee work—encouraging teachers first and foremost to take the time needed to focus on planning and delivering high-quality instruction.

Opportunities to Adjust to Task

This variable is also known as the balance of challenge and skill. Teachers need the skills required to successfully meet the challenges in their classrooms, skills that include maintaining good classroom management, achieving curriculum alignment, and delivering high-quality instruction. Such training must be provided on a timely basis, be aligned directly with teacher needs, and be provided in accordance with high-quality professional development guidelines.

Findings reveal that the skill required for a task or challenge must frequently be only slightly beyond the worker's skill level. When the skill required to complete a task is too far out of reach of the worker, anxiety is experienced. On the other hand, when the worker's skill is well beyond the challenge, boredom is soon experienced—and teachers, like any other workers, check out mentally or refocus on a more interesting job. Neither is a productive or enjoyable state to be in over time (Mitchell, 1988) and may lead to low morale and dissatisfaction. Anxiety and boredom are the states we want to change for teachers.

Immediate Feedback

Teachers need to receive useful and immediate feedback in order to view it as important. Research on teacher evaluations indicates that very little helpful feedback is offered to teachers and that a teacher evaluation is frequently viewed as little more than a ritual required by state lawmakers (Duke, 1995; Haefele, 1993; Nevo, 1994; Scriven, 1981, 1988; Soar et al., 1983).

Teachers benefit from feedback from other teachers and their supervisors, but they benefit most from self-reflection on their performance and effects on students. In doing so, they find their own feedback. Reflection on practice is a necessary element for professional growth and can lead to a greater probability of applying newly learned skills in practice (Norris, Barnett, Basom, & Yerkes, 2002). Frequent reflection on instruction can lead to modification of practice (Downey et al., 2004). In this way, reflection informs instruction, leads to improved instruction, and leads to the development of an internal locus of control (Hill, n.d.). In contrast, traditional evaluation systems often build dependence on external opinions (Frase & Streshly, 1994).

Absence of Distraction

Teaching requires high concentration and direct focus on students. Ringing bells,

discipline disruptions, school announcements, and other undesirable distractions divert teachers from their work and break student concentration. Flow experiences are much less frequent in disruptive environments (Caouette, 1995). All activities other than those directly associated with instruction need to be kept to a minimum. Marzano (2003) reports that studies indicate teachers, on average, spend as little as 3.9 teaching hours per day teaching the required curriculum.

The School Administrator's Role in Creating Work Environments Conducive to Flow Experiences

The primary job of the school principal is to free the educational learning environment of the roadblocks that confront teachers and possibly limit their success. To direct the school's focus on its mission of delivering the curriculum to all students, the school principal needs to be in classrooms frequently and engage teachers in reflective dialogue at faculty and grade level and at individual teacher meetings. Being in classrooms frequently allows principals to monitor delivery of the curriculum, diagnose problems, better understand the teachers' jobs, pursue actions to rectify situations that hinder teaching and learning, and support teachers in doing what they do best. Table 18.4 lists several ideas that school leaders might support to build environments more conducive to teacher flow experiences.

These ideas are not revolutionary. They focus on education's No. 1 job—improving instruction to produce learning—and they place teachers at the apex of importance in this effort. The reason teachers most frequently cite for leaving the field is failure to achieve their No. 1 goal—that of helping students learn. Any ideas that foster student learning are also likely to foster flow experiences for teachers.

Table 18.4   Strategies for Building Environments Conducive to Teacher Flow Experiences

Intervention	*Rationale*
Visit classrooms often	Principal classroom presence is positively correlated with frequency of teacher flow experiences (Frase 2001, 2003; Galloway and Frase, 2003). This practice allows school principals an excellent understanding of the classrooms and teachers' work lives.
Minimize the use of the school bell, intercom, and presentations by outside agencies not directly aligned to the curriculum	Teachers report that flow experiences were broken by such events since they disrupt teaching and concentration and, hence, flow (Caouette, 1995; Gray, 2003).
Provide adequate time for teachers to conduct lesson planning	Caouette's (1995) and Gray's (2003) research revealed that teachers believed that sound preparation was a precedent to flow experiences.
Provide training on the design of high-quality curriculum	Curriculum defines what students are to learn. If the curriculum is not well formed, it is likely that the desired learning is ill defined and the curriculum is difficult for the teacher to use. When these poor conditions are present, it is less likely that teachers will experience success in helping students learn, let alone experience flow (English & Steffy, 2001).
Find time for quality training on instruction	Some instructional practices produce more learning than others. Marzano (2003) in *What Works in Schools: Translating Research Into Action* has compiled a series of effective instructional strategies that are all tied to research in the field. Administrators need to make it a priority to know and understand this research and to make sure all teachers learn about such instructional strategies that have been associated with increased student achievement levels.
Assure that the conditions of the teachers' work environment are conducive to continual development and proud accomplishments	Administrators need to reevaluate the teaching workload to assure that schools have embedded opportunities for collaboration and for ongoing learning in the daily work of the staff and faculty. Teachers should be afforded sustained, content-rich professional development opportunities that link to the school's curriculum and assessment efforts.
Provide well-designed teacher mentoring and induction programs.	Studies have found that well-designed mentoring programs raise retention rates for new teachers by improving their attitudes, feelings of efficacy, and instructional skills.
Provide teachers time to discuss, analyze, and reflect on their classroom successes and failures	Arrange for teachers to observe their own teaching (through video technology) and to observe other teachers teaching Stigler and Hiebert (1999) suggest that teachers organize themselves into teams based on common interests, systematically employ specific techniques for specific lessons, and observe each other's teaching. Veteran teachers could be paired with nonveteran teachers in a mentoring arrangement for modeling and reflection.

THE CHALLENGE
FOR SUPERVISORS AND
OTHER SCHOOL LEADERS

The ultimate question in institutional management is: What conditions promote higher levels of productivity? We must strive for balance in addressing a question that is both scientific and humanistic. In the scientific realm, education is amassing a strong database on instructional practices that yield learning (Downey et al., 2004; Marzano, 2003). However, schools appear to lack purpose, direction, and initiative when it comes to improving the quality of teacher work life as it relates to productivity.

Designing, developing, and maintaining a creative, high-energy learning environment takes tremendous vigor and skill. Teachers cannot do this on their own (Sarason, 1990). Teachers need work conditions that are as free as possible of stumbling blocks, places where they can successfully practice their craft. It is the supervisors' responsibility to ensure that such an environment is available. New information about flow as the ultimate experience, tried and true knowledge about motivating people, and ancient wisdom specifying the spiritual connection between work, life, and satisfaction have been largely ignored, but they potentially provide powerful direction and guidance to supervisors.

Building work environments in schools where teachers and other workers have frequent opportunities to experience flow requires a new view of leadership and supervision. School improvement will depend on principals who can foster the conditions necessary for sustained educational reform in a complex, rapidly changing society (Fullan, 2002).

Fostering intrinsically satisfying work makes sense because it leads to higher levels of commitment and performance. Intrinsically satisfying work also makes sense in and of itself because it is simply right and good for teachers and others to find jobs satisfying and meaningful. This is the moral and humanistic side of the equation. As St. Thomas Aquinas noted, there is an inextricable link between the quality of life and work.

Supervision has suffered many trends and influences, but the main purpose of supervision needs to stand fast—build work environments with teachers where teachers can attain their No. 1 goal, students' learning. It is now clear that dictatorial techniques from administrators will not accomplish this. High-quality supervision, training, and quality work environments are crucial to this endeavor.

Knowledge of flow theory, the educational research related to it, and the variables that predict it can help supervisors who strive to use the instructional strategies described above to create work environments where teachers have greater opportunities to experience this phenomenon. This might very well be the most important function of supervision, in that it is directly linked with student learning. It is time to get about the job of making this possible for teachers.

REFERENCES

American Association of School Administrators. (1957). *AASA thirty-fifth yearbook*. Arlington, VA: Author.

Andrews, R., Soder, R., & Jacoby, D. (1986). *Principal roles, other in-school variables, and academic achievement by ethnicity and SES*. Paper presented at the Annual Meeting of the American Educational Research Association, San Francisco.

Annunziata, J. (1997). Linking teacher evaluation and professional development. In J. Stronge (Ed.), *Evaluating teaching: A guide to current thinking and best practice* (pp. 288–301). Thousand Oaks, CA: Corwin.

Archer, J. (2003). Increasing the odds. *Education Week, 22*(17), 52–56.

Ashton, P., & Crocker, L. (1987). Systematic study of planned variations: The essential focus of teacher education reform. *Journal of Teacher Education, 38*, 2–8.

Ashton, P., & Webb, R. (1986). *Making a difference: Teachers' sense of efficacy and student achievement*. New York: Longman.

Ayer, F. (1954). *Fundamentals of instructional supervision*. New York: Harper and Brothers.

Bandura, A. (1997). *Self-efficacy: The exercise of control*. New York: Freeman.

Basom, M. R., & Frase, L. (2003). Creating optimal work environments: Exploring teacher flow experiences. *Mentoring & Tutoring, 12, 2*, 241–258.

Bass, B. (1998). *Transformational leadership*. Mahwah, NJ: Lawrence Erlbaum.

Begle, E. G. (1979). *Critical variables in mathematics education*. Washington, DC: Mathematical Association of America and National Council of Teachers of Mathematics.

Bennett, J. W. (1986). *What works: Research about teaching and learning*. Washington, DC: U.S. Department of Education.

Berliner, D. C. (1986). In pursuit of the expert pedagogue. *Educational Researcher, 15*(7), 5–13.

Berliner, D. C., & Tikunoff, W. J. (1976). The California beginning teacher study. *Journal of Teacher Education, 27*, 24–30.

Blair, J. (2000). Teacher idealism tempered by frustration, survey finds. *Education Week, 19*(38), 6.

Blase, J. R., & Blase, J. (2004). Handbook of instructional leadership: How successful principals promote teaching and learning. Thousand Oaks, CA: Corwin.

Bolin, F. (1987). On defining supervision. *Journal of Curriculum and Supervision, 2*(4), 368–380.

Boston Town Records. (1710). *Report of the Boston Record Commissions, 8*, 65. Boston: Author.

Bowles, S., & Levin, H. M. (1968). The determinants of scholastic achievement—An appraisal of some recent evidence. *Journal of Human Resources, 3*, 3–24.

Bridge, R. G., Judd, C. M., & Moock, P. R. (1979). *The determinants of educational outcomes: The impact of families, peers, teachers, and schools*. Cambridge, MA: Ballinger.

Brophy, J. E. (1996). *Teaching problem students*. New York: Guilford.

Brown, C., Smith, M., & Stein, M. (1995, April). *Linking teacher support to enhanced classroom instruction*. Paper presented at the Annual Meeting of the American Educational Research Association, New York.

Buckingham, M., & Coffman, C. (1999). *First, break all the rules: What the greatest managers do differently*. New York: Simon & Schuster.

Byrne, C. J. (1983). *Teacher knowledge and teacher effectiveness: A literature review, theoretical analysis, and discussion of research strategy*. Paper presented at the Annual Meeting of the Northwestern Educational Research Association, Ellenville, NY.

Cain, M. (2001). Ten qualities of the renewed teacher. *Phi Delta Kappan, 82*(9), 702–705.

Caouette, A. (1995). *The phenomenon of flow as experienced by classroom teachers: Implications for leadership studies*. Unpublished dissertation, University of San Diego, San Diego, CA.

Chance, P., & Chance, E. (1999, February). *Issues in teacher retention: Supporting new teacher through mentoring and supervision*. Paper presented at the Annual Conference of the American Association of School Administrators.

Choy, S. P. (1993). *America's teachers: Profile of a profession*. (Report No. NCES-93025). Berkeley, CA: MPR Associates. (ERIC Document Reproduction Service No. ED359185)

Cohen, D. K., & Hill, H. (1997, April). *Instructional policy and classroom performance: The mathematics reform in California*. Paper presented at the Annual Meeting of the American Educational Research Association, Chicago.

Coleman, J. (1997). Social capital in the creation of human capital. In A. H. Hasley, H. Lauder, P. Brown, & A. S. Wells (Eds.). *Education: Culture, economy, and society* (pp. 80-95). Oxford, UK: Oxford University Press.

Coleman, J. S., Campbell, E. Q., Hobson, C. J., McPartland, J., Mood, A. M., Weinfeld, F. D., et al. (1966). *Equality of educational opportunity*. Washington, DC: Government Printing Office.

Cothran, D., & Ennis, C. (2000). Building bridges to student engagement: Communicating respect and care for students in urban high schools. *Journal of Research and Development in Education, 33*(2), 106–117.

Cotton, K. (1995). *Effective school practices: A research synthesis. 1995 update* (School Improvement Research Series). Portland, OR: Northwest Regional Educational Laboratory.

Creemers, B. P. (1994). *The effective classroom*. London: Cassell.

Csikszentmihalyi, M. (1990). *Flow: The psychology of optimal experience*. New York: Harper & Row.

Csikszentmihalyi, M. (1997). *Finding flow: The psychology of engagement with everyday life*. New York: Basic Books.

Csikszentmihalyi, M., & Csikszentmihalyi, I. (1988). *Optimal experience: Psychological studies of flow in consciousness.* New York: Cambridge University Press.

Culbertson, J. (1996). *Building bridges: The mission and principals of professional development.* Washington, DC: Department of Education, Government Printing Office. (ERIC Document Reproduction Service No. ED404322)

Cutler, H. (2003). *The art of happiness at work.* New York: Riverhead Books.

Darling-Hammond, L. (2000). Teacher quality and student achievement: A review of state policy evidence. *Education Policy Analysis Archives, 8*(1).

Darling-Hammond, L., Berry, B., & Thoreson, A. (2001). Does teacher certification matter? Evaluating the evidence. *Educational Evaluation and Policy Analysis, 23*(1), 57–77.

Darling-Hammond, L., & McLaughlin, M. (1995). Policies that support professional development in an era of reform. *Phi Delta Kappan, 76*(8), 597–604.

Deming, W. E. (1986). *Out of the crisis.* Cambridge: Massachusetts Institute of Technology.

Deutsch, M. (1949). A theory of co-operation and competition. *Human Relations, 2,* 129–152.

Dimock, M. E. (1958). *A philosophy of administration.* New York: Harper & Row.

Downey, C., Steffy, B., English, F., Frase, L., & Poston, W. (2004). *The three minute classroom walk-through.* Thousand Oaks, CA: Corwin.

Doyle, W. (1986). Content representation in teachers' definitions of academic work. *Journal of Curriculum Studies, 18,* 365–379.

Dreyfus, H., & Rabinow. P. (1983). *Michel Foucault: Beyond structuralism and hermeneutics* (2nd ed.). Chicago: University Press.

Drucker, P. (1974). *Management: Tasks, responsibilities, practices.* New York: Harper & Row.

Druva, C. A., & Anderson, R. D. (1983). Science teacher characteristics by teacher behavior and by student outcome: A meta-analysis of research. *Journal of Research in Science Teaching, 20*(5), 467–479.

Duke, D. (Ed.). (1995). Speculations on the future of teacher evaluation and educational accountability. In *Teacher evaluation policy: From accountability to professional development* (pp. 189–197). Albany: SUNY Press.

Eisner, E. (2002). The kind of schools we need. *Phi Delta Kappan, 83*(8), 576–583.

English, F. W. (1992). *Deciding what to teach and test.* Thousand Oaks, CA: Corwin.

English, F. W., & Steffy, B. (2001). *Deep alignment.* Landham, MD: Scarecrow Press.

Evertson, C., Hawly, W., & Zlotnik, M. (1985). Making a difference in educational quality through teacher education. *Journal of Teacher Education, 36*(3), 2–12.

Feistritzer, C. (1993). *Report card on American education: A state by state analysis, 1972–73 to 1992–93.* Washington, DC: National Center on Education Information.

Ferguson, R. F., & Ladd, H. F. (1996). How and why money matters: An analysis of Alabama schools. In H. F. Ladd (Ed.), *Holding schools accountable: Performance-based reform in education* (pp. 265–298). Washington, DC: Brookings Institution.

Feyerabend, P. (1993). *Against method* (3rd ed.). New York: Verso.

Firth, F., & Pajak, E. (Eds.). (1998). *Handbook of research on school supervision.* New York: Simon & Schuster/Macmillan.

Fowler, W., & Walberg, H. (1991). School size, characteristics, and outcomes. *Educational Evaluation and Policy Analysis, 13*(2), 189–202.

Fox, M. (1994). *The reinvention of work: A new vision of livelihood for our time.* New York: HarperCollins.

Frase, L. (1989). Assessing the effects of intrinsic and extrinsic rewards on teacher recognition and opportunities for job enrichment. *Journal of Educational Research, 83*(1), 53–57.

Frase, L. (1995). Flow: Sagacious thoughts for educational administration: A review of two books. *International Journal of Educational Administration, 4*(4), pp. 510–512.

Frase, L., (1998). *An examination of teachers' flow experiences, efficacy, and instructional leadership in large inner-city school districts.* Paper presented at the Annual Meeting of the American Educational Research Association, San Diego, CA.

Frase, L. (2001). *Impact of school principal classroom presence in large inner city schools.* Paper presented at the Annual Meeting of the American Education Research Association, New York.

Frase, L. (2003). *Policy implications for school work environments: Implications from three research studies regarding frequency of teacher flow experiences, school principal classroom walkthroughs, teacher evaluation, professional development, and three efficacy measures.* Paper presented at the Annual Meeting of the American Education Research Association, Chicago.

Frase, L., & Gray, P. (2003, July 20). *Analysis of teacher flow experiences as they relate to principal classroom walk-throughs.* Unpublished data from report to Shawnee Mission School Board, Shawnee Mission, KS.

Frase, L., & Streshly, W. (1994). Lack of accuracy, feedback, and commitment in teacher evaluation. *Journal of Personnel Evaluation in Education, 8*(1), 47–57.

Frase, L., & Streshly, W. (2000). *The top ten myths in education: Fantasies Americans love to believe.* Landham, MD: Scarecrow Press.

Freedman, B., & Lafleur, C. (2003, January). *Making leadership visible and practical: Walking for improvement.* Paper presented at the Annual Meeting of the International Congress of School Effectiveness and School Improvement, Sydney, Australia.

Fullan, M. G. (1995). The limits and the potential of professional development. In T. R. Guskey & M. Huberman (Eds.), *Professional development in education: New paradigms and practices* (pp. 253–267). New York: Teachers College Press.

Fullan, M. (2002). The change leader. *Educational Leadership, 59*(8), 16–21.

Galloway, F. & Frase, L. (2003). A methodological primer for estimating the effects of teacher flow experiences in the classroom and the factors that foster then. Paper presented at the Annual Meeting of the American Education Research Association, Chicago, IL, April.

Gambrill, B. (1929). A critical review of researches in supervision. *Educational Administration and Supervision, 25,* 179–189.

Gephart, R. R., Jr., Thatchenkery, T. J., & Boje, D. M. (Eds.). (1996). Conclusion: Reconstructing organizations for future survival. In *Postmodern management and organization theory* (pp. 358–364). Thousand Oaks, CA: Sage.

Gergen, K. (1992). Organization theory in the postmodern era. In M. Reed & M. Hughes (Eds.), *Rethinking organizations: New directions in organisation theory and analysis* (pp. 209–226). London: Sage.

Glanz, J. (1998). Histories, antecedents, and legacies of school supervision. In G. Firth & E. Pajak (Eds.), *Handbook of research on school supervision.* New York: Simon & Schuster Macmillan.

Glanz, J. (2001, April 3). Pluto gives weight to Einstein's thesis of negative gravity. *The New York Times,* p. 12.

Glasser, W. (1993). *The quality school teacher.* New York: Harper & Row.

Good, T. L. (1982). How teacher' expectations affect results. *American Education, 18*(10), 25–32.

Good, T. L., & Brophy, J. E. (1986). School effects. In M. C. Wittrock (Ed.), *Handbook of research on teaching* (3rd ed., pp. 570–602). New York: Macmillan.

Good, T., & Brophy, J. (1997). *Looking in classrooms* (7th ed.). New York: Addison-Wesley.

Goodard, R., Hoy, A., & Hoy, W. (2000). Collective teacher efficacy: Its meaning, measure, and impact on student achievement. *American Educational Research Journal, 37*(2), 479–508.

Goodlad, J. (1983). *A place called school.* New York: McGraw-Hill.

Gray, P. (2003). *Analysis of teacher flow experiences as they relate to principal classroom walk-throughs.* Unpublished paper from a Report to the Shawnee Mission School Board, Shawnee Mission, KS, July 20.

Guskey, T. (1994). Teacher efficacy: A study of construct dimensions. *American Educational Research Journal, 31,* 627–643.

Guskey, T. R., & Huberman, M. (Eds.). (1995). *Professional development in education: New paradigms and practices.* New York: Teachers College Press.

Hackman, R. J., & Oldham, G. R. (1980). *Work redesign.* Reading, MA: Addison-Wesley.

Haefele, D. (1993). Evaluating teachers: A call for change. *Journal of Personnel Evaluation in Education, 7*(1), 21–31.

Hanushek, E. A. (1971). Teacher characteristics and gains in student achievement: Estimation using micro-data. *American Economic Review, 61*(2), 280–288.

Hanushek, E. A. (1992). The trade-off between child quantity and quality. *Journal of Political Economy, 100,* 85–117.

Harris, B. (1998). *Paradigms and parameters of supervision in education: Handbook of research on school supervision.* New York: Macmillan.

Hattie, J. A. (1992). Measuring the effects of schooling. *Australian Journal of Education, 36*(1), 5–15.

Hawk, P., Coble, C. R., & Swanson, M. (1985). Certification: It does matter. *Journal of Teacher Education, 36*(3), 13–15.

Heck, R. (1991, April). *The effects of school context and principal leadership on school climate and school achievement.* Paper presented at the Annual Meeting of the American Educational Research Association, San Francisco.

Heck, R. (1992). Principals' instructional leadership and school performance: Implications for policy development. *Educational Evaluation and Policy Analysis, 14,* 21–34.

Heck, R., Larsen, T., & Marcoulides, G. (1990). Instructional leadership and school achievement: Validation of a causal model. *Educational Administration Quarterly, 26,* 94–125.

Herzberg, F. (1959). *The motivation to work.* New York: John Wiley.

Hill, M. (n.d.). *Leadership preparation: Self reflection and self assessment, design for leadership.* Arlington, VA: The Bulletin of the National Policy Board for Educational Administration.

Holloway, J. (2003). Research link. *Educational Leadership, 60*(8), 87–88.

Howell, B. (1981). Profile of the principalship, *Educational Leadership, 38,*333–336.

Huling, L., & Resta, V. (2001). *Teacher mentoring as professional development.* Washington, DC: ERIC Clearinghouse on Teaching and Teacher Education.

Jencks, C., et al. (1972). *Inequality: A reassessment of the effect of family and schooling in America.* New York: Basic Books.

Jenkins, K., Jenkins, D., Hall, H., Ware, A., & Heintzleman, C. (1998, February). *Extracting meaning from stories about teacher attrition.* Paper presented at the Annual Conference of the American Association of School Administrators, San Diego, CA.

Kmetz, J., & Willower, D. (1982). Elementary school principals' work behavior. *Educational Administration Quarterly, 18*(4), 62–78.

Knoblock, G. A. (1986). Continuing professional education for teachers and its relationship to teacher effectiveness. *Dissertation Abstracts International, 46*(2), 3325A.

Kohn, A. (2003). The folly of merit pay. *Education Seek, 23*(3), 44–45.

Kounin, J. S. (1983). *Classrooms: Individual or behavior settings?* (Micrographs in Teaching and Learning). Bloomington: Indiana University, School of Education. (ERIC Document Reproduction Service No. ED240070)

Laflamme, J. G. (1997). The effect of the multiple exposure vocabulary method and the target reading/writing strategy on test scores. *Journal of Adolescent and Adult Literacy, 40,* 372–381.

La Mettrie, J. (1994). *Man a machine* (R. A. Watson & M. Rybalka, Trans.). Indianapolis, IN: Hackett. (Original work published 1748)

Lewin, K. (1952). Group decision and social change. In G. E. Swanson, T. M. Newcomb, & E. L. Hartley (Eds.), *Readings in social psy-*

chology (Rev. ed., pp. 459–473). New York: Holt.

Locke, E. (1997). The motivation to work: What we know. In M. Maehr & P. Pintrich (Eds.), *Advances in motivation and achievement* (Vol. 10). Greenwich, CT: JAI Press.

Luckham, M. (1991). *Increasing reading comprehension and positive attitudes toward reading through improving student vocabulary.* (ERIC Document Reproduction Service No. ED335665)

Martin, W., & Willower, D., (1981). The managerial behavior of high school principals. *Educational Administration Quarterly, 17*(1), 69–90.

Marzano, R. J. (2003). *What works in schools: Translating research into action.* Alexandria, VA: Association for Supervision and Curriculum Development.

Marzano, R. J., Pickering, D., & Pollock, J. (2001). *Classroom instruction that works: Research-based strategies for increasing student achievement.* Alexandria, VA: Association for Supervision and Curriculum Development.

Mauws, M. (1995, June). *Relationality.* Paper presented at the Annual Meeting of the Organization Theory Division, Administrative Sciences Association of Canada, Windsor, Ontario.

Maxcy, S. J. (1994). Introduction. In S. J. Maxcy (Ed.), *Postmodern school leadership: Meeting the crisis in educational administration* (pp. 1–13). Westport, CT: Praeger.

McBer, H. (2000). *Research into teacher effectiveness: A model of teacher effectiveness* (Publication Information: Research Report #216). London: Department for Education and Employment.

McEwan, E. K., & McEwan, P. J. (2003). *Making sense of research.* Thousand Oaks, CA: Corwin.

Medley, D., Coker, H., & Soar, R. (1984). *Measurement-based evaluation of teacher performance: An empirical approach.* New York: Longman.

Meece, J. (1991). The classroom context and students' motivational goals. In M. L. Maehr & P. R. Pintrich (Eds.), *Advances in motivation and achievement: A research annual* (Vol. 7). Greenwich, CT: JAI Press.

Miller, A., Ferguson, E., & Simpson, R. (1998). The perceived effectiveness of rewards and sanctions in primary schools: Adding in the parental perspective. *Educational Psychology, 18*(1), 55–64.

Miller, J. E., McKenna, M. C., & McKenna, B. A. (1998). A comparison of alternatively and traditionally prepared teachers. *Journal of Teacher Education, 49*(3), 165–176.

Mitchell, R. (1988). Sociological implications of the flow experiences. In M. Csikszentmihalyi & I. S. Csikszentmihalyi (Eds.), *Optimal experience: Psychological studies of flow in consciousness.* Cambridge, UK: Cambridge University Press.

Monk, D. H. (1994). Subject area preparation of secondary math and science teachers and student achievement. *Economics of Education Review, 13,* 125–145.

Monk, D. H., & King, J. A. (1994). Multilevel teacher research effects in pupil performance in secondary mathematics and science: The case of teacher subject matter preparation. In R. G. Ehrenberg (Ed.), *Choices and consequences: Contemporary policy issues in education* (pp. 29–58). Ithaca, NY: ILR Press.

Murnane, R., & Phillips, B. (1981). What do effective teachers of inner-city children have in common? *Social Science Research, 10,* 83–100.

Natale, J. (1993). Why teachers leave. *Executive Educator, 15*(7), 14–18.

National Center for Education Statistics. (1993). *America's teachers: Profile of a profession.* Washington, DC: U.S. Department of Education.

National Center for Education Statistics. (1994). *Data compendium for the NAEP 1992 reading assessment of the nation and the states: 1992 NAEP trial state assessment.* Washington, DC: U.S. Department of Education.

National Center for Education Statistics. (1995). *Characteristics of stayers, movers, and leavers: Results from the teacher follow-up survey: 1994/95.* Washington, DC: U.S. Department of Education.

National Center for Education Statistics. (1999). *The condition of education.* Washington, DC: U.S. Department of Education.

National Education Association. (1992). *Status of the American public school teacher: 1990–1991.* New Haven, CT: Author.

Nevo, D. (1994). How can teachers benefit from teacher evaluation? *Journal of Personnel Evaluation in Education, 8*(2), 109–117.

Newlon, J. (1923). Attitude of the teacher toward supervision. *Proceedings of the National Education Association, USA, 548*–549.

Norris, C., Barnett, B. G., Basom, M. R., & Yerkes, D. M. (2002). *Developing educational leaders: A working model: The learning community in action.* New York: Teachers College Press.

Olson, L. (2003a). The great divide. *Education Week, 22*(17), 9–18.

Olson, L. (2003b). Swimming upstream.. *Education Week, 22*(17), 21.

Orlich, D., Remaley, A., Facemyer, K., Logan, J., & Cao, Q. (1993). Seeking the link between student achievement and staff development. *Journal of Staff Development, 14*(3), 2–8.

Payne, W. H. (1875). *Chapters on school supervision.* New York: Wilson, Hinkle.

Perie, M., & Baker, D. (1997). *Job satisfaction among America's teachers: Effects of workplace conditions, background characteristics, and teacher compensation.* Washington, DC: U.S. Department of Education.

PricewaterhouseCoopers. (1998). *School District of Philadelphia operations review.* Fairfax, VA: PricewaterhouseCoopers.

Privette, G. (1983). Peak experience, peak performance, and flow: A comparative analysis of positive human experiences. *Journal of Personality and Social Psychology, 45*(6), 1361–1386.

Public Agenda Foundation. (1995). *Professional development for teachers: The public's view.* New York: Author.

Public Agenda Foundation. (2000). A sense of calling: Who teaches and why: A review of empirical research, 1980–1995. *Educational Administration Quarterly, 32,* 5–44.

Roberts, J., & Moreno, N. (2003, April). *Teacher self-efficacy is not enough!! The problem of interpreting measures of teacher self-efficacy apart from other measures of teacher performance.* Paper presented at the Annual Meeting of the American Educational Research Association, Chicago.

Rosenshine, B. (1983). Teaching functions in instructional programs. *Elementary School Journal, 83*(4), 335–351.

Rosenthal, R., & Jacobson, L. (1968). *Pygmalion in the classroom: Teacher expectations and pupils' intellectual development.* New York: Holt, Rinehart & Winston.

Ross, J. (1992). Teacher efficacy and the effects of coaching on student achievement. *Canadian Journal of Education, 17*(1), 51–65.

Ross, J. (1994). *Beliefs that make a difference: The origins and impacts of teacher efficacy.* Paper presented at the meeting of the Canadian Association of Curriculum Studies, Calgary, Canada.

Rowan, B., Chiang, F. S., & Miller, R. J. (1997). Using research on employees' performance to study the effects of teachers on students' achievement. *Sociology of Education, 70,* 256–284.

Sanders, S. L., Skonie-Hardin, S. D., & Phelps, W. H. (1994). *The effects of teacher educational attainment on student educational attainment in four regions of Virginia: Implications for administrators.* Paper presented at the Annual Meeting of the Mid-South Educational Research Association.

Sanders, W., Collins, J., & Rivers, J. (1996). *Cumulative and residual effects of teachers on future academic achievement.* Knoxville: University of Tennessee, Value-Added Research and Assessment Center.

Sarason, S. (1990). *The predictable failure of school reform.* San Francisco: Jossey-Bass.

Schalock, D. (1979). Research on teacher selection. In D. C. Berliner (Ed.), *Review of research in education* (Vol. 7, pp. 364–417). Washington, DC: American Educational Research Association.

Schmidt, W. H., McKnight, C. C., & Raizen, S. A. (1997). *Splintered vision: An investigation of U.S. science and mathematics education: Executive summary.* East Lansing: Michigan State University, U.S. National Research Center for the Third International Mathematics and Science Study.

Scholastic, Inc. (2000). *Scholastic/CCSSO teacher voices 2000 survey.* Washington, DC: Author.

Scriven, M. (1981). Summative teacher evaluation. In J. Millman (Ed.), *Handbook of teacher evaluation* (pp. 244–271). Beverly Hills, CA: Sage.

Scriven, M. (1988). *Evaluating teachers as professionals.* Nedlands, Western Australia: University of Western Australia. (ERIC Document Reproduction Service No. ED300882)

Sergiovanni, T. (1967). Factors which affect satisfaction and dissatisfaction of teachers. *The Journal of Educational Administration, 5,* 66–82.

Sheldrake, R. (1994). *The rebirth of nature.* Rochester, VT: Park Street Press.

Shernoff, D., Schneider, B., & Csikszentmihalyi, M. (1999, April). *The quality of learning experiences in American classrooms: Toward a phenomenology of student engagement.* Unpublished paper presented at the Annual Meeting of the American Educational Research Association, Montreal, Canada.

Shulman, L. S. (1986). Those who understand: Knowledge and growth in teaching. *Educational Researcher, 15*(2), 4–14.

Soar, R., Medley, D., & Coker, H. (1983). Teacher evaluation: A critique of currently used methods. *Phi Delta Kappan, 65*(4), 239–246.

Stage, S. A., & Quiroz, D. R. (1997). A meta-analysis of interventions to decrease disruptive classroom behavior in public education settings. *School Psychology Review, 26*(3), 333–368.

Stevenson, H. W., & Stigler, J. W. (1992). *The learning gap: Why our schools are failing and what we can learn from Japanese and Chinese education.* New York: Simon & Schuster.

Stigler, J. W., & Hiebert, J. (1999). *The teaching gap: Best ideas from the world's teachers for improving education in the classroom.* New York: Free Press.

Streshly, W. (2001). *Preventing and managing teacher strikes.* Lanham, MD: Scarecrow Press.

Students say: What makes a good teacher? (1997 May/June). *NASSP Bulletin,* pp. 15–17.

Sullivan, S., & Glanz, J. (2000). *Supervision that improves teaching.* Thousand Oaks, CA: Corwin.

Tanner, D., & Tanner, L. (1987). *Supervision in education: Problems and practices.* London: Collier Macmillan.

Turgoose, L. (1996). The relationship of teacher efficacy, mathematics anxiety, achievement, preparation, and years of experience to student IOWA test of basic skills mathematics test scores (Doctoral dissertation, University of Idaho, 1996). *Dissertation Abstracts International, 57-5A,* 1986.

Twain, M. (1948). *The adventure of Huckleberry Finn.* New York: Grosset & Dunlap. (Original work published 1884)

Walberg, H. J., & Waxman, H. C. (1983). *Teaching, learning, and the management of instruction.* (ERIC Document Reproduction Service No. ED237458)

Wang, M. C., Haertel, G. D., & Walberg, H. J. (1993). Toward a knowledge base for school learning. *Review of Educational Research, 63*(3), 249–294.

Wehlage, G. G., Rutter, R. A., Smith, G. A., Leski, N., & Fernandez, R. R. (1989). *Reducing the risk: Schools as communities of support.* New York: Falmer Press.

Watson, D. (1991). A study of the effects of teacher efficacy on the academic achievement of third-grade students in selected elementary schools in South Carolina (Doctoral dissertation, South Carolina State University, 1991). *Dissertation Abstracts International, 53-06A,* 11794.

Wenglinsky, H. (2000). *How teaching matters: Bringing the classroom back into discussions of teacher quality.* Princeton, NJ: Millikan Family Foundation and Educational Testing Service.

Wenglinsky, H. (2002). How schools matter: The link between teacher classroom practices and student academic performance. *Educational Policy Analysis Archives, 10*(12).

Wheatley, M. (1992). *Leadership and the new science.* San Francisco: Berrett-Koehler.

Wiley, D., & Yoon, B. (1995). Teacher reports of opportunity to learn: Analyses of the 1993 California Learning Assessment System. *Educational Evaluation and Policy Analysis, 17*(3), 355–370.

Wright, S., Horn, S., & Sanders, W. (1997). Teacher and classroom context effects on student achievement: Implications for teacher evaluation. *Journal of Personnel Evaluation in Education, 11,* 57–67.

Zhu, N. (2001). *The effects of teacher flow experience on the cognitive engagement of students.* Unpublished doctoral dissertation, University of San Diego, San Diego, CA.

19

Student Misbehavior and Violence

A Reexamination of the Enemy Within

GEORGE J. PETERSEN
California Polytechnic State University, San Luis Obispo

Your children are not your children. Their souls dwell in the house of tomorrow, which you cannot visit, not even in your dreams.

Kahlil Gibran (1923, p. 17)

Numerous scholars have written about the barriers and obstacles faced by children who are poor or of color or from families with little formal education. Children find these barriers and obstacles at home, within the context of their community and the larger society, and remarkably even within the classrooms of our nation's schools. Research has clearly demonstrated that they are often the result of an ongoing and complex interaction between environmental forces and the individual lives of children. Given the enigmatic nature of these factors and their influence, families, school systems, and communities are often unclear on how to substantively resolve such problems.

Respected researchers and practitioners have clearly (and at times passionately) articulated through empirical means the wide array of issues and outcomes that perpetually plague these children. The result of their research is appalling: Children who are poor or of color or from families with little formal education experience a disproportionate level of academic failure, violence, underage pregnancy, drug use, adolescent crime, and incarceration.

Author's Note: *The Enemy Within* is the title of a previous study that I published on the subject of school violence. See Petersen, Pietrzak, and Speaker (1998). In this chapter, I make a deliberate effort to reexamine and redefine some of these issues through the lens of social capital, and I propose a different and more collaborative method to resolve them.

Although some would have us believe these problems are diminishing, a large percentage of my colleagues believe they are not. In fact, they believe the issues facing these children and their families are becoming more severe.

Books and papers have been written, reforms initiated, policies adopted, and programs established to address many of these issues. Rationally, one might think that individuals who are in positions of privilege and power (e.g., politicians, business people, researchers, and professional educators) would understand the influence these issues have in fostering experiences and environments that lead to student misbehavior and school violence. Yet, even with a vast body of literature, the problems persist, and these children, their schools, and their communities somehow remain invisible.

Is it unrealistic to think that there will be a solution? I am unsure. Quite possibly, the problems are too large, complex, and evolving to resolve. Or perhaps the continuous media attention to the ever-widening disparities has gone on for so long that we have become desensitized to it all.

What is clear is that the economic and social inequalities reinforced by social barriers make it difficult, if not impossible, for poor children and their families to escape the crippling whirlpool of failure. However, I am convinced that the substantial impediments and inequalities that face these children need not be perpetuated in our schools. Policies and programs implemented to address the issues of student misbehavior and violence should be representative of all those involved and should clearly be directed to the context within which they occur. No one-size-fits-all program will work.

As a starting point, sweeping policies, myopic curriculum, questionable evaluation processes, and inadequate safety policies and conditions must be ameliorated. We have the collective knowledge and power to rethink educational approaches to meet the needs of *all* students. It should be the mandate of this nation to provide greater resources and visibility for children exposed to these wretched conditions and situations to ensure their academic success and the success of their respective families and communities.

This chapter is organized in three sections. The first section provides the reader with an overview of the extant literature exploring the complex and enigmatic issues that contribute to student misbehavior and violence in our nation's schools. Paying particular attention to both external and internal factors, I argue that both school- and family-related dimensions found in the lives of children actually work in tandem to influence and, at times, compound the problem of misbehavior and violence and to frustrate school leaders' ability to adequately and equitably address them in substantive and effective ways. In the second section, using the conceptual framework of social capital, I examine the most pertinent risk factors faced by children, their families, and schools. This section provides a generative discussion of how the development of social capital among key stakeholders can actually lead to the building of high-quality, participatory, credible, and equitable social institutions—more specifically, schools designed to manage the interests and aspirations of students, families, community members, and school personnel who work there. The third section is devoted to a brief overview of the limitations of some of the commercial violence prevention models and programs. In this final segment, I propose the use of action research to foster social capital among key stakeholders while collaboratively framing and identifying the most pressing problems for those wrestling with these issues on a daily basis—namely teachers, administrators, and students—as well as those interested in gaining insight into this problem. Action research will permit key stakeholders to identify and institute systematic intervention strategies directed at resolving issues and conditions that lead to misbehavior and violence within the context in which they are found.

ANATOMY OF THE ENEMY: COMPLEX SOCIAL AND SCHOOL-RELATED ISSUES THAT FOSTER MISBEHAVIOR AND VIOLENCE

The public school system in the United States has always attempted to represent itself as a hallmark of vital socialization, equality of access, hope for the future, and a sense of community. This picture has changed drastically in the past 30 years. Chaos seems to be replacing community (Lantieri & Patti, 1996). The literature points to a complex interaction between poverty, discrimination, drug addiction, alcoholism, unemployment, inadequate handgun regulation, lack of personal opportunity and responsibility, disinvestment in schools, and domestic violence as playing a crucial role in America's culture of violence (Prothrow-Stith, 1994). The crippling effect these social and school-related issues have on the psyche of our children and their families, as well as the enmity they pose in our efforts to achieve an equitable and quality educational experience, presents us with a formidable opponent. Alone and in concert, these issues form an enigmatic adversary that shifts through time and context, keeping schools and communities off balance and grasping for methods to solve ever more complex problems. The pervasiveness of this multifaceted enemy forces school leaders to resort to piecemeal programs as makeshift ramparts in their attempts to make schools significantly safer than the streets leading to the schoolhouse door, while at the same time attempting to maintain an open atmosphere that emphasizes democratic principles and student learning (Petersen, 1997).

In their work on poverty and youth violence, Vorrasi and Garbarino (2000) offer the term of *social toxicity* to describe forces such as child abuse, community and domestic violence, poverty, depression, drug addiction, homicide, and other pollutants that demoralize families, contaminate the social environment, and endanger the well-being of children. They

stress that these issues are as harmful to the development and success of children as air quality, PCBs in the water, or pesticides in our food.

Of course the social, economic, health, and safety problems facing families and communities represent only some of the stressors children face. McLaren (1998) argues that the current structural constraints and policies that represent traditional schooling also reinforce levels of inequality. McLaren believes schools have been reduced to credentialing mechanisms and protected enclaves that favor the more affluent. Clearly, deteriorating social environments coupled with growing fiscal crises foster a milieu in which children face substantial academic, psychosocial, and physical barriers in their efforts to mature into responsible adults.

In her seminal work on full-service schools, Dryfoos (1994) refers to these barriers as the "new morbidities"—unprotected sex, drugs, violence, and depression—in contrast to the "old morbidities" of chronic diseases, nutritional deficiencies, acne, and infestations of head lice. Needless to say, these new morbidities also create significant problems for schools.

> Today's schools feel pressured to feed children; provide psychological support services; offer health screening; establish referral networks related to substance abuse, child welfare, and sexual abuse; cooperate with the local police and probation officers; add curricula for prevention of substance abuse, teen pregnancy, suicide, and violence; and actively promote social skills, good nutrition, safety, and general health. (Dryfoos, 1994, p. 5)

Student misbehavior and school violence remain central issues for school personnel, researchers, and families (Howard, Flora, & Griffin, 1999; Petersen et al., 1998). Research has shown that violence and misbehavior negatively impact the learning environment (Everett & Price, 1995) and promote a climate and culture of concern and fear among teachers and administrators while at school (Petersen, 1997; Petersen et al., 1998). Violence disrupts schools from functioning, students from learning, and teachers from teaching. It degrades the quality of life and education for children, and it forces some schools to devote many of their already scarce resources to security measures (Berliner & Biddle, 1995).

Family Factors

Being Poor

Probably the most fundamental influence on the attitudes and behavior of children is their family life. For example, family poverty has been repeatedly identified as a significant factor in whether or not students are academically successful, as well as a mediating factor in youth misbehavior and violence (Vorrasi & Garbarino, 2000). Poverty diminishes the capacity of children to access needed resources and creates stressors on already marginalized family units. Changing requirements for skilled and unskilled workers, the globalization and automation of many domestic industries, and the disappearance of work in inner-city neighborhoods and rural areas have created increasingly difficult situations for low-income families (Wilson, 1996), thereby making it nearly impossible to break out of the cycle of poverty.

Yet, job insecurity is only one aspect of this issue. According to the 2000 U.S. Census, the most affluent families are two-parent families. In stark contrast, data on family structure and income revealed that 43.3% of families headed by women with children under 5, and 34.3% with children under 18, were below the poverty line in 1999 (U.S. Bureau of the Census, 2000). This is not to say that single parents do not do a good job in raising children. What these statistics infer is that conditions for many low-income families are becoming more formidable, and given the current socioeconomics of American society, being poor continues to be a good predictor of growing up in a single-parent home (Vorrasi & Garbarino, 2000). Coleman and Hoffer (1987),

in their work on the social networks of families, demonstrated that children in single-parent families tend to receive less attention from adults, which has negative residual effects on their educational outcomes. A national study found that teachers and administrators perceived a lack of adult involvement in the lives of children as a major contributor to student misbehavior and violence in school (Petersen et al., 1998). Other work in this area has also demonstrated that misbehavior increases at home and at school when single-parent families are not able to provide sufficient resources to cope with the demand of primary care for the children (Hyman, 1997).

The relatively low educational achievement of economically disadvantaged children also illustrates that they experience a different reality compared to their more affluent peers. Maruyama (2003) described these children as "educationally poor." They are not emotionally, cognitively, and socially ready when school starts and must always struggle to catch up with their peers. In a study of kindergarten and first-grade math and reading achievement, Denton and West (2002) found twice as many first-grade students from families not considered poor to be proficient in language comprehension and simple multiplication compared to peers identified as being poor.

Domestic Violence

Studies have shown that being raised in a violent home is linked to a variety of interpersonal, emotional, and cognitive deficits (Haugaard & Feerick, 1996). Making more insidious the physical trauma and residual psychological effects of domestic violence are the antisocial behaviors modeled by adults in the home. Children in these situations may perceive violence as an acceptable and appropriate method of handling social conflict. In a national study of school personnel, Petersen et al. (1998) found that teachers and school administrators perceived parental violence and parental drug abuse to be the two most influential contributors to student misbehavior and violence in school. Although abusive homes exist in all socioeconomic classes, research has pointed to the fact that economically disadvantaged families may be more likely to use violence as a coping mechanism (Wolfner & Gelles, 1993), and children from poor homes are more likely to be abused and to witness domestic violence than their affluent peers (Straus & Gelles, 1990). Research looking at adolescent males revealed that exposure to community violence was also a significant predictor of aggressive behavior (O'Keefe, 1997).

Of course, witnessing domestic violence and children's misbehavior and participation in violence are not necessarily in a cause-and-effect relationship. Some research reports significant differences in aggressive behavior in children who have witnessed domestic violence and those who have not (Fantuzzo et al., 1991). Other studies find no differences in these groups of children (Haugaard & Feerick, 1996). Although whether or not exposure to domestic violence has a direct effect on the behavior of children may not be clear, there are strong grounds for concern that family violence is a substantial risk factor in the development and reinforcement of aggressive and antisocial behavior in community and school settings (Vorrasi & Garbarino, 2000).

Child Abuse

The connection between physical abuse of children and school misbehavior and violence is a very complicated one. Research on the influence of child abuse and aggressive behavior has examined the connection to harsh parental discipline (Weiss, Dodge, Bates, & Petitt, 1992), as well as physical abuse and neglect (Howing, Kohen, Gaudin, Kurtz, & Wodarsk, 1992). Scudder, Blount, Heide, and Silverman (1993) concluded that abused children are more likely than nonabused children to participate in antisocial, violent behavior. In their work, they found that adolescent delinquents had experienced a much higher level of childhood victimization than nondelinquent adolescents.

In research on family factors that contribute to misbehavior, Hyman (1997) concluded that "child abuse has a profound impact on students' behavior . . . Children who are physically or emotionally abused at home may present either overly aggressive or sometimes violent behavior in school" (p. 211). Taken together, these studies suggest a relatively strong association between physical abuse and aggressive behavior in children and adolescents. "Although research has shown that some groups of abused children have higher levels of aggression, it is important to note the range of behaviors among abused children is great . . . [therefore] abused children must be considered on an individual basis" (Haugaard & Feerick, 1996, p. 90).

Research has clearly demonstrated that these barriers greatly affect the outcomes of socially disadvantaged families and their capacity to escape the whirlpool of failure (Casella, 2001; Hyman, 1997; Maruyama, 2003). This also compounds the already difficult task for school personnel who attempt to position themselves and establish policies and programs to help these children before they engage in aggressive or violent behavior in school.

School Factors

The Schoolhouse

As social institutions, schools greatly affect the capacity to pursue new and better opportunities and therefore have an enormous influence on the life outcomes of students and their families. Although research points to deplorable societal imbalances experienced by many children, especially those from low-income and poorly educated families, the contextual reality of schooling for these students and their families may not be substantially better. McLaren (1998) argues that the current structural constraints and policies that represent traditional schooling reinforce levels of inequality and reduce schools to credentializing mechanisms and protected enclaves that favor the more affluent.

The search for solutions to the problem of violence in schools has generated a collection of approaches that parallel those used by law enforcement personnel to combat violence and crime in the larger society (Dohrn, 2000; Petersen, 1997). The emphasis on overly punitive and rigidly bureaucratic school rules and policies, coupled with a lack of cooperation with students, their families, and the surrounding communities, fosters an environment that compounds the problem and in some situations makes misbehavior and violence more likely to happen (Casella, 2001; Hyman, 1997; McLaren, 1998; Noguera, 2000; Petersen, 1997; Williams, 2001a).

> Violence occurs as a consequence of inclusion of students in an institutional context in which they have little or no choice, in which they are exposed to forces over which they have no control and as a result, have little chance in gaining what they want and need on their own terms. (Fallis & Opotow, 2003, p. 115)

School Personnel

The expectation that schools will inculcate in young people the values that contribute to a productive and ordered society is not a recent public phenomenon. In 1965, at a White House Conference on Education, then-Vice President Hubert Humphrey said that our country would achieve historical recognition for using its educational system to overcome problems of illiteracy, unemployment, crime and violence, and even war among nations (Lawrence, 1998). Yet, constraints on budgets, schedules, personnel, and resources make it literally impossible for many American schools to focus adequate attention or resources on these problems. Subsequently, teachers and administrators find themselves dealing with these very complex and enigmatic issues in a piecemeal fashion (Petersen et al., 1998). Schools are intricate entities, and understanding how the actions of their members contribute to student misbehavior and violence is not straightforward. Some scholars see efforts to eradicate violence as more *sparring with students* than solving issues of systemic violence (Casella, 2001). Research has demonstrated that issues like teacher and administrator divorce, economic stress, dual employment, and loss of patience (Hyman, 1997) cause a deterioration in the ability of school personnel to empathize and communicate with students and their families. Other work points to poor instruction and teachers' inability to appropriately recognize the instructional needs of their students (Rosenfield, 1987). These issues create school and classroom environments where: students, teachers, and administrators become frustrated; disruptions occur because students are disengaged or worse; students feel marginalized and out of control; teachers want to teach and take formal action to have disruptive students removed, sent to the principal's office, and sometimes sent home.

Williams (2001a, 2001b) focused on the deeper and more veiled issue surrounding the clash of values held by school personnel, students, and the community (social location) about violence and disruptive behavior. In her research, she found that students articulated that fighting or being disruptive and adversarial with teachers and other students made their peers perceive them as tough and thereby helped them avoid future confrontations. Often, students' families expected and accepted the use of violence to resolve social conflict. Administrators and teachers, on the other hand, found any form of violence unacceptable. Because of these vastly different value systems, the needs of students and school personnel regularly clashed, and issues went unresolved.

> Students described to me in a variety of ways of how it was critical for their survival that they never show any vulnerability. Frontin' it was an overall term for acting, walking, and talking as if willing and ready to fight at the slightest provocation and demonstrating no weaknesses. (Williams, 2001a, p. 96)

The absence of student voice (McLaren, 1998), the lack of student and community perspectives (Casella, 2001), moral exclusion (Fallis & Opotow, 2003), and failure to recognize and address contextual factors that influence incidence of violence (Noguera, 2000) by teachers and administrators often result in the adoption and implementation of sweeping policies that inadvertently contribute rather than detract from the problems of misbehavior and violence (Hyman, 1997).

Violence Prevention Policies

Although the creation and implementation of policies to curb student misbehavior and violence are important, bureaucratically implementing a multitude of school rules will have little or no impact on the level of misbehavior or violence a school is experiencing (Petersen, 2002). The limited definition of security policies, particularly zero-tolerance policies for a host of misdeeds inside and outside of schools, has forced school personnel to defer to law enforcement rather than focusing on the teaching potential these behaviors offer (Dohrn, 2000). A body of research indicates that some policies enacted to combat misbehavior and violence may in fact perpetuate the actions they were intended to decrease. For example, a 1998 report entitled *Early Warning, Timely Response: A Guide to Safe Schools* demonstrated that effective and safe schools are places where there is strong leadership and caring faculty and where parents and the community, including police officers

and students, are involved in the design of programs and policies. Yet, many of the current zero-tolerance polices adopted by schools have not included these groups in the development and design stages of the policy. Of equal importance is the fact that these zero-tolerance policies frequently deny superintendents and principals the ability to reasonably exercise professional discretion. In 1999, a Pennsylvania appellate court (*Lyons v. Penn Hills School District*) ruled that a school's zero-tolerance policy exceeded the authority of the school board because it denied the superintendent and students the exercise of discretion specifically articulated in the school code. Addressing issues as behavioral or in ad-hoc fashion overlooks and oversimplifies deeper unaddressed issues (Hyman, 1997). Although these and other measures may be necessary parts of a total system, effective and balanced policies must reflect the context of the organization and provide a caveat for school leaders to make rational and professional decisions when dealing with students.

> Schools, child welfare systems, probation and health services have all made it easier to violate, terminate, exclude, and expel youngsters. Where these youth go for survival, help, socialization development, care, and attention is unclear. One door that always remains open is the gateway to juvenile and criminal justice. (Dohrn, 2000, p. 161)

Amassing Risk

Clearly the interaction between the social contexts of family, communities, and schools, coupled with children's developmental capacities, is implicated in problems of misbehavior and violence. The question arises: Why aren't all children with these experiences and in these situations misbehaving in school and perpetuating violence on their peers? What are the protective factors?

Numerous studies have documented the positive relationships between stress and increased risk. For example, research has shown that individuals who experience too many stressors at one time are at increased risk for becoming violent (Pianta, Egeland, & Sroufe, 1990). In addition, families that experience too many stressors are at risk for experiencing aggravated family crises. In their discussion of social toxicity and its effects on the behavior of children, Vorrasi and Garbarino (2000) present the work of scholars who have examined *accumulated risk* and *opportunity factors* and their influence on the intellectual development of children. The 1987 research of Sameroff, Seifer, Barocas, Zax, and Greenspan (as cited in Vorrasi & Garbarino, 2000) examined eight risk factors for the intellectual development of preschool children. Their investigation found that in the presence of four or more risk factors, children demonstrated maladaptive functioning and a lack of resilience. In 1998, Sameroff extended his work and examined the risk factors and the mental health and development of 13 and 18 year olds. His investigation found children identified as "highly competent" living in high-risk environmental conditions did worse on mental health assessments than similar groups in low-risk conditions. His work also revealed that high-competence children in high-risk environments did worse on these measures than low-competence children in low-risk environments. What this research demonstrates is the overriding influence of environmental adversity and social context, which combine to affect the intellectual and emotional development of children and adolescents.

> The accumulation of risk model is predicated on the idea that almost all children are capable of coping with low levels of risk until the accumulation exceeds a developmentally determined individual threshold. Once accumulated risk moves beyond this threshold, systems of strong compensatory forces (i.e., opportunity factors) are needed to prevent the precipitation of physical and psychological harm. (Vorrasi & Garbarino, 2000, p. 62)

In a 1992 study, Dunst and Trivette (as cited in Vorrasi & Garbarino, 2000) suggested that risk factors might be neutralized or at least partially mitigated if opportunity factors were introduced into other realms of the child's life, even when patterns of risk are thought to be impervious to intervention. For example, although a child might live in a household with inadequate income (risk), if one or more alternative caregivers (opportunity) and parents are responsive and facilitative to the needs of their children (opportunity), developmental risks and family stressors are diminished. In other work looking at issues outside the family, Dunst, Trivette, Davis, and Cornwall (1994) interviewed families about how professionals could help to create a sense of control in the care of their children. Their work revealed that parents identified help-giving attitudes, beliefs, and behaviors of professionals as fostering a sense of control. These behaviors were broadly consistent with identified opportunity factors (Dunst & Trivette, 1994). Given the numerous social and school-related risks faced by children, this theory may have some significance for our discussion. It suggests that although children may be exposed to risk factors, these incidents can be defused or at least partially counteracted by the introduction of opportunity factors both inside and outside the family. The research also clearly demonstrates that the absence of opportunity factors results in maladaptive development and reduced capacity, whereas the presence of counteracting forces (opportunities) within and outside of the family can diminish or even prevent children from becoming involved in antisocial behaviors and activities.

SOCIAL CAPITAL AND THE BUILDING OF SOCIAL INSTITUTIONS

Although there is general agreement that the sources of student misbehavior and youth violence are multifaceted and enigmatic, there are conflicting opinions (Nemeck, 1998) on which criteria should be used to determine the most effective responses (Petersen, Thompson, Gawerecki, & Cauldwell, 2003). In an attempt to explore the interplay of the formal, social, and educational issues and their influence on students' behavior, I offer the conceptual lens of social capital. The use of this lens permits us to examine various dimensions of issues and problems faced by poor children, children of color, and children from families with little formal education and the relationship of these issues to student behavior in the schools and community. It is also my contention that this conceptual lens may also assist us in identifying multifaceted approaches to reduce student misbehavior and violence.

Social Capital

Social capital can be defined as established social networks of trust and relationships that are exercised between individuals in a group, communities, or organization (Putnam, 1995; Spillane, Hallett, & Diamond, 2003). These social networks are composed of social norms, sanctions, trust, and collaboration. Individuals work together to form shared resources for the community and its members. The fundamental elements of social capital are rooted in the social relations and basic social networks of individuals, leading to social trust. "Social capital is productive, making possible the achievement of certain ends that in its absence would not be possible" (Coleman, 1988, p. 81).

Unlike other forms of human capital, social capital inheres in the structure of relations between individuals and among individuals. (Coleman, 1988). Putnam (1995) refers to them as "a dense network of reciprocal social relations" (p. 19). For example, these social networks can reside within and outside of the family structure. Coleman (1988) discusses social capital within the family and its relationship to schooling. He separates social capital into three components: financial capital, human

capital, and social capital. Financial capital is the approximate measure of the family's wealth or income. Human capital is an approximate measure of the parent's education and ability to provide an environment conducive for learning. Social capital is the relations between parents and their children, extended family members, church, community groups, and peers, when they are present. Although each component is important, social capital within the family has been shown to have a tremendous influence on the success of children in the educational setting (see Coleman & Hoffer, 1987).

Social Capital and Education

The acceptance and promotion of education by the family is important for academic performance. Although levels of educational attainment are linked to the socioeconomic status of the family, the presence of financial resources alone does not guarantee positive educational outcomes.

> Successful public education systems require a unique combination of financial, human and social capital that reflects the particular needs of the community they serve. . . . Family, community and state involvement helps to increase the relevance and quality of education by improving ownership, building consensus, reaching remote and disadvantaged groups and strengthening institutional capacity. (World Bank Group, 2003, p. 1)

Social Capital in Communities

The frequency and persistence of interaction among families, neighbors, friends, and members of community groups generate social capital and the ability to work together. The poor can use social capital as a substitute for human and physical capital (Collier, 1998). Interaction can also have a positive impact on the success of the entire community, not only the homes imbued with financial, human, and social capital (Narayan & Pritchett, 1997). Social capital offers many benefits to communities. The relationships among family and neighbors offer safety nets and help develop trust and the capacity to work together. Social capital can reduce problems of violence and "free-riding" by enforcing shared values, norms, and behaviors as well as increasing business opportunities and quality education (World Bank Group, 2003).

> Communities consist of individuals, families, groups and formal and informal organizations that often act independently of one another to promote individual and diverse interests. It is the developed trust in the relationships of diverse groups that create[s] social capital. [Its] creation provides an avenue for successful collaborative participation as well as giving voice to those who may have been locked out of more formal avenues to affect change. (World Bank Group, 2003, p. 1)

Social Institutions

The authors of the 2000/2001 World Development Report, *Attacking Poverty*, focus on economic inequalities and poverty traps faced by individuals in many of the world's developing nations. They document how the cumulative effects of marginal educational and employment opportunities severely weaken the prospects that members of these communities can find gainful employment, while perpetuating the barriers of discrimination and distrust. This dynamic is also amplified by the psychological damage it causes to those who experience it. "Add the physical and financial obstacles to obtaining qualifications and people cease to believe in their abilities and stop aspiring to join the economic and social mainstream" (World Bank, 2000/2001, p. 124).

What is particularly germane to our discussion here is the importance of social capital and its effects on the development of social institutions that aid in removing these barriers, thus permitting individuals a level of personal and

social empowerment and thereby an escape from poverty and its damaging effects. Efforts to reduce social barriers require complementary initiatives to establish and maintain social institutions for the poor and marginalized, particularly members of local community-based organizations. Local organizations can take the form of administrative and political institutions, kinship systems, local organizations, cooperatives, and educational centers (World Bank, 2000/2001). The report indicates that these networks can be more clearly discussed using three different dimensions of social capital:

- *Bonding social capital:* The strong ties connecting family members, neighbors, close friends, and business associates. These ties connect people who share similar demographic characteristics.
- *Bridging social capital:* The weak ties connecting individuals from different ethnic and occupational backgrounds. Bridging implies horizontal connections to people with broadly comparable economic status and political power.
- *Linking social capital:* The vertical ties between poor people and people in positions of influence in formal organizations. This dimension captures a vitally important additional feature of life in poor communities: that their members are usually excluded—by overt discrimination or lack of resources—from participating in major decisions relating to their welfare.

"Constructing high-quality public institutions is essential for ensuring that diverse identities become a developmental asset, not a source of division and violence," the World Bank (2000/2001, p. 127) says. These institutions should be "participatory, credible, and accountable, so that people can see the benefits of cooperation," and they should be supported by "constitutional and legal systems and representative political systems, which allow groups to work out their interests through mechanisms other than violence" (p. 128). If we employ the three dimensions of social capital to examine barriers in the development of building good social institutions (e.g., schools and misbehavior

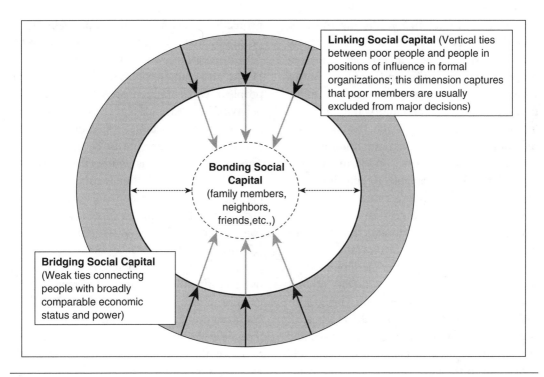

Figure 19.1   Bonding, Bridging, and Linking Social Capital

and violence interventions), the importance of interconnectedness of various individuals and groups is clearly evident (see Figure 19.1).

Beginning with the innermost circle, we see that *bonding social capital* represents the connection of individuals who share similar demographics and underlying norms. This microperspective speaks to the knowledge and skills of people (human capital) and associations of families (social capital) that can either facilitate or impede the development and education of children. The dashed edges represent the openness as well as the vulnerability of the family. Poor and marginalized families are reliant on the larger community and therefore subject to external values and norms.

The next circle offers the second dimension of *bridging social capital* (demonstrated by the dashed horizontal arrows linking families and individuals with the larger community). The dashed arrows represent a loose coupling

connection of community groups (families, local organizations, kinship systems) who have comparable economic status and power. Although some of these relationships may be hierarchical, the concept involves the interactive networks of communities. Membership may offer benefits, but in poorer, less educated, and minority communities, membership offers few opportunities and increased risk factors.

The final dimension, *linking social capital,* speaks to the social and political environment outside of the community and family. This includes formalized institutional relationships (e.g., government or schools). These social institutions have a substantial impact on the ability of families and communities to build capacity for strategic advantage (e.g., procuring education, jobs, and other social benefits). In the case of this figure, the heavily bolded, unidirectional vertical arrows represent issues of power and influence of more affluent groups (e.g., state and local governments, schools, police) and their ability make one-sided policy and programmatic decisions that shape social structures and develop norms within social institutions like schools, many times excluding the community and family.

Social networks at all levels (families, communities, and institutions) are durable and have considerable influence on the amount and type of resources available to individuals to manage risk. The poor, marginalized, and less educated have the greatest risk and the fewest resources (opportunity factors). One method to manage risk factors and increase opportunity is through the development of social institutions, in this case, quality schools and educational policies and programs. Through integration of the dimensions of social capital, the underlying social forces and energy can be used to eliminate barriers and contribute to the development and well-being of children, their families, and the larger community. Historically poor, minority, and undereducated families are not involved in developing larger, more complex social institutions. Their interests and insights have been willfully ignored or misunderstood. Increasing the participation of these individuals, families, and community members enhances levels of trust and interconnectedness (social capital) of institutions. Values, practices, interests, and desires are expressed and incorporated into the norms of the institution, creating an organization that meets the needs of those it is designed to serve.

A key lesson for practitioners and policymakers is the importance of using existing forms of bridging social capital in poor communities as a basis for scaling up the efforts of local community-based organizations (World Bank, 2000/2001, p. 130).

VIOLENCE PREVENTION MODELS

To be effective, violence prevention and intervention efforts hinge on identifying risk and protective factors and implementing a program that is appropriate to children's developmental levels (U.S. Department of Health and Human Services, 2001). Part of the problem with many proposed violence and behavior interventions is that more often than not, they are devised and tested outside of the setting in which they are to be implemented. This is not to say that adherence to proper methods of data collection, analysis, and testing fail to provide components that are generalizable to other settings. Not at all. Yet the context and type of issues that individual schools and districts face make it literally impossible to address these complex issues in one-size–fits-all programs (Petersen, 1997; Petersen et al., 1998). Powell, Muir-McClain, & Halasyamani (1995) estimate that more than 5,000 schools have adopted at least one of more than 3,000 commercially available violence prevention programs. In the United States, more than 90% of secondary schools have reported establishing a policy that prohibits violence, and 96% also implement at least one type of security measure, yet evidence of effective interventions remains sparse (Howard et al., 1999). For example, Noguera's (2000) work in schools looked at students' perceptions of conflict mediation programs as a means of violence prevention. Students perceived them to be unrealistic and impractical, especially in times of intense confrontation. Many of the commercial programs are limited because they are unable to address the substantive issues and problems in every setting.

What we can gather from the extant literature is the paramount importance of familiarity with the issue and knowledge of its context (e.g., community, individuals, and social relations) to fully grasp the problem and to develop ideas and means to resolve it. It is important to take a comprehensive approach to violence prevention because in each setting the social and physical environment may facilitate or mitigate youth victimization and perpetration

(Howard et al., 1999). "The sustainability of violence prevention depends on the degree to which it connects with the environmental, racial and economic bearings of society" (Casella, 2001, p. 151). Often, interventions have languished because they have been add-ons to the regular curriculum and don't have buy-in from teachers and administrators (Burstyn & Stevens, 2001).

> Sometimes we look for solutions to social problems without agreeing on what the problem really is. Identifying the problem is important because each form of school violence deserves a different kind of attention, and by extension a different type of prevention, reform, or intervention strategy. (Casella, 2001, p. 146)

Action Research and the Development of Social Capital

The age-old axiom, "Without data, you're just another person with an opinion," is relevant to our discussion here. Too often, policymakers, consultants, and school personnel are not fully cognizant of the context and complexity of the situation facing schools. They don't have the time, resources, or inclination to collect data when making life-changing decisions that could positively or adversely affect the lives of children. This is particularly true when attempting to address the numerous, complex, and enigmatic issues surrounding student misbehavior and school violence. Although the complexity of these issues makes it difficult to fully comprehend them, let alone propose a "silver bullet" solution, what is clear is that any genuine opportunity for successful intervention rests first and foremost with the faculty, administrators, students, and families that make up the school district. The impact of the school environment on delinquency, violence, and predictors of violence has been demonstrated in numerous studies (Howard et al., 1999). Although numerous scholars have articulated ways

to address these issues, the identification of a realistic and manageable process for addressing an actual problem of practice still seems to elude us.

Rogue Events

Using the metaphor of firefighting to illustrate the work of educational administrators, Weick (1996) speaks to the issue of *fire suppression* and its anchor, the *fire triangle.*

> To produce the flame and combustion of a fire, three things must be mixed together; heat, plus oxygen plus fuel . . . firefighters remove fuel from fires when they build a hand line and clear away debris. They remove oxygen when they drop sticky retardant or shovel dirt onto smoldering embers. (p. 570)

Weick states that the important lesson for administrators and researchers is to know and specify the minimal and sufficient conditions that cause rogue events. For student misbehavior and violence in schools, the fire triangle is (1) the volatile blend of risk factors outside of the school (e.g., poverty, domestic violence, abuse, few opportunity factors); (2) school policies and practices that students perceive as coercive, punitive, and/or unrealistic; and (3) the inability or unwillingness of school personnel to include family and community members in identifying substantive economic, cultural, and contextual issues faced by students and their families and how these factors contribute to misbehavior and violence (See Figure 19.2). "When the perceptions of the students are not taken into account, the policies adopted to help young people often miss the mark and may even generate greater polarization and antipathy toward authority figures" (Noguera, 2000, p. 150). The combination of these factors creates the necessary ingredients that lead to rogue events in schools.

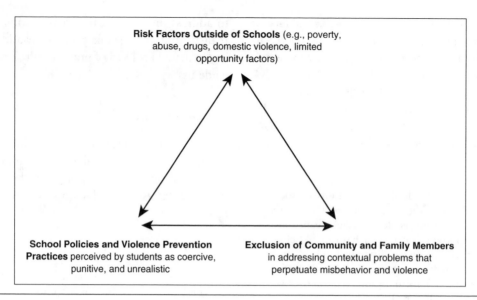

Figure 19.2   The Fire Triangle of Student Misbehavior and Violence

Action Research

For practitioners who work in the school environment daily or researchers who are interested in applied settings, action research is a sound method for systematically investigating social issues in the school setting.

> Action research is a form of inductive, practical research that focuses on gaining a better understanding of a practice problem or achieving a real change or improvement in the practice context. In brief summary, action research, as an approach to research, is essentially a systematic process of practitioner problem posing and problem solving. (Kuhne & Quigley, 1997, p. 23)

Unlike some other forms of empirical investigations, action research focuses primarily on real world issues, looks for change through interventions, seeks active collaborative participation with others, and is conducted in a systematic and cyclical process. It sets out to change matters. Lewin (1946) argues that for action research to be effective, it requires a number of cycles of problem identification, planning and implementing of an intervention, interpretation of the findings, and redefinition of the problem (see Figure 19.3).

Planning. As school personnel, students, and families wrestle with issues (complex components of the fire triangle), they put themselves in a position to develop a clearer understanding of the problem and its context. Action research is designed for these groups to work collaboratively to define issue(s) and problems and determine whether or not they are researchable. Together, they determine and define an intervention that will address the problems and choose appropriate measures for its evaluation and timeline.

Acting. Once the intervention has been established, it is implemented and observed. The investigators stay true to the plan and systematically keep track of the data and its collection. This is also a time for the collaborators to discuss data among themselves and other informed colleagues.

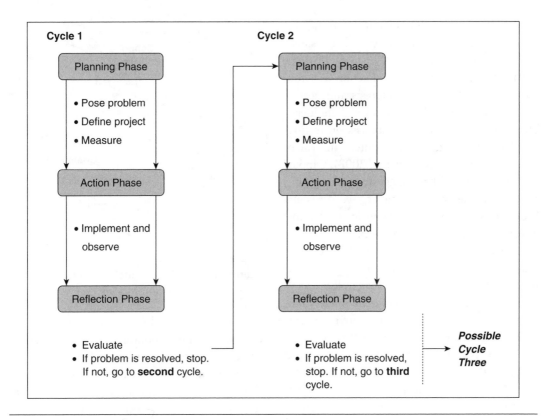

Figure 19.3 Cycles and Phases of an Action Research Project

SOURCE: This figure is an adaptation and modification of Kuhne & Quigley's (1997) model for the phases of an action research project (p. 27). Kuhne, G., & Quigley, A., *Creating Practical Knowledge Through Action Research: Posing Problems, Solving Problems,* and *Improving Daily Practice.* © 1997 by Jossey-Bass. Reprinted by permission of John Wiley & Sons, Inc.

Observing. At the conclusion of the preestablished timeline, the data are dissected and discussed among the collaborators. According to Kuhne and Quigley (1997), this is the most important step in the action research process. Investigators determine what the data reveal about the problem and intervention, whether or not the intervention was successful, and any tangible gains.

Reflecting. Kuhne and Quigley (1997) have pointed out that this is typically the weakest step for practitioners because they feel the need to be always active rather than reflective. Yet, reflecting on the project is essential in determining the results of the project and

the promise of the approach taken by the investigators. More important, in this step, the collaborators determine whether or not another cycle is necessary.

Action Research and Fostering Social Capital to Address Violence

Babe Ruth was once quoted as saying: "The way a team plays as a whole determines its success. You may have the greatest bunch of individual stars in the world, but if they don't play together, the club won't be worth a dime" (BrainyMedia.com, 2004). Reams of research have substantiated the importance and value of networks for sharing knowledge and collaboration resulting in greater productivity and individual job satisfaction with organizations (Cohen & Prusak, 2001). Because the problems of action research are driven by community interests and needs, it makes sense to include all key stakeholders. Of particular note is the emphasis on testing problems within the social context in which they are developed (Maruyama, 2003). Omoto and Snyder (1990) have suggested that a significant characteristic of action research is its "commitment to research as an integral component of social action" (p. 162).

If social institutions are to be effective, they must be trustworthy and participatory. That is, they must continually work to develop social capital. Research has shown that family and community collaboration and involvement with schools help to overcome cultural barriers (Onikama, Hammond, & Koki, 1998), improve the quality of schooling (Griffith, 1996), and increase the academic achievement of children (Peterson, 1989; Xiato, 2001). When considering issues of student misbehavior and violence, numerous scholars have indicated the importance of student voice (McLaren, 1998), student and community values (Williams (2001b), social context (Casella, 2001; Noguera, 2000), family involvement (Petersen, 1997; Petersen et al., 1998), and administrator discretion (Dohrn, 2000; Petersen, 2002) to recognize and address factors that influence these behaviors.

The model shown in Figure 19.4 graphically represents how the development of social capital among families, the community, and school could be accomplished through the implementation of action research directed at issues of student misbehavior and violence. Although each circle symbolizes individualized segments, the true value lies in the extent, density, and reciprocal nature of their relationship and interaction. Issues of violence and misbehavior are not static; rather, they are continually evolving, and the roles and responsibilities of individuals, families, the community, and

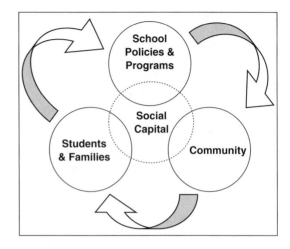

Figure 19.4   Action Research and Social Capital and Violence Prevention Models

school will vary. Ending misbehavior and violence requires continual communication and cooperation among key stakeholders—the development of social capital. The notion of investigating problem behaviors within the context in which they occur is a basic premise of action research. It is also a necessary tenet in developing policies and programs that will be effective. Through such exchanges, social institutions such as schools can strengthen their capacity and better serve the families and children entrusted to their care.

CONCLUSION

When people are provided with the opportunity to expand conflict-coping repertoires, they are in a better position to deal with life circumstances in ways that facilitate their physical and psychological health and well-being rather than being debilitated by circumstances (Frydenberg, 1997). As this chapter has articulated, the problem of student misbehavior and violence is systemic: It is a function of the interaction of risk factors, clashing values systems, and institutional policies that do not address the core issues. I also suggest that given the enigmatic nature of the factors involved in creating misbehavior and violence, families, school systems, and communities are unclear on how to substantively resolve them. Too often, schools rely on policies and programs that may actually exacerbate the behavior they are designed to prevent. Administrators and teachers are then perplexed why families and communities are unresponsive or unsupportive of policies directed at "protecting their children." This clash and misunderstanding of values and ideas foster a cycle in which only a few voices are heard, and no one wins, least of all the children.

With the intention of making schools better places, this chapter deliberately emphasizes the importance of problem context and collaboration and proposes the use of action research to integrate these into the school/community setting. Understanding problem context is paramount in distinguishing the underlying issues; collaboration between families, communities, and schools is equally important when attempting to resolve them. Social capital represents the importance and need of developing trust and personal networks through social interaction. The interactions of key stakeholders enhance efforts to improve the lives and conditions of all students, especially poor and marginalized students. The source, shape, and manifestation of cooperative connections between people foster organizational commitment. Also, empirical evidence clearly demonstrates that social capital in the family and outside it in the adult community surrounding the school provides substantial benefits in the academic achievement of students. Unfortunately, in many current strategies and policies aimed at controlling misbehavior and violence, the social networks between family, community, and schools are weak or absent. The unidirectional nature of many policies creates and perpetuates values, traditions, and norms that are not representative of the students and communities that surround the school and therefore are ineffectual.

To develop practices and policies that will shift the focus from culpability to change, this chapter proposes the use of action research. First, action research is a systematic method requiring the user to identify, investigate, and resolve selected problems of practice. Student violence and misbehavior are influenced by factors both inside and outside of school. Intimate familiarity with the linkages of these factors to student behavior permits the origination of interventions that resonate with the individual nature of each school and community setting.

Second, the development of quality social institutions requires the participation and interconnectedness of numerous stakeholders. Action research is a method that permits and encourages the collaboration of many voices in grasping the actual problem. Through the various stages and cycles of action research, programs and policies reflective of the values, norms, and interests of students, the community, and school can be established and integrated in the school setting. Because such policies have been collaboratively developed and tested within the context in which they occur, there is increased likelihood that they will be more effective in resolving the problems of misbehavior and violence in our nation's schools.

REFERENCES

Berliner, D. C., & Biddle, B. J. (1995). *The manufactured crisis: Myths, fraud, and the attack on America's public schools.* Reading, MA: Addison–Wesley.

BrainyMedia.com. (2004). *BrainyQuote.* Retrieved June 28, 2004, from http://www.brainyquote.com/quotes/quotes/b/baberuth125974.html

Burstyn, J. N., & Stevens, R. (2001). Involving the whole school in violence prevention. In J. Burstyn, G. Bender, R. Casella, H. G. Gordon, D. P. Guerra, K. V. Luschen, R. Stevens, & K. M. Williams (Eds.), *Preventing violence in schools: A challenge to American democracy* (pp. 139–158). Mahwah, NJ: Lawrence Erlbaum.

Casella, R. (2001). *Being down: Challenging violence in urban schools.* New York: Teachers College Press.

Cohen, D., & Prusak, L. (2001). *In good company: How social capital makes organizations work.* Boston: Harvard Business School Press.

Coleman, J. S. (1988). Social capital in the creation of human capital. *American Journal of Sociology, 94, Supplement: Organizations and Institutions: Sociological and Economic Approaches to the Analysis of Social Structure,* 95–120.

Coleman, J., & Hoffer, T. (1987). *Public and private schools: The impact of community.* New York: Basic Books.

Collier, P. (1998). *Social capital and poverty* (Social Capital Initiative Working Paper No. 4). Washington, DC: World Bank.

Denton, K., & West, J. (2002, Spring). Children's reading and mathematics achievement in kindergarten and first grade. *Education Statistics Quarterly, 4*(1), 19–26.

Dohrn, B. (2000). Look out, kid, it's something you did: The criminalization of children. In V. Polakow (Ed.), *The public assault on America's children: Poverty, violence, and juvenile injustice* (pp. 157–187). New York: Teachers College Press.

Dryfoos, J. (1994). *Full service schools: A revolution in health services for children, youth, and families.* San Francisco: Jossey-Bass.

Dunst, C., & Trivette, C. M. (1994). Aims and principles of family support programs. In C. Dunst, C. M. Trivette, & A. G. Deal (Eds.), *Supporting and strengthening families: Volume 1. Methods, strategies and practices* (pp. 30–48). Cambridge, MA: Brookline Books.

Dunst, C. J., Trivette, C. M., Davis, M., & Cornwall, J. C. (1994). Characteristics of effective help-giving practices. In C. J. Dunst, C. M. Trivette, & A. G. Deal (Eds.), *Supporting and strengthening families: Methods, strategies and practices* (pp. 171–186). Cambridge, MA: Brookline.

Everett, S. A., & Price, J. H. (1995). Students' perceptions of violence in the public schools: The MetLife survey. *Journal of Adolescent Health, 17,* 345–352.

Fallis, R. K., & Opotow, S. (2003). Are students failing school or are schools failing students? Class cutting in high school. *Journal of Social Issues, 59*(1), 103–119.

Fantuzzo, J. W., DePaola, L. M., Lambert, L., Martino, T., Anderson, G., & Sutton, S. (1991). Effects of interparental violence on the psychological adjustment and competencies of young children. *Journal of Consulting and Clinical Psychology, 59,* 258–265.

Frydenberg, E. (1997). *Adolescent coping: Theoretical and research perspectives.* London: Routledge.

Gibran, K. (1923). *The prophet.* New York: Knopf.

Griffith, J. (1996, October). Relation of parental involvement, empowerment, and school traits to student academic performance. *Journal of Educational Research, 90*(1), 33–41.

Haugaard, J. J., & Feerick, M. M. (1996). The influence of child abuse and family violence on violence in schools. In A. M. Hoffman (Ed.), *Schools, violence, and society* (pp. 79–100). Westport, CT: Praeger.

Howard, K. A., Flora, J., & Griffin, M. (1999). Violence prevention programs in schools: State of the science and implications for future research. *Applied & Preventive Psychology, 8,* 197–215.

Howing, P., Kohen, S., Gaudin, J., Kurtz, P., & Wodarsk, J. S. (1992). Current research issues in child welfare. *Social Work Research and Abstracts, 28*(1), 5–12.35.

Hyman, I. A. (1997). *School discipline and school violence: The teacher variance approach.* Boston: Allyn & Bacon.

Kuhne, G., & Quigley, A. (1997). Understanding and using action research in practice settings. In A. Quigley & G. Kuhne (Eds.), *Creating practical knowledge through action research: Posing problems, solving problems, and improving daily practice.* San Francisco: Jossey-Bass.

Lantieri, L., & Patti, J. (1996, September). The road to peace in our schools. *Educational Leadership, 54*(1), 28–31.

Lawrence, R. (1998). *School crime and juvenile justice.* New York: Oxford University Press.

Lewin, K. (1946). Action research and minority problems. *Journal of Social Issues, 10,* 34–46.

Lyons v. Penn Hills School District. 723 A.2d 1073 (PA Cmwlth., 1999). Retrieved from http://www.departments.bucknell.edu/edu/ed370/ABSTRACTS%2099/lyons.html

Maruyama, G. (2003). Disparities in educational opportunities and outcomes: What do we know and what can we do? *Journal of Social Issues, 59,* 3.653–3.676.

McLaren, P. (1998). *Life in schools: An introduction to critical pedagogy in the foundations of education* (3rd ed.). New York: Longman.

Narayan, D., & Pritchett, L. (1997, July). *Cents and sociability: Household income and social capital in rural Tanzania.* Washington, DC: World Bank.

Nemeck, S. (1998). Forestalling violence. *Scientific American, 279*(3), 15–17.

Noguera, P. A. (2000). Listen first: How student perspectives on violence can be used to create safer schools. In V. Polakow (Ed.), *The public assault on America's children: Poverty, violence, and juvenile injustice* (pp. 130–153). New York: Teachers College Press.

O'Keefe, M. O. (1997, May). Adolescents' exposure to community and school violence: Prevalence and behavioral correlates. *Journal of Adolescent Health, 20*(5), 368–379.

Omoto, A. M., & Snyder, M. (1990). Basic research in action: Volunteerism and society's response to AIDS. *Personality and Social Psychology, 16*, 152–165.

Onikama, D. L., Hammond, O. W., & Koki, S. (1998). *Family involvement in education: A synthesis of research for Pacific educators.* Honolulu, HI: Pacific Resources for Education and Learning. (ERIC No. ED420446)

Petersen, G. J. (1997, September). Looking at the big picture: School administrators and violence reduction. *Journal of School Leadership, 7*(5), 456–479.

Petersen, G. J. (2002, November). When zero-tolerance goes awry. *Maintaining Safe Schools, 8*(11), 6.

Petersen, G. J., Pietrzak, D., & Speaker, K. M. (1998). The enemy within: A national study on school violence and prevention. *Urban Education, 33*, 331–359.

Petersen, G. J., Thompson, R., Gawerecki, J., & Cauldwell, N. (2003, November). *Seeing the same school through different eyes: A study of stakeholders' perceptions of school violence.* Paper presented at the Annual Conference of the University Council for Educational Administration, Portland, OR.

Peterson, D. (1989). *Parent involvement in the educational process.* (ERIC Digest Series Number EA 43, Portland, OR/ERIC No. ED312776)

Pianta, R., Egeland, B., & Sroufe, L. A. (1990). Maternal stress and children's development: Prediction of school outcomes and identification of protective factors. In J. E. Rolf, A. Masten, D. Cicchetti, K. Nuechterlein, & S. Weintraub (Eds.), *Risk and protective factors in the development of psychopathology* (pp. 215–235). Cambridge, UK: Cambridge University Press.

Powell, K. E., Muir-McClain, L., & Halasyamani, L. (1995). A review of selected school-based conflict resolution and peer mediation projects. *Journal of School Health, 65*, 426–431.

Prothrow-Stith, D. (1994, April). Building violence prevention into the curriculum: A physician–administrator applies a public health model to schools. *The School Administrator, 4*(51), 8–12.

Putnam, R. D. (1995). *Bowling alone: The collapse and revival of American community.* New York: Simon & Schuster.

Rosenfield, S. (1987). *Instructional consultation.* Hillsdale, NJ: Lawrence Erlbaum.

Sameroff, A. (1998). Management of clinical problems and emotional care: Environmental risk factors in infancy. *Pediatrics, 102* (5, suppl), 1287–1292.

Sameroff, A. J., Seifer, R., Barocas, R., Zax, M., & Greenspan, S. (1987, March). Intelligence quotient scores of 4-year-old children: Social-environmental risk factors. *Pediatrics, 79*(3), 343–350.

Scudder, R. G., Blount, W. R., Heide, K. M., & Silverman, I. J. (1993). Important links between child abuse, neglect, and delinquency. *International Journal of Offender Therapy and Comparative Criminology, 37*(4), 315–323.

Spillane, J. P., Hallett, T., & Diamond, J. B. (2003). Forms of capital and the construction of leadership: Instructional leadership in urban elementary schools. *Sociology of Education, 76*, 1–17.

Straus, M. A., & Gelles, R. J. (1990). *Physical violence in American families: Risk factors and adaptation to violence in 8,145 families.* New Brunswick, NJ: Transaction.

U.S. Bureau of the Census. (2000). *People and families in poverty by selected characteristics: Employment, income, poverty status in 1999.* Retrieved from http://www.census.gov/census2000/states/us.html

U. S. Department of Health and Human Services. (2001, November/December). *Youth violence: A report of the surgeon general.* Washington, DC: Author.

Vorrasi, J. A., & Garbarino, J. (2000). Poverty and youth violence: Not all risk factors are created equal. In V. Polakow (Ed.), *The public assault on America's children: Poverty, violence, and juvenile injustice* (pp. 59–77). New York: Teachers College Press.

Weick, K. E. (1996, October). Fighting fires in educational administration. *Educational Administration Quarterly, 32*(4), 565–578.

Weiss, B., Dodge, K. A., Bates, J. E., & Petitt, G. S. (1992). Some consequences of early harsh discipline: Child aggression and a maladaptive social information procession style. *Child Development, 63*, 1321–1335.

Williams, K. M. (2001a). "Frontin' it": Schooling, violence, and relationships in the hood. In J. Burstyn, G. Bender, R. Casella, H. G. Gordon, D. P. Guerra, K. V. Luschen, R. Stevens, & K. M. Williams (Eds.), *Preventing violence in schools: A challenge to American democracy* (pp. 95–108). Mahwah, NJ: Lawrence Erlbaum.

Williams, K. M. (2001b). The importance of ethnography in understanding violence in schools. In J. Burstyn, G. Bender, R. Casella, H. G. Gordon, D. P. Guerra, K. V. Luschen, R. Stevens, & K. M. Williams (Eds.), *Preventing violence in schools: A challenge to American democracy* (pp. 47–60). Mahwah, NJ: Lawrence Erlbaum.

Wilson, W. J. (1996). *When work disappears: The world of the new urban poor.* New York: Knopf.

Wolfner, G. D., & Gelles, R. (1993). A profile of violence toward children: A national study. *Child Abuse and Neglect, 17,* 197–212.

World Bank. (2000/2001). Removing social barriers and building social institutions. In *World development report: Attacking poverty* (pp. 117–128). Retrieved from http://www.worldbank.org/poverty/wdrpoverty/report/toc.pdf

World Bank Group (2003). *Social capital for improvement: Social capital and community.* Retrieved June 28, 2004, from http://www.worldbank.org/poverty/scapital/sources/comm1.htm

Xiato, Z. (2001, Fall). Parental involvement and students' academic achievement: A growth modeling analysis. *Journal of Experimental Education, 70*(1), 27–61.

20

Issues of Teaching and Learning

ERIC HAAS
University of Connecticut

LESLIE POYNOR
University of Connecticut

Teaching is often equated with telling—teachers deliver information that students absorb. This process of teaching and learning and the concomitant relationship between teacher and student have a long tradition of use in the United States. They are, however, based on somewhat outmoded but tenacious understandings of how learning occurs. These understandings also fit well with certain common misconceptions of intelligence and undemocratic but powerful beliefs about how society should be structured.

A minority of educators view teaching and learning differently. Drawing on recent sociopolitical and sociocultural scholarship, advances in science, constructivist learning theory, transaction pedagogy, and inclusive views of democracy, these educators no longer equate teaching exclusively with a teacher telling students information. Such a view of teaching and learning has never gained widespread acceptance in the United States and is in direct conflict with many accepted practices within schools and society. Nevertheless, it

appears to be consistent with how the brain functions and many educators, from teachers to university professors, consider it to be the most effective (not to mention pleasant) method for organizing and operating a school and classroom that enhances learning and promotes democratic citizenship.

This chapter will provide a comparative overview of the concepts and practices of traditional transmission and progressive transaction teaching and learning. It will create a context for the current state of schooling through a review of its history, including a review of the scientific research that contributes to both perspectives. Short vignettes are presented to link concepts with examples of specific practice.

A note of caution as the chapter begins—the authors have a progressive, transactional view of teaching, learning, and schooling that understands knowledge as partially constructed through social interactions, making what one sees in the world and how one interacts with it interrelated. Likewise, the authors do not view

483

social events and interactions as truly separable, including teaching and learning, as well as teachers, students and school administrators. Each embodies parts of the other, each influences and is influenced by the other. These understandings are at least partially at odds with the traditional transmission understandings and practices of teaching, learning, and schooling. Nevertheless, every effort has been made to present traditional transmission schooling in a manner consistent with how one would view it from within that perspective.

TRADITIONAL TRANSMISSION TEACHING AND LEARNING

"Minerva."

"Here."

"Alberto"

"Here."

"Sam."

"Here."

Mrs. Wright sits at her desk in the front of the room carefully marking the attendance register with a black pen.

"Margaret. Margaret?" Mrs. Wright looks up and quickly scans the five rows. Ah! There in the fourth row, the second desk is empty. "Does anyone know where Margaret is?"

"Maybe she's sick," volunteers Jesus.

"Maybe so. Well, take out your social studies homework," answers Mrs. Wright as she picks up her grade book and walks to the center of the room. "Today we are going backwards and since Margaret is absent, Sam, you will be first. Number one. What holiday is celebrated in Mexico at the end of October and beginning of November?"

"Day of the Dead."

"Very good, Sam. Alberto, number 2. How many days does it last and what are they?" Mrs. Wright walks up and down the rows putting a checkmark by each child's name for finishing the homework assignment.

Alberto answers, "3."

"Alberto, remember that you are supposed to say what the days are."

"Day of the Dead."

"And when is it celebrated?" Alberto hesitates. "Who can help Alberto? Juana?"

Juana answers, "October 31, November 1, and November 2."

"Very good, Juana. Alberto, now you try it."

Alberto repeats, "October 31, November 1, and November 2."

"Very good, Alberto," Mrs. Wright is standing beside Eric's desk. "Eric, where is your homework?"

"I forgot."

"Well, that is a minus and you need to write your name on the board. I'm very happy that the rest of you did your homework. Please pass it to the front. Remember, if I give it back to you, you will have to correct it tonight and turn it in tomorrow. Now, blue birds take out your reading books and come to the reading table. The rest of you take out your spelling books and write your new spelling words five times each and do Exercise 3 on page 63."

The preceding vignette about Mrs. Wright gives us a pretty good idea of what traditional, transmission teaching looks like. Mrs. Wright's teaching practices derive from certain fundamental assumptions that she has about learning, people, and the structure of society. Perhaps the most comprehensive and detailed listing of those assumptions is set forth by Constance Weaver. According to Weaver (1994, p. 393), a traditional, transmission teacher:

1. serves to dispense information, assign tasks, and evaluate work;

2. explains lessons and assignments; determines work to be done;

3. creates a climate wherein competition and comparison are encouraged;

4. treats students as incapable and deficient insofar as they have not measured up to preset objectives and norms;

5. rejects and penalizes errors, thus discouraging risk taking and hypothesis formation (thinking); and

6. fosters dependence on external authority to determine what to do and how to do things, as well as to decide what is and is not correct.

Examining the vignette about Mrs. Wright, we can see how these assumptions might have guided her classroom practices. We can assume that for the social studies assignment, she had dispensed the information about the Day of the Dead, assigned the homework, and was evaluating the homework. It was also evident that at the end of the homework review, she explained the next lesson and made assignments; we might reasonably conclude that she was the one who determined what work was to be done. In her interaction with Alberto, it is evident that she fostered competition and comparison by asking for someone else to intervene when Alberto was wrong. We might assume that she considered Alberto deficient for not measuring up to her predetermined ideas about task mastery. She appeared to see her role as one of judging and penalizing errors as well as that of being the authority on what is correct and not correct (Christensen, 2003).

If Mrs. Wright also works for a traditional transmission school administration then her interactions with her school principal would likely be similar to those between Mrs. Wright and her students. In this type of school, the principal would be the "decision-maker, policy-setter, and task master" (Lambert et al., 1995, p. 5), and the teachers would be expected to adhere to the principal's plans, with input generally limited to how best to carry out what the principal had decided (Darling-Hammond, 1997; Lambert et al., 1995). The hierarchal relationship and transmission interactions between the principal and the teachers, including Mrs. Wright, parallel and reinforce similar relationships and interactions between the teachers and the students.

Teachers like Mrs. Wright have been a part of the American educational system for decades. In fact, Cuban (1993) traces their historical participation back for centuries to include European cultures as well. Other researchers generally begin their discussion of the history of U.S. teaching around the 1890s (see, e.g., Callahan, 1962; Cuban, 1993; Kliebard, 1995; Tyack, 1974). Of perhaps greater importance, traditional educators continue to dominate U.S. schooling. So, what is transmission teaching, what is considered to be evidence of learning in this view of teaching, and why are they the traditional and dominant influence on the practice of schooling in the American educational system?

Transmission Practices: An Overview

Traditional transmission teaching is grounded in behaviorist theories of learning and human behavior. Behaviorists such as B. F. Skinner assert that learning can be simple and predictable if it is broken down into a progression of discrete tasks in which positive and negative consequence result from correct and incorrect results. In other words, Skinner believed that learning "was merely the induction of behavior in specific forms upon specific occasions through conditioning and reinforcement. Learning had occurred when rewarded behaviors were repeated" (Darling-Hammond, 1997, p. 48, citations omitted).

Such ideas about learning and behavior have had a profound impact on teaching and school practices. Transmission schooling emphasizes inducing "obedience, respect, loyalty and cooperation" (Lambert et al., 1995, p. 5). Between students and teachers, this means that the teacher presents to the students a curriculum that is a set of predetermined pieces of information to be mastered in an exact, predetermined sequence, along with pre-engineered activities. Learning activities have single, clear correct answers, progress from the simple to the more difficult, and often involve memorization. It is intended that the accumulation of these discrete skills and pieces of information will lead to complex understandings of the subject studied. Students are not permitted to question the importance of what they are doing.

Most educators are familiar with transmission curricula and teaching methods grounded in behaviorist theory. E. D. Hirsch's (1987) core knowledge curriculum, for example, sets out his expert assessment of the information that every student needs to know to be educated and able to participate fully in U.S. society. Hirsch's information is presented in long lists of concepts and facts. Saxon Math requires all students to do the same set of hundreds of similar calculations per week (see, e.g., Hake & Saxon, 2000). Week by week, a new calculation skill is added. Students who struggle with the assignments do more calculations. In *Success for All* (Slavin, 1996), students memorize lists of spelling and vocabulary words in a predetermined sequence. Madeleine Hunter's (1995) teaching method has the teacher model a skill to the whole class; then, the students practice it. The process is repeated until the vast majority of the students have mastered the skill to a certain level of proficiency.

In these programs, as with many transmission-based programs, the emphasis is on teacher-directed work. The student's role is to work diligently on the assigned tasks. Teachers assess student learning by having students repeat what they have practiced, usually in the form of working to get the single correct answer on a paper and pencil test. Standardized tests are a large-scale version of this type of assessment. The assumption in these transmission-based programs and standardized tests is that the ability to repeat the discrete skills is the necessary prerequisite to more complex thinking and that the accumulation of the discrete skills will naturally develop into complex understandings of the subject studied and the world.

Between teachers and principal, the relationship is similar to the one between students and teachers. The principal delivers the curriculum to the teachers, and the teachers are expected to transmit that curriculum, in the manner discussed above, to the students. Teachers practice their delivery of the curriculum, working on individual teaching skills like classroom management, instruction, and discipline. Numerous books, such as *The First Days of School* (Wong & Wong, 1998), provide specific practices and tools that teachers can apply to their classrooms. Books like this assume that teaching involves predominantly the good application of tried and tested methods.

Principals supervise the teachers to ensure that they are delivering the curriculum in the manner prescribed. Principals do classroom observations with lists of good teaching practices and a dated curriculum and watch to see that the teacher is at the right point in the curriculum and implementing the list of accepted teaching practices. Principals may also supplement their observations by checking student test scores. Generally, teachers are not to stray from the basic practices and curriculum put forth by the principal (and higher authorities), though they may alter the positive and negative reinforcements necessary for attracting and maintaining student attention and participation. Some curricula go so far as to require all classrooms to be on the same page each day (Darling-Hammond, 1997). Teachers having great success with other methods, however that success is measured, may be allowed to continue, but a lack of success generally requires greater adherence to the prescribed curriculum and practices. Likewise, principals are expected to strictly follow the mandates of district, state, and federal administrators.

Overall, transmission schooling is characterized by a part-to-whole approach to teaching, learning, and organization in which each part of the school—teacher, student, principal, parent, district personnel—develops separately and interacts via orders and supervision to deliver a predetermined product in a pre-engineered manner.

Scientific Basis for
Transmission Teaching and Learning

Transmission schooling is steeped in "objectivist" science, which posits that we can see and measure the world directly. Objectivist science understands the world as concrete, static, linear, and existing completely outside human control. These understandings have their roots in Plato's concepts of essentialism and Newton's particulate science.

Gould (1996) explains Plato's essentialism this way: "Material objects on earth are immediate and imperfect representations of higher essences in an ideal world beyond our ken" (p. 320). Taken to a logical extreme, this view holds that what scientists "can see and measure in the world is merely the superficial and imperfect representation of an underlying reality" (p. 269). What scientists measure with statistics and tests "express[es] something more real and fundamental than the data themselves" (p. 269); it reveals the true, underlying reality. Thus, human beings can and should work on our world until it more greatly approximates the ideal.

What is generally described as Newtonian physics postulates that certain aspects of the world—such as size, shape, position, motion, and gravitational force—are "physically irreducible primary properties of matter" (Kuhn, 1996, p. 107). Thus, the world can be broken down into its most basic parts, studied, and understood such that knowing the many parts will lead to an understanding of the whole. This is further support for the idea that statistical analyses of large amounts of data reveal the true, unchanging, underlying physical reality of the world. Separately, but more powerfully together, these theories present the existence of an ideal world that is static, separable, and waiting to be discovered or known by human beings.

Applied to knowledge, learning, and schooling, objectivist science supports the belief that large concepts can be broken down into smaller, discrete facts; that students can learn the large concepts through learning the individual facts; and that schooling can be done through systematic programs that can be universally applied to all students, teachers, and schools.

Transmission schooling also has been bolstered by 19th- and early 20th-century research on intelligence. Lacking current medical and scientific equipment that allows scientists to study the brain directly, these scientists attempted to understand intelligence through indirect methods. The most prolific fields during the 19th and 20th centuries were craniometry, sometimes referred to as craniology, and IQ tests. At the outset, the influence of Newtonian and Platonic beliefs must be emphasized. Both craniometry and IQ tests make some basic assumptions about the brain and intelligence. Both assume intelligence to be an innate, concrete, and measurable "thing" that in many respects exists independent of the individual. According to this view, people can learn more things and become more knowledgeable, but their basic intelligence—the ability to learn and comprehend complexity—is fixed, most likely from birth.

Stephen Jay Gould, in his book *The Mismeasure of Man* (1996), provides a comprehensive history and damning critique of both the craniometry and IQ movements. His critiques are important reading; however, what is important for transmission teaching is the initial popularity and influence of both scientific enterprises.

Craniometry is the attempt to determine intelligence by measuring the size of a skull or brain. Craniometry is steeped in the assumption that intelligence is genetic and fixed; it seeks a biological explanation—namely, that larger must be better, and thus a bigger brain equals greater intelligence. These scientists assumed that the world should have a linear predictability, thus they looked for an individual cause (brain size) for a concrete result (intelligence), one that could point to a direct explanation of a larger concept (the social, political, and economic stratification of U.S. society).

Beginning in the early 1800s, scientists began measuring the skull sizes of persons of predetermined intelligence, looking for correlations between the two. Numerous studies with large and small samples were done with various results. Numerous critiques of the methods and conclusions have been done, but in the mid-1800s, an apparent majority of the leading and influential craniometrists of the time passionately believed that the correlation between brain size and intelligence was so strong that brain size must cause intelligence.

By the early 1900s, however, the science of craniometry had fallen into disuse, most likely from its inherent unreliability. Its underlying assumptions of innate, concrete, and measurable intelligence, along with objectivist science, continued untarnished. Rather than reexamine their assumptions about innate intelligence, the majority of scientists looked for new means for determining intelligence, and the IQ test became the method of choice.

Between 1904 and 1911, Alfred Binet developed a series of performances to create a rough guide for identifying students who might be considered mildly retarded or learning disabled in order that they might learn more through special instruction. Binet specifically cautioned against using his test as a measure of intelligence, especially a measure of some form of innate, unalterable intelligence (Gould, 1996). Despite these warnings, the collective work of prominent American psychologists, most notably H. H. Goddard, L. M. Terman, and R. M. Yerkes, expanded Binet's test (known subsequently as the Stanford-Binet) and used it to promote IQ tests as a scientific measure of intelligence. As Gould (1996) explains, Goddard, Terman, Yerkes, and other American psychologists used

IQ tests to bolster and promote a hereditarian theory of intelligence. Relying on the same assumptions as the craniometrists, they equated IQ scores with a fixed, physical entity called intelligence. IQ tests were given to millions of Americans, and American psychologists like Goddard, Terman, and Yerkes concluded that average differences in scores between groups resulted from heredity, dismissing the influence of manifest and profound variation in the quality of life between these same groups (Gould, 1996).

The use of IQ tests as a measure of innate intelligence or anything beyond Binet's original intent has been strongly critiqued, if not debunked (Gould, 1996), but not before IQ tests had been used to determine the intelligence level of probably tens of millions of people throughout the 20th century. Most Americans have taken an IQ test sometime in their life. The Stanford-Binet IQ test is so ingrained in U.S. thinking that it might be considered a cultural marker or artifact. In fact, one can even take an IQ test over the Internet.

Like Newton's belief that a world composed of discrete bits of matter must be simple, linear, and discoverable, behaviorists believe that learning can be maximized by setting out the right set of facts and tasks to be learned and the right set of influences to get the learners to absorb and master them. Like Plato's essential reality, the right set of facts, tasks, and influences can be discovered by experts through statistical studies, independent of what learners think about the learning experience. And, as in the underlying assumptions of the IQ test, intelligence is considered to be an inheritable, innate, and fixed trait of an individual.

Behaviorist theorists such as B. F. Skinner (1954, 1961), Thorndike (1913), and Pavlov (1960) developed theories of learning by studying the behavior of animals as they were induced to run mazes, get food from behind locked doors, and acquire other new, often unnatural behaviors through rewards and punishments. From his studies on a variety of animals, Thorndike (1913) developed the theory of connectivism, which holds that responses to a situation in both animals and humans are learned from the stimuli received during repeated attempts at overcoming a problem. Pavlov (1960) experimented with dogs by ringing a bell at the same time that he gave them meat powder. After several repetitions, he observed that the dogs salivated when they heard the bell, even without the meat powder. From this work, Pavlov developed the theory of classical conditioning, which states that certain stimuli can automatically trigger unconscious responses. Skinner (1954, 1961) studied the behavior of rats and pigeons in mazes and concluded that in animals and humans, "learning was merely the induction of behavior in specific forms upon specific occasions through conditioning and reinforcement" (Darling-Hammond, 1997, p. 48, citations omitted). From these studies on animals, behaviorists "came to believe that children [and arguably adults] too could learn simple skills only through decontextualized drills under conditions of heavy positive and negative reinforcement" (Darling-Hammond, 1997, p. 48). Later, children were tested and observed doing similar discrete, decontextualized activities, such as running mazes and stacking boxes. Darling-Hammond (1997) describes the teaching practices that grew out of behaviorist learning theories:

> [They] included providing small discrete pieces of information to be mastered in a predetermined sequence, short responses to be learned by rote, immediate reinforcement for correct answers, many opportunities for correct performance (achieved by setting tasks at as simple a level as possible), a gradual progression of individual discrete skills intended to cumulate in a more complex performance, and use of reinforcements (rewards and punishments) for maintaining student attention and participation. (p. 48)

Behaviorist theories of knowledge and learning are built on these theories and beliefs about the world. To behaviorists, knowledge, like Newton's matter, is built of individual, unchangeable, brick-like pieces of information or "factoids." As bricks can be used to make different buildings, factoids can be combined in different ways to create different understandings and knowledge, but the factoid, like the brick, is unchangeable and exists independently of the person who finds it and uses it.

To supporters of transmission schooling, there is no difference between the knowledge of a hard science such as physics and a social science such as education. In physics, researchers can capture and measure something, and that measurement is a universal and concrete look at reality. All that is necessary are the right tools to do the job. Following transmission theory, the study of human beings can follow the same model: If the right tool and conditions can be created, then the true, concrete, and universal reality of any human situation can be measured and understood. With schooling, it is believed that a universal program to maximize learning can be developed and applied.

Sociopolitical Influences on Transmission Schooling

While most education historians and scholars begin their study of U.S. schooling with Horace Mann's common school movement of the middle 1800s (Spring, 1986), the initial school system structure was steeped in thousands of years of experience of hierarchal and, in hindsight, behaviorist social relationships. Plato's *Republic* posits that an ideal society is a segregated hierarchy where the natural strengths of each citizen are identified, the citizens are grouped and educated according to these identified natural strengths, and the citizens are placed in the social hierarchy as worker, artisan, soldier, or ruler. Similarly, the Bible describes societies composed of both slaves and masters, kings and commoners, all of whom are ruled by an all-knowing, all-powerful God who created the world, set it in motion, and rewarded and punished the peoples of the world to the extent that they heeded his commandments (Armstrong, 1993). Centuries of European monarchies were legitimated through the divine right of leadership passed down from God.

Western thought is so steeped in the social and religious thought of Plato and the Bible, and the objectivist science of Newton, Plato, and the behaviorists, that it is hard to find a group activity that does not operate through a hierarchy and some sort of behaviorist relations. This has been true for thousands of years. Most families operate this way, as do the vast majority of businesses. Teams have coaches and players: The coaches give orders to the players during games and practices and reward or punish the players based on their performance, in order to get them to play their best. The representative democracy practiced in the United States, a government of, by, and for the people, has its elected and appointed leader minority and its citizen majority followers. Thus, any discussion of current educational theory and practice must begin with the idea that hierarchal and behaviorist relationships are the societal norm and that anything else is a reaction to these accepted, almost unquestionable practices.

All of these ideas, practices, and social relationships helped fuel the growth of the Industrial Revolution in the United States around the beginning of the 20th century. And, they influenced how the Industrial Revolution was (and is) perceived. Looking for ways to organize large amounts of money, labor, and machinery, business and industrial leaders were enchanted with a method of management developed by Frederick W. Taylor (Callahan, 1962; Kliebard, 1995). The Taylor method, which came to be called *scientific management*, was an elaborate system for increasing efficiency in industries and factories. Taylor advocated that to improve efficiency, a scientific accounting of all the tasks

of the factory must be recorded in detail. Then, the workers must be trained in the performance of those tasks and monitored in their performance. Finally, the management must take over all tasks for which they are better suited than the workers (Callahan, 1962). In 1910, when Taylor's scientific management was taking off in the business/industrial world, Frank Spaulding, a well-known superintendent from Massachusetts, was advocating the application of scientific management to schools, particularly by analyzing the efficiency of teaching courses by comparing the cost of recitations in one course (i.e., French) with the cost of recitations in another course (i.e., Greek) (Callahan, 1962). Around the same time, Franklin Bobbitt, an instructor in educational administration at the University of Chicago, was also calling for the application of scientific management to schools, but more along the lines of establishing standards for courses that were being taught. Bobbitt called for the business/industrial leaders of the era to establish standards for schools as a part of their civic duty (Callahan, 1962). When standards were established, teachers would know immediately whether or not a student had succeeded or failed in meeting the standard. Teachers were to fulfill the role of workers in that they would carry out the plan for getting students to meet the standard. The principals and superintendents were to carry out the role of managers, determining who were efficient teachers and who were not, according to how well the students were meeting the standards.

Having settled on scientific management for classrooms and instruction, the question became how these same principles would organize a school. The preferred answer was the bureaucracy formulated by Max Weber. Weber asserted that the most efficient and effective way to coordinate the work of people in an organization was through a pyramidal hierarchy of authority. In this organizing structure, a small number of trained, expert individuals would set the organization's rules and policies and supervise the work of a large number of less trained or untrained workers (Short & Greer, 2002). Short and Greer (2002) describe the application of this structure to education, which should be instantly familiar to everyone:

> Boards of education, superintendents, and central office administrators became the decision makers for all of the schools included in their districts, just as boards of directors, presidents, and headquarters personnel became the decision makers for entire corporations. Bureaucracies, whether they were in education or in private industry, were efficient and therefore good.
>
> Individual schools within a district were also organized as small bureaucracies. Principals were hired as leaders, with teachers and staff members as subordinates. It was the principal's responsibility to carry out the wishes of the central office and to guide the school staff in working with students. (p. 3)

As scientific management and bureaucratic organizations were exploding onto the business/industrial scene as well as onto the educational arena, there was also an explosion of mass circulation journalism. More than at any previous time in history, the general public had access to newspapers and magazines (Kliebard, 1995). This, no doubt, played a huge role in framing the public discussion about schools within the language of the efficiency or inefficiency of education and the appropriateness of the application of scientific management in schools. Furthermore, the news journalists presented schools and schooling as the transmission of knowledge from the teacher to the student with an expectation that students demonstrate mastery of that knowledge according to preestablished standards. This enchantment with mastery and demonstration of discrete, decontextualized bits of knowledge was likely bolstered through the 1920s with the creation of IQ points and with Thorndike's psychological conception of the mind as a machine with numerous independent

connections having little in common with each other (Kliebard, 1995).

With all of these movements coming together from the early 1900s through the 1920s, the ideology of transmission schooling became a force to be reckoned with. Learning was viewed as the mastery of isolated skills to achieve particular standards as defined by business/industry owners and leaders. Administrators were viewed as "plant" managers, teachers as assembly line workers, and students as the products. Although there were other educational movements, specifically, the progressive movement (discussed later), Cuban (1993) notes that only an estimated one in four teachers adopted teaching practices other than those consistent with transmission teaching.

During the 1930s and early 1940s, transmission schooling continued to prevail, but there appeared to be a softening of the rigidity of scientific management, perhaps due in part to the "partial disenchantment with business leadership which accompanied the great depression" (Callahan, 1962, p. 246). More and more elementary school teachers were incorporating progressive practices into their traditional transmission classrooms, creating something of a hybrid (Cuban, 1993; Kliebard, 1995). This changed in the 1940s with the release of the results of the Eight-Year Study, a study of high school students who were released from college admittance requirements of the era (Kliebard, 1995). Kliebard credits the Eight-Year Study with giving strong impetus to the reinfusion of behaviorism in curriculum thinking (Kliebard, 1995). He argues that this gave rise to behavioral objectives, which stated the precise behaviors students were expected to exhibit on mastery of a particular skill. Student behavioral objectives paralleled Taylor's idea of precisely defining the tasks of a factory or business.

In his book, *Basic Principles of Curriculum and Instruction* (1949), Ralph Tyler moves away from Bobbitt's idea that the business and industrial world should determine the standards and therefore the curriculum in schools. Instead, he advocates that schools look to a variety of places for the curriculum, such as the learners themselves, contemporary life, subject specialists, philosophy of education, and psychology of learning. This approach to standards and curriculum is certainly more complex than that of Bobbitt, but it still retains the ideology of traditional transmission teaching—that is, that teachers are transmitters of knowledge and students are receptors who must demonstrate through precise behaviors their receipt and understanding of that knowledge. Behavioral objectives and the traditional transmission ideology of teaching remained constant throughout the 1950s and early 1960s and, except for a brief period between 1965 and 1975, they have remained constant to the present day.

The period between 1965 and 1975 saw the advent of the informal classroom or open education. Cuban (1993) argues that this idea "never took deep hold organizationally among the ranks of educators" (p. 207) but that it did bring to the forefront an alternative ideology, and hybrids once again developed. By the mid-1970s, there was a strong public push for the "back to the basics" movement.

> There was a renewed passion for orderliness, stability, and academic skills captured in symbols that plucked nostalgic strings within the hearts of teachers, parents, taxpayers: rows of desks facing the blackboard, the teacher in front of the room, required homework, detentions, dress codes, spelling bees, letter grades on report cards, tougher promotion standards, and schoolwide discipline rules. (Cuban, 1993, p. 207)

In other words, the ideas and beliefs that formed the underpinnings of scientific management—school standards, behavioral objectives, teacher as transmitter, student as receptor—had once again found its way back into the heart of society. In fact, so powerful was this worldview that some of the education reforms of the 1980s did less to change school practices than to make traditional transmission teaching a more socially acceptable practice (Cuban, 1993). The new progressive education initiatives were little more than slightly altered versions of scientific management. As Giroux and McLaren pointed out in 1986:

> The new educational discourse has influenced a number of policy recommendations, such as competency-based testing for teachers, a lockstep sequencing of materials, mastery learning techniques, systematized evaluation schemes, standardized curricula and the implementation of mandated "basics" (Stedman and Smith, 1983). The consequences are evident not only in the substantively narrow view of the purposes of education, but also in the definitions of teaching, learning and literacy that are championed by the *new* management-oriented policy makers. (p. 219, emphasis added)

As we begin the new millennium, transmission schooling remains the traditional method for organizing schools and teaching students and the method that persists as dominant. No longer compared with factories and industries as they were at the beginning of the 20th century, teachers and schools are compared now with businesses and corporations. Berliner (1990) argues that teachers have less in common with nurturers and information disseminators and more in common with executives. Although Berliner raises the status of teachers by comparing them to executives, he reinforces the traditional transmission understanding of schooling. Under Berliner's metaphor, teachers are now the management, students are the workers, and the knowledge of the students is the product. Everyone has been raised a level, but the transmission model is the same.

Yet, throughout this time period, there were other educational movements, specifically, progressive transaction teaching and learning, which offered an alternative to the tradition of transmission schooling that characterized so much of education. The views of child-centered educators and social reconstructionist educators (Shannon, 1990) that characterizes much of this progressive education movement have coexisted right along with the tradition of transmission education. Yet, the tension that existed between Dewey and Taylor 50 years ago continues to exist as the progressive transaction view of education continues to challenge the status quo.

TRANSACTION
TEACHING AND LEARNING

"Smiles are the same, and hearts are just the same, wherever they are, wherever you are, wherever we are all over the world."

"Read it again!" Mrs. Dyer smiles at Tae-Un, "You like that story, don't you?" Tae-Un nods. Mrs. Dyer continues, "What do you like the best?"

Tae-Un smiles, "I like that page where the mom and the dad and kid are pushing the wheelbarrow. I did that one time in Korea."

Marifer adds, "I like that page where dad and the baby were crying. One time my mom and I cried when my dad had to go to work in Mexico."

Mrs. Dyer picks up her clipboard with her morning checklist and says to Tae-Un and Marifer, "I really like *Whoever You Are*, too. Mem Fox is one of my favorite authors. I tell you what, when we go to centers, why don't the two of you read that book with me again? OK? Right now, I'm going to find out what everyone else will be doing." Looking around the circle, she finds Kelsey. "Kelsey, what are you going to do this morning?"

"I'm gonna work on my Cinco de Mayo report."

"At the writing center?"

"Yeah."

"OK. Jonathon?"

"I'm going to the writing center, too."

"Are you still thinking about a new story?"

"No. I think I'm going to draw pictures for the one my Dad told me about when his great-great-granddaddy was a slave."

"OK. Jayne?"

"I'm going to the reading center."

"Umm. Let's see. Tae-Un, you still want to read with me?" Tae-Un nods.

"OK, then. Gilberto, what are you going to do?"

"Can I work with Kelsey on my Cinco de Mayo report, too?"

"Well, that is up to Kelsey. Kelsey, would that be alright, if you and Gilberto worked together?"

"Sure."

Mrs. Dyer looks around the circle and asks, "Now, Jennifer, what are you going to do this morning?"

This vignette is an interesting contrast to Mrs. Wright's class. Mrs. Dyer's approach to teaching differs greatly from the traditional approach of regimented transmission teaching exemplified by Mrs. Wright. Mrs. Dyer also approaches teaching culturally and linguistically diverse children from a different perspective than Mrs. Wright. Mrs. Dyer's perspective is much more consistent with the stance of progressive transaction teaching, a stance that teachers have been taking for more than 100 years but that has often been ignored for much of that time (Goodman, 1989; Shannon, 1990). Mrs. Dyer's teaching practices derive from fundamental assumptions that are different from those of Mrs. Wright. Again, Constance Weaver (1994) provides a comprehensive and detailed listing of those assumptions. Table 20.1 compares some of the actions of a progressive transaction teacher with those of the traditional transmission teacher already discussed (Weaver, 1994, p. 393).

Thinking about the vignette, we can see that Mrs. Dyer demonstrates she is a literate person who enjoys good literature. She obviously believes that learning is stimulated through discussing and collaborating as she held

Table 20.1   Comparison of Transaction and Transmission Teachers

Progressive Transaction Teacher	Traditional Transmission Teacher
Serves as a master craftsperson, mentor, role model, demonstrating what it is to be a literate person and a lifelong learner	Serves to dispense information, assign tasks, and evaluate work
Stimulates learning by demonstrating, inviting, discussing, affirming, facilitating, collaborating	Explains lessons and assignments; determines work to be done
Creates a supportive community of learners wherein collaboration and assistance are encouraged	Creates a climate wherein competition and comparison are encouraged
Treats students as capable and developing, honoring unique patterns of development and offering invitations and challenges to growth	Treats students as incapable and deficient insofar as they have not measured up to preset objectives and norms
Responds positively to successive approximations, thus encouraging risk taking and hypothesis formation	Rejects and penalizes errors, thus discouraging risk taking and hypothesis formation (thinking)
Shares responsibility for curricular decision making with students, thus empowering them to take responsibility for their own learning	Fosters dependence on external authority to determine what to do and how to do things, as well as to decide what is and is not correct

SOURCE: Adapted from Weaver (1994).

discussions with Tae-Un and Marifer and encourages Kelsey and Gilberto to work together. The process of asking each child what he or she plans on doing illustrates that she shares responsibility for curricular decision making with the students. It does not suggest, however, that Mrs. Dyer abdicates her responsibility as the more competent adult to guide the students' learning. Nor does it suggest that Mrs. Dyer ignores her own responsibilities to the school district, state standards, or upcoming testing requirements. Rather, Mrs. Dyer uses all this information in conjunction with the needs and interests that she elicits from the students to plan and implement her lessons. Thus, students choose activities from a large and changing selection gathered by Mrs. Dyer according to all the requirements above and the interests and needs of her students. Several resources offer practical advice and assistance to teachers who must consider the reality of standardized testing and yet want to include student choice and autonomy in their teaching

practices (see, e.g., Calkins, Montgomery, Santman, & Falk, 1998).

Through her interactions with the students, we get the sense that Mrs. Dyer views them as capable and developing. Thus, a centerpiece of her teaching is assisting the students in learning how to take charge of their own learning. Mrs. Dyer's classroom differs radically from Mrs. Wright's classroom, and only a small percentage of teachers approach teaching from this perspective.

Like Mrs. Wright, Mrs. Dyer probably works for a school administration that shares some of the fundamental assumptions that she does. In this type of school, the principal would expect all members of the school community to act at various points in time as master craftspeople, mentors, role models, and empathetic partners as part of a process of lifelong learning and shared leadership (Lambert et al., 1995). In this school model, leadership is "manifest within the relationships in a community . . . rather than in a set of behaviors performed by an individual leader" (Lambert et al., 1995, pp. 32–33). Teachers, in partnership with school administrators, frequently examine the present school structure and the underlying assumptions about learning and schooling with the goal that the school community will actively construct the best program for their community in light of district, state, and federal requirements. The transactional relationships inherent in the negotiated interactions between the principal and the teachers, including Mrs. Dyer, are expected to support and reinforce similar relationships and interactions between the teachers and the students.

Transactional Practices: An Overview

Transactional teaching and leadership practices are grounded in constructivist learning theory. The work of Piaget and Vygotsky, among others, asserts that learning takes place as the individual internalizes and reshapes information and experiences into new understandings that are enhanced by social interaction. Constructivists believe that learning cannot be mandated or prevented, but it can be invited and enhanced. Brooks and Brooks (1993) offer these examples:

> After gazing at a block of wood for the first three months of his life, an infant who touches the block with his newly acquired grasping skill transforms his cognitive structures, and thus affects his understandings of the block. Virtually all infants do this. On the other hand, many high school students read *Hamlet,* but not all of them transform their prior notions of power, relations, or greed. Deep understanding occurs when the presence of new information prompts the emergence or enhancement of cognitive structures that enable us to rethink our prior ideas. (p. 15)

Viewing learning in this way, constructivists look for school activities that are meaningful, social, and contextual and involve large, overarching concepts. From these activities, constructivists encourage students to create something that not only includes but goes beyond the learning activities themselves.

Adopting a constructivist theory of learning will have a profound impact on one's teaching and the student's learning and school experience. School leadership and learning become manifest in the relationships and spaces within a community, rather than in actions of a person of higher authority directing something toward another of lower status (Lambert et al., 1995). Under this theory, leadership and learning opportunities are seen to exist throughout the school community, and all members are encouraged, expected, and trained to do acts of teaching, learning, and leadership. Ideally, boundaries are diminished, both between groups and between the concepts of leadership, teaching, and learning. Acts of leadership and teaching deemphasize someone being a *sage on the stage* and encourage them to be a *guide on the side*. Interactions, relationships, and acts of leadership and teaching are expected to adhere to professional nonnegotiables that promote participatory democracy, evidence-based practices, meaning construction, and enhanced learning about the world and one's self (Lambert et al., 1995).

Teachers, the principal, students, and other members of the community develop the curriculum together. Outside resources and experts are one source, but they do not trump community interests. Part of the learning involves determining what to learn and how to learn it, so teachers and school administrators learn together and with the community, including the students, in developing the curriculum and in using the curriculum to pursue their interests and questions.

The school community works both within and across interested groups. Opportunities are created, for example, for parents to work as a parent group and for them to participate as members of integrated policy committees, curriculum committees, and classrooms.

Decisions are made by consensus as often as possible, and the entire school community learns and practices how to do group work both as individuals and in the course of their group work.

Assessments across the school community emphasize growth and understanding and emphasize observations and "performances" of work that extend beyond the learning activities themselves. For students, this might include the public presentation of the results of a science investigation or literary work developed by the student after a semester of doing writers' workshop or doing more teacher-directed science experiments. For teachers, this might be facilitating a school committee on curriculum after taking university courses or attending workshops. Self-reflection and multiple opportunities for improved performance are key components of the assessment process.

Scientific Basis for Transaction Schooling

During the early 20th century, scientific understandings of the world began to change, and these affected theories of learning. In the hard sciences, for example, Einstein's theories of relativity set forth the idea that in certain extreme situations, how one experienced the physical world depended on one's relation to what was being studied. Furthermore, the dawn of the nuclear age, embodied in Einstein's famous $E = mc^2$, demonstrated that energy and matter are related and that there may be no fundamental, concrete elements of matter. Relativity, quantum physics, chaos theory, and dissipative structures, to name just a few concepts, began to replace Newton's view that the world was static, linear, and composed of finite, irreducible bits of matter with a perspective that sees the contextual and relational nature of events, bounded disorder as an element of order, and the overlap between matter and energy (Wheatley, 1994).

Similarly, social scientists began to question the idea that the world and knowledge always exist independently of human beings. Although Immanuel Kant in the 18th century claimed that human perceptions of the world are influenced and limited by the innate structures of the mind (Noddings, 1998), objectivist science held sway with the majority of learning theorists through much of the 20th century. Not until Piaget's work in the 1950s and 1960s on the structure of the human mind did large numbers of learning theorists and educators begin to change the way they viewed teaching, learning, and the practice of schooling.

Piaget studied how children of various ages work through different abstract, logical puzzles. Piaget observed that children are able to solve certain types of problems only at certain ages and only after advancing through earlier, less complex problem stages. From his studies, Piaget articulated a theory of knowing or knowledge that is based on the notion of cognitive structures. Kohlberg (1981) advanced a similar theory of the mind, based on stages in moral development.

To Piaget, the human mind is an ever-changing set of cognitive structures that help us make sense of the world. Human beings accumulate knowledge through the interaction of their experiences with their existing cognitive structures or mental systems. Each new experience changes a person in one of two basic ways. When the experience coincides well with the existing cognitive structures, it is assimilated into them in a manner that reinforces these structures. When the experience is at odds with the existing cognitive structure, a dissonance occurs, and the cognitive structure is adjusted to accommodate the new experience. Most often, however, an experience is complex and multilayered, so a combination of the two responses occurs: The new experience is partially assimilated into the existing cognitive structures while also partially altering the cognitive structures.

To Piaget, human beings need to create a state of equilibrium between their cognitive structures and their worldly experiences. It is this need for equilibrium—always temporary—that drives the creation of knowledge. As a person gains experience in the world, experiences dissonance, and makes sense of it by adjusting his or her cognitive structures to achieve equilibrium, his or her cognitive structures become more complex and sophisticated. Brooks and Brooks (1993) offer this example:

> An infant, yet unable to hold or manipulate the cube, defines it by the sides visible to her at that point in time. When the child's musculature and mental structures allow her to touch it, she is presented with new information that must be integrated into her thinking. An important cognitive structure has changed; the initial "nongrasping" structure has been refashioned into a new "grasping" one. This process is called accommodation. The child's newly created structure allows assimilation of the experience to occur within her mind. (p. 26)

Such development of one's cognitive structures occurs at more abstract levels as well. Continuing with this example of the wooden cube, Brooks and Brooks (1993) describe how new abilities and cognitive structures can build on each other, leading this infant to the ability to comprehend rudimentary concepts like "the cube is hard" and then possibly later in life to more complex structures and understanding like "a cube has length, width, and height, and that these three factors combine to determine the cube's volume" (p. 26).

In this Piagetian theory of knowledge, knowledge no longer exists completely outside of human experience; rather, the world and human beings mutually construct each other. Thus, human beings experience, perceive, and interpret the world based on their cognitive structures, and the world that human beings experience, perceive, and interpret is shaped by their cognitive structures. No bright line or one-way arrow could be drawn between one's

knowledge and one's world. This is a profound and difficult concept that has changed and is changing the way many view the human mind in all its aspects, including knowledge, intelligence, and learning.

Piaget's work was groundbreaking, but it appears to have its shortcomings. Other social scientists have questioned Piaget's focus on dissonance resolution and his apparent neglect of the social aspects of learning. For example, the work of Bruner, Chomsky, and Lakoff and Johnson has demonstrated the importance of prior experience, language, and metaphor in the way human beings form cognitive structures. Vygotsky, working separately but at the same time as Piaget, demonstrated the importance of social interactions to the construction of knowledge.

Vygotsky appears to have an especially strong influence on teaching, learning, and school practices. He articulated the idea that people construct the concept of intelligence, as well as meanings and knowledge, through interactions with others and that these understandings accumulate over time, both within the individual and within society. According to Vygotsky (1978), people learn by first doing with others what they cannot do as well by themselves. In this space, known as the "zone of proximal development," people negotiate meaning and co-construct knowledge and the meaning of intelligence. Over time and multiple social interactions, people borrow from the abilities and perceptions of the other people they interact with, reworking it into their own understandings based on their own prior experiences, or, in Piagetian language, their own cognitive structures. Often, people are eventually able to do individually what they could once do only within the group. When this interaction involves someone more capable than another, they both gain, but for the less capable person, great gains in knowledge can occur. Thus, in Vygotsky's view, knowledge, meaning, and intelligence are neither individual nor concrete; rather, each is constructed through a "cumulative experience derived and informed by an individual's and a group's cultural and historical experiences" (Lambert et al., 1995, p. 21).

Research on the metaphorical nature of how people perceive and construct understandings of the world appears to support both Piaget's and Vygotsky's emphasis on the constructed nature of the human mind, how people think, and how they perceive the world. Lakoff and Johnson (1980/2003), two of the leading researchers on the place of metaphor in human thought or metaphor theory, use their own empirical studies on language in combination with "at least seven other types of evidence derived from various empirical methods" (p. 248) to contend that

> Metaphor is not just a matter of language, that is, mere words. We . . . argue that, on the contrary, human thought processes are largely metaphorical. This is what we mean when we say that the human conceptual system is metaphorically structured and defined. (1980/2003, p. 6)

Thus, Lakoff and Johnson later explain, research in metaphor theory points to the idea that our minds process information through metaphors constructed from both our physical and cultural experiences in the world:

> You don't have a choice as to whether to think metaphorically. Because metaphorical maps are part of our brains, we will think and speak metaphorically whether we want to or not. Since the mechanism of metaphor is largely unconscious, we will think and speak metaphorically, whether we know it or not. Further, since our brains are embodied, our metaphors will reflect our commonplace experiences in the world. Inevitably, many primary metaphors are universal because everybody has basically the same kinds of bodies and brains and lives in basically the same kinds of environments, so far as the features relevant to metaphor are concerned.
>   The complex metaphors that are composed of primary metaphors and that make use of culturally based conceptual frames are another matter. Because they make use

of cultural information, they may differ significantly from culture to culture. (1980/2003, p. 257)

Recent neuroscience research on mirror neurons appears to further support the constructed nature of human thought, specifically Vygotsky's emphasis on the social aspects of learning. Studies of the brains of monkeys have revealed that certain clusters of neurons, dubbed "mirror neurons," fire when the monkey does a specific action with its hand, say picking up an object and putting it in its mouth, and that specific neurons correspond to each specific action (Stamenov & Gallese, 2002). These same neurons also fire when the monkey witnesses another monkey or the experimenter perform the same action. Furthermore, the mirror neurons do not fire when a mechanical apparatus performs the action. Thus, it appears that the mirror neurons fire when a monkey performs an action itself and when another living being performs the action. Related studies on human beings strongly suggest that human beings also possess mirror neurons (Ramachandran, 1995).

These findings offer strong support for the social-constructivist theories of learning. As Ramachandran (1995) explains,

> With knowledge of these neurons, you have the basis for understanding a host of very enigmatic aspects of the human mind: "mind reading" empathy, imitation learning, and even the evolution of language. Anytime you watch someone else doing something (or even starting to do something), the corresponding mirror neuron might fire in your brain, thereby allowing you to "read" and understand another's intentions, and thus to develop a sophisticated "theory of other minds." (para. 10)

Thus, the effectiveness of student group work, other cooperative learning activities, and teacher modeling and student practice in developing new skills and language may be due, in part, to mirror neurons.

Taken together, transaction schooling is based on scientific understandings of the world as changing and changeable and of the human mind, knowledge, intelligence, and meaning as constructed and contextual. Given the recent developments in science that appear to support transaction schooling, the question arises, why hasn't it replaced transmission schooling as the dominant model?

Sociopolitical Influences on Transaction Schooling

Unfortunately, the answer to this question is also a complex and difficult one, with no clear answer. One answer is that transmission schooling can help students to learn material when learning is equated with performing well on multiple-choice, standardized tests. Perhaps a better answer is that rarely have the goals of progressive transaction teaching been consistent with the goals of society, business/ industry leaders, politicians, segments of the education and scientific communities, and the public at large (Brooks & Brooks, 1993; Lakoff & Johnson, 1980/2003). In other words, the worldview of progressive transaction schooling has not been consistent with those of either powerful segments of society or the general public. In addition, the assumptions of traditional transmission teaching were bolstered by industrial and scientific developments in the following other fields: (1) scientific management, (2) Thorndike's psychological conception of the mind as a machine conducting numerous isolated activities, (3) the development of IQ points, and (4) the results of the Eight-Year Study, which gave birth to behavioral objectives. Taking reading education as an example, Shannon (1990) points out that while scientific management was on the rise, "three groups tangentially related to literacy lessons became increasingly powerful at the expense of students and teachers" (p. 14). Shannon identifies these groups as (1) reading experts who supported objectivist science

measurements, tests, and methods; (2) basal publishers (who now profit from a $400 million-a-year market); and (3) state departments of education, which became more involved with literacy lessons. With these forces coming together, it is little wonder that traditional transmission schooling has prevailed, but other movements were occurring simultaneously.

Around the turn of the century when the business/industrial world and the public at large were becoming enamored with scientific management, a group of education scholars advocated for a different type of education. G. Stanley Hall and other developmentalists advocated using the nature of the child as a key element in curriculum planning. Hall viewed the tendency of schools to treat students as passive receptacles as contrary to the students' natural predisposition. Instead, he argued for the individualization of instruction based on intellectual ability and gender (Kliebard, 1995). John Dewey staunchly criticized Hall's notion of separate instruction for different ability levels and gender and instead argued that the education of children must center around their interests and their ties to the larger community and must be oriented toward democratic practices as well as other larger social goals (Cuban, 1993; Kliebard, 1995). Shannon (1990) points out that, for Dewey, the larger social goals included reducing the differences among social classes. Dewey argued that the economic and political power of the few made it impossible for the many either to grow as individuals or to have an impact on the social order (Dewey & Tufts, 1908, cited in Shannon, 1990). It was during this time that Dewey opened the Laboratory School, in which the "curriculum centered upon the work that people did rather than upon separate subjects, upon reading and writing learned through activities rather than isolated tasks, and upon group work guided rather than directed by teachers" (Cuban, 1993, p. 41). For Dewey, the underpinnings of progressive transaction education were grounded in the notion that mental processes were social processes. The views of knowledge and learning underlying Dewey's progressive school were quite different from the views of Hall and the developmentalists and from scientific management and traditional transmission teaching.

Constructivist and Deweyian attempts to create more inclusive and democratic schools must be viewed in light of the "mythology around the Founding Fathers" (Zinn, 1997, p. 77). To Zinn, the economic interests of America's founding fathers conflicted with their rhetoric calling for a truly universal democratic society. Alexander Hamilton, for example, recognized that a truly open and fair democracy would likely undermine the privilege of the wealthy colonists. He suggested that the new U.S. government be headed by a president and Senate chosen for life. Considering the views of Hamilton and other founding fathers, historian Zinn (1997) concludes,

> When economic interest is seen behind the political clauses of the Constitution, then the document becomes not simply the work of wise men trying to establish a decent and orderly society, but the work of certain groups trying to maintain their privileges, while giving just enough rights and liberties to enough of the people to ensure popular support. (p. 74)

Boggs (2001) puts it this way:

> Despite its official ideology, liberal capitalism has always stood opposed to genuine forms of democratic governance insofar as such forms present a serious threat to privileged interests; democratization has occurred largely through the energies of popular movements and insurgencies. (p. 19)

It is likely, therefore, that genuine democracy and thus Deweyian and transactional education practices directly conflict with the U.S. capitalist system and the unstated social views of large segments of U.S. society. Classroom teachers who initiate practices based on the concepts of transactional teaching and learning should prepare themselves for negative reactions that range from mere curiosity to misunderstanding, disbelief, anger, and possibly official reprimands (Rothschild, 2003). Changes in school practices as profound as the shift from transmission to transaction teaching will require grassroots organization, collegial support, and educational outreach to all aspects of the school community (Fleischer, 2000). It could require starting one's own school (Glover, 1997). Transaction schooling, then, should be viewed as a radical social movement arrayed against powerful forces that do not want it to succeed.

Although transmission schooling has remained the dominant practice, transaction schooling was not without its influence. From the early 1900s to 1940s, Dewey advocated progressive transaction teaching. For Dewey (1938), progressive education involved placing the child within a community of students, parents, and teachers, all of whom had responsibility for negotiating the curriculum. Dewey did not endorse other methods of the day simply because they were labeled progressive. For example, while Kilpatrick and others were advocating the project method and other child-centered programs, Dewey argued that a child is not isolated and alone but rather lives within a social context that should be considered in educating the child (Dewey, 1930, cited in Shannon, 1990).

As stated earlier, it was also during the 1930s and 1940s that the rigidity of traditional transmission teaching began to loosen due in part to the Great Depression. Suddenly the problems of the United States seemed more social than individual. During this time, the progressive movement moved to the forefront with sharp attacks on both traditional transmission education advocates with their ties to the business and factory community and on the child-centered advocates who ignored the social, economic, and political world of the child (Shannon, 1990). Consequently, more teachers began incorporating progressive transaction teaching practices. Throughout this era, eclecticism in curriculum design and hybrid classrooms were evident, and many of the "alternatives to standard teaching methods were available, widely known, used by a minority of teachers, and considered respectable by professional norms" (Cuban, 1993, p. 145). With the birth of behavioral objectives, as well as the predominance of university reading experts and the near-constant promotion of basal readers, traditional transmission teaching once again regained its prominence as the ideology of choice. Educational protests became an individual matter, but organizational progressive activities during the 1940s and 1950s took a decidedly political turn. Brookwood Labor College and Citizenship Schools undertook the arduous task of eliminating illiteracy in the working and poor classes (Shannon, 1990). These schools had as a focus educating people so that they could successfully read and negotiate labor contracts and, particularly among African Americans in the South, so that they could register to vote. It was not until the mid-1960s that progressive transaction teaching once again gained mainstream attention.

The period between 1965 and 1975 saw the resurgence of Dewey's ideas and progressive transaction schooling, often referred to as open education or informal schooling. Although progressive transaction schooling never took hold to the degree it had in the 1930s and 1940s, it still had a profound impact on the open education reforms of the era. Public schools were criticized for perpetuating the status quo rather than challenging it. In response, free schools were established in an attempt to replace the oppression of public schools. Most public school critics, however, called for a wider choice in what was to be learned, and they used the British primary

schools as their model (Shannon, 1990). Around that same time, psycholinguistics provided empirical evidence for what progressive transaction educators had been claiming. Major centers for curriculum development were established, and experts on human development and learning were included in curriculum projects (Goodlad, 1984). An example of this type of collaboration between experts can be seen in the 1960s reading process work of Smith and Goodman, which built on the language development work of Brown and Bruner as well as the linguistic questions raised by Chomsky (Goodman, 1992). Smith and Goodman (1971, cited in Shannon, 1990) criticized traditional reading instruction based on the principles of scientific management, claiming that an understanding of miscue analysis and the reading process could better help with students' reading proficiency. The primary focus of the reform efforts of this era was "coming to terms with self, acquiring knowledge of the stages of child development, and demonstrating an empathetic relationship with students more as equals than in an authoritarian role" (Grow-Maienza, 1996, p. 511), not unlike the ideological underpinnings of progressive transaction teaching endorsed by Dewey.

By the mid-1970s, schools began a more conservative "back to the basics" movement (see, e.g., the teaching model of Hunter, 1995). Yet, Dewey and progressive education were not entirely forgotten. Some researchers (see, e.g., Halliday, 1978; Heath, 1983) were particularly concerned that the psycholinguistic view of language development ignored the sociocultural aspects of language. These researchers worked to demonstrate the intentionality of language use and the cultural appropriateness of language use (Shannon, 1990). Their work on the sociocultural aspects of language developments was bolstered by the work of Vygotsky (1986), who echoes Dewey's claim that children learn not in isolation but rather in a social context.

Furthermore, according to Vygotsky, learning occurs through interactions with more capable others who support learners as they grow and develop. This is not unlike Rosenblatt's (1978) conceptualization of reading. In the mid-to-late 1970s the term *transaction* began to be used consistently to represent the underlying understandings of progressive teaching. This term comes from Rosenblatt's (1978) reader response theory, which asserts that reading is a transaction between what the reader brings to the text and what the text actually says. In other words, there is no one right way to read a text because each individual reader brings a different set of experiences, interests, and understandings to act on the text. The teacher cannot be the disseminator of knowledge and the student the receptacle because the knowledge is contained not in the teacher or the text but in the transaction between the student and the text. If we extend that beyond the reading of a text to include learning in general, then knowledge is gained through the multiple types of transactions, which occur through the experience of living. Keeping the progressive transaction movement alive in the 1970s and early 1980s was the work on writing by Donald Graves (1983) and others. These researchers of writing development supported the growing understanding that language development and learning were social processes. Thus, in the mid-1980s, the open education movement that had begun in the 1960s and ended in the mid-1970s saw

> a resurgence of interest in neo-progressivism: the integration of reading, writing, and thinking into 'whole language' instruction; the middle school movement that called for team teaching, core curriculum, and cultivating student interests in academic tasks; small group instruction; active learning by students through use of math and science materials; the teaching of practical and critical reasoning; and stronger links between what is learned in school and what occurs in the immediate community. (Cuban, 1993, p. 235)

Since that resurgence and throughout the 1990s, groups of teachers have met together to discuss teaching and learning in general and the teaching and learning of language in particular. These whole-language teacher support groups have grown to well over 100 and are organized under the whole-language umbrella (Goodman, 1989). Furthermore, researchers in the area of sociopsycholinguistics and whole-language theory as well as many others have continued to build on the ideology of progressive transaction teaching (see, e.g., Atwell, 1987; Calkins, 1986; Cambourne, 1988; Edelsky, 1991; Goodman, 1986, 1989; Graves, 1983; Rosenblatt, 1978; Weaver, 1994). During this time of renewed interest in progressive transaction education, critical theorists (see, e.g., Apple, 1990; Aronowitz & Giroux, 1993; Freire & Macedo, 1987; Giroux & McLaren, 1986) were systematically attacking the still prevalent ideology of traditional transmission education. In their attacks, they called for teachers and students to be released from the rigidity of reading programs organized according to principles of scientific management. Rather they advocated that literacy be a way for teachers and students "to understand themselves, to make connections between their lives and the operations of the social structure and to use literacy as a form of social action" (Shannon, 1990, pp. 156–157).

CONCLUSION

The beginning of the 21st century leaves us in pretty much the same place as the beginning of the 20th century. The tradition of transmission schooling still dominates practice. Progressive transaction teaching is persistent but very much on the periphery. As Dewey (1938) said more than 50 years ago,

> When education is based upon experience and educative experience is seen to be a social process, the situation changes radically. The teacher loses the position of external boss or

dictator but takes on that of leader of group activities. (p. 59)

It appears that change of the magnitude that Dewey envisioned and transaction educators push to implement is more than U.S. society is ready to accept. Instead, education reforms, to the extent that they move away from traditional practices, use the language of transaction schooling without replacing the underlying assumptions of objectivist science with those of relativistic science.

The reasons for this disconnect between progressive language (or intention) and underlying assumptions appear to vary. Sometimes, this appears to be a conscious attempt to manipulate public policy (Smith, 2004), while at other times, it appears to be a misunderstanding of how school reform works (House, 1998). At the core in both cases, there appears to be the inability to shake the thousands of years of experience with thinking and living according to an objectivist view of the world. Truly accepting relativistic science and, with it, the construction of knowledge and transaction schooling, would constitute "a profound challenge to many of the traditional ways of thinking about what it means to be human" (Lakoff & Johnson, 1980/2003, p. 273). Such a shift in schooling practice, viewed from a transaction perspective, will require a concomitant sea change in society. That is a monumental task.

REFERENCES

Apple, M. (1990). *Ideology and curriculum.* New York: Routledge.

Armstrong, K. (1993). *A history of God.* New York: Ballantine Books.

Aronowitz, S., & Giroux, H. (1993). *Education still under siege.* Westport, CT: Bergin & Garvey.

Atwell, N. (1987). *In the middle: Writing, reading, and learning with adolescents.* Portsmouth, NH: Boynton/Cook-Heinenmann.

Berliner, D. (1990). If the metaphor fits, why not wear it? *Theory into Practice, 29*(2), 85–93.

Boggs, C. (2001). *The end of politics: Corporate power and the decline of the public sphere.* New York: Guilford Press.

Brooks, J., & Brooks, M. (1993). *The case for constructivist classrooms.* Alexandria, VA: Association for Supervision and Curriculum Development.

Calkins, L. (1986). *The art of teaching writing.* Portsmouth, NH: Heinemann.

Calkins, L., Montgomery, K., Santman, D., & Falk, B. (1998). *A teacher's guide to standardized reading tests: Knowledge is power.* Portsmouth, NH: Heinemann.

Callahan, R. E. (1962). *Education and the cult of efficiency.* Chicago: University of Chicago Press.

Cambourne, B. (1988). *The whole story: Natural learning and the acquisition of literacy in the classroom.* Auckland, NZ: Scholastic.

Christensen, L. (2003). The politics of correction: How we can nurture students in their writing and help them learn the language of power. *Rethinking Schools, 18*(1), 20–24.

Cuban, L. (1993). *How teachers taught: Constancy and change in American classrooms 1880–1990.* New York & London: Teachers College Press.

Darling-Hammond, L. (1997). *The right to learn: A blueprint for creating schools that work.* San Francisco: Jossey-Bass.

Dewey, J. (1938). *Experience and education.* New York: Simon & Schuster.

Edelsky, C. (1991). *With literacy and justice for all.* London: Falmer Press.

Fleischer, C. (2000). *Teachers organizing for change: Making literacy learning everybody's business.* Urbana, IL: National Council of Teachers of English.

Freire, P., & Macedo, D. (1987). *Literacy: Reading the word and the world.* Boston: Bergin & Garvey.

Giroux, H. A., & McLaren, P. (1986). Teacher education and the politics of engagement: The case for democratic schooling. *Harvard Educational Review, 56*(3), 213–238.

Glover, M. K. (1997). *Making school by hand: Developing a meaning-centered curriculum from everyday life.* Urbana, IL: National Council of Teachers of English.

Goodlad, J. (1984). *A place called school.* New York: McGraw-Hill.

Goodman, K. S. (1986). *What's whole in whole language.* Richmond Hill, ON: Scholastic. (Distributed in the U.S. by Heinemann)

Goodman, Y. M. (1989, November). Roots of the whole-language movement. *The Elementary School Journal, 90,* 113–127.

Goodman, Y. M. (1992). A question about the past. In O. Cochrane (Ed.), *Questions and answers about whole language* (pp. 2–6). Katonah, NY: Richard C. Owen.

Gould, S. J. (1996). *The mismeasure of man.* New York: W. W. Norton.

Graves, D. H. (1983). *Writing: Teachers and children at work.* Portsmouth, NH: Heinemann.

Grow-Maienza, J. (1996). Philosophical and structural perspectives in teacher education. In F. B. Murray (Ed.), *The teacher educator's handbook: Building a knowledge base for the preparation of teachers* (pp. 506–525). San Francisco: Jossey-Bass.

Hake, S., & Saxon, J. (2000). *Math 87: An incremental approach.* Norman, OK: Saxon.

Halliday, M. A. K. (1978). *Language as social semiotic: The social interpretation of language and meaning.* Baltimore: University Park Press.

Heath, S. B. (1983). *Ways with words.* Cambridge, UK: Cambridge University Press.

Hirsch, E. D. (1987). *Cultural literacy.* New York: Vintage Books.

House, E. (1998). *Schools for sale: Why free market policies won't improve schools, and what will.* New York: Teachers College Press.

Hunter, M. (1995). *Improved instruction.* Thousand Oaks, CA: Corwin.

Kliebard, H. M. (1995). *The struggle for the American curriculum: 1893–1958* (2nd ed.). New York: Routledge.

Kohlberg, L. (1981). *The philosophy of moral development.* San Francisco: Harper & Row.

Kuhn, T. (1996). *The structure of scientific revolutions* (3rd ed.). Chicago: University of Chicago Press.

Lakoff, G., & Johnson, M. (2003). *Metaphors we live by.* Chicago: University of Chicago Press. (Original work published 1980)

Lambert, L., Walker, D., Zimmerman, D., Cooper, J., Lambert, M. D., Gardner, M., & Szabo, M. (1995). *The constructivist leader.* New York: Teachers College Press.

Noddings, N. (1998). *Philosophy of education.* Boulder, CO: Westview Press.

Pavlov, I. (1960). *Conditioned reflexes: An investigation of the physiological activity of the cerebral cortex.* (G. V. Anrep, Trans., Ed.). New York: Dover.

Ramachandran, V. S. (1995). *Mirror neurons and imitation learning as the driving force behind "the great leap forward" in human evolution.* Inaugural "Decade of the Brain" lecture at the Silver Jubilee Meeting of the Society for Neuroscience. Retrieved September 4, 2003, from http://www. edge.org/3rd_culture/ramachandran/ramachandran_index.html

Rosenblatt, L. (1978). *The reader, the text, the poem: The transactional theory of literary work.* Carbondale: Southern Illinois University Press.

Rothschild, M. (2003). *McCarthyism watch: High school teachers punished in New Mexico.* Retrieved April 28, 2003, from http://www.progressive.org/mcwatch03/mc042803.html

Shannon, P. (1990). *The struggle to continue: Progressive reading instruction in the United States.* Portsmouth, NH: Heinemann.

Short, P., & Greer, J. (2002). *Leadership in empowered schools: Themes from innovative efforts* (2nd ed.). Upper Saddle River, NJ: Merrill-Prentice Hall.

Skinner, B. F. (1954). The science of learning and the art of teaching. *Harvard Educational Review, 24,* 86–97.

Skinner, B. F. (1961). *Cumulative record.* Englewood Cliffs, NJ: Appleton-Century-Crofts.

Slavin, R. (1996). *Every child, every school: Success for all.* Thousand Oaks, CA: Corwin.

Smith, M. L. (2004). *Political spectacle and the fate of American schools.* New York: Routledge Falmer.

Spring, J. (1986). *The American school 1642–1985: Various historic interpretations of foundations and development of American education.* New York: Longman.

Stamenov, M., & Gallese, V. (2002). *Mirror neurons and the evolution of brain and language.* Philadelphia: John Benjamins.

Thorndike, E. L. (1913). *Educational psychology: The psychology of learning.* New York: Teachers College Press.

Tyack, D. B. (1974). *The one best system: A history of urban education.* Cambridge, MA: Harvard University Press.

Tyler, R. W. (1949). *Basic principles of curriculum and instruction.* Chicago: University of Chicago Press.

Vygotsky, L. S. (1978). *Mind in society: The development of higher psychological processes.* Cambridge: MIT Press.

Vygotsky, L. S. (1986). *Thought and language* (A. Kozulin, Trans.). Cambridge, MA: Harvard University Press.

Weaver, C. (1994). *Reading process and practice: From socio-psycholinguistics to whole language.* Portsmouth, NH: Heinemann.

Wheatley, M. (1994). *Leadership and the new science: Learning about organization from an orderly universe.* San Francisco: Berrett-Koehler.

Wong, H., & Wong, R. (1998). *The first days of school.* Mountain View, CA: Harry Wong.

Zinn, H. (1997). *A people's history of the United States* (Abridged teaching edition). New York: The New Press.

21

New Approaches for School Design

JEFFERY A. LACKNEY
University of Wisconsin–Madison

INTRODUCTION AND OVERVIEW

The school facility is a neglected and under-utilized resource in educational planning and administration. Every activity of teaching and learning takes place in a physical setting, and as such, the school facility plays a vitally supportive role in contributing to achieving educational goals. Effective planning, design, and management of school facilities can be a powerful tool for educational leaders in ensuring that the physical settings within which learning takes place are not only adequate but also motivational for both students and teachers. In many cases, stakeholders in key decision-making roles are less interested in how school design can support the changing demands of delivering 21st-century education and more interested in how to deliver school buildings in the shortest time frame and at the lowest possible price for the sake of political expediency. As important as budgeting and scheduling are in educational administration, shortsighted thinking can severely compromise the effectiveness of the school facility in meeting the critical needs of learners now and into the future. Educational leaders and decision makers need to recognize that school facilities are, in effect, a policy statement on the relative importance a community places on education and students. School buildings are cultural artifacts that reflect the values of the community long after the original stakeholders who envisioned, planned, designed, and built them are gone. Indeed, school facilities are more than artifacts; they can influence the behavior, attitudes, and performance of those who work and learn in them. Educational leaders need to be aware of how school facilities affect learning and teaching and how school designs can be created to take full advantage of this knowledge.

The objectives of this chapter are to situate school design as a critical and integral component in educational leadership and to introduce educational leaders to the vital role of school design in supporting teaching and learning. Once the need for educational leadership in school design is established, a brief outline of the relationship between school design and educational reform is presented to place this relationship in historical context. Five emerging and interconnected issues in school design will then be discussed in more depth: (a) school designs for smaller learning communities, (b) collaborative learner-centered environments, (c) learning extensions into the community, (d) technology and school design, and (e) high-performance school design. Finally, the process through which school facilities are delivered and the role of educational leaders in that process are outlined.

THE NEED FOR EDUCATIONAL LEADERSHIP IN SCHOOL DESIGN

A number of interrelated educational trends point to a sense of urgency with respect to the quality of school environments. National and international reports on the current state of the physical infrastructure of schools make it clear that the deteriorating quality of the physical environment is affecting the quality of educational delivery (General Accounting Office, 1995, 2000; Lewis et al., 2000; Organization for Economic Co-operation and Development, 1989). Given that the average age of school buildings in the United States stands at 42 years old (Lewis et al., 2000) and that existing structures do not always contain what are now considered the essential components for a good learning environment, it is critically important to understand the relationship between existing building condition and student performance. There is arguably an ample body of evidence that school environments influence a number of student behaviors and attitudes (Duke, 1998; Earthman, 2002; Gump, 1987; Lackney, 1994; McGuffy, 1982; Schneider, 2002; Weinstein, 1979) that influence educational outcomes (Earthman, 2002; Moore & Lackney, 1993; Weinstein, 1979). Although there is some skepticism about the relationship between building condition and educational outcomes (Frazier; 1993), recent studies (Berner, 1993; Cash, 1993; Cervantes,

1999; Earthman, Cash, & Van Berkum, 1996; Gravelle, 1998; Guy, 2001; Lanham, 1999; Lewis, 2001; Maxwell, 1999; O'Neill, 2000) have found significant correlations between building condition and academic achievement. The emergence of a variety of systemic schoolwide educational reforms in the last quarter of the 20th century (American Institutes of Research, 1999) has placed additional demands on aging school buildings originally designed for an Industrial Age disciplinary mass institution (Huse, 1995). Student population and ethnic diversity continue to increase, creating ever more overcrowded, multicultural, and multilingual schools across the country. The changing nature of family and community life demands that schools continue to open their doors wider to serve the ever growing and diverse educational needs of the community. Finally, information technologies and advances in telecommunication systems have placed a further burden on the educational suitability of existing school facilities. Leadership is required to advance innovations in school design to meet the challenges of these changing paradigms in education.

A variety of reasons can be cited for the lack of attention educational leaders pay to the school environment. Budgetary decisions favor expenditures on educational staffing and programs at the expense of sustaining adequate long-term preventive maintenance programs for facilities. Design professionals and facility managers, who are not directly engaged in educational delivery, focus exclusively on building condition, rarely emphasizing the need or purpose in systematically assessing the educational adequacy or suitability of school facilities. Educational administrators and researchers suggest that the school be "safe, orderly, and conducive to learning" (Lezotte, 1991), referring more explicitly to the social and organizational context of learning than to the quality of the physical setting. Classroom teachers consistently report that they have little control over the quality of their workplace (Johnson, 1990) and take what they have as given, no matter how poorly the environment supports teaching and learning. Arguably, state legislatures, regulatory agencies, and product manufacturers have more of an influence on the school design than educators (Hawkins & Overbaugh, 1988). Educators have not been trained to take advantage of the physical environment as an instructional strategy (Taylor, 1993). There are few practical tools educators can use to integrate the physical settings of the school into their practice, with most of these tools limited to the assessment of school facilities as an adjunct to new school design (Hawkins & Lilley, 1998; Sanoff, 2001) and occasionally classroom management (Weinstein, 1996). Finally, it may be simply that the physical environment is taken for granted by most people, remaining out of awareness as long as it is minimally adequate (Shein, 1997).

SCHOOL DESIGN AND EDUCATIONAL REFORM

School design has continued to change in response to emergent educational reforms through the history of North America. The form, aesthetics, symbolism, and layout of school buildings have been influenced by a complex combination of community culture, educational philosophy, curriculum, and instruction. The general acceptance of innovations in school design usually occurs several years following the innovation, and not without some social and political resistance. Many colonialists did not see the need for a separate schoolhouse; if the objective of education was to learn to read the Bible, or to be apprenticed in the family trade, they reasoned, a child could be adequately educated at home. The progressive movement in education began in the late 19th century but did not significantly influence school design until the middle of the 20th century with the advent of the open education movement

spawning a whole generation of innovation in school design. Today, most social resistance to distance education and Web-based learning has subsided as the youth raised in an era of information technologies are assuming leadership roles in education and society.

Table 21.1 provides a historical framework for understanding broad changes in school design as a response to both sociocultural context and educational philosophy during the agricultural, industrial, and information/knowledge societies (Lackney, 1999). Three useful metaphors for describing changes in school design concepts over the last several hundred years in North America are, namely, the Village, the Factory, and the Learning Community. These metaphors continue to shape the way educators and school designers unconsciously think about the creation of learning environments. Progressive educators often refer to schools critically and pejoratively as factories when advocating for educational reform to influence a shift in thinking toward new pedagogical models.

School Designs for the Village

The one-room schoolhouse best characterizes the typical educational facility of the colonial period, a design response that served the basic educational and social needs of small rural communities for more than 200 years. This single room, with one teacher presiding over instruction, included students of many ages by necessity, due to the relatively small size of the community. Learning was by rote but self-paced depending on the developmental level of the student. Schoolhouses in urban areas were variations on the theme of the country schoolhouse, often containing two, four, or six self-contained rooms, each with separate entrances. The school housed activities such as town meetings, voting, fundraisers, and celebrations that integrated people into their community and provided

Table 21.1 Timeline of Changing School Design as a Response to Changing Societal and Educational Patterns (adapted from Lackney, 1998)

Overarching Patterns	Agricultural Society (The Village)	Industrial Society (The Factory)	Information/Knowledge Society (The Learning Community)
Sociocultural context	Homogeneity Decentralized Egalitarian/autocratic	Institutionalization Centralization Standardization Bureaucratic Mechanization Specialization	Pluralism/diversity Globalization Networks Customization Telecommunication

Educational philosophy response to context	Natural multiage
	  groupings
	Direct instruction
		Common school
		  movement
		Progressive movement
		Carnegie units
		Comprehensive
		  high school
			Middle school philosophy
			Inclusion
			Standards movement
			Interdisciplinary instruction/
			  integrated curriculum
			Project-based,
			  problem-based learning
			Collaborative learning

School design response to educational approaches	Home schooling
	Church as learning
	  environment
	One-room schoolhouse
		Common school
		Factory model/
		  egg-crate schools
			Open schools
			Magnet schools
			Alternative schools
			House plans
			Self-directed learning
			  environments
			Small schools
			Schools-within-a-school
			Distance learning
			Virtual schools
			Home schooling

SOURCE: Adapted from Lackney (1999).

an identity that, to this day, is linked with the metaphorically ideal school (Gulliford, 1996).

Although the one-room schoolhouse was the archetypal school of the agricultural period, as early as the mid-17th century, several Latin grammar schools and universities were established in the Northeast. Most education for the masses, however, took place in the home with the guidance of parents and special tutors or in the shops of craftsmen. In the 18th century, common schools for the working class developed as well as church schools for the poor.

The process of school consolidation in response to rapid urbanization created much resistance in rural communities, where the symbol of the one-room schoolhouse was the focus of rural life and of community spirit. As late as 1913, one half of the schoolchildren in the United States were enrolled in the country's 212,000 one-room schools (Gulliford, 1996). Although such facilities account for less than 1% of all public school buildings in operation today, the one-room country school continues to be a powerful cultural symbol for Americans, as reflected in the current interest in building smaller learning communities.

School Designs for the Factory

As a result of the rise of industrial capitalism after the Civil War, rapid urbanization in the mid-19th century created numerous social problems in cities. From the perspective of the industrialists, the central problem was that of instilling in children of all social classes the values and character traits—such as complying with rules of the workplace, working hard, and obeying authority—that were necessary for employment in industrial settings (DeYoung, 1989). The common school movement took hold in America's cities between 1840 and 1880, with the help of educational reformers such as Horace Mann and Henry Barnard, who argued that public schooling was essential if both the individual and the nation were to fulfill their economic possibilities (DeYoung, 1989). Standardization and centralization in educational programs closely followed the principles of the industrial society. This school was a highly formalized, hierarchical structure designed to sort students who were or were not eligible for promotion to a higher level in the system. An overt curriculum of reading, writing, arithmetic, and history was overlaid on a covert curriculum of punctuality, obedience, rote, and repetitive work.

With the publication in 1838 of his book titled *School Architecture, Or Contributions to the Improvement of School-Houses in the United States,* Henry Barnard is credited with raising the environmental and space standards of school buildings serving the common school movement. Barnard linked architecture with pedagogy by emphasizing school *architecture* over school *building,* which suggested that architects are ultimately concerned with the cultural, spiritual, and humane value of their work, whereas builders are primarily concerned with the physical structure, reasonable cost, and the service of function (McClintock & McClintock, 1970). As the common school movement progressed, school design changed as well. Multiple one-room urban schoolhouse designs were replaced with what was to become known as the factory model for school building design: a repetitive and uniform double-loaded corridor of identical size

self-contained classrooms leading to a centralized administrative area. Urban schools could be found on tight sites of less than a quarter acre with no landscaping. Students were segregated by age into a graded organization. The average classroom was between 600 and 750 square feet, holding a class of up to 50 students, with desks often bolted to floors in row and column arrangements. Toward the end of the 19th century, school buildings began to support other functional considerations. Hallways were widened to accommodate increased traffic flows, auditoriums were built to support whole-school events, administrative offices were included, and cloakrooms were added to classroom layouts. Expanded offerings in art and science begin to dictate the development of specialty classrooms.

As unprecedented numbers of immigrants from Europe arrived in the United States during the first part of the 20th century, hundreds of new schools were needed. During the 1920s, for instance, more than 200 public schools were constructed in New York City alone. This large-scale school building program with its standardized building plans paralleled efforts to further standardize the school curriculum and continuing efforts to "Americanize" the diverse student population (Rieselbach, 1992). Increasingly during this period, sites were set aside for larger school facilities. Buildings designed to specialize in the housing of junior high school and high school educational programs were constructed, and many more types of auxiliary spaces were added. Auditoriums, laboratories, art studios, gymnasiums for physical education, and home arts spaces were routinely added to the educational building program.

At the turn of the 20th century, secondary education had become part of common schooling, giving rise to the development of the comprehensive high school (Herbst, 1996). Simultaneously, in large cities, advocates of vocational education introduced public technical and industrial high schools and established

Figure 21.1   Students preparing a French gourmet lunch in their classroom in John Dewey's Laboratory School, Chicago, 1986–1904

SOURCE: Reprinted by permission of the publisher from Tanner, L. N., *Dewey's Laboratory School: Lessons for Today.* New York: Teachers College Press, © 1997 by Teachers College, Columbia University. All rights reserved.

new forms of school–work relationships through cooperation with industry in areas such as textiles and machine trades (Herbst, 1996). The junior high school, invented at this time as well, had the purpose of easing the transition from elementary school settings to the departmental high schools and simultaneously solved the problem of widespread overcrowding (Rieselbach, 1992).

During the late 19th century, a progressive movement with an emphasis on child-centered education emerged, for example, Friedrich Froebel's development of the kindergarten in Germany and Maria Montessori's educational programs in Italy. In the United States, this movement was expressed by John Dewey as a general critique of the public educational system, the roots of which can be traced back to the early 19th century and the work of Johann Heinrich Pestalozzi, one of the founders of modern pedagogy.

John Dewey established his Laboratory School at the University of Chicago (1896–1904) for testing and verifying new educational theories and principles (Tanner, 1997). Dewey developed the idea of the schoolhouse as a true home in which the activities of social and community life were expressed in the curriculum. The child's interest in the home was used as a vehicle for social activities and learning at school. The physical setting of the Laboratory School was a means through which the developmental curriculum was supported. Children were encouraged to work in their schoolyard garden, cooperate in building and furnishing a clubhouse, make articles in a shop for use in connection with their other work, plan and prepare a French gourmet lunch in their classroom, examine the history of industrialization by working out the process of making cloth, and study the nature of community life with the help of model houses (Figure 21.1).

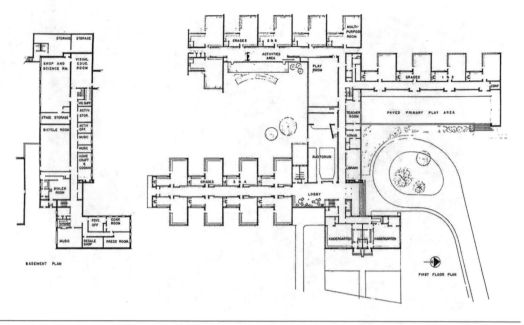

Figure 21.2 "Finger plan" self-contained classrooms of Crow Island School, Winnetka, Illinois, provide a variety of indoor and outdoor learning spaces

SOURCE: Courtesy of Perkins & Will, architects.

Although there were isolated examples in Chicago and New York of schools designed around the ideals of progressive education, it was not until after World War II that a multitude of societal changes, such as the baby boom, created an unprecedented need for school construction (Marks, 2000). A new era of school construction allowed for further experimentation in school design. Along with innovations in educational delivery, school design soon responded with more child-scaled, flexible, and open environmental settings (Brubaker, 1998). The school building that defined modern school design in the United States was Crow Island School in Winnetka, Illinois, which opened in 1940, standing in stark contrast to the traditional, multistory, factory model buildings common at the turn of the 20th century. The most significant contribution of the Crow Island School was the continuous progress curriculum and experientially based learning, and the building was designed to support these innovations (Brubaker, 1998; Meek, 1995). Designed by Eliel Saarinen and

Larry Perkins, the school emphasized child-scaled environments throughout the one-story brick building, with classrooms designed to support a variety of learning activities and provide a sense of belonging. The classroom was designed in an L-shape with an entrance foyer, storage, and an adjacent bathroom; a separate kitchen project area; and a main classroom space with exterior glass walls on two sides of the classroom as well as an exterior door to a semi-enclosed outdoor classroom (Figure 21.2). Crow Island served as a model for many schools after World War II. Although this period marked the beginning of a new age of opportunity to explore innovative school design, many school district leaders missed the trend as they struggled to cope with rapidly increasing enrollments. Inexpensively constructed schools had poorly insulated roofs and walls and poor-quality building systems (Brubaker, 1998). Like the building boom earlier in the century, the 1950s saw a proliferation of standardized plans not optimized for learning.

The 1960s witnessed one of the most dramatic educational reform movements in U.S. history with experimentation involving open education, community education, middle schools, and alternative and magnet schools. In 1958, the Educational Facilities Laboratories (EFL) was created, funded by the Ford Foundation, for the purpose of providing technical assistance to schools and colleges with their physical campuses, stimulating research, and disseminating information related to site selection, planning, design, construction, modernization, equipping, and financing of educational facilities (Marks, 2000). EFL contributed to the institutionalization of progressive thought in school design by advocating community participation in planning of new schools and community schools, providing middle school designs, advancing the development of building technologies, improving school furniture design, and providing options for converting older school buildings.

Arguably one of EFL's most influential innovations was the development of the open-plan school design, a concept that influenced the design of thousands of schools from the late 1950s through the early 1970s. Schools were planned with large, open, flexible spaces adaptable to team teaching and the small-group or individualized instruction that characterized open education. Open education, it was argued, provided more educational opportunities for children, offered freedom and autonomy for self-directed study, required less guidance by the teacher, and helped foster self-responsibility. Almost immediately, however, teachers complained of noise and visual distractions in these open-plan schools. Hundreds of educational research studies were performed to determine the validity of open-plan schools, with inconclusive and controversial results (see Weinstein, 1979, for a review). Permanent wall partitions went up, and traditional instructional methods were reasserted. Reasons given for the failure of the open-plan

school usually centered on concerns related to noise and visual distraction. However, there are more systemic reasons for the failure of the open-plan concept. The ambiguity of the definition of *openness* was never resolved with many educators (Marshall, 1981; Rothenberg, 1989). There was, arguably, a lack of adequate funding for professional training in open education in open-school designs (Ehrenkrantz, 1999). Even if teachers desired to change the program, they had neither the time nor the space to plan together. The full potential of open-plan school design was not realized because open plans were developed totally apart from their users, the educators and students (Bingler & Quinn, 2003). Many of the lessons of open-plan schools have not been lost on school leaders and designers.

School Designs for the Learning Community

The middle school concept, first conceived of in the 1960s, was a philosophy that challenged the junior high school model and advocated for the developmental needs of young adolescents; it sought a balance of the child-centered, supportive instruction of elementary school with the subject-oriented teacher specialization of high school (George & Alexander, 1993). Middle school teachers formed a small interdisciplinary team that served a family of between 100 and 120 students. Gaining popularity in the 1980s and 1990s, the middle school concept spawned a whole new generation of school design that attempted to group students in "families" contained in "pods" or "houses." Pod plans were first developed in the 1960s, whereas the house plan has a more recent history, being most fully developed in the late 1980s. House plans, it is argued, foster a sense of community for academics while providing larger common spaces such as libraries, media centers, administrative offices, gymnasiums, and areas for special programs such as art, music, computer instruction, and language arts. The house may

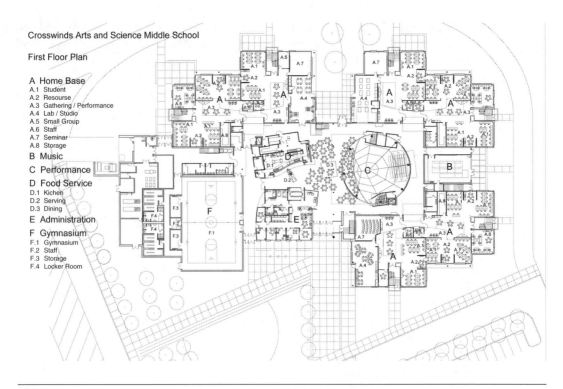

Figure 21.3 Floor plan of Crosswinds Arts and Science Middle School in Woodbury, Minnesota, illustrating a house plan with six home bases for 100 learners each

SOURCE: Courtesy of Cunningham Group Architecture.

include anywhere from four to eight self-contained classrooms oriented toward a centralized resource center and supported with a specialized classroom, teacher offices, small seminar rooms, and other support spaces. Currently, the house plan concept is being applied to secondary environments as well, as a response to advances in self-directed learning, interdisciplinary instruction, and the desire to form smaller learning communities in very large high schools. The residential metaphor of the house has been extended to include the "neighborhoods" and "main streets" in high school design, extending the notion of a community of learners.

Crosswinds Arts and Sciences Middle School in Woodbury, Minnesota (Figure 21.3), provides a recent illustration of school design that interprets the middle school model.

Crosswinds was planned to operate as a year-round school for 600 students. A key conclusion from collaborative facility planning with the community was that the learning process would integrate various individual disciplines through hands-on, project-based learning. Crosswinds includes several learning houses, each designed for 100 students of mixed ages and grade levels and containing a lab and discovery space where students work alone or in small groups exploring subjects. In place of traditional self-contained classrooms, the school offers "home bases" that consist of individual student workstations, resource areas where small groups can meet, and a larger gathering and performance area. Home bases open to a larger central area, the heart of the school, which contains an all-school performance area and social hall.

EMERGING ISSUES
IN SCHOOL DESIGN

School designs continue to respond to changes in education (Brubaker, 1998; Graves, 1993; Lackney, 2003; Tanner & Lackney, 2005). Some innovations in school design, such as self-directed learning environments, are just now finding acceptance in education. Other innovations, such as wireless computing, are completely unprecedented and in many ways driving change. The characteristics of a new 21st-century school facility are starting to emerge as a school that intentionally supports academic achievement (Schneider, 2002); is personalized to the needs of the learner (Washor, 2002); is designed for multiple intelligences of learners (Boer & Karanovich, 2000; Lackney, 1998); authentically engages community (Bingler, Quinn, & Sullivan, 2003; Sanoff, 2002); is flexible to adapt to multiple pedagogies (Wolff, 2001); is sustainable and high performing (Collaborative for High Performance Schools, 2002); acts as a three-dimensional textbook (Taylor, 1993); supports outdoor learning (Stine, 1997); is technology-rich on-site and at a distance (Kleiner & Farris, 2002); and is continuously monitored through evaluation (Sanoff, 2001). Several of the emerging and interconnected themes in school design that are covered here include the advent of school designs for smaller learning communities, collaborative learner-centered environments, the role of community partnerships and joint-use agreements in school planning, the impact of technology on school design, and a trend toward high-performance schools.

Designs for Smaller Learning Communities

The United States is experiencing an intense interest and rapid growth in the creation of smaller school environments, either by building smaller school buildings (Lawrence et al., 2002; Levine, 2002; Nathan & Febey, 2001; Washor, 2002) or by restructuring larger school buildings into a number of schools-within-a-school (SWAS) (Cook, 2000; Davidson, 2001; Duke & Trautvetter, 2001; Raywid, 1996). According to the North Central Regional Educational Laboratory, about three quarters of U.S. high school students attend schools of more than 1,000 students, and more than half of these high school students attend schools with a population of 1,500 of more. The costs associated with new construction and reconfiguring older school buildings runs in the billions of dollars; still the benefits of smaller schools cannot be ignored.

The literature on the effects of school size on a variety of school outcomes is well documented (Cotton, 1996; Garbarino, 1980). Participation in school activities, extracurricular activities, student satisfaction, number of classes taken, and community employment have all been found to be greater in small schools than in large schools (Barker & Gump, 1964; Fowler & Walberg, 1991; Irmsher, 1997; Lashway, 1998–1999; Raywid, 1999). Smaller size may have a positive influence on achievement, school climate, and student connectedness (Oxley, 1994), thereby reducing disciplinary problems; incidents of vandalism, truancy, drug use; and drop-out rates (Fowler & Walberg, 1991). Defining what constitutes the optimal organizational size and structure for SWAS is still an open question (Lee, Ready, & Johnson, 2001). School size research most often refers to the size of the student body, with *large* being defined as anywhere from 1,000 to 2,000 or more students in secondary schools, and *small* being anywhere from 100 to 600 students in elementary and even secondary settings (Lawrence et al., 2002; Nathan & Febey, 2001).

The school design that emerged out of the middle school movement, the house plan (e.g., grouping a small family of 100 to 120 students and their teachers into a grouping of classrooms), serves as the core model for what is now called the neighborhood plan for the learning community. The goal is the same: to break down the scale of the school organization into manageable groups of learners and thus to create a natural sense of belonging, connectedness, and caring. An important characteristic of SWAS is that each school has a distinct administrative entity (Lee et al., 2001). Several models that are emerging include vertical houses, ninth-grade houses, and special curriculum houses (Dewees, 1999; McAndrews & Anderson, 2002). The vertical house plan assigns a few hundred Grades 9 through 12 students and their teachers to a single house. The ninth-grade house plan provides an environment for ninth graders to ease the transition into high school. The special curriculum house plan organizes students into houses based on special interests or needs.

At the main entrance of the school building, a community forum space may be provided where the large groups can come together in formal meetings. This space is often shared with the surrounding community. "Streets" (corridors) not only facilitate circulation but also offer places to meet and socialize. Smaller school buildings, whether by design or due to site limitations, may be designed to eliminate corridors altogether, creating more intimate settings off of classrooms that open on to central gathering spaces. Finally, streets lead to neighborhoods: a smaller group of classroom spaces surrounding a variety of learning and support spaces. Students often spend a large percentage of their academic life in their neighborhoods. Many neighborhood designs are intended to be staffed by an interdisciplinary team of teachers, including a decentralized science teacher and lab. Students often will leave the neighborhood to attend classes in specialized spaces or off-site locations.

Noble High School in North Berwick, Maine, a member of the Coalition of Essential Schools (CES), is representative of new school design for smaller learning communities within a large school building with a capacity for 1,500 learners. This example of school design also serves as an exemplar of other trends to be discussed in following sections of this chapter, including collaborative learner-centered environments and learning extensions into the community. In keeping with CES principles, Noble espouses democratic processes, a collaborative environment, and standards-based curricula. In distinction from the traditional departmental structure of the comprehensive high school, the district uses a project-based, interdisciplinary approach, where teacher teams consisting of a math, science, English, and social studies teacher work within communities of 100 learners. The new facility was designed to decrease anonymity through the SWAS concept, to reflect the concept of teacher as coach and student as worker, to support a collaboratively designed curriculum that is interdisciplinary and project-based, to serve as a community center where community functions are integrated with education functions, and to be flexible in design, material, and function. Fifteen identical learning community environments were designed at Noble, each one including a multipurpose room that functions as a living room for both students and teachers (Figure 21.4). Student lockers adjacent to the multipurpose room reinforce the concept of community. Each community has a variety of room sizes and functions and contains state-of-the art technology to facilitate the project-based curriculum. Each teacher has a direct phone line with voice mail in his or her room, facilitating contact with students outside of class and other staff as well as parents and other community members. More specialized video production labs are located in other areas of the facility, where they are shared by other learning communities. A large classroom can become two when a movable wall is in place. A science lab has movable tables in the middle of the room, with gas and water lines on the sides. A large project room with a sink and a large storage room facilitate student work. Teachers share an office that includes a window into the multipurpose room.

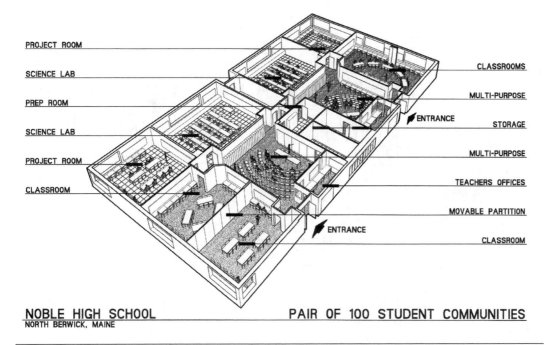

PROJECT ROOM

SCIENCE LAB

PREP ROOM

SCIENCE LAB

PROJECT ROOM

CLASSROOM

CLASSROOMS

MULTI-PURPOSE

ENTRANCE

STORAGE

MULTI-PURPOSE

TEACHERS OFFICES

MOVABLE PARTITION

CLASSROOM

ENTRANCE

NOBLE HIGH SCHOOL
NORTH BERWICK, MAINE   **PAIR OF 100 STUDENT COMMUNITIES**

Figure 21.4   Student learning communities in Noble High School

SOURCE: Courtesy of Harriman Associates & Engineers.

Noble High School's entrance lobby, which has a welcoming appearance and places to sit, has been designed to act as a town square (Figure 21.5). Corridors serve classrooms on one side only with window walls on the opposite side, providing opportunities for benches along windows—all features that avoid the institutional feel of many traditional high schools. The cafeteria contains a small cafe that provides another area available for socializing. In keeping with the school's goal of engendering community, the building includes a community health care clinic, a day care facility, a vocational center located adjacent to the adult education center, a 50-seat public restaurant that provides training for culinary arts students, a 1,000-seat performing arts center, and a community volunteer area within the library for early childhood reading. Finally, when available, athletic fields, gymnasiums, and a fitness-training center are all shared with the community.

Collaborative Learner-Centered Environments

Another educational trend eliciting a response from school designers is classroom environments that emphasize active, self-directed, project-based, collaborative, or cooperative learning strategies over traditional, lecture-oriented, discipline-focused, teacher-centered instruction (Costa & Liebmann, 1997; Johnson & Johnson, 1999). Collaborative learning is a pedagogy that prepares learners for the changing learning expectations in the real world through an active learning process that teaches critical thinking, problem solving, teamwork, negotiation skills, consensus building, technology, and responsibility for one's

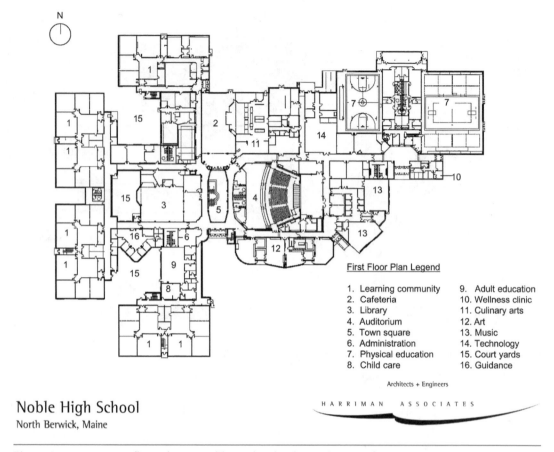

N

First Floor Plan Legend

1. Learning community   9. Adult education
2. Cafeteria   10. Wellness clinic
3. Library   11. Culinary arts
4. Auditorium   12. Art
5. Town square   13. Music
6. Administration   14. Technology
7. Physical education   15. Court yards
8. Child care   16. Guidance

Architects + Engineers

HARRIMAN   ASSOCIATES

Noble High School
North Berwick, Maine

Figure 21.5   First-floor plan in Noble High School, North Berwick, Maine

SOURCE: Courtesy of Harriman Associates & Engineers.

own learning (Wolff, 2001). Self-directed learning, or the process of learning on one's own, has long been seen as a natural and primary mode for adult learning, in which personal growth is the primary goal (Caffarella & O'Donnell, 1987). Grow (1991) outlines the stages of the student-teacher relationship leading to self-directed learning: from dependence on the authority of the teacher, to interest with the teacher as a motivator, to involvement with teacher as facilitator, to fully self-directed with teacher as a consultant or delegator. Public school educators who espouse self-directed learning tend to use teaching tools such as individualized or personalized learning plans, contracts, and advisories (Levine, 2002).

School planners and architects have developed a variety of school designs that support personalized, self-directed learning. Wolff (2001) conducted a series of case analyses of several internationally known innovative school designs, from which she identified a comprehensive list of 32 design features that optimize collaborative, project-based learning experiences. Summarizing Wolff, noteworthy design features that are thought to support learning in groups include: variable size spaces that are easy to change to support several learning activities within the same space, to encourage integration of courses and programs; individual workspaces that can be personalized, providing a sense of ownership and

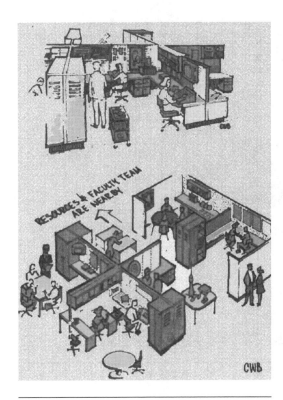

Figure 21.6 Space for individual learning, Perkins and Will, architects

SOURCE: Brubaker, C. W. *Planning and Designing Schools.* © 1998 by McGraw-Hill Professional. Reprinted with permission of the McGraw-Hill Companies.

teaching responsibility for one's own learning; and faculty team spaces with adjacent material preparation areas and meeting space, which encourages team teaching, mentoring of faculty, and collaboration. Functional spaces for collaborative learning activities might include: presentation spaces for individuals and teams to demonstrate their learning and share knowledge acquired with the larger learning community; the continued need for classroom spaces for direct instruction of concepts, content, and skills; process galleries, studios that allow for the display of ongoing projects to showcase concept development; project space that provides a variety of work surfaces, storage areas, and access to technology to

encourage critical thinking, problem solving, and teamwork; home bases for gathering of learners and faculty to seek assistance and resources or hold group discussions; informal, nonclassroom learning spaces such as study spaces, lounges, and outdoor spaces to provide areas for socializing and serendipitous meetings that can foster creative thought and solutions to problems; and a collaboration incubator, idea generation space to support creativity, teamwork, and prototyping of concepts, which can also encourage the involvement of local employers in the development of projects.

The logical extension of designing for self-directed learning may be illustrated in one of the latest high school design trends: the individual student workstation, an assignable desk with pin-up display space and lockable storage. Individual workspace, space students can directly territorialize and take jurisdiction over throughout the year, provides the most tangible demonstration of an authentic learner-centered environment. The individual workstation was an innovation first formally introduced by architect C. William Brubaker of Perkins and Will in Chicago as early as 1959, in what he initially called "space for individual learning" (Figure 21.6); later "Q-space," referring to a student's place for an individual quest; and finally, the "turf concept," in which five students share an office-size home base for individual study, projects, computer work, small-group sessions, and meeting with faculty members (Brubaker, 1998, pp. 35–36). The 1990s saw a number of individual workstation school designs. An individual student workstation may be equipped with a desktop computer, as in the case of Minnesota New Country School in Henderson (Figure 21.7) and High Tech High School in San Diego, California (Figure 21.8, p. 525), or the workstation may be flexible and movable, as is the case with the School for Environmental Studies in Apple Valley, Minnesota.

Figure 21.7   Advisory area workstations at the Minnesota New Country School in Henderson, Minnesota

SOURCE: Courtesy of Minnesota New Country School.

Learning Extensions Into the Community

The belief in the sanctity of the neighborhood community school has been deeply engrained in the American culture for more than 200 years (Allen, 1977). The school is perceived as the center of community life and culture; recall the country school. In stark contrast to this image, many if not most school facilities in operation today were designed to serve as stand-alone, age-appropriate instructional facilities where community access is limited rather than encouraged (Bingler et al., 2003). Movements to bring back the neighborhood community school as well as take learning directly into the community are transforming school design (New Schools, Better Neighborhoods, 2004).

The community school concept, as redefined more than a half century ago, was part of the impetus for the educational reform movements starting in the 1960s and continuing through the 1980s and 1990s (Decker & Romney, 1994). Community schools operate under the assumption that community resources are legitimate sources of education. It is also assumed that the community provides a vast resource for learning not typically taken advantage of by the compensatory educational system. A continuum of community schools can be described to the degree that schools serve as true centers for lifelong learning (adult literacy and family education); reach out to service providers (health and social services); form meaningful partnerships with community organizations, public agencies, and private businesses; encourage parent and community involvement in the educational process; provide an extended school day and day care (elder and child); and practice site-based management and democratic decision making (O'Halloran, 1994).

There are a number of reasons for the trend to create more community-centered schools. Students and their families, especially in underserved urban areas, can benefit from the in-school health, social, and community education services that a community school can provide. A growing number of urban school districts in the United States are returning to neighborhood schools as a strategy for reinvigorating what many district and community leaders see as socially and economically deteriorating urban communities (Beaumont, 2003), although critics charge that the increased interest in returning to the neighborhood school is based primarily on overturning busing and desegregation policies (Orfield, 1996).

As educational leaders face the reality of increasingly limited financial resources, finding innovative ways to deliver education that do not require additional expenditures for facilities has created new possibilities for educational partnerships. Sharing existing facilities and resources with surrounding communities is a relatively new area of exploration for many districts. Because of the increasing costs of public spending for education, it makes sense to share school and community facilities such as gymnasiums, auditoriums, performance spaces, and conferencing facilities to avoid duplicating costs. When facilities are shared with other organizations, long-term maintenance and operating costs are also shared, with savings realized over the life of the building. In addition, sharing school facilities with public, civic, and private organizations may foster meaningful partnerships that can strengthen educational opportunities for learners within and beyond the formal school setting and create opportunities for future employment within the community.

A trend in educational facility planning has been for school leaders to begin viewing whole communities as providing legitimate learning experiences for their students (Bingler et al., 2003). As the school building is seen more and more as a community center, the idea of embracing the whole community as

a learning environment has evolved in a complementary fashion. Community resources exist that cannot be easily brought to or replicated in the school building. To offer students real-world authentic learning experiences not possible in school classrooms, partnerships between schools and community organizations provide a wide variety of community resources for learning including parks, businesses, museums, zoos, hospitals, universities, and government agencies. Educators are increasingly embracing the idea that if learning can take place in spaces other than school buildings, then whole programs of study can take place outside the school, with the school becoming a learning home base. With the rise of school-to-work and school-to-career programs, pairing up students with advisers and mentors from outside the school has become an increasingly valued way to educate students for the real world beyond their classroom (Levine, 2002). In addition, businesses stand to benefit through their partnership with education because learning environments can better prepare students to enter the workforce, potentially decreasing on-the-job training costs and gaining committed and productive parent employees who are more satisfied with their jobs (Galinsky & Bond, 1998).

One example of the diffusion of the school into the community is in Paterson, New Jersey, which is becoming a City of Learning. Floors of commercial buildings, factories, churches, and synagogues are being converted into schools. Renovation of existing buildings, some of them architecturally significant, contributes to a better education for the city's students, historical preservation, and revitalization of downtown. The City of Learning concept coincides with the district's plan to create a number of small career academies to turn around low achievement scores. Because of their small size, schools often form partnerships for sports and afterschool activities with the local park system or youth agencies, to the benefit of both the school and the agencies.

The San Diego Model Schools program applies an innovative, mixed-use, smart-growth development model to school design in a true integration of school and community. Faced with both school overcrowding and a lack of available land for development, San Diego was forced to consider the impact that new school construction would have on surrounding neighborhoods. The demolition of housing necessary to make room for a new school would have a direct impact on the availability of affordable housing in City Heights and displace hundreds of low-income families. A series of community meetings among city and school officials, community representatives, business leaders, and university partners led to an innovative plan called the Model School, proposing a collaborative effort between San Diego City Schools, the City of San Diego, and the Housing Authority and Redevelopment Agency. The Model School proposal included a community school to serve 700 elementary students, 350 multi-family housing units, more than nine acres of open space from underground parking to be dedicated for recreation and pedestrian walkways, health care and day care services, and new retail establishments to serve the community. The San Diego Model School Development Authority was created through state legislation to institutionalize these new municipal relationships and guide project development. The San Diego model provides a good example of the true community school: a school that is developed around the real needs of the neighborhoods it serves and that leverages every available residential, educational, and commercial resource with the goal of building a strong and vibrant community.

When planning educational facilities, these facets of the community school are critical but often overlooked. School leaders often begin with the assumption that various public spaces within the school, such as gymnasiums and auditoriums, can be shared with community organizations. However, a number of other issues need to be addressed when planning a community school, such as clearly identifying community education needs and designing programs that support those needs, pursuing formal legal and financial joint-use agreements with potential partners such as service agencies, and finally, managing parts of the building that will be used and those that will not be used by whom, when, and for what purposes (Testa, 2000). Bingler et al. (2003) cogently summarize a seven-step Citizens' Guide to the process of planning and designing schools as centers of community: (1) build a common understanding, shared beliefs, and a collective vision; (2) determine educational needs; (3) identify resources throughout the community that are capable of meeting these educational needs; (4) prepare a set of recommendations to use the available resources to meet needs; (5) communicate with the larger community through local media and provide a system of gathering and synthesizing feedback; (6) create the facilities master plan that identifies action steps, timetables, resources, and assignment of responsibilities for achieving recommendations; and finally, (7) implement the master plan, maintaining an ongoing community constituency to sustain commitment, manage bond campaigns, develop partnering agreements, and create mechanisms for monitoring and assessing the process and desired outcomes.

The Impact of Technology on School Design

Information technology and telecommunications are essential tools for business and industry and are now firmly established learning tools in education. The use of technology in schools includes an exponentially growing number of software and hardware applications for learning and instruction, school operations, management, and security systems. The U.S. Department of Education, National Center for Educational Statistics (Kleiner & Farris, 2002), reports that as of

2001, the average public school contained 124 instructional computers. About 99% of schools reported having Internet access in 2001, and 55% reported connecting to the Internet through T1/DS1 lines. Instructional rooms with Internet access rose from 50% in 1998 to 85% in 2001. The report indicates that 66% of children use computers at home, with 45% using home computers for schoolwork. The rise in technology use in schools does not necessarily mean that schools are immune to the digital divide. About 53% of white students, compared to 28% of black and 28% of Hispanic students, use computers at home for homework (Kleiner & Farris, 2002).

At its best, computer technology allows students to explore alternative solutions rapidly, produce and revise work quickly, and generate digital portfolios of their work, and it can assist teachers in better assessing the individual learning of their students. Access to the Internet allows students to do original research from the desktop, enhances information sharing and communication between students and teachers, and enables distance learning opportunities for collaborative learning and specialized courses requiring expertise not available at the school site or in the district. Clearly, having access to new information and communication technologies provides educators with new tools to advance learning, but this access does not automatically improve teaching or guarantee learning (Wagner, 2002).

The variation in deployment and use of technology among schools may be greater than would be expected from national surveys. Even with federal and state funding opportunities available, the economic barriers in many districts often limit the quantity and quality of technology and technical service. Organizational cultural barriers may limit the willingness or understanding of teachers to fully integrate technology in curriculum and instruction. At the other end of the spectrum, a small number of schools are well funded, motivated, and technologically literate enough to be well on their way to creating online learning communities, and even virtual schools that offer distance learning via Web-based delivery (Clark, 2001; Freedman, Darrow, & Watson, 2002). Most schools and school districts are somewhere in the middle of these two extremes.

Successful schools have been able to use a wide range of strategies for funding technology outside of the conventional capital and operational budgets by considering charging for services, contacting local outside agencies for seed grant startups, campaigning in the community to raise funds, partnering with other organizations to share costs, soliciting in-kind contributions from private industry for training or equipment, reducing cost through volunteers, marketing a training program or manual designed by the district, and taking full advantage of state and federal funding programs (Ward, 2001).

Having access is only a first step in the effective use of technology for teaching and learning. Ideally, technology should be specified in response to learning objectives of the district as a whole, with technology plans varying from school to school as required to meet local needs. The deployment, access, and effective use of information technology (IT) begin with a needs assessment that examines the needs, capacities, and skills of students and an evaluation as to how technology can support those needs. Along with an assessment of learning goals, an assessment of teacher technology literacy is critical so that needs are matched to the competency of teachers to use technology effectively in instruction. Technology support issues that need to be identified during planning include the creation of technical help desks, instructional support, and purchasing and technical maintenance procedures. Expected modes of communication between students, teachers, and administrators inside the building, as well as parents and community stakeholders outside the building, should be clarified. For instance, will teachers be expected to use e-mail to send and receive materials from students? Will parents be encouraged to communicate electronically with teachers about their child's progress? How does the school administration expect to use technology in communicating with parents and the community?

Continually assessing the effectiveness of the use of technology in schools is a critical ongoing task of school leaders. Making an audit of learning technology needs, knowing the status of the school district's technology infrastructure, and assessing how effectively technology serves school learning, instruction, and operations are critical first steps in strategic long-term technology planning. As the coordination and management of technology become more complex and specialized, the importance of school leaders in establishing a clear vision for the use of technology becomes vitally important to ensure that technology serves the real needs of the district (Arnold, 1997). In addition, educational administrators and planners need to be familiar with technology planning and policies, finance, equipment and infrastructure, technology applications (software and systems), maintenance and technical support, professional development and training, and integration of technology into the curriculum (Goddard et al., 2002).

Technology is precipitating a variety of changes in the organizational and physical form of our schools. At present, technology is often applied in situations that support traditional styles of instruction, such as lecturing with presentation software, rather than using the full potential of technology-enabled instruction to support innovative learning strategies such as self-directed learning and project-based learning. However, as schools become more familiar with the possibilities of technology-enabled instruction, physical layout changes will be required of school designers. Will technology be centrally located in the media center

or distributed throughout all instructional spaces within the building? Which technologies can and need to be distributed throughout the building, and which do not?

One of the earliest changes in the layout of school buildings appeared in the early 1960s with the reconceptualization of the library as an "instructional media center" containing stations for listening to tape recorders and areas for viewing and storing television and videotape machines. A computer room was added to the programming of new school designs in the early 1980s to accommodate the growing addition of stand-alone computers often networked to a shared printer. As computers became less expensive, private sector businesses began donating computers to schools, placing a limited number of stand-alone computers in existing classrooms. In the late 1980s, educational facility planners began to advocate for larger, more flexible, 900 to 1,000 square-foot classrooms to accommodate a half-dozen desktop computers and the associated internal circulation space needed (Hawkins & Lilly, 1998). The introduction of laptop computers and Internet access in the mid-1990s moved technology resources closer to students and teachers. Many new school designs now include a common, shared resource center outside self-contained classrooms to contain computer technology that may be shared by surrounding classrooms. A number of high school designs in the late 1990s have created flexible student workstations outfitted with networked desktop computers.

High Tech High School in San Diego, California, which was occupied in September 2000, provides one illustration of the integration of technology into school design (Figures 21.8, 21.9). High Tech High's goal was to provide students with rigorous and relevant academic and workplace skills, preparing its graduates for careers in a technological society. The school serves 600 students, Grades 7 through 12, and each student has a

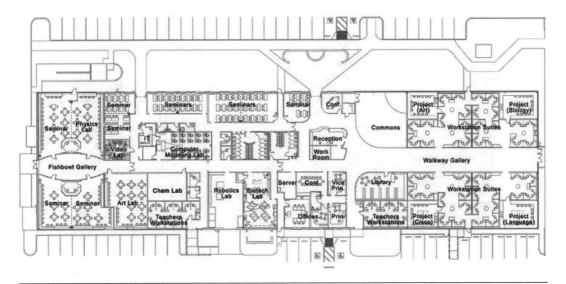

Figure 21.8   Floor plan of Gary and Jerri-Ann Jacobs High Tech High School, San Diego, California

SOURCE: Courtesy of The NTDStichler Design Group.

personalized learning plan and an adviser who remains with the student throughout his or her first 4 years at the school. Students pursue their interests through real-world projects and prepare personal digital portfolios to document their achievement. All students complete academic internships in local workplace organizations during their last 2 years at High Tech High. The school's facilities are unique among high schools in that it is located at the redeveloped Naval Training Center in San Diego in an existing 43,500 square-foot building with multipurpose seminar rooms, labs, project studios, a centralized commons, and a large, high-ceilinged, open area known as the Great Room. Students occupy their own workstations for part of the day and move between seminar, lab, and group project workspace. With much more expansive workstation and project space than commonly found in a conventional school building, High Tech High's facility allows all students to have their own workstation, and it also accommodates classroom, lab, and group project workspace. The building includes nontraditional animation, biochemistry, and engineering laboratories,

all connected to an advanced information technology infrastructure that allows the use of laptops, audio and visual systems, and Smartboards.

Wireless technology and distance learning via Web-based instruction are two recent advances in technology that are influencing educational delivery and will have an enormous impact on school design in the near future.

Wireless Technology

Most new and existing schools, with the help of state and federal funds, have been wired for information technology, and a few schools and school districts have begun to implement wireless computing networks, creating a hybrid of wired and wireless networks and building on the advantages of both. Laptop computers and wireless networks offer an appealing alternative to the billions of dollars that have been invested in wiring schools for desktop computer networks, promising greater access for learners and reduced infrastructure (Fielding, 1999). Initially, wireless

Figure 21.9   Workstation suites in High Tech High School, San Diego, California

SOURCE: Photography by Jeffery A. Lackney

networking was not widely accepted due to concerns with high costs, limited bandwidth for data transmission, interference, security, and reliability. However, as laptops, computer notepads, and personal data assistants quickly overtake desktop computers in popularity, the promise of "anywhere, anytime" wireless computing is becoming more difficult to ignore (Nair, 2002). Wireless computing offers the freedom to work anywhere within the school that is supported by the wireless local area network (WLAN). A WLAN consists of a system of radio transceiver access points and wireless network adapters built into computers that establish communications with the access point via signals that can travel 800 feet and more with add-on antennas. Unlike desktop computers, laptop computers require no specialized furniture, saving space. Wireless technology provides a solution for older facilities where running wires through existing walls can disturb existing construction and create potential environmental hazards

and costs. Laptop rolling carts can provide another level of flexibility in the classroom by being deployed where and when they are pedagogically required. Wireless technology eliminates the clutter of wiring, and the low profile of laptop monitors allows for student-teacher eye contact; laptops are convenient to use when needed, then placed out of the way (Nair, 2002). Wireless networks allow the integration of technology into almost any setting, without the physical constraints imposed by wired data walls or rows.

Some of the disadvantages of wireless technology at present are limited signal bandwidth, interference from materials that either reflect or absorb signals in older buildings, security issues with unauthorized users, and more difficult network administration due to less predictability of system loads. Wireless networks will not completely eliminate the need for high-speed, hard-wired Ethernet networks for specialized computer applications. As bandwidth limitations are surpassed, wireless computing will suffice for most applications used in schools. The near future will see a variety of hybrid systems that use wired backbones for specialized applications while offering a mixture of wired and wireless options.

Wireless computing promises to change the design of many traditional learning environments due to its reach and convenience, with every student having simultaneous access to the Internet and e-mail. Wireless computing may in effect create a culture change by enabling ad-hoc networks among teachers and workgroups among students (Nair, 2002). Wireless technology also complements many of the changes in school design, such as personalized, self-directed learning. Technology appropriate to a learning task can be brought to bear anywhere in the classroom or school, allowing for much more diverse school designs that support group learning, individualized instruction, and informal spaces for learning.

Distance Learning

Distance learning began as a series of correspondence courses broadcast over the television in the 1960s. Starting in the late 1980s, distance learning classroom space with real-time two-way conferencing capabilities has appeared in many new and existing school buildings, especially in rural schools that require access to additional educational resources. Video can take multiple forms beyond videotape and television, such as desktop applications of video (Internet Protocol video) and full-motion, two-way interactive video for distance learning applications. Full-motion video has proven useful in rural schools, offering access to courses they normally could not afford or do not have the staff to teach. Schools often use full-motion video for professional development and staff administration meetings. K–12 schools can also connect with technical colleges and universities for advanced placement courses, professional development, and virtual field trips. Full-motion video requires a dedicated distance education room, which can be expensive for some districts. Strategies schools have used to decrease the cost of distance learning include providing one-way video or Internet Protocol video with mobile video carts and leasing distance education rooms to private business. Leasing not only increases revenue for the school but also provides opportunities for community involvement in the school and awareness of the possibilities of technology education. A final option is to lease existing distance education rooms from other institutions nearby, such as a community college or university, rather than constructing a distance education classroom on-site.

Virtual schooling has been described as the next wave of distance education (Clark & Else, 1998). It may be characterized as a convergence or blending of technologies, centering on use of the Internet and World Wide Web. Online courses use the Web to hold the content, supplemented by e-mail, telephone, and often traditional textbooks and course materials. Part of the promise of the World Wide Web is distributed education within a learning community, where learning can occur anytime, anywhere (Dede, 1996). It is estimated that between 40,000 and 50,000 K–12 students enrolled in an online course, and 14 states had a planned or operational state-sanctioned, state-level virtual school in place in the 2001–2002 school year (Clark, 2001).

Due to the advent of information technology and telecommunications, the school as an organization may become more physically and temporally distributed across the community in libraries, businesses, community centers, and homes in addition to the traditional schoolhouse. Some schools may become smaller in size as functions are relegated to other parts of the community. Media centers, for instance, may become smaller as the majority of knowledge is contained on virtual networks instead of in hard copy.

Learning activities can be liberated from the self-contained classroom, which may become more of a home base to collectively plan learning activities that will take place all over the school site and community. Virtual learning environments and distance learning programs may become complementary to support and supplement the school and community through Community-Area Networks (CANs) that provide digital, audio, and video links within all parts of the school and to tertiary learning centers such as business and community organizations, community colleges, and institutions of higher learning.

As learning becomes increasingly virtual and Web based, it still must take place in a physical place, and student-teacher interactions will continue to be a critically important part of the learning environment for students. Although advocates may overstate technological change, educational leaders must stay alert to the possibilities, as they will be asked to make critical policy decisions regarding technology that will have repercussions on all aspects of education including school design.

High-Performance School Design

A high-performance school (e.g., "green" or sustainable) aims to support students and teachers to perform at their highest potential by being comfortable, healthy, safe, environmentally sound, and economically operational (Collaborative for High Performance Schools, 2002; Sustainable Buildings Industry Council, 2001). The concept of the high-performance school integrates the environmental sustainability and building performance movements, which are concerned ultimately with the sustainability of the human species and the impact of our species on the planet (McDonough & Braungart, 2002; Orr, 1994). Buildings have an enormous impact on our environment and our lives. The total building stock in the United States consumes 36.4% of the total energy consumed, uses 65.2% of

electrical energy, and creates 36% of the carbon dioxide emissions that contribute to global warming, while only 20% to 30% of the building stock is recycled or reused, and the stock contributes 40% of landfill waste (U.S. Green Building Council, 2003). About 90% of our lives are spent indoors, with students and teachers spending more than 2,000 hours a year in school buildings alone (Environmental Protection Agency, 2000).

High-performance buildings can have a direct influence on learning through the design and maintenance of a healthy and safe indoor environment, providing acoustical comfort, optimizing natural light, sharing community resources, and using the school building as a learning tool. Children are the most vulnerable population with regard to the quality of the indoor environment due to their physical and cognitive developmental needs (Evans, Kliewer, & Martin, 1991). Problems with indoor air quality and ventilation, in concert with temperature and humidity, can have profound effects on student and teacher physiology and psychology (Wyon, 1991). Poor indoor air quality has been associated with the rise of a variety of pollutants, mold growth, and chemicals that can spread disease and, in a worst-case scenario, result in sick-building syndrome (EPA, 2000; Miller, 1995). Increases in carbon dioxide simply from human respiration, as well as other contaminants if indoor areas are not ventilated, can cause sleepiness, increased mental fatigue, and decreased alertness leading to a lack of concentration and focus on learning (Schneider, 2002). More than 4.8 million school-age children in the United States suffer from asthma, according to the American Lung Association (2002). Prolonged exposure to the contaminants in a poorly ventilated building may lead to allergies, headaches, dizziness, and asthma, with the result of absenteeism. Students are absent an estimated 10 million school days per year due to illness caused by indoor environmental quality problems in schools (EPA, 2000). Providing proper ventilation through designing increased ventilation rates, as well as providing operable windows in every space, may ameliorate many of the health concerns, enhance performance, and improve teacher retention in many schools.

Acoustics can become an important ambient environmental factor influencing student performance (Evans et al., 1991). Children who are still developing their speech perception have a more difficult time hearing than adults, and nearly 20% of children experience hearing loss, which adds to the problem (Evans et al., 1991). Heating, ventilation, air conditioning, and refrigeration equipment is known to be one of the biggest contributors of noise pollution in buildings (Burt, 2000). Excessive noise, both inside (other students, other classrooms, hallways, and equipment) and outside (street noise) the classroom can cause stress in students, as measured by increased blood pressure, making it difficult to concentrate on cognitive tasks (Evans & Maxwell, 1997). Cumulative effects of excessive noise can be decreased achievement on reading and other tests, along with negative impacts on behavior, attention, and ability to concentrate. Recommendations of the American Society of Heating, Refrigeration and Air Conditioning Engineers, as well as the Acoustical Society of America Working Group on Classroom Acoustics, suggest no more than 35 decibels (dBA) background noise and 0.6 to 0.7 reverberation times with teacher voice at 50–65 dBAs, which means a target signal-to-noise ratio of at least 15 dBA (Nelson, 2003).

Natural light can have positive psychological and physiological affects on humans (Hathaway, 1995) because it stimulates hormones that regulate various body systems and mood. Brighter, continuous spectrum light within a building can increase visibility and can enhance alertness, reduce eyestrain, and improve mood (Tiller, 2000). The physiological and psychology effects of natural light have been found to lead to better performance in a few recent studies (Hathaway, 1995; Heschong & Knecht, 2003).

The slightly higher initial cost of creating a high-performance school is more than offset by the savings in energy costs over the life of the building (see Kats, Alevantis, Berman, Mills, & Perlman, 2003). The U.S. General Services Administration has estimated that initial costs account for only 10% of the total cost of operating and maintaining a building over its life. A very small investment up front can have an enormous impact on the cost of running an organization by decreasing absenteeism due to various building-related sicknesses and improving student and teacher health, satisfaction, teacher retention, and student performance. In addition, high-performance schools are less expensive to operate than conventionally designed schools built in the 1960s through 1990s. Between 35% and 50% of electric power consumption can be saved by taking advantage of daylight in school buildings and refraining from turning on artificial lighting during peak hours. Decreased cooling demands and effectively downsizing heating, ventilating, and air conditioning systems can realize an additional 10% to 20% in energy savings. Finally, water conservation measures, such as water-conserving bathroom fixtures and landscaping strategies, can decrease water consumption by 30%. High-performance buildings are less expensive to operate because they consume less energy (Kats et al., 2003; U.S. Green Building Council, 2003).

Finally, school leaders must model the environmental ethic in their community. As a movement linked to the global environmental sustainability movement, high-performance schools are designed to do their part to protect the environment for future generations through the use of renewable materials and energy, water conservation, and other environmentally sustainable site design strategies (Collaborative for High Performance Schools, 2002). In advocating for a high-performance school building design, school leaders must demand such plans from design and construction professionals, set realistic performance goals, hire professionals that share those goals, and make sure sustainable design philosophy and principles are integrated from the beginning, so that energy-saving opportunities are not lost.

THE PROCESS OF SCHOOL DESIGN

As the school mission is revisited and curriculum and instruction are assessed during the process of educational planning, facility issues often emerge as obstacles or barriers to implementation of desired programs. To assess the scope of space needs, feasibility studies may be required to investigate demographics, building condition and educational suitability, financing options, site acquisitions, and community partnerships. The result may be development of a comprehensive capital improvement program to address unmet facility needs (for a comprehensive review of school facility planning, see Bittle, 1996; Earthman, 2000; Holcomb, 1995; Myers & Robertson, 2004).

Early in the design of a 21st-century school, one of the main objectives should be to involve a wide spectrum of representatives from the community (recall Bingler & Quinn, 2003). In addition to school administrative decision makers, educational leaders should encourage the active participation of parents, business and community leaders, teachers, and even students when possible. Providing for broad community collaboration can be a difficult and frustrating process, but it can also provide a variety of benefits (Sanoff, 1994, 2002). Gaining this wider perspective can avert many roadblocks to implementation later in the process, when financial resources are being committed. Authentic participation can assist in building community support for the passage of bond issues by giving the community a sense of ownership in the process and product. In addition, participation

educates the entire community by initiating and encouraging a dialogue with the school. Finally, participation may defuse politically motivated issues and lay the groundwork for constructive dialogue between divisive groups in the community.

A steering committee appointed by the district superintendent is responsible for selecting consultants, reviewing design options, and reporting recommendations to the school board. Educational planning and architectural consultants, financial consultants, bond counsels, investment bankers, and public relations consultants are retained to conduct pre-referendum planning activities during which project scope, schedule, budget, financing, and legal issues are defined. A public referendum package is presented to the taxpaying public for approval before design and construction can begin in earnest (see Bittle, 1996).

The educational facility planning process for a 21st-century school should ideally begin with a thorough assessment of functional needs and a comparison with the detailed requirements of the educational vision, mission, and program (Myers & Robertson, 2004). The outcome of this assessment process is the development of an educational specifications document that outlines the quantity, quality, and configuration of physical space required to meet the educational program needs. The design phase of the process, which includes schematic design, design development, and construction documents and specifications, can last between 6 months and a year, depending on the complexity of the project. Each step in the design process involves more detailed and specific information about the technical aspects of the building systems, components, and assemblies. The design process requires school board decisions and approval, with each phase offering more detailed descriptions of the scope, budget, and schedule.

Several construction delivery methods are available to the school district: competitive bidding, design/build, construction management, and project management. Each state has evolved its own laws regulating the acceptable forms of construction project delivery, of which competitive bidding is still the most common. It allows contractors in each trade, such as general, mechanical, electrical, and plumbing, to compete for individual prime contracts and form separate contracts with the school district. In principle, it provides the most open and fair competition, which is appropriate for a public sector project; however, project communication and coordination may ultimately affect schedule and budget. Design/build is most popular with private sector owners but is occasionally used in the public sector. Under a design/build contract, the owner contracts with one firm, which completes both design and construction of the project under one contract. Savings in cost and time are possible but often with a loss in quality of the product. Construction management is a service that often is engaged simultaneously with the hiring of the architect. A construction manager's responsibility is to act as project manager throughout the design and construction process, coordinating the project budget and schedule along the way. A fourth form of construction delivery, project management, includes a comprehensive package of financial, legal, and construction management services, extending from pre-referendum through occupancy. Project management services are often entered into with large school districts that have multiple projects.

Following the competitive bidding process, the next phase of the school building process is that of bidding and negotiation. An invitation for bids is publicized to obtain bids from prime construction contractors. Most states require the school district to accept the lowest responsible and responsive bidder. However, the school district reserves the right to reject all bids. Once low bids are accepted, the school district as owner negotiates a contract with each prime contractor. The architect represents the owner in the construction phase, but the contract and legal relationship is between the school district as owner and each prime contractor. The construction of the school can last from 12 to 18 months, depending on the project scope, material selections, lead times for shipment to the site, weather, unforeseen subsurface site conditions, and a variety of other factors. As the use of school buildings is tied to the school year schedule, project phasing is always an issue that needs to be addressed. Other factors that can escalate cost and slow the project are change orders to rectify unforeseen conditions or errors and omissions in the original construction documents. Once the architect is satisfied that the project is complete, a certificate of substantial completion is issued, and the owner can legally occupy the facility.

Once the building is occupied, its long-term maintenance must be a priority. The lack of funding for proper preventive maintenance of school buildings has caused an enormous problem of deferred maintenance across the country in recent years (General Accounting Office, 1995; Lewis et al., 2000; National Education Association, 2000). Management of the facility is often thought to include the maintenance and operations of the physical plant: the mechanical, electrical, plumbing, power, security, and other building systems as well as custodial and maintenance programs and operations. Much of this responsibility is left to district offices; however, many aspects of school management should be the purview of educational leaders. Just as important, if not central, to facility management is the planning for the operation use of the school facility for teaching and learning—scheduling activities, assigning and scheduling space for instruction, making effective use of space, and ensuring the adequacy of the type and size of instructional space as well as the maintenance of an appropriate ambient environment for learning. Educational leaders must ensure that a proactive facility maintenance and management program is in place to anticipate, rather than react to, facility problems when they occur. Design decisions made with an eye toward long-term management and operations will lead to ease in custodial care and maintenance of school building and grounds and will support the flexible scheduling of space for future programs (Association of School Business Officials International, 2002).

SUMMARY

The goal of this chapter was to inform educational leaders about how school buildings have historically reflected the values of the larger community and how school design is of critical importance in supporting everyday teaching and learning activity as well as attaining educational goals. Educational leaders can use the process of planning and school design as a vehicle for motivating the learning community through meaningful participation and collaboration.

School design has responded to the shift from the factory model school to the smaller learning community by generating a variety of physical design solutions from collaborative learner-centered environments to learning extensions into the community through interorganizational partnerships, both physical and virtual. The recognition that environmental quality in schools can have an influence on the comfort, health, and safety of students and teachers has spurred a high-performance "green" schools movement that adds an entirely new dimension to the learning environment and makes the school building site itself a tool for learning and teaching.

Strong, committed leadership is required of educational administrators to advance innovations in school design to meet the challenges of changes in education and society. Without keen insight into the possibilities and potentials of school design, school leaders will continue to take the physical environment of the

school for granted and miss an opportunity to create healthy, comfortable, productive, and motivational places for all learners.

REFERENCES

Allen, I. L. (1977). A retrospective note on urban "neighborhood school" ideology. *Urban Education, 12*(2), 205–212.

American Institutes of Research. (1999). *An educators' guide to schoolwide reform.* Arlington, VA: Educational Research Service.

American Lung Association. (2002). *Asthma in children fact sheet.* New York: Author. Retrieved August 22, 2003, from http://www.lungusa.org/asthma/ascpedfac99.html

Arnold, D. (1997, June). Taking control. *School Planning and Management,* pp. 20–21, 24.

Association of School Business Officials International. (2002). *Planning guide for maintaining school facilities.* Washington, DC: National Forum on Education Statistics and author.

Barker, R. G., & Gump, P. V. (1964). *Big school, small school.* Palo Alto, CA: Stanford University Press.

Beaumont, C. E. (2003, May). *Historic neighborhood schools deliver 21st-century education.* Washington, DC: National Clearinghouse on Educational Facilities.

Berner, M. M. (1993, April). Building conditions, parental involvement, and student achievement in the District of Columbia public school system. *Urban Education, 28*(1), 6–29.

Bingler, S., Quinn, L., & Sullivan, K. (2003, December). *Schools as centers of community: A citizen's guide for planning and design* (2nd ed.). Washington, DC: U.S. Department of Education.

Bittle, E. H. (Ed.). (1996). *Planning and financing school improvement and construction projects.* Topeka, KS: National Organization on Legal Problems in Education.

Boer, H., & Karanovich, F. (2000, September–October). How are your buildings smart? *Illinois School Board Journal.* Springfield: Illinois School Board Association.

Brubaker, C. W. (1998). *Planning and designing schools.* New York: McGraw-Hill.

Burt, T. S. (2000). Acoustic environment: Responses to sound. In J. D. Spengler, J. M. Samet, & J. F. McCarthy (Eds.), *Indoor air quality handbook* (pp. 19.1–19.23). New York: McGraw-Hill.

Caffarella, R. S., & O'Donnell, J. M. (1987). Self-directed adult learning: A critical paradigm revisited. *Adult Education Quarterly, 37*(4), 99–107.

Cash, C. S. (1993). *Building condition and student achievement and behavior.* Unpublished doctoral dissertation, Virginia Polytechnic Institute and State University, Blacksburg.

Cervantes, R. P. (1999). *The relationship between the school building condition and academic achievement and behavior of students in selected Alabama public schools.* Unpublished doctoral dissertation, University of Alabama at Birmingham.

Clark, T. (2001, October). *Virtual high schools: Trends and issues.* Macomb: Western Illinois University, College of Education and Human Services, Center for the Application of Information Technologies.

Clark, T., & Else, D. (1998). *Distance learning, electronic networking, and school policy* (Fastback No. 441). Bloomington, IN: Phi Delta Kappa Educational Foundation.

Collaborative for High Performance Schools. (2002). *High performance schools best practice manual: Vol. 1. Planning.* California: Author.

Cook, A. (2000). The transformation of one large urban high school: The Julia Richman Education Complex. In E. Clinchy (Ed.), *Creating new schools: How small schools are changing American education.* New York: Teachers College Press.

Costa, A. L., & Liebmann, R. M. (Eds.). (1997). *The process-centered school: Sustaining a renaissance community.* Thousand Oaks, CA: Corwin.

Cotton, K. (1996). *Affective and social benefits of small-scale schooling.* (ERIC Document Reproduction Service EDO-RC-96–5)

Davidson, J. (2001, Fall). Innovative school design for small learning communities. *Horace, 8*(1), 1–7, 9, 11–14.

Decker, L. E., & Romney, V. A. (1994). *Educational restructuring and the community education process.* Fairfax, VA: National Community Education Association.

Dede, C. (1996). The evolution of distance education: Emerging technologies and distributed learning. *American Journal of Distance Education, 10*(2), 4–36.

Dewees, S. (1999). *The school-within-a-school model* (ERIC Digest, ED 438 147). Charleston, WV: ERIC Clearinghouse on Rural Education and Small Schools.

DeYoung, A. J. (1989). *Economics and American education: A historical and critical overview of the impact of economic theories on schooling in the United States.* New York: Longman.

Duke, D. (1998). *Does it matter where our children learn?* Unpublished manuscript, University of Virginia, Charlottesville, Thomas Jefferson Center for Educational Design.

Duke, D., & Trautvetter, S. (2001). *Reducing the negative effects of large schools.* Washington, DC: National Clearinghouse on Educational Facilities.

Earthman, G. I. (2000). *Planning educational facilities for the next century.* Reston, VA: Association of School Business Officials International.

Earthman, G. (2002, October). *Planning a research agenda for the next decade.* Paper presented at the Annual Conference of the International Society of Educational Planning, Istanbul, Turkey.

Earthman, G. I., Cash, C. S., & Van Berkum, D. (1996). A statewide study of the relationship between building condition and student achievement. *Journal of School Business Management, 8*(3), 26–37.

Ehrenkrantz, E. (1999, September). Planning for flexibility, not obsolescence. *Designshare, Inc.* Retrieved from http://www.designshare.com/Research/EEK/Enrenkrantz1.htm

Environmental Protection Agency. (2000, August). *Indoor air quality and student performance* (EPA Report 402-F-00–009). Washington, DC: Author. Retrieved August 22, 2003, from http://www.epa.gov/iaq/schools/performance.html

Evans, G. W., Kliewer, W., & Martin, J. (1991). The role of the physical environment in the health and well-being of children. In H. E. Schroeder (Ed.), *New directions in health psychology assessment* (pp. 127–157). New York: Hemisphere.

Evans, G. W., & Maxwell, L. (1997). Chronic noise exposure and reading deficits: The mediating effects of language acquisition. *Environment and Behavior, 29*(5), 638–656.

Fielding, R. (1999, December). *Wired versus wireless: Technology in school computer networks* (a debate between Prakash Nair and Glenn Meeks). Retrieved August 21, 2003, from http://www.designshare.com/Research/Wired/Wired1.htm

Fowler, W., & Walberg, H. J. (1991). School size, characteristics, and outcomes. *Educational*

Evaluation and Policy Analysis, 13(2), 189–202.

Frazier, L. M. (1993, May). *Deteriorating school facilities and student learning.* (ERIC Document Reproduction Service No. ED 356 564)

Freedman, G., Darrow, R., & Watson, J. (2002). *The California virtual school report: A national survey of virtual education practice and policy with recommendations for the state of California* (University of California College Preparatory Initiative). Santa Cruz: University of California, Santa Cruz.

Galinsky, E., & Bond, J. T. (1998). *The 1998 business work-life study: A sourcebook.* New York: Families and Work Institute.

Garbarino, J. (1980). Some thoughts on school size and its effects on adolescent development. *Journal of Youth and Adolescence, 9,* 19–31.

General Accounting Office. (1995). *School facilities: Condition of America's schools* (GAO/HEHS–95–61). Washington, DC: Author.

General Accounting Office. (2000). *School facilities: Construction expenditures have grown significantly in recent years* (GAO/HEHS–00–41). Washington, DC: Author.

George, P. S., & Alexander, W. M. (1993). *The exemplary middle school.* Fort Worth, TX: Holt, Rinehart & Winston.

Goddard, E., Loudat, N. B., Purwin, T., Rogers, A., Schmitt, C., & Vinson, M. (2002). *Technology in schools: Suggestions, tools, and guidelines for assessing technology in elementary and secondary education* (NCES 2003–313). Washington, DC: U.S. Department of Education, National Center for Education Statistics.

Gravelle, C. M. (1998). *The relationship between student achievement and school building conditions in public school districts in Idaho.* Unpublished doctoral dissertation, University of Idaho.

Graves, B. E. (1993). *School ways: The planning and design of America's schools.* New York: McGraw-Hill.

Grow, G. O. (1991). Teaching learners to be self-directed. *Adult Education Quarterly, 41*(3), 125–149.

Gulliford, A. (1996). *America's country schools* (3rd ed.). Washington, DC: Preservation Press.

Gump, P. V. (1987). School and classroom environments. In D. Stokols & I. Altman (Eds.), *Handbook of environmental psychology* (pp. 691–732). New York: John Wiley.

Guy, L. G. (2001). *Student achievement and school condition: Examining the relationship in West Virginia high schools.* Unpublished doctoral dissertation, West Virginia University, Morgantown.

Hathaway, W. E. (1995). Effects of school lighting on physical development and school performance. *Journal of Educational Research, 88*(4), 228–242.

Hawkins, H. L., & Overbaugh, B. L. (1988). The interface between facilities and learning. *The Educational Facility Planner, 26*(4), 4–7.

Hawkins, H. L., & Lilley, E. H. (1998). *Guide to school facility appraisal.* Phoenix, AZ: Council of Educational Facility Planners International.

Herbst, J. (1996). *The once and future school: Three hundred and fifty years of American secondary education.* New York: Routledge.

Heschong, L., & Knecht, C. (2003). Daylighting makes a difference. *Educational Facility Planner, 37*(2), 5–14.

Holcomb, J. H. (1995). *A guide to the planning of educational facilities.* New York: University Press of America.

Huse, D. (1995). Restructuring and the physical context: Designing learning environments. *Children's Environment, 12*(3), 290–310.

Irmsher, K. (1997). *School size.* (ERIC Digest, Number 113). Eugene, OR: ERIC Clearinghouse on Educational Management. (ERICE Document Reproduction Service No. ERICED 414615 97)

Johnson, D. W., & Johnson, R. (1999). *Learning together and alone: Cooperative, competitive, and individualistic learning* (5th ed.). Boston: Allyn & Bacon.

Johnson, S. M. (1990). *Teachers at work: Achieving success in our schools.* New York: Basic Books.

Kats, G., Alevantis, L., Berman, A., Mills, E., & Perlman, J. (2003, October). *The costs and benefits of green buildings: Report to California's Sustainable Buildings Task Force.* Sacramento: California Department of Health Services and Lawrence Berkeley National Laboratory.

Kleiner, A., & Farris, E. (2002). *Internet access in U.S. public schools and classrooms: 1994–2001* (Report No. NCES 2002–018). Washington, DC: National Center for Educational Statistics.

Lackney, J. A. (1994). *Educational facilities: The impact and role of the physical environment of the school on teaching, learning, and educational outcomes.* (Report R94–4). Milwaukee:

University of Wisconsin, Center for Architecture and Urban Planning Research.

Lackney, J. A. (1999, March). *Changing patterns in educational facilities: DesignShare, Inc.* Retrieved December 2004, from http://www.designshare.com/Research/ChangingPatterns/ChangingPatterns1.htm

Lackney, J. A. (2003, February). *Thirty-three educational design principles for schools and community learning centers.* Washington, DC: National Clearinghouse for Educational Facilities.

Lanham, J. W., III (1999). *Relating building and classroom conditions to student achievement in Virginia's elementary schools.* Unpublished doctoral dissertation, Virginia Polytechnic Institute and State University, Blacksburg.

Lashway, L. (1998–1999, Winter). School size: Is smaller better? *Research Roundup, 15*(2). Eugene, OR: ERIC Clearinghouse on Educational Management.

Lawrence, B. K., Bingler, S., Diamond, B. M., Hill, B., Hoffman, J. L., Howley, C. B., Mitchell, S., Rudolph, D., & Washor, E. (2002). *Dollars and sense: The cost effectiveness of small schools.* Columbus, OH: Knowledge Works Foundation.

Lee, V., Ready, D., & Johnson, D. (2001). The difficulty of identifying rare samples to study: The case of high schools divided into schools within schools. *Educational Evaluation and Policy Analysis, 23*(4), 365–379.

Levine, E. (2002). *One kid at a time: Big lessons from a small school.* New York: Teachers College Press.

Lewis, L., Snow, K., Farris, E., Smerdon, B., Cronen, S., & Kaplan, J. (2000). *Condition of America's public school facilities: 1999* (Report No. NCES 2000–032). Washington, DC: National Center for Educational Statistics.

Lewis, M. (2001). *Facility conditions and student test performance in the Milwaukee public schools.* Scottsdale, AZ: Council of Educational Facility Planners International.

Lezotte, L. W. (1991). *Correlates of an effective school: First and second generation.* Okemos, MI: Effective Schools Products.

Marks, J. (2000, June). *The Educational Facilities Laboratories (EFL): A history.* Washington, DC: National Clearinghouse for Educational Facilities.

Marshall, H. H. (1981). Open classrooms: Has the term outlived its usefulness? *Review of Educational Research, 51*(2), 181–192.

Maxwell, L. E. (1999). *School building renovation and student performance: One district's experience.* Scottsdale, AZ: Council of Educational Facility Planners International.

McAndrews, T., & Anderson, W. (2002, January). *Schools within schools* (ERIC Digest 154). Eugene: University of Oregon, Clearinghouse on Educational Management.

McClintock, J., & McClintock, R. (1970). *Henry Barnard's school architecture.* New York: Teachers College Press.

McDonough, W., & Braungart, M. (2002). *Cradle to cradle: Remaking the way we make things.* New York: North Point Press.

McGuffy, C. (1982). Facilities. In H. J. Walberg (Ed.), *Improving educational standards and productivity* (pp. 237–288). Berkeley, CA: McCutchan.

Meek, A. (Ed.). (1995). *Designing places for learning.* Alexandria, VA: Association for Supervision and Curriculum Development.

Miller, N. L. (1995). *The healthy school handbook: Conquering the sick building syndrome and other environmental hazards in and around your school.* Washington, DC: National Education Association.

Moore, G. T., & Lackney, J. A. (1993). School design: Crisis, educational performance, and design patterns. *Children's Environments, 10*(2), 99–112.

Myers, N., & Robertson, S. (2004). *Creating connections: The CEFPI guide to educational facility planning.* Scottsdale, AZ: Council of Educational Facility Planners International.

Nair, P. (2002, October). *The role of wireless computing technology in the design of schools.* Washington, DC: National Clearinghouse on Educational Facilities.

Nathan, J., & Febey, K. (2001). Smaller, safer, saner, successful schools. Minneapolis: Humphrey Institute of the University of Minnesota, Center for School Change.

National Education Association. (2000). *Modernizing our schools: What will it cost?* Washington, DC: Author.

Nelson, P. B. (2003, February). Sound in the classroom: Why children need quiet. *ASHRAE Journal,* pp. 22–25.

New Schools, Better Neighborhoods. (2004, Spring). *Schools as centers of communities* (Knowledgeworks Foundation Concept Paper). Los Angeles: Author.

O'Halloran, K. (1994, Spring). *Why lock the doors at three o'clock? Innovative community uses for the neighborhood school* (Issues in Brief). Philadelphia: Pew Charitable Trusts. (ERIC Document Reproduction Service No. ED372478)

O'Neill, D. J. (2000, August). *The impact of school facilities on student achievement, behavior, attendance, and teacher turnover rate at selected Texas middle schools in Region XIII ESC.* Unpublished doctoral dissertation, Texas A&M University.

Orfield, G. (1996). Turning back to segregation. In G. Orfield, S. Eaton, & The Harvard Project on Desegregation (Eds.), *Dismantling desegregation: The quiet reversal of* Brown v. Board of Education (pp. 1–22). New York: The New Press.

Organization for Economic Co-operation and Development. (1989). *Schools and quality: An international report.* Paris: Author.

Orr, D. (1994). *Earth in mind: On education, environment, and the human prospect.* Washington, DC: Island Press.

Oxley, D. (1994). Organizing schools in small units: Alternatives to homogeneous grouping. *Phi Delta Kappan, 75*(7), 621.

Raywid, M. A. (1996). *Taking stock: The movement to create mini-schools, schools-within-schools, and separate small schools* (Urban Diversity Series No 108). New York: Columbia University, Teachers College, ERIC Clearinghouse on Urban Education. (ERIC Document Reproduction Service No. ED 396 045)

Raywid, M. (1999). *Current literature on small schools.* (ERIC Document Reproduction Service EDO-RC-98–8)

Rieselbach, A. (1992). Building and learning. In *New schools for New York: Plans and precedents for small schools.* New York: Princeton Architectural Press.

Rothenberg, J. (1989). The open classroom reconsidered. *Elementary School Journal, 90*(1), 69–86.

Sanoff, H. (1994). *School design.* New York: Van Nostrand Reinhold.

Sanoff, H. (2001). *School building assessment methods.* Washington, DC: National Clearinghouse for Educational Facilities.

Sanoff, H. (2002). *Schools designed with community participation.* Washington, DC: National Clearinghouse for Educational Facilities.

Schneider, M. (2002, November). *Do school facilities affect academic outcomes?* Washington, DC: National Clearinghouse for Educational Facilities.

Shein, E. H. (1997). *Organizational culture and leadership* (2nd ed.). San Francisco: Jossey-Bass.

Stine, S. (1997). *Landscapes for learning: Creating outdoor environments for children and youth.* New York: John Wiley.

Sustainable Buildings Industry Council. (2001). *High-performance school buildings: Resource and strategy guide.* Washington, DC: Author.

Tanner, K., & Lackney, J. (2005). *Educational architecture: School facilities planning, design, construction, and management.* Needham Heights, MA: Allyn & Bacon.

Tanner, L. N. (1997). *Dewey's Laboratory School: Lessons for today.* New York: Teachers College Press.

Taylor, A. (1993). The learning environment as a three-dimensional textbook. *Children's Environments, 10*(2), 170–179.

Testa, K. C. (2000). *Development of joint-use educational facility agreements between California public school districts and community entities: A cross-case analysis of strategic practices, barriers, and supportive elements.* Unpublished doctoral dissertation, University of La Verne, California.

Tiller, D. K. (2000). Lighting recommendations. In J. D. Spengler, J. M. Samet, & J. F. McCarthy (Eds.), *Indoor air quality handbook* (pp. 18.1–18.22). New York: McGraw-Hill.

U.S. Green Building Council. (2003, February). *Building momentum: National trends and prospects for high-performance green buildings.* Washington, DC: Author.

Wagner, T. (2002). *Making the grade: Reinventing America's schools.* New York: Routledge Falmer.

Ward, D. (2001, April). Sustainable funding: What to do before the money runs out. *School Planning and Management,* pp. 71–72, 74–75.

Washor, E. (2002, August). *Translating innovative pedagogical designs into school facilities designs.* Unpublished doctoral dissertation, Johnson and Wales University, Providence, RI.

Weinstein, C. S. (1979). The physical environment of the school: A review of the research. *Review of Educational Research, 49*(4), 577–610.

Weinstein, C. S. (1996). *Secondary classroom management: Lessons from research and practice.* New York: McGraw-Hill.

Wolff, S. J. (2001, September). *Sustaining systems of relationships: The essence of the physical learning environment that supports and enhances collaborative, project-based learning at the community college level.* Unpublished doctoral dissertation, Oregon State University, School of Education.

Wyon, D. P. (1991). The ergonomics of healthy buildings: Overcoming barriers to productivity. In *IAQ '91: Post-conference proceedings* (pp. 43–46). Atlanta, GA: American Society of Heating, Refrigerating, and Air-Conditioning Engineers.

ONLINE RESOURCES

American Institute of Architects (AIA), Committee on Architecture for Education (CAE). http://www.aia.org/PIA/cae/

Center for Education, Environment and Design Studies (CEEDS) at the University of Washington. http://ceeds.caup.washington.edu/

Center for Health, Environment and Justice. http://www.chej.org

Children, Youth and Environments (CYE). http://cye.colorado.edu/

Children's Environmental Health Network. http://www.cehn.org

Children's Environments Research Group (CERG). http://web.gc.cuny.edu/che/cergfr.htm

Council of Educational Facility Planners International (CEFPI). http://www.cefpi.org

Design Education. http://www.designeducation.org/index.html

Design Share. http://www.designshare.com

EDSPACE. http://www.edspace.school.nz/

Educational Design Institute (EDI). http://www.edi.msstate.edu/

Environmental Protection Agency (EPA). http://www.epa.gov/iaq/schools/tools4s2.html

Funders' Forum on Environment and Education. http://charityadvantage.com/f2e2/AboutUs.asp

Green Schools Program, Alliance to Save Energy. http://www.ase.org/greenschools/

Health and Environmental Funders Network. http://www.hefn.org

Healthy Schools Network (HSN). http://www.healthyschools.org

International Secretariat for Child Friendly Cities. http://www.childfriendlycities.org

Lifelong Kindergarten Group. http://llk.media.mit.edu/

MIG Communications (Moore, Iacofano and Goldman, Inc.). http://www.migcom.com/childdesign/index.html

National Center for Technology Planning (NCTP). http://www.nctp.com/

National Clearinghouse For Education Facilities. http://www.edfacilities.org

North Carolina School Design Clearinghouse. http://www.schoolclearinghouse.org/

Program on Educational Building (PEB), Organization of Economic Cooperation and Development (OECD). http://www.oecd.org

Rural Trust. http://www.ruraledu.org/issues/facilities.htm

San Diego Model School Development Agency http://www.sdmodelschool.net/

School Design and Planning Laboratory. http://www.coe.uga.edu/sdpl/sdpl.html

School Design Research. http://www4.ncsu.edu/~sanoff/schooldesign/home.html

School Design Research Studio. http://schoolstudio.engr.wisc.edu

School Works. http://www.school-works.org

School Designs.com. http://www.schooldesigns.com/

Small Schools Project. http://www.smallschools-project.org/facilities/

Smart Schools Clearinghouse. http://sun6.dms.state.fl.us/smartschools/index.html

Thomas Jefferson Center for Educational Design, Curry School of Education, University of Virginia, Charlottesville. http://www.tjced.org

Urban Educational Facilities for the 21st Century (UEF-21). http://www.designshare.com/UEF.htm

22

Unions, Collective Bargaining, and the Challenges of Leading

TODD A. DeMITCHELL
University of New Hampshire

You can't do that; it violates the contract and I will file a grievance.

I will have to check with the union to see if we can do this.

You cannot implement that change without first going to the union.

These are comments that educational leaders have heard at one time or another. They capture the importance of unions and collective bargaining in our system of bilateral governance when it comes to wages, benefits, and terms and conditions of employment. Educational administrators need to understand the history, the power, the influence, and the limitations of unions and collective bargaining in order to lead and improve their organizations.

In the last fifty years teacher unions have impacted the governance of America's public schools. The two teacher unions have become major policy and political players not only at the local school district level, but also at the national level. In those states that have public sector bargaining laws, governance has become bilateral on issues of wages, benefits, and terms and conditions of employment. Issues of reform and change must cross the bargaining table because they impact terms and conditions of work.

The union's role in school governance, of necessity, impacts the work of educational leaders. The pressures of reform and professionalism are structured in part by the work of the unions and their industrial union labor template. Challenges that unions face in an era of reform are challenges that administrators face as well. Leaders must work with unions. Understanding unions, their work, and their history is important for effective school stewardship in the new century.

Superintendents, principals, and other educational leaders face many challenges as they lead and manage our nation's public schools. They face strong pressures from outside the schoolhouse gate (e.g., legislatures, reports, and groups critical of public education) and inside the schoolhouse gate (e.g., parents, community members, and school boards). One group that has the characteristics of both an outside special interest group and inside constituency is the teacher union. The unions occupy space as both external organizations operating at the state and national level and as internal parts of the governance system by way of the collective bargaining agreement. Teacher unions represent the nation's largest unionized workforce. Wirt and Kirst (1997) wrote that no other group has had "increased influence on education policy in recent decades as much as have teachers. The timid rabbits of 30 years ago are today's ravening tigers in the jungle of school systems" (p. 181). Cooper and Liotta (2001) describe teacher unions as mature institutions. Lieberman (1997) considers unions major components of the educational establishment, playing "an extremely influential role, not just in education but in politics and the economy as well" (p. 1). Clearly, educational leaders must understand the role, function, and impact of unions if they are to lead effectively.

Teachers stand at the crossroads of education. Educational leaders can get nothing done of any lasting value except through the efforts of teachers. If leadership is not focused on teachers and their work, the effort may just be tinkering at the margins of education. Because the true work of the schools is performed by teachers working with students, administrators who wish to lead the efforts of teachers must understand not only leadership, institutions, curriculum, and instruction but also unions and collective bargaining. If the core of the school is the work of the teacher and the work of the teacher is covered by a collective bargaining agreement, it stands to reason that administrators must understand and work effectively with unions as well as teachers.

Unfortunately, the research on collective bargaining and unions is a "surprisingly small body of literature" (Loveless, 2000, p. 1). Michael Kirst likened our understanding of the role of unions in policy making to a "Dark Continent" (Bradley, 1996). Kerchner, Koppich, and Weeres (1997) referred to unions as "the blind spot on the radar scope of educational reform" (p. xi). Little (1993) argued that there is scant knowledge about the "relative salience of the union compared with other sources in shaping teachers' response to or involvement in reform initiatives" (p. 146). DeMitchell and Fossey (1997) posited that with "few exceptions, one will search in vain in the school reform literature for even the appearance of the word union" (p. 191). "A serious gap exists between what we think we know about teachers unions and what we really know" (Loveless, 2000, p. 2).

This chapter will explore the work of unions, the industrial labor union model used in current bargaining, and the impact of collective bargaining on teaching and on efforts to reform education. It will conclude with a discussion of good faith bargaining, grievances, and some points to consider when working with unions.

UNIONS AND THE WORK OF TEACHERS

Early in the history of our nation, work was built around the concept of the artisan or craft guild. As the forces of industrialization in the latter part of the 19th century reshaped the landscape of work by creating factories, a new model of work developed, the industrial model. The new model of work created a new workplace and new types of workers with their own particular needs. The organization and aims of artisan and craft guilds were no longer consistent with the way work was managed and carried out in the newly emerging industrial society. A new labor organization was needed. The model that emerged is our current concept of the industrial union.

What are unions? According to Tannenbaum (1965), "unions are organizations designed to protect and enhance the social and economic welfare of their members" (p. 9). A union is "a continuous association of wage earners for the purpose of maintaining or improving the conditions of their working lives" (Webb & Webb, 1920, p. 1). Lieberman (1997) asserts that a union "exists in whole or in part to represent employees to their employers on their terms and conditions of employment" (p. 9). And, McDonnell and Pascal (1988) posit that unions operate as political interest groups working to obtain benefits from the exterior environment. They have characterized the role of unions in the following manner:

> First, they operate as political interest groups, working to obtain benefits from the external environment. And, second they also function as voluntary organizations that must meet members' demands in the type and level of benefits they obtain and the services they provide. The challenge for the unions is to obtain sufficient benefits to maintain their membership, while also operating effectively in a world of political bargaining and compromise. (p. vii)

As organizations, unions sell a service to specific groups of employees. Because unions can compete for membership—and this is especially true in education—they must be able to demonstrate to members that they receive a value for the dues they pay for the union to represent them (DeMitchell & Cobb, 2003). A major activity of unions is bargaining with management over wages, benefits, and terms and conditions of employment. Potential consumers of union services judge the value received by what is secured through bargaining and other activities that enhance the security of the employee.

A BRIEF HISTORY

Teachers began to organize well before the rise of public-sector collective bargaining. Low pay and low status were precipitating factors (Johnson, 1988). The two major teacher unions, the National Education Association (NEA) and the American Federation of Teachers (AFT), arose in response to these two forces. In some ways, the difference between the two unions can be attributed to whether its energy was focused on status or pay. "The NEA thought collective bargaining would destroy professionalism. . . . In contrast, the AFT pointed out that teachers would gain respect because at last their salaries would be commensurate with their preparation" (Murphy, 1990, pp. 209–210). The NEA, dominated by male college presidents and administrators, focused on professionalizing the teaching force. Johnson (1988) observed that the National Teachers Association, the forerunner of the NEA, was formed in 1857 "to elevate the character and advance the interests of the profession of teaching and to promote the cause of popular education in the United States" (p. 605).

The AFT, from its inception, was a union of teachers. "It was organized by teachers, the membership was composed of teachers, and, most important, the leadership came from classroom teachers" (Streshly & DeMitchell, 1994, p. 9). The AFT aligned itself with national labor. Nicholas Murray Butler, president of the NEA at the turn of the century, called the Chicago Federation of Teachers, the forerunner of the AFT, "insurrectionists" and "union labor grade teachers" (Murphy, 1990, p. 54).

When public-sector collective bargaining marched across the educational landscape in the 1960s, the NEA thought it would destroy professionalism and erode the teacher's status in the community. In contrast, the AFT embraced collective bargaining, arguing that teachers would gain respect because their salaries would finally be commensurate with their preparation. In the 1960s, the NEA started losing members to the AFT primarily over the issue of which union could better represent and protect the self-interest of teachers. The NEA's long-cherished concept of professionalism was seriously challenged. "Teachers wanted higher salaries and better benefits, not necessarily a higher standard of respect" (Streshly & DeMitchell, 1994, p. 10). To remain competitive with the AFT, the NEA changed its philosophy and tactics. It came to look and act more like the AFT.

The transformation of the NEA to a labor union was prompted by the passage of public-sector collective bargaining laws. When these public-sector collective bargaining laws were passed, the predominant labor-management mold was the industrial union of the teamsters, auto workers, and coal miners. "The procedures for conflict resolution, the definition of management and labor, and their respective rights were all borrowed, in many cases word for word, from the private labor sector which embraced the industrial model" (DeMitchell & Streshly, 1996, p. 78). This initial choice of models to use for the public sector has had major consequences for education, given the uniqueness of public schools and a workforce that struggles with the issue of professionalism. "There has always been an imperfect fit, therefore, between collective bargaining and the more fundamental structures and processes of public education itself" (Bacharach, Shedd, & Conley, 1989, p. 103).

THE INDUSTRIAL UNION MODEL

Unions strive to protect the worker from the "whims" of management through a collectively bargained, legally enforceable contract that defines the terms and conditions of employment in addition to the wages and benefits associated with the job. This creates a system with two distinct parties. Consequently, "industrial unionism assumes permanent adversaries" (Kerchner & Caufman, 1993,

p. 15). An "us" and "them" mentality is fostered. Johnson and Kardos (2000) identify three assumptions of the industrial labor model—"labor-management opposition, the value of standardized practice, and the generic treatment of workers [that] underlie the character of industrialism, which is at [the] historical core of teacher unionism" (p. 11). "Industrial-style unionism is organized around anger" (Koppich, 1993, p. 200), which all too often colors the working relationship. Consequently, a great premium is placed on conflict management. This is so fundamental that the absence of conflict actually "arouses anxiety and uncertainty among both union leaders and school managers who fear that they will be seen as having 'gone soft'" (Kerchner & Mitchell, 1988, p. 237).

When the industrial labor model is applied to education, teachers become labor and administrators become management. The fact that both groups are educators with common goals and values is lost in this model. "The separateness of some work activities performed by the teachers and the administrators is emphasized, and not the commonality of purpose, roots, interests, or overlapping functions" (DeMitchell & Fossey, 1997, p. 21). Consequently, the emphasis on separateness places a great premium on conflict management within the labor relations and the contract. This focus on conflict management is further enhanced because collective bargaining is a system for creating agreement when trust is low and union members believe that they must be protected by a legally binding instrument that spells out in some detail the terms and conditions of their work. "As a consequence, contracts must be legally explicit, anticipate contingencies, and provide for policing and enforcement. Such a system may well exaggerate the differences and diminish trust between parties" (Cresswell & Murphy with Kerchner, 1980, p. 479).

With the advent of industrial unionism, workers relinquished control over the outcomes of the product of their work. Decisions about what is produced and how it is produced passed into the hands of management. Workers were divorced from the formation of policy; all they can do is implement it. Kerchner et al. (1997) noted, "collective bargaining invests in the union the obligation to enhance and protect the rights of its members. It implicitly invests in management the responsibility for the health of the educational enterprise" (p. 137). Under the industrial union model, teachers, like factory line workers, are only supposed to perform a labor function; they are not supposed to influence the outcome of the product. We know that this is not the reality of teaching. Classroom teachers' daily work with students is a translation and reconfiguration of policy to meet the highly individualized contexts of their classroom. Educators do not turn out mass-produced widgets; teaching is a highly complex process, calling for the use of judgment. Classroom teachers make and adapt policy with the myriad decisions they make daily. Teachers are not divorced from policy, as the industrial union labor model would have us believe.

Another problem that the industrial union labor model creates for teachers is the proposition that teaching is labor. This viewpoint tries to make labor more easily standardized, so that the work of the union member can be reduced to common contract language, thus making the enforcement of the contract more uniform. Thus, through this process of considering teaching as labor, "the rich texture of a teacher's efforts, those professional and artistic elements which do not fit neatly into the industrial union model, are distorted and often rendered meaningless" (DeMitchell & Streshly, 1996, p. 79). Collegiality and pedagogical technique do not bend easily into strictures of contract language (Johnson, 1987).

The results of collective bargaining are the standardization and centralization of a teacher's work. This standardization is not the same as professional standards developed through rigorous examination of practice, which comports with the accepted literature and forms the core knowledge of the profession. Standardization in collective bargaining occurs because the elements of the contract apply equally to all members of the union. How the contract is interpreted and enforced in one school must be consistent with how it is interpreted and enforced in all of the schools of the district. This need for standardization leads to centralization because the contract must be administered uniformly. Because the contract is between the union and the school board, both parties are charged with its uniform application. Uniformity is enforced at the central office by both union and school district officials through the formal grievance process and the informal and sometimes guarded relationship that often develops between union officials and district-level administrators. Both parties to the contract seek uniform application of the contract; otherwise, instability might ensue, thus endangering the labor peace achieved by the contract. "Both the union and the district office administrators seek to centralize and standardize behavior through consistent rule interpretation, scrutiny, and enforcement" (DeMitchell, 1993, p. 79). Uniqueness or context of teaching environments is typically not accommodated in collective bargaining agreements, which require standardization, centralization, and formalization.

TEACHERS AND THEIR UNIONS

According to Cooper and Liotta (2001), the conundrum is that while "teachers in many communities are union members, they still see themselves and their work as primarily professional—helping children to learn" (p. 109). Even though it can be reasonably argued that the industrial labor model is structural and conceptually misaligned with the professionalism of education, teachers seem to support the protection of unionism, even if at times they do not support the union. Teachers appear to have a "limited level of engagement with their unions" (Farkas, Johnson, & Duffett, 2003, p. 18). Similarly, DeMitchell and Barton (1996) found that teachers were not aligned with their building union representative on issues related to the impact of collective bargaining on educational reform, even though the building representative was a colleague in their school and not a faceless bureaucrat. In the analysis of their data, DeMitchell and Barton observed that "teachers may not see unions and collective bargaining as being related to activities that are at the core of teaching" (p. 376). It should not be inferred, however, that teachers do not see the value of their union in protecting their wages, benefits, and terms and conditions of employment.

In a report on a survey of teachers prepared by Public Agenda, 46% of teachers stated that unions were absolutely essential, 38% considered unions important but not essential, and 12% stated that unions were something you could do without (Farkas et al., 2003, p. 46). About 65% of the teachers said they think the union usually fights for things that would improve education in their district, while 16% thought the union would resist doing things that would improve education. About 19% were unsure (p. 48). On the question, "If the union put more focus on academic issues and student achievement during collective bargaining with your district, would you . . . " the teachers responded:

Welcome this (19%)

Be open to hearing more about it (57%)

Think they were off in the wrong direction (11%)

Not sure (13%) (p. 49)

Teachers in this study supported unionism and believed that unions act in the best interests of improving education. However, they appeared reluctant to see the union focus its energy during collective bargaining on the professional issues associated with academic and student achievement. The explanation may be similar to the findings of McDonnell and Pascal (1988) that a majority of teachers want their union to focus on bread-and-butter issues during bargaining but may be more receptive to union activities outside of bargaining that target improving education. For example, Bob Chase, former NEA president, tells of an incident when he was stumping for support to reinvent the union. He stated, "Speaking to the local NEA leadership in Florida about the union's role in achieving school quality, one union member stated, 'Your job isn't to look out for children; your job is to look out for me!'" (Chase, 1997).

In a preliminary report on a study of teacher perceptions of professionalism and unionism, DeMitchell and Cobb (2003) found that the respondents disagreed with the propositions that quality teaching can be standardized into a contract and that the contract fosters quality teaching. However, the respondents agreed with the statements that the union contract "supports my professional activities" and that "I am better off with a union contract than without a union contract."

Teachers appear to be conflicted about their sense of professionalism and their perceptions about the role of their union. They may not see the union as impacting their professional duties; but they do perceive that they are better off with the union and its contract than without the union. DeMitchell and Cobb (2003) found a recurring theme in their qualitative analysis: Teachers perceive the union as protecting them so they can do their job. In their preliminary analysis, DeMitchell and Cobb also found that this protection is a double-edged sword, with the union protecting mediocrity and incompetence.

LEADING AND EDUCATIONAL REFORM

Administrators lead in an era of reform. There is intense pressure to improve our public schools. Reform in response to accountability impacts the lives of educational leaders. As stated above, real reform must impact the working conditions of teachers, which in turn must pass through the bargaining table.

An early and important line of inquiry looked at the role of unions and reform. A RAND study of educational reform and bargaining (McDonnell & Pascal, 1988) found that union efforts to obtain status benefits such as increased participation in school-site decision making often engendered teacher suspicion, a feeling that the union was "falling down on the job" by not focusing on securing higher wages, better benefits, and more security. The authors concluded that until "a union obtains these bread-and-butter items, a movement toward greater professionalism is not likely" (p. 53). Clearly, teachers expected their union to secure the material benefits of employment first; reform may be a distant second, or even lower, when teachers think of the role of their union. As members perceive it, the job of the union is to protect the self-interests of members and not to secure reform of education. Stated another way, the job of the union is to protect its membership, not the students.

This finding is similar to Bascia's (1994) study, which found that any union movement into new partnerships with administrators that enhance and expand teacher professionalism must be "logically consistent with teachers' historical needs for protection and representation" (p. 98). Taken together, the RAND study and Bascia's research point to an expectation on the part of teachers that their union must take care of the bread-and-butter issues of security, wages, and benefits. If a union must take care of business first, when and under what conditions can it turn to issues of securing reform and greater professionalism, given the fact that the union, like other interest groups, must compete for the district's scarce resources? Can collective bargaining and unionism, which were founded on self-interest,

make the bridge to the reform goal of greater professionalism, which is based on service to another? Kerchner and Mitchell (1988) write of this conundrum: "The legitimation of teacher economic self-interest at the bargaining table has aroused public suspicion that teachers no longer speak for the public interest of schools or represent the real needs of children" (p. 239).

In another line of inquiry, DeMitchell and Barton (1996) conducted a five-state study on the impact of collective bargaining at the school level because that is where reform is truly implemented if it is to mean anything. At each individual school randomly selected for the study, they surveyed the principal, the school's union representative, and the first teacher listed alphabetically who was not the union representative. The study looked at reforms undertaken by the school in the previous 5 years. It also examined, from the perspective of the three groups of respondents, the character of collective bargaining and its impact on their school's educational program.

The character of bargaining section of the research asked three questions. For all three groups, the more the collective bargaining process was viewed as problem solving, the less the contract was considered an obstacle to reform. Similar results were found for the relationship between viewing the collective bargaining process as friendly and viewing it as an obstacle to reform. Bonferroni pairwise contrasts "showed that the union representatives viewed the negotiated contract as less an obstacle to reform than did the principals. Teachers' views were not significantly different from either of the two groups" (DeMitchell & Barton, 1996, p. 372).

The impact section asked two questions: "What impact did collective bargaining have on school reform efforts at your school?" and "What kind of impact has collective bargaining had on the quality of education that your school delivers to its students?" The researchers found a significant statistical difference for the type of impact on school reform efforts, with the union representatives viewing the impact as positive, principals viewing it as negative, and teachers, once again, not significantly different from either group. A similar result was found for the impact of bargaining on the quality of education delivered by the school—union representatives positive, principals negative, and teachers not closely aligned with either group.

The authors concluded that bargaining has little impact on reform efforts at the school level as perceived by union representatives, principals, and teachers. The most surprising finding was two questions that the authors formulated after analyzing the data: "Do teachers care about bargaining and reform?" and "Whom do the union reps represent?" DeMitchell and Barton (1996) expected that there would be disagreement between union representatives and principals on the impact of collective bargaining. They also expected to find that the teachers' views would be closely aligned with their union representatives because the union reps were not distant, bureaucratic functionaries; they worked in the same school as the responding teachers. What the researchers found was that, as a group, teachers stood apart from their union reps' views. They were more moderate than their representatives, and they were not "polarized along the same lines that polarize the management-union debate" (p. 377). The lack of agreement between teachers and their union representatives on the centrality of collective bargaining to reform prompted DeMitchell and Barton to speculate whether "teachers just see collective bargaining as irrelevant to their classrooms" (p. 377).

A final research report on bargaining and educational reform surveyed school superintendents and their perceptions of local school reform that were submitted to collective bargaining. DeMitchell and Carroll (1999) surveyed superintendents from five different states representing five different geographical regions of the United States. The superintendents were

asked questions regarding the impact and ease of bargaining reform in their school district. The 88 respondents stated that a total of 149 reform initiatives were brought to the bargaining table. About 81% of the reforms were successfully bargained, and 19% were not. Small rural school districts had the greatest difficulty in bargaining. The most difficult reform to bargain was an extended school day or school year, and the easiest reform was mentoring. Overall, the superintendents found it difficult rather than easy to bargain reform. However, once a reform was bargained, superintendents perceived that some security was attached to the reform. About 36% of the time, school districts gave money unrelated to the reform to secure the reform initiative. About 26% of the time, school districts gave up language to secure the reform.

These studies raise the issue of whether reform has a favored place at the bargaining table. Can the bargaining table in education, borrowed from the industrial union, meet the challenges of a complex delivery of professional services that relies heavily on context for application of knowledge, as opposed to the rigid prescription often associated with a bargained contract? Is the industrial union bargaining table up to the challenges associated with the implementation of reform to support the delivery of professional services? These studies seem to raise the question formed by Susan Moore Johnson's (1987) study titled "Can schools be reformed at the bargaining table?"

GOOD FAITH BARGAINING

The bread and butter for union members is negotiation over wages, benefits, and terms and conditions of employment. Bargaining assumes a conflict of interest between parties, otherwise there would be nothing to bargain because agreement would already exist. Bargaining also assumes a community of interest. If there is no community of interest that can be served through bargaining, there will be nothing *but* conflict. The concept of good faith bargaining is the bridge between the conflict of interest and the community of interest. A good faith bargaining requirement exists in the private sector as well as the public sector.

There is a mutual obligation on the part of management and labor to bargain in good faith. Typically, the law places a mutual obligation on both management and labor to meet at reasonable times and confer in good faith with respect to wages, hours, and other terms and conditions of employment. This obligation does not compel either party to agree to a proposal or require them to make a concession.

The practical rules for bargaining in good faith are the following:

- Approach bargaining with a mind accessible to persuasion
- Follow procedures that will enhance the prospects of a negotiated settlement
- Be willing to discuss freely and fully your respective claims and demands; when such claims and demands are opposed by the other side, be prepared to justify your claims with reason
- Explore with an open mind proposals for compromise or other possible solutions of differences; make an effort to find a mutually satisfactory basis for agreement

The purpose of collective bargaining is to "bring to the bargaining table parties willing to present their proposals and articulate supporting reasons, to listen to and weigh the proposals and reasons of the other party, and to search for some common ground which can serve as the basis for a written bilateral agreement" (Gorman, 1976, p. 399). Good faith bargaining does not compel either side to meet the other part way. It does not require that concessions be made; the difference between the sides does not have to split so that they meet in the middle. Hard bargaining in which one side says no does not equate to bad faith. Good faith does require that both sides bring to the table a mind accessible to persuasion.

Bargaining in good faith during negotiations is no substitute for good faith dealings during the year. The true measure of success of bargaining is not securing an agreement; it is whether the relationship between the parties improves, or at least does not deteriorate. Good faith should be a description of an ongoing process of good relations between educators.

Good faith bargaining hopefully leads to an "elegant" negotiation solution (a term used by Richard Fossey at the University of Houston). The elegant solution includes the following:

1. The solution is better than any party's best alternative to a negotiated agreement.

2. All parties are committed to making the solution work.

3. The solution produces a good working relationship.

4. The solution is appropriate to long-term goals.

5. The solution can feasibly be implemented.

6. There is a clear understanding between the parties as to the meaning of the solution.

7. No joint interests are remaining to be addressed.

8. The process by which the agreement is achieved is seen by all parties as fair.

WORKING WITH UNIONS

Unions and collective bargaining are here for the foreseeable future. They fulfill a legitimate function, securing benefits and tangible protections for teachers. In my view, unions are neither the great horned devil nor the panacea for public education. They often act as silent allies and public adversaries. Because unions are here to stay, school administrators must be able and willing to work effectively within an organizational climate where unions not only have influence but also can exercise power—even though that power at times only appears to be a veto. Listed below are a few thoughts that I have gathered through my many years of working with unions. Some I learned easily, some I am still learning.

Approach to Unions

Read both *Getting Together: Building Relationships as We Negotiate* (Fisher & Brown, 1988) and *Getting to Yes: Negotiating Agreement Without Giving In* (Fisher & Ury, 1981). Both are classics and worth the time. *Getting Together* provides a framework for understanding relationships with others, and *Getting to Yes* gives a practical, philosophical approach to bargaining that I found helped to ground me while negotiating.

Do not assume that teachers do not support their union. The power of horizontal pressure is at least as strong if not stronger than vertical pressure. What a teacher says to you privately about the union, the teacher may not repeat publicly.

Keep the union informed. Like administrators, its leaders do not like surprises, especially public surprises.

Allow the union, as we do with individuals, to save face as often as practical.

Bargaining

Be prepared and prepare again. My first mistake in bargaining was to underestimate the union's position and to overestimate my ability to think quickly on my feet. An administrator who is well prepared with documentation and an understanding of the issues stands less of a chance of being taken advantage of to the detriment of the school district.

Bargaining is not a contest or a demonstration of your individual skill. You represent a constituency, the school board, and not yourself at the table.

You bargain with three parties. The first is the school board, which you must try to persuade that your recommendations have great merit. The second is your bargaining team, as you hammer out responses during caucuses. The third party sits across from you at the bargaining table.

Take careful notes during bargaining. They may be used later when trying to establish the intent of contract language. In my view, it does little good to watch the other side for telltale signs that give away their thinking. It is better to listen carefully and record what is being said. Doing so is tedious but important.

Grievances

I always wear a narrow, little grievance hat when grievances are presented to me. It is small and narrow because the range of topics is exceedingly small. A grievance is an alleged violation of a specific section of the contract. All conflicts are not grievances. Grievances that access the grievance procedures of the contract must be contained to addressing problems arising from the application or interpretation of the contract. To use the grievance procedure for any and all disagreements is to expand the contract without benefit of bargaining.

Grievances can be our friends. They provide a process for defining what the contract means. Sometimes, it is a difficult process and one that can be overused and abused, but it is a legitimate conflict resolution procedure. All too often administrators react negatively to grievances with displays of anger, embarrassment, and hurt feelings. Although these emotions may be real, they have no place within the administration of the contract. Keep the conversation professional and limit it to the alleged violations of the contract. An emotional response to grievances enables the process to be used as a cudgel to keep administrators off balance and under control. Having a grievance filed is neither a badge of distinction nor a badge of shame. We can use grievances to work through differences of opinion and help to resolve conflict, or we can use them to heighten conflict. We cannot control the union's use of the process; we can control our response to their use of the process. This approach does not mean that we cannot respond firmly and clearly when the process is being abused. It does mean that grievances are not the enemy of good leadership. Good leadership takes those opportunities to respond to conflict to model professional, honest behavior, to improve relationships, and to move the institution forward.

There is no magic bullet or incantation that makes working with the union easy. The public sport of union bashing and administrator trashing will no longer work in a new age of accountability. Confidence in public education is destroyed both inside and outside the schoolhouse gate when the public is left with the impression that the inept are leading the callous and the indifferent. Unions and collective bargaining are here for the foreseeable future. Educational leaders must learn about these two forces and find ways to effectively work with the union within the confines of a collective bargaining environment.

Specifically, we must work to ameliorate the negative impact of the industrial labor model. The challenge for teachers and their unions is to reconcile professionalism and unionism, service to other and self-interest. Administrators face a similar challenge in that they treat teachers as employees during bargaining and contract administration and as valued professionals on curricular and instructional matters. This two-silo approach to management (Rabban, 1991) is fraught with ambiguity and uncertainty. We must find ways through working with teachers and the union to consistently strive to change community perceptions to coincide with the reality that

educators are members of a learned profession. We must find ways to replicate the concept of good faith in bargaining and make it part of the daily work of educators. The challenges abound. The rewards for hard work do not necessarily belong to us educators; rather, the true beneficiaries are the students and the community.

REFERENCES

Bacharach, S. B., Shedd, J. B., & Conley, S. C. (1989). School management and teacher unions. *Teachers College Record, 91,* 97–105.

Bascia, N. (1994). *Unions in teachers' professional lives: Social, intellectual, and practical concerns.* New York: Teachers College Press.

Bradley, A. (1996, December 4). Education's "dark continent." *Education Week,* pp. 25–27.

Chase, B. (1997). *The new NEA: Reinventing teacher unions for a new era.* Remarks before the National Press Club, Washington, DC. Retrieved 1/20/02 from www.nea.org/.

Cooper, B. S., & Liotta, M. (2001). Urban teachers unions face their future: The dilemmas of organizational maturity. *Education and Urban Society, 34,* 101–118.

Cresswell, A. M., & Murphy, M. J., with Kerchner, C. T. (1980). *Teachers, unions, and collective bargaining in public education.* Berkeley, CA: McCutchan.

DeMitchell, T. A. (1993). Collective bargaining, professionalism, and restructuring. *International Journal of Educational Reform, 2,* 77–81.

DeMitchell, T. A., & Barton, R. M. (1996). Collective bargaining and its impact on local educational reform efforts. *Educational Policy, 10,* 366–378.

DeMitchell, T. A., & Carroll, T. (1999). Educational reform on the bargaining table: Impact, security, and tradeoffs. *Education Law Reporter, 134,* 675–693.

DeMitchell, T. A., & Cobb, C. D. (2003, November). *From the industrial union to the professional union? Teacher perceptions of professionalism and unionism.* Paper presented at the Annual Meeting of the Education Law Association, Savannah, GA.

DeMitchell, T. A., & Fossey, R. (1997). *The limits of law-based school reform: Vain hopes and false promises.* Lancaster, PA: Technomic.

DeMitchell, T. A., & Streshly, W. A. (1996). Must collective bargaining be reformed in an era of reform? *International Journal of Educational Reform, 5,* 78–85.

Farkas, S., Johnson, J., & Duffett, A. (2003). *Stand by me: What teachers really think about unions, merit pay, and other professional matters.* New York: Public Agenda.

Fisher, R., & Brown, S. (1988). *Getting together: Building relationships as we negotiate.* New York: Penguin Books.

Fisher, R., & Ury, W. (1981). *Getting to yes: Negotiating agreement without giving in.* New York: Penguin Books.

Gorman, R. A. (1976). *Basic text on labor law: Unionization and collective bargaining.* St. Paul, MN: West.

Johnson, S. M. (1987). Can schools be reformed at the bargaining table? *Teachers College Record, 89,* 269–280.

Johnson, S. M. (1988). Unionism and collective bargaining in the public schools. In N. J. Boyan (Ed.), *Handbook of research on educational administration: A project of the American Educational Research Association* (pp. 603–622). New York: Longman.

Johnson, S. M., & Kardos, S. M. (2000). Reform bargaining and its promise for school improvement. In T. Loveless (Ed.), *Conflicting missions: Teachers unions and educational reform* (pp. 7–46). Washington, DC: Brookings Institution Press.

Kerchner, C. T., & Caufman, K. D. (1993). Building the airplane while it is rolling down the runway. In C. T. Kerchner & J. E. Koppich (Eds.), *A union of professionals: Labor relations and educational reform* (pp. 1–24). New York: Teachers College Press.

Kerchner, C. T., Koppich, J. E., & Weeres, J. G. (1997). *United mind workers: Unions and teaching in the knowledge society.* San Francisco: Jossey-Bass.

Kerchner, C. T., & Mitchell, D. E. (1988). *The changing idea of a teachers' union.* New York: Falmer Press.

Koppich, J. E. (1993). Getting started: A primer on professional unionism. In C. T. Kerchner & J. E. Koppich (Eds.), *A union of professionals: Labor relations and educational reform.* New York: Teachers College Press.

Lieberman, M. (1997). *The teacher unions: How the NEA and the AFT sabotage reform and hold students, parents, teachers, and taxpayers hostage to bureaucracy.* New York: Free Press.

Little, J. W. (1993). Teachers' professional development in a climate of educational reform. *Educational Evaluation and Policy Analysis, 15,* 129–151.

Loveless, T. (Ed.). (2000). *Conflicting missions? Teachers unions and educational reform.* Washington, DC: Brookings Institution Press.

McDonnell, L. M., & Pascal, A. (1988, April). *Teacher unions and educational reform.* Santa Monica, CA: RAND.

Murphy, M. (1990). *Blackboard unions: The AFT and NEA, 1900–1980.* Ithaca, NY: Cornell University Press.

Rabban, D. M. (1991). Is unionization compatible with professionalism? *Industrial and Labor Relations Review, 45,* 97–112.

Streshly, W. A., & DeMitchell, T. A. (1994). *Teacher unions and TQE: Building quality labor relations.* Thousand Oaks, CA: Corwin.

Tannenbaum, A. S. (1965). Unions. In J. March (Ed.), *Handbook of organizations* (pp. 705–734). Chicago: Rand McNally.

Webb, S., & Webb, B. (1920). *History of trade unionism.* New York: Longmans, Green.

Wirt, F. M., & Kirst, M. W. (1997). *The political dynamics of American education.* Berkeley, CA: McCutchan.

23

Finance, Planning, and Budgeting

WILLIAM K. POSTON, JR.
Iowa State University

INTRODUCTION AND OVERVIEW

In the exigencies of educational endeavor, the types and amounts of available resources have always been an integral part of the plans, processes, and productivity of school organizations. How and under what conditions schooling is funded remains a highly complicated situation in every venue where educational programs and activities are provided. The purpose of this chapter is to explore the nature and status of financing public education in the United States and to explicate ways and means of planning and managing the financing process. Ironically, this chapter's title contains some redundancy in that budgeting is actually a form of planning, but the dramatic changes in funding elementary and secondary schools in the past decades have produced developmental responses from school organizations with unusual and different personal, social, economic, and political results.

The political shift in public expectations for schools in the United States has focused in recent times on a national drive to provide education that ensures that all schoolchildren learn and achieve to high standards. This is nothing new: Each generation of Americans has sought a better life for its children. For example, in 1918, the Commission on Reorganization of Secondary Education issued a report citing essential principles of education. Twenty years later, another national organization called for rededication to a set of educational precepts for American youth (Educational Policies Commission, 1938). This has continued with regularity over time, with one of the most visible reports issued under the Reagan administration in 1983, stating that America's schools have placed them at risk in global competition (National Commission on Excellence in Education, 1983). In the 5 years following 1983, no fewer than 32 other reports addressed the needs of schooling and future citizens ("Reports on U.S. Reform," 1988). The call for reform continues unabated.

A new set of national priorities, reflected in the No Child Left Behind Act proposed by President Bush in 2001 and signed into law on January 8, 2002, has now created problems for school boards and educators to meet the political demands placed on them within an economic climate of limited or eroding financial resources. Meeting the financial demands of improvement, reform, and economic temperance is nothing new in the American culture, which has always viewed education as critical for its continued world preeminence and economic survival.

A national desire to ensure that all children learn and achieve to high standards has provoked policymakers and educators to search for better ways to provide schoolchildren with the knowledge and skills they need to function effectively as citizens and workers in a future society that promises to be increasingly complex and globally interconnected (Ladd & Hansen, 2002).

Of course, any organizational activity, public or otherwise, requires resources to function, and a key part of the changes in educational enterprise involves how decisions for financial support are made and how financial support is applied from the more than $300 billion that the United States spends annually on public elementary and secondary education.

The largest piece of budgeted funds of state and local governments in the United States is for the support of education. About $1 in $20 of the U.S. gross domestic product is consumed by education, with about 75% of that going to traditional K–12 education alone. More than 50 million children attend school, and the number of people—educational professionals and support staff—employed in education numbers about 1 for every 10 students. By any measure, education in the United States is an enormous enterprise.

Because education is of such large magnitude, it has been the recipient of much attention in public policy arenas. Recent political and economic demands have been placed on schools, and new state and federal initiatives underscore the high priority on public education across the country. Needs of individuals and needs of society must be met by sound, effective, and efficient educational institutions;

economic and political policies of local, state, and federal governments determine how those needs are met, how they are valued, and how they are financed.

Educational leaders are vested with the responsibility to plan resource procurement and disbursements within the context of maintaining or improving the quality of educational attainment of students. Given the high profile of education and the changing nature of school funding, leaders are at a crossroads of increasing costs, diminishing resources, and rising expectations.

The purpose of this chapter is to visit these challenges, grasp cogent insights into the political and economic forces at work, and fashion some viable options and courses of action to meet and resolve the problems facing school leaders.

THE FINANCIAL CHALLENGE: WHAT ARE THE ISSUES AND SCOPE OF EDUCATIONAL FINANCE?

Responsibility for public education, according to the Tenth Amendment to the U.S. Constitution, was not "delegated to the United States, nor prohibited by it to the States," which made it "reserved to the individual States or to the people." Given the assignment of the function of education to the states, most states have delegated much of the responsibility to local communities as managerial organizations, or school systems or districts. States have created these entities for day-to-day operations of educational programs, but the legal and administrative strictures that guide education are as different as the number of states permits. Generally, a local school system-governing body, elected by the people, operates within the state legislative structure, state rules and regulations, and administrative directives and requirements from state agencies, such as state boards of education.

When compared to the rest of the world, the American educational system is unique. Coupled with the intent to educate *all* individuals, the American system does not finance education for individuals; it finances education for the benefit of society as a whole (Association of School Business Officials, 1990). States define the range and nature of their educational programs, which must be extended to all residents by local school systems. Ironically, this egalitarian principle is confounded by uneven distributions of wealth from community to community. The ability of local communities to offer the state-required programs varies dramatically within states, and the financial strength of states to offer educational programs varies from state to state. In fact, in some states, some local communities have as much as 100 times the wealth to provide education as some other local communities. As a result, a child's educational opportunities can be a function of the wealth, or lack thereof, of his or her resident community (Kozol, 1985).

Despite the highly decentralized school finance systems and the plethora of reforms initiated in school finance for the past three decades, U.S. education is still dominated by huge disparities in education spending, with the differences between states increasing.

The Rise of Shared Governance and State Expectations

Moreover, in recent years, many people have argued for state and federal subsidies, through tax vouchers or tax credits, but in such a plan, the state or federal government financially subsidizes the parent's choice to send a child to a private or religious school. Under voucher or tax credit plans, the individual economic benefit takes precedence over the benefits that occur to society, contrary to historical patterns of funding for schools. Despite this argument, American education, until recently, was never financed based on the residual benefits that may occur to an individual.

Despite many specific state configurations, each state has a legal obligation to see that all

residents who fall in specified age ranges are provided a "basic" educational program. Furthermore, educational opportunity must be evenly distributed so as not to be a function of the wealth or lack of wealth of a local community (Association of School Business Officials, 1990). How well states provide equal access to a "basic" education depends in large part on what the state calls "basic." Each state, usually through its state legislature, prescribes core requirements for all schools, generally defined in terms of statewide graduation standards or in expectations for students. These core requirements take many forms and are difficult to define, resulting in litigation in many state courts (Enrich, 1995).

The Development of National Goals for Education Finance Systems

Given the problem above, the U.S. Congress required the U.S. Department of Education to convene a Committee on Education Finance under a contract with the National Academy of Sciences to evaluate the nature of elementary and secondary educational funding by federal, state, and local governments. The key question posed to the committee was as follows (U.S. Department of Education, 2002b):

> How can education finance systems be designed to ensure that all students achieve high levels of learning and that education funds are raised and used in the most efficient and effective manner possible?

The Committee on Education Finance transformed this question into three preferred effects that educational finance systems should deliver:

1. A substantially higher level of achievement for all students, while using resources in a cost-efficient manner (i.e., improved learning and cost benefits)

2. Efforts to break the nexus between student background characteristics and student

achievement (i.e., elimination of the achievement gap)

3. Generation of revenue in a fair and efficient manner (i.e., funding adequacy and fairness)

With the exception of Goal 2, the results were framed in actual ends or products to be realized, but the second goal points out a difficulty often found in school planning: a commitment to process and not to a product. Effective planning might frame the goal as an "elimination" or "eradication" of the nexus connection that results in the achievement gap, which is an achievable goal according to some researchers (English & Steffy, 2001).

The committee's work was complicated by the structure of American education—most responsibility for educational finance is delegated about equally to local and state levels of government. The committee sought to assess the current condition of education, and Goals 1 and 2 emerged from their assessment. Although schools are not failing as badly as some people charge, they are not producing high levels of learning, especially from economically deprived populations (Ladd & Hansen, 2002).

The achievement gap noted in all contemporary literature is a continual vexation to schools, and it is highly related to socioeconomic factors. Research has clearly established that the higher the economic standing of the student's family, the more achievement scores rise on all high-stakes testing (Downey et al., 2002). This connection between educational attainment and economic well-being has precipitated considerable concern across the nation, particularly in school systems with substantive populations of economically disadvantaged youth.

The third goal of the committee, "raising revenue fairly and efficiently," presents a formidable political challenge, in that the federal role in funding education is very small, with local governments and local property taxes picking up a major portion of the cost. The previously mentioned variances in school

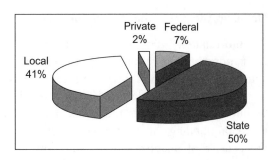

Figure 23.1 Percentage of Educational Funding by Sources, 2003

system wealth and resultant spending produces widespread feelings of unfairness, particularly among low-income taxpayers who may pay more proportionately for education than their wealthier counterparts. The distribution of funding across sources is shown in Figure 23.1.

The need for fairness in revenue acquisition and distribution persistently has prevailed in policy decisions but has been hampered by state legislatures that fail to lift the burdens for funding schools from local communities with limited capabilities. For example, in 1993, the Arizona Supreme Court struck down local property tax support for school construction. Four years later, the Arizona Legislature adopted a program, Schools First, which gave responsibility for school construction, about $250 million a year, to the State of Arizona. Amazingly, the Arizona Legislature failed to provide any funding source—and that spurious measure was supported by the Arizona Chamber of Commerce (Ducote, 2004).

State legislatures have been reluctant to accept responsibility for school funding, but in the past three decades, litigants in many states have been successful in overturning state finance systems on the grounds that they violate equal protection provisions or education clauses. Nearly all states have changed their educational finance systems in the intervening period, but many states have also initiated other reform measures, including a number of categorical programs that address special needs of students and funding inequities (Ladd & Hansen, 2002).

Defining Adequate Educational Funding

Unfortunately, funding disparities across the nation continue to mirror economic characteristics of communities, with levels of educational funding reflecting levels of wealth within and between states and local communities. Confounding this continuing problem is the paucity of understanding about how to translate dollars into student achievement. Empirical studies have failed to show clear connections between variations of resource allocations and differences in student achievement, and what constitutes funding adequacy is not empirically established.

Some researchers have pointed out the connection between the interests of citizens, who care about the value of their homes, and the quality of their educational systems. It is pointed out that most of the court decisions in school finance have rescinded local tax systems but have divorced the value of one's home from the quality of schools, creating less enthusiasm for public education within communities. Moreover, centralization of school finance may result in deteriorating quality in education. For example, two states with almost exclusively state financing, Hawaii and California, have highly problematical schools. No studies have found that high levels of state funding, as opposed to local taxation, have improved academic test performance by students, and some indicate that the shift away from local support for education has made things worse (Fischel, 2002).

Much of the legislation and legislative activity in recent years has focused on providing "adequacy" in funding for every student in the state, but most states have not addressed the question of what is adequate and what is not. In addition, there is no federal mandate or constitutional requirement for equity across or among states. Differences in per-pupil funding are substantial, and variations in per-pupil funding among states have been shown to account for almost two thirds of the total variance nationally in per-pupil spending (Augenblick, Myers, & Anderson, 1997). Even after adjusting for regional cost differences, per-pupil spending varies by as much as 100%. As shown in Figure 23.2, Utah annually spends the least on elementary and secondary education for youth ages 5–17, $4,681, and Alaska spends the most among states, $9,421 (Bureau of the Census, 2002).

Equity is difficult to accomplish at best, and because there is no generally accepted definition of either funding or curriculum adequacy, discussions about equity are not very practicable. However, most states employ some version of a foundation plan, which provides a level of funding for each student within the state based on a political determination of educational goals, student needs, and the availability of tax revenues. The judgment underlying the foundation level is more political than educational, and most states dedicate about one third or more of their total tax resources to elementary and secondary education (Guthrie, 1997).

Using Adequacy to Fund Schools

Replacing the current political systems to determine adequacy and to allocate resources to education accordingly hinges on the perception within the state as to whether the educational system is sufficient to provide appropriate educational services to all the state's students. Some of the basic options are delineated below (Augenblick & Myers, 1994). States have four options to use in determining levels of adequacy in educational funding, with their choice depending in some measure on information available, efficacy of calculation methodologies, and the extent of quality control exercised or sought to be exercised by the state.

1. Historical spending approach. In this approach, the state sets a cost level based on the actual expenditures of the prior year. The

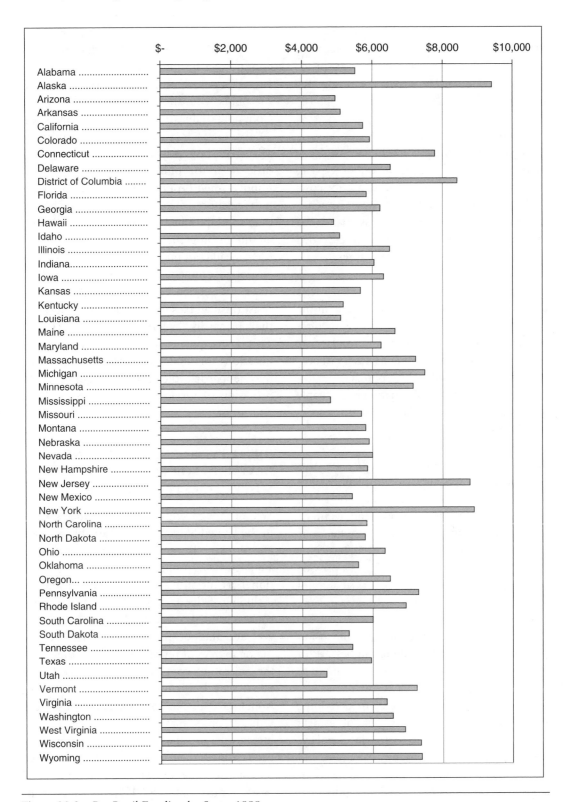

Figure 23.2   Per-Pupil Funding by State, 1999

approach is predictable, adjusts for unspent funding from prior years, and keeps pace with inflation if used properly. However, if spending was inadequate the prior year, it may not keep pace with needs.

2. Expert design approach. In this case, experts are selected from educational finance to determine the needs of a benchmark, or typical, hypothetical school system and to ascribe costs to those needs. This approach assures responding to needs, but the approach was abandoned in Illinois and California because costs exceeded the political will of the state legislatures.

3. Econometric approach. This approach tries to tie educational organizational results in the form of pupil achievement to spending requirements. Complicated regression formulae are used to determine the funding necessary to produce the desired result. This approach is hampered by the dearth of information of a reliable and valid nature to make the performance-based connections across states.

4. Successful schools approach. In this approach, attempts are made to identify optimal school systems—not too large or small, not too wealthy, and so on—and examine the corresponding costs of those systems to be used as a guideline for the cost of a "basic" or "successful" system. Modifications to provide for variances in characteristics of school systems are often needed.

Education is of such enormous dimension in America and needs of communities are of such diversity that it is difficult, if not impossible, for policymakers to define what is adequate. It is even more difficult to determine what adequacy should cost. School leaders need to be prepared to enter into policy-formulating conversations and to provoke and inspire rational people to made funding decisions that contribute to societal and individual well-being within reasonable cost.

Leaders will likely find that building public will in support of education will continue to be increasingly difficult. In the United States, the gap between those who pay for public education and those who benefit from public education has been growing wider (Ward, 1995). In other words, the wealthy can afford to buy private education and have little need for public education, while the impoverished do not have any alternative to public schools. There are those who believe that some political perspectives are directed at diminishing the role of public education for some ulterior purpose, perhaps to reduce the cost of government (Berliner & Biddle, 1996). As a consequence, many wealthy citizens resist raising taxes to pay for public education that primarily benefits the less privileged. This consequence raises very challenging questions for financing public education and may jeopardize the future of equity, or the provision of services according to needs, in education.

IDENTIFYING AND COMPARING REVENUES FOR EDUCATION: WHERE DOES FUNDING COME FROM?

Without the raising of revenue, public schools in the United States would be unable to operate or exist. Revenue is financial and other support (i.e., property) provided to educational organizations from a variety of sources, including federal, state, local, and private sources, and the receipt of revenue varies by type and amount from state to state. The four major sources of revenue include income from the federal government, generally raised from taxes; state legislature appropriations; funding from local efforts or agencies; and other sources. Other sources may include private sources, investments or sales of property, and miscellaneous sources, such as fees or gifts of property.

Total revenue for education on a per-pupil basis approximates $7,067, of which state sources provide about $3,418, local sources about $3,168, and federal sources about $481, as shown in Table 23.1 (U.S. Department of Education, 2002a). State sources provide the most income for schools, and most policy direction for schools comes from the states.

However, with recent federal initiatives and requirements for schools, centralized direction from the federal government is growing but does not carry with it a matching level of support for public schooling.

Table 23.1 Total Revenues (in Cost-Adjusted Dollars) Per Pupil by State

State	Total Revenue		Federal Sources		State Sources		Local Sources	
	Per Pupil	Rank	Per Pupil	Rank	Per Pupil	Rank	Per Pupil	Rank
United States	7,067	-	481	-	3,418	-	3,168	-
Alabama	6,198	44	582	15	3,871	162	1,745	46
Alaska	7,279	22	894	2	4,524	6	1,861	42
Arizona	5,859	49	598	13	2,596	43	2,665	33
Arkansas	6,541	37	706	9	3,773	17	2,061	39
California	5,889	47	482	25	3,545	23	1,862	41
Colorado	6,387	41	324	49	2,773	40	3,289	23
Connecticut	8,378	4	328	48	3,126	30	4,924	5
Delaware	7,977	10	605	12	5,136	4	2,237	38
District of Columbia	8,536	3	1,405	1	0	51	7,131	1
Florida	6,827	29	522	22	3,330	27	2,975	28
Georgia	7,058	25	481	26	3,611	22	2,966	29
Hawaii	6,775	31	585	14	6,027	1	164	51
Idaho	5,873	48	413	37	3,682	20	1,778	45
Illinois	6,883	28	464	30	1,956	49	4,463	9
Indiana	8,143	9	394	41	4,184	12	3,565	19
Iowa	7,572	17	402	39	3,882	15	3,289	24
Kansas	7,452	19	441	32	4,313	9	2,697	32
Kentucky	6,571	36	629	11	4,056	14	1,886	40
Louisiana	6,472	39	729	7	3,263	29	2,479	35
Maine	7,675	14	537	18	3,495	25	3,644	18
Maryland	7,610	15	398	40	2,964	36	4,248	12
Massachusetts	7,097	24	355	45	2,889	38	3,853	15
Michigan	8,283	6	549	17	5,468	2	2,266	37
Minnesota	7,797	13	383	42	4,082	13	3,333	22
Mississippi	5,470	50	771	5	3,030	34	1,670	47
Missouri	6,949	27	434	33	2,760	42	3,755	16
Montana	6,980	26	713	8	3,271	28	2,996	27
Nebraska	7,575	16	504	23	2,510	44	4,561	8
Nevada	6,760	32	310	50	2,150	48	4,299	11
New Hampshire	6,460	40	246	51	604	50	5,610	2
New Jersey	9,158	1	331	47	3,643	21	5,184	4
New Mexico	6,337	43	840	3	4,574	5	923	50
New York	8,652	2	471	28	3,438	26	4,744	6
North Carolina	6,342	42	460	31	4,268	10	1,614	48
North Dakota	6,747	33	834	4	2,771	41	3,143	26
Ohio	7,375	21	429	35	3,040	33	3,905	14
Oklahoma	6,073	45	525	20	3,739	18	1,809	44
Oregon	7,427	20	475	27	4,216	11	2,735	30

(Continued)

Table 23.1 (Continued)

State	Total Revenue		Federal Sources		State Sources		Local Sources	
	Per Pupil	Rank	Per Pupil	Rank	Per Pupil	Rank	Per Pupil	Rank
Pennsylvania	7,975	11	467	29	3,083	31	4,425	10
Rhode Island	7,475	18	406	38	3,000	35	4,069	13
South Carolina	6,796	30	576	16	3,499	24	2,721	31
South Dakota	6,529	38	654	10	2,322	46	3,553	20
Tennessee	5,906	46	522	21	2,820	39	2,564	34
Texas	6,588	35	503	24	2,909	37	3,177	25
Utah	4,998	51	347	46	3,050	32	1,602	49
Vermont	8,220	7	427	36	2,419	45	5,374	3
Virginia	7,207	23	377	43	2,260	47	4,571	7
Washington	6,702	34	430	34	4,421	8	1,851	43
West Virginia	8,209	8	758	6	5,143	3	2,307	36
Wisconsin	8,375	5	376	44	4,495	7	3,504	21
Wyoming	7,891	12	531	19	3,712	19	3,649	17

SOURCE: U.S. Department fo Education, National Center for Education Statistics (2002a).

Federal Revenues

The U.S. government provides about 7% of the total revenue for schools on a per-pupil basis. Although the average amount of federal funding is about $481 per pupil, funding ranges from a low of $324 per pupil in the State of Colorado to a high of $1,405 per pupil in the District of Columbia (U.S. Department of Education, 2002a).

Federal funding comes in many forms but is generally confined to categorical areas such as impact aid for military installations, school lunch-program support, special education, vocational education, block grants, and allocations for low-income students. Most federal funding is distributed through state governments for fiscal control, and it is usually tied to the special needs of certain groups of disadvantaged students.

State Revenues

States provide about 48% of the total revenue for education on a per-pupil basis but generally provide most of the policy and regulatory direction for school systems. Generally, states make appropriations based on information obtained relative to financial, demographic, and historical characteristics of school systems, and those data are used to inform state legislatures as to fiscal capabilities of the state. Legislatures ostensibly use data such as state tax revenue projections, costs of previous year's programs, the number of public schoolchildren, and state financial reserves to make political, economic, and educational decisions and policies for the state.

The bulk of state revenue is accrued from a number of taxes, including property tax levies, income taxes, sales taxes, and other state taxes and fees. Some states do not have income taxes, and some states do not have sales taxes. In those states, other sources of revenue pick up the difference. Some states use nontraditional sources to fund education and other public services, such as lotteries and enterprise (business-like) income.

Local Revenues

After all federal and state funding levels have been determined, local community school boards are left with the responsibility to raise locally the remaining funds needed. In nearly all states, those decisions are constrained by statutory or regulatory directives that limit how much money may be raised, how much the tax rate may be increased, how the decision may be made, or how much the local share may be increased. In a few states, school boards are not allowed to make the revenue determinations, which are reserved for other governmental agencies, that is, county boards of supervisors, city councils, or other intermediate agencies. Nearly all local funds for the support of education are generated through some form of local property tax, but in a few states, boards are allowed to use income surcharge taxes.

Types of Taxes

States use many different configurations of taxes to support education within the state, including taxes on motor vehicles, railroads, mines, utilities, licenses, fines, inheritances, and a host of other areas of human activity. However, the lion's share of educational funding from states is provided by property taxes, sales taxes, income taxes, or combinations of any or all three. It is apparent that income and sales taxes are driven by the wealth of the state as a whole, rather than local communities, and may be used to build equity across the state.

Much controversy surrounds decision making as to which types of taxes to use. Property taxes, which are used extensively by local communities in support of public education, are calculated on a property's assessed value and collected from the property owner. Property tax is controversial in that ownership of property may or may not be an indicator of wealth. Assessment of value varies from location to location, but courts have maintained that "fair market value" is a reasonable assessment tool.

Property taxes are commonly stable, easy to administer, and follow levels of wealth. A difficulty with property tax lies in its uneven distribution across local communities, resulting in unequal spending and unequal tax rates.

Courts across the country have rendered many state financing systems unconstitutional on those grounds. However, unequal tax rates and bases are not themselves indicators of unequal economic burdens (Fischel, 2002).

Income taxes, usually indexed with increasingly larger rates for ascending levels of income, come in two types: individual and corporate. The income tax is a clear example of a progressive tax and cannot be readily shifted to someone else by the individual paying the tax. Income taxes depend on the principles of *social benefit theory* (benefit is to society), *ability to pay* (tax increases along with the tax base), and *elasticity* (yields follow changes in income) (Jones, 1986).

Sales taxes are thought of as regressive taxes and include both general sales taxes, levied against products and services, and excise taxes, levied against specific products such as expensive automobiles, boats, alcoholic beverages, purchases overseas, petroleum, and the like. Some excise taxes may be levied on the producer rather than the consumer directly, and taxes of this kind are levied at both state and federal levels.

Revenue Distribution and Equalization Plans

Educational leaders struggle with conflicting best interests when confronted with financing education in an economical manner with equity in appropriations. Meeting the needs of diverse clientele while trying to limit taxation to reasonable levels often presents a highly difficult set of circumstances. Since the Great Depression, states have increasingly assumed a greater role in financing education, and they have been confronted with four troublesome questions:

1. What is a "basic" or "appropriate" level of education?

2. What should be the state's portion of the cost of education?

3. How much control should the state exercise over the operation of education?

4. What is "equal educational opportunity," and "equitable" educational finance?

For decades, states have tried to equalize educational funding and to equalize educational opportunity for students, and creative taxation systems have been created to balance between state and local funding and to set up fair systems of taxation despite wide variances in taxable wealth across school systems. Gradually, funding formulas were developed that began the slow trend of transferring costs from local educational agencies to the state. By the early 1980s, all states (except Hawaii, which is a state system) had some type of formula distribution system in place, which raised the state share of funding to about 48%. The distribution systems fall into three types:

1. Flat grant, categorical, or entitlement programs

2. State funding programs

3. Equalization programs

Flat Grants

Although each state has its own approach, flat grants or foundation programs are amounts paid to local educational agencies in a uniform manner, usually in dollars per pupil, irrespective of the local taxpayers' ability to pay. Some states have employed a method of "weighting" diverse needs (size, location, demographics, etc.) to provide differentiated allocations to local systems. Few states are using flat grants now due to the determinations by courts and legislatures that the capacities of local systems to support their programs were not considered, violating many of the principles of equity (differential support according to needs) and fairness to poor systems (neutrality of assessed wealth per pupil).

State Funding Programs

In this type of funding, the state assumes the entire cost of public schooling, but Hawaii remains the only state with this system. However, other states, notably California and Texas, have assumed greater shares of funding for schools. In California, the State Supreme Court was the first to require statewide funding equality, and because of *Serrano v. Priest* (1971), tax revenues in nearly all California school districts vary by 5% or less and are controlled almost entirely by the state (O'Sullivan, Sexton, & Sheffrin, 1995). In Texas, the state has placed equalizing limits on revenue rates by requiring wealthier systems to subsidize poorer systems (often referred to as the "Robin Hood" law; see "power equalizing plans" below).

Centralized funding of schools has serious implications, and the trend toward centralized funding may have undermined political support for education and may have caused the quality of public education to get worse (Fischel, 2002).

Equalization Programs

Often called foundation programs, these programs balance the relationship between tax bases, tax rates, educational costs, and discretionary expenditures. There are three types of equalization or foundation plans:

1. Minimum required expenditure per pupil. In these plans, the state requires a minimum tax rate uniformly across all districts, and depending on the assessed tax valuation per pupil, the state's portion is adjusted so that all districts receive a minimal funding level drawn from the local tax and the flexible state portion, which may range from nothing in a wealthy district to a very large portion of the cost in a poor district. To prevent districts from exceeding minimum standards set by the state, most states limit the extent to which a local district can exceed the minimum funding level.

2. Percentage equalizing and guaranteed tax plans. In this type of plan, the formula tries to balance the ability to pay for each district. Percentage equalizing addresses expenditures, and guaranteed tax plans equalize the revenue side–with little difference in the effect. In percentage equalizing, the local district establishes its financial needs, and the state contributes its share based on the wealth of the district. In the guaranteed tax plan, each district also sets an expenditure level, but the state then determines the state guaranteed tax base linked to the wealth of the local district.

3. Power equalizing plans. In these plans, developed in the last few decades, there is a wealth recapture mechanism. A uniform tax rate is guaranteed by the state, and districts with greater assessed valuation than needed to meet the guaranteed rate return the excess to the state, which distributes it to poorer districts. In effect, this resembles the current plan implemented in Texas.

Implications of Revenue Operations

Apart from the type of funding process, no method is perfect, and changes and modifications need to continue to be made. However, some things are unlikely to change. Taxpayers may continue to be treated differently based on their ability to pay, so that regardless of where students live, their community's wealth or lack of it would not determine the quality or quantity of the educational program provided by public schools. With that equal opportunity goal in place, both society and individual students can benefit.

CATEGORIZING EXPENDITURES: WHERE DOES THE MONEY GO?

In large measure, expenditures by public educational agencies follow available revenues, if not in amount, at least in direction. The more money available to school systems, the more

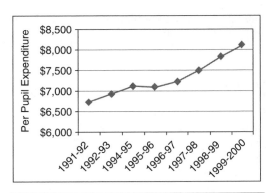

Figure 23.3 Public K–12 Schools' Expenditure Growth, 1991–2000

a school system is likely to spend (U.S. Department of Education, 2002a, 2002b).

Also, expenditures parallel enrollment levels. For example, during the unique enrollment decline from 1972 to 1985, when enrollment in elementary and secondary schools dropped from more than 46 million students to 39 million students, expenditures fell. When enrollment began to grow, with enrollment now more than 44 million, expenditures rose accordingly and more. Expenditures from 1991 to 2000 increased an average of 20.4%, while enrollment grew by 11.2% in the same period (see Figure 23.3).

Total expenditures for elementary and secondary education, which comprise both current and capital expenditures, were $339 billion in 1998–1999, with current expenditures totaling more than $299 billion—or about 88% of total expenditures. All three measures of state wealth—Gross State Product per capita, median family income, and median housing value—were consistently related to all measures of expenditure per pupil except capital expenditures. In other words, wealthier states tended to spend more money per pupil on almost all education functions than poorer states (see Table 23.2).

Expenditure Patterns

Some anomalies have caused the pattern of expenditures to change over the past three

Table 23.2   Total Expenditures for Public Elementary and Secondary Education by Function and State: 1999–2000 (in 1000s)

Category	Amount (dollars)	Percentage
Instruction	199,951,526	52.4
Debt service	43,401,495	11.4
Operations and maintenance	31,162,057	8.2
School administration	18,379,811	4.8
Student support	16,045,679	4.2
Instructional staff	14,639,534	3.8
Transportation	13,006,821	3.4
Food services	12,920,064	3.4
Other support	10,188,315	2.7
Interest on debt	9,135,443	2.4
General administration	6,696,874	1.8
Other current expenditures	5,483,573	1.4
Enterprise operations	818,228	0.2
Grand Total	**381,829,420**	

decades. For example, the different purposes thrust on schools during this period, including special education, limited English programs, at risk programs, desegregation, and so on, have precipitated an increase in per-pupil expenditure with a corresponding decrease in spending for regular education. Special education accounted for the largest amount of the increased spending, consuming more than one third of the new dollars. Special education has grown from 4% of all expenditures in 1967 to about 17% of all expenditures today. Teachers' share of expenditures dropped over the same period, while expenditures for para-professionals grew to nearly 10% of special education funding (Miles & Rothstein, 1995).

Resource disparities within school systems, reflected in expenditure levels, are masked by the per-pupil expenditure figures systemwide, and per-pupil spending levels are misleading. School boards can direct funds to various schools for a plethora of reasons, with inequalities in spending across schools, which affect schools' real capabilities. For example, inexperienced teachers in large numbers at one school will cost less than very experienced teachers, but they may also impact school performance and productivity (Hill, 1994).

(See Figure 23.4 for a summary of total expenditures by state.)

OBSTACLES IN EDUCATIONAL EXPENDITURE PRACTICES

Even in cases where reform is pressuring change, most school systems spend little on quality improvement. Less than 2% of school systems have had their curriculum audited, and school system expenditures on training and development are miserly when compared to training and development expenditures in business.

Another major shortcoming of school system expenditure patterns is the difficulty in understanding clearly where the money goes. School finance plans and reports fail consistently to detail expenditures by program or activity, making meaningful assessment of the effect of spending nearly impossible (Miles & Rothstein, 1995).

School systems and states almost always report expenditures by function and object—a method too general to be of much help— thereby thwarting attempts to evaluate the cost-benefit relationships in activities and expenditures. It seems imprudent and counterintuitive, but

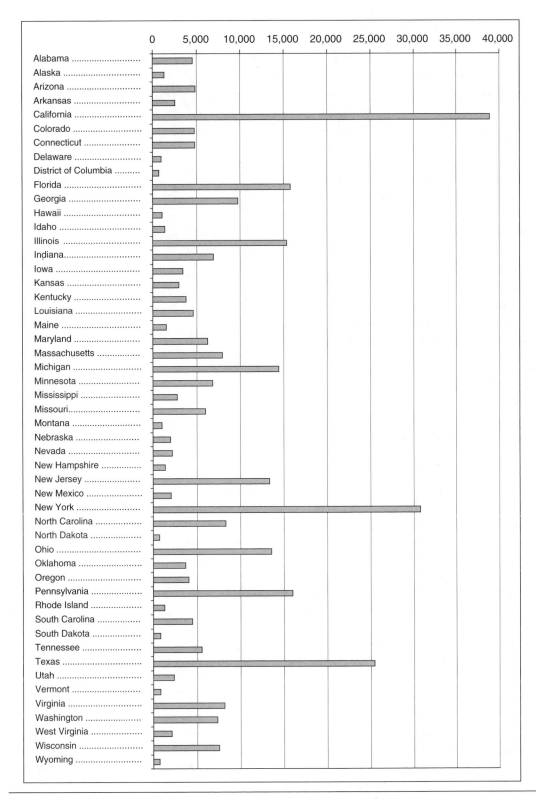

Figure 23.4 Total K–12 Education Expenditures by State, 1999 (in 1000s)

even the prestigious Association of School Business Officials (2000) supports continuing this anomaly. Moreover, capricious or arbitrary expenditure patterns, not focused on results, contribute to a lack of confidence in the schools' economic management structures. When faced withdisparate expenditure patterns in schools, teachers and administrators may view the resource allocation process as unfair, encouraging feelings of suspicion and cynicism (Hill, 1994). With that challenge in mind, the next section on planning and budgeting may provide some answers.

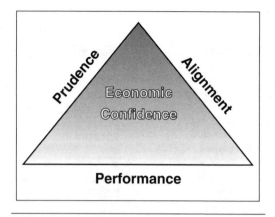

Figure 23.5 Dimensions of Economic Confidence in Education

THE TASK OF FINANCIAL PLANNING: HOW DOES BUDGETING IMPACT THE ORGANIZATIONAL MISSION?

The public's confidence in public schools' economic practices hinges on three factors: prudence, alignment, and performance, as illustrated in Figure 23.5. The three factors, or dimensions, include:

- *Prudence:* Efficiency and maintaining the "financial house" in order
- *Alignment:* Balancing expenditures within revenues, that is, "living within means"
- *Performance:* Demonstrating results tied to organizational goals

Given these three factors, school systems can more readily count on their constituencies for support, particularly in financial areas (Pomerantz, 1992).

Achieving economic confidence entails proper financial controls and sound planning. Planning establishes the goals and objectives, describes ways and means and responsible parties needed to achieve those goals, and establishes a time horizon for accomplishing the goals and objectives. Engaging in short- and long-range planning assures adequate availability of resources and—in the right circumstances—attainment of intended ends.

Defining Budgeting and Financial Planning

Planning in educational finance is essentially budgeting, and vice versa. A budget describes the system in financial terms and provides the yardsticks with which organizational performance can be measured.

Money, it goes without saying, plays a key role in schools, and how it is allocated separates the highly productive school systems from their unproductive counterparts. The primary purpose of a budget is to translate educational priorities into programmatic and financial terms (Thompson, Wood, & Honeyman, 1994).

Aims and Rationale for Budgeting

Rational organizations have goals that translate into activities that are assessed for effectiveness against the goals. Budgets provide benchmarks to define activities and generate information to measure performance, and budgets formulate planning for using available revenues for needed expenditures to accomplish the intentions and purposes of the organization. In effect, budgeting is the process of preparing, compiling, and monitoring financial plans. (See Figure 23.6 for an overview of the budgeting cycle.)

Budgeting provides a number of advantages and operational substance for school systems, including:

- Facilitating the organization and subparts in achieving planned objectives
- Creating a framework within which individuals, departments, and schools can function
- Coordinating and focusing the work and activities of the organization
- Providing a means for evaluating organizational success
- Responding to diagnosed needs of clientele and community
- Reacting to changes in the mission and the nature of clientele
- Providing long-term implementation of objectives
- Measuring results and costs and monitoring performance against needs

Principles of Change With Impact on Budgeting

Budgeting as a form of planning needs to incorporate the best information available in terms of what works and what does not work in planning. In educational planning, there are many factors to take into account to make it successful. For example, even the best of intended strategies have to be tailored to all kinds of circumstances inconceivable in their initial formulation. Planning provides a conceptual tidiness that may provide a better vocabulary for internal communications; planning demands communication with organizational members about the organization's situation, objectives, and clear expressions of policy (Mintzberg, 1994).

Budgeting serves as a control system, facilitating a process to compare expectations with actual performance. Some also believe that just engaging in planning processes builds commitment to the organization, which in turn serves as an effective means of control and change.

Organizational change demands an active initiation of change, support to alleviate anxiety about change, and recognition that both

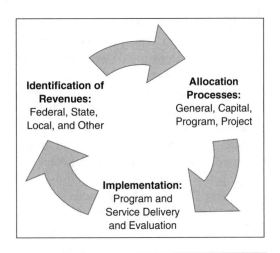

Figure 23.6   Diagram of Budgeting Cycle

practices and beliefs must be changed, but not overnight. Effective ownership and adoption of change takes considerable time (Fullan, 2001).

Types of Budgeting

In budget planning, planners can choose from four types of budgeting, classified to provide conceptual comparisons (Poston, Stone, & Muther, 1992). The four types include the following:

1. Line item budgeting (Answers the question: What is purchased?). In this type of budgeting, sometimes called Level 1, funds are allocated across units (schools, departments, etc.) by function (instruction, support, etc.) and object (salaries, benefits, supplies, etc.). Despite line item budgeting's popularity (about 90% of school system budgets), it does not provide information about activities or programs, usually is formulaic, inadequately addresses diverse individual unit needs, and provides insufficient cost-benefit analysis. The process is highly dependent on prior history, and is prone to using flat percentage increases determined by a closely held process controlled by few people. Most states require fiscal reporting in line item formats.

2. Program budgeting (Answers the question: What activities are provided?). Program, or Level 2, budgeting aggregates requests, descriptions of need, and allocations by program or activity. Program budgeting provides a greater opportunity for matching allocations to specific programmatic needs across buildings and system subunits. Cost-benefit determinations are greatly facilitated, and this method underscores the connection between educational purposes and financial cost. Instead of line items like "salaries, supplies, insurance, and so on," budgeting is based on programs like "kindergarten instruction, fine arts, guidance and counseling, and athletics, and so on," to name a few examples. If coupled with sound data on program needs and results, program budgeting effectively focuses allocations on defined and changing needs of activities and programs and minimizes attention to prior allocation levels—with corresponding increased attention on productivity, or "more bang for the buck." In effect, instead of the budget driving the program, the program drives the budget (English, 1996).

3. Incremental program budgeting (Answers the question: What activities are provided and at what level?). Given the organization and structure of program budgeting, incremental budgeting—Level 3 budgeting—attaches the component of levels of quality with increments of cost. Built on the zero-based budgeting concept, funding is allocated to programs by increments, beginning with a base level, usually less than the prior year's allocation (Wholey, 1979). The program activities are organized across the system, with subunit allocations incorporated within the program increments (sometimes called packages), in ascending levels of quality or quantity and cost. For example, the fine arts program might be organized into three packages as follows:

a. *Recovery or base increment:* (90% of prior year allocation) includes general music and art instruction K–12, instrumental music 7–12, no drama offerings. (This is called

recovery because if funding is done at this level, the system recovers 10% of the previous year's cost, enabling reallocation of those amounts to other programs or retrenchment.)

b. *Current increment:* (100% of prior year allocation) includes general music and art instruction K–12, instrumental music 4–12, and drama 7–12.

c. *Enhancement increment:* (105% of prior year allocation) includes general music and art instruction K–12, instrumental music 4–12, drama 7–12, commercial art 10–12, and strings instruction 7–12.

Note that the quality or extent of program offerings increases with cost, giving the school system considerable latitude in decision making. Costs are tied to purposes and program offerings, giving decision makers and the public an opportunity to compare value and allocate costs to program increments on a priority basis.

4. Performance-based program budgeting. Incorporating the attributes of program budgeting and incremental program budgeting, performance-based budgeting—Level 4 budgeting—adds the enormously important component of results analysis, or performance measurement for value determination. The purpose of a program component is defined, the nature of the operations and structure of the program are delineated, and systematic budget planning extends the credibility, validity, and prudence in cost containment. The components of performance-based program budgeting include the following (Poston et al., 1992):

a. Requests are built on measured value, purposes, and results in incremental form. (See Table 23.3, Sample Performance-Based Budgeting Planning Form.)

b. To enhance the quality of information and enhance decision-making efficacy, teacher and principal participation is encouraged in allocation decisions.

c. To clarify expectations of program component value, results, and extent of costs, public deliberations are used in evaluating components for funding or nonfunding.

Table 23.3 Sample Performance-Based Budgeting Planning Form

Performance-Based Program Budgeting Package Description

(Complete one for each program subcomponent or package)

Program Title: _____ Package Level: _____

Program Package Cost: _____ Manager: _____

1. Describe program activities and services provided by this package.

2. Describe how activities requested in this package will differ from previous year's operation.

3. Describe how the package, if funded, will relate to or support the system's long-range plans.

4. Describe methods/means for assessment of the ends or accomplishments of this package.

5. What organizational results or outcomes will be affected if this package is not funded?

---

d. To establish funding in priority value, program components are rank ordered, and priorities are set by a collaborative team, including personnel recommended in *b* above. (See excerpt of a rank-ordered performance-based budget in Table 23.4.)

With performance-based budgeting, several advantages accrue to the system. For example, tangible connections are initiated between feedback on program results and allocation processes (sometimes referred to as "data-driven" decisions), public participation in the priority-setting process enhances credibility (improving public support) and ownership, program managers initiate new paradigm shifts and innovative approaches based on the feedback and nature of the decision-making process, and the budget purposes and components are more easily understood with the focus on what money produces instead of what things (line items) cost.

LEADERSHIP CHALLENGES IN BUDGETING

Many potential and tough problems await the administrator in the budgeting cycle and process. There is never enough funding to support all of the requests made in any educational organization, and with scarce resources, competition for funding is pervasive regardless of the type of budgeting used. Best interests can conflict—for example, "Do we spend the money on instrumental music for Grades 4–6

Table 23.4   Rank-Ordered Excerpt of Performance-Based Budget

Rank Order	Program/Package Description	Package Cost	Cumulative Cost
1	Media/Technology - 98% Package	$1,366,244	$1,366,244
2	Guidance/Hlth - 98% Package	$2,676,843	$4,043,087
3	Elementary Instruction - 98% Package	$32,035,670	$36,078,757
4	Senior High Instruction - 98% Package	$14,770,359	$50,849,116
5	Custodial/Maintenance - 98% Package	$7,003,545	$57,852,661
6	Junior High Instruction - 98% Package	$13,903,230	$71,755,891
7	Music and Fine Arts - 98% Package	$3,115,830	$74,871,721
8	Elementary Instruction - 99% Package	$326,916	$75,198,637
9	Senior High Instruction - 99% Package	$150,718	$75,349,355
10	Junior High Instruction - 99% Package	$141,832	$75,491,187
11	Elementary Instruction - 100% Package	$326,870	$75,818,057
12	Human Resources - 98% Package	$536,403	$76,354,460
13	ESL - 98% Package	$653,809	$77,008,269
14	Special Education - 98% Package	$9,461,913	$86,470,182
15	Transportation - 98% Package	$7,291,984	$93,762,166
16	Vocational - 98% Package	$1,684,529	$95,446,695
17	Board & Superintendent - 98% Package	$640,374	$96,087,069
18	Talented & Gifted - 98% Package	$687,877	$96,774,946
19	Business Services - 98% Package	$1,955,429	$98,730,375
20	Athletics and Activities - 98% Package	$1,699,756	$100,430,131
21	Media/Technology - 99% Package	$13,941	$100,444,072
22	Junior High Instruction - 100% Package	$141,832	$100,585,904
23	Custodial/Maintenance - 99% Package	$71,465	$100,657,369
24	Senior High Instruction - 100% Package	$150,718	$100,808,087
25	Guidance/Hlth - 99% Package	$27,315	$100,835,402
26	Human Resources - 99% Package	$5,474	$100,840,876
27	Research/Evaluation/Assess - 98% Package	$272,717	$101,113,593
28	Curriculum/Instruction - 98% Package	$1,036,353	$102,149,946
29	Guidance/Hlth - 100% Package	$27,315	$102,177,261
30	Media/Technology - 100% Package	$13,942	$102,191,203

or for keeping libraries open 5 days a week?"—and setting priorities is difficult at best.

Collaborative decision making using sound informational data offers some help to resolving the thorny political issues surrounding where the money goes, and moving to higher level budgeting processes yields higher credibility and, in some cases, additional revenue. The tangible connection between money and results is a powerful motivator to communities needing to provide more support for their schools.

SUMMARY: WHERE DOES THE EDUCATIONAL LEADER GO FROM HERE?

Educational leaders have financial planning responsibilities that, even in times of plenty, have provided difficult challenges. The current national political climate, with an intense debate over educational policy and funding, has created even more challenging opportunities for leaders. It is critical that the positive contributions of education to the economic well-being of the United States remain in focus and that leaders support education as an investment in the future of the country.

Growth in the cost of elementary and secondary education has been unusually robust, but the public's connection between national prosperity and the cost of education is in need of continued vigor as well. The nature of the school client has changed, along with the change in educational resources, with many new and broadened categories of special needs.

Recent reform efforts may have promise, but without adequate financial support, the likelihood of success is minimal. Moreover, the distribution of financial capability is highly variable across states and communities. Some have more wealth than others, which impacts a host of things, from achievement scores to course offerings. A major challenge—to meet the diverse needs of students with differential funding efforts—remains a key struggle for school leaders and policymakers. Students need differential treatment, programs, and services to reach the goals American society holds dear for *all* children.

Another challenge lies in the methods and means of revenue collection. Taxes are generally unwelcome, but taxpayers have been seen to be supportive of additional spending for schools if they see a tangible interest beneficial to their community, real estate values, and society as a whole. If tax systems at all levels continue to inadequately fund educational demands, schools will continue to have funding problems.

The economic confidence of a community in its educational organization requires prudence, alignment, and demonstrated performance from their schools. The enormous pressures on educational leaders originating from government and the citizenry have a powerful effect on financial allocation and resource distribution systems. Different realistic approaches to budgeting offer a variety of advantages, and it is essential for leaders to translate educational priorities into financial terms easily understood by a lay public. It naturally follows that budgeting is the central

hub of the planning process, the vehicle for public approval and implementation of sound education, and an economic and executive tool for financial solvency and successful educational leadership.

REFERENCES

Association of School Business Officials International. (1990). *How public schools are financed*. Reston, VA: Author.

Association of School Business Officials International. (2000). *Government Accounting Standards Board (GASB) Statement No. 34: Implementation recommendations for school districts*. Reston, VA: Author.

Augenblick, J., & Myers, J. (1994). *Determining base cost for state funding systems*. Denver, CO: Education Commission of the States.

Augenblick, J., Myers, J., & Anderson, A. (1997). Equity and adequacy in school funding. *The Future of Children: Financing Schools, 7*(3), 63–78.

Berliner, D., & Biddle, B. (1996). *The manufactured crisis: Myths, fraud, and the attack on America's schools*. Boulder, CO: Perseus.

Bureau of the Census. (2002). *Direct general expenditures of state and local governments for all functions and for education*. Washington, DC: U.S. Department of Commerce.

Commission on Reorganization of Secondary Education. (1918). *Cardinal principles of secondary education*. Washington, DC: Bureau of Education.

Downey, C., Frase, L., Poston, W., Steffy, B., English, F., & Melton, R. (2002). *Leaving no child behind: 50 ways to close the achievement gap*. Johnston, IA: Curriculum Management Systems.

Ducote, R. (2004, January 9). Providing funds to construct schools. *Arizona Daily Star*, p. D1.

Educational Policies Commission. (1938). *Education for all American youth in American democracy*. Washington, DC: Author.

English, F. (1996). *Curriculum management for schools, colleges, and business*. Worthington, OH: Charles C Thomas.

English, F., & Steffy, B. (2001). *Deep curriculum alignment: Creating a level playing field for all children on tests of educational accountability*. Lanham, MD: Scarecrow Education Press.

Enrich, P. (1995). Leaving equality behind: New directions in school finance reform. *Vanderbilt Law Review, 48*(1), 101–194.

Fischel, W. (2002). School finance litigation and property tax revolts: How undermining local control turns voters away from public education. In W. Fowler (Ed.), *Developments in school finance, 1999–2000*. Washington, DC: U.S. Department of Education.

Fullan, M. (2001). *Leading in a culture of change*. San Francisco: Jossey-Bass.

Guthrie, J. (1997). School finance: Fifty years of expansion. *The Future of Children: Financing Schools, 7*(3), 24–38.

Hill, P. (1994). *Reinventing public education* (Report prepared for the Lilly Endowment and the George Gund Foundation). Santa Monica, CA: Rand Corporation.

Jones, T. (1986). Taxation for education. In R. Wood (Ed.), *Principles of school business management*. Reston, VA: Association of School Business Officials International.

Kozol, J. (1985). *Savage inequalities: Children in America's schools*. New York: Harper Collins.

Ladd, H., & Hansen, J. (2002). Making money matter: Financing America's schools. In W. Fowler (Ed.), *Developments in school finance, 1999–2000*. Washington, DC: U.S. Department of Education.

Miles, K., & Rothstein, R. (1995, November 22). Where has the money gone? Understanding the growth in public school spending. *Education Week*, pp. 44, 36.

Mintzberg, H. (1994). *The rise and fall of strategic planning*. New York: Free Press.

National Commission on Excellence in Education (1983). *A nation at risk*. Washington, DC: Author.

No Child Left Behind Act of 2002, Pub. L. No. 107–110.

O'Sullivan, A., Sexton, T., & Sheffrin, S. (1995). *Property taxes and tax revolts: The legacy of Proposition 13*. Cambridge, MA: Cambridge University Press.

Pomerantz, M. (1992). *Remarks to Board of Regents*. Quoted by M. Jischke in address to Faculty Senate, Iowa State University, February 1992.

Poston, W., Stone, P., & Muther, C. (1992). *Making schools work: Practical management of support operations*. Newbury Park, CA: Corwin.

Reports on U.S. reform since *A Nation at Risk*. (1988, April 27). *Education Week* 7:31:21.

Serrano v. Priest, 5 C.3d 584, 487 P.2d 1241 (Serrano I), (1971).

Serrano v. Priest, 557 P.2d 929 (Serrano II), (1976).

Thompson, D., Wood, R., & Honeyman, D. (1994). *Fiscal leadership for schools: Concepts and practices*. New York: Longman.

U.S. Department of Education, National Center for Educational Statistics. (2002a). *Developments in school finance, 1999–2000* (NCES 2002–136) (W. J. Fowler, Ed.). Washington, DC: Author.

U.S. Department of Education, National Center for Education Statistics. (2002b). *Financing elementary and secondary education in the states* (NCES 2002–319) (J. Sherman, E. Rowe, L. Peternick, & F. Johnson, Eds.). Washington, DC: Author.

Ward, J. (1995). *Demographic and economic changes facing schools in the north central region* (Policy Briefs). Oak Brook, IL: North Central Regional Educational Laboratory.

Wholey, J. (1979). *Zero base budgeting: Budgeting and program evaluation*. Lexington, MA: Lexington Books.

Author Index

Adams, D., 340
Adams, L., 395
Adams, M., 60
Adams, N., 340
Adams, R., 218
Adelman, C., 287
Adler, S., 155
Ah Nee-Benham, M. K. P., 382
Ahlstrom, S. E., 49, 50
Akintude, O., 393
Albert, L. R., 60
Alevantis, L., 529
Alexander, T. M., 45
Alexander, W. M., 513
Alinsky, S. D., 239
All Star Directories, 57
Allen, I. L., 520
Allen, K., 154, 348
Allensworth, E., 199, 412
Allison, G., 193, 194, 201, 202, 204
Allman, P., 52
Alston, J. A., 154, 155
Alwood, E., 54
Amanti, C., 242
American Association of School
    Administrators, 432
American Institutes of Research, 507
American Lung Association, 528
Anderson, A., 554
Anderson, G., 57, 58, 149, 297,
    299, 309, 310, 323, 422
Anderson, G. L., 47, 221, 243, 338, 340
Anderson, R. D., 440
Anderson, W., 516
Andrews, R., 131, 448
Andrews, R. L., 111, 131
Annunziata, J., 449, 450
Ansléy, F. L., 342
Anthony, R., 160
Antonio, A., 57
Anyon, J., 192, 306, 317
Apple, M., 422, 502
Apple, M. W., 49, 73
Applebaum, B., 47
Applegate, B., 227

Archer, J., 409, 431, 436
Archibald, J. A., 341
Argyris, C., 195, 196
Armstrong, K., 49, 490
Arnez, N., 154
Arnez, N. L., 53
Arnold, D., 524
Aronowitz, S., 502
Ashton, P., 440, 450
Association of School Business Officials
    International, 532, 552, 564
Astin, A., 57
Atwell, N., 502
Au, K., 241
Au, K. H., 275
Augenblick, J., 554
Axley, S. R., 149
Ayer, F., 432

Baber, C. R., 382
Bacharach, S. B., 541
Baker, D., 431
Bakhtin, M., 385, 388
Bakhtin, M. M., 343
Ball, S., 340
Bamburg, J. D., 199
Bandura, A., 450
Banks, C. M., 156
Banks, J., 411
Banks, J. A., 340, 348, 390, 396
Baquedano-Lopez, P., 384
Barber, B., 395
Barker, J., 309, 323
Barker, R. G., 515
Barker, S. L., 135
Barnett, B. G., 144, 145, 453
Barocas, R., 470
Baron, D., 326
Barth, R., 9, 29, 57, 130, 131, 297, 300, 310
Barth, R. S., 68, 73, 293
Barton, R. M., 543, 544, 545
Bascia, N., 544
Basom, M. R., 111, 453
Bass, B., 437
Bass, B. M., 102

Bates, J. E., 467
Bates, R., 381
Bauman, P. C., 149
Baumgartner, F., 203, 204
Beane, L. A., 73
Beare, H., 323
Beauchamp, G., 422
Beaumont, C. E., 521
Beck, L., 55, 56, 58, 110, 114, 120, 121,
    125-126, 129, 132, 136, 298, 376
Beekley, C., 155
Begle, E. G., 440
Behling, O., 95
Belenky, M., 345
Bell, C., 155, 156
Bell, C. S., 155, 156
Bell, D. A., 342, 343
Bell, L. A., 60
Bell, T., 412
Ben-Avie, M., 243, 298
Benhabib, S., 346
Bennett, H., 408, 410
Bennett, J. W., 441
Bennett, W., 228
Bennion, J. W., 111, 339
Bennis, W., xii, 362
Bennis, W. G., 92
Berla, N., 242
Berliner, D., 233, 492, 556
Berliner, D. C., 442, 444, 466
Berman, A., 529
Berner, M. M., 507
Bernstein, R. J., 352
Berry, B., 440
Berryman, M., 392
Bhabha, H., 385
Bhola, H., 56
Biddle, B., 556
Biddle, B. J., 466
Bidwell, C., 417
Bingler, S., 513, 515, 520, 521, 522, 530
Bishop, R., 341, 391, 392, 396
Bittle, E. H., 530
Björk, L., 144, 147, 150
Bjork, L. G., 158, 159
Björk, L. G., 149, 150
Blackmore, J., 120
Blair, J., 431
Blank, M. J., 74
Blase, J., 57, 58, 149, 298, 299, 450
Blase, J. R., 450
Blignaut, J. N., 60
Blount, J., 110, 113-114, 119, 120,
    124, 125, 128, 150, 151, 152, 153, 155
Blount, J. M., 53, 54, 55, 340, 349
Blount, W. R., 467
Bluhm, W. T., 193

Blunt, P., 365, 373-374
Bobbitt, F., 10, 29, 94, 422, 423
Bode, B., 422-423
Boer, H., 515
Boggs, C., 224, 500
Bogotch, I., 56
Boje, D. M., 434
Boli, J., 90, 100
Bolin, F., 424, 432
Bolman, L., 56
Bolman, L. G., 202, 204, 209
Bond, J. T., 521
Borman, G., 412, 414, 415
Bossert, S. T., 101, 102, 104
Boston Town Records, 433
Bova, B., 79
Bowles, S., 53, 54, 59, 225, 243, 423, 439
Boyd, W., 323
Boyd, W. L., 113, 117, 124, 148
Boyles, D., 227
Boyte, H. C., 242
Bradley, A., 539
BrainyMedia.com, 477
Brantlinger, E., 225, 393
Brashers, D. E., 149
Braungart, M., 528
Bredeson, P., 79, 103
Bredeson, P. V., 79, 129, 131
Brennan, M., 351
Brewer, D. J., 198
Bridge, R. G., 440
Britz, J. J., 60
Britzman, D., 341, 343, 344, 345, 350, 351
Brooks, J., 495, 497, 499
Brooks, M., 495, 497, 499
Brophy, J. E., 441, 444
Broussard, C., 47
Brown, ?, 489
Brown, A., 74
Brown, B., 102
Brown, C., 238, 244, 247, 263, 441
Brown, S., 547
Brubaker, C. W., 512, 515, 519
Bruckerhoff, C., 78
Brunner, C., 340, 350, 351
Brunner, C. C., 144, 150, 153, 154,
    155, 156, 161
Bryk, A., 74, 243, 412
Bryk, A. S., 195, 197, 199, 241, 243
Buber, M., 325, 335, 387, 388
Buckingham, M., 452
Buckley, K., 1
Bullough, R., 300
Burbules, N. C., 388
Bureau of the Census, 554
Burell, G., 339
Burkett, C. W., 132

Burns, J. M., 102, 132, 202, 204, 366
Burroughs, W. A., 146
Burstyn, J. N., 155, 156, 475
Burt, T. S., 529
Bush, L., 273
Bushweller, K., 271-272
Butler, J., 350
Butler, N. M., 11, 30
Butterfield, F., 411
Button, H. W., 118, 119, 121, 123
Butts, R. F., 11, 12, 143, 150
Byrne, C. J., 440

Caffarella, R. S., 518
Cahoone, L., 36
Caine, G., 396
Caine, R. N., 396
Calkins, L., 494, 502
Callahan, D., 193
Callahan, R., x, xi, 7, 16, 53, 55, 94, 118, 119, 121, 219, 422
Callahan, R. E., 144, 145, 146, 147, 148, 339, 364, 485, 490, 491
Cambourne, B., 502
Cambron-McCabe, N., 170
Campbell, J., 309, 323
Campbell, R., 123
Campbell, R. F., 111, 124, 125, 143, 339
Cao, Q., 450
Caouette, A., 434, 446-447, 451, 452, 453
Capper, C., 57, 58
Capper, C. A., 340, 341, 349, 350
Carlson, L. T., 169
Carlson, R. V., 149
Carr, M., 421
Carroll, T., 545
Carroll, W., 367
Carter, G., 129, 132
Carter, G. R., 144
Cartwright, D., 101
Casella, R., 467, 468, 469, 475, 478
Cash, C., 247
Cash, C. S., 507
Casner-Lotto, J., 302
Cassirer, E., 308
Castetter, W. B., 127
Caufman, K. D., 541
Cauldwell, N., 471
Cavanaugh, C., 52
Celce-Murcia, M., 416
Center for Curriculum and Assessment, 420
Center, C., 149
Cervantes, R. P., 507
Chall, J. S., 242
Chambers, J., 198
Chambers, S., 207

Chance, E., 436
Chance, P., 436
Chance, P. L., 149
Chapman, J., 323
Chase, B., 543
Chase, S., 154, 155, 156
Chase, S. E., 155, 156
Chavkin, N. F., 242
Cheng, K., 375
Chiang, F. S., 440
Chodorow, N., 346
Choy, S. P., 431
Christensen, G., 136
Christensen, L., 485
Christman, J. B., 243
Chubb, J., 217, 224, 228, 300, 302
Church, E., 424
Clark, R., 241
Clark, T., 523, 527
Cleary, E. L., 52
Clegg, S. R., 201, 202, 205
Clements, S., 302
Clinchy, B., 345
Coates, L., 386
Cobb, C. D., 540, 543
Cobb, R. W., 204
Coble, C. R., 440
Coburn, C., 412
Coch, L., 99
Cochran-Smith, M., 60
Codd, J. A., 380
Coffman, C., 452
Coggins, K., 275
Cohen, D., 478
Cohen, D. K., 441
Cohen, D. L., 197
Cohen, M. D., 99-100
Cohen, S., 409
Coker, H., 433
Coleman, J., 244, 260, 438, 439, 466, 471
Coleman, J. S., 437, 471
Collaborative for High Performance Schools, 515, 528, 529
College Board's National Task Force on Minority Achievement, 271, 287
Collier, P., 471
Collins, J., 438
Collins, P., 346
Collins, P. H., 341, 346, 348
Comer, J., 243, 247, 298
Commission on Reorganization of Secondary Education, 550
Conley, S. C., 541
Conrad, C., 149
Cook, A., 515
Cook, F., 71
Cooney, M. H., 393

Coons, A. E., 93, 95
Cooper, B. F., 193
Cooper, B. S., 113, 117, 124, 148, 539, 542
Cooper, J. E., 382
Cooper, L., 275
Copland, M., 137
Corcoran, T., 247
Cornwall, J. C., 470
Cortés, E., Jr., 239
Corwin, R., 415
Costa, A. L., 517
Cothran, D., 451
Cotton, K., 441, 515
Counts, G. S., 51, 61, 62
Craft, M., 391
Crampton, F., 157
Crawford, M., 280
Creemers, B. P., 441
Cremin, L. A., 51, 143, 150
Cremins, L., 11, 12
Crenshaw, C. W., 342
Crenshaw, K., 341, 342
Cresswell, A. M., 541
Cribb, J., 228
Crichlow, W., 389
Crocker, L., 440
Croft, D. B., 97
Cronin, J. M., 146
Croninger, R., 197
Croninger, R. C., 192
Crow, G., 57, 117, 118, 321
Crowson, R. L., 90, 127, 148
Csikszentmihalyi, I., 434, 446
Csikszentmihalyi, M., 404, 434, 435,
    445-446, 452
Cuban, L., 1, 7, 9, 55, 57, 68, 70, 71, 80, 81,
    145, 146, 158, 159, 189, 191, 197, 258,
    259, 485, 491, 492, 499, 501, 502
Cubberley, E. P., 94, 114, 116-117
Culbertson, J., 441, 449
Culbertson, J. A., 119, 122, 123, 127, 148, 339
Culp, J. M., 342
Cummings, R., 118
Cummings, T., 384
Cummins, J. P., 391
Cunningham, L., 154
Cunningham, L. L., 143
Cunningham, W., 129, 132
Cunningham, W. G., 144
Cusick, P., 102, 135
Cutler, H., 434

D'Emilio, J., 54
Dahl, R. A., 204, 205
Dalai Lama, 49
Dantley, M., 80, 299, 422
Dantley, M. E., 41, 42, 44, 341

Darder, A., 273
Daresh, J., 56, 57, 116
Darling-Hammond, L., 300, 410-411,
    436, 438, 440, 450, 485, 486, 489
Darrow, R., 523
Davidson, J., 515
Davies, B., 346
Davies, S., 393
Davis, M., 470
Deal, P., xii, xiv
Deal, T., 56, 132, 136
Deal, T. E., 102, 103, 202, 204, 209
DeBevoise, W., 131
Deck, L. L., 160
Decker, L., 31
Decker, L. E., 520-522
Dede, C., 527
DeFelice, M., 134
Delgado Bernal, D., 341, 342, 348
Delgado, G., 239
Delgado, R., 342, 343
Delgado-Gaitan, C., 241
Delpit, L., 242, 270, 384, 396
Deming, E., 418, 422
Deming, W. E., 431, 436, 437, 446
DeMitchell, T. A., 539, 540, 541,
    542, 543, 544, 545
Denton, K., 466
Denzin, N., 339
Derber, C., 218
Derman-Sparks, L., 390
Derrida, J., 343, 346, 390
Deutsch, M., 451
DeVillar, R., 391
Devlin-Scherer, R., 386
Devlin-Scherer, W. L., 386
Dewees, S., 516
Dewey, J., 1, 19, 72, 74, 77, 298, 327,
    328, 500, 502-503
Deyhle, D., 341
DeYoung, A. J., 510
Diamond, J. B., 471
Diamond, S., 52
Dickson, W. J., 96
Dillard, C., 341
Dillard, C. B., 382
Dilley, P., 343-344, 345, 350
DiMaggio, P. J., 90, 100
Dimmock, C., 375, 383
Dimock, M. E., 434, 437
Doble, J., 70, 74
Dodd, L. C., 201
Dodge, K. A., 467
Dohrn, B., 468, 469, 478
Dolby, N., 389
Donahue, H., 396
Donley, M., 411

Donmoyer, R., 58, 338, 339, 340, 341, 348
Doolittle, F., 416
Doolittle, G., 77, 80, 81
Dornbusch, S., 102
Dorrien, G., 52
Dougherty, E., 280
Doughtery, K., 304
Dow, P., 297
Downey, C., 420, 421, 434, 448, 453, 455, 553
Doyle, W., 442
Dreyfus, H., 434
Driscoll, M., 74
Drucker, P., 432, 433, 437
Druva, C. A., 440
Dryfoos, J., 74, 465
DuBois, W. E. B., 273
Ducote, R., 553
Duffett, A., 543
Duke, D., 56, 57, 68, 433, 450, 453, 507, 515
Duke, D. L., 89, 92, 103, 136, 383
Dukerich, J. M., 91
Dunbar, C., 349
Dunham, B., xii
Dunlap, D., 155
Dunn, R. J., 159
Dunst, C., 470
Dunst, C. J., 470
Dutro, E., 409
Dutton, S., 408, 424

Earthman, G. I., 507, 530
Easton, D., 201, 205
Easton, J. Q., 197, 243
Eaton, W. E., 146
Edelman, M., 204, 222-223
Edelsky, C., 502
Edison Schools, 228
Edmonds, R., 275, 293
Education Trust, 272, 287
Educational Policies Commission, 550
Educational Research Service (ERS), 135
Edwards, M., 387, 388
Egeland, B., 470
Ehrenkrantz, E., 513
Ehrlich, S. B., 91
Eidell, T. L., 97-98
Eisner, E., 431, 449
Elementary and Secondary Education Act, 71
Elias, J. L., 52
Ellsworth, E., 346, 351
Elmore, R., 71, 131, 298
Elmore, R. C., 195
Elmore, R. F., 196, 197, 200, 207, 293
Else, D., 527
Emihovich, C., 57
Emmons, C., 247
Encarnation, D. J., 199

Engel, M., 227
English, F., x, xiv, 56, 69, 364, 365, 409, 415, 416, 417, 418, 419, 420, 421, 422, 434, 553, 566
English, F. W., 94, 338, 340, 348, 352, 384, 444
Ennis, C., 451
Enomoto, E., 155
Enomoto, E. K., 154
Enrich, P., 552
Environmental Protection Agency, 528
Epstein, J., 242
Epstein, J. L., 241, 243, 386
Erickson, F., 242
Erickson, R., 300
Evans, G. W., 528, 529
Evans, L., 293
Evans, M. G., 98
Everett, S. A., 465
Evertson, C., 440, 442

Facemyer, K., 450
Fager, J., 197
Fairclough, N., x
Falk, B., 494
Fallis, R. K., 468, 469
Faltis, C. J., 391
Fantuzzo, J. W., 467
Farkas, S., 543
Farquhar, R. H., 110, 127
Farrell, J. P., 396
Farris, E., 515, 522-523
Fatemi, E., 271-272
Febey, K., 515
Feerick, M. M., 466, 467
Feistritzer, C., 441
Feldman, J., 134
Ferguson, E., 442
Ferguson, K. E., 341
Ferguson, M. C., 199
Ferguson, R. F., 440
Fernandez, A., 103, 149
Fernandez, R. R., 451
Feyerabend, P., xiii, 434
Fiedler, F. E., 93, 98
Fielding, R., 525
Fine, L., 271
Fine, M., 253, 263, 340, 387
Fink, D., 72
Finn, C., 228, 302
Finn, C. E., 132
Finnegan, K., 73
Firestone, W. A., 1, 102, 200, 202, 203
Firth, F., 445
Fischel, W., 554, 559, 560
Fischer, F., 202
Fishbaugh, M. S. E., 72, 77
Fisher, R., 547

Fisk, M., 409
Flax, J., 345, 346
Fleischer, C., 500
Fleming, T., 111, 339
Flora, J., 465
Foley, D., 102
Follett, M. P., 96
Fordham, T., xiv
Forester, J., 340, 341
Forsyth, P. B., 341
Fossey, R., 539, 541
Foster, M., 275, 349
Foster, W., x, 36, 40-41, 70-71
Foucault, M., 9, 10, 25, 26, 54, 339,
     344, 346, 347, 350, 351, 392, 434
Fowler, F. C., 157, 191
Fowler, W., 441, 515
Fox, L., xi
Fox, M., 434, 446
Fraaj, H., 80
Frank, T., 225
Frase, L., 416, 421, 433, 434, 436,
     447, 448, 450, 453
Fraynd, D. J., 340, 349, 350
Frazier, L. M., 507
Freedman, B., 421, 422, 448
Freedman, G., 523
Freire, P., 39, 49, 52, 275, 392, 397, 502
French, J. R. P., Jr., 99
Frieberger, P., 92
Fruchter, N., 238, 263
Frydenberg, E., 478
Fuhrman, S., 192, 200, 201, 208
Fuhrman, S. H., 199, 200, 207, 208
Fullan, M., xii, 72, 74, 79, 127, 134, 243, 297,
     298, 300, 310, 326, 421, 431, 455, 565
Fullan, M. G., 159, 441
Fuller, H., 225
Furman, G., 31, 365, 376, 381
Furman, G. C., 72, 77, 387, 395
Furman-Brown, G., 72, 387
Fusarelli, L., 392
Fusarelli, L. D., 95, 148

Gadamer, H. G., 388
Galinsky, E., 521
Gallese, V., 498
Gallimore, R., 275
Galvin, P., 192
Gambrill, B., 432, 438, 439
Gamoran, A., 411
Gamson, D., 200-201
Gamson, W. A., 204
Garbarino, J., 465, 466, 467, 470, 515
Gardiner, M., 155
Gardiner, M. E., 154
Gardner, J. W., 93

Garner, C. W., 1
Gaudin, J., 467
Gaventa, J., 204
Gawerecki, J., 471
Gay, G., 273, 274, 275
Gaylin, W., 308
Geary, L. S., 205
Gee, J., 298
Gehring, J., 272
Gelberg, D., 217
Gelles, R., 467
Gelles, R. J., 467
General Accounting Office, 507, 531
George, P. S., 513
Gephart, R. R., Jr., 434, 436-437
Gergen, K., 435
Getzels, J., 122-123
Getzels, J. W., 148
Gewirtz, S., 221, 224
Gibb, S., 298
Gideon, B. H., 149
Gilbert, N., 11
Giles, H. C., 242, 263
Gill, B. P., 198
Gilligan, C., 346
Gillon, S. M., 193
Gilmer, S., 227
Gintis, H., 53, 54, 59, 225, 243, 423
Giroux, H., 422, 423, 502
Giroux, H. A., 36-37, 492, 502
Gitlin, A., 300, 323
Glanz, J., 117, 431, 432, 447
Glaser, G., 300
Glass, T. E., 146-147, 150, 153, 154, 155, 156,
     157, 158, 160, 161
Glasser, W., 451
Glazer, N., 192, 193, 199
Gleaves-Hirsch, M., 155
Glickman, C., 297, 298, 300, 310, 421
Glover, M. K., 500
Glynn, T., 391
Goddard, E., 524
Golan, S., 304
Gold, E., 238, 243, 244, 247, 263
Goldberger, N., 345
Goldhammer, K., 122
Goldring, E., 57, 71, 74-75, 81
Goldring, E. B., 90
Gonzalez, M., 58
Gonzalez, M. L., 48, 61
Gonzalez, N., 242
Good, T. L., 441, 444
Goodard, R., 451
Goodlad, J., 412, 451, 501
Goodlad, J. I., 74
Goodlad, S. J., 395
Goodman, J., 298, 304, 326, 327

Goodman, K. S., 502
Goodman, R., 54
Goodman, Y. M., 493, 501, 502
Goodson, I., 422
Gootman, E., 262
Gordon, E. W., 340, 348
Gorman, R. A., 546
Gotanda, N., 341
Gotwalt, N., 119
Gould, S. J., 90, 391, 487, 488
Grady, H., 370, 372
Grady, M., 155, 156, 161
Grant, C. A., 348
Gravelle, C. M., 507
Graves, B. E., 515
Graves, D. H., 502
Gray, P., 447, 448, 450
Green, J. M., 396
Greenberg-Walt, C., 384
Greene, M., 385, 396
Greenfield, W., 56, 71, 74-75, 81
Greenleaf, R., 132
Greenspan, S.., 470
Greenwood, J., 385
Greer, J., 491
Gregg, R. T., 113, 122
Grene, D., 368, 371, 376
Gribskov, M., 151
Grieder, C., 144
Griffin, M., 465
Griffin, P., 60
Griffith, J., 478
Griffiths, D., 339
Griffiths, D. E., 122, 123
Grinberg, J., 309, 323, 340
Grogan, M., 56, 59, 131, 144, 150, 153, 154,
     155, 156, 161, 340, 346, 347, 350-351
Gronn, P., 365, 377, 422, 424
Gross, N., 118
Grossman, R., 218
Grow, G. O., 518
Grow-Maienza, J., 501
Grumet, M. R., 391
Guaglianone, C. L., 137
Guba, E. G., 124, 339
Gulick, L., 94
Gullatt, D. E., 169
Gullick, L., 116
Gulliford, A., 509
Gump, P. V., 507, 515
Guo, X., 374, 375
Gurley, D. K., 147
Gur-Ze'ev, I., 385
Guskey, T., 450
Guskey, T. R., 451
Guskin, S. L., 225
Guthrie, J., 56, 115, 412, 554

Gutierrez, K. D., 384, 389
Guy, L. G., 507

Haberman, M., 276, 293
Habermas, J., 70, 187
Hackman, R. J., 434, 436, 437, 446, 452
Haddad, S., 52
Haefele, D., 433, 450, 453
Haertel, G. D., 442
Hafner, M. M., 341
Hake, S., 486
Halasyamani, L., 474
Hale, J. E., 270, 275
Hall, H., 436
Hall, S., 389
Hallett, T., 471
Halliday, M. A. K., 501
Hallinger, P., 56, 130, 131, 334, 338-339, 341,
     348, 383, 425
Halperin, D., 343
Halpin, A. W., 96, 97, 98, 123
Hamilton, D., 408
Hamilton, D. N., 340
Hamilton, L., 413
Hammond, O. W., 478
Handler, J. F., 197
Hansen, J., 551, 553
Hanson, E. M., 130
Hansot, E., 53, 54, 55, 112, 113, 117, 119-120,
     125, 128, 144, 146, 153, 155, 376
Hanushek, E. A., 439
Haraway, D., 346
Harding, S., 346
Hargens, L., 57
Hargreaves, A., 298, 309, 323
Harrington, S., 348
Harris, A. P., 342
Harris, J. J., 171
Harris, R., 438, 439
Harris, T. H., 11, 21-25
Harrison, J., 391
Hart, A., 56
Hartley, M., 97, 98
Hartsock, N., 346
Haste, H., 56
Hatch, T., 199, 200, 247, 298
Hathaway, W. E., 529
Hattie, J. D., 441
Haugaard, J. J., 466, 467
Hausman, C., 130
Hawk, P., 440
Hawkins, H. L., 508, 524
Hawly, W., 440
Hawthorne, R. D., 391
Haycock, K., 272
Haynes, N., 243, 298
Heath, S. B., 242, 501

Heck, R., 56, 377, 409, 425, 448
Heck, R. H., 334, 338-339, 341, 348
Heckman, P. E., 150
Hedges, L. V., 196
Heide, K. M., 467
Heifetz, R. A., 42
Heineman, R. A., 193
Heintzleman, C., 436
Helfrich, J., 57
Helgesen, S., 156, 161
Heller, F., 99
Hemphill, J. K., 93, 95
Henderson, A. T., 241, 242
Henderson, J. G., 391
Heng, C. L., 52
Henig, J. R., 195, 200, 204
Henkin, A. B., 149
Henry, A., 349
Henry, M., 155
Hentges, J., 154
Herbst, J., 510, 511
Herlihy, C., 416
Herman, J., 304
Hermes, M., 341
Herr, K., 54
Herriott, R. E., 118
Herrnstein, R. J., 90
Herzberg, F., 97, 434, 435, 436, 437, 446, 452
Heschong, L., 529
Hess, F. M., 193, 199, 243, 258, 259
Hess, G. A., 207
Hessel, K., xii
Hetzel, R., 421
Hewes, G., 412, 414, 415
Heyerdahl, S., 383
Hickcox, E., 232
Hickman, L. A., 45
Hidalgo, N. M., 242
Hiebert, J., 437
Higgins, D., 70, 74
Hill, H., 441
Hill, H. C., 197
Hill, M., 453
Hill, P., 562
Hill, P. T., 199
Hill, R., 273
Hill-Collins, P., 36
Hilliard, A., III, 275
Hirsch, E. D., 486
Hobsbawm, E., 50
Hodgkinson, H., 154
Hofenberg, W., 297
Hoffer, T., 466, 471
Hofstede, G., 383
Hofstede, G. H., 374
Holcomb, J. H., 530
Holcomb-McCoy, C. C., 393

Holloway, J., xii, 450
Honeychurch, K. G., 344, 345
Honeyman, D., 564
Honeyman, D. S., 157
Hong, Y., 383
Honig, M., 191, 200
hooks, b., 384, 393
Horn, P., 409
Horn, S., 438
Horton, M., 417
Hosking, D. M., 93
House, E., 503
House, R. J., 98
Houston, P., 160
Howard, J., 275
Howard, K. A., 465, 474, 475
Howell, B., 448
Howing, P., 467
Howlett, M., 202, 203
Howlett, P., 148
Hoy, A., xii, 451
Hoy, W., xii, 451
Hoy, W. K., 55, 89, 94, 96, 97-98,
    202, 208, 339
Hoyle, J., 56
Huberman, M., 451
Hudson, W. S., 49, 50, 51
Huerta-Macias, A., 58
Hula, R. C., 204
Huling, L., 450
Hunter, M., 486, 501
Hurley, J., 136-137
Huse, D., 507
Hutchinson, D. L., 47
Hyman, I. A., 466, 467, 468, 469

Iannaccone, L., 159
Iglesias, E. M., 342
Imber, M., 58, 338
Immegart, G. L., 89, 92, 95
Ingersoll, R. M., 196
Ingram, H., 193, 195, 204
Institute for Educational Leadership, 57
Irmsher, K., 515
Irvine, J. J., 270

Jackson, B., 57, 68
Jackson, B. L., 151, 152, 153, 154, 155, 156
Jackson, P., 408
Jacobson, L., 444
Jacobson, S., 57, 232, 348
Jacoby, D., 448
Jantzi, D., 103, 149
Javo, C., 383
Jefferson, T., 175
Jencks, C., 439
Jenkins, D., 436

Jenkins, K., 436
Jenkins-Smith, H. C., 191, 195
Jennings, B., 193, 308
Jermier, J. M., 96
Jeter, L., xi
Jillson, C., 201
Johnson, B., 382
Johnson, B. C., 58, 148
Johnson, C., 11, 28
Johnson, D., 515
Johnson, D. W., 517
Johnson, J., 58, 543
Johnson, K., 342
Johnson, L., 394
Johnson, M., 56, 498, 499, 503
Johnson, R., 517
Johnson, R. A., 341
Johnson, R. S., 272, 277, 279, 293
Johnson, S. M., 508, 540, 541, 542, 545
Johnston, M., 72, 77, 78, 79
Jones, B., 58, 203, 204
Jones, B. A., 135
Jones, B. B., 201
Jones, B. O., 200
Jones, D., 197
Jones, D. R., 192, 193, 201, 203, 205, 207
Jones, M. L., 365, 373-374
Jones, T., 559
Jordan, K. F., 144
Joyner, E., 243, 298
Judd, C. M., 440

Kaba, M., 243
Kahn, R. L., 93
Kahn, S., 239
Kahne, J., 56, 74, 77, 78, 195, 200, 206
Kakabadse, A., 383
Kalvelage, J., 125
Kamler, E., 155, 156
Kane Lewis, S., 227
Kanter, R., 114
Kanter, R. M., 204, 209
Karabenick, S. A., 395
Karanovich, F., 515
Kardos, S. M., 541
Kari, N. N., 242
Katims, D., 59
Kats, G., 529
Katz, D., 93
Katz, J. N., 344
Katz, M., 309
Katz, M. B., 243
Kearny, E. N., 193
Keedy, J. L., 158, 159
Keith, N. Z., 242, 260
Kelley, B., 103
Kellner, D., 36

Kelly, C. J., 73
Kennedy, A. A., 102
Kennedy, D. M., 49, 50
Kerbow, D., 197, 243
Kerchner, C. T., 539, 541, 542, 544
Kerr, D., 194
Kerr, S., 96
Keyes, M. W., 341
Kimborough, R. B., 132
Kincheloe, J., 410
Kincheloe, J. L., 390, 391, 393
King, J. A., 198, 440
King, J. R., 343
King, P. J., 204, 209
King, R. A., 157, 158
Kingdon, J. W., 194, 202, 204, 205, 341
Kirst, M. W., 159, 539
Kleiner, A., 515, 522-523
Kliebard, H., 408, 422
Kliebard, H. M., 485, 490, 491, 499
Kliewer, W., 528
Kmetz, J., 448
Knapp, M., 193, 194, 201
Knapp, M. S., 199, 393
Knecht, C., 529
Knezevich, S. J., 143
Knoblock, G. A., 440
Knott, J., 114, 115, 116, 118
Kochan, F., 56
Kochan, F. K., 68, 70, 74, 75, 76, 77, 78, 79, 80, 81
Koerin, B., 49
Kohen, S., 467
Kohlberg, L., 496
Kohn, A., 416, 436
Koki, S., 478
Konstantopoulos, S., 196
Koppich, J. E., 539, 541
Korn, W., 57
Korostoff, M., 298
Koschoreck, J. W., 340, 349, 350
Kounin, J. S., 444
Kowalski, T. J., 118, 144, 145, 146, 147, 148, 149, 150, 157, 158, 159
Kozol, J., 552
Kranz, J., 196
Kremer-Hayon, L., 80
Krop, C., 198
Kruse, S. D., 102, 243
Kuhn, T., xiv, 338, 352, 487
Kuhne, G., 476, 477
Kunkel, R. C., 74, 75
Kupermintz, H., 409
Kurtz, P., 467
Kuttner, R., 224

La Mettrie, J., 431, 434
Labaree, D., 226

Lackney, J., 515
Lackney, J. A., 507, 508, 515
Ladd, H., 192, 551, 553
Ladd, H. F., 440
Ladson-Billings, G., 270, 273, 275, 324,
    325, 342, 348
Laflamme, J. G., 440
Lafleur, C., 421, 422, 448
Laible, J., 343, 348, 349
Lajuenen, T., 383
Lakatos, I., xiv-xv
Lakoff, G., 498, 499, 503
Lambert, L., 485, 494-495, 498
Lancaster Dykgraaf, C., 227
Laney, J., 155
Lange, E., 52
Lanham, J. W., III, 507
Lantieri, L., 465
Lareau, A., 242
Larsen, T., 448
Larson, C., 58, 59, 348
Larson, C. L., 44, 393, 396
Larson, R., 418
Lashway, L., 515
Lather, P., 346, 351
Lattimore, R., 368, 371, 376
Lauman, E. O., 244
Lauricella, T., xi
Lawrence, B. K., 515
Lawrence, C. R., 342
Lawrence, R., 468
LeCompte, M., 411
Lee, C., 275
Lee, V., 515, 516
Lee, V. E., 192
LeFanu, J., xiv
Leighteizer, V., 393
Leithwood, K., 56, 78, 80, 89, 92,
    102-103, 149, 197, 383
Leo XIII, 50
Leonardo, Z., 275
Leski, N., 451
Levin, B., 204, 209
Levin, H., 226, 227, 297
Levin, H. M., 198, 439
Levine, E., 515, 518, 521
Lewin, K., 451, 476
Lewis, A. C., 238, 263
Lewis, D. A., 197, 206
Lewis, L., 507, 531
Lewis, M., 507
Lezotte, L. W., 507
Lieberman, M., 411, 412, 539, 540
Liebmann, R. M., 517
Lightfoot, S. L., 242
Likert, R., 98
Lilley, E. H., 508, 524

Lincoln, Y., 339
Lincoln, Y. L., 339
Lincoln, Y. S., 339
Lindblom, C., 194
Lindholm, J., 57
Lindle, J. C., 147
Lindorff, D., 229
Lindsay, T., 368, 369
Lindsey, R. B., 293
Linsky, M., 42
Liotta, M., 539, 542
Lipham, J., 123
Lipham, J. A., 93, 95-96
Lipman, P., 221, 275, 309, 323
Lissak, R. S., 50
Little, J. W., 252, 539
Littrell, J., x
Locke, E., 450
Logan, J., 450
Lomotey, K., 57, 58, 154, 348
Long, J. S., 57
Lopez, G., 423
Lopez, G. R., 58
López, G. R., 340, 342, 348-349
Lorentz, E. M., 68, 79
Louis, K. S., 102, 103, 243, 386
Loveless, T., 539
Lubienski, C., 227
Lublin, J., xi
Lucas, C. J., 121
Lucas, S., 423
Luckham, M., 440
Luehe, B., 112
Lugg, C. A., 1, 52, 54, 58, 59, 340, 349-350
Luna, G. T., 342
Lutz, F. W., 159
Lynn, L. E., 195
Lynn, M., 348, 349

Macdonald, J., 423
Macedo, D., 384, 392, 502
Machiavelli, N., 368, 369-370, 371, 372
Macpherson, R., 56
Madaus, G., 304
Madden, J., 76
Maddox, M., 382
Madsen, J., 159
Maguire, S., 74
Maienza, J., 155
Majd-Jabbari, M., 225
Malen, B., 192, 193, 194, 196, 197,
    198, 199, 201, 203, 204, 205, 206,
    207, 243, 309, 323
Mallorie, L. M., 383
Mann, H., 111, 112
Mapp, K. L., 241
Marable, M., 342

March, J. G., 99-100, 201
Marcon, R. A., 241
Marcoulides, G., 448
Margonis, F., 225, 323, 388
Marietti, M., 155
Mark, D., 154
Marks, J., 512, 513
Marshall, C., 58, 156, 339, 340, 341, 345, 422
Marshall, H. H., 513
Martin, J., 102, 528
Martin, W., 448
Martínez, C., 275
Martinez-Flores, M., 100, 197
Maruyama, G., 466, 467, 478
Marx, G., 132
Marzano, R. J., 441, 442, 444, 453, 455
Maslow, A. H., 97
Mathews, D., 1, 69, 70, 71, 72, 74, 81, 264
Matsuda, M. J., 342
Matthews, L., 57
Matthews, L. J., 117, 118
Mausner, B., 97
Mauws, M., 434-435
Maxcy, S., 56
Maxcy, S. J., 35, 433
Maxwell, L., 529
Maxwell, L. E., 507
Maxwell, W., 11, 16-17, 18
May, S., 390
Mayo, P., 52
Mazawi, A. E., 391, 392
Mazzoni, T. L., 201, 202, 203, 204, 205
McAdams, R., 135, 136, 160
McAndrews, T., 516
McBer, H., 440, 442
McCalla, D., 49
McCann, J., 229
McCarthy, C., 389
McCarthy, M., 58, 422
McCarthy, S. J., 197
McCarty, D., 159
McCleary, L., 57
McClintock, J., 510
McClintock, R., 510
McConnell, B., 242
McCormick, K., 135
McDaniel, J., 409
McDonnell, L. M., 540, 543
McDonough, W., 528
McEwan, E. K., 445
McEwan, P., 198
McEwan, P. J., 445
McGregor, D., 96
McGuffy, C., 507
McKenna, B. A., 444
McKenna, M. C., 444
McKinney, W., 409

McKnight, C. C., 437
McLaren, P., 390, 391, 423, 465, 468, 469, 478, 492, 502
McLaren, P. L., 275
McLaughlin, M., 200-201, 412, 450
McLaughlin, M. M., 200
McLeese, P., 206
McMahon, T., 383
McManis, J., 14, 15, 29
McNeil, D., 92
McNeil, L. M., 71, 197, 198
McPherson, R. B., 127, 135, 148
McQuillan, P., 201, 204, 297
Mediratta, K., 238, 263
Medley, D., 433
Medoff, P., 239
Meece, J., 435
Meek, A., 512
Meier, D., 226
Meindl, J. R., 91
Melaville, A., 74
Melby, E. O., 147
Méndez-Morse, S., 343
Mendez-Morse, S. E., 154, 156
Menzies, T., 197
Merchant, B. M., 57, 58
Meron, T., 368, 371
Messerli, J., 408
Metz, M. H., 102
Meyer, J. W., 90, 100
Meyers, R. A., 149
Meza, P., 59
Mickelson, R., 220, 224
Miedel, W. T., 241
Miles, K., 562
Miles, M. B., 103
Miller, A., 442
Miller, F., 340
Miller, G., 114, 115, 116, 118
Miller, J. E., 444
Miller, N. L., 528
Miller, R. J., 440
Mills, E., 529
Mintrom, M., 204
Mintrop, H., 200-201
Mintzberg, H., 565
Mirel, J., 297
Miron, G., 227
Miron, L., 56
Miskel, C., 97, 204
Miskel, C. G., 55, 89, 94, 96, 97, 100, 101, 205, 339
Mitchell, C., 56, 386
Mitchell, D. E., 199, 541, 544
Mitchell, K., 275
Mitchell, R., 453
Mitra, D., 412

Moe, T., 194, 217, 224, 228, 300, 302
Mohatt, G., 242
Mohr, R. D., 47, 48
Moll, L. C., 242
Molnar, A., 227, 231, 232
Monk, D. H., 440
Montenegro, X., 154
Montgomery, K., 494
Montoya, M. E., 342
Moock, P. R., 440
Moodley, K. A., 390
Moore, D. R., 243
Moore, G. T., 507
Moore, H. A., 117, 118, 122, 123
Moran, K. J., 146
Morando Rhim, L., 227
Moreno, N., 451
Morgan, G., 43, 102, 202, 204, 233, 339
Morgenson, G., xi
Moss-Mitchell, F., 409
Moxley, R. S., 384
Moynihan, D. P., 193
Muir-McClain, L., 474
Mulford, W. R., 73
Mullen, C. A., 76
Muncey, D., 197, 201, 204, 206, 207, 297
Murnane, R., 412, 413, 439
Murphy, J., xiv, 56, 57, 73, 110, 114, 120, 121,
    125-126, 127, 129, 130, 131, 132, 133,
    136, 149, 150, 227, 298, 303, 337, 376
Murphy, M., 540
Murphy, M. J., 541
Murray, C., 90
Murrell, P., 275, 293
Murry, J., 56
Murtadha, K., 59, 393, 396
Murtadha-Watts, K., 154, 382, 387
Muther, C., 565
Myers, A., 383
Myers, C., 326
Myers, J., 554
Myers, N., 530

Nachtigal, P., 132
Nagel, S. S., 339
Nair, P., 526, 527
Nakagawa, K., 197, 206
Nanis, B., 362
Narayan, D., 472
Nasaw, D., 53, 54, 55, 59
Nash, R., 391
Natale, J., 436
Nathan, J., 515
National Association of Elementary School
    Principals, 56
National Center for Education Statistics, 115,
    134, 431, 436, 437, 440

National Commission on Excellence in
    Education, 56, 70, 129, 550
National Commission on Teching and America's
    Future, 272
National Commission on Testing and Public
    Policy, 410
National Education Association, 431, 531
National Parent Teacher Association, 231-232
Neff, D., 242
Neill, M., 416
Neill, S., 309
Nelson, B., 425
Nelson, P. B., 529
Nemeck, S., 471
Nevo, D., 433, 450, 453
New Schools for Better Neighborhoods, 520
Newell, L. J., 111, 339
Newlon, J., 433
Newman, F. M., 199
Newmann, F., 409, 412, 424
Newmann, F. M., 246, 396
Nicholson, L., 346
Nieto, S., 289, 390
Noddings, N., 388, 496
Noguera, P. A., 468, 469, 474, 475, 478
Norris, C., 453
Novak, M., 59
Novick, P., 61
Nuland, S., xv
Nuri Robins, K., 293
Nye, B., 196
Nystrand, R. O., 143
Nzelibe, C. O., 373

O'Boyle, T., xi
O'Brien, J., 74
O'Day, J., 199, 418
O'Donnell, J. M., 518
O'Halloran, K., 520
O'Keefe, M. O., 467
O'Loughlin, M., 47
O'Neal, S., 417
O'Neill, D. J., 507
O'Sullivan, A., 560
Oakes, J., 340, 411
Oberman, I., 200-201
Ogawa, R., 97
Ogawa, R. T., 90, 100, 101, 102, 104,
    196, 197, 205, 243
olatoye, s., 263
Oldham, G. R., 434, 436, 437, 446, 452
Oliva, M., 343
Olsen, J. P., 99-100, 201
Olshtain, E., 416
Olson, L., 436
Omoto, A. M., 478
Onikama, D. L., 478

Opotow, S., 468, 469
Orfield, G., 521
Organization for Economic Co-operation and
    Development, 507
Orlich, D., 450
Orr, D., 528
Orr, M., 204
Ortiz, D. J., 154, 156, 348
Ortiz, F., 345
Ortiz, F. I., 128, 154, 155, 156, 348
Osborne, J., 411
Ourada-Sieb, T., 155
Ovando, C., 58
Ovando, C. J., 44
Overbaugh, B. L., 508
Oxley, D., 515

Pabón López, M., 342
Packer, M., 155
Page, A., 227
Page, R., 411
Pajak, E., 445
Pakalov, V., 317
Palmer, D., 391
Palmer, P. J., 385-386, 394
Palmer, T., 229
Parker, D., 383
Parker, L., 41, 225, 340, 341, 342, 348, 349
Parrish, T., 198
Pascal, A., 540, 543
Patri, A., 10, 18-21, 28-29, 31
Patti, J., 465
Patton, M. Q., 196
Pavan, B. N., 155, 156
Pavlov, I., 488, 489
Payne, C. M., 239, 243
Payne, R., 317
Payne, W. H., 432
Pedescleaux, D. S., 204
Peller, G., 341
Peña, R., 348
Perea, J. F., 342
Perie, M., 431
Perina, K., 150
Perlman, J., 529
Peters, M., 224, 351
Petersen, G. J., 48, 144, 145, 465, 466-467,
    468, 469, 471, 474, 478
Peterson, A. L., 52
Peterson, D., 478
Peterson, K., xii, xiv, 132, 136
Peterson, K. D., 103, 132, 136
Peterson, P. L., 197
Peterson, S. A., 193
Petitt, G. S., 467
Petrie, H., 57
Peyton-Caire, L., 154

Pfeffer, J., 91
Phelps, W. H., 440
Phillips, B., 439
Pianta, R., 470
Pickering, D., 442
Pierannunzi, C., 200
Pierce, P., 55
Pierce, P. R., 112-113, 114, 116
Pierce, T. M., 144
Pillow, W. S., 340, 346, 347
Pinar, W., 389, 423
Pinar, W. F., 341, 343
Pini, M., 227
Pitner, N., 156
Pohland, P., 79
Pohland, P. A., 169
Poling, E., 134
Pollock, J., 442
Pomerantz, M., 564
Poole, W., 156, 412
Popkewitz, T. S., 351
Portelli, J. P., 393
Portes, A., 260
Portin, B. S., 135
Portz, J., 201, 205
Post, L., 410-411
Poston, W., 416, 434, 565, 566
Poston, W., Jr., 421
Pounder, D., xiii, 57, 72
Powell, J. A., 342
Powell, K. E., 474
Powell, L. C., 387
Powell, W. W., 90
Preskill, S., 364
Prevost, R., 52
Price, J. H., 465
PricewaterhouseCoopers, 448
Pritchett, L., 472
Privette, G., 446
Prothrow-Stith, D., 465
Prusak, L., 478
Public Agenda Foundation, 431,
    435, 441, 449
Purpel, D. E., 40
Putnam, R., 244, 260
Putnam, R. D., 471

Quantz, R., 299, 322, 323
Quigley, A., 476, 477
Quinn, L., 513, 515, 530
Quinn, T., 74
Quiroz, D. R., 444

Rabban, D. M., 548
Rabinow, P., 434
Rader, D., 391
Radin, B. A., 193

Radin, N., 275
Rains, F. V., 341
Raivetz, M. J., 395
Raizen, S. A., 437
Rallis, S., 57
Rallis, S. F., 160
Ramachandran, V. S., 498
Ramesh, M., 202, 203
Ramsey, C., 159
Randall, E. V., 193
Ransby, B., 239
Rapp, D., 79
Rauch, C. F., 95
Ravitch, D., 110, 411
Rawls, J., 60
Raywid, M., 515
Raywid, M. A., 515
Ready, D., 515
Rebarber, T., 130
Rebore, R., xii
Rebore, R. W., 41
Reed, C. J., 71, 75, 76, 78, 80
Reese, W. J., 50
Reeves, J. E., 103
Reichardt, R., 198
Reid, R. L., 153
Reitzug, U. C., 103, 118
Reller, T. L., 111
Remaley, A., 450
Repa, T., 155, 156, 161
Resta, V., 450
Retallick, J., 72
Revere, A. B., 153, 154
Reyes, P., 58, 155, 340, 348
Reynolds, A. J., 241
Rice, J. K., 196, 198, 199, 201
Richardson, C., 392
Rickover, H. G., 30
Riehl, C., 79
Riehl, C. J., 382
Rieselbach, A., 510, 511
Riis, J., 16
Rivers, J., 438
Rivers, S., 154
Rizvi, F., 348
Robelen, E. W., 228
Roberts, J., 451
Roberts, N. C., 204, 209
Robertson, A. G., 384
Robertson, J. M., 383
Robertson, S., 530
Robinson, J. H., 30
Roe, J., 368, 369-370, 371
Roethlisberger, F. J., 96
Rogers, J., 299
Rogers, R., 422
Rollock, D., 340

Rollow, S., 243
Rollow, S. G., 197
Roman, L. G., 394
Romney, V. A., 520-522
Ronning, J. A., 383
Ropers-Huilman, B., 60
Rorrer, A., 58
Rorty, R., 327
Rosenblatt, L., 502
Rosener, J., 156, 161
Rosenfield, S., 468
Rosenshine, B., 444
Rosenthal, R., 444
Rosiek, J., 348
Ross, J., 450
Ross, M. E., 71, 75, 76
Ross, M. H., 204
Rossman, G., 412
Rost, J. C., 135, 334, 363-364
Rothenberg, J., 513
Rothman, R., 196
Rothschild, M., 500
Rothstein, R., 192, 193, 199, 200, 562
Rousmaniere, K., 54
Rowan, B., 90, 100, 101, 205, 440
Rumbaut, R. G., 260
Rusch, E. A., 68
Russo, C. J., 170, 171
Rutter, R. A., 451
Ryan, J., 335, 381

Saavedra, E., 279
Sabatier, P. A., 201
Sabo, D., 81
Sackney, L., 56, 386
St. Pierre, E., 346, 347, 351
Salinas, K. C., 386
Saltman, K. J., 227, 232
Sameroff, A., 470
Sameroff, A. J., 470
Sandefur, R. L., 244
Sanders, M. G., 241, 243, 386
Sanders, S. L., 440
Sanders, W., 409, 438
Sandholtz, J. H., 100, 197
Sandidge, R., 171
Sanoff, H., 508, 515, 530
Santman, D., 494
Sapon-Shevin, M., 423
Sarason, S., 297, 300, 310, 455
Sarason, S. B., 68, 77, 79, 149, 243
Sartre, J., 319, 325
Sarup, M., 346
Sax, L., 57
Saxon, J., 486
Scalafani, S., 409
Schalock, D., 442

Schattschneider, E. E., 204
Schechter, C., 79, 80
Schein, E. H., 93, 102, 149
Scherr, M., 156
Scheurich, J., 47, 48, 56, 58, 155, 424
Scheurich, J. J., 78, 338, 339, 340, 341, 342, 343, 348, 349, 395
Schlauch, M., 367-368, 369
Schlechty, P. C., 149
Schlesinger, A., 228
Schmidt, W. H., 99, 437
Schmuck, P., 155
Schneider, A., 193, 204
Schneider, B., 243, 435
Schneider, B. L., 241
Schneider, J., 338
Schneider, M., 507, 515, 528
Schoenheit, M. B., 364
Scholastic, Inc., 431
Schon, D. A., 195, 196
Schorr, L. B., 192
Schroth, G., 134
Schubert, W., 422
Schumaker, P., 155
Scoon Reid, K., 272
Scott, J., 346
Scott, W. R., 90, 91, 94, 96
Scribner, A., 58
Scribner, J., 58, 79
Scribner, J. D., 58
Scribner, S., 100
Scribner, S. P., 197
Scriven, M., 433, 450, 453
Scudder, R. G., 467
Sears, J. T., 54
Seashore, D., 57
Sebring, P., 243
Sebring, P. A., 195, 197
Secada, W. G., 246
Seder, R., 228
Sedgwick, E. K., 341, 343, 344, 345
Seifer, R., 470
Seitsinger, R. M., 77, 78, 79
Seltzer, P. A., 387
Selznick, P., 92, 93, 101-102, 104
Senge, P., 73, 75
Sergiovanni, T., xii, 56, 72, 73, 77, 79, 80, 127, 132, 187, 435, 436
Sergiovanni, T. J., 44-45, 97, 158, 293
Sexton, T., 560
Shah, B. P., 74
Shakeshaft, C., 47, 48, 110, 115, 119, 120, 122, 125, 128, 134, 153, 155, 156, 340, 345, 350
Shank, B., 300
Shannon, P., 317, 493, 499, 501, 502
Shapiro, J. P., 60, 348, 349

Shapiro, J. R., 41
Shavelson, R., xiii
Shedd, J. B., 541
Sheffrin, S., 560
Shein, E. H., 508
Sheive, L. T., 364
Sheldrake, R., 434
Shen, J., 135
Shepard, L., 304
Sherman, D., 155, 156, 161
Shernoff, D., 435, 451
Shibles, M. R., 160
Shields, C., 31
Shields, C. M., 381, 387, 388, 391, 392, 395, 396
Shipman, N., 133, 337
Shipps, D., 204, 206, 207, 221
Shirley, D., 241, 242, 244, 247, 263
Shoho, A. R., 47, 55, 58, 59
Short, P., 491
Short, P. M., 48
Shujaa, J. M., 275
Shulman, L. S., 451
Shulman, L. W., 193
Shuman, M., 219
Shumar, W., 242
Sidorkin, A. M., 388
Sielke, C. C., 157
Silins, H. C., 73
Silver, P., 415
Silver, P. F., 124
Silverman, I. J., 467
Simms, J., 58
Simon, B. S., 386
Simon, E., 238, 243, 244, 247, 263
Simpson, R., 442
Singh, B., 56
Sirotnik, K. A., 340
Sittig, L. H., 391
Sizemore, B., 154
Skinner, B. F., 488, 489
Sklar, H., 239
Skonie-Hardin, S. D., 440
Skrla, L., 58, 155, 340, 346, 349, 350, 351, 395, 424
Slattery, P., 410
Slavin, R., 486
Sleeter, C., 390
Sleeter, C. E., 348
Smircich, L., 102
Smith, B., 199, 412
Smith, G. A., 451
Smith, J. B., 192
Smith, M., 199, 418, 441
Smith, M. L., 503
Smith, N., 391
Smith, S. R., 195

Smith, W. F., 111, 131
Smith, W. J., 396
Smith-Maddox, R., 348
Smrekar, C., 78, 208
Smylie, M., 206
Smyth, J., 298, 323
Snipes, J., 416
Snow, C., 242
Snyder, J., 424
Snyder, M., 478
Snyderman, B., 97
Soar, R., 433, 450, 453
Soder, R., 448
Solorzano, D. G., 341, 342, 348, 349, 391
Somerville, J. I., 253
Song, M., 204
Southworth, G., 309, 323
Spaedy, M., 133
Spillane, J., 424-425
Spillane, J. P., 197, 471
Spony, G., 383
Spradley, J., 299, 306
Spreitzer, G., 384
Spring, J., 112, 114, 115, 228, 229,
    289, 411, 489
Spring, J. H., 143, 145
Sroufe, G. E., 204
Sroufe, L. A., 470
Stage, S. A., 444
Stamenov, M., 498
Stanfield, J., 340
Stanley, W., 415, 423
Starratt, J. R., 394
Starratt, R. J., 37-38, 72, 77, 376, 386, 387
Staunton, H., 367, 369, 371
Stefancic, J., 342
Steffy, B., 56, 409, 416, 417, 418, 419,
    421, 434, 444, 553
Stefkovich, J. A., 60
Stein, L., 201
Stein, M., 424-425, 441
Steinberg, L., 102
Steinberg, S., 410
Steinberg, S. R., 390, 391, 393
Stevens, R., 475
Stevenson, H. W., 437
Stevenson, R., 57, 232
Stevenson, R. B., 77, 80, 81
Stewart, G. K., 157
Stiegelbauer, S., 159
Stier, H., 192, 199
Stigler, J. W., 437
Stine, S., 515
Stinebrickner, B., 204
Stogdill, R. M., 92, 95
Stone, C., 10
Stone, C. N., 200

Stone, M., 413-414
Stone, P., 565
Stout, R., 155
Strang, D., 100
Straus, M. A., 467
Strauss, A., 300
Streitmatter, J., 149
Streshly, W., 433, 435, 448, 450, 453
Streshly, W. A., 540, 541, 542
Strike, K. A., 72, 77, 386
Strober, M., 119
Strodl, P., 382
Sulla, N., 298
Sullivan, K., 515
Sullivan, S., 432, 447
Summala, H., 383
Sustainable Buildings Industry Council, 528
Swanson, A. D., 157
Swanson, M., 440
Swasey, M., 292
Sweetland, S., 157
Swidler, A., 102
Swingewood, A., 385
Sykes, G., 195
Symonds, W., 229
Symonds, W. C., 229

Tagiuri, R., 97
Takaki, R., 391
Talbot, D., 321
Tallerico, M., 150, 155, 156, 204, 340
Tannenbaum, A. S., 101, 540
Tannenbaum, R., 99
Tanner, D., 422, 433, 438
Tanner, K., 515
Tanner, L., 422, 433, 438
Tanner, L. N., 511
Tarter, J. C., 202, 208
Tarule, J., 345
Tate, W. F., 341, 342, 348
Tatum, B. D., 348
Taubman, P., 389
Taylor, A., 508, 515
Taylor, F., 422
Taylor, F. W., 94
Teddlie, C., 293
Tejeda, C., 275, 384
Terrell, R. D., 293
Testa, K. C., 522
Tharp, L., 12, 13
Tharp, R. G., 275
Thatchenkery, T. J., 434
Thayer-Bacon, B. J., 387-388
Theobold, P., 132
Thomas, G. M., 90, 100
Thomas, K., 341
Thomas, W. B., 146

Thompson, C. M., 341
Thompson, D., 115, 564
Thompson, D. C., 157
Thompson, J., 416
Thompson, R., 471
Thoreson, A., 440
Thorndike, E., 408-409
Thorndike, E. L., 488-489, 491, 499
Tiakiwai, S., 392
Tienda, M., 192, 199
Tierney, W., 387
Tierney, W. G., 339, 343, 344, 345, 350
Tikunoff, W. J., 442
Tiller, D. K., 529
Tillman, L. C., 348
Tinajero, J., 58
Tollett, J. R., 169
Toole, J. C., 386
Topps, B., 133
Towne, L., xiii
Towns, K., 119
Trautvetter, S., 515
Trimble, K., 149
Trivette, C. M., 470
Trower, C., 57
Trujillo, C., 341
Truman, D. B., 204
Trusty, F. M., 97
Tuchman, B., 8
Turgoose, L., 450
Turner, C., 57
Tyack, D., 1, 7, 53, 54, 55, 68, 69, 70, 71,
     80, 81, 112, 113, 114, 115, 117, 118,
     119-120, 125, 126, 128, 144, 146, 153,
     155, 158, 189, 376, 411
Tyack, D. B., 485
Tyler, R., 423
Tyler, R. W., 491-492
Tyson, C., 47, 48, 348

Uline, C., 68
Underwood, J., 170
U.S. Bureau of the Census, 466
U.S. Department of Education, 129-130,
     552, 557, 558
U.S. Department of Health and Human
     Services, 474
U.S. Green Building Council, 528, 529
Urban, W., 303
Urwick, L., 94
Ury, W., 547
Usdan, M., 258, 259
Usdan, M. D., 143
Useem, E., 243

Vadasy, P., 382
Valdés, F., 342

Valdés, G., 242
Valencia, R. R., 391
Van Berkum, D., 507
Van Meter, E. J., 386
Van Til, W., 147
Varlotta, L., 56
Vasquez, M. A., 52
Vaughan, V. M., 367
Velez, W., 348
Veugelers, W., 73
Vibert, A. B., 393, 396
Villalpando, O., 341, 342, 348
Villenas, S., 341
Vorrasi, J. A., 465, 466, 467, 470
Vroom, V. H., 99
Vygotsky, L. S., 497, 501-502

Wagner, T., 523
Wagstaff, L., 392
Walberg, H., 441
Walberg, H. J., 442, 515
Walker, A., 375, 383
Walker, J., 56
Walker, J. L., Jr., 204
Walker, L., 247
Waller, W., 151
Walsh, M., 228
Wang, M. C., 442
Ward, D., 523
Ward, J., 556
Ware, A., 436
Warren, M., 239, 244, 247, 263
Washor, E., 515
Watson, D., 450
Watson, J., 523
Waxman, H. C., 442
Weaver, C., 484, 493, 502
Webb, B., 540
Webb, N., 409, 417
Webb, R., 450
Webb, S., 540
Webber, C. F., 383
Weber, M., 38, 90, 91-92, 134, 422
Weedon, C., 346
Weeres, J. G., 539
Wehage, G., 200, 208
Wehlage, G. G., 246, 451
Weick, K., 309, 416
Weick, K. E., 99, 475
Weiler, H., 191, 201, 202
Weiler, H. N., 159
Weinberg, M., 128
Weiner, G., 47
Weinstein, C. S., 507, 508, 513
Weis, L., 387
Weise, R., 227
Weiss, B., 467

Weiss, C. H., 196
Weiss, M., 228
Welch, A. R., 217, 219
Wells, R. H., 372
Wendel, F., 57
Wenglinsky, H., 440
Wert-Gray, S., 149
Wesson, L., 155, 156, 161
West, C., 38-39
West, J., 466
Westbury, I., 409
Wheatley, M., 434, 496
Whitaker, K., 136
White, D. A., 47, 48
White, J. A., 200, 208
White, J. L., 247
White, P., 298
White, R. E., 221
Whitney, T., 157
Wholey, J., 566
Wildavsky, A., 192-193, 195
Wiley, D., 441
Wilks, D., 59
Williams, D. L., Jr., 242
Williams, E., 275
Williams, K. M., 468-469, 478
Williams, P. J., 342
Williams, R. C., 135
Willower, D., 448
Willower, D. J., 97-98, 339, 341
Wilmore, E., 56
Wilson, B., 412
Wilson, W. J., 466
Wing, J. Y., 252
Winters, R., 229
Wirt, F. M., 159, 539
Wise, A., 410, 412, 413, 415
Wixon, K., 409
Wodarsk, J. S., 467
Wolcott, H. F., 339
Wolff, S. J., 515, 518
Wolfner, G. D., 467
Wong, H., 486

Wong, K., 56, 375
Wong, P. L., 200-201
Wong, R., 486
Wood, R., 115, 564
Wood, R. L., 244, 247, 263
Woodson, C., 273
Woolverton, S., 393
World Bank, 474
World Bank Group, 471, 472
Wraga, W., 415, 423, 424
Wray, A., 11, 19
Wright, I., 391
Wright, S., 438
Wubbels, T., 80
Wulff, K., 135, 136
Wyon, D. P., 528

Xiato, Z., 478

Yair, G., 411
Yankelovich, D., 326
Yerkes, D. M., 137, 453
Yetton, P. W., 99
Yff, J., 337
Yoon, B., 441
Yosso, T. J., 342, 348, 349
Young, I., 59, 60
Young, M., 48
Young, M. D., 339, 340, 341, 342,
     343, 348, 349, 350
Yukl, G., 89, 92, 93, 99, 323

Zachary, E., 263
Zarins, S., 73
Zax, M., 470
Zelikow, P., 193, 194, 201, 202, 204
Zera, D. A., 77, 78, 79
Zhu, N., 434, 447, 448, 451
Zijlstra, H., 73
Zinn, H., 10, 49, 500
Zlotnik, M., 440
Zollers, N. J., 60
Zumwalt, K., 424

Subject Index

AASA. *See* American Association of School Administrators
Abbott, Jacob, 12
Abell, Aaron, 50
Abood v. Detroit Board of Education, 180
Abuse, physical, 467
Academic excellence, 395-396
   See also Student achievement
Accountability movement
   assumptions, xi, 410-415
   demands on educational leaders, 78, 129, 408
   development, 56, 71-72
   effects on curriculum, 409-410, 415-422
   effects on principals, 127, 129
   focus on standardized tests, 395
   hyperrationalization of schools and, 410-415
   increased state power, 207-208
   mandates, 129
   rational perspective in, 105
   social justice concerns, 58-59
   See also No Child Left Behind Act
Achievement. *See* Student achievement
Action research, 476-478
Actors, 202-203, 204
ADA. *See* Americans with Disabilities Act
Adams, Abigail, 151
Adaptive work, 42
ADEA. *See* Age Discrimination in Employment Act
Advertising in schools, 230-231
African Americans
   aspirations for college going, 280, 287
   civil rights movement, 126
   college prep courses, 287-289
   culturally responsive education, 273-274
   education of, 151
   expulsions, 411
   female administrators, 153
   imprisoned, 411
   principals, 53, 128
   segregated schools, 53, 125, 126, 128, 152, 154, 170, 171
   special education students, 271
   student achievement, 271, 272

   superintendents, 153, 154
   teachers, 53, 152
   See also Racial and ethnic groups
African views of leadership, 373-374
AFT. *See* American Federation of Teachers
Age Discrimination in Employment Act (ADEA), 183
Agostini v. Felton, 174-175
Aguilar v. Felton, 174
Alabama. *See* West Alabama Learning Coalition
Alinsky, Saul, 239
Allen, Jeanne, 227
Alliance Organizing Project (AOP), Philadelphia, 238, 254, 261, 262
Alternative Inc., 227
American Association of School Administrators (AASA), 127, 128, 150, 154, 156, 432
American Federation of Teachers (AFT), 120, 180, 411-412, 540-541
   See also Unions, teacher
Americans with Disabilities Act (ADA), 183
AOP. *See* Alliance Organizing Project
Architecture. *See* School design
Aristotle, 366, 369
Arizona Supreme Court, 553
Art/science binary, xiii-xiv
Arts
   education, 24-25
   See also Literature; Music education
ASCD. *See* Association of Supervision and Curriculum Development
Ashley, Velma, 153
Asian Americans
   college prep courses, 289
   culturally responsive education, 274
   student achievement, 271
   See also Racial and ethnic groups
Asian views of leadership, 374-375
Association of Educators in Private Practice, 227
Association of Masters of Boston Public Schools, 12
Association of Supervision and Curriculum Development (ASCD), 128
Austin Interfaith, 238, 254, 261, 262
Authentic discourses, 323-326
Autonomous schools, 252, 300-309

Bair, Fredrick, 53
Barnard, Chester, x
Barnard, Henry, 28, 510
Bay Area Coalition of Equitable Schools
    (BayCES), 251-252
Becker, Gary, 224
Beecher, Catherine, 151, 152
Behaviorism, 485, 488-489, 490
Bennett, William, 228
Bethel School District No. 403 v. Fraser, 177
Bible, 175-176, 489-490
Binet, Alfred, 488
*Board of Education of Central School District
    No. 1 v. Allen*, 174
*Board of Education of Independent School
    District No. 92 of Pottawatomie v.
    Earls*, 179
*Board of Education of Oklahoma City
    Public Schools v. Dowell*, 171
*Board of Education of the Hendrick Hudson
    Central School District v. Rowley*, 172
*Board of Education of Westside Community
    Schools v. Mergens*, 176
Bobbitt, Franklin, 10, 55, 146, 422, 423, 490
Bode, Boyd, 54
Bolling v. Sharpe, 171
Bond issues, 530
Brain, research on, 487, 498
Brown v. Board of Education (Brown I), 121,
    125, 126, 153, 168, 169, 170-171
*Brown v. Board of Education
    (Brown II)*, 170, 171
Brubaker, C. William, 519
Buckley Amendment, 182
Buckley, James, 182
Budgeting
    challenges, 567-568
    definition, 564
    rationale, 564-565
    types, 565-567
Buildings. *See* School buildings; School design
Bureau of Justice Statistics, 411
Bureaucracies
    business organizations, 35
    characteristics, 415
    educational, 56, 71, 91, 116, 410,
        415, 490-491
    hierarchies, 490-491
    iron cage image, 90
    standardized procedures, 115
    Weber on, 91-92
Burr, Aaron, 433
Bush, George W., 182, 187, 228
Business
    bureaucratic organizations, 35
    interest in public schools, 217, 521
    marketization of public sphere, 217, 222-226

myths about, 232-233
relations with school systems, 120-121,
    218-219, 231-232
scandals, 217
See also Corporations; Management principles;
    Scientific management
Business Roundtable, 220
Butler, Nicholas Murray, 540

California
    school finance, 554, 560
    state legislature, 252-253
    See also Oakland Community Organizations
Canada, teacher unions, 412
Capitalism, 36, 222, 500
Carnegie Foundation for the Advancement of
    Teaching, 30
Carter, James G., 28
Cary, Miles, 54-55
CASA. *See* Committee for the Advancement of
    School Administrators
Catholic Church, 49, 50, 52
Catholic Worker movement, 50
CCSSO. *See* Council of Chief State School
    Officers
*Cedar Rapids Community School District v.
    Garrett F.*, 172
Center for Education Reform, 227
Certification and licensing
    Interstate School Leaders Licensure
        Consortium, 57, 133, 150, 337-338, 365
    of principals, 118, 124, 132, 133
    of superintendents, 124, 150
    of teachers, 440
CES. *See* Coalition of Essential Schools
Channel One, 220, 230
Charlotte (North Carolina), 220-221
Charter schools, 227, 228, 229
Charters, W. W., 35
Chaucer, Geoffrey, 367-368, 369
Chicago
    Logan Square neighborhood, 237-238
    Logan Square Neighborhood Association,
        238, 254, 261, 262
    See also University of Chicago
Chicago Federation of Teachers, 540
Chicago school system
    City Normal School, 14, 15
    corporate influences, 221
    decentralized decision making, 207, 221, 241, 243
    local school councils, 241, 243
    parent and community involvement, 238
    research on elementary schools, 419
    school improvement efforts, 238
    superintendents, 15, 119, 221
    teacher unions, 411
    Young's career in, 14-15, 119

Chicago Teachers Federation, 411
Chicago Teachers Union, Local No. 1, AFT, AFL-CIO v. Hudson, 180
Child abuse, 467
China
  educational leadership, 375
  views of leadership, 374-375
Choice, 223
  See also Vouchers
Chubb, John, 228
Church and state, separation of, 12, 173-176
Cities. *See* Urban schools
Cities in Schools program, 74
City of Learning concept, 521
Civil Rights Act of 1866, 183
Civil Rights Act of 1871, 183
Civil Rights Act of 1964, 182, 183
Civil rights movement, 126
Class. *See* Socioeconomic status
Classroom management, 442-444
Classroom observation
  benefits, 421
  monitoring curriculum, 419-420, 421-422, 453
  objectives, 419-420
  positive effects, 448-449, 453
  relationship to teacher self-efficacy, 450-451
  time spent by principals, 448
  transmission teaching and, 486
Cleveland Board of Education v. Loudermill, 180
Climate
  organizational, 97-98
  school, 97-98, 253, 465, 515
Clinton, De Witt, 11
Coalition of Essential Schools (CES), 516
Cochran v. Louisiana State Board of Education, 173
Cognitive engagement of students, 447-448, 451
Coherence, instructional program, 419
Coleman Report, 437
Collaborative cultures, 323
Collaborative leadership, 68, 72, 73-74, 77-80, 161
Collaborative learning, 517-518
Collective bargaining, 180-181, 540-541, 542, 544-546
  See also Contracts, teacher; Unions, teacher
Collective efficacy, 451
Colleges. *See* Higher education; Normal schools
Color blindness, 393-394
Columbia Teachers College, 118
Commercialization, 217, 229-232
Committee for the Advancement of School Administrators (CASA), 123
Common school movement, 13, 111, 112, 143, 145, 489, 510
Communication, 29-30, 149-150

Communities
  educational responsibilities, 551
  in schools, 72-75
  involvement in school design, 530
  neighborhood schools, 520-522
  partnerships with preparation programs, 81
  power structures, 159
  principals' involvement in, 125-126
  relationships with schools, 69-70, 74, 158, 238, 241, 260, 386, 521
  role of schools, 14
  social problems, 158
  use of school buildings, 408-409, 520-522
  welfare efforts, 21
  See also School boards; Social capital
Communities of difference, 386-387
Communities, learning. *See* Learning communities
Community development, 69, 74
Community organizing
  campaign phases, 256-257
  contributions to school reform, 237-240, 244, 257-260
  groups, 238, 256
  history of, 239
  indicators approach to research, 239-240, 244-248
  lessons from, 263-264
  local contexts, 253, 256
  networks, 256
  purposes, 241
  research on, 262
  small schools campaign (Oakland), 248-253
  social capital development, 244
  variations among groups, 253-257
Community schools, 520-522
Community Schools Movement, 74
Compulsory attendance laws, 115
Computers. *See* Technology
Conflict management, 314-317
Confucianism, 374
Connick v. Myers, 179
Consensus decision making, 311-312
Consolidation of schools, 69, 100, 115, 125, 143, 509
Constitution, U.S.
  Fifth Amendment, 171
  First Amendment, 173, 175-176, 177-178, 179
  Fourteenth Amendment, 170, 172, 173, 218
  Fourth Amendment, 178-179
  Tenth Amendment, 551
Construction projects, 530-531
Constructivist learning theory, 495, 497-498
Consumerism, 229-230, 233
Contingency theories of leadership, 98, 363
Contracting, 228
  See also Outsourcing of school services; Privatization

Contracts, teacher, 127, 229, 545, 547-548
  See also Collective bargaining; Unions, teacher
Corporations
  contributions to schools, 218-219, 226,
    231, 232
  history of, 217-218
  influence on education, 216-217,
    219-222, 226-227
  lack of accountability, 218
  leaders, 365
  legal rights, 218
  myths about, 232-233
  political contributions, 218
  power of, 218
  public subsidies, 218-219
  state charters, 217-218
  tax breaks, 218, 232
  See also Business; Educational management
    organizations
Corporatization, 217
Cosmological constant, 430-431
Cost analysis, 198-199, 413-415
Costs
  difficulty of determining, 413-415
  energy, 529
  of interventions, 197-199
  of technology, 523
  See also Budgeting; Expenditures
Council of Chief State School Officers
  (CCSSO), 133, 143, 337
Council of Great City Schools, 416
Counts, George S., 147
County superintendents, 143, 153
Covello, Leonard, 54
Craniometry, 487-488
Crim, Alonzo, 153
Critical legal theory, 341, 349-350
Critical multiculturalism, 390-391
Critical race theory (CRT), 341-343, 348-349
Critical reflection, 79
Critical self-reflection, 42-43, 45
Critical theory, 35-36, 56, 148, 502
Cross City Campaign for Urban School
  Reform, 238
Cross-cultural leadership, 380, 382-383, 384
  See also Diversity, leadership in context of
Crosswinds Arts and Sciences Middle School
  (Woodbury, Minnesota), 514
Crow Island School (Winnetka, Illinois), 512
CRT. *See* Critical race theory
Cubberley, Ellwood, 10, 55, 146
Cultural diversity. *See* Diversity
Cultural responsiveness, 270, 293
Culturally responsive inquiry strategies, 270
Culturally responsive teaching, 273-275, 293
Culture
  definitions, 102
  hybridity, 384

  of families and communities, 241
  organizational, 102-103
  relationship to communication, 149-150
Cultures, school
  assessing, 279-280, 281-287
  collaborative, 323
  democratic, 73
  lifeworld of, 188
  research on, 102
Curriculum
  accountability environment and,
    409-410, 415-422
  alignment with standardized tests,
    409-410, 417, 418, 444
  behavioral objectives, 491, 492, 501
  classroom instructional design, 444
  coherence, 419
  covering, 409-410
  definition, 408
  development, 409, 495-496
  history of, 408, 422
  hyperrationalization of schools
    and, 410-415
  implementation, 421
  knowledge of leaders, 27-28
  leadership, 419-425
  meaning of, 391
  principal's role, 129, 130, 131
  quality guides, 420-421
  reconceptualism, 423
  reforms in 1960s, 126
  relationship to administrative functions, 408-409
  relevance, 422
  roles of educational leaders, 129, 130, 131, 408
  sequencing, 409
  standardization, 116
  state mandates, 24-25, 78, 420
Curriculum enactments, 424
Curriculum engineering, 423

Dalai Lama, 60
Danforth Foundation, 57
Daoism, 374, 375
*Davis v. Monroe County Board of
  Education*, 173
Davis, Ralph, x
Decision making
  consensus, 311-312
  locus of control, 318
  participatory, 99
  types of procedures, 99
  within schools, 310, 311-314, 321-322, 326-327
Deep democracy, 396
Deficit thinking, 391-392
Deming, W. Edwards, x
Democracy
  deep, 396
  diversity and, 396

economic privilege and, 500
educational leaders' views of, 26, 27
in learning communities, 72, 73
in schools, 242-243, 321
markets as substitute for, 224
purpose of schooling, 121
role of public schools, 1
school reform and, 298, 309-317
social justice and, 327-328
values, 77
Democratic leadership
calls for, 68
collaboration, 68
of principals, 122
of superintendents, 147-148
Desegregation, 53, 125, 126, 170-171
See also Brown v. Board of Education;
Segregation
Dewey, John, 14, 45, 56, 411, 499-500
at University of Chicago, 15, 30, 499, 511
influence, 19, 501, 511
Dialogue, 387-389, 397
Digital divide, 271-272, 523
Disabilities, individuals with, 172, 182, 183
Discipline
due process issues, 178
expulsions, 411
Patri's views, 19
role of administrators, 54
See also Student misbehavior
Discourses, 346, 416
Distance learning, 527-528
Districts, school. *See* School boards;
School districts; Superintendents
Diversity
cultural, 274, 381, 384
dimensions, 381
needs of students, 57
See also Racial and ethnic groups
Diversity, leadership in context of,
381, 396-397
academic achievement and, 395-396
communities of difference, 386-387
creating spaces of encounter, 385-386
democracy and, 396
dialogue, 387-389
identities and difference, 389-390
implications for educational leaders, 395-396
incorporating lived experiences, 392-393, 396
multiculturalism, 390-391
rejecting color blindness, 393-394
rejecting deficit thinking, 391-392
spirituality and, 394
Domestic violence, 466-467
Double-loop learning, 43-44
Downey Walk-through with reflective
questions, 448
Drug testing, 179

EAHCA. *See* Education for All Handicapped
Children Act
Edison Project, 220, 224, 227
Edison Schools, 227, 228, 229, 233
Education Amendments of 1972, Title IX,
173, 182
Education for All Handicapped Children Act
(EAHCA), 172, 182
Education Industry Group, L.L.C., 227
Education Industry Report, 227, 228
Education law
church-state issues, 173-176
collective bargaining, 180-181
courses in, 169-170
development of field, 168
employee rights, 179-181
equal opportunity cases, 170-173
importance in educational leadership, 168-170
Pledge of Allegiance cases, 176
proactive and reactive dimensions, 169
school finance issues, 181
special education issues, 172
student rights, 176-179
See also Federal laws; Supreme Court, U.S.
Education Law Association, 170
Education, science of, 412-413
Educational Facilities Laboratories (EFL), 513
Educational finance. *See* School finance
Educational leadership
corporate influences, 221-222
domains of knowledge, 57
human agency heuristic, 90, 91-93
in China, 375
postmodern context, 365
rational perspective, 94-96
scholarship on, 89, 93-94
social responsibilities, 376
standards, 150
values, 53-54, 55
See also Research on educational leadership
Educational leadership preparation programs.
See Preparation programs
Educational leadership, history of
accomplishments of past leaders, 25-27
dimensions, 27-31
first century of U.S., 8-9, 11
links with higher education, 30
professionalization, 22, 53, 55-56, 112,
114-121, 148
radicalism, 30-31
social activism, 28-29
texts, 7-8
theory-based research, 122, 123, 339
See also Principalship, history of;
Superintendents
Educational management organizations
(EMOs), 220, 227, 228-229, 230, 233
Eduventures.com, 227

Efficiency
    in education, 53, 116, 422
    organizational, 415
    scientific management principle, 34, 35,
        115, 490
    standardization and, 422
EFL. *See* Educational Facilities Laboratories
Eight-Year Study, 51, 491
Einstein, Albert, 430-431, 496
Eisenhower, Dwight D., 181
Elementary and Secondary Education
        Act (ESEA), 71
    Education Amendments of 1972, 182
    passage of, 181
    Title I, 174-175, 182, 305
    Title IX, 173, 182
    titles, 181-182
    See also No Child Left Behind Act
Elementary schools
    female principals, 119-120, 125, 128, 134
    history of, 112
    sizes, 515
Elk Grove Unified School District v.
    Newdow, 176
Ellis v. Brotherhood of Railway, Airline and
    Steamship Clerks, Freight Handlers, Express
    and Station Employees, 180
EMOs. *See* Educational management organiza-
    tions
Employee rights, 179-181
Employment laws, 183
Engel v. Vitale, 175
Enron, 217, 229
Environmental determinism, 90-91
Environmental school design, 528-530
Equal Access Act, 176
Equal opportunity, 170-173
Equal Pay Act, 183
Equality
    access to education, 552
    as goal of public schools, 226
    in school finance, 157-158
    See also Social justice
Equity in school funding, 157-158, 552, 553,
    554, 559, 561-562
ESEA. *See* Elementary and Secondary
    Education Act
Ethics, 45, 128, 366
    See also Moral leadership
Ethnic groups. *See* Racial and ethnic groups
Everson v. Board of Education, 173-174
Existential freedom, 308, 319
Expenditures
    patterns, 561-562
    per pupil, 70, 414, 554, 555
    relationship to enrollment, 561
    reporting, 562-564

state and local, 551, 552, 553, 554, 555,
    556, 557, 558, 563
    See also Budgeting; Costs
External change agents, 305-309, 325

Facilities. *See* School buildings
Factory metaphors, 116, 422, 510-513
Families
    attitudes toward student achievement, 471
    computers in homes, 523
    domestic violence, 466-467
    factors in student misbehavior, 466-467
    low-income, 16, 20, 466, 467
    values, 392
    See also Parents
Family and Medical Leave Act, 183
Family Educational Rights and Privacy Act
    (FERPA), 182
Fayol, Henry, x
Federal government
    education expenditures, 557, 558
    education programs, 126
    expanded role in education, 126, 181
    See also U.S. Department of Education
Federal laws, 181-183
    Age Discrimination in Employment Act
        (ADEA), 183
    Americans with Disabilities Act (ADA), 183
    Civil Rights Act of 1964, 182, 183
    Elementary and Secondary Education Act, 71,
        173, 174-175, 181-182, 305
    Equal Access Act, 176
    Equal Pay Act, 183
    Family and Medical Leave Act, 183
    Family Educational Rights and Privacy Act
        (FERPA), 182
    Individuals with Disabilities Education Act
        (IDEA), 172, 182
    National Defense Education Act, 122, 181
    Rehabilitation Act of 1973, 182
    Stewart B. McKinney Homeless Assistance Act,
        182-183
    See also No Child Left Behind Act
Feminist poststructural theory,
    345-347, 350-351
Feminist theory, 48, 56, 345-346
Feminists, 151
FERPA. *See* Family Educational Rights and
    Privacy Act
Finance, educational. *See* School finance
Financial planning, 564
    See also Budgeting
Finn, Chester, Jr., 224, 228
Fire triangle, 475
Flow, 445-446
    definition, 446
    experiences, 446-448

variables conducive to, 448-452
work environment, 452-453, 455
Follett, Mary Parker, x, 96
Ford Foundation, 513
For-profit school management, 227-229
    See also Educational management organizations
Foundations, 219-220, 224, 227
Frankfurt School, 35-36, 56
Franklin v. Gwinnett County Public Schools,
    172-173
Free speech, 177-178, 179, 218
Freeman v. Pitts, 171
Freire, Paulo, 52
Friedman, Milton, 224
Froebel, Friedrich, 511
Funding. *See* School finance

Gallaudet, Thomas, 12
Gantt, Henry, x
Garvey, Marcus, 273
Gates Foundation, 252, 299
Gays. *See* Homosexuals
*Gebser v. Lago Vista Independent School
    District*, 173
Gender
    bias in educational leadership research, 340
    discrimination based on, 134, 182
    diversity, 381
    identities, 344
    roles, 349
    sexual harassment cases, 172-173, 182
    stereotypes, 114, 119, 120, 151
    technology divide, 272
    See also Feminist theory; Men; Women
Goddard, H. H., 488
Goggin, Catherine, 411
Good News Club v. Milford Central School, 176
Goodlad Coalition for Essential Schools, 74
Goss v. Lopez, 178
Governments. *See* Federal government; States
Greek literature
    Odyssey, 90
    Oedipus, 368, 371, 376
    views of leadership, 368-369
Green school design, 528-530
Grievances, 547-548

Haley, Margaret, 411
Hall, G. Stanley, 499, 500
Hamilton, Alexander, 147, 500
Hamlet (Shakespeare), 370
Harmony Education Center (HEC),
    298-300, 306
Harmony School, 298, 299
Harris, T. H., 16, 17, 21-25, 26, 27, 29, 30, 31
Harris, William T., 14
Hawaii

McKinley High School, Honolulu, 54-55
    school finance, 554, 560
Hawthorne studies, 96, 97
Hazelwood School District v. Kuhlmeier, 177-178
Head teachers, 111, 112
Health, indoor environments of schools, 528-529
HEC. *See* Harmony Education Center
Heteronormativity, 340, 349
Heterosexuality
    assumptions of, 340, 344-345, 349
    bias in educational leadership research, 340
    of administrators, 53-54
High schools
    attendance rates, 116
    buildings, 510, 516-517, 519, 524-525
    climate, 97
    college prep courses, 287-289, 292
    comprehensive, 510
    curricula, 116, 122
    female principals, 134
    history of, 115, 510-511
    sizes, 69, 515
    technical, 510-511
High stakes tests, 304, 395, 415-418, 437
    See also Standardized tests
High Tech High School (San Diego),
    519, 524-525
Higher education
    aspirations to, 280, 287
    See also Normal schools; Preparation programs
High-performance school design, 528-530
Hippocrates, xv
Hispanics
    aspirations for college going, 280, 287
    college prep courses, 287-289
    in Chicago, 237-238
    school segregation and, 171
    student achievement, 271, 272
    student disengagement, 411
    superintendents, 154
    See also Racial and ethnic groups
History of educational leadership. *See*
    Educational leadership, history of;
    Principalship, history of
Homeless children, 182-183
Homophobia, 59, 340, 349, 423
Homosexuals
    gay purges, 54
    queer theory, 343-345, 349-350
    sodomy laws, 59, 350
    teachers, 350
Honig v. Doe, 172
Housing, 16, 20
Hudson Institute, 224, 228
Hughes, Charles Evans, 24
Human agency, 90-93, 95, 96, 99
Human relations school, 96-99, 121-122

Humanities
  lack of attention in leadership studies, 363
  leadership thought, 364
  literature, 366-372
Humphrey, Hubert, 468
Hyperrationalization of schools, 410-415

Iacocca, Lee, 365
IBM, 220-221
IDEA. *See* Individuals with Disabilities
  Education Act
Identities
  construction of, 389-390
  diversity, 389-390
  gender, 344
  sexual, 343, 344
I-it relationships, 387
Immigrants, 12, 54-55, 116, 171
Incremental program budgeting, 566
Indiana University, 298
Individuals with Disabilities Education Act
  (IDEA), 172, 182
Industrial revolution, 115, 146, 432-433, 490
Inequality
  of wealth across communities, 552, 553, 554
  reinforcement of, 465, 468
  See also Equality; Social justice
Influence strategies, 204
Information technology. *See* Technology
Inquiry
  culturally responsive, 270
  in research on educational leadership, 338-341
  See also Whole-school inquiry
Institutional theory, 100-101, 103, 104
Instruction. *See* Curriculum; Teaching
Instructional program coherence, 419
Intelligence
  construction of, 497
  craniometry, 487-488
  IQ tests, 487, 488
Intermediate-level superintendents,
  143-144, 153
Internet
  access in schools, 523
  distance learning, 527-528
  See also Technology
Interstate School Leaders Licensure Consortium
  (ISLLC), 57, 133, 150, 337-338, 365
IQ tests, 487, 488
Irving Independent School District v. Tatro, 172
ISLLC. *See* Interstate School Leaders
  Licensure Consortium
I-thou relationships, 387, 388, 397

Job Characteristics Model (JCM), 452
Johnson, Lyndon B., 181
Journalism, 177-178, 491

Julius Caesar (Shakespeare), 367, 369
Junior high schools
  buildings, 510
  history of, 116, 511
Justice. *See* Social justice

Kant, Immanuel, 308, 496
Kellogg Foundation, 148
*Keyes v. School District No. 1, Denver,
  Colorado*, 171
King John (Shakespeare), 367, 369, 370-371
King Lear (Shakespeare), 368, 369,
  370, 371, 372
King Oedipus, 368, 371, 376
Kingship, 367
Klein, Joel I., 262
Knowledge, construction of, 497-498

*Lamb's Chapel v. Center Moriches Union Free
  School District*, 176
Language
  in politics, 222-223
  metaphor theory, 498
  power of, 35-36
  sanitized, 35
Latin America, social justice issues, 52
Latinos. *See* Hispanics
Law, education. *See* Education law
Laws. *See* Federal laws; States
Leader Behavior Description Questionnaire
  (LBDQ), 96
Leadership
  behavioral theories, 96, 98, 363
  business, 365
  collaborative, 68, 72, 73-74, 77-80, 161
  contingency theories, 98, 363
  cross-cultural, 380, 382-383, 384
  definitions, 92-93, 95
  differences from management, xi-xii
  for common good, 368-369
  heroic, 91, 365
  human relations school, 96-99, 104
  institutional perspective, 101, 103, 104
  kingship, 367
  knowledge of self and others, 371-372
  of culturally responsive schools, 293
  path-goal theory, 98
  rational perspective, 94-96, 104, 105
  relations with subordinates, 98, 99
  relationship to organizational
    culture, 102-103
  relationship to organizational structure, 93
  substitutes, 96
  symbolic, 103, 104-105
  symbolism of, 91
  trait theory, 95, 363
  transactional, 102

transformational, 102-103, 104-105, 130, 132, 321, 322, 323, 363
  See also Diversity, leadership in context of; Educational leadership; Moral leadership
Leadership content knowledge, 425
Leadership preparation programs. *See* Preparation programs
Leadership thought
  critique of traditional, 363-365, 375-377
  domains, 89
  history of, 362, 363-365
  in Western classical literature, 366-372, 376
  international perspectives, 364-365, 372-375
Learning
  behaviorist theories, 485, 488-489, 490
  collaborative, 517-518
  constructivist theory, 495, 497-498
  double-loop, 43-44
  lifelong, 520
  Piaget's theories, 496-497
  self-directed, 518
  single-loop, 43
  transformative, 79
  whole-language theory, 502
  See also Student achievement; Teaching
Learning communities
  democracy in, 72, 73
  professional, 386-387
  school designs for, 513-514, 515-517
Lee v. Weisman, 176
Legal environment. *See* Education law; Federal laws; States
Legalism, Chinese, 374-375
Legitimation crises, 70
Lehnert v. Ferris Faculty Association, 180
Lemon v. Kurtzman, 174, 176
Leo XIII, Pope, 50
Lesbians. *See* Homosexuals
Lexington Normal School, 12-13
Liberation theology, 52
Libraries, 524
Licensing. *See* Certification and licensing
Lifeworld, 187-188
Line item budgeting, 565
Literature, leadership thought in, 366-372, 376
Local education revenues, 551, 553, 556-557, 558-559
Locus of control, 318
Logan Square Neighborhood Association (LSNA), 238, 254, 261, 262
Logical positivism. *See* Positivism
Long, Huey P., 24, 25, 28, 29
Loosely coupled systems, schools as, 99-102, 309, 416
Louisiana

Harris as state schools superintendent, 24-25
  state education laws, 173
Low-income families
  housing problems, 16, 20
  use of violence, 467
  youth misbehavior and violence, 466
Low-income students
  achievement, 272
  homeless, 182-183
  meals in schools, 17
  problems, 463-464, 465
LSNA. *See* Logan Square Neighborhood Association

Macbeth (Shakespeare), 367, 368, 369
Machiavelli, Niccolo, *The Prince*, 368, 369-370, 371, 372
Majority-minority schools, 381
Management
  activities, 116
  differences from leadership, xi-xii
  machine metaphor, 431, 433
Management principles
  criticism of use in education, 14-15, 147
  leadership theory and, 363
  rational, 35
  taught in educational administration programs, 118
  use in educational leadership, x-xi, 9, 53, 217, 221-222, 422
Mann, Horace, 12-13, 30, 31, 111, 112, 408
  common school movement, 13, 489, 510
  influence, 16, 28
  opponents, 13, 29
  view of democracy, 25-26
  view of female teachers, 151
Manpower Demonstration Research Corporation, 416
Marcuse, Herbert, 35-36
Market populism, 225
Marketization, 217, 222-226
Martin, Luther, 433
Martinez v. Bynum, 172
Marxism, 52
Maslow's hierarchy of needs, 49, 60, 97
Massachusetts
  compulsory education, 151
  Lexington Normal School, 12-13, 26
  State Board of Education, 12
  See also Mann, Horace
Massachusetts Bay Company, 217
Maxwell, William H., 9, 15-18, 26, 28, 29, 30, 31
Mayo, Elton, x
McDonald's, 222
McGregor, Douglas, x
McKinley High School, Honolulu, 54-55

McMurry, Frank, 19, 30
Meek v. Pittenger, 174
Melby, Ernest, 147
Men
  domination of preparation program
    faculty, 118, 127
  principals, 113-114, 119-120, 134
  superintendents, 150-151, 152-154,
    349, 350-351
  teachers, 124-125, 128, 151, 152, 153
  See also Gender
Mentors, 120, 434, 450
Metaphor theory, 498
Mexican Americans, 171
  See also Hispanics
Meyerson, Debra, 424
Micropolitics
  meaning of, 297-298
  of school reform, 326
Middle schools
  designs, 513-514, 515
  principals, 128, 134
  purposes, 513
Minnesota New Country School
  (Henderson), 519
Minorities. *See* Racial and ethnic groups
Minoritized groups, 381, 392
Misbehavior. *See* Student misbehavior
Mitchell v. Helms, 174
Modernism, 36-37, 433
  aesthetic, 37
  critics of, 37, 38, 104
  scientific management and, 36-38
  See also Positivism; Postmodernism
Montessori, Maria, 511
Montgomery Ward, 248-249, 251
Moore, Michael, 217
Moral leadership
  Chinese views of, 375
  collaborative leadership and, 72
  critical self-reflection and, 42-43, 45
  dimensions, 44-46
  goals, 45
  importance of social context, 35, 39
  in literature, 376
  issues, 40
  lack of attention to, 366
  of educational leaders, 41-42, 56
  practical art of ruling and, 369-371
  questions for educators, 40-41
  response to modernism and postmodernism,
    39-41
  wholeness, 44
  See also Social justice
Motivation
  intrinsic, 446
  Job Characteristics Model, 452

of teachers, 433-434, 437, 445, 447-448
  theories, 97, 98
  Theory X and Theory Y, 432-433
  See also Flow
*Mt. Healthy City School District Board of
  Education v. Doyle*, 179
Multiculturalism, 274, 390-391
  See also Diversity
Murphy, John, 220
Murray v. Curtlett, 175-176
Music education, 17, 24-25
Mythology, 90

NAEP. *See* National Assessment of
  Educational Progress
NAESP. *See* National Association of Elementary
  School Principals
NASSP. *See* National Association of Secondary
  School Principals
A Nation at Risk, 56, 70, 129-130
National Academy of Sciences, 552
National Assessment of Educational Progress
  (NAEP), 438, 440, 441
National Association of Elementary School
  Principals (NAESP), 57, 128
National Association of Secondary School
  Principals (NASSP), 57, 128
National Commission for the Principalship,
  57, 133
National Commission on Excellence in
  Education, 56, 57
National Conference of Professors of Educational
  Administration (NCPEA), 123
National Conference on Christians and Jews, 176
National Council for the Accreditation of
  Teacher Education (NCATE), 123, 337
National Defense Education Act (NDEA),
  122, 181
National Education Association (NEA)
  administrators included in, 14, 26, 30,
    117-118, 128, 145
  as professional organization, 30, 145, 540
  as union, 541
  conferences, 14, 411
  differences from AFT, 540-541
  history of, 411, 540
  issue positions, 411-412
  male domination of, 120
  membership, 411, 541
  view of collective bargaining, 540-541
  Young as president, 119
National Middle School Association
  (NMSA), 128
National Parent Teacher Association, 231-232
National Policy Board for Educational
  Administration (NPBEA), 57, 133
National School Boards Association, 227

National Science Foundation, System Initiatives, 413
National Society for the Study of Education, 30, 55
National Staff Development Council, 449
Native Americans
  culturally responsive education, 274
  student achievement, 271
  See also Racial and ethnic groups
NCATE. *See* National Council for the
  Accreditation of Teacher Education
NCPEA. *See* National Conference of Professors
  of Educational Administration
NDEA. *See* National Defense Education Act
NEA. *See* National Education Association
Negative gravity, 431
Neighborhood schools, 520-522
  See also Communities
New citizenship discourse, 242, 260, 263, 264
New institutionalism, 100, 101-102
New Jersey v. T.L.O., 178-179
New York ACORN, 238, 261, 262
New York City
  housing problems, 16, 20
  poverty, 29
New York City schools
  budgets, 17
  parent coordinators, 262
  principals, 18, 20, 54
  school construction, 16, 510
  superintendents, 9, 15, 16-17
  teacher unions, 411
  Title I program, 174-175
New York State Board of Regents, 175
New York state school superintendent, 142-143
Newton, Isaac, 487, 490, 496
NMSA. *See* National Middle School Association
No Child Left Behind Act, 182, 387
  data disaggregation, 293, 408
  expectations from, 305, 395
  financial impact, 550-551
  parent involvement, 262
  passage of, 71
  rational perspective in, 105
  requirements, 271, 272, 409, 416
  responses to, 407, 415
  skepticism about, 187
Noble High School (North Berwick, Maine),
  516-517, 518
Noise pollution, 529
Normal schools
  Chicago, 14, 15
  history of, 12-13, 26, 28
NPBEA. *See* National Policy Board for
  Educational Administration

Oakland Community Organizations (OCO), 238,
  248-253, 255, 261, 262
Odyssey, 90

Oedipus, 368, 371, 376
Ohio K-12 English Language Arts Academic
  Content Standards, 420
Ohio State Leadership studies, 96, 98
One-room schoolhouses, 508-509
Open education, 492, 501, 502, 513
Open systems model, 38, 43
Operations research, 434
Organizational culture, 102-103
Organizational ideologies, xii
Organizational structures
  as constraints on human activity, 90, 96, 99
  formal, 94, 96
  informal, 97, 98-99
  leadership and, 93
  See also Bureaucracies
Organizations
  climates, 97-98
  human relations school perspective, 96-99
  institutional theory, 100-101
  rational perspective, 94-96
  rationality of, 415
Outsourcing of school services, 220, 227, 228

Parent associations, 21
Parents
  aspirations for college going, 280, 287
  contributions to school reform, 262
  engagement, 241-243, 264
  involvement in schools, 238, 241-243, 262, 292
  relations with teachers, 242, 243
  single, 466
  training programs, 237-238
  See also Community organizing; Families
Participatory decision making, 99
  See also Democracy
Paterson (New Jersey), 521
Path-goal theory, 98
Pathologizing, 391, 392, 396
Patri, Angelo, 18-21, 26, 27, 28-29, 30, 31
Pedagogy. *See* Teaching
Peirce, Cyrus, 12-13, 26, 28, 31
*People of the State of Illinois ex rel. McCollum v.
  Board of Education of School District No.
  71, Champaign County*, 175
Performance-based program budgeting,
  566-567, 568
Perkins, Larry, 512
Pestalozzi, Johann Heinrich, 511
Pew Charitable Trusts, 337
Philbrick, John, 114
Piaget, J., 495, 496-497, 498
*Pickering v. Board of Education of Township
  High School District*, 179
Pierce v. Society of Sisters, 173
Planning
  facility, 530

financial, 564
   See also Budgeting
Plato, 147, 487, 489, 490
Pledge of Allegiance, 176
Plessy v. Ferguson, 171
Plyler v. Doe, 171-172
Policy advocacy, 80
Policy analysis
   challenges, 191-192
   contexts, 200-201
   education, 192-193
   importance, 192
   political traditions, 201-208, 209
   rational traditions, 194-201, 209, 223, 340
   webs of policies, 199-200
Policy entrepreneurs, 204
Political spectacles, 222-223
Politics
   action on social justice issues, 58
   actors, interests, and arenas, 202-204
   contexts, 204-205
   corporate involvement, 218
   in schools and school systems, 298
   involvement of educators, 29, 51, 58, 127
   involvement of superintendents, 147
   language in, 222-223
   of school reform, 298
   policy analysis, 201-208, 209
   school finance issues, 157-158
   state superintendents and, 24
   See also Micropolitics; Power
Positivism, 35, 41, 56, 339, 365, 432, 434
Postmodernism, 38-39, 56, 104, 365
Poststructuralism, 345, 346
   See also Feminist poststructural theory
Poverty
   relationship to youth misbehavior and
      violence, 466
   urban, 29
   victimization and, 317
   See also Low-income families; Socioeconomic
      status
Power
   abuse of, 368
   corporate, 218
   distribution in school districts, 300-308
   distribution within schools, 309, 316, 320-321
   effects of, 351
   issues for collaboration, 77-78
   of state governments, 207-208
   policymaking and, 201, 202
   sources of, 204, 300-308
   spheres of influence, 316, 318-319
   See also Politics
Preparation programs
   accreditation, 338
   associations, 123-124
   changes in 1960s, 127

changes proposed, 57, 58, 133
communication skills, 150
community partnerships, 81
curricula, 80
democratic leadership, 80-81
education law courses, 169-170
faculty, 57-58, 75, 118, 127
female students, 161
for superintendents, 160
growth of, 127
history of, 55, 117, 118, 124, 132-133, 146
influence, 55
leadership studies, 377
organizational structures, 81
social justice issues in, 55-59, 61, 80
social sciences in, 148
students of color, 161
Principals
   African American, 53, 128
   behaviors that support flow experiences of
      teachers, 451-452
   certification and licensing, 118, 124, 132, 133
   character traits, 117
   characteristics of work, 78
   community involvement, 125-126
   complexity of jobs, 136-137
   curriculum leadership role, 419, 434
   demands of accountability environment, 78, 408
   duties, 17-18, 23, 55, 112-113, 115
   educational requirements, 113, 118-119, 124,
      132, 133
   effects of school reform, 320-322
   evaluations of teachers, 434
   evolving roles, 109-117, 121-129
   former teachers, 128
   future challenges, 134-137
   hiring, 120, 301-302
   in democratic environment, 321
   instructional leadership role, 129, 130, 131
   involvement in contract negotiations, 127
   male dominance of field, 113-114,
      119-120, 134
   management roles, 69
   political activities, 127
   professional organizations,
      117-118, 128, 133
   public scrutiny, 132
   reasons for leaving jobs, 136
   relationships with teachers, 18, 121-122, 485,
      486, 494-495
   religious beliefs, 117
   role in school reform, 301-302, 320-322
   shortage of, 135-136
   social justice responsibilities, 57
   standards, 57, 133
   transformational leadership, 130, 132
   See also Supervision; Women principals
Principals Exchange, 287

Principalship, history of
    anti-intellectual period, 121-125
    constancy and change, 125-129
    emergence, 111-114
    professionalization, 114-121
    reform and restructuring, 129-134
Private schools
    corporate donations, 232
    government subsidies, 173-175, 552
    history of, 226
Privatization, 217, 220, 226-229, 231
    See also Educational management
        organizations
Professional development programs,
    441, 449-450
Professional learning communities, 386-387
Professional organizations, 30, 117-118, 128,
    133, 145
    See also National Education Association
Program budgeting, 566
Progressive education, 50-51, 147, 491, 500, 511
    See also Transaction teaching
Progressive Education Association, 51
Progressive Era, 50, 56
Property taxes, 553, 558, 559
Public schools
    common school movement, 13, 111, 112,
        143, 145, 489, 510
    democratic goals, 1
    goals, 226
    history in United States, 11, 111-112
    public support, 69, 74-75, 112, 556, 564
Public/private binary, x-xi
Purpose-driven leadership. *See* Moral leadership

Quality, xi
    See also Total Quality Management (TQM)
Queer legal theory, 349-350
Queer theory, 343-345, 349-350
Quincy School, 114

Racial and ethnic groups
    aspirations for college going, 280, 287
    college prep courses, 287-289
    computers at home, 523
    digital divide, 271-272, 523
    equal opportunity cases, 170-172
    parental involvement in schools, 242
    problems of children, 463-464
    student achievement, 271, 392
    student misbehavior, 411
    superintendents, 150-151, 153-155, 160-161
    teachers, 53, 152
    underrepresentation in educational leadership,
        53, 120, 128, 150-151
    See also African Americans; Asian Americans;
        Critical race theory; Hispanics;
        Segregation

Racism, 342, 423
Rational choice theory, 224-225
Rational perspective
    criticism of, 101, 195
    educational leadership research, 339, 340
    limitations of, 340
    on leadership and organizations, 94-96,
        104, 105
    policy analysis, 194-201, 209, 223, 340
Rationality
    modernist, 36, 37
    normative, 45
    organizational, 415
    technical, 45
Reader response theory, 502
Reason Foundation, 228
Reciprocity, 325, 326
Reconceptualism, 423
Reconstitution, school, 197, 207
Reflection, 42-43, 45, 79, 421
Reforms
    authentic discourses, 323-326
    autonomous schools, 252, 300-309
    challenges, 317-326
    community organizing and, 237-240, 244,
        257-260
    conflict management, 314-317
    debates on, 158-159
    decision making within schools,
        310, 311-314
    democratic culture and, 298, 309-317
    effects measured by test scores, 305
    external change agents, 305-309, 325
    focus on internal governance, 326-327
    government constraints on, 304-305, 319
    improving quality of students' lives, 314-315
    in 1960s, 126-127
    in 1980s, 56, 129-130, 131
    in 1990s, 130, 131-132, 149
    interest of business in, 227
    leadership, 320, 322-323
    moral purposes, 314-315
    obstacles, 259
    ongoing, 323
    parents' roles, 262
    participation in, 309-310
    politics of, 298
    principal's role, 301-302, 320-322
    relationships among policies, 199-200
    restructuring, 130, 131-132, 149
    school reconstitution, 197, 207
    social justice issues, 58
    standards-based, 197
    superintendents' roles, 149, 159
    teacher unions and, 302-304, 411,
        412, 544-545
    teachers' roles, 300, 311-314, 412
    traditional teaching methods and, 492

views of past educational leaders, 9, 31
See also Accountability movement
Rehabilitation Act of 1973, 182
Religion
  legal cases on church-state issues, 173-176
  liberation theology, 52
  of principals, 117
  of superintendents, 53
  prayer in schools, 175-176
  private schools, 173-175, 552
  social justice and, 49-50
Research for Action, 238
Research on educational leadership
  alternatives to traditional approaches, 341,
    348, 351-352
  blank spots and blind spots, 338-339, 341
  critical race theory, 341-343, 348-349
  debates in, 340
  feminist poststructural approaches, 345-347,
    350-351
  historical development, 338-341
  inquiry in, 338-341
  limitations of, xiii-xiv
  queer theory, 343-345, 349-350
  rational perspective, 339, 340
  theory-based, 122, 123
Revenues for public education
  definition, 556
  distribution and equalization plans, 559-561
  history in United States, 11
  local, 551, 553, 556-557, 558-559
  sources, 556-559
  state, 551, 552, 553, 554, 555, 556, 557, 558
  See also School finance; Taxes
Richard II (Shakespeare), 367, 368, 370,
    371, 372
Rogue events, 475
Rome, ancient, 90, 368-369
Rural schools, 115, 508-509
Rush, Benjamin, 151-152
Ruth, Babe, 477

Saarinen, Eliel, 512
*San Antonio Independent School District v.
    Rodriguez*, 181
San Diego Model Schools, 522
San Diego, High Tech High School, 519, 524-525
Santa Fe Independent School District v. Doe, 176
SASS. *See* Schools and Staffing Surveys
SBI. *See* Site-based management (SBI)
Schmidt, Benno C., Jr., 228
School boards
  history of, 55-56, 111
  power of, 300
  relationships with superintendents,
    144-145, 159-160
  roles of members, 159-160

School buildings
  air quality and ventilation, 528-529
  community use of, 408-409, 520-522
  construction, 530-531
  deteriorating conditions, 507
  facility planning, 530
  funding, 530
  importance, 506
  lighting, 529
  maintenance, 531-532
  noise pollution, 529
  one-room, 508-509
  See also School design
School climate, 97-98, 253, 465, 515
School design
  common school movement and, 510
  community involvement, 530
  contributions to educational goals, 506
  educational leadership and, 507-508
  factory model, 510-513
  for collaborative learning, 517-519
  for learning community, 513-514
  for smaller learning communities, 515-517
  future, 515, 528-530
  high-performance, 528-530
  history in United States, 508-514
  house plan, 513-514
  innovations, 512, 513, 517-519
  neighborhood plan, 515-517
  open-plan, 513
  process, 530
  schools-within-a-school, 515-517
  standardized plans, 510, 512
  student workstations, 519, 525
  technology in, 522-528
*School District of Abington Township v.
    Schempp*, 175-176
School districts
  administrators, 300-302
  autonomy, 207-208
  distribution of power in, 300-308
  See also School boards; Superintendents
School finance
  adequacy of funding, 554-556
  budgets, 564-568
  challenges for superintendents, 157-158
  construction funding, 530
  equity issues, 157-158, 552, 553, 554,
    559, 561-562
  expenditures, 551, 561-564
  goals, 552-553
  impact of No Child Left Behind Act, 550-551
  legal cases, 181
  revenue sources, 553, 556-559
  U.S. system, 551-552
School for Environmental Studies (Apple
  Valley, Minnesota), 519

School law. *See* Education law
School Leaders Licensure Assessment (SLLA), 133
School reform. *See* Reforms
School sizes
  benefits of small schools, 248, 252, 515
  climates, 253, 515
  large high schools, 69, 515
  relationship to student achievement,
      252, 253, 515
  small schools campaign (Oakland), 248-253
  See also School design
School superintendents. *See* Superintendents
School-based management. *See* Site-based
      management (SBI)
Schools and Staffing Surveys (SASS), 437-438
Schools First program, 553
Schools-within-a-school (SWAS), 515-517
Schwarzkopf, H. Norman, 365
Science
  education in, 121, 122, 123, 181
  influence on other fields, 36
  modernist view of, 37
  objectivist, 487
Science of education, 412-413
Scientific management
  in preparation programs, 55
  leadership studies and, 363, 364
  objectives, 115
  relationship to modernism, 36-38
  tenets, 34, 35, 433, 490
Scientific management, application to education
  adoption by educational leaders, x, 94, 490
  critiques of, 9, 16
  effects, 114, 115, 116, 121, 422, 499
  influence, 34, 35
  purpose, 10
  social realities ignored, 39, 40
Search and seizure issues, 178-179
Secondary schools. *See* High schools
Security policies, 469
Segregation
  class, 220-221
  de facto, 220-221
  racial, 53, 125, 126, 128, 152,
      154, 170, 171
  separate but equal doctrine, 171
  See also Desegregation
Self-directed learning, 518
Serrano v. Priest, 560
Sexual harassment cases, 172-173, 182
Sexual identities, 343, 344
Sexual orientation, 53-54
  See also Heterosexuality; Homosexuals
Shakespeare, William
  Hamlet, 370
  Julius Caesar, 367, 369
  King John, 367, 369, 370-371

King Lear, 368, 369, 370, 371, 372
Macbeth, 367, 368, 369
Richard II, 367, 368, 370, 371, 372
  views of leadership, 367, 368-369, 370
Simon, Herbert, x
Single-loop learning, 43
Site-based management (SBI), 73, 100,
    131-132, 197, 206-207, 221, 544
Skinner, B. F., 485, 488, 489
Slaves, 151
SLLA. *See* School Leaders Licensure Assessment
Social capital
  benefits, 472
  bonding, 244, 472, 473
  bridging, 244, 472, 473
  definition, 244, 471
  developing, 74, 244, 477-478
  effects on social institutions, 472-474
  in communities, 471-472, 478
  in families, 471, 478
  linking, 472, 473-474
  relationship to education, 471
Social context, 385
Social gospel movement, 49
Social institutions, 472-474
Social justice
  addressed in preparation programs, 55-59, 61, 80
  community development and, 74
  critical race theory and, 342, 343
  critical theory and, 56, 148
  democracy and, 327-328
  educational leadership and, 53-55
  guiding principles, 60-61
  historical roots, 49-53
  in schools, 396
  injustices of society reflected in schools, 54, 423-424
  interest in, 47
  meaning of, 47-49, 59-61
  religious roots, 49-50
  schools as agents for change, 423-424
  See also Moral leadership
Social service agencies, collaboration with public
    schools, 208
Social toxicity, 465, 470
Society, relationship to education
  historical perspectives, 69-72
  injustices reflected in schools, 54, 423-424
  social structure reflected in schools, 39-40,
      392, 410-411, 422-424
  See also Communities; Social justice
Socioeconomic status
  diversity, 381
  of educational leaders, 53
  relationship to student achievement, 437, 553
  segregation by, 220-221
  social structure reflected in schools, 39-40,
      392, 410-411, 422-424

student pliability and, 411
  See also Poverty
Soviet Union, Sputnik launch, 121, 122, 23, 181
Spaulding, Frank, 490
Special education, 172, 271, 562
Spheres of influence, 316, 318-319
Spirituality, 394
Sputnik, 121, 122, 123, 181
Standardization
  in bureaucracies, 115
  in business, xi
  of curriculum, 116
Standardized tests
  criticism of, 9, 16
  curriculum alignment, 409-410, 417, 418, 444
  disaggregation of results, 293, 408
  high stakes tests, 304, 395, 415-418, 437
  history of, 408
  impact on schools, 415-418
  School Leaders Licensure Assessment (SLLA), 133
  state requirements, 305
  time needed, 410
  transmission teaching and, 486
Standards
  Interstate School Leaders Licensure
      Consortium, 57, 133, 150, 337-338, 365
  state, 420
Stanford School of Education, 55
State school systems, 69, 120
State superintendents
  duties, 142-143
  history in United States, 22-23, 24-25, 142-143
  political roles, 24
  variations among states, 143
States
  aid to private schools, 173-175, 552
  boards of education, 143
  certification and licensing of principals, 118
  constraints on school reform, 304
  control of public school systems, 132
  corporate charters, 217-218
  departments of education, 143, 304
  education expenditures, 551, 552, 553, 554,
      555, 556, 557, 558, 563
  educational laws and regulations, 24-25, 71,
      304, 305, 433, 552, 558
  educational responsibilities, 551
  educational standards, 420
  power over local school districts, 207-208
  school funding equity, 157, 559-562
  sodomy laws, 59, 350
  taxes, 558, 559
  women's voting rights, 153
Statesmanship, 147
Stewart B. McKinney Homeless Assistance
    Act, 182-183
Stigler, George, 224

Stokes, Peter, 227
Stone v. Graham, 176
Strayer, George, 146
Structuralism, 433
Student achievement, factors in
  classroom instructional design, 444
  classroom management, 442-444
  classroom visits by principals, 448
  community organizing indicators, 244-248
  culturally responsive teaching, 275
  family attitudes, 471
  instructional program coherence, 419
  race and ethnicity of students, 271, 392
  reforms, 413
  school building conditions, 507
  school size, 252, 253, 515
  socioeconomic status, 437, 553
  teacher quality, 437-438
  teacher satisfaction, 435
  teacher self-efficacy, 450, 451
  teacher's professional development, 450
  teaching methods, 441-444
Student achievement, in for-profit schools, 229
Student misbehavior
  factors in, 465-470, 478
  family-related factors, 466-467
  impact on learning environment, 465-466
  racial differences, 411
  risk of, 469-470
  rogue events, 475
  school-related factors, 467-469, 515
  See also Discipline; Violence
Students
  cultures, 102
  drug testing, 179
  engagement, 411, 447-448, 451
  free speech rights, 177-178
  homeless, 182-183
  legal rights, 176-179
  low-income, 17, 182-183, 272, 463-464, 465
  perceptions of teacher effectiveness, 442
Superintendents
  annual reports, 14, 15, 30
  certification and licensing, 124, 150
  challenges, 156-160
  communication by, 149-150
  criteria for selecting, 53
  democratic leadership, 147-148
  duties, 17-18, 120
  elected, 53
  financial responsibilities, 157-158
  future research topics, 160-161
  history of, 144-145
  intermediate-level, 143-144, 153
  male dominance of field, 53, 150-151,
      152-154, 349, 350-351
  management roles, 146-147

of color, 150-151, 153-155, 160-161
political involvement, 147
power of, 146
professional organizations, 145
relationships with school boards,
    144-145, 159-160
religious beliefs, 53
role in school reform, 149, 159
roles, 144-150, 160
security policies, 469
shortage of, 160
social issues, 57, 158
standards, 57
urban districts, 144, 145, 146-147
white, 53, 150-151, 154
See also State superintendents; Women
    superintendents
Supervision
classroom management techniques, 442
effects of accountability environment, 127
fallacious philosophies, 432-433
monitoring curriculum, 419-420, 421
pedagogical knowledge, 441
principal's role, 23, 112-113
purposes, 432, 455
reflective dialogue with, 421
research on, 432, 438-445, 448-449
state role, 23-24
teacher evaluations, 433, 434, 450, 453
transmission teaching and, 486
See also Classroom observation
Supreme Court, U.S.
church-state issues, 173-176
collective bargaining cases, 180-181
education law cases, 168, 170
employee rights cases, 179-181
equal opportunity issues, 170-173
school desegregation, 121, 125, 126, 153,
    168, 169, 170-171
school finance issues, 181
search and seizure issues, 178-179
sexual harassment cases, 172-173, 182
special education issues, 172
student rights cases, 176-179
voucher cases, 175
Sustainable school design, 528-530
*Swann v. Charlotte Mecklenburg Board
    of Education*, 171
SWAS. *See* Schools-within-a-school
Symbolic leadership, 103, 104-105
Systemworld, 187-188

Taxes
breaks for corporations, 218, 232
fairness, 560
opposition to use for schools, 11
property, 553, 558, 559

resistance to increases, 556
state, 558, 559
Taylor, Frederick W., x, 55, 94, 115, 490
Taylorism. *See* Scientific management
Teacher evaluations, 433, 434, 450, 453
Teacher training
normal schools, 12-13, 14, 15, 26, 28
professional development, 441, 449-450
See also Normal schools
Teacher unions. *See* Unions, teacher
Teachers
attrition and retention, 431-432, 436
certification, 440
classroom management, 442-444
collaborative activities, 450
competence, 450
content knowledge, 272, 273
cultures, 102
educational backgrounds, 440
employee rights, 179-181
factors that influence student achievement,
    272-273, 435, 437-438, 439-440, 450
female dominance of field, 113, 119, 120,
    128, 151-152, 349
flow experiences, 446-448, 451, 452-453
homosexual, 350
interactions among, 315-316
leadership networks, 73-74
male, 124-125, 128, 151, 152, 153
morale, 431, 436
motivation, 437, 445, 447-448
of color, 53, 152
pedagogical knowledge, 440-441
pliability, 411-412
power of, 309, 318-319
reasons for teaching, 435
reflective dialogue with, 421
relations with parents, 242, 243
relations with principals, 18, 121-122,
    485, 486, 494-495
roles in school reform, 300, 311-314, 412
satisfaction, 431, 435, 437,
    445, 447-448
seen as managers, 492
seen as workers, 221, 542
self-efficacy, 450-451
self-reflection, 453
sexual harassment cases, 172-173
standardized tests and, 416
subject matter knowledge, 440
terminations, 180
treatment by districts, 431
verbal ability, 439-440
victimization feelings, 317-320
working conditions, 431, 435-437, 507-508
See also Classroom observation; Supervision;
    Unions, teacher

Teaching
 classroom instructional design, 444
 corporate influences, 221-222
 culturally responsive, 273-275, 293
 effective practices, 441-444
 history in United States, 485
 impacts of educational leaders, 424-425
 informal classrooms, 492, 501
 open education, 492, 501, 502, 513
 pedagogical knowledge of teachers, 440-441
 transaction approach, 493-502
 transmission approach, 484-493, 499,
  501, 502-503
Technical-rational perspective. See Rational
 perspective
Technology
 benefits, 523
 computers at home, 523
 distance learning, 527-528
 effective use of, 523-524
 funding, 523
 impact on school design, 522-528
 in older school buildings, 507
 modernist view of, 37
 wireless, 525-527
Technology divide, 271-272, 523
Tempered radicals, 424
Tennessee Value Added Assessment System
 (TVAAS), 409
Terman, L. M., 488
Tesseract, 227
Tests, standardized. See Standardized tests
Texts, work, 416
Theories of action, 195-197
Theory
 in social sciences, xiv-xv
 research based on, 122, 123
Theory of change model, 244-248
Thesis of vulnerability, 146
Third International Mathematics and Science
 Study (TIMSS), 437
Thomas Aquinas, St., 434, 455
TIMSS. See Third International Mathematics and
 Science Study
Tinker v. Des Moines Independent Community
 School District, 177-178
Total Quality Management (TQM),
 221-222, 422, 433-434
Tracking, 396, 411
Traditional transmission teaching. See
 Transmission teaching
Transaction teaching
 assessments, 496
 assumptions, 493-494
 challenges, 500
 comparison to transmission approach,
  493, 494

constructivist learning theory,
 495, 497-498
 curriculum, 495-496
 example, 493
 influence, 500
 practices, 495-496
 scientific basis, 496-499
 socio-political influences, 499-502
 student roles, 494
 teacher roles, 494
Transactional leadership, 102
Transactions, 502
Transcendent leaders, 78-80
Transformational leadership, 102-103, 104-105,
 130, 132, 321, 322, 323, 363
Transformative learning, 79
Transmission teaching
 alternatives to, 492-493, 499, 501
 assumptions, 484-485, 499
 behavioral objectives, 491, 492
 comparison to transaction
  approach, 493, 494
 criticism of, 501, 502
 dominance, 492, 499, 501, 502-503
 example, 484
 practices, 485-487
 scientific basis, 487-489
 socio-political influences, 489-493, 499
TVAAS. See Tennessee Value Added
 Assessment System
Tyranny, 367-368

UCEA. See University Council for Educational
 Administration
Unions
 agency or fair-share fees, 180-181
 definition, 540
 history of, 539-540
 industrial, 541-542
 roles, 540
Unions, teacher
 building representatives, 543
 Canadian, 412
 concerns, 302-303
 contracts, 127, 229, 545, 547-548
 contributions, 303-304
 grievances, 547-548
 history of, 411, 540-541
 impact of, 538-539
 negotiating with, 127, 545-546, 547
 research on, 539
 school reform and, 302-304, 411,
  412, 544-545
 seen as obstacle to reform, 302
 strikes, 411
 teachers' relations with, 542-543, 544
 working with, 546-548

See also American Federation of Teachers (AFT); Collective bargaining; National Education Association (NEA)

U.S. Department of Education, 271, 304, 412, 522-523

U.S. General Services Administration, 529

U.S. government. *See* Federal government

U.S. Supreme Court. *See* Supreme Court, U.S.

Universities. *See* Higher education; Preparation programs

University Council for Educational Administration (UCEA), 47, 57, 61, 124, 168-169

University of Chicago
Bobbitt at, 55
Dewey at, 15, 30
economists, 224
Laboratory School, 15, 499, 511
Young at, 15, 30

University of Leiden, 408

University of Michigan, 98, 101

University of Southern California, School of Education, 227

Urban schools
designs, 508, 510
female teachers, 113
leaders, 55
marketization issues, 225
neighborhood schools, 521
problems, 241
superintendents, 144, 145, 146-147
See also Chicago school system; New York City schools

Values
democratic, 77
differences between home and school, 392
educational leadership, 53-54, 55
in cultures, 102

Vernonia School District 47 J v. Acton, 179

Victimization, 317-320

Violence
approaches to combat, 468, 474-475
children exposed to, 466-467
domestic, 466-467
factors in, 465-470, 478
family-related factors, 466-467
impact on learning environment, 465-466
prevention, 469, 474-478
risk of, 469-470
rogue events, 475
school-related factors, 467-469
See also Student misbehavior

Virtual schooling, 527

Vocational education, 219, 510-511

Vouchers, 175, 225, 227, 228, 552
See also Choice

Vygotsky, L. S., 495, 497-498

WALC. *See* West Alabama Learning Coalition

Wallace v. Jaffree, 176

Weber, Max, 38, 490

Webs of policies, 199-200

Webster, Daniel, 11

West Alabama Learning Coalition (WALC), 74, 75-76

Western classical literature, 366-372, 376

Western Electric, Hawthorne plant, 96

Whites
college prep courses, 289
male superintendents, 53, 120, 150-151, 154
preparation program faculty, 118, 127
principals, 113, 120
student achievement, 271
See also Racial and ethnic groups

Whittle, Chris, 228

Whole-school inquiry, 270
components, 275-277
dialogue, 293-294
implementation, 293
outcomes measurement, 278-279
stages, 276-277
tools, 277-280, 287-289, 292-293

Willard, Emma, 152

Wireless technology, 525-527

Wolman v. Walter, 174

Women
discrimination against, 134, 182
education of, 151-152
feminine attributes, 161
labor market participation, 120, 124
restrictions on employment of married, 120
school suffrage, 153
teachers, 113, 119, 120, 128, 151-152, 349
See also Gender

Women principals
activities, 111
barriers, 128, 134
declines in numbers of, 119-120, 125, 128, 133-134
elementary school, 119-120, 125, 128, 134
high school, 134
increases in, 119, 124, 128

Women superintendents
criticism of, 120
declines in numbers of, 53
differences from male, 156
feminist view of, 351
focus on curriculum, 120
history of, 53, 153
increase in, 160-161
lack of research on, 150-151, 154
perceptions of, 156
research on, 155-156, 160-161
Young, 14-15, 119

Work texts, 416

Workers
  education of, 501
  teachers seen as, 221, 542
  training of, 219, 226, 510-511, 521
World Trade Organization, 217

Yerkes, R. M., 488
Young, Ella Flagg, 14-15, 26, 28, 29, 30, 31, 119

ZapMe! Corporation, 231
Zelman v. Simmons-Harris, 175